BUSINESS LAW
in
CALIFORNIA

ELEVENTH EDITION

JAMES B. SMITH, J.D.
of the
California Bar

Author/Coauthor/Contributor

Real Estate in California
(General Educational Publications)

California Commercial Law: II
(Continuing Education of the Bar)

Legal Aspects of Real Estate Transactions
(Continuing Education of the Bar)

GENERAL EDUCATIONAL PUBLICATIONS • 1984
99 South Van Ness Avenue, San Francisco 94103

Published by General Educational Publications,
San Francisco, California

ISBN Number 0-914504-10-X
Library of Congress catalog card number 84-80592

Manufactured in the United States of America

PREFACE

This book presents the basic principles of law upon which business and business transactions are based, together with standard forms representing them.

It presents both general and California law, and emphasizes distinctions where they exist. It covers general law in such manner as to meet the requirements for various national examinations such as the C.P.A. and C.P.C.U. Examinations.

The author expresses appreciation to the following business firms and organizations that have furnished many of the forms used in this book: California Apartment Association, California Association of Realtors, Commissioner of Corporations of State of California, Dried Fruit Association of California, Fireman's Fund Indemnity Company, Founders Title Company, The Hibernia Bank, Howard Terminal Company, Law Printing Co., Office of the Secretary of State of State of California, San Francisco Board of Trade, Standard Forms Bureau, The Recorder, The Travelers Insurance Company, Wolcotts Publishers, and Western Pacific Railroad Company.

To Blaire

and

To Deborah and Cathy

and

Matthew, Allyson and Benjamin

Foreword to Eleventh Edition

The forewords to the eighth, ninth and tenth editions of this book are reprinted below for the reason given in the tenth edition foreword for reprinting the eighth and ninth edition forewords. Forewords can tell a story of their own which it would seem that these do.

Transitionally, while *Wellenkamp* won numerous battles, it lost the war and the due-on-sale clause against which it militated has or will become enforceable in those situations in which it was enforceable before *Wellenkamp*. This will be seen in Chapter 6.

In the field of agency, a growing body of California case law is protecting the at-will employee against discharge without cause. In another, quite distinct area of agency, the California Legislature adopted the uniform durable power of attorney act which allows a principal to appoint an agent whose agency is not terminated by the subsequent incapacity of the principal or, in the alternative, to create an agency which is to take effect upon the subsequent incapacity of the principal; the act also provides for the creation of a durable power of attorney for health care which permits the agent to make health care decisions for the principal. These matters will be seen in Chapter 2.

Presumably so that every person can have a will, the California Legislature adopted provisions for a California Statutory Will and a California Statutory Will with Trust, which are printed forms available from your local stationer. The California Statutory Will is seen in Chapter 9 and the California Statutory Will with Trust is differentiated there. Printed forms were also given an important role in the pleading of the common types of civil actions as will be seen in Chapter 1.

The so-called secondary mortgage market became the mainspring of the machinery for the financing of the purchase and sale of residential real estate and in the process has fielded a colorful cast of characters known variously as Fannie Mae, Ginnie Mae and Freddie Mac. California recently added a character of its own known as Carrie Mac. These players will be seen in the section on real estate financing in Chapter 9.

California adopted the Revised Limited Partnership Act. The Revised Act would attempt to clarify and modernize limited partnership law in ways that will be seen in Chapter 10.

July 1984   JAMES B. SMITH

Foreword to Tenth Edition

The most notable change in the tenth edition is the rewriting of Chapter 14 to provide for the new bankruptcy law, i.e., the Bankruptcy Reform Act of 1978. Very extensive excerpts from the Act are included in the Appendix.

In Chapter 1, material is added on California's new arbitration law for the settlment of civil cases in which the amount in controversy does not exceed $15,000. Immediately following this, in Chapter 1, material is added on administrative law at the federal and California levels.

In Chapter 9, the Real Property chapter, the ever-expanding array of real estate financing devices requried by ever-increasing interest rates is examined. In the same chapter and to some extent relatively to the same problem, the now famous case of *Wellenkamp* v. *Bank of America* is discussed.

The forewords to the ninth and eigth editions of this book are reprinted because they, when coupled with the foreword in this edition, provide the reader with what the author believes to be a brief but quite complete history of the highlights of "business law" for the decade of the 70's.

As the tenth edition of this book was in the production process, a number of notable things happened in the field of real estate financing. A bill to repeal the *Wellenkamp* decision is in committee in the California Legislature. Contrary-wise, California courts of appeal have held that *Wellenkamp* applies to investment as well as residential property and that *Wellenkamp* applies to federally-chartered savings and loan associations. The California Legislature has indicated its intention to pass a bill which would allow state-chartered savings and loan associations to issue variable rate mortgages on the same, higher, terms on which federally-chartered institutions can issue such mortgages. This would be designed to stem the tide of defections from state charter to federal charter among the state's savings and loan associations. Finally, it appears that wraparound mortgages may present sellers with serious income tax difficulties and that tax counsel should be obtained in connection with any such transaction.

Foreword to Ninth Edition

The foreword to the eighth edition is shown below since it seems to be as current now as when it was written late in 1975. Consumer protection law continues to expand and pervade. The major new advancement in the California law since the writing of the eighth edition is the adoption of a new General Corporation Law by which the Californai legislators attempt to simplify and modernize the California law of corporations. This new law is, of course, included in the current edition of this book.

Foreword to Eighth Edition

A major theoretical change has taken place in California's community property law. Where, until 1975, husband had the full and exclusive right to manage and control community property, the wife has now been given equal right of management and control. This makes the marital partnership like a business partnership but with the same basic weakness as a business partnership. If business partners cannot manage the business cooperatively and amicably, there is nothing to do but to dissolve the partnership even though it may have years to run under the agreement of partnership. Similarly, if marital partners cannot manage the marital financial affairs cooperatively and amicably, there is nothing to do but to dissolve the marriage.

Consumerism is the "name of the game" today. Legislatures and courts have been quick to mount this bandwagon on which space is becoming very much at a premium. The consumer is not only one who buys goods but one who buys services—the services of a bank, the services of a hotel, the services of a garage; and is one who leases automobiles as well as buys them; and one who rents real estate; and one who borrows money for personal or family purposes. The list will continue to grow. All of these kinds of people are now receiving kinds of legal protection they did not receive ten years ago; often protection they did not receive five years or three or two years ago. In 1974 residential tenants became protected by the rule of *Green* v. *Superior Court*, 10 C.3d 616, 517 P.2d 1168, under which the California Supreme Court held that the landlord impliedly warranted the habitability of his premises and that the tenant could withhold rent to insure performance of the warranty. Consumer credit is becoming increasingly regulated. The practices of automobile leasing agencies are becoming increasingly regulated. The practices of banks and hotels and garages in the enforcement of liens given to them by law are becoming increasingly regulated. All to the end of protecting the "consumer" of all of the types of commodities with which the consumer is sought to be attracted. Accordingly, much of what is new in this edition will consist of noting this new-found concern for the persons which one court referred to as "Mr. and (Ms.) General Public."

The Real Estate Settlement Procedures Act is in the nature, almost, of a "P.S." regarding new consumer law, since the forms for this Act became available just shortly before this edition went to press, and the Act and its forms are discussed in the chapter on Real Property.

Summary of Contents

Table of Contents

Table of Forms

CHAPTER 1

Law and Court Systems

Introduction

"If an ox gore a man or a woman to death, the ox shall be surely stoned . . . but the owner of the ox shall be quit. But if the ox was wont to gore in time past, and it hath been testified to its owner, and he hath not kept it in, but it hath killed a man or a woman; the ox shall be stoned, and its owner also shall be put to death."—*Old Testament, Exodus,* xxi, 28, 29 (1491 B.C.).

This announces a principle of law, the *one free bite rule,* which is still in force in some states today.[1] The rule is that the owner of a domesticated animal which bites or otherwise injures a person is not liable if the animal has not previously exhibited vicious tendencies; but that the owner is liable if the animal has previously demonstrated viciousness since then the owner is aware of its vicious nature and able to prevent another attack. The penalty, damages, is somewhat less drastic than in the Old Testament, but the principle of law is the same.

This brings out in a small way that much of law is very old, and that the roots of modern law are deeply implanted. Legal history, with which this chapter is primarily concerned, is interesting, and is extremely valuable because it shows the background of and reasons for many rules of law; and to know a rule without knowing the reasons therefor is only half understanding.

● A journey into legal history may begin by asking, "What is *law*?" Law has been defined in many ways: by Cicero as "nothing else but right reason, calling us imperiously to our duty, and prohibiting every violation of it;" by St. Thomas Aquinas as "a regulation in accord with reason, issued by a lawful superior for the common good;" by the California Civil Code in Section 22 as "a solemn expression of the will of the supreme power of the State." Perhaps the best and most workable definition is that it is a body of rules regulating man in his relationships with other men and with society as a whole.

Jewish Law

Law started when society started, but the deepest root of modern law is Jewish Law of roughly 1500 B.C. and thereafter. As was the case with all legal systems to that time, Jewish Law was an inextricable mixture of religious and secular law.

---

[1]Not in California as to dogs at least. C.C. 3342 provides: "The owner of any dog is liable for the damages suffered by any person who is bitten by the dog while in a public place or lawfully in a private place, including the property of the owner of the dog, regardless of the former viciousness of the dog or the owner's knowledge of such viciousness. A person is lawfully upon the private property of such owner within the meaning of this section when he is on such property in the performance of any duty imposed upon him by the laws of this State or by the laws or postal regulations of the United States, or when he is on such property upon the invitation, express or implied, of the owner."

The basic law of the Jewish nation, its "constitution," was the Torah, or first five books of the Old Testament. The heart of the Torah was the Ten Commandments. (Exodus, xx, 117.) Although religious mandates, they are the basis of principles of secular law. "Thou shalt not kill" recognizes the right of personal security. "Thou shalt not covet thy neighbor's house . . . nor his ox, nor his ass, nor anything that is thy neighbor's" recognizes rights of private ownership and the right to be secure therein. "Honor thy father and thy mother . . ." and "Thou shalt not commit adultery" seek to sanctify and protect family institutions and domestic relations.

Chapters xxxxiii of Exodus, the second book, contain a substantial number of purely secular mandates. The opening paragraph of this chapter is an example. Also to be found there is that awesome decree, "Eye for eye, tooth for tooth, hand for hand, foot for foot, burning for burning, wound for wound, stripe for stripe."

In addition, the Jews produced the Talmud or codes, a great mass of detailed law expanding upon the Torah. Modern legal systems develop in the same manner. A constitution becomes implemented by a mass of detailed law, called statutory law.

Each system of law plays a role in the formation of the next, and much of Jewish Law found its way into Roman Law.

Roman or Civil Law System

The Romans have been described as having created "veritable law factories"—the more laws the better. As a result, they were important contributors to the law. They started with the Code of the Twelve Tables prepared by the Decemviri, a committee of ten men appointed in 451 B.C. to formulate a basic written law. This was largely *procedural* as distinguished from *substantive* law, i.e., it dealt at length with how to commence and prosecute actions to enforce legal rights. Substantive law is the "legal rights" end of law; that portion of the law which creates legal relationships and declares the rights, duties and obligations of parties thereto.

Then the lawmakers went to work in earnest until they had conceived the Corpus Juris Civilis (the Body of Civil Law), and the Civil Law, an elaborate and comprehensive set of codes giving immense detail to the law. In part, this came about by legislative process, i.e., a proposition was drafted and passed by the people's Assembly and became law after approval by the Senate. To this extent, it was *statutory law—* law becoming such by the formal enactment of a legislative body. Also it came about by senatorial decree and other methods which have no modern day counterpart.

● The internal structure of the Civil Law deserves examination, for in it is to be found the basic schematic arrangement of every present day system. As today, the law was divided into criminal law and civil law. *Civil law,* in the general sense of the term in which it is used here, refers to that part of the law which fixes the rights, duties and liabilities of private persons in their dealings and relationships: the law of contracts, agency, sales, and so on. Henceforth, "Civil Law Sys-

1

tem" will be used to describe the Roman System of law as distinguished from civil law in its general sense.

Criminal Law

Criminal law is that body of law which prescribes that certain things are offenses against and punishable by society in order that the security of the citizens of the state as a whole may be preserved. Roman statutes made crimes of homicide, kidnaping, bribery, forgery, embezzlement, and other things. Cicero, the greatest of the Roman lawyers and the Clarence Darrow of his day, won his greatest victories in the criminal courts. He first came to public attention by successfully defending a young man accused of murder in the case of *The State* v. *Sextus Roscius*. The case was a dangerous one because powerful political figures were involved, but Cicero showed no fear and climaxed the trial by proving the chief witness for the prosecution to be the murderer.

Civil Law

Civil law embraces all of those fields of law which concern business relationships and property ownership. Here, the Romans had well developed laws of contracts, agency, sales, property, wills and trusts, and suretyship; also, a well established banking system replete with mortgaging and other security arrangements. To a lesser degree, they had a law of commercial paper, corporations, insurance, and bankruptcy.
• Civil law also deals with "civil wrongs," i.e., wrongs by one person against another, for which the injured party is entitled to damages. Civil wrongs are of two general types: breaches of contract, and torts. "Torts" are injuries to the person or property of another, or the obtention or detention of property of another by wrongful means or without right. Torts may be intentional or unintentional, i.e., the result of negligence.

The Romans had a fully developed tort law. Damages were recoverable for any *injuria* or injury to the person of another and any *furtum* (trespass) or injury to his property. The intentional torts of fraud, duress, conversion, malicious prosecution, libel, and slander were actionable. And the law of *negligence* was highly refined.

Negligence was *improvidentia*. While one was liable therefor, "contributory negligence" was a good defense then as now. Thus, if a Roman javelin thrower of 200 A.D. was in the habit of practicing in a place where he knew people might pass, he would be guilty of negligence if he accidentally speared a passerby. But if the passerby knew that the javelinist practiced there, his failure to keep an eye out for flying javelins might be such contributory negligence as to bar recovery.

The modern day distinctions between gross and slight negligence were present in *culpa lata* and *culpa levis sima*. If a flower pot were placed on a window sill in such manner that it might easily fall on the head of a passerby, there would be *culpa lata,* or gross negligence. But if the flower pot were placed on a table in such a position that a child could reach and pull it over, there would be *culpa levis sima,* or slight negligence.

The Roman Civil Law System, then, was a most complete one. It became a main root of the law of Western Europe which continues to be referred to as Civil or Continental Law.
• One further aspect of the Civil Law System is to be noted. In writing and codifying the law, the Romans left very little lawmaking to judges. Their function was almost entirely that of triers of fact, deciding, as between litigants, whose version of the facts was more strongly supported by the evidence. There even developed a requirement of candidates for the bench that they proclaim in advance of election the interpretation they would place on those laws which were susceptible of interpretation. This was a system of "written law," then, as compared to one in which law would result from or be "made" by court decisions.

Feudalism

The decline and fall of the Roman Empire was complete by 471 A.D. A period of one thousand years, known as the Middle Ages, followed, and during this time much of Roman law permeated Western Europe. There also developed in Western Europe the Feudal System which deserves attention because it gave rise to the theory and system of real property law which was adopted in England and eventually found its way into this country, where its basic concepts remain alive. Charlemagne was mainly responsible for the feudal system. During his rule all property was considered to belong to the King in the first instance. As King, it became his prerogative to parcel out the land as he saw fit among noblemen who would be expected to support him. They were said to be *enfeoffed* of the land. They, in turn, subdivided among lesser lords and so on down to the lowest subdivisee on the list, who was said to have the *fee* (income) *od* (of property) or *feud* of his parcel, which he rented to serfs or "tenants" in exchange for a large portion of their crops. In this country today, all real property ownership stems from the state in the first instance. If you own property, the legal name of your ownership is *fee* or *fee simple* ownership, and as fee owner you may create various lesser estates and tenancies in the property—the same nomenclature and basic scheme as in the Feudal System.

English Common Law

Crossing the channel with William the Conqueror, we arrive at the Norman Conquest of England in 1066. The Norman conquerors followed a much different procedure than the Romans in the matter of lawmaking. They established a system of courts and traveling judges, but did not open any "law factories" to provide them with codes. Rather, they were left much to their own devices, and were expected to make law by deciding what the law should be in a particular case as it came before them. Strangely enough, this apparently haphazard system of lawmaking developed a highly rigid system of law. This was due largely to an unwritten rule imposed by the judges upon themselves: the rule of *stare decisis*—to stand by decided cases. It was this simple: Litigants came before a court with a problem of first impression. The court's decision was a "precedent"—an original rule of law. Later, other litigants came before other courts with the same problem. The other courts "stood by the previously decided case;" that is, applied the same rule, whether or not they agreed with it. The result was that a *precedent* became a *law*. Since it was one which would be applied to all persons, it was a law common to all persons or *common law*.

It was in this way that the name *common law* attached, and, while there was some amount of important statutory law, it was upon such common law footings that the great bulk of English law was founded. It was "courtmade law," or "judgemade law," or "case law;" and, although voluminously recorded and in great part "republished" in statutory or code form in later years, it was and continues to be referred to as "unwritten law" because of its origin.

The common law and the Civil Law are the two great systems of law. Our law is patterned after the common law. Before discussing our system, certain other concepts of the

English law which found their way into our law should be examined.

Equity Where Legal Remedy Inadequate

By the Fifteenth Century, the courts which administered the common law were known as common law courts or law courts. Actions brought therein were known as common law actions, actions at law, or legal actions; and the relief or remedies available in such courts were known as common law remedies, remedies at law, or legal remedies. These law courts could give only two general types of relief: money damages for breach of contract or injury to person or property; and restoration of real or personal property to one wrongfully deprived of possession.

This left much "inadequacy" of remedy "at law." For example, as a Fifteenth Century English citizen:

1. You go to a distant part of the country where you contract to buy a farm. You then sell your home and move your family to the new place. At that point, the seller of the farm refuses to complete the contract. Damages would not be an adequate remedy.

2. Because of some misadventure—your horse falls—you are one day late in getting to the appointed place to pay the mortgage on your farm. At law, you would have no remedy.

3. Your neighbor opens a factory which emits great quantities of smoke and soot, which damage your home and cause you great personal discomfort. Your only legal remedy would be periodic lawsuits for money damages.

You had one possibility for adequate remedy, however. If you could reach the King's ear, he could give you relief appropriate to the circumstances. He could order the farmseller to do what he had contracted to do—to perform "in specie" or "specifically perform"—to give you a deed to the farm. In view of the extenuating circumstances, he could permit you to "redeem" your lost farm from the mortgagee. He could "enjoin" your neighbor from continuing his "nuisance," that is, order him to stop it.

This was a royal prerogative, and duty. The King was conceived of as a link between divine authority and man and as such owed it to his subjects to see that "good conscience" prevailed. But the pressure of other duties left little time for these dispensations of "equity," so the King soon turned this element of his royal functions over to a "chancellor," a highly educated high churchman, who would have the intelligence and the moral fibre to see that the right thing was done. It would not do to entrust "the conscience of the King" to mere common law judges, as would seem to us, today, to have been the simple solution. Soon the job got too big for the chancellor and a system of courts of equity, or equity courts, was developed. This produced a divided court system, of law courts and equity courts. The password to equity was inadequacy of legal remedy.

• We had a divided court system in this country for many years. Now, however, in almost every state, one court gives both legal and equitable relief. However, inadequacy of legal remedy is still the key to equitable relief.

• Equitable remedies soon became formalized. The most important became and remain:

1. *Specific performance:* Compelling performance of a contract as distinguished from awarding damages for its nonperformance (the legal remedy).

2. *Relief from forfeiture:* Disallowing strict enforcement of a contract where it would produce "forfeiture" consequences; thus, allowing a mortgagor to redeem his property when late payment of the mortgage was caused by circumstances beyond his control, which eventually became known as the "equity of redemption."

3. *Injunction:* Ordering a person to do or to cease and desist from doing an act.

• Simultaneously, qualifications for equitable relief developed. Equity was not going to give its aid to one whose position was itself not equitable. Therefore, one who sought equity had to be doing equity—had, for example, to be giving an "adequate consideration" if he was seeking specific enforcement of a contract—from which developed the maxim that "he who seeks equity must do equity."

Equity also developed the "clean hands doctrine," that "he who comes into equity must come with clean hands" and must not himself be guilty of fraud or other unconscionable conduct.

Finally, equity said, you must act diligently to assert your rights since this is part of fairness to the other party. From this developed the maxim that "equity aids the vigilant, not those who slumber on their rights." "Laches"—unreasonable delay—will bar a suit in equity, as the statute of limitations will bar a suit at law. Thus, one seeking to rescind a contract must act promptly to do so upon discovering his right and even short delay may be fatal.

Law Merchant

Concurrently with the development of the common law and equity there developed a "law of merchants" or *law merchant* as it came to be called. The law merchant developed separately because, at first, merchants were not allowed access to the common law courts for the settlement of their disputes. Merchants were required to set themselves up in fair towns and, if they had disputes, they were required to set up their own courts for settlement of their disputes; which they did. These courts developed an important body of law regulating the sales transactions of merchants and the "commercial paper" (drafts and notes) by which they were financed. Eventually the merchants were allowed the use of the law courts, which, then, adopted and continued to enforce the "law merchant," such that it continued to retain its separate identity. Out of the law merchant developed the English Sale of Goods Act and the English Bills of Exchange Act and their American counterparts; and, even today, we find the Uniform Commercial Code, the most recent formulation of the law of merchants, telling us that, "unless displaced by the particular provisions of this Act, the principles of law and equity, including the law merchant . . . shall supplement its provisions" (U.C.C. 1103).

United States

General

The English colonists brought with them the principles of the English common law, and ours is a *common law system* in two important respects: (1) The laws of the various states are based upon the English common law, although there are exceptions; e.g., Louisiana has the civil law system, and in a number of western states, including California, the community property law has been adopted with respect to marital property. (2) We have a great body of courtmade law as in the English system and both state and federal courts honor "precedent."

• At this point the term *statutory law* needs to be clarified. In every state, there are thousands of laws consolidated into *codes*. Each code provision is a *statute,* since it is a formal enactment of law by a legislature. But many of these statutes are codifications of common law—formal adoption in statute form of what was originally common law. The remainder embody law which is new or original. When we use the term *statutory law,* we refer to a statute which represents new or original law. To take an example: It became established early in the English common law that one who repaired personal property of another was entitled to hold the property until paid for his services. This was called the *common law possessory lien.* When California adopted its codes in 1872, it was the provision of C.C. 3051 that one who repaired personal property of another was entitled to retain possession until paid. To this extent, there was merely codification of common law. But C.C. 3052 provided further that if the lienholder were not paid for his services within ten days after payment became due, he could sell the property and reimburse himself from the proceeds. Since the lienholder never acquired a right of sale at common law, this was new law. Consequently, we refer to the right of lien given by the combination of C.C. 3051 and 3052 as a *statutory possessory lien.*

United States Constitution and Federal Laws

In this country, we have two levels of government, state and federal. The federal or United States government is what the name implies, a sovereign body created by a federation of states, each of which is a sovereignty, the purpose of which is to represent the states in international matters and to make laws binding on them with respect to matters of common concern. The United States Constitution in Section 8 of Article I gives the federal government the power to make laws on certain subjects and, with respect to these subjects, the federal government has the *exclusive* lawmaking power.
● The United States Constitution is the "supreme law of the land." It divides into:

1. That portion which prescribes a "separation of powers" of government into executive, judicial and legislative departments and the structure and general powers of each.

2. Section 8 of Article I which defines the lawmaking power of Congress by conferring powers, among others, "To lay and collect taxes . . . to pay the debts and provide for the common defense and general welfare of the United States;" "To regulate commerce . . . among the several States;" "To coin money [and] regulate the value thereof;" "To declare war" and "To raise and support armies;" and "*To make all laws which shall be necessary and proper for carrying into execution the foregoing powers. . . .*"

3. The "Bill of Rights," or the ten original amendments which preserve to all persons certain fundamental rights and safeguards such as freedom of speech and freedom of religion.
● Congress exercises its lawmaking power by passage of *Acts* which are compiled in the "United States Code." This constitutes a great body of federal statutory law supplementing the Constitution. Strictly speaking, a law enacted by Congress is an *Act,* while one enacted by a state legislature is a *statute*; and one adopted by a municipal legislative body is an *ordinance*; but the various acts of Congress are commonly referred to as the *federal statutes.*

State Law

General: The Tenth Amendment to the United States Constitution provides that "The powers not delegated to the United States by the Constitution . . . are reserved to the States respectively. . . ." This means that each state may make its own laws with respect to matters which are purely intrastate. So long as the law is "constitutional"; that is, so long as it does not violate a provision of the state constitution

or of the United States Constitution, such as depriving persons of the right of free speech or of due process of law, it is valid.

Despite the fact that each of the fifty states makes its own laws, there is substantial uniformity because of the fact that they follow the common law of England. Not infrequently, however, the law of some states goes one way on a point while the law of other states goes another way. In these situations, it is necessary to refer to a *majority rule* and a *minority rule* on the particular point, or to the "*weight of authority*"— the rule of a numerical majority of states.

Each state has a constitution supplemented by a system of codes. In addition, there is courtmade or case law—judicial decisions interpreting and supplementing statutes, each of which is a binding precedent.

Uniform Laws and Restatements: Since the turn of the century, there have been important efforts to make the laws of the states uniform in certain fields. These are represented by a series of (1) uniform laws, now superseded by the Uniform Commercial Code, and (2) restatements of law, formulated by the National Conference of Commissioners on Uniform State Laws and the American Law Institute.
● The first and second uniform laws were the Uniform Negotiable Instruments Law and the Uniform Sales Act. Uniformity was particularly important here since the instruments and transactions of commerce constantly cross state lines. In all, sixty uniform acts were formulated. The important commercial and business acts in addition to the Uniform Negotiable Instruments Law and the Uniform Sales Act were the Uniform Trust Receipts Act, Uniform Bills of Lading Act, Uniform Warehouse Receipts Act, Uniform Conditional Sales Act, Uniform Partnership Act, Uniform Limited Partnership Act, and Uniform Stock Transfer Act. They are replaced by the Uniform Commercial Code, except the partnership acts, which remain law in California and generally. As of 1984, California is one of sixteen states to have adopted the Revised Uniform Limited Partnership Act.
● The Restatements attempt to bring about uniformity in a different way. They state systematically the principles of particular fields of law as they developed from the common law. Thus, we have a Restatement of Contracts, a Restatement of Torts, a Restatement of Property, and a number of restatements in lesser fields. It is hoped that states and courts will conform their laws and decisions to the rules of the restatements so as to achieve uniformity. The restatements have been given wide recognition by the courts.

Federal Court System

The federal court system is organized as follows:
1. District Courts.
2. Courts of Appeal.
3. United States Supreme Court.

The District Courts are "courts of original jurisdiction" or "trial courts"—the courts in which proceedings are commenced and tried. Among other things, the District Courts have jurisdiction of civil actions where the matter in controversy exceeds $10,000 and arises under the Constitution or laws of the United States or is between citizens of different states. Each state has at least one District Court, with the number ranging to as high as four in California, New York and Texas.

The Courts of Appeal and the United States Supreme Court are courts of review to which appeal may be taken from the District Courts. Appeal must go first to the Court of Appeal which reviews the case on the "record" sent to it from the trial court and either affirms, reverses or modifies the judgment of the trial court. Appeal to the United States Supreme Court is largely a matter of privilege rather than of right. Petition for hearing must be made to the Court, which it may grant or deny.

State Court Systems

State systems have the same general structure as the federal system: (1) Courts of original jurisdiction, or trial courts; (2) intermediate appellate courts; and (3) the highest court of the state as one of final appeal.

1. Courts of original jurisdiction consist of:

a. Inferior courts or courts of limited jurisdiction—city or municipal courts or justices' courts whose jurisdiction is limited to a city or township and which may hea r only criminal cases involving misdemeanors and civil cases for money damages up to certain amounts, e.g., $15,000 in municipal and justice courts in California.

b. Courts of unlimited jurisdiction, i.e., having jurisdiction of all types of actions, in all amounts—law, equity, divorce, probate, felony prosecutions, etc. These are variously called superior courts, county courts, circuit courts or courts of common pleas.

2. Intermediate appellate courts are usually called Courts of Appeal or District Courts of Appeal.

3. The highest court of the state may be called the Supreme Court, Supreme Judicial Court, Supreme Court of Appeals, Supreme Court of Errors, or Court of Errors and Appeals.

Appeal may be made from the highest court in the state to the United States Supreme Court only if there is a constitutional question involved—a state statute or decision asserted to be in violation of the United States Constitution.

California

Law

In its original fundamentals, California law is patterned after the common law of England, although there are exceptions such as the community property law. California is unusual in that, upon attaining statehood, its legal system was converted from that of the Civil Law to that of the common law. These matters are summed up in C.C. 22.2 which provides that "The common law of England, so far as it is not repugnant to or inconsistent with the Constitution of the United States, or the constitution or laws of this State, is the rule of decision in all courts of this State;" and *Fowler* v. *Smith*, 2 C. 568, where the court said: "When the territory now comprised in the state of California was under Mexican dominion, its judicial system was that of the Roman law, modified by Spanish and Mexican legislation. Upon the formation of the present state government, that system was ordained by a constitutional provision to be continued, until it should be changed by the legislature. At the first session of the Legislature an act was passed, adopting the common law of England."

The supreme law of the state is its Constitution which fixes the structure of the state government, the powers of the various arms of government, and the fundamental rights and privileges of citizens of the state. In short, it is to California what the United States Constitution is to the United States, although it is a much more detailed pronouncement of law than the federal Constitution.

The constitution is supplemented by a great body of statutory law enacted by the state legislature and compiled in codes.

California has 28 codes which, with standard abbreviations, are as follows:

Business and Professions Code (B. & P.C.)
Civil Code (C.C.)
Code of Civil Procedure (C.C.P.)
Corporations Code (Corp. C.)
Education Code (Ed. C.)
Elections Code (Elec. C.)
Evidence Code (Evid. C.)
Financial Code (Fin. C.)
Fish and Game Code (F. & G. C.)
Food and Agricultural Code (F. & Ag. C.)
Government Code (Gov. C.)
Harbors and Navigation Code (H. & N. C.)
Health and Safety Code (H. & S. C.)
Insurance Code (Ins. C.)
Labor Code (Lab. C.)
Military and Veterans Code (Mil. & Vet. C.)
Penal Code (Pen. C.)
Probate Code (Prob. C.)
Public Contract Code (Pub. Con. C.)
Public Resources Code (Pub. Res. C.)
Public Utilities Code (Pub. U. C.)
Revenue and Taxation Code (Rev. & Tax. C.)
Streets and Highways Code (Sts. & H. C.)
Unemployment Insurance Code (Unempl. Ins. C.)
Uniform Commercial Code (U. C. C.)
Vehicle Code (Veh. C.)
Water Code (Wat. C.)
Welfare and Institutions Code (W. & I. Code)

The basic and most important codes are the Civil Code, Code of Civil Procedure, Penal Code and Probate Code. The Civil Code states the substantive civil law—torts, contracts, property, etc.—except in cases where, because of development of a sizable body of law or for other reason, a special code has been created, e.g., corporation law was in the Civil Code until creation of the Corporations Code in 1947, and the law of commercial transactions was scattered throughout the Civil Code until its reformulation and reenactment as the Uniform Commercial Code in 1963. The Code of Civil Procedure establishes the procedure for enforcement of rights and redress of wrongs, e.g., how and in what court a civil action may be brought. The Penal Code defines crimes and fixes their punishment. The Probate Code deals with intestate succession, wills and decedents' estates, and with the administration of trusts, decedents' estates and estates of minors and incompetent persons.

Court System

Before going into the court system proper, these general matters may be noted: As in most states, there are no separate courts of law and equity in California. Superior courts, and municipal courts to the extent indicated below, sit as courts of law or equity as the case demands. Since an equitable action is an appeal to the *court,* there is no right to a jury trial. Otherwise, there is a right to a jury trial in both civil and criminal actions, as follows: In felony actions there must be a twelve-man jury. In civil actions and misdemeanor cases the parties may agree on a jury of less than twelve. In civil actions in municipal and justice courts the Legislature may provide that the jury shall consist of eight persons or a lesser number agreed on by the parties. In criminal cases, whether the crime is a felony or a misdemeanor, a unanimous verdict is required for the defendant to be found guilty of the crime. In civil actions a ¾ verdict is sufficient. (Cal. Const. Art. I, § 16.)

• California's inferior courts are Municipal Courts and Justice Courts. Both have jurisdiction of misdemeanors committed within the county within which the municipal or justice court presides and of civil actions where the amount of controversy does not exceed $15,000. They also have various types of equity jurisdiction where the amount involved does not exceed $15,000, e.g., to cancel or declare the rescission of contracts and to issue temporary restraining orders. C.C.P. 86; Pen.C. 1462.

• Small Claims Courts are not separate courts, but municipal courts and justice courts sitting as small claims courts. The parties themselves handle the litigation which is limited to civil matters for damages not exceeding $1,500 and for rent claims not exceeding $1,500 in connection with unlawful detainer proceedings where the term of the tenancy is not greater than month to month. C.C.P. 116.2. Parties may not be represented by attorneys. "No attorney at law or other person than the plaintiff and defendant shall take any part in the filing or the prosecution or defense of such litigation in small claims court . . ." C.C.P. 117.4. This section (C.C.P. 117.4) goes on to provide that "Nothing herein shall prevent an attorney from rendering advice to a party to such litigation, either before or after the commencement of such an action . . ." C.C.P. 117.18 requires each county to establish a small claims court advisory service through which small claims court litigants and potential litigants can obtain free legal advice. The service may be composed of lawyers, law students, paralegals or other persons experienced in resolving minor disputes and familiar with small claims court rules and procedures. C.C.P. 117.5 provides that small claims court claims cannot be prosecuted by assignees.

• The trial court of unlimited jurisdiction is the Superior Court. A Superior Court, having jurisdiction throughout the state, is established in each county. It has exclusive, original jurisdiction of (a) felony prosecutions, (b) actions involving amounts beyond the jurisdictional limits of inferior courts, (c) equity actions, in general, (d) marriage dissolution proceedings and (e) probate proceedings.

• The civil appellate system is as follows:

1. Appellate Department of the Superior Court, for appeals from inferior courts.

2. Courts of Appeal, for appeals from superior courts.

3. Supreme Court of the State of California, for appeal from courts of appeal where necessary to secure uniformity of decision or to settle important questions of law.

Arbitration

Because of the high cost of litigation and the costly delays it may entail, arbitration has emerged as an important substitute for the civil court trial in California. Prior to 1979, arbitration was a permitted remedy in California. As of July 1, 1979, it became the required remedy in civil cases in which the amount in controversy does not exceed $15,000 in these courts and actions: metropolitan courts, i.e., superior courts having 10 or more judges; other superior courts and municipal courts that opt for the program; any action in which the plaintiff agrees that the award will not exceed $15,000. In addition, arbitration is the mandatory procedure, regardless of the amount in controversy, in any case in which both parties so stipulate. All of this is by virtue of C.C.P. 1141.10-1141.20, enacted in 1978 to become effective July 1, 1979. Introductorily, C.C.P. 1141.10 states that "(t)he Legislature finds and declares that litigation involving small civil claims has become so costly and complex as to make more difficult the efficient resolution of such civil claims that courts are unable to efficiently resolve the increased number of cases filed each year, and that the resulting delays and expenses deny parties their right to a timely resolution of minor civil disputes." Section 1141.10 goes on to say that it is the intention of the Legislature that arbitration proceedings "shall provide parties with a simplified and economical procedure for obtaining prompt and equitable resolution of their disputes" and that "(a)rbitration hearings shall be as informal and private as possible and shall provide the parties themselves maximum opportunity to participate directly in the resolution of their disputes, and shall be held during nonjudicial hours whenever possible."

• A superior court judge decides whether the case should go to arbitration, i.e., decides that the amount in controversy will not exceed $15,000.

• C.C.P. 1141.18 provides that "(a)rbitrators shall be retired judges or members of the State Bar, and shall sit individually" but that "(p)eople who are not attorneys may serve as arbitrators upon the stipulation of all parties." Section 1141.18 provides, further, that, unless waived, the compensation for arbitrators shall be $150 per day unless the board of supervisors of a county sets a higher rate of compensation for that county.

• An arbitration award may be in excess of $15,000. C.C.P. 1141.26. An arbitration award is final if a request for a *de novo* trial is not filed within 20 days after the date the arbitrator files the award with the court. C.C.P. 1141.21 provides that if a party who requests a trial *de novo* does not get a more favorable judgment than he did at arbitration, he must pay court costs, arbitrator's compensation and costs of expert witnesses.

• In the counties of Los Angeles, San Bernardino, Santa Barbara and Ventura arbitration is the mandatory procedure in civil cases in which the amount in controversy does not exceed $25,000.

Administrative Law

Much of our lives is regulated by the administrative law process . Administrative agencies administer medicare, social security, tax collection, welfare benefits, workers' compensation and disability benefits and many other things. Regulatory administrative agencies protect us against dangerous foods and drugs and consumer products, regulate with respect to what we are permitted to see on television, regulate the manner in which advertising may be presented, protect us against pollution of the air and the environment and do many other things that are designed to improve the conditions of our lives.

• Administrative agencies are simply agencies created for the purpose of carrying out governmental programs at the federal and state levels. Such agencies abound. In California there are 4 basic administrative agencies: (1) the *agriculture and services agency,* which includes among its subdivisions the department of food and agriculture, the department of consumer affairs, the franchise tax board and the department of veterans affairs; (2) the *business and transportation agency,* which includes among its subdivisions, on the "business" side, the state banking department, the department of corporations, the department of insurance and the department of real estate; (3) the *health and welfare agency*; and (4) the *resources agency.* In addition, there are such completely independent agencies such as the *public utilities commission* and the *fair political practices commission.* Within the basic administrative agency there may be any number of subagencies. Within the California department of food and agriculture, e.g., there are subagencies specifically concerned with the production of milk and dairy products, agricultural pest control, and the activities of livestock dealers, produce dealers and processors of agricultural commodities.

• Administrative agencies perform purely ministerial or administrative functions, adjudicatory or quasijudicial functions and quasilegislative or rulemaking functions.

• The California Administrative Code contains the rules and regulations of most of the California administrative agencies, such as the regulations of the departments of corporations, insurance and real estate. The Code of Federal Regulations is the federal counterpart.

• The judicial function of administrative agencies is accomplished in different ways and with different degrees of elaborateness. In California, e.g., when application is made to the Public Utilities Commission for a rate increase, which will affect the public at large or some segment of it, an elaborate public hearing will be held, in which the Commission as a body acts as the arbiter, and in which extensive introduction of evidence and extensive examination and crossexamination will take place, which may ultimately result in the granting or denial of the application or the partial granting and partial denial. In individual cases, on the other hand, involving, e.g., the granting or revocation of an individual license, California maintains a corps of "hearing officers" whose function it is to adjudicate the disputes that arise out of such actions. Federal administrative agencies may also sit in banc. The federal government also maintains a large corps of "administrative law judges" who preside over and decide much of the important litigation which relates to the operation of federal agencies.

• The judicial action that takes place in the world of administrative agencies is supposed to be less cumbersome than that which takes place in the courts. Administrative hearings come to "trial" much more quickly than do actions in the courts and are not as tightly bound up by technical rules of evidence and procedure as are actions in the courts. Govt. C. 11513(c) says, e.g., with respect to administrative hearings that "(t)he hearing need not be conducted according to technical rules relating to evidence and witnesses. Any relevant evidence shall be admitted if it is the sort of evidence on which responsible persons are accustomed to rely in the conduct of serious affairs, regardless of the existence of any common law or statutory rule which might make improper the admission of such evidence over objection in civil actions. Hearsay evidence may be used for the purpose of supplementing or explaining other evidence but shall not be sufficient in itself to support a finding unless it would be admissible over objection in civil actions."

However, administrative hearings must be fair proceedings and federal[2] and state[3] "administrative procedure acts" are designed to insure this. They demand the presence of the "3 R's" of procedural due process, which are adequate notice of the proceedings, opportunity to be heard and opportunity to test unfavorable evidence. The actions of administrative judicial bodies and officers are subject to court review to insure that due process has been accorded.

Finding Cases and Law

Cases

Generally, only appellate courts write "opinions" setting forth the principles of law upon which their decisions are based. These opinions constitute the body of "case law" of this country. They are published annually in volumes of "Reports" and "Reporters" which are to be found in any law library.

Taking the California System: Opinions of the Supreme Court are found in "California Reports" in chronological or-

[2]5 U.S.C.A. 551 et seq.

[3]Govt. Code 11500 et seq.

der; those of the Courts of Appeal in "California Appellate Reports." Since 1960 both are also found in the "California Reporter."

If you had a reference or "citation" to the California case of *Guy* v. *Brennen*, 60 C.A. 452, you would find it in Volume 60 of the California Appellate Reports at page 452. A citation to *Jameson & Co.* v. *Mayfield*, 118 C.A. 59 would be found in Volume 118 of California Appellate Reports at page 59. The first case is a 1923 case, the second a 1931 case. Usually several volumes are required to cover the cases for a single year, e.g., volumes 103110 cover the opinions of the Courts of Appeal for the year 1930.

If you had the citation *Harding* v. *Robinson*, 175 C. 534, you would find it in Volume 175 of the California Reports at page 534, a Supreme Court case dealing with fraud.

In 1934, a "second series" was started in both the California Reports and California Appellate Reports, so that 4 C.2d 128 refers to the 1935 case of *Brant* v. *California Dairies* in Volume 4 of California Reports, 2d Series; 2 C.A.2d 646 refers to the 1935 case of *Gen. Motors Acc. Corp.* v. *Brown* in Volume 2 of California Appellate Reports, 2d Series.

In 1969, a "third series" was started in California Appellate Reports, and in 1969-1970 a "third series" was started in California Reports. Thus, 2 C.3d 245 refers to the 1970 case of *Price* v. *Shell Oil Co.* in Volume 2 of California Reports, 3d Series.

• Other states have similar sets of "reports."

• To reduce the number of volumes a law library must maintain, the opinions of the California courts are combined with those of Washington, Oregon, Nevada, Arizona and other western states in the "Pacific Reporter" system. Referring to the case of *Harding* v. *Robinson*, above, it would actually be cited as *Harding* v. *Robinson*, 175 C. 534, 166 P. 808. You could then find the case in either of two volumes; in the California Reports as previously explained, or in Volume 166 of the Pacific Reporter at page 808. In 1960 West Publishing Company, publisher of the National Reporter System, introduced the California Reporter, which reports decisions of the California Supreme Court and of the Courts of Appeal, and since 1960 decisions of the California Supreme Court are carried in the California Reporter as well as in California Reports and the Pacific Reporter. Prior to 1960 decisions of Courts of Appeal were carried in Pacific Reporter as well as in California Appellate Reports. They are no longer carried in Pacific Reporter.

Similar reporter systems cover all of the other states by geographical groupings, e.g., the Atlantic Reporter (Atl.) covers Maine, Connecticut and other states; the Northwestern Reporter (N.W.) covers Michigan, Minnesota and others; the Southwestern Reporter (S.W.) covers Texas, Kentucky and others; and each of these reporters now has a second series. This is called the National Reporter System.

• Federal cases are reported in a similar manner—opinions of the Courts of Appeal in the Federal Reporter (Fed.); of the United States Supreme Court in three sets, the United States Reports (U.S.), the Supreme Court Reporter (S.Ct.), and the Lawyer's Edition Supreme Court Reporter (L.Ed.). Thus, the 1954 United States Supreme Court case of *Brown* v. *Board of Education*, holding that the "separate but equal" doctrine in public education violated the equal protection clause of the fourteenth amendment, is cited as 347 U.S. 483, 74 S.Ct. 686, 98 L.Ed. 873; and the 1966 case of *Miranda* v. *State of Arizona*, requiring advice of right to counsel, is cited as 384 U.S. 436, 86 S.Ct. 1602, 16 L.Ed.2d 694.

Law

A wide variety of textbooks and textbook series cover the law according to subject matter, i.e., Agency, Contracts, Negotiable Instruments, Sales. "American Jurisprudence" states general law in all fields of law. It has a local counterpart in many states, e.g., "California Jurisprudence," devoted to the law of California. "Corpus Juris" and "Corpus Juris Secundum," like American Jurisprudence, is a complete coverage of general law. The "Hornbook Series" has a volume by a leading authority in each of the major fields of law, e.g., Calamari and Perillo on Contracts, Prosser on Torts and Burby on Real Property. Williston on Contracts and Corbin on Contracts are classics in that field. Witkin's "Summary of California Law" is a standard reference work on California law. Black's and Bouvier's are the standard law dictionaries. All of these may be found in law libraries.

Nature of Legal Proceedings

In general, legal proceedings are criminal or civil. The former are designed to protect the citizens of a state as a whole, the latter to permit an individual to recover for individual damages suffered by the individual as a result of wrongful conduct of another. The same act may be both a tort or civil wrong, and a crime. D sets fire to P's house. Criminally, this constitutes the felony of arson for which the state in which the crime was committed may bring criminal proceedings. These would be entitled "People of the State of California v. D." They would be designed to protect the security of the citizens of the state and would not be designed to obtain compensation for P. To obtain compensation, P would have to bring a civil action, "P, Plaintiff v. D, Defendant."

Steps in Civil Actions

Major steps in a civil action would be as follows:

Complaint and Summons: A civil action is commenced by the filing of a Complaint with the clerk of the court, who would be the county clerk if the action is a superior court action. The complaint sets forth the "cause of action" i.e., the facts giving rise to the right to sue.

When the complaint is filed, the clerk issues a summons to the plaintiff's attorney who will have a process server serve the summons and a copy of the complaint on the defendant. This will inform the defendant that he is being sued, and why, and the summons will require him to "Answer" within 30 days or suffer judgment by default.

In 1979 the California Legislature undertook to accomplish a much- and long-needed reform by directing the state's Judicial Council to develop printed forms of basic pleadings for the basic causes of action which comprise the civil action agenda, i.e., for causes of action for personal injury, property damage, wrongful death, unlawful detainer, breach of contract and fraud. C.C.P. 425.12. (Form pleadings for dissolution of marriage proceedings have existed for some time and form pleadings exist for probate proceedings.) By 1982 the Judicial Council had established such pleadings. The use of the forms is optional until January 1, 1985, and mandatory thereafter. The complaint forms for breach of contract and for personal injury, property damage and wrongful death (motor vehicle) are shown on pages which follow.

Attachment and Garnishment: Attachment and garnishment are the legal procedures by which property of the defendant is in effect confiscated at the beginning of a lawsuit, to be held by the sheriff pending the outcome of the suit. *Attachment* takes property of the defendant in the possession of the defendant; *garnishment* takes property of the defendant in the possession of a third person, such as the defendant's bank account and wages due the defendant from his employer. Attachment and garnishment are accomplished by a *writ of attachment* obtained from the court clerk after notice and hearing as set forth below. The writ is delivered to the sheriff with instructions to attach or garnish specific property of the defendant, which the sheriff then does. Attachment and garnishment are designed to protect the plaintiff against the dissipation, transfer or concealment of assets while the litigation is pending.

Under earlier law, attachment and garnishment were permitted quite freely and were permitted to be made without prior notice to defendant. Defendant woke up one morning to find that his wages had been "attached" (actually garnished) since attachment was permitted at the time of filing suit and without prior notice to defendant. Beginning in the late 1960's, the courts, including the United States Supreme Court, began to crack down on harshly-operating summary procedures, including attachment. ("Attachment" includes garnishment from here on.) The courts had two thoughts: one, that attachment should not be possible without a hearing, attended by the defendant-debtor, at which consideration was given to the probable validity of the plaintiff-creditor's claim; and, two, that attachment of necessities of life should not be permitted because of the hardships to the defendant-debtor when he is deprived of the use of such necessities.

California set about rewriting its attachment law in such a way as to cause it to conform to these judicial sentiments. The outcome was a new attachment law (C.C.P. 481.010-492.090) which became operative July 1, 1977. These are the principal features of the new law:

Attachment is permitted at all only when the suit is upon an unsecured contract claim in a principal amount of not less than $500 and is a claim against a business organization or is a claim which arises out of the conduct by the individual of a trade, business or profession. C.C.P. 483.010. Attachment may not be issued on a claim against an individual which is based on the sale or lease of property, the furnishing of services, or the loan of money where the property sold or leased, the services furnished or the money loaned was used by the individual primarily for personal, family or household purposes. C.C.P. 483.010. These requirements confine attachment to claims against persons or organizations engaged in commercial activities and to the recovery of business debts and thus indirectly exempt the necessities of life. Necessities of life are more directly exempted by C.C.P. 487.010 which, in effect, confines attachment to business assets of the defendant-debtor.

A hearing, of which defendant-debtor must be given notice and at which defendant-debtor must be given opportunity to be heard, must be had before a writ of attachment may issue. C.C.P. 484.330, 484.370. Pending the hearing, defendant-debtor may file a claim of exemption for the property sought to be attached. C.C.P. 484.070. Every state exempts from attachment, and execution, certain forms of property, principally in the nature of necessities of life.[4] Under the old Cali-

---

[4]C.C.P. 704.010-704.200 make exempt from attachment and execution various kinds of personal property, principally in the way of necessities of life. The following are included:

§ 704.010 exempts motor vehicle equities aggregating $1,200.

§ 704.020 exempts household furnishings, appliances, provisions, wearing apparel and other personal effects if ordinarily and reasonably necessary to, and personally used or procured for use by, the debtor and members of the debtor's family at the debtor's

fornia attachment law, the plaintiff could attach these forms of property and require the defendant to file a claim of exemption to get them back. Under the new law, there can be no attachment until the hearing has determined, among other things, that the property sought to be attached is not exempt property. C.C.P. 484.090. At the hearing, the court must find, before it can permit attachment, that the claim is of the kind that permits attachment (unsecured contract claim for

---

principal place of residence.

§ 704.040 exempts jewelry, heirlooms, and works of art to the extent of an aggregate equity of $2,500.

§ 704.050 exempts health aids and prosthetic and orthopedic appliances.

§ 704.060 exempts tools and equipment of a trade, business or profession by which the debtor earns his or her livelihood to the extent of an aggregate equity of $2,500. A similar $2,500 exemption is made for tools and equipment by which a debtor's spouse earns a livelihood. The exemption is $5,000 if both spouses are engaged in the same trade, business or profession.

§ 704.080 exempts Social Security direct deposits to the extent of $500 for one spouse, $750 for two.

§ 704.100 exempts $4,000 of loan value of insurance policies for an unmarried person; $8,000 of such loan value for a married couple.

§ 704.110 exempts public retirement benefits.

§ 704.115 exempts private retirement plan benefits.

§ 704.130 exempts disability and health insurance benefits.

§ 704.140 exempts personal injury causes of action and personal injury damages or settlements to the extent necessary for the support of the debtor and his or her spouse and dependents.

§ 704.160 exempt workers' compensation claims and awards.

Generally speaking, an exemption must be claimed by filing a claim of exemption on the property within 10 days after notice of levy of execution on the property, and the exemption is lost by failure to do this. C.C.P. 703.520.

Earnings exemption seems to be drawn in an unnecessarily complicated and circuitous manner. C.C.P. 704.070 exempts 75% of earnings during the 30 day period preceding a levy of execution on earnings where the earnings have not already been garnished or subjected to a support order. C.C.P. 706.050 and 706.052(c) confer the protection of the federal Consumer Credit Protection Act noted on the next page. C.C.P. 706.051 would exempt the entirety of the debtor's earnings if necessary for the support of the debtor or his or her family except that the exemption does not apply if the debt is for common necessaries of life, for personal services rendered by an employee of the debtor, for support of spouse or children or for a state tax liability.

Homestead exemption. California allows a dwelling ("homestead") to be protected against execution in two ways: By "*declared homestead*," as provided for in C.C.P. 704.910-704.990 and illustrated on page 19, which acts before judgment is obtained, and by claiming a "*homestead exemption*" as provided for in C.C.P. 704.710-704.850, which acts after judgment is obtained. The declared homestead may have an advantage in protecting the property against clouds on title created by recorded judgment liens. In both cases the exemption is $45,000 if the debtor or spouse is 65 years of age or older or is a member of a "family unit" (debtor and spouse or, per C.C.P. 704.710, debtor and almost any kind of relative who might be living with the debtor); in other cases the exemption is $30,000. If the property is worth more than the homestead exemption, the creditor can have it sold but the debtor must be paid the amount of the homestead exemption out of the proceeds of sale and these funds are then exempt for 6 months. C.C.P. 704.720. The "homestead exemption" may be claimed in condominiums and the like and in mobilehome and boat dwellings as well as in conventional dwellings.

$500 or more); that plaintiff has established the probable validity of the claim for which the attachment is sought; and that the property sought to be attached is not exempt property. C.C.P. 484.090. C.C.P. 487.020 expands the concept of exempt property for the purposes of this matter by providing that "property . . . exempt from attachment" includes "(p)roperty which is necessary for the support of a defendant who is a natural person or the family of such defendant" and "'(e)arnings' as defined by Section 706.011," which defines "earnings" as "compensation payable by an employer to an employee, whether denominated as wages, salary, commission, bonus, or otherwise."

One exception is made to the requirement of a noticed hearing. Attachment can issue without a hearing where plaintiff can show by affidavit that "great or irreparable injury would result to the plaintiff if issuance of the order (or right to attachment) were delayed until the matter could be heard on notice" (C.C.P. 485.010), e.g., where plaintiff can show that there is a danger that the property sought to be attached will become concealed or will become substantially impaired in value if attachment cannot be had without a noticed hearing. C.C.P. 485.010.

Answer: Defendant will file an answer if he has a "defense" to the action, such as fraud. If an answer is filed, the case will be set on the trial calendar and will eventually come to trial.

Judgment: If Defendant does not file an answer, judgment by default may be taken by Plaintiff when the time to answer has expired. If an answer is filed, the case goes to trial, and the court enters judgment at the conclusion of trial.

Execution: Assume judgment for Plaintiff. A judgment is not self-executing. A *writ of execution* is the legal process for enforcing a judgment. A writ of execution directs the sheriff to levy execution on property of the defendant for the purpose of satisfying the judgment against the defendant. The plaintiff must be able to supply the identity of such property however and will not be able to enforce the judgment by execution until he can do so. The order of examination, next considered, may enable the plaintiff to discover the identity of property of the defendant.

Title III of the federal Consumer Credit Protection Act of 1968[5] restricts postjudgment levy of execution on wages of the defendant to certain limited amounts—basically 25% of "disposable earnings." These restrictions were made applicable nationwide.

Order of Examination: If Plaintiff's attorney is unable to discover property of Defendant, he may obtain an *order of examination.* This requires Defendant to appear in court and answer concerning his assets. (Do you have a bank account; when and where did you last have one; do you have a safe deposit box; do you have any stocks, bonds, notes, etc; where do you work; how much are you paid; etc.?) If this reveals anything, it is executed upon.

Renewal of Judgment: If Plaintiff's attorney is unable to effect execution, the judgment will lie dormant until Defendant acquires property. Unless renewed, a judgment expires after some period of time—10 years in California.[6] An indefinite number of renewals is usually permitted. In California, judgments may be renewed for additional periods of 10 years.[7]

---

[5] 15 U.S.C. §§ 1671-1677.

[6] C.C.P. 683.020 bars enforcement of a judgment after 10 years unless it is renewed.

[7] C.C.P. 683.120.

ATTORNEY OR PARTY WITHOUT ATTORNEY (NAME AND ADDRESS):	TELEPHONE:	FOR COURT USE ONLY
RANDALL, TAYLOR & JAMES 100 City Square San Francisco, CA 94903	621-5410	

ATTORNEY FOR (NAME): Plaintiff

Insert name of court, judicial district or branch court, if any, and post office and street address:

SUPERIOR COURT OF CALIFORNIA
COUNTY OF SAN FRANCISCO
CITY HALL, SAN FRANCISCO, CALIFORNIA

PLAINTIFF:

PAUL PLAINTIFF

DEFENDANT:

DANIEL DEFENDANT

☐ DOES 1 TO _____

CONTRACT [X] COMPLAINT ☐ CROSS-COMPLAINT	CASE NUMBER: 0001234

1. This pleading, including attachments and exhibits, consists of the following number of pages: ___12___

2. a. Each plaintiff named above is a competent adult
   ☐ **Except** plaintiff (name):   No exceptions.

   ☐ a corporation qualified to do business in California
   ☐ an unincorporated entity (describe):
   ☐ other (specify):

   b. ☐ Plaintiff (name):
      ☐ has complied with the fictitious business name laws and is doing business under the fictitious name
         of (specify):
      ☐ has complied with all licensing requirements as a licensed (specify):

   c. ☐ Information about additional plaintiffs who are not competent adults is shown in Complaint—Attachment 2c.

3. a. Each defendant named above is a natural person
   ☐ **Except** defendant (name):   No exceptions   ☐ **Except** defendant (name):   No exceptions.

   ☐ a business organization, form unknown   ☐ a business organization, form unknown
   ☐ a corporation   ☐ a corporation
   ☐ an unincorporated entity (describe):   ☐ an unincorporated entity (describe):

   ☐ a public entity (describe):   ☐ a public entity (describe):

   ☐ other (specify):   ☐ other (specify):

   b. The true names and capacities of defendants sued as Does are unknown to plaintiff.
   c. ☐ Information about additional defendants who are not natural persons is contained in Complaint—
        Attachment 3c.
   d. ☐ Defendants who are joined pursuant to Code of Civil Procedure section 382 are (names): None.

(Continued)

If this form is used as a cross-complaint, plaintiff means cross-complainant and defendant means cross-defendant.

Form Approved by the
Judicial Council of California
Effective January 1, 1982
Rule 982.1(20)

COMPLAINT—Contract

CCP 425.12

(Form continued on following page)

SHORT TITLE: PLAINTIFF v. DEFENDANT	CASE NUMBER: 0001234

COMPLAINT—Contract

Page two

4. ☐ Plaintiff is required to comply with a claims statute, **and**
   a. ☐ plaintiff has complied with applicable claims statutes, **or**
   b. ☐ plaintiff is excused from complying because *(specify):*

5. ☐ This action is subject to ☐ Civil Code section 1812.10 ☐ Civil Code section 2984.4.

6. This action is filed in this ☒ county ☐ judicial district because
   a. ☒ a defendant entered into the contract here.
   b. ☒ a defendant lived here when the contract was entered into.
   c. ☒ a defendant lives here now.
   d. ☒ the contract was to be performed here.
   e. ☐ a defendant is a corporation or unincorporated association and its principal place of business is here.
   f. ☐ real property that is the subject of this action is located here.
   g. ☐ other *(specify):*

7. ☐ The following paragraphs of this pleading are alleged on information and belief *(specify paragraph numbers):*
                                                                                    None.

8. ☐ Other: None.

9. The following causes of action are attached and the statements above apply to each: *(Each complaint must have one or more causes of action attached.)*
   ☒ Breach of Contract   ☐ Common Counts
   ☐ Other *(specify):*

10. PLAINTIFF PRAYS
    For judgment for costs of suit; for such relief as is fair, just, and equitable; and for
    ☒ damages of $ 100,000.00
    ☒ interest on the damages ☒ according to proof ☐ at the rate of _____ percent per year
    from *(date):*
    ☒ attorney fees ☐ of $_____ ☒ according to proof.
    ☐ other *(specify):*

PAUL PLAINTIFF   s/ PAUL PLAINTIFF
(Type or print name)   (Signature of plaintiff or attorney)

(If you wish to verify this pleading, affix a verification.)

Page two

NAME AND ADDRESS OF ATTORNEY:	TELEPHONE NO: 621-5410	FOR COURT USE ONLY:
RANDALL, TAYLOR & JAMES 100 City Square San Francisco, CA 94903 ATTORNEY FOR (Name): Plaintiff		

Insert name of court, judicial district or branch court, if any, and Post Office and Street Address:

SUPERIOR COURT OF CALIFORNIA
COUNTY OF SAN FRANCISCO
CITY HALL, SAN FRANCISCO, CALIFORNIA

PLAINTIFF:

PAUL PLAINTIFF

DEFENDANT:

DANIEL DEFENDANT

# SUMMONS	CASE NUMBER: 0001234

NOTICE! You have been sued. The court may decide against you without your being heard unless you respond within 30 days. Read the information below.	**¡AVISO! Usted ha sido demandado. El tribunal puede decidir contra Ud. sin audiencia a menos que Ud. responda dentro de 30 días. Lea la información que sigue.**
If you wish to seek the advice of an attorney in this matter, you should do so promptly so that your written response, if any, may be filed on time.	Si Usted desea solicitar el consejo de un abogado en este asunto, debería hacerlo inmediatamente, de esta manera, su respuesta escrita, si hay alguna, puede ser registrada a tiempo.

1. TO THE DEFENDANT: A civil complaint has been filed by the plaintiff against you. If you wish to defend this lawsuit, you must, within **30** days after this summons is served on you, file with this court a written response to the complaint. Unless you do so, your default will be entered on application of the plaintiff, and this court may enter a judgment against you for the relief demanded in the complaint, which could result in garnishment of wages, taking of money or property or other relief requested in the complaint.

DATED: May 1, 1984 . . . ., Clerk, By ____ s/ JOHN AIDE ____, Deputy

(SEAL)

2. NOTICE TO THE PERSON SERVED: You are served
   a. [X] As an individual defendant.
   b. [ ] As the person sued under the fictitious name of: . . . .
   c. [ ] On behalf of: . . . .

   Under: [ ] CCP 416.10 (Corporation)   [ ] CCP 416.60 (Minor)
            [ ] CCP 416.20 (Defunct Corporation)   [ ] CCP 416.70 (Incompetent)
            [ ] CCP 416.40 (Association or Partnership)   [ ] CCP 416.90 (Individual)
            [ ] Other:
   d. [X] By personal delivery on (Date): May 2, 1984

A written response must be in the form prescribed by the California Rules of Court. It must be filed in this court with the proper filing fee and proof of service of a copy on each plaintiff's attorney and on each plaintiff not represented by an attorney. The time when a summons is deemed served on a party may vary depending on the method of service. For example, see CCP 413.10 through 415.50. The word "complaint" includes cross-complaint, "plaintiff" includes cross-complainant, "defendant" includes cross-defendant, the singular includes the plural.

Form Adopted by Rule 982
Judicial Council of California
Revised Effective January 1, 1979

(See reverse for Proof of Service)

SUMMONS

CCP 412.20, 412.30, 415.10.

(Form continued on following page)

PROOF OF SERVICE

(Use separate proof of service for each person served)

1. I served the
   a. [X] summons [X] complaint [ ] amended summons [ ] amended complaint

   b. On defendant (Name): DANIEL DEFENDANT

   c. By serving (1) [X] Defendant (2) [ ] Other (Name and title or relationship to person served):

   d. [X] By delivery at [X] home [ ] business (1) Date of: May 2, 1984
      (2) Time of: 7:30 p.m. (3) Address: 149 Wildwood Drive
      San Francisco, California

   e. [ ] By mailing (1) Date of: (2) Place of:

2. Manner of service: (Check proper box)
   a. [X] **Personal service.** By personally delivering copies. (CCP 415.10)
   b. [ ] **Substituted service on corporation, unincorporated association (including partnership), or public entity.** By leaving, during usual office hours, copies in the office of the person served with the person who apparently was in charge and thereafter mailing (by first-class mail, postage prepaid) copies to the person served at the place where the copies were left. (CCP 415.20(a))
   c. [ ] **Substituted service on natural person, minor, incompetent, or candidate.** By leaving copies at the dwelling house, usual place of abode, or usual place of business of the person served in the presence of a competent member of the household or a person apparently in charge of the office or place of business, at least 18 years of age, who was informed of the general nature of the papers, and thereafter mailing (by first-class mail, postage prepaid) copies to the person served at the place where the copies were left. (CCP 415.20(b)) **(Attach separate declaration or affidavit stating acts relied on to establish reasonable diligence in first attempting personal service.)**
   d. [ ] **Mail and acknowledgment service.** By mailing (by first-class mail or airmail) copies to the person served, together with two copies of the form of notice and acknowledgment and a return envelope, postage prepaid, addressed to the sender. (CCP 415.30) **(Attach completed acknowledgment of receipt.)**
   e. [ ] **Certified or registered mail service.** By mailing to address outside California (by registered or certified airmail with return receipt requested) copies to the person served. (CCP 415.40) **(Attach signed return receipt or other evidence of actual delivery to the person served.)**
   f. [ ] Other (Specify code section):
      [ ] Additional page is attached.

3. The notice to the person served (Item 2 on the copy of the summons served) was completed as follows (CCP 412.30, 415.10, and 474):
   a. [X] As an individual defendant.
   b. [ ] As the person sued under the fictitious name of:
   c. [ ] On behalf of:
      Under: [ ] CCP 416.10 (Corporation)   [ ] CCP 416.60 (Minor)   [ ] Other:
      [ ] CCP 416.20 (Defunct corporation)   [ ] CCP 416.70 (Incompetent)
      [ ] CCP 416.40 (Association or partnership)   [ ] CCP 416.90 (Individual)
   d. [X] By personal delivery on (Date): May 2, 1984

4. At the time of service I was at least 18 years of age and not a party to this action.

5. Fee for service: $ 10.00

6. Person serving   Sam Server
   a. [ ] Not a registered California process server.
   b. [X] Registered California process server.
   c. [ ] Employee or independent contractor of a registered California process server.
   d. [ ] Exempt from registration under Bus. & Prof. Code 22350(b)

   e. [ ] California sheriff, marshal, or constable.
   f. Name, address and telephone number and if applicable, county of registration and number:
   Sam Server
   1501 Charles St., San Francisco, CA 94105
   Tel: 777-2321
   San Francisco County No. 00415

I declare under penalty of perjury that the foregoing is true and correct and that this declaration is executed on (Date): May 3, 1984 at (Place): San Francisco, California.

(For California sheriff, marshal or constable use only)
I certify that the foregoing is true and correct and that this certificate is executed on (Date): at (Place): , California.

s/ SAM SERVER
(Signature)

(Signature)

A declaration under penalty of perjury must be signed in California or in a state that authorizes use of a declaration in place of an affidavit; otherwise an affidavit is required.

SHORT TITLE:	CASE NUMBER:
PLAINTIFF v. DEFENDANT	0001234

_____FIRST_____ **CAUSE OF ACTION**— Breach of Contract   Page ___1___
  (number)

ATTACHMENT TO [X] Complaint   ☐ Cross-Complaint

(Use a separate cause of action form for each cause of action.)

BC-1. Plaintiff *(name):*

alleges that on or about *(date):*   January 3, 1984,
a [X] written ☐ oral ☐ other *(specify):*
agreement was made between *(name parties to agreement):*   Paul Plaintiff and
                                                               Daniel Defendant.
[X] A copy of the agreement is attached as Exhibit A, **or**
☐ The essential terms of the agreement ☐ are stated in Attachment BC-1 ☐ are as follows *(specify):*

BC-2. On or about *(dates):*   March 1, 1984,
defendant breached the agreement by [X] the acts specified in Attachment BC-2 ☐ the following acts
(specify):

BC-3. Plaintiff has performed all obligations to defendant except those obligations plaintiff was prevented or
excused from performing.

BC-4. Plaintiff suffered damages legally (proximately) **caused by defendant's breach of the agreement**
[X] as stated in Attachment BC-4 ☐ as follows *(specify):*

BC-5. [X] Plaintiff is entitled to attorney fees by an agreement or a statute
       ☐ of $
       [X] according to proof.

BC-6. ☐ Other: None.

ATTORNEY OR PARTY WITHOUT ATTORNEY (NAME AND ADDRESS):	TELEPHONE:	FOR COURT USE ONLY
RANDALL, TAYLOR & JAMES 100 City Square San Francisco, CA 94903	621-5410	

ATTORNEY FOR (NAME): Plaintiff

Insert name of court, judicial district or branch court, if any, and post office and street address:

SUPERIOR COURT OF CALIFORNIA
COUNTY OF SAN FRANCISCO
CITY HALL, SAN FRANCISCO, CALIFORNIA

PLAINTIFF:

PATRICIA PLAINTIFF

DEFENDANT:

DOROTHY DEFENDANT and

[X] DOES 1 TO _5_

COMPLAINT—Personal Injury, Property Damage, Wrongful Death

CASE NUMBER:

0001235

[X] **MOTOR VEHICLE**   [ ] OTHER (specify):
  [X] **Property Damage**   [ ] Wrongful Death
  [X] **Personal Injury**   [ ] Other Damages (specify):

1. This pleading, including attachments and exhibits, consists of the following number of pages: _5_

2. a. Each plaintiff named above is a competent adult
    [ ] **Except** plaintiff (name): No exceptions.
      [ ] a corporation qualified to do business in California
      [ ] an unincorporated entity (describe):
      [ ] a public entity (describe):
      [ ] a minor   [ ] an adult
        [ ] for whom a guardian or conservator of the estate or a guardian ad litem has been appointed
        [ ] other (specify):
      [ ] other (specify):

    [ ] **Except** plaintiff (name): No exceptions.
      [ ] a corporation qualified to do business in California
      [ ] an unincorporated entity (describe):
      [ ] a public entity (describe):
      [ ] a minor   [ ] an adult
        [ ] for whom a guardian or conservator of the estate or a guardian ad litem has been appointed
        [ ] other (specify):
      [ ] other (specify):

  b. [ ] Plaintiff (name):
    is doing business under the fictitious name of (specify):

    and has complied with the fictitious business name laws.
  c. [ ] Information about additional plaintiffs who are not competent adults is shown in Complaint—
    Attachment 2c.   (Continued)

Form Approved by the
Judicial Council of California
Effective January 1, 1982
Rule 982.1(1)

COMPLAINT—Personal Injury, Property Damage,
Wrongful Death

CCP 425.12

(Form continued on following pages)

SHORT TITLE:	CASE NUMBER
PLAINTIFF v. DEFENDANT	0001235

COMPLAINT—Personal Injury, Property Damage, Wrongful Death   Page two

3. a. Each defendant named above is a natural person
   [X] **Except** defendant *(name):* DOE 1   [X] **Except** defendant *(name):* DOE 2

   [ ] a business organization, form unknown   [X] a business organization, form unknown
   [X] a corporation   [ ] a corporation
   [ ] an unincorporated entity *(describe):*   [ ] an unincorporated entity *(describe):*

   [ ] a public entity *(describe):*   [ ] a public entity *(describe):*

   [ ] other *(specify):*   [ ] other *(specify).*

   [ ] **Except** defendant *(name):*   [ ] **Except** defendant *(name)*

   [ ] a business organization, form unknown   [ ] a business organization, form unknown
   [ ] a corporation   [ ] a corporation
   [ ] an unincorporated entity *(describe):*   [ ] an unincorporated entity *(describe):*

   [ ] a public entity *(describe):*   [ ] a public entity *(describe):*

   [ ] other *(specify):*   [ ] other *(specify):*

   b. The true names and capacities of defendants sued as Does are unknown to plaintiff.

   c. [X] Information about additional defendants who are not natural persons is contained in Complaint—
      Attachment 3c.
   d. [ ] Defendants who are joined pursuant to Code of Civil Procedure section 382 are *(names):* None.

4. [ ] Plaintiff is required to comply with a claims statute, **and**
   a. [ ] plaintiff has complied with applicable claims statutes, **or**
   b. [ ] plaintiff is excused from complying because *(specify):*

5. This court is the proper court because
   [X] at least one defendant now resides in its jurisdictional area.
   [X] the principal place of business of a corporation or unincorporated association is in its jurisdictional area.
   [X] injury to person or damage to personal property occurred in its jurisdictional area.
   [ ] other *(specify):*

6. [X] The following paragraphs of this complaint are alleged on information and belief *(specify paragraph numbers):*

   1-4.

                              (Continued)   Page two

(Form continued on following page)

SHORT TITLE:	CASE NUMBER:
PLAINTIFF v. DEFENDANT	0001235

COMPLAINT—Personal Injury, Property Damage, Wrongful Death (Continued)   Page three

7. ☐ The damages claimed for wrongful death and the relationships of plaintiff to the deceased are
☐ listed in Complaint—Attachment 7 ☐ as follows: Not applicable.

8. Plaintiff has suffered
   ☒ wage loss   ☒ loss of use of property
   ☒ hospital and medical expenses   ☒ general damage
   ☒ property damage   ☒ loss of earning capacity
   ☒ other damage (specify):

   Physical pain and suffering and
   mental and emotional distress.

9. Relief sought in this complaint is within the jurisdiction of this court.

10. PLAINTIFF PRAYS
    For judgment for costs of suit; for such relief as is fair, just, and equitable; and for
    ☒ compensatory damages
        ☒ (Superior Court) according to proof.

        ☐ (Municipal and Justice Court) in the amount of $_____
    ☒ other (specify):

        Exemplary damages.

11. The following causes of action are attached and the statements above apply to each: (Each complaint must have
    one or more causes of action attached.)
    ☒ Motor Vehicle
    ☐ General Negligence
    ☐ Intentional Tort
    ☐ Products Liability
    ☐ Premises Liability
    ☐ Other (specify):

PATRICIA PLAINTIFF   s/ PATRICIA PLAINTIFF
(Type or print name)   (Signature of plaintiff or attorney)

SHORT TITLE:	CASE NUMBER:
PLAINTIFF v. DEFENDANT	0001235

<u>   FIRST   </u>   **CAUSE OF ACTION**—Motor Vehicle   Page <u>   1   </u>
(number)

ATTACHMENT TO [x] Complaint [ ] Cross-Complaint

(Use a separate cause of action form for each cause of action.)

Plaintiff *(name)*:   PATRICIA PLAINTIFF

MV-1. Plaintiff alleges the acts of defendants were negligent; the acts were the legal (proximate) cause of injuries and damages to plaintiff; the acts occurred
on *(date)*:   February 6, 1984,
at *(place)*:   San Francisco, California

MV-2. DEFENDANTS
    a. [x] The defendants who operated a motor vehicle are *(names)*:   DOROTHY DEFENDANT

        [ ] Does _____ to _____
    b. [x] The defendants who employed the persons who operated a motor vehicle in the course of their employment are *(names)*:

        [x] Does __1__ to __2__
    c. [x] The defendants who owned the motor vehicle which was operated with their permission are *(names)*:

        [x] Does __1__ to __2__
    d. [x] The defendants who entrusted the motor vehicle are *(names)*:

        [x] Does __1__ to __2__
    e. [x] The defendants who were the agents and employees of the other defendants and acted within the scope of the agency were *(names)*:

        [x] Does __3__ to __5__
    f. [ ] The defendants who are liable to plaintiffs for other reasons and the reasons for the liability are
        [ ] listed in Attachment MV-2f [ ] as follows:
                    None

        [ ] Does _____ to _____

Form Approved by the
Judicial Council of California
Effective January 1, 1982
Rule 982.1(2)   **CAUSE OF ACTION**—Motor Vehicle   CCP 425.12

HOMESTEAD DECLARATION

(SPOUSES AS DECLARED OWNERS)

———— ◄► ————

We, _____ JOHN J. SPOUSE _____ and _____ MARY E. SPOUSE _____,
             (Full Name of Declarant)   (Full Name of Declarant)

do hereby certify and declare as follows:

(1) We are married to each other.

(2) We hereby claim as a homestead, and make ourselves declared homestead owners of, the premises located in the City of

_____ Berkeley _____, County of _____ Alameda _____, State of California,

commonly known as ___ 501 Aspen Street, Berkeley, California 94543, _____
_____,
                                                (Street Address)

and more particularly described as follows: [Give complete legal description]

> Lot 49 in Block 14, as designated on the Map entitled "Tract No. 36
> Berkeley Heights Map No. 6, Alameda County, California," which Map
> was filed in the office of the Recorder of the County of Alameda,
> State of California, on July 24, 1922, in Book 31 of Maps, at p. 40.

(3) I, ___ John J. Spouse _____,
                                  (Name of First Spouse)

own the following interest in the above declared homestead:
> An undivided one-half (1/2) interest
> in said real property as community property.

(4) I, ___ Mary E. Spouse _____,
                                  (Name of Second Spouse)

own the following interest in the above declared homestead:
> An undivided one-half (1/2) interest
> in said real property as community property.

(5) The above declared homestead is the principal dwelling of __ John J. Spouse and Mary E. Spouse __,
                                                (Name of one or both spouses, whichever is applicable)

and ___ we ___ currently reside(s) in that declared homestead.
    (he, she, or we)

(6) The facts stated in this Declaration are true as of our personal knowledge.

                                    s/ JOHN J. SPOUSE _____
                                           (Signature of Declarant)

                                    s/ MARY E. SPOUSE _____
                                           (Signature of Declarant)

STATE OF CALIFORNIA   } ss.

COUNTY OF ___ Alameda _____

On this ___ first ___ day of ___ February ___, in the year 19 84,
before me, the undersigned, a Notary Public in and for said State, personally appeared
___ JOHN J. SPOUSE and MARY E. SPOUSE ___
_____
_____, personally known to me
(or proved to me on the basis of satisfactory evidence) to be the persons whose names
are subscribed to the within instrument, and acknowledged to me that they executed it.

WITNESS my hand and official seal.

                  s/ NANCY NOTARY _____   (SEAL)
                       Notary Public in and for said State.

WOLCOTTS FORM 752—HOMESTEAD DECLARATION (Spouses As Declared Owners)—Rev. 12-83
(price class 3)   © 1983 WOLCOTTS, INC.

CHAPTER 2

Contracts

Introduction

Contracting is the process by which one person places himself under legal obligation to do something for another person. A set of rules developed around this process. M, 12 years old, makes a contract. May he be held to it? A, B and C, who control the country's entire supply of steel, make a contract to maintain prices substantially above those for which they would sell in competition so that each will sell as much steel as before at greater profit. Is the public to be protected against such a contract? S contracts to deliver goods of a certain kind and quality to B. Part of the goods are not according to contract specifications. What is B's position? Rules had to be formulated for these and many other situations. The sum total of these rules is the "law of contracts," with which we are concerned in this chapter.[1]

● Specialization is a natural development in any phase of human activity. Out of medicine has developed neurology, dermatology, toxology, gynecology, cardiography, etc. Out of accounting has developed auditing, controllership, tax accounting, etc. In each case the particular, although having its own set of rules, remains governed by the basic principles of the general field out of which it arose. So it was with contracts. Contracting falls into categories—agency or employment, sales, commercial paper, insurance, suretyship, and so on. The inevitable mitosis occurred. From the main cell of contracts developed the specialized sub-cells of agency, sales, negotiable instruments, etc., with a special body of law growing about each, but with each continuing to be governed by the basic principles of contract law.

● Business law is the study of the fields of law which establish and regulate business transactions and business relationships. These are primarily the law of contracts and its specialized branches. Like the football team, we must first learn fundamentals, Contracts; then go on to more specialized areas.

● Historically, contracting is as old as law. It was seen in Chapter 1 that the Romans had not only contracts generally but many of the specialized kinds of contracts. Through the centuries contracts have undergone a deformalizing process. In the Roman era a contract was like a marriage ceremony. Parties had to go through an elaborate process of play-acting in the presence of witnesses, during which formal promises had to be exchanged ("Do you promise?" and "I promise."). So important was form that a mute person could not make a contract because he could not speak the words of promise. At common law, formality was reduced to the requirement that each party to a contract affix his seal—a waxen wafer impressed with his coat of arms or signet ring; and this had a foundation in practicality. Many persons could not sign their names, and seals insured the genuiness of contracts. Slade's Case in 1603 is generally fixed as the date after which "informal contracts" (without seals) became enforceable. In more recent times, the deformalizing process has been within

contracts, the elimination of superfluous "Whereases" and "Wherefores," and a general streamlining of legal instruments.

● The most dynamic area of contract law today is that in which courts are trying to give people *freedom from contract,* that is to say, in which courts are trying to save people who have no real bargaining power from oppressive contracts which more powerful persons can force on them. These, incidentally, are called *contracts of adhesion* about which we shall see considerably more. The nineteenth century produced a strong doctrine of *freedom of contract* under which a contract became binding if agreed to regardless of the disparity of bargaining power between the parties. Landlords could make tenants accept hard terms. Stores could make customers buying on credit accept hard terms. Today we no longer accept such a point of view. In more and more quarters and in more and more ways the law is coming to protect the little person. We shall see this.

Nature and Essential Elements

There are many definitions of contract, none of which is entirely satisfactory. C.C. 1549 defines a contract as "an agreement to do or not to do a certain thing," but so is an agreement or promise of one person to go to another's house on Saturday night for dinner or to go with him to a basketball game. We know that these are not *contracts* in the legal sense; in the sense of an agreement which imposes a binding obligation.

The definition in *H. Liebes* v. *Klengenberg,* 23 Fed.2d 611, is somewhat better—"an agreement which creates an obligation." But if you do satisfactory work for me on one occasion, and I say: "If I ever have work of this kind done again, I will call you," have I made an agreement which creates an obligation? If I have future work done by someone else, may you sue me for breach of contract? Inherently you know that you cannot; that, contractwise, something is still missing; that a contract should exist only when each party is committed to something. In contract law, this is the requirement of "consideration," which must be satisfied before a contract is formed. Consideration being essential, Blackstone's very old definition of a contract as "an agreement upon sufficient consideration to do or not to do a particular thing," remains one of the best.

Nothing yet discussed takes into consideration certain essential elements of contract.[2] There must be *competent par-*

---

[2]C.C. 1550: "It is essential to the existence of a contract that there should be:

"1. Parties capable of contracting;

"2. Their consent;

"3. A lawful object, and

"4. A sufficient cause or consideration."

C.C. 1567: "An apparent consent is not real or free when obtained through:

"1. Duress;

---

[1]California general contract law is found in C.C. 1549-1701.

AGREEMENT

CONSIDERATION

TO DO OR NOT DO A PARTICULAR THING

COMPETENT PARTIES
REALITY OF ASSENT
LEGAL PURPOSE

ties—persons whom the law recognizes as having capacity to make a binding agreement—not minors or mentally incompetent persons. There must be *reality of assent*; parties must contract voluntarily and with knowledge of the true facts, and an agreement tainted with fraud or duress or entered into by mistake, is not binding. A contract must have a *legal purpose*—one which does not violate statute or public policy or good morals. The price-fixing agreement, suggested earlier, would be invalid on this account.

In addition certain important classes of contracts must be in *writing*. The law which requires this is the Statute of Frauds, discussed on page 44.

In resume it may be said that a contract is an agreement which creates an obligation to do or not to do a certain thing, formed by competent parties, for consideration, and a legal purpose, and which is free of mistake, fraud or other invalidating factor, and which is in writing when required by the Statute of Frauds.[3]

Offer

Offer and *acceptance* are the mechanics of contract making, of reaching the agreement that results in a contract. Once a contract is reduced to writing, it becomes immaterial who made the offer and who accepted. Offer and acceptance become merged in the writing, which thereafter speaks for itself. The only question which may arise is whether it speaks clearly enough on certain points.

● Offers come in many sizes, shapes and forms. They may be formal or informal. They may be written or oral. They may be made by acts unaccompanied by words. All that is required is a commitment to do something for something. Before pursuing this further let us establish certain basic tools with which to work:

1. The party who makes an offer is called the *offeror*; the one to whom it is made, the *offeree*. Only he may accept it since it is only to him that the offer is made.[4]

2. An offer is a *promise*. If I, a retailer, send you, a manufacturer, an order for a carload of furniture, my order is an offer to buy. At the same time, it is a promise to pay the current wholesale prices for the type of furniture ordered.

3. An offer may ask for either of two things: a return promise or the performance of an act. If I will need a carload of lettuce in 30 days, I will write you, a lettuce grower, offering to pay you X dollars a crate if you will promise to ship at the desired time. My offer asks a promise. You accept by promising to ship at the time stipulated. If I need a carload of lettuce presently, I will wire you: "Ship carload Imperial lettuce immediately at $5.00. Wire confirmation upon ship-

ment." Here, I ask the act of shipping. You accept by shipping.[5]

4. It follows from what has been said that an offer is a promise conditioned upon a return promise or the performance of an act.

5. Certain things which look like offers may not be. They may be mere invitations to make offers, or they may be part of preliminary negotiations by which parties attempt to induce offers.

Mere Invitations to Deal

The following is an advertisement from a newspaper:

CALIFORNIA LUMBER COMPANY
1000 Main Street

We are offering the following:

SIZE	SPECIES	8 FT.	10 FT.	12 FT.
2 × 4	Redwood S4S	1.99	2.50	3.00
2 × 6	Redwood S4S	2.56	3.20	3.84
2 × 8	Redwood S4S	5.52	6.90	8.28
4 × 4	Redwood S4S	5.99	7.50	9.00
2 × 12	Redwood S4S	7.92	9.90	11.88
1 × 4	Redwood S4S	1.60	2.00	2.40

Limited Quantities

This appears to be an offer—a commitment to sell plywood at the price stated. But it is well established that newspaper advertisements generally are only invitations to make offers—invitations to the public to make offers to purchase, which the seller accepts by selling. The same is true with respect to catalogs, price lists and the like.

An advertisement may be an offer if it clearly indicates such an intention. This is rare. The plywood ad was selected with reference to this point. It states that the advertiser is "offering" his product. Does this make it an offer rather than a mere invitation to deal? No. The mere use of the word "offer" does not make an ad an offer, and something more specific than the ad in question is required to make an ad an offer.

● The notices on the following page are types of invitations to make offers which are common.

They ask for offers in the form of "bids." Anyone who makes a bid becomes an offeror. As in the case with offers generally, the offeree—the estate's executor in the one case, the City of Oakland in the other—may accept, reject or ignore offers (bids) as it sees fit.

● Auctioneers are mere solicitors of offers, from the bidders (offerors). The offers are revocable and no sale is complete until the auctioneer signifies acceptance of a particular bid by dropping his hammer. The auctioneer, being an offeree, may reject all bids by withdrawing the goods, unless the auction is advertised or announced to be *without reserve* (as in the advertisement below), in which case the highest bid must be accepted.[6]

"2. Menace;
"3. Fraud;
"4. Undue influence; or
"5. Mistake."

[3]The Restatement of Contracts, § 1, defines a contract as a promise (unilateral contract, page 29) or set of promises (bilateral contract, page 29) which the law will enforce. The definition is continued by the Second Restatement.

[4]There may be a "general offer," i.e., one to a class of persons or to the public generally, such as a reward offer. It may be accepted by anyone who, with knowledge of its existence and intent to accept, does the thing requested, e.g., captures the criminal or gives information leading to his arrest.

[5]C.C. 1584: "Performance of the conditions of a proposal . . . is an acceptance of the proposal."

[6]U.C.C. 2328(2)(3).

Offers as Creating Express or Implied Contracts

The following are two illustrations of offers: First, the extreme in informality: You go to your regular barber for a haircut. He knows from past experience how to cut your hair so that no directions are necessary. The haircut completed, you pay and leave. Although less complicated and formed in a different manner, this is as much a contract as an agreement by a manufacturer to manufacture ten million dollars worth of equipment for the United States government. When you got into the barber chair, you impliedly offered or promised to pay the listed price if the barber would cut your hair. By so doing, he accepted your offer, and a contract was formed which resulted in a binding obligation on your part to pay. The noteworthy thing about this contract is that it has been consummated by conduct rather than words. This, and any other contract which results from *conduct*, is called an *implied* contract as distinguished from one stated in words, which is called an *express* contract.[7] Much of the small-scale contracting that goes on in everyday life is of this informal, implied type.

By contrast, a common but very formal type of offer is contained in the real estate purchase contract on page 25. Here, background is required. Real estate, like goods, is sold by contract. S has real property to sell for $500,000. He lists it with R, a real estate broker. R advertises the property and so becomes a solicitor of offers on behalf of S. B is willing to pay the $500,000 which S asks, or perhaps is willing to pay only $450,000. In either case, R will have B sign the real estate purchase contract beneath paragraph 16 that reads, "This constitutes an offer to purchase the described property. Unless acceptance is signed by Seller and the signed copy delivered to Buyer, in person or by mail to the address below, within 3 days, this offer shall be deemed revoked and the deposit shall be returned." This constitutes a formal offer to B, the essence of which is that B offers to purchase for $500,000 (or $450,000, as the case may be) provided S can give clear title as determined by a title insurance company. If S signs beneath the paragraph that begins, "The undersigned Seller accepts and agrees to sell the property on the above terms and conditions," he accepts B's offer. A binding contract is formed. From here, the transaction will go through escrow; title insurance will be issued; a deed will be executed and delivered; and the price paid. This is merely performance of the contract made by execution of the purchase contract.

Certainty of Offer

Material terms of an offer, and of the resultant contract, must be sufficiently certain to be enforceable. Courts are wont to say that they cannot make for parties the contract the parties failed to make. Thus, in *Van Slyke* v. *Broadway Insurance Company,* 115 C. 644, 47 P. 689, it was held that commissions could not be recovered where there was a contract to work for a fixed salary, plus "a contingent commission" of 5%, with no specification of the contingency. But today's courts speak of uncertainty as a "disfavored defense," and, as compared with the California court of 1895 in the *Van Slyke* case, the California court of 1958, in *Sabatini* v. *Hensley,* 161 C.A.2d, 172, 326 P.2d, 622 held that an agreement are stated in words."

C.C. 1621: "An implied contract is one, the existence and terms of which are manifested by conduct."

---

[7]C.C. 1620: "An express contract is one, the terms of which

REAL ESTATE PURCHASE CONTRACT AND RECEIPT FOR DEPOSIT
THIS IS MORE THAN A RECEIPT FOR MONEY. IT IS INTENDED TO BE A LEGALLY BINDING CONTRACT. READ IT CAREFULLY.

CALIFORNIA ASSOCIATION OF REALTORS® STANDARD FORM

_____San Francisco_____, California. _____March 2_____, 19 84

Received from _____Thomas B. Buyer and Helen A. Buyer_____

herein called Buyer, the sum of ___One Thousand and no/100 ----------------------- Dollars $1,000.00___

evidenced by cash ☐, cashier's check ☐, or _____☐, personal check ☒ payable to _____

__Acme Realty Company_____, to be held uncashed until acceptance of this offer, as deposit on account of purchase price of

__One Hundred Eighty-seven Thousand and no/100 --------------------- Dollars $187,000.00__

for the purchase of property, situated in _____The City and_____, County of _____San Francisco_____, California,

described as follows: ___Lot 4, Block 20, Twin Peaks Tract, San Francisco, California,___
                          known as 659 Monterey Avenue, San Francisco, California

1.   Buyer will deposit in escrow with ____Title Insurance Company____ the balance of purchase price as follows:
Within 30 days of acceptance hereof by seller, $18,700.00 cash (including the above
deposit) subject to $149,600.00 30-year 13% first loan, payable $1,654.89 per month,
or more, principal and interest, with loan fee not exceeding 1½%; $18,700.00 second
note and deed of trust to seller with interest at 12%; payable $187.00 or more per
month, interest payments only, interest from close of escrow and first monthly payment one month from close of escrow with entire unpaid balance of principal and
interest, then due, on or before April 30, 1989.

Buyer agrees to make diligent effort to obtain said first loan.

Structural Pest Control Agreement attached is made part of this contract; in no
event shall sellers' liability for corrective repair work under said agreement
exceed the total sum of $1,400.00.

Set forth above any terms and conditions of a factual nature applicable to this sale, such as financing, prior sale of other property, the matter of structural pest control inspection, repairs and personal property to be included in the sale.

2.   Deposit will ☐ will not ☒ be increased by $ _____ to $ _____ within _____ days of acceptance of this offer.

3.   Buyer does ☒ does not ☐ intend to occupy subject property as his residence.

4.   The supplements initialed below are incorporated as part of this agreement.

                                                                        Other

_X_ Structural Pest Control Certification Agreement   ____ Occupancy Agreement   _____ _____

____ Special Studies Zone Disclosure   ____ VA Amendment   _____ _____

____ Flood Insurance Disclosure   ____ FHA Amendment   _____ _____

5.   Buyer and Seller acknowledge receipt of a copy of this page, which constitutes Page 1 of _2_ Pages.

X_____s/THOMAS B. BUYER_____   X_____s/GEORGE S. SELLER_____
  BUYER   SELLER

X_____s/HELEN A. BUYER_____   X_____s/MARY M. SELLER_____
  BUYER   SELLER

A REAL ESTATE BROKER IS THE PERSON QUALIFIED TO ADVISE ON REAL ESTATE. IF YOU DESIRE LEGAL ADVICE CONSULT YOUR ATTORNEY.

THIS STANDARDIZED DOCUMENT FOR USE IN SIMPLE TRANSACTIONS HAS BEEN APPROVED BY THE CALIFORNIA ASSOCIATION OF REALTORS® IN FORM ONLY. NO REPRESENTATION IS MADE AS TO THE APPROVAL OF THE FORM OF SUPPLEMENTS, THE LEGAL VALIDITY OF ANY PROVISION, OR THE ADEQUACY OF ANY PROVISION IN ANY SPECIFIC TRANSACTION. IT SHOULD NOT BE USED IN COMPLEX TRANSACTIONS OR WITH EXTENSIVE RIDERS OR ADDITIONS.

To order, contact—California Association of Realtors®
525 S. Virgil Ave., Los Angeles, California 90020
Copyright © California Association of Realtors® (Revised 1978), 1981)   FORM D-11-1

(Form continued on following page)

REAL ESTATE PURCHASE CONTRACT AND RECEIPT FOR DEPOSIT
The following terms and conditions are hereby incorporated in and made a part of Buyer's Offer

6. Buyer and Seller shall deliver signed instructions to the escrow holder within _____7_____ days from Seller's acceptance which shall provide for closing within ____30____ days from Seller's acceptance. Escrow fees to be paid as follows:
_____By Buyer_____

7. Title is to be free of liens, encumbrances, easements, restrictions, rights and conditions of record or known to Seller, other than the following: (1) Current property taxes, (2) covenants, conditions, restrictions, and public utility easements of record, if any, provided the same do not adversely affect the continued use of the property for the purposes for which it is presently being used, unless reasonably disapproved by Buyer in writing within____10____days of receipt of a current preliminary title report furnished at___Buyer's___expense, and (3)____no other exceptions_____.
Seller shall furnish Buyer at___Buyer's___expense a standard California Land Title Association policy issued by ___a reliable title ins.___Company, showing title vested in Buyer subject only to the above. If Seller (1) is unwilling or unable to eliminate any title matter disapproved by Buyer as above, Seller may terminate this agreement, or (2) fails to deliver title as above, Buyer may terminate this agreement; in either case, the deposit shall be returned to Buyer.

8. Property taxes, premiums on insurance acceptable to Buyer, rents, interest, and____xxxxxxxxxxxx____ shall be pro-rated as of (a) the date of recordation of deed; or (b)____xxxxxxxxxxxx____
Any bond or assessment which is a lien shall be __paid__ by ___Seller___ . ___Seller___ shall pay cost of transfer taxes, if any.

9. Possession shall be delivered to Buyer (a) on close of escrow, or (b) not later than _____days after close of escrow or (c)_____

10. Unless otherwise designated in the escrow instructions of Buyer, title shall vest as follows:_____
____Thomas B. Buyer and Helen A. Buyer, his wife_____

(The manner of taking title may have significant legal and tax consequences. Therefore, give this matter serious consideration.)

11. If Broker is a participant of a Board multiple listing service ("MLS"), the Broker is authorized to report the sale, its price, terms, and financing for the information, publication, dissemination, and use of the authorized Board members.

12. **If Buyer fails to complete said purchase as herein provided by reason of any default of Buyer, Seller shall be released from his obligation to sell the property to Buyer and may proceed against Buyer upon any claim or remedy which he may have in law or equity; provided, however, that by placing their initials here Buyer: (TBB/HAB) Seller: (GSS/MMS) agree that Seller shall retain the deposit as his liquidated damages. If the described property is a dwelling with no more than four units, one of which the Buyer intends to occupy as his residence, Seller shall retain as liquidated damages the deposit actually paid, or an amount therefrom, not more than 3% of the purchase price and promptly return any excess to Buyer.**

13. If the only controversy or claim between the parties arises out of or relates to the disposition of the Buyer's deposit, such controversy or claim shall at the election of the parties be decided by arbitration. Such arbitration shall be determined in accordance with the Rules of the American Arbitration Association, and judgment upon the award rendered by the Arbitrator(s) may be entered in any court having jurisdiction thereof. The provisions of Code of Civil Procedure Section 1283.05 shall be applicable to such arbitration.

14. In any action or proceeding arising out of this agreement, the prevailing party shall be entitled to reasonable attorney's fees and costs.

15. Time is of the essence. All modifications or extensions shall be in writing signed by the parties.

16. This constitutes an offer to purchase the described property. Unless acceptance is signed by Seller and the signed copy delivered to Buyer, in person or by mail to the address below, within____-3-____days, this offer shall be deemed revoked and the deposit shall be returned. Buyer acknowledges receipt of a copy hereof.

Real Estate Broker ___ACME REALTY COMPANY___	Buyer ___s/THOMAS B. BUYER___
___s/MALCOLM D. BROKER___	___s/HELEN A. BUYER___
By_____	
Address ___1514 City Street, San Francisco, CA___	Address ___1402 Carmel Dr., San Francisco, CA___
Telephone ___725-0398___	Telephone ___726-7890___

ACCEPTANCE

The undersigned Seller accepts and agrees to sell the property on the above terms and conditions. Seller has employed_____
_____ACME REALTY COMPANY_____as Broker(s) and agrees to pay for services the sum of
__Eleven Thousand Two Hundred Twenty and no/100__ Dollars ($__11,220.00__), payable as follows:
(a) On recordation of the deed or other evidence of title, or (b) if completion of sale is prevented by default of Seller, upon Seller's default or (c) if completion of sale is prevented by default of Buyer, only if and when Seller collects damages from Buyer, by suit or otherwise and then in an amount not less than one-half of the damages recovered, but not to exceed the above fee, after first deducting title and escrow expenses and the expenses of collection, if any. In any action between Broker and Seller arising out of this agreement, the prevailing party shall be entitled to reasonable attorney's fees and costs. The undersigned acknowledges receipt of a copy and authorizes Broker(s) to deliver a signed copy to Buyer.

Dated: ___March 3, 1984___ Telephone ___725-4321___	Seller ___s/GEORGE S. SELLER___
Address ___659 Monterey Ave., San Francisco, CA___	Seller ___s/ MARY M. SELLER___

Broker(s) agree to the foregoing. Broker ___ACME REALTY COMPANY___   Broker _____
Dated: ___March 3, 1984___ By ___s/MALCOLM D. BROKER___   Dated: _____ By_____

to pay a fixed salary, plus "a bonus" was an agreement to pay a reasonable bonus, which could be determined by the jury. Certain kinds of uncertainty are regularly permitted as follows:

1. Where "reasonable" terms can be supplied. For example, an agreement to buy goods without specifying the price constitutes an agreement to pay a reasonable price, which becomes the market price. And see U.C.C. 2305.

2. Where documents are standard. An agreement to sell real property does not fail because of failure to specify the type of deed to be given. Custom of the community will establish that a warranty deed or a grant deed is the standard document.

3. Where uncertainty relates to minor matters; the kinds of door knobs to be used on the house to be constructed. See also U.C.C. 2311.

Offers Containing Errors

Especially in the contracting business, in the rush to meet a bidding deadline, it is easy for a bidding contractor or a bidding subcontractor to make an adverse clerical error in the compilation of a bid. A subcontract bid to do the plumbing work on a job should have gone in at $30,500. Because of a mathematical error by the clerk who added up the figures, the bid goes in at $30,000. The general contractor to whom the subcontract bid is made notifies the subcontractor that the bid is "accepted." If, on the following day, the subcontractor discovers the $500 error in the compilation of the bid, will he be permitted to withdraw the bid?

Probably not. *Security of contract* was an important fundamental goal to be achieved in contract law and, to this end, it was made difficult to get out of contracts because of mistake or for other reason such as in the cases of impossibility of performance and frustration of purpose, to be seen later. If the general contractor had used the subcontract bid in his general bid, and the general bid had been accepted by the principal, clearly the subcontractor would not be able to get out of his subcontract bid. In such a case the law goes something like this: Where an offer is made that appears to be a true offer, and the offeree, as a reasonable person acting in good faith, accepts the offer and changes position in reliance on the resulting contract, the offer is binding. Suppose the general contractor had not yet used the erroneous subcontract bid in his general bid? Even here it seems likely that the subcontractor would be held. The amount of the error, $500, is very small in relation to the overall size of the bid and, again, security of contract requires that a contract should not be escaped lightly. In fact, cases like this do not get into appellate or supreme courts anymore since the cost of litigation would far exceed the potential recovery.

There is however a type of modern case in which the erroneous bid will be worth litigating and in which there may be relief given to the contractor. This is where the contractor bids on a large scale public works job and the bid contains a serious clerical error which will cause the contractor serious loss if he is required to perform. *Conduit & Foundation Corp. v. Atlantic City*, 64 Atl.2d 382, is the foundation case of American general law, and *M.F. Kemper Const. Co.* v. *Los Angeles*, 37 C.2d 696, 235 P.2d 7, is the foundation case of California law. The cases are essentially similar in facts and results. Contractor works furiously to get a bid together and in by the bidding deadline. By virtue of a clerical error in compiling the bid a large error is made; approximately $300,000 in *Kemper* where the intended bid was approximately $1,100,000 but where, because of the error, the bid

came in as approximately $800,000.[8] The bid is accepted by the municipality before the error is discovered and reported. Modern courts will give relief in such a case if the error is "material," i.e., if a serious financial loss will be suffered by the contractor if the bid is enforced and if the municipality will suffer no loss "but the loss of its bargain," i.e., the loss of its windfall. At this point one needs to know this: public works bidding is usually protected by city ordinance which says that all bids shall remain irrevocable for a period of from sixty to ninety days after bids are opened. Los Angeles had a 90-day ordinance in *Kemper*. Actually the lowest true bid in *Kemper* was approximately $1,050,000, or $50,000 lower than the erring contractor's intended bid. Los Angeles, because of the 90-day ordinance, could go back and get this lowest true bid of $1,050,000 and so come out where it should have come out. So Los Angeles would suffer no loss but the unfair bargain it would gain if the erroneous bid were allowed to be enforced. Security of contract, then, or at least now, gives way to an unwillingness of courts to enforce contracts to an unconscionable degree.[8a]

Written Memorial Contemplated

Suppose oral offer by R and acceptance by E. The oral agreement covers all essential terms of the contract, and the contract is not one of the classes of contracts which is required to be in writing. But the parties agree to execute a formal contract embodying the terms of the oral agreement. Unless the parties clearly indicate that a contract is not to come into existence until a writing is signed, the oral agreement will create a binding contract. The rule and its explanation is stated in *Clarke* v. *Fiedler*, 44 C.A.2d 838, 113 P.2d 275. There, A and B agreed to become partners in the operation of a baseball franchise. Terms were fixed but it was agreed that a written contract would be signed. A refused to go through with the deal. B sued and recovered damages for breach of contract. The court said: "The testimony clearly shows that [A] at no time expressed an intention not to be bound until the writing was executed . . . *After all the formal written contract is not the agreement of the parties, but only evidence of that agreement*. The oral agreement . . . constituted a valid and binding contract . . . (W)here, as in the instant case, the contract is of such nature that the law does not require it to be in writing . . . and where the terms of the contract are definitely agreed upon and complete, then the fact that contemporaneously with the making of their full and complete oral agreement, they decide to evidence the same by a written instrument, the force and effect of the oral agreement is not thereby impaired or interfered with." (Emphasis added.)

---

[8]One cannot take advantage of a known mistake and at all events it is only when the bidder acts in good faith in accepting the bid that the bid can be enforced. The *Kemper* court considered that the discrepancy between the $800,000 erroneous bid and the next lowest bid of $1,050,000 was not so great as to put Los Angeles on notice of error. Presumably this is justified. There can be a wide range of bidding in public works jobs. A contractor may, for example, come in with a very low, nonprofit-making bid, just to keep work crews employed or for some other extraordinary reason. Had the bid in *Kemper* been $300,000, and the error $800,000, Los Angeles would have been on notice.

[8a]Restatement of Contracts 2d, § 295, allows the mistaken general contrator's bid to be escaped, as in *Kemper*, when "enforcement of the contract would be unconscionable."

(margin handwriting: EXPRESS QUALIFIED OR CONDITIONAL COUNTEROFFER ACCEPTANCE)

Duration of Offer

An offer remains in effect until it expires by lapse of time, is terminated by rejection or revocation, or death or insanity, or is accepted and becomes merged in a contract.

● If an offer states that it is to be open for a specified time, it terminates upon expiration of that time. If no time is stated, an offer remains open a reasonable time. Such time is determined by the circumstances of the case. An offer to sell real estate would remain open for a longer period of time than one to sell goods of a perishable nature.

Rejection: Rejection terminates an offer. Three things constitute *rejection*: Express rejection ("Please be advised that your offer is rejected."); counteroffer; and qualified or conditional acceptance.

● If R offers property to E for $200,000, and E replies, "I will give you $180,000 for the property," E's counteroffer constitutes rejection of R's offer and constitutes a new offer, which R, as offeree, may ignore, accept, or reject, or to which he in turn may make a counteroffer. If E says, "Would you be willing to take $180,000," this is a mere inquiry, which leaves the offer open. For a communication to be a counteroffer it must meet the requirements of an offer, that is, it must constitute a promise. "Would you be willing to take $180,000" does not constitute a promise to pay $180,000. A counteroffer may be made which expressly reserves the right to accept the offer. If E says, "I am keeping your offer under advisement, but if you wish to close the deal at once I will give you $180,000," the counteroffer does not constitute a rejection. It is because a counteroffer implies a rejection that it is held to constitute a rejection. If, by expressly reserving the right to accept the offer, a counteroffer shows that the offeree does not intend to reject the offer, the counteroffer does not operate as a rejection.

● Qualified or conditional acceptance is covered in the section on acceptance.

● Rejection in any form *permanently* terminates offer. The offer may not be accepted even though acceptance is communicated within the time originally allowed by the offer. R makes an offer to E which states that it is to remain open for 30 days. E makes a counteroffer which is ignored. Then, before expiration of 30 days, E sends an acceptance. The acceptance is not effective. The original offer was permanently terminated by the counteroffer (rejection).

Revocation: Unless there is an option or a firm offer, an offer may be revoked at any time before acceptance.[9] It makes

---

[9]C.C. 1586: "A proposal may be revoked at any time before its acceptance is communicated to the proposer, but not afterwards."

C.C. 1587 says that "A proposal is revoked:

"1. By the communication of notice of revocation by the proposer to the other party, in the manner prescribed by [C.C. 1583], before his acceptance has been communicated to the former; [C.C. 1583 will be covered in the text.]

"2. By the lapse of the time prescribed in such proposal for its acceptance, or if no time is so prescribed, the lapse of a reasonable time without communication of the acceptance; [This is somewhat unusual in that an offer is more usually thought of as merely 'expiring' from lapse of time rather than being 'revoked' by it.]

"3. By the failure of the acceptor to fulfill a condition precedent to acceptance; [E.g., S offers to sell B real estate within 30 days if B will find a buyer for other property of B's within 5 days after receipt of the offer; B's failure to find a buyer would terminate S's offer. This method of revocation would seldom oc-

no difference that the offer is stated to be open for a time which has not expired. R makes an offer to E on June 1 which states that it is to be open until June 30. On June 9, before acceptance, R revokes. The offer is terminated.[10]

Death or Insanity: Death or insanity of the offeror before acceptance terminates an offer. It makes no difference that the offeree is unaware of the fact at the time of acceptance. It takes two to contract and one no longer exists, either because of death or mental death. Death of the offeree terminates an offer for the reason that only the person to whom an offer is made may accept.

Options: It has been seen that if one party offers to pay money to another if the other will make a promise, a contract is formed if the promise is made and the money paid. If the promise is one which the promisee (offeree) has the election to enforce or not enforce, as he sees fit, the logical name for the contract would be "option contract," which is what an *option* is. An example with which most are familiar is the option to purchase real estate. A has property for sale for $500,000 which B desires. It will take B time to raise the money, and he would like to get a hold on the property for sufficient time to enable him to do so. He agrees to pay A $1000 if A will give him the exclusive right for a period of 30 days to purchase for $500,000, to which A agrees, signing an option of the type illustrated on the following page. The option amounts to a promise by A to convey the property to B for $500,000 at any time within 30 days. In the sense that there is now a contract by A to go through with what was originally merely an offer by him, an option is often described as "a contract, for consideration, to keep an offer open for a specified period of time." It has also been described, perhaps more accurately, as "a contract to contract." The important thing is that it creates an irrevocable offer.

● There are other common options such as the "option to renew" a lease by which the lessee is given the right to release for an additional period upon expiration of the original term. In the original lease, the lessor agrees to lease the property for 5 years and at the same time "promises" to give another lease for 5 years if the lessee wants it. The agreement by the lessee to pay rent is consideration for both the original lease and the promise to renew.

● Options on services of professional athletes, actors, etc., are similar. Mr. Star agrees to work for Movie Studio for three years at $1,000,000 a year. In Star's contract, Star "promises" that if Movie Studio desires, it may avail itself of Star's services for another three years at the same or a different figure.

● Today, stock options, giving a corporate employee the option to purchase stock of the corporation at a price which may, if the option is exercised, yield a handsome profit, often provide an attractive fringe benefit by which to recruit employees.

Firm Offers

U.C.C. 2205 creates "firm offers," as follows:

"An offer by a merchant to buy or sell goods in a signed writing which by its terms gives assurance that it will be held open is not revocable, for lack of consideration, during the time stated or if no time is stated for a reasonable time, but in no event may such period of irrevocability exceed three months; but any such term of assur-

---

cur.]

"4. By the death or insanity of the proposer."

[10]*Bullock* v. *McKeon*, 104 C.A. 72, 285 P. 392.

Option
to Purchase Real Estate

San Francisco, California,...................................July 5,.................19 84

For and in consideration of the sum of

....One thousand & no/100..($.1,000.00..) Dollars

to seller in hand paid, the receipt of which is hereby acknowledged by said seller, to apply on the purchase price, the undersigned

....FRANK S. SELLERS...

herein designated as the seller, hereby grants the right and option to purchase and agrees to sell to

....ARTHUR B. BUYERS...

herein designated as the purchaser, or his assigns, at any time within .... days from the date hereof, the following described
property in the City and County of San Francisco, State of California, to wit:

> Lots 15, 16, 17 and 18, Map of "Sunset Tract", Vol. 2 of
> Maps, page 14, Office of Recorder of City and County of
> San Francisco, California

For the purchase price of

....Two hundred thousand & no/100...($ 200,000.) Dollars

lawful money of the United States of America, payable as follows:

> Cash upon exercise of option.

If said purchaser elects to purchase said property at the price and on the terms herein set forth, and within the time specified,
the said purchaser shall give said seller due notice in writing and shall pay an additional sum of $.199,000.00. for account

of said seller to...............NORTHERN CALIFORNIA TITLE INSURANCE COMPANY...

said sum to apply on the purchase price, whereupon thirty (30) days after the exercising of this option shall be allowed said
purchaser to examine title to said property and report any valid objection thereto, if any, to said seller. If no such objection to
title is reported, the balance of the purchase price shall be paid by said purchaser at or before the expiration of said time and said
seller shall thereupon deliver a properly executed and acknowledged grant deed to said property. If such objection to title is
reported, then said seller shall use due diligence to remove same within ninety (90) days thereafter and if it is so removed the
balance of the purchase price shall be paid within five (5) days after such objection has been removed and upon delivery of said
deed as hereinabove provided; but if such objection to title cannot be removed within the time allowed, all rights and obligations
hereunder, at the election of the purchaser, shall terminate and end and all payments made hereunder shall be returned to the
purchaser unless said purchaser elects to buy the said property subject to such defect in title.

If said purchaser does not give said seller written notice of intention to complete the purchase of said property on or before
the date of expiration of this option or does not make the additional payment on account of purchase price as herein provided,
then seller shall be released from all obligation hereunder and all rights hereunder, legal and equitable, of said purchaser shall
cease and the consideration hereinabove receipted for by seller shall be retained by said seller as liquidated and agreed damages.

All notices required hereunder to be given said seller shall comply herewith if posted U. S. Registered Mail addressed to said

seller at ....200 South Market Street, San Francisco, California...

Taxes for the fiscal year ending June 30, following the date hereof, rents and insurance shall be pro-rated as of the date of
recordation of deed.

Subject to any zoning and set back ordinances of the City and County of San Francisco.

In this agreement, the masculine includes the feminine and neuter, and the singular includes the plural.

Time is of the essence of this agreement.

Witness: Seller:

........s/ ROGER KENNEDY................   ....s/ FRANK S. SELLERS................

....

                                                      Purchaser:

........s/ ELLIOT GOLD................   ....s/ ARTHUR B. BUYERS................

....

(Should be acknowledged by Notary Public.)

ance on a form supplied by the offeree must be separately signed by the offeror."

Most notably, Section 2205 dispenses with the requirement of consideration when the requisite written firm offer is made. This serves the need of merchant-offerees to be able to rely on "firm" offers without need to comply with the technicality of consideration and makes good commercial law as the Uniform Commercial Code is supposed to do.

● In 1980 California enlarged upon U.C.C. 2205 in the manner shown in the Appendix at page 373. The California addition would, subject to the requirements of California subsection (b), make offers by merchants to supply goods to contractors binding without consideration for up to 90 days when the merchant knows the contractor will rely on the offer in making a bid for a construction contract. This complements the rule of the *Drennan* case on page 36 as can be seen when that case is studied.

Acceptance

What Constitutes Acceptance

It has been seen that an offer may ask for either of two things—that something be done, or that a promise be made to do something. Acceptance is simply compliance with the offer—doing the thing requested or making the promise requested. Keeping in mind that an offer is also a promise, if the offer asks for a promise and the offeree accepts by giving the promise, the resultant contract consists of "a promise for a promise." This type of contract is called a *bilateral contract* (two-sided promise contract). Where the offer asks for the performance of an act, it is accepted by the performance of the act. The resultant contract consists of "a promise for an act" and is called a *unilateral contract* (one-sided promise contract). If I write asking you to promise to ship me a carload of lettuce at a specified future date, your promise to do so creates a bilateral contract. If I wire asking you to ship me a carload of lettuce immediately, I am asking you to perform an act, and by so doing you accept and create a unilateral contract.

Offer for Unilateral Contract—Part Performance: A special problem arises at this point. Suppose I have wired for immediate shipment of a carload of lettuce. You put everything else aside and begin work on my order. When the freight car is half filled, you receive a long distance telephone call from me telling you to "forget it." What is your position? You have not *completed* the act requested as yet, so you have not "accepted" my offer. But it would be unjust to leave you without recourse. The courts have evolved the following rule: Where the offeree of an offer for a unilateral contract has entered upon the performance of the act requested by the offeror, and the offer is then revoked, the offeree may recover as damages the profit which he would have made had he been permitted to complete the act, provided he can show that he would have done so within the allotted time. The practical effect is to make an offer for a unilateral contract irrevocable once the offeree has entered upon performance of the act.

Acceptance Must Follow Offer; U.C.C. 2207

It is the common law rule that "the offeror is the master of his offer" and that therefore the offeree cannot deviate from the terms of the offer, even slightly, if he wants to create a contract by acceptance; that the offeree can accept only exactly what is offered. This is sometimes referred to as the "mirror image rule." Under the mirror image rule, if a quantity of goods were offered on particular shipping terms, and

the offeree attempted to accept on different shipping terms, there would be no acceptance of what was offered, and therefore no contract.[11] The purported "acceptance" would be called a *qualified* or *conditional acceptance,* and would be said to operate as a counteroffer which the original offeror could accept or reject as he saw fit. The Uniform Commercial Code rejects the common law rule, in dealings between merchants, in favor of a more commercial rule. The code rule, contained in Section 2207, permits a merchant-offeree to introduce new terms so long as the acceptance is not expressly conditioned on assent to the terms and so long as they are not material new terms. The new terms then become part of the contract unless the merchant-offeror objects to them within a reasonable time. The Code Comments, to Section 2207, give as example the instruction by a merchant-buyer to "Rush" or to "Ship by Tuesday."

● Distinction is made between qualified or conditional acceptance and an unqualified acceptance accompanied by a request. The latter creates a contract. The request may be ignored. If S offers B a single shipment of 2000 tons of steel and B accepts "provided delivery is made in four installments," there is conditional acceptance and no contract. But if B says, "We accept your offer. If possible, please deliver in 4 installments," there is an unqualified acceptance and a contract. S may comply with or ignore the request as it sees fit.

When Effective

Acceptance is effective when put in the course of transmission if the offeree uses the means of communication used by the offeror or other means consistent with business usage.[12] Thus, acceptance by wire of a mailed offer, being consistent with business usage, is effective when deposited with the telegraph company. It makes no difference that the acceptance is lost or delayed in transmission. To protect himself the offeror must stipulate that the offer shall not be effective until received and unless received within a stated time.[13]

● Once a contract is formed it cannot be terminated except by mutual agreement. By weight of authority therefore an acceptance, once communicated, cannot be withdrawn. If the offeree mails acceptance, then sends a wire cancelling acceptance, the wire is not effective even though it reaches the offeror before the letter of acceptance.

Acceptance v. Revocation

Suppose you mail A an offer. The next morning you change your mind and mail a revocation. Before receiving the revocation, A deposits acceptance in the mail. If revocation, like acceptance, is effective when put in transmission, you have revoked the offer, and no contract exists. *But* this is not the rule in the vast majority of states. Except in a few states, including, seemingly, California, it is the rule that revocation

---

[11]C.C. 1585: "An acceptance must be absolute and unqualified, or must include in itself an acceptance of that character which the proposer can separate from the rest. . . . A qualified acceptance is a new proposal."

[12]Restatement of Contracts 2d, §§ 64, 66; U.C.C. 2206.

C.C. 1583: "Consent is deemed to be fully communicated between the parties as soon as the party accepting a proposal has put his acceptance in the course of transmission to the proposer."

[13]C.C.1582: "If a proposal prescribes any conditions concerning the communication of its acceptance, the proposer is not bound unless they are conformed to; but in other cases any reasonable and usual mode may be adopted."

is not effective until received, and unless received prior to the time that acceptance becomes effective. Under this rule, there would be a binding contract, and your revocation would be a nullity.

California: C.C. 1587 provides that "A proposal is revoked: 1. By the communication of notice of revocation by the proposer to the other party, in the manner prescribed by section . . . fifteen hundred and eightythree, before his acceptance has been communicated to the former." C.C. 1583 provides that "Consent is deemed to be fully communicated between the parties as soon as the party accepting a proposal has put his acceptance in the course of transmission to the proposer. . . ." Reading these sections together as C.C. 1587(1) requires, it would appear to be the rule in California that revocation, like acceptance, is effective when put in the course of transmission.

Acceptance After Rejection

A similar problem arises in connection with rejection and acceptance. You make me an offer. I mail rejection, then think better of the matter and telegraph acceptance which reaches you before rejection. A contract is formed. Rejection is not effective until received. Suppose I mail rejection, then acceptance. You receive rejection first. May I claim that, since acceptance is effective when put in transmission, a contract is formed? No. Where an acceptance is put in transmission after a rejection, acceptance is effective only if it is received before the rejection.

Silence as Acceptance

Not infrequently, sellers attempt to induce buyers to buy by sending the product along with the offer of sale. Sometimes this represents a quite legitimate method of doing business, sometimes a high pressure method. In either case, the offer will usually stipulate that if the product is not returned within a specified time, the seller will presume that you have found it satisfactory and will bill you for the price. Suppose you keep the article beyond the stated time but do not want it or intend to accept it. You have simply overlooked its return. May the seller claim that your retention beyond the time specified for return is acceptance? No. A contract is a voluntary agreement into which one may not be forced against his will. Ordinarily, therefore, a person cannot be required to reject an offer on penalty of becoming liable as an acceptor if he does not.[14]

---

[14]Restatement of Contracts 2d, § 72, says silence constitutes acceptance where the offeree remains silent *intending* to accept; also that exercise of dominion over offered goods constitutes acceptance. It has been suggested that this might be true in California under C.C. 1584 and 1589. Section 1584 provides that ". . . acceptance of the consideration offered with a proposal is an acceptance of the proposal." Section 1589 provides that "A voluntary acceptance of the benefit of a transaction is equivalent to a consent to all the obligations arising from it . . ."

C.C. 1716 as a form of consumer protection law, provides: "It shall be unlawful for any person to solicit payment of money by another by means of a written statement or invoice, or any writing that could reasonably be interpreted as a statement or invoice, for goods not yet ordered or for services not yet performed and not yet ordered unless there appears on the face of the billing, invoice or statement in boldface type at least 10 points larger than any other type on the face of the bill, invoice or statement, the following warning:

"'This is NOT a bill, invoice or statement. This is a solicitation for the order of goods or services, or both. You are under

• C.C. 1584.5 provides that unsolicited merchandise may be treated as "an unconditional gift to the recipient who may use or dispose of (it) in any manner he sees fit without any obligation on his part to the sender."
• Silence will operate as acceptance if it has become the custom of the parties. S Company, through salesmen, regularly has taken orders for goods from B. In every case S Company has shipped the goods ordered within a week and without notification to B other than billing him for the goods after shipment. An S Company salesman takes an order from B. S Company receives the order (offer) and remains silent. B refrains from purchasing elsewhere. Because of the custom of the parties, S Company's silence will be deemed acceptance and it will be required to fill the order.

Competent Parties

For various reasons, certain classes of persons are limited in or entirely without the power to contract.[15] As shown in later chapters, corporations and partners are limited by their business purposes. A person convicted of a felony may be deprived of civil rights, including the right to contract. Contracts of minors or mental incompetents may be void or voidable.

Minors

In California, persons under 18[16] are protected against their contracts. They may disaffirm or avoid contracts until they reach 18, and for a reasonable time thereafter.[17] (In many states, minority continues until age 21.) The minor may ratify

---

no obligation to make any payment unless you accept this offer.'

"Any person damaged by noncompliance with this section, in addition to other remedies, is entitled to damages in an amount equal to three times the sum solicited.

"Any person who violates this section shall be liable for a civil penalty not to exceed ten thousand dollars ($10,000) for each violation, which shall be assessed and recovered in a civil action brought in the name of the people of the State of California by the Attorney General or by any district attorney, county counsel, or city attorney in any court of competent jurisdiction.

"If the action is brought by the Attorney General, one-half of the penalty collected shall be paid to the treasurer of the county in which the judgment was entered and one-half to the State Treasurer. If brought by a district attorney or county counsel, the entire amount of the penalty collected shall be paid to the treasurer of the county in which the judgment was entered. If brought by a city attorney or city prosecutor, one-half of the penalty shall be paid to the treasurer of the county and one-half to the city.

"A violation of any of the provisions of this section shall be punishable as a misdemeanor."

[15]C.C. 1556: "All persons are capable of contracting except minors, persons of unsound mind, and persons deprived of civil rights."

[16]C.C. 25: "Minors are all persons under eighteen years of age." C.C. 27: "All other persons are adults."

[17]C.C. 33: "A minor cannot give a delegation of power, make a contract relating to real property, or any interest therein, or relating to any personal property not in his immediate possession or control."

C.C. 34: "A minor may make any other contract than as above specified, in the same manner as an adult, subject only to his power of disaffirmance under [C.C. 35] . . ."

C.C. 35: "In all cases other than those specified in sections thirty-six and thirty-seven, the contract of a minor may be disaffirmed by the minor himself, either before his majority or within a reasonable time afterwards . . ."

the contract upon reaching majority. Ratification may be expressed or implied from continued retention of the benefits of the contract, or acceptance of further benefits after majority.

A minor "disaffirms" by returning what he has received, at which time he becomes entitled to get back that with which he has parted. Where the minor is a buyer of goods, the law of most states gives him exceptional protection. He may return what he has received even though it has depreciated in value or has become worthless, and get back *everything* with which he has parted. Thus, if M, 17 years old but appearing to be 20 or 21, purchases a used car for $2000 from D, who believes M to be an adult, M may return the car and recover his $2000 although, in the interim, he has worn all the rubber off the tires, smashed two fenders, and otherwise made the car worth considerably less than it was worth when it was received.

● Note that it was stated that M was a minor "appearing" to be 20 or 21 and that D *assumed* he was an adult. Where a minor misrepresents his age, the outcome may be different, e.g., if M both is and appears to be 17 but says he is 22. A minor is liable for torts, including the tort of fraud.[18] Such being the case, the adult could sue the minor in fraud for misrepresentation of age and, by recovery of damages for fraud, get back what he has lost in the depreciation of the article sold. Some states deny such a lawsuit as a matter of public policy, for the reason that threat of it may be used to force minors to abide by contracts, and so, permit adults to accomplish indirectly what they cannot do directly—enforce contracts of minors. Other states permit the suit. A third group estops the minor to disaffirm where he has misrepresented his age.[19]

● From the adult seller's standpoint, the solution is to require verification of age and, if the buyer is a minor, to require his parents to guarantee the contract.

● Where a minor *sells* goods, he may avoid the sale until he reaches the age of 18, and for a reasonable time thereafter. He must restore such amount of the purchase price as remains in his possession or, if the money has been used to purchase other things, he must return these. The courts will not permit unjust enrichment of the minor. Where the buyer from the minor has sold to an innocent third person, the third person is protected.[20] Where a minor sells *real property,* there is a special rule as to the time at which he may disaffirm. On the theory that the property will always be there and that the minor may elect to ratify the sale when he reaches majority, it is the rule that the minor cannot disaffirm *until* he reaches majority.

● Property of a minor may be sold by his court appointed guardian. Such sales are usually required to be confirmed by the court and may be made only for certain limited purposes: where necessary to provide funds for support of the minor, or where necessary to preserve the minor's estate. Property of a minor should be purchased only through his guardian and subject to approval of the sale by the court.

● A minor may become an adult in effect by *"emancipation,"* i.e., by being cut free from the control of his parents. In 1978 the California Legislature passed the Emancipation of Minors Act, which is to be found in C.C. 6070. The Act says, first of all, that a person under 18 years of age is an "emancipated minor" if he or she has entered into a valid marriage or is on active duty with the armed forces or has received a declaration of emancipation under C.C. 64. C.C. 64 permits a minor to petition for a declaration of emancipation. The petition must show that the person (1) is at least 14 years of age; (2) is willingly living apart from his or her parents or legal guardian; (3) is managing his or her own financial affairs; and (4) is not deriving income from a criminal activity. The court must conduct a hearing on the petition, after notice to the minor's parents or guardian, and must grant the petition unless it finds that emancipation would not be in the best interests of the minor. C.C. 63 provides that an emancipated minor is to be considered as being over the age of majority for the purposes, among others, of entering into contracts and buying and selling real property and that the minor and his or her earnings are no longer subject to the control of the minor's parents.

Contracts for Necessaries: A minor is liable, to the extent of reasonable value, for necessaries of life furnished him, where they are not made available by a parent or guardian.[21] Necessaries include food, clothing, shelter, medical care, tools of a trade, vocational education and the like, in accordance with the minor's station in life. The minor is liable only if the necessary is actually furnished to (received by) him, so he may disaffirm if he has contracted for but has not received it. He is liable only for "reasonable value," which is not necessarily the seller's price. Certain other contracts of minors are binding.[22]

---

[18]Generally, parents are not liable for torts committed by minor children. Several exceptions are made in California by virtue of the following "anti-juvenile delinquency" statutes:

Educ. C. 48909 makes the parent or guardian of a minor liable to the extent of $5000 where wilful misconduct of the minor results in injury to or death of a fellow pupil or causes damage to school property or personal property of a school employee.

C.C. 1714.1 makes the parent liable for not to exceed $10,000 for "(a)ny act of wilful misconduct of a minor which results in injury or death to another person or in any injury to the property of another . . ."

C.C. 1714.3 makes a parent or guardian liable to the extent of $15,000 for one person injured or killed by the discharge of a firearm by a minor under 18, $30,000 for two or more persons injured or killed, where the parent allows the minor to have or have access to the firearm.

[19]The only California case is *Lee* v. *Hibernia Savings & Loan Society,* 177 C. 656, 171 P. 677, where the court refused to apply estoppel.

[20]See page 91.

[21]C.C. 36: "A contract, otherwise valid, entered into during minority, cannot be disaffirmed upon that ground either during the actual minority of the person entering into such contract, or at any time thereafter, in the following cases:

"1. A contract to pay the reasonable value of things necessary for his support, or that of his family, entered into by him when not under the care of a parent or guardian able to provide for him or them; provided, that these things have been actually furnished to him or to his family."

[22]In many states, a minor is liable on insurance contracts to some extent, e.g., Ins. C. 10112, which declares that the life or disability policy of a minor over 16 is binding. C.C. 63.1 makes all insurance contracts entered into by an emancipated minor binding on the minor.

In many states, it is held that where a minor becomes a partner, he may not disaffirm his partnership agreement and recover his capital contribution until creditors have been satisfied and that the minor's capital contribution is liable for debts incurred prior to time of disaffirmance; also, that his copartners may deduct from the amount to be returned to the minor as his capital contribution such amounts as have been received by the minor as profits or withdrawals.

Entertainers and Professional Athletes: C.C. 36 makes special provision for minors in the sports and entertainment fields. It says a minor cannot disaffirm a contract in the following cases:

"A contract or agreement pursuant to which such person is employed or agrees to render artistic or creative services, or agrees to purchase, or otherwise secure, sell, lease, license or otherwise dispose of literary, musical or dramatic properties (either tangible or intangible) or any rights therein for use in motion pictures, television, the production of phonograph records, the legitimate or living stage, or otherwise in the entertainment field, where such contract or agreement has been approved by the superior court in the county in which such minor resides or is employed or, if the minor neither resides in or is employed in this state, where any party to the contract or agreement has its principal office in this state for the transaction of business. As used in this paragraph, 'artistic or creative services' shall include, but not be limited to, services as an actor, actress, dancer, musician, comedian, singer or other performer or entertainer, or as a writer, director, producer, production executive, choreographer, composer, conductor or designer.

"A contract or agreement pursuant to which such person is employed or agrees to render services as a participant or player in professional sports, including, but without being limited to, professional boxers, professional wrestlers and professional jockeys, where such contract or agreement has been approved by the superior court in the county in which such minor resides or is employed or, if the minor neither resides in or is employed in this state, where any party to the contract or agreement has its principal office in this state for the transaction of business."

• C.C. 36.1 permits the court to require up to one-half of the earnings of such minor to be put into a trust fund for him.

Mentally Incompetent Persons

Contracts of persons wholly without understanding, or who have been judicially adjudged to be incompetent, are void. Contracts of persons who are mentally incompetent to a lesser degree are at most voidable; in many states, if the contract is fair in all respects, the incompetent is held.[23]

Temporarily Incompetent Persons

The contract of an intoxicated person who does not understand the nature of his act is voidable. A contract made by a person who is temporarily incompetent as the result of injury is not binding, e.g., in *Backus* v. *Sessions,* 17 C.2d 380, 110 P.2d 51, a release was not binding where it was signed shortly

---

[23]C.C. 38 and 40 declare void contracts of persons (a) who are insane in fact, i.e., who are entirely without understanding of the nature and import of their acts, but have not been adjudged insane by a court; or (b) who have been judicially declared insane. C.C. 38: "A person entirely without understanding has no power to make a contract of any kind, but he is liable for the reasonable value of things furnished to him necessary for his support or the support of his family."

C.C. 40: "After his incapacity has been judicially determined, a person of unsound mind can make no conveyance or other contract . . . until his restoration to capacity."

Under C.C. 39, contracts of persons who are incompetent in lesser degree are voidable. C.C. 39: "A conveyance or other contract of a person of unsound mind, but not entirely without understanding, made before his incapacity has been judicially determined, is subject to rescission . . ."

after an accident and while the injured person was in a state of shock.

Persons Deprived of Civil Rights

By state statute, a person convicted of a felony is deprived of civil rights to some extent.[24]

Consideration

Nature of Consideration in General

Practically speaking, consideration is value—that for which the parties bargain and for which the contract is formed, its reason or motive, its life blood. The word derives from pleadings of common law lawyers who became accustomed to allege, in contract cases, that P did something, or promised to do something, "in consideration" of D's promise to do something.

Each party to a contract must give consideration if the contract is to be binding. In 999 out of 1,000 cases, consideration is clearly present—consisting of services, goods or property given in exchange for money. In a bilateral contract, consideration is services, goods or property promised for money promised in return; in a unilateral contract, services, goods or property performed, delivered or conveyed in exchange for a promise of payment.

Unfortunately, we have a variety of "1,000th" cases—ones in which consideration is not clear. These are the troublemakers which largely necessitate this section. They are of three general types: (1) Those in which the question is whether there is sufficient consideration to create a contract. (2) Those in which the question is whether there is consideration for a modification of a contract which will confer new benefits upon one of the parties. (3) Those in which the question is whether there is consideration for discharge of a contract in a way which is more favorable to one party than originally agreed. This is substantially the same problem as (2). It is in this order that a variety of "1,000th" cases will be discussed in sections which follow.

Legal Concept of Consideration; Detriment Suffered

The legal concept of consideration is the exact opposite of the lay concept. The layman looks to see if he will obtain a benefit from the contract. The law looks to see if a party to a contract has suffered a detriment. *Detriment suffered* is the legal concept of consideration. If a contract requires a party to do something he was not previously obligated to do, he suffers detriment, and gives consideration. If a person agrees to do something he has a legal right not to do, or in any manner restricts his freedom of action, he has suffered detriment in the legal sense and has given consideration. It is immaterial that there is not a corresponding benefit, or benefit at all, to the other party. You promise to pay me $2000 to paint your brother's house, intending to make a gift to him. Or, to take a ridiculous case but one which will serve to emphasize the point, you agree to pay me $400 if I will remain at home on Sundays for the next 4 months. In neither case

---

[24]Pen. C. 2600 formerly took away civil rights. However, in 1975, Section 2600 was rewritten to provide as follows: "A person sentenced to imprisonment in a state prison may, during any such period of confinement, be deprived of such rights, and only such rights, as is necessary in order to provide for the reasonable security of the institution in which he is confined and for the reasonable protection of the public."

will you be benefited by my performance. In the first case you may receive some sort of spiritual satisfaction, but this is beyond the pale of the legal concept of consideration. In each case, I have suffered detriment. In the first case, by doing the act requested; in the second by giving up my legal right to go where I wish on Sundays. The detriment suffered by me in each case is sufficient to permit me to enforce your promise.[25]

Adequacy of Consideration

S agrees to sell B a truck for $5000. Comparable trucks are selling for $5500 and in some cases as high as $5700 on the open market. Here, the consideration of each party would not balance if placed on an imaginary scale. S's detriment would weigh in at 5500; B's at only 5000. Can S avoid the bargain? The rule is that he cannot.

Contracting—as bargaining—is inherently an activity in which one party comes off second best. Courts are not permitted to set aside contracts merely because consideration does not weigh out evenly. A contrary rule, if carried to logical extreme, would require court approval of all contracts. The axiom is that *"Courts will not inquire into the adequacy of consideration."* If consideration has substantial value, ordinarily the contract will be binding. However, where a party seeks specific performance of a contract, he will be required to show that he has given adequate consideration.[26] If his consideration is substantially inadequate or "so grossly inadequate as to amount to fraud," or to shock the conscience of the court, as courts put it, specific performance will be denied. Specific performance asks a court of equity to act, and "he who seeks equity must do equity."

Sufficiency of Consideration to Create Contract

The first class of "1000th" cases serves only to reemphasize the importance of detriment. Two cases will show the reasoning of all cases. In *Hamer* v. *Sidway,* 124 N.Y. 538, 27 N.E. 256, uncle promised nephew $5000 if he would refrain from drinking, smoking and other vices until he reached 21. Nephew performed. Uncle reneged on his promise, and when sued for the $5000 defended on the grounds that this was not a contract, merely a promise to make a gift; that if it were a contract, it failed for lack of consideration on the nephew's side; that he did not suffer a detriment but was benefited both physically and morally. The court had its greatest trouble with the first defense. Since a contract is essentially a bargain based upon "bargaining intent," the court had to stretch a point to find that it was in such spirit that the parties dealt. Having established that there was such intent, the court had little difficulty in finding consideration. The nephew had given up legal rights—a detriment. As stated by the court: "A valuable consideration, in the sense of the law, may consist either in some right, interest, profit, or benefit accruing to the one party, or some forbearance, detriment, loss or responsibility

given, suffered or undertaken by the other. Courts will not ask whether the thing which forms the consideration does in fact benefit the promisee or a third party or is of any substantial value to anyone. It is enough that something is promised, done, forborne, suffered by the party to whom the promise is made as consideration for the promise made to him. . . . Consideration means not so much that one party is profiting as that the other abandons some legal right in the present, or limits his legal freedom of action in the future, as an inducement for the promise of the first."

• In passing, we note, from the *Hamer* case, that neither economic detriment nor detriment in fact is required; only legal detriment. *Bartlett Springs Co.* v. *Standard Box Co.,* 16 C.A. 671, 117 P. 934 involved the so-called *need* or *requirements contract,* which demonstrates the legal detriment concept in a business contract context. The agreement was that "defendant was to furnish and the plaintiff was to take all the boxes that it would *need* in its business" for a period of one year. Defendant refused to furnish boxes ordered by plaintiff, who was required to obtain them elsewhere. Plaintiff sued for breach of contract. The defense was that since plaintiff had not agreed to buy a given quantity of boxes he had not given consideration. Held, there was consideration and a binding contract for breach of which defendant was liable. The court said: ". . . when one offers to supply another with such goods of a certain kind as he may choose to order or may 'wish' during a certain time and the other accepts the offer . . . there is no consideration for the promise or offer, for the promisee has not bound himself to anything and has incurred no legal liability at all. . . . Where, however, the acceptance does . . . impose any obligation on the acceptor, then a consideration is present and a binding contract results; and this is so wherever the acceptor's freedom of action is in any way limited . . . it is limited where the offer is to supply him with all the goods of a particular kind which he may 'require' or which he may need during a certain time, for here, although it may be that he will neither need nor require any, yet if he does he has bound himself to buy them from the proposer, and has hence *parted with his right to buy them from whom he pleases.*"[27]

Note that the court distinguishes a case in which a party agrees to buy such goods as he "wishes." R writes E: "We offer to sell you all the boxes you may choose to order during 1984" at a fixed price. E replies, "We accept your offer." There is no contract. E has not given up a right to buy elsewhere and fails to suffer detriment. This and any other transaction that creates merely the illusion of contract is called an *"illusory contract."*

• Illusory contracts illustrate the requirement, in bilateral contracts, of *mutuality of obligation.* Each party to a bilateral contract must make a promise that imposes an obligation. The "I will if I want to" type of promise, just noted, is one type that fails to impose an obligation. Another is the "contract" in which one party has an unqualified right to cancel the contract at any time without notice. If a person may cancel his promise at any time, the promise does not really impose an obligation and is therefore an illusory promise. However, if the right to cancel is qualified, it is held that there is sufficient consideration, e.g., as in *Thomas* v. *Anthony,* 30 C.A. 217, 157 P. 823, where 15 days' notice of cancellation was required.

• One exception to the requirement of mutuality of obligation is the voidable promise of the minor or mental incompetent,

---

[25]The detriment must be one that is *bargained for.* For example, if I agree to give you an extension of your lease if you will agree to pay a certain, higher rent, my promise will not become binding if you, without making the rent promise, spend money on plans for improvements you propose to make on the premises. In spending such money, you suffer a detriment, but it is not the one I asked—bargained for. I bargained for your promise regarding rent, and that is the only thing you can give that will make my promise binding.

[26]C.C. 3391: "Specific performance cannot be enforced against a party to a contract in any of the following cases: 1. If he has not received an adequate consideration for the contract. . . ."

[27]Note U.C.C. 2306 (1).

seen earlier. The policy of protecting such persons outweighs the mutuality requirement.

Sufficiency of Consideration to Modify Contract

Now, for illustrations of class (2) of consideration cases—those in which a contract is to be modified in such a way as to confer additional benefits upon one party. For such new benefits there should be offsetting detriment.

Pre-Existing Duty Rule: Suppose an employee who is under contract for 3 years at $3000 a month is promised more money to keep him from breaking this contract by going to work for a competitor who has offered a higher salary for the same period. Since the employee has not suffered new detriment in exchange for the increased compensation, he should not be allowed to recover it. Stated as a legal proposition, this is to say that doing what one is already obligated to do cannot be sufficient consideration for additional benefits. Had the employee agreed to assume new duties or responsibilities, he would have incurred additional detriment sufficient to entitle him to the additional compensation.

Rescission and New Contract: Suppose, in a case of the type above, the parties write on the contract of employment, "We hereby rescind this contract by mutual agreement," and sign their names; then, write a new contract for the same term as the original, but at the higher salary. Many courts say that parties may rescind a contract, then immediately enter into a new one that is the same in all respects except that it confers additional benefits on one party. Some courts require formality of rescission such as outlined. Others "imply" rescission of the old contract and formation of the new.[28]

Modification of Sales Contracts Under the Code: U.C.C. 2209(1) provides that an agreement modifying a contract for the sale of goods "needs no consideration to be binding." The purpose of this provision is "to protect and make effective all necessary and desirable modifications of sales contracts without regard to the technicalities which at present hamper such adjustments," that is, without regard to the technicalities of the law of consideration. U.C.C. 2209, Comment 1.[28a]

---

[28]In *San Gabriel Valley Ready-Mixt* v. *Casillas,* 142 C.A.2d 137, 298 P.2d 76, S agreed to sell B a quantity of cement at a specified price. Thereafter S asked a higher price, which B agreed to pay. Then B changed his mind and said he would get the cement elsewhere which he thought he could do at a lower price, to which S did not object. Being unable to get as good a price elsewhere as S's higher price, he came back to S for the cement. It was held that S could recover the higher price; that the original contract had been "abandoned" and a new one made at the higher price. In *Jura* v. *Sunshine Biscuits,* 118 C.A.2d 442, 258 P.2d 90, S contracted to sell B a quantity of figs at a specified price. Thereafter B asked to be relieved of the contract because it was oversupplied with figs. S told B that B was S's best customer and that S did not want to lose B's business and would therefore forego profit on the deal to be able to supply the figs at a lower price. B then took the figs. It was held that S could recover only the lower price; that the parties had "rescinded" the original contract and had entered into a new one at the lower price.

[28a]California has long had two general statutes regulating modification of contract. They are C.C. 1697, which formerly provided that an *oral* contract could be "altered" by a writing, without new consideration; and C.C. 1698, which formerly provided that a *written* contract could be modified by a written contract or by an executed oral agreement.

These statutes were amended in 1976 to coordinate them with

This does not permit the "holdup case," however, that is, for example, the case of the seller who wants to raise the contract price without any legitimate reason for doing so. The Code requires good faith in all commercial dealings, including this one (U.C.C. 1203), and the seller would have to show some such thing as a market shift which would make performance come to involve a loss. U.C.C. 2209, Comment 2.

Sufficiency of Consideration to Discharge Contract

Class (3) of consideration cases raises the question of the sufficiency of consideration to discharge a contract.

Part Payment plus Other Consideration: D is indebted to C in the amount of $5000 for goods furnished or services rendered by C. D makes the proposition to C that he will assign certain accounts receivable of his business worth $4000 to C or will sell certain assets worth approximately $4000 if C will accept the $4000 in full satisfaction of the $5000 debt, which C agrees to do. Transfer of the accounts receivable to C or payment to him of the $4000 received from sale of the equipment will fully discharge the $5000 debt. Technically, D can be found to have suffered a new, additional detriment in each case. In the first, the act of making the assignment of accounts; in the second, the act of selling the equipment. Again, "the courts will not inquire into the adequacy of consideration," will not say that these acts are not worth $1000 if that is, in effect, the value given them by the parties. Policy considerations are involved here. Compromise of debts is to be favored. It clears the courts of much sterile litigation.

Part Payment and Written Release: By contrast, suppose that D, owing C $1000, offers C $600 cash in full payment, which C accepts. C can still recover the other $400. There is no detriment to offset the $400. In an increasing number of states, however, statutes make an out-and-out exception to the requirement of consideration by providing that an obligation may be discharged by part payment, if a written release is given.[29]

U.C.C. 2209. C.C. 1697 and 1698 now read as follows:
   C.C. 1697: "A contract not in writing may be modified in any respect by consent of the parties, in writing, without a new consideration, and is extinguished thereby to the extent of the modification."
   C.C. 1698: "(a) A contract in writing may be modified by a contract in writing. (b) A contract in writing may be modified by an oral agreement to the extent that the oral agreement is executed by the parties. (c) Unless the contract otherwise expressly provides, a contract in writing may be modified by new consideration. The statute of frauds (Section 1624) is required to be satisfied if the contract as modified is within its provisions. (d) Nothing in this section precludes in an appropriate case the application of rules of law concerning estoppel, oral novation and substitution of a new agreement, rescission of a written contract by an oral agreement, waiver of a provision of a written contract, or oral independent collateral contracts."
   [29]C.C. 1524: "Part performance of an obligation, either before or after a breach thereof, when expressly accepted by the creditor in writing, in satisfaction, or rendered in pursuance of an agreement in writing for that purpose, though without any new consideration, extinguishes the obligation."
   C.C. 1541: "An obligation is extinguished by a release therefrom given to the debtor by the creditor . . . in writing, with or without new consideration."
   Former C.C. 1698, now C.C. 1698(a), both of which are shown in footnote 28a, is deemed to apply when a written contract is modified by an oral agreement, which agrees to accept less than is due under the written contract, and the oral agreement

Composition Agreement: Suppose D owes A $3000, B $2000 and C $1000. Having only $3000, he offers to pay 50 cents on the dollar if each will accept this in full payment. If A, B and C agree to this among themselves as well as with D, the agreement will be binding. D is doing something the law does not require—prorating his assets among his creditors. In addition, it is said that the agreement of each creditor to give up part of his claim is consideration for the like agreement of every other creditor. Such an arrangement is called a "composition of creditors."

Compromise of Disputed or Unliquidated Obligation: There are cases in which parties to a contract have not actually agreed on the consideration to be paid one party, or in which there is a bona fide dispute as to the amount to which one party is entitled. For example, C contracts to do a job for D for $500. Upon completion, C sends a bill for $500 which D refuses to pay, claiming, honestly, that the job is defective to the extent of $150. C agrees to take $350 in full payment. Or, C, an accountant, performs services for D. There has been no agreement as to C's compensation. He bills D for $500. D sends back a check for $350 with a letter stating that he feels that $500 is exorbitant and that the $350 is in full payment. C deposits the check. In these cases it is held that if the parties expressly or impliedly agree on an amount which will discharge the obligation, the agreement will be binding; that the debtor gives up his right to prove that a lesser amount is due. In the first case above, there would be express compromise; in the second, implied compromise resulting from C's acceptance and deposit of the check without objection.[30]

Exceptions—Consideration not Required

In certain cases the requirement of consideration is dispensed with.

Promise Inducing Reliance—Doctrine of "Promissory Estoppel" or "Detrimental Reliance": Sometimes one is held to a promise for which he will receive no consideration. This is so where, in the eyes of the law, the promisee is reasonably justified in relying on the promise and will be injured if it is not enforced. In such circumstances, justice demands that the promise be enforced despite absence of consideration. This is the doctrine of *promissory estoppel* or *detrimental reliance* which may be stated as follows: Where a party makes a promise which he should reasonably expect to induce an act or forbearance on the part of another, the promisor will be *estopped* (not permitted) to escape or withdraw from the promise even though he has received no consideration for it; the promise will be enforced to prevent injustice. Modern writers prefer to refer to the doctrine as the doctrine of *detrimental reliance.*

● The charitable subscription case is a simple example of promissory estoppel at work. You subscribe some amount to

a charity to be paid in installments. The charity incurs obligations on the strength of the subscription. You cannot repudiate the subscription though you will receive nothing in return for the money to be paid. You have induced action by your promise (subscription) and will be held to it.[31]

● *Lusk-Harbison-Jones, Inc.* v. *Universal Credit Company,* 164 Miss. 693, 145 So. 623, is another, quite different type of illustration: D was a Ford dealer. It sold to the consumer public on conditional sale contracts. In accordance with standard business practice, it then assigned the contracts to P financing agency, guaranteeing payment. Five buyers defaulted on their contracts, and D repossessed the cars. D was then obligated to resell for the benefit of P and stand answerable to P for any deficiency. Since the market was poor at the time, D asked permission to hold the cars until the market improved. P agreed on the condition that the cars were to be held at D's "sole risk as to all loss or injury." P, however, told D not to take out insurance on the cars; that P would carry it. Some time thereafter, the cars were destroyed by fire. P had failed to take out insurance on them. P sued D for the balances of the contracts. D set up the failure to insure as a defense. P contended that its promise to insure was not supported by consideration and so not binding on it. Held for D. Said the court: "Upon the point that no consideration is shown for the agreement that [P] would carry the insurance, we bottom our conclusion upon the fact that [D] acted upon the statement made by [P] that the latter . . . would . . . carry it; a very reasonable course on the part of [D] . . . upon the well recognized principle applicable to such a situation which has been summarized in Restatement of the Law of Contracts [Section 90], as follows: 'A promise which the promisor should reasonably expect to induce action or forbearance of a definite and substantial character on the part of the promisee and which does induce such action and forbearance is binding if injustice can be avoided only by enforcement of the promise.' We are mindful that the principle just stated is one to be applied with caution and only when the facts are well within it; but here . . . the statements and representations made were equivalent to a promise to continue that insurance in force; and the promisee having reasonably relied thereon, the promise can only be enforced by casting the loss on the promisor. . . ."[32]

● Other examples of situations in which promissory estoppel is applied are where a debtor induces his creditor to postpone suit by promising not to invoke the statute of limitations: where a mortgagor makes improvements on property in reliance upon the mortgagee's promise not to foreclose; and

---

is then carried out ("executed"). This is illustrated by the *rent reduction case.* Tenant has a 5-year lease at $500 a month rent. While the lease has 3 years to run, business gets bad, and tenant asks landlord to reduce the rent to $400, which landlord agrees to do. Tenant then pays $400 a month. In *Julian* v. *Gold,* 214 C. 74, 3 P.2d 1009, it was held, in accordance with C.C. 1698, that the landlord could not collect the additional $100 a month. In these rent reduction cases, some courts reach the same result by the "implied rescission" theory discussed in the text.

[30]In *Sheldon Builders, Inc.* v. *Trojan Towers* (1967) 255 C.A.2d 781, 63 C.R. 425, it was held that mere retention by the creditor of a check marked "paid in full" without notification that it was not accepted as payment in full operated to discharge the debt.

[31]California will apply the doctrine of promissory estoppel in charitable subscription cases. And in California and a number of states, another theory will be invoked to enforce charitable subscriptions as soon as there are two or more subscribers—the theory that the mutual, reciprocal promises of the various subscribers support and are consideration for each other and give rise to contracts between each and every subscriber of which the charity is a third party beneficiary, with a right of enforcement as discussed on page 51. Under this theory, it is not necessary that the charity incur obligation on the strength of the subscription.

[32]In *Graddon* v. *Knight,* 138 C.A.2d 577, 292 P.2d 632, a bank which was making a home loan promised, as an accommodation to the buyer, to obtain the fire insurance he needed, but failed to do so. The home was destroyed by fire while uninsured. The bank was held liable for its value on the ground of promissory estoppel.

where a donee makes improvements on land in reliance upon a promised gift of the land.[33]

Drennan v. *Star Paving Co.*, 51 C.2d 409, 333 P.2d 757 is an important modern California case because it rejects the theory, widely held at one time at least, that promissory estoppel should not be applied to a bargain promise. A subcontractor's bid is such a promise. It bargains for a promise by the general contractor to hire the subcontractor for the subcontract job if the general contractor wins the general job; such a promise would constitute an acceptance of the subcontractor's bid and make it binding. In *Drennan* the general contractor used a subcontractor's bid without first accepting it in this manner. The general contractor won the job. The subcontractor then undertook to revoke his bid before any formal acceptance by the general contractor. It was held that he could not, the court applying the doctrine of promissory estoppel.[34]

Revival of Barred Debt: Until the enactment of the Bankruptcy Reform Act of 1978, it was the rule that a promise to pay a debt discharged in bankruptcy or barred by the running of the statute of limitations was binding. The debt was regarded as being revived for a new period of limitations. The rationale for the rule came to be that the moral obligation to pay the debt ought to be enough to make the promise to do so enforceable. The rule came to be that a promise to satisfy a moral obligation *arising out of a pre-existing legal obligation* (as distinguished from the "purely" moral obligation involved in the cases in the next section) was sufficiently founded to be enforceable.[35] Some spoke of "moral consideration" in this instance. In fact, courts did not feel sympathetically inclined toward those who escaped debts by technical means.

• The foregoing is still the rule with respect to debts barred by the running of the statute of limitations. Not only will an express promise to pay it revive such a debt but also an unqualified acknowledgment of the debt. It is a companion principle of law that an acknowledgment of a debt implies a promise to pay it and, in this instance, the courts find that the implied promise is as good as an express promise. Some jurisdictions carry the process one step further. In some jurisdictions, part payment alone, not accompanied by an acknowledgment of the debt or a promise to pay it, is enough. The rationale is sometimes said to be that part payment acknowledges the debt, that, as has been seen, acknowledgment of a debt implies a promise to pay it, and that, again as has been seen, an implied promise is sufficient, in this instance, to revive the debt. California requires a *written* promise or acknowledgment to revive a debt barred by the running of the statute of limitations.[36] But part payment before the statute

runs extends the life of the debt.[37] The debt is revived and may be enforced only on the terms and to the extent specified in the new promise. If the new promise is to pay half of the barred debt, that is all that can be recovered.

• The drafters of the Bankruptcy Reform Act of 1978 were of the opinion that many bankruptcy debtors were being pressured into "reaffirming" debts by heavy-handed creditors. Therefore the drafters of the Act included Section 524 in the Act (page 487) which seriously limits the obtainability at least of a new promise to pay a barred debt. Section 524 is not too happily drafted. It appears to say in net effect however that a promise to pay a debt discharged in bankruptcy will not be enforceable unless the debtor has been lavishly warned against and about it [subsection (d)] and that the promise will not be enforceable if the debt is a consumer debt unless the bankruptcy court finds that the promise is in the best interests of the debtor and otherwise meets the requirements of subsection (c)(4).

Moral Obligation Based on Benefit Received: A growing body of case law supports the view that the purely moral obligation involved is sufficient to support a promise to reward a pecuniary benefit gratuitously conferred. If one "blurts out" an idea for a movie, the one to whom the idea is disclosed can use it without obligation; this is a case of benefit gratuitously conferred. Suppose the user then promises to pay for the idea. Relying on the body of case law mentioned, it was indicated in the California case of *Desny* v. *Wilder*, 46 C.2d 715, 299 P.2d 257, that such a promise could be enforced.

A more conventional application of the doctrine is in the "life-saving case" such as *Webb* v. *McGowin*, 168 So. 196 (Ala.). There, P saved D's life by risking his own life and causing a disabling injury to himself in the process. In gratitude, D promised to pay P a small monthly stipend for P's support. The stipend was paid for a period of time and then discontinued. Suit was brought to enforce the continued payment of the stipend and was successful on the ground of the moral obligation owed by D to P based on the benefit that D had received at P's expense.

Legal Purpose

A contract must have a legal purpose and subject matter.[38] Contracts which seek to accomplish a purpose forbidden by statute are illegal and unenforceable. Particular classes of illegal contracts are discussed below.

• Also illegal and unenforceable are contracts contrary to public policy or good morals.[39] Determination of illegality on

---

[33]An interesting modern California application of the doctrine of promissory estoppel is *Morrison* v. *Home S. & L. Assn.*, 175 C.A.2d 765, 346 P.2d 917, where a bank was held to its promise to make a home loan, when the buyer was not able to obtain a loan elsewhere.

[34]Restatement of Contracts 2d, §§ 89B(2) and 295, adopt the *Drennan* view.

[35]C.C. 1606 is a code section to this effect. It says that ". . . a moral obligation originating in some benefit conferred upon the promisor . . . is . . . a good consideration for a promise, to an extent corresponding with the extent of the obligation, but not further or otherwise."

[36]C.C.P. 360: "No acknowledgment or promise is sufficient evidence of a new or continuing contract, by which to take the case out of the operation of . . . [the statute of limitations] . . .

unless the same is contained in some writing, signed by the party to be charged thereby . . ."

But in *Van Cauteren* v. *Forger*, 45 C.A.2d, 388, 114 P.2d 6, where the debtor made a number of payments by check and the creditor sent receipts, it was held that the checks and receipts constituted a writing sufficient to revive the debt.

[37]A promise to pay or an acknowledgment of a debt made *before* the statute of limitations runs, extends the debt for a period of limitations running from the date of the promise. Part payment alone *before* the statute runs does this in California if the obligation is a note. (C.C.P. 360.)

[38]C.C. 1596: "The object of a contract must be lawful . . ."

[39]C.C. 1667: "That is not lawful which is:
"1. Contrary to an express provision of the law;
"2. Contrary to the policy of express law, though not expressly prohibited; or
"3. Otherwise contrary to good morals."

s account is a matter for the judgment of a court in a particular case. It is a matter of "feeling" that a particular agreement is not proper. This is best seen by an examination of ses.

Bacciocco v. *Transamerica Corporation*, 2 C.A.2d 595, 38 2d 417, involved an agreement by an influential individual buy stock of a corporation in order to influence the public buy the stock. The corporation guaranteed the individual ainst loss on the transaction. There was a break in the mar-t, and the individual was forced to sell at a loss. He sued enforce the agreement of the corporation to indemnify him ainst loss. He was denied relief. The court said that the ntract was one for "maintaining in the public market a sell-g price for these stocks above their real value. The contract . was a fraud upon the other stockholders of both corpo-tions and a fraud upon the public generally. By this bargain e individual] sought . . . to lead the public to buy shares the Transamerica Corporation at a fictitious and unfair ice . . . . [He] would lend his name and influence to a udulent scheme to boost the stock on the market to such a ice that he could sell out at a handsome profit to the detri-nt of his friends and business associates who would be left olding the sack.' Such a contract, *being contrary to good rals*, is expressly declared to be unlawful by Section 1667 the Civil Code. . . ."

Trumbo v. *Bank of Berkeley*, 77 C.A.2d 704, 176 P.2d 376 ld that a contract between the promoters of a banking cor-ration and an individual to make the individual a vice-pres-nt of the bank was against public policy and illegal because deprived the directors of the corporation of the power given m by law to appoint officers.

In *Reiner* v. *North American Newspaper Alliance*, 259 N.Y. 0, 181 N.E. 561, a contract to pay $5000 for secret mes-ges on the progress of a flight was held to be against public licy and illegal where exclusive news rights had been sold a newspaper and the person sending secret messages had ned an agreement not to send reports during the flight.

Other types of contracts which have been held to be against blic policy or good morals for obvious reasons are contracts defraud creditors, to fix bidding at public sales, to influence blic officials, and to obstruct justice.

After courts have declared a contract against public policy, legislature may codify the rule. Such has been the case th contracts in fraud of creditors and contracts in restraint trade.

rticular Illegal Contracts or Contract Provisions

Now to be considered are certain types of contracts and ntract provisions which violate statute.

Gambling or Wagering Contracts: Except in Nevada, gam-ng contracts are illegal.[40]

In early days, insurance contracts were sometimes found to "wagers," rather than valid "insurances." *Insurable in-est* is the thing that makes the difference. If there is an surable interest there is a valid insurance contract. Insurable erest is covered in the chapter on insurance.[41]

Usurious Contracts: "Interest" is a charge or rental for the an of money. Statute in every state prescribes the maximum

rate (*contract rate*).[42] To charge in excess of that rate is *usury*, and *usurious contracts* are contracts calling for a higher rate of interest than is permitted by law. The penalty is usually forfeiture of all interest. In some cases even principal is lost.[43]

The contract in these cases is a note, as illustrated on page 116. If I lend money to you, I will have you sign such a note so that I will have written evidence of your indebtedness to me. If I want excessive interest, I will not let that fact appear on the face of the note, but will do it in one of two ways: By having you sign a note for a greater amount than I actually lend, e.g., having you sign a note for $5000 plus a valid rate of interest, but lending you only $4500; or by antedating the note. I lend you $5000 on January 1, 1983, payable on Jan-uary 1, 1984, with interest at the maximum rate, but date the note January 1, 1982, so that I will collect 2 years' interest for the one-year loan. It is when you fail to pay and I sue that the fact of usury will appear. You will be permitted to "go behind the note" to show the usury.

● The *contract rate* must be distinguished from the *legal rate*. The legal rate is that rate of interest which by law attaches to judgments and, after they become delinquent, to obligations which do not expressly provide for interest. In California, the contract rate between private individuals is as shown in foot-note 42. In California, the legal rate is 7% but the Legislature may set a legal rate of up to 10%.[44]

● Certain practices smack of but do not constitute usury:

Collecting interest in advance is valid as long as the amount collected does not exceed the contract rate per annum for the term of the loan.

If you buy an automobile for cash you may pay $7000 for it. If you buy it on time you may pay $10,500. The difference

---

[40]Pen. C. 330 makes gambling a misdemeanor.

[41]California law on *insurable interest* is discussed in the chapter insurance.

[42]California interest law has become increasingly complicated. Earlier on it broke down roughly into three categories: (1) private individuals were limited to 10%; (2) large professional lenders such as banks, were considered self-policing, and were exempted from regulation; (3) smaller classes of professional lenders such as industrial loan companies, personal property brokers and pawnbrokers were regulated by specific statutes according to the degree of risk involved in the lender's form of lending. The pat-tern remains essentially the same but the statutes by which small types of professional lenders are regulated have become increas-ingly complicated. The basic law has always been found in the state constitution. As recently amended, the constitutional pro-vision, which is contained in Article 15, Section 1 of the state constitution is less than clear. Section 1 of Article 15 makes these provisions: (1) Most professional lenders, large and small are exempted from the operation of Section 1. These include banks, building and loan associations, industrial loan companies, credit unions, personal property brokers and pawnbrokers. Exemption is also made of "any loans made or arranged by any person licensed as a real estate broker by the State of California and secured in whole or in part by liens on real property." (2) With respect to nonexempt classes of lenders (a) the maximum rate is 10% "(f)or any loan or forbearance of any money, goods, or things in action, if the money, goods, or things in action are for use primarily for personal, family, or household purposes" ex-cept "purchase, construction or improvement of real property (which) shall not be deemed to be a use primarily for personal, family or household purposes"; (b) for other types of "loans or forbearances," the rate cannot exceed the higher of 10% per annum or 5% per annum plus the prevailing rate on advances by the Federal Reserve Bank of San Francisco to member banks.

[43]For example, under California's Consumer Finance Lenders Law. Fin. C. 24000 et seq.; Fin. C. 24651.

[44]Cal.Const., Art. 15, § 1.

is "time-price differential." Time-price differential is an amount charged for allowing a purchaser to buy on time. Since a *loan* of money is not involved the charge is not interest. Therefore time-price differential is not regulated by interest statutes and may exceed interest rates unless it, specifically, is regulated by statute. In many states it is.[45]

Purchasing commercial paper at discount does not constitute usury. This is discussed in the chapter on Commercial Paper.

Penalty and Forfeiture Provisions: If you and I make a contract, and I fail to perform, your remedy in the usual case is a suit for damages. The damages which you would recover would be called *compensatory damages*—the amount of out-of-pocket loss suffered by you. If I fail to deliver to you, as agreed, 5000 tons of steel at $100 a ton, and you have to buy it elsewhere for $103 a ton, you would have the right to recover $15,000 from me.

• In some cases damages are not so readily computed. I sell you a business. In the contract I agree not to engage in the same business in that city for one year.[46] Two weeks later I open a new business across the street. You have a right to damages but an impossible job of proving them. You should have required a *liquidated damages* clause; a provision prefixing damages. So long as such provision does not assume the proportions of a penalty, it is enforceable where actual damages would be impossible or difficult to ascertain.[47]

---

[45]In California, C.C. 2982(c) expressly limits the timeprice differential in conditional sales of motor vehicles. The limitation depends on whether the precomputed interest basis is used or the simple interest basis.

In 1960 the Unruh Act (C.C. 1801-1812.9) became effective. It regulates time-price differential, "carrying charges," or whatever the item may be called, in installment sales of goods or services (except motor vehicles) of a value of $50 or more. See page 98.

[46]Such agreements are called "*covenants not to compete*," and are generally held to be valid if confined to reasonable geographical limits for a reasonable time. B. & P. C. 16601, 16602 permit them for *exceptionally* long periods of time as follows:

B. & P. C. 16601: "Any person who sells the good will of a business, or any shareholder of a corporation selling or otherwise disposing of all his shares in said corporation, may agree with the buyer to refrain from carrying on a similar business within a specified county or counties, city or cities, or a part thereof, in which the business so sold, or that of said corporation, has been carried on, so long as the buyer, or any person deriving title to the good will or shares from him, carries on a like business therein."

B. & P. C. 16602: "Partners may, upon or in anticipation of a dissolution of the partnership, agree that none of them will carry on a similar business within the same city or town or a specified part thereof, where the partnership business has been transacted."

[47]Until 1977, the California law was as shown in the text, i.e., liquidated damages provisions were valid if actual damages would be extremely difficult to prove and the amount fixed as liquidated damages represented a reasonable effort to estimate actual damages. These criteria are continued in consumer transactions, that is, in contracts for the retail purchase or rental of personal property or services for personal, family or household purposes, and in leases of residential real estate. C.C. 1671. Attempt is made to soften the requirements in other types of transactions, except contracts for the purchase of residential real property, for which there are special rules, shown below. With respect to nonconsumer transactions, C.C. 1671(b) provides that a liquidated damage provision "is valid unless the party seeking to invalidate the provision establishes that the provision was unrea-

• Suppose I sell you a tractor for $10,000 with $1000 dow and the balance to be paid in monthly installments. We use conditional sales contract which says that I retain title un the price is paid, and that if you miss an installment I m repossess and resume ownership of the tractor and keep amounts paid by you—a *forfeiture* provision. After you ha reduced the balance to $3000 you miss an installment, and repossess. I resell the tractor for $5000 so that I make a tot of $12,000 on the deal, $2000 more than I should have mad It would seem that you should be able to recover the $20 from me since $3000 would fully compensate me for yo breach of contract. Unless there is a statute protecting y against such forfeiture, however, there is nothing you can d No matter of damages is involved. I held title all the tim You had only the privilege of getting title by completing t payments. Many states now have statutes protecting buye against this sort of thing, however.[48]

Anti-forfeiture statutes are found in other fields of lav Most states have statutes forbidding cancellation of a life i surance policy with forfeiture of premiums paid. If the insur cannot continue to pay premiums, he must be given a ca surrender privilege and certain other privileges.[49]

Exculpatory Clauses: If A negligently injures B or property, A is liable to B in damages for A's tort. The sar is true if A's employee injures B or his property, since employer is liable for the torts of his employees. Now supp that A and B are going to enter into a contract throughout t term of which A or his employees may cause injury to B his property. A may try to protect himself against liability f such harm by a provision in the contract exempting A fro liability. Such clauses are called *exculpatory clauses*.

Are exculpatory clauses "legal"?

The California law is an interesting study in the develo ment of law. It starts with the 1895 case of *Stephens* v. *Sout ern Pacific Co.*, 109 C. 86, 41 P. 783. In *Stephens*, the ! leased a warehouse to Stephens, located on land adjoining SP depot. The lease provided that SP would not be liable f damages to Stephens' property caused by fire. SP negligent

---

sonable under the circumstances existing at the time the contr. was made." Extreme difficulty in the ascertainment of actu damages is not required and it appears to be enough that t amount fixed as liquidated damages is not punitive.

C.C. 1675-1681 set up special rules for contracts for the pu chase of residential real property, to be occupied as a resident as follows: (i) "If the amount actually paid pursuant to the li uidated damages provision does not exceed 3 percent of the pu chase price, the provision is valid to the extent that payment actually made unless the buyer establishes that such amount unreasonable as liquidated damages." C.C. 1675(c). (ii) "If t amount actually paid pursuant to the liquidated damages pro sion exceeds 3 percent of the purchase price, the provision invalid unless the party seeking to uphold the provision establis es that the amount paid actually is reasonable as liquidated da ages." C.C. 1675(d). (iii) In all cases, "(t)he (liquidated da ages) provision (must be) separately signed or initialed by ea party to the contract" and "(i)f the (liquidated damages) pro sion is included in a printed contract, it (must be) set out eith in at least 10-point bold type or in contrasting red print in at lea eight-point bold type." C.C. 1677.

The foregoing provisions apply only to contracts made on after July 1, 1978.

[48]See Unruh Act, page 98, and U.C.C. 9504(2).

[49]Provisions of the California Insurance Code to this effect w be seen in the chapter on Insurance.

arted a fire which damaged Stephens' property. Stephens
gued that the exculpatory clause was against public policy
d ought not to be enforced. The court held to the contrary.
later cases at least, the court in *Stephens* v. *Southern Pacific*
o. was thought to have held that as long as the contract did
t "affect the public interest" but only the private affairs of
e parties to the contract, the exculpatory clause was valid.
Stephens represented a strong freedom of contract view of
th century and early 20th century courts. Later California
urts were less kindly disposed to exculpatory clauses but
ntented themselves with limiting operation of the *Stephens*
se by the process of strict construction. The doctrine of
rict construction is succinctly stated in *Basin Oil Co.* v.
ash-Ross Tool Co. (1954) 125 C.A.2d 578, 271 P.2d 122,
here the court said: "(T)he law does not look with favor
on attempts to avoid liability or secure exemption for one's
vn negligence, and such provisions are strictly construed
gainst the person relying on them."
Strict construction had its first demonstration in the aggra-
ted negligence cases: *Butt* v. *Bertola* (1952) 110 C.A.2d
8, 242 P.2d 32, and *Barkett* v. *Brucato* (1953) 122 C.A.2d
4, 264 P.2d 978. In *Butt* and *Barkett*, the court thought
at, in each case, the wrongdoer was guilty of active or "af-
mative negligence," which the court thought to be present
hen the wrongdoer was guilty of increasing the probability
harm by extended inaction or by doing an act under cir-
mstances that made it ultra-hazardous. *Butt* and *Bertola*
ere both lease cases. In *Butt*, for a long period of time,
spite frequent request from the lessee, the lessor failed to
pair defective plumbing which eventually caused the prem-
es occupied by the lessee to become flooded. The water
maged the lessee's equipment and property. The lease con-
ined the exculpating provision that "Lessor shall not be li-
le for damages to any goods, property, or effects in or upon
id premises, caused by gas, water, or other fluid from any
urce whatsoever." It was held that this clause did not ex-
erate the lessor. The court said in effect that an exculpatory
ause should not be considered to be intended to include ac-
ve or affirmative negligence of the wrongdoer unless this
as specifically stated in the clause; that an exculpatory clause
the type under consideration should be limited in its oper-
ion to cases in which the wrongdoer was guilty only of or-
nary or passive negligence. In *Barkett,* the lessor removed
e roof of the lessee's flat during the rainy season when not
quired by any emergency. This was part of a course of
rassment designed to get the lessee to vacate the premises.
eakage through the exposed ceiling damaged the lessee's
operty. The lease exculpatory clause provided that lessor
shall not be liable for damage or injury to any person, per-
nal property or effects . . . from any cause whatsoever."
s in *Butt*, it was held that clear intention to include affirm-
ive negligence would have to be shown before an exculpa-
ry clause would be interpreted as extending to such negli-
nce.
Exculpatory clauses are of two general varieties, *exemption*
auses such as have been seen above, in which the exculpator
empts the exculpatee from liability for harm done by the
culpatee to the exculpator, and *indemnity clauses* in which
e one party agrees "to hold and save (the other party) harm-
ss from liability for injury to persons or property." *Vinnell*
o. v. *Pac. Elec. Ry. Co.* (1959) 52 C.2d 411, 340 P.2d 604,
volved an indemnity clause which provided that, "Contrac-
r . . . agrees to indemnify and save Railroad harmless from
d against any and all . . . liability, howsoever same may be
used . . ." Railroad drove a locomotive into Contractor's
xcavation and damaged it and some of Contractor's equip-

ment. Railroad sought escape in the exculpatory clause, which
was held not to save it. Such a clause, said the court, is designed to save the indemnitee (Railroad) from liability to *third
persons* by making the indemnitor (Contractor) his insurer
against such liability. It is not designed to cover an injury by
the indemnitee to the indemnitor unless such an intention is
clearly expressed.

Another major distinction has been drawn in California between exculpatory clauses contained in contracts *affected with
a public interest* and exculpatory clauses contained in contracts not affected with a public interest. The lease cases seen
so far have been deemed to involve "private affairs" only of
the parties to the lease—the lessor and the lessee—and therefore not to be affected with the public interest. *Tunkl* v. *Re-
gents of the University of California* (1963) 60 C.2d 92, 32
C.R. 33, 383 P.2d 441, involved a release that was required
to be signed by a patient to gain admission to the University
of California at Los Angeles Medical Center. The release provided that "patient . . . releases . . . hospital from any and
all liability for the negligent or wrongful acts or omissions of
its employees . . ." The negligence charged was that of the
two physicians employed by the hospital. It was held that this
was a contract or transaction affected with a public interest
and that exculpatory clauses are not good in the cases of such
contracts or transactions. The court laid down as the test of
whether a contract or transaction was affected with a public
interest that it exhibit some or all of the following characteristics:

"It concerns a business of a type generally thought suitable
for public regulation. The party seeking exculpation is engaged in performing a service of great importance to the public, which is often a matter of practical necessity for some
members of the public. The party holds himself out as willing
to perform this service for any member of the public who
seeks it, or at least for any member coming within certain
established standards. As a result of the essential nature of the
service, in the economic setting of the transaction, the party
invoking exculpation possesses a decisive advantage of bargaining strength against any member of the public who seeks
his services. In exercising a superior bargaining power the
party confronts the public with a standardized adhesion contract of exculpation, and makes no provision whereby a purchaser may pay additional reasonable fees and obtain protection against negligence. Finally, as a result of the transaction,
the person or property of the purchaser is placed under the
control of the seller, subject to the risk of carelessness by the
seller or his agents."

The court found that the hospital-patient contract involved
fulfilled all of the characteristics stated as the test of a contract
affected with a public interest.

● The public interest was found to be affected in a more pro-
saic situation in *Akin* v. *Business Title Corp.* (1968) 264
C.A.2d 153, 70 C.R. 287. There, defendant escrow company
undertook to record a chattel mortgage for plaintiff-customer.
The defendant escrow company recorded the chattel mortgage
in the wrong county so that the chattel mortgage was invalid
as against the mortgagor's trustee in bankruptcy. The contract
form which plaintiff was required to sign at the time of employing the services of defendant exempted the defendant
from liability for defendant's negligence. After setting out the
public-interest-affecting criteria of the *Tunkl* case, the court
said: "In comparing these six criteria set forth in *Tunkl* to the
case at bench we find that the transaction before us is also one
that 'affects the public interest.'"

Similar distinctions to those made in California, as shown above, are probably now made in most states.[50]

● Exculpatory clauses in bailment transactions such as the deposit of a car in a parking lot are discussed in the chapter on Personal Property.

● C.C. 2782 and 2784.5 declare void indemnity clauses in construction contracts or hauling, trucking or cartage contracts by which the contractor or hauler exempts himself from liability for injury to person or property resulting from his "sole negligence or willful misconduct."

● A person may limit his liability for failing to complete a contract as distinguished from exempting himself from liability for his negligence. In legal contemplation, these are two quite different sorts of things. Negligent conduct, whether involving only ordinary negligence or involving a greater degree of negligence, is immoral conduct. To allow a person to do a morally wrongful act without liability, as an exculpatory clause does, is inherently objectionable and, as has been seen, we are prepared to at least limit the extent to which it can be done. Failure to complete a contract is not immoral conduct in any of the same sense and therefore there is no objection to allowing a person to limit his liability for such action. *Wheeler* v. *Oppenheimer* (1956) 140 C.A.2d 497, 295 P.2d 128, is a California illustrative case. There, a contract for the sale of real estate provided that the seller would be liable only for costs and expenses incurred by the buyer if the seller did not complete the sale. It was held that the limitation of liability was valid.

Agreements to Eliminate Competition: Ours is designed to be a competitive economy—one which will be self-regulating so long as competition exists. Therefore, arrangements or agreements to eliminate competition would be against public policy. In the last half of the 19th century, our industrial society had developed to the point where competition-eliminating practices were becoming a serious threat to the economy. This induced passage of the Sherman Anti-Trust Act of 1890, which declared to be illegal contracts, combinations and monopolies in restraint of trade or competition.

● If in position to do so, the simplest way to eliminate competition and achieve monopolistic status is to overpower the competition. The early cases under the Act involved this—the Standard Oil Company case (*Standard Oil Company of New Jersey* v. *United States,* 221 U.S. 1, 55 L.Ed. 619, 31 S.Ct. 502) and the American Tobacco Company case (*United States* v. *American Tobacco Company*, 221 U.S. 106, 55 L.Ed. 663, 31 S.Ct. 632). In both cases, competition was simply overwhelmed. In the Standard Oil situation, the final form of monopoly was a holding company, Standard Oil Company of New Jersey, which controlled the stock of the major producers of petroleum products and so could enforce noncompetitive policies. In the American Tobacco case there was a consolidation of the major competitors. In each case, a dissolution was ordered.

● Later, price-fixing agreements and agreements to limit production were attempted. By these, normally competitive business organizations would agree to abide by price or production schedules to eliminate unprofitable competition. These, of course, were equally violative of the Sherman Act.

● The Commerce Clearing House Antitrust Bluebook compiles all cases under the Sherman Act since its enactment. These total in excess of 1000 and read like the roll call of American industry—United States v. American Telephone Telegraph Company, U. S. Rubber Company, General El tric Company, Railway Express Agency, Inc., Internatio Harvester Company, Armour and Company, The Bord Company, E. I. du Pont de Nemours and Company, Sherw Williams Company, Bendix Aviation Corporation, Standa Oil Company of California, National Cash Register Com ny, Continental Can Company, Owens-Illinois Glass Co pany, General Motors Corporation, Safeway Stores, Inc., A sociated Press, International Longshoremen's Assn., F Motor Company, to list but a few in widely diversified fiel

● In 1914, the Federal Trade Commission Act was pass creating the Federal Trade Commission. The Federal Tr Commission is empowered to order the discontinuance of fair methods of competition and is designed to permit "b nipping" of practices and arrangements which may lead monopoly.

● Since the federal government may legislate and regul only with respect to matters which affect interstate commer the state governments must make their own laws with resp to intrastate monopolies and unfair trade practices.[51]

Contracts of Persons Required to be Licensed: Today, most anyone who engages in business is required to have least two licenses, one from the city and one from the sta These are designed to raise revenue and to insure payment city and state sales taxes. In addition, many persons are quired to have a license because of the type of business which they are engaged—insurance agents and brokers, estate salesmen and brokers, accountants, contractors, att neys and others. Here, the license has a different purpose is designed to protect the public by insuring that only quali persons practice in the fields. Now, suppose a contract made by a person who is required to but does not have or more of these licenses. Whether the unlicensed person enforce the contract depends upon the purpose of the licens requirement. If "the object of the statute or ordinance in quiring a license for the privilege of carrying on a cert business is to prevent improper persons from engaging in particular business, or is for the purpose of regulating it the protection of the public . . . [the statute or ordinance] . amounts to a prohibition against doing business without a cense and a contract made by an unlicensed person in vio tion of the statute or ordinance is void." (*Wood* v. *Krep* 168 C. 382, 143 P. 691.) But if the licensing requiremen merely a revenue measure, the contract is enforceable e though the unlicensed person may be subject to penalty by city or state for failure to have a license.

Effect of Illegality

Where a contract is only partly illegal or has only a par ular provision which is illegal, the courts will sever the ille portion and enforce the legal;[52] for instance, will permit covery of principal but not of interest in usurious contrac

---

[50]The exculpation rules of Restatement of Contracts 2d, § 195, are essentially similar to the rules developed by the California courts and illustration 2 to § 195 is the *Stephens* case.

[51]In California, the Cartwright Act (B. & P. C. 16700 et s is a local counterpart of the Sherman Act. It prohibits comb tions or contracts to restrain trade, limit production, fix price eliminate competition.

[52]C.C. 1598: "Where a contract has but a single object, such object is unlawful, whether in whole or in part . . . entire contract is void." C.C. 1599: "Where a contract has eral distinct objects, of which one at least is lawful, and on least is unlawful, in whole or in part, the contract is void a the latter and valid as to the rest."

Where the entire transaction is illegal, the outcome depends on the knowledge of the parties. If both know of the illegality, the courts may "leave the parties where they are," i.e., refuse to entertain legal proceedings in the matter, even though this may leave one party unjustly enriched. In *Holm* v. *Bramwell*, 20 C.A.2d 332, 67 P.2d 114, P entered into a contract with an unlicensed contractor. P paid money to him on account of labor and materials, neither of which materialized. Held, P could not recover his money. Being knowingly a party to an illegal contract, he had no standing in court to seek relief.

Where parties are not *in pari delicto* (not in equal guilt), the innocent party will be given relief. The simple case is that in which one party knows, and the other does not, that the transaction is illegal.

Where a person is a member of a class intended to be protected by a statute, he is usually treated as not *in pari delicto*. In *Tatterson* v. *Kehrlein*, 88 C.A. 34, 263 P. 285, for example, P contracted to purchase stock being sold without a permit from the Corporation Commissioner. Held, that, since the Corporate Securities Act is designed to protect buyers, P could recover payments made in purchase of the stock.

Reality of Assent

To create a contract there must be not only "mutual assent," offer and acceptance, but "real" assent. This is lacking if a party is induced to contract by mistake, fraud, duress or undue influence.[53]

_____

[53]California lists five categories of things which make the assent of a party unreal. C.C. 1567 say that "An apparent consent is not real or free when obtained through:

"1. Duress;

"2. Menace;

"3. Fraud;

"4. Undue influence; or

"5. Mistake."

Most states do not distinguish menace from duress and treat both as duress.

C.C. 1569 says that "*Duress* consists in:

"1. Unlawful confinement of the person of the party, or the husband or wife of such party, or of an ancestor, descendant, or adopted child of such party, husband, or wife;

"2. Unlawful detention of the property of any such person; or

"3. Confinement of such person, lawful in form, but fraudulently obtained, or fraudulently made unjustly harassing or oppressive."

C.C. 1570 says that "*Menace* consists of a threat:

"1. Of such duress as is specified in subdivisions one and three the last section;

"2. Of unlawful and violent injury to the person or property any such person as is specified in the last section; or,

"3. Of injury to the character of any such person."

C.C. 1575 says that "*Undue influence* consists:

"1. In the use, by one in whom a confidence is reposed by other, or who holds a real or apparent authority over him, of such confidence or authority, for the purpose of obtaining an fair advantage over him;

"2. In taking an unfair advantage of another's weakness of mind; or

"3. In taking a grossly oppressive and unfair advantage of another's necessities or distress."

Most California cases involving undue influence have involved contracts between persons in confidential relationships—attorney and client, trustee and beneficiary, etc., where a high degree of good faith is required.

If one of these invalidating factors is present, it has one of two general consequences. It makes the contract at least "voidable" by the injured party. In a few cases, illustrated below, it makes the transaction *void*—a complete nullity—no contract.

When the contract is voidable, the injured party may *rescind*.[54] He must act promptly upon discovering his right to do so and must return the consideration received. In the alternative, he may *affirm* the contract; stand by it and sue for damages. B purchases a business from S. Past earnings of the business are misrepresented, so B has the right to rescind for fraud. He may want to keep the business despite the fraud. The law permits him to do this and to bring an action for damages rather than to rescind. If, because of delay, the right to rescind is lost, the injured party may bring an action for damages.

Mistake

"I certainly made a mistake getting into that deal" or ". . . in buying that thing" are common complaints of persons who have made contracts which have not turned out satisfactorily from their standpoint. Normally, they do not refer to a type of "mistake" for which the law gives relief. That something turns out to be less profitable or efficient than expected is of no avail if it is the thing that was bargained for and there has been no misrepresentation of it. Where there has been misrepresentation, the remedy is an action for fraud.

● What is the nature of the mistake which nullifies a contract? It is not possible to make an all-inclusive statement. First, there may be mistake of such nature that the minds of the parties do not meet. This prevents formation of a contract and renders the transaction void. The classic example is *Raffles* v. *Wichelhaus*, 2 H.&C. 906, where there was a contract to sell cotton to be shipped to the buyer on the "Peerless." Unknown to the parties, there were two ships of this name which had departure dates three months apart, and each party had in mind a different ship. Held, there was never a meeting of minds, and the mistake prevented formation of a contract.

● There may be mistake as to a material fact—some *basic assumption* of the contract.[55] This would be present, for example, when S sells B cotton which S believes to be safely stored in a warehouse in another city, but which actually has been destroyed by fire.

_____

[54]C.C. 1689: "A party to a contract may rescind the same . . .

"1. If the consent of the party rescinding . . . was given by mistake, or obtained through duress, menace, fraud, or undue influence . . ."

[55]C.C. 1576-1579 cover mistake.

C.C. 1576: "Mistake may be either of fact or law."

C.C. 1577: "*Mistake of fact* is a mistake . . . consisting in:

"1. An unconscious ignorance or forgetfulness of a fact past or present, material to the contract; or

"2. Belief in the present existence of a thing material to the contract, which does not exist, or in the past existence of such a thing, which has not existed."

C.C. 1578: "*Mistake of law* . . . [is] . . .

"1. A misapprehension of the law by all parties, all supposing that they knew and understood it, and all making substantially the same mistake as to the law; or

"2. A misapprehension of the law by one party, of which the others are aware at the time of contracting, but which they do not rectify."

Restatement of Contracts 2d, § 151, Comment 6, allows relief for mistake of law as well as for mistake of fact.

Hannah v. *Steinman*, 159 C. 142, 112 P. 1094, is another example of mistake as to a basic assumption. Here, there was a lease of property upon which the lessee was to erect a wooden building for the conduct of his business. Unknown to the parties, a zoning ordinance prohibited wooden structures in the area. Cost of other construction would be prohibitive. Held, the lessee could rescind because of mistake as to a basic fact upon which the contract was predicated.

Materiality: Sometimes it is necessary to decide whether mistake is "*material*," since only material mistake permits avoidance. If I lease you a warehouse which is supposed to contain 10,000 square feet of storage space, but which actually contains only 9000, the mistake would be material and permit rescission because size is of the essence of the transaction. But if I lease you a store building which I mistakenly inform you to be 160 x 220 feet but which is only 160 x 200, there may be no case for rescission. If you intend to use the building as a display room and have examined it and have found it satisfactory for your purposes, there is no mistake which is "material" to you. At most you will be entitled to an adjustment of rent.

Unilateral Mistake: In the cases considered thus far, there has been mutual mistake; that is, mistake on the parts of both parties. Occasionally, there is *unilateral* or one-sided mistake, as in *Lepper* v. *Ratteree*, 98 C.A. 245, 276 P. 1037, where P mistakenly bought Lots 235 and 236 in a tract instead of 225 and 226, as intended. Some courts have denied relief in cases of this kind because the mistake results from negligence. In California, the code makes no distinction between mutual and unilateral mistake, and the courts give relief in either case. In the *Lepper* case, relief was denied because P delayed for over a year after discovering his mistake before taking action to rescind, and, as previously shown, rescission requires prompt action. Even in the states which deny relief for unilateral mistake generally, it may be given where there would be great hardship if it were denied, and the other party would suffer no real harm. Suppose that S owns Lots 5 and 6. B, wishing to purchase what is in fact Lot 5, but thinking it is Lot 6, purchases "lot 6" from S. He then commences construction of a building on what is in fact Lot 5, before discovering his mistake. Here, probably most courts would give him relief, assuming that S is still the owner of Lot 6.

● Actually, the most important kinds of cases in which relief is granted for unilateral mistake are the contractors' bids cases seen on page 26.

Reformation: Where there is a mistake in reducing an agreement to writing, the remedy is *reformation* of the written instrument to state the correct terms. B agrees to purchase Lots 4, 5, 7, 9, 10, 13 and 14 in a tract of land owned by S. The stenographer of an attorney employed by the parties to draft a deed lists "Lots 4, 5, 7, 8, 10, 13 and 14". Neither party catches the error. B is entitled to have the deed reformed.[56]

Fraud

We all know that *fraud* is bad, that it is the antithesis of fair dealing. Fraud as a legal concept is often misconceived,

---

[56]C.C. 3399: "When, through fraud or a mutual mistake of the parties, or a mistake of one party, which the other at the time knew or suspected, a written contract does not truly express the intention of the parties, it may be revised, on the application of a party aggrieved, so as to express that intention, so far as it can be done without prejudice to rights acquired by third persons, in good faith and for value."

however. We buy a used car, and the dealer tells us "You've got a good automobile there" when, in fact, it is a pretty bad automobile. Or you buy a business from a broker who tells you that "It's a gold mine for a good hard-working man," as he says a silent prayer of thanks for someone on whom to unload. These things are generally not frauds in the legal sense. The law writes them off as "seller's talk" or "puffing statements"; or statements of opinion about which you should exercise discretion. The old mandate, *caveat emptor* (let the buyer beware), applies. If, however, the automobile dealer tells us that the automobile is "in good mechanical condition," when he knows it has a cracked block; or the broker says that the business has netted $2000 a month over the past six months, when in fact it has netted $1000, we then have a case of fraud, because the misrepresentation is a misrepresentation of *fact*, and misrepresentation of *fact* is fraud.

Formally defined, fraud is a misrepresentation, concealment or nondisclosure of a material fact, made intentionally or negligently, i.e., without sufficient information to warrant the representation, and with the intent to induce the other party to enter into the contract, which he relies upon to his damage.

This definition would make three classes of acts fraudulent—intentional misrepresentation, negligent misrepresentation, and concealment or nondisclosure.[57] The first of these, intentional misrepresentation, speaks for itself.

---

[57]C.C. 1571-1573 cover fraud.

C.C. 1571 says that "Fraud is either actual or constructive."

Actual fraud is the type discussed in the text. Constructive fraud exists when the result of a transaction is fraudulent as to a person or class of persons, but there is no intent to defraud. This is discussed below:

C.C. 1572 makes five classes of things actual fraud, three of which are discussed in the text. It says that "Actual fraud, within the meaning of this chapter, consists in any of the following acts committed by a party to the contract, or with his connivance, with intent to deceive another party thereto, or to induce him to enter into the contract:

"1. The suggestion, as a fact, of that which is not true, by one who does not believe it to be true: [intentional misrepresentation]

"2. The positive assertion, in a manner not warranted by the information of the person making it, of that which is not true, though he believes it to be true; [negligent misrepresentation]

"3. The suppression of that which is true, by one having knowledge or belief of the fact; [concealment or nondisclosure]

"4. A promise made without any intention of performing it. [This is held to be fraud generally as well as in California, but because of the difficulty of proof, is seldom found. It has been applied to the case of a hopelessly insolvent person who buys on credit.] or,

"5. Any other act fitted to deceive."

C.C. 1573 says that "Constructive fraud consists:

"1. In any breach of duty which, without an actually fraudulent intent, gains an advantage to the person in fault, or anyone claiming under him, by misleading another to his prejudice, or to the prejudice of anyone claiming under him; or,

"2. In any such act or omission as the law specially declares to be fraudulent, without respect to actual fraud."

The first type of constructive fraud is illustrated by cases in which there is a special or confidential relationship between parties, and one party is not informed of pertinent facts, so that while there is no intention to defraud him, the effect is to do so.

In *McFate* v. *Bank of America*, 125 C.A. 683, 14 P.2d 146, a bank made an excessive loan on property. Later it acted as escrow in a sale in which the buyer assumed the loan. It did not inform him of the excessive nature of the loan. He based his price on apparent loan value. Upon discovery of the facts, he was permitted to recover from the bank for constructive fraud.

FRAUD BY STATUTE

Negligent Misrepresentation: Negligent misrepresentation a positive assertion of fact by a party who does not have fficient information on the subject to warrant the represenion. A business is placed in the hands of a broker for sale. he broker, having no knowledge of the earnings of the business, asserts that "It has cleared $2000 a month for the past ear." In fact, it has cleared $1000.

Concealment: Few cases have involved fraud in the form ' concealment. There must be some alteration of an article ot merely for the purpose of improving its looks but to conal a major defect. One of the rare cases is *Herzog* v. *Capitol* o., 27 C.2d 349, 164 P.2d 8, where a house leaked badly cause of defective construction, and the seller patched and ainted it to make it appear to be in good condition.

Nondisclosure: The problem of fraud in the form of nonsclosure arises when one party has special information hich he does not disclose to the other. The early law was pposed to be that if there was no *confidential or fiduciary* *lationship* between the parties—no relationship of principal d agent or partner and copartner or the like—i.e., if the rties were dealing "*at arm's length*," then, in that event, ere was no obligation on the part of the one party to disclose s special information to the other.[57a]

The law has changed, however. Second Torts Restatement, ection 551, which will be the main subject matter of this absection, deals with the matter. Section 551 says that cases presenting a change in the law "have been piling up rapidly, d there are now so many of them that they cannot be ignored."

Nevertheless, Section 551 takes a very cautious approach the matter. Section 551 says there is a duty to disclose facts basic to the transaction" and gives as examples of duty disclose, the duty to disclose that cattle being sold is dis-

---

In *Darrow* v. *Klein & Co.*, 111 C.A. 310, 295 P. 566, a broker ailed to disclose that he was acting as agent for buyer as well as eller and induced the seller to take a second mortgage from the uyer by representing the buyer to be a responsible person, which e was not. The seller was permitted to recover from the broker or constructive fraud.

The second type of constructive fraud is an act made fraudulent y statute; principally a fraudulent conveyance of the type disussed on page 355.

[57a] The distinction between a fiduciary relationship and a condential relationship is described as follows in *Barbara A.* v. ohn G. (1983), 145 C.A.3rd 369, 193 Cal.Rptr. 422:

"(F)iduciary" and "confidential" have been used synonyously to describe "'. . . any relation existing between parties a transaction wherein one of the parties is in duty bound to act ith the utmost good faith for the benefit of the other party. Such relation ordinarily arises where a confidence is reposed by one erson in the integrity of another, and in such a relation the party whom the confidence is reposed, if he (or she) voluntarily ccepts or assumes to accept the confidence, can take no advanage from his (or her) acts relating to the interest of the other arty without the latter's knowledge or consent. . . .'" (Cits.) echnically, a fiduciary relationship is a recognized legal relaonship such as guardian and ward, trustee and beneficiary, prinipal and agent, or attorney and client (Cit.) whereas a "confiential relationship" may be founded on a moral, social, domesc, or merely personal relationship as well as on a legal elationship. (Cits.) The essence of a fiduciary or confidential elationship is that the parties do not deal on equal terms, because he person in whom trust and confidence is reposed and who ccepts that trust and confidence is in a superior position to exert nique influence over the dependent party."

eased and that the basement of a house being sold floods during rains. Section 551 distinguishes "material facts" from such "basic facts." Material facts are ones which "induce" a party to enter into a transaction but which are not "basic" to the transaction. (As Section 551 says, quite honestly, "This is a difficult Section to find language for.") Section 551 gives this as an example of a material, but not basic, fact: "A sells to B a dwelling house, knowing that B is buying in the mistaken belief that a highway is planned which will pass near the land and enhance its value. A does not disclose to B the fact that no such highway is planned. This is not a fact basic to the transaction." In traditional attempts at legal distinction, this appears to attempt to distinguish between a fact which affects the subject matter of the contract directly (diseased; prone to flooding) and one which affects it only collaterally (merely makes it less valuable).

Section 551 sees the law as moving in the direction of an even greater duty of disclosure. It says, "(t)he law may be moving in the direction of requiring disclosure of 'material' facts, but it is not yet sufficiently clear to justify more than 'basic.'"

In support of limiting the duty of disclosure, Section 551 says: "To a considerable extent, fully sanctioned by the customs and mores of the community, superior information and better business acumen are legitimate advantages, which lead to no liability. The (first party) may reasonably expect the (second party) to make his own investigation, draw his own conclusions, and protect himself; and if the (second party) is indolent, inexperienced or ignorant, or his judgment is bad, or he does not have access to adequate information, the (first party) is under no obligation to make good his deficiencies. This is true, in general, where it is the buyer of land or chattels who has the better information and fails to disclose it; somewhat less frequently, it may be true of the seller." This example of these principles is given by Section 551: "A is a violin expert. He pays a casual visit to B's shop, where secondhand musical instruments are sold. He finds a violin which, by reason of his expert knowledge and experience, he immediately recognizes as a genuine Stradivarius, in good condition, and worth at least $50,000. The violin is priced for sale at $100. Without disclosing his information, or his identity, A buys the violin from B for $100. A is not liable to B."

Section 551 continues to this conclusion: "The development of modern business ethics has, however, limited to some extent this privilege to take advantage of ignorance. There are situations in which the (first party) not only knows that his bargaining adversary is acting under a mistake basic to the transaction, but also knows that the adversary, by reason of the relationship between them, the customs of the trade, or other objective circumstances, is relying quite reasonably upon a disclosure of the unrevealed fact if it exists. In such a case good faith and fair dealing may require a disclosure before the bargain is sealed.

"It is extremely difficult to be specific as to the factors which give rise to this known, and reasonable, expectation of disclosure. In general, the bases in which the exceptional rule has been applied have been those in which the advantage taken of the second party's ignorance is shocking to the ethical sense of the community, and is so extreme and unfair as to amount to a form of swindling, in which the (second party) is led by appearances into a bargain which is a trap, of whose essence and substance he is unaware."

Today, nondisclosure cases seem to arise mainly in the real estate field, e.g., in the form of the withholding of an adverse termite report in *Godfrey* v. *Steinpress* (1982) 128 C.A. 3d 154, 180 Cal.Rptr. 95, and in the form of the failure of a subdivider to disclose a property's history of underground water problems and slides in *Barnhouse* v. *Pinole* (1982) 133 C.A. 3d 171, 183 Cal.Rptr. 881, wherein the court said, in quoting from an earlier California case, that "'(i)t is now settled in California that where the seller knows of facts materially affecting the value or desirability of the property . . . and also knows that such facts are not known to, or within the reach of the diligent attention and observation of the buyer, the seller is under a duty to disclose them to the buyer.'"

In an unusual recent California case, *Reed* v. *King* (1983) 145 C.A. 3d 261, 193 Cal.Rptr. 130, the court of appeal held that the purchaser of a house stated a cause of action against the vendor when the vendor failed to disclose that the house had been the site of a multiple murder.

Innocent Misrepresentation: Even though misrepresentation is innocent, the injured party may rescind if it is material.

Contracts Required to be in Writing— Statute of Frauds

If all contracts could be made orally there would be much fraud and perjury; or so the English thought in 1677. It would be unintentional as well as intentional. Dishonest persons would fabricate contracts. Honest persons would color them in their favor. To prevent this the English passed, in 1677, "An Act for the Prevention of Frauds and Perjuries," which quickly came to be known as the Statute of Frauds. It required most important types of contracts to be in writing. Every state in this country has a Statute of Frauds patterned on the English Statute, differing only in that it may require more types of contracts to be in writing.

• A contract for the sale of realty is within the Statute. Suppose we find B in possession of property and that he has made $25,000 of improvements. He claims that A orally agreed to sell the property. It was inevitable that the Statute of Frauds would breed exceptions. The exceptions have a common ground. An extrinsic fact supports a probability that the oral contract was made; in the hypothetical case, the improvements. This reduces the possibility of fraud and allows the purposes of the Statute to be preserved. Where a ground of exception exists the case is said to be "taken out of the Statute." The party claiming the oral contract will be allowed to attempt to prove it. If he is successful the oral contract will be enforced.

Contracts Within the Original Statute

The following types of contracts were required to be in writing by the English statute, and are required to be in writing by the statutes of the various states of this country:[58]

Sale or Lease of Real Property: "*An agreement for the leasing for a longer period than one year, or for the sale of real property, or of an interest therein. . . .*" C.C. 1624(4). Thus, a contract to sell a building or a house or a lot, or to sell a part interest therein, must be in writing. The real estate purchase contract, shown earlier, is the usual writing.

Exception: Where the buyer either takes possession and pays part of the purchase price or makes valuable improvements, the oral contract may be proved i.e., is taken out of the Statute. In some states, which may include California, taking possession alone is enough.

Sale of Goods for Price of $500 or More: "*(A) contract for the sale of goods for the price of $500 or more . . .*" U.C.C. 2201.

These *exceptions* are made:

1. Written confirmation: As between merchants, if one party to the sale sends the other a signed, written confirmation of sale within a reasonable time, the transaction is taken out of the Statute and may be enforced against the sendee unless within 10 days after receipt of the confirmation the sender gives written notice of objection to its contents. U.C.C. 2201(2).

2. Special manufacture: The transaction is taken out of the Statute if the goods are to be specially manufactured for the buyer and are not suitable for sale to others in the ordinary course of the seller's business, and the seller, before notice of repudiation is received and under circumstances which reasonably indicate that the goods are for the buyer, has made either a substantial beginning of their manufacture or commitments for their procurement. U.C.C. 2201(1)(a).[59]

3. Part payment or delivery: The transaction is taken out of the Statute with respect to goods for which the buyer has paid or which he has accepted. U.C.C. 2201(3) (c). This departs significantly from precode law. Under precode Statute, if there was partial payment or partial delivery, the entire contract could be proved and enforced. Thus, if buyer orally contracted for $10,000 of goods and accepted 10% of the goods, the entire contract could be enforced against him if the court could be satisfied that it had been made. Under the code only 10% of the contract can be enforced. The code rule is designed to prevent disputes as to the quality of goods agreed to be bought or sold.

Where the contract is for the sale of *choses in action*, distinguished from goods, it cannot be enforced beyond $500 unless there is a writing. U.C.C. 1206(1). Goods are tangible personal property—automobiles, books, typewriters, etc.— property capable of physical possession. Choses in action are "paper" personal property—rights to money or interests in property, which may be evidenced by such documents as notes and mortgages or stocks and bonds.

Contract Not to be Performed Within Year: "*An agreement that by its terms is not to be performed within a year from the making thereof.*" C.C. 1624(1). Building contracts and longterm distributorship agreements would come within this section, as well as employment contracts which are to extend beyond one year.

• The year is measured from the date of *making* of the contract. In *Kraft* v. *Rooke*, 103 C.A. 552, 284 P. 935, an oral agreement was made on December 24 to employ P for a period of one year, commencing January 1 and ending December 31. Held, the contract was not binding because it could not be performed within one year from the date of *making*.

• It is only a contract which *by its terms* is not to be performed within a year that is within the Statute. Thus it has been held that agreements to employ persons "for life" or "permanently" are not within the Statute.[60] This should not be misconstrued. If I agree to employ you "for two years," the agreement must be in writing, even though you may die within two hours or two days or two months. It is still an agreement that *by its terms* cannot be *performed* within a year. Death operates merely to discharge it.

---

[58]The California Statute of Frauds is set out in footnote 61.

[59]The basis for this rule is sometimes said to be that the transaction is one for the sale of "services" rather than for the sale of "goods."

[60]In California, Lab. C. 2855 limits personal service contracts to 7 years. *De Haviland* v. *Warner Bros.*, 67 C.A.2d 225, 153 P.2d 983.

● It may be found, however, that the *terms* of an agreement prevent performance within a year so as to require a writing, even though a specific period of time is not stated. In *Long v. Cramer Meat Packing Co.*, 155 C. 402, 101 P. 297, an agreement to "always" use land for certain purposes was held to be an agreement which, by its terms, could not be performed within a year, and in *S. F. Brewing Corp.* v. *Bowman* (1959) 52 C.2d 607, 343 P.2d 1, a distributorship for an indefinite term was held to be a distributorship for a "reasonable time," which would have to be in writing if a reasonable time was found to be more than one year.

● Courts have not been in agreement about contracts containing options to terminate or renew. If the contract is to extend beyond a year but is terminable at any time upon, e.g., 30 days' notice, there are as many as 3 views: Some courts hold that the contract is not within the Statute. Some courts hold that the contract is not within the Statute if both parties have the right to terminate. Some courts hold that the contract is within the Statute in all cases. Where the option is to renew, California courts have reached conflicting results, holding in one case that a one-year employment contract renewable by the employer for additional one-year periods was not required to be in writing (*Columbia Pictures Corp.* v. *DeToth*, 26 C.2d 753, 161 P.2d 217), while holding in another case that a one-year lease renewable by the tenant for additional one-year periods was required to be in writing. (*Aaker* v. *Smith*, 87 C.A.2d 36, 196 P.2d 150).

● The *exception* here: The contract is taken out of the Statute if one party fully performs. A and B make an oral contract whereby A is to pay B $10,000 in 30 days, for which B is to render some performance over a period of 2 years. A pays the $10,000 as agreed. The contract is taken out of the Statute.

Suretyship and Guaranty Contracts: These are treated in the chapter on Suretyship and Guaranty.

Personal Contract of Executor or Administrator to Pay Debts of Decedent: The executor or administrator of an estate is usually the same person who is to receive the estate or a substantial part of it. Creditors of a deceased person have the right to have the property of the estate sold if necessary to pay their claims. To keep the property intact, the executor or administrator may agree to pay claims out of his own funds. It is this type of agreement that is contemplated by this section of the Statute.

Contracts upon Consideration of Marriage: Suppose, as in *Hughes* v. *Hughes*, 49 C.A. 206, 193 P. 144, that D agrees to give P $600,000 worth of property, an automobile, an ermine coat, and certain other things, if she will marry him. P's promise to marry D would be consideration for D's promise. The contract may be described, then, as one made "upon consideration of marriage," one in which the consideration of one party is marriage to the other. Such contracts are required by the Statute to be in writing, although an oral agreement may be enforced where actual fraud is shown. In this case there was no writing and it was held for Mr. Hughes. Since agreements of this kind are rather unusual in modern times, this section of the Statute is of little practical importance.

The foregoing are the types of contracts that are required to be in writing by the English Statute. Many states have added others. California additions, which are representative, are shown in footnotes.[61]

---

[61]The California "Statute" is composed of these statutes:

C.C. 1624: "The following contracts are invalid, unless the same, or some note or memorandum thereof, is in writing and subscribed by the party to be charged or by his agent:

Nature of Writing Required by Statute of Frauds

The Statute does not require a formal writing, only "some *note or memorandum . . . in writing and signed by the party to be charged* or by his agent." Letters have been held to be sufficient; in *Steel* v. *Duntley*, 115 C.A. 451, 1 P.2d 999, escrow instructions were held to be sufficient; and the like. The writing must show the essential terms of the agreement, except in the case of a sale of goods, where only the quantity term is essential. See U.C.C. 2201(1).

"1. An agreement that by its terms is not to be performed within a year from the making thereof;

"2. A special promise to answer for the debt, default, or miscarriage of another . . .; [suretyship and guaranty contracts]

"3. An agreement made upon consideration of marriage other than a mutual promise to marry;

"4. An agreement for the leasing for a longer period than one year, or for the sale of real property, or of an interest therein; and such agreement, if made by an agent of the party sought to be charged, is invalid unless the authority of the agent is in writing, subscribed by the party sought to be charged.

"5. An agreement authorizing or employing an agent, broker, or any other person to purchase or sell real estate, or to lease real estate for a longer period than one year, or to procure, introduce, or find a purchaser or seller of real estate or a lessee or lessor of real estate where such lease is for a longer period than one year. [This requires a real estate broker to have a written contract with his client if he wants to get his commission. The writing will be a 'listing' or 'Authorization to Sell,' seen in the chapter on Real Property.]

"6. An agreement which by its terms is not to be performed during the lifetime of the promisor, or an agreement to devise or bequeath any property, or to make any provision for any person by will; [The usual case is one in which a person agrees to leave property by will to one who has taken care of him during lifetime, e.g., *Luders* v. *Security Etc. Bank*, 121 C.A. 408, 9 P.2d 271.]

"7. An agreement by a purchaser of real property to pay an indebtedness secured by a mortgage or deed of trust upon the property purchased, unless assumption of said indebtedness is specifically provided for in the conveyance of such property."

[If the purchaser of mortgaged property is to be personally liable on the mortgage, he must expressly assume it (as by Assumption Agreement, page 213) or accept a deed reciting assumption.]

U.C.C. 2201 (page 372), which covers sales of goods for a price of $500 or more and exceptions.

Prob.C. 737: "No executor or administrator is chargeable upon any special promise to answer in damages or to pay the debts of the decedent out of his own estate, unless the agreement for that purpose, or some memorandum or note thereof, is in writing signed by such executor or administrator, or by some other person by him thereunto specifically authorized in writing."

Beginning January 1, 1985, subsection 6 of the California statute, above, will be reduced to its first clause, i.e., subsection 6 will read "An agreement which by its terms is not to be performed during the lifetime of the promisor." This change is part of a revision of the probate code, discussed at page 237. The probate code revisions will set up specific requirements for making an effective contract to leave property by will. These will read as follows:

"150. (a) A contract to make a will or devise, or not to revoke a will or devise, or to die intestate, if executed after December 31, 1984, can only be established by one of the following:

(1) Provisions of a will stating material provisions of the contract.

(2) An express reference in a will to a contract and extrinsic evidence proving the terms of the contract.

(3) A writing signed by the decedent evidencing the contract.

● The writing must be signed but this may be done informally. A "signature" is the affixation of one's name to a writing with intention to be bound. Intent, not form, is the important thing. A signature may be at any place on a writing and in any form, so long as there is the requisite intention.[62] The "signature" which you authorize the telegraph company to place on a telegram is sufficient, since it is your intention to be bound thereby. *Brewer* v. *Horst and Lachmund Co.*, 127 C. 643, 60 P. 418.

● Lastly, the Statute requires *signing* of a writing only by "the party to be charged," i.e., the party against whom it is sought to enforce the contract. That permits this result: You agree to lease property to me for two years and I promise to pay $500 a month rent. You give me a signed memorandum. I sign nothing. I can enforce the contract against you, but you cannot enforce it against me. This is thought not to be inconsistent with the requirement of mutuality of obligation. The reasoning goes something like this: The writing is not the contract, only evidence of it bearing upon its enforceability. Our lease fulfills the requirements of a contract. Each of us has made a promise that involves a detriment, so there is mutuality of obligation in that sense. Quite independently of this, however, the law makes rules as to when and to what extent a contract may be enforced by legal action. If it is seen fit to frame a law permitting enforcement only by a party who is prudent enough to get a signed memorandum, this may be done. This is what the framers of the Statute of Frauds saw fit to do.[63]

Parol Evidence Rule

A written contract which appears to be intended to cover the entire agreement of the parties cannot be varied by oral agreement made prior to or contemporaneously therewith. This is the parol evidence rule. By written contract A unconditionally promises to pay money to B on June 1. A cannot show a contemporaneous oral agreement giving him until August 1 to pay, or relieving him of his obligation to pay if he does not receive certain moneys from C by June 1, or relieving him of his obligation to pay if B dies before June 1. He can show, however, that there was no consideration for the promise or that it was induced by fraud. Such evidence does not seek to vary the written contract but to invalidate it.

Performance, Breach and Discharge

Performance

In most cases, a contract is performed and that is the end of the matter. In legal parlance, it is *discharged* by performance. This section is concerned mainly with cases of imperfect performance—cases in which one party fails to give the performance called for by the contract—and with the legal consequences thereof.

(b) The execution of a joint will or mutual wills does not create a presumption of a contract not to revoke the will or wills."

[62]C.C. 1624 requires *subscription* rather than *signature*. Ordinarily this would require the instrument to be signed at the end, but the California courts have held otherwise in the case of the Statute of Frauds.

[63]Some states require a writing "signed by the *parties* to be charged," so that neither party may enforce the contract unless both have signed a writing.

Conditions:[64] In one way or another, the obligation of a party to a contract to perform will usually be conditional. The condition may be occurrence of an external event not under control of the parties. B agrees to purchase real property from S if the property is rezoned by the city planning commission for commercial use within sixty days; or provided a bank will lend B a certain amount of the purchase price. A condition of the latter type may be found in a real estate purchase contract.

More important is the fact that the law construes contract performances to be *concurrently conditional* if they are to be rendered at the same time, which is to say that if S is to deliver goods or property to B on a certain date and B is to pay the purchase price at time of delivery, S need not deliver if B is not prepared to perform and B, of course, need not pay if S is not prepared to deliver.

● On the other hand where one performance under a contract is due at an earlier date than the other, the first performance is a *condition precedent* to the other. True, if S is to deliver goods to B on May 1 for which B is to pay on May 15, delivery by S is a condition precedent to B's obligation to pay.

● Conditions may also be subsequent. A *condition subsequent* is an event the occurrence of which discharges a party from his obligation to perform under a contract. The discharging events were held to be conditions subsequent in *Hartman* v. *San Pedro Commercial Co.* (1944) 66 C.A.2d 935, 153 P.2d 212, where an employment contract provided for discharge of the employer if he sold the business and for discharge of the employee if he was drafted.

Satisfactory Performance: One party's performance may be conditioned upon performance by the other to the *satisfaction* of the first party, or of a third person. Where taste or judgment is involved, the test of satisfaction is necessarily a *subjective* one. If I agree to paint a portrait for which you are

---

[64]C.C. 1435: "Conditions may be precedent, concurrent, or subsequent."

C.C. 1436: "A condition precedent is one which is to be performed before some right dependent thereon accrues, or some act dependent thereon is performed."

C.C. 1437: "Conditions concurrent are those which are mutually dependent, and are to be performed at the same time."

C.C. 1438: "A condition subsequent is one referring to a future event, upon the happening of which the obligation becomes no longer binding upon the other party. . . ."

C.C. 1439: "Before any party to an obligation can require another party to perform any act under it, he must fulfill all conditions precedent thereto imposed upon himself; and must be able and offer to fulfill all conditions concurrent so imposed upon him on the like fulfillment by the other party. . . ."

The First Contracts Restatement made the same classification of conditions as does C.C. 1435, above. The Second Contracts Restatement attempts to simplify the law of conditions. Firstly, it eliminates the concept of "condition subsequent" altogether. Matters producing the discharge of a party from a contract are to be collected and given their operation under the heading of "Discharge." Secondly, it deals only in the word "condition" and defines all conditions in the terms in which it formerly defined "conditions precedent." Thus, Second Contracts Restatement, Section 250, which is entitled "Condition Defined," provides that "A condition is an event, not certain to occur which must occur . . . before performance under a contract becomes due." And the Reporter's Note to Section 250 says, "This Section revises former § 250 to eliminate the terms 'condition precedent' and 'condition subsequent.' This terminology has long been criticized . . . Conditions precedent are referred to simply as 'conditions.'"

pay only if satisfied; or to produce a play which you are to finance if you feel that it will be successful, your personal judgment is final.

Where satisfaction depends upon proper installation or mechanical efficiency, the test is an *objective*, or "reasonable man" test, unless it is clearly made subjective. *Bruner* v. *Hegyi*, 42 C.A. 97, 183 P. 369, and *Bryan Elevator Co.* v. *Law*, 1 C.A. 205, 160 P. 170, are examples: In the first case, plaintiff agreed to install tile satisfactory to the building owner; in the second, elevator equipment. In each case, it was held that there was satisfactory performance by reasonable man standards, and that therefore defendant had to pay.

● In building or construction contracts, approval of a third party—an architect or engineer—may be required before there is an obligation to pay or to make the final payment. Since this will relate to proper construction or installation as measured by contract specifications and usual building standards, the architect or engineer cannot arbitrarily refuse to give approval. Thus, in *Coplew* v. *Durand*, 153 C. 278, 95 P. 38, where plaintiff contractor was hired to install the flooring in a building subject to a certificate of satisfaction by the owner's architect, it was held that plaintiff could recover where the certificate was withheld without valid reason.

Substantial Performance: Where one party fails to perform, or his performance falls substantially short of what is called for, the other party may terminate the contract and sue for breach. Since one party has not received what he bargained for, there is said to be a total or material failure of consideration.

By contrast, where there is only partial or slight failure of consideration, there may be no right to terminate the contract, and it is a misconception of the law that a breach by one party, however trivial, permits the other party to escape the contract.

● One important class of cases in which partial failure of consideration will not be fatal is in building or construction contracts, where the *doctrine of substantial performance* is applied. Suppose that P contracts to install the plumbing, heating and ventilating systems in a building for $27,332.66, as was the case in *Haverty Company* v. *Jones*, 185 C. 285, 197 P. 105. "Due to mistakes and misinterpretations of the contract by [P's] employees," there were omissions which could be remedied for $99.21, plus defects which could not be remedied without a greater expense than their importance would justify, which would reduce the value of the building by $2,180.88. These consisted of installations of pipe and fittings other than as called for by the contract. Held, the doctrine of substantial performance applied. Said the court: "According to the testimony . . . the actual cost of the building . . . was about one hundred and eighty-six thousand dollars. The contract price of the work to be done by [P] . . . was $27,332.66. The sum of $99.21 deducted as the cost of remedying the curable defects was, of course, a trivial matter. The sum of $2,180.88 allowed as damages on account of defects which could not be removed or remedied seemed at first to be rather large to come within the rule as to substantial performance. . . . But when the reduction is only $2,180.88 in the value of a building costing one hundred and eighty-six thousand dollars it does not seem so large in comparison. Upon a consideration of the details of the respective failures in performance we find them to be really of trifling character compared to the cost of the building . . . it is settled, especially in the case of building contracts . . . that if there has been a substantial performance thereof by the contractor in good faith, where the failure to make full performance can be compensated in damages to be deducted from the price or allowed as a counterclaim, and the

omissions and deviations were not willful or fraudulent and do not substantially affect the usefulness of the building for the purposes for which it was intended, the contractor may, in an action upon the contract, recover the amount unpaid of his contract price, less the amount allowed as damages for the failure in strict performance." In accordance with this rule, P was given judgment for $10,775.64, the balance due on the contract, less the sums of $99.21 and $2,180.88. It is the doctrine of substantial performance then that where a building contractor is guilty of a non-wilful and insubstantial departure from the terms of the contract, he may recover the amount agreed to be paid him less such amount as will compensate the property owner for the shortcomings of the job.

Timely Performance: Suppose that instead of defective performance there is late performance. One party fails to perform on the day specified by the contract or to complete performance within the time provided. I am to deliver goods to you on December 14 but do not make delivery until the 16th; or I am to complete construction of a building on December 1, but do not finish until the 31st. There is, of course, a breach of contract in each case entitling you to recover damages. But may you cancel the contract if I fail to perform on the exact day? Generally not. The following rules are applied: (1) Unless the nature of the contract is such as to make performance on the exact day of vital importance, or the contract provides that time is of the essence, failure to perform on the exact day does not permit the other party to cancel the contract. (2) In mercantile contracts, performance at the time agreed upon is important, and slight delay may permit the other party to cancel the contract. (3) In contracts for the sale of land, delay must be greater than in mercantile contracts to discharge the duty of a party.

In effect, these rules are: First, the nature of the contract may be such that timely performance is extremely important. If the goods which I was to deliver to you on December 14 were toys to be sold in your department store for Christmas, time would be of great importance. Even though the contract is not one in which time is of the essence, the parties may agree that it is. This they do by inserting the provision that "*time is of the essence*" of this contract.[65] Second, as between mercantile contracts (those for the sale of goods), and contracts for sale of real estate, greater delay is allowed with respect to the latter when there is no time-essence provision. This is because real estate values are ordinarily more stable.

● Contracts especially given to the possibility of delay, such as building contracts and transportation contracts where material shortages, strikes, weather conditions and the like are

---

[65]Where a contract provides that "time is of the essence," a court of equity may give relief to a party who fails to perform at the appointed time if this is not due to negligence and the other party will not be unduly prejudiced. C.C. 3275 so permits:

"Whenever, by the terms of an obligation, a party thereto incurs a forfeiture, or a loss in the nature of a forfeiture, by reason of his failure to comply with its provisions, he may be relieved therefrom, upon making full compensation to the other party, except in case of a grossly negligent, willful, or fraudulent breach of duty."

Restatement of Contracts 2d, § 242, downplays the significance of "time-essence" provisions and would seem not to allow them to be controlling, without more, even though expressly bargained for. Between parties of equal bargaining strength at least, it would seem that many jurisdictions, including California, would probably enforce such a provision where, clearly, it is intended to be enforceable without more being shown and C.C. 3275-type forgiving facts are not present.

always a threat, usually contain a provision excusing delay in performance from such causes.

Installment payment contracts always contain a time-essence provision. Where late payments are accepted without objection, the time-essence provision is waived.

Excuses for Non-Performance or Delay in Performance: In a number of cases, the law excuses failure to perform. The most important of these excuses are various forms of *impossibility of performance*,[66] as follows:

CHANGE OF LAW MAKING LEGAL PERFORMANCE IMPOSSIBLE. I agree to supply you with a certain amount of steel or rubber during the year. Thereafter the government restricts sales of these materials to persons engaged in production of military supplies. Since the law prohibits performance of my contract, impossibility of performance excuses me.

DEATH IN PERSONAL SERVICE CONTRACTS. Where a contract is for personal services or requires the personal skill, judgment or supervision of one party, death excuses performance. This is frequently the case with employment contracts. In other cases, it may present a close question. For example, a building contract: A, an architect, agrees to prepare plans; C, a contractor, to do the construction work. A's death before completion of the plans would excuse performance, since his personal skill and judgment are essential elements of the contract. Death of a building contractor, on the other hand, has been held not to excuse performance, where, as was held to be the case in *Estate of Burke*, 198 C. 163, 244 P. 340, the construction work is of a routine nature and would be performed by a variety of subcontractors so that the personal skill or supervision of the contractor is not really involved. The executor or administrator of the estate of the contractor would be required to see that the contract was completed. C's death, then, may not excuse fulfillment of the construction contract.

ILLNESS. Illness constitutes temporary impossibility of performance in personal service contracts; that is, excuses performance during the period of illness. The employer must be protected however, and if it appears that the illness will be prolonged he will be permitted to terminate the contract.

DESTRUCTION OF MEANS OR SOURCE OF PERFORMANCE. Suppose S agrees to sell and deliver to B 500 pairs of shoes which S proposes to manufacture in his factory in San Francisco. S's factory burns down so that it is impossible for him to make the shoes. Is S excused from performing? It depends on what was contemplated by the parties to the contract. While destruction of the means or source of performance of a contract results in impossibility in fact, it will result in legal impossibility—impossibility which excuses performance—only if it may be said that *both* parties contemplated the continued existence of a particular means or source of performance for the contract, which may be shown by the terms of the contract or by other evidence.

NON-EXISTENCE OF SPECIFIC THING NECESSARY FOR PERFORMANCE. Suppose, as in *Carroll* v. *Bowerstock,* 100 Kan. 560, 164 P. 143, that P contracts to construct a reinforced concrete floor in D's warehouse. After the job is partially completed, the warehouse is destroyed by fire so that P cannot complete performance. The Restatement would describe this as a case of impossibility in the form of the non-existence of a specific thing necessary for performance, the continued existence of which was contemplated by the parties. P would be

---

[66]C.C. 1441: "A condition in a contract, the fulfillment of which is impossible or unlawful . . . is void."

excused from completing performance, and would be permitted to recover for services rendered and materials furnished up to the time of destruction.

UNFORESEEN DIFFICULTY OR EXPENSE. Unforeseen difficulty or expense of an extreme nature will excuse performance, as in the leading case of *Mineral Park Land Co.* v. *Howard,* 172 C. 289, 156 P. 458, where it would have cost one party 10 times as much to perform as he had reason to expect. Held, the increased difficulty of performance "approached" impossibility so nearly as to excuse performance.
● Increases in costs of labor or materials are considered to be forseeable and will not excuse performance. The contractor must protect himself by "cost plus" contract.

COMMERCIAL IMPRACTICABILITY. The Uniform Commercial Code, in Section 2615, makes "*commercial impracticability*" an excuse for nonperformance of a contract for the sale of goods. As to what constitutes such impracticability, Official Comment 4 says:
● "Increased cost alone does not excuse performance unless the rise in cost is due to some unforeseen contingency which alters the essential nature of the performance. Neither is a rise or a collapse in the market in itself a justification, for that is exactly the type of business risk which business contracts made at fixed prices are intended to cover. But a severe shortage of raw materials or of supplies due to a contingency such as war, embargo, local crop failure, unforeseen shutdown of major sources of supply or the like, which either causes a marked increase in cost or altogether prevents the seller from securing supplies necessary to his performance, is within the contemplation of this section."

Official Comment 5 deals with the problem of *third party cooperation,* as illustrated by the famous case of *Canadian Industrial Alcohol Co.* v. *Dunbar Molasses Co.*, 258 N.Y. 194, 179 N.E. 383. In that case, a middleman contracted to supply a buyer with 1½ million gallons of molasses over a period of time. The middleman expected to get the molasses from a refinery with which he had had regular dealings, but did not make a contract with the refinery for the molasses. Midway through the contract with the buyer, the refinery decided to curtail production and as a result the middleman could not fulfill his obligations. It was held that this did not excuse his performance. It was held that, where performance depends on third party cooperation, a party to a contract should not be excused from performing unless, at the very least, he has employed all due measures to assure himself of the requisite for cooperation—in this case, by making a contract with the supplier (refinery) for the amount of the supply. The code approves this position. What is recognized is that problems of impossibility and impracticability are problems of risk allocation and that a party who has not exercised reasonable prudence should not be relieved of the consequences of his lack of prudence.

FRUSTRATION OF OBJECT OR PURPOSE OF CONTRACT. Suppose, as in a famous English case, a newspaper contracts for a suite of rooms in a hotel on a certain day in order to take pictures of a coronation parade. The newspaper, in order to get the rooms for this day, agrees to pay a rate much above the rate usually charged. Then the coronation date is changed. Must the newspaper pay as agreed? It was held that it need not pay; that where the subject matter of a contract is rendered worthless for its intended use by some fortuitous or unforeseeable event, the contract may be terminated. This is not the case of impossibility of performance but of frustration of the object or purpose of the contract which, however, also excuses performance.

Interestingly, many of the contracts for viewing places of the wedding procession accompanying the Charles to Dianne wedding expressly provided for the possibility of cancellation of the procession.

During the war years, there were many cases of this kind in connection with leases. Premises were leased for the sale of automobiles, tires, etc., which then became unobtainable. The courts were strict in their application of the doctrine of frustration. If the frustrating event was reasonably foreseeable, or the premises could be used for other purposes, the lease was held binding. Thus, in *Lloyd* v. *Murphy*, 25 C.2d 48, 153 P.2d 47, where the lease was for the purpose of selling new cars, it was held binding because war priorities were known to be in the offing at the time the lease was made, and the premises could be used for other purposes. And in *Davidson* v. *Goldstein*, 58 C.A.2d Supp. 909, 136 P.2d 665, where the lease was for a tire and battery shop, it was held binding because, although new tires were not obtainable, a retreading and battery business could still be conducted at a profit. But in the somewhat classical case of *20th Century Lites* v. *Goodman*, 64 C.A.2d Supp. 938, 149 P.2d 88, where the lease was of an outdoor neon advertising sign, it was held that the lessee could terminate the contract when the operation of the sign became forbidden by blackout regulations.

PREVENTION AND WAIVER. Impossibility and frustration are not the only excuses from performance. Performance is excused when it is prevented by the other party. And requirements of performance may be waived. Thus, for example, a landlord can accept late rent payments or a bank can accept late loan payments, thereby "waiving" the terms of performance of the contract.

Breach

Here, the rights and liabilities of a party in event of breach of contract are consolidated and discussed in greater detail.

The injured party has three general types of remedies for breach of contract: (1) *Rescission* where there is a material or substantial breach. As discussed earlier, rescission consists of returning what has been received upon becoming aware of the right to rescind. (2) *Damages*. An action for damages may be brought where there is a minor breach, where rescission is not possible, as in the case of a building contract or an employment contract, or where rescission is possible but the injured party prefers to keep what he has received and to sue for damages. (3) *Specific performance* in contracts to purchase property where damages are not an adequate remedy.

Damages: There are many common misconceptions about damages, and they are not given as freely or for as many things as is generally supposed.

General damages are those which anyone should be able to foresee as a consequence of his breach of contract. Should I breach my contract to deliver goods to you at a certain price and can foresee that you may have to purchase elsewhere at a higher price, you can recover this difference from me. But suppose, as was the case in *Mitchell* v. *Clarke*, 71 C. 163, 11 P. 882, that I owe you money which I fail to pay. Unknown to me, you are without funds to pay your creditors, and are relying on payment by me to pay them. Because I do not pay you, they seize your assets and have them sold at great personal loss to you. In *Mitchell*, it was held that you could not recover from me for these *special damages*. Special, as distinguished from general, damages are those resulting from special circumstances causing some unusual injury. Special damages are not recoverable unless it is shown that, at the time of contracting, the breaching party knew of the special

circumstances which might cause special damages and so could foresee them. Foreseeability, then, measures the damages that can be recovered in all cases.[67]

● *Lost profits* may be recovered as damages but they present a special problem. Generally, it must be possible to establish lost profits with reasonable certainty and it is generally held, as it was in *California Press Mfg. Co.* v. *Stafford Packing Co.*, 192 C. 479, 221 P. 345, that where the profits are to come from a new business, their uncertainty and highly speculative character precludes recovery.[68] However, U.C.C. 2708, Comment 2, says, to the contrary of this general rule, that "It is not necessary to a recovery of 'profit' to show a history of earnings, especially if a new venture is involved."

● The innocent party to a breach of contract must take all reasonable steps to minimize or *mitigate damages*, and will not be permitted to recover damages which could have been avoided. If I fail to deliver goods to you, you must obtain substitutes at the nearest available market, or if I breach a contract to employ you for a given period of time, you must seek similar employment elsewhere with reasonable diligence. *Henrici* v. *South Feather Land Co.*, 177 C. 442, 170 P. 1135, is a notable case on this point. There, D breached a contract to supply P with irrigation water. P refused to pay higher prices for water from other sources, and his crops died from lack of water. Held, he could not recover for damage to the crops because reasonableness required the payment of the higher price for water from another source.

● Where a right to damages exists, they are recovered by a lawsuit as outlined in the first chapter.

Specific Performance: In certain cases, courts of equity will compel a party to perform a contract—to give *specific performance*. S refuses to go through with a contract to sell real property to B. The court may order S to give B a deed or go to jail for contempt of court for failing to do so. If, despite this, S persists in his refusal to perform, the court may appoint a commissioner to make a deed in his name and so bring about fulfillment of the contract. The basis for specific performance is that damages are not an adequate remedy, i.e., that they will not repair the injury resulting from the breach of contract.

● Before discussing cases in which specific performance will be decreed, one case in which it will not, the personal service contract, may be noted. You agree to work for me for one year. After 3 months you walk out. A court will not compel you to work for me.[69] Such an order could not be satisfactorily enforced and the employer-employee relationship would not be a harmonious one.

● Specific performance will be given in contracts for the sale of real estate and, in proper cases, in contracts for the sale of goods. Damages will not be an adequate remedy to the buyer if the property or goods are unique or, because of economic or other circumstances, are not obtainable elsewhere.

---

[67]C.C. 3300 is held by the California court to be an adoption of this rule. It provides that "For the breach of an obligation arising from contract, the measure of damages . . . is the amount which will compensate the party aggrieved for all the detriment proximately caused thereby, or which, in the ordinary course of things, would be likely to result therefrom."

[68]C.C. 3301: "No damages can be recovered for a breach of contract which are not clearly ascertainable. . . ."

[69]C.C. 3390: "The following obligations cannot be specifically enforced:
  "1. An obligation to render personal services;
  "2. An obligation to employ another in personal service;"

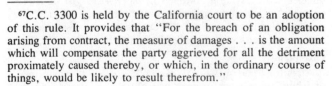

NOT ALL DAMAGES RECOVERABLE

In the case of a contract for the sale of real property, specific performance will be given as a matter of course. In England, land was always looked upon as having special sanctity, a form of property of much greater dignity than mere goods or personal property. Consequently, it came to be held at a very early date that land was inherently "unique"; that if one contracted to sell land and refused to go through with the contract, the other party could never be adequately compensated by damages and should be given specific performance. This led to the presumption that breach of a real estate contract could not adequately be compensated by damages.[70]

Where the contract was for the sale of goods or of an article of personal property, actual uniqueness was required before the adoption of the Uniform Sales Act. Thus, if I failed to perform on a contract to sell you wheat which you could obtain elsewhere, there was no case for specific performances. But if I broke a contract to sell you a painting which was the only one of its kind, or if I contracted to sell you ships' parts and, because of curtailed production or for other reason these could not be obtained elsewhere, specific performance would be granted. The Uniform Sales Act in Section 68 adopted the more flexible rule that in contracts for the sale of goods the court could order specific performance if it "thought fit." The Uniform Commercial Code continues a flexible rule. U.C.C. 2716(1) provides that "(s)pecific performance may be decreed where the goods are unique or in other proper circumstances."

Quasi-Contract Recovery: Suppose that P makes a contract to deliver 2000 tons of steel to D in 4 installments; that after delivery of 1000 tons P is unable to perform further because of inability to get scrap metal to make steel, or for some other reason beyond his control. D, having used the steel received in its manufacturing process is unable to return it. P would have no standing in court to sue on the contract because he is in breach of it. On the other hand, if D were allowed to keep the steel without having to pay for it, he would be unjustly enriched. In a case of this kind, P can bring an action in *quasi-contract*—"as though there were a contract" on the part of D to pay the reasonable value of the steel received. For the purposes of the laws of contracts, then, *quasi-contract* is a remedy which permits a party who cannot enforce a contract to recover the reasonable value of benefits conferred on the other party to prevent unjust enrichment of the other party.

● The remedy of quasi-contract actually extends much beyond the law of contracts and is permitted in any case where one party stands unjustly enriched at the expense of another. For a variety of examples—where, by mistake, P is billed and pays twice for the same goods; where P buys cattle from D at $50 a head and, because of mistake in the count of the herd, pays $1000 too much; where D obtains money from P by fraud.

Quasi-contract is sometimes called "contract implied in law"—a fiction of contract created by the courts—as distinguished from "contract implied in fact"—the type of implied contract considered earlier where an implied contract was made with a barber when the customer got a haircut from him—one intentionally created by conduct.

Discharge

A contract becomes *discharged* when it is fully performed[71] or when, for various reasons, the obligation to perform ceas-

es. The reasons include impossibility of performance,[72] rescission for fraud or other invalidating factor or because of material failure of consideration,[73] termination by mutual agreement where the contract remains wholly unperformed, rescission by mutual agreement after part performance, release for partial performance in states where this is permitted.[74]

Certain other things which will terminate the obligation to perform a contract must be considered in greater detail.

● A contract is discharged by operation of law in two cases—where one party is discharged in bankruptcy, as discussed in a later chapter; and where the statute of limitations runs on a contractual obligation.

● *Statute of limitations* is a law designed to discourage neglect in pressing lawsuits. It says that if you have a "cause of action" (right to sue another), you must commence suit within a specified period of time after the right accrues or forever lose the right to sue. I owe you $1000 on a promissory note payable June 1, 1980. In California, the statute of limitations on written contracts (the note) is 4 years.[75] As of June 2, 1984, you have not yet commenced an action (filed a com-

---

[70]C.C. 3387: "It is to be presumed that the breach of an agreement to transfer real property cannot be adequately relieved by pecuniary compensation."

[71]C.C. 1473: "Full performance of an obligation, by the party whose duty it is to perform it, or by any other person on his behalf . . . extinguishes it."

[72]C.C. 1441: "A condition in a contract, the fulfillment of which is impossible or unlawful . . . is void."

[73]C.C. 1688: "A contract is extinguished by its rescission."
C.C. 1689: "A party to a contract may rescind the same in the following cases only:
"1. If the consent of the party rescinding, or of any party jointly contracting with him, was given by mistake, or obtained through duress, menace, fraud, or undue influence, exercised by or with the connivance of the party as to whom he rescinds, or of any other party to the contract jointly interested with such party;
"2. If, through the fault of the party as to whom he rescinds, the consideration for his obligation fails, in whole or in part;
"3. If such consideration becomes entirely void from any cause;
"4. If such consideration, before it is rendered to him, fails in a material respect, for any cause;
"5. By consent of all the other parties . . . ."

[74]C.C. 1524: "Part performance of an obligation, either before or after a breach thereof, when expressly accepted by the creditor in writing, in satisfaction, or rendered in pursuance of an agreement in writing for that purpose, though without any new consideration, extinguishes the obligation."
C.C. 1541: "An obligation is extinguished by a release therefrom given to the debtor by the creditor, upon a new consideration or in writing, with or without new consideration."

[75]In general, the statute of limitations in California is four years on written contracts, two on oral contracts as per the following code sections:
C.C.P. 335: "The periods prescribed for the commencement of actions . . . are as follows:
C.C.P. 337: "Within four years:
"1. An action upon any contract, obligation or liability founded upon an instrument in writing . . .
"2. An action to recover (1) upon a book account . . .; (2) upon an account stated based upon an account in writing . . .; (3) a balance due upon a mutual, open and current account, the items of which are in writing . . . ."
C.C.P. 339: "Within two years:
"1. An action upon a contract, obligation or liability not founded upon an instrument of writing . . . ."

plaint) to recover the $1000. It is too late to sue. Your action is barred by the running of the statute of limitations, and I am discharged of my obligation.

● A contract may also be discharged by substituted performance, called *accord and satisfaction,* or the substitution of a new party—called *novation.*

Formally defined, an *accord* is an agreement to accept a substitute for the consideration called for by the contract,[76] e.g., to take a tractor in satisfaction of a money debt. Delivery of the tractor is the *satisfaction,* i.e., fulfillment of the accord, at which time the money obligation becomes discharged by accord and satisfaction.[77] Other examples of accord and satisfaction are found on pages 34-35.

Novation is the substitution of a new party for one of the original parties to the contract with the release, simultaneously, of the party for whom the substitution is made, who thereby becomes discharged of the contract.[78]

A novation may take place in connection with the assignment of a lease. R leases premises to E for 5 years. E's business is unsuccessful and, after 2 years he makes a deal with R that he will get a responsible party to take over the lease if R will release him from further liability. The parties would then make a three-cornered agreement which, if prepared by an attorney, would probably be called an "Assignment of Lease and Release." This would recite that E assigns the lease to A and that A "assumes and agrees to perform and fulfill all of the terms, conditions and obligations of said lease"; then the recital that "In consideration of the assumption of the obligations of said lease by A, R hereby consents to said assignment and releases E of all further liability on said lease." When signed by all parties this would constitute a novation in accordance with the definition in the preceding paragraph.

Consent to a novation may be given in advance as in *Chiarello* v. *Axelson,* 25 C.A.2d 157, 76 P.2d 731, where it was agreed in the original contract that assignment of the contract could be made to a corporation to be formed in the future, and that upon assumption of the contract by the corporation, the original party would be discharged of further liability.

Rights of Third Parties

There are two ways in which a person who is not a party to a contract may acquire rights in the contract—by showing

himself to be a third party beneficiary, i.e., a person intended to be benefited by the contract; or by taking an assignment of the rights of one of the original parties.

Third Party Beneficiary Contracts

In the early days of contract law, there developed what came to be known as the doctrine of *privity of contract.* That was the idea, which became the rule, that only the makers of a contract and their assigns could acquire rights under the contract. The doctrine of privity of contract gave rise to this kind of a result in this kind of situation: A owed B $100. C wanted to borrow $100 from A. A loaned it to C on his promise to pay to B the $100 which A owed B. C failed to do this. B sued C for the $100. Under the rule of privity of contract, the court would have had to say to B: "You are a stranger to this contract. We are bound by the rule of privity of contract and cannot recognize you as having any standing in court to enforce the agreement of A and C. A is still your debtor and you must look to him for payment." This was the state of things in the law until 1859 when the New York court, in the famous case of *Lawrence* v. *Fox,* 20 N.Y. 268, changed the rule. In *Lawrence* v. *Fox* the rule was adopted and has since been followed that where the purpose or one of the purposes of a contract is to benefit a third person, he may enforce the contract to the extent that he was intended to be benefited.[79]

Third party beneficiary contracts came to be classified as third party donee beneficiary contracts or *donee beneficiary contracts,* and third party creditor beneficiary contracts or *creditor beneficiary contracts.* If the purpose of the contract is to confer a gift on the third party, it is a donee beneficiary contract and he is a third party donee beneficiary. If the purpose of the contract is to satisfy an obligation owed by the promisee to the third party, as in the hypothetical set of facts in the preceding paragraph, it is a creditor beneficiary contract and he is a third party creditor beneficiary.[80]

Assumption agreements are a common source of creditor beneficiary contracts. In *Central Bank* v. *Wells Fargo Bank,* 18 C.A.2d 559, 64 P.2d 465, it was held, as it regularly is, that a mortgagee was a creditor beneficiary of the contract by the purchaser of mortgaged property to assume the mortgage. Similarly a contract by the buyer of a business to assume the debts of the business, as in *Bryon* v. *Banks,* 98 C.A. 748, 277 P. 1075, makes creditor beneficiaries of the creditors of the business. And the lessor is a third party creditor beneficiary of a lease assumption agreement.

Other examples of creditor beneficiary contracts are *Sublett* v. *Henry's etc. Lunch,* 21 C.2d 273, 131 P.2d 369, in which it was held that an employee was a third party beneficiary of

---

[76]C.C.1521: "An accord is an agreement to accept, in extinction of an obligation, something different from or less than that to which the person agreeing to accept is entitled."

[77]C.C. 1522: "Though the parties to an accord are bound to execute it, yet it does not extinguish the obligation until it is fully executed."
C.C. 1523: "Acceptance, by the creditor, of the consideration of the accord extinguishes the obligation and is called satisfaction."

[78]C.C. 1530: Novation is the substitution of a new obligation for an existing one. C.C. 1531: "Novation is made:
"1. By the substitution of a new obligation between the same parties, with intent to extinguish the old obligation;
"2. By the substitution of a new debtor in place of the old one, with intent to release the latter; or,
"3. By the substitution of a new creditor in place of the old one, with intent to transfer the rights of the latter to the former."
California is exceptional in making substitution of a new obligation a novation, the conventional concept of novation being limited to substitution of party. In California, if parties to a 2 year lease were to cancel it and make a new one for 5 years, the transaction would be a novation.

[79]C.C. 1559: "A contract, made expressly for the benefit of a third person, may be enforced by him at any time before the parties thereto rescind it." But it is generally held, California included, that the contract cannot be rescinded once the third party beneficiary has materially changed position in reliance on it. The word "expressly" as used in C.C. 1559, above, is deemed to have for its purpose merely to exclude incidental beneficiaries from protection.
Where a third party would benefit from a contract but it is not the purpose of the parties to the contract to benefit him, he is called an *"incidental beneficiary."* An incidental beneficiary has no rights. For example, while a contract to build a baseball park would benefit an adjoining property owner who had land he could convert into a parking lot, he could not enforce the contract.

[80]The Second Restatement gives up the terms donee beneficiary and creditor beneficiary in favor of the term *intended beneficiary.* Restatement of Contracts 2d, § 133.

the contract between his union and his employer, and *Lundeen* v. *Nowlin*, 20 C.A. 415, 129 P. 474, in which it was held that a real estate broker was a third party beneficiary of a contract between parties exchanging property which provided for payment of a commission to the broker. Most recently it was held in *Del E. Webb Corp.* v. *Structural Materials Co.* (1981) 123 C.A.3d 593, 176 Cal.Rptr. 824, that a general contractor would be a third party beneficiary of a contract between a roofing subcontractor and a supplier of roofing materials which the latter failed to perform; and in *Zigas* v. *Super. Ct.* (1981) 120 C.A.3d 827, 174 Cal.Rptr. 806, that tenants would be third party beneficiaries of a financing agreement between the federal government and landlords which limited the amount of rent which landlords could charge tenants.

Assignments of Contracts

With two exceptions, it has long been recognized that a party may assign his rights under a contract and that this may be done without consent of the other party.[81] The two exceptions: Assignment requires consent of the other party where the contract expressly forbids assignment without his consent.[82] Assignment also requires consent where the contract involves such a personal relationship or such personal qualities of the assignor that the parties would not have intended it to be assignable, even though they did not say so. Any printed form of lease will provide an example of the first exception. It will contain an express provision that the lessee may not assign the lease without the consent of the lessor. Without this, the vast majority of leases would be assignable without consent since, ordinarily, they do not involve the type of personal relationship which is held to preclude assignment. Insurance contracts on property, e.g., fire insurance, are another class of contracts in which assignment is expressly forbidden without the consent of the other party, the insurance company. Even without this express prohibition against assignment, such contracts would not be assignable. They would then come within the second exception because of the highly personal factors involved. The company enters into the policy because of the good reputation of the insured, as determined from his application and the fact that he has the stamp of approval of a company agent or of a broker known to it, because of his past record of not having fires and upon other very personal considerations.

● The very recent California court of appeal cases have held that clauses in commercial leases prohibiting assignment without the consent of the lessor cannot be enforced arbitrarily. These are the *Schweiso* and *Cohen* cases seen at page 228.

● Contracts for the sale of real property, options on real property and contracts for sale of goods may be assigned by the buyer so long as the seller's risk will not be materially increased. And the right to receive money under a contract may always be assigned. Assignment of an installment purchase contract is a common example of this. Seller sells to buyer on credit, buyer signing an installment purchase contract. Seller then *assigns* or sells the contract to a bank in order to get his money out of the transaction, and the bank collects from the buyer. Of the same nature is the assignment of a simple *account receivable*. I sell goods to you on 60 days' credit. I

need my money immediately, however. With or without your knowledge, I assign my "account receivable" from you—my right to the purchase price—to a financing institution which advances me all or some portion of the purchase price against its pending collection.

Liability of Assignor and Assignee: Perhaps contrary to popular belief, the assignor remains liable on the contract after assignment unless there is a novation, which is rather unusual as a practical matter.[83] While one may assign his rights under a contract, he cannot delegate and thereby escape his duties. To illustrate: R leases to E. E assigns the lease to A with R's consent. R may still collect the rent from E if A fails to pay, unless in connection with the assignment R "releases E of all further liability on said lease," as in the novation on page 51 and, so, discharges E of further liability on the contract.

● As respects the assignee, he becomes liable on the contract by express assumption of its obligations, as in the assignment of lease on page 229. And if he accepts the benefits of the contract, he may be held to have impliedly assumed its obligations.[84]

● Until notified of assignment, the debtor may continue to pay the assignor.

Rights of Assignee: It is a legal cliche that "an assignee steps into the shoes of his assignor"—gets the same rights as the assignor had, no more and no better. This is best illustrated by cases of assignment of a right to receive money—assignment of an installment purchase contract or an account receivable. If the goods sold by the assignor are defective, the buyer has a good defense against the seller-assignor, and also as against his assignee who steps into his shoes.[85] *Iselin & Co., Inc.* v. *Saunders*, 231 N.C. 642, 58 S.E.2d 614, is a typical case. A sold a quantity of slacks to B. While they were enroute to B, A assigned the account receivable to C. B refused to pay for the slacks because they were of inferior quality. C sued B. B won. The slacks were of inferior quality so that B had a good defense against both A and C, as A's assignee.

● It may be noted for future reference that advancing money on accounts receivable is sometimes called *factoring*, or more often *discounting*.

Requirement of Notice of Assignment; Priorities as between Successive Assignees: Suppose C assigns to A an account receivable from D. D, not knowing of the assignment, thereafter pays C. D is protected. An assignee must notify the debtor of assignment of the claim to him.

---

[81]C.C. 1458: "A right arising out of an obligation . . . may be transferred . . ."

[82]Under U.C.C. 9318(4) assignment of an account receivable may not be prohibited. See also U.C.C. 2210, which Restatement of Contracts 2d, § 154, would follow.

[83]C.C. 1457: "The burden of an obligation may be transferred with the consent of the party entitled to is benefits, but not otherwise . . ." While it does not appear to say so, this is held by the California courts to mean that the assignor remains liable after assignment unless the other party to the contract *releases* him of further liability, so the California rule is the same as that stated in the text above, i.e., that the assignor is discharged only if there is a novation.

[84]C.C. 1589: "A voluntary acceptance of the benefit of a transaction is equivalent to a consent to all the obligations arising from it . . ." Accord: Restatement of Contracts, 164; Restatement of Contracts 2d, 160.

[85]C.C. 1459: "A non-negotiable written contract for the payment of money or personal property may be transferred by indorsement, in like manner with negotiable instruments. Such indorsement shall transfer all the rights of the assignor under the instrument to the assignee, subject to all equities and defenses existing in favor of the maker at the time of the indorsement."

Suppose that C assigns an account receivable from D to A-1 who does not notify D of the assignment. C then fraudulently assigns the same account to A-2 who notifies D of the assignment to him before A-1 gives D notice of his assignment. Whom does D pay? Until 1943, there were two rules: (1) the rule of New York and a substantial number of other states that the assignee first in time (A-1) prevailed regardless of who first gave notice to D. This followed the theory that when C transferred to A-1, he divested himself of his interest in the account and had nothing left to transfer to A-2. (2) The rule followed in California and a substantial number of other states that the first assignee (A-2) to notify the debtor prevailed. This followed the theory that A-1, by not giving notice, made it impossible for A-2 to discover the prior assignment by inquiry of D, and that, therefore, A1 made it possible for C to commit the fraud and should be the loser.

A decision of the United States Supreme Court in 1943 (*Corn Exchange Nat. Bank, etc.* v. *Klauder*, 318 U.S. 434, 63 S.Ct. 679) caused rule (2) to be dropped in most states. As a practical matter, much assigning of accounts receivable is on a "non-notice" basis. The seller of goods does not want the buyer to know that he has assigned the buyer's account, and the assignee, a bank or finance company, may agree not to notify the buyer of the assignment. As a result of the *Klauder* decision, the assignee of the account lost his rights to the seller's trustee in bankruptcy if, after making the assignment, the seller went into bankruptcy and the assignee had not notified the buyer of the assignment. This led most states after 1943 to enact legislation, sponsored by banks and finance companies, that either (a) in effect, adopted the New York first-in-time rule, or (b) provided for filing notice of assignments of accounts receivable and protected an assignee who filed notice. California, in 1943, adopted a notice-filing statute—C.C. 3017-3029—under which it became the rule in this state that the first assignee to file notice of assignment of an account receivable prevailed. These various state laws have, in turn, been superseded by the notice-filing rules of Division 9 of the Uniform Commercial Code. These rules will be seen in the chapter on Secured Transactions.

NOTES

CHAPTER 3

Agency & OTHER RELATIONSHIPS

Introduction

In this chapter the relationships in which one person is employed or engaged to do something for another are discussed. While the chapter title is "Agency,"[1] this is but one of three relationships that are covered: principal and agent, employer and employee, and principal or employer and independent contractor.[2] Of the three, the principal-agent relationship gives rise to the greatest number of legal problems.

● The earliest type of relationship in which one person performed services for another was known as "master and servant." This began in the very early days when industry was in the home. The head of the house was the master, and those who moved into his home to assist in the industry were his servants. Later, as the factory system developed, the persons who lived at home and came to the factory for daily work became known as *employees* by distinction. The language of master and servant is little used today, having been replaced by that of *employer and employee,* which is used hereafter.[3]

Concurrently, there developed that class of persons who were engaged to do a given job—to build factories, provide transportation systems for their output, and the like. Being experts in their respective fields, they were hired only to produce a given result, and reserved the right to use their own methods and discretion as to the manner in which it was accomplished. They became and continue to be known as *independent contractors.*

An *agent* is a legal representative appointed to represent another in business affairs or transactions with third persons. His is a position of greater dignity and responsibility than that of an employee, and his function of *representation* is essentially different from that of an employee or an independent contractor. Agency has always existed to some extent, but it received great impetus as economies and business organizations became more complex and it became increasingly necessary to transact business through representatives. Further impetus was given by the advent of the corporation which, as a fictitious "person," could conduct its business only through agents—its directors and officers.

---

[1]In California, the general law of agency is found in C.C. 22952356. In addition, the entire Labor Code is devoted to the employer-employee relationship. It is primarily concerned with working conditions and workers' compensation, however, and its discussion will be deferred until the last section of this chapter.

[2]The one who employs an independent contractor is usually called his *principal,* but may be called his *employer.* There is no strict rule in the matter.

[3]In the law, the word "servant" has never meant what it is generally considered to mean in a non-legal sense—a maid or butler or other household employee. Legally, it has always been more or less synonymous with "employee," it being used in older cases to describe anyone from the president of the corporation to the janitor or night watchman.

More recently, there has developed a corps of professional agents—real estate brokers, stock brokers, food brokers, insurance brokers, etc.

● The agent may make or negotiate contracts on behalf of his principal. Much litigation has involved the question of the extent of the authority of an agent in a particular case and with the consequences of an unauthorized act. It is with these matters that much of this chapter is concerned. Since the function of employees and independent contractors is to do a particular job and no more, these problems do not arise with respect to them. In other respects, the rules of law governing agents apply with equal force to employees and independent contractors with the one important exception, to be discussed later, that a principal is liable for torts of his agents and employees, but not for those of an independent contractor or his employees. It may be assumed, then, that what is said for agency applies to independent contractorship and employment unless otherwise indicated.

● It is often important, however, to decide into which category a person falls. (1) In tort cases, for the reason indicated above. (2) Because state unemployment insurance laws, federal income tax laws and the Social Security Act require records to be kept and withholdings from wages to be made as to an employee, but not as to an independent contractor. (3) Because state workers' compensation laws require an employer to carry compensation insurance for an employee but not for an independent contractor.

● The distinctions among the three classes and how the courts have dealt with them are now considered.

Independent Contractor, Employee and Agent Distinguished

Employee or Independent Contractor?: In the classical sense, an *independent contractor* is one employed to produce a given result and having complete discretion as to the manner of its accomplishment[4]—the building contractor, the firm of accountants called in periodically to make an audit, and so on. The *employee,* in the usual sense at least, is one engaged to perform certain duties in a manner directed and supervised by the employer, and who remains under the control of the employer at all times—the factory worker, the stenographer, etc.

Today, the concept of independent contractor has a somewhat different meaning, particularly in connection with matters of taxation and insurance; and, as a practical matter, there is necessarily much flexibility in classifying persons as agents, employees or independent contractors.

Today, we have many relationships that do not fall squarely within the classical concepts. The real estate salesman in Cal-

---

[4]Lab. C. 3353, defining an independent contractor for the purposes of the workers' compensation law, says that he is "any person who renders service for a specified recompense for a specified result, under the control of his principal as to the result of his work only and not as to the means by which such result is accomplished."

ifornia is an example. We have real estate *brokers* and *salesmen* as the two classes of persons whose business it is to find buyers of real estate for sellers. Both must be licensed. The broker's license permits him to engage in business for himself. The salesman, on the other hand, must "work for" a broker and cannot operate on his own. But this is largely a technical relationship which comes about only because it is required by law. It is not "employment" in the usual sense. In many cases at least, the broker's office serves only as a sort of headquarters for the salesmen. They depend for compensation on some percentage of commissions received from sales of property assigned to them. They have great, if not entire, freedom of action. On the other hand, these salesmen are not independent contractors in the usual sense. While they have the freedom or *discretion* of independent contractors, it is not technically true that they are "employed to produce a given result," at least from the standpoint of the broker for whom they "work." The federal and state governments require, e.g., that employers withhold income taxes from wages of *employees* and that employers carry workers' compensation insurance for *employees,* but these things are not required with respect to independent contractors. How is the real estate salesman classified for these purposes? What the courts have done in these cases is to place the party in the category into which he most nearly fits. Real estate salesmen having substantial freedom of action have been classified as independent contractors. *California Employment Stabilization Commission* v. *Morris,* 28 C.2d 812, 172 P.2d 497, is a typical case. It raised the question of whether real estate salesmen were independent contractors or employees for the purposes of unemployment insurance taxes, the broker being liable for such taxes if the salesmen were employees. The court said that the salesmen could be either, depending upon all of the circumstances surrounding the relationship to the broker; that the salesmen here were *independent contractors* because they paid their own office expenses, had no fixed hours, obtained their own "leads," were paid only out of commissions, were not employed for any definite period of time, and had no instruction manual or set of rules to follow as to the manner of doing their work. The court said, however, that if the broker paid all office expenses, required the salesmen to work fixed hours, etc., they might be held to be employees.

As applied to situations of this kind, then, independent contractorship means primarily freedom of action in doing one's work, whatever it may be, and the borderline between it and employment lies in the extent to which the employer has the right to control the details of the work.[5]

---

[5]*Twentieth Century Lites, Inc.* v. *Calif. Dept. of Employment,* 28 C.2d 56, 168 P.2d 699, raised the question of whether a group of neon sign salesmen were employees or independent contractors for unemployment insurance tax purposes. The salesmen were paid only commissions and had no drawing accounts, had no regular hours and had the right to take business obtained by them to other companies if they chose, although customarily it was first offered to Twentieth Century Lites. On the other hand, pointing to employment were the facts that the company supplied office space, a substantial number of "leads" and certain tools and equipment required by the salesmen, the company could terminate the relationship at any time, every order for sale or lease of a sign had to be approved by the company, and no price adjustments could be made without the consent of the company. Held, the salesmen were employees. In addition to the facts above favoring employment, the court said that the salesmen were "*not engaged in a distinct occupation*" but carried on the regular business of the company," thereby stressing the classical concept of

Employee-Agent Combination: The function of the *agent* is *representation.* He is usually defined as one who represents another, his principal, for the purpose of bringing him into legal relationships—contracts—with third persons.[6] Except for the professionals, however, an out-and-out agent is rare. The usual case is that of an employee acting as an agent—a person serving primarily as an employee but functioning as an agent on particular occasions or for particular purposes—the store manager who is an employee as to the internal management of the store but becomes the owner's representative for the purpose of buying goods to replenish inventory; or the corporation president who is a salaried employee for the purposes of supervision of the internal operation of the corporation, but its agent to make contracts in its name. The lines, then, are not clearly drawn, and a person may move in and out of the one or the other of these two categories quite readily, depending upon which of his functions he is performing at a given time.

Independent Contractor-Agent Combination: From the general standpoint of the client by whom he is employed the real estate broker is an independent contractor. He is employed to produce the given result of finding a buyer and the client will not expect to attempt to tell him how to do the job. But in dealing with prospective buyers he *represents* the client, which is the badge of *agency.* If he or the salesman to whom he assigns the listing misrepresents the property to the buyer, the client may be charged with the fraud to the extent at least that the buyer may be permitted to rescind. To this extent therefore the characteristics of agency relationships attach to the relationship.

As mentioned earlier, flexibility in making these classifications is necessary. A person cannot be placed definitely, completely and exclusively into a particular category in every case. He may fall into one category or another at a given time, depending upon what he is doing and for whom. To properly classify a person at a particular time, the important thing is to understand the characteristics of each classification and be able to analyze each situation according to the nature of the act in question.

Particular Agents

Various types of agents have come to be known by particular names which indicate the nature and extent of their agency powers or the agency function to be performed.

General and Special Agents: All agents are either general or special. The distinction is one of degree—a *general agent* having broad powers, a *special agent* relatively limited powers, or being appointed only for a particular transaction.[7]

Suppose you are going to Europe for a year. You own various properties which you wish to leave in my hands, giving me complete power of management and control during your absence. In short, you wish to make me your general agent with respect to these properties. To this end, you will give me a *power of attorney* which is simply a written instrument

---

an independent contractor as one engaged in a business with which the employer has no connection, such as, the plumber or the accountant called in to do a plumbing job or an audit by a department store.

[6]C.C. 2295: "An agent is one who represents another, called the principal, in dealings with third persons. Such representation is called agency."

[7]C.C. 2297: "An agent for a particular act or transaction is called a special agent. All others are general agents."

by which agency authority is conferred.[8] Since you desire to make me your general agent, it will be a *general power of attorney* in the form of that on page 58.

Or, suppose you are retired and living in Florida but still own a piece of real estate in California. I have been your attorney in past years. I am offered a good price for your California property and communicate it to you. You wish to sell. Here, you may give me a *special power of attorney* to act as your agent for the sole purpose of carrying out the details of the sale, executing a deed to the property and collecting the price. This would be a special or limited agency, as distinguished from the broader general one created in the first case.

• In the field of insurance, "general agent" is used in contradistinction to "agent." Here, *general agent* means one through whom all applications for insurance and all policies in a particular area must flow to and from the insurance company, a general agent being the processor of all of the company's business in a given area. In addition, it will have some degree of authority to pass upon applications, i.e., to determine whether or not a particular policy should be issued. For its services it will receive an overriding commission on the business that passes through it. *Agents*, on the other hand, are those who sell insurance to the public, and who channel business to the next higher level, the general agency. The agent operates his own place of business at his own expense, and his only compensation is commissions[9] on the business procured which is acceptable to the company. He has, however, a contract which permits him to *bind* the company until the company acts upon an application, i.e., issues a formal policy or notifies the agent that a policy will not be issued to the applicant. His, then, is a special or limited agency as compared to the general agency. The "Agency Agreement" on page 59 is a standard form and one which is deemed to confer the power to bind the company.

Brokers: A *broker* is a negotiator between parties who serves as a "middleman" to bring together supply and demand. In most cases, he seeks a buyer on behalf of a seller and fulfills his job when he finds someone ready, willing and able to buy—real estate and business opportunities brokers who attempt to find buyers for properties and businesses listed with them, or food brokers who attempt to find purchasers for products of a manufacturer or producer. A broker may also attempt to find a seller for a buyer, however, and this is essentially the function of an insurance broker—finding a company willing to sell insurance to a person who comes to the broker seeking coverage.[10]

Factors: A *factor* or commission merchant is one who obtains goods on consignment for resale by him on a commission basis, or at some markup which will allow him a profit.[11] He is an *agent* in the sense that he is selling goods—acting as retail outlet—for another. He differs from the broker in that he deals with the goods in his own name, the goods appearing to be his so far as customers are concerned. When you buy appliances, for example, you may assume that they are owned by the retailer from whom you buy. Actually, however, he may be holding them only on consignment and be selling as a factor. The broker, by contrast, deals only in the names of the parties between whom he negotiates, and the parties themselves make the ultimate contract. The factor fully consummates the transaction, making the sale and receiving the price in his own name, and then reimburses his principal, the manufacturer or producer.[12]

FACTOR UNDER DEL CREDERE COMMISSION. Factors may sell for cash or on credit.[13] When they sell on credit, they may assume absolute responsibility for the price of the goods, i.e., agree to pay the principal for the goods within a specified time even though they, in turn, are not paid by credit purchasers. Where a factor does this, he is called a *factor under a del credere commission* or *del credere agent*. He may demand a higher rate of commission for assuming this additional risk.[14]

"FACTORING." The word factor is also used in another sense—to describe a financing agency which engages in the business of "*factoring*"—buying or "discounting" accounts receivable pending payment. Suppose you are a retail seller who sells on short term credit, 6090 days, and cannot afford to have your capital tied up. A factor may advance you money, taking an assignment of your credit accounts as security pending payment and charging you some rate of interest on the moneys advanced.

Creation of Agency

Who May Appoint or Be Agent

Anyone may appoint an agent to negotiate or make contracts on his behalf, but the contracts of persons who lack general capacity to contract—minors and mental incompetents—are no more binding when made through an agent than when made directly.[15]

---

[8]The word "attorney" means simply *agent* or *deputy*—"one who acts in the place or stead of another." The person appointed as agent by a power of attorney is customarily called an *attorney in fact* and may be anyone—a relative, friend or attorney at law. An *attorney at law*, as distinguished from an attorney in fact, is one engaged for the special purpose of representing another in legal proceedings and having the license required by law to engage in such representation.

[9]To this there is one exception. The life insurance agent—salesman—usually works out of the company itself and is paid a salary plus commissions.

[10]The difference between an insurance *broker* and the insurance *agent* discussed in the preceding paragraph of the text lies in the fact that the *broker* is the agent of the person seeking insurance while the *agent* is the agent of the person selling insurance—the insurance company. Legal consequences of this distinction are discussed in the chapter on Insurance.

[11]C.C. 2026: "A factor is an agent who, in the pursuit of an independent calling, is employed by another to sell property for him, and is vested by the latter with the possession or control of the property . . ."

[12]The principal will not be permitted to repossess the goods from the consumer if the factor fails to remit the purchase price. This is because the principal has participated in an arrangement which makes the factor *appear* to be the owner of the goods, and, so, is *estopped* to recover them from the consumer-purchaser. This is discussed in detail in the chapter on Sales.

[13]C.C. 2028: "A factor may sell property consigned to him on such credit as is usual . . ."

[14]C.C. 2029 is designed to cover the factor under a del credere commission. It does not describe him as such, however, but rather as a "factor under guaranty commission." It says that "A factor who charges his principal with a guaranty commission upon a sale, thereby assumes absolutely to pay the price when it falls due, as if it were a debt of his own, and not as a mere guarantor for the purchaser . . ."

[15]C.C. 2296: "Anyone having capacity to contract may appoint an agent, and any person may be an agent."

POWER OF ATTORNEY

_____ OSCAR B. OWNER _____ , Principal,

appoints _____ HENRY A. BUDDIE _____ , Attorney,

TRUE AND LAWFUL ATTORNEY for Principal and in the name, place and stead and for the use and benefit of Principal, to ask, demand, sue for, recover, collect and receive all such sums of money, debts, dues, accounts, legacies, bequests, interests, dividends, annuities and demands whatsoever as are now or shall hereafter become due. owing, payable or belonging to Principal, and have, use and take all lawful ways and means to recover the same by legal process, and to compromise and agree for the same, and grant releases or other sufficient discharges for the same, and for and in the name of Principal to make, seal and deliver; to bargain, contract, agree for, purchase, receive and take lands, tenements, hereditaments and accept the seizin and possession of all lands and all deeds and other assurances, in law therefor; and to lease, let, demise, bargain, sell, remise, release, convey, mortgage and hypothecate lands, tenements and hereditaments, upon such terms and conditions, and under such covenants as Attorney shall think fit. Also to bargain and agree for, buy, sell, mortgage, hypothecate and in any and every way and manner deal in and with goods, wares and merchandise, choses in action, and other property in possession or in action; and to make, do and transact all and every kind of business of every kind and nature whatsoever, and also, for and in the name of Principal to sign, seal, execute, deliver and acknowledge such deeds, leases and assignment of leases, covenants, indentures, agreements, mortgages, hypothecations, bottomries, charter-parties, bills of lading, bills, bonds, notes, receipts, evidences of debt, releases and satisfaction of mortgage, judgments and other debts, and such other instruments in writing of every kind and nature as may be necessary or proper in the premises.

GIVING AND GRANTING unto said Attorney full power and authority to do and perform all and every act and thing whatsoever requisite and necessary to be done in and about the premises, as fully to all intents and purposes as Principal might or could do if personally present, with full power of substitution or revocation, hereby ratifying and confirming all that said Attorney shall lawfully do or cause to be done by virtue of these presents.

We, and each of us, jointly and severally, have hereunto set our hands this ___9th___ day of _____ March _____ , 19 _84_ .

_____ s/ OSCAR B. OWNER _____

_____

_____

(Must be acknowledged by Notary Public.)

AGENCY AGREEMENT

THIS AGREEMENT, made this ___4th___ day of ___September___, 19 _84_, by and between ___California Insurance Company, a California Corporation,___ hereinafter referred to as the Company and ___William T. Insuranceman___ of ___San Rafael___

in County of ___Marin___ and State of ___California___, hereinafter designated as the Agent:

WITNESSETH THAT:

Pursuant to request that the underwriting facilities of the Company be made available to the undersigned, as Agent, the Company hereby grants authority to Agent to receive and accept proposals for such contracts of insurance covering risks on properties located in ___County of Marin,___

___State of California,___

as the Company has authority lawfully to make; subject, however, to restrictions placed upon such Agent by the laws of the state or states in which such Agent is authorized to write insurance business and to the terms and conditions hereinafter set out.

IT IS HEREBY AGREED:

(1) Agent has full power and authority to receive and accept proposals for insurance covering such classes of risks as the Company may, from time to time, authorize to be insured; to collect, receive and receipt for premiums on insurance tendered by the Agent to and accepted by the Company and to retain out of premiums so collected, as full compensation on business so placed with the Company, commissions as may be from time to time mutually agreed upon.

(2) In the event of termination of this Agreement, the Agent having promptly accounted for and paid over premiums for which he may be liable, the Agent's records, use and control of expirations shall remain the property of the Agent and be left in his undisputed possession; otherwise the records, use and control of expirations shall be vested in the Company.

It is a condition of this Agreement that the Agent shall refund ratably to the Company, on business heretofore or hereafter written, commissions on cancelled liability and on reductions in premiums at the same rate at which such commissions were originally retained.

(3) Accounts of money due the Company on the business placed by the Agent with the Company are to be rendered monthly so as to reach the Company's office not later than the twentieth day of the following month; the balance therein shown to be due to the Company shall be paid not later than forty-five (45) days after the end of the month for which the account is rendered.

(4) Company shall not be responsible for Agency expenses such as rentals, transportation facilities, clerk hire, solicitors' fees, advertising, exchange, personal local license fees, adjustment by the Agent of losses under policies issued by the Agent, or any other Agency expenses whatsover.

(5) Any policy forms, maps, map corrections and other like Company supplies furnished to the Agent by the Company shall always remain the property of the Company and shall be returned to the Company or its representatives promptly upon demand.

(6) This Agreement supersedes all previous agreements, whether oral or written, between the Company and Agent and may be terminated by either party at any time upon written notice to the other.

Executed by the parties hereto on the day and year first above written.

CALIFORNIA INSURANCE COMPANY

By /s/ ARNOLD E. OFFICER

Vice-President

By /s/ WILLIAM T. INSURANCEMAN

(Agent)

Conversely, anyone may be an agent except a mental incompetent or "infant of tender years"—a minor too young to appreciate the legal consequences of a contract.[16] It is felt that one who makes contracts as the agent of another should understand the legal import of such transactions, and, since neither of the classes mentioned qualify in this respect, they are not proper agents.

Methods of Creation

The function of the agent is to negotiate or make contracts on behalf of the principal. If the contract is or *appears* to be within the scope of the agent's authority, it binds the principal. In addition, the principal may subsequently approve or *ratify* a contract that was not within the authority of the agent to make. This makes it possible for agency to become established or be "created" in 3 ways—intentionally or by "appointment;" by "estoppel;" and by "ratification," and it is these various methods of creation that are now discussed.

Appointment: Most of agency originates from express authorization or *appointment,* specific authority being given to the agent who then, by the exercise of his given powers, binds the principal. The only problem here is that in some cases the law requires the agent's authority to be conferred by written instrument if contracts made by him are to be enforceable. There are two rules on the matter. Probably the general rule is that an agent must have written authority only where he is to enter into a contract for the sale of real property. In a number of states including California, however, a much broader requirement is made—that the agent's authority must be conferred by written instrument in any case in which the agent will enter into any of the types of contracts required by the Statute of Frauds to be in writing—sales of real property, sales of goods for a price of $500 or more, etc.[17] This is called the *equal dignities rule*—that if the agent is to make contracts which are required by law to be in writing, his authority must be created by a method of equal dignity—a written instrument.

Where the agency is created by appointment and the *agent* is exercising granted powers, he is called an *actual agent* as distinguished from the *apparent* or *ostensible agent,* next considered.

Estoppel: In Contracts, one application of the doctrine of estoppel was shown. There it took the special form of *promissory estoppel*—which was that if one person made a promise to another, which the promisee justifiably relied on to his detriment, the promisor would not be permitted (would be *estopped*) to escape the promise, even though he had received no consideration in return.

There is a broader general concept of *estoppel,* however, which is encountered here for the first time but which will be encountered again. Whenever one person leads another to believe that something is true which is not true, the person creating the false impression will be estopped to show the true facts as to one who has been misled and who would be injured if the true facts could be shown.

Applying this principle to the law of agency, *agency by estoppel* occurs when third persons have been led to believe

that a person is an agent who is not or that a person has been invested with agency powers which he does not have. There are two general types of agency by estoppel situations:

1. Where no agency at all exists, but one party, the apparent or ostensible principal, leads third persons to believe that a particular individual, the apparent or ostensible agent, is his agent, and the third person deals with the ostensible agent in reliance upon the ostensible agency.[18] In such case, the ostensible principal will be estopped to deny the existence of an agency relationship and will be held liable as though an actual agency existed.

This occurrence is rare. One business practice out of which it might arise is this: The seller of a business may agree to make it appear, for some time after the sale, that the buyer has merely become associated with him in the operation of the business. This gives the buyer opportunity to meet and become acquainted with the established customers of the business. After the buyer has had the opportunity to conduct a number of transactions with customers, enabling him to gain their respect and confidence, the seller withdraws from the picture. This assures the buyer of the seller's customers. During the period in which the seller makes it appear that the buyer is an employee or associate, the seller runs the risk of agency by estoppel.[19]

2. Where an actual agency exists and the principal leads third persons to believe that the agent has greater or broader powers than he has. In this case, the actual agent becomes an ostensible agent to the extent of the larger powers that he is made to appear to possess.[20]

This is the more likely estoppel situation. The cases that follow are illustrative. In *Robinson* v. *American Fish etc. Co.,* 17 C.A. 212, 119 P. 388, an agent was authorized to purchase fish on consignment, but not to make outright purchases. He was held out as the company's *general agent,* however, and was authorized to do all of its buying throughout a large territory. The principal did not notify sellers with whom it knew the agent was negotiating of the limitation upon his authority, i.e., that he could purchase only on consignment. Thereafter, the agent made contracts for outright purchases from such persons. Held, the principal was bound; that by presenting the agent as a general agent who would seem to have authority to make outright purchases, it had contrived to give a false impression of the agent's authority and was estopped to show its limitations.[21]

---

[16]While C.C. 2296 does not exclude these classes, the courts would probably do so since this is recognized general law. There are no California cases on this point since, as a practical matter, such persons are not made agents.

[17]C.C. 2309: "An oral authorization is sufficient for any purpose, except that an authority to enter into a contract required by law to be in writing can only be given by an instrument in writing."

[18]C.C. 2300: "An agency is ostensible when the principal intentionally, or by want of ordinary care, causes a third person to believe another to be his agent who is not really employed by him."

[19]If buyer were held out as associate or partner of seller it might be held that there was *partnership by estoppel,* which involves the same idea as agency by estoppel. Partners are *mutual agents,* i.e., each partner is agent of and principal to every other partner, and has the same liability as does a principal for an agent generally. An ostensible partnership or partnership by estoppel would exist, then, when persons make it appear that they are in business as partners.

[20]C.C. 2334: "A principal is bound by acts of his agent, under a merely ostensible authority, to those persons only who have in good faith, and without want of ordinary care, incurred a liability or parted with value, upon the faith thereof."

[21]Some courts decide cases of this kind by stating simply that a principal may not place secret limitations on the powers of agents so as to reduce their powers below those of other agents similarly placed. Although stated in this manner, the rule is still one of estoppel.

In *Leavens* v. *Pinkham & McKevitt*, 164 C. 242, 128 P. 399, the principal placed limitations upon prices to be paid by its general agent for fruit purchased from growers during a particular season. In previous years, the agent had been authorized to make purchases at such prices as it felt proper. The principal did not inform growers with whom the agent had regularly dealt of the newly imposed limitations. Thereafter, the agent made contracts to purchase at prices in excess of the limitations. Held, the principal was bound since the agent continued to have ostensible authority to do what it had done in the past, until parties with whom it had regularly dealt were expressly advised to the contrary.

Ratification: Agency by estoppel rests upon the theory that the principal has led third persons to believe that another is his agent, or, being his agent, has broader powers than he actually has. Agency by *ratification* is a reciprocal to this. It covers the case where a person, having no authority to do so, purports to act as agent, and the purported principal has done nothing to lead third persons to believe the person is an agent; or, the more likely case, where an actual agent exercises an authority which he does not have, and the principal has done nothing to lead third persons to believe that he possesses such authority. In neither case is the rule of estoppel applicable. Therefore, the "principal" is not bound upon the contract as of the time it is made. But the law permits him to approve or *ratify* it if he sees fit, and thereby cure the defect of lack of authority. An agency authority is created retroactively by such ratification.[22]

Ratification may be express or implied from acceptance of the benefits of the contract.[23] Until the contract is ratified, the third person may withdraw from it. Once he ratifies it, the principal is, of course, bound to perform on the contract.

As an example, suppose the secretary of a corporation finds a stock of goods of a type which he knows the corporation needs. Secretaries of corporations do not have the authority to make purchases on behalf of corporations, and everyone is charged with knowledge of this fact. Immediate action is required, however, so the secretary makes a contract to purchase in the name of the corporation. Since this was a wholly unauthorized act and since there was no legal justification for it on the part of the seller for believing that the secretary had the power which he purported to exercise, the corporation cannot be held on the contract if it chooses not to honor it. But assuming that it does, that it accepts and is pleased to get the goods, it then ratifies and becomes bound upon the contract.

● Ratification may build into estoppel. Suppose that the secretary of a corporation makes several unauthorized purchases.

In each case, however, the corporation ratifies the transaction and does not caution the seller that the secretary is acting without authority. Under such circumstances, the seller would probably be justified in believing that authority to make purchases had been conferred upon the secretary, and as to subsequent purchases of the same nature the corporation might be estopped to deny the secretary's authority.

Powers, Duties and Liabilities of Agents

Powers

In general, an agent has such powers as are expressly conferred upon him, plus, impliedly, such powers as are necessary, proper or usual to enable him to accomplish the purpose of the agency,[24] e.g., an agent to purchase goods would have implied authority to arrange transportation to the principal's place of business; an agent to operate and manage a business would have implied authority to employ necessary help, replenish inventory, etc.

Powers of Selling Agents: Agents to sell goods are said to have implied authority to warrant the quality of the goods and the title of the principal,[25] and to sell on credit if it is customary in the trade. If they are entrusted with the goods and sell them as their own, as do factors, they may collect the purchase price.[26] If they are ordinary "salesmen," they may collect the price in connection with a delivery of the goods but not afterwards or in other connections.[27]

Agents for the sale of real property—real estate brokers—are considered to have only the authority to find a purchaser. They have no authority to make a sales contract or to collect the purchase price.

Power to Execute Negotiable Instruments: An agent may be expressly authorized to execute negotiable instruments, usually checks, in the name of his principal e.g., the treasurer of a corporation. If such an agent abuses his authority for personal advantage, the loss will fall upon the principal so long as persons dealing with the agent are not on notice of the fact that he is misappropriating funds. This is discussed in the later chapter on Commercial Paper.

In *implying* power to an agent to deal with negotiable instruments in the name of the principal, however, the courts become very strict. Only in very exceptional cases will such a power be implied, as where the agent is authorized to borrow money for the principal. In such case, it must be implied that the agent has authority to execute a note in the name of the principal in return for the loan. Beyond such rare instances as this, the power will not be implied.

Emergency Powers: The powers of an agent or employee are broadened in an emergency situation, i.e., the principal may be held for acts of an agent or employee in emergency circumstances which are not within the scope of his authority under ordinary circumstances, and for which the principal

---

[22]C.C. 2307: "An agency may be created, and an authority may be conferred, by a precedent authorization or a subsequent ratification."

[23]There is an important qualification upon this in California. C.C. 2310 says that "A ratification can be made only in the manner that would have been necessary to confer an original authority . . ." This would extend the *equal dignities rule* to ratification, and require ratification by written instrument where an agency by appointment to make the type of contract made by the agent would have required a writing. *Kadota Fig Assn.* v. *Case-Swayne Co.*, 73 C.A.2d 815, 167 P.2d 523, is a case in which there was an express ratification. There a surety bond was improperly executed at the time it was filed. Later, however, the bonding company filed a supplemental instrument in which it expressly stated that it ratified the bond as of date of execution, and this was held to be binding.

[24]C.C. 2319: "An agent has authority: 1. To do everything necessary or proper and usual, in the ordinary course of business, for effecting the purpose of his agency . . ."

[25]C.C. 2323: "An authority to sell personal property includes authority to warrant the title of the principal, and the quality and quantity of the property."

[26]C.C. 2325: "A general agent to sell, who is entrusted by the principal with the possession of the thing sold, has authority to receive the price."

[27]C.C. 2326: "A special agent to sell has authority to receive the price on delivery of the thing sold, but not afterwards."

would not be held in ordinary circumstances. Suppose that an employer goes on vacation leaving an employee in charge of the business during his absence. The employee has never been given power to borrow money in the name of the employer. While the employer is away, a carload of goods arrives which the employer has purchased but for which he has forgotten to make provision for payment. The employer's whereabouts are not known so that he cannot be reached. Unless the goods are paid for immediately, the railroad company will start to assess substantial demurrage charges for the detention of its freight car, and the seller will have the right to recall the goods and ultimately sue the employer-buyer for breach of contract. Under these circumstances, the employee in charge would have the power to borrow money in the name of the employer to pay for the goods. This set of facts would fulfill the requirements for an *emergency situation* which are said to be (1) that immediate action is necessary to protect the principal against serious liability, and (2) that it is not possible or practicable to communicate with the principal before taking action. When this is shown, the agent has authority to do whatever is reasonably necessary to protect the interests of the principal.[28]

Duties

An agent must use reasonable skill, care and diligence in what he does, but will be excused for errors of judgment.

He must obey to the letter the instructions of his principal. If he wishes to perform in a manner or at a time not in accordance with the principal's instructions, he must secure the principal's consent to the change. If, without the consent of the principal, he deviates from his given instructions, he will be held liable for any loss that results, even though the deviation is in good faith and for the best interests of the principal. To this there is one exception, however—the emergency situation discussed above.

• The agent must account to the principal for all moneys or property received by the agent on behalf of the principal.

Fiduciary Duty: An agent has a fiduciary relationship to his principal which imposes additional duties on him. It requires him to observe a high degree of loyalty and good faith to the principal and to refrain from competing with the principal in any way or making any secret profits in connection with the agency.[29] Certain cases may be specially noted:

[28]C.C. 2320: "An agent has power to disobey instructions . . . in cases where it is clearly for the interest of his principal that he should do so, and there is not time to communicate with the principal."

[29]The California law provides this in a rather circuitous way. C.C. 2322(3) says that an agent does not have authority "To do any act which a trustee is forbidden to do by . . . [C.C. 2228-2239] . . .", which set out the fiduciary obligations of trustees. C.C. 2228 says that "a trustee is bound to act in the highest good faith toward his beneficiary, and may not obtain any advantage therein over the latter by the slightest misrepresentation, concealment, threat, or adverse pressure of any kind." The following sections forbid a trustee to use trust property for his own advantage, to use his position to personal advantage, or to purchase trust property unless the beneficiary, with full knowledge of all facts and with no influence on the part of the trustee, permits him to do so.
California cases illustrating the application of these principles are *Kinert* v. *Wright*, 81 C.A.2d 919, 185 P.2d 364, where an agent was given $1200 to buy a parcel of land; the agent got it and a larger tract for $500 and attempted to keep the balance of land and money for himself; held, the principal was entitled to the balance of the land and the difference in the price. And *Sands*

Where the agency is to sell property of the principal, the agent may purchase the property himself, but the principal may avoid the sale if there is the slightest unfairness, even though the price appears to be adequate. To this, one exception is generally recognized. Real estate brokers may take "net listings" on property, particularly business property. This means that the broker gets as his compensation everything above a specified net price, e.g., if a broker agrees to sell a hotel lease at a net price of $50,000, he gets $5000 if he sells it for $55,000, $2000 if he sells for $52,000. It is generally held that the broker may himself purchase the property at the stipulated net figure in such cases, since the seller gets the full amount desired. The broker may purchase where the time of the listing is about to run out, and he feels that, given more time, he can sell at substantially above the net figure.[30]

• An agent may not secretly contrive to act as agent for both parties to a transaction. Their interests necessarily conflict and the agent cannot do full justice to both. In such case, it is held that the agent may not recover compensation from either party even though the contract is fair in all respects; and that either of the principals may rescind even though no injury is shown. If both principals have full knowledge of it, however, such *dual agency* is permissible. The better practice is to have both principals approve in writing the agency and its commissions.

• The duty of loyalty requires the agent, or more specifically an employee in this case, to use the employer's time for the employer's purposes and interests. This may give rise to a question of whether or not an employer has any right to claim ownership of an invention of an employee, the idea for which arises in connection with the employment or which is developed during working hours. It is generally held that the employee is entitled to his invention unless it has been developed during working hours and with company materials, in which case it has been held that the principal is entitled to it.[31]

Delegation of Powers or Duties

As a basic proposition, it may be said that an agent cannot delegate to others—*subagents*—such parts of his duties as involve his personal skill, judgment or discretion. There are a number of cases, however, in which an agent may appoint subagents and delegate duties to them: (1) Where this has been expressly authorized by the principal. (2) Where the duties delegated to a subagent are of a purely mechanical or ministerial nature, e.g., one hired to plan or construct a building could delegate to another the job of collecting the routine data which would have to be assembled. (3) Where it is customary or necessary to carry out the agency, e.g., a bank which receives a check drawn on a bank in another city may forward the check to a correspondent bank in that city as its subagent

v. *Eagle Oil & Ref. Co.*, 83 C.A.2d 312, 188 P.2d 782, where the agent was engaged to obtain a lease on service station property; he purchased the property himself and leased it to the principal through a dummy owner at a rent $25 a month higher than it could have been obtained otherwise; held, the lease was not binding on the principal.

[30]In *Rattray* v. *Scudder*, 28 C.2d 214, 169 P.2d 371, however, where a broker, having a prospect who would purchase for $13,500, took and exercised an option to buy for $10,250 without disclosure, it was held that there was such fraudulent conduct on the part of the broker as to justify revocation of his license by the Real Estate Commissioner.

[31]*Union Die Casting Co.* v. *Anderson*, 25 C.A.2d 195, 76 Pac.2d 703.

for collection; the manager of a business may hire employees necessary to operate it; and a collection agency may employ an attorney to prosecute a lawsuit for collection of an account turned over to the agency for collection.[32]

● If the case is a proper one for appointment of a subagent, and the subagent has been selected with reasonable care, it is the general rule that the subagent becomes the agent of the original principal. Under this rule, liability for acts of the subagent rests with the original principal rather than with the agent, and the original principal suffers the loss if there is any dereliction of duty on the part of the subagent.[33]

Liabilities

There are a number of cases in which an agent may become personally liable to third persons because he has acted in excess of his authority, has failed to disclose that he is acting on behalf of a principal, or for other reason.

Lack of Authority: Every agent impliedly *warrants* his authority, i.e., guarantees that he is authorized by the principal to do what he is doing.[34] If it develops that he has acted without or in excess of his authority, he is liable for breach of *warranty of authority* for any damages suffered by the third person with whom he has dealt. If he is in doubt as to the extent of his authority, the agent may protect himself by making full disclosure of its nature and terms. If this is done, the third person cannot be said to have relied upon the usual implied warranty. Instead, he relies upon his own evaluation of the agent's authority and may not hold the agent if his evaluation proves to be wrong.

Incompetency of Principal: There is an academic dispute as to whether or not an agent warrants the competency of his principal, i.e., warrants that the principal is not a minor or mental incompetent. The majority rule seems to be that he does not. Under this majority rule, however, the agent has the duty to advise the third person of incompetency of his principal, and is liable for *fraud* in the form of nondisclosure if he does not. The result is the same as though the agent had warranted competency.

Torts Committed by Agent: In a following section, it is shown that a principal is liable for torts committed by an agent or employee within the scope of his agency or employment. This does not relieve the agent or employee of liability, however. A person is liable for torts committed by him even though someone else may also be liable.[35] Thus, if a truck

driver negligently hits a pedestrian in a crosswalk, he is liable to the injured party even though his employer is also liable.

● In one case at least, an agent may incur liability for tort where he acts at the direction of the principal and without knowledge that the act is wrongful. Suppose that a principal, a seller of goods, directs an agent to repossess an article sold, telling the agent that it has not been paid for, when in fact it has. In ignorance of the wrongful nature of his act, the agent repossesses. In so doing, he will have committed the tort of *conversion*—the wrongful taking or detention of property of another. This is a tort which does not require intent. Hence, it has been held that the agent is liable for damages even though he is ignorant of his wrongdoing.[36] By contrast, it has been held that an agent who innocently passes on false information given to him by the principal which he has reasonable cause to believe to be true, is not liable for the tort of fraud because it is a tort which requires intent, or at least some amount of negligence on the part of the agent.[37]

● Where the innocent agent is required to pay damages for a tort committed at the direction of the principal, he is entitled to reimbursement from the principal. Conversely, where the principal is compelled to answer for the tort of the agent, he is entitled to recover from the agent.

Undisclosed Principal: On occasion, an agent may enter into transactions on behalf of a principal without disclosing to the third party that he is acting only as an agent, i.e., by making the contract in his own name as ostensible principal. A usual case is this: P knows that T wants to sell his factory for $5,000,000. P wants it but, being a prominent and wealthy person, believes that T may raise the price if he knows that P is interested. So, P has A make the purchase, A holding himself out as a principal and making the contract in his own name without disclosing that he is acting only as agent. This is all perfectly legitimate. It would be a case of an agent making a contract on behalf of an *undisclosed principal*. The following rules apply in such case: (1) The contract may be enforced by the undisclosed principal even though the third person was unaware of his existence at the time the contract was made. (2) The third party may enforce the contract against *either* the agent or the undisclosed principal when his existence is discovered.[38] This is the calculated risk of the agent of an undisclosed principal. As a practical matter, however, the third person would pursue the discovered principal, since he would be the one with the money. The third person cannot hold both principal and agent, but must make an election to hold the one or the other. Obtaining a judgment against

---

[32]C.C. 2349: "An agent, unless specially forbidden by his principal to do so, can delegate his powers to another person in any of the following cases, and in no others:

"1. When the act to be done is purely mechanical;

"2. When it is such as the agent cannot himself, and the subagent can lawfully perform;

"3. When it is the usage of the place to delegate such powers; or

"4. When such delegation is specially authorized by the principal."

[33]C.C. 2351: "A sub-agent, lawfully appointed, represents the principal in like manner with the original agent; and the original agent is not responsible to third persons for the acts of the subagent."

[34]C.C. 2342: "One who assumes to act as an agent thereby warrants to all who deal with him in that capacity, that he has the authority which he assumes."

[35]C.C. 2343 makes an agent liable for his torts by its provisions that "an agent is responsible to third persons as a principal . . . [w]hen his acts are wrongful in their nature."

---

[36]Restatement of Agency 2d, § 349.

[37]Restatement of Agency 2d, § 348.

Thus, in *Graham* v. *Ellmore*, 135 C.A. 129, 26 P.2d 696, it was held that a real estate broker was not liable for fraud where he incorrectly informed a prospective purchaser of the balance due on a mortgage on the property to be sold, the information having been given to the broker by his principal (the seller).

[38]There are no California code sections on the rules of undisclosed principal presented in the text, but the California cases follow the rules stated, which are the rules of the Restatement of Agency.

In *W. W. Leasing* v. *Commercial Standard Title Ins.*, 149 C.A.3d 792, 197 Cal.Rptr 118, it was held that it is not the third person's duty to seek out the identity of the principal and that therefore, when the principal does business under a fictitious trade name, it is the duty of the agent to disclose the actual identity of the principal if the agent wishes to escape personal liability.

the one constitutes an election to hold that one and a bar to recovery from the other.

DISCLOSED AGENCY BUT UNDISCLOSED PRINCIPAL. Suppose an agent signs a contract, "John Deaux, Agent," i.e., indicates in the contract that he is acting as an agent but without disclosing the name of his principal. The rule of the Restatement of Agency 2d in Section 323 is that oral evidence may be introduced to show that the parties intended to bind only the principal, even though his name was not disclosed.[39]

Principal and Third Persons

Contracts of Agent

The principal is liable for contracts made by the agent within the scope of his actual or apparent authority; and, as just discussed, the principal is liable even though his existence was not known to the third person at the time the contract was made.

Torts of Agent—"Respondeat Superior"

At an early date in the law, it was felt that a principal or employer should be made responsible for torts committed by his agent or employee in the course of his agency or employment activities. The rationale was that the principal had placed the agent or employee in position to commit the tort and that, as a practical matter, only the principal would be financially able to answer in damages in most cases.[40] *Respondeat superior*—that the principal must respond in damages for the wrongs of his agent or employee—became and is the rule.[41]

Formally stated, the rule is that a principal or employer is liable for torts of an agent or employee committed within the scope of his agency or employment.[42] The problem in every case is whether the agent or employee was acting "within the

scope" of his agency of employment or was "on a frolic of his own," as Justice Cardozo once phrased it, so that the principal is not liable. These scope of employment problems are best discussed in terms of three general types of torts committed by agents or employees—negligence, intentional torts, and fraud.

Negligence: The common case here is of negligent operation of a vehicle by an employee, resulting in injury to the person or vehicle of another. In these cases, the courts find that the employee was within the scope of his employment if he was on duty during working hours and pursuing the activities that he was directed or employed to perform. In short, the employer is liable in virtually all cases of this kind. Occasionally, however, the accident happens in an area of deviation from a direct route which should have been followed. Suppose a truck driver starts out on the direct route from his employer's place of business to a railroad depot to which he is to deliver a quantity of goods. He decides to stop at his home which is only a block off this direct route and halfway between the employer's place of business and the railroad depot. Just after turning the corner, he has an accident which is caused by his negligence. The employer will still be liable. The courts have held that mere *deviations* or minor deflections from the direct route are not enough to place the employee outside the scope of his employment. On the other hand, suppose that a truck driver delivers goods and then goes on to his home which is several miles beyond the place of delivery. Here, the courts would probably say that he had made a *departure* from the scope of his employment, or was "on a frolic of his own," and that the employer is not liable for an accident occurring in the area of departure. This, of course, may become a close question. In *Gordoy* v. *Flaherty*, 9 C.2d 716, 72 P.2d 538, the employee went about three blocks beyond his proper destination, and the court held that there was a *departure* and that the employer was not liable. The court laid great stress on the fact that the destination had been reached and passed, and indicated that this action was considerably more serious than a deviation en route.[43]

● The "*going and coming rule*" may also be noted. Ordinarily, while an employee is going to or coming from his place of work, he is outside the scope of his employment. However, if it is an express or implied condition of the employment that the employee use his own vehicle in attending to his duties, the employer will be liable.

Intentional Torts: In earlier days, cases of intentional torts caused considerable difficulty. The courts felt that they had to be able to say that the employee intended to further or protect the interests of his employer in some way before they could hold the employer for such overzealous activities of the employee as assault and battery. This was difficult to do in a case where, e.g., as the result of an argument between a female customer and a clerk in a grocery store, the clerk hit and kicked the customer. In the later cases, however, e.g., *Stansell* v. *Safeway Stores*, 44 C.A.2d 822, 113 P.2d 264, which involved the facts just described, the courts said that the employer was liable if the tort was merely *connected with* the employment.

---

[39]The California cases seem to adopt a contrary and very strict view here—that the agent is personally liable on the contract unless the name of the principal is disclosed on its face and in such a way as to show that it was intended to bind him. In *Otis Elevator Company* v. *Berry*, 28 C.A.2d 430, 82 P.2d 704, where a contract was offered to "Hotel Berry Systems" and was signed by "B. S. Berry," whom both parties knew intended to sign only as agent, it was held that Berry was nevertheless personally liable on the contract because it did not show on its face that he was acting only as agent.

[40]Another justification is suggested in *Johnston* v. *Long*, 30 C.2d 54, 181 P.2d 645: "The principal justification for the application of the doctrine of respondeat superior in any case is the fact that the employer may spread the risk through insurance and carry the costs thereof as part of his costs of doing business. . . ."

[41]Ordinarily, a principal is not liable for torts of an independent contractor or his employees. There are a few exceptions, however. For the most part, they are cases in which the principal is himself guilty of some degree of negligence, e.g., (1) where he employs an incompetent contractor, (2) where he employs the contractor to do something which is inherently dangerous or wrong, or (3) where he is otherwise negligent as in *Wise* v. *Maxwell Hardware Company*, 94 C.A. 765, 271 P. 918, where uncrated metal roofing material purchased by the property owner was with his knowledge unloaded and left on the sidewalk by the delivery company.

[42]C.C. 2338: ". . . a principal is responsible to third persons for the negligence of his agent in the transaction of the business of the agency, including wrongful acts committed by such agent in and as a part of the transaction of such business, and for his willful omission to fulfill the obligations of the principal."

---

[43]An interesting case of a different type was *George* v. *Bekins Van & Storage Co.*, 33 C.2d 834, 205 P.2d 1037, where property stored in a warehouse was destroyed by fire commenced by employees carelessly smoking. The defense was that smoking was an act done for personal pleasure and therefore not within the scope of employment. Held, otherwise.

Where the tort results from a personal grudge which originates in some matter outside of and unrelated to the employment, the principal will not be held if the matter happens to be settled on his premises during the; employee's working hours.

Fraud: Selling agents may misrepresent their wares in order to make a sale. Here, the tort of fraud is committed for which the principal may be liable, but here, again, the courts have had difficulty. They have felt that the principal should not be held for all types of misrepresentations that an agent may make, particularly where he is a professional engaged only for the one transaction. The difficulty has been in framing a rule to express this. The rule so framed and as it exists today is the rather tenuous one that the principal is liable for representations of a type which are normally incident to sales but not for unusual or exceptional representations.[44] Suppose that S lists a restaurant for sale with R, a business opportunities broker. To make a sale, R represents to B, the buyer, (1) that the net income of the business has been $2000 a month for the past year when in fact it has been $1000, and (2) that Acme Company, a large industrial organization, has purchased the entire next block and will shortly erect a factory there, employing several thousand persons from whom B should get much business. Both of these representations are false. Misrepresentation (1) would be of the type for which a principal could be held liable; (2) for which he would not be held liable.

Knowledge of Agent Imputed to Principal

In general, it may be said that "what the agent knows, the principal knows." This is an abbreviated way of stating the rule of agency law that notice to or knowledge of an agent is *imputed* to the principal, i.e., that the principal is charged with it even though the agent does not pass it on to him.

There are limitations on the rule. One is that the information acquired by the agent must be within the scope of the agency, i.e., must relate to matters with which the agency is concerned. To illustrate the point, suppose that A is P's agent to collect rents from P's various properties. If A were notified of a tenant's intention to terminate his tenancy in 30 days, this would be notice to P even though A did not inform him, since this would be information within the scope of or pertaining to the subject of A's agency; hence, P would be precluded from collecting further rent from the tenant on the ground that he had not been notified of the termination. But suppose, as in *People ex rel. Carr, County Collector* v. *Guilborg,* 324 Ill. 538, 155 N.E. 324, that A is mailed notice that the assessed value of one of P's apartment buildings has been raised from $80,250 to $110,250, and that P must appear for a hearing on a certain date if he wishes to contest the reassessment. A does not inform P so that the time to contest passes without P's knowledge. Here, it was held that the notice to the agent was with respect to a matter that was outside the scope of his agency and that, therefore, the principal was not bound by it and could have the matter reopened.

Along the same lines was *Lorenz* v. *Rousseau,* 85 C.A. 1, 258 P. 690. In California, leased property may become subject to a lien for repairs made by a lessee, even though the lessor-owner has not authorized them in any way, if the lessor, upon learning that repairs are being made, does not file a *notice of non-responsibility* disclaiming liability for the repairs.[45] This was the situation in the *Rousseau* case. The own-

er's rent collector knew that repairs were being made in one of the principal's buildings, but did not inform him, so that notice of non-responsibility was not filed. The contention was that since the agent-rent collector knew that repair work was being done, the principal-owner had notice, and since he had failed to file notice of non-responsibility, a lien could be enforced against the building. Held, that a lien could not be enforced; that this was information not within the scope of the agency and so not chargeable to the principal.

● The rule that the principal is charged with knowledge of what the agent knows proceeds on the theory that the agent has merely forgotten to give the principal the information and that this is negligence of the agent for which, like other negligence, the principal ought to be made to stand liable. Therefore if the case is one in which it is clear that the agent would not have passed on the information, the principal may not be charged with the agent's knowledge. This is so where the agent is acting adversely to the principal, and in his own interests, and is not acting in a representative capacity. *McDonald* v. *Randall,* 139 C. 246, 72 P. 997, illustrates the point. There, a bank officer sold a note to the bank without notifying it that there was a defense to the note. The purchase of the note was authorized by the bank's board of directors. The bank was not charged with the officer's knowledge of the defense. By contrast, in *McKenney* v. *Ellsworth,* 165 C. 326, 132 P. 75, where a bank president sold a defensible note to his bank, it was held that the bank was charged with knowledge of the defense. In *McKenney,* the bank president was the authorizing force for the purchase of the note, and this was the basis on which the California court distinguished the cases. The California court would not charge the principal with knowledge of the adversely acting agent where he is not acting in a representative capacity in connection with the transaction, as in *McDonald,* but would charge the principal where, while the agent is acting adversely to the interests of the principal, he is also nevertheless acting as the representative of the principal in connection with the transaction, as in *McKenney.*

Termination of Agency

Certain matters with respect to termination of *employment* contracts as distinguished from *agencies* are discussed in the next section. Considered here are methods of terminating the authority of an agent, and *agency or power coupled with an interest*—a form of agency authority which may not be terminated.

Methods of Termination

Unless it is agreed that agency will exist for a specified period of time, it may be terminated at any time by either party by notice to the other. If it is for a fixed time, it expires at the end of that time. Even though it is for a fixed time, either party may wrongfully terminate it before the expiration of that time but, of course, becomes liable in damages to the other for so doing.

In addition, agency is terminated by death or incapacity of the principal or agent; and, where the agency is to sell particular property, by impossibility in the form of destruction of the property or bankruptcy of the principal, which automatically vests title to his property in his trustee in bankruptcy.

Notice to Third Persons

Even though an agency has been terminated, third parties with whom the agent has dealt may not know of this fact and may continue to honor him as agent. As to them, he remains *ostensibly* or *apparently* an agent. Hence, in one class of cases

---

[44]Restatement of Agency 2d, § 258.

[45]C.C. 3129.

at least, the principal to protect himself fully will have to give notice of termination to third parties. Where termination is by revocation by the principal, the general law requires that he give notice to third persons with whom the agent has dealt in the past. This must be *personal notice*, i.e., a communication to such persons by letter or other direct means. In addition, the principal should give *public or newspaper notice* in the locality in which the agency was established as to persons who may know of the agency. If these things are not done, the agent can still make contracts in the name of the principal for which the principal will be bound.

Where termination is by death or incapacity of the principal, on the other hand, the agent may not bind the principal or his estate to third persons, even though they have no notice of the fact. This is for the rather technical reason, seen in contracts, that it takes two existing, competent parties to make a contract. When the principal dies or becomes incompetent to contract, this ceases to be possible. Since the agent is but the "alter ego" of his principal, it must be the case that it is no longer possible for the agent to make a contract for the principal if it would no longer be possible for the principal to make a contract for himself.

California Exceptions

The foregoing rules regarding termination of agency and notice to third persons represent the general law on the subject. California makes these important exceptions:

1. Death or incapacity of the principal does not terminate an agency in California, as respects the third person, unless the third person contracting with the agent has "actual knowledge" of such death or incapacity. C.C. 2356(a). Death or incapacity of a principal who has executed a written power of attorney does not terminate an agency until the agent (attorney in fact) has actual knowledge of it. C.C. 2403.

2. California protects third persons dealing with agents of "absentee" principals. An "absentee" principal is a serviceman or governmental employee who is determined to be in "missing status" by appropriate government authority. Prob. C. 1403. Until the third person is given notice of the absentee's death by appropriate government authority, the third person is protected in his contracts with the absentee principal's agent.

3. In 1981 California adopted the *uniform durable power of attorney act* in C.C. 2400-2407. So far this act has been adopted only by a handful of other states. In general the act allows a person to appoint an agent ("attorney in fact") whose agency is not terminated by the subsequent incapacity of the principal or, in the alternative, to create an agency which is to take effect upon the subsequent incapacity of the principal. C.C. 2400. The agency must be created in writing which contains the words "This power of attorney shall not be affected by subsequent incapacity of the principal" or "This power of attorney shall become effective upon the incapacity of the principal" or "similar words showing the intent of the principal that the authority conferred shall be exercisable notwithstanding the principal's subsequent incapacity." C.C. 2400(a). Where the power of attorney is created by a printed form to be signed by a principal who does not have the advice of legal counsel, the printed form must have a 10-point bold face type "WARNING TO PERSON EXECUTING THIS DOCUMENT" warning the principal that such a document may grant broad powers to deal with the principal's property, that the grant of powers is for an indefinite period of time unless its duration is expressly limited and that the powers will continue to exist notwithstanding the principal's subsequent incapacity or disability. C.C. 2400(b). The "warning"

must also tell the principal that he or she has the right to revoke or terminate the durable power of attorney at any time. C.C. 2400(b).

C.C. 2402 allows a court-appointed conservator of the estate of the principal to revoke or amend the power of attorney. C.C. 2402(a). The conservator must first obtain a court order authorizing or requiring revocation or amendment. C.C. 2402(a). The principal may nominate, in the durable power of attorney, a person to serve as conservator of his estate and the court is required to respect such a nomination unless it finds that the appointment of the nominee would not be in the best interests of the proposed conservatee. C.C. 2402(b); 1810. Since the durable power of attorney would be designed to bridge the gap in the management of the principal's estate from competency to incompetency, the nomination of a conservator would be apt to be found and would, of course, in most instances be the same person nominated to serve as attorney in fact.

In 1983 California added provisions to the durable power of attorney act authorizing the creation of a separate "durable power of attorney for health care" which permits the agent to make health care decisions for the principal. C.C. 2432 prescribes the requirements for the creation of such a power of attorney.

Agency Coupled With Interest

Suppose that D owns real estate. He wants to borrow money from C which C is willing to lend if D will give him a mortgage on the property as security, which D does. The mortgage will provide that if D fails to repay the loan, C may sell the property and take the amount due from the proceeds of sale. If C sells, he will have to give the purchaser a deed to the property. This he will do by executing a deed in D's name by himself, C, as "agent." This whole arrangement is an "agency" or "power coupled with an interest." It has nothing to do with *agency* as has been discussed to this point but is a technical application of the concept of agency. Formally defined, an *agency or power coupled with an interest* is an interest in specific real or personal property created to secure performance of an obligation and conferring upon the secured party the power, as agent of the party creating the security, to sell the property to enforce the security. The only examples of consequence would be the mortgage with power of sale above, and the other security devices of a similar nature seen in later chapters. Such "agencies" are said to be *irrevocable* which means simply that they may not be revoked by the debtor and are not affected by his death or insanity.

● Distinguished from agency coupled with an interest is *agency or power coupled with a security or obligation*, which consists of an authorization to collect a sum of money for the purpose of applying it to a debt. T is indebted to D and D, in turn, is indebted to C for a similar amount. If D authorizes C to collect from T and apply the money to D's debt to C, this creates in C an "agency or power coupled with a security or obligation." It differs from an agency coupled with an interest to this extent: It is the law of some states that while an agency coupled with a security or obligation cannot be revoked by other methods, it is terminated by the death of the creator.

Statutory Regulation of the Employer-Employee Relationship

In this section are treated certain special phases of employer-employee law: (1) Termination of employment; (2) workers' compensation; and (3) labor legislation. The first two matters are discussed in terms of California law which, howver, is generally representative of the law to be found in ther states. The California law covering the employer-employee relationship is the Labor Code, which is designed to eal with all phases of the matter. It regulates working hours, ayment of wages, health and safety requirements of the orking premises, and termination of employment; sets up a abor Commission which, among other things, determines e validity and enforces payment of wage claims of employes; and provides for workers' compensation and sets up a orkers' Compensation Appeals Board as the agency through hich it may be recovered.

ermination of Employment

Lab. C. 2922 provides that "An employment, having no ecified term, may be terminated at the will of either party notice to the other. Employment for a specified term means employment for a period greater than one month." This rmits either party, employer or employee, to terminate onth-to-month employment at any time by notice to the oth-. Contrary to common belief, there is no requirement of wo weeks' notice," at least in the case of non-union employees. A union contract with the employer may modify ese statutory rules.

Collective bargaining agreements customarily stipulate that employee can only be discharged for "just cause" and ovide for arbitration of disputes on the subject. As will be en below, recent case law is beginning to impose substantial nitations on the rule of Labor Code 2922.

Lab. C. 2924 provides that "An employment for a specified rm may be terminated at any time by the employer in case any wilful breach of duty by the employee in the course of s employment, or in case of his habitual neglect of his duty continued incapacity to perform it." This says that where e employee is a contract or fixed term employee, the emyer may terminate the employment before the end of the m only "for cause," i.e., because of misconduct or inca-city of the employee. Lab. C. 2925 provides, reciprocally, at the employee may quit if the employer is guilty of "any lful or permanent breach" of his obligations as employer. b. C. 2926-2927 provides that the employee is entitled to ages to the date of dismissal or quitting.

Lab. C. 2921 says that death or insanity of the employer minates the employment in every case as soon as the emyee has notice of it, except that, under Lab. C. 2923, a ntract employee must stay on for a reasonable time to per-t the executor or administrator of the deceased employer to e control.

dicial Limitations on Discharge of Employee

Recent California cases have imposed important limitations the right of an employer to discharge an at-will employee o is not protected by a collective bargaining agreement. ere are (1) a *public policy limitation* and (2) *contract limi-ions*. Tamemy v. *Atlantic Richfield Co.* (1980) 27 Cal.3d 7, 164 Cal.Rptr. 839, held that discharge of an employee precluded when it "violates fundamental principles of pub-policy" and that therefore a complaint which alleged that employee was discharged because he refused to participate activity which would have constituted a violation of the itrust laws stated a cause of action. The public policy lim-ion prevents the harm to the public that would be caused such a discharge. *Pugh* v. *See's Candies* (1981) 116 A.3d 311, 171 Cal.Rptr. 917, sees two types of contract itations, an implied-in-fact contract limitation and an im-ed-in-law contract limitation. In *Pugh*, the employee had rked for See's for 32 years, had risen from dishwasher to

vice-president in charge of production and member of the board of directors. He had regularly received promotions and raises and bonuses and a commendation for the quality of his work. The company had a long-established policy of not terminating administrative personnel except for good cause. *Pugh* held that from such a set of facts an *"implied-in-fact promise"* for permanent employment could be found. *Pugh* continued on to say that there is an *"implied-in-law covenant of good faith and fair dealing inherent in every contract,"* including every employment contract, and that the "termination of such a long-time employee arbitrarily, i.e., without *some* legitimate reason, (is not) compatible with either good faith or fair dealing."

● Where the employer is engaged in interstate commerce and has an "employee pension benefit plan," the employee is protected by ERISA (Employee Retirement Income Security Act, 29 U.S.C.A. § 1001 et seq.) against discharge "for the purpose of interfering with the attainment of any right to which (the employee) may become entitled under the plan . . ." ERISA preempts state law on its subject. *Johnson* v. *Trans World Airlines, Inc.* (1983) 149 C.A. 3d 548, 196 Cal.Rptr. 896.

Workers' Compensation

Before the various states enacted workers' compensation laws, the employee who suffered an "industrial accident"—an injury on the job—was in a difficult position. To recover from his employer he was required to show negligence of the employer and lack of negligence on his part. In addition, the "fellow servant rule" exempted the employer from liability if injury was caused by another employee. Need was felt for laws which would enable the employee to obtain compensation without regard to negligence, either of the employer or the employee. Workers' compensation laws are such laws. They require an employer to procure, maintain and pay for insurance which will pay compensation to an injured or disabled employee for any on-the-job injury, however caused, except self-inflicted injuries and those occurring while the employee is intoxicated. In California, workers' compensation is covered by Lab. C. 3201-6002.

Lab. C. 3700 requires persons employing one or more employees, except those listed in the next paragraph, to procure compensation insurance for his employees from a private insurance company or from the State Compensation Insurance Fund, or to maintain a plan of self-insurance for this purpose. This must be paid for entirely by the employer, and Lab. C. 3751 makes it a misdemeanor for an employer to require any contribution to the insurance premium from the employee. If insurance is properly obtained, the employer has no liability for the employee's injury.[46] But if the employer is guilty of serious and willful misconduct, the compensation award may be increased by one-half.[47]

Under the California law, insurance need not be carried on the following classes of persons, among others, (a) independent contractors;[48] and (b) a person employed by the owner or occupant of a residential dwelling whose duties are incidental to the ownership, maintenance, or use of the dwelling, including the care and supervision of children, or whose duties are personal and not in the course of the trade, business, profession, or occupation of such owner or occupant, and who was employed to be held liable for less than 52 hours during

---

[46]Lab. C. 3755.

[47]Lab. C. 4553.

[48]Lab. C. 3353.

the 90 calendar days immediately preceding the date of injury or who earned less than $100 from the employer during the 90 calendar days immediately preceding the date of injury (i.e., casual or temporary employees such as gardeners, household domestics and baby sitters, who conform to the foregoing definition).[49]

Compensation is recoverable for injuries suffered "in the course of the employment,"[50] and this is broadly construed in favor of the employee. There are exceptions, however, e.g., there is no recovery where the injury is self-inflicted or arises from intoxication or out of an altercation in which the employee is the initial physical aggressor;[51] or where it results from "horseplay," as in *Dalsheim* v. *Ind. Acc. Com.*, 215 C. 107, 8 P.2d 840, where an employee ignited cleaning fluid to see if it would explode. And compensation may be reduced 50% where the injury is due to serious or willful misconduct of the employee.

Compensation is awarded by the Workers' Compensation Appeals Board after a hearing before one of its referees. Awards include medical expenses, compensation for lost earnings predicated upon average earnings and the nature and degree of injury, and death benefits to the employee's family where the injury results in death.[52]

Labor Legislation

Labor and management were left pretty much to their own devices until 1932. Labor could strike as and when it saw fit,

---

[49]Lab. C. 3351-3352.

[50]Lab. C. 3600.

[51]Lab. C. 3600(d) (e).

[52]An across-the-board overhaul of the provisions for workers' compensation benefits took place in 1982.

For 1983, temporary and permanent total disability benefits were increased from a range of $73-262 per week to a range of $125-294 per week, and for 1984 such benefits were increased in turn to a range of $168-336 per week. Lab. C. 4453, 4460.

For 1983, permanent partial disability benefits were increased from a range of $45-105 per week to a range of $75-195 per week, and for 1984 such benefits were increased in turn to a range of $105-210 per week. Lab. C. 4453, 4659.

Maximum death benefits (two or more total dependents) were increased from $75,000 in 1982 to $85,000 in 1983 and to $95,000 in 1984. Lab. C. 4702.

Where a nonemployment connected disability is suffered, as where an employed person falls while at home and is injured, disability compensation may be recovered under the Unemployment Insurance Code.

but injunctions against picketing were rather liberally issued by the courts and the "yellow dog contract"—a contract in which an employee was required to agree not to join a union—was considered valid.

The Norris-LaGuardia Act of 1932 outlawed the yellow dog contract. In addition, it clarified the matter of picketing by declaring certain types of acts to be peaceful picketing and not subject to injunction.

In 1935, Congress passed the National Labor Relations Act (Wagner Act) setting up the National Labor Relations Board to prevent "unfair labor practices." The most important of these, as declared by the Act, consists of attempting in any way to prevent an employee from joining a union and of refusing to bargain collectively with representatives of the union of one's employees.

The Labor-Management Relations Act of 1947 (Taft-Hartley Act) imposed important restrictions on unions in their dealings with employers. It made collective bargaining by the union mandatory. The Wagner Act required it only of the employer. It required "cooling-off" periods before strikes and strikes of an industry-wide character could be enjoined for up to 80 days. Various unfair union practices were made illegal such as the secondary boycott, which is a strike against an employer because of his refusal to stop doing business with another employer who is having a labor dispute, and "featherbedding," which is requiring an employer to hire stand-by employees.

The Labor-Management Reporting and Disclosure Act of 1959 (Landrum-Griffin Act) was addressed to problems of corruption within the union leadership. It imposed important controls on union officials in their relationship with union members. Extensive fiscal information is required to be filed with the Secretary of Labor by the union, and various safeguards are set up to prevent mishandling of union funds and to insure union members of an effective voice in the governance of the union.

The National Labor Relations Act, Taft-Hartley and Landrum-Griffin are generally what are contemplated by references to "labor law." In the main, however, their concern is only with matters relating to the unionization of employees and there is much law that has developed and is developing regarding the employment relationships, as such, such as wage and hour laws, safety laws and laws barring discrimination in employment on the basis of sex or race. The space limitations of this book preclude an extended treatment of such laws.

CHAPTER 4

Introduction to the Uniform Commercial Code and to Commercial Transactions

Introduction to the Uniform Commercial Code

Background

Commercial transactions are sales of goods at the various [sta]ges of the marketing process and the transactions that sup[po]rt and otherwise relate to sales of goods such as the financ[ing], shipment and storage of goods.

[B]eginning at the start of this century, sales and related [tran]sactions came to be regulated by a series of uniform [law]s—the Uniform Sales Act, the Uniform Negotiable Instru[me]nts Law, the Uniform Bills of Lading Act, the Uniform [wa]rehouse Receipts Act, the Uniform Trust Receipts Act, [and] others. These laws were drafted and enacted at different [tim]es, by different draftsmen, in differing commercial set[tin]gs, over the period of half a century. One result was that [the]y were not uniform as among themselves to the extent that [the]y might have been. In addition, most of them required [mo]dernization by the middle of the 20th century. The Uni[for]m Commercial Code, which is the new commercial law of [the] 1960's and of the second half of the 20th century, is the [ans]wer. It puts all of the laws regulating commercial trans[act]ions under one roof, rewrites them, makes them an inte[gra]ted, uniform body of law within themselves, and modern[ize]s, simplifies and clarifies the whole system of the commer[cial] law.[1]

[T]his chapter is designed to introduce the Uniform Com[me]rcial Code (technically, the Uniform Commercial Code, [196]2 Official Text), hereafter referred to as "the code," and [tog]ether with the next three chapters, will comprise the ["co]de" chapters of this text.

Code Concept

[T]he code states its concept as follows:

[The concept of the present Act (the code) is that 'com[mer]cial transactions' is a single subject of the law, notwith[stan]ding its many facets.

[A single transaction may very well involve a contract for [sale], followed by a sale, the giving of a check or draft for a [par]t of the purchase price, and the acceptance of some form [of s]ecurity for the balance.

[The check or draft may be negotiated and will ultimately [pas]s through one or more banks for collection.

[If the goods are shipped or stored the subject matter of the [sale] may be covered by a bill of lading or warehouse receipt [or b]oth.

[Or it may be that the entire transaction was made pursuant [to a] letter of credit either domestic or foreign.

"Obviously, every phase of commerce involved is but a part of one transaction, namely, the sale of and payment for goods.

"If, instead of goods in the ordinary sense, the transaction involved stocks or bonds, some of the phases of the transaction would obviously be different. Others would be the same. In addition, there are certain additional formalities incident to the transfer of stocks and bonds from one owner to another.

"This Act purports to deal with all the phases which may ordinarily arise in the handling of a commercial transaction, from start to finish."[2]

Coverage, Organization and Structure of the Code

"Commercial transactions" are sales of *goods*, and attendant transactions. Real estate transactions are not "commercial transactions" as the term has come to be understood, but are just that, by contrast—real estate transactions. The code is not concerned with and does not regulate real estate transactions, only transactions dealing in goods or personal property. Thus, very important Article 2 of the code, dealing with Sales, deals only with sales of goods; and very important Article 9 of the code, dealing with Secured Transactions, deals only with transactions involving the use of personal property as security.

● The code is divided into 11 parts, called "Articles," which treat all phases of the commercial transaction as conceived by the code concept, stated above. There are three main articles: Article 2, Sales; Article 3, Commercial Paper; and Article 9, Secured Transactions. Each of these is the subject of a chapter which follows. Articles 1 and 10 are special purpose articles. Article 1 states general principles and definitions that apply throughout the substantive articles (Articles 2-9), and provides the glue that insures internal uniformity. Articles 10 and 11 are technical and will not receive further attention. The remaining articles, Articles 4-8, are treated in this and the next three chapters, to an extent consistent with the objectives of this text, and by grouping them with major articles to which they bear relationship. Thus, bulk transfers, the subject of Article 6, are, among other things, extraordinary sales of goods as compared with the ordinary sales of goods covered by Article 2. Therefore, Article 6 is covered at the end of Article 2, that is, bulk transfers are covered at the end of the chapter dealing with sales. Where Article 3 deals with "money paper," Article 7 is said to deal with "commodity paper" and Article 8 to deal with "investment paper,"[3] and each of these articles is, in major part at least, a "negotiable instruments law." Therefore, they have much in common and it is appropriate to discuss Articles 7 and 8 at the end of Article 3, as is done in Chapter 6. The bills of lading of Article 7 also receive considerable attention later in this chapter. Arti-

---

[U].C.C. 1102(2)(a). The code has now been adopted in all [stat]es except Louisiana.

[2]Uniform Commercial Code, Comment to Title.
[3]U.C.C. 7104, Official Comment.

cle 4 augments Article 3 and is dealt with in connection with Article 3. Article 5, lastly, receives its coverage later in this chapter.

● Code Articles are divided into major subdivisions called "Parts." The code adopts a section-numbering system under which the first digit, followed by a hyphen, designates the article in which the section is located and under which the first digit following the hyphen designates the "Part" of the article in which the section is located. Thus, Section 2-105 is located in Article 2, Part 1, and contains a definition of "goods;" Section 3-404 is found in Article 3, Part 4, and relates to unauthorized signatures on commercial paper; and Section 7-202 is located in Article 7, Part 2, and is concerned with the form and terms of a warehouse receipt.

California Variations in Substance and in Form

Uniform laws, even the most successful ones, seldom remain entirely uniform. Because of its scope, this is especially true of the code. Many states felt the need to make variations from the code when they adopted it. In the case of some states, the variations were few and slight. In others, including California, they were greater in number and often quite substantial. Many of the California variations are noted in the chapters that follow. The code, as drafted by its national draftsmen, is referred to as the Official Text. Where it is necessary to point out a California variation from the Official Text, the terminology "California code," or the like, and Official Text, are used to make the distinction.

The code's divisional term, "Article," and its hyphenated section-numbering system are not compatible with the divisional terminology and the section-numbering system of the California codes. "Division" is the divisional term that California uses throughout its codes and which therefore it uses in place of "Article" in its commercial code. None of the California codes has a hyphenated section-numbering system so California does not include the hyphen in its commercial code section numbering. Thus, in California, Article 2 is Division 2 and Section 2-105 is Section 2105; Article 3 is Division 3 and Section 3-404 is Section 3404; and so on. The California (no hyphen) section-numbering system is used in the text, except where there is occasion to refer to the Official Text, in which cases its hyphenated section-numbering system is used.

From time to time, California *omits* a provision that is contained in the Official Text. For examples, California omits entirely Sections 2302[3a] and 2318 of the Official Text. The California Uniform Commercial Code, which is the version of the code included in the Appendix, shows this by designating the section as "Reserved." On other occasions, California omits a subsection or part of a subsection which is contained in the Official Text. For example, California omits part (c) of subsection (1) of Section 4213 and omits part (e) of subsection (1) of Section 9302, and omits subsection (2) of Section 9307. Some of these omissions are shown by use of the word "Reserved," as in the case of the omission of part (c) of subsection (1) of Section 4213. Others are noted only by the simple fact of omission, as with the omission of part (e) of subsection (1) of Section 9302 and the omission of subsection (2) of Section 9307. The reader should be aware that these latter forms of omissions and other inconsistencies in numbering and lettering do not constitute printing errors in this publication.

[3a]But later adopted the rule of 2-302 verbatim in C.C. 1670.5 as part of the California general contract law.

The Code Comments

Each section of the Official Text is accompanied by "Comments" of the draftsmen, referred to as Official Comments, most of which are quite detailed and designed to clarify and explain the meaning of, and the interpretation to be placed on, the terms of the section in question. The Comments are an aid in the interpretation of the code and reference is made to them from time to time in the chapters that follow. Since the Comments are considerably greater in length than the code itself, it has not been possible to reproduce them in this text. The Official Text with Comments may be found in law libraries.

The Anatomy of a Commercial Transaction

For the purposes of orientation and to make the chapters that follow more easily understood, the broad details of a commercial transaction as it occurs at the manufacturer-retailer level are now examined.

F.O.B. Point of Shipment; Sight Draft and Order or Negotiable Bill of Lading

The basic domestic transaction at the manufacturer-retail level of the marketing process is the transaction commercially designated as "F.O.B. point of shipment; sight draft and order bill of lading." To understand it, it is first necessary to come to an understanding of bills of lading.

Bills of Lading: The bill of lading (originally, bill of lading) is the document given by the carrier to the shipper or consignor upon receipt of goods for shipment. It is several things. First of all, it is a *receipt* for the goods. Secondly, it is a *contract of carriage*, that is, a contract between the consignor and the carrier fixing the terms upon which the goods are transported. Note that on the reverse side of each of the specimen forms of bills of lading which appear on the following pages there are extensive "Contract Terms and Conditions." Finally, it is either a *negotiable document of title* or a *nonnegotiable document of title*.

The bill of lading on page 73 recites on its face:

Consigned to ORDER of _____

and the bill of lading on page 71 recites on its face merely

Consigned to _____

It is the two words—"order of"—that make the difference between a *negotiable or order bill of lading* and a *nonnegotiable or straight bill of lading*.[4]

The negotiable bill of lading is "negotiable" in the important sense, for present purposes, that it is capable of transferring title to the goods and that the carrier cannot surrender the goods without getting it back. If the carrier surrenders the goods without getting back the negotiable bill of lading, it will be liable to the person who holds it. A nonnegotiable bill does not possess this degree of sanctity. The goods may be delivered to the named consignee without surrender of the nonnegotiable bill of lading and no penalty attaches to the carrier for failure to obtain surrender of the nonnegotiable bill.

The negotiable character of the order bill of lading permits it to be used as a security device, which is what is important

(Continued on page 75)

---

[4]U.C.C. 7104.1.

Form C-93   **1st Sheet**

orm Domestic Straight Bill of Lading, adopted by Carriers in Official, Southern, Western and Illinois Classification Territories, March 15, 1922, as amended August 1, 1930, and June 15, 1941.)

THE WESTERN PACIFIC RAILROAD COMPANY
UNIFORM STRAIGHT BILL OF LADING
(Original—Not Negotiable)

Shipper's No._____

Agent's No._____

EIVED, subject to the classifications and tariffs in effect on the date of the issue of this Bill of Lading,

_____19____

M_____

roperty described below, in apparent good order, except as noted (contents and condition of contents of packages unknown), marked, consigned, and destined as indicated below which said any (the word company being understood throughout this contract as meaning any person or corporation in possession of the property under the contract), agrees to carry to its usual place of ry at said destination, if on its own road or its own water line, otherwise to deliver to another carrier on the route to said destination. It is mutually agreed, as to each carrier of all or of said property over all or any portion of said route to destination, and as to each party at any time interested in all or any of said property, that every service to be performed hereunder shall bject to all the conditions not prohibited by law, whether printed or written, herein contained, including the conditions on back hereof, which are hereby agreed to by the shipper and accepted nself and his assigns.

Mail or street address of consignee—For purposes of notification only.

SIGNED TO_____

KINATION_____ STATE OF_____ COUNTY OF_____

TE_____

VERING CARRIER_____ CAR INITIAL_____ CAR NO._____

ackages	Description of Articles, Special Marks and Exceptions	★ Weight (Subject to Corr.)	Class or Rate	Check Column	
					Subject to Section 7 of conditions, if this shipment is to be delivered to the consignee without recourse on the consignor, the consignor shall sign the following statement:
					The carrier shall not make delivery of this shipment without payment of freight and all other lawful charges.
					(Signature of consignor)
					If charges are to be prepaid, write or stamp here, "To be Prepaid."
					Received $_____ to apply in prepayment of the charges on the property described hereon.
					Agent or Cashier.
					Per_____ (The signature here acknowledges only the amount prepaid.)
					Charges Advanced:
					$_____

o shipment moves between two ports by a carrier by water, the law requires that the bill of lading shall state whether it is "carrier's or shipper's weight."
—Where the rate is dependent on value, shippers are required to state specifically in writing the agreed or declared value of the property.
greed or declared value of the property is
y specifically stated by the shipper to be not exceeding_____ per_____

_____ Shipper.   **1**   _____ Agent

_____   Per_____

anent post-office address of shipper_____

(This Bill of Lading is to be signed by the shipper and agent of the carrier issuing same.)

(Reverse side of this form on following page)

CONTRACT TERMS AND CONDITIONS

Sec. 1. (a) The carrier or party in possession of any of the property herein described shall be liable as at common law for any loss thereof or damage thereto, except as hereinafter provided.

(b) No carrier or party in possession of all or any of the property herein described shall be liable for any loss thereof or damage thereto or delay caused by the Act of God, the public enemy, the authority of law, or the act or default of the shipper or owner, or for natural shrinkage. The carrier's liability shall be that of warehouseman, only, for loss, damage, or delay caused by fire occurring after the expiration of the free time (if any) allowed by tariffs lawfully on file (such free time to be computed as therein provided) after notice of the arrival of the property at destination or at the port of export (if intended for export) has been duly sent or given, and after placement of the property for delivery at destination, or tender of delivery of the property to the party entitled to receive it, has been made. Except in case of negligence of the carrier or party in possession (and the burden to prove freedom from such negligence shall be on the carrier or party in possession), the carrier or party in possession shall not be liable for loss, damage, or delay occurring while the property is stopped and held in transit upon the request of the shipper, owner, or party, entitled to make such request, or resulting from a defect or vice in the property, or for country damage to cotton, or from riots or strikes. Except in case of carrier's negligence, no carrier or party in possession of all or any of the property herein described shall be liable for delay caused by highway obstruction faulty or impassable highway, or lack of capacity of any highway, bridge or ferry and the burden to prove freedom of such negligence shall be on the carrier or party in possession.

(c) In case of quarantine the property may be discharged at risk and expense of owners into quarantine depot or elsewhere, as required by quarantine regulations or authorities, or for the carrier's dispatch at nearest available point in carrier's judgement, and in any such case carrier's responsibility shall cease when property is so discharged, or property may be returned by carrier at owner's expense to shipping point, earning freight both ways. Quarantine expenses of whatever nature or kind upon or in respect to property shall be borne by the owners of the property or be a lien thereon. The carrier shall not be liable for loss or damage occasioned by fumigation or disinfection or other acts required or done by quarantine regulations or authorities even though the same may have been done by carrier's officers, agents, or employees, nor for detention, loss, or damage of any kind occasioned by quarantine or the enforcement thereof. No carrier shall be liable, except in case of negligence, for any mistake or inaccuracy in any information furnished by the carrier, its agents, or officers, as to quarantine laws or regulations. The shipper shall hold the carriers harmless from any expense they may incur, or damages they may be required to pay, by reason of the introduction of the property covered by this contract into any place against the quarantine laws or regulations in effect at such place.

Sec. 2. (a) No carrier is bound to transport said property by any particular schedule, train, vehicle or vessel; or in time for any particular market or otherwise than with reasonable dispatch. Every carrier shall have the right in case of physical necessity to forward said property by any carrier or route between the point of shipment and the point of destination. In all cases not prohibited by law, where a lower value than actual value has been represented in writing by the shipper or has been agreed upon in writing as the released value of the property as determined by the classification or tariffs upon which the rate is based, such lower value plus freight charges if paid shall be the maximum amount to be recovered, whether or not such loss or damage occurs from negligence.

(b) As a condition precedent to recovery, claims must be filed in writing with the receiving or delivering carrier, or carrier issuing this bill of lading, or carrier on whose line the loss, damage, injury or delay occurred, or carrier in possession of the property when the loss, damage, injury or delay occurred, within nine months after delivery of the property (or, in the case of export traffic, within nine months after delivery at port of export) or, in the case of failure to make delivery, then within nine months after a reasonable time for delivery has elapsed; and suits shall be instituted against any carrier only within two years and one day from the day when notice in writing is given by the carrier to the claimant that the carrier has disallowed the claim or any part or parts thereof specified in the notice Where claims are not filed or suits are not instituted thereon in accordance with the foregoing provisions, no carrier hereunder shall be liable, and such claims will not be paid.

(c) Any carrier or party liable on account of loss of or damage to any of said property shall have the full benefit of any insurance that may have been effected upon or on account of said property, so far as this shall not avoid the policies or contracts of insurance: PROVIDED, That the carrier reimburse the claimant for the premium paid thereon.

Sec. 3. Except where such service is required as the result of carrier's negligence, all property shall be subject to necessary cooperage and baling at owner's cost. Each carrier over whose route cotton or cotton linters is to be transported hereunder shall have the privilege, at its own cost and risk, of compressing the same for greater convenience in handling or forwarding, and shall not be held responsible for deviation or unavoidable delays in procuring such compression. Grain in bulk consigned to a point where there is a railroad, public, or licensed elevator, may (unless otherwise expressly noted herein, and then if it is not promptly unloaded) be there delivered and placed with other grain of the same kind and grade without respect to ownership (and prompt notice thereof shall be given to the consignor), and if so delivered shall be subject to a lien for elevator charges in addition to all other charges hereunder.

Sec. 4. (a) Property not removed by the party entitled to receive it within the free time (if any) allowed by tariffs, lawfully on file (such free time to be computed as therein provided), after notice of the arrival of the property at destination or at the port of export (if intended for export) has been duly sent or given, and after placement of the property for delivery at destination has been made, or property not received, at time tender of delivery of the property to the party entitled to receive it has been made, may be kept in vessel, vehicle, car, depot, warehouse or place of business of the carrier, subject to the tariff charge for storage and to carrier's responsibility as warehouseman, only, or at the option of the carrier, may be removed to and stored in a public or licensed warehouse at the point of delivery or other available point, or if no such warehouse is available at point of delivery or at other available point, then in other available storage facility, at the cost of the owner and there held without liability on the part of the carrier, and subject to a lien for all freight and other lawful charges, including a reasonable charge for storage. In the event consignee cannot be found at address given for delivery, then in that event, notice of the placing of such goods in warehouse shall be mailed to the address given for delivery and mailed to any other address given on the bill of lading for notification, showing the warehouse in which such property has been placed, subject to the provisions of this paragraph.

(b) Where nonperishable property which has been transported to destination hereunder is refused by consignee or the party entitled to receive it upon tender of delivery, or said consignee or party entitled to receive it fails to receive or claim it within 15 days after notice of arrival shall have been duly sent or given, the carrier may sell the same at public auction to the highest bidder, at such place as may be designated by the carrier:

PROVIDED, That the carrier shall have first mailed, sent, or given to the consignor notice that the property has been refused or remains unclaimed, as the case may be, and that it will be subject to sale under the terms of the bill of lading if disposition be not arranged for, and shall have published notice containing a description of the property, the name of the party to whom consigned, or, if shipped order notify, the name of the party to be notified, and the time and place of sale, once a week for two successive weeks, in a newspaper of general circulation at the place of sale or nearest place where such newspaper is published. PROVIDED That 30, days shall have elapsed before publication of notice of sale after said notice that the property was refused or remains unclaimed was mailed, sent or given.

(c) Where perishable property which has been transported hereunder to destination if refused by consignee or party entitled to receive it, or said consignee or party entitled to receive it shall fail to receive it promptly, the carrier may, in its discretion, to prevent deterioration or further deterioration, sell the same to the best advantage at private or public sale: PROVIDED, That if time serves for notification to the consignor or owner of the refusal of the property or the failure to receive it and request for disposition of the property, such notification shall be given, in such manner as the exercise of due diligence requires, before the property is sold.

(d) Where the procedure provided for in the two paragraphs last preceding is not possible, it is agreed that nothing contained in said paragraphs shall be construed to abridge the right of the carrier at its option to sell the property under such circumstances and in such manner as may be authorized by law.

(e) The proceeds of any sale made under this section shall be applied by the carrier to the payment of freight, demurrage, storage, and any other lawful charges and the expense of notice, advertisement, sale, and other necessary expense and of caring for and maintaining the property, if proper care of same requires special expense, and should there be a balance it shall be paid to the owner of the property sold hereunder.

(f) Property destined to or taken from a station, wharf, landing or other place at which there is no regularly appointed freight agent shall be entirely at risk of owner after unloaded from cars, vehicles or vessels or until loaded into cars, vehicles or vessels and, except in case of carrier's negligence, when received from or delivered to such stations, wharfs, landings, or other places, shall be at owner's risk until the cars are attached to and after they are detached from locomotive or train or until loaded into and after unloaded from vessels, or if property is transported in motor vehicle trailers or semi-trailers, until such trailers or semi-trailers are attached to and after they are detached from power units. Where a carrier is directed to unload or deliver property transported by motor vehicle at a particular location where consignee or consignee's agent is not regularly located the risk after unloading, or delivery, shall be that of the owner.

Sec. 5. No carrier hereunder will carry or be liable in any way for any documents, specie or for any articles of extraordinary value not specifically rated in the published classification or tariffs unless a special agreement to do so and a stipulated value of the articles are endorsed hereon.

Sec. 6. Every party, whether principal or agent, shipping explosives or dangerous goods, without previous full written disclosure to the carrier of their nature, shall be liable for and indemnify the carrier against all loss or damage caused by such goods, and such goods may be warehoused at owner's risk and expense or destroyed without compensation.

Sec. 7. The owner or consignee shall pay the freight and average, if any, and all other lawful charges accruing on said property; but, except in those instances where it may lawfully be authorized to do so, no carrier shall deliver or relinquish possession at destination of the property covered by this bill of lading until all tariff rates and charges thereon have been paid. The consignor shall be liable for the freight and all other lawful charges, except that if the consignor stipulates, by signature, in the space provided for that purpose on the face of this bill of lading that the carrier shall not make delivery without requiring payment of such charges and the carrier, contrary to such stipulation shall make delivery without requiring such payment, the consignor (except as hereinafter provided) shall not be liable for such charges. PROVIDED, That, where the carrier has been instructed by the shipper or consignor to deliver said property to a consignee other than the shipper or consignor, such consignee shall not be legally liable for transportation charges in respect of the transportation of said property (beyond those billed against him at the time of delivery for which he is otherwise liable) which may be found to be due after the property has been delivered to him, if the consignee (a) is an agent only and has no beneficial title in said property, and (b) prior to delivery of said property has notified the delivering carrier in writing of the fact of such agency and absence of beneficial title, and, in the case of shipment reconsigned or diverted to a point other than that specified in the original bill of lading, has also notified the delivering carrier in writing of the name and address of the beneficial owner of said property; and, in such cases the shipper or consignor, or, in the case of a shipment so reconsigned or diverted, the beneficial owner shall be liable for such additional charges. If the consignee has given to the carrier erroneous information as to who the beneficial owner is, such consignee shall himself be liable for such additional charges. Nothing herein shall limit the right of the carrier to require at time of shipment the prepayment or guarantee of the charges. If upon inspection it is ascertained that the articles shipped are not those described in this bill of lading, the freight charges must be paid upon the articles actually shipped.

Sec. 8. If this bill of lading is issued on the order of the shipper, or his agent, in exchange or in substitution for another bill of lading, the shipper's signature to the prior bill of lading as to the statement of value or otherwise, or election of common law or bill of lading liability, in or in connection with such prior bill of lading shall be considered a part of this bill of lading as fully as if the same were written or made in or in connection with this bill of lading.

Sec. 9. (a) If all or any part of said property is carried by water over any part of said route, such water carriage shall be performed subject to all the terms and provisions of, and all the exemptions from liability contained in, the Act of the Congress of the United States, approved on February 13, 1893, and entitled "An act relating to the navigation of vessels, etc.," and of other statutes of the United States according carriers by water the protection of limited liability, and to the conditions contained in this bill of lading not inconsistent therewith or with this section.

(b) No such carrier by water shall be liable for any loss or damage resulting from any fire happening to or on board the vessel, or from explosion, bursting of boilers or breakage of shafts, unless caused by the design or neglect of such carrier.

(c) If the owner shall have exercised due diligence in making the vessel in all respects seaworthy and properly manned, equipped and supplied, no such carrier shall be liable for any loss or damage resulting from the perils of the lakes, seas, or other waters, or from latent defects in hull, machinery, or appurtenances whether existing prior to, at the time of, or after sailing, or from collision, stranding, or other accidents of navigation, or from prolongation of the voyage. And, when for any reason it is necessary, any vessel carrying any or all of the property herein described shall be at liberty to call at any port or ports, in or out of the customary route, to tow and be towed, to transfer, tranship, or lighter, to load and discharge goods at any time, to assist vessels in distress, to deviate for the purpose of saving life or property, and for docking and repairs. Except in case of negligence such carrier shall not be responsible for any loss or damage to property if it be necessary or is usual to carry the same upon deck.

(d) General Average shall be payable according to the York-Antwerp Rules of 1924, Section 1 to 15, inclusive, and Sections 17 to 22, inclusive, and as to matters not covered thereby according to the laws and usages of the Port of New York. If the owners shall have exercised due diligence to make the vessel in all respects seaworthy and properly manned, equipped and supplied, it is hereby agreed that in case of danger, damage or disaster resulting from faults or errors in navigation, or in the management of the vessel, or from any latent or other defects in the vessel, her machinery or appurtenances, or from unseaworthiness, whether existing at the time of shipment or at the beginning of the voyage (provided the latent or other defects or the unseaworthiness was not discoverable by the exercise of due diligence), the shippers, consignees and/or owners of the cargo shall nevertheless pay salvage and any special charges incurred in respect of the cargo, and shall contribute with the shipowner in general average to the payment of any sacrifices, losses or expenses of a general average nature that may be made or incurred for the common benefit or to relieve the adventure from any common peril.

(e) If the property is being carried under a tariff which provides that any carrier or carriers party thereto shall be liable for loss from perils of the sea, then as to such carrier or carriers the provisions of this section shall be modified in accordance with the tariff provisions, which shall be regarded as incorporated into the conditions of this bill of lading.

(f) The term "water carriage" in this section shall not be construed as including lighterage in or across rivers, harbors, or lakes, when performed by or on behalf of carriers other than water.

Sec. 10. Any alteration, addition, or erasure in this bill of lading which shall be made without the special notation hereon of the agent of the carrier issuing this bill of lading, shall be without effect, and this bill of lading shall be enforceable according to its original tenor.

(Uniform Domestic Order Bill of Lading adopted by Carriers in Official, Southern, Western and Illinois Classification Territories, March 15, 1922, as amended August 1, 1930, and June 15, 1941.)

THE WESTERN PACIFIC RAILROAD COMPANY
UNIFORM ORDER BILL OF LADING
(ORIGINAL)

Shipper's No._____

Agent's No._____

RECEIVED, subject to the classifications and tariffs in effect on the date of the issue of this Bill of Lading,

_____, 19____

M_____

the property described below, in apparent good order, except as noted (contents and condition of contents of packages unknown), marked, consigned, and destined as indicated below, which said company (the word company being understood throughout this contract as meaning any person or corporation in possession of the property under the contract), agrees to carry to its usual place of delivery at said destination, if on its own road or its own water line, otherwise to deliver to another carrier on the route to said destination. It is mutually agreed, as to each carrier of all or any of said property over all or any portion of said route to destination, and as to each party at any time interested in all or any of said property, that every service to be performed hereunder shall be subject to all the conditions not prohibited by law, whether printed or written, herein contained, including the conditions on back hereof, which are hereby agreed to by the shipper and accepted for himself and his assigns.

The surrender of this Original ORDER Bill of Lading properly indorsed shall be required before the delivery of the property. Inspection of property covered by this bill of lading will not be permitted unless provided by law or unless permission is indorsed on this original bill of lading or given in writing by the shipper.

(Mail or street address of consignee—For purposes of notification only.)

Consigned to ORDER of_____

Destination_____ State of_____ County of_____

City_____

_____ State of_____ County of_____

Route_____

Delivering Carrier_____ Car Initial_____ Car No._____

Packages	Description of Articles, Special Marks and Exceptions	*Weight (Subject to Corr.)	Class or Rate	Check Column	
					Subject to Section 7 of conditions, if this shipment is to be delivered to the consignee without recourse on the consignor, the consignor shall sign the following statement:
					The carrier shall not make delivery of this shipment without payment of freight and all other lawful charges.
					(Signature of consignor.)
					If charges are to be prepaid write or stamp here, "To be Prepaid."
					Received $_____ to apply in prepayment of the charges on the property described hereon.
					Agent or Cashier.
					Per_____ (The signature here acknowledges only the amount prepaid.)
					Charges Advanced:

If the shipment moves between two ports by a carrier by water, the law requires that the bill of lading shall state whether it is "carrier's or shipper's weight."

NOTE—Where the rate is dependent on value, shippers are required to state specifically in writing the agreed or declared value of the property.

The agreed or declared value of the property is hereby specifically stated by the shipper to be not exceeding_____ per_____

$_____

_____ Shipper

1

_____ Agent

Per_____

Permanent post-office address of shipper:_____

(This Bill of Lading is to be signed by the shipper and agent of the carrier issuing same.)

(Reverse side of this form on following page)

CONTRACT TERMS AND CONDITIONS

Sec. 1. (a) The carrier or party in possession of any of the property herein described shall be liable as at common law for any loss thereof or damage thereto, except as hereinafter provided.

(b) No carrier or party in possession of all or any of the property herein described shall be liable for any loss thereof or damage thereto or delay caused by the act of God, the public enemy, the authority of law, or the act or default shipper or owner, or for natural shrinkage. The carrier's liability shall be that of warehouseman, only, for loss, damage, or delay caused by fire occurring after the expiration of the free time allowed by tariffs lawfully on file (such free time computed as therein provided) after notice of the arrival of the property at destination or at the port of export (if intended for export) has been duly sent or given, and after placement of the property for delivery at destination, or tender of d of the property to the party entitled to receive it, has been made. Except in case of negligence of the carrier or party in possession (and the burden to prove freedom from such negligence shall be on the carrier or party in possession), the or party in possession shall not be liable for loss, damage, or delay occurring while the property is stopped and held in transit upon the request of the shipper, owner, or party entitled to make such request, or resulting from a defect or vice property, or for country damage to cotton, or from riots or strikes.

(c) In case of quarantine the property may be discharged at risk and expense of owners into quarantine depot or elsewhere, as required by quarantine regulations or authorities, or for the carrier's dispatch at nearest available point in co judgment, and in any such case carrier's responsibility shall cease when property is so discharged, or property may be returned by carrier at owner's expense to shipping point, earning freight both ways. Quarantine expenses of whatever or kind upon or in respect to property shall be borne by the owners of the property or be a lien thereon. The carrier shall not be liable for loss or damage occasioned by fumigation or disinfection or other acts required or done by quarantin ulations or authorities even though the same may have been done by carrier's officers, agents, or employees, nor for detention, loss, or damage of any kind occasioned by quarantine or the enforcement thereof. No carrier shall be liable, except i of negligence, for any mistake or inaccuracy in any information furnished by the carrier, its agents, or officers, as to quarantine laws or regulations. The shipper shall hold the carriers harmless from any expense they may incur, or damage may be required to pay, by reason of the introduction of the property covered by this contract into any place against the quarantine laws or regulations in effect at such place.

Sec. 2. (a) No carrier is bound to transport said property by any particular train or vessel, or in time for any particular market or otherwise than with reasonable dispatch. Every carrier shall have the right in case of physical necessity to said property by any carrier or route between the point of shipment and the point of destination. In all cases not prohibited by law, where a lower value than actual value has been represented in writing by the shipper or has been agreed u writing as the released value of the property as determined by the classification or tariffs upon which the rate is based, such lower value plus freight charges if paid shall be the maximum amount to be recovered, whether or not such loss or d occurs from negligence.

(b) As a condition precedent to recovery, claims must be filed in writing with the receiving or delivering carrier, or carrier issuing this bill of lading, or carrier on whose line the loss, damage, injury or delay occurred, within nine month delivery of the property (or, in case of export traffic, within nine months after delivery at port of export) or, in case of failure to make delivery, then within nine months after a reasonable time for delivery has elapsed; and suits shall be ins against any carrier only within two years and one day from the day when notice in writing is given by the carrier to the claimant that the carrier has disallowed the claim or any part or parts thereof specified in the notice. Where claims filed or suits are not instituted thereon in accordance with the foregoing provisions, no carrier hereunder shall be liable, and such claims will not be paid.

(c) Any carrier or party liable on account of loss of or damage to any of said property shall have the full benefit of any insurance that may have been effected upon or on account of said property, so far as this shall not avoid the policies tracts of insurance: **Provided,** That the carrier reimburse the claimant for the premium paid thereon

Sec. 3. Except where such service is required as the result of carrier's negligence, all property shall be subject to necessary cooperage and baling at owner's cost. Each carrier over whose route cotton or cotton linters is to be transported under shall have the privilege, at its own cost and risk, of compressing the same for greater convenience in handling or forwarding, and shall not be held responsible for deviation or unavoidable delays in procuring such compression. Grain consigned to a point where there is a railroad, public or licensed elevator, may (unless otherwise expressly noted herein, and then if it is not promptly unloaded) be there delivered and placed with other grain of the same kind and grade respect to ownership (and prompt notice thereof shall be given to the consignor), and if so delivered shall be subject to a lien for elevator charges in addition to all other charges hereunder.

Sec. 4. (a) Property not removed by the party entitled to receive it within the free time allowed by tariffs, lawfully on file (such free time to be computed as therein provided), after notice of the arrival of the property at destination or at th of export (if intended for export) has been duly sent or given, and after placement of the property for delivery at destination has been made, may be kept in vessel, car, depot, warehouse or place of delivery of the carrier, subject to the tariff for storage and to carrier's responsibility as warehouseman, only, or at the option of the carrier, may be removed to and stored in a public or licensed warehouse at the place of delivery or other available place, at the cost of the owner, and ther without liability on the part of the carrier, and subject to a lien for all freight and other lawful charges, including a reasonable charge for storage.

(b) Where nonperishable property which has been transported to destination hereunder is refused by consignee or the party entitled to receive it, or said consignee or party entitled to receive it fails to receive it within 15 days after no arrival shall have been duly sent or given, the carrier may sell the same at public auction to the highest bidder, at such place as may be designated by the carrier: **Provided,** That the carrier shall have first mailed, sent, or given to the co notice that the property has been refused or remains unclaimed, as the case may be, and that it will be subject to sale under the terms of the bill of lading if disposition be not arranged for, and shall have published notice containing a desc of the property, the name of the party to whom consigned, or, if shipped order notify, the name of the party to be notified, and the time and place of sale, once a week for two successive weeks, in a newspaper of general circulation at the pl sale or nearest place where such newspaper is published: **Provided,** That 30 days shall have elapsed before publication of notice of sale after said notice that the property was refused or remains unclaimed was mailed, sent, or given.

(c) Where perishable property which has been transported hereunder to destination is refused by consignee or party entitled to receive it, or said consignee or party entitled to receive it shall fail to receive it promptly, the carrier may, in cretion, to prevent deterioration or further deterioration, sell the same to the best advantage at private or public sale: **Provided,** That if time serves for notification to the consignor or owner of the refusal of the property or the failure to receive request for disposition of the property, such notification shall be given, in such manner as the exercise of due diligence requires, before the property is sold.

(d) Where the procedure provided for in the two paragraphs last preceding is not possible, it is agreed that nothing contained in said paragraphs shall be construed to abridge the right of the carrier at its option to sell the property unde circumstances and in such manner as may be authorized by law.

(e) The proceeds of any sale made under this section shall be applied by the carrier to the payment of freight, demurrage, storage, and any other lawful charges and the expense of notice, advertisement, sale, and other necessary expense caring for and maintaining the property, if proper care of the same requires special expense, and should there be a balance it shall be paid to the owner of the property sold hereunder.

(f) Property destined to or taken from a station, wharf, or landing at which there is no regularly appointed freight agent shall be entirely at risk of owner after unloaded from cars or vessels or until loaded into cars or vessels, and, ex case of carrier's negligence, when received from or delivered to such stations, wharves, or landings shall be at owner's risk until the cars are attached to and after they are detached from locomotive or train or until loaded into and after un from vessels.

Sec. 5. No carrier hereunder will carry or be liable in any way for any documents, specie, or for any articles of extraordinary value not specifically rated in the published classifications or tariffs unless a special agreement to do so and ulated value of the articles are indorsed hereon.

Sec. 6. Every party, whether principal or agent, shipping explosives or dangerous goods, without previous full written disclosure to the carrier of their nature, shall be liable for and indemnify the carrier against all loss or damage caus such goods, and such goods may be warehoused at owner's risk and expense or destroyed without compensation.

Sec. 7. The owner or consignee shall pay the freight and average, if any, and all other lawful charges accruing on said property; but, except in those instances where it may lawfully be authorized to do so, no carrier by railroad shall or relinquish possession at destination of the property covered by this bill of lading until all tariff rates and charges thereon have been paid. The consignor shall be liable for the freight and all other lawful charges, except that if the consigno ulates, by signature, in the space provided for that purpose on the face of this bill of lading that the carrier shall not make delivery without requiring payment of such charges and the carrier, contrary to such stipulation, shall make delivery w requiring such payment, the consignor (except as hereinafter provided) shall not be liable for such charges. Provided, That, where the carrier has been instructed by the shipper or consignor to deliver said property to a consignee other than the or consignor, such consignee shall not be legally liable for transportation charges in respect of the transportation of said property (beyond those billed against him at the time of delivery for which he is otherwise liable) which may be found due after the property has been delivered to him, if the consignee (a) is an agent only and has no beneficial title in said property, and (b) prior to delivery of said property has notified the delivering carrier in writing of the fact of such agenc absence of beneficial title, and, in the case of a shipment reconsigned or diverted to a point other than that specified in the original bill of lading, has also notified the delivering carrier in writing of the name and address of the beneficial of said property; and, in such cases the shipper or consignor, or, in the case of a shipment so reconsigned or diverted, the beneficial owner, shall be liable for such additional charges. If the consignee has given to the carrier erroneous infor as to who the beneficial owner is, such consignee shall himself be liable for such additional charges. On shipments reconsigned or diverted by an agent who has furnished the carrier in the reconsignment or diversion order with a notice of c and the proper name and address of the beneficial owner, and where such shipments are refused or abandoned at ultimate destination, the said beneficial owner shall be liable for all legally applicable charges in connection therewith. If the signor or diverter has given to the carrier erroneous information as to who the beneficial owner is, such reconsignor or diverter shall himself be liable for all such charges.

If a shipper or consignor of a shipment of property (other than a prepaid shipment) is also the consignee named in the bill of lading and, prior to the time of delivery, notifies, in writing, a delivering carrier by railroad (a) to deliver such erty at destination to another party, (b) that such party is the beneficial owner of such property, and (c) that delivery is to be made to such party only upon payment of all transportation charges in respect of the transportation of such property delivery is made by the carrier to such party without such payment, such shipper or consignor shall not be liable (as shipper, consignor, consignee, or otherwise) for such transportation charges but the party to whom delivery is so made shall event be liable for transportation charges billed against the property at the time of such delivery, and also for any additional charges which may be found to be due after delivery of the property, except that if such party prior to such de has notified in writing the delivering carrier that he is not the beneficial owner of the property, and has given in writing to such delivering carrier the name and address of such beneficial owner, such party shall not be liable for any adc charges which may be found to be due after delivery of the property; but if the party to whom delivery is made has given to the carrier erroneous information as to the beneficial owner, such party shall nevertheless be liable for such add charges. If the shipper or consignor has given to the delivering carrier erroneous information as to who the beneficial owner is, such shipper or consignor shall himself be liable for such transportation charges, notwithstanding the foregoing pro of this paragraph and irrespective of any provisions to the contrary in the bill of lading or in the contract of transportation under which the shipment was made. The term "delivering carrier" means the line-haul carrier making ultimate de

Nothing herein shall limit the right of the carrier to require at time of shipment the prepayment or guarantee of the charges If upon inspection it is ascertained that the articles shipped are not those described in this bill of lading, the charges must be paid upon the articles actually shipped.

Where delivery is made by a common carrier by water the foregoing provisions of this section shall apply, except as may be inconsistent with Part III of the Interstate Commerce Act.

Sec. 8. If this bill of lading is issued on the order of the shipper, or his agent, in exchange or in substitution for another bill of lading, the shipper's signature to the prior bill of lading as to the statement of value or otherwise, or election o mon law or bill of lading liability, in or in connection with such prior bill of lading, shall be considered a part of this bill of lading as fully as if the same were written or made in or in connection with this bill of lading.

Sec. 9. (a) If all or any part of said property is carried by water over any part of said route, and loss, damage or injury to said property occurs while the same is in the custody of a carrier by water the liability of such carrier shall be mined by the bill of lading of the carrier by water (this bill of lading being such bill of lading if the property is transported by such water carrier thereunder) and by and under the laws and regulations applicable to transportation by water. water carriage shall be performed subject to all the terms and provisions of, and all the exemptions from liability contained in the Act of the Congress of the United States, approved on February 13, 1893, and entitled "An act relating to the n tion of vessels, etc.," and of other statutes of the United States according carriers by water the protection of limited liability, as well as the following subdivisions of this section; and to the conditions contained in this bill of lading not inconsisten this section, when this bill of lading becomes the bill of lading of the carrier by water.

(b) No such carrier by water shall be liable for any loss or damage resulting from any fire happening to or on board the vessel, or from explosion, bursting of boilers or breakage of shafts, unless caused by the design or neglect of such c

(c) If the owner shall have exercised due diligence in making the vessel in all respects seaworthy and properly manned, equipped, and supplied, no such carrier shall be liable for any loss or damage resulting from the perils of the lakes, or other waters, or from latent defects in hull, machinery, or appurtenances whether existing prior to, at the time of, or after sailing, or from collision, stranding, or other accidents of navigation, or from prolongation of the voyage. And, when f reason it is necessary, any vessel carrying any or all of the property herein described shall be at liberty to call at any port or ports, in or out of the customary route, to tow and be towed, to transfer, trans-ship, or lighter, to load and dis goods at any time, to assist vessels in distress, to deviate for the purpose of saving life or property, and for docking and repairs. Except in case of negligence such carrier shall not be responsible for any loss or damage to property if it be nec or is usual to carry the same upon deck.

(d) General Average shall be payable according to the York-Antwerp Rules of 1924, Sections 1 to 15, inclusive, and Sections 17 to 22, inclusive, and as to matters not covered thereby according to the laws and usages of the Port of New Y the owners shall have exercised due diligence to make the vessel in all respects seaworthy and properly manned, equipped and supplied, it is hereby agreed that in case of danger, damage or disaster resulting from faults or errors in navi or in the management of the vessel, or from any latent or other defects in the vessel, her machinery or appurtenances, or from unseaworthiness, whether existing at the time of shipment or at the beginning of the voyage (provided the latent o defects or the unseaworthiness was not discoverable by the exercise of due diligence), the shippers, consignees and/or owners of the cargo shall nevertheless pay salvage and any special charges incurred in respect of the cargo, and shall con with the shipowner in general average to the payment of any sacrifices, losses or expenses of a general average nature that may be made or incurred for the common benefit or to relieve the adventure from any common peril.

(e) If the property is being carried under a tariff which provides that any carrier or carriers party thereto shall be liable for loss from perils of the sea, then as to such carrier or carriers the provisions of this section shall be modified in ance with the tariff provisions, which shall be regarded as incorporated into the conditions of this bill of lading.

(f) The term "water carriage" in this section shall not be construed as including lighterage in or across rivers, harbors, or lakes, when performed by or on behalf of rail carriers.

Sec. 10. Any alteration, addition, or erasure in this bill of lading which shall be made without the special notation hereon of the agent of the carrier issuing this bill of lading, shall be without effect, and this bill of lading shall be enfor according to its original tenor.

Revised June 15, 1941

UNIFORM STRAIGHT CLASSIFICATION

out it at this point. A sight draft and order bill of lading transaction such as the one we are supposing is a cash transaction, that is, one in which the seller is not prepared to extend credit to the buyer and wants cash on delivery. The sight draft and order bill of lading transaction permits such a transaction to be accomplished very neatly. When the seller deposits the goods with the carrier for delivery to the buyer, the seller has the bill of lading made out to his, the seller's, order, thusly:

Consigned to ORDER of Seller

This leaves seller in control of the goods. Buyer cannot get them without the bill of lading and carrier cannot deliver them without obtaining surrender of the bill of lading. Now, seller introduces the order bill of lading into the banking system. He selects, to be his agent for the purpose of collecting the purchase price, a bank which has a branch office or a correspondent bank in the buyer's city. Seller indorses the order bill of lading in blank and gives it to the collecting bank with instructions to deliver it to the buyer when the bank receives the purchase price from the buyer. (It is to accommodate this procedure that the back of the order bill of lading has a space at the top for "Endorsements." See page 74. A person to whom an order bill of lading indorsed in blank is transferred—here, the buyer when he pays the purchase price—becomes the owner of the bill of lading, entitled to receive from the carrier the goods that it represents.[5]) Upon receipt of the order bill of lading indorsed in blank, the collecting bank calls the buyer and says in effect, "Bring in your money and we will give you the bill of lading." If buyer delivers the money, he will get the bill of lading and that will end the matter. If buyer does not deliver the money, seller will still have control of the goods by virtue of his continued control of the bill of lading and, although he may suffer a loss on the transaction, will be able to sell the goods elsewhere or have them returned and, thus, at least minimize his loss. It is in this respect—that the order bill of lading permits the seller to hold the goods until he is paid—that the order bill of lading operates as a security device. For future reference, another way of characterizing the sight draft and order bill of lading transaction is to describe it as a "cash against documents" transaction.

The Sight Draft; Commercial Drafts: The *sight draft* which goes with the order bill of lading is now considered.

When seller delivers the hypothetical order bill of lading to the collecting bank, it will not be alone but will be accompanied by a sight draft drawn on the buyer for the purchase price, which is a document that will look like the specimen shown below.

A sight draft is one of two general types of commercial drafts. A *commercial draft* is an order drawn by the seller of goods on the buyer for the purchase price (as distinguished, for example, from the bank draft, seen later). The commercial draft is the way in which, at a very early date, it became customary for the seller of goods to call upon the buyer for the purchase price. It is a very concise, precise way, and therefore a very businesslike way, to do that act (call on the buyer for the price). If it is a sight draft form of commercial draft, it calls upon the buyer to pay "at sight," that is, immediately. Now, what the collecting bank will actually do when deputized to act as the seller's agent in a sight draft and order bill of lading transaction is, upon receipt of the documents, to call the buyer and say, "Come in and pay the sight draft drawn on you for the purchase price and we will give you the bill of lading."

Documentary Sight Drafts: Frequently, the sale of goods will involve such documents as an insurance policy covering the goods against loss in transit and an inspection certificate assuring their quality. The sight draft then may be accompanied by an invoice, an insurance policy, an inspection certificate, and the bill of lading. A sight draft to be accompanied by such documents is called a *documentary sight draft*.

Risk of Loss in Transit: While the draft and bill of lading are moving forward through banking channels to the buyer's city for collection, the goods are moving forward by rail or motor or air carrier, to the buyer's city. During this period the goods are subject to damage or loss by fire, theft, accident or from other cause. This raises the question of the location of risk of loss during transit. Even though the goods are insured, this may still present a problem. The insurance may be payable to the person having risk of loss, without regard, so far as the insurer is concerned, to whether this is the seller or the buyer, making it necessary for seller and buyer to determine this between themselves.

San Francisco, California   February 1   ,19 84
(PLACE OF DRAWING)

                     At sight   PAY TO THE ORDER OF

SELLER COMPANY $ 10,000.00

Ten Thousand and no/100 - DOLLARS

TO   BUYER COMPANY

AT   801 South First Street

Denver, Colorado   SELLER COMPANY

                         BY: *Mary Thompson*

---

[5] U.C.C. 7502(1).

The code enumerates a set of rules on risk of loss, seen beginning at page 85. Where, as in the hypothetical case considered here, the sale is f.o.b. point of shipment,[6] the rule is that risk of loss passes to the buyer when the goods are deposited with the carrier for shipment.[7]

Risk of loss is on the buyer in a f.o.b. point of shipment transaction, even though the seller takes a bill of lading to his (seller's) order. The order bill of lading creates merely a security interest in the seller and, although it is a "document of title," does not affect the location of risk of loss.[8]

Time Draft (Trade Acceptance) and Order or Negotiable Bill of Lading

The transaction of time draft and order bill of lading, now considered, permits the seller to get his money immediately while at the same time allowing the buyer to have a credit period.

The transaction, "F.O.B. point of shipment; sixty-day trade acceptance and order bill of lading," may be used as a working example.

This transaction would be the same in all respects as the transaction, "F.O.B. point of shipment, sight draft and order bill of lading," except for the substitution of the sixty-day trade acceptance for the sight draft.

Sixty-day trade acceptance means that the buyer would have 60 days to pay but would have to sign an instrument (trade acceptance) immediately, which would oblige him to pay the purchase price in 60 days. The instrument that the buyer would be called upon to sign would look like the one shown on page 77.

Note, first, that whereas the sight draft called for payment "At sight"—meaning on demand, or immediately—the basis of its description as a "sight draft," the sixty-day trade acceptance calls for payment "60 days after sight," or at a date 60 days in the future. This would make the trade acceptance a *time draft* as distinguished from a *sight draft,* that is, a draft which is payable at a future time rather than a draft which is payable presently. Sight drafts and time drafts are the two general types of *commercial drafts.*

Note, secondly, that the trade acceptance makes provision, in the lower left-hand corner, for "*acceptance*" by the buyer. When the trade acceptance reaches the collecting bank's branch or correspondent in the buyer's city, that bank calls buyer in, this time however not to pay cash in exchange for the bill of lading but to "accept" the trade acceptance in exchange for the bill of lading. Buyer dates and signs the trade acceptance in the lower left-hand corner. This constitutes acceptance of the draft. It makes the buyer obligated on the draft—to pay the face amount of the draft in sixty days from the date of acceptance. It is like the buyer's promissory note to pay the amount for which the draft is drawn in sixty days, and the legal effect is the same—the same, that is, as if the buyer had given a sixty-day promissory note for the purchase price.

The instrument that has been discussed is called a *trade acceptance,* as it has been referred to here, and not a time draft, although it is also that for reasons that have been shown. The "trade acceptance" is an "acceptance" for the

---

[6]A mercantile term meaning "free on board" at place of shipment and which requires the seller to bear the expense and risk of putting the goods into the possession of the carrier at that place. U.C.C. 2319(1)(a). See also U.C.C. 2509(1)(a).

[7]U.C.C. 2509(1)(a); 2319(1)(a).

[8]U.C.C. 2509(1)(a). See also U.C.C. 2401(2).

reason and in the sense just seen. It is a "trade" acceptan because it is issued in connection with trade or commer The recital that, "The transaction which gives rise to t instrument is the purchase of goods by the acceptor from drawer," is notable. Early in this century, a movement w undertaken to popularize the trade acceptance as a commerc device. The Federal Reserve Board was an important spons of the movement. Federal reserve banks are bankers' ban They perform services for banks as banks perform servic for the public. The seller will deal with the buyer on a tra acceptance basis if the seller can "*discount*" the trade ceptance with a bank, i.e., sell the trade acceptance to bank—the collecting bank—so as to enable the seller to his money immediately. The seller's bank will discount trade acceptance for the seller, or will discount it for h more readily, if it can "*rediscount*" the trade acceptance roughly, resell the trade acceptance to a federal reserve ban To make this possible, the Federal Reserve Act of 1913 a thorized federal reserve banks to rediscount trade acceptanc under certain conditions, which were then prescribed by Fe eral Reserve Board Regulation to be as follows: "A tra acceptance must bear on its face, or be accompanied by, e dence in form satisfactory to the Federal Reserve Bank, t it was drawn by the seller of the goods on the purchaser such goods. Such evidence may consist of a certificate on accompanying the acceptance to the following effect: 'T obligation of the acceptor of this bill arises out of the purcha of goods from the drawer.'" It would now be apparent w this legend is printed on the trade acceptance.

If the seller expects to get his money by discounting a tra acceptance with his bank, he will set up the arrangement the outset of the transaction—before he commits himself the buyer. Then when the goods are shipped and the bill lading is obtained, the seller will, when he takes the bill lading to the bank, complete a trade acceptance form like t on page 77, except that the seller's bank rather than the sell will be designated as the payee.

This will save the bank the necessity of shuffling funds ba and forth between it and the seller. The bank will credit t seller's account with the amount of the trade acceptance for with, and the bank will collect the trade acceptance for own account at the end of the sixty-day period.

International Transactions: Commercial Letters of Credit; Banker's Acceptances

From the seller's end, international transactions invol problems that are not found in domestic transactions. On the goods are at sea they cannot be stopped, and if the buy does not pay for them when they reach the foreign port, res may be of the distress sale variety. If the seller has to sue t buyer for damages, he will be required to do so in a forei and possibly hostile jurisdiction. Therefore, the seller wa definite assurance that the goods will be paid for before allows them to leave home port.

The commercial letter of credit provides this. To illustra suppose a domestic seller and a foreign buyer in a cash de In the domestic transaction, the seller would deposit the goo with the carrier in exchange for an order bill of lading, exchange for which—the order bill of lading—the buy would be required to pay the purchase price; meanwhile, t goods would be moving forward to the buyer; all as has ready been seen. In the foreign transaction, the seller wa absolute assurance of payment before the goods move. To this, he requires a commercial letter of credit. A *commerc letter of credit* is a promise by a bank to pay a documenta sight draft of a certain description when it is drawn and wh

METROPOLITAN BANK

DETROIT, MICHIGAN _____ June 1, ____ 19 84

To: BUYER COMPANY _____ 1000 Blank St., San Francisco, CA

60 days after sight _____ PAY TO ORDER OF ___ SELLER COMPANY

Fifty Thousand and no/100 - - - - - - - - - DOLLARS $50,000.00

THE OBLIGATION OF THE ACCEPTOR OF THIS BILL ARISES OUT OF THE PURCHASE OF GOODS FROM THE DRAWER.

ACCEPTED San Francisco, CA

June 5, 1984

PAYABLE AT Bank of San Francisco

San Francisco, CA

BUYER COMPANY

By *Thomas Brown*

SELLER COMPANY

By *Henry Jones*

(Sixty-Day Trade Acceptance)

is presented to the bank with the prescribed documents.[9] Then, what happens is this: The buyer deposits the purchase price in his bank. His bank then pays a like sum to a domestic bank in the seller's country and city, designated by the seller. That bank then issues a letter of credit to the seller which in effect says to the seller that if he presents at that bank a sight draft for the purchase price of the goods, accompanied by a bill of lading and any other required documents, the bank will pay the sight draft. The seller is now willing to proceed. His payment is guaranteed by a bank in his own city. Seller deposits the goods with the ocean carrier in exchange for an order bill of lading (called an ocean order bill of lading in this case). Seller takes the bill of lading, together with his sight draft for the amount of the purchase price and any other required documents to the bank that has issued the letter of credit. That bank must pay him the purchase price in exchange for the documents.

A commercial letter of credit is shown on the following page. Letters of credit will not receive further treatment in this text. Division 5 of the code is devoted to letters of credit but purports to establish only a "theoretical frame" on which law of letters of credit can develop.[10] Commercial letters of credit have long been governed by the "ICC Uniform Customs," that is, the Uniform Customs and Practices for Documentary Credits of the International Chamber of Commerce, which originated in 1929 and which have undergone several revisions, the most recent in 1962. New York has rejected Article/Division 5 in favor of the Uniform Customs. In view of the importance of New York's role in international finance, this action should sharply restrict the impact of Article 5. The reasons given by New York for its action are that the Customs have been established for a long period of time and have been found to fill all needs and to work well; that legislation is not required in the field; and that legislation, if it is to be adopted, should not be unilateral.

● *Banker's acceptances* are a counterpart in international trade of the trade acceptance and order bill of lading in domestic trade. Here, the domestic bank does not promise to pay the domestic seller's sight draft for the purchase price of the goods, but rather to accept a time draft for the amount of the purchase price, payable in some period of time—30, 60, 90 days. The draft, bearing as it does the acceptance of a bank and not merely that of the buyer, is gilt-edged and can easily be discounted by the seller if he wishes.

● So-called "*standby*" *letters of credit* are gaining widespread use in domestic transactions. Examples are to be found in the purchase and leasing of real estate. A buyer of real estate which is still under construction can avoid tying up his money in a down payment deposit by having a bank, for a relatively small fee, issue a letter of credit guaranteeing the builder payment of the amount of the down payment when construction is completed. The lessee of real property may be required by the lessor to provide a letter of credit guaranteeing payment of the rent. Standby letters of credit are now also used to back up such things as corporate commercial paper and municipal bonds. This will improve their ratings and therefore their salability.

Financing at the Buyer's End

For the sake of simplicity, it has been assumed thus far that sales to retail buyers are for cash or on short term credit and that if they are for cash, the buyer has the cash on hand. Most retail buyers finance their inventories, however, and the consumer buyer may in his turn require financing, so that there evolves at the buying end of the sale of goods an elaborate scheme of financing and subfinancing. This aspect of the commercial transaction is examined briefly at this time to complete a broad survey of the commercial transaction.

If a retail merchant buying goods on sight draft and order bill of lading or other cash terms needs financing, he will arrange with a financer—bank or other financing agency—to pay the purchase price on his behalf. In such case, if the transaction is sight draft and order bill of lading, for example,

---

[9] A traveller's letter of credit, by contrast, guarantees payment of checks cashed by foreign banks for a traveller, up to some limit stated in the letter.

[10] U.C.C. 5101, Official Comment. See also, U.C.C. 5102(3) and Official Comment 2.

(Continued on page 81)

INTERNATIONAL
DIVISION

CALIFORNIA BANK

CABLE ADDRESS: CALBANK

IRREVOCABLE
LETTER OF CREDIT
NO. 0000
AMOUNT US$12,345.00**

Dec. 30, 19 83

[X] This credit has been advised by airmail through:

Foreign Sellers
Stockholm, Sweden

Goteborgs Bank
Stockholm, Sweden

[ ] This is the confirmation of the credit opened today by cable through our
above named correspondent.
It is only available for such amount as has not already been availed of
under such cable advice and may not be availed of at all unless attached to
and as a part of our correspondent's notification of such cable advice, the
two jointly constituting evidence of the outstanding amount of this credit.

Gentlemen:

We hereby authorize you to draw on California Bank, San Francisco, California

at ---30 days---   sight for account of U.S. Importer, San Francisco, California

up to an aggregate amount of US$12,345.00
(U.S. Dollars Twelve Thousand Three Hundred Forty Five only).

Drafts to be accompanied by:

1. Commercial Invoice in triplicate, stating that Cases are marked
   "U.S.I. - S.F.".
2. Special Customs Invoice in duplicate.
3. Insurance Policy or Certificate in duplicate, covering Marine
   and War Risks, including all Risks clause, for 110% of invoice
   value; claims payable in USA in US currency.
4. Inspection Certificate in duplicate.
5. Full set of clean on board ocean bills of lading, to order of
   shipper, blank endorsed, marked "Freight Prepaid" and notify
   U.S. Customs Brokers, San Francisco, California.

Evidencing shipment of: One drilling machine, Model E-7-50.
CIF San Francisco, Shipment to be effected not later than
May 15, 1981 from Sweden to San Francisco, California.
Partial shipments are not allowed.
Transhipment is not allowed.

```
              *
            *
          *
        *
      *
    *
```

Drafts drawn hereunder must specifically mention the number and date of this letter of credit.

The amount of each draft negotiated, together with the date of negotiation, must be endorsed on the reverse side of
this Letter of Credit.

We hereby agree with the drawers, endorsers and bona fide holders that the drafts drawn under and in accordance
with the terms of this credit shall be duly honored upon presentation to the drawee, if negotiated on or before

June 1, 1984

Sincerely,

AUTHORIZED SIGNATURE   AUTHORIZED SIGNATURE

Except as otherwise stated herein, this credit is subject to the Uniform Customs and Practice for Documentary Credits (1962 Revision) International Chamber of
Commerce Brochure No. 222.

TO: **CALIFORNIA BANK**   LETTER OF CREDIT APPLICATION AND SECURITY AGREEMENT

Please issue your irrevocable Letter of Credit as follows: [X] Airmail   [ ] Cable   L/C No. 0000

IN FAVOR OF (name and address)

FOREIGN SELLERS, Stockholm, Sweden

FOR ACCOUNT OF (person or firm requesting this credit)

U.S. IMPORTER, San Francisco, California

(check only one)

TENOR OF DRAFTS

30 Days Sight

AMOUNT

DRAWINGS FOR **100** % OF INVOICE VALUE   [X] NOT TO EXCEED   [ ] APPROXIMATELY   **$12,345.00**

DRAFTS TO BE ACCOMPANIED BY THE FOLLOWING DOCUMENTS: (Which the negotiating bank is authorized to forward to you in one mailing.)

[X] COMMERCIAL INVOICE(S) (indicate number of copies) **3**   [X] SPECIAL CUSTOMS INVOICE(S)

[X] INSURANCE POLICY(IES) COVERING THE FOLLOWING RISKS (such as marine and war risk, etc.) **all risks, including war risk**

INSURANCE EFFECTED BY OURSELVES (name of ins. co. and policy no.)   I/We agree to furnish you, upon request, such policy.

[X] OTHER DOCUMENTS **Inspection Certificate in Duplicate**

[X] FULL SET OF CLEAN ON BOARD OCEAN BILLS OF LADING, TO ORDER OF SHIPPER, BLANK ENDORSED

PERSON OR FIRM TO BE NOTIFIED BY CARRIER UPON ARRIVAL OF SHIPMENT

NOTIFY: **U.S. Customs Brokers, San Francisco**

[ ] AIRWAY BILL/AIR CONSIGNMENT NOTE CONSIGNED TO

[ ] RAILROAD/TRUCK BILL OF LADING CONSIGNED TO

EVIDENCING SHIPMENT OF:

COMMODITY (omit details of price, quality, etc.) **One Drilling Machine, Model E-7-50**

FROM (country or port of shipment)	DESTINATION (port of arrival)	SHIPPING TERMS (check one)			
Sweden	**San Francisco**	[ ] FAS	[ ] FOB	[ ] C&F	[X] CIF
SHIPMENT TO BE MADE NO LATER THAN	DATE THIS CREDIT TO EXPIRE	TRANSHIPMENT		PARTIAL SHIPMENTS (check one)	
May 15, 1984	**June 1, 1984**	[ ] ALLOWED [X] NOT ALLOWED		[ ] ALLOWED [X] NOT ALLOWED	

SPECIAL INSTRUCTIONS

Cases to be marked: "U.S.I. - S.F."

We, and each of us, agree that the terms and conditions set forth on this and the reverse page hereof are hereby made a part of this application and are hereby accepted and agreed to by us.

January 11, 1984   **U.S. IMPORTER**

DATE   APPLICANT'S NAME

FOR BANK USE ONLY	CUSTOMER'S CURRENT LIABILITY
	*
OFFICE NO.	SIGNATURE OF LOAN OFFICER AUTHORIZING CREDIT

AUTHORIZED SIGNATURE   TITLE

LETTER OF CREDIT AND SECURITY AGREEMENT

In consideration of your opening at our request a letter of credit in accordance with the terms stated on the reverse side hereof, and you or your correspondents' accepting or paying drafts at our request or for our account, we, and each of us, hereby represent, warrant and agree, as follows:

1. We will pay you in lawful money of the United States of America at your office, on demand in the case of sight drafts, and at such time before maturity as you may require to enable you to meet payment at least one business day before maturity in the case of time drafts, an amount sufficient to pay all monies to be paid by you or your correspondents to meet disbursements of any kind or character made or to be made pursuant to said letter of credit, together with interest, commissions, charges and any and all other amounts owing you or paid or to be paid by you in connection therewith. We also authorize you to charge any accounts any of us may have with you for all such payments to be made by us.

2. We hereby grant to you a security interest in all goods and documents, and the proceeds or products thereof, which shall come into our possession or control, or in which we may acquire an interest, or which shall come into the possession or control of you or uny of our correspondents as a result of opening or in connection with any transactions under said letter of credit or otherwise, as security (a) for all payments made or to be made by you or your correspondents pursuant to said letter of credit; (b) for all interest, commissions or other charges in relation to said letter of credit; (c) for any other obligations of any of us to you. At any time and from time to time, on demand, we agree to deliver, convey, transfer, or assign to you, as security, for any and all of our liabilities hereunder or otherwise, which are now or may at any time hereafter be owing by any of us to you, additional property of a value and character satisfactory to you, or to make such payment as you may require. We will, at our expense, do, make, procure, execute and deliver all acts, things, writings and assurances as you may at any time require to protect, assure or enforce your interests, rights and remedies created by, provided in or emanating from this agreement, including but not limited to execution of writings, documents and instruments required by you to perfect this security interest under the California Uniform Commercial Code.

3. Any changes or modifications with respect to the terms or provisions of said letter of credit or any of the matters or things herein contained must be in writing and signed by us, shall be effective only after receipt thereof and agreement thereto by you and all other concerned parties and shall have no effect upon actions taken by you or by your correspondents prior to such receipt and shall have no effect upon the remaining terms or provisions of the said letter of credit or this agreement. Any such changes or modifications made by any of us shall be deemed to have been made by all of us.

4. We represent and warrant that any and all necessary import, export or other licenses for the import, export or shipping of any and all goods shipped under or pursuant to or in connection with credit have been obtained and that all foreign and domestic governmental regulations in regard to the shipment of any and all such property or the financing thereof have been or will be complied with. We will obtain or cause to be in existence insurance satisfactory to you on any goods described in said letter of credit. You are hereby authorized and empowered to collect the amount due under any such insurance and apply the same against any of our obligations to you arising under said letter of credit or otherwise.

5. To indemnify and save you and/or your correspondents harmless against and from and to pay to you and/or your correspondents on demand any and all loss, liability, damage, costs and expense, including reasonable attorneys' fees, arising out of the issuance by you or any of your correspondents of letters of guaranty or indemnity to enable us or our agents to obtain delivery of the property or any portion thereof in the absence of the relative documents. We also agree to take immediate steps upon the issuance by you or any of your correspondents of any such letters of guaranty or indemnity to cause the prompt delivery to you or your correspondents, as the case may be, of the missing documents covered by such letters of guaranty or indemnity, in order that you or your correspondents may surrender the same to the addressee of such letters. If, upon receipt of such documents covering any of the property, you find such documents to be incorrect, defective, or not in conformity with the terms of the said letter of credit, you are nevertheless authorized to accept and/or pay the draft(s) covering said documents with the same force and effect as though such documents were in full and exact compliance with the terms of the said letter of credit.

6. Upon any default by any of us in any of the undertakings herein set forth, or upon the failure of any of us forthwith, with or without notice, to furnish satisfactory additional collateral or to make payments on account as herein agreed or to perform or comply with any of the other terms or provisions of this agreement, or in the event of the failure in business, dissolution, termination of existence or insolvency of any of us, or in case any petition in bankruptcy should be filed by or against any of us, or any proceeding in bankruptcy or under any Acts of Congress relating to the relief of debtors should be commenced for the relief or readjustment of any indebtedness of any of us either through reorganization, compostition, extension, arrangement, or otherwise, or if any of us should make an assignment for the benefit of creditors or take advantage of any insolvency law, or if a receiver of any of our property should be appointed at any time, or if any of our funds or other property which may be in or come into your possession or control or that of any third party acting on your behalf as aforesaid should be attached or distrained or should be or become subject to any mandatory order of court or other legal process, then, or at any time after the happening of any such event, any or all of the aforesaid obligations and/or liabilities of each of us shall, at your option, become due and payable immediately, without demand or notice; and you shall have the remedies of a secured party under the California Uniform Commercial Code and full power and authority are hereby given you to the full extent permissible by law to sell, assign, and deliver all or any of the property hereinbefore referred to, or any substitutes therefor, or any additions or accessions thereto, or any other property upon which you have hereinbefore been given a lien or security interest, at any public or private sale, at your option, either for cash or on credit or for future delivery, without assumption of any credit risk, and to the full extent permissible by law, without either demand, advertisement or notice of any kind, all of which are hereby expressly waived. At any such sale, you may, at your sole discretion, to the full extent permissible by law, purchase the whole or any part of the property sold, free from any right of redemption on our part, all such rights being also hereby waived and released. In the event of any sale or other disposition of any of the property as aforesaid, after deducting all costs or expenses of every kind for retaking, holding, care, safekeeping, collection, preparation for sale, sale, delivery or otherwise, including reasonable attorneys' fees and legal expenses incurred by you in connection therewith, you may apply the residue of the proceeds of the sale or other disposition thereof to the payment or reduction, either in whole or in part, of all or any of our obligations and/or liabilities, whether then due or not due, making proper allowance for the interest on obligations or liabilities not then due, and returning the surplus, if any, to us or to the person or persons entitled thereto; all without prejudice to your rights against us with respect to any and all amounts which may be or remain unpaid on any of our said obligations and/or liabilities. No delay on your part or that of any assignee or transferee hereunder in exercising any rights or options under this agreement shall operate as a waiver of any such rights or options or prejudice your rights as against us.

7. You are hereby authorized, at your option and without any obligation to do so, to transfer to and/or register in the name of your nominee all or any part of the property which may be held by you as security at any time hereunder, and to do so before or after the maturity of any of the said obligations and/or liabilities and with or without notice.

8. You shall not be deemed to have waived any of your rights hereunder unless you or your duly authorized agent shall have signed such waiver in writing. No such waiver, unless expressly so stated therein, shall be effective as to any transaction which occurs subsequent to the date of such waiver nor as to any continuance of a breach after such waiver.

9. Said letter of credit shall be subject to and performance by you, your correspondents and the beneficiaries thereunder shall be governed by the "Uniform Customs and Practice for Documentary Credits (1962 Revision), International Chamber of Commerce, Brochure No. 222."

10. You may assign or transfer this agreement, or any instrument and/or document evidencing all or any of the aforesaid obligations and/or liabilities, and may deliver all or any of the property then held as security therefor to the transferee, who shall thereupon become vested with all the powers and rights in respect thereto given you herein or in the instrument and/or document transferred, and you shall thereafter be forever relieved and fully discharged from any liability or responsibility with respect thereto, but you shall retain all rights and powers hereby given with respect to any and all instrument, documents, rights or property not so transferred.

11. We hereby authorize and appoint you to act as our agent in obtaining and cancelling insurance and adjusting and settling losses under the insurance on any of the property referred to in this agreement and in endorsing and negotiating any documents or instruments necessary to permit collection of proceeds of collateral.

12. This agreement shall be binding upon us as well as upon our legal representatives, successors and/or assigns, shall be construed as the joint and several obligation of each of us where there is more than one, and shall be deemed to be made under and shall be governed by the laws of the State of California in all respects, including matters of construction, validity and performance. If this agreement is signed by one individual, the terms "we", "our", and "us" shall be read throughout as "I", "my" and "me" as the case may be.

the sight draft will be presented to and paid by the financer in exchange for the bill of lading.

Prior to the code, the financer would give the buyer the bill of lading, to enable the buyer to get the goods, in exchange for a *trust receipt*, executed by the buyer to the financer, giving the financer a security interest in the goods and in the proceeds of sale thereof until the amount advanced by the financer on behalf of the buyer was paid.

Under the code, the trust receipt and other old forms of security devices are replaced by the *security agreement*, seen in detail in Chapter 7, which today therefore is the form of security device that would be entered into between retailer and his financer.

If retailer's customer, consumer, requires financing, which he will for more expensive items, the security agreement will also be the document used for that purpose.

NOTES

CHAPTER 5

Sales

Basic Concepts

Introduction

Technically speaking, a *"sale"* is a transfer of title to personal property. Technically, only personal property is "sold." Technically, real property is "conveyed," although it is common practice to speak of "selling" real property. Division 2 of the code, and this chapter, use the word "sell" in its technical sense, and Division 2 of the code and this chapter are concerned only with sales of personal property, and, more specifically, only with sales of tangible personal property or *"goods."*[1]

Goods may be the subject of gift as well as sale. The thing that makes the difference between sale and gift is *consideration*. A sale is a transfer of title to goods for consideration,[2] whereas a gift is a transfer of title to goods without consideration.

• Precode law took a "property approach" to the subject of the sale of goods. This required, first, location of title. That being done, everything else fell into place automatically because, by locating title all of the "incidents of title"—risk of loss, insurable interest, tax liability, liability of the goods to creditors, etc.—were located. Thus, if it was determined that title had passed to the buyer, he had risk of loss, he had the insurable interest in the goods, he was liable for property taxes on the goods, the goods were subject to the claims of his creditors, and so on, even though he had not yet paid for the goods or taken possession of them. Although it makes very little difference in the end results, the code abandons the precode "title pea" approach and undertakes to take what it calls a "contractual approach" to the subject of the sale of goods.[2a] Under this approach, it deals with the incidents of title on an individual basis and on terms that are considered to make good commercial law.

• Chapter 1 of Division 2 establishes the basic concepts upon which the Division is built. These are now considered.

Sale; Contract for Sale; Present Sale; Contract to Sell

It has been seen that a *sale* is a transfer of title to goods for a consideration called the price, and the code so defines it.[3] While such title-passing is a property concept, the transaction which gives rise to it necessarily has its origin in contract. Thus, the code has every sale originate in a *contract for sale*.[4]

The contract for sale and the completion of that contract may occur almost simultaneously as it does with the millions of everyday over-the-counter transactions. When this is so, the code calls the transaction a *present sale*, which the code defines as "a sale which is accomplished by the making of the contract."[5]

If the transaction is not to be complete—title is not to pass—until a future time, the transaction is called a *contract to sell*.[6]

Existing and Identified Goods; Future Goods

The law conceives that a person can transfer, presently, only something that he owns and that a person can own only something that exists. You can neither own nor transfer, for example, a book to be published next week. You can *contract to* sell it but you cannot *sell* it.

This leads to the rules of the Uniform Commercial Code, which merely continue rules of the Uniform Sales Act, and, before that, of the law merchant, that only *existing and identified goods* can be the subject of a present sale.[7] Goods that are not both existing and identified specifically as the subject matter of the contract are *future goods*.[8] Future goods can be the subject only of a contract to sell.[9] Thus, if, after making the contract for sale, the seller must manufacture the goods or obtain them from a supplier or segregate them from inventory and identify them to the contract, the goods are future goods and cannot be the subject of a present sale.

Special Forms of Goods

Certain things are sufficiently unusual that their character as "goods" is notable, or, although they might be thought of as goods, they require special rules because of exceptional characteristics.

• Goods to be *specially manufactured* by the seller for the buyer are "goods,"[10] although, because they are not existing goods, they cannot be the subject matter of a present sale. The importance of declaring that specially manufactured goods are "goods" is that it removes room for the argument that a contract for specially manufactured goods is a contract for "services" rather than for goods and that therefore it is not controlled by Division 2.

• Although it may not be widely known, there is a market in the *unborn young of animals*, for example, in spring lambs, and the code declares that the "unborn young of animals" are "goods."[11]

• A contract for the sale of *crops* or of *fixtures* that can be severed without material harm to the land is a contract for the sale of goods and there can be a present sale of such things without severance from the land to which they are attached.[12]

---

[1]U.C.C. 2102.

[2]U.C.C. 2106(1).

[2a]U.C.C. 2509, Official Comment 1.

[3]U.C.C. 2106(1).

[4]U.C.C. 2106(1).

[5]U.C.C. 2106(1).

[6]U.C.C. 2106(1).

[7]U.C.C. 2105(2).

[8]U.C.C. 2105(2).

[9]U.C.C. 2105(2).

[10]U.C.C. 2105(1).

[11]U.C.C. 2105(1).

[12]U.C.C. 2105(1), 2107(2).

• A contract for the sale of *timber* or *minerals* (including oil and gas) or of a *structure or its materials* to be removed from land is a contract for the sale of goods, provided, in the cases of minerals or a structure or its materials, that severence is to be made by the seller.[13] If minerals or a structure or its materials are to be severed by the buyer, the transaction is treated as the sale of an interest in land, outside of Division 2 and subject to the rules of law regulating the sales of interests in land.[14] Even the timber or minerals or structure or structure materials that is to be severed by the seller is treated as a special transaction to the extent that the sales contract involving such subject matter must be recorded in order for it to be good as against a subsequent innocent purchaser from the seller.[15]

• *Fungible goods* are goods of which any unit is, by nature or usage of trade, the equivalent of any other like unit,[16] or which by agreement are treated as fungible.[17] By nature, such goods as grain and oil are fungible. By usage of trade or by agreement such goods as sacks of sugar or cases of eggs may be treated as fungible. There may be a present sale of an undivided share of a stock of fungible goods, and the sale may take the form of a sale of a percentage of the bulk, or it may be by number, weight or other measure.[18] Thus, there may be a sale of "ten per cent" of a fungible bulk, or of "twenty tons" or "one hundred bushels" to be drawn from a fungible bulk. Until the buyer's purchase is withdrawn from the fungible bulk, the seller and buyers are owners in common of the mass of fungible goods in accordance with their proportionate ownership interests.[19]

Sale of Interest in Goods

There may be a sale of an interest in an existing and identified stock of goods as distinguished from a sale of goods.[20] In such case, the goods need not be fungible. For example, there could be a sale of "fifty per cent" of a stock of furniture consisting of assorted (nonfungible) pieces.

Merchant

Merchant is a defined term under the code. It means "a person who deals in goods of the kind or otherwise by his occupation holds himself out as having knowledge or skill peculiar to the practices or goods involved in the transaction or to whom such knowledge or skill may be attributed by his employment of an agent or broker or other intermediary who by his occupation holds himself out as having such knowledge or skill."[21]

This conceives of a merchant as a "professional in business"[22] and one may be a merchant either under the "goods" aspect of the definition—because he has specialized knowledge as to the goods involved in the transaction—or under the "practices" aspect of definition—because he has

specialized knowledge as to the business practices involved in the transaction.

• Special provisions regarding merchants appear only in Division 2. They are of three kinds. (1) Sections 2201(2), 2205, 2207 and 2209, which deal with the statute of frauds, firm offers, confirmatory memoranda and modification of the contract, which rest on normal business practices which would be familiar to anyone in business. (2) Sections which require the merchant to be a "dealer in goods of the kind," such as Section 2314 which imposes a warranty of merchantability upon a seller who is such a merchant, and Section 2403(2). (3) Sections which impose obligations of various kinds on merchant-parties, such as Section 2103(1)(b) which requires a merchant-party to observe reasonable commercial standards of fair dealing in the trade in order to satisfy an obligation to act in "good faith." See, for further examples of this third category of cases, 2327(1)(c) and 2603.

Contractual Aspects of the Sales Contract

Chapter 2 of Division 2 and part of Chapter 3 of the code deal with the contractual aspects of a sales contract. Much of this material has been covered in the chapter on Contracts where it was more appropriate to discuss it.

These sections of Chapter 2, which comprise most of the sections of Chapter 2, are covered in the chapter on Contracts, at the pages indicated:

Firm offers; etc. (U.C.C. 2205), page 27;
Offer and acceptance (U.C.C. 2206), page 29, n. 12;
Additional terms in acceptance (U.C.C. 2207), page 29;
Modification of contract (U.C.C. 2209), page 34;
Statute of Frauds (U.C.C. 2201), page 44; and
Delegation of performance and assignment of rights (U.C.C. 2210), page 52, n. 82.

• It is the philosophy of the code that the law of commercial transactions should be accommodated to the practices of the commercial world so far as this can be done without violence to legal concepts. This spirit is evident in many of the sections recalled above. Examples are the firm offer statute; Section 2207 which recognizes that merchants sometimes introduce small new terms into the transaction without intending to engage in the technical process of "counteroffer;" and Section 2209 which recognizes that in the commercial world it may be desirable to permit modification of contract without regard to the technicalities of the law of consideration.

• The code's commercial attitude is demonstrated by other groups of provisions which are now considered.

Open Terms and Unspecified Terms

The code softens the certainty requirement of the law of contracts (page 23) in that it allows terms of a sales contract to be left open to some degree and to the extent that it supplies a series of rules for filling gaps that may be left by the parties regarding such things as the time and place of delivery.

A policy statement is made in this regard by Section 2204(3), which provides: "Even though one or more terms are left open a contract for sale does not fail for indefiniteness if the parties have intended to make a contract and there is a reasonably certain basis for giving an appropriate remedy."

The Official Comments to Section 2204 say this about subsection (3):

"Subsection (3) states the principle as to 'open terms' underlying later sections of the Article. If the parties intend to enter into a binding agreement, this subsection recognizes that agreement as valid in law, despite missing terms, if there is

---

[13]U.C.C. 2105(1), 2107(1)(2).

[14]U.C.C. 2107, Official Comment 1.

[15]U.C.C. 2107(3).

[16]U.C.C. 1201(17).

[17]U.C.C. 1201(17). California omits the provision of the Official Text that goods may be treated as fungible by agreement.

[18]U.C.C. 2105(4).

[19]U.C.C. 2105(4).

[20]U.C.C. 2105(3).

[21]U.C.C. 2104(1).

[22]U.C.C. 2104, Official Comment 2.

any reasonably certain basis for granting a remedy. The test is not certainty as to what the parties were to do nor as to the exact amount of damages due the plaintiff. Nor is the fact that one or more terms are left to be agreed upon enough of itself to defeat an otherwise adequate agreement. Rather, commercial standards on the point of "indefiniteness' are intended to be applied, this Act making provision elsewhere for missing terms needed for performance, open price, remedies and the like.''

Open Price Term: Section 2305 permits an *open price term.* Under Section 2305, the parties may intentionally leave price to future agreement or to a market or other standard set or recorded by a third person. If, thereafter, the parties fail to agree or the market or other standard is not set or recorded, the price is a reasonable price at the time for delivery.

Options Respecting Particulars of Performance: Section 2311 permits the parties to leave particulars of performance to be specified by one of the parties without causing the contract for sale to be fatally uncertain. The buyer, on the one hand, could be given an option regarding assortment, for example, the number of each of gallon, quart and pint-sized Mason jars to be furnished in an order for a carload of Mason jars. The seller, on the other hand, could be given an option regarding shipping arrangements.

Gap-filling Rules Regarding Time and Place of Shipment or Delivery and Payment

If a contract for sale does not specify the *time for shipment or delivery* or other action required by the contract, the action must be taken within a reasonable time.[23]
● If the contract does not specify the *place for delivery*, that place is the seller's place of business, except that if the sale is of identified goods which to the knowledge of the parties at the time of contracting are at some other place, that is the place for delivery.[24]
● If the contract is silent as to *time and place of payment*, payment is due at the time and place at which the buyer is to receive the goods even though the place of shipment is the place of delivery.[25] Very commonly, the "place at which the buyer is to receive the goods" and the "place of delivery" are not the same. The place of delivery is ordinarily the seller's place of business which might be in Los Angeles. The place at which the buyer is to receive the goods is ordinarily, as between merchants, the buyer's place of business which might be in San Francisco. Section 2310(b) protects the seller as to the purchase price in such circumstances by permitting him to ship "under reservation," that is, by bill of lading drawn to the seller's order, permitting him to withhold delivery until payment. At the same time, Section 2310(b) protects the buyer by permitting him to inspect the goods before paying, except where he has agreed otherwise (as in "cash against documents," page 75).

The Code's Approach to Problems Arising Under the Contract for Sale

After a contract for sale has been entered into and before it has been completed, many kinds of questions regarding the legal status of the goods can arise.

---

[23]U.C.C. 2309(1).
[24]U.C.C. 2308.
[25]U.C.C. 2310(a).

The goods may be destroyed accidentally, or stolen. The question will then arise as to the location of *risk of loss.* Is it still the seller or has it shifted to the buyer?

The question may arise as to whether the buyer has yet acquired an *insurable interest.* The question may arise as to where property *tax liability* for the goods lies. The question may arise as to whether the goods remain an asset of the seller, liable to the *claims of his creditors,* or have become an asset of the buyer, subject to the claims of his creditors.

If the goods are *damaged by a third party,* the question arises as to whether the seller or the buyer has the cause of action for the damages.

If one party or the other, seller or buyer, defaults on the contract, a question may arise as to the *remedy or form of remedy* to which the injured party may resort if he is the seller, whether he may sue for the purchase price or whether he must bring an action for breach of contract for failure to take delivery; if he is the buyer, whether he may recover the goods themselves or whether he must be content to bring an action for damages for the seller's failure to deliver.

The precode law took a property approach to the whole matter. When the "property in the goods" or "title" was located, everything else followed. Risk of loss was an incident of title and went with it. Who had title, had risk of loss. Title gave insurable interest and imposed tax liability. If the seller still had title, his creditors could still levy on the goods. And remedy turned on title. An action for the price by the seller required that there have been a "sale," i.e., a passage of title. Short of this the seller generally could only sue for damages for breach of contract if the buyer failed to complete the contract.

The code abandons this "title pea" approach in favor of what it calls a "contractual approach," which has been described perhaps more satisfactorily in another way as the "narrow issue approach." Under the code specific statutory rules are stated for each of the kinds of problems that has been noted. These rules directly solve the problem in each case, without regard to the location of title.

These statutory rules are now examined, as they deal with the problems that have been mentioned—the problems of passage of title, risk of loss, insurable interest, rights of creditors, and remedies of seller and buyer.

Passage of Title and Risk of Loss

Risk of Loss

While, as has been seen, the code treats passage of title and passage of risk of loss as separate issues, it is convenient for our purposes to consider them together. This is because, despite the code's technical divorcement of risk of loss from title, risk of loss passes at the same time as title except in one instance. Therefore, except in the one instance, it will be the case that when title passes, under the title-passing rules set forth below, risk of loss will also pass.

The exception is where shipment is not required and the buyer is to take delivery of the goods at the seller's place of business or at the situs of the goods. The case is an interesting study in the differences between the property approach of the precode law and the commercial, analytical approach of the code. Assume that parties have agreed to sell and buy identified goods of which the buyer is to take delivery at the seller's place of business. The precode law reasoning was this: Since there was nothing left for the seller to do, there was no reason to postpone passage of title; therefore it passed even though transfer of possession, as distinguished from title, was to be postponed. It also did not matter that the purchase price had not been paid. That was a neutral factor, not bearing on the question of passage of title one way or the other. If there were parties, identified goods, and a contract for their sale without any agreement to postpone passage of title, title should be considered to pass at once. Since risk of loss accompanied title, it should also be deemed to pass at once and despite the fact that, temporarily, the goods were to remain in the possession of the seller. This, as stated, was the precode law reasoning. The code approach by contrast is to separate passage of title and passage of risk of loss in such a case and to have title pass but not risk of loss. The code postpones transfer of risk of loss in such a case until the buyer takes delivery of the goods if the seller is a merchant; until tender of delivery in other cases.[26] The code explains its position and demonstrates the specific approach it takes to problems, thusly: "The underlying theory of this rule is that a merchant who is to make physical delivery at his own place continues meanwhile to control the goods and can be expected to insure his interest in them. The buyer, on the other hand, has no control of the goods and it is extremely unlikely that he will carry insurance on goods not yet in his possession." [27]

• Where the goods are held by a bailee (warehouseman) to be delivered without being moved, risk of loss passes to the buyer (a) on his receipt of a negotiable document of title covering the goods; or (b) an acknowledgment by the bailee of the buyer's right to possession of the goods; or (c) after his receipt of a nonnegotiable document of title or other written direction to deliver.[28]

• Again, dealing with specific problems specifically, the code, in Section 2510, lays down rules regarding the effect of breach of the sales contract, by the seller or by the buyer, which rules are as follows:

1. Where delivery of goods so fails to conform to the contract as to give the buyer a right of rejection, risk of loss remains on the seller until cure or acceptance.

2. Where the buyer rightfully revokes acceptance he may to the extent of any deficiency in his insurance coverage treat risk of loss as resting on the seller.

3. Where the buyer repudiates the contract or is otherwise in breach before risk of loss has passed to him, the seller may to the extent of any deficiency in his insurance coverage treat risk of loss as resting on the buyer for a commercially reasonable time.

Passage of Title

Agreement of Parties: In no case can title to goods pass until their identification to the contract for sale.[29] Beyond this, parties can make any agreement they wish regarding passage of title.[30] If the goods are identified at the time the contract is made they may agree that title and risk of loss shall pass at that time, or that risk of loss but not title shall pass at that time, or that title but not risk of loss shall pass at that time. This does not often happen. Parties to a sales transaction are concerned with the practicalities—quantity, price, shipping terms, shipping dates, etc.—and tend to ignore the legalities. The California Dried Fruit Association contract (Fig Contract) that follows is one of the exceptions. Paragraph 6 (re-

verse side) provides for immediate passage of title,[31] but leaves risk of loss in the seller until delivery.

Once goods are identified to the contract the buyer has an insurable interest.[32]

Intention Not Expressed: If parties do not express their intention regarding passage of title, rules of law control. These are now examined.

IDENTIFIED GOODS; SHIPMENT NOT REQUIRED. If the seller is not required to ship the goods to the buyer title passes at the time the goods become identified to the contract.[33] If this occurs at the time the transaction is entered into, title passes at that time, except that if the seller is to deliver a document of title to the goods title passes on delivery of the document.[34] If identification does not occur until a later date, title passes at that time.[35] In this connection U.C.C. 2501(1)(b) provides that identification occurs when goods are marked or otherwise designated by the seller as the goods to which the contract refers. Upon identification the buyer, if he has paid part of the price, is given the protection of U.C.C. 2502 in case the seller becomes insolvent.

SHIPMENT REQUIRED. The code lays down passage of title rules for those cases in which the seller is required to ship the goods to the buyer. These are shown below under the heading, General Rules. In addition Chapter 3 of Division 2, in Sections 2319-2324, states the obligations of the seller in various well defined types of mercantile contracts. For our purposes it is convenient to consider the two sets of rules together, which is done below.

General Rules. (1) [*Shipment Contracts*] If the contract requires or authorizes the seller to send the goods to the buyer but does not require him to deliver them at destination, title and risk of loss pass to the buyer at time and place of shipment.[36] (2) [*Destination Contracts*] If the contract requires delivery at destination, title and risk of loss pass on tender there.[37]

F.O.B. and Other Mercantile Contracts: Certain symbols or "mercantile terms" have acquired well defined meanings in the commercial world. The Code codifies the generally established rules governing such terms.

1. *F.O.B. Terms:* F.O.B. means "free on board" a particular place,[38] which means the seller must pay the costs of moving the goods forward to the named place.[39] He has risk of loss until the goods reach the place designated.[40] If the term is F.O.B. point of shipment, the seller bears the expense and risk of putting the goods into possession of the carrier.[41] If it is, in addition, F.O.B. vessel, car or other vehicle, point of shipment, the seller bears the expense and risk of loading the

---

[26]U.C.C. 2509(3).

[27]U.C.C. 2509, Official Comment 3.

[28]U.C.C. 2509(2).

[29]U.C.C. 2401(1).

[30]U.C.C. 2401(1).

---

[31]Note U.C.C. 2501(1)(c) [identification of future crops occurs "when the crops are planted or otherwise become growing crops"].

[32]U.C.C. 2501(1).

[33]U.C.C. 2401(1), 2501(1).

[34]U.C.C. 2401(3).

[35]U.C.C. 2401(1) and Official Comment 2, 2501(1).

[36]U.C.C. 2401(2)(a), 2509(1)(a).

[37]U.C.C. 2401(2)(b), 2509(1)(b).

[38]U.C.C. 2319(1).

[39]U.C.C. 2319(1).

[40]U.C.C. 2319(1).

[41]U.C.C. 2319(1)(a).

FIG CONTRACT

...., Cal., ... 19............

...., hereinafter called Seller, whose post office

address is ...., California, has sold and .... hereinafter

called Buyer has bought, upon the terms and conditions stated below and on the back hereof, which are hereby referred to and made a part hereof, all the crops of figs of the varieties specified below, grown or to be grown during

the current year, on the .... acre tract of land, known as the ....

ranch, leased or owned by Seller, situated on .... Road, ... County, California.

The quantity (estimated by Seller), the varieties sold and the prices (subject to adjustment as below provided) are as follows:

QUANTITY	VARIETY OF FIGS	BASIS PRICE PER TON

Should the tests provided for on the reverse side hereof indicate that any of the lots tendered exceed the 10% tolerance named by the United States Department of Agriculture, and provided that such lots shall in all other respects conform to the requirements of this contract unless otherwise specified herein, Buyer shall accept them at the reduced price determined as follows:

For all figs testing less than 90% passable, deduct 1% of the basis price per ton for each test point below 90%. (Unless otherwise specified herein, sunburn and puff ball figs to be paid for at 75% of such reduced price.)

Seller hereby guarantees said fruit to be Seller's sole and absolute property, free from all encumbrances except

.... hereby affirms that Seller has not contracted to sell, nor sold any thereof to others, and hereby agrees that all fruit deliverable hereunder shall be the product of clean, sound, mature fruit, thoroughly and properly cured by sun-drying or dehydration, unbleached, in original condition, not stored at any time loose in bins, or sacked, ungraded as to size, of choice quality, of good color, free from defective fruit or damage of any kind (except as otherwise provided), and in good marketable and merchantable condition, as

a whole or in deliverable lots, at the earliest possible date and not later than the .... day of ...., 19......

(unless Buyer shall in writing extend the time for delivery) at

Buyer's Packing House at .... } California
F. O. B. Cars ....

(Strike out one.)

TIME OF DELIVERY: Buyer reserves the right to regulate time of delivery to packing house, such regulation to be so exercised as to allow Seller to deliver within contract time.

Payment shall be made upon basis of tests made at point and time of delivery only.

.... Buyer

By ....

.... Seller.

(Reverse side of this form on following pages)

FIG CONTRACT

1. Should any of the fruit tendered under this contract not conform to the requirements of this contract, it shall be optional with Buyer to accept same at the reduced price herein provided for, to reject same or take in, assort, weigh back and reject, at Seller's expense, any portion not so conforming, and such partial or complete rejection by Buyer shall not invalidate this contract or release Seller from any obligations hereunder.

2. Should the quantity of fruit of any crop sold exceed Seller's estimate herein stated, Buyer agrees to accept delivery of and pay for such excess up to, but not exceeding ten per cent of said estimated quantity, at the price herein fixed. In consideration thereof Seller agrees that Buyer may, at its option, demand delivery of the whole of such crop at the price herein fixed, although such total crop may exceed by more than ten per cent the quantity estimated by Seller.

3. Figs delivered hereunder shall be free from active infestation, and (except as herein provided for) shall not contain over ten per cent (10%) of defective fruit (within the meaning of the rules and practice of the Food and Drug Administration, Federal Security Agency) to be ascertained promptly after tender of figs by Seller at point of delivery specified herein. Inspection and tests to be made by Dried Fruit Association of California.

4. Certificates of Dried Fruit Association of California on figs tendered hereunder relating to defects defined in regulations of the Food and Drug Administration of the United States Department of Agriculture shall be final and binding on the parties hereto. but unless expressly provided herein shall not determine finally or at all the quality or merchantability of such figs in other respects.

5. No inspection, receipt or other handling by Buyer of figs tendered on delivery hereunder prior to receipt of certificate of test herein provided for and adjustment as herein provided on the basis thereof, shall be deemed an acceptance of such goods.

6. This contract is intended and understood by both parties to pass title to said fruit, and to constitute an absolute sale, but until delivery has been completed, Seller agrees to and does assume all risk of loss of or damage to undelivered fruit.

7. Buyer shall have the right to the possession of any fruit as and when the same shall be dried and cured and may at any time thereafter enter upon the premises where such fruit is and remove the same; but nothing herein contained shall affect Seller's obligation to deliver such fruit as herein provided.

8. If any part of the fruit sold shall, before its delivery, be destroyed by fire, frost or other like unavoidable cause, Seller shall be released from obligation to deliver the fruit so destroyed. If the packing house of Buyer at or nearest the point of delivery specified herein shall be destroyed by fire or other cause before delivery hereunder is completed, Buyer may at its option by written notice to Seller either terminate this agreement as to all fruit then undelivered or designate another reasonable place for its delivery, such added expense, however, as may be involved in making delivery at such other designated delivery point shall be paid by Buyer. If, before delivery hereunder is completed, quarantine, embargo or other laws, regulations or restrictions of any governmental authority or any strike of employees of Buyer or of transportation companies or other labor disturbance or failure of transportation companies to provide cars sufficient for Buyer's business or the Panama Canal being closed to passage of vessels or any other cause beyond Buyer's control shall prevent or substantially interfere with the business of the Buyer or with its receiving, handling, packing or shipping such fruit (or fruit of like kind) or would prevent or substantially interfere with the admission of such fruit into any substantial European market or into any ten or more states of the United States, or would render any such fruit subject to detention, seizure or condemnation, Buyer at its option by written notice to Seller may either postpone the time for delivery hereunder for such period, not exceeding ninety days, as such causes of prevention or interference shall operate or terminate this contract as to all fruit then undelivered. If before delivery hereunder is completed, any strike of employees of Seller or of transportation companies or other labor disturbance or any other cause beyond Seller's control shall prevent or substantially interfere with Seller completing delivery hereunder, the time for completion of such delivery shall be deemed extended for such period not exceeding ninety days, as such cause of prevention or interference shall operate. If in any case above provided for, delivery cannot be made or received within ninety days after the time specified for such delivery, the rights and obligations of both parties hereunder shall terminate (without liability on either party) with respect to any fruit not then delivered.

9. Should the Federal Government fix a maximum price for any kind of fruit herein contracted for (a) to be paid to the grower or (b) to be charged to itself or to the jobbing trade, which shall be or represent less than the price herein specified then the price in this contract is to be reduced, in case (a) to the price so fixed and in case (b) to a price based on and having proper relation to the price so fixed.

10. BOXES (CONTAINERS): If Buyer has furnished boxes or other containers to be used for delivery of dried figs covered by this contract, Seller hereby agrees that such containers will be used for no other purpose, and further agrees, unless otherwise specified, to return all such containers at the time and point of completion of delivery hereunder. Title to containers shall remain in the name of Buyer at all times. Seller to be charged the reasonable cost to Buyer of all containers lost, damaged or destroyed by any cause whatsoever or not returned at the time of payment for the dried figs covered by this contract, also expense which may be incurred by Buyer in repairing, replacing, recovering or attempting to recover the same, said cost and expense to be payable when delivery is completed.

11. Should the State or Federal Government limit the quantity or quality of fruit Seller may deliver or Buyer may accept, then the provisions of this contract shall be modified in accordance with such limitations.

12. Figs delivered hereunder shall be certified as "Marketable Figs" and shall be deliverable to processors in conformance with the rules and regulations of the Marketing Program for Figs as issued by the Program Committee of Fig Zone Number One. Buyer shall not pay for figs which are not so certificated as "Marketable Figs," and is authorized to hold such figs for disposition in accordance with Rules and Regulations of the Marketing Program for Figs. In accordance with rules and regulations governing the operation of the Surplus Pool under the Marketing Program for Figs, the Seller hereby transfers and conveys title to 50% of the certificated Black Mission figs to the Program Committee and authorizes said Committee to take possession of same in accordance with rules and regulations of said Marketing Program for Figs. Buyer shall not be liable for any loss or damage to figs with respect to which title passes to the Program Committee unless occasioned by his own act.

13. Buyer agrees to make payment for the figs accepted hereunder (and not deliverable to Program Committee of Fig Zone No. 1 under paragraph 11 hereof) upon completion of delivery in full.

14. Time is of the essence of this contract.

15. If any controversy shall arise hereunder between the parties hereto, such controversy shall be determined by arbitration before the Dried Fruit Association of California in accordance with its rules, and the determination thereof on such arbitration shall be binding and conclusive upon the parties hereto.

16. If, when any fruit is delivered by Seller, any Federal or State law, or any marketing agreement, code, license or other action, made, adopted, issued or taken under any such law, shall by its terms or operation require Buyer or Seller to withhold from immediate sale, or to hold for or deliver to any Control Board or other agency, any part or percentage of such fruit, or any weight of other or like fruit, or to make any payment out of the purchase price or otherwise to any such agency, this contract shall be subject to such requirements, and any such withholding, holding, delivery or payment may be done or made by Buyer at Seller's expense and for Seller's account, except as otherwise provided in paragraph 13 hereof.

17. In making settlement for any lot or lots of certificated figs delivered hereunder, Seller hereby authorizes Buyer to make deductions in the amounts and for the purposes specified below and to remit same to the designated agencies:

(1) One dollar and seventy-five cents ($1.75) per ton to the California Fig Institute to promote the general welfare of the California Fig industry, and to develop research in improved cultural practices and by-products utilization.

(2) One dollar and twenty-five cents ($1.25) per ton to the Marketing Programs for Figs for the issuance of Secondary Certificates as required for "Marketable Figs."

(3) Sixty cents ($.60) per ton to the California Fig Institute as Seller's portion of industry advertising fund.

---

goods on the carrier.[42] If the term is F.O.B. point of destination, the seller bears the expense and risk of transporting the goods to and tendering delivery of them at destination.[43]

2. *F.A.S. Terms:* F.A.S. ("free alongside") vessel at a named port requires the seller at his expense and risk to deliver the goods alongside the vessel at the named port of embarkation in the manner usual in that port or on a dock designated by the buyer.[44]

3. *Ex-Ship:* A term for delivery of goods "ex-ship" ("from the carrying vessel") requires the seller to see the goods through unloading at the named port of destination at his expense and risk.[45]

4. *C.I.F. and C. & F. Terms:* These are used in international trade. C.I.F. means the price includes in a lump sum the cost of the goods and the insurance and freight to the named destination.[46] The seller has risk of loss until the goods are loaded on the carrier and he has paid freight and obtained insurance in favor of the buyer to destination.[47] The buyer may prefer to place the insurance himself. Here C. & F. is used. The rules are the same as for C.I.F. contracts except that the price does not include and the seller is not required to obtain insurance.[48] Under C.I.F. and C. & F. terms, unless otherwise agreed the buyer must pay for the goods upon presentation to him of proper documents by the seller; that is, upon presentation of a bill of lading, freight receipt, and in C.I.F. contracts, an insurance certificate.[49] This means the buyer may be required to pay for the goods substantially in advance of receipt.

• As indicated above, the ordinary CIF contract is a "cash against documents" transaction, requiring the buyer to pay on presentation of the documents although the goods are still at sea. The parties may agree, however, that the buyer need not pay until arrival of the goods. In such case, unlike the ordinary CIF contract, the buyer is entitled to inspect the goods before paying.[50]

5. *No Arrival, No Sale:* Under a term "no arrival, no sale," the seller bears risk of loss to destination but is not liable for non-delivery resulting from hazards of transportation, and, if he is a reselling seller (a seller reselling goods bought by him as shipped by another) and this fact is known to the buyer, he is not liable for the failure of the underlying seller to ship or for the failure of the underlying seller to ship conforming goods.[51] If the goods are partially destroyed in transit, the buyer at his option may accept the balance and pay a prorated price.[52]

Other Transactions: The Code establishes rules for passage of title in a variety of special cases, as shown below. Presumably risk of loss passes on delivery of goods, under Section 2509(3), except in the cases of bailed goods and sales on approval and sale or return, which have their special rules, shown below.

GROWING CROPS AND YOUNG OF ANIMALS. Title may be passed to future crops as of the time they are planted or otherwise become growing crops; to young of animals as of the time they are conceived.[53]

GOODS TO BE SEVERED FROM REALTY. (1) If they are to be severed by the seller, title may be passed to minerals or to a structure or its materials to be removed from realty as of the time of severance.[54] (2) Title to identified timber may be passed at the time of contracting.[55] (3) The transaction must be recorded if the buyer is to be protected against good faith purchasers.[56]

FUNGIBLE GOODS. Title may be passed to an undivided share of identified fungible goods.[57] A seller may sell "2,000 bushels from" or "one-third of" a quantity of corn.[58] Seller

---

[42]U.C.C. 2319(1)(c).

[43]U.C.C. 2319(1)(b).

[44]U.C.C. 2319(2)(a).

[45]U.C.C. 2322.

[46]U.C.C. 2320(1).

[47]U.C.C. 2320(2).

[48]U.C.C. 2320(1)(3).

[49]U.C.C. 2320(4).

[50]U.C.C. 2321(3).

[51]U.C.C. 2324(b) and Official Comment 1, 2613.

[52]U.C.C. 2613(b).

[53]U.C.C. 2105(1), 2501(1)(c).

[54]U.C.C. 2107(1).

[55]U.C.C. 2107(2).

[56]U.C.C. 2107(3).

[57]U.C.C. 2105(4).

[58]U.C.C. 2105(4).

and buyer become owners in common of the quantity in proportion to their interests.[59]

PART INTEREST IN IDENTIFIED GOODS. Title may be passed to a part interest in existing identified goods,[60] for example, to a one-third interest in a mixed lot of furniture. The underlying theory here, and in the case of fungible goods, is that the sale is not of goods but of an *interest in* goods.

BAILED GOODS. Goods may be in possession of a third party bailee at the time of sale, for example, a warehouseman or processor. Risk of loss passes when a document of title covering the goods is delivered to the buyer or the bailee "attorns" to the buyer, that is, recognizes him as owner, as by doing something to the goods on the buyer's behalf such as cleaning or packaging them at the buyer's direction.[61]

SALE ON APPROVAL AND SALE OR RETURN. If goods are delivered to a purchaser for use rather than resale, on terms allowing him a trial period or permitting him to return the goods if he decides not to buy them, the transaction is a *sale on approval.*[62] Title and risk of loss do not pass to the buyer until he accepts the goods, which he does if he accepts part of them, or if, within the time agreed, or if no time is agreed within a reasonable time, he fails to notify the seller of election to return the goods.[63] If the buyer elects to return the goods, return is at the seller's risk and expense.[64] Ordinarily goods held on approval are not subject to claims of the buyer's creditors until acceptance.[65]

• If goods are delivered to a purchaser for resale on terms allowing him to return the goods or the unsold portion thereof, which is a transaction referred to as "on consignment" or "on memorandum," the transaction is a *sale or return.*[66] Risk of loss is on the buyer until return of the goods, which is at the buyer's expense.[67] The goods are subject to claims of the buyer's creditors unless they know he is accustomed to receive goods on consignment or a financing statement is filed under Division 9 of the code.[68]

Insurable Interest in Goods

The buyer obtains an insurable interest in goods when they are identified to the contract. In the absence of explicit agreement, identification occurs: (1) When the contract is made if it is for the sale of goods already existing and identified; (2) When goods are shipped, marked or otherwise designated by the seller as goods to which the contract refers, if the contract is for the sale of future goods; (3) When crops are planted or otherwise become growing crops, or the young are conceived, if the contract is for the sale of unborn young of animals to be born within 12 months after contracting or for the sale of crops to be harvested within 12 months or the next normal harvest season.[69]

---

[59]U.C.C. 2105(4).

[60]U.C.C. 2105(3).

[61]U.C.C. 2509(2).

[62]U.C.C. 2326(1)(a).

[63]U.C.C. 2327(1)(a)(b), 1204(3).

[64]U.C.C. 2327(1)(c).

[65]U.C.C. 2326(2).

[66]U.C.C. 2326(1)(b).

[67]U.C.C. 2327(2)(b).

[68]U.C.C. 2326(3). See page 137 re financing statements.

[69]U.C.C. 2501(1).

• The seller retains an insurable interest in goods so long as title to or any security interest in the goods remains in him, and when identification is by seller alone he may, until default or insolvency or notification to the buyer that the identification is final, substitute other goods for those identified.[70]

Good Faith Purchasers and Creditors

Basically one can transfer only such title to goods as he has. If B steals goods from A and sells them to C, C, although he is a good faith purchaser, will not get title because B does not have title.

• Sometimes one makes it appear that another is the owner of goods, which the apparent owner then sells to a good faith purchaser. In such case the owner may be estopped to assert his rights. This is the doctrine of *apparent ownership*, which is another application of the doctrine of estoppel. This requires guilty conduct on the part of the owner sufficient in the eyes of the law to warrant shifting the loss to him. A lends an article to B who sells it to C, a good faith purchaser. A will be permitted to recover from C. As a matter of social policy it would be unreasonable to make A suffer the loss in such a case, although admittedly, by entrusting the article to B, A has created the appearance of ownership in B. But if, in the presence of A and C, B represents himself to be the owner of the article and A remains silent, A will probably be estopped to assert his rights if, subsequently, B sells the article to C. There is now a plus factor, sufficient as a matter of social policy to warrant shifting the loss to A.

• U.C.C. 2403 is the code provision covering the protection of good faith purchasers, which is analyzed below. It is supplemented by Section 1103, which preserves the doctrine of estoppel, and of apparent ownership, discussed above; also the doctrine of ostensible agency, by which a principal will be estopped to assert lack of authority of an agent to sell property where the agent has been invested with apparent authority to do so.[71]

Purchase From One Without Title

Here, as shown above, the purchaser, even though acting in good faith, gets no title in the absence of estoppel.[72] Thus the purchaser from a thief gets no title and the purchaser from a borrower or other bailee gets no title in the absence of estoppel.

Purchase From One With Voidable Title

U.C.C. 2403 provides:

"(1) A person with voidable title has power to transfer a good title to a good faith purchaser for value. When goods have been delivered under a transaction of purchase the purchaser has such power even though

"(a) The transferor was deceived as to the identity of the purchaser, or

"(b) The delivery was in exchange for a check which is later dishonored, or

---

[70]U.C.C. 2501(2).

[71]U.C.C. 2403(1), Official Comment 1 ["the policy of this Act expressly providing for the application of supplementary general principles of law to sales transactions wherever appropriate (U.C.C. 1103) joins with the present section (U.C.C. 2403) to continue unimpaired all rights acquired under the law of agency or of apparent agency or ownership or other estoppel, whether based on statutory provisions or on case law principles."] See note 75.

[72]U.C.C. 2403(1).

"(c) It was agreed that the transaction was to be a 'cash sale,' or
"(d) The delivery was procured through fraud punishable as larcenous under the criminal law."

These provisions are now examined.

Goods Purchased From Minor or Incompetent: Where goods are purchased from a minor or mental incompetent, the latter generally may avoid the transaction. The buyer therefore gets voidable title. If he sells to a good faith purchaser, the purchaser is protected under U.C.C. 2403(1), above. The policy of protecting minors and incompetents is made to give way to the need to preserve the security of commercial transactions.

Impostors: U.C.C. 2403(1)(a), above, deals with the impostor case. To induce A to sell goods, B represents himself to be C, a responsible person. The precode law was that the seller, A, had a "dual intention" in such case, to sell to C, but also to sell to the person he thought was C, B; that if there was face-to-face imposture the "dominant intention" of the seller was to sell to the person standing before him, B, who therefore got voidable title and could transfer good title to a good faith purchaser. If imposture were by mail, on the other hand, it was held that the seller's "dominant intention" was to sell to the person he thought B to be, C; that therefore B did not get title and could convey none. Unfortunately, U.C.C. 2403(1)(a) does not make it clear whether it applies to imposture by mail as well as face-to-face imposture.[73] Where B merely represents himself to be the agent of C, precode law was that the impostor got and could pass no title. Presumably this would continue to be the rule under the code.

Payment by Worthless Check; "Cash Sale": A sells goods to B, "terms cash." The commercial understanding in this case is that A may take a check. A does so, and immediately presents the check, which proves to be worthless. Meantime B has sold the goods to C, a good faith purchaser. U.C.C. 2403(1)(b)(c) protects the good faith purchaser.

Fraud Punishable as Larceny: Prior to the code, some courts held that where goods were obtained by fraud which amounted to larceny under criminal law, the person acquiring the goods by fraud got no title and therefore could pass none. Subsection (1)(d) of Section 2403 is designed to reject such decisions, and the good faith purchaser for value from the fraud-committing party gets title.

Purchase From Dealer

U.C.C. 2403 provides further:

"(2) Any entrusting of possession of goods to a merchant who deals in goods of that kind gives him power to transfer all rights of the entruster to a buyer in the ordinary course of business.
"(3) 'Entrusting' includes any delivery and any acquiescence in retention of possession *for the purpose of sale, obtaining offers to purchase, locating a buyer, or the like,* regardless of any condition expressed between the parties to the delivery or acquiescence and regardless of whether the procurement of the entrusting or the possessor's disposition of the goods have been such as to be larcenous under the criminal law."

• A deposits an item of goods with B, a merchant who deals in such goods, new and used. Deposit is subject to the agreement that B is to seek a purchaser of the goods but is not to sell them without A's approval of the sale and price. Without

consulting A, B sells to C, a buyer in the ordinary course of business.[74] C prevails under U.C.C. 2403(2)(3), above.[75]
• A "consigns" goods to B, or deposits them with him "on memorandum," for sale by B. Under U.C.C. 2403(2)(3), a buyer in the ordinary course of business takes free of any claim of A.
• California varies significantly from the Official Text here. The italicized words in the quotation of Section 2403 are a California addition, and a limitation of the code. The italicized words are not included in the Official Text. The difference is demonstrated by a case of bailment: A deposits grain in B's warehouse. B warehouses and buys and sells grain. B wrongfully sells A's grain to C. C would prevail under the Official Text[76] but not under the California variation.

Creditors of Seller

Where the buyer leaves the seller in possession of goods purchased by the buyer, state law may make the transaction a fraud on the seller's creditors and void. Section 2402(2) recognizes this. It makes the exception that retention of possession by a merchant-seller for a commercially reasonable time after sale is not fraudulent.

Rights and Remedies of Seller and Buyer in the Event of Failure or Prospective Failure of Performance

The code provides extensive protection to each party, seller and buyer, against the other's default or prospective default. The rights and remedies accorded by the code are now considered.

Rights and Remedies of Seller

The code attempts to make its rights and remedies "commercial," that is, of a kind that provide intelligent solutions for the problems of the commercial world. In this connection the code gives the seller the right to "cure" a nonconforming delivery, seen below, which is a novel statutory right. It also gives the seller the right of resale, also seen below, which permits the seller, in the event of the buyer's default, to resell the goods and to recover from the buyer the difference between the resale price and the contract price.

Anticipatory Repudiation: If either party repudiates the contract before time for performance arrives the other may bring an action for anticipatory breach.[77] The repudiating party may retract his repudiation unless the aggrieved party has materially changed position or has indicated that he considers the repudiation final (by suing for anticipatory breach).[78]

Assurance of Performance: When either party has reasonable grounds to believe that the other party may not perform,

---

[73]Compare U.C.C. 3405(1)(a), which deals with the same problem in negotiable instruments and spells out the fact.

[74]See U.C.C. 1201(9) for definition of buyer in ordinary course of business. Note that purchase may be for cash or on credit.

[75]The same result is reached under modern agency law. If one "delivers a chattel to a dealer in such chattels to be sold or exhibited for sale, an unauthorized sale of the chattel by such dealer in accordance with normal business practices to one who reasonably believes the dealer to be the owner, binds the owner, although the dealer was not authorized to sell it without the consent of the owner or was not authorized to sell it to the person to whom it was sold or at the price at which it was sold." Restatement of Agency 2d, §§ 175, 201.

[76]U.C.C. 2403(2)(3), Official Comment 2; U.C.C. 7205.

[77]U.C.C. 2610.

[78]U.C.C. 2611(1).

he may make written demand for adequate assurance of performance and may suspend performance until he receives it.[79] The code does not attempt to define "adequate assurance." Its official comments offer various guidelines.[80] The matter is to be determined by commercial rather than legal standards. In a given case a buyer's submission of a good credit report from his banker may be sufficient. In another case a party may be entitled to the posting of a guaranty of performance. Failure to provide adequate assurance of performance within a reasonable time after receipt of justified demand constitutes repudiation of the contract.[81]

Insolvency of Buyer: Where the seller discovers that the buyer is insolvent he may refuse delivery except for cash, including payment for all goods theretofore delivered, and stop delivery.[82]

Where the seller discovers that the buyer has received goods on credit while insolvent he may reclaim the goods upon demand made within 10 days after the receipt.[83] The 10-day limitation does not apply if, within 3 months of delivery, the buyer has, in writing, misrepresented his solvency to the seller.[84]

Stoppage in Transit: Upon discovery of the buyer's insolvency, the seller (or a financing agency which has a security interest in the goods[85]) may stop delivery of the goods in the possession of a carrier or warehouseman.[86] Also he may stop delivery of carload lots if the buyer repudiates the contract or fails to make a payment due before delivery.[87] If a negotiable document of title has been issued for the goods, the carrier or warehouseman is not obliged to obey a stop order until surrender of the document.[88] The "transit" period within which a stop order may be given is defined by U.C.C. 2705(2).

"Cure": Where the seller delivers nonconforming goods, U.C.C. 2508 gives him an opportunity to avoid breach by substituting conforming goods. U.C.C. 2508 provides that (1) when a nonconforming tender is made and rejected and time for performance has not expired, the seller may notify the buyer of intention to cure and may then within the contract time make a conforming delivery; (2) if the seller had reasonable grounds to believe that the nonconforming tender would be acceptable, he may cure the tender within a reasonable time even though the time for performance has expired.

Remedies Upon Wrongful Rejection by Buyer: The seller has the following remedies in the case of wrongful rejection of goods by the buyer:

RESALE. Under U.C.C. 2706, whether or not title has passed to the buyer, the seller may resell the goods if the buyer wrongfully refuses to accept them. If the seller resells in a commercially reasonable manner, he may recover from the buyer the difference between the resale price and the contract price. The seller is not accountable to the buyer for profit made on such resale. (This is the seller's counterpart of the buyer's remedy of "cover," infra.)

DAMAGES FOR NONACCEPTANCE OR REPUDIATION. The seller need not resort to the remedy of resale, just considered, if the buyer fails to accept delivery or repudiates the contract. Instead, the seller may, if the sale is of a specific lot of goods, recover from the buyer damages equal to the difference between the market price at the time and place of delivery and the contract price.[89] If the sale is from a constant and recurring inventory of goods rather than a sale of a specific lot of goods, the seller may recover the profit he would have made on the sale.[90]

ACTION FOR PRICE. Where the buyer fails to pay for goods, the seller can recover the purchase price of (1) goods theretofore delivered to the buyer or to which risk of loss has passed to the buyer; and (2) goods identified to the contract if, after reasonable efforts, the seller is unable to resell them.[91]

Rights and Remedies of Buyer

Buyer, like seller, is given a full complement of rights and remedies, as shown below. The most dynamic area of the modern law of sales is the area of "products liability," which involves the matter of the seller's liability for injuries suffered by the buyer as the result of defective goods supplied by the seller. While the warranty provisions of the code, not yet seen, are designed to deal with this matter, the modern California law, which is a leader in the field, goes much beyond them. For this reason the discussion of warranty and of the California law of products liability is placed at the end of the material on sales, following the present topic of the rights and remedies of the buyer.

Anticipatory Repudiation: As shown earlier, under seller's rights and remedies, the buyer, like the seller, has an action for anticipatory breach if the seller repudiates the contract before the time for performance arrives.[92]

Assurance of Performance: Like the seller, the buyer is given the right to adequate assurance of performance when he has reasonable grounds to believe that he may not receive performance. See the discussion of this matter at page 91-92.

Insolvency of Seller: If the buyer has paid part of the price and the goods have been identified to the contract, the buyer may recover the goods by tendering the balance if the seller becomes insolvent within 10 days after receipt of the part payment.[93]

Inspection: Except where the transaction is C.O.D. or cash against documents (C.I.F.), the buyer has the right to inspect the goods before accepting or paying for them.[94] If the goods do not conform to the contract, the buyer may reject them.[95]

Rejection of Nonconforming Goods: If goods tendered by the seller fail in any respect to conform to the contract, the buyer may reject the whole, accept the whole, or accept any commercial unit or units and reject the rest.[96] This is the

[79]U.C.C. 2610.

[80]U.C.C. 2609, Official Comments 3, 4.

[81]U.C.C. 2609(4). See 2610-2611 re "repudiation."

[82]U.C.C. 2702(1).

[83]U.C.C. 2702(2).

[84]U.C.C. 2702(2).

[85]U.C.C. 2707.

[86]U.C.C. 2705(1).

[87]U.C.C. 2705(1).

[88]U.C.C. 2705(3)(c).

[89]U.C.C. 2708(1).

[90]U.C.C. 2708(2).

[91]U.C.C. 2709(1).

[92]U.C.C. 2610.

[93]U.C.C. 2502.

[94]U.C.C. 2513(1)(3).

[95]U.C.C. 2601. See 2603-2604 re buyer's rights and duties after rejection.

[96]U.C.C. 2601.

code's "*perfect tender rule*" which, except in installment contracts,[96a] requires the goods to conform exactly, not merely substantially, to the contract.

• U.C.C. 2602-2604 set out the following requirements for rightful rejection: (1) Rejection must be within a reasonable time after delivery of the goods. (2) Seasonable notice must be given to the seller. (3) If the buyer has taken possession of the goods before rejection, he must hold them with reasonable care at the seller's disposition. (4) A merchant-buyer must follow reasonable instructions of the seller to reship, store, or resell. If no instructions are given, the buyer must make reasonable efforts to sell for seller's account if the goods are perishable or threaten to decline in value. If the goods are not perishable and are not threatening to decline in value speedily, the buyer may resell them for the seller's account or return them to the seller or store them for the seller's account.

Acceptance and Revocation of Acceptance: "*Acceptance*" of goods occurs when the buyer after reasonable opportunity to inspect signifies that the goods are conforming or that he will take or retain them in spite of nonconformity; fails to make an effective rejection; or does any act inconsistent with the seller's ownership.[97] Acceptance of a part of any commercial unit is acceptance of that entire unit.[98]

Upon acceptance, the seller becomes entitled to the contract price.[99] However the buyer may revoke his acceptance in certain cases, shown below, and acceptance does not take away from the buyer his right to damages for breach of contract or for breach of warranty.[100]

Revocation of acceptance by the buyer is permitted with respect to any nonconforming lot or commercial unit whose nonconformity substantially impairs its value to the buyer if the buyer has accepted it on the reasonable assumption that nonconformity would be cured and it has not been, or without discovery of the nonconformity if acceptance was reasonably induced either by difficulty of discovery before acceptance or by the seller's assurances of conformity.[101] Revocation of acceptance must occur within a reasonable time after the buyer discovers or should have discovered grounds for it and before any substantial change in condition of the goods not caused by their own defects.[102] It is not effective until the buyer notifies the seller of it.[103] A buyer who revokes has the same rights and duties with regard to the goods as a buyer who rejects.[104]

The right to revoke acceptance is, potentially, important consumer law as it is quite slowly coming to be realized. Potentially, the right to revoke acceptance is an important "antilemon" remedy in favor of the consumer who gets the lemon automobile, which can never be made right, or some other form of incurably unsatisfactory merchandise. Case law has been coming to recognize that the consumer can give back the lemon and get back his money under Section 2608.

"Cover": If the seller fails to make delivery or repudiates the contract or the buyer rightfully rejects goods or justifiably revokes an acceptance of them, the buyer may "*cover*" by purchasing substitute goods, and may then recover from the seller, as damages, the difference between the contract price and the cost of the substitute goods.[105]

Damages for Nondelivery or Repudiation: Instead of "covering," buyer may recover from the seller damages equal to the difference between the market price and the contract price.[106]

Specific Performance: The buyer may obtain specific performance where goods are unique or in other proper circumstances, for example, where the buyer is not able to "cover."[107]

Right of Action Against Third Party for Injury to Goods

Where a third party wrongfully injures goods identified to a contract for sale, the third party may be sued by the party having title to the goods or a party having a security interest or an insurable interest in them.[108] If the party suing did not have risk of loss at the time of the injury, he holds the amount recovered for the benefit of the party having risk of loss to the extent that the party actually suffers loss as a result of the injury to the goods.[109]

Warranties and Products Liability Law

In the law of sales, a *warranty* is an obligation incurred by the seller with respect to the character or quality of or title to the goods. Warranties may be express, resulting from a representation or promise concerning the goods, or implied. Implied warranties are warranties which the law attaches to a sale without regard to whether the seller has made a representation or promise concerning the goods.

In earlier times the doctrine of *caveat emptor* (let the buyer beware) was followed,[110] under which one bought goods at his risk, having no recourse if they proved defective, unless the seller was guilty of fraud. By the time of the adoption of the Uniform Sales Act the doctrine had become a disfavored one and the contrary doctrine, *caveat venditor*, was adopted by the Sales Act by the inclusion of implied warranties of quality. These are continued and enlarged by the code.

Warranty law, as it has developed in American law, has dealt with two quite distinct kinds of problems—the case of the buyer who is cheated in some way because the goods do not measure up to reasonable expectations, and the case of the buyer, or other person, who is injured in some way because the goods are defective. Under the code, warranty doctrine continues to be extended to both kinds of cases. Under the code a buyer may recover for any "injury to person or property proximately resulting from any breach of warranty,"[111] as may members of his family or household and guests

[96a]U.C.C. 2612.
[97]U.C.C. 2606(1).
[98]U.C.C. 2606(2).
[99]U.C.C. 2607.
[100]U.C.C. 2607.
[101]U.C.C. 2608(1).
[102]U.C.C. 2608(2).
[103]U.C.C. 2608(2).
[104]U.C.C. 2608(3).

[105]U.C.C. 2712.
[106]U.C.C. 2713(1).
[107]U.C.C. 2716(1).
[108]U.C.C. 2722(a).
[109]U.C.C. 2722(b).
[110]But also, no doubt then as now, the practical doctrine that "the customer is always right."
[111]U.C.C. 2714-2715.

in his home.[112] However modern American law is rapidly developing a body of tort law to deal with products liability, that is, liability for persons or property injured by defective goods, and this *products liability law* is rapidly leaving behind the more cumbersome and less satisfactory law of warranty. The California Supreme Court has been a leader in the development of products liability law and it is case law and not the code that is the important products liability law of this state.

In the sections that follow conventional warranty doctrine, as it is enunciated by the code, is examined, then products liability law as it has been conceived by the California court.

Express Warranties

These are provided for by U.C.C. 2313, as follows:

"(1) Express warranties by the seller are created as follows:

"(a) Any affirmation of fact or promise made by the seller to the buyer which relates to the goods and becomes part of the basis of the bargain creates an express warranty that the goods shall conform to the affirmation or promise.

"(b) Any description of the goods which is made part of the basis of the bargain creates an express warranty that the goods shall conform to the description.

"(c) Any sample or model which is made part of the basis of the bargain creates an express warranty that the whole of the goods shall conform to the sample or model.

"(2) It is not necessary to the creation of an express warranty that the seller use formal words such as 'warrant' or 'guarantee' or that he have a specific intention to make a warranty, but an affirmation merely of the value of the goods or a statement purporting to be merely the seller's opinion or commendation of the goods does not create a warranty."

U.C.C. 2313, above, provides for four kinds of express warranties; warranties by affirmation, promise, description and sample.

Promissory Warranties ["promise(s) relat(ing) to the goods"]: These consist of guarantees of quality, life or performance, and are identified by formal words such as "warrant" or "guarantee," but need not be. U.C.C. 2313(2), above. They are common in sales of hard goods and automobiles, where they take the form of a document which will be entitled "Warranty" or "Warranty Contract," for example, the new car warranty, which provides in essential part: "The .... Motor Company warrants all such parts of new automobiles, except tires, for a period of .... months from the date of original delivery to the purchaser or before such vehicle has been driven .... miles, whichever event shall first occur, as shall, under normal use and service, appear to have been defective in workmanship or material."

Other Express Warranties: "Any affirmation of fact" is an express warranty, says U.C.C. 2313(1)(a), above, which makes possible an infinite variety of such warranties—oral statements of fact concerning the goods; written statements on containers, labels or tags attached to goods; representations made in advertisements. So long as the affirmation is one of *fact* it is a warranty—"sterling silver," "100% wool," "sanforized"—and if the article is not as represented the seller is guilty of breach of warranty. In most cases, these would also constitute "description(s) of the goods," which would qualify them as express warranties on that account.

Oral Representations in Connection with Written Contracts: As has been indicated, express warranties may be made orally. This raises a problem where the contract is finalized in writing. Suppose that, in negotiations for sale, S informs B that a machine will produce X units per hour. The sale is consummated by written contract that says nothing about this. The machine does not produce X units per hour for B. May he rescind? Not unless he can show fraud; that S knew the machine would not perform as represented. The *parol evidence rule*[113] is applicable, which forbids variation of a written contract by oral agreement. It is only when the writing is intended to operate as the entire agreement of the parties that the parol evidence rule is a bar, however, and the fact that writings attend the transaction, for example, a letter ordering and a bill for goods, does not preclude evidence of an oral warranty.

Opinions and Commendations: Mere opinions and commendatory statements do not constitute warranties. U.C.C. 2313(2), above. Sellers are given considerable latitude in the matter of "puffing talk" or "seller's talk"—this is the "best on the market;" this will "sell like hot cakes." So long as they do not misrepresent fact they are on safe ground. In case of doubt however a statement will be treated as one of "fact," as in *Turner* v. *Central Hardware Co.*, 353 Mo. 1182, 186 S.W.2d 603, where advertisement of ladders as "safe" and "strong" was held to give rise to an express warranty of safety and soundness.

Warranty of Title and Against Infringement

A seller warrants good title to the goods sold and, if he is a dealer in such goods, that no claim of infringement of a patent or trademark by a third party will mar the buyer's title.[114]

Implied Warranty of Merchantability

U.C.C. 2314 provides for and defines this warranty as follows:

"(1) Unless excluded or modified (Section 2316), a warranty that the goods shall be merchantable is implied in a contract for their sale if the seller is a merchant with respect to goods of that kind. Under this section the serving for value of food or drink to be consumed either on the premises or elsewhere is a sale.

"(2) Goods to be merchantable must be at least such as

"(a) Pass without objection in the trade under the contract description; and

"(b) In the case of fungible goods, are of fair average quality within the description; and

"(c) Are fit for the ordinary purposes for which such goods are used; and

"(d) Run, within the variations permitted by the agreement, of even kind, quality and quantity within each unit and among all units involved; and

---

[112]U.C.C. 2318 (not adopted in California).

The Official Text offers two alternative versions of Section 2318, one or the other of which has been adopted in a number of states. Under these alternatives warranty liability is extended to "any person" who may reasonably be expected to "use, consume or be affected by the goods," and is not limited to family members, household members and household guests as it is by the original version of Section 2-318. Under one of these alternatives, warranty liability is made to include liability for both personal injuries and property damage; under the other, it is made to include liability only for personal injuries. Under these alternatives, warranty liability would extend to "bystanders" (as discussed later in the text), which it does not under the original version.

---

[113]Page 46.

[114]U.C.C. 2312. While this warranty attaches automatically and is therefore an "implied" warranty, the code refrains from calling it such because it would then become subject to the rule of U.C.C. 2316(3)(a), which is not intended.

"(e) Are adequately contained, packaged, and labeled as the agreement may require; and

"(f) Conform to the promises or affirmations of fact made on the container or label if any."

The predecessor of this warranty under the Uniform Sales Act has been important and highly versatile. It has been given wide application by the courts and is considered to require goods to be free of defects and harmful elements, of usual quality and fit for the general purposes for which sold. It has been applied to such a variety of defects, to mention but a few, as defective parts in machinery, failure of cloth to hold color, a pin in a loaf of bread, and injurious pharmaceuticals and cosmetics. If anything, the code's warranty is broader and will therefore be at least as versatile.

Implied Warranty of Fitness for Particular Purpose

U.C.C. 2315:

"Where the seller at the time of contracting has reason to know any particular purpose for which the goods are required and that the buyer is relying on the seller's skill or judgment to select or furnish suitable goods, there is unless excluded or modified under the next section an implied warranty that the goods shall be fit for such purpose."

Where the warranty of merchantability warrants the general utility of goods, the warranty of fitness assures their suitability for a particular purpose for which they are known to be purchased. Thus cable capable of carrying 110 volts, though of the best quality, is not fit for the purposes of a buyer who announces that he wants cable for "220 wiring." A furnace capable of heating 5 rooms, although of the finest construction is not fit for the purpose of a buyer who asks for "a furnace capable of heating a 7 room house." The warranty of fitness has also been given wide application.[115]

Merchantability and Fitness Compared Further

Sometimes both warranties are breached. This is the case with defective food and drugs. Contaminated food or food containing an injurious substance such as glass is not merchantable and is not fit for its particular purpose, human consumption.

Sometimes neither warranty is breached. For example, in *Smith Company* v. *Fisher Plastics Corp.*, 76 Fed.Supp. 641, B purchased plastic from S to manufacture arctic boots. B did not tell S of the intended use. The plastic cracked in subzero weather. B had no action for breach of warranty. There would be no breach of the warranty of merchantability because the plastic was suitable for ordinary purposes such as the manufacture of toys or of women's purses. On the other hand, there would be no breach of the warranty of fitness because the seller did not know of the buyer's particular purpose, which knowledge is a condition of the warranty of fitness.

Food and Drugs; Privity

As shown above both the warranties of merchantability and fitness apply to sales of food and drugs. Large personal injury awards have been recovered for breach of warranty in this area, and more recently large recoveries have been made where new pharmaceuticals or serums have caused injury.[116]

● California has followed the *"foreign substance doctrine"* in sales of foods, which holds that the warranty of fitness is not breached by the presence in canned or packaged foods of something that is part of the product in its natural state, for example, by the presence of an olive pit in a can of pitted olives, or a piece of oyster shell in a can of oysters.[117] Under prior law this was justified on the ground that the warranty of fitness of the Uniform Sales Act required only that goods be "reasonably fit" for the buyer's purpose.[118] Since the code requires that the goods be "fit" (U.C.C. 2315, above) this doctrine may be rejected in future cases.

● The doctrine of "privity of warranty" has caused much difficulty in the field of warranty. Early in the development of the law of warranty it became established that only a party (the buyer) to the transaction which gave rise to the warranty could acquire warranty rights. Only he had "privity." This was an extension of the doctrine of privity of contract[119] to the field of warranty. Thus, while the consumer had privity with the retailer, he did not have privity with the manufacturer and could not recover from the manufacturer for breach of warranty although he could recover from the retailer. If the consumer served contaminated food to friends who were injured, they lacked privity with both retailer and manufacturer and could not recover from either for breach of warranty. They could recover from the manufacturer if they could show *negligence* in the preparation of the food but this is a more difficult case than one for breach of warranty, which requires only the showing of contamination and injury.

Later courts began to see the food and drugs case as an exceptional one; one in which personal injury, not mere money damage, would result from a defective product. To make recovery easier and thereby create a sanction which would induce careful preparation of food and drugs, they created artifices to overcome the privity requirement. The consumer bought the food as "agent" for his friends who therefore, as "principals," were the real parties to the transaction. The friends were "third party beneficiaries"[120] of the contract between retailer and consumer. Finally they declared openly, as a public policy rule in this area, that a person injured by foods or drugs would be permitted to recover from retailer or man-

---

[115]Animals. 224 N.W.93 (cows for dairy purposes).

Animal feed. 231 P. 621 (moldy feed).

Building materials. 192 S.W.2d 759 (roof coating for leaks).

Fixtures. 155 S.W.2d 892 (equipment for freezing and preserving ice cream).

Furnaces and heating equipment to provide heat for a given space. 136 Fed.2d 271; 51 N.E.2d 594.

Machinery or equipment for specific purposes or to perform to certain efficiencies. 57 Atl.2d 442; 230 N.Y.S. 529; 3 N.W.2d 471; 247 N.W.558; 148 S.W.2d 917.

Minerals. 59 N.Y.S.2d 547; 107 Atl. 713 (steel for manufacture of tools).

Paper products. 188 N.E. 223 (cardboard for candy boxes).

Seeds or plants. 50 Atl.2d 45 (seed potatoes).

Toiletries. 19 N.E.2d 697 (powder with irritants).

Vehicles. 167 Fed.2d 1005 (oil tank trailers).

[116]*Gottsdanker* v. *Cutter Laboratories* (1960) 182 C.A.2d 602, 6 C.R. 320 (defective polio vaccine).

[117]*Mix* v. *Ingersoll Candy Co.*, 6 C.2d 674, 59 P.2d 144 (no breach of warranty where chicken pie contained chicken bone), and *Silva* v. *Woolworth Co.*, 28 C.A.2d 649, 83 P.2d 76 (no breach where turkey bone in order of turkey and dressing). Compare: *Lane* v. *C. A. Swanson & Sons*, 130 C.A.2d 210, 278 P.2d 723 (description "Boned Chicken" on label, accompanied by advertising stating "no bones," held express warranty guaranteeing absolutely against bones).

[118]Uniform Sales Act, § 15(1).

[119]Page 51.

[120]Page 51.

ufacturer for breach of warranty, though lacking privity with such party.[121]

The Official Text abolishes the privity requirements to the extent of Section 2318, discussed earlier.

Disclaimer of Warranty

In an effort to limit or eliminate warranty liability, sellers insert disclaimer clauses in contracts of sale or print them on the containers in which their products are sold. Typical of the type of disclaimer that may be found on a container is the recital that "No warranties of any kind, express or implied, are made unless written hereon."

Basically this is permissible, but disclaimer clauses are not looked upon with favor by the courts and modern cases have ground them down considerably.

U.C.C. 2719 permits the seller to expressly limit remedies or damages but presumes that a limitation of damages for personal injuries suffered in the use of consumer goods is unconscionable and therefore unenforceable.

In the widely followed case of *Henningsen* v. *Bloomfield Motors, Inc.* 32 N.J. 358, 161 A.2d 69, it was held on grounds of public policy that a limitation of warranty liability to parts replacement in a new automobile warranty did not exonerate the manufacturer from liability to the purchaser's wife where, shortly after purchase, she was injured as the result of a defective steering mechanism.

U.C.C. 2316 lays down various rules as to what constitutes a disclaimer and what is necessary to effect a disclaimer. Its provision relieving the seller of defects which examination ought to have revealed is not to be taken very seriously. The Uniform Sales Act had a similar provision and it seldom operated to deprive the buyer of his warranty cause of action.[122] Courts have taken the position that the complex nature of modern goods is such that the layman is seldom capable of discovering defects by that degree of "reasonable examination" that he is able to make. Of course if he discovers a defect he does not buy.

Song-Beverly Consumer Warranty Act

In California, the Song-Beverly Consumer Warranty Act, contained in C.C. 1790-1795.7, imposes an implied warranty of merchantability on the *manufacturer* of consumer goods in favor of the retail buyer of such goods. The warranty arises either when the consumer goods are a new mobilhome, motor vehicle, machine, appliance, or like product sold for personal, family or household purposes, or when it is any other form of new goods or product, except soft goods or consumables, bought for personal, family or household purposes, the retail sale of which is accompanied by an express warranty. This warranty can be disclaimed only by a conspicuous writing attached to the goods which clearly informs the buyer, prior to the sale, in simple and concise language of each of the following: (1) The goods are being sold on an "as is" or "with all faults" basis; (2) the entire risk as to the quality and performance of the goods is with the buyer; and (3) the buyer assumes the entire cost of service or repair if the goods prove defective. The manufacturer cannot disclaim the implied warranty of merchantability at all if it has given an express warranty. The Song-Beverly Act provides that its provisions ov-

erride those of the California Uniform Commercial Code, where the two are in conflict, so the Song-Beverly manufacturer's implied warranty of merchantability cannot be avoided by a U.C.C. 2316 type of disclaimer. 1982 amendment of the Song-Beverly Act requires express warranties under the Act to conform to Magnuson-Moss requirements for disclosure of warranty terms and conditions, below.

Song-Beverly gives the buyer injured by breach of the manufacturer's implied warranty of merchantability, the breach of warranty remedies accorded by the Commercial Code, which would include the damages remedies provided for in U.C.C. 2714 and 2715. If the buyer prevails in a breach of warranty action, the buyer may recover attorney's fees in addition to damages and if the breach of warranty is proved to be wilful the buyer can recover a penalty of up to two times the amount of actual damages. C.C. 1794.

Song-Beverly also requires manufacturers of consumer goods who expressly warrant such goods sold in California to maintain, within the state, adequate service and repair facilities to carry out the terms of such warranties and to commence service and repair within a reasonable time after the goods have been presented for service or repair. If service and repair facilities are not maintained, the consumer purchaser may return the goods to the retail seller for repair or service and if repair or service cannot be obtained from the retail seller, the consumer purchaser is entitled to get back the purchase price of the goods. If the retail seller provides the repair or service, he is entitled to recover its cost from the manufacturer. If service and repair facilities are not maintained, the consumer purchaser may also, as an alternative to seeking service or repair from the retail seller, secure the services of an independent repair or service facility for the service or repair when service or repair can be economically accomplished. This alternative applies, however, only with respect to goods which have a wholesale price to the retailer of at least $50. The manufacturer is then liable to the independent repair or service facility for the reasonable value of the repairs or service.

If the manufacturer cannot service or repair the goods to conform to applicable express warranties after a reasonable number of attempts, the manufacturer must either replace the goods or reimburse the buyer in an amount equal to the purchase price paid by the buyer, less the amount attributable to use by the buyer prior to discovery of the nonconformity. C.C. 1793.2(e), enacted in 1982, sets up a special and somewhat complicated rule with respect to what constitutes "a reasonable number of attempts" to conform a new motor vehicle to applicable express warranties. A reasonable number of attempts is to be presumed if within one year from delivery to the buyer or 12,000 miles, whichever occurs first, either (1) the same nonconformity has been subject to repair four or more times by the manufacturer or its agents and the buyer has at least once directly notified the manufacturer of the need for repair of the nonconformity or (2) the vehicle is out of service by reason of repair of nonconformities by the manufacturer or its agents for a cumulative total of more than 30 calendar days since delivery of the vehicle to the buyer. However, the manufacturer may, under Section 1793.2(e) be able to force the buyer to participate in an arbitration-like procedure for settlement of the matter. "Nonconformity" is specially defined by Section 1793.2(e) to mean "a nonconformity which substantially impairs the use, value, or safety of the new motor vehicle" and, consistently with the Song-Beverly Act's operation as a consumer protection law, "new motor vehicle" is specially defined to mean "a new motor vehicle which is used or bought for use primarily for personal, fam-

---

[121]*Klein* v. *Duchess Sandwich Co.*, 14 C.2d 272, 93 P.2d 799, is the first California case to take this stand.

[122]*Grass* v. *Steinberg*, 331 Ill.App. 378, 73 N.E.2d 331, is one of the rare cases in which it did; but there, before purchase, the buyer had a lathe examined by some 8 different experts.

ily, or household purposes, but does not include motorcycles, motorhomes, or off-road vehicles.''

Truth in Warranties Act

The Magnuson-Moss Warranty Act of 1975 (15 U.S.C.A. §§ 2301-2312), popularly called the Truth in Warranties Act, is a federal statute designed mainly to require the consumer to be given accurate information regarding the quality of the warranty that the consumer is getting. The Act has had a profound effect on the *form* of warranties that are now issued in connection with the sales of consumer goods.

● The Act is designed to work in cooperation with state laws and not to the exclusion of such laws. In this regard, the Act provides that "Nothing in this (Act) . . . shall . . . supersede any provision of State law regarding injury, "thereby preserving such very important features of state law as the provisions of U.C.C. 2719(3)," as noted more fully below.

● The Act applies to sales of "consumer products" costing more than $10, sold by "suppliers" to "consumers" and accompanied by a written warranty. *Consumer product* is defined as personal property normally used for personal, family or household purposes. *Supplier* is defined as a "person engaged in the business of making a consumer product directly or indirectly available to consumers," and so avoids the so-called "vertical privity" problem by making both manufacturers and retailers liable to consumers as warrantors. The so-called "horizontal privity" problem is avoided, on the other hand, by defining *consumer* to include not only the original purchaser but also transferees from the original purchaser during the life of the warranty and persons, such as "bystanders" (page 94, note 112), who would have rights against the supplier under state law.

● In its most important provision, the Act requires every written warranty to be designed either as a *full (statement of duration) warranty* (i.e., full one-year warranty, full two-year warranty, etc.) or as a *limited warranty*, and we now see all written warranties so labeled.

● If the warrantor designates its warranty to be a *full (statement of duration) warranty*, these important requirements must be met and these important restrictions are imposed:

1. Defects in the product must be remedied within a reasonable time without charge.

2. If, after a reasonable number of attempts, a defect cannot be remedied, the warrantor must give the consumer, at the consumer's option, a replacement or a refund of the purchase price. This is popularly referred to as the "*anti-lemon provision*" of the Act.

3. If liability for consequential damages is disclaimed by the supplier, that is, for damages for personal injuries or property damage caused by a defective product, the disclaimer must be "conspicuously (printed) on the face of the warranty." If state law invalidates such a disclaimer, as U.C.C. 2719(3) is regarded as doing with respect to personal injury damages, Magnuson-Moss would, presumably, give way to state law under the provision, previously noted, that "Nothing in this (Act) . . . shall . . . supersede any provision of state law regarding consequential damages for injury to the person or other injury."

4. Implied warranties cannot be disclaimed under a full (statement of duration) warranty.

The Act also has remedial provisions which permit consumers to bring both individual actions and class actions to recover damages for breach of warranty and for violations of the Act and to recover attorneys' fees in addition to damages.

California Products Liability Law

As early as 1944, in *Escola* v. *Coca Cola Bottling Co. of Fresno* (1944) 24 C.2d 453, 150 P.2d 436, involving an exploding Coca Cola bottle, California's Justice Traynor attempted to get the California Supreme Court to adopt a doctrine of strict liability in tort in products liability cases. It was not until almost twenty years later, in 1963, that he was successful, with a court whose membership had changed considerably and which had become increasingly consumer-protection oriented.

In 1963, in *Greenman* v. *Yuba Power Products, Inc.* (1963) 59 C.2d 57, 27 C.R. 697, involving a defective power tool that caused injury, the California Supreme Court, in an opinion written by Justice Traynor, made this historic statement: "A manufacturer is strictly liable in tort when an article he places on the market knowing that it is to be used without inspection for defects, proves to have a defect which causes injury to a human being."

Greenman ushered in a new era of California products liability law, as will be seen.[123]

Strict tort liability is to be distinguished from tort liability based on negligence. Tort liability based on negligence requires it to be shown that it was because of negligence of the seller that the defect was present in the goods. Strict tort liability requires it to be shown only that the defect was present in the goods, actually or potentially, at the time of sale, without any need to show that negligence of the seller was responsible for its presence.

Warranty liability is also strict liability, often described as "strict liability in contract" to distinguish it from "strict liability in tort" (although this is actually erroneous, since properly speaking warranty is a form of liability, distinct from either contract or tort). Since warranty liability is also strict liability, it would not seem necessary to conceive a doctrine of strict liability in tort as the court did in *Greenman*. However, it was necessary and was very important for at least three reasons:

1. *Notice of breach of warranty:* To recover for breach of warranty, notice of breach of warranty must be given by the buyer to the seller within a reasonable time after the breach is or should have been discovered.[124] Failure to give notice bars the buyer from any remedy.[125] Frequently a buyer will not be aware of this requirement and will not discover it until it is too late to satisfy it; until, at a later date, he consults a lawyer for the first time about recovering for his injuries. No such requirement exists, on the other hand, as a condition precedent to a suit in tort.

2. *Disclaimer clauses:* Disclaimer clauses may still have some effect in warranty suits. They can have none at all, on the other hand, in tort suits since they are at most effective to exempt the seller from warranty liability and do not exempt him from tort liability.

3. *Privity of warranty:* The privity of warranty requirement, to whatever extent it continues to be effective in a particular jurisdiction, does not apply to tort actions, and therefore does not serve as a limitation on such actions.

Greenman imposed strict liability on the *manufacturer*. *Vandermark* v. *Ford Motor Co.* (1964) 61 C.2d 256, 37 C.R. 896, involving a defect in the manufacture or assembly of the

---

[123]On the national level, the Restatement Second of Torts.2d, § 402A, adopts the rule of manufacturer's strict liability.

[124]U.C.C. 2607(3)(a).

[125]U.C.C. 2607(3)(a).

master cylinder of the braking system of an automobile, extended the *Greenman* doctrine to the retailer and by implication others in the distributive chain, and to defects in the "design, manufacture, assembly, or adjustment" of the product.

Seely v. *White Motor Co.* (1965) 63 C.2d 9, 45 C.R. 17, involved a truck purchased for use in a transportation business. The truck "galloped" because of some defect that, as it developed, it was never possible for the manufacturer to isolate. Eventually the truck was involved in an accident but it was not possible to show that the "galloping" caused the accident. It was held that if this could be shown there would be recovery for the damage to the *truck* under the *Greenman* doctrine. To this extent there was, by dictum, an extension of the *Greenman* doctrine to damages to *goods* resulting from a defective condition of the goods. At the same time the court imposed its first major limitation on the *Greenman* doctrine. The court held that the buyer could not recover under the *Greenman* doctrine for merely *commercial or economic loss*— in this case the profits lost by the buyer because of loss of service of the truck. The doctrine of strict liability in tort was designed to govern and is limited to the governance of the problem of "physical injuries" to person or property, said the court. On the other hand, said the court, the "economic relations" of the parties—the purely "commercial aspects" of the matter—may and should be left to the law of sales warranty, permitting among other things, disclaimer clauses to operate as to those aspects of the matter.

Read v. *Safeway Stores* (1968) 264 A.C.A. 472, 70 C.R. 454, extended the *Greenman* doctrine to containers (bottle which exploded when removed from vending machine).

Elmore v. *American Motors* (1969) 70 A.C. 615, 75 C.R. 652 (defectively connected automobile driveshaft) was a major extension of the *Greenman* doctrine—to "*bystanders*" injured by the defective product.

Toole v. *Richardson-Merrell Inc.* (1967) 251 C.A.2d 689, 60 C.R. 398, is an application of the *Greenman* doctrine to pharmaceuticals, wherein the court said that if a drug manufacturer did not prepare the drug properly or failed to give warning of its dangerous propensities he could be held strictly liable in tort.

Hanberry v. *Hearst Corporation* (1969) 276 C.A.2d 680, 81 C.R. 519, held that the Good Housekeeping magazine's seal of approval of a brand of shoes could make Hearst Corporation, the publisher of the magazine, liable for injuries suffered by a purchaser of a pair of the shoes who slipped and fell allegedly because of a low coefficient of friction of the soles of the shoes on vinyl floor coverings.

Kriegler v. *Eichler Homes, Inc.* (1969) 269 C.A.2d 224, 74 C.R. 749, applied the strict liability doctrine to a mass producer of homes, holding him liable under that doctrine for physical damage suffered as the result of the installation of a defective radiant heating system.

Price v. *Shell Oil Co.* (1970) 2 C.3d 245, 85 C.R. 178, applied the strict liability doctrine to a "commercial lessor." In *Price*, Shell Oil Company leased to Flying Tiger Line, Inc. a gasoline tank truck with a movable ladder mounted on it for refueling aircraft. An employee of Flying Tiger was injured when, while he was using the ladder, the ladder broke because of a defect in its construction. The employee was held to be entitled to recover from Shell on the *Greenman* doctrine.

The tank truck lease contained an indemnity clause which provided that "Lessee (Flying Tiger) shall indemnify Shell against any and all claims and liability for injury or death of persons or damage to property caused by or happening in connection with the equipment or the condition, maintenance, possession, operation or use thereof." Shell contended that this clause obligated Flying Tiger to indemnify Shell, that is to pay for the injuries suffered by the Flying Tiger employee. In accordance with the rule of strict construction of exculpatory clauses, discussed at page 39, the court held that since the clause did not expressly purport to cover the lessor's (Shell's) own negligence or to cover strict liability in tort (as distinguished from negligence) it should not be construed to cover such things.

The *Greenman* doctrine will continue to grow and, with the high degree of consumer protection consciousness that exists today, the law of products liability will remain a dynamic area of development of the law. The traditional law of transactional warranties, on the other hand, being confined as it now is to commercial problems, will be expected to lead a quiet existence.

Most recently on the horizon has been a spate of "handgun suits" against manufacturers of "Saturday night specials" which proceed on both negligence and strict liability theories. The negligence approach sees the manufacture and sale of the cheap handgun as the marketing of an unreasonably dangerous product for which tort liability in negligence should lie. The strict liability theory is that the ready availability, concealability and capacity of such a gun to inflict lethal harm make it a defectively designed product. California lawyers would seek to find support for this in a new standard of product defectiveness formulated by the California Supreme Court in *Barker* v. *Lull Engineering Co.* (1978) 20 C.3d 413, 143 C.R. 225. This new standard, called the "risk-versus-utility test," is that "a product (can be found to be) defective even if it satisfies ordinary consumer expectations, if through hindsight (it is determined) that the product's design embodies 'excessive preventable danger'." Some commentators have regarded such suits as "stretching tort law to the breaking point" and laws are being proposed at both the federal and California levels which would halt such suits.

After the foregoing was written, California did in fact enact such a law in the form of C.C. 1714.4 which provides:

"(a) In a products liability action, no firearm or ammunition shall be deemed defective in design on the basis that the benefits of the product do not outweigh the risk of injury posed by its potential to cause serious injury, damage, or death when discharged.

"(b) For purposes of this section:

"(1) The potential of a firearm or ammunition to cause serious injury, damage, or death when discharged does not make the product defective in design.

"(2) Injuries or damages resulting from the discharge of a firearm or ammunition are not proximately caused by its potential to cause serious injury, damage, or death, but are proximately caused by the actual discharge of the product.

"(c) This section shall not affect a products liability cause of action based upon the improper selection of design alternatives.

"(d) This section is declaratory of existing law."

California Statutory Consumer Protection Law

Unruh Act (C.C. 1801-1812.20)

This Act became effective in California on January 1, 1960, as California's first major consumer protection law. It is not repealed by the Uniform Commercial Code.[126] It is a comprehensive regulation of retail installment sales, including conditional sales, and installment charge accounts. It applies to all retail installment sales of goods to which a finance charge is added, except sales of motor vehicles. (C.C. 2982

---

[126]U.C.C. 9203(2).

egulates the finance charge on conditional sales of motor vehicles, as shown in footnote 45 on page 38, and makes requirements similar to those seen here regarding form and contents of conditional sales contracts for the sale of motor vehicles.) The Unruh Act also applies to services to be paid for on an installment basis and involving a finance charge, including repair of goods or motor vehicles and services rendered in connection with the improvement of real property. Services rendered for commercial or business use are excluded however, as are those of doctors and dentists.

The Act requires every such retail installment contract to be in writing and to contain the disclosures required by Federal Reserve Board Regulation Z promulgated under the Truth in Lending Act, discussed below. In effect this requires the financial details of the transaction to be set forth in elaborate detail. The contract must be labeled "Security Agreement" in 12-point boldface type if a security is retained in the goods sold or a security interest is taken in other goods or in real property. If a security interest in real property is taken, a 14-point boldface type "foreclosure warning" warning of the possibility of foreclosure by sale (i.e., without court action) must be set out immediately below the title of the contract and must be alluded to immediately above the buyer's signature line; otherwise the security interest is void and unenforceable. If no security interest in goods or real property is to be taken, the contract is to be labeled "Retail Installment Contract" in 12-point boldface type. In addition, the contract must contain a notice in at least 10-point bold type advising the buyer not to sign the contract if it has any blanks, that he is entitled to a completely filled-in copy of the contract and that he has a right to prepay and obtain a proportionate refund of the finance charge. The contract must show the price, down payment, trade-in, insurance, finance charge, and balloon payments, if any. See the form on page 138 for a contract form that complies with the requirements of the Unruh Act. The buyer must be given or mailed a copy. If insurance is included it must show who is to procure it and, if it is the seller, he must mail the buyer a copy of the policy or a certificate of insurance.

The entire agreement of the parties must be contained in a "single document" which must contain any promissory note which evidences the indebtedness created by the transaction. If the buyer gives the seller a negotiable promissory note for the balance of the purchase price, an assignee of the note, from the seller, takes the note subject to all defenses of the buyer against the seller so that if the goods are defective the assignee of the note cannot enforce it against the buyer any more than the seller could. This changes the ordinary rule regarding the position of a transferee of a negotiable instrument. See pages 111-113, showing that ordinarily the transferee of a negotiable instrument takes free of defenses of the maker (buyer, here) against the payee-transferor (seller, here).

C.C. 1805.1 sets out rather complicated formulas for the determination of maximum finance charges.

The buyer may pay in full at any time and will be entitled to a refund credit on the finance charge. (The conditional buyer of a motor vehicle has the same privilege under C.C. 2982, except that the seller may make a charge of $25 for the privilege of prepayment.)

If the buyer defaults on the contract, the seller may repossess the goods. He must then notify the buyer that he intends to retain the goods in satisfaction of the balance due or that he intends to resell them. In either case the buyer has 10 days to redeem the goods, and may redeem them until time of sale if the notice is of intention to resell. If the seller elects to resell, he is accountable to the buyer for any excess realized over the balance due on the contract. He may not recover a deficiency.

Automobile Sales and Leasing Acts

The Rees-Levering Motor Vehicle Sales and Finance Act (C.C. 2981-2984.4) imposes cost of credit disclosure requirements in connection with sales of motor vehicles. Its requirements conform it to the federal Truth in Lending Act, seen below. A form of automobile sales contract conforming to the Rees-Levering Act is shown on page 100. The Moscone Automobile Leasing Act (C.C. 2985.7-2990) imposes disclosure requirements in connection with leases of motor vehicles, in particular with respect to the lessee's liability at the end of the lease period.

More Recent California Statutory Consumer Protection Law

Legislators everywhere have become increasingly aware of the need to protect the consumer public against harsh and unfair business practices and of the popularity to be gained in championing consumer protection legislation. Consequently, such legislation now appears with ever-increasing frequency, almost to the point of being unable to assimilate it.

The California Legislature is gaining a prolific record in this regard, as evidenced by the following laws of this decade which are only some of the recent consumer protection laws:

Consumer Affairs Act (B.P.C. 300-336): This Act creates the Department of Consumer Affairs to study and investigate matters affecting the interests of consumers; recommend consumer protection legislation; represent consumer interests before federal and state legislative hearings and executive commissions; hold public hearings regarding consumer interests; receive complaints from consumers concerning unfair or deceptive business practices, unfair methods of competition, and the sale of dangerous goods; and disseminate to the public information regarding goods and services which are unsafe or unhealthful, test results of consumer products, and trade practices which are detrimental to consumers.

Song-Beverly Credit Card Act of 1971 (C.C. 1747-1748.5): Two of the important things done by this Act are that (1) it exempts the cardholder from liability for unauthorized use of the card if he notifies the card issuer of loss or theft within a reasonable time after discovery, and it limits the cardholder's liability for unauthorized use to $50 at all events; (2) it preserves to the cardholder as against the card issuer, such as MasterCard or BankAmericard, the defense of the cardholder against a retail seller where the retail seller has sold defective goods to the cardholder in a California transaction for a purchase price of more than $50, the cardholder has made written demand on the retail seller with respect to the purchase and has attempted in good faith to obtain reasonable satisfaction from him, and the cardholder gives written notice of the facts of the situation to the card issuer.

Consumer Credit Reporting Agencies Act (C.C. 1785.1-1785.35): This Act undertakes to protect a member of the consumer public against harmful erroneous information regarding his credit. It requires a credit reporting agency to disclose to a person whose credit is reported upon the information it has regarding him and the sources of such information. Additionally, if the accuracy of the credit report information is disputed by the person reported upon, the credit reporting agency must reinvestigate its information, and if the information continues to be disputed, the credit reporting agency must show this fact (that is, that the information is

(Continued on page 104)

SIMPLE INTEREST   MOTOR VEHICLE CONTRACT AND SECURITY AGREEMENT

BUYER'S NAME		DATE OF AGREEMENT	Stock No.
			Source
BUYER'S RESIDENCE OR PLACE OF BUSINESS	ZIP CODE	AGREEMENT NO.	Salesman
			Date
CO-BUYER'S NAME AND ADDRESS			Bus. Phone
			Res. Phone

In this contract the words "we," "us" and "our" refer to the creditor (seller) named below. The words "you" and "yours" refer to the buyer and co-buyer if any named herein.

We sell you the motor vehicle described below on credit. The credit price is shown below as the "Cash Price." The "Cash Price" is also shown below. By signing this contract you choose to buy the motor vehicle on credit and agree to pay us the total sale price in the amounts and under the terms and agreements shown on the front and back of this contract. You agree you have accepted the vehicle in good order. If this contract is signed by a buyer and co-buyer each is individually and together responsible for all agreements in the contract.

YEAR	NEW	USED	MAKE	TRADE NAME	CYL	DIESEL	GAS	OTHER	BODY STYLE	MODEL	ODOMETER READING		I.D. NUMBER
☐ AIR CON-DITIONING	☐ DISC BRAKES	☐ VINYL TOP	☐ POWER SEATS	☐ POWER BRAKES	TRIM			☐ POWER STEERING	☐ POWER WINDOWS	☐ 8 TRACK ☐ CASSETTE	☐ AM ☐ AM/FM	☐ RADIO ☐ STEREO	
☐ TINTED GLASS	☐ UNDER COATING	☐ BUCKET SEATS	COLOR							TIRES	TRANS	☐ REAR SPEAKER	KEY NO LIC. NO
												R.O.S. No.	

Total Sale Price
The total cost of your purchase on credit, including your down payment of $ _____ (e)

DISCLOSURES PURSUANT TO TRUTH-IN-LENDING ACT

ANNUAL PERCENTAGE RATE The cost of your credit as a yearly rate. _____%	**FINANCE CHARGE** The dollar amount the credit will cost you. $ _____ (e)	**Amount Financed** The amount of credit provided to you or on your behalf $ _____ (e)	**Total of Payments** The amount you will have paid after you have made all payments as scheduled. $ _____ (e)

YOUR PAYMENT SCHEDULE WILL BE:

Number of Payments:	Amount of each Payment:	When Payments Are Due:
One payment of		Payments are due on:
One payment of payments		Monthly, beginning
One Final Payment		

The Finance Charge, Total of Payments, Total Sale Price and Final Scheduled Payment are estimated.
SECURITY: You are giving a security interest in the goods or property being purchased.
LATE CHARGES: ( ) Applies only if checked: If any payment is more than 10 days late you will be charged 5% of the payment.
PREPAYMENT: If you pay early, you may be charged a minimum finance charge.
See your contract documents for any additional information about nonpayment, default, any required prepayment in full before the scheduled date and any minimum finance charge payable upon prepayment.

STATEMENT OF INSURANCE

NOTICE: No person is required as a condition to financing the purchase of a motor vehicle to purchase, or negotiate any insurance through a particular insurance company, agent or broker.

You have requested Seller include in the balance due under this agreement the following insurance. Insurance is to expire WITH ☐ BEFORE ☐ AFTER ☐ the due date of the final installment.

You are requested to insure the described property against fire, theft and collision for the term of this agreement. Any insurance will not be in force until accepted by the insurance carrier.

WARNING — UNLESS A CHARGE IS INCLUDED IN THIS AGREEMENT FOR PUBLIC LIABILITY OR PROPERTY DAMAGE INSURANCE, PAYMENT FOR SUCH COVERAGE IS NOT PROVIDED BY THIS AGREEMENT.

	BUYER(S)	
S/S		Premium
S/S	BUYER(S)	
$ _____	DED. COMP. FIRE & THEFT	Mos: $ _____
$ _____	DEDUCTIBLE COLLISION	Mos: $ _____
	LIMITS	Mos: $ _____
	BODILY INJURY	

ITEMIZATION OF THE AMOUNT FINANCED

1.
A. Cash Price (Motor Vehicle) $ _____ (A)
B. Accessories $ _____ (B)
C. Documentary Preparation Charge (not a governmental fee) $ _____ (C)
D. Sales Tax (on A+B+C) $ _____ (D)
E. Service contract (optional) $ _____ (E)
F. Amount Paid to Others $ _____ (F)
    To whom paid:

CASH PRICE (A to F) .... $ _____ (1)

AMOUNTS PAID TO PUBLIC OFFICIALS

2.
A. License .... $ _____ (A)
B. Certificate of Title ...... $ _____ (B)
C. Registration .... $ _____ (C)

TOTAL OFFICIAL FEES (A+B+C) $ _____ (2)

PROPERTY DAMAGE $ _____ LIMITS _____ Mos: $ _____

MEDICAL _____ Mos: $ _____

_____ Mos: $ _____

TOTAL VEHICLE INSURANCE PREMIUMS: _____ (A)

The foregoing declarations are hereby acknowledged.

_____
Date   Seller

_____
Date   Buyer

CREDIT INSURANCE AUTHORIZATION AND APPLICATION

You voluntarily request the credit insurance checked below, if any, and understand that such insurance is not required. You acknowledge disclosure of the cost of such insurance and authorize it to be included in the balance payable under the security agreement. Only the persons whose names are signed below are insured.

CREDIT LIFE _____ Mos. Premium $ _____

JOINT LIFE _____ Mos. Premium $ _____

CREDIT DISABILITY _____ Mos. Premium $ _____

TOTAL CREDIT INSURANCE PREMIUMS _____ $ _____ (B)

☐ You want Credit Life Insurance
☐ You do not want Credit Life Insurance
☐ You want Credit Disability Insurance (Primary Buyer only)
☐ You do not want Credit Disability Insurance
☐ You want Joint Credit Life Insurance

You are applying for the credit insurance marked above. Your signature below means that you agree that:
1. You are not eligible for insurance if you reached your 65th birthday.
2. You are eligible for disability insurance only if you are working for wages or profit 30 hours a week or more on the Effective Date.
3. Your co-buyer is not eligible for disability insurance.

_____   _____   Age _____
Date   Primary-Buyer

_____   _____   Age _____ ID-1
Date   Co-Buyer

TOTAL INSURANCE PREMIUMS (A+B) ARE DESCRIBED IN ITEM 3.

NOTICES: The names and addresses of all persons to whom the notices required or permitted by law are to be sent are set forth below.

SEE OTHER SIDE FOR ADDITIONAL TERMS AND CONDITIONS

Buyer acknowledges that: [1] before signing this agreement Buyer read both sides of this agreement and received a legible, completely filled-in copy of this agreement, and: [2] Buyer has received a copy of every other document that Buyer signed during the contract negotiation.

Buyer
sign here **X** _____

Address _____

_____   Zip _____   Phone _____

Seller _____

NO. 553 (Rev. 12/82) © 1982 LAW PRINTING CO., INC.

The Printer makes no warranty, express or implied, as to content or fitness for purpose of this form.

---

3. **AMOUNTS PAID TO INSURANCE COMPANIES:**
   (Total premiums per Statement of Insurance) _____ $ _____ (3)

4. Smog Cert. Fee Paid to State .... _____ $ _____ (4)

5. **TOTAL (1 to 4)** .... _____ $ _____ (5)

   A. Trade-in (Description)
      Yr. _____ Make _____ (A)
      Model _____ $ _____
      I.D. NO. _____
      ODOMETER _____

   B. Less Pay Off .... $ _____ (B)
   C. **TRADE-IN** (A less B) .... $ _____ (C)
   D. Deferred downpayment due before second installment payment ...... $ _____ (D)
   E. MFR'S Rebate .... $ _____ (E)
   F. Remaining cash downpayment .... $ _____ (F)

6. **TOTAL DOWNPAYMENT** (6C+D+E+F) _____ $ _____ (6)

7. **AMOUNT FINANCED** (5 less 6) _____ $ _____ (7)

OFFICIAL FEES (Not Financed): The Buyer will pay the estimated fee(s) of $ _____ to the appropriate public authority in order to transfer registration after full payment under this agreement.

SERVICE CONTRACT (Optional). You request the cost of a service contract written with the following company for the term below. The cost is shown in item 1(E) above.

Company _____ Term _____ Months

Buyer _____

SELLER ASSISTED LOAN

Proceeds of Loan — From _____ Finance Charge _____ Total $ _____

Amount $ _____ installments of $ _____

Payable _____ from this loan is described in 6(D) above.

$ _____

NOTICE TO BUYER ON SELLER ASSISTED LOAN — BUYER MAY BE REQUIRED TO PLEDGE SECURITY, WHICH SECURITY MUST BE MUTUALLY AGREED TO BY BUYER AND LENDER. BUYER WILL BE OBLIGATED FOR THE INSTALLMENT PAYMENTS ON BOTH THE SECURITY AGREEMENT AND THE LOAN.

Buyer
sign here **X** _____

Address _____

_____   Zip _____   Phone _____

Address _____

By _____   Title _____

ORIGINAL

(Form continued on following pages)

ADDITIONAL TERMS AND AGREEMENTS

A. PROMISE TO PAY: You promise to pay the Amount Financed disclosed on the reverse side hereof, plus finance charges, in addition to the down payment, at the times and in the amounts set forth in the Payment Schedule on the reverse side of this contract. The finance charges are computed as simple interest and will be calculated on a daily basis based upon the Annual Percentage Rate disclosed on the reverse side hereof. Finance charges will accrue on the unpaid balance of the Amount Financed until all sums due under this contract are fully paid. Each payment will be applied first to any unpaid deferred downpayment, then to finance charges and the remainder to the Amount Financed.

B. SIMPLE INTEREST CONTRACT: This is a simple interest contract. The Finance Charge, Total of Payments and Payment Schedule set forth in the disclosures on the reverse side hereof were computed, as permitted by state and federal law, upon the expectation of payment exactly as disclosed. Even if payments are made exactly as disclosed the final payment may differ. The final payment will have the effect of reducing your final payment, while late payments will cause your final payment to be higher. Your promise requires you to pay the final payment on the date due, which payment will be equal to all unpaid sums due under this contract, even if the amount of final payment differs from the amount of final payment disclosed on the reverse side hereof.

C. SECURITY INTEREST: You give us a security interest under the California Uniform Commercial Code in the vehicle and all parts or accessories put on the vehicle and in all insurance premiums financed for you or rebates from insurance premiums, service contracts, and in the proceeds of any insurance policies covering the vehicle or insuring your life or health, which security interest secures all sums which may become due under this contract.

D. USE OF VEHICLE: You agree to keep the vehicle free of all taxes and liens, except in favor of Seller, and not to use the vehicle illegally, improperly, or for hire, and not to make any material change in the vehicle or remove it from this State for a period in excess of 30 days or transfer any interest in the vehicle. You agree not to remove the vehicle from this country. If we must, although not obligated to do so, pay any liens or taxes you will reimburse us upon demand.

E. INSURANCE: You agree to keep the vehicle insured in favor of us with a policy satisfactory to us for comprehensive and collision insurance insuring the vehicle against loss by fire and theft in amounts not less than the unpaid sums owed under this contract. If you fail to maintain such insurance, we may, at our option, procure such insurance and you agree to pay for the insurance we procure in accordance with the law. At our option, we may insure only our interest or your interest as well. If insurance has been purchased in connection with this contract, any difference between the amounts shown in the Statement of Insurance or premiums which may arise from errors in computation, classification, grouping or zoning, or changes in the type of insurance shall be payable by you on demand. You agree that we can use any proceeds from insurance to either repair or replace the vehicle or to reduce your debt under this contract as we may decide. Whether or not the vehicle is insured, you must pay for it if is lost, damaged, or destroyed.

F. PREPAYMENT OF AMOUNTS OWED: You may prepay all amounts due under this contract at any time. In addition, if you fail to make any payment when due or perform any other agreement provided for in this contract, we may, in addition to other remedies, declare all sums immediately due and payable. If you prepay a portion of your balance payment will be credited first to interest and the balance to the unpaid Amount Financed. Your next payment will be due on the next regular installment date. If you prepay in full you agree that we are entitled to a minimum finance charge as follows: (1) $25, if the original Amount Financed does not exceed $1,000 (2) $50, if the original Amount Financed is more than $1,000, but not more than $2,000, or (3) $75, if the original Amount Financed is more than $2,000. Your obligation will be determined, as applicable as of the date we are paid in full, or as of the date we recover the vehicle's value through its disposition, or upon entry of a court judgment for what you owe under this contract, or if we elect to keep the vehicle in satisfaction of what you owe under this contract, as of the date we take possession of the vehicle.

G. CHANGE IN PAYMENT SCHEDULE: If we receive two or more payments after their due dates and we have not taken action under the "default" section you agree that upon our request you will make an extra payment that reduces the unpaid balance of the Amount Financed to the amount it would have been had all installment payments been received on time.

H. DEFAULT: If you default in the performance of any of the terms and conditions of this agreement, including, but not limited to, making of any payment when due, or become insolvent, or file any proceeding under the U.S. Bankruptcy Code, or upon your demise, we may at our option and without notice or demand (1) declare all unpaid sums immediately due and payable (2) file suit against you for all unpaid sums (3) take immediate possession of the motor vehicle. Upon taking possession of the motor vehicle and giving notice as provided for by law, if you do not redeem the vehicle we will sell it at public or private sale. We may purchase the vehicle at any sale. The proceeds of sale will be applied first to the expenses of retaking, reconditioning, storing and selling the property, and the remainder will be applied to the unpaid sums owing under this contract. Attorney fees and court costs are allowed too. If there is any money left over (surplus) it will be paid to you. If a balance still remains owing, you promise to pay the same upon demand. Our remedies are cumulative and taking of any action shall not be a waiver or prohibit us from pursuing any other remedy. You promise to pay reasonable collection costs and attorney fees in the event we prevail in any action to enforce the terms of this contract. If you prevail we agree to pay reasonable attorney's fees and court costs. If the motor vehicle is repossessed we may store any personal property found in the vehicle for your account and at your expense and if you do not claim the property within 90 days after the repossession, we may dispose of the personal property in any manner we deem appropriate without liability to you. If checked in the disclosure on the reverse hereof, and your payment is more than 10 days late you will be charged 5% of each late payment.

I. WARRANTIES OF BUYER: You promise that you have given true and correct information in your application for credit and understand that we have relied upon the correctness of that information in entering into this agreement, that you have given us a true payoff amount on any vehicle traded in and you promise that if it is not correct and is greater than the amount shown in this contract, you will pay the excess to us upon demand.

J. OTHER AGREEMENTS OF BUYER: (1) In the event the estimated Department of Motor Vehicles fees are greater than the amount shown, you will pay the excess to us on demand. If they are less, we will refund the excess to you. (2) You agree that if we accept monies in sums less than those due or make extensions of due dates of payments under this contract, doing so will not be a waiver of any later right to enforce the contract terms as written. (3) You will allow us to inspect the motor vehicle at any reasonable time and notify us of any change of your address within 30 days. (4) If you are married, and sign this agreement, you agree that your separate property shall be liable for all unpaid sums due. (5) If we transfer this contract to an assignee you will be given notice thereof and you agree that the assignee will have all of our rights and remedies under the contract and you agree to pay all that is still owed under this contract at the times, and in the amounts, to the assignee. (6) That all of the agreements between us and you are set forth in this contract and no modification of this contract shall be valid unless it is made in writing and signed by you and us. (7) That any provision of this contract which may be held invalid shall not mean that this contract is unenforceable and the remaining provisions of this contract shall continue to be binding.

K. DELAY IN ENFORCEMENT: We can delay or waive enforcement of any of your rights under this contract without losing them.

L. LIABILITY OF PARTIES: Each person who signs this contract is a maker and agrees to be individually and jointly obligated to repay the contract in accordance with its terms and conditions.

M. WARRANTIES: YOU AGREE THAT THERE ARE NO WARRANTIES, EXPRESS OR IMPLIED, REPRESENTATIONS, PROMISES OR STATEMENTS AS TO THE CONDITION, FITNESS FOR MERCHANTABILITY OF THE VEHICLE THAT HAVE BEEN MADE BY US UNLESS THEY ARE STATED IN THIS CONTRACT. ANY STATEMENT AS TO THE YEAR MODEL OF THE VEHICLE IS FOR IDENTIFICATION ONLY AND IS NOT A REPRESENTATION OR WARRANTY BY US.

... DEBTOR COULD ASSERT AGAINST THE SELLER OF GOODS OR SERVICES OBTAINED PURSUANT HERETO OR WITH THE PROCEEDS HEREOF. RECOVERY HEREUNDER BY THE DEBTOR SHALL NOT EXCEED AMOUNTS PAID BY THE DEBTOR HEREUNDER.

Complaints concerning unfair or deceptive practices or methods by the seller shall be referred to the seller and, if the complaint is not resolved may be referred to the Department of Motor Vehicles, Division of Compliance, 2570 24th Street, Sacramento 95818.

NOTICE TO BUYER: (1) Do not sign this agreement before you read it or if it contains any blank spaces to be filled in. (2) You are entitled to a completely filled-in copy of this agreement. (3) You can prepay the full amount due under this agreement at any time. (4) If you default in the performance of your obligations under this agreement, the vehicle may be repossessed and you may be subject to suit and liability for the unpaid indebtedness evidenced by this agreement.

ASSIGNMENT WITH RECOURSE

FOR VALUE RECEIVED, the Agreement herein assigned (on the reverse side) between the Purchaser and the undersigned, and the property described, and all the rights, title and interest thereon of the undersigned are hereby sold, assigned and transferred to

its successors or assigns. The undersigned jointly and severally hereby guarantee full performance of said Agreement in all its terms and the prompt payment of any and all sums provided therein, together with collection expenses, costs and attorney's fees, and agrees to pay any attorney's fees and costs incurred in enforcing this guaranty. That undersigned has not assisted the Buyer in obtaining a loan from any third party to be used as a part or all of the down payment or any other payment on the within agreement, except as specifically indicated on the reverse hereof. Undersigned warrants and represents that all requirements of the Federal Truth in Lending Law and any other consumer credit laws relating to the within agreement have been properly satisfied and Undersigned hereby agrees to indemnify said Assignee against and hold said Assignee harmless from all claims, actions, suits, proceedings, costs, expenses, loss, damages, and liabilities, including attorney's fees, arising out of, connected with, relating to or resulting from any contention, whether well-founded, baseless or otherwise, that there has been a violation of, or failure to comply with, any such laws in connection with the within agreement. The Undersigned jointly and severally hereby agree that in the event of the non-compliance with any of the conditions of said agreement, whether or not repossession has been made or undertaken, suit may be brought by the holder against any one or more or all of the parties herein, whether or not suit has been commenced against the party or parties to said Agreement and without waiving any rights as to time of repossession. The Undersigned jointly and severally hereby agree in the event of repossession or default by the Purchaser, the entire balance outstanding under said Agreement shall become immediately due and payable. Seller waives all rights and defenses as such guarantor (including, without limitation, its rights under the provisions of sections 2845, 2849 and 2850 of the California Civil Code and any amendments thereof) and all demands and notices whatsoever. The Undersigned agrees to indemnify the holder of this contract from all claims, demands, loss and liability, including attorney's fees, howsoever arising from the goods sold hereunder or the making of this contract. The Undersigned jointly and severally hereby waive any and all notice of non-payment, demand, presentment or protest, which may be required under this Agreement or in connection therewith, and agree that any extensions or impairments of remedies which may be granted by the holder hereof to the parties to said Agreement shall not in any manner release the Undersigned. In the event that suit is instituted to enforce any of the terms of this Agreement the Undersigned jointly and severally hereby waive the right to change place of trial from the court originally acquiring jurisdiction. The Undersigned warrants that application has been made for California registration with said assignee as legal owner.

Dated _____ at _____

_____   _____
(Name of Dealer)   (Dealer's Town and State)

                                          (Seal)

Signed _____ By _____
                                    (Officer, Firm Member or Owner)

ASSIGNMENT WITHOUT RECOURSE

FOR VALUE RECEIVED, the undersigned (assignor) does hereby sell, assign and transfer to

his, its or their right, title and interest to the within agreement, the property described therein, and the monies to become due hereunder, such assignment made WITHOUT RECOURSE in consideration of the following representations and warranties: (a) that said agreement represents a bona fide sale and was actually executed in good faith by the purchaser therein named and this assignor; (b) that at the time of such execution said purchaser was of legal age and competent to execute said agreement; (c) that the property which is subject of said agreement is truly and accurately described therein, and has been delivered into the possession of said purchaser, and that application has been made for California registration with said assignee as legal owner; (d) that the amount recited as having been received as a down payment was actually paid in cash and not its equivalent, that undersigned has not assisted the Buyer in obtaining a loan from any third party to be used as a part or all of the down payment or any other payment on the within agreement, except as specifically indicated on the reverse hereof; that merchandise taken in trade was received at not more than the reasonable market value thereof at the time of its receipt and that the terms of sale and statements set forth in the agreement and in the statement of transaction are true and correctly set forth; (e) that the assignor has the full and complete title to the property sold, subject only to the rights of said purchaser; (f) that there are no recoupments, counterclaims or set-offs on the part of the purchaser against the amounts payable, and that there have been no representations or warranties made to said purchaser not contained in the agreement; (g) that the information concerning the purchaser, given on blank provided for that purpose, is truly set down therein, and that said information is true and correct as to the purchaser's address and occupation; (h) that the assignor has no information or reason to suspect that any provision of the agreement will be violated and that the purchaser is not a good moral and financial risk; (i) said contract, and the transaction evidenced thereby, and all disclosures to purchaser and other matters in connection with said contract are in all respects made as required by and in accordance with, all applicable federal and state laws and regulations governing the same; (j) seller agrees not to accept or take possession of payments on said property, without prior written consent to the holder of this contract; (k) Undersigned warrants and represents that all requirements of the Federal Truth in Lending Law and any other consumer credit laws relating to the within agreement have been properly satisfied and Undersigned hereby agrees to indemnify said assignee against and hold said assignee harmless from all claims, actions, suits, proceedings, costs, expenses, loss, damages, and liabilities, including attorney's fees, arising out of, connected with, relating to or resulting from any contention, whether well-founded, baseless or otherwise, that there has been a violation of, or failure to comply properly with, any such laws in connection with the agreement.

Should any of the representations or warranties be false, the assignor agrees to pay the assignee or holder, upon demand, the full unpaid balance of the within agreement, whether or not possession of the property covered hereby has been taken by assignee or suit has been instituted against the purchaser or the assignor, or both. Assignor agrees that the taking of possession of said property shall not be deemed an election of remedies, and assignor agrees to pay any deficiency thereafter remaining. If assignee is required to bring action against assignor as a result of the breach of any representation or warranty contained in this assignment, assignor agrees to pay reasonable attorney's fees and court costs incurred by assignee in such action. The assignor consents to extensions of payment or alterations of said agreement or impairments of remedies which may be granted by the holder hereof, and waives any and all notice of nonpayment, demand, presentment or protest, which otherwise might be required under this assignment or in connection therewith. Seller hereby waives all statutes of limitation and the defense thereof.

Dated _____ at _____

_____   _____
(Name of Dealer)   (Dealer's Town and State)

                                          (Seal)

Signed _____ By _____
(Rev. 12/82)   (Officer, Firm Member or Owner)

disputed by the person reported upon) in future credit rating reports.

Consumer Legal Remedies Act (C.C. 1750-1784): This Act allows a consumer, as to whom there has been an unfair or deceptive act or practice in connection with the sale or lease of goods or services, to sue for damages and punitive damages, and, if similar harm has occurred to other consumers similarly situated, to bring a class action on behalf of himself and such other consumers.

"Home Solicitation Contract" Law (C.C. 1689.5-1689.13): This gives a person who contracts with a door-to-door salesman for goods or services in an amount of $25 or more a "cooling off period," i.e., a 3-day right of cancellation of the contract. If a down payment is made, the seller may retain out of the payment, as a cancellation fee, 5% of the cash price of the goods or services but in no event may the seller retain more than $15.

Still More Recent Legislation

Consumer protection law proceeds apace, to the point where only brief noting seems possible. During the 1975-1977 period, since the prior edition of this book, additional legislation has been enacted regarding the collection, reporting and dissemination of credit information, and legislation has been enacted regarding contracts for discount buying services and regarding debt collection practices.

The preceding paragraph was written with respect to the ninth edition of this book, published in 1978. Since that publication, these are notable public or consumer protection laws: The "standards for warranty work" statute (C.C. 1796-1796.5) requires that a person or firm which engages in the business of installing new or used consumer goods, or in the business of servicing or repairing consumer goods, must perform its services "in a good and workmanlike manner." The "home equity sales contracts" statute (C.C. 1695-1695.14) is designed to protect persons whose homes are being foreclosed and who contract to sell their home equity to an "equity purchaser" for an inadequate price. The statute forbids misrepresentation regarding the value of the home by the equity purchaser and requires that the home equity seller be given a conspicuously-noticed 5-day right of cancellation in the equity purchase contract. The "contracts for seller-assisted marketing plans" statute (C.C. 1812.200-1812.220) is designed to protect purchasers of marketing plans in such fields as vending machines, racks and work-at-home paraphernalia by requiring plan sellers to make disclosures regarding such things as the seller's previous experience with the plan and the amount of money the purchaser can reasonably be expected to earn with the plan.

Other Important Consumer Protection Law

Much additional consumer protection law has issued forth in the last decade, both statutory law and decisional law.

Truth in Lending Act (15 U.S.C.A. §§ 1601 et seq.)

The federal Truth in Lending Act, which requires disclosure of the cost of credit, is part of the larger Consumer Credit Protection Act, which also regulates such things as consumer credit reporting and the extent to which wages can be garnisheed for credit defaults (on the theory that if there are no restrictions on wage garnishment predatory extensions of credit are encouraged).

● The Truth in Lending Act covers consumer credit transactions, which are installment purchases and installment loans

for personal, family, household, or agricultural purposes does not apply to credit transactions involving extension credit for business or commercial purposes or to credit tr actions, other than real property transactions, in which total amount to be financed exceeds $25,000.

● The Act requires the credit seller or creditor to state *"annual percentage rate"* applicable to an extension of cre which is to say in effect that the credit seller or creditor n show its interest charges in terms of simple annual interes the outstanding balance. The Act defines "finance char expansively so as to include things that might not otherw be included (amounts payable under a point or discount tem; service or carrying charges; loan fees; credit invest tion and reporting fees; credit insurance premiums) and requires inclusion in the interest rate of things that might otherwise be included in the computation of the rate of ir est.

● The Act requires extensive disclosure of all of the finar aspects of the transaction, e.g., in connection with a consu credit sale: price; down payment; trade-in allowance; all o charges, individually itemized, which are included in amount of credit extended but which are not part of the nance charge; total amount to be financed; finance cha finance charge expressed as an annual percentage rate; ment schedule; and delinquency and default charges.

● The Act exempts from its requirements credit transact within a state if the law of the state subjects the transactio requirements substantially similar to those imposed by the and has adequate provision for the enforcement of its requ ments. The Unruh Act (page 98) is such a state law. security agreement on page 138 and the conditional sale c tract on page 100 demonstrate the disclosure requirement the Unruh Act which, in turn, demonstrate and satisfy disclosure requirements of the Truth in Lending Act.

● The Truth in Lending Act is concerned only with disclos of credit costs and is not a "usury law," i.e., it does regulate interest rates.

Uniform Consumer Credit Code

The Uniform Consumer Credit Code, or U-Triple C is called, is a uniform act which is seeking adoption companion piece to the Uniform Commercial Code. It w undertake to be all things to consumer *"credit transactio* as the Uniform Commercial Code is all things to *"commer transactions,"* and as it is "(t)he concept of the (Unif Commercial Code) that 'commercial transactions' is a si subject of the law, notwithstanding its many facets" (p 69), it is "(t)he concept of the (Uniform Consumer Cr Code) that 'credit transactions' is a single subject of the notwithstanding its many facets (emphasis added)." Comn to UCCC Title. The proponents of the UCCC advance m convincing arguments for its adoption: Uniform laws on subject of consumer credit legislation will benefit both consumer and the consumer credit industry. The consu credit industry operates across state lines and uniform cr legislation will reduce the industry's costs of operation will promote competition within the industry. In a mobile ciety, uniform legislation will produce maximum consu understanding of credit transactions.

● The UCCC does in fact undertake to regulate all aspect consumer credit transactions, as follows: Basically, it re lates consumer credit sales and consumer loans. Consu credit sales include installment sales and charge account sa Consumer loans include simple loans and the use of cr cards as the means of gaining the use of money. Inte charges are regulated both with respect to sales and lo

closure requirements are made, similar to those prescribed
the Truth in Lending Act, and it is one of the purposes of
UCCC to provide an adopting state with a state law which
exempt it from the requirements of the Truth in Lending
as the Unruh Act does for California. Advertising regard-
credit transactions and interest rates is regulated. Agree-
ts regarding credit insurance are regulated. "Home Solic-
on Sales" are regulated in the manner of the California
on page 104, and the buyer is given a 3-day right of
cellation as under the California law.

dditionally, the UCCC regulates various kinds of agree-
ts and practices which undertake to take advantage of the
tion of or to deceive the consumer buyer or borrower.
se include prohibition of the following:

. Negotiable instruments for purchase price balances in
nection with consumer credit sales. Additionally, the as-
ee of the seller's right to the balance of the purchase price
s subject to defenses of the buyer against the seller. These
s correspond to the Unruh Act rules discussed on page 99.

. Security agreements in connection with consumer credit
s which take a security interest in property other than the
perty sold, e.g., a security agreement in connection with
sale of furniture which takes a security interest in the
er's automobile. Certain exceptions are made, however.
ross-collateral" agreements are permitted. This means that
he buyer has previously purchased goods from the seller
ch are not yet fully paid for, the seller may make the old
ds as well as the new goods security for the new purchase.
ne goods sold are to be annexed to other goods or to land,
seller may take a security interest in the other goods if the
t to be secured is $300 or more, in the land if the debt to
secured is $1000 or more.

. Wage assignments for payment or as security for pay-
t of a debt arising out of a consumer credit sale.

alifornia has not shown interest in the U-Triple C because
lready covers most of the same bases by means of the
ruh Act and other statutory provisions, which have been
n earlier.

onscionable Contracts; Herein Adhesion Contracts

ontemporary courts have taken militant stands against un-
scionable contracts. The term covers a multitude of sins
m the illusory Big Three new car warranty in *Henningsen*
Bloomfield Motors, 161 A.2d 69 (N.J.), which at that time
effect said, "If you are killed or disabled because of a
ect in this automobile, return the defective part to the fac-
y in Detroit and we will replace it," to the badly put upon
er in *Jones* v. *Star Credit Corp.*, 298 N.Y.S.2d 264, who
s induced to sign a contract which would have required
a to pay $1500 for a freezer worth $300.

he Official Text of the Uniform Commercial Code con-
s what has become a quite famous provision relative to
onscionable contracts, Section 2302, which is entitled
nconscionable Contract or Clause" and which provides, as
lows:

"(1) If the court as a matter of law finds the contract or
clause of the contract to have been unconscionable at the
e it was made the court may refuse to enforce the contract,
it may enforce the remainder of the contract without the
onscionable clause, or it may so limit the application of
unconscionable clause as to avoid any unconscionable re-
t.

"(2) When it is claimed or appears to the court that the
tract or any clause thereof may be unconscionable the par-
shall be afforded a reasonable opportunity to present evi-

dence as to its commercial setting, purpose and effect to aid
the court in making the determination."

The court relied directly upon Section 2-302 in finding the
price term unconscionable in the *Jones* case and referred to it
in the *Henningsen* case where the code had not yet become
law in New Jersey at the time of the case.

● The California Uniform Commercial Code does not contain
Section 2-302. The California legislators elected to omit it on
the ground that California courts had already recognized such
a doctrine and therefore did not need a statutory base for it,
a determination that is quite possibly questionable. However,
in 1979 the California legislature did an about-face and adopted the language of U.C.C. 2-302 verbatim but not as part of
the Uniform Commercial Code but as part of the California
general contract law in C.C. 1670.5.

● Certainly much mileage may be expected to be obtained
from the doctrine of unconscionability in the future.

● At the consumer level, most unconscionable contracts are
also *contracts of adhesion* or *adhesion contracts*. The term is
not one of precise definition but the adhesion contract is easily
recognized by its characteristics which are that it is a standardized or form contract for which the buyer has no alternative but to "take it or leave it," to "adhere" to it or not
have a contract at all; that it involves no bargaining and no
real possibility for bargaining regarding terms other than the
financial terms; that the terms other than the financial terms
are dictated solely by the seller; that the buyer cannot shop
around for a better form of contract because other sellers will
have essentially the same form; and that the contract or contract terms in question is unduly oppressive or "unconscionable." The printed terms, and especially some fine print
terms, of the adhesion contract are apt to be unconscionable
and if they are they can be struck down by the court as was
the illusory, and unconscionable, automobile warranty in
Henningsen. For another example of an adhesion contract, see
the *Tunkl* case at page 39.

Bulk Transfers

Introduction

Bulk sales laws or acts, as they have been called heretofore,
have been in the law for a long time. The code chooses the
new expression, *"bulk transfer,"* to describe its law on the
subject. A bulk sale is the opposite of an ordinary sale. An
ordinary sale is a retail sale out of inventory of one or more
units of inventory. A bulk sale is ordinarily the sale of the
inventory itself. Thus, the sale of ten kitchen ranges by an
appliance dealer to an apartment house owner is, while it may
be a large sale, not a "bulk sale." Ordinarily a merchant does
not sell his entire inventory except in connection with the sale
of his business. Therefore ordinarily a "bulk sale" is a sale
of a business.

● Bulk sales laws were enacted to prevent fraud upon the
seller's creditors in connection with the sale of a business.
Without such laws, a dishonest merchant could sell an inventory obtained on credit and abscond with the proceeds. Bulk
sales laws prevent this by requiring creditors to be given advance notice of sale and opportunity to impound the proceeds,
so it is the function of bulk sales law to warn creditors of a
proposed sale of a business.

● Precode bulk sales laws also regulated "bulk mortgages"—
mortgages of the fixtures and equipment of a business. Under
the code, bulk mortgages are regulated by Division 9, covered
in Chapter 7.

● There were several variations of bulk sales acts under precode law. Some were "actual notice" statutes, requiring the

seller of the business to furnish a list of his creditors and for such creditors to be notified of the proposed sale by mail. Others, including California's, were "public notice" statutes, which required notice of the proposed sale to be published in the newspaper for some period of time in advance of sale. Some merely required creditors to be given notice. Others imposed an obligation on the buyer to see that they were paid, and to pay the seller only the net purchase price for the business; that is, the balance of the agreed purchase price remaining after the seller's creditors were paid. California did not require that the seller's creditors be paid, but as a matter of legal practice this was always done, through the establishment of an escrow, as described below, and continues to be done. These variations continue under the code so that Article 6 has several major variations.

• The penalty for not complying with a bulk sales act, both prior to the code and under the code, is that the sale is not good as against the seller's creditors, who can still enforce their claims against the assets of the business in the hand of the buyer.[127]

• Some of the main provisions of California's Division 6 are now examined.

California's Division 6

Transfers Subject to Division 6: The evil at which bulk sales acts were aimed was found mainly in connection with sales of businesses dealing in merchandise, which purchased inventory on open credit. Only a few types of service businesses were offenders. The official text of the code does not regulate the sale of service businesses at all, only the sale of a business "whose principal business is the sale of merchandise from stock, including those who manufacture what they sell." California's Section 6102(3) regulates not only the sales of these kinds of businesses but also sales of bakery, restaurant, garage and cleaning businesses.

Exempt Transactions: Section 6103 lists eight types of exempt transactions, which generally speaking are exempt either because they are, under the code, regulated by Division 9

rather than Division 6, or because they are not bulk sal the understood sense of that term, which is that a bulk sa a voluntary transfer, which the transactions covered by divisions (2), (4) and (5) of Section 6103 essentially are

Form of Notice to Creditors; and Publication: Sec 6107 states the required contents of notice to creditors anc requirement that such notice be (1) *recorded* in the offic the county recorder of the county in which the property t transferred is located at least 12 business days before the transfer is to be consummated, (2) *published* in the ma required by subdivision (2)(b) of Section 6107 at least 12 t ness days before the bulk transfer is to be consummated, (3) be delivered or sent by registered or certified mail at 12 business days before the bulk transfer is to be cons mated to the county tax collector in the county or countie which the property to be transferred is located.

An illustrative form of the kind of notice that would recorded and published in California is shown on the foll ing page.

Escrows: In the sale of a California business it is stand legal practice to establish an escrow out of which the sell creditors who file claims with the escrow agent are paid. crow is required where the sale includes an onsale liquo cense.[128]

Sale of a business ordinarily starts with a written cont for sale, prepared by an attorney serving one of the part or both of them. The escrow is one of the things agreed t the contract. Commonly, the attorney is agreed on as the crow agent, although it may also commonly be a bank or broker who has produced the sale. The attorney or the esc sees that notice to creditors is recorded and published obtains various clearances—for such things as sales taxes unemployment and disability insurance contributions. At conclusion of the notice period, the escrow agent pays cla of creditors who have filed claims within the allowed ti The buyer takes free of claims of creditors who have not f claims within this period.

---

[127]U.C.C. 6105 makes this so under the code.

[128]B.P.C. 24073, 24074.

NOTICE TO CREDITORS OF BULK TRANSFER
(Secs. 6101-6107 U.C.C.)

Notice is hereby given to creditors of the within named transferor(s) that a bulk transfer is about to be made on personal property hereinafter described.

The name(s) and business address of the intended transferor(s) are:

The location in California of the chief executive office or principal business office of the intended transferor is: (If 'same as above", so state.)

All other business names and addresses used by the intended transferor within three years last past so far as known to the intended transferee are: (If "none", so state.)

The name(s) and business address of the intended transferee(s) are:

That the property pertinent hereto is described in general as:

and is located at:

The business name used by the said transferor(s) at said location is:

That said bulk transfer is intended to be consummated at the office of:

_____ , _____ , California_____

on or after _____ , 19_____ .

This bulk transfer _____ subject to California Uniform Commercial Code Section 6106.
                        is/is not

The name and address of the person with whom claims may be filed is_____

_____ ,

and the last day for filing claims by any creditor shall be _____ ,

which is the business day before the consummation date specified above.

Dated _____ , 19_____   _____

                                                            _____

                                                            _____

                                                            _____
                                                                  Intended Transferee(s)
                                                            (Please Sign and Print or Type Name)

ESCROW INSTRUCTIONS
FOR TRANSFER OF ALCOHOLIC BEVERAGE LICENSE
SEPARATELY OR INCLUDING SALE OF BUSINESS

California Bank

_____, 19___

Gentlemen:

In consideration of your acting as escrow holder herein, it is agreed that you shall in no case or event be liable for the failure of any of the conditions of this escrow or damage caused by the exercise of your discretion in any particular manner, or for any other reason, except gross negligence or willful misconduct with reference to the said escrow, and you shall not be liable or responsible for your failure to ascertain the terms or conditions, or to comply with any of the provisions of any agreement, contract or other document filed herewith or referred to herein, nor shall you be liable or responsible for forgeries or fraudulent impersonations.

It is further agreed that if any controversy arises between the parties hereto or with any third person, with respect to the subject matter of this escrow, its terms or conditions, you shall not be required to determine the same or take any action in the premises, but you may await the settlement of any such controversy by final appropriate legal proceedings or otherwise as you may require, notwithstanding anything in the following instructions to the contrary, and in such event you shall not be liable for interest or damage.

IT IS UNDERSTOOD that the fees and usual charges agreed upon for your services hereunder shall be considered compensation for your ordinary services as contemplated by these instructions, and in the event that the conditions of this escrow are not promptly fulfilled or that you render any service hereunder not provided for in the following instructions, or that there is any assignment of any interest in the subject matter of this escrow or modification hereof, or that any controversy arises hereunder or that you are made a party to, or intervene in, any litigation pertaining to this escrow or the subject matter thereof, you shall be reasonably compensated for such extraordinary services and reimbursed for all costs, attorney fees and expenses occasioned by such default, delay, controversy or litigation and you shall have the right to retain all documents and/or other things of value at any time held by you hereunder until such compensation, fees, costs and expenses shall be paid, the undersigned hereby jointly and severally promising to pay such sums upon demand.

The undersigned Transferor-Licensee in this escrow is: _____
_____
_____ :
Soc. Sec. # or Fed. I.D. # _____ : who will hand you a Bill of Sale of the transfer of stock in trade, fixtures, equipment, good will and_____ of that certain
_____ business known as _____
indicated at the address below and _____
_____
_____
_____
_____

The undersigned, Transferee in this escrow, _____
_____
_____

Soc. Sec. # or Fed. I.D. # _____ will hand you, or cause to be handed you,
a Notice of Intended Transfer of Liquor License(s) covering that certain _____
license issued for the premises at _____
(and, or combined with, a Notice to Creditors) and the full amount of the purchase price or consideration, totaling $_____
for the above described Alcoholic Beverage License: said purchase price or consideration shall be made up as follows:
_____
_____
_____
_____

The said Transferee will additionally hand you $_____ total consideration for the subject business, including inventory of stock in trade not to exceed $_____ ; said purchase price or consideration shall be made up as follows:
_____
_____
_____

If a Security Agreement is to secure part of the purchase price, Transferee will also hand you a Financing Statement duly executed. You are authorized and instructed to prepare, accept, hold and disburse or use the above documents and funds as follows:

1.   Record the Notice(s) in the Office of the County Recorder of_____
County(ies) immediately and at least 10 days before date specified in paragraph 4.

2.   Publish a copy of such notice(s) in a newspaper of general circulation in the appropriate Judicial District (if no Judicial District, then in such county) wherein the above referred to personal property is located. Said Notice shall be published not less than 10 days before date specified in paragraph 4.

(Form continued on following pages)

3.   Send a copy of such Notice(s) by Registered or Certified Mail to the County Tax Collector in the County or Counties in which the above referred to personal property is located, at least 10 days before date specified in paragraph 4.

(STRIKE PARAGRAPHS 2 AND 3 IF TRANSFER OF LICENSE ONLY)

4.   Hold the Bill of Sale, if any, cash deposited, and other documents until the_____day of_____, 19___, (at least 15 days after date of escrow), and if you have not received a notice in writing from the Department of Alcoholic Beverage Control on or before said date, of its approval of the transfer of said license, continue to hold the same until you receive such notice in writing.

5.   On or after said date, and after your receipt of such notice from said Department in writing, you are hereby authorized to pay such taxes and amounts specified in Business and Professions Code §24049 as are required by the Department of Alcoholic Beverage Control to be paid as a condition precedent to the transfer of the license, after which you will close this escrow, unless bills of creditors have been filed in excess of the deposited total of the cash portion of the purchase price for the transfer of the license and the cash portion of the consideration for the other property involved herein, and providing Transferee and Transferor-Licensee have complied with their respective requirements, deliver said Bill of Sale, if any, and _____

_____

_____

to the Transferee and deliver to Transferor-Licensee, or order, the Note secured by the Security Agreement, if any, and other documents to which he may be entitled. File the Financing Statement, if any, in the Office of the Secretary of State at Sacramento. If the said total of the cash portion of the purchase price for the transfer of the license and the cash portion of the consideration for the other property involved herein is sufficient to do so, you will pay escrow fees and claims of bona fide creditors of Transferor-Licensee which are filed prior to the time you are notified by the Department of Alcoholic Beverage Control of its approval of the transfer of the license and which are approved by the Transferor-Licensee, and pay the balance over to the Transferor-Licensee. If the cash portion of the purchase price or consideration involved herein is not sufficient to pay said claims in full, you will distribute said total of the cash portions in accordance with the priorities established by Business and Professions Code §24074 to such creditors of the licensee within a reasonable time after the completion of the transfer of said license. You are also authorized to retain the promissory note, if any, to collect the payments thereon as become due and to distribute the proceeds of the collections in accordance with the same priorities.

If the Transferor-Licensee disputes any claim, the amount or pro rata amount thereof shall be retained by you for a period of twenty five days from the date the consideration in escrow would otherwise be available for distribution to the Transferor-Licensee or his creditors and, if not attached during that period, thereafter paid to the Transferor-Licensee.

6.   After all bills are paid or adjusted, pay the balance to transferor.

It is understood that the within instructions, authorizations and agreements are for the benefit of the parties hereto only and are not intended to constitute an assignment either legal or equitable to or in favor of any person or persons not a party to this escrow or to create in any person or persons not a party hereto any interest either legal or equitable in the property being transferred through this escrow or the consideration paid therefore.

YOU WILL ASSUME NO LIABILITY FOR THE PAYMENT OF ANY INSURANCE, PERSONAL PROPERTY TAX, SALES TAX, BEVERAGE TAX, SOCIAL SECURITY OR UNEMPLOYMENT INSURANCE DEDUCTIONS, OR ANY OTHER TAX, IT BEING UNDERSTOOD THAT SUCH MATTERS WILL BE PAID OR ADJUSTED OUTSIDE OF THE ESCROW. IT IS FURTHER UNDERSTOOD THAT SHOULD YOU BE DIRECTED TO MAKE ANY SUCH PAYMENTS OF TAXES OR INSURANCE, SAME MAY OR MAY NOT CONSTITUTE FULL OR FINAL PAYMENT THEREOF.

Transferee may at his option instruct you in writing before delivery of documents or disbursement of funds not to deliver any documents or disburse any funds until such time as transferee herein advises you that he has satisfied himself that transferor-licensee has obtained releases or waivers, or authorized payment through escrow, of taxes affecting business described herein.

It is understood that you are to make no examination of the property nor of the title thereto, and that unless otherwise provided herein you are not concerned with any conditional sale contract, lease contract, or security agreement that may affect the herein referred to personal property, and are not to be responsible for the delivery of any papers other than described herein.

Regardless of the consummation of this transaction, without limiting the joint and several liability of the undersigned for all compensation, fees, costs and expenses herein, the transferor-licensee and transferee each agree to pay one-half, unless otherwise provided, of all of your usual charges.

Unless otherwise expressly provided, prorations herein, if any, are to be made on basis of a 30 day month, as follows: personal property taxes on figures to be furnished you by the transferor and approved by the transferee and such figures to be construed as covering the period from July 1 to June 30, inclusive; principal and interest on encumbrances or contracts based on statements by the secured party, or holder thereof or holder for collection; interest on new encumbrances by endorsement on notes; and, rents on basis of statement furnished by transferor and approved by transferee. Assume that insurance premiums are paid and transfer on behalf of the parties hereto any insurance policies (except Employe's Liability) as handed you. Forward such policies, upon close of escrow to agent with the request that insurer consent to such transfer or attach secured party's clause or other additions or corrections, and that agent thereafter forward such policies to parties entitled thereto.

The expression "close of escrow," as used herein, shall mean the date you are authorized to disburse funds and deliver documents pursuant to the provisions of paragraph 5.

The following adjustments only are required in this escrow: Prorate

Disposition of transferor's funds (indicate by "X"):

( ) a. Credit _____ account of _____ at your
_____Branch.

( ) b. Mail check to address below.

( ) c. Other:

In the event that the conditions of this escrow have not been fulfilled on the date designated in paragraph 4 hereof, by reason of the fact that you have not received notice in writing from the said Department of its approval of the transfer of said license(s) or for any other reason, you are instructed, nevertheless, to complete the escrow at any time thereafter as soon as the conditions (except as to time) have been fulfilled and without recording and publishing a new notice to creditors unless otherwise specifically instructed herein, or the undersigned, or either of them, shall have made written demand upon you for the return of money and instruments deposited by them.

Each of the undersigned states that he has read the foregoing instructions and understands and agrees to them.

_____	_____
TRANSFEROR-LICENSEE	TRANSFEREE
_____	_____
TRANSFEROR-LICENSEE	TRANSFEREE

Address: _____   Address: _____

Telephone: _____   Telephone: _____

CHAPTER 6

Commercial Paper

Negotiability

Negotiable instruments are another special type of contract—private contracts for the payment of money—notes, drafts and checks drawn by private individuals, as distinguished from government contracts to pay money in the form of currency.[1]

Negotiable instruments are the most famous and important product of the *law merchant*,[2] and have been in existence for many centuries, since there has long been need for and use of such contracts to make possible credit transactions, and as a general substitute for money. The best known of these, the check, is actually the most recent, its development being concurrent with that of the great chain banking systems of today.

As in sales, and for the same reason—that negotiable instruments do not know boundary lines—a uniform law was desirable. Such a law was drafted at the turn of the century, was first presented to the states for adoption in 1907, and was adopted by all states: the "Uniform Negotiable Instruments Law." In California, and elsewhere, it is superseded by Division 3/Article 3 of the Uniform Commercial Code.

What Is Negotiability?

Today, we take negotiable instruments for granted, particularly the check, and seldom have occasion to consider their "negotiable" character. There is good reason for this. The idea of *negotiability* was conceived with reference to private contracts for the payment of money that might be expected to pass through a succession of hands, and is particularly important where that is what happens. Today, this would be the exception rather than the rule. If you give B a check for $100 for goods sold to you, and B wishes to buy $100 worth of goods from S, the normal procedure is for B to deposit the check in his account and write his own check to S, so that he incurs an obligation directly to S. At the time negotiable instruments were conceived, however, when the banking conveniences of today were not available, it might well have been the case that B would transfer or indorse your instrument to S, provided S was agreeable. But S would have to reason this way: If this is a mere contract that I am taking, my status will be that of an assignee, and I will have no better rights than my assignor had; if he sold defective goods to the maker of this instrument so that the maker has a defense of failure of consideration against him, that defense will be good against me also. The person assigning this contract to me comes from another part of the country, to which I would have to go to recover from him; so perhaps I had better insist on cash.

If this line of reasoning were multiplied by many thousands of times, this would be the result: commerce would be greatly retarded because it would be neither safe nor practical to carry on commercial transactions entirely with money. It would be the ideal situation if private instruments for payment of money could be made to circulate freely in lieu of money, but to bring this about it would be necessary to give them characteristics not possessed by ordinary contracts.

A simple enough idea was evolved, which provided an excellent solution to the whole problem. It was this: Certain special qualities were to be given to such "instruments," provided they were in certain form.[3] It was to be the rule that such instruments were to pass to a transferee (1) free from the most likely defenses of the maker, and (2) free of claims of intermediate holders, provided that the transferee gave value for the instrument and took it without notice of the defense to the maker or claim of the intermediate party. In short, the transferee was to be entitled to get better rights than his transferor had—a radical departure from the theory of *assignment* of contracts. These special qualities—this capacity to pass free of defenses and claims of intermediate parties—was to be known as *negotiability*, and instruments so endowed were to be known as *negotiable instruments*. To avoid the nomenclature of contracts, the transfers of such instruments were to be called *negotiations* rather than assignments, and one who took such an instrument for value and without notice of defenses or claims to it, and so got the benefit of its special qualities, was to be called a *holder in due course*. In brief, this is the story of negotiability and negotiable instruments.[4] There is much more, of course, and as a first step into and through it, fuller inquiry may be made into the matter of the defenses and claims from which such instruments are freed. To make this inquiry, suppose the following fact situation:

M makes and gives his negotiable instrument for $100 to P in payment of the purchase price of goods. Unknown to P, the goods are defective in some way so as to make them worthless, so that while there was no intention on his part to defraud, there was failure of consideration as between him and M which gives M a defense to the enforcement of the instrument by P.

P transfers the instrument to A, who, in turn, transfers it to B. There is fraud as between A and B in that B takes the instrument in exchange for goods which he fraudulently misrepresents to A. As between A and B, A is an intermediate holder who has a claim to the instrument because of the fraud which has been practiced on him. B transfers the instrument to C, who gives value for it and takes it without knowledge of the various wrongdoings that have occurred.

Graphically, the situation is this:

```
|— Defect No. 1 —|              |— Defect No. 2 —|
M ——————— P ——————— A ——————— B ——————— C
    (FAILURE OF                    (FRAUD)
    CONSIDERATION)
```

---

[1] An item of paper money, or currency, constitutes a promise of the government to pay money. It may be in the form of a certificate of deposit, as in the case of a dollar bill, or in the form of a note, as in the case of fivedollar bills and upwards.

[2] See page 3 for discussion of the law merchant.

[3] The formal requirements for negotiable instruments are discussed in following sections.

[4] This did not happen in a short time, but developed over a period of several centuries.

Defect No. 1 is a *defense*, the right of a maker to refuse to make payment of the instrument because of a wrong practiced on him. Defect No. 2 is a claim to the instrument of a third person, an intermediate holder, because of a wrong practiced on him; an *adverse claim*.

Defenses—Real and Personal

Discussing Defect No. 1, suppose C attempts to collect on the instrument from M, who raises his defense of failure of consideration. This will not be good as against C, a holder in due course. As stated, one of the attributes of negotiability is that a holder in due course takes a negotiable instrument free of certain important defenses of the maker. Failure of consideration is one of those defenses. This is very important because of all the defenses that a maker is apt to have to an instrument, *failure of consideration* is apt to be the most likely. For every case of some other defense, there will be a hundred cases of the defense of failure of consideration, real or imagined. So by freeing negotiable instruments of this defense, much was done to promote their negotiability.

C would be able to collect from M even if P had intentionally defrauded M, because *fraud as to the consideration* is another defense which is not good against a holder in due course. This would give added stimulus to the negotiability of such instruments.

There were and are certain defenses for which even negotiability is not a cure, however. Suppose P had raised the amount of M's instrument from $100 to $300 before transferring it. Even in the hands of C, a holder in due course, M would have a defense against payment of the amount by which the instrument had been raised. He would have to pay its original amount of $100, but no more. It would be carrying negotiability too far to make a person liable for an instrument that was not his. The same would be true if M had not issued an instrument at all, but P had forged his name to an instrument. A forgery is a complete nullity and something for which the person whose signature was forged could not possibly be held, any more than the government could be required to issue good money to replace a counterfeit bill.

The various defenses that a maker might have against an instrument came to be classified as *real* and *personal*. *Real defenses* are those which are good against everyone including holders in due course—the defenses of *material alteration* and *forgery* discussed in the preceding paragraph, together with a few others considered later. *Personal defenses* are those which are not good against a holder in due course—the failure of consideration and fraud as to the consideration mentioned above, together with others to be considered. When it is said, then, that a negotiable instrument passes free of certain important defenses of the maker, it is meant that it passes free of *personal defenses*.

Adverse Claims

Defect No. 2 in the hypothetical case above involves a "claim" to the instrument by A because of fraud committed upon him by B. Now, suppose A tells M about the fraud. Later, C demands payment. M refuses to pay on the ground that, since A was defrauded, he remains the true owner of the instrument. M is not raising a *defense* because he is not asserting a wrong practiced upon him. M is asserting a right or claim of a third person, A. But it is no more effective against C than M's defense of failure of consideration. C is entitled to recover from M despite the claim of A. A negotiable instrument passes free of *adverse claims* as well as of defenses.

Just as there are real defenses, however, there is one type of adverse claim that is good even as against a holder in due course—a claim based on the fact that the instrument was transferred by a forgery of the claimant's indorsement. To understand this, it is necessary to become familiar to some extent with the methods of transferring negotiable instruments which, in turn, requires some knowledge of the distinction between *order paper* and *bearer paper*.

Bearer and Order Paper

M might give P a negotiable instrument in either of the following forms:

(1) "On June 1, 1984, I promise to pay *bearer* $100.

                                                  (Signed) M."

                          or

(2) "On June 1, 1984, I promise to pay *to the order of P* $100.

                                                  (Signed) M."

Both would be negotiable notes, but would differ in the fact that the first is a bearer instrument or *bearer paper*, while the second is an order instrument or *order paper*.

Bearer paper is what the name implies—paper which is payable to the holder of the instrument. Since such instruments are not identified to a particular individual they are transferable by "delivery alone," i.e., by being handed to a transferee. To make such an instrument is a dangerous thing. The law says that it has a quality of negotiability not yet considered—a sort of supernegotiability or *full negotiability* as it is usually called. By this is meant that if a bearer instrument finds its way into the hands of a holder in due course, it is enforceable by him regardless of how his transferor came into possession of the instrument. Using the bearer instrument above as an example, if M, after writing and signing it, had lost it, and F, the finder, had transferred it to C who gave value for it without knowledge of F's lack of title, M would have to pay C the amount of the instrument. Or, if M had delivered it to P but it had been stolen from P by F and transferred to C, a taker for value and without knowledge of the theft, C would again be protected. P would have no right to recover the instrument from C, and M would have to pay C its amount. By way of summing up this matter of full negotiability, it is often said that it means that "even a thief" may transfer good title to bearer paper—thus indicating that even the most serious of wrongdoers may effectively transfer it.[5]

Order paper, however, is protected by being identified to a particular person, P in instrument (2) above, so as to require *indorsement* of such person, i.e., transfer by the signature of such person. If P loses the order instrument or it is stolen from him, the only way in which F, the finder or thief, can transfer it is to forge the signature of P. Just as forgery of the signature of the maker will not create an instrument, forgery of indorsement will not transfer it. Even though C, the transferee, is a holder in due course, P may recover the instrument from him. This is one instance, then, in which the right of an adverse claimant is superior to the right of a holder in due course—when the instrument has come into the hands of a holder in due course through forged indorsement.

---

[5]Currency is payable to "bearer," and so has this supernegotiability; and currency has it to an even greater degree in the practical sense that one would never question currency but might be reluctant to take a negotiable instrument even though it was a bearer instrument.

● Let us start anew with the order instrument. P proposes to transfer it to A. There are two general types of indorsements by which he may do so. (1) He may simply sign his name on the back of the instrument. This is called a *blank indorsement*—one which names no particular person as indorsee—and converts to bearer paper[6] this instrument which up to this point has been order paper. If this is done, all the consequences of bearer paper follow, i.e., anyone into whose hands it falls may effectively transfer it. So, if after indorsing but before delivering the instrument to A, P loses it or it is stolen from him, the finder or thief may pass good title to a holder in due course. Or, if P delivers it to A, and A loses or has it stolen from him, the finder or thief may pass title. (2) P may write on the back of the instrument "Pay to the order of A" and then sign his name. This is a *special indorsement*—one which names a particular person as indorsee. This perpetuates the "order" nature of the instrument, i.e., requires the indorsement of A for further negotiation. So, if A loses the instrument or it is stolen from him, the finder or thief cannot pass title since he must forge A's indorsement to effect transfer, and forged indorsement does not pass title.

Summary

What has been discussed to this point will be of great importance throughout the chapter.

1. Negotiable instruments are private contracts for the payment of money which meet certain formal requirements (to be discussed in the next two sections). The distinctive characteristic of a negotiable instrument is that it passes to a holder in due course free of certain important (personal) defenses of the maker and of adverse claims, and it is in this respect that a negotiable instrument differs from an ordinary contract.

2. Negotiable instruments may be written in the form of bearer paper or in the form of order paper. In the latter case they require the genuine indorsement of the holder for negotiation. If written as bearer paper or converted into bearer paper by blank indorsement, they have the exceptional quality of "full or absolute negotiability," which means they may be transferred even by a finder or thief.

Nature and Types of Negotiable Instruments

Section 3528 of the California Civil Code says that "The law respects form less than substance." This is one of a number of Maxims of Jurisprudence set out at the end of the Civil Code—broad propositions of legal philosophy. Generally speaking this is true.

Negotiable instruments are the exception—here form is more important than substance. It was felt that this was necessary; that if these contracts for the payment of money were to be given the exceptional quality of negotiability, they should be required to be in particular form and that this requirement should be enforced with considerable strictness. This was so under the law merchant, continued to be so under the Uniform Negotiable Instruments Law, and remains so under the code. U.C.C. 3104(1) sets out the formal requirements of a negotiable instrument, as follows:

"(1) Any writing to be a negotiable instrument within this division must
  "(a) Be signed by the maker or drawer; and
  "(b) Contain an unconditional promise or order to pay a sum certain in money and no other promise, order, obligation or power given by the maker or drawer except as authorized by this division; and

"(c) Be payable on demand or at a definite time; and
"(d) Be payable to order or to bearer."

● These are absolute requirements, and instruments which do not conform are *non-negotiable*—mere *contracts* which may be assigned, but in which the transferee gets no better rights than his transferor had.

● U.C.C. 3104(1) recognizes three alternatives in the matter of form, however: That negotiable instruments may be instruments containing a "promise *or* order;" that they may be made payable "on demand *or* at a definite time;" and that they may be made payable "to order *or* to bearer." Alternatively, then, they may be:

1. *Promise* or *order* instruments.
2. *Demand* or *time* instruments.
3. *Order* or *bearer* paper.

● The first of these alternatives is the most important since it concerns the basic structural nature of the instrument—whether it represents the making of a promise or the issuance of an order.

Promise Instruments

Notes[7] are by far the most important type of promise instruments. A note is simply a written promise by one person to pay money to another. Ordinarily, it is given in return for a loan, and serves as written evidence of the obligation to make repayment—(1) M borrows $1000 from J, a friend, and gives him his note by which he promises to pay J in 30 days; (2) M borrows $2000 from her credit union and gives her note promising to pay in installments of $100 a month; (3) H and W borrow $10,000 from a bank for home improvements, and give the bank a note for $10,000, payable in installments of $213.00 a month for 5 years. At the same time, H and W give the bank a second deed of trust on the property so that the bank has security for its loan—something which it can sell if H and W fail to pay. Each of these transactions is basically the same, but the note may grow progressively more elaborate, the money more difficult to borrow, and the demands for security more stringent.

1. M's note to J for the $1000 loan might look like this:

```
                                                June 1, 1984
   30 days from date, I promise to pay to the order of
John Jones the sum of $1000, without interest. If action
is instituted on this note, I promise to pay such sum as
the court may fix as attorney's fees.
                              (Signed) MICHAEL MAKER
```

It might be written on a blank piece of paper or be on a form purchased at a stationery store. It contains all of the essentials of a negotiable instrument. It is in writing and signed; contains an unconditional promise—"I promise;" is for a sum certain in money; is payable at a determinable future time—by the computation of 30 days from June 1, 1984; and is payable to order—"to the order of John Jones." In addition, it calls for payment of attorney's fees if Jones is required to sue to recover his money. This brings up a new point. While the code requires that certain things *must* be in the instrument if it is to be negotiable, it does not say that other things cannot be included. In general, other provisions are permissible so long as they do not make the promise conditional.

---

[6]U.C.C. 3204(2).

[7]Prior to the code, called "*promissory notes.*" In the interests of streamlining legal language the code drops "*promissory.*" U.C.C. 3104(2)(d).

2. M's note to her credit union for the $2000 loan might look like the note on page 115. Here, M is entering into a business transaction and the note becomes more "business-like" in form.

3. H and W's note to the bank for the $10,000 loan for home improvements might look like the note on page 116.

It might recite that it is "secured by a Deed of Trust," which means that H and W are creating a *lien* upon real property as security for the loan, the lender having the right to sell the property if the debt is not paid. Whenever a loan assumes substantial proportions, the lender will require substantial security and, in addition, as a safeguard against depreciation, will require that the value of the security exceed considerably the amount of the debt. The lien may be in the form of a *mortgage* or *deed of trust* on real estate, as above, or in the form of a *security agreement* granting a security interest in personal property owned by the note-makers, such as an automobile. It may also consist of a *pledge* of stocks or bonds. These various security devices are discussed in Chapter 7.

• Banks issue another kind of "promise instrument"[8] called a *certificate of deposit*, an illustration of which appears on page 116. (The "promise" is thought to be "implied" in this instrument, i.e., the instrument taken as a whole is considered to imply a promise on the part of the bank to pay the holder at maturity of the instrument.) Today, certificates of deposit are generally used only for large, generally short-term deposits, by business concerns. Today, with the great proliferation of "savings account"-like term deposit arrangements that are available to individuals, individuals do not generally use certificates of deposit. The idea of the two things is basically the same, however, except that in the case of certificates of deposit the interest rate increases not only with the length of the term for which the money is left on deposit but also with the amount of money that is placed on deposit.

Drafts

A negotiable instrument is "a '*draft*' ('bill of exchange') if it is an order.[9] It is "a '*check*' if it is a draft drawn on a bank and payable on demand."[10] Since checks are familiar they are considered first. For the sake of convenience checks and drafts are referred to as "order instruments" in this section, meaning that they are orders rather than promises. This should not be confused with the distinct requirement that a negotiable instrument must be *payable to* order or bearer, which is designed to require an instrument to show on its face that it is intended to be transferable.

Checks: Every order instrument consists of an order by one person to another directing him to pay money to a third per-

son. The personal check is the most familiar illustration. (See top of page 118.)

Like all order instruments, the check is built around a one word order—"*Pay.*" In the case of a check, this order is made to a bank and directs the bank to pay immediately—"on demand." Correctly speaking, the one who gives the order in an order instrument, the depositor in the case of the check, is called the *drawer*, but in everyday and banking practice he is commonly referred to as the *maker*. The party to whom the order is given, the bank in the case of the check, is called the *drawee*; and the party to whom payment is to be made, the *payee*. Like the check, all order instruments are *three party instruments*.[11] In legal theory a check reads: "Pay . . . . . to the order of David Deaux." "Pay" is the "order" we are talking about here. It is the primary or prime order directed to the bank. It is of the very concept of the instrument. On the other hand, "to the order of David Deaux," and note that this part of the instrument is to be read together in the manner given, has reference only to the party payable. The bank is ordered to pay the specified sum to David Deaux or to such person as he may see fit to transfer his rights, (to the order of David Deaux), by indorsing the instrument to another.

Cashier's Checks: While a cashier's check is in form an order by a bank upon itself to pay money to a third person, it is in effect a promise by the bank to pay the money, and is designed to provide an instrument of unimpeachable integrity to satisfy persons not willing to take personal checks. (Second form, page 118.)

Certified Checks: These serve the same purpose as cashier's checks, the bank certifying the personal check of its depositor as in the form at the bottom of page 118, thereby making the check its own obligation.[12] It immediately charges the account of its depositor with the amount of the check and credits this amount to its own "Certified Check Account" from which it will pay this and other checks certified by it.

Certified checks have greatly declined in use in recent years. Banks are reluctant to issue them because they are more susceptible to alteration than cashier's checks and, since it makes little difference to the depositor, he will usually be satisfied to take a cashier's check.

Commercial Drafts: As has been shown in Chapter 4, beginning at page 75, where one person sells goods to another, his method of collecting the purchase price may take the form of an instrument which "orders" the buyer to pay the price to the seller or to a bank which is acting as the seller's agent to make collection. These are the instruments called *commercial drafts* and are either *sight drafts* or *time drafts*.

SIGHT DRAFTS. A specimen form of sight draft is shown on page 75. That form contains all of the essential elements of a negotiable instrument—is in writing and signed by the drawer, contains an unconditional order to pay a sum certain in mon-

---

[8]"A 'promise' is an undertaking to pay and must be more than an acknowledgment of an obligation." U.C.C. 3102(1)(c). A certificate of deposit is a negotiable instrument. U.C.C. 3104(1)(2)(c). "A 'certificate of deposit' . . . is an acknowledgment by a bank of receipt of money with an engagement to repay it." U.C.C. 3104(2)(4). IOU's and "due bills" ("Due John Jones $100") are mere acknowledgments of obligations [U.C.C. 3102(1)(c), above] and therefore are not negotiable instruments.

[9]U.C.C. 3104(2)(a). "Bill of exchange" was the law merchant term for the "draft," the original negotiable instrument. Before banks, and still to a large extent in Europe, drafts passed hand to hand, or were "exchanged," and were an important medium of exchange. As has been noted, under today's banking system persons in this country deposit the other man's check and write their own.

[10]U.C.C. 3104(2)(b).

---

[11]This does not mean that the instrument must involve three separate and distinct persons. The same "person" may and often does serve in two capacities on an order instrument; e.g., a bank may be both drawee and payee on checks sent to it for monthly installments on a loan. All that *three party instrument* signifies is that in order instruments there are the three distinct legal capacities of drawer, drawee and payee to be occupied. The same individual may occupy two of these. See U.C.C. 3110 (1)(a)(b)(c).

[12]Certification of a check by a bank is the equivalent of the "acceptance" of a commercial draft, discussed in the next section. U.C.C. 3411(1).

LOAN AGREEMENT, SECURITY AGREEMENT, AND
FEDERAL DISCLOSURE STATEMENT
(FEDERAL CREDIT UNION)

In this agreement, the words I, ME, MY and MINE mean each and all of those who sign this agreement. The words YOU, YOUR, and YOURS mean the Credit Union.

BORROWER'S NAME AND ADDRESS:	CREDIT UNION'S NAME AND ADDRESS:

Date of Loan:	Account No.:	Note No.:

ANNUAL PERCENTAGE RATE The cost of my credit as a yearly rate %	FINANCE CHARGE The dollar amount the credit will cost me. $	Amount Financed The amount of credit provided to me or on my behalf. $	Total of Payments The amount I will have paid after I have made all payments as scheduled. $

My payment schedule will be:

Number of Payments	Amount of Each Payment	When Payments Are Due

Insurance: Credit life insurance and credit disability insurance are not required to obtain credit, and will not be provided unless I sign, agreeing to pay the additional cost.

Type	Premium	Signature
Credit Life	$	I want credit life insurance X
Credit Disability	$	I want credit disability insurance X

I may obtain property insurance from anyone I want that is acceptable to you.

Penalty for Late Payment: If my payment is more than 7 days late I will be charged a late charge of 20% of the FINANCE CHARGE due, but not less than $0.05.

Prepayment: If I pay off early, I will not have to pay a penalty.

Security Interest: ☐ If this box is checked, this loan is secured by the following described personal property:

Collateral Type: _____   Year _____   Make _____   I.D. Number _____

Share Pledge: _____   Account Number(s) _____   Amount(s) _____

Other (specify): _____

See the Note and Security Agreement for any additional information about security interests, nonpayment, default, any required repayment in full before the scheduled date, and prepayment refunds and penalties.

_____

e means an estimate

ITEMIZATION OF AMOUNT FINANCED

Itemization of Amount Financed of $ _____

1.   Amount given to me directly   (1) $ _____
2.   Amount paid on my account   (2) $ _____
3.   Amount paid on my behalf

_____ $ _____
_____ $ _____
_____ $ _____
_____ $ _____
_____ $ _____

☐ If this box is checked, the following fee has been paid by me separately and is **not** included in the Amount Financed.
To _____ $ _____.

NOTE AND SECURITY AGREEMENT

Payment Schedule: To repay my loan, I, jointly and severally, promise to pay you or to your order, the Amount Financed (shown above) plus FINANCE CHARGE (shown above), in lawful money of the United States. I will pay this sum at your office as set forth in the payment schedule (shown above). I understand that each payment is applied first to collection costs and late charges, if any, then to FINANCE CHARGE and then to the Amount Financed.

Security Agreement: If the security interest box is checked above, I understand that to protect you if I default on my loan, I give you a security interest under the Uniform Commercial Code in the property described above or on the attached exhibits, if any. I understand that my loan is also secured by any insurance proceeds or any insurance premium refunds. I also understand and agree to the additional security agreement terms on the reverse hereof.

NOTICE: SEE OTHER SIDE FOR ADDITIONAL TERMS

Copy Received: I acknowledge receipt of a copy of this Loan Agreement, Security Agreement (and Exhibits, if any) and Federal Disclosure Statement and accept and agree to the terms thereof.

CU 8-9 (REV. 10/82) LAW PRINTING CO., INC.   ©COPYRIGHT 1982

The Printer makes no warranty, express or implied, as to content or fitness for purpose of this form. Consult your own legal counsel.

Signature _____   Date _____

Signature _____   Date _____

INSTALLMENT NOTE
(INTEREST INCLUDED)

$ 10,000.00   San Francisco, California   June 26 , 1984

FOR VALUE RECEIVED, we   promise to pay in lawful money of the United States of America, to

CALIFORNIA BANK

or order, at San Francisco, California   the principal sum of

Ten thousand and no/100   Dollars,

with interest in like lawful money from date   , 19   at ten (10%) per cent
per annum on the amounts of principal sum remaining unpaid from time to time.

Principal and interest payable in monthly   installments of

two hundred thirteen and no/100   Dollars,

or more each, on the   first   day of each and every   month

beginning on the   first   day of August   1984

Each payment shall be credited first on interest then due and the remainder on principal; and interest shall thereupon cease upon the principal so credited. (Should interest not be so paid it shall thereafter bear like interest as the principal, but such unpaid interest so compounded shall not exceed an amount equal to interest on the unpaid principal at the maximum rate permitted by law.) Should default be made in payment of any installment of principal or interest when due the whole sum of principal and interest shall become immediately due at the option of the holder of this note. If action be instituted on this note I promise to pay such sum as the Court may fix as attorney's fees. This note is secured by a Second Deed of Trust bearing even date herewith.

                                                          s/THOMAS B. BUYER

                                                          s/HELEN A. BUYER

00-1 California Bank 00-1   No. 9628

                                        OAKLAND, CALIFORNIA_____ June 1,   19 84

THIS CERTIFIES THAT

                    DANIEL DEPOSITOR   HAS DEPOSITED IN THIS BANK

            5000 dols 00 cts   DOLLARS $5,000.00

PAYABLE ON _____ November 30, 1984 _____ TO _____ DANIEL DEPOSITOR _____ OR ORDER

UPON PRESENTATION AND SURRENDER OF THIS CERTIFICATE PROPERLY ENDORSED.
THIS DEPOSIT WILL BEAR SIMPLE INTEREST AT THE RATE OF ___ nine ___ PER CENT PER ANNUM FROM DATE HEREOF.
NO INTEREST WILL BE PAID ON THIS DEPOSIT AFTER MATURITY.

CERTIFICATE OF DEPOSIT   _Thomas Teller_

                                                          AUTHORIZED SIGNATURE

ey, is payable on demand, and is payable to order. Technically, it is a negotiable instrument of the order type. In reality, however, it is merely an established and convenient method of billing a buyer for the price of goods.

TIME DRAFTS—TRADE ACCEPTANCES. These have been discussed in Chapter 4, beginning at page 76.

Other Types of Drafts: There are other types of drafts than commercial drafts, but they are not important for our purposes. There is the *bank draft* drawn by a bank upon itself to pay what it owes another bank, determined by a balancing of the clearances of each bank against the other through the clearinghouse. Insurance companies use drafts rather than checks for some purposes, such as for the payment of claims. These are made "payable through" a bank, and so in practical effect are checks.

Essential Elements

U.C.C. 3104 provides:

"(1) Any writing to be a negotiable instrument within this division must
"(a) Be signed by the maker or drawer; and
"(b) Contain an unconditional promise or order to pay a sum certain in money and no other promise, order, obligation or power given by the maker or drawer except as authorized by this division; and
"(c) Be payable on demand or at a definite time; and
"(d) Be payable to order or to bearer."

Writing

Any medium or combination of mediums is permissible.[13] In his book, Uncommon Law, A. P. Herbert alludes to his story The Negotiable Cow, which has a negotiable instrument painted on the side of a cow. As a practical matter, most instruments are a combination of print and ink as in checks, of print and type as in notes, and so on. Obviously, forms of writing which constitute a "permanent memorial" and thus minimize the possibility of alteration are the most desirable; hence, pencil, though permissible, is not desirable.
• Conflicts sometimes occur in the writing—between the amount as expressed in words and figures or between written and printed provisions. U.C.C. 3118 sets out "rules of construction" which cover these matters. Section 3118(c) says that "Words control figures except that if the words are ambiguous figures control." So, if the figures on a check read "$10.00," but the words read "One Hundred DOLLARS," the bank can properly pay $100. *Nuzum* v. *Sheppard*, 87 W.Va. 243, 104 S.E. 487, illustrates ambiguous figures. It was held that $365 was properly payable on a check calling for payment of "Three sixty five . . . DOLLARS" in words and "$365" in figures.
• U.C.C. 3118(b) says that "Handwritten terms control typewritten and printed terms, and typewritten control printed." Thus, if a printed note had a provision for interest in the body and the parties were to write in at the end of the note "no interest shall be charged on this note," the written addendum would control.

Signature

A negotiable instrument must "be signed by the maker or drawer."[14] "*Signature*" is any symbol executed with intent

to authenticate a writing.[15] It may consist of a trade or assumed name, a printed or stamped signature, initials, mark or thumbprint.[16]
• "Unless the instrument clearly indicates that a signature is made in some other capacity it is an indorsement,"[17] so it must be clear that one is signing as a maker or drawer if he is to be held as such. Ordinarily, however, this is perfectly clear. Intent to sign in a capacity other than indorser is made out clearly by signing in the place customary for maker or drawer; in the lower right-hand corner. Extrinsic evidence is not admissible to show the capacity in which one has signed; U.C.C. 3402, above, says that "*the instrument*" must clearly indicate that the person has signed in another capacity if he is to be other than an indorser.

Signature in Representative Capacity: If one signs a negotiable instrument in a representative capacity, i.e., as agent, corporate officer, executor, administrator, or trustee, or the like, he must show this fact *on the instrument* or be personally liable. U.C.C. 3403 lays down these rules in these matters:
1. If both the name of the principal and the fact of representation appear, the representative is not personally liable:

Peter Piper
By Adam Archer, Agent

2. If the name of an organization (which includes corporation, partnership, estate, trust) is preceded or followed by the name and office of the representative, he is not personally liable:

Peter Piper Corporation
Adam Archer, Treasurer

Adam Archer, Administrator of the
Estate of Peter Piper, Deceased

3. If neither the name of the principal nor the fact of representation is shown, the representative is personally liable:

Adam Archer

4. If the name of the principal appears but not the fact of representation,

Peter Piper Corporation
Adam Archer

or the fact of representation but not the name of the principal,

Adam Archer, Agent

the representative may, as between the original parties to the instrument (maker and payee), show that he signed in a representative capacity.

Unconditional Promise or Order

Here are two requirements within the one: (1) That the instrument contain a promise or order; and (2) that the promise or order be unconditional. The first has been covered in prior sections.[18]

Negotiable instruments were conceived as a substitute for money. It was thought that certain things should be required of them, which would make them approximate money as near-

[13]U.C.C. 1201(46)
[14]U.C.C. 3104(1)(a).
[15]U.C.C. 1201(39).
[16]U.C.C. 3401(2), 1201(39), and Official Comments.
[17]U.C.C. 3402.
[18]See pages 113-117.

BY ENDORSEMENT THIS CHECK WHEN PAID IS ACCEPTED
IN FULL PAYMENT OF THE FOLLOWING ACCOUNT

DATE		AMOUNT
TOTAL OF INVOICES		
LESS % DISCOUNT		
LESS		
TOTAL DEDUCTIONS		
AMOUNT OF CHECK		

GENERAL EDUCATIONAL PUBLICATIONS   1392
99 SO. VAN NESS AVE.   621-5410
SAN FRANCISCO, CALIF.   94103

19_____   00-1

PAY
TO THE
ORDER OF _____ $_____

_____ DOLLARS

California Bank

⑈001392⑈ ⑆1210⑈0123⑆ 02606⑈00502⑈

DELUXE CHECK PRINTERS - SVA

00-1   **California Bank**   00-1   No. 86945

OAKLAND, CALIFORNIA ___May 15,___ 19_84_

PAY TO THE
ORDER OF ___HENRY DEAUX -___ $1,000.00

1000dols00cts _____ DOLLARS

CASHIER'S CHECK   *Carl Cashier*
                                          ASST. CASHIER - MANAGER

BY ENDORSEMENT THIS CHECK WHEN PAID IS ACCEPTED
IN FULL PAYMENT OF THE FOLLOWING ACCOUNT

DATE		AMOUNT

CERTIFIED

PAYABLE ONLY IF PRESENTED WITHIN THREE MONTHS FROM THIS DATE IF UNALTERED SINCE ISSUANCE AND IF PROPERLY ENDORSED

July 6, 1984
$10,000.00 ONLY

CALIFORNIA BANK

Ben Bankteller   TELLER

PAY

DO NOT DESTROY

TOTAL OF INVOICES
LESS   % DISCOUNT
LESS
TOTAL DEDUCTIONS
AMOUNT OF CHECK

GENERAL EDUCATIONAL PUBLICATIONS   1393
99 SO. VAN NESS AVE.   621-5410
SAN FRANCISCO, CALIF.   94103

         July 3,   19_84_   00-1

PAY
TO THE
ORDER OF ___NATIONAL PRINTING COMPANY - - - - - - -___ $10,000.00

10000dols00cts   DOLLARS

California Bank

                           Dorothy Drawer

⑈001393⑈ ⑆1210⑈0123⑆ 02606⑈00502⑈

DELUXE CHECK PRINTERS - SVA

ly as possible. They should carry the general credit of the maker and not be limited to payment from a particular fund. They should be "couriers without luggage," i.e., like money, "clean" instruments. The obligation of the instrument should be "contained within its four corners;" one should be able to take the instrument at face value and not have to look elsewhere to ascertain the obligation assumed by the maker. Some concessions had to be made. While drafts could be clean instruments it was in the nature of notes to have luggage, and an ever-increasing amount: interest provisions, acceleration clauses, security clauses, attorney's fees provisions. Since these would promote negotiability they could hardly be found to be objectionable. The Uniform Negotiable Instruments Law established provisions which permitted a good deal of luggage. The code, particularly as it is adopted in California, goes further.

Under the code there are only two things that cannot be done with an instrument. It cannot be made "payable only out of a particular fund or source"[19] (with exceptions, shown below) and it cannot be made "subject to or governed by" another agreement.[20] Today we are not concerned so much with substitutes for money as with an orderly system of commercial paper. This is why the code shows the considerable disregard that it does for the courier without luggage ideal.

Designation of Fund for Payment: As shown above, the instrument may not be limited to payment from a particular fund or source, except that "entity" instruments (instruments of partnerships, associations, estates, trusts) may be limited to the assets of the entity.[21] Examples of instruments limited to particular funds, held nonnegotiable on that account under the Uniform Negotiable Instruments Law, are *Tomlin* v. *Neale*, 76 C.A. 726, 245 P. 800 (from "cotton returns" from certain ranch) and *Glendora Bank* v. *Davis*, 204 C. 220, 267 P. 311 ("This note is given in payment of merchandise and is to be liquidated by payments received on account of sales of such merchandise.")

Permitted Luggage: U.C.C. 3105(1) provides that none of these facts or provisions destroys negotiability:

1. Security recitals; that the instrument is secured by mortgage, reservation of title, or otherwise: (a) "This note is secured by a second deed of trust," as in the note on page 124. (b) "This note is given as per security agreement of even date herewith, and it is agreed that title to the goods covered by said agreement shall remain in the payee hereof until this note is paid."

2. Statement of transaction which gave rise to instrument: "The transaction which gives rise to this instrument is the purchase of goods by the acceptor from the drawer," as in the trade acceptance on page 77.

3. Recital that instrument given "as per" underlying transaction, as in title-retention recital in paragraph 1(b), above.

4. Recital of executory consideration: "This note is given for goods to be delivered by payee to maker."

5. Recital that instrument matures in accordance with underlying transaction: "The obligation of the acceptor hereof arises out of the purchase of goods from the drawer, maturity being in conformity with original terms of purchase" (*West-*

lake Merc. Finance Corp v. *Merritt,* 204 C. 673, 269 P. 620, which held instrument bearing such recital nonnegotiable under the Uniform Negotiable Instruments Law).

6. Reference to separate agreement for rights as to prepayment or acceleration: "This note is secured by a security agreement of even date herewith, to which reference is hereby made for rights of the holder to accelerate the time of payment hereof."

7. Fact that instrument is subject to implied or constructive conditions, e.g., note and security agreement, with perforations for detachment of the one instrument from the other, as in *Commercial Credit Corp.* v. *Orange County Mach. Works*, 34 C.2d 766, 214 P.2d 819.

● In addition, U.C.C. 3112(1)(c) permits "A promise or power to maintain or protect collateral, *to furnish financial information or to do or refrain from doing any other act for the protection of the obligation expressed in the instrument* . . ." (Emphasis added.) The italicized portion of the section is not contained in the Official Text. It is a New York addition which California has adopted.

This permits a covenant to absorb depreciation in security: a provision, where a note is secured by a pledge of stock, which requires the maker to furnish additional collateral (stock) if the original collateral depreciates in value during the term of the note, on penalty that if additional collateral is not supplied the note will become immediately due and payable.

It also permits other types of covenants that modern lenders require in connection with commercial loans: covenants to furnish periodic financial statements, to establish sinking funds, to suspend dividends, and the like.

Any of these provisions may be contained in a separate agreement.[22]

Sum Certain in Money

Here, again, are two requirements within the one—that the instrument be for a "sum certain" and that it be made payable "in money."

Sum Certain: U.C.C. 3106(1) covers "sum certain." It says that the sum is certain even though the instrument "is to be paid."

"(a) With stated interest or by stated installments; or

"(b) With stated different rates of interest before and after default or a specified date; or

"(c) With a stated discount or addition if paid before or after the date fixed for payment; or

"(d) With exchange or less exchange, whether at a fixed rate or at the current rate; or

"(e) With costs of collection or an attorney's fee or both upon default."

Provisions for increase in interest rate if the instrument is not paid at maturity, for reduction in interest rate if promptly paid, or for discount on the principal if paid within specified time, e.g., a note payable in 6 months but with a 5% discount if paid within 30 days, are permitted by this section.

● A recent innovation in residential real estate financing by savings and loan associations is the *adjustable or variable interest rate* note under which the interest rate may be raised

---

[19]U.C.C. 3105(2)(b).

[20]U.C.C. 3105(2)(a).

[21]U.C.C. 3105(1)(h). Instruments issued by governmental agencies, which this text does not consider, may be limited to particular funds, e.g., proceeds of particular taxes. U.C.C. 3105(1)(g).

---

[22]U.C.C. 3119.

or lowered semi-annually by not more than ¼ of 1%,[23] to accord with generally prevailing interest rates. The "negotiability" of such notes seems somewhat in doubt. In keeping with the notion that the whole story of a negotiable instrument ought to be told on its face, Official Comment 1 to Section 3-106 of the Uniform Commercial Code says that "The computation (of interest) must be one which can be made from the instrument itself without reference to any outside source, and this section (3-106) does not make negotiable a note payable with interest 'at the current rate.'" The adjustable or variable rate note calls for interest, up or down from time to time, to be determined from, e.g., statistical averages "as shown by statistics prepared by (the) Federal Home Loan Bank"—clearly an "outside source" of reference. It would, of course, not really be important to the lender whether such a note was negotiable. The lender has taken the note purely in exchange for money—loaned to the maker of the note. There is no possible defense to the note and the lender would not expect to transfer it, and "negotiability" is only important when defenses against a transferee become involved.

Money: Under the code, the test of "money" is government sanction. "'*Money*' means a medium of exchange authorized or adopted by a domestic or foreign government as a part of its currency.[24]

"An instrument is payable in money if the medium of exchange in which it is payable is money at the time the instrument is made. An instrument payable in 'currency' or 'current funds' is payable in money."[25]

Instruments payable in foreign money are negotiable; they are payable at the exchange rate at date of payment unless it is expressly specified that payment is to be made in the foreign currency.[26]

Demand or Definite Time

Demand: A demand instrument is one which becomes payable as soon as it is issued. U.C.C. 3108 says that demand instruments include those payable "at sight or on presentation and those in which no time for payment is stated." Notes are sometimes made payable *on demand*. Sight drafts, being payable *at sight*, are demand instruments. The form *on presentation* is not used. Checks are payable on demand since they are instruments "in which no time for payment is stated."

Definite Time: U.C.C. 3109 defines "definite time," as follows:

"(1) An instrument is payable at a definite time if by its terms it is payable

"(a) On or before a stated date or at a fixed period after a stated date; or

"(b) At a fixed period after sight; or

"(c) At a definite time subject to any acceleration; or

"(d) At a definite time subject to extension at the option of the holder, or to extension to a further definite time at the option of the maker or acceptor or automatically upon or after a specified act or event.

"(2) An instrument which by its terms is otherwise payable only upon an act or event uncertain as to time of occurrence is not payable at a definite time even though the act or event has occurred."

This permits all types of acceleration.

Acceleration by Maker: Many notes read: "On or before [some specified date], I promise to pay . . ." This is permitted by U.C.C. 3109(1)(a), and would allow acceleration by the maker—payment by him at any time prior to the fixed maturity date should he desire to make payment at an earlier date. This would permit the maker to reduce the amount of interest paid by him.

● A *prepayment charge* or "*penalty*" will be assessed against the maker who pays early. The reasoning on behalf of the lender is that prepayment will defeat the purpose of the transaction from the lender's standpoint and require it to bear the administrative cost of replacing the money at interest. A common prepayment charge was 1% of original principal or, e.g., $500 if a balance was being paid off on a $50,000 loan. The past tense was just used because C.C. 2954.9 now places these limitations on and grants these privileges with respect to prepayment charges on residential loans: There cannot be a prepayment charge after the fifth year of a loan; (2) during the first 5 years of the loan, the borrower must be given the privilege of prepaying an amount equal to 20% of the original principal of the loan without prepayment charge; and (3) the prepayment charge on prepayment in excess of the free 20% during the first 5 years cannot exceed an amount equal to 6 months' advance interest on the excess amount paid.[26a]

Acceleration by Holder: Notes will always give the holder the option to accelerate for default in payment of an installment, as in the notes on pages 115-116. The right to accelerate may be given for breach of any covenant, e.g., the covenant to furnish financial statements and other covenants, above. It may be given for failure to absorb depreciation in the value of security (above) and upon occurrence of events increasing the holder's risk, as in the trade acceptance in *People's Finance & Thrift Co.* v. *Shaw-Leahy Co.*, 214 C. 108, 295 P. 1072, which provided, as older forms of trade acceptances commonly did, that the holder had the right to accelerate, "upon the acceptor . . . suspending payment, giving a chattel mortgage, suffering a fire loss, disposing of his business or failing to meet at maturity any prior acceptance." An instrument may be made accelerable "whenever the holder deems himself insecure" but it may be accelerated under such a clause only if the holder in good faith believes that the prospect of performance is impaired.[27]

● The Uniform Negotiable Instruments Law permitted an instrument to be made payable on occurrence of an event certain to happen but uncertain as to the time of happening. This permitted the post-obituary note, i.e., a note payable on or at some period after death. Death is an event certain to happen. The code reverses this non-commercial rule.[28]

---

[23]C.C. 1916.5 places these restrictions on adjustable or variable rate note loans on residential property: (1) The change in interest rate cannot exceed ¼ of 1% in any semiannual period or 2½% over the life of the loan; (2) the interest cannot be changed more than once during a semiannual period; (3) if the interest rate is increased, the life of the loan must be extended (but not beyond 40 years) to permit the borrower to continue to have the same monthly payment; (4) provision must be made for possible reduction as well as possible increase in the interest rate; (5) the borrower must be permitted to prepay the loan in whole or in part without prepayment charge within 90 days of notification of any increase in the interest rate; and (6) the note and mortgage must each contain this warning legend in 10 point type: Notice to Borrower: This Document Contains Provisions for a Variable Interest Rate.

[24]U.C.C. 1201(24).

[25]U.C.C. 3107(1).

[26]U.C.C. 3107(2).

[26a]C.C. 2954.10 forbids the exaction of a prepayment penalty if a due-on-sale clause (next considered) is being enforced.

[27]U.C.C. 1208.

[28]U.C.C. 3109(2).

• As will be seen in the chapter on Real Property, the funds required to purchase real estate are obtained by borrowing them from an institutional lender and giving the lender a note for the amount of the loan and a mortgage (deed of trust in California) on the property as security for the note. Such a note and mortgage are assumable by a purchaser of the property unless the loan instruments (note and mortgage) provide otherwise. It has long been the practice to have them do so. Modern real estate loan instruments (except FHA and VA instruments, which are not permitted to do so) contain *"due-on-sale" clauses*. These permit the lender to require the loan to be paid in full if the property is sold, which the lender will do if interest rates have gone up in the meantime. This permits a lender to upgrade its loan portfolio in a rising interest rate market.

In 1978, in *Wellenkamp* v. *Bank of America* (1978) 21 Cal.3d 947, 582 P.2d 970, which was to become a celebrated case nationally, the California Supreme Court struck down the due-on-sale clause. The decision came at a time when mortgage interest rates were beginning to soar and the housing market was drying up. The court stressed the public's interest in having a housing market as healthy as possible. Preserving the mortgage assumption possibility as far as possible would serve this purpose. Therefore, the court held, it would be an unreasonable restraint on alienation to allow due-on-sale clauses to be enforced unless it could be specifically shown that enforcement of the clause would be reasonably necessary to protect the lender against impairment of the security or against increased risk of default. To show the first, the lender would have to show that the buyer was a person more likely to commit waste on the property than was the mortgagor-seller. To show the second, the lender would have to show that the buyer was a less creditworthy person than was the mortgagor-seller. Only in a very rare case would it be possible to show either of these things.

Subsequently to *Wellenkamp* it was determined that the *Wellenkamp* rule did not apply to federally-chartered savings and loan associations, and this caused many of the state-chartered organizations to seek federal charters.

While *Wellenkamp* won a battle, it lost the war. In 1982, federal legislation which became effective on October 15, 1982 (Garn-St. Germain Depository Institutions Act) struck the death knell for the *Wellenkamp* rule. Under the Garn Act, only certain "window period" loans may be assumed. The "window period" is a grace period for loans obtained and transfers made in reliance on state law holding due-on-sale clauses unenforceable. The window period runs from the date of such state law to the date of the Garn Act. As to institutional loans, the date of California state law holding due-on-sale clauses unenforceable would be August 25, 1978, the date of the *Wellenkamp* decision, so the California window period would run from that date, as to institutional loans, to October 15, 1982, the date of the Garn Act.[28a] In the absence of any state law to the contrary in the interim, window period loans may be assumed for a period of 3 years after the date of enactment of the Garn Act. The assumer must be able to meet the creditworthiness standard applied by the lender for

similar loans. Window period loan restrictions do not apply to loans by federal savings and loan associations and federal savings banks and such loans are not assumable if a due-on-sale clause is contained.

The Garn Act exempts certain kinds of transactions from the enforcement of due-on-sale clauses: These include (1) transfers which are mere changes in the form of holding title such as transfers by spouses from themselves as joint tenants to themselves as community property; (2) transfers which are not motivated by economic factors such as transfers at death; and (3) the creation of junior liens on the propery (second mortgages). Regulations issued by the Federal Home Loan Bank Board in 1983 for the purpose of implementing the Garn Bill undertake to place substantial limits on the foregoing exemptions. The regulations limit the exemptions to owner-occupied residences. Thus, e.g., if a residence were transferred by parent to child upon death, it would appear that the child would have to take occupancy of the home to escape enforcement of the due-on-sale clause. And second mortgaging by one other than the owner of an owner-occupied residence would appear to be capable of triggering a due-on-sale clause.

FHA and VA loans are not subject to due-on-sale clauses and such loans may be assumed in any state by creditworthy buyers.

Words of Negotiability: Order or Bearer

An instrument must be payable to order or to bearer. This is the requirement of *"words of negotiability,"* the requirement of words showing intent to make the instrument transferable.

Order Paper: An instrument is payable to order when it is payable to the order or assigns of a person (Pay to the order of John Deaux; Pay John Deaux, or assigns); or to a person or his order (Pay to John Deaux, or order); or when it is designated "exchange" and names a payee.[29]
• It may be payable to the order of the maker, drawer, drawee, or a third person.[30] It may be payable to an entity (estate, trust, partnership or association) or an office or officer.[31] It may be payable to two or more persons together (A and B) or in the alternative (A or B).[32] If payable to them together it can be negotiated only by all of them.[33]

Bearer Paper: An instrument is payable to bearer when it is payable to (1) bearer (Pay bearer); or a specified person or bearer (Pay John Deaux or bearer); or the order of bearer (Pay to the order of bearer);[34] or the order of specified person or bearer (Pay to the order of John Deaux or bearer), if the bearer words are handwritten or typewritten;[35] or (2) "Cash" or the order of "cash" or other indication which does not purport to designate a specific payee (Pay "bills payable").[36]

Other Matters Not Affecting Negotiability

U.C.C. 31123114 cover various matters not affecting negotiability. Two warrant discussion.

[28a]*Dawn Investment Co.* v. *Superior Court* (1982) 30 Cal.3d 695, 180 Cal.Rptr. 332, was the first case to decide that the *Wellenkamp* rule applied to financing by non-institutional financers, i.e., to seller financing in which the seller provides first or second mortgage financing. The *Dawn* case was decided on February 4, 1982, and that date would seem to be the opening date for the window period as to non-institutional financing.

[29]U.C.C. 3110(1).
[30]U.C.C. 3110(1)(a)(b)(c).
[31]U.C.C. 3110(1)(e)(f)(g).
[32]U.C.C. 3110(1)(d).
[33]U.C.C. 3116(b).
[34]U.C.C. 3111(a)(b).
[35]U.C.C. 3110(3).
[36]U.C.C. 3111(c).

• Negotiability is not affected by antedating or postdating.[37] Time of payment is determined by the stated date of the instrument.[38]

• A law intended for the advantage or protection of the obligor may be waived, which permits waiver of the statute of limitations, except that in California such waiver is limited to 4 years.[39] The exemption statutes[40] may not be waived in California.[41]

• The rules of construction of U.C.C. 3118 should be noted.

Negotiation

General

"*Negotiation*" is transfer of an instrument in a manner prescribed by the code.[42] Bearer paper is negotiated by delivery; order paper by indorsement and delivery.[43] This is important because one must take an instrument by "negotiation" to become a holder in due course. If order paper is transferred without indorsement, which is necessary to the negotiation of such paper, the transferee has a right to indorsement; negotiation takes effect when the indorsement is obtained, and the transferee must qualify as a holder in due course at that time.[44]

• Indorsement must be on the instrument or on a paper so firmly affixed as to become part thereof (called an "allonge").[45]

• Indorsement must convey the entire instrument or its unpaid residue.[46] A $5000 note cannot be indorsed "Pay X $3000 and Y $2000." This is an application of the broad rule that causes of action cannot be split so as to impose on an obligor a greater burden than he assumed.

Indorsement

The code provides for four kinds of indorsements: *special*, *blank*, *restrictive* and *nonrecourse*.

Special: A *special indorsement* specifies the person to whom or to whose order it makes the instrument payable:[47]

Pay to   Pay to the order of
Henry Holder   (or)   Henry Holder
(signed) Paul Payee   (signed) Paul Payee

The special indorsee's indorsement (Henry Holder's indorsement) is necessary to further negotiation of the instrument.[48] He may indorse specially or in some other manner.

Words of Guaranty, etc.: U.C.C. 3202(4) says that words of guaranty, waiver, assignment, condition or limitation, or disclaimer of liability accompanying an indorsement do not affect its character as an indorsement. This is designed to resolve conflicts under the Uniform Negotiable Instruments Law over indorsements such as

Payment guaranteed
(signed) Paul Payee

Under the Uniform Negotiable Instruments Law some courts said this was a guaranty, not an "indorsement;" that therefore it constituted mere transfer, not "negotiation," of the instrument.

It is common to obtain waiver of presentment and notice of dishonor in connection with indorsement of a note, as follows:

Presentment and notice of dishonor waived
(signed) Paul Payee

And to combine the two:

Payment guaranteed
Presentment and notice of dishonor waived
(signed) Paul Payee

However, this is not necessary under the code. U.C.C. 3416(5) provides that "when words of guaranty are used presentment, notice of dishonor and protest are not necessary to charge the user."

Blank: A *blank indorsement* specifies no indorsee and consists of a mere signature:[49]

Paul Payee

It converts the instrument to bearer paper.[50] It may be converted back to order paper by special indorsement.[51]

Paul Payee   (bearer paper)

Pay to
Thomas Transferee
(signed) Henry Holder   (restored to
order paper)

• Bearer paper may also be converted to order paper by writing a special indorsement over a blank indorsement.[52] If Paul Payee indorses in blank, Henry Holder, the transferee, may write "Pay to Henry Holder" over the blank indorsement and convert it into a special indorsement. This protects Holder in event of theft since his indorsement is now necessary to the transfer of the instrument.

Restrictive: U.C.C. 3205 makes these indorsements "restrictive":

1. *Conditional indorsements*:

Pay to
Peter Piper Corporation
on completion of building
repairs at 200 Blank St.,
San Francisco, Calif.
(signed) Paul Payee

Suppose Peter Piper Corporation sells the instrument to Henry Holder, indorsing:

Pay to
Henry Holder
Peter Piper Corporation
(signed) By Adam Archer, President

---

[37]U.C.C. 3114(1).

[38]U.C.C. 3114(2).

[39]C.C.P. 360.5.

[40]Page 8.

[41]*Industrial Loan Co.* v. *Super. Ct.*, 189 C. 546, 209 P. 360.

[42]U.C.C. 3202(1).

[43]U.C.C. 3202(1).

[44]U.C.C. 3201(3) and Official Comments.

[45]U.C.C. 3202(2) and Official Comments.

[46]U.C.C. 3202(3).

[47]U.C.C. 3204(1).

[48]U.C.C. 3204(1).

---

[49]U.C.C. 3204(2).

[50]U.C.C. 3204(2).

[51]U.C.C. 3204(2).

[52]U.C.C. 3204(3).

Under the Uniform Negotiable Instruments Law, Holder took the instrument subject to Payee's rights, i.e., Payee was entitled to the proceeds of the instrument, as against Holder, if the condition (building repairs) was not fulfilled. Not so under the code.[53]

2. *Indorsements which purport to prohibit further transfer*:

Pay to
Henry Holder only
(signed) Paul Payee

These do not prevent further transfer[54] and so are restrictive in form only.

3. *Deposit and collection indorsements*:

For deposit Paul Payee	For collection Paul Payee
Pay to the order of State Bank for deposit only Paul Payee Co.	Pay to the order of State Bank for collection and credit to account of Paul Payee Co.

4. *Trust indorsements*:

Pay Thomas Trustee in trust for Ben Beneficiary (signed) Paul Payee	Pay Thomas Trustee for Ben Beneficiary (signed) Paul Payee
Pay Thomas Trustee for account of Ben Beneficiary (signed) Paul Payee	Pay Thomas Trustee as agent for Ben Beneficiary (signed) Paul Payee

An indorsee from the "trustee" (Thomas Trustee) must, to become a holder in due course, pay or apply value given by him consistently with the trust indorsement.[55] This means in effect that he may not take it in satisfaction of a personal debt of the trustee to him. Payment of cash to a fiduciary is consistent with the terms of a trust indorsement.[56]

Nonrecourse: Indorsement may be made *"without recourse"*:[57]

Paul Payee Without recourse	or	Without recourse Paul Payee	or	Pay to Fred Firstindorsee Paul Payee Without recourse

When a transferor makes a nonrecourse indorsement, his purpose is to limit his liability on the instrument—essentially to escape liability to his transferee in case the maker becomes insolvent and is not able to pay the instrument at maturity. To understand this it is necessary to become acquainted with the nature and types of liabilities incurred by the transferor of a negotiable instrument.

---

[53]U.C.C. 3206(3), Official Comments.

[54]U.C.C. 3206(1).

[55]U.C.C. 3206(4).

[56]U.C.C. 3304, Official Comments.

[57]U.C.C. 3414(1), 3417(3). Under the Uniform Negotiable Instruments Law, such indorsements were classified as "qualified indorsements," a term not adopted by the code.

Transferor's Liability

Every negotiator of a negotiable instrument, whether a transferor by delivery alone of bearer paper or an indorser of order paper, incurs some liability to at least his transferee. If he is a transferor by delivery alone of bearer paper or a nonrecourse indorser, he warrants certain things about the instrument which make him liable if, for instance, the instrument is forged or has been altered. If he is a general indorser, that is, uses some form of indorsement other than the nonrecourse indorsement, he does more—he warrants the instrument and, in addition and very importantly, he guarantees it, i.e., he says that if the instrument is not paid, he will pay it so that he is liable for its amount if, because of insolvency, the maker is not able to pay.

If he is a transferor by delivery alone of bearer paper, his liability (as warrantor) extends only to his immediate transferee. If he is a transferor by indorsement, his liability as warrantor in the case of a nonrecourse indorsement, or as warrantor and guarantor in case of a general indorsement, extends to all subsequent transferees.

U.C.C. 3414(1) and 3417(2)(3) cover transferor's liability.

U.C.C. 3414(1) establishes the *guaranty* of a general indorser by providing:

"Unless the indorsement otherwise specifies (as by such words as 'without recourse') every indorser engages that upon dishonor and any necessary notice of dishonor and protest he will pay the instrument according to its tenor at the time of his indorsement to the holder or to any subsequent indorser who takes it up, even though the indorser who takes it up was not obligated to do so."

This is a *conditional guaranty* to the extent that the indorser is relieved of it if there is not due presentment of the instrument and due notice to the indorser of its dishonor, matters covered on page 122.[58]

U.C.C. 3417(2)(3) establish the *warranties* of transferors, as follows:[58a]

"(2) Any person who transfers an instrument and receives consideration warrants to his transferee and if the transfer is by indorsement to any subsequent holder who takes the instrument in good faith that

"(a) He has a good title to the instrument or is authorized to obtain payment or acceptance on behalf of one who has a good title and the transfer is otherwise rightful; and

"(b) All signatures are genuine or authorized; and

"(c) The instrument has not been materially altered; and

"(d) No defense of any party is good against him; and

"(e) He has no knowledge of any insolvency proceeding instituted with respect to the maker or acceptor or the drawer of an unaccepted instrument.

"(3) By transferring 'without recourse' the transferor limits the obligation stated in subdivision (2)(d) to a warranty that he has no knowledge of such a defense."

● The foregoing rules of transferor's liability may be summarized as follows:

---

[58]U.C.C. 3502(1)(a).

[58a]If the instrument is a check which has entered the bank collection process, the warranty and guaranty liabilities are those imposed by U.C.C. 4207(2).

Method of transfer	Warranties	Guaranty
General or recourse indorsement (special, blank, restrictive). [U.C.C. 3414(1), 3417(2)]	1. Good title. 2. Signatures genuine. 3. No alteration. 4. No defense. 5. No knowledge of insolvency of obligor.	"Engages" that if, on due presentment, instrument not paid, he will pay if given due notice of dishonor.
Nonrecourse indorsement. [U.C.C. 3417(2)]	Same as above except no *knowledge of* defense.	NONE
Delivery alone (bearer paper). [U.C.C. 3417(2)]	Same as general indorser *but* only to immediate transferee.	NONE

● Let us observe these rules at work. Warranties are designed to protect the transferee in case there is a real defense to the instrument or an adverse claim based on forged indorsement, such that the transferee cannot collect on the instrument. The transferee need not be concerned about personal defenses; as a holder in due course, he will take free of them. The general indorser's guaranty, again, is designed to protect the transferee in case the maker is or becomes insolvent. The following fact situations will demonstrate these principles:

Thomas Transferor transfers an instrument to Theodore Transferee. The following things are wrong with or about it, of which Transferor is without knowledge (the first four being *real defenses*):

1. The signature of the maker is a forgery. (*Forgery.*)

2. The amount of the instrument has been raised from $2000 to $3000. (*Material alteration.*)

3. The maker is a blind person who was induced by a trusted friend to sign the instrument on the representation that it was a letter to her son. (*Fraud in the procurement.*)

4. The maker is a minor. (*Incapacity.*)

5. The instrument has been transferred by forged indorsement. (*Forged indorsement.*)

6. The instrument is genuine and valid in all respects but the maker has become insolvent. (*Insolvency of maker.*)

Upon what grounds, if any, may Transferee recover from Transferor if Transferor is a (1) general indorser, (2) nonrecourse indorser, (3) negotiator by delivery?

In Cases 1 and 2 the warranties of genuineness of signature and against alteration are breached by all types of transferors.[59]

In Cases 3 and 4 the warranty against defenses is breached by the general indorser and the negotiator by delivery.

In Case 5 all types of transferors breach the warranty of title.

In Case 6 the general indorser is liable on his guaranty; others, on warranty, only if, at time of transfer, they had knowledge of insolvency proceedings instituted against the obligor.

In brief, warranties protect against *legal defects* in the instrument, guaranty against the *insolvency* of the maker or drawer.

---

[59]The general indorser is also liable on his guaranty in these cases and the cases that follow, provided that due presentment is made and notice of dishonor is duly given.

Holder in Due Course

The preceding section was concerned with the methods of negotiation and the liability of the negotiator; this section is concerned with the rights of the transferee. These depend upon whether or not he qualifies as a *holder in due course*—essentially a good faith purchaser for value and without notice of any defect in the instrument or wrongdoing in connection with it. If the transferee qualifies as a holder in due course, he may enforce the instrument free of personal defenses. Real defenses are good against him, however. If he does not meet the requirements for due course purchase, he takes the instrument subject to all defenses, real and personal.

It is to be noted, as previously discussed, that under modern law the doctrine of holder in due course is not allowed to operate against a *consumer purchaser*. See discussion of this fact under Unruh Act on page 98 and under U-Triple C on page 104.

Requirements for Due Course Purchase; Qualified Persons

U.C.C. 3302 establishes requirements for due course status and designates classes of persons capable of occupying that satus, as follows:

"(1) A holder in due course is a holder who takes the instrument
"(a) For value; and
"(b) In good faith; and
"(c) Without notice that it is overdue or has been dishonored or of any defense against or claim to it on the part of any person.
"(2) A payee may be a holder in due course.
"(3) A holder does not become a holder in due course of an instrument:
"(a) By purchase of it at judicial sale or by taking it under legal process; or
"(b) By acquiring it in taking over an estate; or
"(c) By purchasing it as part of a bulk transaction not in regular course of business of the transferor."

Value

"Value": Value is agreed consideration to the extent it has been performed.[60] On May 1 P indorses a $5000 note to H in consideration of H's promise to pay P $3000 on June 1 and $2000 on July 1. H is not yet a holder for value. On June 1, without notice of a defense to the instrument,[61] H pays P $3000. H is now a holder for value to the extent of $3000. On July 1, without notice of a defense to the instrument,[62] H pays P $2000. He is now a holder for value to the extent of the full amount of the instrument.

Antecedent Debt: Value is given when an instrument is taken in payment of or as security for an antecedent claim whether or not the claim is due.[63] P owes H $5000 due July 1. On May 1 P receives a $5000 note from M, which he transfers to H as security for his obligation to H. H takes M's note for value.

Negotiable Instrument; Irrevocable Commitment to Third Person: U.C.C. 3303(c) makes an executory undertaking in two cases: (1) When it takes the form of a negotiable instru-

---

[60]U.C.C. 3303(2), 1201(44)(d).

[61]Value must be paid without notice of a defense if the purchaser is to become a holder in due course. U.C.C. 3303(1), Official Comments.

[62]Note 61.

[63]U.C.C. 3303(b)

ment and (2) when it takes the form of an irrevocable commitment to a third person.

H makes a note for $5000, payable to P on July 1, and, on May 1, gives it to P in exchange for a $5000 note of M, payable June 1, held by P. H takes M's note for value. P can transfer H's note to a third person so as to cut off defenses which H may have to the note. This is the reason for the rule of U.C.C. 3303(c) making H's note "value."

• A letter of credit issued when an instrument is taken is an example of an irrevocable commitment to a third person which would constitute value.

Purchase at Discount: Purchase "at discount," that is, purchase of an instrument for less than face value is purchase for value;[64] for example, purchase of a $5000 note for $4000. There is nothing wrong with this. A negotiable instrument is merely a form of property and must be sold for what it will bring. If the holder needs money, he may sacrifice to some extent to get it. If he sells the instrument for less than face value, he has received what it is worth to him, and the purchaser is a purchaser for value for the full face amount of the instrument. Severe discount may be evidence of bad faith, however, and disqualify the purchaser from becoming a holder in due course on that account. And purchase must be made without notice that the instrument is overdue.

Limited Value: In three cases, one of which has been seen, one may become a purchaser for value only to a limited extent and therefore only a limited or partial holder in due course:

1. *Executory Promise as Value Only to Extent Agreed Consideration Performed.* This has been seen in the section, above, entitled "Value."

2. *Pledgee as Holder for Value Only to Extent of Lien.* A pledgee or other lienholder is a holder for value only to the extent of his lien. P borrows $3000 from H, pledging M's $5000 note as security. H is a holder for value of M's note to the extent of $3000.

3. *Bank Credit as Value Only to Extent of Actual Credit or to Extent Credit Made Available for Withdrawal as of Right.* Bank credit is value only to the extent that, in accordance with the first in, first out rule, or "fifo," a customer is permitted to draw against an item or is given a credit against which he may draw as a matter of right.[65]

On June 1, C receives a $400 check from M in a transaction in which C has defrauded M. On June 2, M gives his bank notice to "stop payment"—refuse to pay the check when it is presented for payment. On the same day C deposits the check in his bank. He has $100 on deposit at the time. The bank will provisionally credit the $400 check to his account and will then send it through the clearinghouse for collection. Now, suppose that on the morning of June 3 C cashes a check at his bank for $250. Later in the day, M's check is returned to the bank unpaid and with the notice "Payment Stopped" attached. C's bank has the right to "charge back" to (deduct from) C's account what is owed it, but this will get back only the $100 that was in his account originally, and will leave the bank $150 short. Therefore the bank is a holder for value of M's check to the extent of $150, and may recover that amount from him.

Notice

To qualify as a holder in due course, one must take the instrument without notice (1) that it is overdue or (2) of a defense or adverse claim.[66]

Overdue Instrument: A purchaser has notice an instrument is overdue if he has reason to know:

1. An installment of principal is overdue,[67] but not interest;[68] or that there is an uncured default in payment of another instrument of the same series.[69]

2. Acceleration of the instrument has been made.[70]

3. He is taking a demand instrument more than a reasonable length of time after issue, which, in the case of a domestic check, is presumed to be 30 days.[71]

Defense or Claim: A purchaser has notice of a defense or claim if:

1. The instrument is so incomplete, bears such visible evidence of forgery or alteration, or is otherwise so irregular as to call into question its validity, terms or ownership or to create an ambiguity as to the party to pay.[72] This replaces the absolute requirement of the Uniform Negotiable Instruments Law that, to become a holder in due course, one had to take the instrument "complete and regular on its face." The code considers that an instrument may be blank as to some unnecessary particular or contain a minor erasure or show a change, e.g., on a check of the date from "January 2, 1983" to "January 2, 1984," without exciting suspicion, and that such things should not be fatal to due course status.

2. He has notice that the obligation of any party is voidable.[73] If the purchaser has notice that the obligation of the maker, or of an intermediate party, is voidable for fraud or failure of consideration or for other reason, such as mistake, illegality or duress, he is not a purchaser in due course.

3. He has notice of misappropriation by an agent or fiduciary, in which case he has notice of the claim of the principal.[74] He has such notice when he has notice that an agent or fiduciary is negotiating the instrument in payment of or as security for his own debt or in any transaction for his own benefit or otherwise in breach of duty.[75] This may involve close questions. The situation is this: (1) Agents may be given authority to write checks in the name of their principals, e.g., a corporation, as principal, may authorize one of its officers, the treasurer, to write checks in the name of the corporation for payment of its obligations; and (2) fiduciaries—trustees and executors or administrators of estates—are, by law, authorized to write checks in the name of the estate which they represent for payment of its obligations, these checks being drawn on an account in which the fiduciary has deposited the funds of the estate. The agent or fiduciary, as the case may be, abuses his authority by writing checks in the name of the principal to pay his personal obligations and, in this way,

---

[64]U.C.C. 1201(32).

[65]U.C.C. 4208-4209.

[66]U.C.C. 3302(1)(c); see Requirements for Due Course Purchase, supra.

[67]U.C.C. 3304(3)(a).

[68]U.C.C. 3304(4)(f).

[69]U.C.C. 3304(3)(a).

[70]U.C.C. 3304(3)(b).

[71]U.C.C. 3304(3)(c).

[72]U.C.C. 3304(1)(a).

[73]U.C.C. 3304(1)(b).

[74]U.C.C. 3304(2).

[75]U.C.C. 3304(2).

misappropriates the principal's funds. If the taker of the check is not on notice of misappropriation, he is protected, the loss falling on the principal under the rules of agency law that the principal suffers the wrongful conduct of his agent. On the other hand, if the taker has sufficient notice of misappropriation, he must pay back the money received. What constitutes notice of misappropriation may be a close question. Two cases illustrate the point:

a. A, treasurer of P Corporation, owes a personal debt of $5000 to H. He draws a check for $5000 in the name of the corporation made payable to H and signed, "P Corporation, By A, Treasurer," and delivers this to H in payment of his debt. Here, H may well have notice of misappropriation.

b. A makes the check payable to *himself* and for only $3000, and then *indorses* it to H on account of his indebtedness to H. There is nothing wrong with the treasurer of a corporation writing to himself a check for his salary, or for dividends payable to him if he is also a stockholder of the corporation. It has been held, therefore, that since H could legitimately reason that it was for such a purpose that A had drawn the check, he may be without notice of misappropriation in this case. A slight change in the form or mechanics of the transaction, then, may deprive it of its tendency to indicate misappropriation sufficiently to permit purchase without notice, and each case must be judged on its own circumstances.

• U.C.C. 3304(4)(5) provide that knowledge of the following facts *does not* of itself give the purchaser notice of a defense or claim:

1. Antedating or postdating.

2. Consideration for the instrument remains executory, unless there is knowledge of failure of consideration. H purchases M's instrument from P. H knows M gave P the instrument for goods yet to be delivered by P to M. This does not prevent H from becoming a holder in due course. But if, at time of purchase, H knows that P has failed to deliver the goods within the agreed time, of failure of consideration, he has notice of a defense and fails to qualify as a holder in due course.

3. Accommodation status of a party.

4. Incomplete instrument has been completed, unless the purchaser has notice of improper completion.

5. Negotiator is or was a fiduciary. But notice of misappropriation by a fiduciary gives notice of the rights of his principal, as shown above.

6. Constructive notice of recording. The pre-code California case of *Ross*. v. *Title Guaranty & Trust Co.*, 136 C.A. 393, 29 P.2d 236, illustrates this. Recording notice of action to cancel a note and mortgage did not give notice to a purchaser of the note and mortgage.

Shelter Rule

One who derives title through a holder in due course gets the rights of a holder in due course even though he cannot qualify as such in his own right.[76] This is called the "*shelter rule.*" One can transfer what he owns and a holder in due course owns the rights of a holder in due course.

To illustrate: M gives a note to P who indorses to H1, a holder in due course. H-1 indorses to H-2 who takes (a) after maturity or (b) as a gift from H-1 or (c) with knowledge of a defense of fraud between M and P. H-2, then, cannot qualify as a holder in due course because of his failure to (a) take before maturity or (b) give value or (c) take without notice, as the case may be. Nevertheless he gets H-1's rights, and so

has the rights of a holder in due course. Like H-1, he holds the instrument free of personal defenses.

• There is an exception. One who has been a party to fraud or illegality affecting the instrument or who as a prior holder had notice of a defense or claim against it cannot improve his position by "shooting the instrument through a holder in due course."[77] A payee-*reacquirer* is an obvious example. Take the same case as above, but have H-1 sell back to P at a later date. P still holds the instrument subject to the defense. It was his dishonesty that gave rise to the defense to the instrument.

The exception applies to anyone who participated in or was responsible for the transaction which gave rise to the defense. *McCredie* v. *Elmer*, 132 Ore. 368, 284 P. 573, is a good example. M gave a note to C Corporation for the purchase price of machinery. The note was indorsed by C Corporation and by P, its president, as guarantor, and sold to H Bank. The machinery was not delivered, and M refused to pay the note. The bank then collected the amount of the note from P, as guarantor, and transferred the note to him. P then sought to recover from M, contending that he (P) had the rights of a holder in due course since he had derived title to the instrument from a holder in due course, H Bank. Held, P could not recover; that as president and chief executive of the corporation, the failure of the corporation to deliver the machinery was attributable to him; that, therefore, he was a party to fraud or illegality affecting the instrument within the meaning of the exception.

Defenses

Defenses are *real*, good even as against a holder in due course, or *personal*, good against anyone but a holder in due course. Real defenses are enumerated by U.C.C. 3305(2). The following is a summary of the real and personal defenses to which this section is devoted:

Real

Fraud in the procurement
Material alteration
Unauthorized signature of maker
Incapacity

Personal

Fraud as to the consideration
Nondelivery
Failure of consideration

Illegality and duress may be either real or personal.

Fraud and Failure of Consideration

Fraud in the Procurement: This is also called essential fraud, fraud in the inception, fraud in the execution, and fraud in the factum. It might better be called fraud as to the instrument, as distinguished from fraud as to the consideration, discussed below. It is present where a person has no intent at all to become liable on a negotiable instrument, i.e., where he is induced to sign an instrument on the representation that it is some other type of document; or where he intends to sign one instrument but is fraudulently deceived into signing another.[78] Since there is no intention to enter into the contract signed in either case, and since intention to make a contract is essential, the courts say that no contract ever comes into existence in

---

[76]U.C.C. 3201(1), 3306.

[77]U.C.C. 3201(1).

[78]U.C.C. 3305(2)(c).

such a case—that the transaction is a complete nullity—void. This type of fraud is rare.

Examples of fraud in the procurement where the party has no intention at all to enter into a negotiable instrument: P writes letters for M, a blind person, which M signs. One day, P has M sign a note, which he represents to be a letter, and sells it to a holder in due course. Or an illiterate person is induced by a friend to sign a note on the representation that it is a contract for building repairs, as in *C.I.T. Corporation* v. *Panac*, 25 C.2d 547, 154 P.2d 710. The holder in due course loses because of fraud in the procurement.[79]

Gate City Nat. Bank v. *Bunton*, 316 Mo. 1338, 296 S.W. 375 is an example of intention to sign an instrument other than the instrument signed. There M agreed to sign a $5000 note for the accommodation of a friend. M read it and was about to sign when an associate of the friend diverted his attention long enough to permit substitution of a $25,000 note for the $5000 note. M signed the $25,000 note without noticing the substitution. Held, fraud in the procurement was perpetrated because M was induced to sign an instrument which he had no intention of signing.

Fraud as to the Consideration: This is also called fraud in the inducement. It is present where the maker understands the nature of and intends to become liable on the instrument signed but is deceived as to the nature, quality or value of the consideration which he is to receive in exchange; for example, M gives a note in part payment of the purchase price of a worthless piece of desert property represented to be fine orchard land complete with orange groves.

Failure of Consideration: Failure of consideration is closely akin to fraud as to the consideration. Failure of consideration is present whenever a party to a contract receives less than he bargained for even though there was no intent to defraud him. This is the *defense most likely to arise*, so it is an important feature of the negotiable instrument that it passes to a holder in due course free of this defense.[80]

Nondelivery

The Uniform Negotiable Instruments Law distinguished between nondelivery of a complete instrument and nondelivery of an incomplete instrument. If you filled out and signed a check, made payable to "Cash," and it was stolen from you and passed to a holder in due course, you suffered the loss under the Uniform Negotiable Instruments Law. If, under that law, on the other hand, you signed a check in blank and it was stolen, completed by the thief and passed to a holder in due course, the holder in due course did not get good title.

The code abolishes this distinction. Nondelivery of an incomplete instrument as well as of a complete instrument is a *personal* defense.[81] In the case above you are liable to a holder in due course on the signed blank check, for whatever amount the thief completes it.

"Conditional Delivery": Suppose M gives P a negotiable note. The note remains in P's hands at all times. As in *Oakland Med. Bldg. Corp.* v. *Aureguy*, 41 C.2d 521, 261 P.2d 249, M wants to show an *oral* agreement between him and P, at the time of delivery of the note, that he was not to have to pay the note unless, by the time of its maturity, he had received certain moneys from a third person. May he show this as against P? (In no case can he show it as against a holder in due course.) No. Such a showing would violate the *parol evidence rule*.[82] M is seeking to show an oral agreement varying the terms of a written contract, which is what the parol evidence rule forbids. Or, as in *Security First Nat. Bank* v. *Rospaw*, 107 C.A.2d 220, 237 P.2d 76, M wants to show an oral agreement that he is to be discharged on the note if P, the payee, dies. Here, again, it was held the parol evidence rule would be violated by admission of the evidence sought to be introduced.

But, as between himself and the payee (but not as against a holder in due course), M can show a so-called "condition precedent" to the effectiveness of the instrument, e.g., that it was not to be effective until signed by another person as co-maker; or, as in *Boies* v. *Wylie*, 113 C.A.2d 243, 248 P.2d 76, that it was a complete sham. Here, M is not trying to vary the terms of a contract but to show that no contract came into existence, which is not forbidden by the parol evidence rule.[83]

Unauthorized Signature

Unauthorized signature of maker is a real defense.[84] "Unauthorized signature" includes a signature by an agent or employee without authority as well as forgery in the more usual sense.[85] Forgery may be ratified, however,[86] and one who by negligence permits a forgery may be estopped to assert it.[87] The Official Text gives as an example one who is negligent in caring for an automatic signing device.[88]

● Forged indorsement gives rise to an adverse claim rather than a defense[89] and is considered in the section on adverse claims, below. Payment by a bank of a forged check or check bearing a forged indorsement is considered in later sections.

Alteration

Material alteration is a real defense to the extent of the alteration, and a holder in due course may enforce the instrument only according to its *original tenor*.[90] As in the case of forgery, the instrument is simply not that of the maker to the

---

[79]It may be reasoned that the maker was negligent and should be *estopped* to assert his defense here; that he should have called in someone to read the instrument to him before signing. The courts have held otherwise—that it is not negligence to fail to call in an outsider where such person is not conveniently available; and that even where such person is available, he need not be called in where the signer is justified in reposing confidence in the person who induces him to sign, such as a relative or trusted friend. Official Comments to U.C.C. 3305 seem to support these views.

[80]U.C.C. 3408.

[81]U.C.C. 3305(2), 3306(c), 3407(3), 3115(2).

[82]Page 46.

[83]U.C.C. 3306(c).

[84]U.C.C. 3404(1).

[85]U.C.C. 1201(43).

[86]U.C.C. 3404(2).

[87]U.C.C. 3406.

[88]U.C.C. 3406, Official Comments.

[89]M gives P a note payable to the order of P. F steals the note from P, forges his indorsement and negotiates to H, a holder in due course. When H seeks to recover from M on the note, he will not be able to do so, as stated in the text above. M will not really be asserting a "defense" here, however, because that word has reference to a right of the maker to refuse payment because of a wrong practiced on him, the maker. Here, the wrong is to someone else (P), an intermediate party. M, when he refuses to pay, is asserting a superior *claim* or *equity of ownership* in another or *"jus tertii"* (the right of a third person) as it is also called, as distinguished from a defense.

[90]U.C.C. 3407.

extent to which it has been altered. Such alteration may consist of a change in amount, interest, maturity date, or any other material term of the instrument. If the amount is raised, the holder in due course may enforce the instrument only for its original amount; if the rate of interest is raised, only at the original rate, and so on. Like forgery, alteration may be ratified.[91] One who, by negligence, facilitates alteration, as by leaving blank spaces in which words or figures may be inserted, may be estopped to assert the alteration.[92] The case of the liability of a bank which pays the materially altered check of its depositor is considered in a later section.

Incapacity

The contract rules with respect to minors and mentally incompetent persons carry over to negotiable instruments. Minors may avoid negotiable instruments just as they may avoid contracts generally.[93] A mental incompetent is not bound on an instrument if the transaction is one which is void as to the mental incompetent.[94] Thus, the negotiable instrument of a person who has been judicially adjudged incompetent is not enforceable even by a holder in due course.[95] In these respects incapacity is a real defense. Minors may disaffirm their negotiable instruments and need return only such of the consideration as remains in their possession, as in the case of other contracts.

Illegality

Illegality is a real defense where statute declares *void* an instrument issued in connection with a particular type of illegal transaction; in other cases, it is a personal defense.[96] For example, New York statute declares *void* an instrument given in payment of a gambling debt. Such being the case, there is nothing which can be enforced even by a holder in due course. In California, by contrast, while the Penal Code prohibits gambling, there is nothing which says that instruments given in payment of gambling debt are void. So, in California, illegality because of gambling is a mere personal defense.

Duress

Duress less than threat of immediate great bodily injury or death is a personal defense;[97] e.g., P, an unscrupulous person, threatens to expose M's past criminal record to M's employer unless M gives P a note for $5000. M would have only a personal defense. But if P were to place the note in front of M, and with a gun in his hand threaten to shoot M unless he signed the note, M would have a real defense. Here, again, M would be completely without intent to contract.

Adverse Claims

A holder in due course takes free of all adverse claims except one resulting from forged indorsement.[98] To illustrate: M gives P a note. P indorses to H^1, who indorses to H^2. Between H^1 and H^2 there is fraud, mistake, duress or illegal-

---

[91]U.C.C. 3407(2)(a).

[92]U.C.C. 3406.

[93]U.C.C. 3305(2)(a).

[94]U.C.C. 3305(2)(b).

[95]See page 32.

[96]U.C.C. 3305(2)(b).

[97]U.C.C. 3305(2)(b).

[98]U.C.C. 3305(1), 3404(1).

---

ity; or H^1 lacks capacity. H^2 negotiates to H^3, a holder in due course. H^3 takes free of the claim of H^1 based on any of the things mentioned.[99] By contrast, F steals a note from P, the payee, forges his indorsement and negotiates to H, a holder in due course. P may recover the note from H. *Forged indorsement* is the one adverse claim to which a holder in due course is subject.

Liabilities of Parties

To some extent, certain aspects of the liabilities of parties to negotiable instruments have already been discussed, e.g., that a drawee becomes liable on the instrument when he accepts, and that a general indorser is both a warrantor and guarantor. In this section, these matters are considered in greater detail, in addition to matters not yet considered.

Maker and Acceptor

A maker or acceptor is primarily or unconditionally liable on an instrument. The instrument is his and he must pay it.[100] His liability is not subject to the conditions of due presentment or notice of dishonor, as is that of a drawer and a general indorser on his guaranty, each of whom therefore is a "secondary party."[101] The maker or acceptor remains liable until the statute of limitations has run on his obligation. There is one exception. If a note or draft is made payable at a bank and the maker or acceptor has funds there to cover it on its due date, the maker or acceptor, in the event of delay in presentment, is discharged to the extent that the bank becomes insolvent during the period of delay and will be unable to pay.[102] This is illustrated in the section on drawer, below.

Guarantor

U.C.C. 3416 spells out the liability of a guarantor, which is of the same quality as that of a maker or acceptor in that it is not conditioned on due presentment or notice of dishonor.

Accommodation Parties

Accommodation parties are liable in the capacity in which they sign to the same extent as a party of the same capacity who has received value for the instrument. Thus, an accommodation maker, or *comaker* or *cosigner* as he is more commonly described, has the same unconditional liability as the real maker, and a general accommodation indorser has the same conditional liability as guarantor as do general indorsers generally; and it makes no difference that the holder knows the party to be merely an accommodation party at the time that he takes the instrument.[103]

Suretyship defenses, such as extension of time,[104] are available to an accommodation party, however, except as to a holder in due course without notice of the accommodation.[105]

Transferor

This is covered at pages 123-124.

---

[99]U.C.C. 3305(1) and Official Comments; 3207 and Official Comments.

[100]U.C.C. 3413(1).

[101]U.C.C. 3102(1)(d).

[102]U.C.C. 3502(1)(b).

[103]U.C.C. 3415.

[104]See page 367.

[105]U.C.C. 3415(3).

Drawer

The liability of the drawer of a check or other draft is conditioned on due presentment and notice of dishonor.[106] But the drawer of a check is discharged by delay in presentment only to the extent that the drawee bank becomes insolvent during the period of delay so that funds are lost which could have paid the check.[107] M gives P a $100 check. P delays presentment beyond the permitted time. Thereafter the bank becomes insolvent and will pay only 60¢ on the dollar. M is discharged of his liability to P to the extent of the other 40¢ on the dollar and may discharge his liability for the 60¢ on the dollar by assigning to P his, M's, claim against the bank for that amount.[108]

Discharge of Drawer by Certification: One other special rule with respect to drawers of checks, which also applies to indorsers, bears note. The holder of a check may go to the drawee bank and ask to have the check certified. The bank may do this or not as it sees fit, since its only obligation is to pay the check. Suppose that it elects to certify. U.C.C. 3411(1) then applies. It says that "where holder procures certification the drawer and all indorsers are discharged." The theory of this is that the holder, by procuring certification, evinces willingness to rely on the financial responsibility of the bank alone since, by certification, it becomes his debtor. It is only when the *holder* procures certification, however, that the drawers and indorsers are discharged. If the *drawer* obtains certification, U.C.C. 3411(1) does not apply, and the drawer and indorsers have their ordinary liability.

Presentment and Notice of Dishonor

Unless excused, presentment is necessary to charge secondary parties.[109] Unless excused, notice of dishonor is necessary to charge secondary parties, except that a drawer is discharged only to the extent that he is discharged by failure duly to make presentment.[110]

Presentment: U.C.C. 3503-3506 detail the time for and mechanics of presentment. These are some of the more important rules: An instrument having a fixed maturity date must be presented on that date.[111] A demand instrument must be presented within a reasonable time after the party whom it is sought to hold became liable thereon.[112] With respect to the drawer of a check this is presumed to be 30 days after issue;[113] with respect to an indorser, 7 days after his indorsement.[114] Presentment must be made at the place specified in the instrument; if there is none, at the place of business or residence of the obligor.[115] The presenter must be prepared to receipt for payment on the instrument and surrender it on payment.[116]

---

[106]U.C.C. 3413(2), 3502(1)(b).

[107]U.C.C. 3502(1)(b).

[108]U.C.C. 3502(1)(b).

[109]U.C.C. 3501(1).

[110]U.C.C. 3501(2). See section on drawers, above, re extent to which drawer is discharged by failure duly to make presentment.

[111]U.C.C. 3503(1)(c).

[112]U.C.C. 3503(1)(e).

[113]U.C.C. 3503(2)(a).

[114]U.C.C. 3503(2)(b).

[115]U.C.C. 3504(2)(c).

[116]U.C.C. 3505(1)(d).

Notice of Dishonor: U.C.C. 3508 states the rules of notice of dishonor. It must be given by a person other than a bank before midnight of the third business day after dishonor or receipt of notice of dishonor. The holder may give it only to his immediate transferor and rely on him to pass it on down the line, but if the holder does this he takes the chance that his transferor will fail to give notice to those below him in the chain of transfer; therefore to be certain of preserving his rights against them, the holder should give notice to all prior parties. Notice may be oral but should of course be written, and sent by registered or certified mail so there will be proof of noticegiving. The notice need not be in particular form. It need only identify the instrument and state that it has been dishonored.

Waiver and Excuse: Presentment and notice of dishonor may be waived or excused. U.C.C. 3511 covers this. Waiver may be made before or after the instrument, or notice, has become due. It may be oral or written, or by conduct as in *Vigen* v. *Castle Bldg. Co.*, 19 C.A.2d 704, 65 P.2d 1340, where a promise of an indorser to substitute a new note was deemed a waiver of presentment and notice of dishonor. A waiver embodied in the instrument binds all parties.

● Delay in making presentment or giving notice is excused when it is caused by circumstances beyond the control of the holder and he acts promptly to make presentment or give notice after the cause of delay ceases to exist. Presentment or notice is entirely excused when, after the exercise of reasonable diligence, it cannot be made or given. Presentment is excused when the maker or acceptor is dead or is in insolvency proceedings instituted after issue of the instrument.

Protest: Protest is formal presentment and certification of dishonor by a notary public. It is required only in the case of a draft drawn or payable in a foreign country.[117] The usual procedure for protest is for the bank through which the draft is to be presented for payment to have a notary make presentment and make a certificate of dishonor in the form of that shown on page 130 when presentment fails to obtain payment. The notary then sends copies to all parties who should be given notice of dishonor.

Bank and Customer

It is only when he *accepts* it or, in the case of a bank, when it *certifies*, that a drawee becomes liable on the instrument itself, i.e., becomes a party to the instrument.

In the case of checks, however, a drawee bank incurs liability to a customer by virtue of an implied contract that is deemed to be made between a bank and its customer. A bank impliedly contracts with its customer that it will pay out his money only on and in accordance with his order (check) and to persons to whom the order validly runs.[118] Payment of a forged check breaches this contract because a forged order is no order at all. Payment of an altered check breaches it to the extent that the payment is otherwise than in accordance with the customer's order, i.e., to the extent of the alteration. Payment of a check bearing a forged indorsement breaches it because payment is not to one to whom the order runs, which is to the payee and subsequent persons validly acquiring title.

Subject to exceptions noted below, the bank will be liable to the customer in each of the above cases for the damages suffered by him. In the forged check and forged indorsement cases it will have to recredit his account with the amount

---

[117]U.C.C. 3501(3); 3509.

[118]See U.C.C. 4401. See also 3419(1)(c).

Protest

United States of America
State of California   } ss.
County of

BY THIS PUBLIC INSTRUMENT OF PROTEST

Be it Known that on   at the

request of the holder of the negotiable instrument hereto attached, I, the undersigned, a duly qualified

Notary Public in and for said County, during business hours of said day and at the place of payment

therein named, in the City of   , did duly present said instrument to and demand

payment thereof from

which was refused, giving as reason for such refusal

Whereupon, I, the said Notary Public, did PROTEST, and by these presents do publicly and
solemnly PROTEST, as well against the maker of said instrument as against all other parties thereto,
for all loss of any kind that may have been, or may be sustained, by reason of the non-payment of the
same.

And I Hereby Certify that the parties to said instrument have been duly notified of the
protest thereof by letters deposited by me in the United States Postoffice in said City with postage
thereon prepaid, addressed in the manner required under the provisions of Section 3189 of the Civil
Code of California.

Thus Done And Protested in said County and State on the day and year aforesaid.

In Witness Whereof, I have hereunto set my
hand and affixed my official seal of office in said
County.

....
Notary Public in and for said County and State

Form N.P. — Sam Hopkins Legal Form Printing Service, 4125 East 17th St., Oakland 1, Calif.

charged to it; in the altered check case, with the amount of the overpayment.

Forged Checks: As shown, a bank must recredit its depositor's account if it charges it with a forged check. There are however these limitations on the bank's liability:

1. The customer must with reasonable promptness examine his statement and cancelled checks and report forgeries to the bank.[119] If he does not he will be estopped to assert the forgery if the bank can show that, by reason of the delay, it lost an opportunity to recover from the forger.[120] Precode California cases required a strong showing by the bank in this regard; a showing of more than the mere theoretical possibility that the bank might have recovered if it had been notified promptly.[121]

Banks have attempted to limit liability by the "10 day" provisions that are put in signature cards, monthly statements and authorizations to mail statements. Such provisions customarily state that *errors* (which banks consider to include payments on forged checks) must be reported within 10 days after receipt of the monthly statement and cancelled checks. The courts have consistently found grounds upon which to defeat such provisions—that they were not specifically called to the customer's attention and that therefore he did not know of or intend them to be part of his contract with the bank; that they are too indefinite; that they do not permit a reasonable time for examination of returned checks; etc. The code permits exculpatory clauses but leaves it to local law to determine their validity.[122]

2. The customer is estopped to assert the forgery if his negligence permitted it, as where he was negligent in caring for an automatic signing device.[123]

● The bank may not recover from the party paid on the forged check if he was innocent of knowledge of the forgery at the time of taking the check and at the time of obtaining payment.[124] This restates the "rule of *Price* v. *Neal*," a famous early English case in which it was so held. The rule of *Price v. Neal* was adopted by the Uniform Negotiable Instruments Law and is continued by the code.

Altered Checks: Here again the customer may lose his rights by failure to discover and report the alteration.[125] He may also lose his rights if negligent execution has facilitated alteration, as where he has left spaces in which words or figures have been inserted.[126]

Here, unlike in the forged check case, the bank may recover from the party paid unless it has certified the check.[127]

Forged Indorsement: Here the code clarifies two matters that were controversial under the Uniform Negotiable Instruments Law.

1. *Fictitious Payee Case.* A dishonest employee of a large plant, having charge of personnel records and the payroll, sets up a fictitious employee in the personnel records, draws checks payable to that name, which he has the employer sign along with the other payroll checks, then "indorses" and cashes the checks until the deception is discovered—the so-called "*padded payroll case.*" Under the Uniform Negotiable Instruments Law, in most states this would have been a case of forged indorsement and the employer would have been entitled to recover from the bank. The code reverses the rule.[128] The employer suffers the loss.

2. *Impostor Case.* If an impostor by use of the mails or otherwise induces a person to give him a check, payable to the person impersonated, the impostor has the capacity to indorse the check (such indorsement is not a "forgery") and the party defrauded suffers the loss.[129]

● Where a bank pays a check on a forged indorsement it may recover from the party paid.[130]

Other Matters: The code establishes rules in connection with other aspects of the bankcustomer relationship, as follows:

1. *Wrongful Dishonor.* The bank is liable for actual or out-ofpocket damages suffered by the depositor by virtue of its failure to honor his proper check, for which he has sufficient funds.[131] The Official Text permits the customer also to recover damages for an arrest or prosecution of the customer. The California code deletes this provision.

2. *Overdrafts.* A bank may pay a check even though it creates an overdraft and may then recover the amount of the overdraft from the customer.[132] The bank may not recover from the party paid on an overdraft if he was unaware of the fact of overdraft.[133]

3. *Stop Orders.* A California bank must honor a written stop payment order delivered to the branch on which the check is drawn.[134] The Official Text permits oral stop payment orders good for 14 days.

4. *Stale Checks.* A bank may but is not required to pay an uncertified check which is more than 6 months old.[135]

5. *Death or Incompetence of Customer.* A bank may pay checks of a customer presented within 10 days after his death unless notified to stop payment by an heir.[136] And, in the absence of such stop order, a bank may pay checks of an incompetent customer drawn prior to incompetence.[137]

Discharge of Parties

General

U.C.C. 3601 lists grounds of discharge of a party to a negotiable instrument. Two are self-explanatory: payment and tender. Two have been seen: certification of a check procured by the holder and unexcused delay in presentment or notice of dishonor.[138] Others are now examined.

---

[119]U.C.C. 4406(1).

[120]U.C.C. 4406(2)(a).

[121]*Glassell Devp. Co.* v. *Citizens' Nat. Bank*, 19 C.2d 375, 216 P. 1012.

[122]U.C.C. 4103(1), 1102(3).

[123]U.C.C. 3406 and Official Comments.

[124]U.C.C. 3418, 3417(1)(b)(iii); 4207(1)(b)(iii).

[125]U.C.C. 4406(1)(2).

[126]U.C.C. 3406 and Official Comments.

[127]U.C.C. 3417(1)(c)(iii); 4207(1)(c)(iii).

[128]U.C.C. 3405(1)(c).

[129]U.C.C. 3405(1)(a).

[130]U.C.C. 3417(1)(a); 4207(1)(a).

[131]U.C.C. 4402.

[132]U.C.C. 4401(1). Recently adopted C.C. 1719 makes a person who writes a bad check liable to the payee for $100-500 damages if the check is not paid in cash within 30 days of a certified mail demand for payment.

[133]U.C.C. 3418.

[134]U.C.C. 4403; 4105(g), 4106 (branch as separate bank).

[135]U.C.C. 4404.

[136]U.C.C. 4405(1)(2).

[137]U.C.C. 4405(1)(3).

[138]U.C.C. 3601(1)(g)(i).

Cancellation or Renunciation

A party is discharged if the holder cancels the instrument, or the party's signature, as by destroying the instrument or mutilating it or striking out the signature.[139] A party is discharged if the holder renounces his rights by a signed writing delivered to the party to be discharged or by surrender of the instrument to him.[140]

Impairment of Recourse or Collateral

A party is discharged if the holder impairs his rights against a prior party, as by discharging the prior party.[141] A party is discharged pro tanto if the holder impairs collateral for the instrument, as by releasing the collateral, or some part of it, to the debtor.[142]

Nonnegotiable Instruments

A note which lacks words of negotiability—is not payable to order or bearer—is not negotiable, even though it meets the other requirements of a negotiable instrument. The transferee takes it subject to personal as well as real defenses of the maker.

What are the liabilities of an indorser of such an instrument? What are the obligations of the holder with respect to presentment and notice of dishonor? These, and like questions, were not answered by the Uniform Negotiable Instruments Law. The cases have usually answered them by analogy to the Uniform Negotiable Instruments Law. The code codifies such a rule. The rules of Division 3 apply to such an instrument, except that there cannot be a holder in due course, i.e., it is subject to all defenses of the maker.[143] The general indorser is a guarantor of payment as he is of a negotiable instrument. Duties of presentment and notice of dishonor are the same as for negotiable instruments.

---

[139]U.C.C. 3605(1)(a) and Official Comments.

[140]U.C.C. 3605(1)(b).

[141]U.C.C. 3606(1)(a).

[142]U.C.C. 3606(1)(b).

[143]U.C.C. 3805.

Negotiable Documents of Title

These are negotiable bills of lading and negotiable warehouse receipts, regulated by Division 7 of the code.[144] Neither represents an obligation to pay money and so is not a negotiable instrument; the one, bill of lading, represents a right goods from a carrier; the other, warehouse receipt, a right t goods from a warehouse.

Divisions 3, 7 and 8[145] of the code are like a big negotiable instruments law (Division 3) and two little negotiable instruments laws (Divisions 7 and 8), dealing with three kinds c paper sometimes described as *money paper* (drafts, check and notes), *commodity paper* (documents of title), and *invest ment paper* (investment securities).

The quality of "*negotiability*" that is common to all three types of paper is that if they are issued to bearer or, being order paper, become bearer paper by blank indorsement the can be effectively negotiated by a finder or thief to a du course purchaser.[146]

A document of title is negotiable if by its terms the good are to be delivered to bearer or to the order of a named perso (hence, "order bill of lading," page 73).[147] Any other docu ment is nonnegotiable ("straight bill of lading," page 71.)[148] The Official Text requires negotiation of a document of titl to be "in the regular course of business," suggesting that on ought not to be able to get good title from "a tramp or professor."[149] California deletes this requirement, but th purchaser must take the document in good faith and withou notice of a defense or claim.[150]

---

[144]Federal law dealing with transportation and storage of good is extensive, and Division 7 is subject to such law where it applicable, e.g., where interstate transportation of goods is in volved.

[145]Division 8 is covered in Chapter 11.

[146]U.C.C. 7501, 7502, as regards documents of title.

[147]U.C.C. 7104(1)(a).

[148]U.C.C. 7104(2).

[149]U.C.C. 7501(4) and Official Comments.

[150]U.C.C. 7501(4).

Approved by the California Warehousemen's Association.

WAREHOUSE RECEIPT N? 42

Howard Terminal
95 MARKET STREET
OAKLAND. CALIF.

_____19 __

𝕿𝖍𝖎𝖘 𝖎𝖘 𝖙𝖔 𝕮𝖊𝖗𝖙𝖎𝖋𝖞, that this Company has received in Storage Warehouse,

_____for the account of

_____Ex_____

in apparent good order, except as noted hereon (contents, condition and quality unknown) the following described property, subject to all the terms and conditions contained herein and on the reverse hereof, such property to be delivered to_____order, upon the payment of all storage, handling and other charges and the surrender of this Warehouse Receipt properly endorsed.

NUMBER	PACKAGES	SAID TO BE OR CONTAIN	MARKS

(vertical text, right margin:) THIS RECEIPT IS VALID ONLY WHEN SIGNED BY ONE OF THIS COMPANY'S DULY AUTHORIZED OFFICERS

(watermark:) NEGOTIABLE

Lot No._____

*Storage_____per_____per_____

from_____19__

*Handling_____per_____in and out inclusive.

Advances have been made and liability incurred on such goods in the amount of

$_____

*Rates for storage and handling charges are as published in Tariffs filed with the Railroad Commission of California and in our office.

HOWARD TERMINAL

claims a lien for all lawful charges for storage and preservation of the goods, also for all lawful claims for money advanced, interest, insurance, transportation, labor, weighing, coopering, and other charges and expenses, in relation to such goods.

No delivery of goods specified upon this receipt will be made unless written order is accompanied by this warehouse receipt properly endorsed.

Endorse here

The goods mentioned below are hereby released from this receipt for delivery from warehouse. The unreleased balance of the goods is subject to a lien for unpaid charges and advances on the released portion.

DATE	QUANTITY RELEASED	SIGNATURE	QUANTITY DUE ON RECEIPT

STANDARD TERMS AND CONDITIONS

These goods are stored and handled subject to the rules, regulations, rates and charges as published in our warehouse schedules on file with the Railroad Commission of California and in our office, and such amendments thereto as may hereafter be filed.

Rates do not include fire or other insurance. Warehousemen do not arrange for insurance unless instructed to do so in writing.

Warehousemen are not responsible for loss or damage caused by fires (from any cause), frost or change of weather, riots, strikes, insurrections, or from inherent or perishable qualities of the merchandise, or other causes beyond their control; and are not responsible for loss or damage caused by leakage, pilferage, ratage, theft, vermin or water, unless such loss or damage be caused by the failure of the warehousemen to exercise the ordinary care and diligence required of them by law.

Rates are subject to limited liability as provided by the Tariff.

Goods in Bonded Warehouses are subject to all Federal Government regulations and cannot be delivered without the authority of the Collector of Customs.

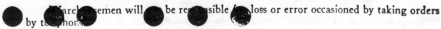 Warehousemen will not be responsible for loss or error occasioned by taking orders by telephone.

CHAPTER 7

Secured Transactions

Introduction

Division 9 is thought to be the most important part of the ⁀e. So much so that when for a time it appeared that the ⁀e as a whole might not be accepted, some states were ⁀pared to adopt Division 9 as a separate statute.

⁀rior to the code, personal property security devices and ⁀ laws governing them developed unsystematically. The re-⁀ was a jumble of devices and laws involving different the-⁀s, different terminology, different forms and different ⁀rding or filing requirements, although all were designed ⁀serve the same purpose and generally speaking could as ⁀l have been regulated by one law, one form and one filing ⁀uirement.

⁀he differences were due to the fact that the various devices ⁀ laws were conceived at different times by different authors ⁀rating in different kinds of commercial environments or ⁀ponding to different kinds of commercial pressures.

⁀our important types of precode security devices demon-⁀te the point—the conditional sale, the chattel mortgage, ⁀ trust receipt, and the assignment of accounts receivable.

⁀he *conditional sale* was used to finance the consumer in ⁀installment purchase of goods—his automobile, household ⁀liances, television set. The theory was title retention—that ⁀ seller retained "title" to the goods until the purchase price ⁀s paid in full—although everyone understood that what the ⁀er really had was merely a security interest in the goods. ⁀e seller assigned the conditional sale contract to a financ-⁀house which paid him off and actually carried the paper—⁀, of course, the interest it bore.) Some states required ⁀ording of the contract for its perfection; most, including ⁀ifornia, did not.

⁀he *chattel mortgage* was also used to finance consumer ⁀chases. The consumer-purchaser was loaned the money to ⁀ke the purchase and then immediately gave back to the ⁀der a mortgage on the chattel purchased. Here the theory ⁀ mortgage or "lien"—that the lender got a lien on the ⁀perty as security for the loan until it was paid. Here ⁀ording was required to perfect the security interest.

⁀he *trust receipt* was a contrivance necessitated by the ⁀'s failure to keep up with the commercial times. Chattel ⁀rtgages on inventory of a merchant were not permitted as ⁀an early date[1] in the belief that the merchant who could ⁀row money on his inventory might be tempted to defraud ⁀ecured creditors. He could get inventory on credit, then ⁀row money on it by giving the lender a chattel mortgage ⁀he inventory. If, after that, the merchant's business failed, ⁀ unpaid suppliers, who would be unsecured creditors, ⁀uld have no source of assets from which to recover on their ⁀ims, since the person to whom the chattel mortgage had ⁀n given would be secured and, as a secured creditor, ⁀uld be entitled to the merchant's remaining inventory to ⁀ exclusion of the merchant's unsecured creditors. But re-

tailers needed inventory financing which manufacturers were not able to give and for which banks and other lenders had to be the source. The trust receipt circumvented the bar on chattel mortgages. Theoretically the bank took title to the goods by taking an order bill of lading for the goods and paying the accompanying sight draft for the purchase price.[2] In exchange for a trust receipt, the bank then gave the merchant the bill of lading to enable him to get the goods from the carrier to put on the floor of his place of business (hence the term "*flooring*" by which trust-receipting is better known). The trust receipt, quite ingeniously, borrowed from the law of trusts. Under it, the bank, as "entruster," entrusted the goods to the merchant, as "trustee." The merchant then held the goods, and, as they were sold, their proceeds, "in trust" for the bank. The effect was to give the bank a security interest in the goods and their proceeds until it was paid, with interest, the purchase price it had advanced on behalf of the merchant. Since this was a "trust" rather than a "mortgage," it did not violate laws against chattel mortgages on inventory. All of this was fully legitimatized by the Uniform Trust Receipts Act (adopted in California) under which notice of the trust receipt interest had to be filed in the office of the Secretary of State.

● *Field-warehousing*, discussed at page 161, was another device by which the ban on chattel mortgages by a merchant could be circumvented.

● Merchants also wanted and got *nonnotification financing of accounts receivable*. The merchant sold on short term credit to customers but could not afford to carry their paper. His solution would be to borrow money on these accounts receivable, but he didn't want his customers to know that this was necessary. So a financing house would lend him money and take an "assignment" of the accounts receivable as security for the loan, agreeing at the same time not to notify the merchant's customers that their accounts had been assigned. This was dangerous for financing houses, however, because under much of existing law this left the security interest in the accounts unperfected. Perfection would require notice to the account debtors that the account had been assigned, which was the very thing that the assignee had agreed not to do. This caused accounts receivable statutes to be adopted in the 1940's under which assignments could be perfected by filing notice of the assignment in the office of the Secretary of State. This allowed the transaction to remain confidential while at the same time protecting the position of the lender. California adopted such a statute. Instead of taking an assignment of the accounts "as security," the lender might "buy" them. Ordinarily this would make the difference one of form only for the reason that ordinarily the merchant would be required to guarantee payment of the accounts (this being "recourse" financing of accounts receivable, as distinguished from "nonrecourse" financing under which there would be no recourse against the merchant if the accounts were not paid). The fact that as a practical matter there is no distinction between an

---

Former C.C. 2955.

[2]See explanation of this transaction at pages 77 and 70.

assignment of accounts receivable for security and a purchase of accounts with recourse is an important basic concept in connection with Division 9, as shown in the next section.

• Division 9 does not do anything revolutionary. It brings all personal property security devices under one roof, and it simplifies form and notice-giving procedure as far as it is possible to do so. Its ideal, substantially accomplished, is one form of instrument and one form of filing. The instrument, which would replace the conditional sales contract, the chattel mortgage, the trust receipt, and other precode forms, is called a *security agreement*. It creates a *security interest* in the *collateral* in favor of the *secured party* and against the *debtor*. It is perfected, generally, by *filing* a *financing statement* in the office of the Secretary of State.

• Forms of security agreements appear on pages 100 (motor vehicle purchase), 138 (household goods purchase), and 142 (dealer financing).

Transactions Covered; Excluded

Division 9 covers two general kinds of transactions: (1) Any transaction intended to create a security interest in personal property and (2) any sale of accounts or chattel paper.[3]

In early drafts of the code it was proposed to distinguish between outright sales of accounts and assignments for security but, as has been shown above, there is not really any difference if the "seller" of the accounts is required to guarantee their payment, that is, if the assignment is with recourse, as it usually is. Therefore the draftsmen of the code decided to include all assignments of accounts, whether admittedly for security or purporting to be "sales."

• Section 9104 excludes from the coverage of Division 9 a variety of transactions which do not constitute commercial financing transactions.

• The California code makes a significant departure from the Official Text at this point. California adds a subdivision (4) to Section 9102, which provides: "Notwithstanding anything to the contrary in this division, no nonpossessory security interest, other than a purchase money security interest, may be given or taken in or to the inventory consisting of durable goods having a unit retail value of at least five hundred dollars ($500) or motor vehicles, house trailers, semitrailers, farm and construction machinery and repair parts thereof, or aircraft."

This preserves the precode rule in California, under the Uniform Trust Receipts Act. The U.T.R.A. permitted a merchant to finance *new* inventory but, shades of the rule that a chattel mortgage could not be given on stock in trade of a merchant, did not allow a merchant to borrow money on *old* inventory, that is, inventory that he already owned. So if the merchant bought some new inventory and if in the process a bank technically took title to it and then "entrusted" it to the merchant in exchange for a trust receipt giving the bank a security interest in the stock, that was all right. But if a merchant wanted to borrow money on inventory which he already owned, that is, which he had bought with his own funds at an earlier date, he could not use a trust receipt to do so. This would be so much like giving a chattel mortgage on stock in trade as to be objectionable. Eventually, however, California amended this U.T.R.A. rule to permit trust receipting of *old* inventory of the very expensive per unit types that subdivision (4) of U.C.C. 9102 refers to, that is, durable goods of $500 or more per unit value (for examples, perhaps, color televi-

sion sets, pianos, boats, cars, airplanes, trailers, and farm construction machinery).

This was a concession to the commercial reality that heavy investment in inventory required of merchants of kind, and the extraordinary financial stresses placed on th as a result, might be justification for giving them special tr ment.

When the time came for adoption of the code in Californ the Legislature decided to continue the same rule, althoug would now be a limitation rather than an indulgence since Official Text did not restrict security interests to new inv tory.

The Special Terminology of Division 9

Drafters of the code wanted to use a set of terms that wo not run the danger of implying some connection with terms or forms such as the conditional sale and the cha mortgage.[4] Therefore they conceived and adopted the foll ing terms to designate the parties to and elements of a secu transaction, which the student of Division 9 must master which will be used hereafter in this text:[5]

Security agreement means an agreement by which a secu interest is created.

Secured party means the seller or lender in whose favo security agreement runs, that is, the party having the secu interest.

Debtor means the person who owes payment of the o gation secured by the security agreement.

Collateral means the property subject to a security agr ment, and includes accounts which have been sold.

Collateral may consist of goods, commercial specialties intangibles.

• "*Goods*" are, according to Section 9109:

Consumer goods if they are used or bought for use prim ily for personal, family or household purposes.

Farm products if they are crops or livestock or supp used or produced in farming operations and if they are in possession of a debtor engaged in farming operations.

Inventory if they are held for sale or lease or to be furnis under contracts of service, or if they are raw materials, w in process or materials used or consumed in a business.

Equipment if they are used or bought for use primaril business and do not fall within one of the foregoing de tions.

• *Commercial specialties* consist of documents, instrume and chattel paper, defined as follows by Section 9105(1):

Document means a document of title (bill of lading or w house receipt).

Instrument means a negotiable instrument (Division 3 investment security (Division 8). It also includes other wri evidences of indebtedness such as nonnegotiable promiss notes.

Chattel paper means a writing or writings which com a money obligation with a security interest. The most c spicuous example of chattel paper would be a Division 9 curity agreement. A security agreement may be used as curity for another security agreement. A holds a secu agreement from B giving A a security interest in pers property of B. A wants to borrow money from C wh willing to take the security agreement between A and security for C's loan to A. The AB security agreement

---

[3]U.C.C. 9102(1).

[4]U.C.C. 9105, Official Comment 1.

[5]These definitions are to be found in U.C.C. 9105.

nstitute "chattel paper" security when taken by C as col-
eral for C's loan to A.

Intangibles consist of accounts and general intangibles, deed by Section 9106 as follows:

Account means any right to payment for goods sold or
sed or for services rendered which is not evidenced by an
trument or chattel paper; what would be called, in more
mmon usage, an "account receivable."

General intangible means intangible property not falling
thin one of the foregoing categories, which may be used as
curity, such as goodwill, copyrights, trademarks, patents
d literary rights.

Perfection of Security Interest

A security interest is perfected when it has attached and
en the steps required for perfection by Sections 9302, 9304
d 9305 have been taken.[6]

tachment: Agreement, Value and Collateral

"Attachment" is a word coined by the code to describe the
int at which property becomes subject to a security interest.
requires three things: (1) A written security agreement,
gned by the debtor, if the secured party does not take pos-
ssion of the collateral; (2) the giving of value by the secured
rty; and (3) the acquisition of rights in the collateral by the
btor if he does not already have them.[7] The requirement of
written security agreement for a nonpossessory security in-
est is "in the nature of a Statute of Frauds."[8]

The security agreement must "contain a description of the
llateral."[9] The description need not be exact and detailed
t only a description which is sufficient to reasonably identify
hat is described.[10]

Section 9105 defines a security agreement as "an agreement
hich creates or provides for a security interest." In Ameri-
n Card Co. v. H.M.H. Co. (1963) 196 A.2d 150 (R.I.), it
as held that this required a document which "granted" a
curity interest and that since a financing statement did not
this (see form on page 148) it could not serve as a security
reement.

ling Financing Statement or
aking Possession of Collateral

The other requirement for perfection of a security interest,
addition to attachment, is that the steps required for per-
ction by Sections 9302, 9304 and 9305 be taken.

Sections 9302, 9304 and 9305 provide for four possibilities
ith respect to perfection of an attached security interest, as
llows:

1. Automatic Perfection: Transactions Exempt from Re-
uirement of Filing or Taking Possession. Section 9302(1)
empts certain types of transactions from the requirements
filing or taking possession. The important transaction for

our purposes is "a purchase money security interest[11] in consumer goods," excepted by subdivision (1) (d) of Section
9302. Consumer goods are goods "used or bought for use
primarily for personal, family or household purposes."[12] This
exemption means that the retailer who sells a stove or a re-
frigerator or a television set on time and who takes a security
agreement for the balance of the purchase price is not required
to file a financing statement to protect his security interest
against other creditors of the buyer. To make him do so would
be to impose a prohibitively expensive and onerous requirement.

2. Possession Only. A security interest in instruments can
be perfected only by taking possession of the collateral.[13] This
rule is necessary in order to protect innocent purchasers of
such collateral. If, for example, the holder of commercial paper could borrow money on it as security without surrendering
possession of it, the holder could then sell the paper to someone else. If the buyer then took subject to the security interest
if notice of it was filed, the "negotiability" of the commercial
paper would mean nothing.

3. Filing Only. The concept of possession is not apposite
to intangible collateral, not represented by a writing; therefore
filing is the only way in which a security interest can be perfected in intangibles, that is, in accounts and general intangibles.[14]

4. Filing or Possession. A security interest can be perfected
in goods, negotiable documents, and chattel paper by filing or
by taking possession.[15] Field warehousing, discussed on page
161, would be a commercial financing transaction using goods
as collateral, perfected by taking possession of the goods. Our
purposes in studying Division 9 are served by considering
only those transactions in which filing is the means of perfecting the security interest and the discussion in the remaining sections of this chapter will be devoted to such transactions.

● In some instances the code comes into conflict with and may
give way to other kinds of filing requirements. The example
for our purposes is the motor vehicle registration statute. Under the law of California, and that of many other states, the
only way in which a security interest in an automobile which
is not inventory may be perfected is to have the security interest recorded on the ownership certificate ("pink slip").[16]
Thus, if a car is purchased on time and the buyer gives a
security agreement by way of creating a security interest in
the car for the balance of the purchase price, the seller (secured party) must have the security interest recorded on the
ownership certificate to perfect it.

● Most cases involving the filing of a financing statement to
perfect a security interest will be cases involving the financing
of a merchant by a bank or other financing agency, which

---

[6]U.C.C. 9303.

[7]U.C.C. 9203(1)(2).

[8]U.C.C. 9203, Official Comment 5.

[9]U.C.C. 9302(1)(a).

[10]U.C.C. 9110 and Official Comment.

[11]U.C.C. 9107 defines a purchase money security interest as
follows: "A security interest is a 'purchase money security interest' to the extent that it is

"(a) Taken or retained by the seller of the collateral to secure
all or part of its price; or

"(b) Taken by a person who by making advances or incurring
an obligation gives value to enable the debtor to acquire rights in
or the use of collateral if such value is in fact so used."

[12]U.C.C. 9109(1).

[13]U.C.C. 9304(1).

[14]U.C.C. 9305, Official Comment 1.

[15]U.C.C. 9302, 9304 and 9305.

[16]U.C.C. 9302(1)(d), (3)(b), (4).

takes a security interest in the inventory, equipment and/or accounts receivable of the merchant. The formal requirements of a financing statement are set forth in Section 9402. An illustrative form follows. Section 9401 specifies the place at which the financing statement must be filed, ordinarily in the office of the Secretary of State. This is known as a *central filing* system (one office for the entire state) as distinguished from a local filing system (filing with county officers).

• The kind of filing required by the code is called *notice-filing* as distinguished from the filing of a copy of the document which creates the security interest (the security agreement) although the secured party may, if he wishes, file a copy of the security agreement and allow it to serve as the amount of paper which is required to perfect and maintain public records and security interests, and that, plus the incident saving of expense, is its purpose.[17] Instead of filing a copy of a three or four page document (the security agreement), the secured party files the one page form shown on page 145, which, from the standpoint of giving public notice, serves the purpose equally as well. Notice-filing was introduced by the Uniform Trust Receipts Act and is one of the good features of that act that has been preserved by the code.

• A financing statement may be filed before a security agreement is made or a security interest otherwise attaches.[18]

• A filed financing statement is effective for a period of 5 years from the date of filing, after which it lapses unless a *continuation* statement is filed prior to lapse.[19]

The office of the Secretary of State of California has prepared a booklet which sets forth and explains the Division 9 filing procedures in full detail and exhibits Division 9 forms which are approved by the office of the Secretary of State, which, if used, will expedite filing. On the following pages are shown the financing statement form, and the request for information or copies form by which any person may obtain from the filing officer information as to whether a financing statement has been filed against any person and by which he may obtain a copy of a financing statement on file.

Priorities

The important and difficult problems under Division 9 are priority problems. Secured parties may find themselves in competition with (1) other secured parties, (2) creditors of the debtor, and (3) buyers from the debtor. Each case presents problems of priorities to be settled, which are discussed more fully below, after certain preliminary considerations which follow next.

Preliminary Considerations: After-Acquired Property Clauses; Future Advance Clauses; "Proceeds"

Many priorities problems result from certain devices that accompany security agreements, namely, after-acquired property clauses and future advances clauses. They also result from the fact that the right to collateral includes the right to proceeds of collateral.[20]

Inventory financing is common. It is an arrangement whereby a financing agency, the inventory financer, will in effect subsidize the business operation of a merchant by providing

him with the funds necessary to maintain a stock of invento The inventory financer will want a comprehensive lien on assets of the merchant as security for the loan.

The basic lien will be a security agreement giving the ventory financer a security interest in the original invent of the merchant. But the original inventory will soon be s and replaced by new inventory, which in its turn will be so and so on, and the inventory financer will want his secu interest to attach to each of these turnovers in inventory occurs. The inventory financer can accomplish this to the le extent to which it can be accomplished[21] by including an *aft acquired property clause* in the security agreement that takes from the merchant. An after-acquired property clause simply a provision that a security agreement includes coll eral of a certain type, in this case inventory, then owned thereafter acquired by the debtor, the merchant in this ca Such clauses are permitted by Section 9204(1) of the co Where a security interest is designed to attach to new inv tory as it replaces old, the secured party is said to have "*floating lien*" on the inventory. Section 9302(3) automa cally extends a security interest to "*proceeds*" of collater Section 9306 defines proceeds and lays down important ru regarding the recovery of proceeds which have been comm gled with other funds of the debtor, as follows: If the deb has not become insolvent, Section 9306(1) provides that perfected security interest in proceeds "continues in any ide tifiable proceeds." This means that if, by tracing (first-first-out, and the like), the secured party can identify p ceeds, he can recover them even though they have been co mingled with other funds of the debtor. Where insolver proceedings have been instituted by or against the debtor. S tion 9306(4) limits the secured party's pursuit of procee commingled with other funds to cash proceeds received the debtor within ten days before the institution of the ins vency proceedings.

• The inventory financer may expect to make additional vances—so-called "*future advances*"—to the debtor fr time to time. The inventory financer will want these advanc to be covered by all available collateral, both old and ne that is, by the original collateral to the extent that it still exi and by substitutions for it or additions to it which are includ in the security agreement. A *future advances clause* is device by which old collateral is made to cover new advanc Such clauses are permitted by Section 9204(3). It has be held that the security agreement must contain a future vances clause in order for future advances to be covered b security interest.[22]

The inventory financer may demand collateral other th inventory, present and future, and proceeds of inventory. T inventory financer may demand, as well, that his lien exte to equipment of the debtor, both present and future, there giving itself in effect a blanket lien on the assets of the debt

Conflicting Security Interests in the Same Collateral: The Rules of Section 9312

Section 9312 is a major provision of Division 9. It la down rules regarding priorities among conflicting security terests in the same collateral. Its major rules for our purpos are concerned with (1) competition for the same collate

---

[17]U.C.C. 9402(1).

[18]U.C.C. 9402(1).

[19]U.C.C. 9403(2)(3).

[20]U.C.C. 9203(3). See Section 9306(1) for what constitute "proceeds."

[21]This caveat is included because, as will be seen, the aftera quired property clause may be subordinate to a purchase mon security interest in collateral.

[22]*Coin-O-Matic Service Co.* v. *Rhode Island Hospital Trust C* (1966) 3 U.C.C. Rep. 1112 (R.I. Super. Ct.).

etween a purchase money security interest and a nonpurchase money security interest and (2) competition for the same collateral between nonpurchase money security interests. A purchase money security interest increases the debtor's assets by an amount equal to the lien of the purchase money security interest. For example, if purchase money secured party lends debtor $5000 to buy a piece of equipment, debtor's assets will have been enhanced by the sum of $5000 when he purchases the piece of equipment, which is an amount equal to the amount of the purchase money security interest lien. Consequently, debtor's prior creditors, secured and unsecured, have not been harmed by the transaction. They are as well secured as they were before the transaction. Therefore it is appropriate to give the purchase money secured party a prior lien in the asset which he has generated, which is basically what the law does.

1. *Purchase Money Security Interest v. Non-Purchase Money Security Interest.* The rules of Section 9312 distinguish between purchase money security interests in non-inventory collateral and purchase money security interests in inventory collateral, as follows:

a. *Purchase Money Security Interest in Non-Inventory Collateral v. Non-Purchase Money Security Interest*: A purchase money security interest in non-inventory collateral prevails over a non-purchase money security interest in the same collateral provided that the purchase money security interest is perfected at the time the debtor receives possession of the collateral or within ten days thereafter.[23] It does not matter that the purchase money secured party knows of the nonpurchase money security interest or that the nonpurchase money security interest has been filed.[24]

Example: Debtor gives Secured Party-1 a non-purchase money security interest in collateral which includes Debtor's equipment; the security agreement contains an after-acquired property clause. Subsequently, Debtor borrows money from Secured Party-2 to purchase equipment and gives Secured Party-2 a purchase money security interest in the equipment. If the purchase money security interest is perfected at the time Debtor receives possession of the collateral or within ten days thereafter, it prevails over the after-acquired property interest of Secured Party-1.

b. *Purchase Money Security Interest in Inventory Collateral v. Non-Purchase Money Security Interest:* A purchase money security interest in inventory collateral must meet two requirements to gain priority over a conflicting security interest in the same collateral: (1) The purchase money security interest must be perfected at the time the debtor receives possession of the collateral (without grace period); and (2) the purchase money secured party must, before the debtor receives possession of the collateral, give notice of the purchase money security interest to all prior secured parties who have filed financing statements covering the same types of inventory. Official Comment 3 to Section 9312 explains the notice requirement as follows:

"The reason for the additional requirement of notification is that typically the arrangement between an inventory secured party and his debtor will require the secured party to make periodic advances against incoming inventory or periodic releases of old inventory as new inventory is received. A fraudulent debtor may apply to the secured party for advances even though he has already given a security interest in the inventory to another secured party. The notification requirement protects the inventory financer in such a situation: if he has re-

ceived notification, he will presumably not make an advance; if he has not received notification (or if the other interest does not qualify as a purchase money interest), any advance he may make will have priority. Since an arrangement for periodic advances against incoming property is unusual outside the inventory field, no notification requirement is included in subsection (4)."

2. *Non-Purchase Money Security Interest v. Non-Purchase Money Security Interest.* Here, the first to file prevails.[25]

Example: Secured Party-1 files against Debtor on May 1. Secured Party-2 files against Debtor on May 5. Secured Party-2 makes a non-purchase money advance against certain collateral on May 10. Secured Party-1 makes a non-purchase money advance against the same collateral on May 15. Secured Party-1 has priority even though Secured Party-2's advance was made earlier and was perfected when made. It makes no difference whether or not Secured Party-1 knew of Secured Party-2's interest when he made his advance.[26]

3. *Accounts Financer v. Other Financer.* A prior inventory financer, who is on file, takes priority over a subsequent accounts financer by virtue of its, the inventory financer's, automatic right to proceeds.[27]

Example: Secured Party-1 finances Merchant's inventory, taking a security interest therein and filing a financing statement. Thereafter, Secured Party-2 lends Merchant money on the security of Merchant's accounts, taking a security interest in the accounts. Thereafter, Merchant develops accounts from the sale of the inventory. Secured Party-1 has priority in the accounts by virtue of its right to proceeds of inventory.

If, on the other hand, accounts financing comes first and is filed first, the accounts financer has priority over the subsequent inventory financer.[28] In one case, however, a subsequent financer will take priority over a prior accounts financer. This is where the accounts come from the sale of non-inventory collateral, such as equipment, in which the subsequent financer has taken and duly perfected a purchase money security interest.[29] This is because such non-inventory collateral is not expected to be sold and it is appropriate, therefore, to prefer the secured party as to the proceeds.[30]

Example: Secured Party-1 takes and duly files a security interest in Merchant's accounts. Thereafter, Merchant borrows money from Secured Party-2 in order to finance the purchase of new equipment. Secured Party-2 takes and duly files a purchase money security interest in the equipment. Thereafter, Merchant sells some of the equipment, producing "accounts." Secured Party-2 has priority in the accounts.

4. *Chattel Paper Purchaser v. Competing Security Interests.* U.C.C. 9308 protects the innocent purchaser for value of chattel paper left in the hands of the debtor against a secured party who has a security interest in the chattel paper perfected by filing. The secured party, in such case, makes it possible for its debtor to commit a fraud which the secured party could prevent by stamping or noting on the chattel paper that the chattel paper has been assigned to the secured party.[31]

Example: Debtor gives Secured Party a security interest in chattel paper which is left in Debtor's hands without notation on the paper

---

[23]U.C.C. 9312(4).

[24]U.C.C. 9312, Official Comment 3.

[25]U.C.C. 9312(5).

[26]U.C.C. 9312, Official Comment 5.

[27]U.C.C. 9312, Official Comment 8.

[28]U.C.C. 9312, Official Comment 8.

[29]U.C.C. 9312(4).

[30]U.C.C. 9312, Official Comment 3.

[31]U.C.C. 9308, Official Comment 3.

that Secured Party has been given a security interest in it. Secured Party files a financing statement showing its security interest in the paper. Thereafter, without knowledge of Secured Party's security interest in the chattel paper, Chattel Paper Purchaser purchases the paper. Chattel Paper Purchaser has priority in the chattel paper.

U.C.C. 9308 also gives priority to the chattel paper purchaser against an inventory financer who claims the chattel paper merely as "proceeds." Here, the chattel paper purchaser prevails even though he knows of the prior security interest. Presumably this is because the purchaser of chattel paper provides an important type of financing. Such financing is important because it enables a merchant to obtain necessary current operating funds. Such financing therefore deserves to be protected.

The Secured Party and Creditors of the Debtor: Unperfected Security Interest v. Lien Creditor

Throughout the law it is customary to protect unsecured "attaching or execution creditors" of a debtor against an unrecorded lien on his assets. This is because the judicial lien creditor, after searching the records and finding no such lien and thinking therefore that the debtor's assets are clear, is induced to spend the money necessary to attach or execute on the assets. The secret lienholder—the person having the unrecorded lien—should not be allowed to then step forward, show his hand and take precedence over the judicial lien creditor.

This makes the judicial lien creditor a special breed—the highest form of *unsecured* creditor.

The code adopts and applies these principles in Section 9301. It creates a defined term for the purpose—the term *"lien creditor."* A lien creditor is a creditor who has acquired a lien on the property involved by attachment or levy of execution and also is a trustee in bankruptcy from the date of the filing of the petition in bankruptcy.

● Section 9301(1)(b) provides that an unperfected security interest is subordinate to the rights of "a person who becomes a lien creditor before it is perfected."

Example: On May 1, Debtor gives Secured Party a security interest in certain collateral, which attaches at that time. On May 5, C, an unsecured creditor of Debtor, levies execution on the collateral. On May 8, Secured Party files a financing statement. C would have priority in the collateral.

The Secured Party in the Debtor's Bankruptcy

Security is designed to protect a creditor against his debtor's bankruptcy. If the creditor is protected by a fixed security, he will, generally speaking, have the protection of the security if the debtor takes bankruptcy.

● The Bankruptcy Reform Act of 1978 imposes a new, significant limitation on the security of a creditor who is a floating lien holder. To prevent such creditor from being preferred, Section 547(c)(5) limits the creditor's secured position in the manner illustrated on page 379.

The Secured Party and Purchasers of the Collateral

1. *Buyer from Dealer.* Goods must pass in the market place to consumer purchasers free of liens of inventory financers. A contrary state of the law would be intolerable. Section 9307(1) protects the consumer purchaser against the inventory financer. It provides that a buyer in the ordinary course of business [defined in Section 1201(9) as a person who "buys in the ordinary course from a person in the business of selling goods of that kind"] takes free of a security interest created by his seller even though the buyer knows of its existence.

Example: Department Store finances its inventory, through Inventory Financer, giving Inventory Financer a security interest in its inventory, present and future. Inventory Financer files a duly executed financing statement. Thereafter Department Store sells an item of inventory to Consumer, a buyer in the ordinary course of business. Consumer takes free of Inventory Financer's lien on the item of inventory.

2. *Buyer from Private Party.* At this point the Official Text has a subsection which the California Code omits. In the Official Text, Section 9307 contains a subsection (2) which provides that "In the case of consumer goods . . . , a buyer takes free of a security interest even though perfected if he buys without knowledge of the security interest, for value and for his own personal, family or household purposes . . . unless prior to the purchase the secured party has filed a financing statement covering such goods."

Example: Same facts as in previous example as regards the financing of Department Store by Inventory Financer. Department Store sells the item of inventory, which is an item of consumer goods, to Consumer on time, taking a security interest in the item of consumer goods as security for the purchase price. Department Store does not file a financing statement covering its security interest. Consumer sells the item to Private Party who buys it for personal use. Private Party should take free of Inventory Financer's lien on "shelter" principles as seen in the chapter on Commercial Paper.[32] Under the Official Text of the Code, if Private Party did not know of Department Store's lien, it would take free of that lien because of Department Store's failure to file a financing statement.

The result is the opposite under the California Code because of the omission of subsection (2) to Section 9-307. This preserves the pre-code rule in California under which conditional sales were not required to be recorded to be good against a buyer from the conditional buyer.

Rights and Duties of Parties After Default

Chapter 5 of Division 9 deals with the rights and duties of secured party and debtor after default by debtor. "Default" is not defined by the code and it is left to the parties to define it in the security agreement. The usual default of course is the failure of the debtor to make a payment owed to the secured party and secured by the security agreement, but other acts may also constitute defaults, such as failure to insure the collateral, unauthorized removal of the collateral from the state and allowing legal seizure of the collateral by a third party.

The secured party is entitled to take possession of the collateral on default.[33] He may then resell it, or he may elect to retain it in satisfaction of the debtor's obligation provided that he gives the debtor and, except in the case of consumer goods, other secured parties 21 days' written notice of intention to do so and does not receive written objection to such action.[34] In California, the provisions of the code give way to the provisions of the Unruh Act with respect to retail installment sales, and under that Act the repossessing seller has 10 days to elect to resell or to retain the goods in satisfaction of the obligation.

Resale is compulsory where the collateral is consumer goods and the debtor has satisfied 60% of the obligation for which the security interest has been given, but the debtor may waive his right after default.[35] If the secured party elects to

---

[32]Page 126.

[33]U.C.C. 9503.

[34]U.C.C. 9505(2).

[35]U.C.C. 9505(1).

sell, he is given wide latitude regarding the manner of conducting the sale. See Section 9504(3). It is thought that this is likely to obtain the best price and therefore to serve the best interests of the debtor. Resale must, in every respect, be conducted in a commercially reasonable manner.[36]

If there is a resale, the debtor is liable for a deficiency, except that if the collateral is accounts, the security agreement must expressly provide that the debtor is to be liable for a deficiency.[37] This is because accounts are presumed to be assigned without recourse unless recourse against the assignor is preserved. In California, the Unruh Act bars deficiency judgments with respect to the transactions which it regulates—retail installment sales—and this takes precedence over the code.

The debtor and other secured parties have a right of redemption pending resale or expiration of the time for objection where the secured party gives notice of intention to retain the collateral in satisfaction of the obligation.[38]

If the secured party fails to proceed in accordance with the provisions of Chapter 5, that is, in accordance with the procedures described above, the debtor can recover from the secured party any loss caused by such failure, and, if the collateral is consumer goods, the debtor can recover interest plus an amount equal to 10% of principal.[39]

---

[36]U.C.C. 9504(3).
[37]U.C.C. 9504(2).

[38]U.C.C. 9506.
[39]U.C.C. 9507(1).

LINE UP COMPUTER/PRINTER SQUARELY WITH BRACKET BELOW ↓

SECURITY AGREEMENT
DISCLOSURES PURSUANT TO TRUTH-IN-LENDING ACT

BUYER'S NAME

DATE OF AGREEMENT	Salesman:
ZIP CODE AGREEMENT NO.	To be delivered to the following address:

BUYER'S RESIDENCE OR PLACE OF BUSINESS

In this contract the words "we," "us" and "our" refer to the creditor (seller) named below. The words "you" and "yours" refer to the buyer and co-buyer if any named herein.

We sell you the goods and services described below on credit. The credit price is shown below as the "Total Sale Price". The "Cash Price" is also shown below. By signing this contract you choose to buy the goods and services on credit and agree to pay us the total sale price in the amounts and under the terms and agreements shown on the front and back of this contract. If this contract is signed by a buyer and co-buyer, each is individually and together responsible for all agreements in the contract.

NEW/USED	MODEL	SERIAL NO.	DESCRIPTION OF GOODS/SERVICES

Address where goods purchased will be located:

ANNUAL PERCENTAGE RATE: The cost of your credit as a yearly rate.	FINANCE CHARGE The dollar amount the credit will cost you.	Amount Financed The amount of credit provided to you or on your behalf.	Total of Payments The amount you will have paid after you have made all payments as scheduled.	Total Sale Price The total cost of your purchase on credit, including your down payment of $ _____
%	$	$	$	$

YOUR PAYMENT SCHEDULE WILL BE:

Number of payments:	Amount of payments:	When payments are due:
One payment of		
One payment of		
payments		☐ Wkly. ☐ Semi Mthly. ☐ Mthly. Payments beginning
One Final Payment		

SECURITY: You are giving a security interest in the goods or property being purchased.

LATE CHARGES: If any payment is more than 10 days late you will be charged 5% of the payment or $5.00, whichever is less, but in no event less than $1.00.

PREPAYMENT: If you pay early you may be entitled to a refund of part of the finance charge

See your contract documents for any additional information about nonpayment. default. any required prepayment in full before the scheduled date and prepayment refunds.

STATEMENT OF INSURANCE

NOTICE: No person is required as a condition to financing the purchase of goods or services to purchase, or negotiate any insurance through a particular insurance company, agent or broker.

You voluntarily request us to include in the balance due under this agreement the following insurance. Said insurance is to expire WITH ☐ BEFORE ☐ AFTER ☐ the due date of the final installment.

ITEMIZATION OF THE AMOUNT FINANCED

1. (A) Cash price of goods and services .... $ _____
   (B) Taxes on sale .... $ _____
   (TOTAL CASH PRICE AND TAXES .... $ _____

———— (1)

$ _____ DED. COMP. FIRE & THEFT — Mos: $ _____ Premium
$ _____ OTHER (DECLARE) _____ Mos: $ _____
$ _____ TOTAL INSURANCE PREMIUMS: $ _____ (A)

The foregoing declarations are hereby acknowledged.

_____ Seller
_____ Buyer

CREDIT INSURANCE AUTHORIZATION AND APPLICATION

You voluntarily request the credit insurance checked below, if any, and understand that such insurance is not required. You acknowledge disclosure of the cost of such insurance and authorize it to be included in the balance payable under the security agreement. Only the persons whose names are signed below are insured.

CREDIT LIFE _____ Mos. Premium $ _____
JOINT LIFE _____ Mos. Premium $ _____
CREDIT DISABILITY _____ Mos. Premium $ _____
TOTAL CREDIT INSURANCE PREMIUMS _____ $ _____ (B)

☐ You want Credit Life Insurance
☐☐ You do not want Credit Life Insurance
☐☐ You want Credit Disability Insurance (Primary Buyer only)
☐☐ You do not want Credit Disability Insurance
☐☐ You want Joint Credit Life Insurance

You are applying for the credit insurance marked above. Your signature below means that you agree that:
1. You are not eligible for insurance if you reached your 65th birthday.
2. You are eligible for disability insurance only if you are working for wages or profit 30 hours a week or more on the Effective Date.
3. Your co-buyer is not eligible for disability insurance.

Date _____ Primary-Buyer _____ Age _____
Date _____ Co-Buyer _____ Age _____ ID-1

TOTAL INSURANCE PREMIUMS (A+B) ARE DESCRIBED IN ITEM 3.

SEE THE BACK OF THIS CONTRACT FOR ADDITIONAL TERMS AND CONDITIONS

Buyer acknowledges that: (1) before signing this agreement Buyer read both sides of this agreement and received a legible, completely filled-in copy of this agreement; and (2) Buyer has received a copy of every other document that Buyer signed during the contract negotiation.
Buyer sign here **X** _____
Address _____ Zip _____ Phone _____

Seller _____
NO. 164 (REV. 10/82) © 1982 LAW PRINTING CO. INC
The Printer makes no warranty, express or implied, as to content or fitness for purpose of this form. Consult your own legal counsel.

(**AMOUNTS PAID TO PUBLIC OFFICIALS**
(A) Recording fee _____ $ _____
(B) Other (described) _____ $ _____
2. { **TOTAL OFFICIAL FEES** _____ $ _____ (2)

3. **AMOUNTS PAID TO INSURANCE COMPANIES**
(total premiums per statement of insurance) _____ $ _____ (3)

4. **TOTAL (1+2+3)** _____ $ _____ (4)

(A) Agreed value of Property Traded in _____ $ _____
Describe _____
5. (B) Deferred downpayment due before second installment payment _____ $ _____
(C) Manufacturer's rebate _____ $ _____
(D) Remaining cash downpayment _____ $ _____
TOTAL DOWNPAYMENT (5A+B+C+D) _____ $ _____ (5)

6. **AMOUNT FINANCED (4 less 5)** _____ $ _____ (6)

PREPAYMENT REFUND: (Check box which applies) Any refund for prepayment will be calculated according to :
☐ The Rule of 78.
☐ The sum of the periodic time balance method.

NOTICES: The names and addresses of all persons to whom the notices required or permitted by law are to be sent are set forth below.

Notice to buyer: (1) Do not sign this agreement before you read it or if it contains any blank spaces to be filled in. (2) You are entitled to a completely filled-in copy of this agreement. (3) You can prepay the full amount due under this agreement at any time and obtain a partial refund of the finance charge if it is $1 or more. Because of the way the amount of this refund will be figured, the time when you prepay could increase the ultimate cost of credit under this agreement. (4) If you desire to pay off in advance the full amount due, the amount of the refund you are entitled to, if any, will be furnished upon request.

Buyer sign here **X** _____
Address _____ Zip _____ Phone _____

Address _____
By _____ Title _____

(Form continued on following pages)

ADDITIONAL TERMS AND CONDITIONS

A. SECURITY INTEREST: You give us a security interest under the California Uniform Commercial Code in the goods sold and all parts or accessories and in all insurance premiums financed for you or rebates from insurance premiums and in the proceeds of any insurance policies covering the goods for insuring your life or health, which security interest secures all sums which may become due under this contract. You agree that you will keep the goods free from all taxes and liens and will not use them improperly and not make any material change in the goods. We may pay any taxes or liens and you agree to reimburse us on demand.

B. PREPAYMENT AND ACCELERATION: You may prepay all amounts due under this agreement at any time. If you default in making any payment when due, or in the performance of any term or condition of this agreement, we may, in addition to our other remedies, declare all unpaid sums immediately due and payable. In either event, any unearned finance charge will be credited or refunded to you in accordance with Civil Code #1806.3. In no event shall the minimum finance charge be less than $12.00 unless the due date of the last installment is 8 months or less from the date of this agreement, in which case the minimum finance charge is $10.00. No refund credit of less than $1.00 will be made. The refund will be calculated according to Rule of 78's.

C. INSURANCE: You agree to keep the property insured in favor of us by a policy of insurance which includes comprehensive coverage insuring against loss by fire, theft and related damage in a company satisfactory to us in amounts not less than the total unpaid sums due under this agreement. If you fail to secure or maintain said insurance, we may, but need not insure your interest. You agree to pay for any such insurance on demand. If you fail to do so the insurance premium will be added to your unpaid balance and you agree to pay finance charges thereon at the annual percentage rate shown on the reverse. The proceeds of any insurance whether paid by reason of loss, injury, return premium, or otherwise, shall be applied toward the replacement or repair of the property or as payment against the unpaid sums due under this agreement. Any difference between the amounts stated in the Statement of Insurance for premiums which may arise from errors in computation, classification, grouping or zoning, or changes in the type of insurance shall be payable by you on demand.

D. CREDIT INFORMATION: You warrant that all information contained in your application for Credit is true and correct and acknowledge that we and if applicable, our assignee, have relied upon the accuracy thereof in connection with this agreement.

E. LATE CHARGES: If you default in the payment of any installment for a period of 10 days or more, we will collect a late charge in a sum equal to 5% of such delinquent installment or $5.00, whichever is less, but in no event less than $1.00.

F. RIGHTS UPON DEFAULT: 1) If you default in the performance of any of the terms and conditions of this agreement, including but not limited to the making of any payment when due; b) becomes insolvent or is the subject of bankruptcy proceedings; c) or dies; d) or the property purchased is damaged or destroyed; we at our option and without notice may: a) declare all unpaid sums due under this agreement immediately due and payable; b) file suit against you for all unpaid sums due under this agreement; c) without prior demand, we may take immediate possession of the property wherever the same may be found. Within 10 days of taking such possession, we shall give written notice to you: i) of our intention to retain the property in satisfaction of all unpaid sums due under this agreement; (ii) that the property will be sold at public sale. In either event, you shall have the right to redeem the property within 10 days by paying or tendering all unpaid sums due under this agreement, together with delinquency and extension charges, plus any expense reasonably incurred by us in good faith for repairing, reconditioning, or preparing the property for sale, and if such redemption is not made, said amounts and the expenses of the subsequent sale shall be payable from the proceeds thereof: (d) in the event that you shall fail to notify us of any change of address or shall not communicate with us for a period of 45 days after any default in paying installment due under this agreement, or if you shall remove the property from this state, we may collect reasonable costs of collection. 2) In the event that any action to enforce the terms or conditions of this agreement is brought, the prevailing party shall be entitled to reasonable attorney's fees and court costs.

G. WARRANTY: NO WARRANTIES, EXPRESS OR IMPLIED, REPRESENTATIONS, PROMISES OR STATEMENTS AS TO THE CONDITION, FITNESS OR MERCHANTABILITY OF THE PROPERTY HAVE BEEN MADE BY SELLER UNLESS STATED IN THIS AGREEMENT.

H. OTHER AGREEMENT OF BUYER: 1) You agree that if we accept monies in sums less than those due or make extension of due dates of payments under this contract, doing so will not be a waiver of any later right to enforce the contract terms as written. 2) We may, at your request, and at our option, add subsequent purchases to this contract. 3) You will allow us to inspect the goods at any reasonable time and notify us of any change of your address within 30 days. 4) If you are married, and sign this agreement, you agree that your separate property shall be liable for all unpaid sums due. 5) If we transfer this contract to an assignee, you will be given notice thereof and you agree that the assignee will have all our rights and remedies under the contract and you agree to pay all that is still owed under this contract at all times, and in the amounts, to the assignee. 6) That all of the agreements between us and you are set forth in this contract and no modification of this contract shall be valid unless it is made in writing and signed by you and us. 7) That any provision of this contract which may be held invalid shall not mean that this contract is unenforceable and the remaining provisions of this contract shall continue to be binding;

NOTICE

ANY HOLDER OF THIS CONSUMER CREDIT CONTRACT IS SUBJECT TO ALL CLAIMS AND DEFENSES WHICH THE DEBTOR COULD ASSERT AGAINST THE SELLER OF GOODS OR SERVICES OBTAINED PURSUANT HERETO OR WITH THE PROCEEDS HEREOF. RECOVERY HEREUNDER BY THE DEBTOR SHALL NOT EXCEED AMOUNTS PAID BY THE DEBTOR HEREUNDER.

Notice to buyer: (1) Do not sign this agreement before you read it or if it contains any blank spaces to be filled in. (2) You are entitled to a completely filled-in copy of this agreement. (3) You can prepay the full amount due under this agreement at any time and obtain a partial refund of the finance charge if it is $1 or more. Because of the way the amount of this refund will be figured, the time when you prepay could increase the ultimate cost of credit under this agreement. (4) If you desire to pay off in advance the full amount due, the amount of the refund you are entitled to, if any, will be furnished upon request.

SELLER'S ASSIGNMENT WITHOUT RECOURSE

For value received, Seller assigns to _____ all of Seller's interest in the foregoing agreement and the property described in paragraph A of the foregoing agreement.

Seller warrants:
1. Seller has not helped the Buyer get a loan to make any of the payments required under the agreement.
2. Seller has done everything required to perfect assignee's security interest in the property according to the laws of the state in which the property is to be situated. All persons who will be registered owners of the property have signed the agreement.
3. No one else has or will have a security interest in the property referred to in paragraph A of the agreement.
4. Seller has complied with all laws and/or regulations applicable to the agreement.
5. The agreement evidences a bona fide sale of the property, shows all the terms of the agreement, and is not rescindable except if assignee and Buyer mutually and voluntarily so agree.
6. The property has been delivered to the Buyer.
7. Buyer is bound to all of the terms and conditions of the agreement, and has no claims against Seller that Seller has breached the agreement violated any laws and/or regulations applicable to the agreement, or that the property is defective.
8. The information contained in Buyer's Application for Credit is true and correct and Seller has no information or reason to believe that the property will be used in connection with any violation of federal or state law.

Seller agrees:
1. Seller will repurchase the agreement from assignee, on assignee's demand, paying assignee the then unpaid balance (which includes any amount advanced by assignee in connection with the agreement), if any of the warranties are breached, or if the agreement is rescinded by operation of law or otherwise.
2. Seller will indemnify and hold assignee harmless from all claims, suits, costs, expenses, losses, damages and liabilities, and will pay assignee's legal expenses (whether incurred if assignee hires independent counsel or assignee uses its own salaried attorneys), if any of these warranties are breached as a result of any contention, valid or otherwise.
3. Assignee may grant extension as to the time and amounts of payments due from Buyer, without affecting Seller's liability to assignee and without seller's consent.
4. Assignee does not have to take any action against the Buyer before calling on Seller to carry out Seller's obligations to assignee.

Dated _____ at _____
                              (Seller's Town and State)

Signed _____ (Seal) By _____
                                    (Officer, Firm Member or Owner)

WITH RECOURSE (Additional Term)

In addition to the warranties (paragraphs 1 through 8 above) and agreements (paragraphs 1 through 4 above) to which Seller expressly warrants and agrees to be bound, Seller also agrees to repurchase the agreement, on assignee's demand, paying assignee the then unpaid balance (which includes any amounts advanced by assignee in connection with the agreement) if the Buyer does not make any or all payments under the agreement as agreed.

Dated _____ at _____
                              (Seller's Town and State)

Signed _____ (Seal) By _____
       (Name of Seller)   (Officer, Firm Member or Owner)

CALIFORNIA BANK

SECURITY AGREEMENT AND NOTE
(FLOORING)

DEALER (DEBTOR)	OFFICE	DATE	SECURITY AGREEMENT NO
INVOICE(S) FROM (DISTRIB. OR SELLER)	INVOICE NUMBER(S)		DATE DUE

$_____, _____, California, _____, 19___, For new value received, the undersigned as Debtor holds in trust for California Bank (Bank) the following described property, complete with all attachments and equipment, to wit:

MAKE	TYPE (REFRIGERATOR, AUTO) MODEL	SERIAL NUMBER	INVOICE PRICE	RELEASE PRICE*	DATE PAID OFF	DUE	DUE	DUE
1						1		
2						2		
3						3		
4						4		
5						5		
6						6		
7						7		
8						8		
9						9		
10						10		
11						11		
12						12		
			TOTALS					

* INVOICE PRICE LESS DOWN PAYMENT APPLICATION. TOTAL OF THIS AMOUNT MUST AGREE WITH AMOUNT OWING, AS STATED BELOW.

Debtor hereby acknowledges that a security interest, pursuant to the California Uniform Commercial Code, in the property described above and in the proceeds of said property is hereby granted to Bank as security for the payment of moneys due Bank, and Debtor promises to pay Bank or order on _____, 19___, or at Bank's option, on demand, at its _____ office in this city the sum of _____ Dollars with interest thereon from _____, 19___, at the rate of _____ percent per annum. Should the interest not so be paid, it shall bear interest as the principal. This Security Agreement and Note also secures all other indebtedness of Debtor, if any, to Bank, now in existence or hereafter arising. The conditions and agreements set forth on the reverse side hereof constitute a part of this Security Agreement and Note. Debtor has received a copy of this agreement.

_____
DEBTOR

_____
BY (OFFICIAL TITLE IF COMPANY)

_____
BY (OFFICIAL TITLE IF COMPANY)

INSTRUCTIONS
1 TYPE IN TRIPLICATE.
2 GOLDENROD COPY TO DEALER
3 WHITE, PINK COPIES TO BANK

(Form continued on following page)

The Debtor agrees to deliver all or any portion of said property to Bank on demand in good order and unused.

The Debtor represents that said property is free from liens of every kind and agrees at its own expense to hold said property, together with attachments and equipment, in trust for Bank. Debtor shall not create a security interest in or otherwise encumber said property, but shall have the right to sell for cash, or on terms approved in advance in writing by Bank, to buyers in the ordinary course of business, any of said property at prices not less than the sums, under the heading "Release Price", set opposite the respective items in the above schedule. However, no sale or delivery shall be made to any one who, prior to sale or delivery, has any claim or outstanding account which might be valid against the Debtor as a set-off or defense, unless Debtor shall have obtained the Bank's specific authorization in writing, to make such sale or delivery.

Immediately upon receipt of the proceeds of any sale the Debtor shall deliver said proceeds in whatever form received to the Bank. The Debtor shall not commingle said property, or any part of the proceeds of the sale thereof, with any other property, nor hypothecate or otherwise dispose of the same or any interest therein. All cash proceeds of sales shall be applied to the indebtedness of the Debtor secured hereby. Proceeds in other form shall not be applied until collected in cash, and the Bank may sell or discount the same without notice and apply the proceeds.

The Bank may at any time examine said property and the books and records of the Debtor with reference thereto. At any time, either before or after the due date, the Bank may require Debtor to assemble the property and make it available to Bank at a place designated by Bank and may repossess said property or the proceeds of such property without notice or demand of any kind, and for such purpose Bank, or its representative may with or without legal process enter any premises in which said property or proceeds are located.

The Debtor acknowledges that the property is complete and satisfactory. Debtor at its own expense shall properly house said property, and keep the same insured against all hazards to their full value. The risk of loss of or damage to said property is assumed by the Debtor, who agrees to hold the Bank harmless from any loss resulting therefrom whether or not insurance be had on said property.

The Debtor agrees to indemnify and save harmless the Bank for any expense incurred, and on demand to pay all costs and expenses, including attorneys' fees, incurred by the Bank in the protection or enforcement of its rights or in the collection of any moneys due under this agreement.

In event of repossession of any of said property, the Bank may sell at either public or private sale upon legal notice to Buyer. At public sale the Bank may itself be a purchaser.

The proceeds of such sale shall be applied first to the payment of expenses of retaking, keeping, storing and selling said property, including all attorney fees incurred by Bank, and then to satisfaction of any and all of Debtor's obligation to Bank. After satisfying all obligations of the Debtor to Bank, any surplus shall be paid to Debtor. Debtor shall be liable for any deficiency.

If the Debtor, or any guarantor of the obligations of the Debtor at any time fails or becomes insolvent or commits an act of bankruptcy, or if any deposit account of the Debtor or of any such guarantor with Bank, or if any other property of the Debtor or of any such guarantor held by Bank be attempted to be obtained or held by writ of execution, garnishment, attachment or other legal process, or if any representations made by the Debtor of the financial condition of the Debtor prove to be untrue or if the Debtor fails to notify Bank of any material change in the financial condition of the Debtor, or if any material change occurs, then and in any such case all obligations of Debtor in connection herewith shall immediately become due and payable without demand or notice.

In the event of any default on the part of the Debtor, the Debtor's interest therein may be forfeited, in lieu of sale, at the election of Bank, to the extent of the Debtor's then remaining indebtedness. Bank shall not be deemed to have elected to declare a forfeiture unless Bank notifies Debtor in writing to such effect.

Debtor agrees that Bank assumes no responsibility for the correctness, validity or genuineness of any documents released to Debtor in connection herewith nor for the existence, character, quantity, quality, condition, value or delivery of any goods purported to be represented by any such documents.

On default of the Debtor and in the event of Debtor's failure to deliver any of said property on demand, Debtor shall, until delivery or repossession thereof, or until payment in full in cash of all principal, interest and costs or expense involved, pay as damages for retention a sum equal to one percent (1%) per month of the total indebtedness against such property.

Time and each of the terms, covenants and conditions hereof are of the essence of this agreement, and acceptance by Bank after it is due shall not constitute a waiver by Bank of this or of any other provision of this agreement. No waiver of any existing default shall be deemed to waive any subsequent default and all of Bank's rights hereunder are cumulative and not alternative, and in addition to those otherwise created. Debtor hereby waives all statute of limitations and the defense thereof, in any way affecting the time in which Bank may enforce its rights hereunder. No waiver of any rights or powers of Bank or consent by it shall be valid unless in writing and signed by it.

This FINANCING STATEMENT is presented for filing pursuant to the California Uniform Commercial Code.

1. DEBTOR (LAST NAME FIRST—IF AN INDIVIDUAL)		1A. SOCIAL SECURITY OR FEDERAL TAX NO.	
1B. MAILING ADDRESS	1C. CITY, STATE		1D. ZIP CODE
2. ADDITIONAL DEBTOR (IF ANY) (LAST NAME FIRST—IF AN INDIVIDUAL)		2A. SOCIAL SECURITY OR FEDERAL TAX NO.	
2B. MAILING ADDRESS	2C. CITY, STATE		2D. ZIP CODE

3. DEBTOR'S TRADE NAMES OR STYLES (IF ANY)	3A. FEDERAL TAX NUMBER

4. SECURED PARTY	4A. SOCIAL SECURITY NO., FEDERAL TAX NO. OR BANK TRANSIT AND A.B.A. NO.
NAME MAILING ADDRESS CITY STATE ZIP CODE	
5. ASSIGNEE OF SECURED PARTY (IF ANY)	5A. SOCIAL SECURITY NO., FEDERAL TAX NO. OR BANK TRANSIT AND A.B.A. NO.
NAME MAILING ADDRESS CITY STATE ZIP CODE	

6. This FINANCING STATEMENT covers the following types or items of property **(include description of real property on which located and owner of record when required by instruction 4).**

7. CHECK IF APPLICABLE ☒	7A. ☐ PRODUCTS OF COLLATERAL ARE ALSO COVERED	7B. DEBTOR(S) SIGNATURE NOT REQUIRED IN ACCORDANCE WITH INSTRUCTION 5(a) ITEM: ☐ (1) ☐ (2) ☐ (3) ☐ (4)
8. CHECK IF APPLICABLE ☒	☐ DEBTOR IS A "TRANSMITTING UTILITY" IN ACCORDANCE WITH UCC § 9105 (1) (n)	

9.		CODE	10. THIS SPACE FOR USE OF FILING OFFICER (DATE, TIME, FILE NUMBER AND FILING OFFICER)
▶ SIGNATURE(S) OF DEBTOR(S)	DATE:		
TYPE OR PRINT NAME(S) OF DEBTOR(S)		1	
▶		2	
SIGNATURE(S) OF SECURED PARTY(IES)		3	
		4	
TYPE OR PRINT NAME(S) OF SECURED PARTY(IES)		5	
11. *Return copy to:*		6	
NAME		7	
ADDRESS		8	
CITY		9	
STATE		0	
ZIP CODE			

FORM UCC-1—FILING FEE $3.00
Approved by the Secretary of State

SECURED TRANSACTIONS

149

This **STATEMENT** is presented for filing pursuant to the California Uniform Commercial Code

1. FILE NO. OF ORIG. FINANCING STATEMENT	1A. DATE OF FILING OF ORIG. FINANCING STATEMENT	1B. DATE OF ORIG. FINANCING STATEMENT	1C. PLACE OF FILING ORIG. FINANCING STATEMENT

2. DEBTOR (LAST NAME FIRST) | **2A.** SOCIAL SECURITY OR FEDERAL TAX NO.

2B. MAILING ADDRESS | **2C.** CITY, STATE | **2D.** ZIP CODE

3. ADDITIONAL DEBTOR (IF ANY) (LAST NAME FIRST) | **3A.** SOCIAL SECURITY OR FEDERAL TAX NO.

3B. MAILING ADDRESS | **3C.** CITY, STATE | **3D.** ZIP CODE

4. SECURED PARTY | **4A.** SOCIAL SECURITY NO., FEDERAL TAX NO. OR BANK TRANSIT AND A.B.A. NO

NAME

MAILING ADDRESS

CITY   STATE   ZIP CODE

5. ASSIGNEE OF SECURED PARTY (IF ANY) | **5A.** SOCIAL SECURITY NO., FEDERAL TAX NO. OR BANK TRANSIT AND A.B.A. NO.

NAME

MAILING ADDRESS

CITY   STATE   ZIP CODE

6.

A ☐ CONTINUATION—The original Financing Statement between the foregoing Debtor and Secured Party bearing the file number and date shown above is continued. If collateral is crops or timber, check here ☐ and insert description of real property on which growing or to be grown in Item 7 below.

B ☐ RELEASE—From the collateral described in the Financing Statement bearing the file number shown above, the Secured Party releases the collateral described in Item 7 below.

C ☐ ASSIGNMENT—The Secured Party certifies that the Secured Party has assigned to the Assignee above named, all the Secured Party's rights under the Financing Statement bearing the file number shown above in the collateral described in Item 7 below.

D ☐ TERMINATION—The Secured Party certifies that the Secured Party no longer claims a security interest under the Financing Statement bearing the file number shown above.

E ☐ AMENDMENT—The Financing Statement bearing the file number shown above is amended as set forth in Item 7 below. (Signature of Debtor required on all amendments.)

F ☐ OTHER

7.

8.

(Date)_____ 19___

By:_____
SIGNATURE(S) OF DEBTOR(S)   (TITLE)

By:_____
SIGNATURE(S) OF SECURED PARTY(IES)   (TITLE)

CODE: 1 2 3 4 5 6 7 8 9

9. This Space for Use of Filing Officer
(Date, Time, Filing Office)

10. **Return Copy to**

NAME
ADDRESS
CITY AND STATE

STANDARD FORM—FILING FEE $3.00   UNIFORM COMMERCIAL CODE—FORM UCC-2
Approved by the Secretary of State

REQUEST FOR INFORMATION OR COPIES. Present in Duplicate to Filing Officer

1. ☐ INFORMATION REQUEST. Filing officer please furnish certificate showing whether there is on file any presently effective financing statement naming the Debtor listed below and any statement of assignment thereof, and if there is, giving the date and hour of filing of each such statement and the names and address of each secured party named therein.

1 A. DEBTOR (LAST NAME FIRST) | 1 B. SOC. SEC. OR FED. TAX NO.

1 C. MAILING ADDRESS | 1 D. CITY, STATE | 1 E. ZIP CODE

1 F.

Date_____19____   Signature of Requesting Party_____

2. CERTIFICATE:

FILE NUMBER	DATE AND HOUR OF FILING	NAME(S) AND ADDRESS(ES) OF SECURED PARTY(IES) AND ASSIGNEE(S), IF ANY

The undersigned filing officer hereby certifies that the above listing is a record of all presently effective financing statements and statements of assignment which name the above debtor and which are on file in my office as of_____19___ at____ ___M.

_____19____
(DATE)

_____
(FILING OFFICER)

By:_____

3. ☐ COPY REQUEST. Filing officer please furnish _____ copy(ies) of each page of the following statements concerning the debtors listed below ☐ Financing Statement ☐ Amendments ☐ Statements of Assignment ☐ Continuation Statements ☐ Statement of Release ☐ Termination Statement ☐ All Statements on file.

FILE NUMBER	DATE OF FILING	NAME(S) AND MAILING ADDRESS(ES) OF DEBTOR(S)	DEBTORS SOC. SEC. OR FED. TAX No.

Date_____19____   Signature of Requesting Party_____

4. CERTIFICATE:

The undersigned filing officer hereby certifies that the attached copies are true and exact copies of all statements requested above.

_____19____
(DATE)

_____
(FILING OFFICER)

By:_____

5. **Mail Information or Copies To**

NAME
MAILING
ADDRESS
CITY AND
STATE

UNIFORM COMMERCIAL CODE—FORM UCC-3 N/S

CHAPTER 8

Personal Property

Introduction

Personal and Real Property Distinguished

Personal property is defined by the process of elimination of real property. *Property* is that which is subject to ownership, and ownership is the right to possess and use a thing to the exclusion of others.[1] Property is of two general types—real and personal.[2] *Real property* is land, things permanently attached to land, and appurtenances to land such as easements.[3] All other property is personal property.[4] Both real

---

[1]C.C. 654:"The ownership of a thing is the right of one or more persons to possess and use it to the exclusion of others. In this code, the thing of which there may be ownership is called property."

While this is the stock definition of "ownership," it has never been an entirely satisfactory one because it does not exclude mere "leasing" or "renting" of property which also confers the right to "possess and use it to the exclusion of others," but by contract rather than by reason of ownership, and leasing or renting must be excepted from the concept of ownership.

C.C. 669: "All property has an owner, whether that owner is the state, and the property public, or the owner an individual, and the property private . . ."

[2]C.C. 657: "Property is either:
"1. Real or immovable; or
"2. Personal or movable."

[3]C.C. 658: "Real or immovable property consists of:
"1. Land;
"2. That which is affixed to land;
"3. That which is incidental or appurtenant to land;
"4. That which is immovable by law; except that for the purposes of sale, emblements, industrial growing crops and things attached to and forming part of the land, which are agreed to be severed before sale or under the contract of sale, shall be treated as goods and be governed by the provisions of the title of this code regulating the sales of goods."

C.C. 659. *Land.* "Land is the material of the earth, whatever may be the ingredients of which it is composed, whether soil, rock, or other substance, and includes free or occupied space for an indefinite distance upwards as well as downwards, subject to the limitations upon the use of airspace imposed, and rights in the use of airspace granted, by law." To make way for the condominium, discussed on page 176, this section was amended in 1963 to include airspace.

C.C. 660. *Fixtures.* "A thing is deemed to be affixed to land when it is attached to it by roots, as in the case of trees, vines, or shrubs; or imbedded in it, as in the case of walls; or permanently attached to what is thus permanent, as by means of cement, plaster, nails, bolts, or screws. . . ."

C.C. 662. *Appurtenances.* "A thing is deemed to be incidental or appurtenant to land when it is by right used with the land for its benefit, as in the case of a way, or watercourse, or of a passage for light, air or heat from or across the land of another."

See page 168 and footnote 30 on page 168 on "easements appurtenant," and page 167 on "riparian rights," which are examples of appurtenances.

[4]C.C. 663: "Every kind of property that is not real is personal."

---

and personal property may be owned either individually or jointly with others in the various forms of "concurrent" or coownership discussed in the next chapter on Real Property. Jointly owned stocks and bonds and the joint bank account are common examples of joint ownership of personal property.[5]

● Personal property consists of choses in possession or chattels, and choses in action. ("Chose" is French for thing.) A chose in possession or *chattel* is personal property which is capable of manual possession—tangible, physical property such as an automobile or furniture. A *chose in action* is "paper property"—property in the form of a document or instrument which confers rights on a person[6]—notes, bonds or judgments giving him a right to a sum of money, mortgages and deeds of trust giving him a lien against property as security for a debt, and stock certificates giving him an ownership interest in a corporation and the right to share in its earnings.

Special Cases

Certain forms of property are somewhat hybrid in nature, partaking of the nature of both real and personal property to some extent. Some of these are sometimes referred to as "mixed" property, but this description has largely been eliminated, and in the final analysis these forms of property, like others, are either real or personal.

Crops: In the first instance, crops are real property—part of the land which produces them. Once they have been sold or contracted to be sold, however, they are converted into personal property.

Fixtures: Fixtures are items of personal property which are attached to real property, ranging from the various materials which go into and become a building upon the property to such things as light fixtures and heating units which are, in turn, attached to the building.[8] Where things are attached to the property by a tenant or lessee, a special rule pertains

---

[5]If these things are owned in "joint tenancy," as is usually the case by reasons of provisions to that effect in the instrument or in the signature card, the "right of survivorship" of joint tenancy ownership attaches and the property passes to the survivor on death of one coowner. Right of survivorship is discussed at page 170.

While parties may have "joint access" to a safe deposit box, joint tenancy ownership of the contents is forbidden by C.C. 683.1.

[6]A chose in action is sometimes defined in the more limited sense of a right or "cause of action" against another, and this is the definition of the California code which says in C.C. 953 that "A thing in action is a right to recover money or other personal property by a judicial proceeding." For our purposes, the broader concept suggested in the text is more satisfactory.

[7][Deleted.]

[8]See C.C. 660 in footnote 3.

the property by a tenant or lessee, a special rule pertains which is discussed in the later section on landlord and tenant.[9] Where attachment is by the owner of the property, the fixtures are deemed to be converted into real property if his intention is to make a permanent attachment. *Intention* must be determined from the circumstances of the case—the general nature and apparent permanency of the attachment, such as a concrete foundation; whether the article is "tailor made" to fit the property, as would be the case with, e.g., venetian blinds specially cut to fit particular windows, or wall-to-wall carpeting. Usually the intention is clear, but close cases may arise. In *Los Angeles* v. *Klinker*, 219 C. 198, 25 P.2d 826, it was held that newspaper printing presses were fixtures which would go with the property in a condemnation proceeding. In *People* v. *Church*, 57 C.A.2d Supp. 1032, 136 P.2d 139, on the other hand, it was held that a service station building was removable by a lessee in a condemnation proceeding. Other general types of cases in which the fixture question may arise are where the property is sold without understanding between seller and buyer as to whether or not particular items are fixtures and to go with the property, and where the property is mortgaged and, since a mortgage is a lien on the real property, whether particular items are fixtures, and so, covered by the mortgage, e.g., as in *Bell* v. *Bank of Perris*, 52 C.A.2d 66, 125 P.2d 829, where it was held that a pump set on a concrete foundation was a fixture covered by the mortgage. The problem of priority as between a mortgagee and an unpaid seller of things which have been attached to real property is treated in a later section.[10]

Leases—Chattels Real: A contract is a chose in action—personal property—and, since a lease is a contract giving one the right to use real property for some period of time, it is to that extent personal property. Insofar as a lease grants the use of real property, however, it is in the nature of real property. To indicate its dual nature, a lease is sometimes called a *chattel real*.[11] When it becomes necessary to place it in the one category or the other, a lease is legally classified as personal property, e.g., upon death of the lessee, a lease is treated as personal property in his estate.

Evidences of Ownership

Most transfers of title to personal property are by sale, and if the property is of any substantial value, the transfer is usually accompanied by a written instrument ranging from a mere *receipt* to the formal *bill of sale* of the type shown on the next page which is used, e.g., in the sale of a business and its stock and equipment. While customary, a written instrument is not necessary to transfer title or to evidence ownership in the transferee. Delivery alone is sufficient in the case of personal property. Even in the case of a sale of goods for the price of $500 or more, covered by the statute of frauds, the transaction is binding, without a writing, if delivery has been made to the buyer.

● In certain special cases, ownership of personal property is represented by a *document of title*, e.g., the certificate of title to a motor vehicle or the order bill of lading previously discussed. In these cases, the document *is* the goods or controls the goods, and transfer of it is necessary to transfer the property represented by it.

Methods of Acquisition of Title

Sale and Conditional Sale

The most important methods of transfer of title to personal property and, hence, of acquisition of title are by sale or conditional sale, covered in Chapters 5 (sale) and 7 (conditional sale).

Intestate Succession and Will

When a person owning personal property dies, title necessarily passes to another—the one designated by the decedent's will to receive it, or, if he leaves no will, to his heirs in accordance with rules of intestate succession. These matters are discussed in detail in a later section.[12]

Possession

Where personal property has been abandoned, title may be acquired simply by taking possesion of it. Personal property is said to be abandoned when it is discarded by the owner with no intention of reclaiming it, a question of fact in each case.[13]

Finding

The base rule at common law was that the finder of property became entitled to possession against everyone but the true owner. Certain distinctions were made, however. The property had to be *lost* as distinguished from *mislaid*, and it had to be lost in a *public* place rather than a *private* place.

● Property is *lost* when it has been involuntarily parted with; *mislaid* when it has been voluntarily laid down and forgotten—again, a question of fact in each case. Thus, something voluntarily put down and left behind on a bank counter by a customer would be mislaid property. Something found in the street, by contrast, would probably be lost property—dropped unknowingly or having slipped from the owner's pocket unobserved and, so, involuntarily parted with.

● A *public place* is one which is freely accessible or open to the general public, and it is only when the loss occurs in such place that the finder is entitled to retain possession of the property. Thus, something found in the lobby of a bank, being lost in a public place, would go to the finder, but not something found on the floor of the bank's safe deposit vault—a private place to which only boxholders have the right of access. Where property is either mislaid or lost in a private place, the owner of the premises on which it is found is entitled to it as against the finder. The original idea was that this would provide the loser with a better opportunity to locate his property. An unfortunate result followed, however, which was probably not intended by the original framers of the rule. At common law, the person entitled to custody of lost or mislaid goods pending return of the true owner never did himself become the owner. He was only a sort of permanent custodian. What should have been done was to fix some period of time within which the owner could reclaim the property, and if he did not claim it within the allowed time, to then turn it over to the actual finder, but this was not done. The result was that if custodianship were given to the owner of the prem-

---

[9]See the discussion of removal of "trade fixtures" on page 230.

[10]See "mortgage and security interest in fixtures" on page 218.

[11]Leases create estates or tenancies for years, as seen in a later section, and C.C. 765 says that ". . . estates for years are chattels real. . . ."

[12]See page 230 et seq.

[13]California has no general statute on abandoned property but follows the general rules stated in the text. Under the Uniform Disposition of Unclaimed Property Act (C.C.P. 1500 et seq.) adopted in 1959, the state becomes permanent custodian of such forms of abandoned property as bank accounts and life insurance benefits.

BILL OF SALE

HENRY S. SELLERS , Vendor,

for the sum of Fifty thousand and no/100 Dollars ($50,000.00),

paid by ROBERT B. BEYERS , Vendee,

receipt whereof is hereby acknowledged, do es GRANT, BARGAIN, SELL AND CONVEY to Vendee, his

executors, administrators and assigns:

That certain florist shop known and designated as "Acme Florists", located at 240 Green Street in the City and County of San Francisco, State of California, together with the fixtures, furnishings, equipment, stock on hand, per inventory attached and made part hereof, good will, including right to name, and all other assets of said business, excepting cash on hand or in banks, accounts receivable, and items held on consignment per said inventory.

TO HAVE AND TO HOLD the same unto the Vendee, his executors, administrators and assigns forever. And Vendor does for his heirs, executors and administrators covenant and agree to and with the said Vendee, his executors, administrators and assigns, to warrant and defend the sale of the said property, goods and chattels hereby made unto the Vendee, his executors, administrators and assigns, against any and all persons whomsoever lawfully claiming or to claim the same.

We, and each of us, jointly and severally, have hereunto set our hands this 10th day of August, 1984.

s/ HENRY S. SELLERS

(Should be acknowledged by Notary Public.)

ises on which the article was found, he kept it indefinitely even though the true owner did not return, and, for all practical purposes, became the owner. Since this was unfair to the actual finder, some courts came to hold that the actual finder was entitled to recover the article from the owner of the premises on which it was found if the true owner did not appear to claim it after a reasonable time; other states enacted statutes to this effect.[14] And many states have changed the common law rule by making the finder owner of the goods if the loser does not appear after a specified time.[15]

Accession

Accession, as the term is used in the law of personal property, means *adding* to the property of another by labor or materials. The old case of *Wetherbee* v. *Green*, 22 Mich. 11, 7 Am.Rep. 653, is a rather classical example. There, by mistake, D took a quantity of timber worth $25 belonging to P. D made the timber taken from P into barrel hoops, which increased its value to $700. P then sought to recover the barrel hoops on the ground that they were still his property, although in a new and far more valuable form. It was held for D. The court invoked the rule of accession—that where, by mistake, labor or property of one person is added to the property of another so as to substantially increase its value, the one contributing the principal value to the resultant product acquires *title by accession* upon reimbursing the other party.[16] In the

---

[14]California has no statute dealing with the matter, and the only California case bearing upon it is *Burns* v. *Clark,* 133 C. 634, 66 P. 12, holding that as against an employer an employee is entitled to property found on the employer's premises.

[15]C.C. 2080-2080.3 deal with finding. They require the finder to notify the owner, if known, and to return the property without compensation except a reasonable charge for saving and taking care of the property. If the owner is not known and the property is of a value of $50 or more, the finder must deposit it with the police department of the city where found. If the owner does not appear within 90 days, the police department must advertise the finding in the newspaper. If within 7 days after such advertisement, the owner does not appear, title vests in the finder if he pays the cost of the newspaper advertisement. If the value of the property is less than $50, advertising is not required but deposit with the police department is if the value of the property is $10 or more. The finder gets title if the owner does not appear within 90 days.

C.C. 2080.7 provides that "The provisions of this article [i.e., the code sections above] have no application to things which have been intentionally abandoned by their owners," thus recognizing the distinction between lost and abandoned property and inferring that title to abandoned property may be acquired immediately upon abandonment, as discussed in the text.

[16]C.C. 1025-1029 and 1031-1033 deal with accession in considerable detail. Section 1025 covers accession by adding property to property: "When things belonging to different owners have been united so as to form a single thing, and cannot be separated without injury, the whole belongs to the owner of the thing which forms the principal part; who must, however, reimburse the value of the residue to the other owner, or surrender the whole to him."

C.C. 1028 covers the addition of labor to property: "If one makes a thing from materials belonging to another, the latter may claim the thing on reimbursing the value of the workmanship, unless the value of the workmanship exceeds the value of the materials, in which case the thing belongs to the maker, on reimbursing the value of the materials."

C.C. 1032 gives the party whose property has been taken the option of demanding its cash value in any case, and C.C. 1033

Wetherbee case, then, D became the rightful owner of the timber and the hoops into which they had been converted by paying P $25.

Where there is a willful or intentional taking—*conversion*—of the property of another, the converter's position is not the sympathetic one that it is in the *Wetherbee* type case. Accordingly, some courts have given the resultant product to the person whose property was converted with no obligation on his part to reimburse the converter for the increase in value.[17] This gives the party whose property was converted a windfall, however, and violates the rule that ordinarily "the law intends compensation for a wrong done and not a penalty," i.e., that a civil action should not do more than reimburse the injured party and should not impose a penalty upon the wrongdoer. Courts adhering to this concept would permit the party substantially increasing the value of the other's property to keep the property upon reimbursing the other, even though the conversion was wilful.

Confusion

Confusion, as distinguished from accession, consists of the intermixing or *commingling* of the goods of two or more persons in a common mass so that their separate identities are lost. It may be by consent of the parties, as where farmers throughout a farming community deposit their grain in a grain elevator where it is weighed, and then mixed together indiscriminately, by accident, by mistake, or by wrongful conduct of one party. Where it is by other than wrongful conduct, the parties are considered to acquire a new title as *tenants in common* in the "fused" mass, each owning a share proportionate to his contribution.[18] Where it is by wrongful conduct, some courts permit the wrongdoer to retain his portion if he can reasonably approximate it, applying again the philosophy that "the law intends compensation for a wrong done and not a penalty;" others, including California, hold that the wrongdoer loses everything.[19]

Gift

Nature and Types: C.C. 1146 states the stock definition that a *gift* is "a transfer of personal property, made voluntarily, and without consideration."[20] A gift differs from a sale in that the sale is a transfer for, a gift a transfer without, consideration. The absence of consideration does not make the gift subject to recall and, once made, a gift cannot be revoked unless it is a gift *causa mortis*, discussed below.

---

provides that "One who wrongfully employs materials belonging to another is liable to him in damages, as well as under the foregoing provisions of this chapter."

[17]C.C. 1031 adopts this rule.

[18]C.C. 1030: "When a thing has been formed by the admixture of several materials of different owners, and neither can be considered the principal substance, an owner without whose consent the admixture was made may require a separation, if the materials can be separated without inconvenience. If they cannot be thus separated, the owners acquire the thing in common, in proportion to the quantity, quality, and value of their materials; but if the materials of one were far superior to those of the others, both in quantity and value, he may claim the thing on reimbursing to the others the value of their materials."

[19]C.C. 1031 makes this the California rule.

[20]A gift may also be made of real property, and this is done by a gift deed of the type shown on page 180.

• Gifts are classified as (1) gifts *inter vivos* and (2) gifts *causa mortis*. A gift *inter vivos* is one made under ordinary circumstances, i.e., not under fear of death. It is irrevocable.[21]

• A gift *causa mortis* is one made in fear of death from some existing cause or peril,[22] such as a gift made immediately after a serious heart attack. It may be revoked at any time before death and is automatically revoked by recovery or escape from the illness or peril by which it was prompted.[23]

• A gift may also be called a "gift to take effect at death" and a "gift in contemplation of death," neither of which is a gift *causa mortis*. A *gift to take effect at death* is simply another way of describing a disposition of property by will, since that is what a will is—an instrument by which gifts of property are made to others upon death.

• A *gift in contemplation of death* is one which may be said to have been made in general anticipation of death but without immediate fear of death as in the case of the gift *causa mortis*; e.g., a gift designed to effect an orderly and tax free distribution of property by an elderly but healthy person who is not prompted by immediate peril of death, but who is acting in general anticipation of death. The term is primarily a tax term used to distinguish between gifts which are tax free and gifts made within a certain time prior to death (3 years at present) which are made taxable. A gift in contemplation of death would fall into the broader category of gifts *inter vivos* and would not be revocable.

• Somewhat different than any of the foregoing but interesting to note is a gift in contemplation of marriage, which is generally held to be revocable if the marriage does not take place.[24]

Essential Elements: First, there must be *intention* to make a present transfer of title to the donee, and if the statements or circumstances surrounding the making of the gift indicate

---

[21]C.C. 1148: "A gift, other than a gift in view of death, cannot be revoked by the giver."

[22]C.C. 1149: "A gift in view of death is one which is made in contemplation, fear, or peril of death, and with intent that it shall take effect only in case of the death of the giver." While the California code sections use the description "gift in view of death," the customary description of such gifts is gift *causa mortis*, as in the text.

C.C. 1150: "A gift made during the last illness of the giver, or under circumstances which would naturally impress him with an expectation of speedy death, is presumed to be a gift in view of death."

[23]C.C. 1151: "A gift in view of death may be revoked by the giver at any time, and is revoked by his recovery from the illness, or escape from the peril, under the presence of which it was made . . . but when the gift has been delivered to the donee, the rights of a bona fide purchaser from the donee before the revocation, shall not be affected by the revocation." The latter half of this section speaks for itself. It also raises an interesting question. If the donee has transferred the gift to a bona fide purchaser so that it may not be recovered, is the donee liable to the donor for its value? If the donee still has the money that he received from the purchaser of the gift, this may be recovered by the donor. If he has dissipated it? There are no cases answering the question.

[24]C.C. 1590: "Where either party to a contemplated marriage in this State makes a gift of money or property to the other on the basis or assumption that the marriage will take place, in the event that the donee refuses to enter into the marriage as contemplated or that it is given up by mutual consent, the donor may recover such gift or such part of its value as may, under all of the circumstances of the case, be found by a court or jury to be just."

---

that it is not to be effective until the donor dies, there is no effective gift. The donor may reserve a life interest in the subject matter of the gift, however, e.g., one may make a gift of stock, but reserve the right to dividends until his death. And, in one class of gifts, a trust created during lifetime, the gift is valid even though a power to revoke is reserved.[25]

Secondly, there must be *delivery* of the property to complete a verbal gift. If a written instrument is executed and delivered to the donee, it is held that there is an effective gift though not accompanied by the property itself or some symbol of it. Where the gift is verbal, and so must be accompanied by a delivery of the property, there must be manual or physical delivery of the property itself if this is reasonably possible, but a constructive or symbolical delivery will suffice where manual delivery is not possible or practicable,[26] e.g., where the donor is bedridden. Thus, in *Braun* v. *Brown*, 14 C.2d 346, 94 P.2d 348, it was held that delivery of the key to a safe deposit box was a sufficient constructive or symbolical delivery; and in *White* v. *Bank of America*, 53 C.A.2d 831, 128 P.2d 600, delivery of a savings account passbook was held to be sufficient. But in *Knight* v. *Tripp*, 121 C. 674, 54 P. 267, it was held that there was not a sufficient delivery where a key to a strong box was given, and the box itself was available and might have been delivered.

• Delivery may be to the donee directly or through an intermediary. Where delivery is attempted to be made through an intermediary, a problem may arise. If the intermediary is an agent of the donor, such as a secretary, and the donor dies before the intermediary reaches the donee with the gift, the gift will fail for lack of delivery. If, however, the intermediary may be found to be an agent for the donee or at least a trustee and not really an agent of the donor, then the gift will be good, as where the intermediary is merely a mutual friend of the parties. This latter case also raises the point of *acceptance*. Technically, there must be acceptance of a gift by the donee before it is complete, but most courts will presume acceptance where the property has been placed in the hands of one who may be said to hold it as agent of or trustee for the donee, even though the donee does not have knowledge of the gift, and the donor dies before such knowledge is received.

Bailments

Nature

A *bailment* is the most common of all legal transactions.[27] It exists in any case in which one person rightfully obtains *possession* of personal property belonging to another. The person having possession is called the *bailee*, the one to whom

---

[25]This would be an *inter vivos* trust as discussed on pages 238-240. And as pointed out on page 240, such a trust may be made revocable and is always revocable in California unless expressly made irrevocable.

[26]C.C. 1147: "A verbal gift is not valid, unless the means of obtaining possession and control of the thing are given nor, if it is capable of delivery, unless there is an actual or symbolical delivery of the thing to the donee."

[27]The word "bailment" derives from the French *bailler*—to deliver or put in the hands of another.

In California, bailments are dealt with in C.C. 1813 et seq. The California code does not use the word "bailment," however, but rather "deposit," "loan," and "hiring," and these are to be construed as referring to bailments in the California code sections throughout the footnotes to follow.

the property belongs is called the *bailor*. Everyone has entered into countless transactions of this kind. You borrow something, you lend something to another, you leave something with another for repair or cleaning or for transportation or storage. All of these transactions constitute bailments while possession rests with the one who is not the owner. And a finder is at one and the same time a bailee, as is one with whom property has been deposited as security, e.g., a pawnbroker with whom a watch is left or a bank with which stocks or bonds are deposited as security for a loan, such *pledges* as they are called also being classified as bailments for security.

For purposes of definition, then, it may be said most broadly that a bailment is the rightful possession of personal property by one who is not the owner; or, in terms of a business transaction, that it is a transfer of possession of personal property to another for the purpose of repair, transportation, storage, safekeeping, or other business purpose.

Distinguished from Sale

Sale, gift and bailment are the three important transactions in personal property. Sale and gift are alike in that they are transfers of title and differ only in that the one is with, the other without, consideration. Sale and bailment differ in three basic respects:

1. Sale is a transfer of title. Bailment is a transfer of possession only.

2. Sale requires consideration. A bailment may be for consideration or it may be gratuitous.

3. Sale contemplates a permanent change of possession, bailment contemplates a temporary change only.

● Cases involving returnable containers may raise close questions with respect to the distinction between a bailment and a sale. *Consolidated Paper Co.* v. *Nims*, 306 Mich. 216, 10 N.W.2d 833, is a noted case. Carton manufacture sold beer cartons to breweries. Breweries packed beer in the cartons and sold it directly to the public. A consumer-purchaser was required to pay a deposit on a carton, which he could get back if he returned the carton. The question was whether a sale of cartons by the manufacturer to a brewery was a sale or a sale for resale. This would depend on whether the transactions between breweries and consumers were, as to cartons, sales or bailments. If sales, the transactions between manufacturer and breweries would be sales for resale and not taxable to the manufacturer. If bailments, the transactions between manufacturer and breweries would be simple sales on which the manufacturer would have to pay sales tax. Because return was optional and not mandatory, the court held that the transactions between breweries and consumers were sales of the cartons rather than bailments. The extent of the obligation to return is the test in these cases. If the reasonable construction of the transaction is that return of the container is required, then the transaction is a bailment. If the reasonable construction of the transaction is that return of the container is optional, with the forfeiture of a deposit if return is not made, the transaction is, as to the container, a sale.

● Other problem situations: Goods are delivered to another who is to return them in a different form or who will satisfy his obligation by returning similar goods, e.g., wheat is taken to a mill to be ground into flour and returned, or wheat is deposited in a grain warehouse, with the warehouseman being required to return a like quantity of wheat on demand of the depositor but not necessarily the same wheat deposited. Where the same goods are to be returned, even though in different form, the transaction is a bailment. So, the wheat-into-flour case is a bailment. Where the deliveree is required to return only similar goods, the transaction may be a sale as

it was held to be in the famous old case of *Carpenter* v. *Griffin et al.*, 37 Am.Dec. 396, where there was a five year lease of a farm and a herd of cows, with the provision that the lessee should return "cows of equal age and quality" at the expiration of the lease.[28] But it is a well established exception that where there is a *confusion* of goods with the consent of the owners, the party holding the confused goods is a mere bailee, not a buyer, even though he is obliged only to return a like quantity of goods of equal quality to the various depositors, and this would make the wheat-in-the-warehouse case a bailment.

● In the case of deposits in a bank, on the other hand, they are not considered to be bailments, at least if the deposit is the ordinary *general deposit* in a checking or savings account. The bank is deemed to become the owner of the money and a debtor to the depositor of the amount of the deposit, and the relationship is that of creditor and debtor. If, however, it is a *special deposit*, that is, a deposit for a particular purpose, the bank is considered to be a *bailee* of it. For example, a bank may act as "escrow" in the sale of a business. The buyer deposits the purchase price with the bank. The seller then gives notice of intended sale of the business in the newspaper as the law requires. When this is done, the seller gives the bank a bill of sale of the business made out to the buyer, and the bank gives the seller the purchase price. Until this time, the purchase price deposited with the bank is a special deposit which the bank holds as bailee, despite the facts that the money will not be returned to the party from whom it was received and that the bank will not pay out the same money that it received, so that the bailment is not a true one. The fact that a special deposit is a bailment is important in the event of insolvency of the bank while the money is being held. Special depositors are preferred creditors and entitled to full return of their money before anything is paid to general depositors who are mere general creditors.

Types and Liability of Bailee

Duty of Care in General: Suppose that you lend your automobile to F to make a trip from San Francisco to Los Angeles. It is purely an act of friendship on your part and you are not to receive any compensation for F's use of the car. En route to Los Angeles, F has an accident which does substantial damage to the car. May you hold F for the damages? First, it should be clearly understood that in no case is an ordinary bailee[29] an *insurer* or absolute guarantor of the safety of the bailed property. It is only when the bailed property is damaged through *negligence on the part of the bailee* that he is liable to the bailor. Hence, unless negligence of F was responsible for or at least contributed to the accident, he would not be held.

---

[28]Several California code sections are aimed at this situation. C.C. 1818 says that "A deposit for exchange is one in which the depositary is only bound to return a thing corresponding in kind, to that which is deposited." C.C. 1902: "A loan for exchange is a contract by which one delivers personal property to another, and the latter agrees to return to the lender a similar thing at a future time, without reward for its use." C.C. 1904: "By loan for exchange the *title* to the thing lent *is transferred* to the borrower . . ."

[29]"Ordinary bailee" is used in contradistinction to certain types of "quasi-public bailees"—carriers, warehousemen and hotel-keepers—considered in later sections and upon whom exceptional liability may be imposed, e.g., the carrier, which is made virtually an insurer of the goods.

• The early cases assessed different degrees of duty of care to bailees, according to whether the bailment was for the benefit of the bailee or for the benefit of the bailor or for mutual benefit.

• In the case of the loan of the automobile, the bailment is entirely for the benefit of F, the bailee. You, the bailor, gain nothing from it. Where such is the nature of the bailment, it is called, appropriately, a "bailment for the sole benefit of the bailee." In the early days of the law, the courts reasoned that the bailee should be required to exercise *great care* in such case or, conversely, that he should be held liable to the bailor if the property were damaged through even *slight negligence* on his part. This became the general rule and is a rule which still receives lip service at least in many quarters.[30] F's liability to you for the damage to your automobile would be determined by this test.[31]

• Suppose, by contrast, that you are going on a trip and ask F to store your automobile in his garage during your absence. He does so as an act of friendship. You leave the keys with him so that he can start the engine periodically to keep the battery charged. Here, the bailment is entirely for the benefit of you, the bailor, and such a bailment is called a "bailment for the sole benefit of the bailor." The same judges who rea-

soned the duty of care in the first type of bailment reasoned that just the reverse should be true here—that in a bailment for the sole benefit of the bailor, the bailee should have the duty of only *slight care* or, conversely, should be held liable only if damage or loss was due to *gross negligence* on his part.[32] Suppose, then, that F leaves the garage in which your car is stored unlocked one night after running the engine that afternoon. During the night the car is stolen, the theft being facilitated somewhat by the unlocked garage. Is F liable to you? It does not seem likely that this amount of lack of care would be sufficient to constitute gross negligence. Suppose that F not only leaves the garage unlocked but also leaves the keys in the car so as to greatly facilitate theft. Here, it would seem that he could be guilty of the kind of gross negligence for which he could be held.[33]

• Lastly, suppose that you take your car to a garage for repair. This would create a "bailment for the mutual benefit of the bailor and the bailee." You, as bailor, will get your property back in an improved condition. The garage as bailee will make a profit by doing the repair work. For such a bailment, a middle ground was struck. It was held that the bailee must exercise *ordinary care* for the protection of the bailed property and would be liable for loss of or damage to it resulting from *ordinary negligence* on his part.[34]

---

[30]C.C. 1886: "A borrower for use must use great care for the preservation in safety and in good condition of the thing lent."

C.C. 1889: "A borrower for use must repair all deteriorations or injuries to the thing lent, which are occasioned by his negligence, however slight."

[31]As a related matter, it may be noted that the bailee is not an *agent* of the bailor and, so, is not liable for injuries inflicted upon third persons by the bailee in his use or handling of the bailed property. *Menge* v. *Manthey*, 200 Wis. 485, 227 N.W. 938 is a good illustration of this: There D had a wreck on the highway at night. He called E Garage which sent a tow truck. The operators of the tow truck negligently swung the automobile out over the highway while hoisting it so that the automobile of P approaching on the highway smashed into it. P sued D and E. E, of course, was liable, but D was not because his car was in the control of E as bailee at the time of the accident, and, as stated at the outset, a bailor is not responsible for torts committed by the bailee.

To this there is one important exception, however. Most states have *imputed negligence* statutes where motor vehicle operation is concerned, i.e., statutes which impose some degree of liability on the owner where he allows another to use his automobile. The following California statutes are typical:

Veh. C. 17700 et seq. make the parent liable to the extent of $5000-15,000-30,000 where the parent signs for the license of a minor child, i.e., to the extent of $5000 for damage to property by the child, $15,000 for one person injured in an accident, and $30,000 (total) for two or more persons injured in an accident. And if the child operates the vehicle as *agent* or employee of the parent rather than for his (child's) own purposes, the parent has the unlimited liability of principal for agent. Veh. C. 17150-17151 imposes the same liability on the owner, and with the same monetary limitations, where he lends the car to any other person. Where restrictions are placed on the use, however, and the person to whom the automobile is given exceeds these restrictions, the owner is not liable, at least if there is a substantial deviation from the restricted use. In *Henrietta* v. *Evans*, 10 C.2d 526, 75 P.2d 1051, e.g., a used car dealer allowed a proposed purchaser to take a car home overnight and to come back the following day to sign papers and complete the purchase. The sole use to be made of the car was to drive to the purchaser's home and back to the dealer's place. The purchaser used it for other purposes and had an accident while doing so. Held, there was a substantial deviation from the restricted use, and the dealer was not liable.

[32]The California code classifies a bailment for the sole benefit of the bailor as a *gratuitous bailment*; i.e., one in which the bailee receives no compensation. C.C. 1844: "Gratuitous deposit is a deposit for which the depositary receives no consideration beyond the mere possession of the thing deposited." C.C. 1846 imposes upon a *gratuitous bailee* the duty of care specified in the text by providing that "A gratuitous depositary must use, at least, slight care for the preservation of the thing deposited."

The term "gratuitous bailment" is not peculiar to California, however, and is commonly used generally as a synonym for both bailments for the sole benefit of the bailor and bailments for the sole benefit of the bailee.

[33]Even here there is some doubt, however, because of a general reluctance of the law to hold a person liable for the supervening *criminal* act of a third person.

[34]Where the bailment for the mutual benefit of both parties consists of the *hiring* of a thing by the bailee, e.g., renting an automobile, or storing an automobile in a garage at a daily rate, it is often referred to as a *bailment for hire*; and these are the only types of mutual benefit bailments specifically provided for in the California code. C.C. 1851: "A deposit not gratuitous is called storage. The depositary in such case is called a depositary for hire." C.C. 1852: "A depositary for hire must use at least ordinary care for the preservation of the thing deposited." C.C. 1928: "The hirer of a thing must use ordinary care for its preservation in safety and in good condition"; and C.C. 1929: "The hirer of a thing must repair all deteriorations or injuries thereto occasioned by his want of ordinary care."

Bailments are often classified more simply than has been done so far as *bailments for hire*—meaning bailments in which consideration passes—and *gratuitous bailments*—meaning bailments in which consideration does not pass.

C.C. 1858-1858.3 provide that a person who is in the business of repairing or altering personal property must notify the customer bailor from whom he takes property that the property is not insured against theft, fire, and vandalism while it is in the hands of the bailee if such is the case. This is limited to personal property used for or intended for personal, family, or household purposes and does not include motor vehicles. If the bailee fails to give notice, he is "strictly liable" to the customer for any loss occasioned by theft, fire, or vandalism.

• The rules of slight, ordinary and great care discussed above are referred to as the "classical rules" on duty of care, i.e., the rules established early in the common law and which have come down through the centuries. A number of courts have abandoned them in favor of a more flexible *reasonable care* test—that is, that in every case the bailee must exercise reasonable care in the light of all of the circumstances of the particular case.

Liability for Unauthorized Use: Where the bailee uses the bailed property in an unauthorized manner, the picture changes. A majority of courts make the bailee an "insurer" of the property in such case, their rule being that the bailee is liable for any damage to the property which occurs during the period of unauthorized use, even though it occurs without fault on the part of the bailee.[35] The case of storage of your car in F's garage may be used as an example. Assume that you gave F no permission to use the car in any way, but that he uses it to make a trip of about 50 miles and has an accident en route. The accident is entirely the fault of the other party. Under the general rule, you would be able to hold F for the damage to your car because of the unauthorized use (also, of course, the third party who caused the accident). A substantial number of courts reject this rule and hold the bailee only if he is negligent or if the unauthorized use can be shown to be the cause of the damage.[36]

Exculpatory Clauses: Suppose that C parks his car in a parking lot operated by P. Somewhere on the lot is a sign saying "Not responsible for loss of or damage to cars from any cause. All parking entirely at risk of owner." While C's car is on the lot, P or his employee moves another car and negligently smashes a fender on C's car. C demands reimbursement from P, who points to the sign and to the ticket which C received when he parked his car, which contains the same provision. May P validly escape his bailee's liability in this way?

The sign and ticket represent attempts on the part of the bailee (P) to limit his liability by special contract—by a special liability-limiting provision engrafted upon the general contract of bailment.

There is some division of authority as to whether this can be done.[37] Even where it is permitted, it must be shown that the bailor knew of the limitation of liability at the time the bailment was created, or that the instrument which he received at that time was one which he should have understood to be a "contract." Otherwise, he cannot be said to have *intended* the special contract, and intention to contract is necessary to a valid contract unless one *should* know that he is entering into a contract, in which case his apparent intention to do so will be sufficient. Applying this to the parking lot case, unless it can be shown that C saw or should have seen the sign at the time he parked, or that P pointed it or the ticket provision out to C at that time, the limitation of liability is not effective because of C's lack of intention to contract on special terms. As to the ticket, C could reasonably consider it a mere token of identification and not a contract. This is the general approach of the law to signs and ticket provisions.

Suppose that a shipper deposits goods for transportation with a railroad company, which gives the shipper a *bill of lading* stipulating that it will have only limited liability for goods damaged or lost. The shipper does not read the bill of lading or ask for an explanation of its terms. Here, the bill of lading is the shipper's contract with the carrier-bailee covering the transportation-bailment of the goods, and knowledge that the bill of lading is a contract is presumed under the law, i.e., the courts would hold that the shipper *should* know that he is making a contract. Therefore, the shipper is bound by the limitation of liability. This is discussed more fully in the section on carriers as bailees.

Enlargement of Liability by Special Contract: Just as the liability of a bailee may be reduced by special contract, so also it may be enlarged. In *Kaye* v. *M'Divani*, 6 C.A.2d 132, 44 P.2d 371, a furnished house was leased, and the lease provided that the lessee "assumes all liability" for furnishings. A rug was stolen without negligence of the lessee-bailee of the furniture. Held, the lessee had assumed the absolute liability of an insurer for the furnishings and was liable for loss of the rug.

---

[35]The California law is not clear. C.C. 1930 says that "When a thing is let for a particular purpose, the hirer must not use it for any other purpose; and if he does, he is liable to the letter for all damages resulting from such use . . ."

C.C. 1836, dealing with *depositaries* as distinguished from the *hirers* above, says that "A depositary is liable for any damage happening to the thing deposited, during his wrongful use thereof, *unless such damage must inevitably have happened though the property had not been thus used.*" The italicized portion of Section 1836 has not been clarified by cases. Reading it for what it says, if F wrongfully uses your car for a trip, he should still be liable because the damage would not have occurred at all had the property "not been thus used." The type of case to which the italicized portion of Section 1836 would seem to apply would seem to be one like this: You lend your car to F for the express purpose of making a trip from San Francisco to Los Angeles (400 miles). Unknown to either you or F the steering mechanism is defective. Instead of going to Los Angeles, F travels in the opposite direction to Sacramento (100 miles). En route, the steering mechanism fails and the car crashes. Assuming the same quality of highway in each direction, this would seem to be a case in which the damage would have been inevitable.

[36]See footnote 35 as to the California law.

[37]C.C. 1630 allows parking lot ticket exculpatory clauses by providing: "Except as provided in Section 1630.5, a printed contract of bailment providing for the parking or storage of a motor vehicle shall not be binding, either in whole or in part, on the vehicle owner or on the person who leaves the vehicle with another, unless the contract conforms to the following:

(a) 'This contract limits our liability—read it' is printed at the top in capital letters of 10-point type or larger.

(b) All the provisions of the contract are printed legibly in 8point type or larger.

(c) Acceptance of benefits under a contract included within the provisions of this section shall not be construed a waiver of this section, and it shall be unlawful to issue such a contract on condition that provisions of this section are waived.

A copy of the contract printed in large type, in an area at least 17 by 22 inches, shall be posted in a conspicuous place at each entrance of the parking lot.

Nothing in this section shall be construed to prohibit the enactment of city ordinances on this subject that are not less restrictive, and such enactments are expressly authorized."

C.C. 1630.5 provides: "The provisions of any contract of bailment for the parking or storage of a motor vehicle shall not exempt the bailee from liability, either in whole or in part, for the theft of any motor vehicle, when such motor vehicle is parked or stored with such bailee, and the keys are required by such bailee to be left in the parked or stored vehicle."

Failure to Redeliver; Misdelivery: Except in certain cases discussed below, the bailee has absolute liability for failure to redeliver the bailed property to the bailor upon termination of the bailment. Thus, if he delivers the bailed property to the wrong person he will be liable, as in *Clark* v. *Burns Hamman Baths*, 71 C.A. 571, 236 P. 152, where D's employee delivered P's valuables to an impostor.

In two types of cases, the bailee may give the goods to a person other than the bailor: (1) Where the goods are taken by legal process while in the bailee's possession, e.g., attached by the sheriff on account of a debt of the bailor. (2) Where someone other than the bailor is the true owner of the goods and claims them while they are in the hands of the bailee. This may place the bailee in a difficult position. He is confronted with two persons claiming the goods. If he delivers the goods to the one who is not the rightful owner, he will be liable to the rightful owner for their value. The law will protect the bailee in this case by allowing him to *interplead* the parties, i.e., to surrender the goods to a court and require the claimants to establish their rights there, or by requiring the party who claims the goods and who was not the bailor to indemnify the bailee against any liability to the bailor.[38]

Special Bailees

Common Carriers of Freight

Common carriers of goods or freight—railroads and motor carriers—are "persons" who, being authorized by the state to do so, hold themselves out as carrying freight for compensation.[39] As common carriers, they must afford their services to all members of the public who wish to avail themselves of them, and must not discriminate among shippers.[40] Since their authority stems from the state, and from the federal government if they are engaged in interstate transportation, they are subject to regulation as to rates by the appropriate governmental authority—the Interstate Commerce Commission if engaged in interstate transportation, or the corresponding state authority if engaged in intrastate transportation, e.g., the Public Utilities Commission in California.

Exceptional Liability: Where the state confers exceptional privileges on a person, it may impose exceptional liabilities on him. Since common carriers were given virtually monopolistic powers in early days, it was appropriate to impose upon them an extraordinary liability for goods carried by them (which, however, they could substantially limit by *special contract*, as seen in the next section). This so-called *common law liability* of a carrier was and is as follows: With five exceptions, the carrier is liable for any loss of or damage to the goods in transit, i.e., liable irrespective of whether its negligence is in any way responsible for the loss or damage. Since it approximates the liability of an insurer, the carrier's common law liability is described as that of an *insurer*.

The five exceptions are that the carrier is not liable where loss of or damage to the goods is caused by:[41]

1. Act of God, i.e., violent, unforeseen, superhuman events or catastrophes, such as fire caused by lightning, or severe floods.

2. Act of public enemy, i.e., of enemy nation or force in time of foreign or civil war. This does not exempt the carrier of liability where goods are stolen by criminals.

3. Act of state or of public authority, e.g., attachment of the goods by the sheriff or confiscation by pure food authorities.

4. Act of the shipper, e.g., improper packing (but if this is apparent upon visual inspection, and the carrier nevertheless accepts the goods, it has full liability for them).

5. Inherent nature of the goods, e.g., shrinkage consisting of the normal percentage of evaporation of oil or other liquid in transit.

Comparing the ordinary bailee with the carrier, the ordinary bailee would not be liable for loss of goods if they were stolen from him without his fault or if they were destroyed by fire set by an arsonist. The carrier would be liable in each of these cases, on the other hand, since they do not come within the exceptions; hence, we can see that a carrier's liability is indeed that of an insurer.

● Even though damage is from one of the excepted causes, the carrier will be liable if it has unnecessarily exposed the goods to the cause as by erroneous routing.[42]

● The carrier's liability as an insurer begins as soon as the goods are received for shipment. There are two general rules concerning termination of liability as an insurer: Under one rule, liability as an insurer ceases and liability as a warehouseman begins when the goods reach destination and the consignee is notified of the fact.[43] Under the other rule, liability as an insurer continues until the consignee has had a reasonable time after notice of arrival within which to pick up the goods.

Limitation of Liability by Special Contract: A common carrier cannot, by special contract, exempt itself from liability for loss of goods caused by negligence of its employees but, by weight of authority, the carrier can limit its liability for such loss. For example, the carrier may obtain an agreement

---

[38]In California, the general *interpleader* statute, C.C.P. 386, gives the bailee the right to interplead the parties in all cases by its provision that ". . . whenever conflicting claims are or may be made upon a person for or relating to personal property . . . such person may bring an action against the conflicting claimants to compel them to interplead and litigate their several claims among themselves."

C.C. 1826 is an *indemnity* statute, providing that unless the third party claimant does "sufficiently establish his right thereto, and indemnify the depositary against the claim of the depositor," the bailee (depositary) may return the property to his bailor without liability to the third party claimant.

[39]C.C. 2168: "Everyone who offers to the public to carry persons, property, or messages, excepting only telegraphic messages, is a common carrier of whatever he thus offers to carry." They are generally required to have state authority to operate, however—usually called a "certificate of public convenience and necessity," as in the California Public Utilities Code.

[40]C.C. 2169. And C.C. 2170 prohibits discrimination among shippers.

[41]C.C. 2194 makes the same exceptions by its provision that "Unless the consignor accompanies the freight and retains exclusive control thereof, an inland common carrier of property is liable, from the time that he accepts until he relieves himself from liability . . . for the loss or injury thereof from any cause whatsoever, except:

"1. An inherent defect, vice, or weakness, or a spontaneous action, of the property itself;

"2. The act of a public enemy of the United States, or of this state;

"3. The act of the law; or

"4. Any irresistible superhuman cause."

[42]C.C. 2195: "A common carrier is liable, even in the cases excepted by the last section, if his want of ordinary care exposes the property to the cause of the loss."

[43]C.C. 2120 adopts this rule.

with the shipper that the carrier will be liable only up to the maximum amount of $250, even though the goods shipped are worth $1000. In this way, the carrier is able, in large measure, to accomplish indirectly what it cannot do directly—contract away liability for negligence. To make such *declared value clauses* valid, two requirements must be met: (1) Since the law requires the carrier to ship with full common law liability if the shipper so requires, it must be shown that the shipper has had this *option* made available to him. But this will always be true, i.e., the carrier will always have such an arrangement available if the shipper wants to require it, and it will make no difference that the shipper does not know about it. (2) Since the shipper is "giving up" his right to ship under a common law liability contract (even though unknowingly), he must receive a *consideration* in exchange for the right surrendered, which will take the form of a lower freight rate.[44]

The *contract* by which liability is limited is the bill of lading given in exchange for the goods, and the extent of the carrier's liability will be fixed by the "class or rate" column.[45]

Liability for Misdelivery: As in the case of ordinary bailees, discussed on page 159, and subject to the same exceptions as made there, the carrier is absolutely liable for delivery of the goods to the wrong person.

Common Carrier of Passengers

Only property may be bailed, and a carrier of passengers is not a *bailee* of them, nor is it an insurer of their safety. Its only duty is to use reasonable care in the operation and maintenance of its equipment for their protection. It is, however, an insurer of a reasonable amount of baggage.[46]

Warehousemen

In general, a warehouseman has the liability of a bailee for hire, i.e., the obligation to use ordinary care for the safety of goods. If the goods are lost or damaged without violation of this duty on the part of the warehouseman, he is not liable.

Like a carrier he may limit his liability by a declared value clause.[47]

Hotel and Innkeepers

At common law, hotel and innkeepers had the same exceptional liability as a carrier of goods as to luggage of a guest, i.e., were absolutely liable for loss of or damage to it unless caused by one of the five exceptions from which the carrier of goods was saved. Most states have now changed this, and a variety of rules exist today—some states adding to the five exceptions a sixth of accident, others making the hotel or innkeeper liable only if it is negligent, and still others regulating the matter by statute, as is done in California.[48]

Liens and Personal Property as Security

Bailee's Possessory Lien

At common law, one who added value to personal property by repairing or improving it was given a *possessory lien*[49]—the right to refuse to return the property until he was paid. The property became the improver's security for payment. This *common law possessory lien* lacked effect, however, in that it did not permit sale of the property however long the services went unpaid. The only thing the lienholder could do was to bring suit, get a judgment, and then execute upon the property held under the right of lien.
● Most states have enlarged upon the common law lien in two ways: (1) By extending it to anyone who performs services upon or in connection with the property, whether or not value is added—storers, transporters, etc., and (2) by giving the lienholder the right to sell the property if payment is not made within a specified time.[50] Such liens are called *statutory possessory liens*, as distinguished from the common law lien.

---

[44]U.C.C. 7309(2): "Damages may be limited by a provision that the carrier's liability shall not exceed a value stated in the document if the carrier's rates are dependent upon value and the consignor by the carrier's tariff is afforded an opportunity to declare a higher value or a value as lawfully provided in the tariff, or where no tariff is filed he is otherwise advised of such opportunity; but no such limitation is effective with respect to the carrier's liability for conversion to its own use."

[45]See bill of lading on page 71.

[46]C.C. 2180: "A common carrier of persons . . . must receive and carry a reasonable amount of baggage for each passenger without charge . . ." C.C. 2181: "Luggage may consist of whatever the passenger takes with him for his personal use and convenience, according to the habits or wants of the particular class to which he belongs, either with reference to the important necessities or to the ultimate purposes of his journey. . . ." C.C. 2182: "The liability of a carrier for baggage received by him from a passenger is the same as that of a common carrier of property." But liability has been limited by later statutes.
C.C. 2178 limits the liability of a railroad to $100 for a trunk and contents, $50 for a suitcase and contents, and $10 for a bundle or package. C.C. 2205 limits the liability of a stageline, transfer company, or other highway carrier to $500 for a trunk and contents and $250 for a suitcase and contents or a bundle or package. But the carrier may "consent in writing to assume a greater liability" in every case.

[47]U.C.C. 7204(2).

[48]C.C. 1859-1860 cover the matter. C.C. 1859 states that hotel, apartment, boarding house, innkeeper, and others of like nature, have the liability of a "depositary for hire," i.e., are liable only if loss or damage is caused by ordinary or greater negligence on their part. But C.C. 1859 imposes a $500 limitation of liability for trunks and a $250 limitation of liability apiece for suitcases and other forms of belongings, with an aggregate liability of $1000, unless, in writing, a greater liability is assumed. And C.C. 1860 makes a special rule for valuables—that if the hotel, etc., posts notice that it keeps a safe and will not be liable for money, documents, jewelry, furs or "other articles of unusual value and small compass" unless placed therein, it is not liable if such articles are not deposited in the safe. Section 1860 further provides that in no case (apparently including that of deposit of valuables) is the hotel, etc., liable to any one guest for more than $500 unless a "receipt in writing" is given whereby the liability is expressly increased.

[49]This may also be called an *artisan's lien*.

[50]C.C. 3051 gives the lien to all persons—those who repair, alter, improve, store, transport or otherwise perform services on or in connection with the property. Section 3051a imposes the special limitation that a lien for services is not good for more than $300 and that a lien for safekeeping is not good for more than $200 unless the owner of property is notified of the proposed work, where the property is brought in by someone other than the owner. C.C. 3067 et seq. make the same rules as to motor vehicles but with a $500 limit on services and a $400 limit on storage, safekeeping or parking space rental. Warehousemen are given liens by U.C.C. 7209; carriers by U.C.C. 7307. C.C. 1861-1861a give hotel, apartment house, boarding house keepers, etc. a lien upon baggage and property of guests and upon "other property belonging to or legally under the control of" the guest,

• The improver's lien was good only against the property upon which the services were performed and to the extent of the services performed upon it. Thus, a garage could not hold a truck for costs of making repairs upon other trucks of the same owner. Because of this, the improver's lien is called a *special lien.* By contrast, a few persons such as bankers and factors have *general liens*, which means that they may hold all property or moneys of the depositor or principal for all amounts owed them. So, if one is indebted to a bank on two distinct obligations—a personal loan and an automobile loan—it may hold all of his deposits and the certificate of title to the automobile for either obligation if it becomes delinquent.[51]

• The lien is lost if possession is relinquished, unless there is an express agreement of the parties to the contrary, and it is not revived by subsequent reacquisition of the property.[52]

---

but this may not be sold if it does not belong to the guest and the hotel, etc. receives notice of such fact at any time before sale.

C.C. 3052 provides for enforcement of the lien given by § 3051 and provides that if the lienholder's charge is not paid within 10 days after it comes due, he may then give 10 days' notice of sale and sell the property. C.C. 3053.5 makes exception from these requirements with respect to items of nominal value. Section 3052a sets up a special rule for jewelers because of the exceptional value of the property handled by them. The jeweler must wait until his charge has been unpaid for one year and may then sell after giving 30 days' notice by registered mail to the owner, or by posting notice if the owner's address is not known. Section 3066 sets up a special rule for cleaners, pressers and launderers, requiring them to wait 90 days and then give 30 days' notice by registered mail to the owner. To have this right, they must keep posted on the premises two signs, one stating that "All articles cleaned, pressed, glazed, laundered, washed, altered or repaired and not called for in 90 days shall be sold to pay charges;" the other that "All articles stored by agreement and charges not having been paid for 12 months will be sold to pay charges," the latter sign covering a case in which a cleaner, presser, etc. agrees to store the goods temporarily after completion of his services.

The liens given by C.C. 3051 take precedence over prior liens such as chattel mortgages, so that, e.g., a garage keeper may hold a car as against a party having a chattel mortgage on it. The theory of this is that the improver adds value to the property commensurate with the amount of the lien claimed for his services, so that there is no actual prejudice to the prior lienholder, and that it is not possible to expect the improver to examine the records for prior liens every time he repairs a chattel.

[51]C.C. 2874: "A general lien is one which the holder thereof is entitled to enforce as a security for the performance of all the obligations, or all of a particular class of obligations, which exist in his favor against the owner of the property." C.C. 2875: "A special lien is one which the holder thereof can enforce only as security for the performance of a particular act or obligation, and of such obligation as may be incidental thereto." C.C. 3051 gives the laundryman and cleaner a general lien; C.C. 3053, a factor; C.C. 3054, a banker or savings and loan association; and the warehouseman's lien in footnote 50 is a general lien if the warehouse receipt so provides; see U.C.C. 7209(1).

[52]C.C. 2913: "The voluntary restoration of property to its owner by the holder of a lien thereon dependent upon possession extinguishes the lien as to such property, unless otherwise agreed by the parties, and extinguishes it, notwithstanding any such agreement, as to creditors of the owner and persons, subsequently acquiring a title to the property or a lien thereon, in good faith, and for value." C.C. 3070 states the rule that if a garageman's lien is lost through trick or fraud, he may revive it by regaining possession of the car, but subject to the rights of an intervening bona fide purchaser or encumbrancer.

• Various of the personal property security liens have come under heavy fire lately in another form of development of consumer protection law. *Klim* v. *Jones*, 315 Fed. Supp. 109, involved California's Innkeeper's Lien Law (C.C. 1861-1861a, footnote 50, page 160). Hotel proprietor padlocked boarder's room and belongings for alleged failure to pay rent. The federal district court held that "Section 1861 (footnote 50, page 160) is constitutionally infirm . . . for its failure to provide for any sort of hearing prior to the imposition of the innkeeper's lien thereunder, thus depriving the boarder of property without due process of law." This is part of a movement on the part of courts to abolish or severely restrict prejudgment remedies which do not provide for notice and hearing in advance of being exercised, of which the remedy of attachment is the prime example, as seen earlier (page 8). Other recent decisions have held against the banker's lien (C.C. 3054, footnote 51, below) and the towkeeper's lien given by Vehicle Code, Section 22851, on constitutional grounds. In one instance the legislature responded to the new order in an effort to head off another form of confrontation. In 1974, the legislature amended the garage keeper's lien law (C.C. 3067-3075, footnote 50, page 160) to require the garage keeper, before conducting a lien sale, either to get a judgment on the claim giving rise to the lien or to get authority from the Department of Motor Vehicles to conduct a sale. The Department of Motor Vehicles has only very limited authority in this regard. If its authority to conduct a lien sale is sought by a garage keeper, it must notify the car owner of this fact and must leave the garage keeper to his judicial remedy if the car owner returns a form, with which the Department must supply him along with its notice, in which the car owner states that he wishes to have a court hearing on the matter.

Security Transactions in Personal Property

The lien just discussed is called a lien *created by operation of law*, i.e., conferred by statute without regard to any agreement of the parties. The liens now to be discussed are, by contrast, intentionally created or *contractual* liens, arrangements by which property is made security for a debt by express agreement of the parties.

Pledges: A pledge is a deposit of personal property by way of security with the creditor, as *pledgee*, or with a third party, as *pledge-holder* for the benefit of the creditor. The pledgor retains title, the pledgee having a lien only. Common pledges are the pawnshop transaction, *pawn* and *pledge* being synonymous, and the deposit of securities—stocks and bonds[53]—with a bank as security for a loan. The essence of the pledge is change of possession, but in one case—*field warehousing*—a sort of constructive change only is required, as follows: A manufacturer wants to borrow money on his inventory. He segregates it within his own plant, and then "leases" that part of the plant to a warehouseman for a nominal "rent," e.g., $1. The warehouseman then issues warehouse receipts on the inventory to the lending agency (pledgee) as security for its loans to the manufacturer. As the manufacturer sells his stock of inventory, the moneys received are used to "buy back" the warehouse receipts from the financing agency, the goods sold being obtainable from the "warehouse" only by paying the bank and obtaining the warehouse receipts from it.

---

[53]This is by indorsement or assignment to the pledgee "as pledgee."

• The pledgee has the right to profits or increases accruing to the pledged property during the term of the pledge,[54] e.g., to dividends on pledged stock,[55] but must apply them to satisfaction of the debt for which the pledge is security. Where notes are pledged as security, the pledgee has the right, and duty, to collect them when due, the pledgee having a general duty to preserve and protect the security pledged. A pledgee may re-pledge the property to the extent of his lien.[56]

---

[54]U.C.C. 9207(2)(c).

[55]But the corporation will be required to pay dividends to the pledgee only if there has been a transfer of the stock to the pledgee on the books of the corporation, as discussed in the chapter on Corporations.

[56]U.C.C. 9207(2)(e).

• The pledgee's rights in event of default by the pledgor are covered by Division 9 of the Uniform Commercial Code.[57]

Security Agreements: The pledge is unique among the contractual liens in that it is the only one in which the security is created by a transfer of possession from the debtor to the creditor. Other contractual liens both on personal property and on real property—the real estate mortgages and deeds of trust—are *paper* liens, i.e., liens imposed upon property by an instrument of which the whole world is given notice by recording or filing. In the case of personal property, these paper liens take the form of the security agreements seen in Chapter 7.

---

[57]U.C.C. 9501 et seq.

CHAPTER 9

Real Property

Introduction

The general nature of ownership and of real property, as distinguished from personal property are discussed at the beginning of the preceding chapter. As seen there, real property is land and everything permanently attached to it. Ownership interests in land are called *estates*, which is the origin of the more familiar term real estate, used synonymously with real property.

● Broadly speaking at least, our general theory of real property ownership stems from the feudal system which evolved in Europe in the Middle Ages and was carried over into England. The theory and pattern of feudalism was that the state owned all property in the first instance and that it was the prerogative of the King, as chief of state, to parcel out the land in a just manner which, as far as the King was concerned, consisted of dividing much of it among the high ranking noblemen from whom he would receive support. They, in turn, divided parts of their grants among other persons. The ultimate subdivisees were said to have the *fee* of the land which was then and ever since has been synonymous with ownership. As the final step down the ladder, the fee owners leased or rented their lands to tenant farmers in exchange for a portion of their crops. These farmers had mere *tenancies*—possessory interests—as distinguished from ownership.

● Our pattern is roughly the same. The breakdown is into ownership interests, on the one hand, and possessory interests or tenancies on the other. Ownership stems from the state in the first instance, as seen in a later discussion of the origin of California land titles. The highest form of ownership interest is called the *fee* or *fee simple* ownership.

The general outline is as follows:[1]

---

[1]With some minor variations in language, C.C. 761 and 762 adopt the same scheme. Section 761 says that "Estates in real property . . . are either:
"1. Estates of inheritance or perpetual estates;
"2. Estates for life;
"3. Estates for years; or
"4. Estates at will."
Section 762 says that "Every estate of inheritance is a fee, and every such estate, when not defeasible or conditional, is a fee simple or an absolute fee."
While the California code sections above call both ownership and possessory interests "estates," the more usual terminology is that of estates and *tenancies*, followed in the text. The distinction is not of importance, however. The language of "tenancy" is used in the text because it is the more usual usage and because it seems more appropriate to the section heading of "Landlord and Tenant," under which tenancies are discussed.
Certain other fundamental nomenclature may be noted. A *freehold interest* in real property is an interest of uncertain duration, which makes all estates freehold interests. (C.C. 765: "Estates of inheritance and for life are called estates of freehold; estates for years are chattels real; and estates at will are chattel interests . . .") Fees, simple and defeasible, are *estates of inheritance*, in that they pass to heirs of the owner on his death.

1. Ownership interests or *estates*:
  a. Fee simple estates.
  b. Fee simple defeasible estates.
  c. Life estates.
2. Possessory interests or *tenancies*:
  a. Tenancies for years.
  b. Tenancies at will.

● The ownership interests listed above are discussed in the next section. In connection with them are discussed rights incidental to ownership and rights that may be acquired in the land of another. Tenancies are discussed in the section on landlord and tenant.

Ownership Interests or Estates

Fee Simple

"*Fee simple*" is the highest type of ownership of real property that it is possible to have.[2] It is described as absolute, unconditional and perpetual ownership. It is perpetual ownership in the sense that it passes to the heirs of the immediate owner upon his death, and so has a duration equal to that of the property itself. Virtually everyone who buys property, whether a home or business property, acquires fee simple ownership.[3]

● To explain fee simple ownership more simply, it is that degree of ownership that permits the owner to do anything with, on or to the land that he sees fit, subject only to three general limitations which are limitations upon all ownership of property regardless of degree. These limitations are that (1) a nuisance may not be committed upon the property; (2) the state, in the exercise of its police power, may regulate the use of the property; and (3) the state or federal government, by exercise of the right of eminent domain, may take all or part of the property.

● A *nuisance* is the use of one's property in such a way as to interfere with another landowner in his use and enjoyment of his property, e.g., the operation of a factory which emits great quantities of smoke which discolors surrounding homes, leaves deposits of soot and causes personal discomfort to the home owners. Injured parties may obtain relief by injunc-

---

[2]Fee simple ownership may be called merely *fee* ownership, or more elaborately, and for the purpose of distinguishing it fully from fee simple defeasible ownership, *fee simple absolute* ownership.

[3]The fact that you have a "mortgage" (deed of trust in California) on your property does not mean that you have less than fee simple ownership. When you buy property you borrow part of the purchase price from a lending institution to which you give a deed of trust on the property as security. At the same time the vendor gives you a deed to the property, which gives you the ownership interest in fee. The deed of trust is merely a *lien* on the property which does not affect ownership, although of course the lending institution can foreclose its deed of trust and take away ownership if you do not pay the deed of trust.

tion—a court order prohibiting continuance of the nuisance.[4] Even though a person is the fee simple owner of property, then, he cannot maintain a nuisance.

• The *police power* of the state is the power of the state or its political subdivisions—cities, counties, etc.—to pass laws reasonably calculated to promote the health, safety and general welfare of its citizens. The *zoning ordinance* is an example of its exercise in such a way as to limit the use of real property.[5] Essentially, a zoning ordinance divides a city into certain "zones"—heavy industrial, light industrial, business or commercial, multiple dwelling residential and single family residential—and property falling within a particular zone may not be used for purposes beyond those allowed. Since this keeps industrial and commercial activities out of residential areas, it promotes health and safety and, so, is a valid exercise of the police power. Even though R is fee simple owner of property, then, he may not use it commercially or industrially if it is within a zone confined to residential use.

---

[4]C.C. 3479: "Anything which is injurious to health, or is indecent or offensive to the senses, or an obstruction to the free use of property, so as to interfere with the comfortable enjoyment of life or property, or unlawfully obstructs the free passage or use, in the customary manner, of any navigable lake, or river, bay, stream, canal, or basin, or any public park, square, street, or highway, is a nuisance." C.C. 3480 says further that a *public nuisance* is one which "affects . . . an entire community or neighborhood or any considerable number of persons," and C.C. 3481, that any other is a *private nuisance.* C.C. 3491-3503 prescribe the remedies for nuisances—criminal or civil proceedings in case of a public nuisance, civil proceedings in case of a private nuisance. C.C. 3502 provides for *abatement* of a private nuisance—"A person injured by a private nuisance may abate it by removing, or, if necessary, destroying the thing which constitutes the nuisance, without committing a breach of the peace, or doing unnecessary injury." C.C. 3503 qualifies the right of abatement by providing that "Where a private nuisance results from a mere omission of the wrongdoer, and cannot be abated without entering upon his land, reasonable notice must be given to him before entering to abate it."

In modern times, however, the likelihood of a nuisance subject to injunction is not very great. First, there is the doctrine of "balancing of equities" or "balancing the conveniences," which holds that a court of equity may refuse to exercise its power to enjoin where the injury suffered would be small and injunction would require the shutting down of a large industrial plant performing an important public service. Secondly, in conjunction with the zoning ordinances next discussed in the text, state statutes now usually provide that if a business is operated within its proper zone it will not constitute a nuisance, e.g., C.C.P. 731a which provides that where a zoning law permits certain manufacturing, commercial or airport activities in a particular zone, it will not constitute a nuisance or be enjoinable unless the operation is conducted in such a way as to unnecessarily magnify the nuisance effects; or the operation is a cannery, refinery or the like and produces offensive odors, in which case it is excluded from the provisions of Section 731a. It is held in California and many other states that there is no nuisance where the offense is to aesthetic senses only, as in *Dean* v. *Powell Undertaking Co.,* 55 C.A. 545, 203 P. 1015, where it was held that operation of an undertaking parlor in a residential area would not be enjoined merely because it caused mental depression to those in the neighborhood.

[5]Others are city ordinances or city building codes, setting out various safety regulations in the construction, wiring, etc., of buildings.

• The power of *eminent domain* is the power of the federal government and of the state, its subdivisions and certain "quasi-public" bodies—public utilities—to take (condemn) private property for public purposes upon compensating the owner in the amount of the fair market value of the property taken, e.g., of the state to condemn property needed for a highway.[6] Fee simple ownership is always subject to this exercise of sovereign authority.

In 1975 California rewrote its eminent domain law so as, among other things, to allow "property," not merely real property, to be taken for public use. At bottom it is this fact that the City of Oakland relies on in bringing its suit to acquire the Los Angeles Raiders, nee Oakland Raiders, football team franchise. California's "Eminent Domain Law" is to be found in C.C.P. 1230.010-1273.050.

Fee Simple Defeasible

Fee simple ownership always originates in the "sovereign"—the government; in this country, the government of the state in which the property is situated. Taking California as a case in point, the first fee simple titles date from the period 1849-1850, the ending of the war with Mexico by the signing of the Treaty of Guadalupe Hidalgo. Under this treaty, it was agreed that certain lands theretofore owned by Mexican nationals should continue to be owned by these persons under the government of the State of California. While this was a "rubber-stamping" of much of the existing ownership, it does mark the point of origin of the fee simple titles to this land as "California" rather than "Mexican" land, and, figuratively speaking, is the "Year One" of the ownership history of such lands. The remainder of the land was largely laid open to the first claimant—the first party to get a patent[7] from the government. These patentees became the first fee simple owners of their respective lands. This, briefly, was the way it all began.

• Suppose now that R became the first fee simple owner of a tract of California land by government patent in 1850. Thereafter, someone would always be required to have the fee simple interest in the land. R until he sells it, and, so, vests it in another, or until he dies and it passes to his heirs. Say that R dies and the property passes to A, his heir. A, as the new fee simple owner, has the same rights that R had. He may sell the property, or keep it and pass it to his heirs upon death. Now suppose that by a succession of heirships the property passes A-B-C-D and that it comes to rest in D as of 1910. It being larger than he needs, D decides to sell a portion of the property to E. Wishing to protect the portion retained against the inroads of business however, D stipulates in his deed to E that he conveys the property to E "on condition that said property never be used for business, commercial or industrial purposes; (and that) breach of any of the foregoing conditions

---

[6]*Dedication* may be noted in connection with eminent domain. A governmental subdivision—city or county—gets property from private individuals in two general ways: (a) By eminent domain as discussed in the text, which takes property from the owner involuntarily. (b) By dedication which is the voluntary gift of property from a private individual for stipulated public uses, such as park or library. Such gifts would be made in the will of the owner or, during lifetime, by a gift deed to the city or county in the form of that on page 180.

[7]A *patent* is simply an instrument by which the government confers a right of ownership upon a private individual, whether it be the more familiar grant of the exclusive right to manufacture a new invention or, as used in connection with real property, a grant of such property to an individual.

shall cause to be forfeited all right, title and interest of the grantee, his heirs, successors and assigns in and to said property, and (that) the same shall thereupon revert to the grantor, his heirs, successors and assigns, each of whom shall have the right of immediate entry upon said property in the event of any such breach."

It must follow that E has something less than D had. In D's hands, the use of the property was subject only to the three general limitations discussed above (no nuisance, police power, and eminent domain). In E's hands, however, it stands subject to a fourth limitation—no business, commercial or industrial use. It is a fourth limitation of this or some other sort that makes the difference between fee simple absolute and *fee simple defeasible*. The significance of the word "defeasible" should now be apparent. It means that D may repossess the property and terminate E's ownership if the condition is ever violated by E or anyone who succeeds to the property from him or to whom he sells. It must also mean that D has retained some type of interest in the property since he has parted with something slightly less than the full and entire fee simple ownership. D's is a *future interest*—called technically a "*right of re-entry for condition broken*"—as opposed to E's *present interest*, and it is always the case that there must be a future interest in one person if less than full fee simple ownership is conveyed to another.[8] Such future interests are property and, like other property, pass to one's heirs upon death. Thus, upon D's death, the right of re-entry passes to D's heirs and upon their deaths to their heirs.[9] So long as E complies with the condition, however, he is entitled to enjoy the property in the same manner as a fee simple owner—he may sell, lease or mortgage it and use it otherwise than as specially forbidden.[10]

---

[8]Fees simple defeasible are usually sub-classified into (a) fees on condition subsequent, and (b) fees on conditional limitation. It is entirely a question of the exact language used in the deed. If I convey to you "*on condition that* the property never be used for business purposes," as in the text above, I will have created a *fee on condition subsequent*—a fee subject to a right on my part to re-enter and retake the property if, at any time subsequent to the conveyance, the condition is broken. If, by contrast, I were to convey the property to you "for *so long as* it is used for residential purposes," I would have created a *fee on conditional limitation*. Here, the qualifying language, "so long as," serves as the criterion by which to measure the duration of the estate, which extends in length as the grantee continues to observe the limitation. There is this technical difference between the fee on condition subsequent and the fee on conditional limitation: The fee on conditional limitation is deemed to terminate automatically, if the limitation is violated, and the property is deemed thereupon to revert automatically to the grantor or his heirs. The future interest in the property is called the "possibility of reverter." The "right of re-entry for condition broken" which accompanies the fee on condition subsequent, on the other hand requires affirmative action to reclaim the property if the condition is broken and the right of re-entry will be lost if it is not exercised within the time permitted by the statute of limitations.

[9]One may eliminate a condition by getting a *quitclaim deed* from the person owning the right of re-entry. Suppose R conveys to E on condition that intoxicating liquors never be sold on the premises, as in *Wedum-Aldahl Co. v. Miller*, 18 C.A.2d 745, 64 P.2d. 762. Several generations later, X has succeeded to the right of re-entry, Y to the fee simple defeasible. X does not care whether liquor is sold on the premises. Y may pay X a small sum for a quitclaim deed relieving the property of the condition.

[10]Anyone to whom E sells or leases the property or who inherits it from him must, of course, observe the condition just as

---

• The law abhors a forfeiture and will therefore strictly construe such conditions. This means that the courts will, if possible, avoid construing them as conditions. For example, a recital in a deed that "Said property shall be used for a cemetery" may be construed to be a mere "declaration" of the purpose for which the property may be used rather than as a "condition" permitting forfeiture in the event of other use. Therefore, if a use restriction is intended as a condition, it should be expressly stated to be a "condition" and the right of re-entry for condition broken should be expressly reserved.

• Modern day zoning ordinances eliminate the necessity for the "no business use" type of condition illustrated above. But the idea of the fee simple defeasible persists to the extent of *building restrictions* designed to regulate property more strictly than it is regulated by the applicable zoning ordinance. For example, S is about to subdivide a tract of land for an area of expensive homes. The local zoning ordinance classifies the tract as single family residence. But this would not prevent erection of cheap houses. So S records a set of "restrictions" requiring architect approval of any house built in the tract, requiring that construction cost shall be not less than $500,000, etc., and subjects each deed of a lot within the tract to these restrictions. B, a purchaser of a lot in the tract, would acquire a fee simple defeasible, an estate of which he could be divested for violation of the restrictions.[11]

• In *Los Angeles Land & Water Co. v. Kane*, 96 C.A. 418, 274 P. 380, the limitation was as to the type of business to be carried on, the deed reciting that it was "subject to the condition subsequent that no part of said property shall be used for the manufacture or sale of crushed rock, gravel or sand . . ." for a period of 10 years. The court said that "It is the settled law of California that a condition subsequent prohibiting the carrying on of a particular business upon property conveyed is valid and will be upheld where the question of monopoly is not involved or the purpose of the condition is not unlawful. . . ."[12]

E was required to, and R or his heirs may retake the property if anyone, E or another deriving his rights from E, violates the condition.

[11]Such restrictions will ordinarily be "*covenants running with the land*," that is, restrictions upon the use of land which bind successors of the person who originally purchased subject to the restrictions and enforceable by successors of the one who originally imposed the restrictions.

[12]This brings to bear the possibility of an illegal condition. If the condition is illegal, the conveyance becomes a fee simple, i.e., the condition is treated by the courts as being void and the grantee gets the property as though the condition had not been imposed. Thus, if the purpose of the condition in the *Los Angeles Land & Water Co.* case was to stifle competition and, so, be illegally in restraint of trade, it would be void. Various California statutes expressly declare certain types of conditions to be illegal and void, such as conditions against marriage. So, if R conveys property to E "on condition that E never marries," the condition is void and E has fee simple ownership and may marry without losing the property. A technicality enters here, however. If, instead, the conveyance is to E "for so long as he remains unmarried"—a fee on conditional limitation—it is recognized as valid on the technical ground that it does not restrain marriage but only makes unmarried status the yardstick of duration of the estate. Accordingly, C.C. 710, which deals with conditions against marriage, says that "Conditions imposing restraints upon marriage, except upon the marriage of a minor, are void; but this does not affect limitations where the intent was not to forbid marriage, but only to give the use until marriage." The reason for the rule against conditions prohibiting marriage is that it is felt to be

• Also, gifts of property to a city or to a private organization may be conditioned upon the use of the property for a particular purpose—park, library, hospital, etc.

Life Estates

Because of their relatively short duration, life estates may be thought of as the lowest rung on the ladder of ownership interests. Actually, the life estate differs basically from either of the fee type interests. As its name infers, it is ownership of property for the period of a lifetime only. The fee, on the other hand, is the perpetual estate in the land, the interest of a duration equal to that of the land itself. As stated earlier, someone must always hold the fee interest in the land, and this is true even though a life estate has been created. The fee interest continues, but as a future interest during the period of the life estate. This will be seen more clearly in connection with the discussion of reversions and remainders which follows.

Types: There are two general types of life estates classified as conventional or intentionally created life estates, and life estates created by operation of law.

Life estates are *conventional* or intentionally created in two general types of situations:

1. W is an elderly widow who owns her home. F, a younger friend, comes to live with her and serve as a companion. Wishing to assure F of a home for life, W writes in her will, "I devise my real property at 2010 Elm Street, San Diego, California to my friend, F, for life." Upon W's death, F would have a life estate in the property—the exclusive right to use and possess the property for the balance of her life.

What happens to the property upon F's death? Since no one is named to succeed to it at that time, it must go to the heirs of W. Where a life estate is created without naming anyone to succeed to the property upon the death of the life tenant,

the property is said to revert to the heirs of the creator of the life estate upon the death of the life tenant, and a *reversion in fee* is said to rest in them during the continuance of the life estate.[13] Again, the fee must always lie in someone, and this is the way in which it is located or accounted for during a life estate.

As a practical matter, however, W would probably have written something like this in her will: "I devise my real property at 2010 Elm Street, San Diego, California, to my friend, F, for life, remainder in fee to my nephew, N." Here, the situation and the legal nomenclature that attaches to it is different. A specific person, N, has been named to take the fee, and where this is done, the future interest holder is said to have a *remainder in fee* as distinguished from the reversion in fee, and to be the *remainderman* instead of the *reversioner.*[14]

By this theory of co-existing present and future interests in property, it is possible to uphold the basic concept of a *fee* interest in the land existing in some person at all times even though the *present estate*—the present use and enjoyment of the property—is in another person during some part of that time.

2. Life estates may also be created to avoid the necessity of probate proceedings to get property from its owner to his heirs.[15] For example, W is an elderly widow who owns a home which she wishes to go to her son, S, upon her death. W may deed the property to S during her lifetime, with the deed providing that the "Grantor (W) reserves to herself a life estate in said property." This will transfer the fee ownership to S, but subject to a life estate in W. It will accomplish W's objective of avoiding the necessity or probate proceedings upon her death because she will die without ownership of the property. Her life estate will terminate at the moment of death, and the fee will already be owned by S; and it is only when a person owns something at and through the moment of death that probate proceedings are necessary. S, again, will have the remainder in the property while W lives.

• The second general category of life estates—life estates created *by operation of law*—are interests given by statute to a spouse in real property owned by the other spouse at the time of his or her death. These are called dower and curtesy. *Dower* is the right of a wife to a life estate in ⅓ of her husband's real property upon his death. *Curtesy*, while a reciprocal, entitles the husband to a life estate in all the wife's real property upon her death. Curtesy exists in only a very few states today, however, and in place of it the husband is usually given outright a portion of the wife's property upon her death, ordinarily ⅓. Dower, on the other hand, still exists in many states. Neither dower nor curtesy exists in the community property states, of which California is one,[16] and the rights

---

against public policy to restrain marriage.

C.C. 715.2 enacts the American common-law rule against perpetuities which requires an interest in real property to vest not later than 21 years after some life in being at the time of creation of the interest.

Racial conditions were common until made unconstitutional in 1948. Their history may be noted briefly. They came about in two general ways: The subdivider of a tract of land would sell all lots on condition that a lot never be sold to persons of certain races; or property owners in a certain area would sign and record a *restrictive covenant* in which they agreed that they would not sell to persons of certain races. In subsequent sales, these were expressly made conditions of the deeds or automatically became conditions by reason of the fact that the recorded document was notice of the condition to any purchaser and binding upon him. Then, the U.S. Supreme Court held that conditions forbidding *sale* of property violated the rule against restraints on alienation. Thereafter, the conditions were re-worded to prohibit only the *use* of the property by persons of the named race so that, while R could not convey to E "on condition that the property never be *sold* to a member of the . . . race," he could validly convey to E "for so long as" or "on condition that the property never be *used* by a member of the . . . race." E could still sell to anyone, but a member of the designated races, even though the purchaser of the property, could not use it. This distinction was eliminated in the 1948 case of *Shelley* v. *Kraemer,* 334 U.S. 1, 68 S.Ct. 836, where the U.S. Supreme Court held that the enforcement of such use restrictions by state courts was a violation of the equal protection clause of the Fourteenth Amendment. This made them no longer enforceable by legal action and, so, meaningless. Restrictive covenants are now forbidden by C.C. 53, 782.

[13]C.C. 768: "A reversion is the residue of an estate left by operation of law in the grantor or his successors, or in the successors of a testator, commencing in possession on the determination of a particular estate granted or devised."

[14]C.C. 769: "When a future estate, other than a reversion, is dependent upon a precedent estate, it may be called a remainder . . ."

[15]Probate proceedings are discussed at page 236.

[16]C.C. 5129 expressly abolishes dower and curtesy in California by its provision that "No estate is allowed the husband as tenant by curtesy upon the death of the wife, nor is any estate in dower allotted to the wife upon the death of her husband." But the probate homestead gives a similar right. See page 237.

of husband and wife upon death are determined by rules discussed in later sections of this chapter.

Rights and Duties of Life Tenants: Theoretically, a life tenant may sell or lease the property,[17] but since he cannot transfer more than he has—the use of the property for his own lifetime—he would have a difficult time doing so. If he were to give a 5-year lease and then die two months later, the lease would come to an end at that time. A short term lease or month-to-month rental of the property would be about the only possibility. Theoretically also, he can mortgage the property to the extent of his interest, but the same difficulty is present, and, unless the property is income-producing, it would not have any value as security.

● A life tenant must pay the annual taxes on the property during his life tenancy, together with the interest on any mortgage existing upon the property at the time he receives his life estate. He must also keep the property in ordinary repair.[18] Failure to do so constitutes *waste* for which the reversioner or remainderman may take action against him.[19]

Rights Incidental to Ownership

Every owner has certain miscellaneous rights arising out of his ownership of land. These are often referred to as *natural rights*, which are as follows:

1. The right, already seen, to enjoy one's land free of nuisances created by adjoining landowners.[20]
2. The right to *minerals* beneath the land on the theory that one owns to the center of the earth.[21] Removal of minerals which constitute natural resources—gas and oil—may be controlled by the state as a valid exercise of its police power, with the state limiting annual production and/or regulating methods of production in order to prevent waste.[22]
3. The *riparian right*, which is the right of a person whose land abuts upon a river or other body of water to extract water for agricultural or other purposes. This, too, may be regulated by the state in places where agricultural demands are heavy and the water supply limited, the state permitting each land-

owner to extract only a limited gallonage annually based upon needs, past usage, and other factors.[23]

4. The right to *lateral support*, which is the right of a landowner to have his land continue to receive the support which it receives naturally from adjoining lands. The common law rule was that this right extended only to land in its natural state, however, and that if the weight of buildings placed upon land caused it to subside when excavations were made on adjoining land, the excavator was not liable for the damage to the land or to the building, provided that there was no negligence on his part. Statutes in many states have modified the common law rule.[24]

Certain other matters of contention between adjoining landowners are discussed in footnotes below.[25]

---

[17]C.C. 818: "The owner of a life estate may use the land in the same manner as the owner of a fee-simple, except that he must do no act to the injury of the inheritance," i.e., must not commit "waste" as next discussed in the text and in the footnote following.

[18]C.C. 840: "The owner of a life estate must keep the buildings and fences in repair from ordinary waste, and must pay the taxes and other annual charges, and a just proportion of extraordinary assessments benefitting the whole inheritance."

[19]*Waste* may be *passive*—simply failing to care for the property—or it may be *active* or affirmative waste, consisting of the destruction of improvements upon the property. There may also be another form of active waste. Suppose a life tenancy is given in timber or mineral-bearing lands. The creator of the life estate has regularly taken out a certain number of feet or tons of the timber or mineral annually in the past. The life tenant may continue to cut timber or extract ore at the same annual rate, but not at an increased rate. If he takes out more in any year, he will be guilty of and liable for waste.

[20]See page 163 for earlier discussion of nuisances.

[21]C.C. 829: "The owner of land in fee has the right to the surface and to everything permanently situated beneath or above it."

[22]The Public Resources Code in Sections 3000 et seq. regulates methods of removal of gas and oil and places the regulatory power in the Department of Conservation.

[23]The Water Code deals with this in detail. Sections 100-101 recognize riparian rights but provide that removal of water "shall be limited to such water as shall be reasonably required for the beneficial use to be served." Sections 2000 et seq. place regulatory power in the Department of Water Resources and the State Water Resources Control Board and provide for settlement of controversies by court-appointed referees. Sections 4050 et seq. provide for the appointment of "*watermasters*" to regulate extraction in areas and at times when the water supply is limited.

[24]C.C. 832 is the California statute on lateral support. It makes a number of changes in the common law rule. A summary of the provisions of Section 832 is as follows:

a. Where there is no building on the adjoining land, the excavator must give notice to his neighbor of the proposed excavation and must take reasonable precautions to sustain the adjoining land. If notice is given and there is no violation of the duty to take reasonable precautions, the excavator is not liable for damage to the adjoining land. Theoretically at least, this is a lesser liability than that imposed by the common law rule, because under the common law rule the excavator is liable in such case irrespective of how careful he is, i.e., has absolute liability. As a practical matter, however, it is difficult to imagine a case in which the excavator could be said to have taken the reasonable precautions to sustain the land required by Section 832 and still have the land fall. Particularly in view of California cases holding, e.g., that the taking of reasonable precautions requires foreseeing and allowing for the possibility of heavy rains. (*Conlin* v. *Coyne*, 19 C.A.2d 78, 64 P.2d 1123.) It may be noted that the owner of the land on which the excavations are made is not excused from liability because the work is done by an independent contractor, as normally the employer of an independent contractor would be. This is another case in which a principal is held liable for wrongs of his independent contractor, on the ground that one cannot escape an express statutory duty by delegating the job to an independent contractor.

b. If the adjoining land has a building on it (1) if excavations are to go deeper than the foundations of such building, the adjoining landowner must be given at least 30 days to protect his building; (2) if they are to go deeper than the standard depth of foundations (12 feet below curb level) and the foundation of the building on the adjoining property goes to such depth, the excavator must protect the building on the adjoining land and is absolutely liable for any damage to it except "minor settlement cracks."

[25]*Line trees.* C.C. 833 provides that "Trees whose trunks stand wholly upon the land of one owner belong exclusively to him, although their roots grow into the land of another." This would make it the duty of such landowner to maintain the trees. The cases have held that if the branches overhang onto the adjoining property, they constitute a *nuisance* since they interfere with the adjoining landowner's right to the airspace above his property. Also that the adjoining landowner may *abate* the nuisance by

Incidental Rights in Land

One may obtain a *right* in land as distinguished from an ownership interest. There are three types of such rights: easements, profits and licenses.

Easements: An *easement* is the right to *use* the land of another in a particular way; to use a road crossing it; or to be a party to a "community driveway" arrangement in which neighbors each confer on the other the right to use a portion of the other's land for their mutual benefit, which actually creates cross-easements.[26]

● Easements are classified as easements appurtenant and easements in gross. An *easement appurtenant* is the use of one parcel of land for the benefit of another, ordinarily adjoining, parcel, such as the use of a roadway across one parcel of land to get to another.[27] An *easement in gross*, by contrast, is the use of land without reference or benefit to other land, such as a railroad's right to run tracks through land.

● An easement is an interest in land within the meaning of the statute of frauds and, so, must be created by a written instrument, except in certain exceptional cases discussed below.

● The writing creating an easement may grant an easement or reserve an easement. If A and B are neighbors and A wants to allow B to cross A's land, A would give B a writing entitled "Easement" in which A would grant B the right to cross A's land to B's. This would create an *easement by express grant*. If, by contrast, A is selling part of a tract of land to B over which A wishes to continue to have the right to pass, A, in the deed to B, would insert the stipulation that "grantor (A) reserves the right to use that certain roadway (describing it)." This would create an *easement by express reservation*.

● Easements may be created for such time as the parties see fit—perpetually or in fee, for a lifetime, or for a period of years. Easements appurtenant are transferable and will pass automatically with the land receiving the benefit of the easement, but the general rule seems to be that a non-commercial

easement in gross is not transferable unless a contrary intent appears.[28]

● There are two cases in which easements can be created without a writing:

1. *Easements by Implied Grant.* Suppose, again, that A is going to sell part of his property to B. On it is a house which A has rented up to now. Crossing A's land is a road which leads to the house and which has been used by the tenants as a means of access. B takes it for granted that he will have the right to use the road when he buys the property, and nothing is said about B's use of the road in A's deed of the property to B. Thereafter, A attempts to stop B from using the road. He may not do so. B would have an *easement by implied grant*. A purchaser of property receives with it easements which are being used at the time of his purchase and which he would reasonably expect to have the right to use.[29] Essentially, this is another application of the principle of estoppel.

2. *Easements by Prescription.* These are interesting and quite unusual. Suppose that, with no right or permission, A openly and regularly uses a road across B's land for a period of years and that B takes no steps to prevent the use. If A continues this for a sufficient time, called the *prescriptive period* (which is 5 years in California but 15-20 years in most states), he will acquire the permanent right to do so—an *easement by prescription*—with which B cannot interfere thereafter. This sort of legitimized piracy has come down from the common law where it was the theory that one held land only by grace of the King, and that if he failed to protect it should suffer the penalty of having others acquire rights in it.

● Four requirements must be met to acquire such an easement. There must be (1) open and notorious, (2) continuous (3) adverse (non-permissive) use, (4) for the prescriptive period, whatever it may be in the particular state. At any time before the prescriptive period has run, the owner may prevent the acquisition of an easement by getting an injunction prohibiting the continued trespass.[30]

cutting off the branches. It has also been held, however, that if the adjoining landowner cuts back his neighbor's tree and, by so doing, kills a valuable tree, he may be liable to him in damages. C.C. 834 provides, on the other hand, that "Trees whose trunks stand partly upon the land of two or more coterminous owners, belong to them in common" so that there is an equal obligation to maintain such trees, and neither has the right to cut them down.

Line fences. C.C. 841 requires adjoining owners to contribute equally to the maintenance of line fences "unless one of them chooses to let his land lie without fencing; in which case, if he afterwards incloses it, he must refund to the other a just proportion of the value, at that time, of any division fence made by the latter" (adjoining owner).

C.C. 841.4 makes "spite fences"—fences more than 10 feet high and erected to annoy the neighbor—a nuisance which may be abated by the adjoining owner.

Ditches, pipelines, etc. Wat. C. 7001 requires that joint users of ditches, pipelines or other conduits for conveyance of water or of a pumping plant share maintenance expenses.

[26]C.C. 845 requires the one having an easement in the form of a right of way to keep it in repair, and those jointly sharing an easement to contribute equally to its maintenance.

[27]The land benefitted by an easement appurtenant is called the "*dominant tenement;*" the land burdened by it, the "*servient tenement;*" and C.C. 803 so provides.

[28]C.C. 1104 makes easements appurtenant transferable by its provision that "A transfer of real property passes all easements attached thereto . . ." Easements in gross would be transferable in California under the broad provision of C.C. 1044 that "Property of any kind may be transferred, except as otherwise provided by this article," which does not forbid transfer of easements in gross.

[29]C.C. 1104 would make this so: "A transfer or real property passes all easements attached thereto, and creates in favor thereof an easement to use other real property of the person whose estate is transferred in the same manner and to the same extent as such property was obviously and permanently used by the person whose estate is transferred, for the benefit thereof, at the time when the transfer was agreed upon or completed."

[30]The duration of an easement by prescription is measured by the interest of the owner of the servient estate if the easement by prescription is *appurtenant*. If A gets an easement by prescription through your land and you have fee ownership, A's easement is in fee; if you have only a life estate, A's easement is only for your life. If the easement is in gross, it must necessarily end with the lifetime of the one acquiring it. In California, it is lost by abandonment for the prescriptive period. C.C. 811: "A servitude is extinguished . . . [w]hen the servitude was acquired by enjoyment [prescription], by disuse thereof by the owner of the servitude for the period prescribed for acquiring title by enjoyment."

An easement by prescription cannot be enlarged upon. If A acquires a prescriptive easement through your land by his individual use of your land, A cannot thereafter open a hotel on his land and give the guests the right to use the road. C.C. 806

California enacted what might be called an "antiprescrip-ive easement statute" in 1965, C.C. 1008, which provides that no use, no matter how long continued, of any land, shall ripen into an easement by prescription, if the owner of the property posts at each entrance to the property or at intervals of not more than 200 feet along the boundary a sign reading substantially as follows: "Right to pass by permission, and subject to control, of owner: Section 1008, Civil Code."

● Another, even more startling, concept of property law which is of a related nature is the concept of *title by adverse possession*. It is the adverse possession rule that if you (1) openly and notoriously, (2) continuously, (3) adversely (non-permissively) take possession of, as distinguished from mere-ly use, the land of another, (4) for the prescriptive period, you acquire *title* to the land, and thereby divest the owner of his title.[31] If he had fee simple title, you get fee simple title, and if he comes on the land after you have acquired title by adverse possession, you can have him put off as a trespasser. However, the California law makes one more requirement of one attempting to acquire title by adverse possession—(5) that he must pay the annual taxes on the property during the 5-year prescriptive period.[32] California is exceptional in this respect and most states do not have this requirement. One may sell ownership acquired by adverse possession, but title by adverse possession is not a "marketable title," which is to say that, because it is not a record title, it is not a title which a title company will insure.

Profits: A *profit* is the right *to take something from* the land of another, such as water or timber.[33] The rules as to easements apply with equal force to profits.[34]

"The extent of a servitude is determined by the terms of the grant, or the nature of the enjoyment by which it was acquired."

[31]C.C. 1007 recognizes title by adverse possession. It says that "Occupancy for the period prescribed by the Code of Civil Procedure as sufficient to bar any action for the recovery of the property confers a title thereto, denominated a title by prescription, which is sufficient against all . . ." The section then goes on to provide that such title cannot be acquired in government owned lands. C.C.P. 318 says that actions to recover real property must be brought within 5 years, and it is this statute that makes the *prescriptive period* 5 years in California.

[32]C.C.P. 325 is the section which requires the payment of taxes, and it requires payment of "all the taxes, State, county, or municipal, which have been levied and assessed upon such land."

[33]The California code does not distinguish between easements and profits but lumps them together as *servitudes* upon land. They are provided for by C.C. 801-802 which list some 17 types. Among these are right of way; of pasture; of taking water, wood or minerals; to discharge water on the land of another; to use a party wall (a wall used in common to support buildings of adjoining owners); and the right to receive light and air from adjoining land.

The last of these—an easement of light and air—is of some interest. Suppose you have a one story home on your land. The adjoining land has not previously been built upon, but the owner builds a three story apartment house which restricts the light and air to which you have become accustomed. Do you have any right against him? Not in this country where it is held that there is no right to an easement of light and air created by such facts, and it was so held in *Kennedy* v. *Burnap*, 120 C. 488, 52 P. 843. However, by virtue of C.C. 801.5, adopted in 1978, there may, in California, be an *express* "solar easement," defined as "the right of receiving sunlight across the real property of another for any solar energy system."

[34]Profits, like easements, are appurtenant or in gross and may

Where one has land which is found to contain valuable minerals, such as oil or gas, the usual arrangement is to *lease* the subsurface of the land to a professional producer for a percentage of the profits realized from what is removed. The oil and gas lease on a royalty basis is a common example.

Licenses: A *license* is a right or permit to go on the land of another for a particular purpose—to consummate a business transaction or to enjoy entertainment, a movie or a football game, in which latter case a consideration is given for it. A license is said to differ from an easement in that it is of relatively short duration, is not such an interest in land as requires a writing for its creation, is not assignable[35] and may be revoked at any time. It may be noted that the landowner has the duty to keep his property in safe condition for licensees or invitees upon his premises.

Concurrent Ownership

The discussion so far has been entirely in terms of acquisition of ownership of real property by a single individual—A deeds property to B, B to C, and so on. More often than not, however, A may be called upon to deed to B *and* C or to H *and* W, husband and wife, i.e., to deed property as an undivided whole to two or more persons collectively. When this happens, *concurrent ownership* or *cotenancy* is created—ownership of one piece of property by two or more persons at the same time. Four forms of concurrent ownership are discussed in this section—joint tenancy, tenancy by the entirety, tenancy in common and community property ownership.[36] Community property ownership is considered last to permit discussion not only of its basic nature but also of the general rules of community property law.

● In the next section, condominiums, as a modern form of common ownership, are discussed.

Joint Tenancy

A *joint tenancy* is defined as a conveyance to two or more persons in which there is an expressed intention to create a joint tenancy and in which the *four unities* of time, title, interest and possession are present.[37] The requirement of *ex-*

---

be obtained by prescription, although there is little practical likelihood of a profit by prescription. Thus, if A pipes water from your land onto his adjoining land for irrigation, A has a profit appurtenant (and also an easement appurtenant to the extent that the pipe is run across your land). On the other hand, if A draws spring water from your land for bottling and sale, he has a profit in gross.

[35]See footnotes 28 and 29 for transferability of easements.

[36]C.C. 682: "The ownership of property by several persons is either:
"1. Of joint interests;
"2. Of partnership interests; [Discussed in the later chapter on Partnerships.]
"3. Of interests in common;
"4. Of community interests of husband and wife."

[37]C.C. 683: "A joint interest is one owned by two or more persons in equal shares, by a title created by a single will or transfer, when expressly declared in the will or transfer to be a joint tenancy, or by a transfer from a sole owner to himself and others, or from tenants in common or joint tenants to themselves, or some of them, or to themselves or any of them and others, or from a husband and wife when holding title as community property or otherwise to themselves or to themselves and others or to one of them and to another or others, when expressly declared in the transfer to be a joint tenancy . . . A joint tenancy in personal

pressed intention to create a joint tenancy is satisfied by the words "as joint tenants" in the specimen form of joint tenancy deed on page 171. The four unities, while a technical requirement, are present rather as a matter of course. Using the specimen deed on the following page as an example: The unities of time and title require that the parties receive their interests at the same time and by the same instrument, which is obviously the case. Unity of interest requires that each receives the same degree of ownership interest which is necessarily the case where nothing is said to the contrary. The parties would jointly receive fee simple ownership, since that is what passes when there is an unqualified conveyance of property.[38] Unity of possession is really synonymous with *concurrent ownership* or *cotenancy*. It is present wherever persons are given "undivided interests" in property. This must be the case whenever they receive the property in a lump sum, as they do in the specimen deed.

• The right of survivorship attaches automatically to every joint tenancy, and it is for this reason that a joint tenancy is created. *Right of survivorship* means that when a joint tenant dies his interest passes to the surviving joint tenants rather than to his heirs. This eliminates the need for probate proceedings with respect to the property. Ordinarily one enters into joint tenancy with a spouse or close relative who would be the one who would succeed to his property upon death at all events.

• Joint tenants have equal rights of use and possession of the property. In addition, they are entitled to share equally in profits such as rents and crops. All are required to contribute equally to expenses of maintenance, annual taxes and any mortgage payments on the property.

• A joint tenancy may be broken; once created it is not indestructible. Any joint tenant may sell his *undivided interest* at any time. Thus, if A and B own property as joint tenants, A may sell his undivided one-half interest to T if he sees fit. Between T and B, there would be no joint tenancy because there could be no conveyance by A designating B and T joint tenants (B has the right to choose his joint tenants), and, while further reasons are not required, there is neither unity of time nor unity of title, since B and T would have received their interests at different times and by different instruments. Hence, conveyance of his interest by a joint tenant will destroy a joint tenancy. In the case above, T and B would become tenants in common.

• Joint tenancy may also be terminated at any time by any joint tenant by *partition*. This consists of a division of a property into parcels with each joint tenant taking a parcel as his own. This being done, concurrent ownership would cease to exist. Partition may be voluntary or involuntary. Joint tenants A and B may agree upon a boundary line splitting the property, then make a deed from themselves to A of the western one-half and a deed from themselves to B of the eastern one-half, and thereby effect a *voluntary partition*. If they cannot reach an agreement, either party may go to court at any time and obtain *involuntary partition*.[39] If the property is susceptible of physical division, the court may divide it and give a specific one-half to each; if not, e.g., if it has a house on it,

the court will order the property sold and split the proceeds of sale between the parties. Involuntary partition proceedings are expensive, however, because of costs of legal proceedings and attorneys' fees and because the property is sold at auction and may not realize its fair value; hence, they are usually avoided. Creditors of a joint tenant may compel an involuntary partition in order to permit them to reach this asset of their debtor.

Tenancy by the Entirety

Eight states have the community property law. In them, conveyance of property to a husband and wife gives rise to community property ownership. In other states, conveyance of real property to a husband and wife may create a *tenancy by the entirety*, which closely resembles joint tenancy. Like joint tenancy, tenancy by the entirety has the right of survivorship. Like joint tenancy, tenancy by the entirety requires the four unities for its creation. However, there is no requirement of expressed intention to create tenants by the entirety. So long as the four unities are present, tenancy by the entirety is automatically created by a conveyance to husband and wife. Tenancy by the entirety differs from joint tenancy in the important respect that neither tenant by the entirety can sell his interest without the consent of the other, and a sale without consent is void.

In many non-community property states a conveyance to the husband and wife creates only a joint tenancy or tenancy in common.

Tenancy in Common

Into this category falls every case in which two or more persons acquire undivided interests in a parcel of land but in which one or more of the requirements for joint tenancy, tenancy by the entirety or community property ownership is not met.[40] Suppose a deed simply to "A, B, and C" (brothers). Since there is no expressed intention to create a joint tenancy, that form does not result. Since A, B, and C are not husband and wife, tenancy by the entirety or community property ownership is not possible. The parties do acquire undivided interests in the land, however, so they must have the only remaining form of concurrent ownership—*tenancy in common*. It is by such a process of elimination that this form of concurrent ownership is found.

• Tenancy in common often results from a will. Suppose that W makes a will in which he says "I devise my real property at 3020 Elm Street, Sacramento, California to my sisters, S and T." Using the elimination test, it is seen that S and T are not joint tenants because, again, there is no expressed intention to make them such. Since they are sisters, tenancy by the entirety and community property ownership are not possible. Hence, nothing remains but tenancy in common.

• Tenancy in common also results when a joint tenant conveys his interest to a third person. Since the remaining joint tenant and the third person do not acquire their interests in accordance with the requirements for creation of a joint tenancy, but since they do have undivided interests in the property, they must become tenants in common.

• Tenancy in common differs importantly from joint tenancy and tenancy by the entirety in that there is *no right of survivorship*. Upon death of a tenant in common, his interest goes to his heirs rather than to the surviving tenant in common.

---

property may be created by a written transfer, instrument or agreement."

[38]C.C. 1105: "A fee simple title is presumed to be intended to pass by a grant of real property, unless it appears from the grant that a lesser estate was intended."

[39]C.C.P. 872.010 et seq. provide for involuntary partition proceedings by a joint tenant or tenant in common.

---

[40]C.C. 685 says that "An interest in common is one owned by several persons, not in joint ownership or partnership," and C.C. 686, "unless acquired as community property."

Joint Tenancy Grant Deed

ALL

PTN.

The undersigned grantor(s) declare(s):

Documentary transfer tax is $..........................

(   ) computed on full value of property conveyed, or

(   ) computed on full value less value of liens and encumbrances remaining at time of sale.

(   ) Unincorporated area: (   ) City of.., and

(   ) Realty not sold.

FOR A VALUABLE CONSIDERATION, receipt of which is hereby acknowledged,

hereby GRANT(S) to

, AS JOINT TENANTS,

the following described real property in the

County of   , State of California:

Mail tax statements to_____

Dated_____

STATE OF CALIFORNIA

COUNTY OF_____ } SS.

On_____ before me, the under-

signed, a Notary Public in and for said State, personally appeared

_____

_____

_____, known to me

to be the person_____whose name_____subscribed to the within

instrument and acknowledged that_____executed the same.

WITNESS my hand and official seal.

Signature_____ _____

_____ _____

Name (Typed or Printed)

(This area for official notorial seal)

MAIL TAX STATEMENTS AS DIRECTED ABOVE

Community Property

In California and a number of other states, the community property law governs the ownership and control of marital property. The community property law derives from the Civil Law and came to those states which were most heavily influenced by it because of pre-statehood history—Louisiana by reason of the French influence; the western states by reason of the Spanish influence by way of Mexico. There are differences in the community property laws of the states that have adopted such laws, but essentially they are the same. The following discussion is based upon the California law.[41]

What is Community Property?: First, it does not include property owned by one spouse or the other before marriage. Thus, if W buys a house and then later marries H, the house is not converted into community property by the fact of marriage. Property owned by either spouse before marriage remains the *separate property* of that spouse,[42] and the house would remain the separate property of W. H would acquire no rights in the property during W's lifetime unless, as by making a deed of it from herself to herself and H after marriage, she makes a gift of it to the community and, so, converts it into community property. (H's rights in the property upon W's death are discussed in the later section on wills and intestate succession.) Secondly, profits or increments to separate property are separate property and become the separate property of the spouse to whose property they accrue. Thirdly, property remains separate property even though it undergoes some change in form. Thus, if, after marriage, W sells her house and buys stocks with the proceeds, the stocks remain her separate property since they represent a mere change in form of separate property. At least this is so if W takes ownership of the stocks in her name only. If she takes them in the names of herself and her husband, the stocks may be converted into community property, since the courts are rather quick to presume a gift of separate property to the community and have little difficulty in so doing where ownership is placed in the names of both parties. Fourthly, assuming that W took the stocks in her own name, the dividends paid to her on them would be her separate property since they are profits or increments to separate property. Here, again, there is a good possibility that separate property status may be lost. If the dividends are put into a bank account with other moneys of the parties which are community property, it is a rule of community property law that separate property becomes community property if it is *commingled* with community property in such a manner as to lose its identity as separate property.

---

[41]In 1969 California enacted The Family Law Act under which it consolidated in Part 5 of the Civil Code all of the law relating to marriage and married persons. Part 5 fixes the rules for the solemnization of marriage (C.C. 4100-4309); the circumstances in which a marriage is void or voidable and may be annulled (C.C. 4400-4457); the events by which marriage is "dissolved" and the procedure for obtaining the dissolution of a marriage (C.C. 4501-4531); the rules regarding custody and support of children (C.C. 4600-4800); and the rules determining the property rights of married persons (C.C. 4800-4813, 5100-5138).

Prior to 1969, the California community property law, now found in C.C. 5100-5108, was found in C.C. 161-172a.

[42]C.C. 5107: "All property of the wife owned by her before marriage and that acquired afterwards by gift, bequest, devise, or descent, with the rents, issues, and profits thereof, is her separate property . . ." C.C. 5108 says the same thing with respect to the husband.

Community property, then, is only that property which is acquired *after* and during marriage,[43] and not even all of it is community. Property acquired by one spouse or the other after marriage by gift, will or inheritance is not community property but is the separate property of the spouse to whom it is given or by whom it is inherited.[44] The usual community property is the husband's earnings and what has been acquired with them.

To summarize what has been said to this point, *community property* is all property acquired after and during marriage, except property acquired by either spouse by gift, will or inheritance. Property acquired before marriage and its profits and changes in form remain separate property.

● Certain special problems arise in connection with the determination of what constitutes community property. Suppose that at the time of marriage husband owns a business worth $15,000, as in *Pereira* v. *Pereira*, 156 C. 1, 103 P. 488. After marriage, he continues to operate the business. The earnings are community property, since the main source of community property is the productive ability of the husband as translated into earnings. It is only "self-productive" profits realized from separate property that continue to be separate property, as in the case of the stock dividends previously discussed which do not represent any personal effort of the spouse. But a more difficult problem is involved. As in the *Pereira* case, the business increases in value to $70,000 over a period of years. The parties then dissolve their marriage. As part of the dissolution proceeding the court will be required to divide the community property between the parties. The wife contends that the $55,000 increase in the value of the business is due in large part to the husband's efficient management and to the fact that he devoted all of his time and energy to the business; that, therefore, a large part of this increase in value should be classified as community property. It was so held in the *Pereira* case, where the court announced the rule of *apportionment* in cases of this kind—that where separate property is increased in value after marriage as a result of the time and energy devoted to it by the owning spouse, the increase in value should be fairly apportioned between separate and community property wherever reasonably possible; that a proper apportionment would be to allocate to separate property the original investment ($15,000) plus the reasonable return (interest) to be expected on a conservative long-term investment, and this was done in the *Pereira* case where 7% was fixed as a reasonable return. An alternative approach in some California cases led by *Van Camp* v. *Van Camp*, 53 C.A. 17, 199 P. 885, has been to determine the reasonable value of the services of the spouse operating the business and award that as community property while treating the rest of the earnings of the business as separate property.

● Separate and community property interests may exist in the same property. Suppose H buys a house which he has half paid for when he marries W. He pays the balance out of his earnings after marriage, that is, from community property. At the time of final payment, H would own a half interest in the property as his separate property. The other half, having been acquired with his earnings after marriage, would be community property in which H would also have a half interest, and this would be the status of ownership of the property under such circumstances unless at some time after marriage H

---

[43]C.C. 687: "Community property is property acquired by husband and wife, or either, during marriage, when not acquired as the separate property of either."

[44]See footnote 42.

made a deed from himself to himself and W, thereby making a gift of his separate property-half interest to the community.

● C.C. 5126(a) makes personal injury damages received by a spouse the separate property of that spouse if the cause of action for such damages arose after rendition of a decree of legal or final judgment of dissolution of marriage, or while the injured spouse is living separate from the other spouse.

● The California codes state two instances in which earnings which ordinarily are community property, are separate property: (1) Under C.C. 5118-5119, where the spouses are living apart, whether or not there has been any legal separation proceeding. (2) Under C.C.P. 1811-1821, a married woman may go through proceedings to have herself declared a *sole trader* where the husband fails to provide proper support. When declared a sole trader, she may invest not more than $500 of community property in a business to be operated by her. Profits are her separate property and not liable for debts incurred by the husband.

● Suppose husband and wife acquire personal property in a non-community property state, then move to California bringing the property with them. Is it community property after they establish a residence in this state? An attempt was made to make it so in 1917 by amending former C.C. 164 to provide that "personal property wherever situated, heretofore or hereafter acquired while domiciled elsewhere, which would not have been . . . separate property . . . if acquired while domiciled in this state, is community property. . . ." The California Supreme Court held this unconstitutional in *Estate of Thornton*, 1 C.2d 1, 33 P.2d 1, as a deprivation of vested property rights. Every state may set up its own rules of succession, however, and to some extent what was attempted unsuccessfully in C.C. 164 was able to be accomplished by adding § 201.5 to the Probate Code in 1935 to provide that if a husband or wife dies without leaving a will and leaving property which was separate property in the state where acquired but which would have been community property if it had been acquired in this state, such property goes to the survivor in the same manner as community property.

● In 1961 California went a step further by adopting a concept of "*quasi-community property*." This is now defined by C.C. 4803 as "all real or personal property, wherever situated, heretofore or hereafter acquired in any of the following ways: (a) By either spouse while domiciled elsewhere which would have been community property if the spouse who acquired the property had been domiciled in this state at the time of its acquisition. (b) In exchange for real or personal property, wherever situated, which would have been community property if the spouse who acquired the property so exchanged had been domiciled in this state at the time of its acquisition." In dissolution of marriage proceedings such quasicommunity property may be divided by the court in the same manner as community property (C.C. 4800), and quasi-community property may be homesteaded.[45] If a spouse dies intestate, quasi-community property passes in the same manner as community property.[46]

● Except for the forms of separate property described above, property acquired by a husband and wife is presumed to be community. Thus, if real property is deeded simply to "John Jones and Mary Jones, his wife," they are presumed to acquire it as community property. But a husband and wife may own or take property otherwise than as community if this intention is shown.[47] So, if a deed is to "John Jones and Mary Jones, his wife, as joint tenants," they would take the property as joint tenants. In California it may be shown, however, that the parties did not intend to create a joint tenancy, but under the most recent cases it appears that *both* parties must admit that this is so and that the joint tenancy form was used only for convenience.

California's Community Property Rules: The rules regulating California community property were changed quite drastically in 1973, becoming effective January 1, 1975. The changes were in response to increasing criticism of the existing law and were designed to bring the California law in line with changes in law that were being made in other community property states.

● The main objectives of the changes were to equalize the management rights of the parties in community property and to establish uniform rules for both spouses. Prior to 1975, the husband had the exclusive management and control of the community property. Prior to 1975, the community property was liable for debts incurred by the husband but not, generally speaking, for debts incurred by the wife. Now all of this is changed.

MANAGEMENT AND CONTROL. Former C.C. 5105 provided that "The respective interests of the husband and wife in community property during continuance of the marriage relation are present, existing and equal interests *under the management and control of the husband* . . ." Revised C.C. 5105 deletes the italicized words. This combines with revised C.C. 5125(a), which says that "either spouse has the management and control of the community *personal* property," and revised C.C. 5127, which says that "either spouse has the management and control of the community *real* property," to make the spouses general partners in the management and control of the community property, with each spouse having power to bind the entire community.

1. *Restrictions on Powers of Management and Control.* Various restrictions that were placed upon the husband's powers of management and control under pre-1975 law are now placed upon the powers of both parties. The most important of these are as follows:

a. *Sale, Conveyance, Encumbrance or Lease of Community Real Property.* Revised C.C. 5127 requires both spouses to execute any instrument by which community real property is sold, conveyed, encumbered or leased for more than one year. Revised C.C. 5127 undertakes to protect good faith purchasers by providing that, if record title to community real property stands in the name of one spouse alone, a sale, conveyance, encumbrance or lease by that spouse shall be presumed to be valid in favor of a good faith purchaser.

b. *Gift.* Revised C.C. 5125(b) forbids a spouse to make a gift of community personal property without the written consent of the other spouse. Revised C.C. 5127, seen above, produces the same result with respect to community real property by its requirement that both spouses execute any deed to such property.

● Suppose the donor spouse dies before the prohibited gift is set aside? Since, as will be seen, each spouse is entitled to give away one-half the community property at death, by will, California case law has held that the prohibited gift should be allowed to stand to the extent of one-half thereof. *Blethen* v. *Pac. Mutual Life Ins. Co.*, 198 C. 91, 243 P. 431, is an illustration of the application of the gift rule. There, the hus-

---

[45]C.C. 1238.
[46]Prob. C. 201.5.

[47]C.C. 5104: "A husband and wife may hold property as joint tenants, tenants in common, or as community property."

band without knowledge of the wife, used part of his earnings to pay premiums on a life insurance policy in which he named his sister as beneficiary. The wife did not discover this until after his death and payment of the policy proceeds by the insurance company to the sister. Held, the wife would recover one-half the proceeds from the sister.

c. *Sale, Conveyance or Encumbrance of Household Furnishings, Etc.* Revised C.C. 5125(c) forbids either spouse to sell, convey or encumber the household furniture, furnishings, or the clothing or wearing apparel of the other spouse or minor children which is community personal property, without the written consent of the other spouse. A 1983 amendment to Section 5125(c) also forbids the sale, conveyance or encumbrance of community personal property used as a family dwelling, such as a mobilehome, without the written consent of the other spouse.

2. *"Business Exception."* Revised C.C. 5125(d) provides that "A spouse who is operating or managing a business or an interest in a business which is community personal property has the sole management and control of the business or interest." This exception to the equal management rule is necessary to allow the business being managed by one spouse to be operated in an orderly manner.

3. *Significance of Equal Management and Control Rule and Practical Problems Presented.* The management of the matrimonial household is not a very apt subject for legislative fiat. Obviously, the extent to which the equal management rule will work will depend on the extent to which the spouses in question will be able to work together cooperatively. Revised C.C. 5125(e) requires the spouses to act in "good faith" with respect to each other in the management and control of the community property, and this will give some sort of legal protection to a spouse against mismanagement or overreaching by the other spouse.

● Third parties dealing with marital communities will have to be on guard against the equal management rule. Suppose, for example, that husband wants to open a security account in his name alone and to buy and sell on the stock market on his direction alone. Can the stock broker safely go along with this? It would seem not and that the broker had better get the consent of both spouses to all transactions. The effect is to translate equal management and control into joint management and control.

DEBT AND TORT LIABILITY OF COMMUNITY AND SEPARATE PROPERTY.

Separate property is liable for the debts of the spouse who owns it, whether the debts are contracted before or after the marriage. Revised C.C. 5121. Separate property is not liable for any of the debts of the other spouse except debts for necessaries of life in cases where there is no community or quasi-community property. Revised C.C. 5121, 5132.

● In keeping with the "limited partnership" nature of the pre-1975 marital community, in which the husband had the management and control of the community property and in which the wife had an ownership interest in the community property but generally speaking no management powers, the community property had full liability for the debts and torts of the husband but only very limited liability for the debts and torts of the wife. Now, with equally shared management—a "general partnership" relationship—*community property* is made liable for debts of either spouse contracted after marriage. Revised C.C. 5116. Community property consisting of the earnings of a spouse is not liable for debts of the other spouse contracted before marriage. Revised C.C. 5120.

● Community property is liable for *torts* committed by a spouse according to whether or not the act or omission constituting the tort was being performed for the benefit of the community. If it was, then liability for the tort must first be satisfied from community property. To the extent that community property is insufficient to satisfy the liability, it may be satisfied from the separate property of the spouse committing the tort. Revised C.C. 5122(b)(1). If the act or omission constituting the tort was not being performed for the benefit of the community, then liability for the tort must be satisfied, first, from the separate property of the spouse committing the tort and, second, from community property. Revised C.C. 5122(b)(2).

TERMINATION OF COMMUNITY PROPERTY OWNERSHIP BY DISSOLUTION OF MARRIAGE[48] AND DEATH.

There are only three ways in which community property ownership may be terminated and, of these, one is ordinarily used only in connection with one of the others: (1) By voluntary agreement of the parties; (2) in connection with an action for dissolution of marriage or legal separation; and (3) upon death of one party. Possibility (1) usually takes the form of a "property settlement agreement" and is ordinarily found only in connection with (2). There is no right of "partition" of community property, i.e., no right of a spouse to go into court and have his one-half interest set aside as his separate property.

● In dissolution of marriage or legal separation proceedings,[49] there are two possibilities: (1) Prior to or during the dissolution or separation proceedings, the parties may enter into a property settlement agreement, which is simply a voluntary division of the community property, making part thereafter the separate property of each spouse. Such contracts are binding.[50] (2) If there is no property settlement, then the court must make an appropriate division of the community property and quasi-community property. With minor exceptions, C.C. 4800 requires the court to divide the community property and quasi-community property equally. Ordinarily, community property personal injury damages are to be assigned to the

---

[48]Until 1969, "divorce" was the proceeding in California by which a marriage was terminated. The 1969 Family Law Act abolished the terminology of "divorce" and the concept of fault in divorce was abolished by eliminating the requirement that one spouse be found responsible for the breakup of the marriage. "Dissolution of marriage" replaces "divorce." "Legal separation" is an alternative for those who, for religious or other reasons, do not wish to dissolve the marriage but who otherwise wish to end their relationship. C.C. 4506 provides that, "A court may decree a dissolution of the marriage or legal separation on either of the following grounds . . .: (1) Irreconcilable differences, which have caused the irremediable breakdown of the marriage. (2) Incurable insanity. C.C. 4507 provides that, "Irreconcilable differences are those grounds which are determined by the court to be substantial reasons for not continuing the marriage and which make it appear that the marriage should be dissolved."

[49]What is said here for marriage dissolution proceedings applies to legal separation proceedings.

[50]C.C. 4802 and 5103 recognize the validity of such contracts. The parties having as community property a house, bank account, automobile and business operated by the husband, a typical property settlement agreement might provide that the house and bank account "shall hereafter be the sole and separate property of W," and the automobile and business that of H.

C.C. 5134 requires all contracts for marriage settlements to be in writing and acknowledged.

party who suffered the injuries. C.C. 4800. If the parties have declared a homestead, C.C. 4808 states these rules for its disposition: "(a) If a homestead has been selected from the community property or the quasi-community property, it may be assigned either absolutely or for a limited period to either party, subject, in the latter case, to the future disposition of the court, be divided, or be sold and the proceeds divided. (b) If the homestead has been selected from the separate property of either, it shall be assigned to the former owner of such property, subject to the power of the court to assign it to the other party for a limited period not to exceed the life of such party."

C.C. 4800.1 provides that, for the purposes of division of property on dissolution of marriage or legal separation, property held in joint tenancy shall be presumed to be community property. Section 4800.1 goes on to provide that the presumption may be rebutted by "(a) (a) clear statement in the deed or other documentary evidence of title by which the property is acquired that the property is separate property and not community property; (b) (p)roof that the parties have made a written agreement that the property is separate property." A companion section, C.C. 4800.2 enacted in 1983, is designed to protect a spouse who has put separate property funds into the acquisition of community property. Section 4800.2 provides that upon the division of community property on dissolution of marriage or legal separation, unless waived, a spouse who has contributed separate property to the acquisition of the community property shall be reimbursed for such contribution and that "contributions to the acquisition of the property" shall "include downpayments, payments for improvements, and payments that reduce the principal of a loan used to finance the purchase or improvement of the property." Section 4800.2 represents an important change in California law which, prior to the adoption of Section 4800.2, presumed that separate property contributions to the acquisition of community property were intended as gifts to the community property.

● Each spouse has the right to dispose of one-half of the community property by will. If this is not done, the share of the spouse who dies without leaving a will goes to the surviving spouse.[51] Disposition of separate property is discussed in a later section.[52]

Joint Tenancy vs. Community Property

A question of practical importance arises as to whether a husband and wife should hold real property in joint tenancy or as community property. Some amount of background is necessary to appreciate the problem. It is only when a person continues to be the owner of property at and through the moment of death that he leaves an *estate*, and it is only when a person leaves an estate that a *probate proceeding* is necessary after death, the probate proceeding being the method by which the property which constitutes the estate is transmitted to those entitled to it after the death of the owner. It is part of the *right of survivorship* theory of joint tenancy that the interest of the joint tenant who dies passes to the survivor at the *exact moment* of death and that, therefore, he leaves no estate to be probated. Community property, on the other hand, is owned

through the moment of death and so constitutes *estate*. Until 1975, community property, like other property owned through the moment of death, had to go through probate to get to the wife if the husband died and so bore the expense and delay of probate proceedings, which joint tenancy property escaped. Coordinately with the new, equal management rules, seen above, the California Legislature adopted new Probate Code rules (Sections 650-659) whereby community property, and more recently quasi-community property, was permitted to pass without probate proceedings.

● *However, important tax considerations are involved in determining how to hold title to marital property, especially in view of the dramatic increases in real estate values in recent years, and legal counsel should be obtained in every case.*

Property Rights in Nonmarital Relationships

In the widely reported "palimony" case of *Marvin* v. *Marvin* (1976) 18 Cal.3d 660, 134 Cal.Rptr. 815, 557 P.2d 106, plaintiff Michelle Marvin brought an action against defendant Lee Marvin, with whom plaintiff had lived for approximately six years. Plaintiff alleged "that she and defendant entered into an oral agreement that during the time they lived together they would combine their efforts and earnings and share equally property acquired and that plaintiff would render services to defendant as companion, housekeeper and cook, give up her career as an entertainer and that defendant would support her for life." The question was the enforceability of such an agreement. The California Supreme Court held that such agreements were enforceable so long as they were not "expressly and inseparably based upon an illicit consideration of sexual services," and that if they were not, they would "fail only to the extent that they rest(ed) upon a consideration of meretricious sexual services." Justice Tobriner, who wrote the opinion in *Marvin* had these things to say about changing times:

"In summary, we believe that the prevalance of nonmarital relationships in modern society and the social acceptance of them, marks this as a time when our courts should by no means apply the doctrine of the unlawfulness of the so-called meretricious relationship to the instant case. As we have explained, the nonenforceability of agreements expressly providing for meretricious conduct rested upon the fact that such conduct, as the word suggests, pertained to and encompassed prostitution. To equate the nonmarital relationship of today to such a subject matter is to do violence to an accepted and wholly different practice.

"We are aware that many young couples live together without the solemnization of marriage, in order to make sure that they can successfully later undertake marriage. This trial period, preliminary to marriage, serves as some assurance that the marriage will not subsequently end in dissolution to the harm of both parties. We are aware, as we have stated, of the pervasiveness of nonmarital relationships in other situations.

"The mores of the society have indeed changed so radically in regard to cohabitation that we cannot impose a standard based on alleged moral considerations that have apparently been so widely abandoned by so many. Lest we be misunderstood, however, we take this occasion to point out that the structure of society itself largely depends upon the institution of marriage, and nothing we have said in this opinion should be taken to derogate from that institution. The joining of the man and woman in marriage is at once the most socially productive and individually fulfilling relationship that one can enjoy in the course of a lifetime."

---

[51]Prob. C. 201: "Upon the death of either husband or wife, onehalf of the community property belongs to the surviving spouse; the other half is subject to the testamentary disposition of the decedent, and in the absence thereof goes to the surviving spouse. . . ."

[52]See page 230.

• At various California lower court levels, attempts have been or are being made to extend the principles of the *Marvin* case to homosexual and lesbian relationships.

• Most recently, in *Butcher* v. *Super. Ct.* (1983) 139 C.A.3d 58, 188 Cal.Rptr. 503, it was held that a "spouse" in a nonmarital cohabitation arrangement could sue for loss of consortium when the other "spouse" was injured by a third party. Ironically, the quite ancient concept of a right to "consortium" laid in the very sexist notion that the wife was a servant or chattel of the husband and that injury to the wife deprived the husband of his property rights in the services and society of the wife. The court in *Butcher* said that we no longer hold such an archaic view of the concept of consortium but rather regard it as a "relational interest" and that "interference with the continuance of the relation (whether it be between a married or unmarried couple) may be redressed by a tort action."

Even more recently, however, another California court of appeal held to the contrary in *Butcher*. In *Hendrix* v. *General Motors Corp.* (1983), 146 C.A.3d 296, 193 Cal.Rptr. 922 a prospective wife living with her prospective husband sought to recover on the theory of loss of consortium for injuries suffered by the prospective husband in an automobile accident. The court denied recovery. It pointed out that at common law an action for loss of consortium required a legal marriage; that the "cause of action for loss of consortium presupposes that upon entry into a marriage a party is entitled to expect not only financial support or services but also comfort, companionship, sexual relations and more (and that) injury to one spouse thus interferes with the other spouse's enjoyment of these benefits;" that "marriage continues to be the foundation of this nation's family life . . . the basic unit of social order;" that "a cause of action for loss of consortium (should not be permitted) whenever there is (an) injury to a legally recognized relationship;" that " '(s)ocial policy must at some point intervene to delimit liability';" and that (a)bsent legislative authority, we think the line must be drawn to exclude a nonmarital cohabitant." The California Supreme Court has granted a petition to hear the *Hendrix* case.

Condominiums

California passed a condominium ("own your own apartment") law in 1963. Major provisions are as follows:
• A *condominium* is an estate in real property, in fee, for life, or for years, which consists of a common interest in the land and the common areas of the condominium project (stairways, halls, etc.) and a separate and exclusive interest in the airspace occupied or to be occupied by the condominium owner. C.C. 783, 1353. A "condominium" is the composite of these rights of its owner. A "unit" is part of a condominium, the area, above, in which the condominium owner has a separate and exclusive interest. A "project" is the total of the individual condominiums that go to make up the building. C.C. 1350.
• Having exclusive rights within his unit, the condominium owner may decorate it as he pleases. C.C. 1353.
• The condominium owner has an easement in the common areas of the project, that is, stairways, halls, etc. C.C. 1353.
• To qualify property as a condominium project, there must be previously recorded a diagrammatic plan of the project and certificates of the owner of the property and persons, if any, having security interests therein, consenting to such recordation. C.C. 1351.
• C.C. 1355 provides that prior to sale of condominiums within a project a declaration of restrictions relating to the project must be recorded, which may provide, among other things:

(a) For the management of the project by one or more of the following management bodies: the condominium owners, a board of governors elected by the owners, or a management agent elected by the owners or the board or named in the declaration; for voting majorities, quorums, notices, meeting dates, and other rules governing such body or bodies; and for recordation from time to time, as provided for in the declaration, of certificates of identity of the persons then composing such management body or bodies, which certificates shall be conclusive evidence thereof in favor of any person relying thereon in good faith.

(b) As to any such management body:

(1) For the powers thereof, including power to enforce the provisions of the declaration of restrictions;

(2) For maintenance by it of fire, casualty, liability, workers' compensation and other insurance insuring condominium owners, and for bonding of the members of any management body;

(3) For provision by it of and payment by it for maintenance, utility, gardening and other services benefiting the common areas; for employment of personnel necessary for operation of the building, and legal and accounting services;

(4) For purchase by it of materials, supplies and the like and for maintenance and repair of the common areas;

(5) For payment by it of taxes and special assessments which would be a lien upon the entire project or common areas, and for discharge by it of any lien or encumbrance levied against the entire project or common areas;

(6) For payment by it for reconstruction of any portion or portions of the project damaged or destroyed;

(7) For delegation by it of its powers;

(8) For entry by it or its agents into any unit when necessary in connection with maintenance or construction for which such body is responsible;

(9) For an irrevocable power of attorney to the management body to sell the entire project for the benefit of all of the owners thereof when partition of the project may be had under Section 1354 of the Code of Civil Procedure, which said power shall: (i) be binding upon all of the owners, whether they assume the obligations of the restrictions or not; (ii) if so provided in the declaration, be exercisable by less than all (but not less than a majority) of the management body; (iii) be exercisable only after recordation of a certificate by those who have power to exercise it that said power is properly exercisable hereunder, which certificate shall be conclusive evidence thereof in favor of any person relying thereon in good faith.

(c) For amendments of such restrictions, which amendments, if reasonable and made upon vote or consent of not less than a majority in interest of the owners in the project given after reasonable notice, shall be binding upon every owner and every condominium subject thereto whether the burdens thereon are increased or decreased thereby, and whether the owner of each and every condominium consents thereto or not.

(d) For independent audit of the accounts of any management body.

(e) (1) For reasonable assessments to meet authorized expenditures of any management body, and for a reasonable method for notice and levy thereof, each condominium to be assessed separately for its share of such expenses in proportion (unless otherwise provided) to its owner's fractional interest in any common areas; (2) For the subordination of the liens securing such assessments to other liens either generally or specifically described.

(f) For the conditions upon which partition may be had of the project pursuant to Section 1354 of the Code of Civil Procedure. Such right to partition may be conditioned upon failure of the condominium owners to elect to rebuild within a certain period, specified inadequacy of insurance proceeds, specified damage to the building, a decision of an arbitrator, or upon any other reasonable condition.

• C.C. 1356 makes an assessment under a declaration of restrictions a lien on the condominium charged, as follows: A reasonable assessment upon any condominium made in accordance with a recorded declaration of restrictions permitted by Section 1355 shall be a debt of the owner thereof at the time the assessment is made. The amount of any such assessment plus any other charges thereon, such as interest, costs (including attorneys' fees), and penalties, as such may be provided for in the declaration of restrictions, shall be and become a lien upon the condominium assessed when the management body causes to be recorded with the county recorder of the county in which such condominium is located a notice of assessment, which shall state the amount of such assessment and such other charges thereon as may be authorized by the declaration of restrictions, a description of the condominium against which the same has been assessed, and the name of the record owner thereof. Such notice shall be signed by an authorized representative of the management body or as otherwise provided in the declaration of restrictions. Upon payment of said assessment and charges in connection with which such notice has been so recorded, or other satisfaction thereof, the management body shall cause to be recorded a further notice stating the satisfaction and the release of the lien thereof.

Such lien shall be prior to all other liens recorded subsequent to the recordation of said notice of assessment except that the declaration of restrictions may provide for the subordination thereof to any other liens and encumbrances. Unless sooner satisfied and released or the enforcement thereof initiated as hereafter provided such lien shall expire and be of no further force or effect one year from the date of recordation of said notice of assessment; provided, however, that said one-year period may be extended by the management body for not to exceed one additional year by recording a written extension thereof.

Such lien may be enforced by sale by the management body, its attorney or other person authorized to make the sale, after failure of the owner to pay such an assessment in accordance with its terms, such sale to be conducted in accordance with the provisions of Sections 2924, 2924b and 2924c of the Civil Code, applicable to the exercise of powers of sale in mortgages and deeds of trust, or in any other manner permitted by law. Unless otherwise provided in the declaration of restrictions, the management body shall have power to bid in the condominium at foreclosure sale and to hold, lease, mortgage and convey the same.

• C.C. 1357 relieves a condominium owner from mechanic's lien liability for work done on other condominiums, but makes each condominium liable pro tanto and subject to lien for work done in common areas under the authority of the management body.

• With respect to property taxation, Revenue & Taxation Code 2188.3 provides that (a) each condominium owned in fee shall be separately assessed to the owner thereof, and the tax on each such condominium shall constitute a lien solely thereon; (b) each condominium not owned in fee shall be separately assessed, as if it were owned in fee, to the owner of the condominium or the owner of the fee or both (and the tax on each such condominium shall be a lien solely on the interest of the owner of the fee in the real property included in such condominium and on such condominium), if so agreed by the assessor in a writing of record; such an agreement shall be binding upon such assessor and his successors in office with respect to such project so long as it continues to be divided into condominiums in the same manner as that in effect when the agreement was made.

• The partition referred to in C.C. 1355(b)(9), above, requires a showing that (1) three years after damage or destruction to the project which renders a material part thereof unfit for its use prior thereto, the project has not been rebuilt or repaired substantially to its state prior to its damage or destruction, or (2) that ¾ or more of the project has been destroyed or substantially damaged, and that condominium owners holding in aggregate more than a 50% interest in the common areas are opposed to repair or restoration of the project, or (3) that the project has been in existence in excess of 50 years, that it is obsolete and uneconomic, and that condominium owners holding in aggregate more than a 50% interest in the common areas are opposed to repair or restoration of the project, or (4) that conditions for such a partition by sale set forth in restrictions entered into with respect to such project have been met. A condominium owner may commence partition proceedings for these reasons if the management body does not. C.C.P. 1354.

Deeds

Ownership of real property may be transferred to another in two general ways or, perhaps more accurately, at two different times—during lifetime of the owner and upon his death. Deed is the method of transfer during lifetime. Upon death, ownership passes according to the will of the owner or, if he leaves no will, by rules of intestate succession, which are considered in a later section.

Nature and Types of Deeds

A *deed* may be defined as the written instrument by which an ownership interest in real property—fee simple or life estate—is transferred from one person to another during lifetime. The maker of the deed is called the grantor, the transferee of the property, the grantee.

• Deeds are of three general types—warranty, grant and quitclaim[53]—from highest to lowest in terms of liability incurred by the grantor to the grantee. Broadly speaking, a warranty deed is one in which the grantor *absolutely guarantees* title to the grantee—guarantees absolutely that title is free of defects and that there are no liens or encumbrances upon the property. A grant deed is one in which the grantor warrants only that he *knows of* no defects in his title.[54] A quitclaim deed is one in which the grantor makes *no warranties* at all concerning his title, the grantee buying at his own risk.

Warranty and Grant Deeds: Warranty and grant deeds are used in the everyday sales of real estate. In earlier days, there

(Continued on page 181)

---

[53]Deeds are sometimes called by other names, e.g., the "Joint Tenancy Grant Deed" on page 171, but this is nothing more than a grant deed to two persons in joint tenancy. And the "Gift Deed" on page 180, which is just what its name implies.

[54]This is the net result of C.C. 1113, which says that the only covenants which are to be implied in a grant deed are that "the grantor has not conveyed the same estate . . . to any person other than the grantee" and that the "estate is . . . free from encumbrances done, made, or suffered by the grantor, or any person claiming under him."

Warranty Deed

KNOW ALL MEN BY THESE PRESENTS:

That..

....

of..for and in consideration of the

sum of...DOLLARS,

to.........................in hand paid by..

....

ha............conveyed and warranted, and by these presents do............convey and warrant

unto the said...

all that certain premises situated in...County, State of Arizona,

described as follows, viz:...

....

....

....

....

....

....

....

TO HAVE AND TO HOLD, the above described premises, together with all and singular

the rights and appurtenances thereto in any wise belonging unto the said..............................

....heirs and assigns forever.

And.................... hereby bind.................... ....heirs, executors and administrators,

to warrant and forever defend, all and singular, the premises unto the said.............................

....heirs and assigns,

against every person whomsoever, lawfully claiming or to claim the same or any part thereof.

....

....

....

....

With usual covenants of warranty

Witness.......... hand......... this.......................day of........................, A. D. 19......

Signed, sealed and delivered in the presence of ⎫ ....(SEAL)

.... ⎪ ....(SEAL)

.... ⎬ ....(SEAL)

.... ⎭ ....(SEAL)

(Must be acknowledged by Notary Public.)

Quitclaim Deed

The undersigned grantor(s) declare(s):

Documentary transfer tax is $.........................

(   ) computed on full value of property conveyed, or

(   ) computed on full value less value of liens and encumbrances remaining at time of sale.

(   ) Unincorporated area: (   ) City of.., and

(   ) Realty not sold.

FOR A VALUABLE CONSIDERATION, receipt of which is hereby acknowledged,

hereby REMISE(S), RELEASE(S) AND FOREVER QUITCLAIM(S) to

the following described real property in the

County of   , State of California:

Mail tax statements to _____

Dated _____

STATE OF CALIFORNIA

COUNTY OF_____ } SS.

On_____ before me, the under-

signed, a Notary Public in and for said State, personally appeared

_____

_____

_____

_____ , known to me

to be the person_____ whose name_____ subscribed to the within

instrument and acknowledged that_____ executed the same.

WITNESS my hand and official seal.

Signature _____

_____
Name Typed or Printed)

(This area for official notorial seal)

MAIL TAX STATEMENTS AS DIRECTED ABOVE

Gift Deed

, the first part   ,

for and in consideration of the love and affection which   he   ha   for the second party   ,

does   hereby give and grant unto

, the second party   ,

all that real property situate in the

County of   , State of California, described as follows:

WITNESS............hand......this.................day of ...., 19..........

....

....

STATE OF CALIFORNIA } SS.   On.., 19........, before me, the undersigned, a Notary Public in and for said County

COUNTY OF...} and State, personally appeared...

person........ whose name...subscribed to the within instrument, and acknowledged to me that.........he......... executed the same.

NOTARY'S SIGNATURE...

TYPE OR PRINT NOTARY'S NAME...

was no such thing as the grant deed. Sales of real estate were by warranty deed, and this continues to be true today in many states. There were no title insurance companies, and the warranty deed was the grantee's only "insurance" against defects in title. There were "abstracters" who prepared abstracts of title, but this was quite different from the title insurance arrangement of today. If E wanted to buy property from R, he might hire A, an abstracter, to "search" R's title—to go through the public records and trace the complete history of the property—all deeds by which the property had been transferred from hand to hand,[55] all transfers by reason of death of an owner, all mortgages placed upon the property from time to time, all satisfactions of mortgage showing payment of mortgages, etc. A would make copies of these various documents from the first title to the property down to R, the present owner, and these, bound in chronological order, constituted the *abstract of title*. From this, E had to decide whether or not he would get clear title from R. He might consult an attorney for an opinion, or A, the abstracter, might be an attorney and give the opinion, called a *certificate of title*. It was only an opinion in any case, however. If it proved wrong, E would have no recourse against the person giving it. He would demand a warranty deed from R, therefore, to have someone from whom to recover in case the opinion was incorrect.

● Eventually the procedure was placed on a more businesslike basis by the formation of business organizations which would search title and charge a substantial fee for it but which, in return for this fee, would guarantee their work—would say in effect that "It is our opinion that you will get a clear title, and we will back this up with a guarantee. If it is determined that your title is defective in some way, we will reimburse you for damages suffered. And, further, we have established a fund of money for this purpose so that you may rest assured that you will obtain reimbursement." These business organizations became and are known as "title insurance and guaranty companies," or, more simply, as title companies, as they will be called hereafter. They issue title insurance policies by which they guarantee or insure the buyer of good title.[56] A specimen policy is on page 200.

● With the advent of title insurance, the warranty deed lost its importance. The buyer was no longer concerned with a guarantee of title from the seller. He would get title insurance and expect to look to the title company if some defect of title appeared. At this point, the grant deed replaced the warranty deed in California and some of the other states, it being fairer to the grantor than the warranty deed while at the same time satisfying the grantee's needs. A grant deed is shown on page 189.

● The original warranty deeds were quite elaborate in form, setting out in full 5 warranties of title, the sum total of which was the absolute guarantee discussed above. In modern times,

warranty deeds have been very much streamlined as shown by the one on page 178. The 5 warranties which were once set out in full in the deed are now simply implied by the provision that the deed is with "usual covenants."[57]

● Deeds may be identified by their *granting clauses* or *words of conveyance* which (1) in the warranty deed is the recital that the grantor "conveys and warrants" to the grantee; (2) in the grant deed the recital that he "grants" to the grantee or sometimes, more elaborately, that he "grants, bargains and sells;" (3) in the quitclaim deed the recital that he "quitclaims" or "remises, releases and quitclaims" to the grantee "all of his right, title and interest" in the property.

Quitclaim Deeds: These are used only for certain limited purposes: (1) Where one person is selling property of another in a public or representative capacity and, so, does not wish to incur personal liability, e.g., where a sheriff or other public official is selling property on execution sale to satisfy a judgment or at a tax sale for delinquent taxes. While these are often referred to as "sheriff's deeds" or "tax deeds," they are quitclaim deeds in form, employing the quitclaim words of conveyance or quitclaim language of sale of the "right, title and interest" of the person whose property is being sold, as discussed in the preceding paragraph. (2) The other use of quitclaim deeds is to clear up "clouds on title"—abandoned easements, boundary line disputes and the like. (See footnote 9, page 165.)

Delivery

Requirement of Unconditional Delivery: A deed is not effective until delivered and unless delivered with intention, by the delivery, to pass title immediately.[58]

The California case of *Kimbro* v. *Kimbro*, 199 C. 344, 249 P. 180, is a classic example of lack of intention to pass title despite an act of delivery. There, a wife wanted her husband to sign a deed. Finally, he said, "Well, I will sign it, but it won't benefit you any for it is not acknowledged." While the husband was in error, his words nullified the deed. He was in error because, while a deed must be acknowledged before it can be recorded, acknowledgment is not necessary to pass title. But the husband's words clearly indicated that he considered the deed to be worthless and, so, that he did not intend to pass title by it.

● More difficult cases arise, such as cases in which there is delivery of the deed to a third person. Suppose, as in *San Filippo* v. *Vita*, 80 C.A.2d 290, 186 P.2d 163, that R, owner of property, makes a deed to his son and leaves it with a realtor in an envelope with instructions that "This envelope contains papers which are to be delivered to me on demand or in event of my death then to be delivered to my son . . ." Here, R negates an intention to pass title by the delivery by reason of his reservation of right to recall the deed "on de-

---

[55]Each transfer of real property is by a new deed. There is not one deed which passes from hand to hand or is indorsed from one person to another as is sometimes believed, although this was so in the very early periods of the English law.

[56]In many states, title insurance companies have never developed, and it is unlikely that they will at this late date because of the tremendous cost that would be involved in setting up a title company "plant," which is, in effect, a complete history of every piece of property within the area in which the title company operates. In these states, the abstract or certificate of title, coupled with a warranty deed from the seller, continue to be the extent of "insurance" of title that the buyer gets.

[57]This implies 5 warranties or covenants as follows: the covenant of title (grantor has title to the property), covenant of right to convey (grantor has the right to convey the property), covenant against encumbrances (that the property is free of liens or encumbrances), covenant of quiet enjoyment (grantee shall not be disturbed in his possession or enjoyment of the premises), and covenant of general warranty (grantor will forever warrant and defend the title)—adding up to the absolute guarantee for which the warranty deed is described to stand in the text.

[58]C.C. 1054: "A grant takes effect, so as to vest the interest intended to be transferred, only upon its delivery by the grantor."

C.C. 1056: "A grant cannot be delivered to the grantee conditionally. . . ."

mand." If he dies without doing so, the document, if it is to be effective, must be made effective as a "will," because a deed is a method of transferring title during lifetime. But a will must be executed with certain formalities with which a deed is not executed so that it is not possible to treat or qualify a deed as a will. Such a deed must fail, therefore, because of lack of delivery with intention to pass title.[59]

If a right to recall the deed is not reserved, the doctrine of *Bury* v. *Young* may save the transaction. In *Bury* v. *Young*, 98 C. 446, 33 P. 338, R delivered a deed to T to be given to E upon R's death. R did not retain any right to recall the deed. The court held that this constituted an immediate transfer of the fee interest to E with a life estate reserved to R, just as though the transaction were in the form of that described in paragraph 2 on page 163; that it may be implied that such was the intention of the grantor. The doctrine of *Bury* v. *Young* is followed in states other than California and it is said to be the prevailing rule.

• Another type of transaction that occurs in this area is the *cross-deeds* transaction in which survivorship is made the condition. H and W, to avoid the necessity of probate proceedings upon the death of the one or the other, make deeds to each other of their interests in their home. The understanding is that when one dies, the survivor will record the deed given him. Here, again, there is no intention to transfer title during lifetime and no valid delivery; merely *conditional delivery.*

Escrows: There is one exception to the requirement of unconditional delivery, the delivery of a deed in escrow. This is important because it is the method of delivery in practically every transfer of real estate in modern times. Escrow operates in this manner: B wants to buy property from S but does not want to part with his money until he has had a title company examine S's title and commit itself to issuance of a title policy. The parties make a contract accordingly. B then has the title company make its title search. S deposits a deed to B with the title company to be delivered to B only at such time as the title company is prepared to deliver to S the purchase price received from B, which will be when the title search is completed and the title company has found S's title to be clear. In this general sense, S's is a conditional delivery of the deed. Such *escrows* are fully effective for all purposes,[60] and even if S dies before the title search is completed, the transaction must be consummated.

• Escrows are the mechanics of real estate transfer. An escrow comes about and operates in this manner:[61]

Buyer (B) and seller (S) are brought together by real estate broker (R), with whom S has listed the property, under a

listing such as that shown on page 184.[62] R has them execute a real estate purchase contract in the form of that shown on page 24, under which B agrees to buy, i.e., finally complete the purchase, provided he can get the requisite loan, and in which it is agreed that B shall receive clear title except for stated exceptions. This constitutes a binding contract to buy and sell and the transaction is ready to "*go into escrow.*" R opens an escrow with the title company selected for the search of S's title and issuance of a title policy.

At this point, the title company takes over as "*escrow agent*" for the parties, i.e., as agent to receive, hold and disburse the documents and moneys that must be exchanged. First, it will search S's title and issue a "*preliminary report*" of the type shown on page 185. This will set out anything that should not exist if B is to get the clear title that he is bargaining for, i.e., defects of title in the form of defective instruments or transactions in the chain of title, and liens or encumbrances of any kind against the property. In this connection suppose that J has a judgment for $20,000 against S which J has recorded; also, that M has recorded a mechanic's lien[63] against the property; that S has not mentioned either of these things. The preliminary report would disclose them, and it is against such things as these that the title company protects the buyer. As agent of B, the title company will require that these claims be paid or that an amount sufficient to pay them be withheld from the purchase price.

After completion of the preliminary search and finding that there are no defects of title so serious that they cannot be cleared, the title company will have S sign a deed to B; also, "*sellers escrow instructions*" of the type shown on page 188 by which S authorizes the title company to deliver the deed to B when it has received the purchase price.

The title company will have B pay in the cash required to be paid by B and to deliver the first and second notes and deeds of trust called for by the transaction and shown on pages 191-195. B will also sign escrow instructions, of the type on page 190 ("*buyers escrow instructions*"), authorizing the title company to pay his money to S when it has determined that S's title is clear.

The title company will then have the lender (L), California Bank here, pay or commit itself to the payment of the $149,600 on B's behalf, and L will deposit escrow instructions authorizing payment of the money paid or pledged by it when the title company has determined that S's title is clear and has received the proper note and deed of trust from B.

The escrow is now ready to be "*closed.*" The title company will do these things in connection with closing (1) Pay R his commission.[64] (2) Prepare and send closing statements to S and B to show them the disposition of funds. (3) Issue its title

---

[59]After finding that the delivery was a conditional one and not effective to pass title, the court ultimately found that title passed in the *San Filippo* case for another reason—that R had subsequently confirmed or ratified the conveyance.

[60]C.C. 1057: "A grant may be deposited by the grantor with a third person to be delivered on performance of a condition, and, on delivery by the depositary, it will take effect. While in the possession of the third person, and subject to conditions, it is called an escrow."

[61]In this hypothetical sale, the title company to issue the title insurance is made the escrow holder. This is the practice in Northern California. In Southern California, it is the practice to have a bank or escrow company act as escrow holder independently of the title insurance company whose sole function, under such practice, is to search title and provide title insurance.

[62]This is an *exclusive listing* by which the broker is given the exclusive right to sell the property for some period of time, 30, 60, 90 days. A *multiple listing,* by contrast, allows sale by a broker other than the broker who obtains the listing, with, in such case, the commission being divided on some agreed basis between the listing broker and the selling broker.

[63]A "*mechanic's lien*" is the right of anyone who performs services on real property—builds, repairs, alters, etc., the building on it—to record a lien against the property as a means of getting his money if he is not paid. It is also a lien right in favor of one who supplies materials for any such purposes, but the supplier's lien is more usually called a "materialman's lien." Further discussion of such liens is found at page 203 and in footnotes 69 and 70 on that page.

[64]Highly negotiable on California real property today.

policy insuring B of good title.[65] (4) Send the $149,600 note to L. (5) Send the deeds of trust to the county recorder's office for recording. This completes the escrow.

***Real Estate Settlement Procedures Act of 1974* (12 U.S.C.A. 2601-2616):** This Act, which immediately became known as RESPA, became operative on June 20, 1975. The Act is a form of consumer protection law, designed to do several things: To acquaint home purchasers with the nature of settlement or closing costs in connection with real estate purchases; to show them how much real interest they will be paying; and to give them an opportunity to "shop around" for the most favorable settlement charges. Basically what the Act does is to require a mortgage lender to disclose both in advance and at the time of settlement what closing costs in a particular transaction will be. However, "in advance" merely means at the time the mortgage lender makes its loan commitment. Mortgage lenders are required to provide mortgage borrowers with a booklet which explains the Act quite comprehensively, and which illustrates the disclosure forms that mortgage lenders are required to use. A copy of the disclosure statement form appears on pages 186-187.

Recording

Upon arrival at the recorder's office, the deed and deeds of trust are stamped as received for recording at the hour and minute received. Photographic copies are made. They are then bound with other similar documents in books of "Official Records" in the recorder's office, which are there for the public to inspect. By an alphabetical index, one may find the proper page of these records to consult for a particular document. Officially, recording takes effect at the moment a document is received in the recorder's office. After documents are recorded, they are returned to parties entitled to them; in this case, the deed is returned to B and the mortgage to L.

● Of what significance is *recording*? Recording gives constructive notice of the rights of persons in property.[66] It tells the world who owns the property, who has a mortgage on it, and most everything else that is to be known about the property. Everyone is bound by this information. If you buy a lot from S against which there is a judgment lien and you take a chance on buying without a title search and do not check the public records, you are "charged with" knowledge of whatever the records would have shown—have "*constructive notice*" of such information. Conversely, if you have some right in property and do not record it, your right will be cut off by a right acquired by another person without knowledge of yours—a *subsequent bona fide purchaser or encumbrancer.*"[67] To illustrate with the S-B-L case: If the title company

delivered the deed and deed of trust directly to B and L without recording, and L delayed in recording its deed of trust, B could immediately record his deed and then give a deed of trust on the property to someone else for another $50,400. This subsequent deed of trust would outrank L's deed of trust since L's deed of trust would not be discoverable upon the public records (at least if the subsequent deed of trust was recorded before L's[68]). Recording, then, is an orderly system of establishing ownership rights in and lien rights against the property. By sending the deed and deed of trust to the recorder simultaneously, the title company prevents the possibility of an occurrence of the type suggested above, and protects L's security interest in the property.

Title Insurance

When we talk about title insurance companies, it is natural to think of issuance of a title insurance policy as their important function. Actually it is not, and the fact is that the title policy is relatively unimportant. The important thing done by the title company is to search the records and discover defects of title and liens before the buyer is allowed to part with his money. Take the S-B-L case again: If B had purchased from S for $187,000 cash and had not had a title search, he would have parted with his money before discovery of the liens of J and M. B would have to pay J and M to prevent sale of the property to enforce their liens. He would have a right to recover from S— if S could be found. The title company's search saves B from this, and, again, this is the really important function of the title company. When it finally issues its policy, it is certain that S's title is clear. Title companies seldom make mistakes.

● Title insurance policies exempt themselves from liability in the types of cases set forth in Schedule B of the title policy on page 200.

● There is danger to the buyer in these exceptions. Suppose six months or a year after buying, B discovers that the house which he purchased is five feet on the neighboring lot. Its owner wishes to build and wants B to move his house back on his own lot, which will be very costly. B may believe that his title insurance will pay the cost of moving the house, but since this is a matter that can be ascertained only by a survey, it is not insured against by the policy. B has no recourse against S if S gave him a grant deed, since, assuming S did not *know* of the encroachment upon the neighboring property, S has not breached the warranty of such deed. If there seems a possibility that a house or building to be purchased encroaches on other property, the buyer should condition his purchase on a survey.

● Suppose that on January 2, 1984, S employs M, a contractor, to build a patio on his property. M starts the job on

(Continued on page 203)

---

[65]Who pays the cost of title insurance—seller or buyer—is a matter of local custom. In the San Francisco area, the buyer pays; in the Los Angeles area, the seller.

[66]C.C. 1213: "Every conveyance of real property acknowledged . . . and recorded as prescribed by law from the time it is filed with the recorder for record is constructive notice of the contents thereof to subsequent purchasers and mortgagees. . . ."

C.C. 1215: "The term 'conveyance' as used in section twelve hundred and thirteen and twelve hundred and fourteen, embraces every instrument in writing by which any estate or interest in real property is created, aliened, mortgaged, or encumbered, or by which title to any real property may be affected, except wills."

[67]C.C. 1214: "Every conveyance of real property, other than a lease for a term not exceeding one year, is void as against any subsequent purchaser or mortgagee of the same property, or any part thereof, in good faith and for a valuable consideration, whose conveyance is first duly recorded, and as against any judg-

ment affecting the title, unless such conveyance shall have been duly recorded. . . ." Note again the definition of "conveyance" in C.C. 1215 set out in footnote 66. An unrecorded deed or mortgage is good as against creditors unless the person receiving the deed or mortgage intentionally withholds it from record to deceive creditors, in which case he will be estopped to assert his rights as against creditors who rely upon the property as an asset of the debtor (grantor or mortgagor). (*Breeze* v. *Brooks*, 71 C. 169. Glenn on Creditors' Rights, pp. 162-164.)

[68]Some states, including California, protect the subsequent bona fide purchaser or encumbrancer only if he records before the prior purchaser or encumbrancer. These are called "race" ("race to the recorder's office") statutes. See C.C. 1214 in footnote 67.

EXCLUSIVE AUTHORIZATION AND RIGHT TO SELL

THIS IS INTENDED TO BE A LEGALLY BINDING AGREEMENT— READ IT CAREFULLY.
CALIFORNIA ASSOCIATION OF REALTORS® STANDARD FORM

1. **Right to Sell.** I hereby employ and grant _____ ACME REALTY CO. _____ hereinafter called "Agent," the exclusive and irrevocable right commencing on _____ February 8 _____, 19 84 _____, and expiring at midnight on _____ May 8 _____, 19 84 _____, to sell or exchange the real property situated in _____ the City and _____, County of _____ San Francisco _____, California described as follows:

_____ 659 Monterey Avenue, San Francisco, California _____

2. **Terms of Sale.** The purchase price shall be $ 187,000.00 _____, to be paid in the following terms:
_____ All cash to sellers _____

(a) The following items of personal property are to be included in the above-stated price:
_____ None _____

(b) Agent is hereby authorized to accept and hold on my behalf a deposit upon the purchase price.

(c) Evidence of title to the property shall be in the form of a California Land Title Association Standard Coverage Policy of Title Insurance in the amount of the selling price to be paid for by _____ Buyer _____

(d) I warrant that I am the owner of the property or have the authority to execute this agreement. I hereby authorize a FOR SALE sign to be placed on my property by Agent. I authorize the Agent named herein to cooperate with sub-agents.

3. **Notice: The amount or rate of real estate commissions is not fixed by law. They are set by each broker individually and may be negotiable between the seller and broker.**

Compensation to Agent. I hereby agree to compensate Agent as follows:

(a) _____ 6 _____ % of the selling price if the property is sold during the term hereof, or any extension thereof, by Agent, on the terms herein set forth or any other price and terms I may accept, or through any other person, or by me, or _____ 6 _____ % of the price shown in 2, if said property is withdrawn from sale, transferred, conveyed, leased without the consent of Agent, or made unmarketable by any voluntary act during the term hereof or any extension thereof.

(b) the compensation provided for in subparagraph (a) above if property is sold, conveyed or otherwise transferred within _____ 90 _____ _____ days after the termination of this authority or any extension thereof to anyone with whom Agent has had negotiations prior to final termination, provided I have received notice in writing, including the names of the prospective purchasers, before or upon termination of this agreement or any extension hereof. However, I shall not be obligated to pay the compensation provided for in subparagraph (a) if a valid listing agreement is entered into during the term of said protection period with another licensed real estate broker and a sale, lease or exchange of the property is made during the term of said valid listing agreement.

4. If action be instituted to enforce this agreement, the prevailing party shall receive reasonable attorney's fees and costs as fixed by the Court.

5. In the event of an exchange, permission is hereby given Agent to represent all parties and collect compensation or commissions from them, provided there is full disclosure to all principals of such agency. Agent is authorized to divide with other agents such compensation or commissions in any manner acceptable to them.

6. I agree to save and hold Agent harmless from all claims, disputes, litigation, and/or judgments arising from any incorrect information supplied by me, or from any material fact known by me concerning the property which I fail to disclose.

7. This property is offered in compliance with state and federal anti-discrimination laws.

8. Other provisions:
_____ None _____

9. I acknowledge that I have read and understand this Agreement, and that I have received a copy hereof.
Dated _____ February 8 _____, 19 84 _____ San Francisco _____, California

Owner _____ s/GEORGE S. SELLER _____ Address _____ 659 Monterey Avenue _____

Owner _____ s/MARY M. SELLER _____ City, State, Phone _____ San Francisco, CA _____ 725-4321 _____

10. In consideration of the above, Agent agrees to use diligence in procuring a purchaser.
Agent _____ ACME REALTY CO. _____ Address _____ 1514 City Street _____ City _____ San Francisco, CA _____

By _____ s/MALCOLM D. BROKER _____ Phone _____ 725-0398 _____ Date _____ February 8, 1984 _____

NO REPRESENTATION IS MADE AS TO THE LEGAL VALIDITY OF ANY PROVISION OR THE ADEQUACY OF ANY PROVISION IN ANY SPECIFIC TRANSACTION. IF YOU DESIRE LEGAL ADVICE, CONSULT YOUR ATTORNEY.

To order, contact—California Association of Realtors®
525 South Virgil Avenue, Los Angeles, California 90020
Copyright © 1978 by California Association of Realtors® (Revised, 1980)   FORM A-11

Reprinted by permission, CALIFORNIA ASSOCIATION OF REALTORS. Endorsement not implied.

TITLE INSURANCE COMPANY

PRELIMINARY REPORT

Issued for the sole use of: CALIFORNIA BANK

THOMAS B. BUYER and HELEN A. BUYER

Our Order No.   123456

Reference   78135

When Replying Please Contact:
Shirley Grace

Property Address: 659 Monterey Avenue, San Francisco, California

In response to the above referenced application for a policy of title insurance, Founders Title Company hereby reports that it is prepared to issue, or cause to be issued, as of the date hereof, a Policy or Policies of Title Insurance describing the land and the estate or interest therein hereinafter set forth, insuring against loss which may be sustained by reason of any defect, lien or encumbrance not shown or referred to as an Exception below or not excluded from coverage pursuant to the printed Schedules, Conditions and Stipulations of said policy forms.

The printed Exceptions and Exclusions from the coverage of said Policy or Policies are set forth in Schedule I and Schedule I (continued) attached. Copies of the Policy forms should be read. They are available from the office which issued this report.

This report (and any supplements or amendments hereto) is issued solely for the purpose of facilitating the issuance of a policy of title insurance and no liability is assumed hereby. If it is desired that liability be assumed prior to the issuance of a policy of title insurance, a Binder or Commitment should be requested.

Dated as of _____February 9_____, 1984, at 7:30 A.M.

TITLE INSURANCE COMPANY

_____XXXXXXXXXXXXXXX_____
Title Officer

The form of policy of title insurance contemplated by this report is:
a California Land Title Association Standard Coverage Policy-1973, owner's policy; and an American Land Title Association Loan Policy-1970 with A.L.T.A. Endorsement Form 1 Coverage(Ammended 10-17-70), loan policy.

The estate or interest in the land hereinafter described or referred to covered by this Report is: a fee

Title to said estate or interest at the date hereof is vested in:

GEORGE S. SELLER and MARY M. SELLER, his wife

The land referred to in this Report is situated in the State of California/County of   City and San Francisco
and is described as follows:

Lot 4 in Block 20, as designated on the map entitled "Twin Peaks Tract, City and County of San Francisco, State of California", filed in the Office of the Recorder of the City and County of San Francisco, State of California, on August 5, 1909, in Volume 3 of Maps, at page 8.

At the date hereof exceptions to coverage in addition to the Exceptions and Exclusions in said policy form would be as follows:

Deed of trust securing payment of $35,000.00 and other obligations from GEORGE S. SELLER and MARY M. SELLER, his wife, to TITLE INSURANCE COMPANY, trustee, and CITY NATIONAL BANK, beneficiary, dated March 10, 1971, and recorded March 14, 1971, recorded in Book 6150, at page 82, Official Records of the County Recorder of the City and County of San Francisco.

PAGE 1

A. U.S. DEPARTMENT OF HOUSING AND URBAN DEVELOPMENT SETTLEMENT STATEMENT	B. TYPE OF LOAN

TITLE INSURANCE COMPANY

B. TYPE OF LOAN

1. ☐ FHA   2. ☐ FMHA   3. ☐ CONV. UNINS.

4. ☐ VA   5. ☒ CONV. INS.

6. FILE NUMBER: 7. LOAN NUMBER:

8. MORT. INS. CASE NO.:

C. NOTE: This form is furnished to give you a statement of actual settlement costs. Amounts paid to and by the settlement agent are shown. Items marked "(p.o.c.)" were paid outside the closing; they are shown here for informational purposes and are not included in the totals.

D. NAME OF BORROWER:	E. NAME OF SELLER:	F. NAME OF LENDER:
THOMAS B. BUYER HELEN A. BUYER	GEORGE S. SELLER MARY M. SELLER	CALIFORNIA BANK

G. PROPERTY LOCATION:	H. SETTLEMENT AGENT: TITLE INSURANCE COMPANY	I. SETTLEMENT DATE:
659 Monterey Avenue San Francisco, CA 94105	PLACE OF SETTLEMENT: San Francisco, CA	March 23, 1984

J. SUMMARY OF BORROWER'S TRANSACTION:		K. SUMMARY OF SELLER'S TRANSACTION:	
100. GROSS AMOUNT DUE FROM BORROWER		400. GROSS AMOUNT DUE TO SELLER	
101. Contract sales price	187,000.00	401. Contract sales price	187,000.00
102. Personal property		402. Personal property	
103. Settlement charges to borrower (line 1400)	4,295.50	403.	
104.		404.	
105.		405.	
Adjustments for items paid by seller in advance		Adjustments for items paid by seller in advance	
107. County/taxes 3/23/84 to 7/1/84	509.04	407. County/taxes 3/23/84 to 7/1/84	509.04
108. Assessments to		408. Assessments to	
109.		409.	
110.		410.	
111.		411.	
112.		412.	
113		413	
114		414	
120. GROSS AMOUNT DUE FROM BORROWER	191,804.54	420. GROSS AMOUNT DUE TO SELLER	187,509.04
200. AMOUNTS PAID BY OR IN BEHALF OF BORROWER		500. REDUCTIONS IN AMOUNT DUE TO SELLER	
201. Deposit or earnest money	23,504.54	502. Settlement charges to seller (line 1400)	13,619.00
202. Principal amount of new loan(s)	149,600.00	503. Existing loan(s) taken subject to	
203. Existing loan(s) taken subject to		504. Payoff of first mortgage loan *	29,009.00
204. Prin. amount of new 2nd loan	18,700.00	505. Payoff of second mortgage loan *	
205.		506. Mortgage loan to Borrower 2nd	18,700.00
206.		507.	
207.		508.	
208.		509.	
209.			
Adjustments for items unpaid by seller		Adjustments for items unpaid by seller	
211 County taxes to		511. County taxes to	
212. Assessments to		512. Assessments to	
213.		513.	
214.		514.	
215.		515.	
216.		516.	
217.		517.	
218		518	
219		519	
220. TOTAL PAID BY/FOR BORROWER	191,804.54	520. TOTAL REDUCTION AMOUNT DUE SELLER	61,328.00
300. CASH AT SETTLEMENT FROM OR TO BORROWER		600. CASH AT SETTLEMENT TO OR FROM SELLER	
301. Gross amount due from borrower (line 120)	191,804.54	601. Gross amount due to seller (line 420)	187,509.04
302. Less amounts paid by/for borrower (line 220)	(191,804.54)	602. Less reduction amount due seller (line 520)	(61,328.00)
303. CASH (☐ FROM) (☐ TO) BORROWER	--	603. CASH (☒ TO) (☐ FROM) SELLER	126,181.04

* See Page 2 for Breakdown of these items

(Form continued on following page)

PAGE 2

L. SETTLEMENT CHARGES		PAID FROM BORROWER'S FUNDS AT SETTLEMENT	PAID FROM SELLER'S FUNDS AT SETTLEMENT
700.	TOTAL SALES/BROKER'S COMMISSION based on price $ 187,000.00 @ 6 %		
	Division of commission (line 700) as follows:		
701.	$ 11,220.00 to Acme Realty Co.		
702.	$ to		
703.	Commission paid at Settlement		11,220.00
704.			
800.	ITEMS PAYABLE IN CONNECTION WITH LOAN		
801.	Loan Origination Fee 1½% California Bank	2,244.00	
802.	Loan Discount %		
803.	Appraisal Fee to California Bank	100.00	
804.	Credit Report to California Bank	20.00	
805.	Lender's Inspection Fee		
806.	Mortgage Insurance Application Fee to		
807.	Assumption Fee		
808.	Tax Service Fee California Bank	28.00	
809.			
810.			
811.			
900.	ITEMS REQUIRED BY LENDER TO BE PAID IN ADVANCE		
901.	Interest from to @ $ /day		
902.	Mortgage Insurance Premium for mo. to		
903.	Hazard Insurance Premium for 1 yrs. to Northern Insurance Company	700.00	
904.	Flood Ins. Premium yrs. to		
905.	yrs. to		
906			
907.			
908.			
1000.	RESERVES DEPOSITED WITH LENDER FOR		
1001.	Hazard insurance mo. @ $ /mo.		
1004.	County property taxes mo. @ $ /mo.		
1005.	Annual assessments mo. @ $ /mo.		
1006.	mo. @ $ /mo.		
1007.	mo. @ $ /mo.		
1100.	TITLE CHARGES		
1101.	Settlement or closing fee to Title Insurance Company	288.35	
1102.	Abstract or title search to		
1103.	Title examination to		
1104.	Title insurance binder to		
1105.	Document preparation to Title Insurance Company	20.00	10.00
1106.	Notary fees to Title Insurance Company	15.00	10.00
1107.	Attorney's fees to		
	(includes above items No.:)		
1108.	Title insurance to Title Insurance Company	770.15	
	(includes above items No.: 1102 and 1103)		
1109.	Lender's coverage $ 116.40		
1110.	Owner's coverage $ 653.75		
1111.			
1112.			
1113.			
1114.			
1200.	GOVERNMENT RECORDING AND TRANSFER CHARGES request for notice $4.00		
1201.	Recording fees: Deed $ 4.00 ; Mortgage $ 12.00 ; Releases $ 4.00	20.00	4.00
1202.	City/county tax/stamps: Deed $ 935.00 : Mortgage $		935.00
1204.			
1205.			
1206			
1300.	ADDITIONAL SETTLEMENT CHARGES		
1302.	Pest inspection to Bugg Pest Control	90.00	
1303.	Reconveyance fee to Title Insurance Company		40.00
1304.	Held in escrow for termite work		1,400.00
1305.			
1306			
1307			
1308			
1309			
1310			
1311			
1400.	TOTAL SETTLEMENT CHARGES (enter on lines 103 and 502, Sections J and K)	4,295.50	13,619.00

SELLER'S INSTRUCTIONS

TITLE INSURANCE COMPANY OF

Office _____ Phone No. _____

Property Address _____ 659 Monterey Avenue _____ Escrow No. ____ 123456 ____

_____ San Francisco, CA 94105 _____ Date _____ 3/4/84 _____

The following are handed to you herewith, and you are authorized to deliver or record them when you can comply with the instructions herein. From the amounts due seller you are authorized, as required, to pay or deduct all debits against seller in accordance with the Seller's Statement included herein.

Deed to ___ Thomas B. Buyer and Helen A. Buyer, his wife ___ describing the property covered in the above referenced escrow. ___

As of _____ closing _____ prorate on the basis of a 30 day month: ☒ Taxes (Based on the most recent tax bill available)

  Assessments   ☐ Fire insurance premiums (if acceptable to buyer); ☐ Interest on existing loan; ☐ Mortgage insurance; ☐ Rents;

☐ Credit existing loan trust funds, if any, to seller. ☐ _____

ADDITIONAL INSTRUCTIONS:

Funds withheld from seller for termite work to be released upon receipt of notice of completion.

Obtain 2nd Note and 2nd Deed of Trust from buyer to seller for $ 18,700.00 _____ naming Payee and Beneficiary as _____
George S. Seller and Mary M. Seller, his wife

_____ , said Note shall be payable $ 187.00 _____ or more per month plus/ including (strike one) interest at ___ 12%
per cent per annum from ___ date of closing ___. The first payment shall be due ___ 30 days after closing of escrow. ___
Due in full: ___ April 30, 1989. Title company to complete terms of note at closing

Record said Deed of Trust when you can issue your Standard Form Title Insurance Policy to said seller showing said Deed of Trust subject to the exceptions in your Preliminary Report which are to be shown in buyer's Title Insurance Policy, and any other Deeds of Trust of buyer securing principal amounts not to exceed a total of $ _____ , and the following: _____

	SELLER'S STATEMENT ITEMS	CHARGES	CREDITS	
(1)	SALE PRICE		187,000.00	(1)
(2)				(2)
(3)	EXISTING LOAN BALANCE TO: ( ) Pay			(3)
(4)	INTEREST @ FROM TO			(4)
(5)	INTEREST @ FROM TO			(5)
(6)	PREPAYMENT CHARGE			(6)
(7)	RECONVEYANCE/FORWARDING FEE			(7)
(8)	LOAN TRUST FUND			(8)
(9)				(9)
(10)				(10)
(11)	DEMAND OF: City National Bank	29,009.00		(11)
(12)				(12)
(13)				(13)
(14)				(14)
(15)				(15)
(16)	LOAN DISCOUNT FEE (POINTS)			(16)
(17)	DEED OF TRUST (Buyer to Seller) (2nd)	18,700.00		(17)
(18)	TRANSFER TAX (X) CITY (X) COUNTY	935.00		(18)
(19)	PREPARING DOCUMENTS $ 10.00 NOTARY FEES $ 10.00	20.00		(19)
(20)	RECONVEYANCE FEES	40.00		(20)
(21)	RECORDING	4.00		(21)
(22)	ESCROW AND/OR TITLE FEES			(22)
(23)	TERMITE REPORT			(23)
(24)	TERMITE WORK Bugg Pest Control	1,400.00		(24)
(25)	COMMISSION TO: Acme Realty Co. (6%)	11,220.00		(25)
(26)				(26)
(27)	PAY ASSESSMENT			(27)
(28)	PRO RATA ASSESSMENT			(28)
(29)	PAY TAXES			(29)
(30)	PRO RATA TAXES as of closing		509.04	(30)
(31)	PRO RATA INSURANCE			(31)
(32)	PRO RATA MORTGAGE INSURANCE			(32)
(33)	PRO RATA INTEREST			(33)
(34)	RENTAL DEPOSITS			(34)
(35)	PRO RATA RENTS			(35)
(36)	Title company to record a request for notice of default			(36)
(37)	and sale for the undersigned at closing at buyer's expense.			(37)
(38)				(38)
(39)	ESTIMATED BALANCE TO SELLER	126,181.04		(39)
(40)	TOTALS	187,509.04	187,509.04	(40)

These instructions shall remain in full force and effect until rescinded in writing. See reverse hereof for additional escrow provisions.

Sellers _____ s/GEORGE S. SELLER _____ Sellers _____ s/MARY M. SELLER _____

Received ___ March 4, 1984 _____ Address ___ 659 Monterey Avenue _____
    TITLE INSURANCE COMPANY   San Francisco, CA 94105
By: _____ s/JOHN A. COUNTERMAN Telephone ___ 725-4321 _____

OFC - 1045 - Rev. 5/77

Grant Deed

The undersigned grantor(s) declare(s):

Documentary transfer tax is $..935..00......

(X) computed on full value of property conveyed, or

(   ) computed on full value less value of liens and encumbrances remaining at time of sale.

(   ) Unincorporated area: (X) City of........................San Francisco........................,

(   ) Realty not sold.

FOR A VALUABLE CONSIDERATION, receipt of which is hereby acknowledged,

> GEORGE S. SELLER and MARY M. SELLER, his wife

hereby GRANT(S) to

> THOMAS B. BUYER and HELEN A. BUYER, his wife

that property in   San Francisco   County, State of California, described
as:

> Lot 4 in Block 20, as designated on the map entitled "Twin Peaks Tract,
> City and County of San Francisco, State of California", filed in the
> office of the Recorder of the City and County of San Francisco, State
> of California, on August 5, 1909, in Volume 3 of Maps, at page 8.

Mail tax statements to___Thomas B. Buyer and Helen A. Buyer, 659 Monterey Avenue
                                                       San Francisco, CA 94105

Date _____March 4, 1984_____   _____

                                              _____s/GEORGE S. SELLER_____

                                              _____s/MARY M. SELLER_____

                                              _____

STATE OF CALIFORNIA
                                    } ss.
COUNTY OF _San Francisco_____

On this _4th_ day of __March____, in the year 19_84_, before me, the undersigned, a Notary Public in and for said State,

personally appeared ___George S. Seller and Mary M. Seller, his wife,_____

_____

personally known to me (or proved to me on the basis of satisfactory evidence) to be the person whose name is subscribed to the within

instrument, and acknowledged to me that _the_ executed it.

WITNESS my hand and official seal.

                                    _____s/NANCY N. NOTARY_____
                                    Notary Public in and for said State.

MAIL TAX STATEMENTS AS DIRECTED ABOVE

BUYER'S INSTRUCTIONS

FOUNDERS TITLE COMPANY

Office _____   Phone No. _____

Property Address _____ 659 Monterey Avenue _____   Escrow No. ____ 123456 _____

San Francisco, CA 94105   Date _____ 3/4/84 _____

The following are handed to you herewith: ☒ _____

☒ Note and 2nd ☒ deed of trust from buyer for $ __18,700.00__   Payable to: __George S. Seller and Mary M. Seller,__

☐ Note and ☐ deed of trust from buyer for $ _____   Payable to: ____ his wife

Title Company is authorized and instructed to fill in dates on the last above mentioned Note as follows: Interest to commence __close of escrow__
@ ___12___ % per annum. First payment due ____30 days after close of escrow____ in the amount of $ __187.00__
or more per month. Final payment due __April 30, 1989. Title company to complete terms of note at closing.__

You are authorized to deliver all of said documents and disburse all of said funds, together with the proceeds of any loan deposited with you, in accordance with the instructions herein, and the buyer's statement included herein, when you can provide a Title Insurance Company of Minnesota _____ CLTA Standard
_____ Form Title Insurance Policy in the amount of $__187,000__ insuring title to the property described in your report under the above number to be vested of record
in _____ Thomas B. Buyer and Helen A. Buyer, his wife
subject to the printed provisions, exceptions and stipulations in said Policy, and subject to: _____

☒ Taxes for the year 19 _83_ - 19 _84_. both installments paid.
☒ Supplemental Taxes accrued for the year 19 _83_ - 19 _84_ if any.
☐ Assessments not delinquent, and Covenants, Conditions, Restrictions, Rights of Way, Easements and Reservations shown in your Title Report.
☐ Existing   ☒ New Deed of Trust in favor of __California Bank $149,600.00__
☐ Existing 2nd ☒ New Deed of Trust in favor of __seller $18,700.00__
☐ _____

As of ____ closing ____ prorate on the basis of a 30 day month: ☒ Taxes (Based on the most recent tax bill available)
☐ Assessments;   ☐ Fire Insurance premiums; ☐ Interest on existing loans; ☐ Mortgage insurance ☐ Credit
existing loan trust funds, if any, to seller. ☐ Rents _____

ADDITIONAL INSTRUCTIONS:

	BUYER'S STATEMENT ITEMS	CHARGES	CREDITS	
(1)	PURCHASE PRICE	187,000.00		(1)
(2)	DEPOSIT		1,000.00	(2)
(3)	EXISTING LOAN			(3)
(4)	LOAN TRUST FUND			(4)
(5)	ASSUMPTION/FORWARDING FEE			(5)
(6)				(6)
(7)	FIRST DEED OF TRUST TO: California Bank LOAN #		149,600.00	(7)
(8)	INTEREST @ From to $			(8)
(9)	LOAN FEE $ 2,244.00			(9)
(10)	TAX SERVICE FEE $ 28.00 MORTGAGE INS. $			(10)
(11)	TAX RESERVES $ INSURANCE RESERVE $			(11)
(12)	CREDIT REPORT $ 20.00 APPRAISAL FEE $ 100.00	2,392.00		(12)
(13)				(13)
(14)				(14)
(15)				(15)
(16)				(16)
(17)	DEED OF TRUST 2nd to seller		18,700.00	(17)
(18)	CITY CONVEYANCE TAX			(18)
(19)	PREPARING DOCUMENTS $ 20.00 NOTARY FEES $ 15.00	35.00		(19)
(20)	RECORDING FEES	20.00		(20)
(21)	ESCROW FEE	288.35		(21)
(22)	TITLE INSURANCE CLTA $ 653.75 ALTA $ 116.40	770.15		(22)
(23)	ENDORSEMENT INSPECTION			(23)
(24)	TERMITE REPORT Bugg Pest Control TERMITE WORK	90.00		(24)
(25)	NEW FIRE INSURANCE POLICY (homeowners)	700.00		(25)
(26)	PAY ASSESSMENT			(26)
(27)	PRO RATA ASSESSMENT			(27)
(28)	PAY TAXES			(28)
(29)	PRO RATA TAXES as of closing	509.04		(29)
(30)	PRO RATA INSURANCE			(30)
(31)	PRO RATA MORTGAGE INSURANCE			(31)
(32)	PRO RATA INTEREST			(32)
(33)	RENTAL DEPOSITS			(33)
(34)	PRO RATA RENTS			(34)
(35)				(35)
(36)				(36)
(37)				(37)
(38)				(38)
(39)	ESTIMATED FUNDS DUE TO CLOSE (Enclosed Herewith)		22,504.54	(39)
(40)	TOTALS	191,804.54	191,804.54	(40)

These instructions shall remain in full force and effect until rescinded in writing. See reverse hereof for additional escrow provisions.

Buyers _____ s/THOMAS B. BUYER _____   Buyers _____ s/HELEN A. BUYER _____

_____

Received _____ March 4, 1984 _____   Address _____ 1402 Carmel Drive _____
TITLE INSURANCE COMPANY   _____ San Francisco, CA 94104 _____
By: _____ s/JOHN A. COUNTERMAN _____   Telephone _____ 726-7890 _____

OFC - 1044

NOTE

No. _____5432_____ $ _149,600.00_____

San Francisco, California, _____March 4, 1984_____

For Value Received, the undersigned, jointly and severally, hereby promise to pay to the order of CALIFORNIA BANK,

a California banking corporation, the sum of _One Hundred forty-nine thousand six hundred and_

_no/100 ---------------_ Dollars with interest thereon from date until paid at the rate of _____

per centum per annum, principal and interest, being payable in lawful money of the United States of America in the manner and at the times following, to wit:

An installment of _Eighteen Hundred ninety-one and 62/100 ------------_ Dollars, on the

___15___ day of _____April, 1984_____ , an equal installment of _Eighteen Hundred ninety-one_

and 62/100 ------------------ Dollars on the ___15___ day of each and every succeeding month thereafter

until the ___15___ day of _March, 2014_____ , on which day the entire unpaid balance of said principal sum with interest thereon shall be due and payable. Each of said installments when paid shall be applied by the holder hereof, first so much thereof as shall be required to the payment of interest accrued as above specified and the balance thereof to the payment of said principal sum. In case default be made in the payment of any of said installments, or in case any change is made in the title to all or any part of the property described in the Deed of Trust securing this note, the entire unpaid balance of said principal sum, together with the interest that shall have accrued thereon, shall at the election of the holder of this note become immediately due and payable, of which election notice is hereby waived. And if said interest is not paid when the same becomes due, interest on overdue interest shall thereafter be paid at the same rate.

The principal amount of this note may be prepaid in whole or in part at any time. If such prepayment or prepayments are made within five years of the date of the execution of this note, there shall be a prepayment fee equal to six months' interest on the amount prepaid in any twelve months' period which exceeds twenty per cent on the original principal amount of the loan.

If any of said installments be not paid within fifteen days from the date it becomes due, the undersigned, jointly and severally, promise to pay a reasonable late or collection charge of two percent of the amount unpaid.

In case suit is instituted to collect this note or any portion thereof, the undersigned, jointly and severally, promise to pay such additional sum as the court may adjudge reasonable as attorney's fees in said suit.

This note is secured by a Deed of Trust of even date herewith.

_____
s/THOMAS B. BUYER

_____
s/HELEN A. BUYER

This Deed of Trust, made in the State of California this   4

day of   March   , 19 84 , between

THOMAS B. BUYER and HELEN A. BUYER, his wife

as and hereinafter called Trustor;

CALIFORNIA NATIONAL BANK, a corporation

as and hereinafter called Trustees, and   CALIFORNIA BANK   ; a corporation, as and hereinafter
called Beneficiary,

WITNESSETH:

WHEREAS, Trustor is indebted to the Beneficiary in lawful money of the United States in the sum of
One Hundred forty-nine thousand six hundred ------------------ Dollars,
as evidenced by   promissory note   of even date herewith, executed by the trustor to the
beneficiary, and has agreed to pay the sum with interest to the beneficiary or order in like lawful money, according
to the terms of said note.

NOW, THEREFORE, for the purpose of securing (a) the payment of said note and all extensions or renewals
thereof (b) the payment of all sums hereafter loaned by Beneficiary to Trustor or any successor in interest of the
Trustor with interest thereon (c) any present or future demands of any kind or nature which the Beneficiary or its
successor may have against the Trustor or any successor in interest of the Trustor, whether created directly or acquired
by assignment, whether absolute or contingent, whether due or not, whether otherwise secured or not or whether
existing at the time of the execution of this instrument, or arising thereafter (d) the payment of all sums of money
with interest thereon which may be paid or advanced by or may otherwise be due to Trustees or Beneficiary under
the provisions of this instrument, and (e) the discharge and performance of each agreement of Trustor herein
contained, Trustor does hereby grant to Trustee, in trust, with power of sale, that property and the

improvements thereon in the   City and   , County of   San Francisco

State of California, described as follows:

Lot 4 in Block 20, as designated on the map entitled "Twin Peaks
Tract, City and County of San Francisco, State of California", filed
in the office of the Recorder of the City and County of San Francisco, State of California, on August 5, 1909, in Volume 3 of Maps,
at page 8.

TOGETHER with the rents, issues and profits thereof, the hereditaments and appurtenances thereunto belonging, all water
rights and stock appurtenant thereto or connected therewith, and all the estate which Trustor now has or may hereafter
acquire in said property.
  1.   Trustor agrees:
  (a)   To pay, at least ten days before delinquency, all taxes and assessments affecting said property, including assessments
on appurtenant water stock, and to pay, when due, all incumbrances, charges and liens, with interest, on said property or any
part thereof, which appear to be prior or superior hereto, and all costs, fees and expenses of this Trust.
  (b)   To keep said property in good condition and repair; not to remove or demolish any building thereon; to complete
or restore promptly and in good and workmanlike manner any building which may be constructed, damaged or destroyed
thereon and to pay when due all claims for labor performed and materials furnished therefor; to comply with all laws affecting
said property or requiring any alterations or improvements to de made thereon; not to commit or permit waste thereof; not to
commit, suffer or permit any act upon said property in violation of law; to cultivate, irrigate, fertilize, fumigate, prune and do
all other acts which from the character or use of said property may be reasonably necessary, the specific enumerations herein
not excluding the general.
  (c)   To provide, maintain and deliver to Beneficiary fire insurance satisfactory to, and with loss payable to, Beneficiary.
The amount collected under any fire or other insurance policy may be applied by Beneficiary upon any indebtedness secured

hereby in such manner as Beneficiary may determine, or at option of Beneficiary the entire amount so collected or any part thereof may be released to Trustor. Such application or releasee shall not cure or waive any default or notice of default hereunder or invalidate any act done pursuant to such notice.

(d)   To appear in and defend any action or proceeding purporting to affect the security hereof or title to said property or the rights or powers of Beneficiary or Trustee; and to pay all costs and expenses, including cost of evidence of title and attorneys' fees in a reasonable sum, in any such action or proceeding in which Beneficiary or Trustee may appear.

2.   Should Trustor fail to make any payment or to do any act as herein provided, then Beneficiary or Trustee, but without obligation so to do and without notice to or demand upon Trustor and without releasing Trustor from any obligation hereof, may make or do the same in such manner and to such extent as either may deem necessary to protect the security hereof, Beneficiary or Trustee being authorized to enter upon, and take possession of said property for such purposes, to appear in and defend any action or proceeding purporting to affect the security hereof, or title to said property or the rights or powers of Beneficiary of Trustee, to pay, purchase, contest or compromise any incumbrance, charge or lien which in the judgment of either appears to be prior or superior hereto, and, in exercising any such powers, to pay necessary expenses, employ counsel and pay their reasonable fees. Trustor agrees to repay immediately and without demand all sums so expended by Beneficiary or Trustee, with interest from date of expenditure at eight per cent per annum.

3.   Any award of damages in connection with any condemnation for public use of or injury to said property, or any part thereof, is hereby assigned and shall be paid to Beneficiary, who may apply or release the money received by him, in the same manner and with the same effect as above provided for the disposition of the proceeds of fire or other insurance.

4.   By accepting payment of any sum secured hereby after its due date, Beneficiary will not waive or in any manner affect his right to require prompt payment when due of all other sums so secured, and to declare a default for failure of Trustor so to pay.

5.   At any time and from time to time, without liability and notice, upon the written request of Beneficiary and the presentation of this deed of trust and all promissory notes secured hereby, and without affecting the personal liability of any person for payment of the indebtedness secured hereby, Trustee may (a) reconvey all or any part of said property, (b) consent to the making of any map or plat thereof, (c) join in granting any easement thereon, or (d) join in any extension agreement or any agreement subordinating the lien and charge thereof.

6.   In the event all sums secured hereby have been paid and upon surrender of this deed of trust and all promissory notes secured hereby to Trustee for cancellation, and upon payment to Trustee of its fees, then Trustee shall, at the request and cost of Trustor, reconvey without warranty, the property then held hereunder. The grantee in any reconveyance may be described as "the person or persons legally entitled thereto."

7.   Trustees may at any time, at the request of the Beneficiary, reconvey to Trustor, or successors or assigns, any portion of said property without affecting the personal liability of any person for the payment of any of said indebtedness, and trusts shall continue in force as to the property not reconveyed.

8.   The recitals of any matters or facts in any instrument executed by Trustees hereunder shall be conclusive proof of the truthfulness thereof.

9.   Trustor hereby declares that this conveyance is irrevocable and that if two or more persons be named as Trustees herein, this deed of trust shall be construed as a conveyance to them as joint tenants with right of survivorship. Any one of Trustees hereunder named may perform any act, exercise any power, execute any trust and make any conveyance or reconveyance hereunder with the same effect as if all said Trustees had so acted. Beneficiary may, from time to time, in the manner provided by law, appoint a new trustee, or trustees to act in lieu of Trustee named above. Any such appointment by Beneficiary, duly acknowledged before a notary public, when recorded in the County in which the property, or any part thereof is situated, shall be conclusive proof of the proper appointment of such new trustee or trustees.

10.   Should more than one person execute this deed of trust as Trustor, the undertakings of Trustor herein contained shall be deemed to be their joint and several undertakings.

11.   Unless directed in writing by Trustor or Beneficiary to do so, Trustee is not obligated to request a copy of any notice of default and of election to sell or of any notice of sale under any other deed of trust, nor to notify any party hereto of any pending sale under any other deed of trust or of any action or proceeding to which Trustor, Beneficiary or Trustee shall be a party, unless such action or proceeding be brought by Trustee.

12.   Whenever Trustor shall be in default in the payment of any indebtedness secured hereby, Trustee and/or Beneficiary shall be entitled to do any or all of the following: (a) to take possession of said property or any part thereof; (b) to operate said property or any part thereof; (c) to do such acts as may be necessary to conserve the value of said property or any part thereof, and (d) to collect the rents, issues and profits from said property or any part thereof, either with or without taking possession. In addition and without prejudice to such rights, Beneficiary shall have the right to have a receiver appointed to do any or all of the aforesaid things during any such default. Beneficiary's legal expense in procuring the appointment of a receiver shall be chargeable to Trustor. If a net profit be realized from the exercise of the powers herein conferred, it shall be applied upon the indebtedness secured hereby in such manner as Beneficiary may determine; if a net loss be realized, Trustor hereby agrees to pay the amount thereof to Trustee and/or Beneficiary, as their interests appear.

13.   In the event that any change or changes occur in the title to all or any part of the said property, then the whole of the principal sum named in the said promissory note, and the interest that shall have accrued thereon, shall become and be immediately due and payable at the election of Beneficiary without demand or notice. Upon default by Trustor in the payment of any indebtedness secured hereby, or in the performance of any agreement herein contained, Beneficiary may, at his option, declare all indebtednesses, obligations and sums secured hereby to be immediately due and payable by delivery to Trustee of a written declaration of default. If Beneficiary desires said property to be sold, he shall deposit with Trustee this deed of trust and all promissory notes and documents evidencing expenditures secured hereby, and shall deliver to Trustee a written notice of default and of election to cause the property to be sold, in form required by law, which shall be duly filed for record by Trustee or Beneficiary.

When not less than three months shall have elapsed after recordation of such notice of default and election, Trustee shall give notice of sale as then required by law and, without demand upon Trustor, shall sell said property at the time and place of sale fixed in said notice of sale. Beneficiary may, without liability on his part, designate whether said property shall be sold as a whole or in separate parcels and, if in separate parcels, the order in which said parcels shall be sold. The property shall be sold at public auction to the highest bidder for cash. The purchase price shall be payable at the time of the acceptance of the bid. The sale shall take place at some place in the county wherein the said property is situated, an, if situated in different counties, then in any county in which any part of the property is situated. Trustee may act through an attorney, auctioneer of other agent in all proceedings connected with the sale. Any person, including Trustor. Trustee and Beneficiary, may purchase at the sale. Trustee may postpone the sale of all or any portion of said property from time to time by public announcement at the time and place of sale as fixed in said notice of sale or as fixed by public announcement of postponement. Upon payment of the full purchase price, Trustee shall deliver to the purchaser its deed

(Form continued on following page)

conveying the property so sold, but without any covenant or warranty, express or implied. The recitals in such deed of any matters, proceedings and facts shall be conclusive proof of the truthfulness and regularity thereof. The receipt for the purchase money contained in any such deed shall discharge the purchaser from all obligation with reference to the proper application of the purchase money by Trustee.

14. After deducting all costs, fees and expenses of trustee and of this trust, including reasonable compensation to counsel employed by Trustee or Beneficiary for the purpose of exercising the power of sale hereunder, or for any other purpose in connection with this instrument, and the cost of evidence of title in connection with the sale, Trustee shall apply the proceeds of sale, first, to payment of all sums expended under the terms of this instrument, not then repaid, with accrued interest at eight per cent (8%) per annum, and secondly, to the payment of all other sums then secured hereby, in such order and manner as may be designated by Beneficiary; the remainder, if any, to be paid to the person or persons legally entitled thereto.

15. In case of suit being commenced for the foreclosure of this deed of trust, the Trustor agrees to pay to Beneficiary or Trustee (whichever may be the plaintiff in said foreclosure suit) for counsel fees therein the sum of One Hundred Dollars ($100.00) and also an amount equal to five per cent of the amount then unpaid upon the said promissory note, whether the said suit be brought to a decree or not, and also such further sums, if any, as Beneficiary or Trustee shall have paid for procuring an abstract of, or for search of, the title to said premises subsequent to the execution of this deed of trust, and also a reasonable fee for Trustee; and in such suit of foreclosure, the plaintiff therein shall be entitled, without notice, to the appointment of a receiver to take possession of and operate said property and to collect and receive the rents, issues and profits of said property, and to exercise such other powers as the court shall confer. All moneys herein agreed to be paid shall be secured hereby.

16. In addition to any of the powers or remedies conferred upon the Trustee and the Beneficiary or either of them under this instrument, either the Trustee or Beneficiary or both may bring an action in the proper court for the foreclosure of this instrument as a mortgage, and obtain all the remedies in such action that are given by any statute or law of the State of California. No power or remedy herein conferred is exclusive of, or shall prejudice any other power or remedy of Trustee or Beneficiary. Each such power and remedy may be exercised from time to time, as often as is deemed necessary.

17. Trustee and Beneficiary shall be entitled to enforce any indebtedness or obligation secured hereby and to excersise all rights and powers under this deed of trust or under any other agreement or any law now or hereafter in force, although some or all of the indebtedness and obligations secured hereby are now or shall hereafter be otherwise secured, whether by mortgage, deed of trust, pledge, lien, assignment or otherwise. Neither the acceptance of this deed of trust nor its enforcement, whether by court action or pursuant to the power of sale or other powers herein contained, shall prejudice or in any manner affect Trustee's or Beneficiary's right to realize upon or enforce any other security now or hereafter held by Trustee or Beneficiary, it being agreed that Trustee and Beneficiary shall be entitled to enforce this deed of trust and any other security now or hereafter held by Beneficiary or Trustee in such order and manner as they or either of them may in their uncontrolled discretion determine.

18. If any change or changes occur in the title to all or any part of the said property, Beneficiary may, from time to time, (a) take, exchange, or release security for any of the obligations now or hereafter secured hereby. (b) extend the time for payment of the said obligations; (c) otherwise change the terms of said obligations; all without notice to, or consent of Trustor, and without in any way impairing or releasing the obligations of Trustor hereunder.

19. Any Trustor who is a married woman and who has joined in the execution of the said promissory note hereinabove set forth hereby expressly agrees to the liability of her separate property for all the indebtednesses and obligations hereby secured, but without hereby creating a present or any lien or charge thereon.

20. The provisions of this deed of trust are hereby made applicable to, and shall inure to the benefit of and bind all parties hereto and their heirs, legatees, devisees, administrators, executors, successors and assigns (including a pledge of any indebtedness secured hereby). The masculine gender includes the feminine and/or neuter, and the singular number includes the plural.

The undersigned Trustor requests that a copy of any notice of default and of any notice of sale hereunder be mailed to him at his mailing address set opposite his signature hereto.

IN WITNESS WHEREOF, Trustor has executed this agreement at Richmond, County of Contra Costa, State of California, on the date first above written

Signature of Trustor: Mailing Address for Notices:

s/THOMAS B. BUYER   659 Monterey Avenue

                                                          San Francisco, CA 94510

s/HELEN A. BUYER   659 Monterey Avenue

                                                          San Francisco, CA 94105

(Must be acknowledged by Notary Public.)

Escrow No.   123456

INSTALLMENT NOTE - INTEREST INCLUDED
(Balloon Payment)

$ 18,700.00   San Francisco , California   March 4   , 19 84

FOR VALUE RECEIVED, we, or either of us, promise to pay in lawful money of the United States of America, to

GEORGE S. SELLER and MARY M. SELLER, his wife

or order, at place designated by payee, the principal sum of   Eighteen Thousand Seven Hundred and
no/100-- dollars
with interest in like lawful money from   March 4   , 19 84   at 12   per cent
per annum on the amounts of principal sum remaining unpaid from time to time.
Principal and interest payable in   monthly   installments of   One Hundred Eighty-
seven and no/100-- dollars
or more each, on the   4th   day of each and every   month   beginning on the
     4th   day of   April   , 19 84 and continuing until April 30, 1989
at which time the entire unpaid balance of principal and interest hereunder shall be due and payable.

This note is subject to Section 2966 of the Civil Code, which provides that the holder of this note shall give written notice to
the trustor, or his successor in interest, of prescribed information at least 90 and not more than 150 days before any balloon
payment is due.

Each payment shall be credited first on interest then due and the remainder on principal; and interest shall
thereupon cease upon the principal so credited. Should default be made in payment of any installment of
principal or interest when due the whole sum of principal and interest shall become immediately due at the
option of the holder of this note. If action be instituted on this note I promise to pay such sum as the Court may
fix as attorney's fees. This note is secured by a Deed of Trust in which the maker of this note is referred to as
"Trustor."

_____   _____

                                                     s/THOMAS B. BUYER

_____   _____

                                                     s/HELEN A. BUYER

SHORT FORM DEED OF TRUST AND ASSIGNMENT OF RENTS

This Deed of Trust, made this   4   day of   March, 1984   , between

THOMAS B. BUYER and HELEN A. BUYER, his wife, herein called TRUSTOR,

whose address is 659 Monterey Avenue, San Francisco, California 94105 ,
(number and street)   (city)   (state)   (zip)

Title Insurance Company, a California corporation, herein called TRUSTEE, and

GEORGE S. SELLER and MARY M. SELLER, his wife, herein called BENEFICIARY,

Witnesseth: That Trustor IRREVOCABLY GRANTS, TRANSFERS AND ASSIGNS to TRUSTEE IN TRUST, WITH POWER OF SALE,
that property in   San Francisco   County, California, described as:

Lot 4 in Block 20, as designated on the map entitled "Twin Peaks Tract, City and County of San Francisco, State of California", filed in the office of the Recorder of the City and County of San Francisco, State of California, on August 5, 1909 in Volume 3 of Maps, at page 8.

This is a second deed of trust subject to a first deed of trust dated March 4, 1984, in favor of California Bank, a California banking corporation, in the sum of $149,600.00.

TOGETHER WITH the rents, issues and profits thereof, SUBJECT, HOWEVER, to the right, power and authority given to and conferred upon Beneficiary by paragraph (10) of the provisions incorporated herein by reference to collect and apply such rents, issues and profits.

For the Purpose of Securing: 1. Performance of each agreement of Trustor incorporated by reference or contained herein. 2. Payment of the indebtedness evidenced by one promissory note of even date herewith, and any extension or renewal thereof, in the principal sum of $18,700.00 executed by Trustor in favor of Beneficiary or order. 3. Payment of such further sums as the then record owner of said property hereafter may borrow from Beneficiary, when evidenced by another note (or notes) reciting it is so secured.

To Protect the Security of This Deed of Trust, Trustor Agrees: By the execution and delivery of this Deed of Trust and the note secured hereby, that provisions (1) to (14), inclusive, of the fictitious deed of trust recorded in Santa Barbara County and Sonoma County October 18, 1961, and in all other counties October 23, 1961, in the book and at the page of Official Records in the office of the county recorder of the county where said property is located, noted below opposite the name of such county, viz.:

COUNTY	BOOK	PAGE	COUNTY	BOOK	PAGE	COUNTY	BOOK	PAGE	COUNTY	BOOK	PAGE
Alameda	435	684	Kings	792	833	Placer	895	301	Sierra	29	335
Alpine	1	250	Lake	362	39	Plumas	151	5	Siskiyou	468	181
Amador	104	348	Lassen	171	471	Riverside	3005	523	Solano	1105	182
Butte	1145	1	Los Angeles	T2055	899	Sacramento	4331	62	Sonoma	1851	689
Calaveras	145	152	Madera	810	170	San Benito	271	383	Stanislaus	1715	456
Colusa	296	617	Marin	1508	339	San Bernardino	5567	61	Sutter	572	297
Contra Costa	3978	47	Mariposa	77	292	San Francisco	A332	905	Tehama	401	289
Del Norte	78	414	Mendocino	579	530	San Joaquin	2470	311	Trinity	93	366
El Dorado	568	456	Merced	1547	538	San Luis Obispo	1151	12	Tulare	2294	275
Fresno	4626	572	Modoc	184	851	San Mateo	4078	420	Tuolumne	135	47
Glenn	422	184	Mono	52	429	Santa Barbara	1878	860	Ventura	2062	386
Humboldt	657	527	Monterey	2194	538	Santa Clara	5336	341	Yolo	653	245
Imperial	1091	501	Napa	639	86	Santa Cruz	1431	494	Yuba	334	486
Inyo	147	598	Nevada	305	320	Shasta	684	528			
Kern	3427	60	Orange	5889	611	San Diego	Series 2 Book 1961, Page 183887				

(which provisions, identical in all counties, are printed on the reverse hereof) hereby are adopted and incorporated herein and made a part hereof as fully as though set forth herein at length; that he will observe and perform said provisions; and that the references to property, obligations, and parties in said provisions shall be construed to refer to the property, obligations, and parties set forth in this Deed of Trust.

The undersigned Trustor requests that a copy of any Notice of Default and of any Notice of Sale hereunder be mailed to him at his address hereinbefore set forth.

STATE OF CALIFORNIA
COUNTY OF San Francisco } SS.

On this 4th day of March, in the year 19 84, before me, the undersigned, a Notary Public in and for said State, personally appeared Thomas B. Buyer and Helen A. Buyer, his wife, —————————————, personally known to me (or proved to me on the basis of satisfactory evidence) to be the persons whose names are subscribed to the within instrument, and acknowledged to me that they executed it.

WITNESS my hand and official seal.

s/MARY MILLS
Notary Public in and for said State.

s/THOMAS B. BUYER

s/HELEN A. BUYER

—— DO NOT RECORD ——

The following is a copy of provisions (1) to (14), inclusive, of the fictitious deed of trust, recorded in each county in California, as stated in the foregoing Deed of Trust and incorporated by reference in said Deed of Trust as being a part thereof as if set forth at length therein.

To Protect the Security of This Deed of Trust, Trustor Agrees:

(1) To keep said property in good condition and repair; not to remove or demolish any building thereon; to complete or restore promptly and in good and workmanlike manner any building which may be constructed, damaged or destroyed thereon and to pay when due all claims for labor performed and materials furnished therefor; to comply with all laws affecting said property or requiring any alterations or improvements to be made thereon; not to commit or permit waste thereof; not to commit, suffer or permit any act upon said property in violation of law; to cultivate, irrigate, fertilize, fumigate, prune and do all other acts which from the character or use of said property may be reasonably necessary, the specific enumerations herein not excluding the general.

(2) To provide, maintain and deliver to Beneficiary fire insurance satisfactory to and with loss payable to Beneficiary. The amount collected under any fire or other insurance policy may be applied by Beneficiary upon any indebtedness secured hereby and in such order as Beneficiary may determine, or at option of Beneficiary the entire amount so collected or any part thereof may be released to Trustor. Such application or release shall not cure or waive any default or notice of default hereunder or invalidate any act done pursuant to such notice.

(3) To appear in and defend any action or proceeding purporting to affect the security hereof or the rights or powers of Beneficiary or Trustee; and to pay all costs and expenses, including cost of evidence of title and attorney's fees in a reasonable sum, in any such action or proceeding in which Beneficiary or Trustee may appear, and in any suit brought by Beneficiary to foreclose this Deed.

(4) To pay: at least ten days before delinquency all taxes and assessments affecting said property, including assessments on appurtenant water stock; when due, all incumbrances, charges and liens, with interest, on said property or any part thereof, which appear to be prior or superior hereto; all costs, fees and expenses of this Trust.

Should Trustor fail to make any payment or to do any act as herein provided, then Beneficiary or Trustee, but without obligation so to do and without notice to or demand upon Trustor and without releasing Trustor from any obligation hereof, may: make or do the same in such manner and to such extent as either may deem necessary to protect the security hereof, Beneficiary or Trustee being authorized to enter upon said property for such purposes; appear in and defend any action or proceeding purporting to affect the security hereof or the rights or powers of Beneficiary or Trustee; pay, purchase, contest or compromise any incumbrance, charge or lien which in the judgment of either appears to be prior or superior hereto; and, in exercising any such powers, pay necessary expenses, employ counsel and pay his reasonable fees.

(5) To pay immediately and without demand all sums so expended by Beneficiary or Trustee, with interest from date of expenditure at the amount allowed by law in effect at the date hereof, and to pay for any statement provided for by law in effect at the date hereof regarding the obligation secured hereby any amount demanded by the Beneficiary not to exceed the maximum allowed by law at the time when said statement is demanded.

(6) That any award of damages in connection with any condemnation for public use of or injury to said property or any part thereof is hereby assigned and shall be paid to Beneficiary who may apply or release such moneys received by him in the same manner and with the same effect as above provided for disposition of proceeds of fire or other insurance.

(7) That by accepting payment of any sum secured hereby after its due date, Beneficiary does not waive his right either to require prompt payment when due of all other sums so secured or to declare default for failure so to pay.

(8) That at any time or from time to time, without liability therefor and without notice, upon written request of Beneficiary and presentation of this Deed and said note for endorsement, and without affecting the personal liability of any person for payment of the indebtedness secured hereby, Trustee may: reconvey any part of said property, consent to the making of any map or plat thereof; join in granting any easement thereon; or join in any extension agreement or any agreement subordinating the lien or charge hereof.

(9) That upon written request of Beneficiary stating that all sums secured hereby have been paid, and upon surrender of this Deed and said note to Trustee for cancellation and retention and upon payment of its fees, Trustee shall reconvey, without warranty, the property then held hereunder. The recitals in such reconveyance of any matters or facts shall be conclusive proof of the truthfulness thereof. The grantee in such reconveyance may be described as "the person or persons legally entitled thereto." Five years after issuance of such full reconveyance, Trustee may destroy said note and this Deed (unless directed in such request to retain them)

(10) That as additional security, Trustor hereby gives to and confers upon Beneficiary the right, power and authority, during the continuance of these Trusts, to collect the rents, issues and profits of said property, reserving unto Trustor the right, prior to any default by Trustor in payment of any indebtedness secured hereby or in performance of any agreement hereunder, to collect and retain such rents, issues and profits as they become due and payable. Upon any such default, Beneficiary may at any time without notice, either in person, by agent, or by a receiver to be appointed by a court, and without regard to the adequacy of any security for the indebtedness hereby secured, enter upon and take possession of said property or any part thereof, in his own name sue for or otherwise collect such rents, issues and profits, including those past due and unpaid, and apply the same, less costs and expenses of operation and collection, including reasonable attorney's fees, upon any indebtedness secured hereby, and in such order as Beneficiary may determine. The entering upon and taking possession of said property, the collection of such rents, issues and profits and the application thereof as aforesaid, shall not cure or waive any default or notice of default hereunder or invalidate any act done pursuant to such notice.

(11) That upon default by Trustor in payment of any indebtedness secured hereby or in performance of any agreement hereunder, Beneficiary may declare all sums secured hereby immediately due and payable by delivery to Trustee of written declaration of default and demand for sale and of written notice of default and of election to cause to be sold said property, which notice Trustee shall cause to be filed for record. Beneficiary also shall deposit with Trustee this Deed, said note and all documents evidencing expenditures secured hereby.

After the lapse of such time as may then be required by law following the recordation of said notice of default, and notice of sale having been given as then required by law, Trustee, without demand on Trustor, shall sell said property at the time and place fixed by it in said notice of sale, either as a whole or in separate parcels, and in such order as it may determine, at public auction to the highest bidder for cash in lawful money of the United States, payable at time of sale. Trustee may postpone sale of all or any portion of said property by public announcement at such time and place of sale, and from time to time thereafter may postpone such sale by public announcement at the time fixed by the preceding postponement. Trustee shall deliver to such purchaser its deed conveying the property so sold, but without any covenant or warranty, express or implied. The recitals in such deed of any matters or facts shall be conclusive proof of the truthfulness thereof. Any person, including Trustor, Trustee, or Beneficiary as hereinafter defined, may purchase at such sale.

After deducting all costs, fees and expenses of Trustee and of this Trust, including cost of evidence of title in connection with sale, Trustee shall apply the proceeds of sale to payment of: all sums expended under the terms hereof, not then repaid, with accrued interest at the amount allowed by law in effect at the date hereof, all other sums then secured hereby; and the remainder, if any, to the person or persons legally entitled thereto.

(12) Beneficiary, or any successor in ownership of any indebtedness secured hereby, may from time to time, by instrument in writing, substitute a successor or successors to any Trustee named herein or acting hereunder, which instrument, executed by the Beneficiary and duly acknowledged and recorded in the office of the recorder of the county or counties where said property is situated, shall be conclusive proof of proper substitution of such successor Trustee or Trustees, who shall, without conveyance from the Trustee predecessor, succeed to all its title, estate, rights, powers and duties. Said instrument must contain the name of the original Trustor, Trustee and Beneficiary hereunder, the book and page where this Deed is recorded and the name and address of the new Trustee.

(13) That this Deed applies to, inures to the benefit of, and binds all parties hereto, their heirs, legatees, devisees, administrators, executors, successors and assigns. The term Beneficiary shall mean the owner and holder, including pledgees, of the note secured hereby, whether or not named as Beneficiary herein. In this Deed, whenever the context so requires, the masculine gender includes the feminine and/or neuter, and the singular number includes the plural.

(14) That Trustee accepts this Trust when this Deed, duly executed and acknowledged, is made a public record as provided by law. Trustee is not obligated to notify any party hereto of pending sale under any other Deed of Trust or of any action or proceeding in which Trustor, Beneficiary or Trustee shall be a party unless brought by Trustee.

—— DO NOT RECORD ——

REQUEST FOR FULL RECONVEYANCE

To be used only when note has been paid.

To TITLE INSURANCE COMPANY, Trustee: Dated _____

   The undersigned is the legal owner and holder of all indebtedness secured by the within Deed of Trust. All sums secured by said Deed of Trust have been fully paid and satisfied; and you are hereby requested and directed, on payment to you of any sums owing to you under the terms of said Deed of Trust, to cancel all evidences of indebtedness, secured by said Deed of Trust, delivered to you herewith together with said Deed of Trust, and to reconvey, without warranty, to the parties designated by the terms of said Deed of Trust, the estate now held by you under the same.

MAIL RECONVEYANCE TO:

_____   _____

_____   _____

_____   By _____

_____   By _____

Do not lose or destroy this Deed of Trust OR THE NOTE which it secures. Both must be delivered to the Trustee for cancellation before reconveyance will be made.

REQUEST FOR COPY OF NOTICE OF DEFAULT

IN ACCORDANCE WITH SECTION 2924B, CIVIL CODE OF THE STATE OF CALIFORNIA, REQUEST IS HEREBY MADE
THAT A COPY OF ANY NOTICE OF DEFAULT AND A COPY OF ANY NOTICE OF SALE UNDER THE DEED OF TRUST

RECORDED   : March 23, 1984
IN BOOK/REEL   : 7350 ——————————— of official records
AT PAGE/IMAGE   : 210
SERIES NUMBER   : P59160
COUNTY OF   : San Francisco ——————————, State of California
EXECUTED BY   : Thomas B. Buyer and Helen A. Buyer, his wife, —— as Trustor/s
IN WHICH   : California National Bank, a corporation, —— is named Trustee
AND   : California Bank, a California banking corp., is named Beneficiary
BE MAILED TO   : George S. Seller and Mary M. Seller
WHOSE ADDRESS IS   : 334 Summit Drive, Monterey, CA 93940

s/GEORGE S. SELLER

s/MARY M. SELLER

STATE OF CALIFORNIA

COUNTY OF _____ San Francisco _____ } ss.

On this ___23___ day of _____March_____, in the year 19_84_, before me, the undersigned, a Notary Public in and for said State,

personally appeared __George S. Seller and Mary M. Seller__

personally known to me (or proved to me on the basis of satisfactory evidence) to be the persons whose name is subscribed to the within

instrument, and acknowledged to me that they executed it.

WITNESS my hand and official seal.

s/NANCY N. NOTARY
Notary Public in and for said State.

FULL RECONVEYANCE

Title Insurance Company , a California corporation, as duly appointed Trustee under Deed of Trust hereinafter referred to, having received from holder of the obligations thereunder a written request to reconvey, reciting that all sums secured by said Deed of Trust have been fully paid, and said Deed of Trust and the note or notes secured thereby having been surrendered to said Trustee for cancellation, does hereby RECONVEY, without warranty, to the person or persons legally entitled thereto, the estate now held by it thereunder. Said Deed of Trust was executed by

GEORGE S. SELLER and MARY M. SELLER, his wife,   Trustor,

and recorded in the official records of   San Francisco   County, California, as follows:

RECORDED	AS INSTRUMENT NO.	IN BOOK	PAGE
March 14, 1971	P34671	6150	82

TITLE INSURANCE COMPANY , as Trustee

Dated: March 27, 1984   By XXXXXXXXXXXXXXXXXX

President

Dated: By XXXXXXXXXXXXXXXXX

Secretary

STATE OF CALIFORNIA
COUNTY OF   } SS.

On   March 27   , 19 84,
before me, the undersigned, a Notary Public in and for said County
and State, personally appeared _____
(above-named officers)   personally
known to me (or proved to me on the basis of satisfactory evidence) to be
President and Secretary
of Title Insurance Company , the corporation that executed the
foregoing instrument as such Trustee, and known to me to be the
person who executed said instrument on behalf of the corporation
therein named, and acknowledged to me that such corporation
executed the same as such Trustee.
WITNESS my hand and official seal.
s/NANCY N. NOTARY
Notary Public in and for said County and State.

Nancy N. Notary
(Notary's name shall be typed or legibly printed - Gov't. Code 8205)

FOR NOTARY STAMP OR SEAL

POLICY OF TITLE INSURANCE

ISSUED BY

TITLE INSURANCE COMPANY

SUBJECT TO SCHEDULE B AND THE CONDITIONS AND STIPULATIONS HEREOF, TITLE INSURANCE COMPANY   , a corporation, herein called the Company, insures the insured, as of Date of Policy shown in Schedule A, against loss or damage, not exceeding the amount of insurance stated in Schedule A, and cost, attorneys' fees and expenses which the Company may become obligated to pay hereunder, sustained or incurred by said insured by reason of:

1. Title to the estate or interest described in Schedule A being vested other than as stated therein;

2. Any defect in or lien or encumbrance on such title;

3. Unmarketability of such title; or

4. Any lack of the ordinary right of an abutting owner for access to at least one physically open street or highway if the land, in fact, abuts upon one or more such streets or highways;

and in addition, as to an insured lender only:

5. Invalidity of the lien of the insured mortgage upon said estate or interest except to the extent that such invalidity, or claim thereof, arises out of the transaction evidenced by the insured mortage and is based upon

   a. usury, or

   b. any consumer credit protection or truth in lending law;

6. Priority of any lien or encumbrance over the lien of the insured mortgage, said mortgage being shown in Schedule B in the order of its priority; or

7. Invalidity of any assignment of the insured mortgage, provided such assignment is shown in Schedule B.

IN WITNESS WHEREOF, Title Insurance Company   has caused its corporate name and seal to be hereunto affixed by its duly authorized officers on the date shown in Schedule A.

Countersigned:

                                              TITLE INSURANCE COMPANY

                                              By   XXXXXXXXXXXX

                                                                    President

By_____XXXXXXXXXXXX_____   By   XXXXXXXXXXXX
         Validating Officer
                                                                    Secretary

CLTA Standard Coverage Policy—1973

SCHEDULE A

Policy No: 000000
Order No:

Date of Policy: March 31, 1984

Amount of Insurance: $ 187,000.00

Premium: $ 653.75

1.   Name of Insured: CALIFORNIA BANK,   THOMAS B. BUYER   and   HELEN A. BUYER

2.   The estate or interest referred to herein is at Date of Policy vested in:

   THOMAS B. BUYER   and   HELEN A. BUYER,   his wife

3.   The estate or interest in the land described herein and which is covered by this policy is a fee.

SCHEDULE B

This policy does not insure against loss or damage, nor against costs, attorneys' fees or expenses, any or all of which arise by reason of the following:

PART I

1. Taxes or assessments which are not shown as existing liens by the records of any taxing authority that levies taxes or assessments on real property or by the public records.
   Proceedings by a public agency which may result in taxes or assessments, or notices of such proceedings, whether or not shown by the records of such agency or by the public records.

2. Any facts, rights, interests or claims which are not shown by the public records but which could be ascertained by an inspection of the land or by making inquiry of persons in possession thereof.

3. Easements, liens or encumbrances, or claims thereof, which are not shown by the public records.

4. Discrepancies, conflicts in boundary lines, shortage in area, encroachments, or any other facts which a correct survey would disclose, and which are not shown by the public records.

5. (a) Unpatented mining claims; (b) reservations or exceptions in patents or in Acts authorizing the issuance thereof; (c) water rights, claims or title to water.

6. Any right, title, interest, estate or easement in land beyond the lines of the area specifically described or referred to in Schedule C, or in abutting streets, roads, avenues, alleys, lanes, ways or waterways, but nothing in this paragraph shall modify or limit the extent to which the ordinary right of an abutting owner for access to a physically open street or highway is insured by this policy.

7. Any law, ordinance or governmental regulation (including but not limited to building and zoning ordinances) restricting or regulating or prohibiting the occupancy, use or enjoyment of the land, or regulating the character, dimensions or location of any improvement now or hereafter erected on the land, or prohibiting a separation in ownership or a reduction in the dimensions or area of the land, or the effect of any violation of any such law, ordinance or governmental regulation.

8. Rights of eminent domain or governmental rights of police power unless notice of the exercise of such rights appears in the public records.

9. Defects, liens, encumbrances, adverse claims, or other matters (a) created, suffered, assumed or agreed to by the insured claimant; (b) not shown by the public records and not otherwise excluded from coverage but known to the insured claimant either at Date of Policy or at the date such claimant acquired an estate or interest insured by this policy or acquired the insured mortgage and not disclosed in writing by the insured claimant to the Company prior to the date such insured claimant became an insured hereunder; (c) resulting in no loss or damage to the insured claimant; (d) attaching or created subsequent to Date of Policy; or (e) resulting in loss or damage which would not have been sustained if the insured claimant had been a purchaser or encumbrancer for value without knowledge.

PART II

(Exceptions of trust deeds to CALIFORNIA BANK
and SELLERS would be shown here.)

SCHEDULE C

The land referred to in this policy is situated in the County of __San Francisco,_____
State of California, and is described as follows:

   Lot 4 in Block 20, as designated on the map entitled "Twin
   Peaks Tract, City and County of San Francisco, State of
   California", filed in the Office of the Recorder of the
   City and County of San Francisco, State of California,
   on August 5, 1909, in Volume 3 of Maps, at page 8.

(Form continued on following page)

CONDITIONS AND STIPULATIONS

1. DEFINITION OF TERMS

The following terms when used in this policy mean:

(a) "insured": the insured named in Schedule A, and, subject to any rights or defenses the Company may have had against the named insured, those who succeed to the interest of such insured by operation of law as distinguished from purchase including, but not limited to, heirs, distributees, devisees, survivors, personal representatives, next of kin, or corporate or fiduciary successors. The term "insured" also includes (i) the owner of the indebtedness secured by the insured mortgage and each successor in ownership of such indebtedness (reserving, however, all rights and defenses as to any such successor who acquires the indebtedness by operation of law as described in the first sentence of this sub-paragraph (a) that the company would have had against the successor's transferor), and further includes (ii) any governmental agency or instrumentality which is an insurer or guarantor under an insurance contract or guaranty insuring or guaranteeing said indebtedness, or any part thereof, whether named as an insured herein or not, and (iii) the parties designated in paragraph 2 (a) of these Conditions and Stipulations.

(b) "insured claimant": an insured claiming loss or damage hereunder.

(c) "insured lender": the owner of an insured mortgage.

(d) "insured mortgage": a mortgage shown in Schedule B, the owner of which is named as an insured in Schedule A.

(e) "knowledge": actual knowledge, not constructive knowledge or notice which may be imputed to an insured by reason of any public records.

(f) "land": the land described, specifically or by reference in Schedule C, and improvements affixed thereto which by law constitute real property; provided, however, the term "land" does not include any area excluded by Paragraph No. 6 of Part One of Schedule B of this Policy.

(g) "mortgage": mortgage, deed of trust, trust deed, or other security instrument.

(h) "public records": those records which by law impart constructive notice of matters relating to the land.

2(a). CONTINUATION OF INSURANCE AFTER ACQUISITION OF TITLE BY INSURED LENDER

If this policy insures the owner of the indebtedness secured by the insured mortgage, this policy shall continue in force as of Date of Policy in favor of such insured who acquires all or any part of the estate or interest in the land described in Schedule C by foreclosure, trustee's sale, conveyance in lieu of foreclosure, or other legal manner which discharges the lien of the insured mortgage, and if such insured is a corporation, its transferee of the estate or interest so acquired, provided the transferee is the parent or wholly owned subsidiary of such insured; and in favor of any governmental agency or instrumentality which acquires all or any part of the estate or interest pursuant to a contract of insurance or guaranty insuring or guaranteeing the indebtedness secured by the insured mortgage. After any such acquisition the amount of insurance hereunder, exclusive of costs, attorneys' fees and expenses which the Company may be obligated to pay, shall not exceed the least of:

(i) the amount of insurance stated in Schedule A;

(ii) the amount of the unpaid principal of the indebtedness plus interest thereon, as determined under paragraph 6 (a) (iii) hereof, expenses of foreclosure and amounts advanced to protect the lien of the insured mortgage and secured by said insured mortgage at the time of acquisition of such estate or interest in the land; or

(iii) the amount paid by any governmental agency or instrumentality, if such agency or instrumentality is the insured claimant, in acquisition of such estate or interest in satisfaction of its insurance contract or guaranty.

(b). CONTINUATION OF INSURANCE AFTER CONVEYANCE OF TITLE

The coverage of this policy shall continue in force as of Date of Policy, in favor of an insured so long as such insured retains an estate or interest in the land, or owns an indebtedness secured by a purchase money mortgage given by a purchaser from such insured, or so long as such insured shall have liability by reason of covenants of warranty made by such insured in any transfer or conveyance of such estate or interest; provided, however, this policy shall not continue in force in favor of any purchaser from such insured of either said estate or interest or the indebtedness secured by a purchase money mortgage given to such insured.

3. DEFENSE AND PROSECUTION OF ACTIONS — NOTICE OF CLAIM TO BE GIVEN BY AN INSURED CLAIMANT

(a) The Company, at its own cost and without undue delay, shall provide for the defense of an insured in litigation to the extent that such litigation involves an alleged defect, lien, encumbrance or other matter insured against by this policy.

(b) The insured shall notify the Company promptly in writing (i) in case of any litigation as set forth in (a) above, (ii) in case knowledge shall come to an insured hereunder of any claim of title or interest which is adverse to the title to the estate or interest or the lien of the insured mortgage, as insured, and which might cause loss or damage for which the Company may be liable by virtue of this policy, or (iii) if title to the estate or interest or the lien of the insured mortgage, as insured, is rejected as unmarketable. If such prompt notice shall not be given to the Company, then as to such insured all liability of the Company shall cease and terminate in regard to the matter or matters for which such prompt notice is required; provided, however, that failure to notify shall in no case prejudice the rights of any such insured under this policy unless the Company shall be prejudiced by such failure and then only to the extent of such prejudice.

(c) The Company shall have the right at its own cost to institute and without undue delay prosecute any action

or proceeding or to do any other act which in its opinion may be necessary or desirable to establish the title to the estate or interest or the lien of the insured mortgage, as insured; and the Company may take any appropriate action, whether or not it shall be liable under the terms of this policy, and shall not thereby concede liability or waive any provision of this policy.

(d) Whenever the Company shall have brought any action or interposed a defense as required or permitted by the provisions of this policy, the Company may pursue any such litigation to final determination by a court of competent jurisdiction and expressly reserves the right, in its sole discretion, to appeal from any adverse judgment or order.

(e) In all cases where this policy permits or requires the Company to prosecute or provide for the defense of any action or proceeding, the insured hereunder shall secure to the Company the right to so prosecute or provide defense in such action or proceeding, and all appeals therein, and permit the Company to use, at its option, the name of such insured for such purpose. Whenever requested by the Company, such insured shall give the Company, at the Company's expense, all reasonable aid (1) in any such action or proceeding in effecting settlement, securing evidence, obtaining witnesses, or prosecuting or defending such action or proceeding, and (2) in any other act which in the opinion of the Company may be necessary or desirable to establish the title to the estate or interest or the lien of the insured mortgage, as insured, including but not limited to executing corrective or other documents.

4. PROOF OF LOSS OR DAMAGE — LIMITATION OF ACTION

In addition to the notices required under Paragraph 3 (b) of these Conditions and Stipulations, a proof of loss or damage, signed and sworn to by the insured claimant shall be furnished to the Company within 90 days after the insured claimant shall ascertain or determine the facts giving rise to such loss or damage. Such proof of loss or damage shall describe the defect in, or lien or encumbrance on the title, or other matter insured against by this policy which constitutes the basis of loss or damage, and, when appropriate, state the basis of calculating the amount of such loss or damage.

Should such proof of loss or damage fail to state facts sufficient to enable the Company to determine its liability hereunder, insured claimant, at the written request of Company, shall furnish such additional information as may reasonably be necessary to make such determination.

No right of action shall accrue to insured claimant until 30 days after such proof of loss or damage shall have been furnished.

Failure to furnish such proof of loss or damage shall terminate any liability of the Company under this policy as to such loss or damage.

5. OPTIONS TO PAY OR OTHERWISE SETTLE CLAIMS AND OPTIONS TO PURCHASE INDEBTEDNESS

The Company shall have the option to pay or otherwise settle for or in the name of an insured claimant any claim insured against, or to terminate all liability and obligations of the Company hereunder by paying or tendering payment of the amount of insurance under this policy together with any costs, attorneys' fees and expenses incurred up to the time of such payment or tender of payment by the insured claimant and authorized by the Company. In case loss or damage is claimed under this policy by the owner of the indebtedness secured by the insured mortgage, the Company shall have the further option to purchase such indebtedness for the amount owing thereon together with all costs, attorneys' fees and expenses which the Company is obligated hereunder to pay. If the Company offers to purchase said indebtedness as herein provided, the owner of such indebtedness shall transfer and assign said indebtedness and the mortgage and any collateral securing the same to the Company upon payment therefor as herein provided. Upon such offer being made by the Company, all liability and obligations of the Company hereunder to the owner of the indebtedness secured by said insured mortgage, other than the obligation to purchase said indebtedness pursuant to this paragraph, are terminated.

6. DETERMINATION AND PAYMENT OF LOSS

(a) The liability of the Company under this policy shall in no case exceed the least of:

(i) the actual loss of the insured claimant; or

(ii) the amount of insurance stated in Schedule A, or, if applicable, the amount of insurance as defined in paragraph 2 (a) hereof; or

(iii) if this policy insures the owner of the indebtedness secured by the insured mortgage, and provided said owner is the insured claimant, the amount of the unpaid principal of said indebtedness, plus interest thereon, provided such amount shall not include any additional principal indebtedness created subsequent to Date of Policy, except as to amounts advanced to protect the lien of the insured mortgage and secured thereby.

(b) The Company will pay, in addition to any loss insured against by this policy, all costs imposed upon an insured in litigation carried on by the Company for such insured, and all costs, attorneys' fees and expenses in litigation carried on by such insured with the written authorization of the Company.

(c) When the amount of loss or damage has been definitely fixed in accordance with the conditions of this policy, the loss or damage shall be payable within 30 days thereafter.

7. LIMITATION OF LIABILITY

No claim shall arise or be maintainable under this policy (a) if the Company, after having received notice of an alleged defect, lien or encumbrance insured against hereunder, by litigation or otherwise, removes such defect, lien or encumbrance or establishes the title, or the lien of the insured mortgage, as insured, within a reasonable time after

receipt of such notice; (b) in the event of litigation until there has been a final determination by a court of competent jurisdiction, and disposition of all appeals therefrom adverse to the title or to the lien of the insured mortgage as insured, as provided in paragraph 3 hereof; or (c) for liability voluntarily admitted or assumed by an insured without prior written consent of the Company.

8. REDUCTION OF INSURANCE; TERMINATION OF LIABILITY

All payments under this policy, except payment made for costs, attorneys' fees and expenses, shall reduce the amount of the insurance pro tanto; provided, however, if the owner of the indebtedness secured by the insured mortgage is an insured hereunder, then such payments, prior to the acquisition of title to said estate or interest as provided in paragraph 2 (a) of these Conditions and Stipulations, shall not reduce pro tanto the amount of the insurance afforded hereunder as to any such insured, except to the extent that such payments reduce the amount of the indebtedness secured by such mortgage.

Payment in full by any person or voluntary satisfaction or release of the insured mortgage shall terminate all liability of the Company to an insured owner of the indebtedness secured by the insured mortgage, except as provided in paragraph 2 (a) hereof.

9. LIABILITY NONCUMULATIVE

It is expressly understood that the amount of insurance under this policy, as to the insured owner of the estate or interest covered by this policy, shall be reduced by any amount the Company may pay under any policy insuring (a) a mortgage shown or referred to in Schedule B hereof which is a lien on the estate or interest covered by this policy, or (b) a mortgage hereafter executed by an insured which is a charge or lien on the estate or interest described or referred to in Schedule A, and the amount so paid shall be deemed a payment under this policy. The Company shall have the option to apply to the payment of any such mortgage any amount that otherwise would be payable hereunder to the insured owner of the estate or interest covered by this policy and the amount so paid shall be deemed a payment under this policy to said insured owner.

The provisions of this paragraph 9 shall not apply to an owner of the indebtedness secured by the insured mortgage, unless such insured acquires title to said estate or interest in satisfaction of said indebtedness or any part thereof.

10. SUBROGATION UPON PAYMENT OR SETTLEMENT

Whenever the Company shall have paid or settled a claim under this policy, all right of subrogation shall vest in the Company unaffected by any act of the insured claimant, except that the owner of the indebtedness secured by the insured mortgage may release or substitute the personal liability of any debtor or guarantor, or extend or otherwise modify the terms of payment, or release a portion of the estate or interest from the lien of the insured mortgage, or release any collateral security for the indebtedness, provided such act occurs prior to receipt by such insured of notice of any claim of title or interest adverse to the title to the estate or interest or the priority of the lien of the insured mortgage and does not result in any loss of priority of the lien of the insured mortgage. The Company shall be subrogated to and be entitled to all rights and remedies which such insured claimant would have had against any person or property in respect to such claim had this policy not been issued, and the Company is hereby authorized and empowered to sue, compromise or settle in its name or in the name of the insured to the full extent of the loss sustained by the Company. If requested by the Company, the insured shall execute any and all documents to evidence the within subrogation. If the payment does not cover the loss of such insured claimant, the Company shall be subrogated to such rights and remedies in the proportion which said payment bears to the amount of said loss, but such subrogation shall be in subordination to an insured mortgage. If loss should result from any act of such insured claimant, such act shall not void this policy, but the Company, in that event, shall as to such insured claimant be required to pay only that part of any losses insured against hereunder which shall exceed the amount, if any, lost to the Company by reason of the impairment of the right of subrogation.

11. LIABILITY LIMITED TO THIS POLICY

This instrument together with all endorsements and other instruments, if any, attached hereto by the Company is the entire policy and contract between the insured and the Company.

Any claim of loss or damage, whether or not based on negligence, and which arises out of the status of the lien of the insured mortgage or of the title to the estate or interest covered hereby, or any action asserting such claim, shall be restricted to the provisions and conditions and stipulations of this policy.

No amendment of or endorsement to this policy can be made except by writing endorsed hereon or attached hereto signed by either the President, a Vice President, the Secretary, an Assistant Secretary, or validating officer or authorized signatory of the Company.

No payment shall be made without producing this policy for endorsement of such payment unless the policy be lost or destroyed, in which case proof of such loss or destruction shall be furnished to the satisfaction of the Company.

12. NOTICES, WHERE SENT

All notices required to be given the Company and any statement in writing required to be furnished the Company shall be addressed to it at its Main Office, San Francisco, California 94104.

13. THE FEE SPECIFIED IN SCHEDULE A IS THE ENTIRE CHARGE FOR TITLE SEARCH, TITLE EXAMINATION AND TITLE INSURANCE.

January 5, 1984, and completes it on February 2, 1984. S does not pay him, and then sells to B without mentioning this. The escrow on the sale is closed on February 3, 1984. M is a "mechanic," as is anyone who performs work on real property, and the law gives such a person a *mechanic's lien* if he is not paid for his services.[69] These mechanic's liens are given special protection in many states including California. Under the California Mechanic's Lien Law, M would have at least 60 days after the completion of his job to record a lien.[70] The lien would then *date back* and become effective as of the date work was *commenced*, and would take priority over the rights of intervening parties.[71] Suppose, then, that M records a mechanic's lien on March 10, 1984, well within the 60-day time limit but 5 weeks after purchase of the property by B. When this is done, M's lien dates back and becomes effective as of January 5, 1984, a date which is a month before B's purchase, and takes precedence over B's rights. B holds the property subject to this now recorded mechanic's lien and must pay the lien to save the property from sale. This is a lien which was not on the public records as of the time of issuance of title insurance and so is not insured against by the title company. B, of course, has a right to recover from S. About the only way B can protect himself against this possibility is by examining the property for signs of recent construction or repairs and, if found, asking to see receipts for payment.

---

[69]C.C. 3082-3267 is the California Mechanic's Lien Law. C.C. 3110 confers the right of lien upon every type of person who performs services upon or furnishes materials for services performed upon real property.

[70]As a condition to enforcing a lien, a subcontractor must give a *prelien notice* to the owner, the general contractor ("original contractor") and the construction lender within 20 days of the first furnishing of labor, equipment or materials. C.C. 3114.

C.C. 3115 gives an "original contractor" 60 days to record a lien if the owner of the property records a "Notice of Completion" of the work within 10 days after it is completed. If this is not done, the original contractor has 90 days after completion of the work to record his lien. C.C. 3116 gives one other than an original contractor, i.e., a subcontractor or laborer, only 30 days to record a lien if notice of completion is recorded, but 90 days if it is not. To preserve the lien, C.C. 3144 requires legal action to be commenced for the unpaid services within 90 days after the recording of the lien.

The "mechanic" has still another form of protection. Within the time that he may record a lien, a mechanic may serve a *stop notice* on the party who is to pay for the job—the property owner, if he is paying; or the construction lender if a bank or other lender is lending the property owner the money for the job. C.C. 3158-3159. By the stop notice the mechanic is able to block payment to the general contractor of funds in the amount owed to the mechanic for his work. If the general contractor is not bonded and the property owner is paying for the construction work, the property owner must withhold the amount claimed by the stop notice. C.C. 3161. If the general contractor is not bonded and a construction lender is paying for the construction work, the lender may withhold the amount claimed by the stop notice; *must* withhold it if served with a bonded stop notice, that is, a stop notice accompanied by a bond protecting the lender against the general contractor. C.C. 3162. Suit to enforce a claim stated in a stop notice must be commenced within 90 days after the expiration of the period within which a claim of lien must be recorded. C.C. 3172.

[71]C.C.P. 1188.1 provides this. Osborne on Mortgages, 2d, pp. 394, 397, indicates that the mechanic is given a lien from date of commencement of work in about half the states.

● The foregoing is intended to show that title insurance is not fool-proof. Again, the important function of the title insurance company is to discover defects of title and liens of record *before* a buyer parts with his money. Title companies will, if requested, issue a policy which will protect the buyer against encroachments and mechanics' liens, but will charge a higher premium since they will then have to survey the property for encroachments and inspect it for repairs or new construction to discover mechanics' liens.

Mortgages and Deeds of Trust

While it is more properly a real estate mortgage, as distinguished from the chattel mortgage previously seen, the single word "mortgage" is invariably associated with real estate, and is used hereafter to describe the real estate mortgage. Mortgages and deeds of trust are contractual liens on real property. The word "gage" is a Teutonic word meaning "pledge" or pawn—something put up as security. In very early mortgages, the mortgagee (the one given the mortgage) took possession of the property and got, as a sort of bonus, the profits accruing to the property during the term of the mortgage. This arrangement came to be known as a "*mort gage*" or dead pledge in the sense that the property was "dead" to the mortgagor during the term of the pledge. The word eventually came to be applied to the mortgage as we know it today.

● A *mortgage* is defined as the hypothecation (putting up) of real property as security for an obligation[72]—ordinarily, the obligation to repay the money borrowed from a lender to enable one to buy the property on which the mortgage is given, as seen in the escrow transaction. Parties to the mortgage are the *mortgagor* (borrower and giver of the mortgage) and *mortgagee* (lender and taker). While it is referred to simply as a "mortgage," there are actually the two documents of *note* and *mortgage* involved. Theoretically, at least, the note is the primary document, the evidence of the debt, while the mortgage is but secondary or *incident to* the note, security for the note. As a practical matter, of course, the mortgage is more important in that it gives the lender a solid, valuable asset to sell, if necessary. The importance of the note as the primary document is demonstrated by *Adler* v. *Sargent*, 109 C. 42, 41 P. 799. There, E held a note and mortgage. He sold the genuine note and a forged copy of the mortgage to X and sold the genuine mortgage and a forged copy of the note to Y. The question was which party had the security of the land. It was properly held that X did. Since the mortgage was an incident of the note, the one who got the note got the security of the mortgage.

● One other point of law which rests on the theory that the mortgage is an incident of the note is the doctrine of *imparted negotiability*—that if the note is negotiable and, so, passes to a holder in due course free of defenses of the maker, the mortgage securing the note also passes to him free of such defenses, the negotiable quality of the note being imparted to the mortgage which secures it and which is its incident.

● As seen in the escrow transaction, the buyer-mortgagor becomes the owner or titleholder of the property and, simultaneously, gives the mortgagee a lien (the mortgage) on the

---

[72]C.C. 2920: "Mortgage is a contract by which specific property is hypothecated for the performance of an act, without the necessity of a change of possession."

C.C. 2922: "A mortgage can be created, renewed, or extended, only by writing, executed with the formalities required in the case of a grant of real property."

property as security, so the mortgagor has possession of and title to the property, while the mortgagee only a lien against the property as security.[73]

Mortgage, Mortgage with Power of Sale and Deed of Trust

There are three general variations of mortgaging, i.e., of putting up real property as security—the mortgage, mortgage with power of sale, and deed of trust.

• Despite its rather formidable appearance, the *mortgage* is a very simple thing. Using R and E for mortgagor and mortgagee, the whole essence of the mortgage is simply that: The property is put up as security for the note. R will pay taxes when due and carry fire insurance covering E's interest. E will have the right to foreclose by action if any installment of the note is not paid or any other covenant (pay taxes; carry insurance) is breached.

• This was the original mortgage, the *mortgage without power of sale* as distinguished from the mortgage with power of sale. One serious disadvantage was the fact that court proceedings, *foreclosure action*, were necessary to enforce it. This was (1) slow, and (2) expensive, at least temporarily. It was expensive because it was necessary to employ an attorney to prosecute the proceeding. The mortgage gave the right to recover attorney's fees from the proceeds of sale, but in most cases there were no proceeds. The mortgagee may always "bid in" the amount owed him at such sales, that is, declare a bid in that amount without putting up any cash. If no higher bid is received, he becomes the "buyer" at the foreclosure sale, and this is usually what happens. Eventually, the mortgagee will sell the property and get his money, but this may not happen for some time.

• Before long, mortgagees conceived an idea which was designed to avoid these disadvantages. They began inserting *power of sale* provisions in their mortgages, that is, provisions authorizing sale by the mortgagee, without court proceedings.

A mortgage providing this remedy became known as a *mortgage with power of sale*, to distinguish it from the simple mortgage or mortgage without power of sale heretofore considered. Except that it affords the power of sale remedy, there are no differences between the two. To distinguish them, these remedies are hereafter referred to as "foreclosure by action" and "foreclosure by sale." A specimen form of mortgage with power of sale is set out on page 205. Mortgages are probably no longer used anywhere in California and the form on page 205 is an old form which would now be quite extinct in California.

Foreclosure by sale met with mixed reaction. In many states, it did not gain acceptance because of the belief that only through *foreclosure by action* and sale of the property under court decree could a marketable title be obtained. Some of these states passed statutes forbidding foreclosure by sale. Other states passed statutes expressly permitting it.[74] As of today, it is in use in probably less than half the states, and

foreclosure by action is still required or used in the others.[75]

• As stated in several California cases, the *deed of trust*, or *trust deed* as it is also called, is "little more than a mortgage with power of sale." It has become virtually the exclusive form of transaction used in California and is in use in a number of other states. The differences between it and the mortgage with power of sale are purely formal. They may be summed up as follows:

The *deed of trust* introduces a new, third party—a trustee—for whom there is no counterpart in the mortgage. Theoretically, the borrower transfers *title* to the property *in trust* to this trustee who holds it for the benefit of the lender. Hence, the statement that R "grant(s)" the property to the trustee in the specimen form of deed of trust on page 192—language of deed or transfer, as distinguished from that of mortgage or lien—R "hereby mortgages"—found in the mortgage. In the law of trusts, *trustor* is used to describe the one creating a trust, *beneficiary* the one for whose benefit it is created, and this nomenclature is used in the deed of trust in keeping with the theory that it is a trust transaction. Thus, the borrower who makes the transfer in trust becomes the trustor rather than *mortgagor*, and the lender becomes the beneficiary rather than *mortgagee*.

The only power given to the trustee by virtue of the transfer of title to him, is the power to sell the property upon the demand of the beneficiary if the trustor fails to pay the note which the deed of trust secures.[76] Accordingly, his *title* is spoken of as a "mere security title," another way of saying that the deed of trust is really just a lien like the mortgage, or that it is really nothing more than a mortgage with power of sale.

As seen later in this section, the mechanics of foreclosure by sale are the same in a deed of trust as in a mortgage with power of sale, except that in a deed of trust, sale is made by the trustee.

Contract of Sale of Real Property

One other type of financing device is a transaction called variously *contract of sale, contract to sell, agreement of sale, conditional sale* and *land contract* (see form, page 214). All of these terms are synonymous. The theory of the contract of sale is that the seller retains *title* until the purchase price is paid in full. Thus, the seller sells a house but retains title to it until the full purchase price is paid, perhaps 20 years later, at which time he gives the buyer a deed.[77]

The contract of sale is used for very low down payment transactions. Down payment being low, monthly payments must be high to compensate, and this is a disadvantage to the buyer.

(Continued on page 208)

---

[73]C.C. 2927: "A mortgage does not entitle the mortgagee to possession of the property . . ." C.C. 2888: ". . . a lien . . . transfers no title to the property subject to the lien."

[74]C.C. 2932: "A power of sale may be conferred by a mortgage upon the mortgagee or any other person, to be exercised after a breach of the obligation for which the mortgage is security."

[75]Osborne on Mortgages, 2d, pp. 724-727, indicates that foreclosure by sale is used in only 18 states and that foreclosure by action is still used in the others.

[76]Foreclosure by action is also permissible under the deed of trust, however. The specimen form of deed of trust at page 202 does not expressly provide for the remedy of foreclosure by action, because in California C.C.P. 725a automatically gives this remedy whether or not it is provided for in the deed of trust. C.C.P. 725a says that "The beneficiary or trustee named in a deed of trust . . . shall have the right to bring suit to foreclose the same in the manner and subject to the provisions, rights and remedies relating to the foreclosure of a mortgage . . ."

[77]There is no statutory authorization for such transactions in California, but not being forbidden, they are permitted.

MORTGAGE

WITH POWER OF SALE AND ASSIGNMENT OF RENTS

THIS INDENTURE, *made this   day of   , by and between*

hereinafter referred to in the singular as Mortgagor, and BANK, *a banking corporation, duly organized and existing under the laws of the State of California, and whose office and principal place of business is in the City and County of San Francisco, State of California, hereinafter referred to as Mortgagee.*

WITNESSETH: *Mortgagor has received from Mortgagee the sum of*

Dollars as a loan, and has executed and delivered to Mortgagee a Promissory Note of even date herewith for said sum and interest thereon, said principal and interest payable as in said Promissory Note provided.

Mortgagor hereby mortgages to Mortgagee the real and personal property hereinafter described, and also mortgages and assigns to said Mortgagee all of the rents, issues and revenues of said property, and of every part thereof as security for the payment of said Promissory Note and the performance of all of the terms, provisions and conditions thereof, for the payment to Mortgagee of all additional sums advanced by it to Mortgagor or his successor in interest, not to exceed the sum of $500.00 and the interest thereon and for the payment of all sums paid hereunder for the account of Mortgagor.

Said real property is located in the City and County of San Francisco, State of California, and is described as follows:

Said real property shall specifically include all machinery, equipment or other articles used in connection with said property, any part of which is fastened thereto by nails, screws, pipes, wires, cables, cement, glue or posts, all of which the Mortgagor hereby declares to be a part of the realty and subject to the lien of this Mortgage, and also any and all lands adjacent to and which are within the enclosure of or occupied by buildings, fences or other structures principally upon said real property.

Mortgagor shall keep all of the mortgaged property in good condition and repair and shall keep the buildings located upon the real property herein described insured against loss by fire and against such other risks and hazards in such amounts as Mortgagee shall require and demand, each such policy shall be in a company or agency acceptable to Mortgagee, and loss under each such policy shall be payable to Mortgagee as its interest may appear under this Mortgage and shall be delivered to and retained by Mortgagee until the obligations represented by this Mortgage and said Promissory Note are paid in full; should Mortgagor fail to effect such insurance and deliver to Mortgagee policies evidencing the same, Mortgagee may and it is hereby authorized to obtain all such insurance and pay the premium due thereof for the account of Mortgagor

Mortgagor shall pay, when due, all taxes and assessments that may be levied or assessed or become a lien upon the mortgaged property, this Mortgage or the money or debt secured hereby

Mortgagee is hereby empowered for the account of Mortgagor, and without any notice to Mortgagor, to purchase any adverse claims to and to pay and discharge any and all liens upon the mortgaged property, or any part thereof, including any claim or lien arising from or relating to any tax or assessment that may be levied, imposed or assessed upon the mortgaged property, this Mortgage or the money or debt secured hereby; the fact of such payment shall conclusively establish the validity and legality of all such claims or liens, Mortgagee is further empowered to maintain or defend any action or proceeding affecting the title to the mortgaged property, and upon the Mortgagee's appearance in any such action or proceeding there shall be due to Mortgagee and thereupon secured hereby a sum equal to three per cent. of the amount due under the terms of this Mortgage and said Promissory Note as and for attorney's fees therein.

Mortgagor shall and hereby promises to pay to Mortgagee on demand all expenses incurred by it in and about the making of the loan secured hereby, including counsel fees, and Mortgagee is hereby authorized to pay such expenses for the account of Mortgagor.

(Form continued on following pages)

All moneys which may be paid by Mortgagee for the account of Mortgagor, as herein provided, shall bear interest from the respective dates of payment at the rate provided in said Promissory Note, shall be immediately secured hereby and shall be immediately due and payable; and Mortgagor hereby promises to pay all said sums and interest to Mortgagee in lawful money of the United States.

Upon the breach of any of the terms, conditions or provisions of this Mortgage and assignment, or said Promissory Note, or in the event that Mortgagor fails to repay any future advances hereunder strictly in accordance with his promise so to do, or if any change be made in the title to or the record title to the mortgaged property, or any part thereof, the principal sum of said Promissory Note and all interest due thereon, together with all sums paid hereunder to or for the account of Mortgagor, or his successors in interest, shall become immediately due and payable at the option of Mortgagee, and notice of the election to exercise said option is hereby expressly waived; at any time after said sums have become due and payable Mortgagee herein may foreclose this Mortgage by suit in the manner provided by law, or sell a part or all of the property herein mortgaged under and in accordance with the power of sale hereinafter contained; upon the filing of any such foreclosure suit or the recordation of a notice of default hereunder as a step in the exercise of said power of sale, there shall be due to Mortgagee and thereupon secured hereby a sum of money equal to five per cent. of the debt due from Mortgagor under this Mortgage and said Promissory Note as and for attorneys' fees, together with the costs of such abstracts of title, title reports and title policies, covering the property mortgaged hereby as Mortgagee may require.

Mortgagor hereby empowers Mortgagee to sell and convey the property herein mortgaged, or any part thereof, at any time after said Promissory Note has become due and payable in accordance with the terms, provisions and conditions of this Mortgage or said Promissory Note; any such sale may be public or private at the option of the Mortgagee, may be conducted by Mortgagee, its agent or attorney, and may be for such price and on such terms as to payment or otherwise as Mortgagee may deem proper; at any such sale, Mortgagee, in its own name or in the name of any other person, shall have the right to purchase, and Mortgagor hereby authorizes and empowers Mortgagee to execute, acknowledge and deliver, in the name of Mortgagor, a good and sufficient Deed and Bill of Sale of said property, or any part thereof; any recitals contained in any Deed or Bill of Sale of the mortgaged property which may be made by Mortgagee shall be deemed conclusive evidence of the facts recited, before making any sale under the provisions of this paragraph, Mortgagee shall cause to be filed and given all notices required by Sections 2924 and 2924-B of the Civil Code of the State of California, and thereafter and after expiration of the time required by said Section 2924 shall cause notice of time and place of said sale to be given in the manner and for a time not less than that required by law for sale of similar property on execution. Proceeds of such sale shall be applied, first, to the payment of the expenses of the sale and the balance to the payment in whole or in part of the amount due Mortgagee upon this Mortgage and said Promissory Note; attorneys' fees due, payable and secured as hereinbefore provided, together with cost of all necessary Revenue Stamps required by law to be affixed to any Deed or Bill of Sale hereunder, shall be charged as a part of the expenses on such sale.

At the time and place appointed for any sale under the provisions of this Mortgage, Mortgagee, if it so elects, may continue said sale to a subsequent date, and thereafter continue the same from time to time; to effect such continuance Mortgagee, its agent or attorney shall, at the time and place appointed for said sale, publicly announce, in an audible tone of voice, the fact of such continuance and the time to which the same is continued, and no other or further notice of said sale, or of said continuance need be given.

At any sale held under the terms of this Mortgage, irrespective of whether this Mortgage shall be foreclosed by suit, sale under the power or by any other means, the mortgaged property need not be within view of those attending such sale and Mortgagee may sell the mortgaged property as a whole, or in separate parcels, as it may direct and may sell any personal property mortgaged hereby, together with said real property at a single sale or separately at a separate sale as it may see fit.

Should default or breach occur in the performance of any of the terms, provisions or conditions of this Mortgage or said Promissory Note, Mortgagee herein by itself, its agent, or Receiver appointed by Court in appropriate legal proceedings, and Mortgagor hereby consents to the appointment of such Receiver without previous notice or any notice to him, shall be and it is hereby empowered and authorized to take possession of all of the property mortgaged to it hereunder, and to collect all income and revenue therefrom, and to manage, operate and lease the same, or any part thereof, and to make such repairs and replacements thereto and carry such insurance thereon as it may deem necessary; the income and revenue so derived shall be applied, first, to attorneys' fees, costs and expenses of such operations and proceedings, including fees of Receiver, if appointed, and the balance thereof shall be applied on account of any indebtedness secured hereby. Mortgagee may accumulate income for application as herein specified.

Mortgagor hereby expressly waives the right to plead all statutes of limitation and all homestead statutes, which may now or hereafter exist, as a defense to any action based upon said Promissory Note or this Mortgage, or as a bar to the exercise of said power of sale, and also waives the right to move for a dismissal under the present provisions or any future provisions of Section 581a and 583 of the Code of Civil Procedure of the State of California in any action instituted on said Note or this Mortgage, and also waives any and all defenses which may now or hereafter exist to any action based upon said Promissory Note or this Mortgage, or to the exercise of power of sale herein, except the sole defense of payment.

Failure of Mortgagee to exercise or promptly exercise any right or option herein shall not be or be deemed to be a waiver of such right or option, and the waiver by Mortgagee of any breach of any of the terms, provisions or conditions hereof shall not constitute a waiver of any subsequent breach of the same, or any other term, provision or condition hereof or consent thereto.

Each and every term, provision and condition hereof shall inure to and be binding upon the heirs, administrators, successors and assigns of the parties hereto with the same effect as if such person was a party hereto. The use of the singular person herein shall include the plural, the plural shall include the singular, and the masculine shall include the feminine and the neuter.

Mortgagor requests that a copy of any notice of default and a copy of any notice of sale hereunder be mailed to the undersigned at the address set opposite their respective signatures hereto.

WITNESS *the hand and seal of the Mortgagor.*

Number, Street, City and State:

Signature:

_____   _____

_____   _____

_____   _____

STATE OF CALIFORNIA

COUNTY OF _____ } ss.

On this _____ day of _____, in the year 19____, before me, the undersigned, a Notary Public in and for said State, personally appeared _____ _____ _____, personally known to me (or proved to me on the basis of satisfactory evidence) to be the persons whose names are subscribed to the within instrument, and acknowledged to me that they executed it.

WITNESS my hand and official seal.

_____
Notary Public in and for said State.

(This area for official notorial seal)

The advantage of this transaction to the seller or the financing agency to which he may sell the contract is that it gives a swift, rather drastic remedy if any of the monthly installments of the purchase price are missed. As seen later, the law of most states gives a mortgagor some period of time within which to *reinstate* the mortgage or deed of trust if he becomes delinquent, and may also give him some period of time within which to *redeem* the property if there is a foreclosure sale. The contract of sale avoids these things. If an installment payment is missed, the seller or his transferee may simply *repossess* the property since he still owns it, and evict the buyer, whose equity in the property is forfeited. But a court of equity may give relief from such forfeiture where there are extenuating circumstances. California decisions have been particularly generous in this regard.[78]

Real Estate Financing

This discussion is confined to the financing of residential real estate, i.e., to home loans. *The information on lending policies, interest rates and other aspects of home loans, contained herein, is subject to frequent change, and the reader should consult with his bank or other lender for current information.*

Historical Perspective

As of 1934, America was becoming a nation of renters. While a home could be purchased for only two or three thousand dollars, few persons had the money to make the down payment which might be $500 or $1000. In addition, amortized financing did not exist. If you borrowed $2000 to buy the $3000 house, you would have to do so by means of a "straight note," i.e., a loan which would call for lump sum payment of principal and interest in 3 to 5 years. At that time you might not be able to refinance the purchase in which case you would lose the house and your investment in it.

FHA-Insured Loans: In 1934 the National Housing Act[79] was passed which was one of the great pieces of social legisltion. The National Housing Act created the Federal Housing Administration and its FHA-Insured Loan which was a long term, fixed rate, level payment, fully amortized mortgage loan. Now you could buy the $3000 home with a low down payment and a long term loan because the federal government was guaranteeing payment of the loan on your behalf. This was enough to overcome the lender's fears that you might at some point default on the loan or that the property might in the future decline in value. Now, America was on its way to becoming a nation of homeowners.

The FHA Loan was surrounded with a variety of consumer protection-type safeguards. Purchase price was limited to fair market value as determined by FHA appraisal. The buyer had to be making enough money to afford the payments. A small, but respectable down payment was required so that the buyer had a serious stake in the property. Secondary financing (second mortgage to seller) was forbidden so that the down payment requirement could not be circumvented in this manner. A low interest rate, originally 4½%, was required to be accepted by the lender. It was hoped that lenders would want the FHA Loan business enough to tolerate a low interest rate

permanently but lenders invented "points" to defeat this goal.[80] Finally, a "mutual mortgage insurance fund" was created to which each borrower was required to become a contributor in an amount equal to 1/2 of 1% of the loan. This fund was designed to cover defaults which produced deficiencies on foreclosure sale.

As this is written, FHA's maximum loan guarantee is $90,000. Interest rate is about 13½%. Minimum down payment is required. Loans are at fixed or adjustable rates, are fully assumable and ordinarily run for 30 years. FHA has recently introduced a 15-year loan which permits a great saving in interest if it can be handled. The 15-year loan is said to be proving very popular. FHA has also introduced a graduated payment mortgage plan which permits young, first-time home buyers to have reduced, but gradually increasing monthly payments during the first 5 years of the loan after which payments level off.

In December of 1983 the FHA Loan was deregulated as to the interest rate it could bear and the interest rate is now entirely a matter of negotiation between the lender and the borrower. Some lenders are now offereing a schedule of rates tied to the number of points the buyer is willing to pay at time of purchase, e.g., 8 points might bring and 11½% loan, 4 points a 12½% loan and zero points a 13½% loan.

VA-Guaranteed Loans: The Servicemen's Readjustment Act of 1944,[81] or "G.I. Bill," was designed to give World War 2 veterans, and, later, Korean and Vietnam war veterans, a package of benefits, including, in addition to the home loan guarantee considered here, the educational benefits that were so important to so many veterans, and loans to start businesses.

Whereas the FHA-Insured Loan guaranteed "the loan," the VA-Guaranteed Loan guaranteed a specific number of dollars of the loan. Originally, this was $7,500. Over the years it has climbed to its current level of $25,000. Otherwise, the principles of the VA-Guaranteed Loan were pretty much the same as those of the FHA-Insured Loan. Purchase price was limited to the fair market value of the property as determined by VA appraisal. A down payment was required. Secondary financing was not allowed. The original interest rate was a low 4%.

Cal Vet Loans: California passed its own "G.I. Bill" following World War 2 which gave California veterans educational benefits and farm and home loan benefits. The latter became known as Cal Vet Loans (CVL).

The Cal Vet Loan (CVL) is for veterans who were born in California or who were residents of the state at the time of entering the service, and for widows of such veterans who have not remarried. A fairly detailed system of priorities is established by the loan law. First priorities are given to wounded and disabled veterans, prisoners of war and wives of servicemen killed or missing in action; then priorities are given on the basis of the length of separation from the service and monthly earnings.

The form of the CVL is unique in the field of government guaranteed loans. The state raises the money for CVLs from

---

[78]*Barkis* v. *Scott*, 34 Cal.2d 116, 208 P.2d 367; *Baffa* v. *Johnson*, 35 C.2d 36, 216 P.2d 13; *Freedman* v. *Rector*, 37 C.2d 16, 230 P.2d 629; *Peterson* v. *Ridenour*, 135 C.A.2d 720, 287 P.2d 848; *Ward* v. *Union Bond & Trust Co.*, 243 Fed.2d 476.

[79]12 U.S.C.A. 1701-1743.

[80]*"Points"* compensate lenders for the difference between prevailing interest rates and the lower interest rates required by government guaranteed loans. A "point" is an amount equal to 1% of the amount of the loan. If the loan is $90,000 and the lender requires 5 points, the cost of points is $4,500.

When the FHA Loan had a regulated interest rate, the seller had to pay the points since the buyer could not, through points or otherwise, pay a greater rate of interest than the loan law permitted.

bond issues. The state, from the bond money, buys for the veteran the home of the veteran's choice and then sells it to the veteran in a transaction in the form of the contract of sale discussed on page 204.

The state can spend up to $75,000 for a home. The veteran can pay the difference between that amount and a higher price being charged for the home. Secondary financing is permitted. The basic contract term is 25 years.

The interest rate must be redetermined annually by the state. It started out at the unheard of low of 3%. Presently it is at 8%. A valuable package of fringe benefits accompanies the loan, including low-cost fire and hazard insurance, low-cost term life insurance which pays the balance of the loan if the borrower dies, and low-cost disability insurance which takes care of monthly payments during a period of disability.

The home must become the personal residence of the veteran and cannot be bought and then rented out at a profit or resold so as to pass on the veteran's beneifts to a non-veteran. Reasonable exceptions are made, however. For example, if the veteran suffers a job transfer or is required to relocate for reasons of health or requires a larger home, sale is permitted and new Cal Vet financing can be obtained but all of the proceeds of the sale of the old home must be put into the new home and non-veteran purchaser of the old home does not get the veteran's advantaged position.

The Cal Vet program allows the state to spend up to $75,000 for the construction of a home for a veteran and to pay up to $200,000 for the purchase of a farm for a veteran. The state may also spend up to $75,000 for a mobile home to be sited on a lot owned by the veteran and up to $55,000 for a mobile home to be sited in a mobile home park.

The law regulating Cal Vet Loans is to be found in Military & Veterans Code § 987.50-987.94.

Conventional Loans: "Conventional loan" is the real estate industry term for a loan which is not guaranteed by a government agency. It is the loan for those who for some reason cannot get a government-guaranteed loan or do not want one. Until the very recent advent of the "adjustable rate mortgage," it would be a long term, fixed rate, level payment, fully amortized loan. The conventional loan so described will differ from the government-guaranteed loan only in the respects that down payment requirements will be higher and interest rate will be higher. *Private* mortgage guaranty insurance is now widely available under which the guarantor guarantees the top 20-25% of the loan which makes the lender willing to lend a higher percentage of the purchase price.

Turn of the Decade

In 1980 America was again on the road to becoming a nation of renters. At least its younger generations were. Real estate prices were astronomically high as were interest rates, monthly payment requirements and down payment requirements. A climax came in September of 1981 when FHA interest rates reached their all time high of 17½%.

1979-1982 ushered in the era of *"creative financing."* We had the buyer who wanted the house but couldn't make the down payment or couldn't handle the monthly payments, or both. So things were invented which overcame these obstacles; not necessarily to the best advantage of the buyer.

• The simplest and most common form of creative financing would hardly deserve to be called "creative." It consisted simply of having the seller take a second mortgage for part of the purchase price because the buyer could not meet the difference between the purchase price and the first loan. Sometimes a third party lender paid the difference and took

the second mortgage in which case it was called a "hard money second." Sometimes a second mortgage was not enough and we might have a first mortgage, a hard money second, and the seller taking a third mortgage. Such a second mortgage is apt to be quite sizable and it invariably calls for a very hefty "balloon payment" at its maturity which is apt to be in 3 to 5 years. For example, a seller might take a $25,000 second mortgage on which only $5,000 of principal was to be paid during its 5-year term, leaving a "balloon payment" of $20,000 at maturity. Many foreclosures are threatening to result as the result of the inability of buyers to meet these sorts of balloon payments.

• The *"wraparound,"* or *"all-inclusive loan"* as it is known in California, has enjoyed some popularity. It requires an assumable first loan at a favorable rate of interest. The presence of these circumstances may tempt the seller to finance the buyer. Suppose, for example, that property will be sold for $100,000. The property has an existing first mortgage on it with an assumable loan balance of $50,000 at 8% interest. The current rate of interest is 13%. Seller could profitably agree to finance the purchase to the extent of $80,000 at 11% interest, which from the buyer's standpoint would be conceived to be "wrapping around" the existing first mortgage with its balance of $50,000. Seller would make the payments on the existing first mortgage out of the payments on the "wrap." This enables the seller to get 11% interest on $80,000 while paying only 8% on $50,000. If the seller does not want to finance the deal, a third party lender may find the wraparound sufficiently attractive to take it. Wraparounds involve the danger to the buyer that payments may not be made on the existing first mortgage. This can be overcome by requiring payments on the wraparound to be made to a neutral third party who will assume responsibility for making a proper allocation of the payments to the first mortgage. Wraparounds involve the dangers to the seller that they must not violate usury laws and that they may involve income tax problems.

• *Graduated payment mortgages* exist which are designed to be sort of "easy starter" loans by allowing lower monthly payments during the early years of the loan. Akin are loans which permit interest-only payments during the early years. There are also graduated payment mortgages which have the whole different and virtually opposite purpose of permitting the buyer to accelerate payment of the loan. For example, payments might be increased by 4% a year so as to permit the loan to be paid in 12 years rather than 30 years. This arrangement effects a huge saving in interest but requires a high income borrower.

• The *"payment-capped adjustable loan"* is one of the more insidious inventions of the modern lender. Payments are at a fixed rate for a period of years, e.g., 3 years, but interest is adjusted at, e.g., 6-month intervals. If interest rates fall, a larger portion of the monthly payments goes to principal but if interest rates rise the deficit in interest payments is added to the principal of the loan so that the buyer's equity decreases. This is called "negative amortization." It has been calculated that if a capped mortgage home buyer had had an original loan balance of $100,000 in 1975, his loan balance today would be $105,000 because of increases in interest rates.

• *"Equity-sharing"* or SAMs, for shared appreciation mortgages, are for buyers who can't afford the down payment. A lender puts up all or part of the down payment in exchange for part of the gain which is realized when the home is sold. This allows the lender to profit from the expected long-term appreciation in the value of the property.

● Developers may offer *"buy down" financing* to make their houses more affordable. Here, the developer pays a lump sum to a lender in exchange for the lender's agreement to finance sales at several points under prevailing interest rates for several years. For example, a buyer might be given a loan at 3 points under the going interest rate for the first 3 years of the loan.

California's Creative Financing Disclosure Law: In 1982, California adopted a law designed to protect buyers against some of the more deadly pitfalls of creative financing. The law consists of C.C. 2956-2967. It is operative as of July 1, 1983.

The law applies to cases in which a seller takes a second mortgage arranged for through an "arranger of credit" who ordinarily would be the real estate broker who negotiates the second mortgage along with the other terms of the transaction.

Before signing the note and second mortgage, the buyer must be given a written disclosure statement by the arranger of credit which shows, among other things (1) the terms of senior mortgages; (2) the date and amount of any balloon payment and the fact that new financing or a loan extension may not be available at the time that the balloon payment becomes due; (3) "(i)f negative amortization is possible . . ., a clear disclosure of this fact and an explanation of its potential effect;" and (4) who is responsible for making payments on the first mortgage if an all-inclusive loan is involved "and a warning that, if that person is not a neutral third party, the parties may wish to agree to have a neutral third party designated for" that purpose. C.C. 2963.

If a balloon payment note and second mortgage is involved, the holder of the note must give the mortgagor a written notice at least 60 and not more than 150 days before the balloon payment becomes due, showing the amount of the payment, when it is due, to whom it is to be paid, and refinancing rights, if any. Failure to give timely notice extends the due date of the balloon payment to a date 60 days from the date notice is actually given but interest continues to be payable in the interim. C.C. 2966. The balloon payment note must contain a statement informing the mortgagor that he is entitled to written notice of the balloon payment at least 60 and not more than 150 days before the payment is due. C.C. 2966(d).

The California form of disclosure statement is not required when the buyer is entitled to receive a disclosure statement pursuant to the Real Estate Settlement Procedures Act (page 183) or various other acts or laws requiring disclosure. C.C. 2958.

● C.C. 2924i adds a balloon payment notice requirement as to all balloon payment loans executed on or after January 1, 1984.

Today

Starting in 1982, lending institutions became awash with funds from the new "money market accounts" they were allowed to offer, for which each institution has invented a name, interest rates began a return to saner levels, and real estate prices stabilized; and there began to be a living, breathing real estate market again. Not a robust one but at least a moderately healthy one. FHA has become a principal actor in this turn of events and joins with characters known as Fannie Mae, Freddie Mac and Ginny Mae to put on a hit play which seems headed for along run.

● Today, as always, we have, basically, conventional loans and government guaranteed loans. Conventional loans are principally either fixed (interest) rate loans or adjustable (interest) rate loans. The adjustable rate loan will be explained in detail, below. Lending institutions sell probably at least two-thirds of these loans to Fannie, Freddie and Ginny who are middlemen whose function it is to provide a bridge between lending institutions who want to sell their mortgages and institutional investors who want to buy them. Institutional investors get what for them is an attractive investment. Lending institutions get fees for writing the loans and fees for servicing them which they continue to do even after they are sold. This resale market in mortgages, which is becoming a huge, *trillion* dollar business, is known as the *"secondary mortgage market."* The secondary mortgage market is the backbone of today's mortgage loan industry.

● Now let us examine in greater detail the nature of the adjustable rate mortgage and the nature of the secondary mortgage market.

Adjustable Rate Mortgage: The *"adjustable rate mortgage"* came on the scene in the 1980s and now shares honors with the *"fixed rate mortgage"* in providing real estate financing. The adjustable rate mortgage provides for the interest on a loan to be adjusted up or down at periodic intervals in accordance with an economic indicator which reflects the prevailing interest rate. If the interest rate goes up from 12% to 14%, a +2% adjustment on the loan's interest rate will be made eventually. This gives lenders an instrument that responds to the cost of money and will save lenders from getting caught with their rates down as they did in the late 1970s when they had portfolios full of 8% loans at a time when they were having to pay 12% to attract deposits. While the adjustable rate mortgage was first thought of as another form of creative financing, it has now transcended its character as such and like the fixed rate mortgage is a "convention" which is here to stay.

"Adjustable rate mortgage" seems to have become the general usage and therefore is adopted here but the California Civil Code uses the term "variable interest rate" mortgage. C.C. 1916.5 imposes various restrictions on the frequency with which and the extent to which interest rates can be changed during the life of an adjustable rate mortgage. These are binding on state-chartered banks and savings and loan associations but not on federally-chartered banks, which can adjust rates by up to 1% every 6 months, or federally-chartered savings and loan associations which can make adjustments as frequently as they wish. The restrictions imposed by C.C 1916.5 are shown in footnote 23 at page 120.

At a given time, when interest rates are down, the adjustable rate mortgage may be carrying an interest rate which is several points lower than that of the fixed rate mortgage. This may permit a buyer to qualify for an adjustable rate loan who could not qualify for a fixed rate loan.

The adjustable rate mortgage may be tied to any one of a number of economic indicators for the determination of its interest rate. These include the national mortgage interest rate computed weekly by the Federal Home Loan Bank Board and a 3- and 6-month and 3- and 5-year treasury securities indexes.

● Akin to the adjustable rate mortgage is the *"renegotiable rate mortgage."* "Renegotiable" is really a misnomer because there really isn't any "negotiating" involved. C.C. 1916.8-1916.9 provide for renegotiable rate mortgages in California which are really nothing more than adjustable rate mortgages in which the adjustment period is 3, 4 or 5 years rather than 6 months. If the mortgage is a 5-year renegotiable rate mortgage, then at the end of 5 years, the lender must offer to renew the mortgage with the increase in interest, if any, called for by certain Federal Home Loan Bank Board economic indicators.

Secondary Mortgage Market: The backbone of the mortgage system is the *"secondary mortgage market."* This is where we find the characters named "Fannie Mae" (for Federal National Mortgage Association), "Freddie Mac" (for Federal Home Loan Mortgage Corporation) and "Ginnie Mae" (for Government National Mortgage Association).

These organizations act as intermediaries between lending institutions which have mortgages which they don't want to warehouse and the "secondary mortgage market" which consists of investors such as insurance companies, pension funds and mutual funds who want to buy the mortgages the lending institutions want to get rid of.

Keeping it simple, this is how the system works: Lender Savings & Loan Association makes a fixed rate, 30-year, $100,000 mortgage loan to Homebuyer. Lender S & L sells this and other like mortgages to Freddie Mac. Freddie Mac then sells securities secured by this and other blocs of mortgages (called, appropriately, "mortgage-backed securities") to private investors to whom they represent an attractive investment because of their interest rates and because the securing mortgages carry a guarantee of payments by Freddie Mac. Specifically, the Freddie Mac securities are called *"participation certificates."*

Lender S & L is happy because it will collect fees for making the loan and will service the loan throughout its life for which it will enjoy a continuing income.

Ginnie Mae pools FHA and VA mortgages which back securities sold to investors. It is estimated that almost 90% of all FHA and VA loans made by lenders are going into the Ginnie Mae hopper. The Ginnie Mae security is called a "mortgage backed certificate" and recites by way of guarantee that it is guaranteed by the Government National Mortgage Association and that "The full faith and credit of the United States is pledged to the payment of all amounts which may be required to be paid under this guaranty."

Purely private organizations have entered the secondary mortgage market, primarily to purchase mortgages which Fannie Mae and Freddie Mac are not allowed to buy such as "jumbos" or mortgages exceeding $108,300. (Fannie Mae and Freddie Mac are not government entities as such but do enjoy special privileges such as having government lines of credit and holding exemption from many of the securities laws. Freddie Mac is also exempt from federal taxation.)

Legislation introduced in Congress in the Fall of 1983 (Trust for Investment in Mortgages Act and Secondary Mortgage Market Enhancement Act) would encourage private competition with Fannie Mae and Freddie Mac, thereby making more mortgage money available and, hopefully, reducing interest rates on mortgages. Trusts for Investment in Mortgages (TIMs) would resemble mutual funds but with the investment being in pools of mortgages. Investors in TIMs would qualify for various tax law and securities law advantages, including preferential capital gains treatment.

Recent California Entries into the Real Estate Financing Field: The Cal-First Home Buyer's Program, born of Proposition 5 in 1982 and being carried out by the California Housing Finance Agency is a tax exempt revenue bond program designed to provide first-time homebuyers of limited price homes with low interest rate loans (starting rate of 9.5%). Thus far the program has suffered heavily from lack of lender and investor interest.

• "Carrie Mac" (for California Association of Realtors Mortgage Assistance Corporation) is the newest Mac on the block. It is a program started in mid-1982 which provides a secondary mortgage market for seller-financed first and second mortgages. The seller who takes such a mortgage is, through the program, able to discount it immediately with such organizations as Fannie Mae and Freddie Mac and thereby to cash out the deal. The seller's concession is to provide financing at 1 or 2 points below prevailing interest rates which may be important especially to the first-time homebuyer.

Enforcement of Mortgage and Deed of Trust

This is an area in which state statutes vary considerably, and local law must be consulted in each case. The following generalizations may be made (mortgage includes deed of trust and mortgagor and mortgagee include trustor and beneficiary in the following discussion):

Right of Reinstatement: The mortgagor is usually given the *right of reinstatement* at any time up to foreclosure sale of the property, i.e., the right to pay delinquent installments—to bring the note up to date—and thereby restore it to good standing. The mortgagee must then dismiss the foreclosure proceedings even though the note contains an acceleration clause, as it always does.[83]

One-Action Statutes: A number of states have *one-action statutes* which make sale of the security mandatory[84]—not that the mortgagee would do otherwise. Recourse may be had against the mortgagor personally only if a deficiency exists after such sale.

Sale Cuts Off Junior Liens: The purchaser of the property at foreclosure sale takes the property free of second mortgages or other liens attaching to the property subsequent to the mortgage being foreclosed.

Deficiency Judgment: In most states, a deficiency judgment can be obtained if the property sells for less than the balance due on the note, whether the remedy exercised is foreclosure by action or foreclosure by sale.[85]

Anti-Deficiency Judgment Statutes: During the depression years, many states adopted statutes placing limitations on deficiency judgments. The most widely adopted of these were *fair value statutes* which limited a deficiency judgment to the difference between the balance due on the note and the fair market value of the property.[86] Thus, if there was a balance due of $7000 and the property was sold for $4000, deficiency judgment would be limited to $1000 if it could be shown that the fair market value of the property at time of sale was $6000. In some states, statutes were passed denying deficiency judgments altogether in certain cases.

Right of Redemption: Twenty-four states give the mortgagor a *right of redemption* after foreclosure sale, for periods ranging from 6 months to as long as 2 years in one state, Alabama.[87] The usual period is one year. The right of redemption permits the mortgagor to recover the property by paying to the purchaser at foreclosure sale the amount paid

---

[81]38 U.S.C.A. 1501-2105.

[82][*Deleted*]

[83]California law follows.

[84]C.C.P. 726 is such a statute.

[85]California law follows.

[86]C.C.P. 726 is such a statute.

[87]Osborne on Mortgages, p. 95, says the right of redemption is given in 24 states. The California law is covered in the next section.

by him for the property, plus taxes, insurance premiums, and costs of repair paid by the purchaser prior to redemption. In the great majority of the 24 states giving a right of redemption, the right exists whether foreclosure is by action or by sale. In all but 4 states, the mortgagor is entitled to remain in possession during the redemption period, but an express provision in the mortgage giving the mortgagee the right of possession is valid and enforceable. The right may be exercised by junior encumbrancers—second mortgagees—to preserve their security, as may the right of reinstatement discussed above.[88]

Foreclosure of Junior Encumbrance: Second mortgagees may foreclose subject to the first mortgage. Suppose property worth $100,000 on which there is a $60,000 first mortgage and a $25,000 second mortgage. The first mortgage is being paid but not the second. The second mortgagee may sell the property subject to the first mortgage, bid in the amount of his second mortgage for the purchase price and become purchaser of the property if no higher bid is made. He must then make the payments on the first mortgage until he is able to find someone willing to purchase the property by taking over the first and paying him $25,000 plus what he has paid on the first mortgage.

California: The California law[89] is as follows:

1. If a deficiency judgment is desired, the remedy of foreclosure by action must be employed because C.C.P. 580d does not permit a deficiency judgment after foreclosure by sale. *But* C.C.P. 580b does not permit a deficiency judgment in any case if the mortgage or deed of trust is a *purchase money mortgage* or *purchase money deed of trust.* A purchase money mortgage or deed of trust is one given to obtain or make up the original purchase price of property. For example, S has property for sale for $70,000. R purchases, paying $10,000 cash and giving E Bank a first mortgage for $55,000 borrowed from it, and S a second mortgage for the remaining $5000. Both of these are purchase money mortgages, and R cannot be held for a deficiency judgment in either case. Since most mortgages are of this type, there would seldom be occasion to bring a foreclosure action for the purpose of obtaining a deficiency judgment.

Where foreclosure by action is used, the mortgagor or trustor is given the *right of reinstatement* prior to sale by C.C. 2924c[90] and a *right of redemption* for one year after sale if

---

[88]C.C.P. 701 permits redemption by junior encumbrancers.

[89]This will be subject to the federal laws on G.I. and F.H.A. loans where applicable.

[90]C.C. 2924c: "(a) Whenever all or a portion of the principal sum of any obligation secured by a deed of trust or mortgage on real property hereafter executed has, prior to the maturity date fixed in such obligation, become due or been declared due by reason of default in payment of interest or of any installment of principal, or by reason of failure of trustor or mortgagor to pay . . . taxes, assessments, premiums for insurance . . . the trustor or mortgagor . . . at any time within three months of the recording of notice of default under such deed of trust or mortgage if the power of sale therein is to be exercised, or otherwise at any time prior to entry of the decree of foreclosure, may pay to the beneficiary or the mortgagee . . . the entire amount then due . . . (including reasonable costs and expenses, subject to the provisions of subdivision (c) of this section, which are actually incurred in enforcing the terms of such obligation, deed of trust or mortgage, and trustee's or attorney's fees, subject to the provisions of subdivision (d) of this section), other than such portion of principal as would not then be due had no default occurred, and thereby cure the default . . . and thereupon, all proceedings

the proceeds of sale are not sufficient to pay the mortgage debt; for only 3 months if they are.[91]

2. Where the remedy exercised is foreclosure by sale, the following procedure must be followed (C.C. 2924[92]):

a. The secured party must first record a "Notice of Default" in the form of that on page 216. This states in general that the mortgagor or trustor has defaulted and that the mortgagee or beneficiary intends to sell the property to get his money. C.C. 2924(b) requires that a copy of the notice of default be mailed to the mortgagor or trustor if request for a copy is made in the mortgage or deed of trust, as it is, for example in the last paragraph of the deed of trust beginning on page 192; or if a separate request for a copy of notice of default form is recorded. C.C. 2924c(b) requires the notice of default to contain a notice, in statutory form, advising the mortgagor or trustor of his right of reinstatement.

b. The secured party must then wait 3 months during which time the trustor or mortgagor has the *right of reinstatement.*[93]

c. If the mortgage or deed of trust is not reinstated, the mortgagee—or trustee in the case of a deed of trust—sells the property. There is no right of redemption after the sale.[94]

Satisfaction and Reconveyance: When a note secured by a mortgage is fully paid, the mortgagee returns the note stamped "Paid" and, at the same time, gives the mortgagor a "Satisfaction of Mortgage" in the form of that on page 217. By recording this, the mortgagor is able to show of record that the lien on the mortgage has been discharged and that he now owns the property free and clear. The same procedure is followed as to the deed of trust, except that the instrument

(Continued on page 218)

. . . shall be dismissed or discontinued and the obligation and deed of trust or mortgage shall be reinstated and shall be and remain in force and effect, the same as if no such acceleration had occurred."

Subdivision (c) of Section 2924c limits costs and expenses to "costs incurred for recording, mailing, publishing, and posting notices required by this article and for a trustee's sale guarantee."

Subdivision (d) of Section 2924c allow trustee's or attorney's fees of $150 on the first $50,000 of unpaid principal, 1/2% on the next $100,000 of unpaid principal, 1/4% on the next $350,000 and 1/8% on any unpaid balance of principal over $500,000.

[91]C.C.P. 729.030: the mortgagor is entitled to possession during the period of redemption, but C.C.P. 729.030 gives the purchaser at foreclosure sale the right to rents during the period of redemption. These must be credited to the amount required to redeem, however, if the mortgagor redeems, i.e., he must be given credit for any rents collected.

[92]C.C. 2924: There shall be no sale under a mortgage with power of sale or deed of trust "until (a) the trustee, mortgagee, or beneficiary, shall first file for record . . . a notice of default . . .; (b) not less than three months shall thereafter elapse; and (c) after the lapse of the three months the mortgagee [or] trustee . . . shall give notice of sale, stating the time and place thereof, in the manner and for a time not less than that set forth in Section 2924f." Section 2924f requires notice of sale to be posted in a public place and a conspicuous place on the property for 20 days before the sale and to be published in a newspaper once a week for the same period.

[93]See C.C. 2924c in footnote 90.

[94]This is because C.C.P. 729.030, the redemption statute, applies only to "judicial sales"—sales by a public officer under court order. The sale under the power of sale in the mortgage or deed of trust, being by the mortgagee or trustee, is not a judicial sale. Hence, C.C.P. 729.030 does not apply to it.

ASSIGNMENT AND ASSUMPTION AGREEMENT

To: CALIFORNIA BANK

I   For value received the undersigned hereby transfer and assign to _____
_____ANTHONY L. ASSUMER and MARIA J. ASSUMER, his wife_____
                                                    Purchaser
all of the interest of the undersigned in any refunds or credits which may at any time be available by reason of the
provisions of the deed of trust described in the following described agreement or the contract of insurance thereof by
the Federal Housing Administration.

Dated: _____February 3, 1984_____   s/PETER L. TRUSTOR_____
                                                                     Maker – Seller
                                                    s/CATHERINE D. TRUSTOR_____
                                                                     Maker – Seller

To: CALIFORNIA BANK

II   The undersigned having heretofore assumed or being the maker(s) or guarantor(s) of the promissory note and
deed of trust described in the following Assumption Agreement, Section III below in consideration of the execution
and acceptance thereof, hereby jointly and severally agree that the liability of the undersigned on the said note shall not
be affected thereby. The undersigned further jointly and severally waive presentation, demand of payment, protest and
notice of non-payment of the said indebtedness and expressly consent to delay or change in the time of payment of
principal or any instalment thereof or in the amount of one or more instalments or performance of any of the
provisions of the deed of trust, to partial releases of the property covered by the said deed of trust, to the acceptance of
additional security for said note, to the increase or reduction of the interest rate payable under said note; to the
reduction of principal thereof, and to subsequent assumption agreements all without notice to the undersigned and
without affecting the liability of the undersigned thereon.

Dated: _____February 3, 1984_____   s/PETER L. TRUSTOR_____
                                                                     Original Maker
                                                    s/CATHERINE D. TRUSTOR_____
                                                                     Original Maker

                                                    _____
                                                                  Seller or Guarantor

To: CALIFORNIA BANK

III   The undersigned having acquired title to that certain real property described in a deed of trust dated _____
September 20, 1971 executed by Peter L. Trustor & Catherine D. Trustor, his wife_,
which deed of trust was given to secure a promissory note of even date in the principal sum of $_17,000.00_____
_____ , and having agreed as part of the purchase price of said property to assume and pay
the indebtedness evidenced by said note, does hereby assume and agree to pay the indebtedness evidenced by the said
promissory note (or as the same may be modified or extended) and to be bound by and to perform all of the covenants
of the said deed of trust at the time and in the manner provided therein. The undersigned further agrees that the
property described in said deed of trust shall be held as security for the payment of any and all obligations and
liabilities, whatsoever, whether primary, secondary, direct, indirect, fixed or contingent, which are now due or may
hereafter become due from the undersigned (or any of them or any successor in interest to the undersigned or any of
them) whether created directly or acquired by assignment if the document evidencing any such other obligation or
liability or any other writing signed by the undersigned (or any of them or any successor in interest to the undersigned
or any of them) specifically provides that said obligation is secured by said deed of trust. Any married woman who
signs below as Purchaser hereby expressly agrees that her separate property shall be liable for any and all indebtedness
which is or which may hereafter be secured by said deed of trust.

Dated: _____February 3, 1984_____   s/ANTHONY L. ASSUMER_____
                                                                     Purchaser
                                                    s/MARIA J. ASSUMER_____
                                                                     Purchaser

                                                    _____
                                                                  Mailing Address

INSTRUCTIONS:
   (a) The immediate sellers should sign Sections I and II.
   (b) Guarantors, if any, and original makers should then sign Section II, except that if the obligation is on an FHA or VA form of
       note and original makers are not readily available, their signatures need not be obtained, (FHA and VA note forms contain
       waivers and consent to extensions.) In all other cases signature of original maker should always be obtained (before obtaining
       signatures of purchasers) except that when makers have once signed this form, it is not necessary that they sign subsequent
       agreements.
   (c) Purchasers should then sign Section III.

CONTRACT OF SALE OF REAL PROPERTY

Contract of sale of real property made and entered into by and between _____

_____ STEPHEN M. SELLER _____, hereinafter called vendor,

and ___ BERNARD A. BUYER and BEVERLY D. BUYER ___, hereinafter called purchaser:

In consideration of the promises, agreements, and covenants contained herein, and subject to the terms and conditions set forth herein, the parties agree as follows:

1. Vendor agrees to sell to purchaser and purchaser agrees to purchase from vendor

the following described real property situated in the City of _____ Richmond _____,

County of _____ Contra Costa _____, State of California:

> Lot 9 in Block 6, as designated on the map entitled
> "Richmond Park Tract, Contra Costa County, California,"
> filed in the Office of the Recorder of the County of
> Contra Costa, State of California, on March 17, 1923,
> in Book 7 of Maps, at page 25.

2. Purchaser agrees to pay vendor for said real property the sum of _one hundred_

thousand & no/100 Dollars ($100,000.00), which sum shall be payable as

follows, with interest at the rate of _____ thirteen _____ per cent (13%)
per annum on the unpaid balance of principal:

> Ten thousand & no/100 dollars ($10,000.00) at the
> time of execution of this contract and the balance
> of ninety thousand & no/100 dollars ($90,000) in
> monthly installments of nine hundred ten & no/100
> ($910.00) per month, principal and interest,
> commencing May 1, 1984.

3. Possession shall be delivered by vendor to purchaser on the date hereof.

4. Purchaser shall pay taxes and assessments from date hereof assessed and levied against the property hereafter. Taxes for the current fiscal year shall be prorated as of the date hereof.

5. Purchaser, at his expense, shall maintain fire insurance upon the property in amounts and with companies satisfactory to purchaser. The policies evidencing such insurance shall insure vendor and purchaser as their interests may appear and shall be deposited with and held by vendor. Should purchaser fail to keep the property insured, as aforesaid, vendor may insure it. In such case, purchaser upon demand, shall pay vendor the amount paid as premiums for such insurance, together with interest on said sum at the rate payable on the unpaid balance of the purchase price.

6. Should purchaser fail to make any of the installment payments required by this contract, or to fulfill any of the promises, agreements, or covenants contained herein, or to comply with any of the terms or conditions hereof, the amounts paid hereon may be

retained by vendor as consideration for making this contract and vendor shall be released from all obligation in law or equity to convey said real property.

7. Waiver by vendor of any promise, agreement, or covenant contained herein, on one or more occasions, or of any term or condition hereof, on one or more occasions, shall not vitiate the same or any other promise, agreement, covenant, term, or condition hereof.

8. Time is of the essence of this agreement.

9. In case it becomes necessary for vendor to commence suit to enforce this contract, or any of the promises, agreements, covenants, or terms hereof, or to recover possession of said real property, purchaser agrees to pay costs of suit and reasonable attorney's fees incurred by vendor.

10. The words used in this contract shall be construed to include the plural number as well as the singular and the feminine gender as well as the masculine. If the "purchaser" consists of more than one person, the liability of the persons constituting the "purchaser," for each and all of the promises, agreements, and covenants contained herein, and for each and all of the terms and conditions hereof, shall be joint and several. This contract, and each of the promises, agreements, and covenants contained herein, and each of the terms and conditions hereof, is binding on the parties, their heirs, successors, personal representatives, and assigns.

11. Upon payment in full of all sums due from purchaser to vendor hereunder, vendor shall execute and deliver to purchaser a grant deed to said real property and shall, at the same time, furnish purchaser, at vendor's expense, with a standard California Land Title Association policy if title insurance insuring title in purchaser subject only to liens, encumbrances, easements, restrictions, rights, or conditions set forth herein or created or suffered by purchaser. Provided, however, that vendor reserves the right to deliver said deed and furnish such policy of title insurance at any time during the term hereof, in which case, purchaser, in lieu of this contract, shall execute and deliver to vendor a note for all amounts of money then unpaid, which note shall be secured by a first deed of trust upon said real property, in usual form and with provisions requiring purchaser to maintain fire insurance upon the property in favor of vendor, which first deed of trust shall be executed and delivered by purchaser to vendor concurrently with the delivery of said note.

Executed at _____Richmond_____, California, on _____April 16_____, 19_84_.

EACH PARTY HEREBY ACKNOWLEDGES THAT HE UNDERSTANDS THAT THIS IS A BINDING CONTRACT.

_____/s/ STEPHEN M. SELLER_____

_____/s/ BERNARD A. BUYER_____

_____/s/ BEVERLY D. BUYER_____

(Should be acknowledged by Notary Public.)

NOTICE OF DEFAULT AND ELEC-
TION TO SELL UNDER DEED OF
TRUST

Loan No. 40469
T.S. No. 16205-2-80
IMPORTANT NOTICE

IF YOUR PROPERTY IS IN FORE-
CLOSURE BECAUSE YOU ARE BE-
HIND IN YOUR PAYMENTS, IT MAY
BE SOLD WITHOUT ANY COURT
ACTION, and you may have the legal
right to bring your account in good
standing by paying all of your past
due payments plus permitted costs
and expenses within three months
from the date this notice of default
was recorded.

This amount is $7,500.00 as of
March 31, 1984 and will increase until
your account becomes current. You
may not have to pay the entire unpaid
portion of your account, even though
full payment was demanded, but you
must pay the amount stated above.

After three months from the date of
recordation of this document (which
date of recordation appears hereon),
unless the obligation being foreclosed
upon permits a longer period, you
have only the legal right to stop the
foreclosure by paying the entire
amount demanded by your creditor.

To find out the amount you must
pay, or to arrange for payment to stop
the foreclosure, or if your property is
in foreclosure for any other reason,
contact:

Lorna Gray, 500 Gough Street, San
Francisco, CA 94109; (415) 201-1221.

If you have any questions, you
should contact a lawyer or the government agency which may have insured
your loan.

Remember, YOU MAY LOSE LE-
GAL RIGHTS IF YOU DO NOT TAKE
PROMPT ACTION.

In addition to the amount stated
above, should any prior taxes, liens,
or encumbrances be delinquent or become delinquent, and the loan can be
reinstated, said delinquencies must
be cured as a condition of reinstatement.

Notice is hereby given: That MAR-
TIN TITLE INSURANCE COMPANY,
a California corporation, is duly appointed Trustee under the following
described deed of trust: AN ALL-IN-
CLUSIVE DEED OF TRUST.

TRUSTOR: JAMES GERARD, a
single man.

BENEFICIARY: LORNA GRAY, a
single woman.

Recorded August 4, 1982, as Instrument No. CO 67676 in Book C 915,
page 104, of Official Records in the
office of the Recorder of San Francisco County.

Said deed of trust describes the following property: PROPERTY DE-
SCRIBED THEREIN.

Said deed of trust secures certain
obligations including one note for the
sum of $200,000.00.

That the beneficial interest under
such deed of trust and the obligations
secured thereby are presently held by
the undersigned; That a breach of,
and default in, the obligations for
which such deed of trust is security
has occurred in that payment has not
been made of:

The installment of principal and interest which became due January 1,
1984, and all subsequent installments
of principal and interest.

That by reason thereof, the undersigned, present beneficiary under
such deed of trust, has executed and
delivered to said duly appointed Trustee, a writ⁺   Declaration of Default
and Der   .u for sale, and has deposited wiui said duly appointed Trustee,
such deed of trust and all documents
evidencing obligations secured thereby, and has declared and does hereby
declare all sums secured thereby immediately due and payable and has
elected and does hereby elect to
cause the trust property to be sold to
satisfy the obligations secured thereby.

Dated April 13, 1984.

LORNA GRAY
No. 4657   Apr 15-4t-F-R

SATISFACTION OF MORTGAGE

The mortgage dated the   eighth   **day of**   January,   19 74

made and executed by DOUGLAS R. MORTGAGOR and FRANCES H. MORTGAGOR, his wife,

to   EDWARD J. MORTGAGEE

which mortgage was recorded on the   fifteenth   day of   January,   19 74

in the office of the County Recorder of the   City and   County of

San Francisco   , State of California

in Book   5230   of Official Records at page   217   , Recorder's Serial No. P34567,

together with the debt thereby secured, is fully paid, satisfied and discharged, and the property

therein described is hereby released from the lien of said mortgage.

WITNESS   my   hand   this   9th   day of   January   , 19 84

_____/s/ EDWARD J. MORTGAGEE_____

_____

For Recorder's Use Only	STATE OF CALIFORNIA }ss.
	COUNTY OF ___ San Francisco ___
	On this __9th__ day of __January__, in the year 19 __84__, before me, the undersigned, a Notary Public in and for said State, personally appeared _____ Edward J. Mortgagee _____ _____, personally known to me (or proved to me on the basis of satisfactory evidence) to be the person__ whose name__ __is__ subscribed to the within instrument, and acknowledged to me that __he__ executed it. WITNESS my hand and official seal. _____NANCY A. NOTARY_____ Notary Public in and for said State.

given is a "Deed of Reconveyance," the language of "deed" being used in both directions in keeping with the concept that the deed of trust is a transfer of "title." A deed of reconveyance is set out on page 199.[95]

Priorities Between Mortgages and Other Liens

It is often the case that two or more of the various types of liens attach to property at the same time, a mortgage or deed of trust on the one hand as against one or more of the various types of liens created by law on the other—mechanics' liens, attachment or judgment liens, or tax liens; or that different liens are designed to charge different values offered by the property, e.g., to charge the lands and improvements, on the one hand, and to charge the crops on the other.

These create questions of priority which are discussed briefly at this point. As used throughout the balance of this discussion, the word "mortgage" is to be taken to include deed of trust.

Mortgage and Crop Mortgage: Crops may be mortgaged independently of the land. Crop mortgages are usually required by statute to be executed with certain formalities and to be recorded as a "crop mortgage" to be an effective lien. Hence, while the ordinary real estate mortgage usually covers not only the land but also the "rents, issues and profits," this is not enough to constitute it a crop mortgage, and a crop mortgage in the required form takes precedence over the real estate mortgage as to the crops, even though it was given and recorded subsequently to the real estate mortgage. If the real estate mortgagee wants a mortgage on the crops as well, he should take a separate crop mortgage.[96]

Mortgage and Security Interest in Fixtures: U.C.C. 9-313[97] states rules for priorities between mortgages and other real estate interests and security interests in fixtures. Until 1981, California did not have a 9-313 and the rules regulating priorities between mortgages and security interests in fixtures were the product of California case law. California was one of a number of states which had rejected 9-313. Rejection was for a number of reasons including the feeling that 9-313 was too much of an invasion of real estate law and because of sharp differences between the rules of 9-313 and existing California rules in various particulars. In 1980, California finally adopted 9-313, to become effective January 1, 1981. California was the last holdout against 9-313 and some version at least of 9-313 is now the law in all 49 of the code states.

U.C.C. 9313 gives the secured party, holding a security interest in fixtures, priority over a real estate mortgage in these instances:

1. Purchase money security interest in fixtures v. *prior* real estate mortgage: Except when the prior real estate mortgage is a "construction mortgage," as defined in 9313(1)(c), a purchase money security interest in fixtures has priority over a *prior* real estate mortgage when the security interest is perfected (by filing a financing statement with the Secretary of State's office, as discussed in Chapter 7) and when, in addition, there is a "fixture filing" before the goods become fixtures or within 10 days thereafter. U.C.C. 9313(4)(a). A "fixture filing" is a filing of a financing statement in the county recorder's office of the county in which a real estate mortgage

would be recorded. So, two financing statements must be filed to establish priority, one in the secretary of state's office and one in the county recorder's office.

2. Fixture security interest v. *subsequent* real estate mortgage: The fixture security interest has priority if there is a fixture filing before the real estate mortgage is recorded. In other words, the ordinary rule of priority in conveyancing applies, which is that the first to file or record prevails.

3. "Soft fixtures": Readily removable fixtures are referred to as "soft fixtures." U.C.C. 9313(4)(c) gives a perfected security interest in readily removable factory or office machines and replacement domestic appliances priority over competing real estate mortgages.

4. "Trade fixtures":[98] U.C.C. 9313(5)(b) would give a party having a security interest in trade fixtures priority over a conflicting real estate mortgage interest.

● Prior to its adoption of Section 9313, California had the rules, as did some number of other states prior to adoption of the code fixtures rule, that, as against a real estate mortgage, fixtures had to be removable without material injury to the real estate improvements and without causing a material reduction in the value of the mortgage security. U.C.C. 9313(8) rejects these rules. Under 9313(8) the party holding the security interest in fixtures can remove them even though removal will cause physical injury to the real estate and diminution in value of the real estate. But the fixtures secured party must reimburse the real estate mortgagee for the cost of repair of the physical injury. U.C.C. 9313(8).

Mortgage and Mechanic's Lien: By reason of the special privilege of "relation back" given to it, the mechanic's lien may obtain priority over a mortgage recorded before the mechanic's lien but after commencement of the work for which the "mechanic" is entitled to his lien, and the property may be sold to enforce the mechanic's lien despite the mortgage. The mechanic's lien extends to the entire property and not merely the particular part of it on which the work was done. See page 203 for a general discussion of mechanics' liens and the doctrine of "relation back."

Mortgage and Attachment or Judgment Lien: A recorded mortgage is, of course, good against subsequent creditors of the mortgagor. As noted in footnote 67, on page 183, even an unrecorded mortgage is good against subsequent creditors who, it is said, "stand in the shoes of the debtor" (against whom the unrecorded mortgage is good), unless the mortgage was withheld from record for the express purpose of deceiving the subsequent creditors. Since the prior mortgage is good as against the creditors, it is good as against their liens by attachment or judgment. In many states, but not California, an *execution creditor* prevails over a prior unrecorded mortgage. An execution creditor is one who has spent money to bring about a sheriff's sale of property of a debtor to get satisfaction of the judgment. Since he would not have incurred this additional expense had he known of the mortgage, it is felt that fairness requires that he be permitted to sell the property free of the mortgage.

● If an attachment or judgment lien is recorded prior to a mortgage, it takes precedence, but, of course, a mortgagee will not lend money and knowingly take a partially or totally worthless mortgage as security, so there is little likelihood of this happening.

---

[95]If the note is paid early, there will be a *prepayment charge* or "*penalty*," as discussed on page 120.

[96]This appears to continue to be the California law under the Uniform Commercial Code. U.C.C. 9102(1)(c).

[97]See Appendix for U.C.C. 9313.

---

[98]See page 230 for definition and discussion of "trade fixtures."

Mortgage and Tax Lien: The government—federal and state—has the power to give tax liens priority over private liens, but unless this is done by the taxing statute there is no such priority. For example, since the Internal Revenue Code does not give priority to tax liens for unpaid income taxes, they have no superiority over the liens of prior mortgages or deeds of trust. Taxes on the property itself, i.e., annual real property taxes, are usually given priority over private liens,[99] it being the right of the city or county to sell the property free of private liens if such taxes are not paid.

• In other cases, as in the case of the income tax lien mentioned above, or, in California, in the case of a lien for delinquent state sales taxes, the lien may be recorded by the taxing authority and becomes effective from the date of recording, taking priority over subsequent liens but being subordinate to prior recorded liens.

Landlord and Tenant

The landlord-tenant relationship is one in which use and possession of property, as distinguished from title or ownership, is transferred to another for some period of time in exchange for a consideration called rent. The landlord remains owner of the property, but the tenant has the exclusive right to use and possess it for the agreed period. The history of this relationship has been discussed earlier, and the word "landlord" is self-explanatory.

Types of Relationships

The various types of landlord-tenant relationships are usually called *tenancies.* Originally, there were two general types of tenancies—tenancies for years and tenancies at will.[100]

Tenancies for Years: "Tenancy for years" is misleading. It sounds like an arrangement that must exist for *years.* It is not. *Tenancy for years* is the term used to distinguish a tenancy of certain duration, i.e., a tenancy for a fixed term, from a tenancy not of certain duration, i.e., the tenancy at will or the periodic tenancy, seen below. Since most fixed term tenancies exist for a year or more, the term, tenancy for years, is not inappropriate. A tenancy for more than one year is within the statute of frauds and must be evidenced by a writing. This becomes the writing we call a *lease.*

Tenancies at Will and Periodic Tenancies: Originally, all tenancies which were not tenancies for years were *tenancies at will,* and tenancy at will meant the opposite of tenancy for years, i.e., a tenancy of uncertain duration. Tenancies at will were terminable by either party at any time, without advance notice. Today, statutes require advance notice for a period equal to the rental period. Therefore, there is no longer any such thing as a true tenancy at will. These tenancies which, by statute, require notice of termination, have come to be known as *periodic tenancies.* Where the period is one month, as it almost always is, they are called *month-to-month tenancies.* Home rentals comprise the great bulk of month-to-month tenancies. Fixed term tenancies are more likely to be found in connection with commercial properties.

• If a month-to-month tenant "holds over"—stays on the premises—after he has been properly notified to vacate, or if a lessee holds over after the expiration of his lease, he is called a *tenant at sufferance.* One of three things may be done at this point—the landlord may enter into a new tenancy arrangement with him; the landlord may take legal proceedings to evict him; or the landlord may accept further rent from him without having any understanding regarding his status. If the last is done, C.C. 1945 provides that, "If a lessee of real property remains in possession thereof after the expiration of the hiring, and the lessor accepts rent from him, the parties are presumed to have renewed the hiring on the same terms, and for the same time, not exceeding one month when the rent is payable monthly, nor in any case one year." This is modified by C.C. 1945.5 which is designed to save a residential property lessee from being trapped into a long term lease renewal by fine print in the original lease and which does this by providing that automatic renewal, for holding over or failing to give notice of intention not to renew, is void unless the renewal provision appears in at least 8-point bold-face type in the body of the lease and immediately above the lessee's signature line.

Residential Tenancies

The discussion in the next section is devoted to *leases,* the instruments that create "tenancies for years," and in the main therefore the next section is devoted to *commercial tenancies.* Certain important law regarding *residential tenancies* should first be considered, as follows:

Rent: Rent is payable in advance only if agreed or established by custom between the parties. Since the one thing or the other is invariably the case, rent is almost always payable in advance.[101]

Discriminatory Rental Practice: Mostly under the Unruh Civil Rights Act (C.C. 51-53), which is regarded as prohibiting all types of arbitrary discrimination by "business establishments," a number of recent cases have struck down various types of restrictions on residential occupancy attempted to be imposed by landlords and condominium associations. The leadoff case is *Marina Point, Ltd.* v. *Wolfson* (1982) 30 Cal.3d 721, 180 Cal.Rptr. 496, 640 P.2d 115. Marina Point, the landlord, was a large apartment complex. It brought an unlawful detainer action against tenants who refused to vacate the premises at the conclusion of a lease. The ground for refusing to renew the lease was the presence of a minor child on the premises in violation of a no-children policy. The California Supreme Court held that "the provisions of the Unruh Act, in light of its broad application to 'all business establishments,' have been held to apply with equal force to the business of renting housing accommodations;" that, while a business owner may adopt reasonable rules regulating the conduct of patrons or tenants and may exclude individuals who violate such rules, "an individual who has committed no such mis-

---

[99]See Rev. & Tax. C. 2192.1.

[100]See footnote 1 on page 163.

[101]C.C. 1947: "When there is no usage or contract to the contrary, rents are payable at the termination of the holding, when it does not exceed one year. If the holding is by the day, week, month, quarter, or year, rent is payable at the termination of the respective periods, as it successively becomes due."

Right of landlord to hold tenant's property for rent. In England, the landlord had the right to seize the property of the tenant located on the premises to enforce payment of rent due and payable. This was called "distraint" or the right to "distrain for rent." Such a right has not generally been recognized in this country, and, in California, was denied in *Gruber* v. *Pacific States Sav. & Loan Co.*, 13 C.2d 144, 88 P.2d 137. But apartment house, boarding house, hotel keepers and the like are given a lien upon property of guests for rent by C.C. 1861-1861a. However, the constitutionality of C.C. 1861-1861a has been questioned in the federal case of *Klim* v. *Jones* (1970) 315 Fed. Supp. 109.

NOTICE TO PAY RENT OR QUIT

TO: _____ ROBERT D. RENTER and RUTH B. RENTER, his wife _____

All residents (tenants and subtenants) in possession (full name) and all others in possession

WITHIN THREE DAYS after the service on you of this notice, you are hereby required to pay to the undersigned or ___ X X X X X X X X X X X X X X X X X ___ , his authorized agent, the rent of the premises hereinafter described, of which you now hold possession amounting to the sum of one thousand four hundred & no/100 ---------------- dollars ($ 1,400.00) enumerated as follows:

$ 700.00 ___ Due From ___ April 1 ___ 19 84 ___ To ___ April 30 ___ 19 84

$ 700.00 ___ Due From ___ May 1 ___ 19 84 ___ To ___ May 31 ___ 19 84

$ XXXXX ___ Due From ___ XXXXX ___ 19 XX ___ To ___ XXXXX ___ 19 XX

OR QUIT AND DELIVER UP THE POSSESSION OF THE PREMISES.

The premises herein referred to are situated in the city of ___ San Francisco ___ ,

County of ___ San Francisco ___ , State of California, designated by the number and street as ___ 410 Terrace Street, San Francisco, Calif. ___ , apt. ___ xxx ___ .

YOU ARE FURTHER NOTIFIED THAT, the owner/landlord does hereby elect to declare the forfeiture of your lease or rental agreement under which you hold possession of the above-described premises and if you fail to perform or otherwise comply, will institute legal proceedings to recover rent and possession of said premises which could result in a judgement against you including costs and necessary disbursements together with treble damages as allowed by law for such unlawful detention.

DATE: ___ June 1, 1984 ___   ___ s/ HENRY H. MOMONER ___

                                        OWNER/~~AGENT~~

                                        Henry H. Homoner

UNAUTHORIZED REPRODUCTION OF THIS FORM IS ILLEGAL

---

conduct cannot be excluded solely because he falls within a class of persons whom the owner believes is more likely to engage in misconduct than some other group;" that "(w)hether the exclusionary policy rests on the alleged undesirable propensities of those of a particular race, nationality, occupation, political affiliation, or age, in this context the Unruh Act protects individuals from such arbitrary discrimination;" and that therefore the alleged fact that "(c)hildren are rowdier, noiser, more mischievous and more boisterous than adults" could not provide a non-discriminatory basis for the landlord's action.

● In *Hubert* v. *Williams* (1982) 133 C.A.3d Supp. 1, 184 Cal. Rptr. 161, plaintiff, a quadriplegic who required a 24-hour attendant, sued his landlord alleging that plaintiff had been evicted from the landlord's rental housing because plaintiff's attendant was a lesbian and because plaintiff associated with persons of homosexual orientation. The Appellate Department of the California Superior Court held that these facts, if proven by the landlord, would not justify eviction. The Court said, in part, "We find the discussion in (*Marina Point Ltd.* v. *Wolfson*) to be fully dispositive of the issue presented by the instant case. Accordingly, we hold that under the Unruh Act, landlords may not refuse to rent an apartment to a homosexual solely because of that person's sexual preference."

● In *Hess* v. *Fair Employment and Housing Commission* (1982) 138 C.A.3d 232, 187 Cal.Rptr. 712, landlords, after agreeing to rent a duplex to tenants, refused to go through with the rental agreement when landlords learned that tenants were an unmarried couple. The California Court of Appeal held that "(t)he California Fair Employment and Housing Act (Govt.C. 12900-12996) prohibits discrimination based on marital status, including that against unmarried couples." In particular, Govt.C. 12955 "provides in pertinent part, 'It shall be unlawful (a) For the owner of any housing accommodation to discriminate against any person because of the . . . marital status . . . of such person'"

O'Connor v. *Village Green Owners Assn.* (1983) 33 Cal.3d 790, 191 Cal.Rptr. 320, found the Supreme Court echoing its opinion in *Marina Point, Ltd. O'Connor* involved an apartment complex converted to a condominium development with a condominium association rule forbidding residency by anyone under the age of 18. Plaintiffs bought a condominium unit in 1975. In 1979 a son was born. The condominium association gave plaintiffs notice that the presence of the son constituted a violation of the association rules and directed them to discontinue having the son live there. Being unable to find other housing, plaintiffs filed suit to have the age restriction declared invalid and were successful. The Court had somewhat more difficulty in finding that the condominium association was a "business establishment" (C.C. 51) than it did with the landlord-for-profit in *Marina Point, Ltd.* But the Court worked it out. It noted that the Legislature in using the words "all business establishments *of every kind whatsoever*" intended "the term 'business establishments' (to be) used in the broadest sense reasonably possible." It went on to say that "(a)lthough our cases so far have all dealt with profit-making entities, we see no reason to insist that profit-making to be a *sine qua non* for coverage under the act." The Court noted that while hospitals are often nonprofit organizations they would clearly be "business establishments" for the purposes of the act. The Court concluded by finding that "(the association) has sufficient businesslike attributes to fall within the scope of the act's reference to 'business establishments of every kind whatsoever' . . . the association performs all the customary business functions which in the traditional landlord-tenant relationship rest on the landlord's shoulders."

Repairs; Modern California Statutory Law and the New Judicial Doctrine of Implied Warranty of Habitability: It was, and is, the common law rule that the residential landlord does not have a duty to maintain or repair leased premises. Many states, including California, gave the residential tenant some relief from this rule by "*repair and deduct*" statutes which allowed the tenant to use one month's rent to make repairs when the landlord failed to do so. California's repair and deduct statute is the combination of C.C. 1941 and 1942. C.C. 1941 requires the landlord to make repairs of conditions that render residential premises "untenantable." C.C. 1942 provides that if, "within a reasonable time after notice," the landlord fails to make repairs, the tenant may use up to one month's rent for that purpose and may deduct the moneys so used from his rental obligation to the landlord; or, in the alternative, the tenant may vacate the premises and terminate the lease.

C.C. 1942 goes on to provide, further, that 30 days is the "reasonable time" within which the landlord must act and that the tenant cannot use his repair and deduct remedy more than twice in a 12-month period.

C.C. 1942.1 provides that lease provisions waiving C.C. 1941 or 1942 are void as against public policy. Leases continue to contain waiver provisions, however. See, e.g., paragraph 5 of specimen lease.

C.C. 1941.1 provides that residential premises are "untenantable for the purposes of section 1941" if they are substantially lacking in housing code-conforming plumbing, heating or electrical lighting facilities, water supply, effective waterproofing or weather protection of roof and exterior walls, clean surrounding grounds as regards those areas which are under the control of the landlord, adequate receptacles for the disposition of garbage and rubbish, or safe floors, stairways and railings.

● Landlords were prone to retaliate against tenants who took advantage of their repair and deduct rights or who attempted to improve their lot by other means, as by reporting housing code violations of the landlord. Retaliation took the form of terminating the tenancy or increasing the rent and then evicting the tenant when he did not pay the increased rent. This landlords' practice became known as the practice of "*retaliatory eviction*," that is, the practice of terminating a tenancy for the purpose of retaliating against a tenant for some act of the tenant which did not constitute a breach of the rental agreement such as exercising the repair and deduct remedy or reporting housing code violations. The California Supreme Court put its foot down on this practice in 1970 in the case of *Schweiger* v. *Bonds*, 3 C.3d 507, 90 Cal.Rptr. 729, where it held that the "doctrine of retaliatory eviction" was a defense to a tenant who refused to pay a rent increase which was prompted by the tenant's exercise of his repair and deduct remedy. In the course of the decision, the California Supreme Court approved an earlier federal case, *Edwards* v. *Habib*, 397 Fed.2d 687, which refused to allow the eviction of a tenant who had reported a housing code violation. The California Legislature responded to this decisional law by enacting C.C. 1942.5 which provides that a tenant may not be evicted, or have his rent increased, for 60 days after he has exercised his repair and deduct rights or has complained to a governmental agency about the untenantability of the premises. It is possible that the Supreme Court will find that C.C. 1942.5 does not go far enough in protecting tenants.

● In 1974, the California Supreme Court made a landmark ruling in *Green* v. *Superior Court*, 10 C.3d 616, 111 Cal.Rptr. 704. In *Green*, the Court decided that the repair and deduct remedy was not the exclusive remedy of the residential tenant but that he should, in addition, be entitled to an *"implied warranty of habitability"* which would ensure him of substantial compliance with building and housing code requirements with respect to matters which materially affected his health or safety. In *Green* the landlord failed to remedy housing code violations which included the collapse of the bathroom ceiling, plumbing blockages, faulty wiring, an illegally installed and dangerous stove, lack of heat, and the continued presence of rats, mice and cockroaches on the premises. Clearly the landlord's implied warranty was violated and the breach of warranty was held to be a defense to an eviction action for nonpayment of rent. So long as the landlord refused to repair the condition of the premises, the Court said, the tenant could not be evicted for nonpayment of rent. The landlord could and should be protected, the Court said, by requiring the tenant to pay the agreed-upon rent into court, but if the tenant proved his case he should get damages in an amount equal to the difference between the fair rental value of the premises as they should have been maintained and the fair rental value of the premises as they were in fact maintained. *Green* leaves many loose ends which must await further decisions of the California Court. *Green* involved an apartment house tenant, but surely no distinction can be made between an apartment house tenant and the tenant of a single family dwelling. *Green* deals with housing code violations but it does not seem that any other forms of threats to a tenant's health or safety would be any the less reprehensible. A troublesome problem will be that of the premises which are uninhabitable at the time of the inception of the tenancy, a problem with which the *Green* Court did not have to deal. The *Green* Court did however note that someday it might have to decide whether a tenant ought to be considered to have "assumed the risk" of premises which were uninhabitable at the time of the inception of the tenancy. One major answer to this is that the doctrine of assumption of risk is not supposed to apply to persons who incur risks only because they are so lacking in bargaining power as to be unable to do otherwise.[102] Still another question is that of the extent to which the doctrine of retaliatory eviction may come into play when the landlord makes the demanded repairs and then raises the rent to a level which is beyond the means of the tenant to pay.

● C.C. 1942.5 was rewritten in 1979 to protect the tenant for a period of 180 days and to protect him from eviction or rent increase because he has organized or participated in a tenants' association or has lawfully and peaceably engaged in acts which he has a right to do, presumably such as publicly demonstrating against or picketing a landlord.

Termination: Statutes in most states require that 30 days' notice of intention to terminate a periodic tenancy be given by the party terminating the tenancy whether it be the landlord or the tenant.[103]

---

[102]For other answers, see The Implied Warranty of Habitability: A New Doctrine Raising New Issues (1975) 62 Cal. Law Review 1444, 1451, and see this article generally for a comprehensive discussion of the warranty of habitability by one of the lawyers for the tenant in the *Green* case.

[103]C.C. 789 and 1946 require 30 days' written notice, but Section 1946 permits this to be reduced to 7 days if the parties expressly so agree at the time the tenancy is created.

If the tenant does not vacate at the expiration of the notice period, the landlord may commence "unlawful detainer proceedings" under C.C.P. 1161 et seq., this being a special, speedy remedy designed to permit the landlord to recover the property in a very short time. This is by virtue of C.C.P. 1179a which says that the court "shall give such actions precedence over all

Leases

From here on, the discussion is confined to tenancies for years, and the leases that document them. Some of the rules shown apply with equal force to tenancies at will and periodic tenancies, such as those dealing with the right to remove fixtures and with liability for injuries to persons coming on the premises. A printed form of lease is set out on pages 223-226. It is representative and contains the usual provisions of such forms. If it is desired to provide for matters not covered by the printed terms, additional provisions may be typed in at the end, as is illustrated by paragraphs 24-26 at the end of the specimen form. In leases, it is customary to refer to the parties as *lessor* and *lessee*, which is done throughout the following discussion.

● Limits are placed on the duration of leases of certain types of property. C.C. 717 prohibits a lease of land for agricultural or horticultural purposes for a period of more than 51 years. C.C. 718 prohibits the lease of property within a city or town for more than 99 years. C.C. 718f prohibits the lease of land for the purpose of producing minerals, oil or gas for more than 99 years.

Purposes; Noncompetition Clause: The purposes for which the leased premises may be used should be expressly stipulated in the lease—restaurant, hardware store, etc., as the case may be. Otherwise, the lessee may use the premises for any purpose not materially different from that for which they are usually employed or for which they are constructed or adapted.

● By way of protecting himself against competition, the lessee may require a provision against a lease of another portion of the same premises to a competing business, as in paragraph 24 of the specimen form. Suppose that R has a building with 7 or 8 ground floor stores. E leases one for a restaurant. Obviously, he does not want competition next door or 2 or 3 doors away, and a provision of this kind gives him the protection needed. Although this is "in restraint of trade" to some extent, it is permitted.

Rent: Rent is always set out as shown in the printed form, that is, total rent first; then the monthly or other installments in which it is to be paid.

● Often, lessor will require lessee to pay one or more of the last months' rent in advance (as in the printed form), or to deposit cash security that will cover breaches of the lease, including failure to pay rent. How this provision reads is important for tax purposes. If it reads in such a way as to make what is paid prepaid rent, the lessor must include it in his income tax return in the year of receipt—the year the lease is made—even though it applies to the last months of the lease.

(Continued on page 227)

---

other civil actions."

Where a tenant is delinquent in rent, the landlord may bring unlawful detainer proceedings after giving tenant 3 days' notice to pay the rent.

C.C. 789.3, provides that a landlord may not interrupt or terminate any utility service to residential premises for the purpose of terminating a tenancy. The section makes the landlord liable for damages in the amount of $100 per day for each day that the tenant is deprived of the utility service, plus actual damages of the tenant, and attorney's fees. In 1979, C.C. 789.3 was enlarged to include acts intended to evict a tenant such as locking him out, removing doors or windows, and the act of removing the tenant's furnishings or property from the premises, each of which acts also carries a $100 per day damages liability.

𝕿𝖍𝖎𝖘 𝕴𝖓𝖉𝖊𝖓𝖙𝖚𝖗𝖊, Made and executed in duplicate this   first   day of   June   ,1984

𝕭𝖞 𝖆𝖓𝖉 𝕭𝖊𝖙𝖜𝖊𝖊𝖓 LEO LESSOR, 1408 Wellington Way, Santa Ana, California,

hereinafter called the Lessor, and EDWARD LESSEE, 916 State Street, Los Angeles, California,

hereinafter called the Lessee,

𝖂𝖎𝖙𝖓𝖊𝖘𝖘𝖊𝖙𝖍: That for and in consideration of the sum of $2,000.00 .... to the Lessor paid by Lessee, receipt of which is hereby acknowledged by Lessor, and for and in the further consideration of the payment of the rents and the performances of the covenants contained herein on the part of the Lessee and in the manner hereinafter stated, the Lessor does hereby demise, lease and let to the Lessee, and in consideration of the premises, the Lessee does hereby lease, hire, and take from the Lessor upon the terms and conditions hereinafter set forth, the following described property and its appurtenances, situate in the City of ....and................, County of Los Angeles...., State of .California....., particularly described as follows, to-wit:

2100 Capitol Street, Los Angeles, California;

For the term of   three (3) years

commencing on the   first   day of   June   ,1984,

and ending on the   thirty-first   day of   May   ,1987,

at and for the total rent or sum of   thirty-six thousand & no/100   DOLLARS,
including the sum of two thousand dollars heretofore paid to Lessor, as aforesaid,
payable monthly in advance, in installments of
                                 one thousand and no/100   DOLLARS

each in lawful money of the United States of America, on the   first   day of each and every calendar month. In the event Lessee has paid the rental hereunder, as herein provided, and has duly complied with the terms and provisions hereof, Lessee may occupy and enjoy the leased premises for the final two (2)........ months of the term, free from obligation to pay any rental for such ....two..(2)..... months.

This lease is made subject to the following terms and conditions:

1. Said Lessee agrees to pay said rents to said Lessor at the time and in the manner herein provided, without any deduction whatever and free of and from any and all claims and demands against said Lessor of any kind or character.

2. Should said Lessee fail to pay any part of the rents herein specified, at the times or in the manner herein provided, or fail faithfully to comply with or perform any other of the terms, conditions, covenants and agreements of this lease on the part of said Lessee to be performed or complied with, then and in that event, said Lessor may, at the option of said Lessor, either enter into and upon and take possession of said leased premises as the agent and for the account of said Lessee, and if said Lessor so elects to lease or rent the whole or any part of said premises for the balance or any part of the term of this lease, and retain all rents thus received, and, after deducting therefrom all expenses incurred in and about the renting of the same and all costs and expenses incurred in the collection of said rents, apply the balance to the payment of the rents payable hereunder by said Lessee, but the performance of all or any of the said acts by the said Lessor shall in nowise release or discharge said Lessee from a full and strict compliance with and performance of all the terms, conditions and covenants of this lease on the part of said Lessee to be performed, including the payment of the total amount of rent which said Lessee by the express terms of this lease agrees and promises to pay as rental for

said leased premises for and during the whole of the term of this lease; or else said Lessor, at the option of said Lessor, may terminate this lease, or said Lessor may pursue any remedy whatsoever provided for by law, and in any of said events, said Lessor shall be forthwith entitled to the possession of said leased premises, and may enter into and upon said leased premises, without notice to said Lessee, and exclude said Lessee therefrom and from in any manner having access thereto, and remove all persons and property therefrom, and by process of law, or otherwise, take and resume possession of said leased premises, and in the removal of such property, said Lessor shall in nowise be responsible or liable either to said Lessee, or to any other person whomsoever for such property or the safe keeping thereof, or for any damage whatsoever thereto or to any part thereof, and said Lessor is hereby further authorized to store such removed property in any warehouse or other place at the expense and for the account of said Lessee.

3. That said leased premises shall be used, occupied and conducted exclusively as and for restaurant
* *
and for no other purpose, and shall be used, occupied and conducted in a thoroughly orderly and respectable manner, without let, hindrance, annoyance, disturbance, detriment, injury or offense to the Lessor; that said Lessee shall not maintain or commit, nor suffer to be maintained or committed any nuisance or waste in or about said leased premises; that said Lessee shall not do or permit anything to be done in or about the said leased premises, nor bring or keep anything therein, which will in any way affect fire or other insurance on said building or any of its contents, or which shall in any way conflict with any law, ordinance, rule or regulation affecting the occupancy and use of said premises which are or may hereafter be enacted or promulgated by any public authority.

Lessee shall not construct, maintain or permit to be constructed or maintained, any sign or bill board on the roof of the building located on said demised premises, nor paint, nor hang, nor permit or authorize others to paint or hang, any sign on the outside walls thereof, unless written permission to do so be first obtained from the Lessor.

4. Said Lessee hereby agrees not to assign this lease or any interest therein, nor let or underlet the whole or any part of said leased premises without the written consent of said Lessor first had and obtained, and that neither this lease, nor any interest therein shall be assigned or assignable, either by operation of law or otherwise.

PROVIDED ALSO, and these presents are upon this covenant, that if the Lessee do or shall neglect or fail to perform or observe any of the covenants contained in these presents and on its part to be observed and performed for ten (10) days after notice by the Lessor, or if the estate hereby created shall be taken on execution, and such execution shall not be satisfied, cancelled or otherwise removed within thirty days after notice by Lessor, or if the Lessee shall be adjudicated bankrupt or insolvent according to law, or if any assignment of its property shall be made for the benefit of creditors, then and in any of said cases the Lessor lawfully may enter into and upon the said premises or any part thereof in the name of the whole, and repossess the same as of the former estate of the Lessor and expel the Lessee and those claiming under and through it and remove its effects (forcibly if necessary) without being deemed guilty of any manner of trespass, and without prejudice to any remedies which might otherwise be used for arrears of rent or preceding breach of covenant, and upon entry as aforesaid this lease shall determine, and the Lessee covenants that in case of such termination it will indemnify the Lessor against all loss of rent which the Lessor may incur by reason of such termination, during the residue of the term above specified.

5. Said Lessee agrees that the said leased premises are now in tenantable and good order and condition and that said Lessee shall keep and maintain said premises in good and sanitary order and condition, and that no alteration, repair or change whatever shall be made in or about said leased premises without the written consent of the Lessor, said Lessee hereby waiving all rights under the provisions of Section 1942 of the Civil Code of the State of California to make repairs at the Lessor's expense, and that unless otherwise provided by written agreement, all alterations, improvements and changes that may be required shall be done by or under the direction of the Lessor but at the cost of the Lessee; that all alterations, additions and improvements made in and to said leased premises shall, unless otherwise provided by written agreement be the property of the Lessor and shall remain upon, and be surrendered with said leased premises; that said Lessee shall not mar or deface in any manner the walls, woodwork, or any other part of said leased premises; that all damage or injury done to the premises or property of said Lessor by said Lessee, or by any person who may be in or upon the premises, with the consent of the Lessee, shall be paid for by the Lessee at the time the damage or injury is inflicted; and that said Lessee shall, at the termination of this lease, surrender said leased premises to the Lessor in as good order and condition as reasonable and proper use thereof will permit.

6. In the event of the inability of the Lessor to deliver possession of said leased premises at the time herein fixed for the commencement of the term of this lease, neither the Lessor nor the agent of said Lessor shall be liable for any damages caused thereby, nor shall this lease thereby become void or voidable, but in such event the Lessee shall not be liable for any rent until such time as the Lessor can deliver possession.

7. Said Lessee shall at least thirty days before the date of the expiration of this lease give to said Lessor a written notice of intention to surrender said leased premises on said date; if such notice is not given, then said Lessee shall be liable for rent of one additional month in the event that he shall have vacated said leased premises, at the expiration of the term of this lease.

8. If said Lessee holds possession of the said premises after the expiration of the term of this lease, such Lessee shall become a tenant from month to month only upon the terms herein specified, but at a monthly rental of

two thousand & no/100   Dollars ($ 2000.00   ) per month
payable monthly in advance in said lawful money of the United States on the first
day of each month and shall continue to be such tenant until such tenancy shall be terminated by the Lessor, or until

(Form continued on following pages)

said Lessee shall have given to said Lessor a written notice at least one month prior to the date of the termination of such monthly tenancy of his intention to terminate such tenancy and shall at the expiration of such month have vacated and surrendered possession of said leased premises to said Lessor.

9. That if the said building or the said leased premises shall be destroyed by fire or other cause or be so damaged thereby that they become untenantable and cannot be rendered tenantable within ninety (90) days from the date of the injury this lease may be terminated by the Lessor; that in case said premises shall be so damaged as not to require a termination of the lease as above provided, then a proportionate allowance shall be made to the Lessee for the rent hereinbefore reserved corresponding to the time during which and to the portion of the premises of which the Lessee shall be so deprived. The Lessee expressly waives the provisions of Section 1932 and Subdivision 4 of Section 1933 of the Civil Code of the State of California. The Lessor shall be sole judge as to whether such damage has caused said building or premises to be untenantable, and as to whether they can be rendered tenantable within ninety days from the date of the injury.

10. Said Lessor shall have the right at all times during the term of this lease to enter said leased premises for the purpose of examining or inspecting the same, and of making such repairs or alterations therein or in other parts of said building as said Lessor shall deem necessary in connection with said premises, or said building.

11. Lessee agrees to pay during the term hereof, all charges made against said premises for water rates, gas, electric lights, power, heat, telephone and garbage disposal services, and for any other commodities furnished or supplied or used in or upon or about said premises.

12. The Lessor agrees to maintain the roof over said demised premises in good order and repair and repairs to said roof shall be made by and at the expense of the Lessor, but without liability for failure so to do unless first notified by Lessee in writing of the necessity thereof.

13. Said Lessee hereby waives all claims for damages that may be caused by the Lessor in re-entering and taking possession of the said leased premises as herein provided or for loss or injury of, by or arising out of theft, burglary, fire, steam, gas, electricity, or defect in the building, or by or out of the breaking, leakage, or overflow of the roof, or of any pipe, sewer or plumbing, or by or out of the destruction or injury of the building, or any part thereof, or by or out of the making of any repairs, alterations, additions, or improvements to said building, or any part thereof, or by reason of loss of property, or injury or damage to person or property occurring in said leased premises or in or about said building no matter how caused.

14. This lease shall be subject and subordinate at all times to the lien of any mortgage or mortgages or trust deed or deeds which may now exist upon or which may be placed upon the demised premises or the property of which the demised premises are a part and the Lessee covenants that it will execute and deliver to the Lessor or to the nominee of the Lessor proper subordination agreements to this effect at any time upon the request of the Lessor and without payment being made therefor.

15. Each and every covenant and term hereof to be kept and performed by the Lessee is expressly made a condition, upon breach whereof said Lessor may terminate this lease and exercise all rights of entry and re-entry upon said leased premises, herein provided for.

16. The failure or omission of said Lessor to terminate this lease, for any violation of any of its terms, conditions or covenants shall in nowise be deemed to be a consent by the Lessor to such violation, and shall in nowise bar, estop or prevent said Lessor from terminating this lease thereafter, either for such or for any subsequent violation of any such term, condition or covenant. The acceptance of rent hereunder shall not be, or be construed to be, a waiver of any breach of any term, covenant or conditions of this lease.

17. That in each suit brought for the recovery of any rent due hereunder, or for the recovery of the possession of said demised premises, or for the breach of any of the terms, conditions or covenants of this lease, wherein said Lessor shall prevail, said Lessee shall pay said Lessor a reasonable sum as and for attorney's fees therein, the amount of which shall be determined by the court in such suit and added to and become part of the judgment therein.

18. The servive of any and all notices of any nature and description given by said Lessor to said Lessee, when given to said Lessee in the manner now prescribed by the provisions of Section 1162 of the Code of Civil Procedure of the State of California, or else when mailed to said Lessee addressed to said Lessee to said leased premises, shall be deemed to be and constitute full and complete notice to said Lessee and shall constitute full compliance with any of the provisions of this lease or of the laws of the State of California requiring personal service of notice upon said Lessee and shall constitute notice to said Lessee for any purpose whatsoever.

19. It is further covenanted and agreed by said Lessee that nothing herein contained and no security or guarantee which may now or hereafter be furnished said Lessor for the payment of the rent herein reserved or for the performance by said Lessee of the other terms or covenants of this lease, shall in any way be a bar or defense to any action in unlawful detainer, or for the recovery of said premises, or in any action which said Lessor may at any time commence for breach of any of the terms or covenants of this lease.

20. The word "Lessor" and the word "Lessee" as used herein include the plural as well as the singular. The neuter gender where used here, shall include the masculine and feminine.

21. This lease shall include and inure to and bind the heirs, executors, administrators, successors and assigns of the respective parties hereto, but nothing in this paragraph contained shall be construed to modify or impair in any manner

any of the provisions and restrictions of this lease relating to the assignment of this lease or of any interest therein, or to the subletting or underletting of said leased premises or any part thereof.

22. The Lessee agrees that this instrument contains all of the provisions of the agreement between the parties hereto, and that no promise or agreement not contained herein shall be binding on the Lessor.

23. Time is the essence of this agreement.

24. Throughout the term of this lease or any extensions or renewals hereof, lessor agrees not to lease, rent or use for the purposes of a restaurant, cafe, soda fountain or like business any of the store buildings on the ground floor of or any of the space within or in the basement of that certain building known as the California Building, 2100 Capitol Street, Los Angeles, California.

25. Lessee shall have the right, at its option, to renew this lease for a period of three (3) years from the date of expiration hereof upon the same terms and conditions as herein stated, except that lessee shall pay a monthly rental of fifteen hundred and no/100 dollars ($1500.00) throughout the term of such renewal. Lessee shall give lessor notice of intent to renew at least sixty (60) days before the expiration of this lease. Said notice shall be in writing and shall be communicated to the lessor in accordance with the provisions of paragraph 18 herein.

26. Lessee shall have a period of ten (10) days after the expiration of this lease or any extension or renewal hereof to remove such fixtures as lessee shall have installed in or upon or attached to the said premises; provided, however, that lessee shall restore to a condition of good repair any portion or portions of said premises from which fixtures shall have been so removed or detached.

IN WITNESS WHEREOF, said parties have executed this lease the day and year first above written.

.... s/ EDWARD LESSEE .... s/ LEO LESSOR ....
                Edward Lessee   Leo Lessor

....

....

....
                                        Lessee.   Lessor.

If it is a true security deposit provision, on the other hand, lessor need not include the amount in his return at any time, except so far as it is actually applied to unpaid rent.[104]

• *Percentage rentals* have become common. In a percentage rental lease the lessor agrees to take a percentage of the gross receipts of the lessee's business in lieu of a fixed rental. If the business is successful, the lessor profits from the arrangement; otherwise he loses to some extent. From the lessee's standpoint, it enables him to hold down his overhead during the first months of the business, and throughout its life if it proves to be unsuccessful. The percentage rental is usually combined with a "minimum guaranteed rental," i.e., the lessee agrees to pay at least some minimum fixed rental monthly. For example: R leases property to E for 5% of E's gross sales, with a minimum guaranteed rental of $500 a month. R would have leased at a fixed rental of $800 a month. E expects to have gross sales of $25,000 a month when his business is established. During the first month, his gross sales are only $6000. On the percentage rental basis, this would come to only $300, but R will be entitled to $500 since that is the minimum guaranteed rental. During the second month, gross sales are $12,000. R will be entitled to $600 since this is the percentage rental, and it exceeds the minimum guaranteed rental. During the third month, E's sales increase to $20,000. R will be entitled to $1000 percentage rental. If E's sales stay at this level, the percentage rental terms will ultimately prove to be more profitable to R than fixed rental terms would have been. The percentage rental lease will require the lessee to furnish the lessor with financial statements, usually quarterly, so that the lessor can be assured that he is receiving the proper amount of rent. The lease will also give the lessor the right to inspect the lessee's books of account at any time. The percentage varies according to the greater or lesser speculativeness of the business and other factors. According to the Realtors National Marketing Institute, in its most recent survey in 1973, representative percentage rentals were: Department Stores, .25-6.5%; Drug Stores, 1.0-7.0%; Furniture Stores, 1.0-6.5%; Hardware Stores, .50-6.0%; Household Appliances, 1.0-5.0%; Liquor Stores, 1.0-6.0%; Movie Theatres, 5.0-17.0%; Parking Lots (Attended), 45.0-85.0%; Restaurants, 3.0-12.0%; Supermarkets, 1.0-2.5%.

Today, the minimum guaranteed rental is fixed at an amount which approximates the estimated percentage rental. The effect of this is to make the lessor, so far as profitsharing is concerned, a "partner" of the lessee to the extent of the percentage/minimum guaranteed rental.

Termination of Obligation to Pay Rent: There are several instances in which the lessee's obligation to pay rent may cease before the lease runs its course. (1) In cases of *destruction* of the premises as discussed below. (2) Where there is an *eviction* of the lessee, e.g., because of foreclosure of a

mortgage. In this connection, it may be noted that if the lease was made after the mortgage was placed upon the property, the lease is subject to the mortgage and the lessee may be evicted upon foreclosure. If, however, the lease antedates the mortgage, the lease is good against the mortgage unless there is an express provision in the lease that it is subordinate to subsequent mortgages, as in paragraph 14 of the specimen form. One may mortgage only what he owns and, without such a provision, the lessor may mortgage only leased property. Because a long term lease may make subsequent mortgaging of the property difficult, a subordination clause of the type contained in paragraph 14 is included in a lease. (3) Where there is a "*constructive eviction*" of the lessee by reason of an untenantable condition of the premises for which the lessor is responsible, e.g., where the lessor, being under obligation to do so, fails to provide proper heat for the premises or fails to repair a badly leaking roof.

• Suppose the lessee wrongfully abandons the leased premises before the expiration of the lease and discontinues payment of rent. For example, E takes a 2-year lease. His business fails, and, after a year, he vacates the premises and fails to pay further rent. In an earlier day, the lessor had two alternatives: to allow the premises to remain idle and sue for installments of rent as they become due;[105] or to re-rent and hold the original lessee for any deficiency, that is, for any difference between the original lessee's rent and the rent obtained from the new tenant. This was changed by C.C. 1951.2 and C.C. 1951.4, which became operative in 1971. Under C.C. 1951.4, the lessor may allow the premises to remain idle and continue to collect rent from the original lessee only if the lease gives the lessee a reasonable right to assign the lease or to sublet the property. If no such right is given, C.C. 1951.2 in effect limits the lessor's recovery to such amount as his damages would be reduced by good faith effort to mitigate damages by reletting. Lease forms have not come to reflect the provisions of C.C. 1951.4 and 1951.2.

Insurance: The lessee may be required to carry one or more types of insurance for the protection of the lessor such as fire and plate glass insurance, payable to the lessor; and liability insurance protecting both lessor and lessee against liability for persons injured on the premises. Inasmuch as he is paying the premiums for insurance that would otherwise be carried by the lessor, as owner, the lessee is actually paying additional rent.

Repairs; Destruction: Paragraph 5 of the specimen lease requiring the tenant to make repairs is customary. Despite this, the lessor usually voluntarily makes repairs as a matter of good will.

• Where leased premises are partially or totally destroyed by fire or other mishap, most states have statutes designed to protect the lessee, e.g., C.C. 1932(2) and 1933(4), which are held to apply in such cases and which provide that the "hirer"

---

[104]C.C. 1950.5, 1950.7 expressly require the refund of such amount of security deposit (or advance rent payment) as exceeds the amount reasonably necessary to remedy tenant defaults. The refund must be made within two weeks after the termination of the tenancy and the landlord may be charged with punitive damages in an amount of up to $200, in addition to actual damages, for bad faith retention of deposit moneys that should be refunded. Section 1950.5 limits security deposits to two months' rent in the case of unfurnished residential property where the term of the lease is less than six months, to three months' rent in the case of furnished residential property where the term of the lease is less than six months, and to six months' rent where the term of the lease is six months or longer.

---

[105]This was held not to violate the rule of *mitigation of damages* discussed at page 49 in Contracts. (*Phillips-Hollman* v. *Peerless Stages*, 210 C. 253, 291 P. 178.) As discussed on page 152, a lease is a *chattel real*—in part a contract but also in part an estate or interest in land. To the extent that it is an estate in land, it is deemed to vest in its entirety in the lessee at the time the lease is created. At the same time, the lessee incurs an obligation to pay the entire amount of the agreed purchase price—the total rent for the lease—even though he is permitted to pay this in monthly installments. If the strict letter of theory is followed, the fact that the lessee does not choose to use what he has purchased would not excuse him from his obligation to pay for it.

of a thing may terminate his further obligation to pay for it upon "destruction of the thing hired" or of "the greater part of the thing hired." Leases will expressly provide for the contingency of destruction, however, as does the specimen lease in paragraph 9, and such provisions are controlling.

Liability for Injuries: It is a common misconception that a lessor or landlord is liable for every injury suffered on rented premises which is caused by some condition of disrepair. Actually, much the opposite is true. Only in these cases is he liable:[106]

1. When the lease requires him to make repairs, he has been notified by the tenant of the need for repairs, and he fails to take prompt steps to make them.

2. Where, having no obligation to do so, he nevertheless voluntarily makes repairs and does a defective job, as in *Janofsky* v. *Garland*, 42 C.A.2d 655, 109 P.2d 750, where the landlord voluntarily undertook to replaster the ceiling but did a defective job and injuries were sustained from falling plaster.

3. Where there are latent (concealed) defects of which the lessor, but not the lessee, is aware.

Even in these cases, the lessor may escape liability by requiring the lessee to carry liability insurance protecting the lessor and by exculpatory clauses as in paragraph 13 of the specimen lease (but see discussion on page 38 regarding exculpatory clauses). And C.C. 1953 invalidates exculpatory clauses in residential leases.

● The related matter of liability for injuries on sidewalks is discussed in the footnote below.[107]

● In multi-unit premises, the landlord must maintain in reasonably safe condition the common areas of the building over which the landlord retains control for the use of the tenants, such as lobbies and passageways.

Assignment and Sublease: An *assignment* is a transfer by the lessee of his *entire* remaining interest in the leased premises. A *sublease* is a transfer of less than his entire interest, with the lessor retaining some part of or interest in the leased premises—in effect, a lease within a lease with the lessee playing the dual role of lessee as to the original lessor and sublessor as to his sublessee.

● The ordinary lease is not considered to be such a "personal" contract as to be non-assignable on that account. Therefore, assignment or subletting (in effect, partial assignment) is permissible if not expressly forbidden by the lease. Paragraph 4 of the specimen lease does this, and every lease will contain a similar provision. This is important from the lessor's standpoint since, without it, he would have no control over the identity of the occupant. However, there is a growing tendency to invalidate and cut down on anti-assignment claus-

es. The Bankruptcy Reform Act of 1978 makes them invalid as against the trustee in bankruptcy of a bankrupt lessee. And a number of courts have held that, even in the case of an unconditional anti-assignment clause, the lessor would still have to show cause why he objected to the assignment. California adopted this view in 1983 in the court of appeal case of *Cohen* v. *Ratinoff* (1983) 147 C.A. 3rd 321, 195 Cal.Rptr. 84. In *Cohen* a commercial lease forbad assignment without written consent of the lessor, as in paragraph 4 of the specimen lease. The lessor contended that this permitted him to refuse consent to assignment arbitrarily, i.e., without showing cause why he should be entitled to do so. The court disagreed. It first pointed out, as noted on page 152, supra, that a lease is both a conveyance and a contract; that to the extent that it is a contract, it embodies the "implied covenant of good faith and fair dealing" previously seen in connection with employment contracts, at page 67; that this covenant militates against the arbitrary or unreasonable withholding of consent to assignment. "(A) lessor," said the court, "may refuse consent only where he has a good faith reasonable objection to the assignment or sublease, even in the absence of a provision prohibiting the unreasonable or arbitrary withholding of consent to an assignment of a commercial lease. Examples of bases for such good faith reasonable objection would be inability to fulfill terms of the lease, financial irresponsibility or instability, suitability of premises for intended use, or intended unlawful or undesirable use of premises. No such bases were raised by the lessor." *Cohen* was followed by the 1984 court of appeal case of *Schweiso* v. *Williams* (1984) 150 C.A.3d 883, 198 Cal.Rptr. 238. Both *Cohen* and *Schweiso* involved commercial leases where the hardship on the lessee is apt to be at its greatest if consent to assignment can be denied. Ordinarily a commercial lease will be assigned only as part of the package of selling the business which is being conducted on the leased premises so that refusal to permit assignment of the lease will prevent sale of the business with large adverse economic consequences to the lessee. It remains to be seen whether a comparable rule will be adopted when it is a residential lease for which consent to assignment is sought.

● Even though the lessor consents to an assignment, the original lessee remains liable for rent unless the lessor expressly releases him, in which case there is a novation. If the assignee *assumes* the lease, he becomes liable for the rent for the balance of the term of the lease. The lessor may enforce the assumption agreement as a third party beneficiary. A form of assignment and assumption agreement is set out on the next page.

● In some leases, the lessee may expressly be given the privilege of subletting; usually, where the sublessee will set up a type of business which will complement the lessee's business. The lessee of premises for an automobile agency, e.g., might reserve the right to sublease parts of the premises to persons who would set up repair and parts departments. Since there is no privity of contract between the sublessee and the original lessor, the lessor has no rights against the sublessee unless the sublease provides that the sublessee assumes the original lease to an extent coextensive with the sublease, and that he will pay rent directly to the lessor. If this provision is made, the lessor may enforce the assumption agreement directly against the sublessee as a third party beneficiary.

Option to Renew: A lessee usually desires to have the right to renew the lease for another term so that if, during the original term, he has developed a successful business, he can be assured of being able to continue it. An option to renew is

---

[106]There are no California statutes on this matter. These are rules of the Restatement of Torts 2d., Sections 355 et seq. The California courts have followed the same rules.

[107]The landlord-landowner is *not* liable for injuries suffered by reason of a defective condition of the sidewalk fronting the premises unless statute imposes such liability. In California, under Streets & Highway Code, Section 5611 et seq., the landowner must repair defective sidewalks after notice from the superintendent of streets to do so and the superintendent of streets may cause the repairs to be made at the landowner's expense if the landowner fails to make them. However, the landowner is not liable for injuries suffered by sidewalk users unless the injury results from a defect caused by the landowner or from an alteration of the sidewalk made for the benefit of the landowner's property.

ASSIGNMENT OF LEASE

EDWARD LESSEE hereby assigns to ALBERT ASSIGNEE all of his right, title and interest in and to the following lease:

Lease dated June 1, 1984, between LEO LESSOR, as lessor, and EDWARD LESSEE, as lessee, and being a lease for a period of three (3) years of the premises known as 2100 Capitol Street, Los Angeles, California; said lease being at a monthly rental of One Thousand Dollars ($1000.00) per month, for the purposes of a "restaurant" and none other.

In consideration of said assignment of lease, ALBERT ASSIGNEE hereby assumes and agrees to perform all of the terms and conditions of said lease and to fulfill all of the obligations imposed thereby.

ALBERT ASSIGNEE further agrees to pay to EDWARD LESSEE the sum of Two Thousand Dollars ($2000.00) at the date of execution hereof as and for the last two (2) months' rent of said lease prepared by EDWARD LESSEE.

This agreement shall not become effective and said lease shall not be deemed assigned unless and until LEO LESSOR, the lessor in said lease, shall give written consent to such assignment.

Dated:_____December 1, 1984_____

s/ EDWARD LESSEE
_____
Edward Lessee

s/ ALBERT ASSIGNEE
_____
Albert Assignee

CONSENT TO ASSIGNMENT

In consideration of the assumption of said lease by ALBERT ASSIGNEE, LEO LESSOR, lessor therein, hereby consents to assignment to ALBERT ASSIGNEE. This consent shall not constitute a release of EDWARD LESSEE from the obligations of said lease for any purpose or to any extent.

Dated:_____December 1, 1984_____

s/ LEO LESSOR
_____
Leo Lessor

added to the lease for this purpose. It will usually provide that the lessee may renew the lease for the same period of time as was given by the original lease, and that renewal shall be "on the same terms and conditions" as in the original lease except that a higher monthly rental may be charged during the renewal period to protect the lessor against inflation. See paragraph 25 of the specimen lease for an option to renew.

Trade Fixtures—Removal: Fixtures attached by a lessee for the purposes of trade or manufacture are called *trade fixtures.* It is generally held that they may be removed by the lessee if this will not cause substantial damage to the premises, and provided that removal is completed before the lease expires. If these requirements are not met, the fixtures become the property of the lessor.

• C.C. 1019 is a typical statute on trade fixtures. It provides that "A tenant may remove from the demised premises, any time during the continuance of his term, anything affixed thereto for purposes of trade, manufacture, ornament, or domestic use, if the removal can be effected without injury to the premises, unless the thing has, by the manner in which it is affixed, become an integral part of the premises." The courts have construed the words "without injury" to mean *without substantial injury,* particularly where valuable fixtures are involved. Thus, it has been held in California cases that a refrigeration system installed in a hotel could be removed although holes would have to be cut in the wall and replastered to disconnect and remove piping,[108] but that a refrigeration system could not be removed where it consisted of rooms built into the building;[109] that a "portable gasoline station" nailed to 2 × 4's set in concrete together with gas pumps on a concrete pier could be removed,[110] but that a steel service station building on a cement foundation was not detachable.[111] That a marble false front attached to the face of a leased building could not be removed, that it had "become an integral part of the premises."[112] In short, it becomes a matter for the judgment of the court. To eliminate controversy, the lease may and should expressly provide for removal where the lessee is to install fixtures of substantial value. In addition, the lease may provide that the lessee shall have some period of time, a week or ten days, after expiration of the lease to remove the fixtures so that he does not have to devote the last week of the lease to their removal. See paragraph 26 of the specimen lease for a provision of this type.

Estates, Trusts and Administration

The principal methods of transfer of title during lifetime—by deed in the case of real property, by sale in the case of goods or personal property—have been discussed. Title to one's property, both real and personal, must pass to another upon death. The owner may leave a will disposing of the property, in which case he is said to have died *testate.* If he dies *intestate*—without leaving a will—the law must and does set up rules or statutes providing for the disposition of his property. These are called *rules of intestate succession.* In either case, the property left at death is called the decedent's *estate* and must go through a *probate proceeding* to get to the

persons entitled to it, although there are a few exceptions to this. The probate proceeding is necessary to determine, where a will has been left, that the will is valid; in order to give creditors of the decedent an opportunity to obtain payment of their claims; and to establish the transfer of title from the decedent to those who succeed to his estate.

In this section are discussed intestate succession, wills, and administration of decedents' estates—the probate proceeding. Where an estate is large and there are young children, a trust may be set up in the will to withhold large sums of money from the children until they become sufficiently mature to deal with it intelligently. Hence, trusts and their administration are also discussed in this section.

Rules of Intestate Succession

In a general way, these rules stem from the English law, as does most of our other law, but the original English rules have been substantially modified. In England, the "rules of primogeniture" were followed under which male children inherited to the exclusion of female and the eldest son inherited to the exclusion of the younger sons. In this country, children have always been treated equally regardless of sex or age.

Special Rules as Between Husband and Wife: Most of these have been discussed in the section on concurrent ownership, and are summarized at this point as follows:

1. In community property states, the community property rules govern that form of property. The California rule is that each spouse may dispose of his or her one-half of community and quasi-community property by will. If he or she does not, it goes to the survivor.

2. In non-community property states (a) tenancy by the entirety or other rules govern jointly owned property; (b) dower and curtesy, where followed, apply to separately owned real property of the spouses; and (c) as to property not covered by the foregoing, the surviving spouse is usually given ⅓ of the property of the deceased spouse.

Rules in Other Cases: In California, Prob. C. 221-226 set up rules of succession to the separate estate of a married person and the estate of an unmarried person.[113] With some exceptions, noted as they arise, these rules are generally representative of those to be found in noncommunity property states for like types of property:

1. Spouse and one child: If the decedent leaves a spouse and one child or issue of a deceased child, ½ goes to the surviving spouse and ½ to the child or issue.[114] California gives more to the surviving spouse than most states, which give only ⅓.

Children of children usually take the share of their deceased parents by *right of representation,* i.e., divide equally among them the share which their parent would have received if the parent had not predeceased the decedent. This is what is meant by the provision for "issue of a deceased child" in paragraph 1 above and 2 below.

2. Spouse and two or more children: If the decedent leaves a spouse and more than one living child, or one or more living

[108]*Woodward* v. *Lazar,* 21 C. 448.

[109]*Yokohama Specie Bank* v. *Higashi,* 56 C.A. 2d 709, 133 Pac.2d 487.

[110]*Murr* v. *Cohn,* 87 C.A. 478, 262 P. 768.

[111]*R. Bancroft & Sons Co.* v. *Cullen,* 217 C. 708, 20 P.2d 665.

[112]*Alden* v. *Mayfield,* 163 C. 793, 127 P. 44.

[113]These rules do not apply to real property situated in another state. This is because the law of the *situs* (the state where the property is located) determines ownership of real property, and succession thereto. Thus, if D, who dies in California, has real estate in Wisconsin, the Wisconsin law determines who gets it and in what proportion. Not so with personal property, which is deemed to "follow" the owner wherever he goes and is distributed according to the law of his residence.

[114]Prob. C. 221.

children and issue of one or more deceased children, ⅓ goes to the surviving spouse and ⅔ goes to the children in equal shares. Issue of deceased children take the parents' share by right of representation, as discussed above.[115] To illustrate: H dies leaving W, his wife; S-1, a living child; S-2, a deceased child who has 2 living children, C-1 and C-2; and S-3, a deceased child who has 3 living children, C-3, C-4 and C-5. Distribution of H's separate property would be as follows:

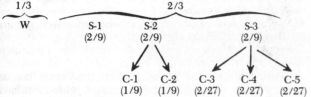

3. Children and no surviving spouse: If the decedent leaves no surviving spouse, but leaves issue, all goes to the issue in equal shares, or to their living descendants by right of representation.[116]

4. Surviving spouse and no issue: If the decedent leaves a spouse and no issue, ½ goes to the surviving spouse; the other ½ goes to the decedent's parents in equal shares or to the survivor, or, if both are dead, to their issue—the brothers and sisters of the decedent—in equal shares, with descendants of deceased brothers and sisters taking by right of representation.[117]

5. Surviving spouse and no issue, parents, brothers or sisters: If the decedent leaves a spouse, and neither issue, parent, brother, sister, nor descendant of a deceased brother or sister (niece or nephew), all goes to the surviving spouse.[118]

6. No surviving spouse or issue: If the decedent leaves neither issue nor spouse, all goes to his parents in equal shares, or to the survivor; or, if both are dead, in equal shares to his brothers and sisters and descendants of deceased brothers and sisters by right of representation.[119]

7. No surviving spouse, issue or immediate family: If the decedent leaves neither issue, spouse, parent, brother, sister, nor their descendants, the estate goes to the *next of kin* in equal degree—aunts and uncles, cousins, etc.—those claiming through the nearest ancestor of decedent being preferred claimants.[120]

8. No blood relatives: If the decedent leaves no one to take his estate, it *escheats* to the state.[121]

Certain other rules are noted in the footnotes.[122]

---

[115]Prob. C. 221.

[116]Prob. C. 222.

[117]Prob. C. 223.

[118]Prob. C. 224.

[119]Prob. C. 225.

[120]Prob. C. 226.

[121]Prob. C. 231-236.

[122]Adopted children inherit from their adoptive parents but not from their natural parents. (Prob. C. 257.) An illegitimate child is substantially protected by the rules of the Uniform Parentage Act (C.C. 7000-7018) which are made to apply to the law of succession by Prob. C. 255. Through the Uniform Parentage Act, the child would, among other things, have rights of inheritance from its natural mother in all cases, would have rights of inheritance from both natural mother and her husband if born during wedlock, and would have rights of inheritance from a man who

Wills

A *will* is a legal declaration by which a person makes a disposition of his property to take effect at death. The person making a will is called the *testator.*[123] Dispositions of real property by will are called *devises*; of personal property, *bequests*; of money, *legacies.* The recipients of these may be called devisees or legatees or, more generally, distributees, as they are referred to here. A will is not required to be notarized and need to be executed only with the formalities discussed below. Since it is an ambulatory instrument—one which may be revoked at any time—it is not recorded.

● With certain exceptions,[124] a person may give his property, including his half interest in community property, to anyone he wishes—his spouse, his children, his friends, his charities.

● Writings existing at the time a will is executed may be incorporated by reference into a will. T may make a will on June 1, 1981, in which he declares that "I bequeath to my sister, S, the securities listed in that certain inventory of securities dated March 1, 1981, contained in my safe deposit box at Bank of San Jose, San Jose, California."

● A will may be revoked at any time by destruction or cancellation[125] and is automatically revoked by a subsequent, inconsistent will.[126]

---

receives the child into his home and holds the child out as his natural child. "Kindred of the half blood [having only one parent in common] inherit equally with the whole blood in the same degree," unless the property came to the intestate by gift, will or inheritance from an ancestor, in which case it goes to those of the whole blood. (Prob. C. 254.)

Prob. C. 229 sets up special rules where the *surviving* spouse dies, designed to protect members of the family of the predeceased spouse. Suppose H dies and community property passes to W, his wife, who does not remarry. Then W dies. There are no children of the HW marriage. W's heirs are brothers and sisters. H also has brothers and sisters living. Prob. C. 229 provides that one-half the community property which vested in W by reason of H's death goes to H's heirs—his brothers and sisters. If the property passing to W had been separate property of H's, Prob. C. 229, would return all of it to H's relatives. Nothing would go back in either case if the surviving spouse had left issue or spouse, i.e., had remarried. Prob. C. 229 also provides that if the decedent leaves neither spouse nor issue and part of the estate was created by gift, descent, devise, or bequest from the separate property of a parent or grandparent, it reverts to the parent or grandparent, or if the parent or grandparent is dead, to the heirs of the parent or grandparent.

[123]Prob. C. 2021 permit wills to be made by persons "of sound mind, over the age of eighteen years."

[124]The surviving spouse and/or minor children are entitled to the homestead right and family allowance discussed on page 249, despite the will. And C.C. 205 makes the estate liable if the decedent leaves children who would become a public charge, providing that "If a parent chargeable with the support of a child dies, leaving it chargeable to the county, and leaving an estate sufficient for its support, the supervisors of the county may claim provision for its support from the parent's estate by civil action, and for this purpose may have the same remedies as any creditors against that estate, and against the heirs, devisees, and next of kin of the parent."

[125]Prob. C. 74 so provides.

[126]Prob. C. 72: "A prior will is not revoked by a subsequent will unless the latter contains an express revocation, or provisions wholly inconsistent with the terms of the prior will. In other cases the prior will remains effectual so far as consistent with the provisions of the subsequent will . . . ."

• Wills are of these various types:

Oral or Noncupative Wills: Most states permit a person to dispose of a very limited amount of property under very special circumstances by this type of will. Until 1972, California permitted a solider in the field or a sailor at sea or person who had suffered an injury on the same day to make this type of will; he had to be in fear or peril of death at the time of making the will; 2 witnesses had to be present; the will was permitted to dispose of personal property only, of a value not exceeding $1000; and probate proceedings had to be commenced within 6 months after the making of the will. All of these provisions were repealed in 1982.

Holographic Wills: An *holographic will* is a handwritten will. Prior to 1982, Prob. C. 53 required such a will to be "*entirely* written, dated and signed" in the handwriting of the testator. Courts took a hard line on the requirement of *entirety* of handwriting and refused to rewrite the statute by saying that *"entirely"* required only that material part of the will be in writing as lawyers argued for. This resulted in some invalid wills in some large estates where only some small and inconsequential part of the will was not in handwriting. In 1982 the Legislature amended Prob. C. 53 to reduce the requirements for a valid holographic will to "signature" and "material provisions" in the handwriting of the testator; in other words, to what the lawyers had argued for—and more since the dating requirement was deleted. However dating is still very important because new Prob. C. 53 says that if the will is not dated (1) it gives way to an inconsistent, competing will of the testator unless the holographic will can be proved to have been executed after the date of execution of the inconsistent, competing will; and (2) it requires proof of testamentary capacity at the time the holographic will was executed if it is established that the testator lacked testamentary capacity at any time during which the will might have been executed. Since a will in the testator's own handwriting is necessarily genuine, no witnesses are required.[127] Such a will may dispose of any type or size of estate to the same extent as the formal or witnessed will. It need not be in any particular form and need only show clearly the intention to dispose of the property to particular persons. Holographic wills are permitted in about half the states.

Formal or Witnessed Wills: This type of written will is usually prepared by a lawyer in typewritten form. California requirements for such a will are as follows:[128] (1) It must be subscribed at the end by the testator himself, or some person in the testator's presence and by his direction must subscribe his name thereto. (2) The subscription must be made, or the testator must acknowledge it to have been made by him or by his authority, in the presence of 2 attesting witnesses, present at the same time. (3) The testator, at the time of subscribing

or acknowledging the instrument, must declare to the attesting witnesses that it is his will. (4) There must be at least 2 attesting witnesses, each of whom must sign the instrument as a witness, at the end of the will, at the testator's request and in his presence. The witnesses should give their addresses but a failure to do so will not invalidate the will. The witnesses need not read the will nor have knowledge of its contents. To be valid, this or any other type of will must have been executed freely and voluntarily, without fraud, duress or undue influence, and the testator must have been of sound mind at the time of execution.

• Two other points with respect to witnessing may be noted. (1) Distributees should not be witnesses because of the rule designed to preclude undue influence, that where a distributee named in a will is a witness, he may not receive more than he would have received if the testator had died intestate where it is necessary to count the distributee-witness to make the requisite number of witnesses.[129] Thus, if T wills ½ of his estate to A, and A would have received only ⅓ of the estate if T had died intestate, A gets only ⅓ if A and B are the only witnesses to the will. (2) Even though only 2 witnesses are required in California and a number of other states, some states require 3 witnesses and it is advisable to have 3 since the law of wills of the state of the situs of real property determines whether or not a will is sufficient to dispose of the real property. So, if T, a Californian owning real property in another state, makes a will purporting to dispose of the property, and the will is signed by only 2 witnesses, it will not be effective to dispose of the real property if the law of situs requires 3 witnesses for a formal will.[129a]

• The major purpose of the lawyer-drawn will may be to reduce estate taxes in some way. For example, if the principal of an estate is willed directly to children in trust but with the income reserved to the surviving spouse for life, double taxation may be avoided, on transfer by deceased spouse to surviving spouse and then again, on the deceased spouse's share on transfer from surviving spouse to children.

Codicils: If the testator wishes to make minor changes in a will, it is not necessary to rewrite the will. He may merely add a *codicil*, which is the name for an instrument which alters or amends a will. A codicil must be executed with the same formalities as a will, but there may be a holographic (handwritten) codicil to a formal will or a statutory will.

California Statutory Wills: These are a 1982 invention of the California Legislature. The idea would appear to be to make relatively simple will and will with trust forms available to Californians who need or want such forms. One set of statistics says that 43% of California adults are without will and that 68% of adults with children are without wills.

• Probate lawyers have given mixed reviews to the new forms, mostly negative. The gist of criticism is that testamentary planning is too complicated and too sophisticated to permit of its being handled in this way and therefore runs the risk of being mishandled. One eminent probate lawyer sees the statutory will primarily as a "stop-gap measure" for a young married person with what he calls "modest assets," described as house, furniture, car, bank account and a few

---

Prob. C. 7071 may also be noted. They provide that if a person makes a will and thereafter marries, the will is revoked as to the spouse or issue unless they have been anticipated and provided for in the will, or by codicil.

Prob. C. 80, adopted in 1980, applicable to wills executed after January 1, 1981, provides that if a person divorces after making a will and if, in connection with the divorce, there has been a property settlement agreement in which one spouse waives rights in the other's estate, the spouse waiving rights is cut off from the will.

[127]New Prob. C. 53 expressly dispenses with the need for witnessing as did old Prob. C. 53. But it is permissible to have witnesses.

[128]Prob. C. 50.

[129]Prob. C. 51 so provides. Some states do not have such statute, however.

[129a]In 1979 California adopted the Uniform International Will Act in Prob. C. 60-60.8. This makes a foreign will valid in California if it has 2 witnesses and is certificated by "a person authorized to act in connection with international wills."

shares of stock, who wants to leave everything to his spouse and children. Clearly the Legislature (consisting mostly of lawyers) was not entirely comfortable with its inventions as witness the warning required to be prominently displayed, that "It may be in your best interest to consult with a California lawyer because this statutory will has serious legal effects on your family and property," and that "If there is anything in this will that you do not understand, you should ask a lawyer to explain it to you."

● The California Statutory Will form is set forth on the pages that follow. (Probate Code 56.7 provides for this form.) Then the differences between it and the California Statutory Will with Trust form are shown. (Probate Code 56.8 provides for the will with trust form.) Finally various California Probate Code sections that bear on the statutory will forms are set forth or described and explained.

● The California Statutory Will with Trust leaves the entire "residuary estate," in effect the entire estate, in trust rather than outrightly and, so, paragraph 2.3 of the will with trust says the following as compared with paragraph 2.3 of the straight will:

"ALL OTHER ASSETS (MY RESIDUARY ESTATE). I adopt only one property Disposition Clause in this paragraph 2.3 by writing my signature in the box next to the title of the property Disposition Clause I wish to adopt. I sign in only one box. I write the words "not used" in the remaining boxes. If I sign in more than one box or if I fail to sign in any box, the property will be distributed as if I did not make a will.
PROPERTY DISPOSITION CLAUSES (Select one.)

(a) TO MY SPOUSE IF LIVING; IF NOT LIVING THEN IN ONE TRUST TO PROVIDE FOR THE SUPPORT AND EDUCATION OF MY CHILDREN AND THE DESCENDANTS OF ANY DECEASED CHILD UNTIL

   I HAVE NO LIVING CHILD UNDER 21 YEARS OF AGE.

(b) TO MY CHILDREN AND THE DESCENDANTS OF ANY DECEASED CHILD IN ONE TRUST TO PROVIDE FOR THEIR SUPPORT AND EDUCATION UNTIL I HAVE NO LIVING CHILD UNDER 21 YEARS OF AGE. I LEAVE NOTHING TO MY SPOUSE, IF LIVING.

(c) TO BE DISTRIBUTED AS IF I DID NOT HAVE A WILL. "

The will with trust also, of course, contains a provision for naming a trustee of the trust.
● Various Probate Code sections which explain and expand upon the will form sections are important.
● First, Probate Code 56.3 tells us that the "statutory wills" consist *not only of the forms that we* have seen but *also of various other things*. The first of these is the set of 11 "notices" that we see on page 234. Thse are declared by Section 56.3 to be an "included" part of the will. In addition, a number of things are declared to be "included" parts of the will *"by reference."* That means they become *part of the will* even though they do not appear in it. These are:
1. "The definitions and rules of construction set forth in Section 56." Section 56 provides, as follows: "For the purposes of this chapter, the following definitions and rules of construction apply unless, in a particular case, the context clearly requires otherwise:
(a) 'Testator' means any person choosing to adopt a California statutory will.
(b) 'Spouse' means the testator's husband or wife at the time the testator signs a California statutory will.
(c) 'Executor' means both the person so designated in a California statutory will and any other person acting at any time as the executor or administrator under a California statutory will.

(d) 'Trustee' means both the person so designated in a California statutory will and any other person acting at any time as the trustee under a California statutory will.

(e) 'Descendants' means children, grandchildren, and their lineal descendants of all degrees.

(f) A class designation of 'descendants' or 'children' includes (1) persons legally adopted into the class during minority and (2) persons naturally born into the class (in or out of wedlock). The references to "descendants" in the plural includes a single descendant where the context so requires.

(g) Masculine pronouns include the feminine, and plural and singular words include each other, where appropriate.

(h) If a California statutory will states that a person shall perform an act, the person is required to perform that act. If a California statutory will states that a person may do an act, the person's decision to do or not to do the act shall be made in the exercise of the person's fiduciary powers.

(i) Whenever a distribution under a California statutory will is to be made to a person's descendants, the property is to be divided into as many equal shares as there are then living descendants of the nearest degree of living descendants and deceased descendants of that same degree who leave descendants then living; and each living descendant of the nearest degree shall receive one share and the share of each deceased descendant of that same degree shall be divided among his or her descendants in the same manner.

(j) 'Person' includes individuals and institutions."

2. "The clause set forth in Section 56.9." Section 56.9 says in effect that paragraph 2.1 of the will form, disposing of "personal and household items," is actually an abbreviated statement of that disposition and that the "full text" of paragraph 2.1 (in effect that paragraph 2.1 really says) is this: "If my spouse survives me, I give my spouse all my books, jewelry, clothing, personal automobiles, household furnishings and effects, and other tangible articles of a household or personal use. If my wife does not survive me, the executor shall distribute those items among my children who survive me, and shall distribute those items in as nearly equal shares as feasible in the executor's discretion. If none of my children survive me, the items described in this paragraph shall become part of the residuary estate."

3. "The mandatory clauses set forth in Sections 56.12 and, if applicable, 56.13." Here again "by reference" we have things that are *part of the will* even though they are not set forth in the will form. Among other things, Section 56.12 sets forth powers of executors' and guardians appointed by the will forms. Section 56.13 applies to the will with trust and sets forth powers of trustees appointed by that will form.

● Probate Code Sections 56.10 and 56.11 are additional "full text," or "this-is-what-they-really-say," sections giving us "full texts" of the "property disposition" clause of the straight will (56.10) and the "property disposition" clause of the will with trust (56.11). Sections 56.10 and 56.11 are too lengthy to permit reproduction. Section 56.11 provides, it may be noted, that "Consistent with the trustee's fiduciary duties, the trustee may distribute trust income or principal *in equal or unequal shares* and *to any one or more of the beneficiaries to the exclusion of the other beneficiaries.* In deciding on distributions, the trustee may take into account, so far as known to the trustee, the beneficiaries' other income, outside resources, or sources of support, including capacity for gainful employment of a beneficiary who has completed his or her education." (Emphasis supplied.)

CALIFORNIA STATUTORY WILL

NOTICE TO THE PERSON WHO SIGNS THIS WILL:

1. IT MAY BE IN YOUR BEST INTEREST TO CONSULT WITH A CALIFORNIA LAWYER BECAUSE THIS STATUTORY WILL HAS SERIOUS LEGAL EFFECTS ON YOUR FAMILY AND PROPERTY.

2. THIS WILL DOES NOT DISPOSE OF PROPERTY WHICH PASSES ON YOUR DEATH TO ANY PERSON BY OPERATION OF LAW OR BY ANY CONTRACT. FOR EXAMPLE, THE WILL DOES NOT DISPOSE OF JOINT TENANCY ASSETS OR YOUR SPOUSE'S SHARE OF COMMUNITY PROPERTY, AND IT WILL NOT NORMALLY APPLY TO PROCEEDS OF LIFE INSURANCE ON YOUR LIFE OR YOUR RETIREMENT PLAN BENEFITS.

3. THIS WILL IS NOT DESIGNED TO REDUCE DEATH TAXES OR ANY OTHER TAXES. YOU SHOULD DISCUSS THE TAX RESULTS OF YOUR DECISIONS WITH A COMPETENT TAX ADVISOR.

4. YOU CANNOT CHANGE, DELETE, OR ADD WORDS TO THE FACE OF THIS CALIFORNIA STATUTORY WILL. YOU MAY REVOKE THIS CALIFORNIA STATUTORY WILL AND YOU MAY AMEND IT BY CODICIL.

5. IF THERE IS ANYTHING IN THIS WILL THAT YOU DO NOT UNDERSTAND, YOU SHOULD ASK A LAWYER TO EXPLAIN IT TO YOU.

6. THE FULL TEXT OF THIS CALIFORNIA STATUTORY WILL, THE DEFINITIONS AND RULES OF CONSTRUCTION, THE PROPERTY DISPOSITION CLAUSES, AND THE MANDATORY CLAUSES FOLLOW THE END OF THIS WILL AND ARE CONTAINED IN THE PROBATE CODE OF CALIFORNIA.

7. THE WITNESSES TO THIS WILL SHOULD NOT BE PEOPLE WHO MAY RECEIVE PROPERTY UNDER THIS WILL. YOU SHOULD CAREFULLY READ AND FOLLOW THE WITNESSING PROCEDURE DESCRIBED AT THE END OF THIS WILL. ALL OF THE WITNESSES MUST WATCH YOU SIGN THIS WILL.

8. YOU SHOULD KEEP THIS WILL IN YOUR SAFE-DEPOSIT BOX OR OTHER SAFE PLACE.

9. THIS WILL TREATS MOST ADOPTED CHILDREN AS IF THEY ARE NATURAL CHILDREN.

10. IF YOU MARRY OR DIVORCE AFTER YOU SIGN THIS WILL, YOU SHOULD MAKE AND SIGN A NEW WILL.

11. IF YOU HAVE CHILDREN UNDER 21 YEARS OF AGE, YOU MAY WISH TO USE THE CALIFORNIA STATUTORY WILL WITH TRUST OR ANOTHER TYPE OF WILL.

CALIFORNIA STATUTORY WILL OF

_____

(Insert Your Name)

Article 1. Declaration

This is my will and I revoke any prior wills and codicils.

Article 2. Disposition of My Property

2.1. PERSONAL AND HOUSEHOLD ITEMS. I give all my furniture, furnishings, household items, personal automobiles and personal items to my spouse, if living; otherwise they shall be divided equally among my children who survive me.

2.2. CASH GIFT TO A PERSON OR CHARITY. I make the following cash gift to the person or charity in the amount stated in words and figures in the box which I have completed and signed. If I fail to sign in the box, no gift is made. If the person mentioned does not survive me, or the charity designated does not accept the gift, then no gift is made. No death tax shall be paid from this gift.

FULL NAME OF PERSON OR CHARITY TO RECEIVE CASH GIFT (Name only one. Please print.)..	AMOUNT OF GIFT: $_____ AMOUNT WRITTEN OUT: _____ _____ Dollars _____ Signature of Testator

2.3. ALL OTHER ASSETS (MY "RESIDUARY ESTATE"). I adopt only one Property Disposition Clause In this paragraph 2.3 by writing my signature in the box next to the title of the Property Disposition Clause I wish to adopt. I sign in only one box. I write the words "not used" in the remaining boxes. If I sign in more than one box or if I fail to sign in any box, the property will go under Property Disposition Clause (c) and I realize that means the property will be distributed as if I did not make a will.

PROPERTY DISPOSITION CLAUSES (Select one.)

(a) TO MY SPOUSE IF LIVING; IF NOT LIVING, THEN TO MY CHILDREN AND THE DESCENDANTS OF ANY DECEASED CHILD............................

(b) TO MY CHILDREN AND THE DESCENDANTS OF ANY DECEASED CHILD. I LEAVE NOTHING TO MY SPOUSE, IF LIVING...............................

(c) TO BE DISTRIBUTED AS IF I DID NOT HAVE A WILL...

Article 3. Nominations of Executor and Guardian

3.1 EXECUTOR (Name at least one.)

I nominate the person or institution named in the first box of this paragraph 3.1 to serve as executor of this will. If that person or institution does not serve, then I nominate the others to serve in the order I list them in the other boxes.

FIRST EXECUTOR   ....

SECOND EXECUTOR ....

THIRD EXECUTOR   ....

3.2. GUARDIAN (If you have a child under 18 years of age, you should name at least one guardian of the child's person and at least one guardian of the child's property. The guardian of the child's person and the guardian of the child's property may, but need not, be the same. An individual can serve as guardian of either the person or the property, or as guardian of both. An institution can serve only as guardian of the property.)

If a guardian is needed for any child of mine, then I nominate the individual named in the first box of this paragraph 3.2 to serve as guardian of the person of that child, and I nominate the individual or institution named in the second box of this paragraph 3.2 to serve as guardian of the property of that child. If that person or institution does not serve, then the others shall serve in the order I list them in the other boxes.

FIRST GUARDIAN OF THE PERSON

FIRST GUARDIAN OF THE PROPERTY

SECOND GUARDIAN OF THE PERSON

SECOND GUARDIAN OF THE PROPERTY

THIRD GUARDIAN OF THE PERSON

THIRD GUARDIAN OF THE PROPERTY

3.3. BOND

My signature in this box means that a bond is not required for any individual executor or guardian named in this will. If I do not sign in this box, then a bond is required for each of those persons as set forth in the Probate Code.................

I sign my name to this California Statutory Will on _____
                                                                                                    (Date)

at _____, _____.
                              (City)   (State)

_____
Signature of Testator

STATEMENT OF WITNESSES (You must use two adult witnesses and three would be preferable.)

Each of us declares under penalty of perjury under the laws of California that the testator signed this California statutory will in our presence, all of us being present at the same time, and we now, at the testator's request, in the testator's presence, and in the presence of each other, sign below as witnesses, declaring that the testator appears to be of sound mind and under no duress, fraud, or undue influence.

Signature _____   Residence Address: _____

Print Name Here: _____   _____

Signature _____   Residence Address: _____

Print Name Here: _____   _____

Signature _____   Residence Address: _____

Print Name Here: _____   _____

• It would now be clear that what the legislators have done is to try to give us a brief basic will *form* and then to embellish it with these outside things, i.e., these "full texts" and "mandatory provisions," which are made part of the will form "by reference."

• Probate Code 56.4 tells us that if we botch paragraph 2.3 of the will form, our property will pass by the rules of intestate succession. Specifically, Section 56.4 says: "If more than one property disposition clause appearing in paragraph 2.3 of a California Statutory Will Form is selected, or if none is selected, the property of a testator who signs a California statutory will shall be distributed to the testator's heirs as if the testator did not make a will." Related to this, each of Probate Code Sections 56.11 and 56.12, seen in other connections, above, tells us that "If the testator has not made an effective disposition of the residuary estate, the executor shall distribute it to the testator's heirs at law . . . according to the laws of the State of California in effect on the date of the testator's death . . ."

• Probate Code 56.1 tells us who may execute a California statutory will which is "(a)ny person of sound mind and over the age of 18."

• Probate Code 56.2 tells us how we execute a California statutory will. It says: "The only method of executing a California statutory will is for the following to occur:

(a) The testator shall do the following:
(1) Complete the appropriate blanks.
(2) Sign the will.
(b) The witnesses shall do the following:
(1) Observe the testator's signing.
(2) Sign their names in the presence of the testator.

The execution of the attestation clause provided in the California statutory will by two or more witnesses shall satisfy Section 329."

Section 329 sets up simplified procedure for proving the proper execution of a will in order to gain its admission to probate. Basically, Section 329 allows the will to be proved by an *affidavit* of *one* of the witnesses which means that a witness does not even have to appear in court to prove the will.

• As a point of information, an *executor* is one appointed by will to administer the estate of a deceased person and to carry out the terms of the will. An *administrator*, by contrast, is one appointed by the probate court to administer the estate of a person who leaves no will or who, having left a will, has failed to name an executor. Fees of executors and administrators are statutory in California.[130]

---

[130]Prob. C. 901 and 910 give the following fees to both the executor or administrator and the attorney for the executor or the administrator:

4% on the first $15,000;
3% on the next $85,000;
2% on the next $900,000; and
1% on all above $1,000,000.

Thus, if the value of the estate is $20,000, each party—executor or administrator and attorney—gets a fee of $800; if $50,000, a fee of $2000, etc.

Section 910 provides that an attorney may charge a reasonable fee for representing a person seeking to obtain community property under Sections 650-659 (note 131, below), subject to approval by the court.

Estate of Getty (1983) 143 C.A.3d 455, 191 Cal.Rptr. 897, involved the largest estate ever left subject to probate in California, an estate of $1,357,877,342.00. At the statutory rates, above, this would produce executors' and attorneys' fees of

Probate Proceedings—Administration of Decedents' Estates

With certain exceptions discussed in the footnote,[131] below, including the new *community property exception* discussed there, a decedent's estate must go through *probate proceedings*, whether he leaves a will or dies intestate. Originally, "probate" had reference to the proving of a will, i.e., showing that it had been properly executed, but the word is now used broadly to describe the entire proceeding by which a decedent's estate is administered and distributed. Probate proceedings are designed to give creditors of the decedent an opportunity to get their claims satisfied and to establish of record the persons acquiring title to his property by reason of his death.

• In 1975 California adopted an act which it entitled the Independent Administration of Estates Act. The act is found in Probate Code Sections 591-591.7. The purpose of the act is to simplify probate procedures. The act allows the personal representative to do many things without court approval that formerly required such approval. Without court approval, formerly required, the personal representative can now continue the decedent's business for up to 6 months, pay a family allowance for up to 12 months, pay creditors' claims, compromise claims by and against the estate, sell listed securities, and invest estate funds in savings accounts and short-term obligations of the United States. Court approval is still required for sales of estate real property and of accountings and distributions. A third class of acts requires "advice of proposed action" to heirs before they are done, to enable the heirs to object. These acts include the continuance of business of the decedent for a period of more than 6 months and the payment of a family allowance for a period of more than 12 months.

$27,179,846.00. The California Attorney General contended that the probate court "was free to depart from the 'literal language' of Probate Code sections 901 and 910, and to interpret them 'so as to avoid requiring the payment of . . . fees which so far exceed the reasonable value of services rendered as to create a monumental windfall, unjustly enriching fiduciaries at the expense of the estate, a result which is both absurd and contrary to the statutory purpose to protect estates against excessive . . . fees." The Court of Appeal held that Probate Code Sections 901 and 910 were clear and unambiguous and used the mandatory word "shall," that nothing in the sections indicates that selective application of the fee schedules was contemplated or intended by the Legislature, and that applying the schedules to this case did not produce results that were either absurd or unconscionable.

[131]California: (1) Where the estate consists entirely of personal property or money not exceeding $30,000 in value or amount, probate is not required. The heir entitled to it may obtain it from the custodian by giving him an affidavit showing the right to it. (Prob. C. 630.) (2) Where the estate does not exceed $20,000, it may be set aside to a surviving spouse or minor children by the court. Expenses of last illness and funeral expenses of the deceased spouse must be paid, however, before this is done, and the estate is liable to that extent. The recipient of the estate is personally liable for the unsecured debts of the decedent, up to the amount of the value of the estate, for the period of one year after receiving the estate. (Prob. C. 640-646.) In each case, joint tenancy interests of the decedent are not included in computing the value of the estate. (Prob.C. 632, 647.) (3) Prob. C. 650-659 allow community property and quasi-community property which will pass to a surviving spouse on the death of a spouse to be set aside to the surviving spouse without the formality of probate proceedings. See further discussion of these sections at page 175.

• A probate proceeding is commenced in the probate court of the county of which the decedent was a resident at the time of his death.[132] The following are major steps in a California proceeding and of probate proceedings generally:

1. *Petition and Probate of Will.* Where a will is left, the executor files a "petition for probate of will and for letters testamentary."[133] At a hearing on the petition, the genuineness and due execution of the will is first established by the testimony of at least one of the subscribing witnesses who must testify that the will was executed with the proper legal formalities,[134] i.e., properly published and witnessed, that the testator was of sound mind, and that the will was executed freely and voluntarily. This is called the "probate of the will"—the proving of due execution. In the case of a holographic will, all that is required to be proved is the handwriting of the testator, by some witness to it. "*Letters testamentary*" are then issued to the executor. These constitute official recognition of his status by the court and are a badge of office that authorize him to carry out administration proceedings.

Where the person has died intestate, a "petition for letters of administration" must be filed by a party entitled to them.[135] Testimony is introduced to establish the fact of death, and "*letters of administration*" are then issued to the petitioner which authorize him, as administrator of the estate, to carry out the administration proceedings. Statutes prescribe an order of priority to letters of administration, e.g., Prob. C. 422, which gives priority in this order: Surviving spouse, children, grandchildren, parents, brothers and sisters, next of kin and public administrator.[136]

2. *Homestead and Family Allowance.* Most states have statutes requiring the probate court to set aside the family home to a surviving spouse and/or minor children of the decedent for some period of time, usually for the life of the spouse or until majority of the children.[137] This is called the *probate homestead* and takes priority over any disposition which the decedent may have made of his estate. Statutes usually provide for a *family allowance* during the period of administration—monthly payments to the surviving spouse and/or minor children for their support during this period.[138]

3. *Duties of Executor or Administrator.* From here through the decree of distribution, the probate proceeding is the same whether conducted by executor or administrator. Their administration duties are as follows:

a. Immediately upon appointment, take custody of all assets of the decedent.[139] Permission may be obtained from the court to continue the operation of the decedent's business.

b. Publish notice to creditors to file their claims against the estate.[140] Statutes prescribe a time within which claims must be presented, after which they become barred. In California, they must be presented within 4 months after the first publication of notice to creditors.[141]

c. During this waiting period for the presentation of claims, the executor or administrator files an inventory of the estate. Prob. C. 600 requires that this be done within 3 months after appointment.

d. Pay claims after they have been approved by the court.[142]

e. Sell property of the estate if necessary to raise money to pay claims.[143]

f. Bring or defend against lawsuits which the decedent might have brought or which have been commenced against him.[144]

4. *Account and Distribution.* After the time for filing claims has expired and all of the foregoing duties have been fulfilled, the executor or administrator files a final account and petition for distribution.[145] The final account sets out all moneys and property received by the executor or administrator and all expenditures for expenses of administration and payment of claims.

If the court finds the final account to be in order and that all inheritance and property taxes have been paid, it makes a decree of distribution of the remaining property of the estate to the persons designated in the will to receive it, or, if there is no will, to the persons entitled to it under the rules of intestate succession.

The executor or administrator must then make distribution in accordance with the decree, obtaining receipts from the distributees. When all receipts have been obtained and filed with the court, it enters an order discharging the executor or administrator. This concludes the probate proceedings.[146]

Pending Changes in Probate Law and Procedure

A bill contemplating a rather major reorganization of the probate code was passed into law in 1983 to become appli-

---

[132]Prob. C. 301.

[133]Prob. C. 323, 326.

[134]Prob. C. 329 requires the testimony or affidavit of a witness to the will but says that if this cannot be procured, the will may be admitted to probate upon proof of the handwriting of the testator and one of the witnesses.

[135]Prob. C. 440.

[136]Prob. C. 422.

[137]Prob. C. 660 et seq. make the establishment of a probate homestead permissive rather than mandatory. Sec. 664 permits the court to "select as a homestead the most appropriate property available that is suitable for use as a dwelling." See footnote 4, page 9 for discussion of homestead, and page 19 for form of declaration of homestead.

[138]Prob. C. 680-683 provide for such a family allowance.

[139]Prob. C. 571.

---

[140]Prob. C. 700.

[141]Prob. C. 707 bars forever claims not presented within the 4 months' period unless the claimant is out of the state and does not have notice, in which case the claim may be filed at any time before the decree of distribution is rendered.

[142]Prob. C. 713.

[143]Prob. C. 750 so provides. Section 754 says there is no priority as between real and personal property. Section 755 requires confirmation (court approval) of sales before they become final.

[144]Prob. C. 573.

Causes of action for breach of contract and torts against property survive and may be brought by the executor or administrator. In general, torts against the person (negligent personal injuries, false imprisonment, etc.) or reputation (libel or slander) die with the person injured or the person committing the tort, i.e., no action may be brought after death for such wrongs. Wrongful death statutes (C.C.P. 377 in California) give the heirs of a person killed by the wrongful conduct of another a cause of action against the wrongdoer. In California, exceptionally, by virtue of Prob. C. 573, causes of action for personal injuries survive both the death of the person committing the tort and the death of the person injured by the tort, except that if the person injured by the tort is the one who dies recovery may not be had against the wrongdoer for pain, suffering or disfigurement.

[145]Prob. C. 1020-1021.

[146]Prob. C. 1066.

cable to estates of decedents who die after January 1, 1985. The purpose would seem to be to attempt to establish a more logical and better coordinated arrangement of the substantive law provisions of the code.

The substantive law itself will be changed in various significant respects. Among changes which affect provisions talked about in the immediately preceding sections of the text are the following:

• Dispensed with are the requirements of "publication" of a formal will, i.e., of a declaration by the testator to the witnesses that the instrument is his will, and of a request by the testator to the witnesses that they sign the will. It will suffice that the witnesses understand that the instrument they sign is the testator's will. Also dispensed with is the requirement that the signatures of the testator and the witnesses be at the end of the will.

• The rule limiting the share of an "interested witness" to the amount he would have received under the rules of intestate succession is softened. The new rule would not disqualify such a witness from taking under the will but would create a presumption that the interested witness was guilty of duress, menace, fraud or undue influence which the interested witness would be required to rebut.

• Some ability is given to an adopted child to inherit from its natural parents.

• Issue of a predeceased spouse are preferred over next of kin of a decedent more remote than grandparents and issue of grandparents.

• Under present law, seen in footnote 126, page 231, divorce has only a limited effect on a will. Under the new law, divorce or annulment of marriage will revoke the will as to the former spouse except where it appears that the testator intended the will provisions to remain in effect as to the former spouse, or the parties remarry.

Trusts and Administration

Trusts are of two general types: express or intentionally created trusts, and trusts implied or imposed by law.[147]

• An *express or intentionally created trust* may be defined as a transfer of legal title to property (called the *trust estate*, trust res or corpus or trust property) by one person, called the *trustor* or settlor, to himself or another as *trustee*, to be held and administered by the trustee for the benefit of designated *beneficiaries*.

• Transfers in trust of real property are held to come within the section of the statute of frauds requiring transfers of real property to be in writing.[148] Since there is no statute requiring a writing, trusts of personal property may be created orally.

• There are three *essential elements* of an express trust: (1) Definite trust property; (2) beneficiaries sufficiently identified; and (3) trust intention and purposes.[149] Trust intention is indicated simply by the statement in the trust instrument that the property is being transferred in trust. Occasionally in a homemade will or trust, the person making it will say that he "hopes" that something will be done with certain property or money. Such language is generally held to be precatory rather than mandatory and not sufficient to create a trust. Trust purposes will be either charitable, as discussed below, or private, i.e., for "support, maintenance and education" of the named

beneficiaries, and ordinarily no problem is encountered in this connection.

• Any person or corporation may be a trustee, and if the trustor neglects to name a trustee or the named trustee dies or declines to act, the court may appoint a trustee.[150]

Classifications of Trusts: Express trusts are classified:

1. With respect to time of taking effect, as *inter vivos* or *living* trusts and *testamentary* trusts. An *inter vivos* or living trust is one which is to go into operation immediately—during the lifetime of the trustor. A testamentary trust is one which is to go into effect upon the death of the trustor. Testamentary trusts are usually made part of a will. Most trusts are testamentary, although inter vivos trusts are becoming increasingly common because of their value as income-shifting devices for income tax purposes.

2. With respect to method of creation, as *transfers in trust* and *declarations of trust*. A person may create a trust by a transfer of property in trust to a third person, in which case the trust is said to be created by a transfer in trust. This is the usual method. Or, in the case of an *inter vivos* trust, by transferring the property from himself to himself as trustee for the designated beneficiaries (who cannot be himself), in which case the trust is said to be created by declaration of trust.

3. With respect to purposes, as *private* or *charitable*. A private trust is any trust which is not a charitable trust. A charitable trust is one which (a) has a charitable purpose, which means simply any socially beneficial purpose such as advancement of education or medicine or the establishment of a hospital or library; and (b) does not have specifically named persons as beneficiaries, but, rather, a class of persons. Thus, a trust created "for the education of worthy students at Henley University" would fulfill the second requirement, but not one "for the education of Jane Doe and Richard Roe, worthy students at Henley University."

Powers, Duties and Liabilities of Trustee: As mentioned above, any person or corporation may be a trustee. Usually it is a bank, since this is one of the functions of banks, and they are better able to make the diversified type of investment of trust funds that should be made by a trustee.

• The trustee has such powers as are expressly conferred by the trust instrument and, impliedly, such powers as are necessary to carry out the trust[151]—invest the trust funds in securities, vote the securities,[152] pay expenses of the trust, etc. Actually, the trust instrument will give the trustee wide-ranging and highly discretionary power to administer the trust estate—to sell, lease or mortgage trust property, to pay the income to beneficiaries in such amounts as he sees fit, etc. Trusts have been wont to give trustees "absolute" power or "absolute discretion" in the management and administration of the trust and courts have kept hands off except in clear cases of abuse. By 1981 amendment of C.C. 2269 the reins were tightened somewhat however. Section 2269 says, among other things, that "a discretionary power conferred upon a trustee is presumed not to be left to his or her arbitrary discretion but shall be exercised reasonably;" that the exercise of a discretionary power is subject to court review; and that "where a trust instrument confers absolute, sole, or uncon-

---

[147]Trusts created by law are discussed on page 240 (Constructive and Resulting Trusts).

[148]C.C. 852 expressly requires trusts of real property to be in writing.

[149]C.C. 2221 requires these three elements.

[150]C.C. 2289.

[151]C.C. 2267: "A trustee is a general agent for the trust property. . . ."

[152]C.C. 2270 expressly confers this power.

trolled discretion upon a trustee, the trustee shall act in accordance with fiduciary principles and shall not act in bad faith or in disregard of the purposes of the trust."

• The trustee always has the power to sell the property which comes to him in trust in order to put the proceeds in more desirable investments[153] unless the trust expressly forbids sale of particular property, in which case the trustee must abide by the trust instrument.[154] Unless he is given the power in the trust instrument, which he almost always is, the trustee may not mortgage or otherwise encumber trust property.[155]

• The trustee occupies a fiduciary position of the highest confidence and must not use his position for personal advantage or gain.[156] With respect to his management of the trust estate, he must use reasonable skill, prudence and diligence.[157] Accordingly, he must dispose of poor investments and unproductive property immediately upon taking over as trustee and invest the funds in proper investments producing a normal rate of return for trust funds. The trustee is personally liable for any loss suffered by reason of his failure to do so.[158] There are certain legal standards for making investments as follows:

1. Most states follow the *legal list rule* which permits a trustee to invest only in certain "blue chips": generally, only in government securities, first mortgages, corporate bonds, and preferred stocks.

2. Other states, including California,[159] follow the *prudent man rule* under which a trustee may invest in any property or securities in which a prudent man would invest his own funds for a long term conservative investment. The difference, from the legal list rule, is that the trustee may invest in investment grade common stocks.

• The general rule is that the trustee is personally liable on contracts or other obligations incurred in the administration

---

[153]Restatement of Trusts 2d, Section 189.

[154]C.C. 2258: "A trustee must . . . follow all the directions of the trustor . . ."

[155]Restatement of Trusts 2d, Section 191.

[156]See footnote 29, page 62.

[157]C.C. 2259: "A trustee . . . must use at least ordinary care and diligence in the execution of his trust."

[158]C.C. 2262: "If a trustee omits to invest the trust moneys according to the last section [C.C. 2261 in the next footnote], he must pay simple interest thereon, if such omission is negligent merely, and compound interest if it is willful."

[159]The *prudent man rule* was adopted in California in 1943 by an amendment of C.C. 2261 to provide: "(1) In investing, reinvesting, purchasing, acquiring, exchanging, selling and managing property for the benefit of another, a trustee shall exercise the judgment and care, under the circumstances then prevailing, which men of prudence, discretion and intelligence exercise in the management of their own affairs, not in regard to speculation, but in regard to the permanent disposition of their funds, considering the probable income, as well as the probable safety of their capital. Within the limits of the foregoing standard, and subject to any express provisions or limitations contained in any particular trust instrument, a trustee is authorized to acquire every kind of property, real, personal or mixed, and every kind of investment, specifically including, but not by way of limitation, corporate obligations of every kind, and stocks, preferred or common, which men of prudence, discretion and intelligence acquire for their own account."

C.C. 2261(2) may be noted. It permits the trustee to retain trust property in the form received by him if "in the exercise of good faith and of reasonable prudence, discretion and intelligence," he considers it "in the best interests of the trust."

of the trust unless he expressly exempts himself from such liability upon entering into the contract or obligation.[160]

Administration of the Trust: The trustee must keep complete records and accounts of all trust funds and transactions, and must render accountings to the beneficiaries as required by the trust instrument. Where a testamentary trust is created by will, its legal existence stems from the court's validation of the will, and the court has continuing jurisdiction of the trust in order to require the trustee to make periodic accountings.[161]

• In his administration of the trust, the trustee may encounter certain problems of allocation and apportionment of receipts and disbursements upon which, in turn, will depend the propriety of his accounts. This may be illustrated by a hypothetical case: Suppose H dies leaving a will creating a testamentary trust of apartment houses, securities and money. There are mortgages on some of the apartment houses. The trust directs T, the trustee, to retain the apartment houses in the trust estate. As is quite common, the trust provides that W is to receive the income from the trust estate for her life and that, upon her death, A and B are to receive the corpus or principal when they reach certain ages. During the first year of T's administration of the trust, he receives as income (1) rents from the apartment houses, (2) dividends on stocks, and (3) interest on bonds. He has to pay the following expenses on the apartment houses: (1) fire insurance premiums; (2) real estate taxes; (3) principal and interest on the mortgages; (4) costs of miscellaneous routine repairs; and, in addition, he has to pay (5) his own trustee's fee. The amount of income to be paid to W, the income beneficiary, will depend upon which of these expenses are paid out of the income received. A Uniform Principal and Income Act provides for these matters.[162] It makes payable out of income (1) regular annual taxes, (2) interest on encumbrances, (3) costs of ordinary repairs, (4) insurance premiums, and (5) the trustee's fee for his annual services;[163] out of the principal or corpus of the

---

[160]Restatement of Trusts 2d, §§ 261-265.

[161]Prob. C. 1120 provides, to the contrary of the text statement, that "(a) trust created by a will is not subject to the continuing jurisdiction of the superior court unless the testator provides otherwise."

Prob. C. 1138-1138.13, allow a trustee, beneficiary, or remainderman of an *inter vivos* trust to petition the court for various purposes, such as for instructions as to how to administer the trust, to determine the distribution of the trust property upon termination of the trust, and to compel an accounting by the trustee where the trustee fails to make an accounting within 60 days after written request of a beneficiary or remainderman and no accounting has been made within 6 months preceding such request.

[162]California has not adopted this uniform act but has an act (C.C. 730730.17) which is substantially the same.

Income to trust estate as income or principal. Both the uniform act and the California law deal in detail with the allocation of income received from the trust property. In general, ordinary income—rents, cash dividends and the like—is income and goes to the income beneficiary. Various special problems arise, however, as where, e.g., there are extraordinary dividends on stock or discounts on bonds, for which reference may be made to the uniform act or the California law (C.C. 730-730.17).

[163]The trustee is entitled to compensation for his services. Under C.C. 2274 and Prob. C. 1122, he is entitled to the amount specified in the trust, if the trust specifies his compensation; otherwise to reasonable compensation upon the settlement of each account. In California, half the annual fee is paid from income, half from principal.

trust (1) assessments for permanent improvements—sewers, etc.—as distinguished from the annual property taxes, (2) principal on encumbrances, (3) costs of capital improvements or extraordinary repairs, such as a new roof on one of the apartment houses, (4) costs of litigation to protect or recover trust property, (5) costs of opening and closing the trust, and (6) the trustee's fees for other services. In short, it attempts as far as possible to charge the income beneficiary with current operating expenses and the corpus beneficiaries, who will be primarily benefitted by them, with capital expenditures.

Termination of Trust: A trust normally terminates when its terms have been fulfilled,[164] i.e., when the corpus beneficiaries have reached the age when the corpus of the trust is to be distributed to them and this has been done. In the case of an *inter vivos* trust, the trust may be terminated by the trustor at any time by revocation, provided that he expressly reserves the right to revoke in the trust instrument.[165]

Constructive and Resulting Trusts

When one person holds money or property which rightfully belongs to another—money obtained by fraud or mistake, secret profits made by an agent or any other of the multitude of circumstances in which this would be possible—he is said to be a *constructive trustee* of the money or property so held.[166] The person rightfully entitled to the money or property may bring a lawsuit against the wrongdoer as such constructive trustee and recover what is rightfully his. The constructive trust is an implied trust or trust imposed by law, as distinguished from the intentionally created trusts considered to this point. Constructive trust is really a remedy rather than a "trust."

● Where an express trust fails, e.g., because it violates the rule against perpetuities or because the trustor has failed to describe the beneficiaries with certainty, the courts consider that the trust property should be restored to the trustor. They express this by saying that a trust "results" in favor of the trustor, and this is the concept of the *"resulting trust."*

● Where, because of impossibility, inexpediency, or changed conditions, the purpose of a charitable trust cannot be carried out, a court of equity may apply the property to a purpose as nearly like that of the original purpose as is possible, e.g., where a trust was created to found a home for deaf children but did not contain sufficient funds for this purpose, the trust funds were applied to the support of an existing school for deaf children. This is called the *cy pres doctrine* ("as near as [possible]" doctrine).

---

[164] C.C. 2279.

[165] C.C. 2280 states the opposite of this general rule. It says that the trust may be revoked *unless* the power to revoke has been expressly given up in the trust.

---

[166] C.C. 2223-2224 so provide.

CHAPTER 10

Partnerships

Partnership and Corporation Compared

This section is devoted to an introduction to the business organizations of partnership and corporation, discussing broadly the features, advantages and disadvantages, and various types of each of these types of organizations.

Any person wishing to start a business is faced with the choice of one of the three general types of business organizations—sole proprietorship, partnership, and corporation. If his capital is sufficient, he will probably choose sole proprietorship. There, he will have absolute control of the business operation, and all profits will go to him alone.

If he does not have enough money to finance the venture and cannot borrow the required funds, he will have to resort to the alternatives of partnership or corporation, with which this and the next chapter are concerned. Here, choice may be governed by various factors—the amount of money needed, the more or less speculative nature of the business.

Partnership

A *partnership* is simply an agreement between or among two or more persons to carry on a business together and to share the profits. It is best adapted to moderate-sized businesses where substantial capital is needed and where the persons contributing the capital will be able to devote their time and services to the business and all derive a satisfactory income.

● It has several bad features. First, partners have *unlimited liability*. This means that if the business is unsuccessful and ends up in debt, all members of the partnership will be personally liable to the unpaid creditors for the amount of the deficit. So, if one partner has invested $50,000 of his $100,000 life savings in the partnership and it ends up $70,000 in debt, the partnership creditors may sue and recover from him the other $50,000. He may recover proportionately from his copartners, but this will not be of much value if they have no money.

● Second, while the contract of partnership may provide that the business is to continue for one year or two years or some other minimum fixed period of time, this has little meaning if the partners have a falling out. One partner may break up a partnership virtually at will, and even though he may be acting wrongfully in doing so, the expense and delay of litigation to enforce his rights will usually cause the other partner or partners to buy out the dissatisfied partner or to sell the business. As a practical matter, then, a partnership contract is only as good as the parties who make it.

Corporation

Many business ventures must be launched with large capital. The partnership is not adapted to this. It is difficult to find a small number of persons who can put together such a fund or who would be willing to do so. The solution is to induce a large number of persons to make relatively small contributions, and this is the concept of the corporation. The law permits the total fund raised to be put into the hands of another,

artificial "person" called a *corporation* created by those who promote the fund. The fund becomes the *capital* of the corporation which enables it to proceed with the business venture for which it was formed. The persons who contribute the capital become the owners of the corporation in proportion to their contributions.[1] To evidence their ownership, they receive certificates showing that they own a certain number of *shares* of the corporation—*stock certificates* as they are familiarly known. Being its owners, they are entitled to the profits of the corporation, which they receive in the form of *dividends* on their shares.

● Stockholders are given a specially privileged status by the law. If the corporation is unsuccessful, they are not personally liable for its losses or deficits. If a corporation is started with a capital of $1,000,000 and, after a year of operation, is $500,000 in debt and forced into bankruptcy, the $500,000 deficit may not be recovered from the stockholders. They lose their investments in its stock but have no further liability. In this respect, they are not like the owners of a partnership business who have unlimited liability.

● The corporation presents *tax problems*, however, particularly where incorporation of a small business is contemplated which, alternatively, could operate as a partnership. Net earnings are subject to double taxation in the sense that income tax must be paid upon them by the corporation as the "person" which earns them and by the stockholders who receive them as dividends. A small corporation that can qualify can now enjoy the same tax treatment as a partnership, however. Where incorporation of a small business is contemplated—two or three persons to contribute all capital and be both owners and operators[2]—corporation versus partnership must be carefully weighed. Although partnership involves unlimited liability, as previously discussed, responsible partners largely eliminate this danger. Tort liabilities (auto accidents, etc.) can be protected against by insurance. And even if a corporation is formed, the incorporators may be required by creditors to personally guarantee major obligations so that, as to these, personal liability exists anyway. On the other hand, if all

(Continued on page 247)

---

[1]Such persons are called *shareholders* or stockholders. The terms are used interchangeably in this chapter and in the next chapter.

[2]The corporation may be a small as well as a big venture. Where, as in the case above, a small number of persons are to furnish all capital and own and operate the corporation, it is called a "*closed corporation.*" The articles of such a corporation will usually require an owner-stockholder who desires to sell his stock to first offer it to the remaining stockholders. And a corporation may be a "*one man corporation*" in which one person owns all or all but token shares.

The "closed corporation" is to be distinguished from "*close corporations,*" provided for by the new California Corporations Code and designed to permit qualifying corporations to have the separate entity status of a corporation while maintaining the informal structure of a partnership. Close corporations are discussed at page 264.

AGREEMENT OF GENERAL PARTNERSHIP

HOWARD J. SMITH, ROBERT L. JOHNSON, and THOMAS W. GREEN, hereby form a general partnership under the following terms and conditions:

Article I.

The name of the partnership shall be ACME TRANSPORTATION COMPANY. The principal place of business of the partnership shall be at 200 South Market Street, San Francisco, California, or at such other localities as the partners may hereafter select.

Article II.

The partnership shall continue until terminated by mutual agreement of the partners or pursuant to provisions for dissolution hereinafter set forth.

Article III.

The partnership shall engage in the business of motor transportation, warehousing and storage, and such other business of a similar nature or related thereto as shall be agreed upon by the partners.

Article IV.

1. The initial capital of the partnership shall be the sum of $1,250,000, consisting of the sum of $500,000 to be contributed by Smith, $500,000 to be contributed by Johnson, and $250,000 to be contributed by Green, each of which sums shall be contributed in cash forthwith by each of said partners.

2. An individual capital account shall be maintained for each partner.

3. Except by agreement of the partners, or on dissolution, or as hereinafter provided, the capital contributions of the partners shall be subject neither to withdrawal nor addition. No partner shall be entitled to interest other than for express loans or advances to the partnership.

Article V.

1. The net profits or net losses of the partnership shall be distributable or chargeable, as the case may be, to the partners in the same relative proportions as their capital contributions.

2. An individual Income Account shall be maintained for each partner. Profits and losses shall be credited or debited to the individual Income Accounts as soon as practicable after the close of each fiscal year.

3. "Net profits" are defined as follows:

In determining the net profits of the partnership for any accounting period the deductions from gross receipts of the partnership shall include: disbursements made by or on behalf of the partnership for the usual and customary expenses of conducting the business; taxes chargeable to the partnership as such and paid by it; adequate reserves for taxes accrued or levied but not yet payable; interest on all interest-bearing loans of the partnership; salaries paid to employees and to partners; adequate reserves for depreciation on partnership property and for contingencies, including bad accounts; proper allowance for all liabilities accruing; and also any and all other disbursements made by the partnership during such accounting period incidental to the conduct of the business, except payments to partners on account of partnership profits.

4. Salaries or drawing accounts of the partners shall be a first charge against partnership profits in the division of profits between the partners.

5. If there be no balance in the individual Income Accounts, net losses shall be debited to the individual Capital Accounts. If the Capital Account of a partner shall have been depleted by the debiting of losses under this paragraph, future profits of that partner shall not be credited to his Income Account until the depletion shall have been made good, but shall be credited to his Capital Account. After such depletion in his Capital Account shall have been made good, his share of the profit thereafter shall be credited to his Income Account.

6. The partnership shall keep full and accurate accounts and shall follow the accounting methods and practices customarily employed in businesses of like character. At least once each year an inventory shall be taken and an accounting made. The fiscal year of the partnership business shall be from February 1 to January 31, and the annual accounting shall be made as of the close of business on January 31 of each year. Unless the partners otherwise agree, all accounting shall be made by certified public accountants.

Article VI.

Each of the partners shall have an equal voice in the management and conduct of the partnership business. All decisions shall be by a majority vote and each partner shall be entitled to one vote. Each partner shall devote his full time and attention to the partnership business. Each partner shall receive such salary as shall from time to time be agreed upon, but the payment of salaries shall be an obligation of the partnership only to the extent that there are partnership assets available therefor, and shall not be an obligation of the partners individually.

Article VII.

Any partner may retire from the partnership upon 60 days' prior written notice to the other partners.

Article VIII.

A majority in interest of the partners may at any time require any partner to retire involuntarily from the partnership on the ground of inactivity, disability for a period exceeding 4 months, neglect of business, misconduct, breach of partnership articles, conflicting outside interests or shrinkage of business, by delivering a written notice to him 2 months prior to the effective date of his retirement. As of such effective date settlement shall be made with him by the firm for all of his interest in the partnership in the manner hereinafter set forth for settlement upon the death, bankruptcy, insanity or voluntary retirement of a partner.

Article IX.

1. Retirement, bankruptcy, or insanity of a partner shall work an immediate dissolution of the partnership. Upon death of a partner, the partnership shall not dissolve immediately but shall continue until the end of the calendar month in

(Form continued on following pages)

which such death shall have occurred, when it shall dissolve, and for all purposes of this agreement, including the sharing of profits and losses, said deceased partner, or his representative, shall be considered to have continued as a member of the firm until the end of said month. The provisions in this paragraph shall be subject, however, to the provisions of Paragraphs 3 and 4 of this Article IX.

2. In the event of dissolution of the partnership, a proper accounting shall be made of the Capital and Income Accounts of each partner and of the net profit or net loss of the partnership from the date of the last previous accounting to the date of dissolution.

3. In the event of the retirement, bankruptcy, death or insanity of a partner, the remaining partners shall have the right to continue the business of the partnership under its present name by themselves or in conjunction with any other person or persons they may select, but they shall pay to the retiring or expelled partner, or to the legal representative of the deceased or insane partner, or trustee in bankruptcy, as the case may be, the value of his interest in the partnership as provided in paragraph 5 hereof. Written notice of such election shall be given within 30 days after the event giving rise to such election, or within the same number of days after appointment of the legal representative, or trustee. If the remaining partners do not desire to continue the partnership, it shall be liquidated in accordance with Article X hereof.

4. It is agreed that if any partner leaves the firm by retirement, voluntary or involuntary, or bankruptcy, and the other partners continue the business under the firm name, as above provided, he will not divulge the trade secrets thereof nor enter into competition with the firm for a period of 2 years thereafter in the same city or town or portion thereof wherein the partnership business has been transacted; nor use a trade name similar to that of the firm.

5. In the event the remaining partners elect to continue the business, the value of the interest of a retiring, bankrupt, deceased or insane partner, as of the date he is no longer a member of the firm, shall be the sum of:

 a) His Capital Account;
 b) His Income Account;
 c) Any earned and unpaid salary due him;
 d) His proportionate share of the profits.

If a net loss has been incurred to the date of dissolution, his share of such loss shall be deducted.

Inventory for purposes of this determination shall be valued at cost or market value, whichever is lower. Other assets shall be valued at book value.

No value for good will or firm name shall be included in any computation of a partner's interest under these provisions.

6. In the event the remaining partners elect to continue the business, payment for the interest of the partner so leaving the partnership shall be made as follows:

By paying to such partner or his representative an amount equal to the value of such interest computed in accordance with the terms of Paragraph 5 of this Article IX. The payment of said amount shall be made in four equal annual installment

the first of which shall be due on or before six months following the date of the
partner's separation from the firm, and the following three instalments shall become due and payable on each of the next three anniversary dates of said first
payment, respectively.

In addition to the foregoing payments, but not as a part of the purchase
price of any interest of said former partner in the assets of the partnership,
said former partner or his estate or representative shall be entitled to one-
third (1/3) of the profits which he would have been entitled to, had he continued
as a partner, for a period of two years following the date of his separation from
the partnership.

Article X.

1. Unless dissolved by the retirement, bankruptcy, death or insanity of a
partner, the partnership shall continue until dissolved by the majority of the
partners. Upon any such voluntary dissolution by agreement, the affairs of the
partnership shall be liquidated forthwith. The assets of the partnership shall
first be used to pay or provide for all debts of the partnership. Thereafter,
all moneys in the Income Accounts of the partners, and all amounts due for earned
or unpaid salaries of the partners, shall be paid to the partners respectively
entitled thereto. Then the remaining assets shall be divided according to the
proportionate interests of the partners on the basis of their respective Capital
Accounts as they stood upon the date of such dissolution, after crediting or debiting thereto the net profit or net loss accrued or incurred, as the case may be,
from the date of the last accounting to the date of dissolution.

2. Upon the termination of the partnership, no further business shall be
done in the partnership name, unless the business is being continued by certain
of the partners under the provisions of Article VIII or IX, except the completion
of any incomplete transactions and the taking of such action necessary for the
winding up of the affairs of the partnership and the distribution of its assets.
The maintenance of offices to effectuate the winding up of the partnership affairs
shall not be construed a continuance of the partnership.

3. The surviving partner or partners giving his or their personal attention
to the winding up of the partnership affairs shall receive reasonable compensation
for such services, and may employ such agent or agents as reasonably necessary to
effectuate the winding up of the affairs.

Article XI.

1. No partner may, without the consent of the other partners:

a) Borrow money in the firm name or utilize collateral owned by the
partnership as security for a loan;
b) Assign, transfer, pledge, compromise or release any of the claims
of or debts due the partnership except upon payment in full, or arbi-
trate or consent to the arbitration of any of the disputes or controversies of the partnership;
c) Make any assignment for the benefit of creditors or give any
bond, confession of judgment, chattel mortgage, deed, guarantee, indemnity bond, surety bond, or contract to sell or contract of sale
of all or substantially all of the property of the partnership;
d) Lease or encumber any partnership real estate or any interest
therein or enter into any contract for such purpose;

(Form continued on following page)

e) Pledge, hypothecate or transfer his interest in the partnership, except to the other parties to this agreement;

f) Become a surety, guarantor, or accommodation party to any obligation other than that of the firm;

g) Purchase for, or sell property of, the partnership of a value greater than $1,000;

h) Lend money of the firm;

i) Borrow money for personal use in excess of the total sum of $1,000 except for the purchase of a home or permanent investment.

2. Each partner agrees:

a) To keep his personal debts and financial affairs in good order;

b) To inform the other partners of all of his work and transactions in behalf of the partnership and to disclose to them his knowledge of the partnership business and affairs.

Article XII.

1. A commercial account in the name of the partnership shall be maintained in such bank or banks as the partners may from time to time select. All funds of the partnership shall be deposited in the bank account or accounts of the partnership, and all checks or orders of withdrawal shall be signed in the firm name. Checks or orders of withdrawal shall be signed by any two of the partners.

2. All notices provided for in this agreement shall be sent to the last known address of the party to whom such notice is to be given, by registered mail.

3. The parties agree to execute any further instruments and to perform any further acts which are or may become necessary to effectuate and carry on the partnership created by this agreement.

Article XIII.

Upon dissolution of this partnership by death, bankruptcy, retirement or insanity of a partner, or otherwise, a notice of dissolution shall be published, and an affidavit shall be published, and an affidavit of publication filed, as set forth in Section 15035.5 of the California Corporations Code.

This agreement shall become effective as of the date of execution.

IN WITNESS WHEREOF, the parties hereunto have set their hands on the day

of _____ , 19____ .

_____
Howard J. Smith

_____
Robert L. Johnson

_____
Thomas W. Green

probable earnings can be consumed by proper salaries to the incorporators for their services as operators (officers) of the corporation, the tax problems are largely eliminated. In the final analysis, all that can be said is that an attorney must be consulted when formation of a corporation is contemplated.
● Other, relatively inconsequential disadvantages of the corporation are expenses of incorporation and management formalities required—a board of directors and regular meetings thereof, to be seen later.

Intermediate Forms

Certain intermediate forms of business associations may be noted briefly: the limited partnership, the business or Massachusetts trust, and the joint stock company. The limited partnership is the only one of these in wide use today.

Limited Partnerships: In one instance, the law permits a member of a partnership to have limited liability similar to that of a stockholder in a corporation: where a limited partnership is formed and the person becomes a limited partner. A and B wish to start a business which requires $300,000 capital. They can raise $200,000 between them. C is approached and agrees to invest $100,000 in return for ⅓ of the profits, but he does not intend to take an active part in the business and wants to limit his liability as far as possible. The limited partnership is made to order for this situation. If certain recording requirements are complied with,[3] C will have the desired limited liability so long as he does not participate in the management of the business. If the business fails, he will lose his $100,000 but no more.

Joint Stock Companies and Business Trusts: These were forerunners of the corporation. Described briefly, the joint stock company is a corporation with unlimited liability of stockholders.
● The business or Massachusetts trust approaches very closely the corporation. Capital is raised and turned over to *trustees* who invest it in a business which they operate, occupying a position comparable to that of the board of directors of a corporation. Profits are paid to the contributors of the capital, the shareholders. Shareholders have limited liability provided they do not have too large a measure of control of the trustees. What measure of control is fatal varies among the states. In some, there must be no control at all—the trustees must be a self-perpetuating body with complete control of the business operation. In others, shareholders may be given the right to replace a trustee who dies or retires. In a liberal group, including California, the trustees may be elected annually at a meeting of shareholders,[4] just as the board of directors of a corporation is elected.

Summary of Partnership-Corporation Distinctions

Major partnership-corporation distinctions are as follows:

Partnership	*Corporation*
1. Formed by mutual agreement of parties.	1. Requires state approval to come into existence.
2. Association of individuals.	2. Separate legal entity.
3. Unlimited liability of owners-partners.	3. Limited liability of owners-stockholders.
4. Direct management by owners-partners as agents of the partnership.	4. Indirect management through directors elected by owners-stockholders.
5. Ownership interest may not be transferred without consent of all owners- partners.	5. Ownership interests, represented by stock certificates, freely transferable.
6. Limited existence—death, etc., of owner-partner dissolves.	6. Perpetual existence—death, etc., of owner-stockholder does not affect.

Nature and Formation of Partnership

Definition and Formation

Uniform Partnership Act 6(1) says that "A *partnership* is an association of two or more persons to carry on as coowners a business for profit."[5] Two or more persons agree to pool their resources and energies in the operation of a business with the net profits of their endeavor being shared among them.

Such an arrangement is ordinarily brought about by the execution of a written contract in the form of that on page 242. This will state the important essentials of the agreement: the business purposes, i.e., the business that the partnership will carry on; the capital contributions of the partners—what each of them will put into the business, which may consist of money, property or merely services; the profit sharing ratio which may be equal or in such percentages as the partners agree; the duration of the partnership; and provision for purchase by the remaining partners of the interest of a partner who dies or withdraws from the partnership.

Partnership comes into existence as soon as the agreement of partnership is signed, and this is one of the basic differences between partnership and corporation. A corporation must be approved by the state before it can do business. Partnership comes into existence simply by the agreement of the parties. State approval is not required before doing business.

Joint Venture Distinguished

A partnership contemplates the co-management or co-operation of a business of a permanent or continuing character. Not infrequently, parties join forces for a single project, with profits to be split. These associations are joint adventures, or *joint ventures*, as distinguished from partnerships. As stated in *Keyes* v. *Nims*, 43 C.A. 1, 184 P. 695, "a partnership [differs] from a joint venture . . . in the fact that, while a partnership is ordinarily formed for the transaction of a general business of a particular kind, a joint adventure relates to a single transaction, although the latter may [cover] a period of years." In the *Keyes* case, there was held to be a joint venture where the parties agreed to pool their money to purchase a franchise for the sale of a tractor, form a corporation to make a going business of it, and then sell the business and divide the profit. Other common examples are agreements to pool funds to purchase property to be resold immediately and the profit split, and agreements of two or more contractors to join forces to develop a subdivision.

While they differ in their basic nature, there is little difference otherwise between partnership and joint venture. As stated in *McSherry* v. *The Market Corporation*, 129 C.A. 330, 18 P.2d 776, "the resemblance is so close that the rights of

---

[3]Discussed on page 258.

[4]So held in *Goldwater* v. *Oltman*, 210 C. 408, 282 P. 624.

[5]The Uniform Partnership Act, adopted in 30 states, is the general partnership law. It is set out in the Appendix, and is referred to throughout this chapter as the "U.P.A." In California, it is Corp. C. 15001-15045, as shown in the Appendix.

the parties are governed by practically the same rules . . ."[6] There is the same general profit and loss sharing as in a partnership, and members of a joint venture may be held liable for torts of co-joint venturers just as partners are held liable for torts of their copartners. It is said that the power of a co-joint venturer to bind the joint venture on a contract is narrower than that of a partner to bind the partnership, but even this seems a questionable statement. It is generally held that the co-joint venturer may make contracts reasonably necessary to carry on the venture and for which he has actual or apparent authority. In the final analysis, a partner can do no more.

Other Arrangements Distinguished

There are many profit sharing arrangements which cannot be classified either as partnerships or as joint ventures, such as deals in which one party is to put up money to back a scheme or business venture and another is to develop or operate it, or in which one party has property which another is to exploit. These are not partnerships because *co-management*, or at least the right to participate in the management, of a business enterprise is not present. They are not joint ventures because even in a joint venture the parties must have a voice in the management, or share in the control of the venture, and it is held that if a party has no interest in a scheme beyond a share of the profits and is to have *no liability for losses*, there is no joint venture. The courts have frequently pointed to the fact that there is no liability for losses as the basis for finding that there is no joint venture.

● The question of whether or not there is a partnership or joint venture will be determined by looking to see if one party would be chargeable for the contracts or torts of the other. In the controversial cases, the parties usually do not name their agreement; they enter into some kind of written contract but do not call it a partnership or joint venture, designating it perhaps only an "Agreement." This is not of great importance because if, in fact, it is a partnership or joint venture, the court will so hold. Conversely, even though the parties may have called it a "partnership," if it is not, the court will hold that it is not.[7]

● A number of these controversial cases are considered below. First, however, must be noted U.P.A. 7, which attempts to clarify U.P.A. 6 by listing a number of arrangements which are *not* partnerships (and which also would not be joint ventures for the same reason—that they do not involve comanagement or joint control of a business enterprise). These rules of U.P.A. 7 provide a solution in most of the cases discussed.

● U.P.A. 7. *Rules for Determining the Existence of a Partnership.*

"In determining whether a partnership exists, these rules shall apply:

"(1) Except as provided by section 16, persons who are not partners as to each other are not partners as to third persons. [This says that unless a partnership by estoppel is created, persons who are not partners as to each other are not partners as to third persons. This rule is not involved in the present discussion.]

---

[6]Or, as stated in the recent case of *Milton Kauffmann, Inc.* v. *Superior Court*, 94 C.A.2d 8, 210 P.2d 88, "The resemblance between a partnership and a joint venture is so close that the rights as between adventurers are governed practically by the same rules that govern partners. . . ."

[7]If they call it a partnership, however, and hold it out as such to the public, a partnership by estoppel may arise, as discussed on page 249.

"(2) Joint tenancy, tenancy in common, tenancy by the entireties, joint property, common property, or part ownership does not of itself establish a partnership, whether such co-owners do or do not share any profits made by the use of the property.

"(3) The sharing of gross returns does not of itself establish a partnership, whether or not the persons sharing them have a joint or common right or interest in any property from which the returns are derived.

"(4) The receipt by a person of a share of the profits of a business is prima facie evidence that he is a partner in the business, but no such inference shall be drawn if such profits were received in payment:

"(a) As a debt by installments or otherwise;
"(b) As wages of an employee or rent to a landlord;
"(c) As an annuity to a widow or representative of a deceased partner;
"(d) As interest on a loan, though the amount of payment vary with the profits of the business;
"(e) As the consideration for the sale of the good-will of a business or other property by installments or otherwise."

● Now considered is a variety of cases in which there was held not to be a partnership.

In *Fischer* v. *Carey*, 173 C. 185, 159 P. 577, D owned a majority, P a minority interest, in a ship which carried lumber cargoes. D alone operated the ship, and P did not receive any portion of the profits of the operation. P brought an action for sale of the ship and an accounting and distribution of the proceeds on the theory that the parties were partners. Held, no partnership existed merely by reason of the *joint ownership* of the property, and that, therefore, the action was not a proper one.

In *Krenz Copper & Brass Works, Inc.* v. *England*, 109 C.A. 747, 293 P. 689, P had control of patents on paint spraying equipment. He made a deal with D in which he, as "licensor," gave D, as "licensee," the exclusive right to manufacture and distribute the equipment. P was to receive 50% of the profits in return. The agreement did not give P a right to participate in the business or management in any way. Held, no partnership. The court: ". . . it has been held that although the sharing of profits is one of the elements of the partnership relation a *mere participation in profits* does not necessarily constitute a partnership relation . . . there must be such community of interest as empowers each party to make contracts, incur liabilities, manage the whole business . . . The association must be one for the purpose of jointly carrying on the business."

In *Dickenson* v. *Samples*, 104 C.A.2d 311, 231 P.2d 530, where the owner of a building was to receive ⅓ of the profits of the business carried on in return for the use of the building, it was held that this was merely "*rent to a landlord*" and did not create a partnership.[8]

In *In re Mission Farms Dairy*, 56 Fed.2d 346, parties made a written agreement as follows: D was to give H and W $7400 to be used by them to purchase land, cattle and equipment to open a dairy. H and W were to give D a note for the $7400. Out of the profits, H and W were first to get specified salaries. The balance of profits was to be paid to D until the note was paid in full. D was to have a lien on the property purchased as security until the note was paid. After that, H and W were to have a right to purchase a 49% interest in the property

---

[8]This would be a "percentage rental" arrangement as discussed on page 227.

The entire management and operation was to be in the hands of H and W. The writing expressly stated that "This agreement shall not be deemed a partnership between the parties . . ." The business was not successful and ended in bankruptcy. This action was brought to determine whether there was a partnership so as to permit D to be held for the unpaid debts of the business. The court first pointed out that a "mere declaration in the agreement that the relationship established is not that of a partnership is not controlling, if the agreement actually establishes a partnership relationship." It then went on to find that there was no partnership, saying that "The record is convincing that there was no intention . . . to form a partnership. Very few of the indicia of partnership were present, and most of them were absent. This was the only property they had a common interest in; there was no firm name, no firm funds, no firm accounts, no firm letterheads, no firm bank account, no commingling of funds or property, no certificate of partnership filed,[9] no agreement as to losses, no time fixed when it would expire;" that the profits paid to H and W for salaries were mere "*wages of an employee*," those to D, "*interest on a loan*."

In *Spier* v. *Lang*, 4 C.2d 711, 52 P.2d 138, P sued D as a partner of L for materials furnished to L for drilling operations. D owned land containing gas and oil. L was a free lance driller. D agreed to provide $3000 for L to conduct drilling operations. Out of profits, D was to be repaid his $3000 and the balance was to be split. All drilling equipment was furnished by L, and he had complete control of the drilling operations. The enterprise was operated under the name of the "Lang-Wall Company," Lang and Wall being L and D. L ran up bills for several thousand dollars in excess of D's $3000 advance, and P was one of the unpaid creditors. Held, no partnership. The court: "The main reliance of plaintiffs is on the provisions of the contract that the defendants were to share in a division of the profits. But this feature of the agreement has long been held not to require a conclusion that a partnership relation existed where also there was no joint participation in the management and control of the business, and the proposed profit sharing was contemplated only as *compensation or interest for the use of the money advanced*."

● Finally may be noted the case of *Nelson* v. *Abraham*, 29 C.2d 745, 177 P.2d 931, which is something of a switch in that the court found that, while there was no partnership in fact, equity required treating the relationship as a partnership in order to give one party the ⅓ of the proceeds of the sale of the business that he deserved. The situation was this: D was owner and operator of a large ice company in Alameda County. P worked for him as a salesman. P felt that a like business could be operated successfully in the San Francisco area. D agreed to let P try. P was to receive a salary and ⅓ of the profits realized by the San Francisco enterprise. D furnished money for a plant and equipment in San Francisco. The San Francisco business was developed by P. Shortly after it had become successful, a competitor offered to buy it, and D sold it to him. P then sued D for ⅓ of the profit realized from the sale of the business. Held for P. The court said that while there was no partnership, there was more than mere employment—an "operation" from which, in equity, P should be entitled to a share of the profit realized from the sale.

The language of the court: "Something more than mere direction to perform a particular task in return for salary or wages was inherent in the agreement and in the minds of the parties. The establishment of the business entailed more than merely selling merchandise. To establish the ice routes in the new and competitive territory required effort, skill, management and tact beyond the mere delivery of ice over an already established route. That the time and effort expended by the plaintiff in these respects were successful is evidenced by the eagerness of the competitors and the return to the defendant on the sale of the business. The profits taken by the defendant . . . may . . . be deemed at least an undue benefit to the defendant, and therefore a profit in which the plaintiff was entitled to share. . . . Considering the relationship which the defendant had assumed toward the plaintiff . . . the principles of equity might best be served by treating the San Francisco business . . . as an 'operation.'[10] To that end the defendant should not be permitted to say that he intended to profit from the plaintiff's labor and at the same time deprive the plaintiff of the fruits of the agreement."

Partnership by Estoppel

A partnership is a *mutual agency*—an association of persons in which each party is agent of and principal to every other party. Just as agency by estoppel arises when a person is made to appear to be one's agent, or, being one's agent, is made to appear to have greater powers than he has in fact, so also partnership by estoppel arises when a person is made to appear to be a partner or, being a partner, is made to appear to have greater powers than he actually possesses. U.P.A. 16 so provides. Examples are few, however. The same situation that is interpreted as giving rise to an agency by estoppel may also be held to give rise to a partnership by estoppel. About the only California case of any consequence is *Associated Piping & Engineering Co.* v. *Jones*, 17 C.A.2d 107, 61 P.2d 536. There, defendant was a friend of members of a partnership. The partnership wanted to obtain materials and services from plaintiff on credit and told plaintiff that the partnership had the financial backing of defendant. Defendant added to this by expressly authorizing plaintiff to extend credit to the firm. Held, defendant was liable as a partner by estoppel for the credit extended by plaintiff.

Fictitious Name Statutes

Many states, including California, have statutes requiring persons or partnerships doing business under a fictitious name to record and publish notice of the fact. These are customarily called *fictitious name statutes*. The penalty for non-compliance is denial of the use of the courts to recover on obligations owed to the person or partnership. In California, the matter is covered by Business and Professions Code, §§ 17900-17930.

● California requires a person who transacts business for profit under a fictitious name to file a *fictitious business name statement* within 40 days from the time he commences to transact such business. B.P.C. 17910. The statement must be filed with the clerk of the county in which the registrant has his principal place of business in the state or, if he has no place of business in the state, with the Clerk of Sacramento County. B.P.C. 17914. ("Registrant" means a person who is filing or has filed a fictitious business name statement. B.P.C. 17903.) There must, additionally, be newspaper publication of the fictitious business name statement within 30 days after the statement has been filed, and an affidavit showing such publication must be filed with the county clerk within 30 days after the completion of the publication. B.P.C. 17917.

---

[9]This has reference to the certificate of doing business under a fictitious name discussed below.

[10]The court's description of the arrangement as an "operation" is a novel one.

● B.P.C. 17900 defines fictitious business name, as follows:
"(a) As used in this chapter, 'fictitious business name' means:

(1) In the case of an individual, a name that does not include the surname of the individual or a name that suggests the existence of additional owners.

(2) In the case of a partnership or other association of persons, a name that does not include the surname of each general partner or a name that suggests the existence of additional owners.

(3) In the case of a corporation, any name other than the corporate name stated in its articles of incorporation.

(b) A name that suggests the existence of additional owners within the meaning of subdivision (a) is one which includes such words as 'Company,' '& Company,' '& Son,' '& Sons,' '& Associates,' 'Brothers,' and the like, but not words that merely describe the business being conducted."

● B.P.C. 17910.5 forbids the adoption of a fictitious business name which indicates corporate status ("Corporation", "Corp.", "Incorporated", or "Inc.") except by a corporation.

● The county clerk must furnish fictitious business name statement forms without charge. B.P.C. 17924. A copy of the appropriate form, as prescribed by B.P.C. 17913, appears on the following page.

● B.P.C. 17918 prescribes the penalty for failing to comply with the fictitious business name statement requirements, as follows: "No person transacting business under a fictitious business name contrary to the provisions of this chapter, or his assignee, may maintain any action upon or on account of any contract made, or transaction had, in the fictitious business name in any court of this state until the fictitious business name statement has been executed, filed, and published as required by this chapter."

● A fictitious business name expires at the end of 5 years from December 31 of the year in which it was filed in the office of the county clerk (B.P.C. 17920) and a new statement must be filed before the old expires. B.P.C. 17910. A fictitious business name statement also expires if there is any change in the facts set forth in the statement, except information with respect to residence address. B.P.C. 17920.

Rights and Duties of Partners in General

Sections 18-22 of the Uniform Partnership Act state the general rights and duties of partners—to participate in management, share in profits, contribute to losses, etc. Some of these will be restated in the agreement of partnership, e.g., the profit sharing right, even though this is not necessary unless there is to be other than an equal division of profits. But the partners prefer this to be stated in writing. The partners do not require the inclusion of other matters covered by Sections 18-22, but take them for granted, e.g., the right to participate in management. The balance of this section is devoted to the rules of Sections 18-22.

Management; Unanimous Consent Cases

Each partner is entitled to an equal voice in the management, i.e., an equal right to decide what transactions shall be entered into and what business policies will be followed, and, as in other democratic institutions, the majority controls.[11] However, Section 9(3) requires unanimous consent to the following exceptional actions:

---

[11]U.P.A. 18(e)(h).

1. Assignment of the partnership property in trust for creditors.
2. Disposition of the good will of the business.
3. Acts making it impossible to carry on the business.
4. Confession of judgment.[12]
5. Submission of a partnership claim or liability to arbitration.

● As indicated above, these are all things of an exceptional nature which might be done by a partnership.

The first, assignment of the property in trust for creditors or "assignment for the benefit of creditors," as it is more commonly known,[13] is something that is done only by a business which is insolvent and beyond redemption, which may be a matter of opinion depending upon the owners' inclination or disinclination to give up—certainly a thing for which unanimous consent might be required. The only example of the second and third exceptions would be a sale of the partnership business—clearly a matter for the concurrence of all. The fourth and fifth exceptions are primarily matters which would make all partners liable for some wrongful act or breach of contract—again, a matter of exceptional concern to all partners. These things are also exceptional in another way—they almost never happen.

Profits and Losses; Compensation

In the absence of agreement to the contrary, profits are divided equally.[14] It makes no difference that capital contributions are in different amounts, e.g., that one partner has contributed $200,000 and the other $100,000. Profits are still shared equally unless there is an express agreement to apportion them in the ratio of 2 to 1.

● Just as profits are shared equally, losses must be borne equally in the absence of agreement to the contrary. However, if there is an express agreement for dividing profits in other than equal proportion, losses must be borne in the same proportions, as in *Monson* v. *Rahlmann*, 7 C.2d 506, 61 P.2d 456, where the agreement was that one partner should receive ⅔ and the other ⅓ of the profits, and it was held that the parties had to contribute to a deficit in the same proportions. This is the rule of Section 18(a) which says that a partner "must contribute toward the losses . . . according to his share in the profits" and was, of course, the rule applied in the *Monson* case.

● The partner's reward for his participation in the business is his share of profits and there is no right to a salary or other compensation for this.[15] Quite frequently, however, the partnership setup is one in which it is agreed that one partner will devote little or no time to the business or considerably less time than the others. In such case, it may be agreed that the active partner or partners shall first receive a salary or fixed amount from the profits, after which the balance will be divided equally with the inactive partner. Unless there is an agreement of this type, the fact that one party expects to and

---

[12]A "confession of judgment" is a written instrument authorizing a creditor to take a judgment in a particular matter without contest. It is seldom encountered today.

[13]An assignment for the benefit of creditors is simply a transfer by an insolvent business of its assets to some person or organization as *assignee*, to liquidate the assets of the business and distribute the proceeds pro rata among the creditors of the business. See page 355 for further discussion.

[14]U.P.A. 18(a).

[15]U.P.A. 18(f).

FICTITIOUS BUSINESS NAME STATEMENT

FILE NO. _____ FILING FEE — $10.00 FOR FIRST NAME. $2.00 FOR EACH ADDITIONAL NAME.

THE FOLLOWING PERSON (PERSONS) IS (ARE) DOING BUSINESS AS:

A   (★) FICTITIOUS BUSINESS NAME _____

B   at (★★) _____

C

1 (★★★) _____	2 _____
FULL NAME - TYPE/PRINT	FULL NAME - TYPE/PRINT
STREET ADDRESS	STREET ADDRESS
CITY STATE ZIP	CITY STATE ZIP
IF CORPORATION, SHOW STATE OF INCORPORATION	IF CORPORATION, SHOW STATE OF INCORPORATION
3 _____	4 _____
FULL NAME - TYPE/PRINT	FULL NAME - TYPE/PRINT
STREET ADDRESS	STREET ADDRESS
CITY STATE ZIP	CITY STATE ZIP
IF CORPORATION, SHOW STATE OF INCORPORATION	IF CORPORATION, SHOW STATE OF INCORPORATION

D   (★★★★) This business is conducted by ☐ an individual; ☐ a general partnership; ☐ a limited partnership; ☐ an unincorporated association other than a partnership; ☐ a corporation; ☐ a business trust. (CHECK ONE ONLY)

If Registrant a corporation sign below.

Corporation name _____

Signed _____

Signature & Title _____

Typed or Printed _____

Type or Print
Officer's Name & Title _____

This statement was filed with the County Clerk of the City and County of San Francisco, California, on the date indicated by file stamp above.

Certification

I hereby certify that the foregoing is a correct copy of the original on file in my office . . . .

_____
COUNTY CLERK

By _____
DEPUTY

CARL M. OLSEN
County Clerk
of the City and County of
San Francisco

**SEE REVERSE
SIDE FOR
INSTRUCTIONS**

FORMS FURNISHED BY: **The RECORDER**

The officially designated newspaper
(ch. X, sec. 5, rules of Superior Court)
in and for the City and County of San Francisco

99 South Van Ness Avenue
San Francisco, California 94103
PHONE: 621-5400, ext. 47

(Reverse side of this form on following page)

does all or a greater portion of the work does not entitle him to a greater share of the profits.

Indemnity or Reimbursement; Contribution

A partner is entitled to be indemnified or reimbursed for personal expenditures made in carrying out the partnership business or preserving partnership property.[16]

● As mentioned earlier and discussed in detail later, a partner has unlimited personal liability for debts and liabilities of the partnership, including liabilities resulting from wrongful acts of a partner in the course of the partnership business. Thus, any partner may be compelled to satisfy a judgment against the partnership. An example of this is given in the section on partner's liability on page 255. Where one partner is required to satisfy a partnership obligation, he is entitled to contribution from his copartners.[17]

Books; Information; Accounting

A partner has the right, at all times, to inspect and copy partnership books,[18] and to full and complete information on partnership affairs.[19]

● Since he has access to the books, a partner is in position to apprise himself of partnership finances and financial affairs. Accordingly, it is the rule of U.P.A. 22 that a partner is not entitled to a formal accounting, except in connection with the dissolution and winding up of the partnership, unless (1) he is excluded from the business, and so does not have access to the books; (2) the right is given in the partnership contracts,

---

[16]U.P.A. 18(b)(c).

[17]U.P.A. 18(a).

[18]U.P.A. 19.

[19]U.P.A. 20.

as it always is, e.g., paragraph 6 of Article V in the specimen agreement on page 242; (3) the right exists by virtue of U.P.A. 21 which says that partners are fiduciaries and must account to each other for any secret profits made in the course of partnership business; or (4) "other circumstances render it just and reasonable." The matter is of little practical importance for the reason that when partners reach such a state of discord that formal accountings are demanded, they will either voluntarily dissolve or one of them will force a dissolution under U.P.A. 32(c)(d) or (f).

Repayment of Capital and Advances

U.P.A. 18(a)(c) provide that a partner is entitled to repayment of his capital contribution, and, with interest, of any loans or advances made to the partnership. Problems which may arise in this connection are discussed in the later section on dissolution and winding up.[20]

Fiduciary Duty

Partners have a fiduciary relationship—a relationship of special trust, confidence, loyalty and good faith which prohibits a partner from taking advantage of his copartners in any transaction related to the partnership business or of secretly profiting from partnership business or affairs. This is the rule of U.P.A. 21(1) which says that "Every partner must account to the partnership for any benefit, and hold as trustee for it any profits derived by him without the consent of the other partners from any transaction connected with the formation, conduct, or liquidation of the partnership or from any use by him of its property."[21]

Business Opportunity Doctrine: The *business opportunity doctrine* is an extension of the doctrine of fiduciary obligation. The business opportunity doctrine is an extension to partnerships of the *corporate opportunity doctrine* of the law of corporations. In the law of corporations it is the rule that if a director learns of a business opportunity which the corporation can undertake, he must inform the corporation of it and cannot take advantage of it for himself alone. The same rule was applied in the field of partnerships for the first time in California in the 1947 case of *MacIsaac* v. *Pozzo*, 81 C.A.2d 278, 183 P.2d 278. Two partnerships entered into a joint venture to construct a housing project, the agreement being that they would continue to work together on other like ventures upon completion of the first. During the final stages of the job, one of the partnerships obtained another construction job on the merits of the one about to be completed. It represented to the other partnership that the job had been obtained entirely through its own efforts and reputation, and persuaded it to take 15% rather than 50% of the profits, which had been the division on the first job. Later, when the true facts were discovered, the deceived partnership sued for an additional 35% which was awarded to it. The court first stated the business opportunity rule of the law of corporations discussed above and then said that it applied here and to any business association. In its words: ". . . if there is presented to a corporate officer or director a business opportunity which the corporation is financially able to undertake, [and] is, from its nature,

in the line of the corporation's business . . . the law will not permit him to seize the opportunity for himself. And, if, in such circumstances, the interests of the corporation are betrayed, the corporation may elect to claim all of the benefits of the transaction for itself, and the law will impress a trust in favor of the corporation upon the property, interests and property so acquired. The facts bring the case within the stated rule. While it has been applied so generally in corporation cases as to have become known as the doctrine of corporate opportunity it is founded in the doctrine of loyalty in business which applies in all situations in which trust is reposed."

Property Rights

Partnership Property

U.P.A. 8 says that *partnership property* consists of the money or property originally contributed by the partners to launch the partnership plus all property subsequently acquired by the partnership with partnership funds or otherwise. The cases have extended upon this by saying that, in addition, any property which parties intend to become and treat as partnership property is such property. In *Perelli-Minetti* v. *Lawson*, 205 C. 642, 272 P. 573, ranches were owned by parties as tenants in common. Later, they formed a partnership rather informally, it being based entirely upon oral agreement. Nothing was actually said about the ranch lands becoming property of the partnership, but they were used thereafter for the partnership business. In fact they were the partnership business, the partnership being engaged in raising grapes and making wine. At no time was the property changed over to the partnership name, being left in the names of the partners as individuals. It was carried on the books of the partnership as an asset, however, was shown in partnership tax returns as an asset, and was used as security for loans to the partnership. Held, it was partnership property; that where the parties by their conduct and course of dealing indicate an understanding that certain property is partnership property, it becomes such whether or not acquired with partnership funds or held in the partnership name.

Property Rights of Partners

U.P.A. 24-28 confer certain property rights on partners, these sections being designed to define the nature and scope of a partner's proprietary or ownership interest in the partnership business and its assets.

● Section 24 says that a partner has three *property rights*: "(1) his rights in specific partnership property, (2) his interest in the partnership, and (3) his right to participate in the management."

● The third right, the right to participate in the management, has been covered in the preceding section.

● The second right is defined by U.P.A. 26 which says that "A partner's interest in the partnership is *his share of the profits and surplus*, and the same is personal property."

● The first right—the partner's right in specific partnership property—requires extended discussion. By *specific partnership property* is meant simply the physical, tangible assets of the partnership—its factory, equipment, fleet of trucks, office equipment, stock of merchandise, etc. U.P.A. 25(1) states that the partners own this as *tenants in partnership*, another form of concurrent ownership like the joint tenancy and tenancy in common forms, discussed in Real Property and, like each of them, having its own special features or "incidents," as Section 25(2) calls them, listing 5 such incidents. Section 25(2)(a) says that the partners have the equal right to use and possess the various items of partnership property "subject to

---

[20]See page 256.

[21]*Donleavey* v. *Johnston*, 24 C.A. 319, 141 P. 229, is an example of violation of the fiduciary duty. There P and D were partners in a grocery business, having a monthtomonth tenancy of the premises on which the business was operated. P wanted the partnership to buy the building, but D discouraged this because he was secretly negotiating to buy the building for himself.

. . . any agreement between the partners," but for partnership purposes only.[22] This is nothing new; it is the concept of unity of possession of the real property cotenancies, seen earlier. The other incidents are peculiar to partnership and must be discussed in greater detail. All are designed for the mutual protection of the partners—to prevent or minimize injury or prejudice to a partnership by reason of the act or upon the death of a single partner.

Not Assignable: Section 25(2)(b) says that "A partner's right in specific partnership property is not assignable . . ." This statement is somewhat deceiving. Suppose A, B and C form a partnership. Later, C would like to sell to D and have D replace him in the partnership. The law of contracts presents an objection to this—that the partnership contract is a highly *personal* one since it is based upon the business experience and acumen, financial resources, personal integrity and reputation of those who agree to associate together as partners; that therefore a partner should not be able to assign or sell his part of the partnership contract without the approval of his copartners. The Uniform Partnership Act does not have a provision that says this squarely. However, the courts have always found this to be the rule from the combination of Sections 25(2)(b) above, and 27(1). The statement of Section 25(2)(b) that the "partner's right in specific partnership property is not assignable" prevents a partner from selling his right to share in the use and possession of the tangible property of the partnership. Section 27(1) is a kind of negative-positive. It says that "A conveyance by a partner of *his interest in the partnership* does not of itself dissolve the partnership, nor, as against the other partners in the absence of agreement, entitle the assignee, during the continuance of the partnership, to interfere in the management or administration of the partnership business or affairs, or to require any information or account of partnership transactions or to inspect the partnership books; but it merely entitles the assignee to receive in accordance with his contract the profits to which the assigning partner would otherwise be entitled." Since, as seen earlier, a partner's "interest in the partnership" is only his right to a share of the profits, this is all that is covered by Section 27(1). The obvious intention and purpose of the two sections (25(2)(b) and 27(1) is to prohibit the sale by a partner of his interest in the sense of his entire ownership or proprietary interest, and this is the well established law. In summation, by virtue of Sections 25(2)(b) and 27(1), a partner may not sell his participating interest without the consent of his copartners.

Not Subject to Attachment or Execution: Section 25(2)(c) says that "A partner's right in specific partnership property is not subject to attachment or execution, except on a claim against the partnership. . . ." What this means is that personal creditors of a particular partner may not have his interest in partnership assets sold to recover what is owed them. So, if A, B and C are partners and C owes T a personal debt, T may not attach or have execution sale of ⅓ of the partnership's fleet of trucks or ⅓ of the partnership's stock of merchandise to obtain his money.

While this may appear unjust to personal creditors, it is not really so because (1) partnership assets should be preserved primarily for the benefit of partnership creditors, and (2) personal creditors are protected by other provisions of law: (a) Under U.P.A. 28, they may get a judgment against the partner and then secure a *charging order* under which a receiver will

be appointed to collect from the partnership the share of profits of the debtor-partner, paying this over to the personal creditors until they are satisfied. (b) If the debtor-partner is in bankrupt condition, the partnership is automatically dissolved, and the remaining partners must immediately proceed to liquidate the business and pay over to the trustee in bankruptcy the share of the bankrupt partner for distribution to his creditors in the course of the bankruptcy proceeding.

Not Subject to Dower, Curtesy, etc.: This is best developed in terms of a factual situation. Suppose A, B and C are partners. C dies. If his interest in the partnership were ordinary property, two consequences would follow immediately:

(1) There would vest in the surviving spouse and children of the deceased partner dower rights, rights to a family allowance, etc., discussed in the earlier sections on succession and decedents' estates. This might result in confusion and dissension and the clouding of title to the partnership property. To prevent these consequences, U.P.A. 25(2)(e) provides that "A partner's right in specific partnership property is not subject to dower, curtesy, or allowances to widows, heirs, or next of kin," and California adds: "and is not community property" to prevent clouding of the title by virtue of operation of the rules of community property law in this state.[23]

(2) The executor or administrator of the deceased partner would be entitled to take custody of the partner's interest, probably resulting in confusion, difficulty and dissension. Again, the U.P.A. provides a solution. Under Section 25(2)(d), the deceased partner's right in the partnership property vests in the surviving partners who continue to have the exclusive right of possession of the partnership property. This does not mean that the surviving partners become owners of the deceased partner's interest, however. To the contrary, they must immediately proceed to liquidate the partnership assets and pay over the deceased partner's share to his executor or administrator.[24] But, giving the surviving partners the exclusive possession of the partnership property during this period for this purpose permits liquidation to be accomplished more efficiently and satisfactorily.

Partnership and Third Persons

Mutual Agency

A partnership is a *mutual agency* in which each partner is an agent of the partnership and of his fellow partners, and each partner is principal to and bears unlimited liability for the acts of every other partner. All of the ordinary rules of agency law apply, e.g., notice to and admissions of one partner bind the other partners, and the partnership is liable for contracts made and torts committed by a partner in the ordinary course of the partnership business.

Contracts and Instruments

U.P.A. 9(1) states the rule of agency and of the power to bind the partnership on contracts and instruments as follows: "Every partner is an agent of the partnership for the purpose

---

[22]U.P.A. 25(2)(a).

[23]This does not mean that the deceased partner's interest is his separate property; only that the surviving spouse does not have rights in it immediately upon death and during the course of administration of the decedent's estate, which he or she would have if this provision were not included to disallow such rights.

[24]This would not be required, of course, if arrangements had been made for purchase of the deceased partner's interest by the surviving partner(s) through "partnership insurance" or otherwise.

of its business, and the act of every partner, including the execution in the partnership name of any instrument, for apparently carrying on in the usual way the business of the partnership of which he is a member binds the partnership, unless the partner so acting has in fact no authority to act for the partnership in the particular matter, and the person with whom he is dealing has knowledge of the fact that he has no such authority."

● What contracts and instruments are "for apparently carrying on in the usual way the business of the partnership" is of course a question of fact in each particular case. Distinction is made between a *trading partnership*, one engaged in manufacturing or buying or selling goods or property, and a nontrading partnership, one rendering services such as a partnership of professional persons. A partner in a trading partnership has broader implied or apparent authority than one in a nontrading partnership. He will have implied or apparent authority to buy and sell property in which the partnership deals; to borrow money on behalf of the partnership; and to execute negotiable instruments in the partnership name.

● In *Jackson* v. *Lamb*, 91 C.A. 405, 267 P. 114, a partnership was engaged in the transportation business. One of the partners signed notes totaling $24,000 in the partnership name, giving as the reason for the loans that the partnership was "expanding." The partner then "disappeared," and the notes were discovered. The court held that there was enough evidence to hold the partnership on all of the notes; that a partner in a trading partnership has the power to borrow money for the purpose of the business and that, therefore, the transaction was "within the ordinary and usual course of the conduct of business" even though there had been no conduct on the part of the other partner to indicate that the loan was authorized and no inquiry had been made of him.

● A partnership is not bound upon a guarantee of obligations of others unless it is shown that this is necessary to accomplish the purposes of the partnership business, or at least that it is directly in furtherance of the business of the partnership.[25] In *Stauffer* v. *Ti Hang Lung & Co.*, 29 C.A.2d 121, 84 P.2d 209, a partner signed the partnership name in guarantee of a note of a corporation which was a sales outlet of the partnership. The partnership disclaimed liability on the note when it was not paid by the corporation. The partnership business was the sale of rice which it sold through the corporation. Held, the guarantee was in the "ordinary course of business" and within the power of the partner under the circumstances; that it would "contribute to the financial stability and credit" of the corporation and, so, was in furtherance of the partnership business since it was important to the partnership to maintain the corporation as a sales outlet.

● In *Cowan* v. *Tremble*, 111 C.A. 458, 296 P. 291, one partner made a contract to sell the business. There was substantial conflict in the evidence as to whether the other partner had authorized the contract or, at least, had ratified it after it was made. Held, the evidence was not sufficient to find authorization or ratification; that, without this, the contract was clearly one which was not enforceable; that since it was not one for carrying on the business in the usual way, it required unanimous consent so that the would-be purchaser of the business was on notice of the partner's lack of authority.

Conveyances of Real Property

U.P.A. 10 deals with this in detail, the important rules of which are as follows:

1. If title to the property stands in the name of the partnership, an unauthorized conveyance by a partner is not binding on the partnership unless (a) the conveyance *appears* to be within his authority, about the only possibility for which would be the case of a partnership engaged in the business of selling real estate; or (b) the buyer from the partner acting without authority in turn *sells to* a bona fide purchaser for value.[26]

2. If title stands in the name of one or more partners, a conveyance by the partners in whose names it stands is binding if it appears to be within their authority, or the *buyer* is a bona fide purchaser for value.

Torts

In accordance with the agency theory of *respondeat superior*, the partnership is liable for torts committed by a partner within the scope of the partnership business. U.P.A. 13 imposes such liability by its provision that "Where, by any wrongful act or omission of any partner acting in the ordinary course of the business . . . loss or injury is caused to any person . . . the partnership is liable therefor . . ."

Thus, it was held in *Madsen* v. *Cawthorne*, 30 C.A.2d 124, 85 P.2d 909, that the partnership was liable for personal injuries inflicted upon a third person in an automobile accident which occurred while one partner was operating an automobile in the course of the partnership business.

And in *Siebold* v. *Berdine*, 61 C.A. 158, 214 P. 658, the partnership was held liable for fraud in the form of misrepresentations as to profits and income by one partner in connection with the sale of the partnership business. The other partner was entirely innocent. The buyer elected to affirm the contract (keep the business) and sue for damages for the fraud. Judgment for damages was entered against both partners.

● U.P.A. 14 makes the partnership liable for misapplication or misappropriation by a partner of money or property received from third persons in connection with the partnership business.

Extent of Partner's Liability

In General—Unlimited Liability: Partners have *unlimited liability*, i.e., each partner is liable to the full extent of his personal assets for all obligations and liabilities incurred by the partnership whether arising out of contract or tort. In this respect, the partnership may prove to be a dangerous association. Every partner is, of course, entitled to have the partnership assets applied to the satisfaction of obligations and liabilities[27] but has full individual liability to the extent to which the same remain unsatisfied after partnership assets have been exhausted.

Section 13 of the act says that the partners are "jointly" liable in the case of debts or contracts, "jointly and severally" liable for torts, but this is a procedural distinction rather than a practical one, and even procedurally it means little. Suppose ABC Partnership makes a note. Partnership assets are not sufficient to pay it at maturity. That the partners are *jointly* liable in this instance means only that all of the partners must be sued or joined in any action by the noteholder to recover what

---

[25]See page 285 for the same rule on corporations.

[26]Note that California amends U.P.A. 10(1) so as to protect the original buyer if he is a bona fide purchaser. (See Corp. C. 15010 in Appendix and Note following that section in Appendix.) Note also Corp. C. 15010.5 which is not found in the Official Text of the Uniform Partnership Act.

[27]U.P.A. 38(1).

is due him, and that if an action is brought against less than all the partners, they may halt the proceedings temporarily until the others are joined, i.e., also made defendants in the action. If, on the other hand, A of ABC Partnership commits a tort, an action may be brought against any one or more of the partners, since *joint and several* liability means that parties so liable have both collective and full individual liability. As a practical matter, the attorney for the party suing the partnership will name all partners as defendants in every case; and the ultimate liability is the same in either case in that once judgment is obtained, it may be satisfied in full from the personal assets of any partner who has been sued after partnership assets have been exhausted. Thus, if a judgment for $50,000 is obtained in the action on the note above mentioned, and partnership assets satisfy only $20,000 of this, the noteholder obtaining the judgment is not confined to recovering $10,000 each from A, B and C, but may recover the entire amount of $30,000 from A, B or C. The partner paying must then seek proportionate contribution from his copartners.

Silent Partners: That one is a *silent partner*, i.e., does not actively engage in partnership affairs and is not even known to be a partner to those dealing with the partnership, does not exempt him from liability. Only where a limited partnership is formed and a party becomes a limited partner may he limit his liability to partnership assets. Thus, as held in *Bissell* v. *King*, 91 C.A. 420, 267 P. 356, a silent partner may be held liable to the same extent as any other partner when his existence is discovered, even though his association with the partnership was unknown to the person doing business with the partnership at the time the business was transacted. As stated by the court in the *Bissell* case, ". . . a partner's liability is measured not by the impression a third party dealing with the partnership may have respecting his interest, but is measured by the fact of whether or not he is a partner. Thus in cases of secret partnership and dormant partners, a creditor is entitled to recover from all the partners when discovered, though the debt was not originally charged to all, and even though one partner holds himself out as the sole owner . . ."[28]

Incoming and Outgoing Partners: Suppose, again, ABC Partnership. With the consent of the other partners, C sells his interest to D who takes over as partner in C's place. The partnership business is continued without interruption. Questions may arise as to the liability of C and D for obligations existing at the time of sale of C's interest. If D assumes these, as is ordinarily the case, he becomes fully liable for them. This does not relieve C of liability, however, unless there is a novation with partnership creditors, i.e., unless they agree to look only to D and to release C of all liability.[29]

If D does not assume, the partnership act in Section 17 states a rule which is fair to all parties concerned. Under Section 17, the incoming partner, D, does not become personally liable for obligations existing at the time of his entry into the partnership, but all of the partnership assets, including the share purchased by the incoming partner continue to be liable. This gives the creditors everything they bargained for—the liability of partnership assets and the personal liability of three individuals at all times: the liability of C's ⅓ interest in the partnership assets transferred to D, and the personal liability of C for everything up to the time of the transfer and of D for everything after the transfer.

---

[28]In one instance a silent partner escapes liability. U.P.A. 35(2) exempts him from personal liability on contracts wrongfully made after dissolution of the partnership.

[29]U.P.A. 36.

Dissolution and Winding Up

Dissolution

Nature: Technically, *dissolution* of a partnership occurs automatically in any case in which one partner ceases his association with the partnership—dies, retires or sells his interest.[30] Dissolution does not necessarily mean that the partnership comes to an end, however.[31] That is another step, *winding up*, which may but need not follow upon dissolution. Take the cases above, for example. Where a partner sells his interest with the consent of his copartners, the business will continue without interruption, with the creditors of the "old" or "dissolved" partnership simply continuing as creditors of the "new" partnership composed of the balance of the original partners and the new, incoming partner.

When a partner retires, he usually sells his interest to the other partners or makes some arrangement which will allow the business to continue. When he dies, his interest will usually be purchased by the surviving partners. The partnership agreement usually provides in some way for the matter of death:

(1) In earlier days, by providing for purchase by the surviving partners at, for example, "market value, according to standard accounting procedure," as was the provision in *Wood* v. *Gunther*, 89 C.A.2d 718, 201 P.2d 874, where the court said that "It is well settled that partners may agree in their contract of copartnership or by subsequent agreement that the firm shall not be dissolved[32] by the death of a partner; that the interest of the deceased partner may be purchased by the surviving partners for a stated sum, or for an amount arrived at by a process or formula . . ."[33]

(2) In modern times, by requiring partnership insurance to provide funds for the purchase of a deceased partner's interest.

Causes: Sections 31-32 of the Uniform Partnership Act provide for three general types of causes or grounds for dissolution, which may be summarized as follows:

1. By the expiration of the time agreed upon in the partnership agreement; or, if no time has been agreed upon or the partnership is continued beyond the agreed time,[34] at any time that one partner demands dissolution and winding up; or, at any time by mutual agreement of the partners (as illustrated on the next page).

2. Automatically upon death[35] or bankruptcy of a partner or of the partnership.

3. By court decree (a) because of the inability of a partner to carry out his part of the partnership contract—where a partner becomes insane or physically incapacitated; or (b) because of misconduct of a partner: in the language of U.P.A. 32(c),

---

[30]U.P.A. 29. California amended U.P.A. 31 (Section 15031, page 442) to add subdivision (7), which permits partners to agree in writing, before withdrawal of a partner or admission of a new partner, that such event shall not dissolve the partnership.

[31]U.P.A. 30.

[32]The court uses the word "dissolved" here in the broad sense that liquidation need not follow upon technical dissolution.

[33]California amended U.P.A. 31(4) (Section 15031(4), page 443) to permit partners to agree that death of a partner will not dissolve the partnership.

[34]Where a partnership continues in business beyond the time fixed in the partnership agreement, it is called a *partnership at will*.

[35]See note 33.

DISSOLUTION OF COPARTNERSHIP

BY MUTUAL CONSENT of the undersigned, PAUL PARTNER and CARL COPARTNER, the parties to that certain partnership agreement dated January 2, 1970, the partnership thereby formed is hereby wholly dissolved except so far as it may be necessary to continue the same for the final litigation and settlement of the business thereof, and said partnership agreement is to continue in force for such purpose until such final litigation and dissolution be made, and no longer.

DATED May 1, 1984

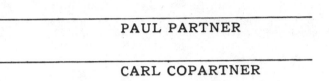

PAUL PARTNER

CARL COPARTNER

because "A partner has been guilty of such conduct as tends to affect prejudicially the carrying on of the business," and 32(d), because "A partner wilfully or persistently commits a breach of the partnership agreement, or otherwise so conducts himself in matters relating to the partnership business that it is not reasonably practicable to carry on the business in partnership with him."

Where dissolution is caused by the wrongful conduct of one of the partners, Section 38(2)(b) attempts to protect the innocent partners by providing that they may continue the business and retain possession of the partnership assets until expiration of the agreed term of the partnership "provided they secure the payment by bond approved by the court, or pay to any partner who has caused the dissolution wrongfully, the value of his interest in the partnership at the dissolution, less any damages [to which the innocent partners may be entitled by reason of the wrongful dissolution], and . . . indemnify him against all present or future partnership liabilities."

Power of Partner to Bind Copartners: U.P.A. 33-35 deal with this. Section 33, dealing with the "general effect" of dissolution on the authority of a partner to make further contracts or enter into further business transactions, says that "Except so far as may be necessary to wind up partnership affairs or to complete transactions begun but not then finished, dissolution terminates all authority of any partner to act for the partnership." In other words, a partner is not supposed to make contracts or enter into transactions after dissolution has occurred.

However, two types of problems arise. (1) Suppose a partner makes a contract without knowing that dissolution has occurred, e.g., without knowing that one of the partners has died or become bankrupt. Section 34 protects the partner who has acted innocently in such instances by making the contract binding upon all partners.

(2) Suppose a partner knows that a dissolution has occurred and, despite this, makes further contracts. The element of estoppel enters here. Until third persons are given some kind of notice of the fact that the partnership has been dissolved, there still *appears* to them to be a partnership. Hence, Section 35 says that contracts made by a partner after dissolution, although made wrongfully, are binding upon the partnership until:

a. In the case of actual creditors—those who have done business with the partnership in the past—they are given *ac-tual notice* of the dissolution—are mailed or otherwise given the information that the partnership has been dissolved so that they know that the partners no longer have authority to enter into contracts on behalf of the partnership.

b. In the case of other persons, there is *public notice* of the fact of dissolution, that is, until notice of dissolution is published in the newspaper.[36]

Winding Up

If winding up is to follow dissolution, the partnership assets must be liquidated and distributed to creditors and partners in accordance with rules laid down by U.P.A. 40.

Rules for Distribution: Section 40 says that partnership liabilities shall be satisfied in the following order:

1. Payment of creditors other than partners.
2. Payment of loans or advances by partners.
3. Payment of capital contributions by partners.
4. Distribution as profits of any balance remaining.

Section 40(d) says that the partners must make "contribution" to the extent necessary to satisfy these liabilities.

Section 40(h)(i) states the rule of *marshaling of assets*[37] where the partnership or a partner is insolvent or in bankruptcy. This is the rule that partnership assets must always be applied first to the satisfaction of the claims of partnership creditors and that individual or personal assets of a partner must be applied first to the satisfaction of the claims of his individual or personal creditors, with any balance of the personal estate of a partner then going to the satisfaction of partnership creditors.

Illustrative Problems:

1. Suppose a partnership of A, B and C with capital contributions of $25,000, $15,000 and $10,000 respectively, profits and losses to be shared 50%, 30% and 20%. During the life of the business, A makes an advance of $5000. The firm has assets of $80,000 and liabilities to creditors of $20,000. Liquidation would be as follows under the rules of Section 40:

---

[36]Note Corp. C. 15035.5 in the Appendix, which is a California addition to the U.P.A.

[37]This is a general principle of equity that whenever there are two sets of creditors and two funds against which they have recourse, each set of creditors should be given first satisfaction out of the fund which, in equity and fairness, primarily belongs to it.

Liquidated assets				$80,000
Creditors				20,000
				60,000
A, Advance				5,000
A, Capital			$25,000	
B, Capital			15,000	
C, Capital			10,000	
				50,000
				5,000
A, Surplus			2,500	
B, Surplus			1,500	
C, Surplus			1,000	
				5,000
				0

2. Suppose the same facts as in problem 1, except that the assets upon liquidation bring only $65,000:

		A	B	C	
Liabilities					
Creditors					$20,000
Advances		$ 5,000			5,000
Capital		25,000	$15,000	$10,000	50,000
					75,000
Liquidated assets					65,000
Loss					−10,000
Loss distribution					
A (50%)		5,000			
B (30%)			3,000		
C (20%)				2,000	
		25,000	12,000	8,000	
Cash distribution					
Creditors					20,000
A, Advance		5,000			
A, Capital		20,000			
B, Capital			12,000		
C, Capital				8,000	45,000
		0	0	0	$65,000

Limited Partnerships

In the one instance of a limited partnership, a person may become a member of a partnership without having unlimited liability for the obligations and liabilities of the partnership. By becoming a *limited partner* in a limited partnership, the person's liability is limited to his agreed capital contribution so that his position is substantially the same as that of a stockholder in a corporation. A limited partner may not participate in the management or control of the business, so there must be at least one *general partner* in every limited partnership, i.e., one partner who can manage the business. The general partner will have the unlimited liability of a partner in a general partnership.

Uniform Limited Partnership Act (ULPA), Revised Uniform Limited Partnership Act (RULPA), and California Revised Limited Partnership Act

ULPA has been the general law on the subject of limited partnerships and, until recently, the California law. In 1976 the Commissioners on Uniform State Laws completed the drafting of a revised act (RULPA) and presented it to the states for adoption. Adoption was delayed by the IRS ruling, originally, that RULPA partnerships were to be treated as "associations" and therefore taxed as corporations rather than as partnerships with tax consequences of activities being "passed through" to partners. This would have resulted in double taxation of income, at the patnership or entity level

and again at the individual partner level, and would have had other adverse tax consequences such as preventing partners from taking deductions for partnership losses. IRS has reversed its original position and will now treat RULPA partnerships as partnerships for tax purposes. This removed the barrier to adoption of RULPA and California adopted the revised act in 1981, to become operative January 1, 1984. Fifteen other states have adopted the revised act to date and it would seem that other states which had ULPA will adopt RULPA. California has added touches of its own to the revised act and has chosen to call its act the California Revised Limited Partnership Act. The California Act is set out in the Appendix and provides the statutory profile for the treatment of limited partnerships in this section.[38]

● Chiefly, the revised act attempts to clarify and modernize the original act in various respects. The original act, in section 7, made a limited partner liable as a general partner if he took part in "the control of the business." Debate waged as to when the line was crossed. Corp. C. 15632(a) makes a limited partner who participates in the control of the business without being named as a general partner liable at all events only as to "persons who transact business with the limited partnership . . . with actual knowledge of (the) partner's participation in control and reasonably believing (the) partner to be a general partner." In addition, Corp. C. 15632(b) contains a number of so-called "safe-harbor" provisions. These allow some kinds of "business-like" transactions and relationships to take place or exist between a limited partner and the partnership which might have caused the limited partner trouble under the original act.[39]

● Modern limited partnerships often involve sizable numbers of limited partners especially where they are designed to create tax shelter investments. The revised act takes this fact into consideration in a number of connections. The provisions of Corp. C. 15537 regarding limited partnership meetings has a very corporations-like flavor.

● The original act called for filing of the certificate of limited partnership with the county recorder of the counties in which the partnership was doing business. This imposed a burden on partnerships doing business in numerous counties. The revised act, in Corp. C. 15621(a), calls for central filing, i.e., filing in the office of the secretary of state, rather than for the original act's local filing. This relieves the partnership of the burden of multiple filing and also gives persons who would do business with the partnership a central source of information regarding the partnership.

● The original act did not provide for foreign limited partnerships. The revised act does so in Corp. C. 15691-15698.

Special Requirements

Certain special requirements must be met and adhered to if one is effectively to obtain and retain the privileged status of limited partner:

1. In connection with the formation of the partnership, *a certificate of limited partnership* must be filed in the office of the Secretary of State in conformance with the requirements of Corp. C. 15621(a). The limited partnership is formed at the time of the filing of the certificate.[40]

2. The name of a California limited partnership, as set forth in the certificate of limited partnership, must contain without

---

[38]The California Act as presented in the Appendix consists of sections 15611-15721, beginning at page 428 of the Appendix.

[39]In addition to Corp. C. 15632(b), see Corp. C. 15617.

[40]Corp. C.15621(b).

abbreviation the words "a California limited partnership" at the end of its name.[41] With minor exceptions, the limited partnership name may not contain the name of a limited partner.[42] Violation of this rule makes the limited partner liable for the obligations of the limited partnership to persons without actual knowledge or notice that the limited partner is not a general partner.[43]

3. If a limited partner participates in the control of the business, the limited partner is liable to persons who transact business with the partnership with actual knowledge of the limited partner's participation in control and reasonably believing the limited partner to be a general partner.[44]

• Corp. C. 15632(b) lists things that a limited partner may do without being guilty of participating in the control of the business. These include being a contractor for or an agent or employee of the limited partnership, consulting with and advising a general partner with respect to the business of the limited partnership, and voting on a variety of things that are concerned with the internal affairs of the partnership. The list is not intended to be exclusive.[45]

Rights of Limited Partners

A limited partner has rights, as follows:

1. A limited partner has the right to the profits allocated to him by the partnership agreement.[46] If the partnership agreement omits to allocate profits, they are to be allocated in proportion to the contributions of each partner.[47]

2. A limited partner has quite extensive rights to financial information regarding the partnership. Corp. C. 15615 requires the partnership to keep at its office the partnership's books and records for at least the current and past three fiscal years, the partnership's financial statements for the six most recent fiscal years and copies of federal, state and local income tax returns for the six most recent taxable years. Corp. C. 15634(b)(1) gives a limited partner the right to inspect and copy any of these records. Corp. C. 15634(b)(2) gives the limited partner the right to copies of the annual federal, state and local income tax returns. Corp. C. 15634(c)(1) provides that if the limited partnership consists of more than 35 limited partners, the limited partners are entitled to an annual report containing a balance sheet as of the end of the fiscal year and an income statement of changes in financial position for the fiscal year. Corp. C. 15634(c)(2) gives limited partners representing 5% or more of the interests of limited partners the right to require, retroactively, quarterly income statements.

3. Limited partners are protected against extraordinary actions of the general partners by Corp. C. 15636(f) which requires the affirmative vote of a majority in interest of limited partners for such actions as admitting or removing a general partner, changing the nature of the partnership business, the extraordinary incurrence of indebtedness, the sale, exchange or mortgage of all or a substantial part of the assests of the limited partnership other than in the ordinary course of business, and the dissolution of the partnership before its expiration. In addition, Corp. C. 15636(f) requires the unanimous

vote of the limited partners to continue the business of the limited partnership after the retirement, death or insanity of a general partner.

4. Corp. C. 15663 gives a limited partner the right to withdraw from a limited partnership as follows: "A limited partner may withdraw from a limited partnership at the time or upon the happening of events specified in the partnership agreement. If the partnership agreement does does not specify the time or the events upon which a limited partner may withdraw or a definite time for the dissolution and winding up of the limited partnership, a limited partner may withdraw upon not less than six months' prior written notice to each general partner at his address set forth in the certificate."

5. A limited partnership interest is assignable unless forbidden by the partnership agreement.[48] Assignment does not dissolve the limited partnership.[49] The assignee becomes a substituted limited partner if the partnership agreement permits him to do so or all partners consent;[50] otherwise the assignment only entitles the assignee to receive the distributions to which the assignor would have been entitled.[51] An assignee who becomes a limited partner has the rights and liabilities of the limited partner he replaces.[52]

Dissolution and Winding Up

Corp. C. 15681-15682 make provision for nonjudicial dissolution, i.e., dissolution not involving legal action, and judicial dissolution.

• Section 15681 says that nonjudicial dissolution occurs upon the happening of the first to occur of the following: (1) The happening of events specified in the partnership agreement which bring about termination of the partnership. The most obvious event would be the expiration of the time fixed for the duration of the partnership where its duration is a fixed time such as 3 years or 5 years. (2) The general partners and a majority in interest of the limited partners agree in writing to terminate the partnership. (3) There is no general partner left to manage the business.

• Under Section 15682 a partner may sue to terminate the partnership whenever any of the following occurs: (1) The partnership business cannot be carried on in conformity with the partnership agreement. (2) The general partners have been guilty of fraud or abuse of authority or unfairness toward a partner or have misapplied or wasted partnership property. (3) Dissolution is reasonably necessary for the protection of the rights or interests of the complaining partners.

• Dissolution is to be followed by winding up, for which general partners have power to bind the partnership for acts appropriate for winding up partnership affairs or completing unfinished transactions.[53] Upon winding up, assets are to be distributed, first, to creditors, including partner-creditors, in satisfaction of partnership liabilities to creditors; then, to partners, generally in accordance with the rules of Corp. C. 15654.

• Upon dissolution a certificate of dissolution must be filed in the office of the Secretary of State in accordance with the requirements of Corp. C. 15623.

---

[41]Corp. C. 15612.

[42]Corp. C. 15612.

[43]Corp. C. 15632(d).

[44]Corp. C. 15632(a).

[45]Corp. C. 15632(c).

[46]Corp. C. 15653.

[47]Corp. C. 15653.

---

[48]Corp. C. 15672.

[49]Corp. C. 15672.

[50]Corp. C. 15654(a).

[51]Corp. C. 15672.

[52]Corp. C. 15674(b).

[53]Corp. C. 15683, 15685.

Foreign Limited Partnerships

The revised act makes provisions for foreign limited partnerships which have no counterpart in the original act.

• A foreign limited partnership is one organized under the laws of another state or country. The laws of the state or country of organization govern the organization and internal affairs of the foreign limited partnership and the liability of its limited partners, and a foreign limited partnership cannot be denied registration in California because of differences between those laws and the laws of the State of California.[54]

• Before transacting intrastate business in California, a foreign limited partnership must register with the Secretary of State in accordance with the requirements of Corp. C. 15692.

---

[54]Corp. C. 15691.

• If 25% or more of the limited partners of a foreign limited partnership are residents of California, the California-resident limited partners must be given the same kind of financial information and the same kind of access to financial information that limited partners in California limited partnerships must be given.[55]

• If a foreign limited partnership transacts intrastate business in this state without registration, it cannot sue in a court of this state until it has registered, is subject to monetary penalty, and may be restrained from transacting business in the state.[56]

---

[55]Corp. C. 15694.
[56]Corp. C. 15697, 15698.

CHAPTER 11

Corporations

Introduction

The basic idea of a corporation—as an organization of many persons making up a capital fund to put into operation a business concern operated by a representative management in the form of a board of directors—has been with us for many centuries. The great English "joint stock companies" of the 17th and 18th centuries were just that. They issued shares of stock to their many investors just as does the corporation of today, and stock exchange trading was fully as vigorous then as now.

● The *limited liability* feature of the corporation is of relatively recent origin, however. In England, it dates from the Limited Liability Act of 1855, which required the word "Limited," or its abbreviation "Ltd." to accompany the business name in order to indicate the special status of the business concern, a practice still followed in English corporations. In this country, at least in many states, it came much later; not until 1929 in California.

● The California law was revised in the period 1929-1931, with two important changes being made: Stockholders were given limited liability. Corporations were allowed to have perpetual existence; previously, 50 years was the maximum duration. In 1947, the corporation law of California was removed from the Civil Code and made the subject of a separate Corporations Code. The California General Corporation Law and the California Corporate Securities Law are set forth in the Appendix.[1]

Beginning in the 1970's the California Corporations Code was rewritten with an eye to simplifying and modernizing it. Among other things, the form of articles of incorporation was simplified; cumbersome terminology regarding capital structure was eliminated; and the close corporation, in effect a partnership allowed to operate as a corporation, was provided for. This puts California corporations law in advance of that of a considerable number of states, but the California law will be used as an example of statutory law in the field where it seems appropriate to do so. The rewriting of the California code was completed and enacted into law in 1975, to become operative on January 1, 1977, and it is this 1975/1977 law that is referred to throughout this chapter.

Promotion

Promotion is the activity necessary to bring a corporation into existence. The extent of promotional activity varies greatly. In the case of a small, closed[2] corporation it amounts to very little—one or more informal meetings of those who will become the incorporators. In a large enterprise, where large issues of stock are to be sold to the public, the promotional activity will be extensive.

Capitalization?

In promoting a large corporation, the usual procedure today is to first incorporate—go through the mechanics of bringing the corporation into existence—and then set about selling the stock which will provide the working capital. Even before the corporation is formed, however, the incorporators must decide what kind or kinds of stock will be issued because this information must be stated in the *articles of incorporation* which must be filed with the State in order to become a corporation and obtain the right to sell stock. A plan of capitalization, then, will be one of the first things to be accomplished during the promotional phase. There are two general possibilities. The incorporators may decide to issue all *common stock* or part common and part *preferred stock*, these being the two general classes of stock which a corporation may issue.

● Preferred stock is given two types of preferences, a *dividend preference* and a *liquidation preference*. By the dividend preference, preferred stock is given the right to a fixed return annually before any return can be paid on the common stock. By the liquidation preference, the preferred stockholder is given the right, upon liquidation, to the return of a fixed sum per share before the common stockholder is paid anything.

● Preferred stock, then, is a relatively safe or conservative type of stock, and if the incorporators decide to issue preferred stock it will be for the purpose of appealing to conservative investors. Common stock is of a more speculative nature. Theoretically, its buyers are willing to gamble that the corporation will be successful, will make large profits and accumulate large assets. If this proves to be the case, they will make more money out of the corporation than the preferred stockholders since they will get as dividends all of the profits to be distributed after the preferred stockholders have been paid their fixed percentage[3] and they will profit from the growth in asset value of the corporation. Hence, in the vernacular of today, common stocks are "growth stocks."

● Depending upon whether the incorporators wish to appeal entirely to the more speculative investor or partly to him and partly to the more conservative investor in preferred stock, they will decide upon a plan of capitalization of all common or partly common and partly preferred stock.

---

[1]Provisions of the Corporations Code are referred to as sections of the "Corp. C." throughout this chapter.

[2]Occasional reference in this chapter to a "*closed corporation*" may cause confusion in view of the new California code's adoption of the concept of "*close corporation*," discussed at page 264. "Closed corporation" is an informal expression designed to describe any corporation which is owned by a small number of persons and does not offer its stock to the public. "Close corporation" is a technical concept, as explained at page 264.

[3]A substantial portion of corporate earnings will be used to acquire additional equipment, property, inventory, etc., i.e., for expansion and increasing assets, and to establish various reserves. And the corporation will attempt to establish a long range program under which it will pay regular, fixed amounts dividends on the common stock, reserving some of the profits which might be paid out as dividends in highly profitable years against less profitable years when such funds can be used to keep up the regular payment of dividends.

Pre-incorporation Subscriptions

Having decided upon a plan of capitalization, the promoters have other important things to accomplish. Before the corporation is formed, they may decide to see if they can get people to pledge themselves to buy its stock when it is formed. To do this, they must first secure a permit from the State to take *pre-incorporation subscriptions*; then they may solicit prospective investors for subscriptions (agreements to purchase).

Usually, however, no attempt is made to get pre-incorporation subscriptions. The more usual procedure is to form the corporation and then seek buyers for its stock.

● Where pre-incorporation subscriptions are obtained, the problem arises that they must be mere *offers* to purchase stock, since the corporation is not yet in existence. The corporation may accept these offers after coming into existence, and in many states it is the rule that the corporation accepts them by the mere fact of coming into existence; in others, an affirmative act of the corporation after coming into existence is required—a resolution of the board of directors adopting the subscriptions. The problem is to avoid the consequence that, as offers, they can be revoked prior to formation or formal acceptance by the corporation. This has been accomplished in the following ways:

1. In some states, as soon as there is more than one subscriber, the fiction is resorted to that the mutual, reciprocal promises of the various subscribers support and are consideration for each other, and give rise to contracts between each and every subscriber of which the corporation is a third party beneficiary with a right of enforcement if the corporation is formed within a reasonable time after the subscriptions are made. Essentially it is the same fiction as in the charitable subscription case discussed on page 35.

2. A "trustee" may be designated with whom the subscription agreements are made in order to supply the necessary two parties to a contract immediately upon the making of the subscription. A binding contract is deemed to be created between the subscriber and the trustee as soon as the subscription is made. The trustee then "assigns" the contracts to the corporation when it is formed.

3. In some states, pre-incorporation subscriptions are declared binding and irrevocable by statute. Corporations Code § 410(a) does this.

● For the protection of subscribers, subscription agreements provide that they will not be binding unless some minimum amount, e.g., 80%, of the proposed capitalization is subscribed to within some specified period of time—3 to 6 months after the taking of subscriptions is commenced.

Contracts and Options

Promoters may line up contracts to be taken over by the corporation when it is formed, or may get options to purchase property on its behalf.[4] Care must be taken in making contracts, however. The corporation, when it is formed, cannot be held unless it adopts them by resolution of the board of directors. In many states, it is the rule that the promoters are personally liable on contracts if the corporation does not adopt them, unless it has been expressly stipulated in the contract that the other party shall look only to the corporation to be formed for performance of the contract. To protect themselves against the possibility of personal liability, the promoters should make such a stipulation in any contracts entered into.

---

[4]See discussion of options on page 27.

Promoters' Compensation—Promotion Stock, Etc.

To illustrate the possibilities connected with large scale promotion, suppose a corporation issuing 1,000,000 shares of common stock at $1 par value a share. When the corporation is formed and a permit to issue stock is secured from the Commissioner of Corporations, the promoters may get a permit which will allow them to take for themselves as much as one share of stock for every nine shares sold to the public, as reimbursement for their services as promoters. They can sell 900,000 shares to the public for $900,000 and keep the other 100,000 shares, worth $100,000 on paper, as *promotion stock* or *promoters' stock*. This means, of course, that the corporation will start out with "watered stock"—stock which is worth less than its face value—since it will have $1,000,000 worth of stock outstanding and only $900,000 in assets (the cash received from the cash purchasers). But, if the venture is successful and asset value is increased, the water will be "squeezed out" and the promoters' stock will become worth its face value of $100,000. Pending this, the Corporation Commissioner will require promoters to "waive" dividend rights on their promotion stock to some extent, e.g., until cash purchasers have received as dividends an amount equal to their cash investment in the stock. And, the Corporation Commissioner will impose an *escrow* upon the stock until the "water is squeezed out," i.e., will require the stock to be held in escrow and will require any transfers of it to be made through the Commissioner's office so that the transferee may be fully informed of all facts concerning the stock.[5] This will prevent the promoters from making a quick profit by reselling the stock. In short, the corporation will have to be successful if the promoters are to realize a profit from their promotional labors. The Corporation Commissioner will not permit promotion to be used merely for the purpose of enriching the promoters.

● There are rewards other than promotion stock which promoters usually seek. They may expect to become permanent officers at substantial salaries or be given a long term management contract, which, when coupled with the stock interest acquired, makes the effort worthwhile.[6]

Fiduciary Obligation of Promoters

Promoters' activities may be motivated by another purpose, the sale to the corporation after it is formed of property owned or controlled by the promoters. The board of directors determines the value of property to be purchased by the corporation. The directors could easily overvalue property, particularly if they were also the promoters selling it to the corporation. This type of fraudulent manipulation is prevented in two ways: by the intervention of the Corporation Commissioner and by the well established rule of law that promoters

---

[5]See Corp. C. 25141.

[6]Salaries fixed by directors for themselves as officers may not be exorbitant. So long as they are not, the salaries fixed are valid despite the personal interests of the directors involved. (Ballantine on Corporations, p. 174.)

Promoters may be reimbursed for their out-of-pocket expenses in connection with the promotion by a resolution of the board of directors to that effect when the corporation is formed. Since the promoters are usually the first directors, this resolution will be forthcoming automatically, but should others than the promoters have control of the corporation at the outset and should they not see fit to reimburse the promoters, the promoters would have no remedy since they are not entitled to reimbursement as a matter of right, but only if the corporation sees fit to make it.

have a fiduciary relationship to the corporation which prohibits them from making secret or fraudulent profits in sales of property to the corporation. If this is done, the defrauded stockholders may recover the improper profits from the promoters either by an action brought by the corporation or by a stockholder's suit brought by them if the corporation fails or refuses to take action.

Mechanics of Incorporation

The last thing to be done by the promoters is the actual formation of the corporation. In California, as in most states, this is done by preparing and filing *articles of incorporation* with a designated state official, the Secretary of State or the Corporations Commissioner; in California, the Secretary of State. The drafting of articles is done by an attorney employed by the promoters or incorporators to handle the legal mechanics of incorporation.

Articles of Incorporation

State law requires that articles contain certain information. California's recently simplified law requires less information in the articles than do most states. All of the requirements are set forth in Corp. C. 202 which provides that "The articles of incorporation shall set forth:

"(a) The name of the corporation; . . .

"(b) The applicable one of the following statements:

"(1) The purpose of the corporation is to engage in any lawful act or activity for which a corporation may be organized under the General Corporation Law of California[7] other than the banking business, the trust company business or the practice of a profession permitted to be incorporated by the California Corporations Code; . . .

The articles shall not set forth any further or additional statement with respect to the purposes or powers of the corporation, except by way of limitation or except as expressly required by any law of this state other than this division or any federal or other statute or regulation. . . ."

"(c) The name and address in this state of the corporation's initial agent for service of process in accordance with subdivision (b) of Section 1502.

"(d) If the corporation is authorized to issue only one class of shares, the total number of shares which the corporation is authorized to issue.

"(e) If the corporation is authorized to issue more than one class of shares, or if any class of shares is to have two or more series:

"(1) The total number of shares of each class the corporation is authorized to issue, and the total number of shares of each series which the corporation is authorized to issue or that the board is authorized to fix the number of shares of any such series.

"(2) The designation of each class, and the designation of each series or that the board may determine the designation of any such series; and

---

[7]The California law has had an interesting history on this point. Prior to 1949, a corporation simply was required to state "The purposes for which it is formed," which is the type of provision found in the statutes of most states. Thereafter the California law was amended to require identification of a specific business in which the corporation was primarily to engage. The amendment was aimed at controlling broad statements of purpose which essentially allowed the corporation to engage in any kind of business. The new code provision set forth above is as liberal as it possibly could be, surpassing even the lenient requirements of the pre-1949 provision.

"(3) The rights, preferences, privileges and restrictions granted to or imposed upon the respective classes or series of shares or the holders thereof."

Section 203 completes the capital structure picture by providing that "Except as specified in the articles or in any shareholders' agreement, no distinction shall exist between classes or series of shares or the holders thereof . . . ."

Section 204 permits various optional provisions. It provides that "The articles of incorporation may set forth:

"(a) Any or all of the following provisions, which shall not be effective unless expressly provided in the articles:

"(1) Granting . . . the power to levy assessments upon the shares or any class of shares;

"(2) Granting to shareholders preemptive rights . . . [Preemptive rights are the rights of existing stockholders to have first opportunity to purchase new stock of the corporation. California is an exception to the general rule here. Most states automatically confer preemptive rights. California stockholders have them only if expressly given by the articles.][8]

"(3) Special qualifications of persons who may be shareholders;

"(4) A provision limiting the duration of the corporation's existence to a specified date;

"(5) A provision requiring, for any or all corporate actions (except as provided in Section 303, subdivision (b) of Section 402.5, subdivision (c) of Section 708 and Section 1900) the vote of a larger proportion or of all of the shares of any class or series, or the vote or quorum for taking action of a larger proportion or of all the directors, than is otherwise required by this division;

"(6) A provision limiting or restricting the business in which the corporation may engage or the powers which the corporation may exercise or both;

"(7) A provision conferring upon the holder of any evidences of indebtedness, issued or to be issued by the corporation, the right to vote in the election of directors and on any other matters on which shareholders may vote[9];

"(8) A provision conferring upon shareholders the right to determine the consideration for which shares shall be issued;

"(9) A provision requiring the approval of the shareholders (Section 153) or the approval of the outstanding shares (Section 152) for any corporate action, even though not otherwise required by this division.

Notwithstanding this subdivision, in the case of a close corporation any of the provisions referred to above may be validly included in a shareholders' agreement . . .

"(b) Reasonable restrictions upon the right to transfer or hypothecate shares of any class or classes or series, but no restriction shall be binding with respect to shares issued prior to the adoption of the restriction unless the holders of such shares voted in favor of the restriction.

"(c) The names and addresses of the persons appointed to act as initial directors.[10]

"(d) Any other provision, not in conflict with law, for the management of the business and for the conduct of the affairs of the corporation, including any provision which is required

---

[8]See Corp. C. 1106 and discussion of preemptive rights at page 300.

[9]This provision is rather exceptional. It permits a corporation to create bonds with voting power.

[10]Under former Section 301(d), this information was required rather than optional.

or permitted by this division to be stated in the bylaws." This last is intended as a blanket clause permitting any other valid provision to be included in the articles. Such additional provisions were infrequent under the former code and can be expected to be even less frequent under the new code because of the breadth of the specific optional provisions enumerated in Section 204."

• The articles must be signed and acknowledged by each incorporator and each director named in the articles[11] and then filed with the designated state officer (Secretary of State in California) together with incorporation fees. A specimen set of articles of incorporation ready for filing is set out on page 265.[12] Assuming that the articles are in proper order, the corporation's existence officially begins when they are filed.[13] The Secretary of State or other designated state officer will return to the attorney for the incorporators some form of certification as official evidence of incorporation and corporate existence. This may be referred to as the corporate charter, i.e., the state's official recognition of the corporation and grant of authority to engage in business as a corporation in accordance with the terms and provisions of its articles of incorporation.

• When the attorney for the corporation receives this official notification that the corporation is authorized to do business, states usually require the filing of a copy of the articles in the office of the county clerk of the county in which the corporation has its principal office. In California, under the new code, this filing no longer is required. The attorney then advises the incorporators to fix a date for an *incorporation meeting* or first meeting of the board of directors.

Incorporation Meeting—Bylaws, Appointment of Officers, Etc.

A number of important things are accomplished at this incorporation meeting.

1. In California and many other states, a set of *bylaws* is adopted by the directors. Bylaws are rules for the internal government of the corporation. Adoption of bylaws must be

---

[11]Corp. C. 200(b), and note Corp. C. 210.

[12]The specimen form of articles of incorporation set out in the text contain the minimum requirements under the new law. In this respect, they demonstrate how simple articles may be under that law. However, as the text indicates, a very considerable number of optional provisions are possible. Two types of optional provisions that might be expected to be found in many California articles are *preemptive rights provisions* and *first-right-of-purchase provisions*. The following would be examples of these:

Each shareholder shall be entitled to full preemptive rights to subscribe to, purchase and acquire any share which may be issued subsequent to the original issue in the same proportion, ratio or fractional amount as the number of shares owned and held by such shareholder bears to the total number of shares issued and outstanding immediately prior to such new issue and sale and held by shareholders who elect to exercise their right to subscribe to, purchase and acquire additional shares.

In case any shareholder desires to sell his share or shares of the stock of this corporation, he shall first offer them for sale to the remaining stockholders of the corporation at book value, including good will. Any sale or attempted sale in violation of this provision shall be null and void. A stockholder desiring to sell his said share or shares shall file notice in writing of his intention with the secretary of the corporation, and unless one or more of the other shareholders shall exercise their right to purchase as aforesaid within 30 days thereafter, they shall be deemed to have waived their privilege of purchasing, and he be at liberty to sell to anyone else.

[13]See Corp. C. 110(a), 200(c).

---

deferred until a later date in other states where statute requires that the bylaws be approved by the shareholders.[14] A typical set of bylaws, showing the matters covered by them, such as time, place and conduct of meetings of stockholders and directors, number and designation of officers and their powers, and method of execution of share certificates, is shown on pages 267-278.[15]

2. Officers are appointed by the directors.[16]

3. If there have been any expenditures by the promoters, a resolution may be passed to reimburse them, and if any contracts have been entered into by the promoters for the corporation, a resolution adopting them is passed.[17]

4. A resolution is passed to apply to the proper state officer—in California, the Corporations Commissioner—for a permit to issue stock, or to otherwise qualify stock for issuance.

Minutes which might be made of the incorporation meeting are shown on pages 279-281.

A copy of the form of Certificate of Filing of articles of incorporation, issued by the office of the Secretary of State, is shown on page 266.

Issuance of Stock

When the permit to issue stock is received or stock is otherwise qualified for issuance, stock will be issued and sold in accordance with the plan of capitalization. (1) If the corporation is a small closed one, this will be a mere formality, the various members of the corporation taking the amount of stock agreed upon. (2) If the corporation is a large corporation, promotion stock will be taken by the promoters. If pre-incorporation subscriptions have been obtained, the subscribers will be called upon to honor their subscriptions; pay in their money and take their stock. If pre-incorporation subscriptions have not been obtained, the stock will be offered for sale directly or through investment brokers who will receive commissions on sales for their services.

Close Corporations

For the first time in the history of California, the status of *close corporations* has been given independent recognition with the 1975 enactment of the revisions of California's corporation code. Corp. C. 158 is the basis for this newly acknowledged corporate form. The reason for this change was to allow certain qualifying California corporations to have the separate entity status of a corporation while maintaining the informal structure of a partnership.[18]

• In a close corporation, management and control of corporate affairs may be conducted by way of a shareholders' agreement, eliminating the traditional functions of the board of di-

(Continued on page 281)

---

[14]There are 3 rules on adoption, amendment and repeal of bylaws: (1) This may be done by the directors alone; (2) may be done only by the stockholders; (3) may be done by the directors subject to modification or repeal by the stockholders. Corp. C. 211 follows the last rule.

[15]Corp. C. 212(b) states the matters which may be covered by bylaws.

[16]Corp. C. 312; note also 300(a).

[17]*Resolutions* are the formal process by which the board of directors of a corporation acts and records its acts, and every act elected to be done by the board should be evidenced by a formal written resolution signed by the directors.

[18]Briggs, *California Close Corporations*, 8 U.W.L.A. Law Review 185 (1976).

ARTICLES OF INCORPORATION

OF

CALIFORNIA CONSTRUCTION COMPANY, INC.

ARTICLE ONE: The name of this corporation is CALIFORNIA CONSTRUCTION COMPANY, INC.

ARTICLE TWO: The purpose of this corporation is to engage in any lawful act or activity for which a corporation may be organized under the General Corporation Law of California other than the banking business, the trust company business or the practice of a profession permitted to be incorporated by the California Corporations Code.

ARTICLE THREE: The name and address in the State of California of this corporation's initial agent for service of process is: CALIFORNIA SERVICE CORPORATION, 2011 West Montgomery Street, San Francisco, California 94106.

ARTICLE FOUR: This corporation is authorized to issue only one class of shares of stock; and the total number of shares which this corporation is authorized to issue is one hundred thousand (100,000).

Dated: June 1, 1984.

_____
HENRY L. WADSWORTH, Incorporator

I hereby declare that I am the person who executed the foregoing Articles of Incorporation, which execution is my act and deed.

_____
HENRY L. WADSWORTH

State of California

OFFICE OF THE SECRETARY OF STATE

I, March Fong Eu, Secretary of State of the State of California, hereby certify:

That on the   day of   , 19   ,

became incorporated under the laws of this State by filing its Articles of Incorporation in this office.

In Witness Whereof, I execute this certificate and affix the Great Seal of the State of California this day of

March Fong Eu

Secretary of State

BYLAWS

OF

CALIFORNIA CONSTRUCTION COMPANY, INC.

ARTICLE 1.   APPLICATION OF GENERAL CORPORATION LAW
OF CALIFORNIA CORPORATIONS CODE

These bylaws are intended to follow and conform to the provisions and requirements of the General Corporation Law of the California Corporations Code.
With respect to the matters covered by these bylaws, the construction of these
bylaws shall be governed by the general provisions and definitions of said
General Corporation Law. With respect to any matter not covered by these
stated bylaws, the provisions of said General Corporation Law shall be deemed
to apply and to govern the matter.

ARTICLE 2.   DIRECTORS AND MANAGEMENT

Section 1.   CORPORATE POWERS TO BE EXERCISED BY BOARD OF DIRECTORS. The
business and affairs of this corporation shall be managed and all corporate
powers shall be exercised by or under the direction of the board of directors.
The board of directors may delegate the management of the day-to-day operation
of the business of the corporation to a management company or other person
provided that the business and affairs of the corporation shall be managed and
all corporate powers shall be exercised under the ultimate direction of the
board of directors.

Section 2.   NUMBER OF DIRECTORS. The number of directors of the corporation shall not be less than five (5) nor more than nine (9). The exact number
of directors shall be five (5) until changed by amendment of the bylaws.

After the issuance of shares, a bylaw specifying or changing a fixed number of directors or the maximum or minimum number or changing from a fixed to
a variable board of directors or vice versa may only be adopted by the vote or
written consent of holders of a majority of the outstanding shares entitled to
vote; provided, however, that a bylaw or amendment of the articles reducing
the fixed number or the minimum number of directors to a number less than five
cannot be adopted if the votes cast against its adoption at a meeting or the
shares not consenting in the case of action by written consent are equal to
more than 16 2/3 percent of the outstanding shares entitled to vote.

In no case shall the stated maximum number of directors be greater than
two times the stated minimum minus one.

Section 3.   ELECTION OF DIRECTORS AND TERM OF OFFICE. At each annual
meeting of shareholders, directors shall be elected to hold office until the
next annual meeting. Each director, including a director elected to fill a
vacancy, shall hold office until the expiration of the term for which elected
and until a successor has been elected and qualified.

(Form continued on following pages)

Section 4.   REMOVAL OF DIRECTORS.   The board of directors may declare vacant the office of a director who has been declared of unsound mind by an order of court or convicted of a felony.

Any or all of the directors may be removed without cause if such removal is approved by the vote or written consent of holders of a majority of the outstanding shares entitled to vote; provided, however, that no director may be removed (unless the entire board of directors is removed) when the votes cast against removal, or not consenting in writing to such removal, would be sufficient to elect such director if voted cumulatively at an election at which the same total number of votes were cast (or, if such action is taken by written consent, all shares entitled to vote were voted) and the entire number of directors authorized at the time of the director's most recent election were then being elected.

Section 5.   FILLING VACANCIES ON BOARD OF DIRECTORS: RESIGNATION OF DIRECTORS.   Vacancies on the board of directors, including vacancies occurring in the board of directors by reason of the removal of directors, may be filled by a majority of the directors then in office, whether or not less than a quorum, or by a sole remaining director.

The shareholders may elect a director at any time to fill any vacancy not filled by the directors.   Any such election by written consent, other than to fill a vacancy created by removal, requires the consent of a majority of the outstanding shares entitled to vote.

A director may resign effective upon giving written notice to the chair-person of the board of directors, the president, the secretary or the board of directors of the corporation, unless the notice specifies a later time for the effectiveness of such resignation.   If the resignation is effective at a future time, a successor may be elected to take office when the resignation becomes effective.

Section 6.   DIRECTORS' MEETINGS; NOTICE AND WAIVER OF NOTICE; QUORUM; ACTION BY WRITTEN CONSENT.   Meetings of the board of directors may be called by the chairperson of the board of directors or the president or any vice-president or the secretary or any two directors.

Regular meetings of the board of directors may be held without notice if the time and place of such meetings are fixed by the board of directors. Special meetings of the board of directors shall be held upon four days' notice by mail or 48 hours' notice delivered personally or by telephone or telegraph. A notice, or waiver of notice, need not specify the purpose of any regular or special meeting of the board of directors.

Notice of a meeting need not be given to any director who signs a waiver of notice or a consent to holding the meeting or an approval of the minutes thereof, whether before or after the meeting, or who attends the meeting with-out protesting, prior thereto or at its commencement, the lack of notice to such director.   All such waivers, consents and approvals shall be filed with the corporate records or made a part of the minutes of the meeting.

A majority of the directors present, whether or not a quorum is present, may adjourn any meeting to another time and place.   If the meeting is adjourned for more than 24 hours, notice of any adjournment to another time or place shall be given prior to the time of the adjourned meeting to the directors who were not present at the time of the adjournment.

Meetings of the board of directors may be held at any place within or without the state which has been designated in the notice of the meeting or, if not stated in the notice or there is no notice, designated by resolution of the board of directors.

Members of the board of directors may participate in a meeting through use of conference telephone or similar communications equipment, so long as all members participating in such meeting can hear one another. Participation in a meeting pursuant to this provision constitutes presence in person at such meeting.

A majority of the authorized number of directors constitutes a quorum of the board of directors for the transaction of business.

Every act or decision done or made by a majority of the directors present at a meeting duly held at which a quorum is present is the act of the board of directors.

A meeting at which a quorum is initially present may continue to transact business notwithstanding the withdrawal of directors, if any action taken is approved by at least a majority of the required quorum for such meeting.

Any action required or permitted to be taken by the board of directors may be taken without a meeting, if all members of the board of directors shall individually or collectively consent in writing to such action. Such written consent or consents shall be filed with the minutes of the proceedings of the board of directors. Such action by written consent shall have the same force and effect as a unanimous vote of such directors.

The provisions of this section apply also to committees of the board and action by such committees mutatis mutandis.

Section 7. COMMITTEES OF DIRECTORS. The board of directors may, by resolution adopted by a majority of the authorized number of directors, designate one or more committees, each consisting of two or more directors, to serve at the pleasure of the board of directors. The board of directors may designate one or more directors as alternate members of any committee, who may replace any absent member at any meeting of the committee. The appointment of members or alternate members of a committee requires the vote of a majority of the authorized number of directors. Any such committee, to the extent provided in the resolution of the board of directors, shall have all the authority of the board of directors, except with respect to (a) the approval of any action for which shareholders' approval or approval of the outstanding shares is required; (b) the filling of vacancies on the board of directors or in any committee; (c) the fixing of compensation of the directors for serving on the board of directors or on any committee; (d) the amendment or repeal of bylaws or the adoption of new bylaws; (e) the amendment or repeal of any resolution of the board of directors which by its express terms is not so amendable or repealable; (f) distribution to the shareholders of the corporation, except at a rate or in a periodic amount or within a price range determined by the board

(Form continued on following pages)

of directors; and (g) the appointment of other committees of the board of directors or the members thereof.

ARTICLE 3.   OFFICERS

Section 1.   REQUIRED OFFICES; SELECTION OF OFFICERS; RESIGNATION OF OFFICERS. The corporation shall have a chairperson of the board of directors, a president, a secretary, a chief financial officer and such other officers with such titles and duties as shall be determined by the board of directors and as may be necessary to enable it to sign instruments and share certificates. Any number of offices may be held by the same person.

Officers shall be chosen by the board of directors and serve at the pleasure of the board of directors, subject to the rights, if any, of an officer under any contract of employment. Any officer may resign at any time upon written notice to the corporation without prejudice to the rights, if any, of the corporation under any contract to which the officer is a party.

Section 2.   CHAIRPERSON OF THE BOARD OF DIRECTORS. The chairperson of the board of directors shall preside at meetings of the board of directors and exercise and perform such other powers and duties as may be from time to time assigned to him or her by the board of directors.

Section 3.   PRESIDENT. The president shall be the chief executive officer of the corporation and shall have general supervision, direction, and control of the business and the officers of the corporation. The president shall preside at all meetings of the shareholders and, in the absence of the chairperson of the board of directors at all meetings of the board of directors. The president shall have the general powers and duties of management usually vested in the office of president of a corporation.

Section 4.   VICE-PRESIDENTS. In the event of the absence or disability of the president, a vice-president designated by the board of directors shall perform the duties of the president. The vice-presidents shall have such other powers and duties as may from time to time be prescribed for them by the board of directors, the president or the chairperson of the board of directors.

Section 5.   SECRETARY. The secretary shall keep, at the principal executive office of the corporation, a book of minutes of all meetings and actions of directors, committees of directors, and shareholders, with the time and place at which the meeting was held or the action was taken, whether, in the case of meetings, the meeting was regular or special, and, if special, how authorized, the notice given, the names of those present at directors' meetings or committee meetings, the number of shares present or represented at shareholders' meetings, and the proceedings.

The secretary shall keep at the principal executive office of the corporation or at the office of the corporation's transfer agent or registrar, as determined by resolution of the board of directors, a share register showing the names and addresses of shareholders, the number and classes of shares held by each shareholder, the number and date of certificates issued for shares, and the number and date of cancellation of every certificate surrendered for cancellation.

The secretary shall give notice of all meetings of shareholders and of the board of directors required by the bylaws or by law to be given. The secretary shall maintain custody of the seal of the corporation. The secretary shall have such other powers and duties as may be prescribed by the board of directors.

Section 6. CHIEF FINANCIAL OFFICER. The chief financial officer shall keep and maintain books of account and records of the properties and business transactions of the corporation, including accounts of its assets, liabilities, receipts, disbursements, gains, losses, capital, retained earnings, and shares. The books of account shall be open to inspection by any director at all reasonable times.

The chief financial officer shall deposit moneys, checks and other valuables in the name and to the credit of the corporation with such depositaries as the board of directors shall designate. The chief financial officer shall disburse the funds of the corporation as ordered by the board of directors. The chief financial officer shall render to the president and directors, whenever requested, an account of his or her transactions as chief financial officer and of the financial condition of the corporation. The chief financial officer shall have other powers and duties as may be prescribed by the board of directors.

ARTICLE 4. SHAREHOLDERS' MEETINGS AND CONSENTS

Section 1. PLACE AND TIME OF MEETINGS. All meetings of shareholders shall be held at the principal executive office of the corporation which is located at 100 Center Street, San Francisco, California.

An annual meeting of shareholders for the election of directors shall be held at the principal executive office of the corporation on the third Tuesday in January of each year, at the hour of ten o'clock a.m.; provided that when said day shall fall upon a legal holiday, such meeting shall be held on the next business day at the same hour and place. Any other proper business may be transacted at the annual meeting.

Special meetings of the shareholders may be called by the board of directors, the chairperson of the board of directors, the president or the holders of shares entitled to cast not less than 10 percent of the votes at the meeting.

Section 2. NOTICE OF MEETINGS; WAIVER OF NOTICE. Whenever shareholders are required or permitted to take any action at a meeting a written notice of the meeting shall be given not less than 10 nor more than 60 days before the date of the meeting to each shareholder entitled to vote thereat. Such notice shall state the place, date and hour of the meeting and, in the case of a special meeting, the general nature of the business to be transacted, and no other business may be transacted; or, in the case of the annual meeting, those matters which the board of directors, at the time of the mailing of the notice, intends to present for action by the shareholders, but, subject to the provisions of the paragraph next following, any proper matter may be presented at the meeting for such action. The notice of any meeting at which directors are to be elected shall include the names of nominees intended at the time of the notice to be presented by management for election.

If action is proposed to be taken at a meeting for the approval of a contract or transaction in which a director has a direct or indirect financial

(Form continued on following pages)

interest, an amendment of the articles of incorporation of the corporation, a reorganization of the corporation, a voluntary dissolution of the corporation or a distribution in dissolution other than in accordance with the rights of outstanding preferred shares, the notice of the meeting shall state the general nature of the proposal.

Notice of a shareholders' meeting shall be given either personally or by first-class mail or other means of written communication, addressed to the shareholder at the address of such shareholder appearing on the books of the corporation or given by the shareholder to the corporation for the purpose of notice; or if no such address appears or is given, at the place where the principal executive office of the corporation is located or by publication at least once in a newspaper of general circulation in the county in which the principal executive office is located. The notice or report shall be deemed to have been given at the time when delivered personally or deposited in the mail or sent by other means of written communication. An affidavit of the mailing or other means of giving notice of a shareholders' meeting shall be executed by the officer or assistant officer giving the notice, and shall be filed and maintained in the minute book of the corporation.

If any notice or report addressed to a shareholder at the address of such shareholder appearing on the books of the corporation is returned to the corporation by the United States Postal Service marked to indicate that the United States Postal Service is unable to deliver the notice or report to the shareholder at such address, all future notices or reports shall be deemed to have been duly given without further mailing if the same shall be available for the shareholder upon written demand of the shareholder at the principal executive office of the corporation for a period of one year from the date of the giving of the notice or report to all other shareholders.

Upon request in writing to the chairperson of the board of directors, president, vice-president or secretary by any person (other than the board of directors) entitled to call a special meeting of shareholders, the officer forthwith shall cause notice to be given to the shareholders entitled to vote that a meeting will be held at a time requested by the person or persons calling the meeting, not less than 35 nor more than 60 days after the receipt of the request. If the notice is not given within 30 days after receipt of the request, the persons entitled to call the meeting may give the notice.

When a shareholders' meeting is adjourned to another time or place, except as hereinafter expressly provided, notice need not be given of the adjourned meeting if the time and place thereof are announced at the meeting at which the adjournment is taken. At the adjourned meeting the corporation may transact any business which might have been transacted at the original meeting. If the adjournment is for more than 45 days or if after the adjournment a new record date is fixed for the adjourned meeting, a notice of the adjourned meeting shall be given to each shareholder of record entitled to vote at the meeting.

The transactions of a meeting of shareholders, however called and noticed, and wherever held, are as valid as though had at a meeting duly held after regular call and notice, if a quorum is present either in person or by proxy, and if, either before or after the meeting, each of the persons entitled to vote, not present in person or by proxy, signs a written waiver of notice or a consent to the holding of the meeting or an approval of the minutes thereof.

All such waivers, consents and approvals shall be filed with the corporate records or made a part of the minutes of the meeting. Attendance of a person at a meeting shall constitute a waiver of notice of and presence at such meeting, except when the person objects, at the beginning of the meeting, to the transaction of any business because the meeting is not lawfully called or convened and except that attendance at a meeting is not a waiver of any right to object to the consideration of matters required to be included in the notice but not so included, if such objection is expressly made at the meeting. Neither the business to be transacted at nor the purpose of any regular or special meeting of shareholders need be specified in any written waiver of notice, consent to the holding of the meeting or approval of the minutes thereof, except that the general nature of the action approved must be stated in the waiver, consent or approval, where the action approved consists of the approval of a contract or transaction in which a director has a direct or indirect financial interest, an amendment of the articles of incorporation of the corporation, a reorganization of the corporation, a voluntary dissolution of the corporation or a distribution in dissolution other than in accordance with the rights of outstanding preferred shares.

Section 3. QUORUM OF SHAREHOLDERS. A majority of the shares entitled to vote, represented in person or by proxy, shall constitute a quorum at a meeting of shareholders. If a quorum is present, the affirmative vote of the majority of the shares represented at the meeting and entitled to vote on any matter shall be the act of the shareholders.

The shareholders present at a duly called or held meeting at which a quorum is present may continue to transact business until adjournment notwithstanding the withdrawal of enough shareholders to leave less than a quorum, if any action taken (other than adjournment) is approved by at least a majority of the shares required to constitute a quorum.

In the absence of a quorum, any meeting of shareholders may be adjourned from time to time by the vote of a majority of the shares represented either in person or by proxy, but no other business may be transacted.

Section 4. ACTION BY WRITTEN CONSENT WITHOUT MEETING. Any action which may be taken at any annual or special meeting of shareholders may be taken without a meeting and without prior notice, if a consent in writing, setting forth the action so taken, shall be signed by the holders of outstanding shares having not less than the minimum number of votes that would be necessary to authorize or take such action at a meeting at which all shares entitled to vote thereon were present and voted.

Unless the consents of all shareholders entitled to vote have been solicited in writing (a) notice of any shareholder approval of a contract or transaction in which a director has a direct or indirect financial interest, of the indemnification of a corporate agent, a reorganization of the corporation or of a distribution in dissolution other than in accordance with the rights of outstanding preferred shares, without a meeting by less than unanimous written consent shall be given at least 10 days before the consummation of the action authorized by such approval; and (b) prompt notice shall be given of the taking of any other corporate action approved by shareholders without a meeting by less than unanimous written consent, to those shareholders entitled to vote who have not consented in writing. Such notice shall be given in the manner set forth in Section 2 of Article 4 of these bylaws.

(Form continued on following pages)

Any shareholder giving a written consent, or the shareholder's proxyholders, or a transferee of the shares or a personal representative of the shareholder or their respective proxyholders, may revoke the consent by a writing received by the corporation prior to the time that written consents of the number of shares required to authorize the proposed action have been filed with the secretary of the corporation, but may not do so thereafter. Such revocation is effective upon its receipt by the secretary of the corporation.

Except in the case of filling vacancies not filled by the directors, directors may not be elected by written consent except by unanimous written consent of all shares entitled to vote for the election of directors.

ARTICLE 5.   VOTING OF SHARES

Section 1. VOTING RIGHTS IN GENERAL. Each outstanding share, regardless of class, shall be entitled to one vote on each matter submitted to a vote of shareholders.

Any holder of shares entitled to vote on any matter may vote part of the shares in favor of the proposal and refrain from voting the remaining shares or vote them against the proposal, other than elections to office, but, if the shareholder fails to specify the number of shares such shareholder is voting affirmatively, it will be conclusively presumed that the shareholder's approving vote is with respect to all shares such shareholder is entitled to vote.

Voting rights of shares held by a fiduciary, of shares standing in the name of a minor, of shares held by another corporation and of shares standing in the names of two or more persons shall be determined in accordance with the provisions of Sections 702-704 inclusive of the California Corporations Code.

Section 2.   RECORD DATE FOR SHAREHOLDERS OF RECORD FOR PURPOSES OF NOTICE AND VOTING AND FOR OTHER PURPOSES. In order that the corporation may determine the shareholders entitled to notice of any meeting or to vote or entitled to receive payment of any dividend or other distribution or allotment of any rights or entitled to exercise any rights in respect of any other lawful action, the board of directors may fix, in advance, a record date, which shall not be more than 60 nor less than 10 days prior to the date of such meeting nor more than 60 days prior to any other action.

If no record date is fixed (a) the record date for determining shareholders entitled to notice of or to vote at a meeting of shareholders shall be at the close of business on the business day next preceding the day on which notice is given or, if notice is waived, at the close of business on the business day next preceding the day on which the meeting is held; (b) the record date for determining shareholders entitled to give consent to corporate action in writing without a meeting, when no prior action by the board of directors has been taken, shall be the day on which the first written consent is given; and (c) the record date for determining shareholders for any other purpose shall be at the close of business on the day on which the board of directors adopts the resolution relating thereto, or the 60th day prior to the date of such other action, whichever is later.

A determination of shareholders of record entitled to notice of or to vote at a meeting of shareholders shall apply to any adjournment of the meeting unless the board of directors fixes a new record date for the adjourned meeting, but the board of directors shall fix a new record date if the meeting is adjourned for more than 45 days from the date set for the original meeting.

Shareholders at the close of business on the record date are entitled to notice and to vote or to receive the dividend, distribution or allotment of rights or to exercise the rights, as the case may be, notwithstanding any transfer of any shares on the books of the corporation after the record date, except as otherwise provided by agreement.

Section 3. PROXIES. Every person entitled to vote shares may authorize another person or persons to act by proxy with respect to such shares.

No proxy shall be valid after the expiration of eleven (11) months from the date thereof unless otherwise provided in the proxy. Every proxy continues in full force and effect until revoked by the person executing it prior to the vote pursuant thereto, except as otherwise provided in this Section. Such revocation may be effected by a writing delivered to the corporation stating that the proxy is revoked or by a subsequent proxy executed by the person executing the prior proxy and presented to the meeting, or by attendance at the meeting and voting in person by the person executing the proxy.

A proxy is not revoked by the death or incapacity of the maker unless, before the vote is counted, written notice of such death or incapacity is received by the corporation.

The revocability of a proxy which states on its face that it is irrevocable shall be governed by the provisions of subdivisions (e) and (f) of Section 705 of the California Corporations Code.

Section 4. CUMULATIVE VOTING FOR DIRECTORS AND OTHER RULES REGULATING ELECTION OF DIRECTORS. Every shareholder complying with the provisions of the next paragraph and entitled to vote at any election of directors may cumulate such shareholder's votes and give one candidate a number of votes equal to the number of directors to be elected multiplied by the number of votes to which the shareholder's shares are normally entitled, or distribute the shareholder's votes on the same principle among as many candidates as the shareholder thinks fit.

No shareholder shall be entitled to cumulate votes (i.e., cast for any candidate a number of votes greater than the number of votes which such shareholder normally is entitled to cast) unless such candidates' names have been placed in nomination prior to the voting and the shareholder has given notice at the meeting prior to the voting of the shareholder's intention to cumulate the shareholder's votes. If any one shareholder has given such notice, all shareholders may cumulate their votes for candidates in nomination.

In any election of directors, the candidates receiving the highest number of votes of the shares entitled to be voted for them up to the number of directors to be elected by such shares are elected.

Elections for directors need not be by ballot unless a shareholder demands election by ballot at the meeting and before the voting begins.

(Form continued on following pages)

ARTICLE 6.   RECORDS AND REPORTS AND
RIGHTS OF INSPECTION THEREOF

Section 1.   All records made subject to inspection by the provisions of
this Article 6 of these bylaws shall be maintained in written form.

Section 2.   LOCATION OF BYLAWS AND SHAREHOLDERS' RIGHTS OF INSPECTION.
The corporation shall keep, at its principal executive office in this state,
the original or a copy of the bylaws as amended to date, which shall be open
to inspection by the shareholders at all reasonable times during office hours.

Section 3.   SHARE REGISTER AND SHAREHOLDER'S RIGHT TO INSPECT AND COPY AND
TO OBTAIN COMPILATION THEREOF.   The corporation shall keep at its principal
executive office, or at the office of its transfer agent or registrar, a
record of its shareholders, giving the names and addresses of all shareholders
and the number and class of shares held by each.

A shareholder or shareholders holding at least five percent (5%) in the
aggregate of the outstanding voting shares of the corporation shall have the
absolute right to do either or both of the following: (a) inspect and copy
the record of shareholders' names and addresses and shareholdings during usual
business hours upon five business days' prior written demand upon the corporation, or (b) obtain from the transfer agent for the corporation, upon written
demand and upon the tender of its usual charges for such a list, a list of the
shareholders' names and addresses, who are entitled to vote for the election of
directors, and their shareholdings, as of the most recent record date for which
it has been compiled or as of a date specified by the shareholder subsequent to
the date of demand.   The list shall be made available on or before the later of
five business days after the demand is received or the date specified therein
as the date as of which the list is to be compiled.

The record of shareholders shall also be open to inspection and copying by
any shareholder or holder of a voting trust certificate at any time during
usual business hours upon written demand on the corporation, for a purpose
reasonably related to such holder's interests as a shareholder or holder of a
voting trust certificate.

Any inspection and copying under this Section may be made in person or by
agent or attorney.

Section 4.   ACOUNTING BOOKS AND RECORDS AND MINUTES OF PROCEEDINGS AND
SHAREHOLDERS' RIGHTS OF INSPECTION.   The accounting books and records and
minutes of proceedings of the shareholders and the board and committees of the
board of directors shall be kept at the principal executive office of the corporation and shall be open to inspection upon the written demand on the corporation of any shareholder or holder of a voting trust certificate at any reasonable time during usual business hours, for a purpose reasonably related to such
holder's interests as a shareholder or as the holder of such voting trust certificate.   The right of inspection created by this subdivision shall extend to
the records of each subsidiary of a corporation subject to this provision.

Such inspection by a shareholder or holder of a voting trust certificate
may be made in person or by agent or attorney, and the right of inspection
includes the right to copy and make extracts.

Section 5. DIRECTOR'S RIGHT TO INSPECT BOOKS, RECORDS AND DOCUMENTS AND PHYSICAL PROPERTIES. Every director shall have the absolute right at any reasonable time to inspect and copy all books, records and documents of every kind and to inspect the physical properties of the corporation and also of its subsidiary corporations, domestic or foreign. Such inspection by a director may be made in person or by agent or attorney and the right of inspection includes the right to copy and make extracts.

Section 6. WAIVER OF REQUIREMENT OF ANNUAL REPORT TO SHAREHOLDERS: SHAREHOLDERS' RIGHTS TO FINANCIAL STATEMENTS. The annual report to shareholders referred to in Section 1501 of the California Corporations Code is expressly waived. The board of directors may, however, issue such annual or other periodic reports to shareholders as it deems appropriate.

If no annual report for the last fiscal year has been sent to shareholders, the corporation shall, upon the written request of any shareholder made more than 120 days after the close of such fiscal year, deliver or mail to the person making the request within 30 days thereafter the financial statements required for such year by subdivision (a) of Section 1501 of the California Corporations Code.

A shareholder or shareholders holding at least five percent (5%) of the outstanding shares of any class of shares of the corporation may make a written request to the corporation for an income statement of the corporation for the three-month, six-month or nine-month period of the current fiscal year ended more than thirty (30) days prior to the date of the request and a balance sheet of the corporation as of the end of such period and, in addition, if no annual report for the last fiscal year has been sent to shareholders, the statements required by subdivision (a) of Section 1501 of the California Corporations Code for the last fiscal year. The statements shall be delivered or mailed to the person making the request within thirty (30) days thereafter. A copy of the statements shall be kept on file in the principal office of the corporation for twelve (12) months and they shall be exhibited at all reasonable times to any shareholder demanding an examination of them or a copy shall be mailed to such shareholder.

The quarterly income statements and balance sheets referred to in this Section shall be accompanied by the report thereon, if any, of any independent accountants engaged by the corporation or the certificate of an authorized officer of the corporation that such financial statements were prepared without audit from the books and records of the corporation.

ARTICLE 7. SHARE CERTIFICATES

Section 1. RIGHT TO SHARE CERTIFICATE. Every holder of shares in the corporation shall be entitled to have a certificate signed in the name of the corporation by the chairperson or vice chairperson of the board of directors or the president or a vice-president and by the chief financial officer or an assistant secretary, certifying the number of shares and the class or series of shares owned by the shareholder. Any or all of the signatures on the certificate may be facsimile. In case any officer, transfer agent or registrar who has signed or whose facsimile signature has been placed upon a certificate shall have ceased to be such officer, transfer agent or registrar before such certificate is issued, it may be issued by the corporation with the same effect as

(Form continued on following page)

if such person were an officer, transfer agent or registrar at the date of issue.

Section 2. REPLACEMENT OF LOST, STOLEN OR DESTROYED CERTIFICATES. The corporation may issue a new share certificate or new certificate for any other security in the place of any certificate theretofore issued by it, alleged to have been lost, stolen or destroyed, and the corporation may require the owner of the lost, stolen or destroyed certificate or the owner's legal representative to give the corporation a bond (or other adequate security) sufficient to indemnify it against any claim that may be made against it (including any expense or liability) on account of the alleged loss, theft or destruction of any such certificate or the issuance of such new certificate.

ARTICLE 8. AMENDMENT OR REPEAL OF BYLAWS OR ADOPTION OF NEW BYLAWS

These bylaws may be amended or repealed or new bylaws may be adopted by the vote or written consent of the holders of a majority of the outstanding shares of the corporation entitled to vote. Subject to the foregoing rights of the shareholders to adopt, amend or repeal bylaws, bylaws may be adopted, amended or repealed by the board of directors. The board of directors may adopt a bylaw or an amendment of a bylaw changing the authorized number of directors only for the purpose of fixing the exact number of directors within the limits specified in Section 2 of Article 2 of these bylaws.

The undersigned, being all of the directors of CALIFORNIA CONSTRUCTION COMPANY, INCORPORATED, hereby assent to the foregoing bylaws.

_____   _____
HENRY L. WADSWORTH   LOUIS B. CONTI

_____   _____
THOMAS A. JONES   JAMES B. SMITH

_____
CHARLES L. JOHNSON

CERTIFICATE OF SECRETARY

I, the undersigned, do hereby certify that I am the duly elected and acting secretary of CALIFORNIA CONSTRUCTION COMPANY, INC., a California corporation, and that the foregoing bylaws, comprising twelve (12) pages, including this page, constitute the bylaws of said corporation as duly adopted at a meeting of the board of directors thereof duly held on July 17, 1984.

IN WITNESS WHEREOF, I have subscribed my name and affixed the seal of the corporation on July 17, 1984.

_____
JAMES B. SMITH, Secretary

(CORPORATE SEAL)

MINUTES OF FIRST MEETING OF BOARD OF DIRECTORS

OF

CALIFORNIA CONSTRUCTION COMPANY, INC.

The first meeting of the Board of Directors of CALIFORNIA CONSTRUCTION COMPANY, INC. was held at the principal executive office of the corporation at 100 Center Street, San Francisco, California, on July 17, 1984 at 2:00 o'clock p.m.

The following were present: HENRY L. WADSWORTH, THOMAS A. JONES, CHARLES L. JOHNSON, LOUIS B. CONTI, and JAMES B. SMITH.

HENRY L. WADSWORTH, the incorporator, called the meeting to order and upon motion duly made, seconded and carried, HENRY L. WADSWORTH was appointed chairperson and JAMES B. SMITH was appointed secretary of the meeting.

The chairperson reported that the Articles of Incorporation of the corporation had been filed in the office of the Secretary of State of the State of California on June 1, 1984 by James B. Smith, as attorney for the corporation. The chairperson presented a certified copy of the Articles of Incorporation which was ordered to be inserted in the minute book.

The following named persons were elected as directors of the corporation, to serve until the first annual meeting of the corporation: HENRY L. WADSWORTH, THOMAS A. JONES, CHARLES L. JOHNSON, and JAMES B. SMITH.

The secretary presented proposed bylaws for the regulation of the affairs of the corporation, which were read, article by article, and unanimously adopted. A copy thereof was ordered inserted in the minute book.

Upon motion duly made, seconded and carried, the following officers were unanimously elected to hold office as provided in the bylaws:

Chairperson of the Board and President: HENRY L. WADSWORTH
Vice-President: THOMAS A. JONES
Secretary: JAMES B. SMITH
Chief Financial Officer: LOUIS B. CONTI

The Chairperson of the Board thereupon took the chair.

Upon motion duly made, seconded and carried, the seal, an impression of which is affixed in the margin hereof, was adopted as the corporate seal of the corporation.

(CORPORATE
   SEAL)

The attached form of stock certificate was presented and on motion duly made, seconded and carried, was approved and adopted.

(Form continued on following pages)

It was moved, seconded and carried that the principal executive office of the corporation be established and maintained at 100 Center Street, San Francisco, California.

It was moved, seconded and carried that the SIXTH NATIONAL BANK OF SAN FRANCISCO, located at 210 Center Street, San Francisco, California, be and it is hereby designated as the principal depositary for the funds of the corporation and that all checks, drafts and other instruments obligating the corporation to pay money shall be signed on behalf of the corporation by its chief financial officer except that any and all promissory notes signed on behalf of the corporation shall be signed by its president and countersigned by its chief financial officer. In connection therewith, the following resolution was unanimously adopted:

"RESOLVED, that SIXTH NATIONAL BANK OF SAN FRANCISCO, a corporation, be and it is hereby selected as depositary for the funds of CALIFORNIA CONSTRUCTION COMPANY, INC., that said account shall be governed by the rules, regulations, bylaws and practices, present and future, of the bank, including interest, service charges and all other matters whether the same as or different therefrom, and that, as hereinafter specified, the following officer of this corporation, who has been duly and regularly elected and/or appointed:

LOUIS B. CONTI, Chief Financial Officer

be and he is hereby authorized to withdraw said funds from said depositary on the check of the corporation, signed as aforesaid, and that the said officer authorized to withdraw funds be and he is hereby authorized to indorse and receive payment of bills and notes payable to the corporation, and the said bank is hereby authorized to pay any such instruments so indorsed and presented to it for payment, and be it

FURTHER RESOLVED, that said authority hereby conferred shall remain in force until written notice of the revocation thereof by the board of directors of CALIFORNIA CONSTRUCTION COMPANY, INC. shall have been received by said depositary, and that the secretary be and he is hereby authorized and directed to deliver to the said bank a certified copy of this resolution and to certify to said bank the true and correct signature of the above-named officer."

It was moved, seconded and carried that the shares of the capital stock of the corporation be sold and issued in the manner and to the persons and in the amounts and for the consideration set forth in the following resolutions:

"RESOLVED, that CALIFORNIA CONSTRUCTION COMPANY, INC. shall sell and issue an aggregate of not to exceed twenty thousand (20,000) shares of its capital stock at a purchase price of fifty and no/100ths dollars ($50.00) per share, in consideration of money paid to the corporation, as follows:

(Form continued on following page)

Name of Purchaser	Number of Shares	Amount of Money
HENRY L. WADSWORTH	5,000	$250,000.00
THOMAS A. JONES	5,000	$250,000.00
CHARLES L. JOHNSON	5,000	$250,000.00
LOUIS B. CONTI	5,000	$250,000.00

"RESOLVED FURTHER, that the appropriate officers of the corporation be and they are hereby authorized and directed to take such actions and execute such documents as they may deem necessary or appropriate to effectuate the sale and issuance of such shares for such consideration."

"RESOLVED FURTHER, that the shares of capital stock authorized at this meeting to be sold and issued by CALIFORNIA CONSTRUCTION COMPANY, INC. shall be offered and sold strictly in accordance with the terms of the exemption from qualification provided for in Section 25102(h) of the California Corporations Code, so that counsel for the corporation will be in a position to sign and file with the California Commissioner of Corporations the form of notice specified in said Section."

Upon motion, duly made, seconded and carried, the meeting was thereupon adjourned.

JAMES B. SMITH, Secretary

rectors.[19] Section 186 defines a *shareholders' agreement* as a written agreement among all of the shareholders of a close corporation. A shareholders' agreement may concern "any" phase of the affairs of a close corporation and is valid even if it interferes with the discretion of the board of directors.[20] Section 300(d) relieves directors of a close corporation of liability for acts which are performed or omitted pursuant to a shareholders' agreement. Thus a shareholder in a close corporation has the shield of limited liability as well as the right to participate in the management and control of the corporation in a dual director-shareholder capacity. Additionally a close corporation, like other corporations, is perpetual in nature and does not lose that status when one party ceases to be a shareholder.

• The articles of a close corporation must contain two statements: (1) that all of the corporation's issued shares of all classes shall be held by not more than a specified number of persons, not to exceed 35 in number; and (2) that "This corporation is a close corporation."[21] In addition, the share certificates are required to contain a prominent statement warning prospective purchasers of the nature of the corporation.[22] If the election to be treated as a close corporation is made after the issuance of shares, the articles must be amended accordingly and the affirmative vote of all the issued and outstanding shares of all classes is required regardless of limitations or restrictions on voting rights.[23]

• In the event a close corporation acquires more than 35 shareholders, it will lose its status as a close corporation. Loss of that status does not mean dissolution, but rather that the corporation thereafter will be treated as a public issue corporation.[24] Section 158(d) sets forth the guidelines for determining the number of shareholders in a close corporation. Under that section, a husband and wife are considered to be a single shareholder. A partnership (or trust) holding shares is considered a unit unless the primary purpose of the partnership is the acquisition or voting of shares. In that case the voting of shares will be counted according to the number of beneficial interests therein. Finally, a corporation holding shares of a close corporation is counted as a single shareholder. A corporation also may elect to eliminate its close corporation status.[25] An affirmative vote of two-thirds of each class of outstanding shares is required for such a change unless the articles specify a lesser vote.[26]

• A single shareholder of a close corporation may file a complaint for involuntary dissolution pursuant to Section 1800(a)(2). Section 1800(b)(5) permits such a filing where the liquidation is reasonably necessary for the protection of the rights or interests of the complaining shareholder. The two

---

[19]Corp. C. 300.
[20]Corp. C. 300(b).
[21]Corp. C. 158(a).
[22]Corp. C. 418(c).

[23]Corp. C. 158(b).
[24]Corp. C. 158(e).
[25]Corp. C. 158(c) & (e).
[26]Corp. C. 158(c).

sections give a single, dissatisfied shareholder significant power over the corporation's future. Inclusion of a buy-out or option provision in the shareholders' agreement is one solution to safeguard a corporation against dissolution by a disgruntled shareholder.[27] An arbitration provision in the shareholders' agreement is another method which can be used to resolve intracorporate controversy and to spare the close corporation from involuntary dissolution.[28]

Defective and Fraudulent Corporations

A corporation may be partially or totally defective by reason of failure properly to comply with required incorporation procedure. Or, a corporation may have been fraudulently conceived. Legal problems that arise in these connections are now considered.

De Facto Corporations; Corporations by Estoppel

A *de jure* corporation is one that has been more perfectly formed than a *de facto* corporation; that is, one in which there has been more complete compliance with statutory requirements. A *de jure* corporation is said to result from substantial compliance with the statutory requirements. A *de facto* corporation is said to come into existence when (1) there is a valid statute under which such a corporation can be formed; (2) there has been an attempt in good faith to comply with such statute; and (3) there has been a user of corporate powers; that is, business has been transacted as a corporation. Good examples are rare. It has been held in California, in *Westlake Co.* v. *Jordan*, 198 C. 609, 246 P. 807, that a *de facto* corporation was formed when the articles of incorporation provided for a class of stock which was not permitted by law; and in *Midwest Air Filters* v. *Finn*, 201 C. 587, 258 P. 382, that at least a *de facto* corporation resulted when there was failure to file a copy of the corporation's articles with the county clerk of the county in which the principal office was located. The distinction is not of practical importance because transactions entered into by a *de facto* corporation are fully binding on both parties. The fact that a corporation is only a *de facto* corporation has this technical significance: (1) The state can forfeit the corporate charter if, after warning the corporation to do so, it fails to remedy the defect and (2) it has been held that pre-incorporation subscribers cannot be held on their subscriptions unless a *de jure* corporation is formed.

Corporations by Estoppel: Where there is serious or complete failure to comply with incorporation procedure, a *corporation by estoppel* may nevertheless result. Suppose that several persons start doing business as a corporation without any attempt to comply with the required incorporation procedure—without even filing articles of incorporation. The "corporation" then enters into a transaction with X, who assumes that he is dealing with a valid corporation, and sells and delivers goods to X. X then discovers that there is no properly formed corporation and holds back payment thinking that, because no corporation has been formed, no effective action can be taken to recover the purchase price from him. The "corporation" sues X who asserts as a defense that the corporation lacks existence and therefore has no standing to sue. X will lose. The court will hold that, because X dealt with the other party as a corporation, he is estopped to deny

that it is a corporation. This is one more of the many applications of the principle of estoppel.[29]

● Conversely, suppose the "corporation" attempts to escape liability upon the contract with X. This will not be permitted. The operators of the corporation will be held to be estopped to deny that they have formed a corporation. As regards liability, they will be held to have the unlimited personal liability of partners if the assets of the "corporation" are not sufficient to answer for the obligations incurred in its name.[30]

Disregard of Corporate Entity

Where a corporation is formed to perpetrate a fraud or to accomplish a wrongful or inequitable purpose, the corporate entity will be disregarded, or, as the courts often state it, they will "pierce the corporate veil." Stockholders will be charged with personal liability for the obligations of the corporation, or a new corporation will be held for debts of an old corporation whose assets it buys, where the new corporation is but a continuation of the old and the entire transaction is part of a fraudulent scheme. In short, the courts will not permit the corporate privilege to be abused.

Specific examples: (1) In *Minifie* v. *Rowley*, 187 C. 481, 202 P. 673, D borrowed money on his personal note. When the note came due, he induced the holder to accept in its place a note signed by the "Rowley Investment Co.," a one man corporation formed by D. Held, the holder of the note could recover from D personally; that to hold otherwise would "sanction a fraud or promote injustice." (2) In *Blank* v. *Olcovich Shoe Corp.*, 20 C.A.2d 456, 67 P.2d 376, Olcovich Shoe Co. sold stock in violation of law. Being liable in damages, it went into bankruptcy. In the course of the bankruptcy proceeding, a corporation called Olco Shoe Co. was formed by the operators of the Olcovich Shoe Co. and Olco Shoe Co. bought the assets of the Olcovich Shoe Co. from the trustee in bankruptcy. The new corporation had the same directors as the old and sold its stock to the stockholders of the old corporation at nominal prices. Held, the new corporation was "but a continuation of the old" and could be held for the damages for which the old corporation was liable in connection with its illegal sales of stock. (3) In *Shea* v. *Leonis*, 14 C.2d 666, 96 P.2d, 332, a corporation wanted to break a lease. The stockholders formed a new corporation with nominal assets to which the lease was assigned. Held, unpaid rents could be collected from the stockholders of the old corporation. This case applies the somewhat broader *inadequate capitalization rule* followed by the courts, which is that if a corporation enters into business with only nominal or insubstantial capital and then incurs obligations which it knows it cannot meet, its operators will be held liable personally for its obligations.

While a corporation may be formed for the express purpose of limiting liability, then, it cannot be created to defeat or defraud existing creditors, or, as in the last case, with such inadequate capital that it is not prepared to undertake normal obligations.

---

[27]Briggs, *California Close Corporations*, 8 U.W.L.A. Law Review 185 (1976).

[28]Id.

---

[29]In *California Fruit Exchange* v. *Buck*, 163 C. 223, 124 P. 824, it was held that a mortgage could be foreclosed by a "corporation" despite failure to file articles, and, in *Ehrlich etc. Co.* v. *Slater*, 183 C. 709, 192 P. 526, that a contract could be enforced.

[30]Ballantine on Corporations, p. 92, finds this to be the majority rule.

Directors and Officers

Directors

Appointment and Removal: Except for the first directors, who are self-appointed, directors are elected for a one-year term at the *annual meeting* of stockholders which is fixed for the same date each year by the bylaws.[31] The directors are the chosen agents of the stockholders or, as in the case of any election, of such of the stockholders having a right to vote as chose to exercise the right. Indifference to this right often permits a few large, but minority, stockholders to control elections.

• In many states, directors must be stockholders, and in some states, both residents and stockholders. In California, no such requirement exists.

• Directors are not entitled to compensation for their ordinary services in the absence of a bylaw provision awarding compensation.

• In most states, statute provides that the majority of the voting stockholders may remove any one or more of the directors from office at any time with or without cause.[32] In a few states, statutes permit a lawsuit by some relatively small percentage of the stockholders to remove directors for cause—fraud, dishonesty or gross abuse of authority or discretion—e.g., California and Pennsylvania permit an action by 10% of the stockholders.[33]

Function and Powers: The board of directors is the supreme authority of the corporation.[34] The function of the board of directors is to set major policies and to fix and direct the business and operational program of the corporation. Details of the business program can be left to the operating management, the officers. In some corporations, the directors may reserve to themselves almost entirely the contract-making authority; in others, a greater measure of authority may be delegated to officers to make contracts and enter into transactions in aid of the general business program.

• In addition to directing the business program of the corporation, the directors have the power and duty to select, supervise and fix the compensation of officers and to determine dividend payments, financing, and capital changes.

• Certain fundamental or organic actions are generally required to have the approval of some percentage of the stockholders, usually ⅔. These include: (1) amendment of articles; (2) increase or decrease of stock; (3) consolidation; (4) sale of entire assets; and (5) dissolution.

Formal and Informal Action: Normally directors would be expected to perform their function in a formal manner, i.e., at duly scheduled meetings and by formal resolutions. The bylaws usually provide for regular monthly meetings of which notice is not required.[35] Special meetings may be called by the president of the corporation at any time upon giving the notice required by statute.[36] A valid meeting requires the presence of a *quorum* (majority) of directors.[37] Acts or decisions by a majority of the directors attending a meeting at which a quorum is present are binding and effective.[38]

• The new California Corporations Code goes to considerable lengths to allow *informal action* by directors. Section 307(a)(3) dispenses with notice of a meeting of the board with respect to a director who signs a waiver of notice or a consent to holding the meeting or an approval of the minutes of the meeting, whether before or after the meeting, or who attends the meeting without protesting, prior thereto or at its commencement, the lack of notice. Section 307(a)(6) permits a "meeting" to be conducted by conference telephone. Finally, Section 307(b) dispenses with the requirement of a meeting entirely if *all* of the members of the board consent in writing to an action. Section 307(c) allows similar informal action by committees of the board of directors.

• Since their duties call for a high degree of personal judgment, directors may not delegate them to others.

The new California code is exceptional in the extent to which it allows directors to appoint committees and to delegate authority to them.[39]

Liability for Incompetence, Mismanagement, Improper Dividends, etc.: Directors are required to exercise reasonable skill and diligence in the performance of their duties, but the courts are usually lenient when it is sought to charge a director with some loss on the grounds of incompetence or neglect of duty. While the courts will say that a director is required to exercise the skill and diligence that "an ordinarily prudent man would exercise in the management of his personal business affairs" or that "a normally prudent director would exercise in like circumstances," they largely nullify this by saying that it must exclude liability for "honest errors of judgment." The result is that it will take a strong case of lack of prudence before directors will be held, such as leaving everything in the hands of a completely unsupervised officer, serious failure to maintain adequate insurance resulting in a heavy loss to the corporation, or the like.

• Statutes in all states provide that directors are personally liable for improper payment of dividends, i.e., payment at a time when there is no surplus from which dividends may properly be declared.[40]

• Directors who approve an "*ultra vires*" transaction, i.e., a transaction beyond the granted power of the corporation, may be held personally for damages suffered by the corporation.

• To exempt himself from personal liability for improper dividends, *ultra vires* transactions or other wrongful acts of the board, a director should at least register a formal dissent to the particular act and see that it is entered in the minutes of the meeting at which the transaction is approved by the other directors. In addition, it may be incumbent upon him to take affirmative action, as where he becomes aware of the fact that dishonest or fraudulent schemes are being perpetrated by his co-directors.

Fiduciary Position of Directors:

TRANSACTIONS WITH CORPORATION. Like other agents, a director has a fiduciary duty to his principal, the corporation—a duty to act in the best interests of the corporation and not in his personal interests.

• A director may have conflicting interests. Interlocking directorates are common. Suppose D is a director of Corpora-

---

[31]Corp. C. 301.

[32]Corp. C. 303 (note the limitation). Note also Corp. C. 302, 305.

[33]Corp. C. 304.

[34]Corp. C. 300(a).

[35]Corp. C. 307(a)(2).

[36]Corp. C. 307(a)(1)(2).

[37]Corp. C. 307(a)(7)(8).

---

[38]Corp. C. 307(a)(8).

[39]Corp. C. 311. Note also Corp. C. 300(a) and Corp. C. 300(b) re close corporations.

[40]Corp. C. 316(a).

tion 1, which is a manufacturing business, and also of Corporations 2 and 3, which supply raw materials that could be used in the manufacturing process of Corporation 1. This is perfectly legitimate, but a somewhat delicate situation arises if D attempts to secure Corporation 1's contracts for raw materials for Corporations 2 and 3, and to get Corporations 2 and 3 to use the product of Corporation 1. The courts have taken a realistic attitude here, however, and have adopted as a general rule that if the common directorship is known and if the particular transaction is generally fair and reasonable, it is valid and binding.

• There is another type of situation in which the personal interest of the director is even more pronounced. Director Joseph Brown owns, as sole proprietor, a business which could supply certain needs of the corporation; or the corporation is looking for a piece of property for a factory site, and Joseph Brown happens to own property which he is willing to sell. Here, the general rule is a little more strict. The general rule is that all directors must know of Brown's personal interest, and that the transaction must be approved by an independent majority of the directors, i.e., by a vote in which Brown does not participate or in which his vote is not necessary to constitute a majority. The new California code appears to adopt a more lenient rule.[41]

"CORPORATE OPPORTUNITY RULE." The fiduciary duty of the director to the corporation has another facet. The "Pepsi-Cola case" (*Guth* v. *Loft, Inc.*, 23 Del. Ch. 255, 5 Atl. 2d 503) presents the situation. There, a corporation was engaged in the manufacture and sale of soft drinks and candy. Its president bought the Pepsi-Cola formula from a bankrupt concern and then used the corporation's money, plant and employees to manufacture Pepsi-Cola which he sold to the corporation at a 10% profit. Held, the president had misappropriated a business opportunity which belonged to the corporation, together with the profits derived therefrom; that directors and officers of a corporation have the duty to advise and give the corporation opportunity to take advantage of profitable business deals which are in the corporation's field and may not appropriate such opportunities for themselves.[42]

TRANSACTIONS WITH STOCKHOLDERS. Since an agent's fiduciary duty is to his principal, the courts took the position at an early date that a director's fiduciary duty was only to the corporation and that he was not bound to observe fiduciary standards in his dealings with stockholders. Therefore, in early days, a director with "inside information" of something extraordinarily profitable in view for the corporation could, with relative impunity, buy up stock without disclosing his inside information and reap the benefit thereof. The United States Supreme Court undertook to require disclosure of inside information in *Strong* v. *Repide*, 213 U.S. 419, 29 S.Ct. 521.

Federal and state statutes now regulate the matter with so-called "insider-trading" laws. At the federal level, Section 10(b) of the Securities Exchange Act of 1934 (page 308), and SEC Rule 10b-5 promulgated thereunder, makes it unlawful to use inside information in connection with the purchase and sale of stock. In addition, under Section 16(b) of the Securities

Exchange Act of 1934, directors and officers of a corporation with more than 500 shareholders and $1,000,000 in assets, and beneficial owners of more than 10% of the stock of such a corporation, may be required to disgorge "short-swing profits," i.e., profits made from purchases and sales of the corporation's stock within the period of six months. At the state level, Corp. C. 25402 makes it unlawful to take advantage of inside information and Corp. C. 25502 prescribes the damages of the victim of such unlawful conduct.

California has approved the special facts doctrine in several cases. In *Hobart* v. *Hobart Estate*, 26 C.2d 412, 159 P.2d 958, a director and officer of a closed corporation sought to deal at arm's length in the purchase of stock from an heir of a deceased member of the corporation. It was held that he could not do so, the court saying that a "confidential relationship arises as a result of the officer's possession of special knowledge gained in his capacity as a corporate fiduciary. An officer, in buying or selling to a shareholder, must inform him of those matters relating to the corporate business of which the officer has knowledge and which the shareholder has a right to know about, so that the latter may have the benefit of such information in judging the advantages of the deal."

• *Schwab* v. *Schwab-Wilson Machinery Corp.*, 13 C.A.2d 1, 55 P.2d 1268, presents the broader principle that directors and majority stockholders occupy a fiduciary position in exercising or using corporate powers and are supposed to do so only in good faith and for legitimate purposes. In the *Schwab* case, two directors-stockholders in a closed corporation issued additional stock sufficient to give them voting control while the third director-stockholder was ill. Held, that this was a violation of fiduciary obligation and that the transaction could be set aside.

Officers

Typical corporations are required to have a president, a vice-president, a secretary and a treasurer, all chosen by the board of directors. Additionally a corporation may have such other officers as it deems necessary. Generally two or more offices, except those of president and secretary, may be held by the same person.

The new California provisions contained in Corp. C. 312 are somewhat atypical. Section 312(a) requires that a corporation "have a chairman of the board *or* a president *or* both, a secretary, a chief financial officer and such other officers with such titles and duties as shall be stated in the bylaws . . ." and provides that "Any number of offices may be held by the same person unless the articles or bylaws provide otherwise."

• In general, officers have such powers as are conferred upon them by the bylaws as well as such powers as they are made to appear to possess.

President: The president is, of course, an agent of very high dignity. He may or may not also be chairman of the board of directors. If he is, he is the chief executive officer of the corporation. If not, he is second in importance to the chairman of the board if the latter is the controlling figure in the corporation, as is often the case. The president's real power will depend on the internal structure of the particular corporation. At one extreme, he may be a mere figurehead; at the other, the real controlling power. As chief executive, he has general charge and control of the corporation's business and affairs. In a large corporation, he is usually a broadly presiding officer with the detailed management of the business being placed in the hands of a "general manager."

• Questions as to the extent of the president's power to bind the corporation to contracts may arise in connection with the

---

[41]Corp. C. 310(a)(3) and (b)(2) appear to make the "justice and reasonableness" of the transaction the ultimate test, howsoever it is approved.

[42]See the quotation in the case of *MacIsaac* v. *Pozzo*, 81 C.A.2d 278, 183 P.2d 278, on page 265. It is a quotation from the case of *Guth* v. *Loft, Inc.*, which is considered to be the leading case on the *corporate opportunity rule.*

dealings between the corporation and third persons. It is not possible to announce a precise formula. Certainly, the president has at least apparent authority to consummate ordinary business transactions on behalf of the corporation—purchases of goods and equipment, etc. It will be up to a court to decide whether a contract is within the scope of the actual or apparent authority of the president in the light of such considerations as the extent to which the president has been allowed to act in the past, the size of the corporation, etc. The president should, of course, have the authorization of the board of directors in all transactions of an extraordinary nature.

Vice-President: A vice-president is just what the name infers—one who assists the president and serves as a substitute for the president as occasion or necessity requires. In large corporations, however, there are usually a number of vice-presidents whose functions are to act as department heads.

Secretary: The secretary makes and maintains records of corporate transactions—minutes of meeting of directors and stockholders, sets up and maintains stock and stock transfer records, and acts as stock transfer agent in smaller corporations.

Chief Financial Officer: In most states, the corporation's fiscal officer is called the treasurer, as was formerly the case in California. The new code chooses to call the fiscal officer the "chief financial officer," as is seen in Section 312(a) above. Curiously, it refers to "assistant treasurer" in Section 313. The chief financial officer has charge of financial records and disbursement of funds. In larger corporations, there is usually a controller in addition to the chief financial officer, in which case the controller keeps the books of account while the chief financial officer handles the money.

Corporate Powers

General Powers

In general, a corporation may do the same things that a natural person may do with the limitation that its powers must be exercised for the attainment of its corporate purposes.[43]
● Before statutes were enacted in every state expressly conferring such powers,[44] every corporation was held to have certain inherent or implied powers to (1) appoint necessary officers and agents, (2) enter into contracts, (3) acquire and dispose of property, (4) borrow money and pledge its assets as security, and (5) sue and be sued.

Special Problems

Purchase of Own Stock: It is now the rule in all states that a corporation may purchase its own stock out of *earned surplus*, the profits produced by successful operation of the corporation.[45] There is seldom a really legitimate reason for this, however, at least for purchases of its own shares in substantial quantities. It has been held that such purchase is justified on occasion as a means of adjusting financial structure, to repur-

chase stock sold to employees under an employees' stock purchase plan, and for other like reasons.

There is danger that the power to purchase its own shares may be used by the corporation for improper purposes, e.g., to manipulate voting control or buy off opposition to current management. If it is clear that such is the case, a court of equity may provide a remedy to the injured stockholders since, as mentioned earlier,[46] both the directors and the majority stockholders have the duty to deal fairly with the minority stockholders.

● Shares of stock reacquired by a corporation are ordinarily called *treasury shares.* Treasury shares are a kind of neutral quantity until retired or resold. While held by the corporation, they have no voting or dividend rights and may not be included as assets in computing surplus available for dividends. They may be retired by the corporation or resold for whatever they will bring. "Treasury shares" was the terminology and the foregoing were the rules regarding treasury shares under Section 1714 of the old code. The new code eliminates the concept of treasury shares. Section 510(a) of the new code provides that "(w)hen a corporation purchases or redeems or otherwise acquires its own shares, such shares are restored to the status of authorized but unissued shares, unless the articles prohibit the reissuance thereof."

Purchase of Stock of Other Corporations: The general rules on this are uncertain, but seem to be as follows: (1) A corporation may purchase stock of another corporation where the other is engaged in a related or allied line of business and the purchase is to enable the first corporation better to accomplish its business purposes, i.e., to obtain the products and facilities of an affiliate or subsidiary. (2) In some states, statute permits the purchase or other acquisition of shares of another corporation. This would probably broaden the circumstances under which stock of another corporation could be acquired, but even here the acquisition must be the means of accomplishing a legitimate end. Thus, a corporation might acquire stock of another corporation as a temporary investment of idle funds or in payment or compromise of a debt, but not for speculation. Former California code section 802(d) expressly allowed the acquisition of the "securities of any corporation." The new code does not contain a comparable provision.

Becoming Surety or Guarantor: Like everything else, the credit and responsibility of a corporation should be used only for the accomplishment of its corporate purposes. Suppose that the president, with approval of the directors, signs the corporation's name on a note as guarantor to enable the maker, a friend of the president or of one of the directors, to obtain a loan. If the corporation will not benefit from the transaction, its credit is being used for an improper purpose, and it may not be held on the guaranty. The courts will hold that the taker of the note is on notice that a corporation cannot make and is not bound upon a guaranty which is not designed in any way to enable the corporation to achieve its corporate purposes.

But suppose, by contrast, that a corporation engaged in the canning business guarantees the note of a farmer to enable him to obtain a bank loan which he will use to raise a crop which he has contracted to sell to the corporation when harvested. Here, the guaranty is reasonably related to the accomplishment of the corporate purposes and will be binding.

---

[43]Corp. C. 207.

[44]Corp. C. 207.

[45]In California, Corp. C. 500 is the section to look to in determining whether or not a corporation may purchase its own stock. Section 500 refers to "distributions to shareholders" and Section 166 defines that term to include the purchase or redemption of the corporation's own stock. Because of California's elimination of the concept of par value, *earned surplus* has no application in California.

---

[46]See *Schwab* case, page 284.

The rule, then, is that the suretyship or guaranty contract of a corporation is binding only if it will in some tangible way enable the corporation to achieve its corporate purposes.[47]

Becoming Partner: The general rule is that a corporation may not enter into a partnership unless its articles permit it to do so. The theory is that partnership takes too much of the management function out of the hands of the board of directors of the corporation where it is supposed to rest exclusively.

Section 207(h) of the new California code adopts the very liberal rule here that a corporation may "(p)articipate with others in any partnership, joint venture or other association, transaction or arrangement of any kind, whether or not such participation involves sharing or delegation of control with or to others."

A corporation would rarely have occasion to enter into a partnership. On occasion two or more corporations will enter into a *joint venture* for a particular project or transaction, e.g., two corporations engaged in the building construction business might join forces to build a tract of houses. Such joint venture transactions have been held not to violate the rule against entering into a partnership.

Making Donations: Generally corporations are not permitted to make donations which do not benefit the corporation. The new California code, in Section 207(e), allows corporations, subject to limitations in the articles, to "(m)ake donations, regardless of specific corporate benefit, for the public welfare or for community fund, hospital, charitable, educational, scientific, civic or similar purposes."

Ultra Vires Transactions

Where a corporation enters into a transaction which is outside the line of business in which it is authorized to engage, the transaction is described as *ultra vires* or "beyond its powers."

Such transactions may range from the very obvious to those which present a close question. It would be obvious that the contract of a shoe manufacturing concern to purchase a gold mine would be *ultra vires*. On the other hand, it would seem to be quite clear that a corporation formed to manufacture and sell automobiles could buy and operate a tire manufacturing business to supply tires for its automobiles. Most of these cases are covered in the articles of incorporation by the simple expedient of broadening the language of the "purposes clause" to permit the corporation to engage in every conceivable line of business related to or in any way connected with its main line.

● Some *ultra vires* cases still arise, however, and a variety of rules is applied. Suppose that on May 1, a corporation engaged in the frozen foods business makes an *ultra vires* contract to purchase a quantity of grain on speculation. The grain is to be delivered to the corporation on May 15, and the corporation is to pay for it on May 30.

1. On May 7, delivery and payment are still pending. That makes the contract still *executory on both sides*. It is the general rule that as long as an *ultra vires* transaction remains executory on both sides, it may be avoided by either party. If a substantial number of stockholders discover and object to the transaction, they may be able to register their objection in time to prevent its perfection.

2. On May 16, the grain is delivered to and accepted by the corporation. Payment remains to be made on May 30.

Now the contract is *executed on one side*. Two conflicting rules are applied here: (a) Some states hold that the contract may still be avoided by either party. (b) Others hold that the contract is binding provided it was not clearly outside the corporation's field of business endeavor so that the party who dealt with the corporation should have known that it was ultra vires.

3. Payment is made on May 30. The contract is now *executed on both sides*. The general rule with respect to an executed transaction is that the courts will not disturb it. It stands, and neither party may have it set aside.

● *California* has abolished the doctrine of *ultra vires*. Corp. C. 208(b) makes *ultra vires* transactions binding on both parties even though they have not yet been executed on either side. The theory of the California statute is that third persons should have the right to assume that the directors of a corporation are acting in an authorized manner and that, even if they are not, the stockholders who have selected the directors should not be protected at the expense of third persons. A few other states have enacted statutes similar to that of California.

● *Ultra vires* applies only to transactions which are beyond the scope of the business purposes of the corporation as stated in its articles (in jurisdictions where business purposes must be specifically stated). Other acts or transactions may be improper but for different reasons, that is, because they are illegal or fraudulent, e.g., unauthorized dividends or sales of stocks.

● As a related matter, the corporation is liable for torts of officers and employees committed in the course of the corporation's business and may be liable for fraud or misrepresentation by directors in dealing with third persons on behalf of the corporation. An officer or director is not liable for torts of other officers, employees, or directors unless he directs or authorizes the act constituting the tort or may be said to have participated in it.

Stocks and Bonds

Stocks and bonds are the instruments by which a corporation obtains its initial operating capital and such additional capital as it may need for other purposes for which profits are insufficient. As discussed earlier, a corporation sells its ownership to some number of persons by issuing to them shares of its stock as evidence of their proportionate ownership. Shares of *stock* are ownership interests in a corporation, and a corporation's stockholders are its owners. Where stock issues are "equity issues" or "equity securities," bond issues are, by contrast, "debt issues" or "debt securities." *Bonds* are really long term notes of a corporation issued to some number of persons who are willing to lend money to a corporation.[48] The bonds are their evidence of the corporation's obligation to repay them at a future time. The difference between stockholders and bondholders, then, is that the former are *owners*, the latter *creditors*, of the corporation. Bonds and preferred stocks are described as "senior securities" since each in its way has priority over common stock (as bonds have priority over preferred stock).

Common Stock

As discussed earlier, there are two types of stock and stockholders—common and preferred.[49] As its name implies, *com-*

---

[47]Corp. C. 207(d) appears to adopt a liberal approach to contracts of guaranty and suretyship.

[48]Extraordinarily, Corp. C. 204(7) allows a corporation to issue bonds having the right to vote.

[49]See Corp. C. 400.

mon stock represents ownership of the corporation by numerous persons who have no special rights or privileges, as distinguished from *preferred stock* which is specially privileged. The common stock is usually the voting stock, which makes the common stockholders the electors of the board of directors. The theory is that even though the preferred stockholders are owners, their primary interest is the fixed return (dividend) which they are entitled to receive and that they are not greatly concerned about management as long as their dividends are paid regularly; that the common stockholder is an owner in the full sense of the word since he gambles to the fullest extent on the success of the corporation; that therefore the choice of management should be left to him. The preferred stockholders are usually given voting rights in a special case, however—when one or more dividends on the preferred stock are missed or "passed," the word used to describe the failure to pay a dividend. A dividend will be passed only if the corporation has failed to make profits during the dividend period. This may indicate poor judgment in the selection of management and, protective of their interests, the preferred stockholders should become vitally concerned with the management at this point. The usual provision in the articles is that if two consecutive dividends on preferred stock are passed, the preferred stockholders shall have the right to elect a majority of the board of directors until such time as the passed dividends are made up and the corporation is again on a dividend-paying basis.[50]

● Despite the fact that all common stockholders have an equal interest in the choice of management, all of them may not have voting rights. Stock, both common and preferred, may be further refined into classes—Class A Common Stock, Class B Common Stock, etc. Voting rights may be confined to one class of common stock. Such arrangements are closely scrutinized by the Corporations Commissioner and will be disallowed where they would produce unfairness, as where they represent manipulations by promoters to perpetuate control. By contrast, suppose that a large, long-established corporation proposes a new issue of common stock. Here common stock without voting rights will be allowed. This preserves the position of those who have grown up with the corporation, and here it will not be unfair to withhold voting right from new stockholders.

● See page 288 for a common stock form.

Par and No Par Common Stock

In the early period of the history of corporations in this country, stock was required to have a *par value*—a specific dollar sign on its face. The face value and the real value of the stock, its *book value*, seldom coincided however, and this became the main justification for *no par stock*. Suppose that 100,000 shares of stock of $10 par value are issued—90,000 for cash and 10,000 taken by the promoters in payment for their services. At this point, the real or book value of each share is $9 as against its par or face value of $10. Now suppose that the corporation has been in business for a time, has been successful, and now has net assets of $2,000,000. At this point, the par value remains $10 a share but the book value has become $20 a share. If the corporation is successful, book value exceeds par value; if the corporation is unsuccessful, par value exceeds book value.

Those advocating no par stock, i.e., stock without an assigned dollar value, had two arguments: (1) That par value

seldom bore a true relation to book value; and (2) that if potential investors were not given an assigned value, they would have to ascertain book value and would be better informed and protected by being required to do so. These arguments were successful, and it has long since been permissible to issue no par stock or par stock, as the corporation sees fit.

● The new California code eliminates the par value concept entirely.

Preferred Stock

Preferred stock has been discussed to some extent.[51] Again the preferences are (1) dividend preference and (2) liquidation preference. Dividends on preferred stock must be paid to the preferred stockholders before any dividend may be paid to common stockholders.

● See page 290 for a preferred stock form.

Cumulative and Noncumulative: Since dividends are distributions of profits, there can be no dividend in a particular year if there are no profits. This raises the question of what happens when a dividend on preferred stock is passed for this reason. Preferred may be *noncumulative*, in which case the dividend is lost, but it is almost invariably *cumulative*, so that if one or more dividends is passed, they accrue and both back and current dividends must be paid before dividends can be paid on common stock.[53]

Participating Preferred: Preferred stock may be made *participating*, in which case (1) preferred is first paid a specified dividend rate; (2) common is then paid a specified rate; (3) preferred and common then share equally or in some other specified proportions in the balance of profits available for dividends.[54]

Redemption and Conversion Features: The corporation may give itself a right to *redeem* (buy back) preferred stock at some figure which will give the preferred stockholder a small premium, e.g., to repurchase $100 par value preferred at $105.[55] This permits the corporation, if successful, to eliminate the relatively fixed charge which preferred stock represents.

● To make preferred stock more attractive and to offset the redemption privilege of the corporation, the preferred stock may be given conversion rights or stock purchase rights.[56]

● The *conversion right* permits the preferred stockholder to convert his preferred into common at a certain rate of exchange and within a limited period of time. This permits the preferred stockholder, if the corporation is successful, to convert his preferred stock to common and take advantage of the appreciation in market price enjoyed by the common stock. In fairness to those who take common at the beginning, however, the conversion ratio is often at a graduated annual rate

---

[51]See page 261.

[52](*Deleted*)

[53]Ballantine on Corporations, p. 505, says that in the absence of an express provision to the contrary in the stock certificate, preferred dividends are cumulative since this would be the assumption made by a purchaser. In other words, preferred stock is noncumulative only if it is expressly declared to be so.

[54]Ballantine on Corporations, p. 506, says that preferred stock is not participating unless it is expressly made participating by the certificate.

[55]Corp. C. 402.

[56]Corp. C. 403.

---

[50]In one other case, the class vote situation discussed on page 299, preferred stock will have voting rights by statute.

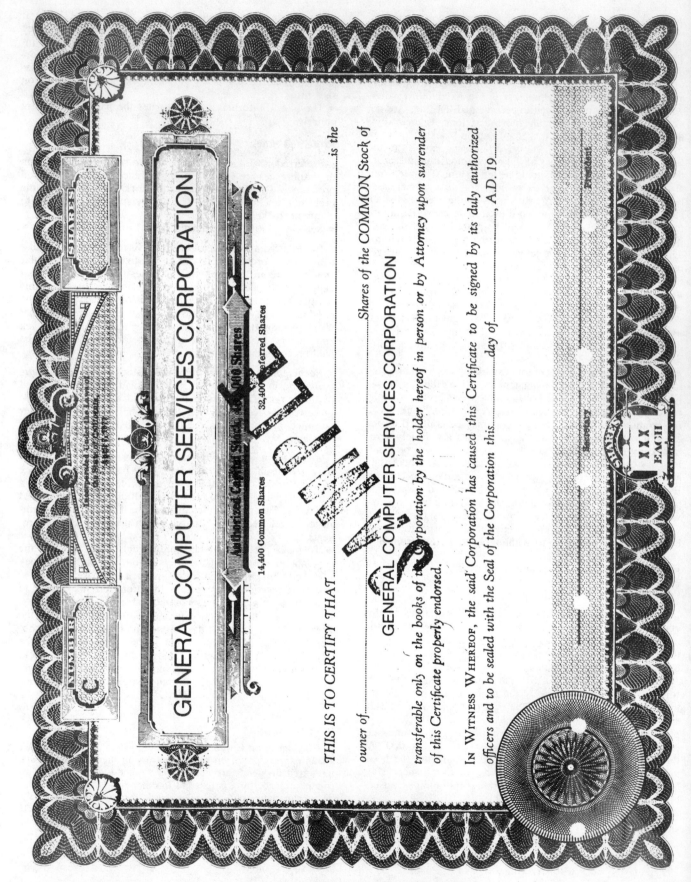

GENERAL COMPUTER SERVICES CORPORATION

A statement of the rights, preferences, privileges and restrictions granted to or imposed upon each class or series of shares authorized to be issued by the Corporation, and upon the holders thereof, may be obtained by any shareholder, upon request and without charge, from the Secretary of the Corporation at the principal executive office of the Corporation at 500 South Montgomery Street, San Francisco, California.

For value Received,...............*hereby sell, assign and transfer unto*

....

....*Shares of*

the Common Stock of the within named Corporation, represented

by the within Certificate and do hereby irrevocably constitute and

appoint ....*Attorney to*

transfer the said shares of said Common Stock on the books of

the said Corporation, pursuant to the provisions of the By-Laws

thereof, with full powers of substitution in the premises.

Dated.......................................*A.D. 19*........

....

In Presence of:

....

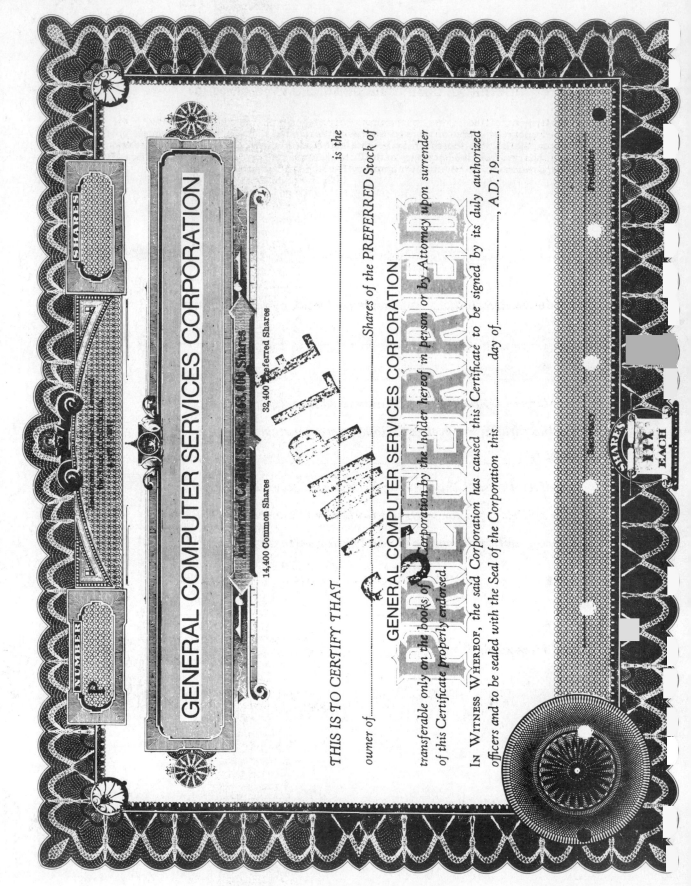

(Reverse side of this form on following page)

GENERAL COMPUTER SERVICES CORPORATION

A statement of the rights, preferences, privileges and restrictions granted to or imposed upon each class or series of shares authorized to be issued by the Corporation, and upon the holders thereof, may be obtained by any shareholder, upon request and without charge, from the Secretary of the Corporation at the principal executive office of the Corporation at 500 South Montgomery Street, San Francisco, California.

For value Received,..............hereby sell, assign and transfer unto

....

....*Shares of*

the Common Stock of the within named Corporation, represented

by the within Certificate and do hereby irrevocably constitute and

appoint .... Attorney to

transfer the said shares of said Common Stock on the books of

the said Corporation, pursuant to the provisions of the By-Laws

thereof, with full powers of substitution in the premises.

Dated..A.D. 19.........

....

In Presence of:

....

NOTICE: The si.... ture to this assignment ...st strictly correspond wi... the name as written upo.. ...he face of the Certificate in every particular and without alteration or enlargement or any change whatever.

so that it will cost the preferred stockholder more each year to convert. This prevents him from speculating at the expense of the corporation and common stockholders for an unduly long period of time.

• The *stock purchase right* permits the preferred stockholder to purchase a specified quantity of common stock within a specified time and at a specified price in order to permit him to participate in the growth that will be realized by common stock if the corporation is successful.

Bonds

Bonds are the long term notes of a corporation given in exchange for loans of money to it, the lenders becoming the bondholders and being creditors of the corporation. Bond issues occur after a corporation has been in business for some time and requires additional capital for expansion for other purposes. Bonds are usually issued in the denominations of $1000 or more.

Bonds, like notes, are simply promises to pay money at a future date with interest to be paid in the meantime. Accordingly, a bond reads just like a note with respect to the manner in which it frames its obligation. See the specimen bond on pages 294-295 and compare it to the note on page 116. (Dates and interest rates have been omitted from the specimen bond form because of the technical difficulties that would be presented in attempting to change dates and interest rates in successive editions of this book.)

Bearer and Registered Bonds; Negotiability: The specimen bond is payable "to bearer or if this bond is registered, then to the registered holder," which is a customary provision. The person to whom the bond is issued may "register" it with the corporation which will then show on its books that he is the owner. This will also be shown on the bond, which will have a space on it for this purpose as follows:

NOTICE: No writing below except by the bond registrar		
Date of registration	Name of registered owner	Signature of registrar

If the bond is registered, it may be transferred only by written assignment of the registered owner, and, like the *order* negotiable instrument, it is protected against loss or theft. If the bond is not registered, it remains payable to bearer and, like the *bearer* negotiable instrument, title may be passed to a good faith purchaser by the finder or thief if it is lost or stolen.

Coupons: Coupons are attached to bonds to represent the installments of interest payable on them. There is one coupon for each installment of interest. In the specimen bond, if interest were at 6 percent payable semiannually on March 1 and September 1 and the bond had been issued on September 1, 1983, there would be a coupon for $30.00 payable on each of these dates throughout the life of the bond. These would read as follows:

"On the first day of March, 1983, the California Gas & Electric Corporation will pay to bearer . . . Thirty and no/100ths Dollars ($30.00) . . ."

"On the first day of September, 1984, the California Gas & Electric Corporation will pay to bearer . . . Thirty and no/100ths Dollars ($30.00) . . ."

"On the first day of March, 1984, the California Gas & Electric Corporation will pay to bearer . . . Thirty and no/100ths Dollars ($30.00) . . ."

Being payable to bearer, the coupons are negotiable.

Mortgages Securing Bonds: Bonds are usually secured by a mortgage or trust deed on property of the corporation, in which case they are like notes secured by mortgages or deeds of trust, seen previously. The mortgage or deed of trust is called the *mortgage indenture* or *trust deed indenture*. Accordingly, such bonds are called *indenture bonds*. There will be one mortgage securing the entire issue of bonds with each bond making reference to it as in the specimen form on page 294.

• A trustee named in the bonds will be empowered to sell the mortgaged property if the installments of interest are not paid when due, as in the deed of trust seen earlier. Usually the trustee is a bank or trust company.

Sinking Fund Provision: As further security, bonds may be protected by a sinking fund provision. This will require that the corporation set aside a certain amount of money each year during the life of the bonds to provide a fund with which to pay them at maturity. This fund will be required to be deposited with and placed under the control of the trustee.

Open and Closed End Mortgage Bonds: In its own interests, as against future needs of money, a corporation may wish to make its mortgage bonds *open ended*. This means that the corporation may float additional issues of bonds under the same security. In a *closed end* bond issue, by contrast, no further bonds may be issued under the security of the mortgage or deed of trust.

Redemption Privilege: The corporation may give itself the privilege of calling in or redeeming bonds before they reach maturity. The bondholder is usually given a premium if the bond is called in early. Thus, a $1000 bond might call for payment of $1050 if the corporation elects to redeem it in advance of its maturity date.

Serial Bonds: To ease the burden on itself, the corporation may stagger the maturity dates of bonds in a particular issue— make ⅓ of them payable in 1990, ⅓ payable in 1991, and ⅓ payable in 1992. Such bonds are called *serial bonds*.

Debenture Bonds: Debenture bonds are the opposite of mortgage or secured bonds. They are unsecured bonds and approach more nearly the speculative nature of stock.

Advantages and Disadvantages of Bond Financing: The use of bonds is confined almost entirely to government agencies—federal, state and municipal; quasipublic corporations— utility companies; and industrial corporations of national reputation. This is because bonds, being for loans of money, require the borrowing corporation to have substantial assets and/or a "name" which connotes solidity or unimpeachable integrity, and it is only the types of organizations described that will meet these requirements.

• An advantage of bonds may be that they require a lower rate of interest than preferred stocks. In the case of govern-it agencies, there is another advantage—bond interest can made tax free. This permits the investor to realize a higher ctive rate of return on his money.

Another advantage from the standpoint of private corporat.s is that they may deduct the amount paid as interest on ds from their income for income tax purposes, but not punts paid as dividends on preferred or common stock.

The big disadvantage of the bond is that it is a *fixed charge*. d interest must be paid regularly each year even though profits are made, whereas dividends on stock are payable y if profits are made. The strain of meeting bond interest ing a period of recession may be very great for the cor ation. If the interest payments are not made, the bond ers will require the trustee to sell the property on which bond mortgage has been given—the principal assets of the poration—thereby wiping out the corporation. For this rea corporations which could issue "debt issues," or bonds, prefer to issue "equity issues," or stock, as the means btaining additional capital.

Stock Issuance; Certificates; Transfer

nce—Investor Protection Laws

ate Blue Sky Laws: Before a corporation may solicit sale or issue its stock, it is required to qualify its stock for ance before one or more government agencies whose pur e is to protect the public against stock frauds. State laws very state except Nevada require such qualification before ate agency usually called the Commissioner of Corpora s, as in California.[57] Based on the description in a famous that they are designed to prevent "speculative schemes ch have no more basis than so many feet of blue sky," e laws are called *blue sky laws*. The Corporations Com sioner will grant a stock permit only if he finds that the posed business venture and its securities are *bona fide* and vide a fair arrangement for investors.[57a] Such is the nature he Corporate Securities Law in California, which is the sky law of this state.[57b]

he Corporations Commissioner may "*escrow*" stock ch has some "water" in it such as promotion stock or k issued for property which may be overvalued.[58] stock is sold without a permit or in violation of escrow rictions, the person buying it may recover the considera paid for it.[59]

ederal Investor Protection Laws: The Securities Act of 3, or "Truth-in-Securities" Act, and the Securities Ex ge Act of 1934 are federal laws which complement the blue sky laws. The Securities Act of 1933 prohibits the ring of securities of a corporation in a state outside the of incorporation until an elaborate *registration statement* led with the Securities and Exchange Commission. This ents incorporation in a state having a weak blue sky law then selling the stock in other states as a means of avoid their more stringent laws. The registration statement is

designed to require the corporation to present a complete and accurate picture of the proposed stock issue. A prospectus which is required to make a similar disclosure must be deliv ered to a purchaser of the stock. The S.E.C. cannot flatly prohibit the issue of a particular stock, but the disclosure re quirements furnish a powerful restraint on speculative and in secure schemes.

● The Securities and Exchange Act of 1934 covers a wide variety of matters. Pertinent here is that it requires an addi tional registration statement if the stock is to be listed on a stock exchange, and that it regulates the conduct of stock brokers by giving the S.E.C. the power to expel them from an exchange and revoke their licenses for fraudulent or uneth ical practices, such as conspiring to manipulate prices of stock or selling stock in excess of current market prices. It also regulates proxy solicitation and insider trading.

Stock Certificates

A corporation must issue certificates for shares when they are paid for.[60] The certificate must show the number of shares and the class or series of shares owned by the shareholder and the rights, preferences, privileges and restrictions granted to or imposed upon each class or series.[61] See the specimen forms on pages 288 and 290.

● A corporation may issue certificates for shares which are only partly paid where shares are sold on an installment basis, as is permitted to be done. If it is, the certificates will be required to show on their face the amount remaining to be paid.[62]

● A single certificate may be issued for the entire number of shares purchased by a particular buyer. A purchaser of 250 shares of the stock of a corporation may get but one certificate for the entire number of shares. If he wishes to sell part, say 100 shares, he must surrender the certificate to the corpora tion's transfer agent who will then issue two new certificates, one for 150 shares in the shareholder's name, the other for 100 shares in the name of his purchaser.

Stock Transfer and Negotiability; Division 8 of Uniform Commercial Code

Division 8 of the code is "a negotiable instruments law dealing with securities."[63] It covers methods of transfer of securities, the extent to which a transferee takes free of de fenses and claims to the security, and the obligation of the issuer to register transfer.

● "*Security*" is defined by U.C.C. 8102(1). The main thing is that the instrument is a *traded* security; form is not impor tant as it is with Division 3's commercial paper. Mainly Di vision 8 would apply to stocks and bonds since they are the principal forms of traded securities, but it would also apply to such things as stock warrants and equipment trust certifi cates if they are traded.

● The rules on transfer are essentially the same as those on transfer of commercial paper. A registered security may be transferred by indorsement on the instrument or by separate

---

Corp. C. 25113.

Extensive excerpts from the California Corporate Securities of 1968, which replaced the original California Corporate rities Law, are set out in the Appendix. They are Corp. C. 0 et seq.

Corp. C. 25140(b).

Corp. C. 25141. Note also §§ 25149, 25133, 25151, 25142, 7, 25148.

Corp. C. 25503.

---

[60]Corp. C. 416(a).

[61]Corp. C. 416, 417. Note also § 418.

[62]Corp. C. 409(d).

[63]U.C.C. 8101, Official Comments.

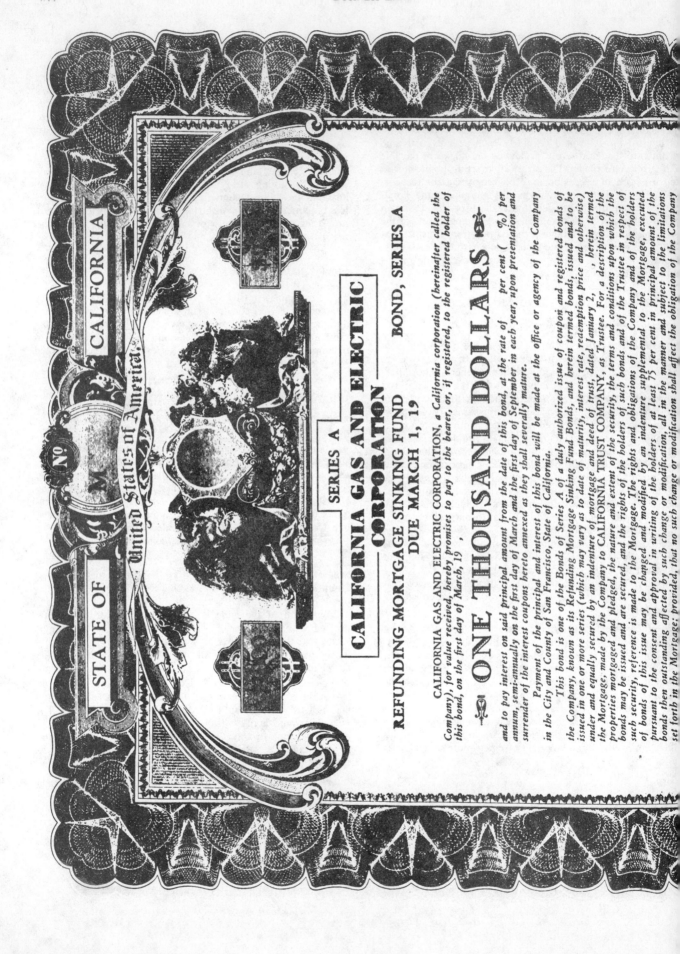

STATE OF

CALIFORNIA

No.

United States of America

SERIES A

CALIFORNIA GAS AND ELECTRIC CORPORATION

REFUNDING MORTGAGE SINKING FUND   BOND, SERIES A
DUE MARCH 1, 19

CALIFORNIA GAS AND ELECTRIC CORPORATION, a California corporation (hereinafter called the Company), for value received, hereby promises to pay to the bearer, or, if registered, to the registered holder of this bond, on the first day of March, 19 ,

and to pay interest on said principal amount from the date of this bond, at the rate of   per cent (%) per annum, semi-annually on the first day of March and the first day of September in each year, upon presentation and surrender of the interest coupons hereto annexed as they shall severally mature.

Payment of the principal and interest of this bond will be made at the office or agency of the Company in the City and County of San Francisco, State of California.

This bond is one of the Bonds of Series A of a duly authorized issue of coupon and registered bonds of the Company, known as its Refunding Mortgage Sinking Fund Bonds, and herein termed bonds, issued and to be issued in one or more series (which may vary as to date of maturity, interest rate, redemption price and otherwise) under and equally secured by an indenture of mortgage and deed of trust, dated January 2,   , herein termed the Mortgage, made by the Company to CALIFORNIA TRUST COMPANY, as Trustee. For a description of the properties mortgaged and pledged, the nature and extent of the security, the terms and conditions upon which the bonds may be issued and are secured, and the rights of the holders of such bonds and of the Trustee in respect of such security, reference is made to the Mortgage. The rights and obligations of the Company and of the holders of bonds of this issue may be changed and modified by an indenture supplemental to the Mortgage, executed pursuant to the consent and approval in writing of the holders of at least 75 per cent in principal amount of the bonds then outstanding affected by such change or modification, all in the manner and subject to the limitations set forth in the Mortgage: provided, that no such change or modification shall affect the obligation of the Company

ONE THOUSAND DOLLARS

by operation of the Sinking Fund provided in the Mortgage for the Bonds of Series A.

In case any default as defined in the Mortgage shall occur, the principal of all the bonds may become or be declared due and payable in the manner and with the effect provided in the Mortgage.

This bond shall pass by delivery unless registered in the name of the owner at the office or agency of the Company in the City and County of San Francisco, State of California, such registration being noted hereon by the Company. After such registration no transfer shall be valid unless made at such office or agency by the registered owner in person, or by his attorney duly authorized and similarly noted hereon, but the same may be discharged from registration by a transfer in like manner to bearer, and thereupon transferability by delivery shall be restored; but this bond may again, from time to time, be registered or transferred to bearer as before. Such registration, however, shall not affect the negotiability of the coupons, which shall continue to be transferable by delivery.

Series A Bonds with coupons are issuable in the denominations of $1,000 and $500 each. Series A Bonds fully registered without coupons are issuable in the denominations of $1,000, $5,000 and $10,000, and authorized multiples of $10,000. In the manner prescribed in the Mortgage and upon payment of the charges therein provided, coupon bonds of this Series, of either denomination, with all unmatured coupons attached, may be exchanged for a like aggregate principal amount of coupon bonds of this Series of the other denomination, with all unmatured coupons attached, and coupon bonds of this Series of either denomination, with all unmatured coupons attached, in the aggregate principal amount of $1,000, or multiples thereof, may also be exchanged for a like aggregate principal amount of registered bonds without coupons of this Series. Any such registered bond in like manner and upon payment of the charges provided in the Mortgage may in turn be exchanged for a coupon bond or bonds of this Series for the same aggregate principal amount and bearing all unmatured coupons.

No recourse shall be had for the payment of the principal of or interest on this bond or any part thereof, or for any claim based thereon or otherwise in respect thereof, or of the indebtedness represented thereby or of the Mortgage, against any incorporator, stockholder, officer or director, past, present or future, of the Company, or of any successor corporation, either directly or through the Company or such successor corporation, whether by virtue of any statute or constitutional provision or by the enforcement of any assessment or otherwise, all such liability being by the acceptance hereof and as part of the consideration for the issue hereof expressly released, as provided in the mortgage.

This bond shall not be entitled to any benefit under the Mortgage, and shall not become valid or obligatory for any purpose, until it shall be authenticated by the execution of the certificate hereon endorsed by the Trustee under the Mortgage.

IN WITNESS WHEREOF, California Gas and Electric Corporation has caused this bond to be signed in its name by its President or one of its Vice-Presidents, and its corporate seal to be hereunto affixed or imprinted, and to be attested by its Secretary or one of its Assistant Secretaries, and coupons for said interest with the facsimile signature of its Treasurer to be attached hereto.

Dated the 1st day of March, 19

CALIFORNIA GAS AND ELECTRIC CORPORATION

By _____
President

Attest Seal:

Secretary

(Corporate Seal)

document of transfer.[64] Indorsement may be in blank or special.[65]

• Securities have the negotiability of commercial paper and in one respect even greater negotiability; if a security passes by forged indorsement a bona fide transferee who, without notice of the forgery, obtains issuance of a new security obtains good title.[66] A bona fide purchaser takes free of other adverse claims.[67]

• The "shelter rule" pertains.[68]

• Realistically speaking, there is, in California, only one "defense" to a security: forgery of the security. Even this is not a defense if the unauthorized signature is by a person entrusted with execution or "responsible handling" of securities.[69]

• U.C.C. 8202(2) makes unconstitutional issue a defense to a private issuer as against the issuee. This is without meaning in California because issuance of private securities is not regulated by the constitution.

• Overissue is a defense to the extent that a person entitled to a security cannot compel issuance if it would result in overissue or require issuance of additional securities. However, if the security is available on the market, the issuer must buy and deliver it.[70]

• U.C.C. 8401-8406 cover the duty of the issuer of securities to register transfer.

Shareholder of Record: This is important to the transferee of shares. Until he informs the corporation that he has become the owner by surrendering the certificate purchased and getting a new one in his name, the corporation may continue to treat the old owner as continuing to be the owner. Dividends may still be paid to him, and he can be allowed to cast the votes to which the shares are entitled, and the transferee has no rights against the corporation if either of these things occur.[71] In order to get his dividends and voting rights, therefore, the transferee should immediately surrender the old and get a new certificate in his name so that the corporation's transfer agent will at the same time enter his name as *shareholder of record* in the share records of the corporation.

Dividends

Sources

Earned Surplus: This is the normal source of dividends. *Earned surplus* is the net earnings or accumulated profits of the corporation. Since dividends are a distribution of profits, this is their natural source.

• Former Corp. C. 1500(a) provided, consistently with general law on the subject, that dividends could be paid "(o)ut of earned surplus." The new code abandons the term "earned surplus" and substitutes the formula for when dividends may be paid which is found in Section 500. Corp. C. 500 provides that dividends (which the California code refers to as "distri-

butions")[72] cannot be paid unless the retained earnings e the amount of the dividend or unless after the dividend sum of the assets of the corporation . . . would be at equal to 1½ times its liabilities . . . and . . . (t)he cu assets of the corporation would be at least equal to its cu liabilities . . ."

THE INSOLVENCY LIMITATION. Even though a corporatio an earned surplus, it may not be in condition to pay a dend. A corporation may have assets which substantiall ceed its liabilities in value.[73] But its assets may be non-l assets such as plant and equipment (called *fixed asset* business needs liquid assets (called *current assets*), i.e., and potential cash from sales of inventory, to meet its cu obligations. If it does not have sufficient current funds to current liabilities as they mature, it is called "insolven the "equity sense." It is a general limitation on the pay of dividends that they may not be paid if, as a resul corporation would not be able to meet its liabilities as mature. Corp. C. 501 so provides.

Paid-in Surplus: A corporation may have other form surplus than earned surplus. If, as is often the case, it se stock for more than par value, it will have a surplus o *paid-in surplus* at the outset, which is defined as the e over par value paid to a corporation for its stock.

Assume that at the end of the first year of operatio corporation has no earned surplus from which dividend be paid because all of the earnings have been used to expenses. Statutes of most states permit the paid-in surp be used to pay a dividend. However, a dividend from p surplus is a kind of liquidating dividend—a return of cap and as a matter of policy should not be paid except po to cumulative preferred stockholders if the corporatio such. Preferred stockholders are in a sufficiently differe sition from common stockholders to warrant the use o fund for payment of a dividend to them. Theirs is more a fixed obligation of the corporation. In a number of sta recent years, statutes have been adopted or amended to vide that it is only to preferred stockholders that divi may be paid from paid-in surplus.

• California's elimination of the concept of par value, s earlier,[74] carries with it the elimination of the concept of in surplus.

Revaluation Surplus: This is another form of surplu may arise. Surplus other than earned surplus is called c surplus, and paid-in surplus and revaluation surplus cons two forms of capital surplus. A *revaluation surplus* c when assets of the corporation appreciate in value as the of inflationary or other economic forces. The corporatio then "write up" the value of the assets to show their enh value. Suppose that certain assets of a corporation hav preciated in value from $200,000 to $300,000 as the res economic forces, while its liabilities have remained con This would create a surplus of $100,000 on paper, to be to whatever other surplus the corporation has. But the g rule is that an unrealized appreciation in the value of ass

---

[64]U.C.C. 8301(1).

[65]U.C.C. 8301(2). Note 8307, which, as in the case of commercial paper, gives the transferee the right to an indorsement if a registered security is transferred without indorsement.

[66]U.C.C. 8311(a) and Official Comments.

[67]U.C.C. 8201(2).

[68]U.C.C. 8301(1).

[69]U.C.C. 8205.

[70]U.C.C. 8104.

[71]U.C.C. 8207(1); Corp. C. 700(d).

[72]Section 500 refers to "distributions" to shareholders than "dividends." But, under the new code, dividends a form of the broader concept of "distributions to sharehol defined in Section 166.

[73]It may be noted that the amount by which assets excee bilities is called the *net worth* or *shareholders' equity* in th poration.

[74]See page 287.

proper fund to be taken into account in determining
her a corporation is in condition to pay a dividend.
lifornia had the general rule in former Corp. C. 1502
ncluded it in the original version of Section 500 of the
code, but then amended it out of Section 500 in 1977.

s

vidends may be paid in cash, property or stock of the
oration.[75] Usually they are paid in cash. Cash dividends
be regular or *ordinary dividends,* usually paid quarterly
arge corporations, or *extraordinary dividends,* extra or
s dividends paid because of exceptional earnings of the
oration. Property dividends are very rare. One of the in-
ent examples was a distribution to its stockholders of its
uct, bottled in quarts and fifths, by a distiller which, be-
 of difficult times, had been unable to pay cash dividends
ome time. It was thought that the dividend would put the
holders in a better frame of mind.

ck Dividends: Share dividends, or *"stock dividends"* as
more popular to call them, are very common. The des-
ion "dividend" is something of a misnomer, however.
stock dividend is in fact a device used by a corporation
ep shareholders happy when the corporation has earnings
h it wishes to use for some form of corporate develop-
 rather than for dividends.

 illustrate the workings and consequences of stock divi-
s, suppose shareholder S owns 100 shares of the stock of
rporation and that S's equity in C by virtue of S's own-
p of the 100 shares is $1000. Now suppose that the 1977
ings of C are such as to increase S's equity to $1100. S's
es are now worth $1100, or when thought of in terms of
tential dividend, they are worth $1000 plus $100 of po-
al dividend. If C wants to keep the potential dividend
r than distribute it to S, it can give S a 10 share stock
end. This will mean that S now owns 110 shares worth
 instead of 100 shares worth $11. But in either form S
s only an $1100 asset. So, by virtue of the stock dividend,
erely has a larger number of shares to represent the same
unt that a lesser number of shares previously represented.
e issuance of a stock dividend in lieu of a cash dividend
lled a *capitalization of surplus,* i.e., a conversion of sur-
(earnings) into capital (additional assets).

stock dividend is not without real value. A stock dividend
rally indicates a healthy condition of the corporation
g with an ambitious corporation. It promises expansion,
 increased sales and increased earnings. This will reflect
rably in the market price of the stock, causing it to rise.
 will permit the shareholder, if he wishes, to sell some
ber of his dividend shares, and in this indirect way to
ze a cash dividend, without decreasing the dollar value
s predividend equity in the corporation.

ock splits[76] generate the same kinds of psychological re-
ns as stock dividends. Stock is split when it is so suc-
ful that its market price gets out of hand, e.g., the market
e of a stock jumps from $50 a share to $250 a share. This
ows the investment potential for the stock. But if each 1
e of the stock is split into 5 shares now worth, again, $50
, the potential for investment will have been restored and
use of the success which the corporation has enjoyed,

Corp. C. 166 defines "distributions to shareholders" to in-
e distributions of cash or property but to exclude share div-
ds. This recognizes, by implication, the possibility of share
ends, however, as would Section 188.

See Corp. C. 188.

investment interest will be strong. The investment public will
see the corporation as repeating its successes, as many, many
corporations have done.

Declaration and Payment

Discretion of Directors: Since the directors are the chosen
representatives of the stockholders, the courts have always
taken the position that the stockholders should have confidence in their judgment and be willing to abide by their decisions on whether dividends should be paid; that if the directors feel that surplus funds should be retained for purpose of
expansion or to set up reserves, their judgment should be re-
spected; that, therefore, the stockholders should not be allowed to force the directors to pay dividends unless the directors abuse their discretion, e.g., use all of the earnings for
expansion purposes for a long period of time without paying
dividends. Abuse of discretion was found in the famous case
of *Dodge* v. *Ford Motor Co.,* 204 Mich. 459, 170 N.W. 668,
where Ford Motor Co. had a surplus of $112,000,000 but
would pay no dividends. Henry Ford, who controlled the
board of directors, proposed to put the money back into the
business for expansion as had been done for a number of years
previously. Ten percent of the stockholders brought an action
to compel the distribution of approximately $40,000,000 as
dividends and the court held for them to the extent of ordering
payment of $32,000,000 as dividends.

Declaration and to Whom Payable: The usual procedure in
the declaration and payment of dividends is as follows: The
dividend is *declared* by a resolution of the board of directors,[77] e.g., on February 1. The resolution will stipulate, however, that the dividend will be paid to *stockholders of record*
on a specified future date, e.g., February 15, called the *record
date,*[78] and that the dividend will be paid at an even later date,
e.g., on March 1. The dividend will go to the person who
owns the stock on the record date so that if there is a transfer
between the declaration date and the record date, the transferee is entitled to the dividend.[79]

● This may arise here: Corporations usually "close" their
books to transfers of stock between the record date and payment date to give them time to determine who is entitled to
dividends and to prepare checks for their payment. Suppose
that after declaration but before the record date, A sells his
stock to B. B does not record the transfer before closing of
the stock transfer books, and the corporation sends the dividend check to A who continues to be the stockholder of record
on its books. B may recover the dividend from A, but has no
right against the corporation since it is bound to recognize
only stockholders of record.[80] It has been held, however, that
if the corporation has actual knowledge of an unrecorded
transfer, it must pay the dividend to the person to whom it
knows the stock has been transferred.[81]

---

[77]At which time it becomes a "debt" of the corporation and
cannot thereafter be revoked by the directors.

[78]Corp. C. 701(a).

[79]Corp. C. 701(d) provides that, so far as the corporation is
concerned, the transferor is entitled to the dividend.

[80]Corp. C. 701(d). Note also U.C.C. 8207(1).

[81]Corp. C. 701(d) is to the contrary, providing that the *transferor* is entitled to the dividend even though there is an actual
transfer on the books of the corporation after the record date.

Stockholders

Investment in General

Then: First and foremost, a person with a substantial amount of money to invest wants security. He will put a substantial part of his funds in blue chip investments which will assure him of a lifetime income. A substantial portion of the balance may go into young but established and strong ventures whose shares show promise of substantial appreciation in value. Lastly, he may invest in a new venture which is relatively speculative in nature. Here, he ceases to be an investor and becomes a speculator. He may, for example, put a little money in a corporation formed to develop and market a new soft drink. It may prove to be a complete failure or it may turn out to be another "Coca Cola," in which case the stock may return several thousand dollars for each dollar invested, as was the case with Coca Cola stock.

A man with only $5000 to $20,000 to invest may not wish to expose his savings to risk of loss and may keep them in a bank where they will produce a small return. Or, he too may want the higher return of stocks. A "mutual fund," which operates as follows, may attract him: He turns his money over to a business organization—the *mutual fund*—operated by professional investors. They give him in return a "certificate" for the amount received. The fund gets thousands of similar amounts from other investors, giving each a certificate. Its operators invest the funds received in various corporate securities—some in securities of highly conservative and established corporations, others in sound new ventures or young corporations. By this diversification, they can get a good rate of return on the money invested. Part of this they keep for their services. The rest they pay to certificate holders as their return on their money. This arrangement has two advantages from the certificate holder's standpoint. (1) It puts his money in the hands of professional investors whose skill and judgment in such matters surpass his own, and (2) it gives him diversification of investment. Were he to put his $5000 in a single corporation which failed, all would be lost. In the mutual fund, if a particular corporation in which part of the funds are invested becomes insolvent, the effect on the individual certificate holder is usually slight. Such losses are distributed among and absorbed by the whole body of certificate holders so that each suffers but slight loss.

Finally, there is the real speculator. He is the man who is able to take advantage of short term fluctuations in the market price of stock brought about by current economic trends—the man who buys on the "bull (rising) market," sells when it turns into a "bear (falling) market," and purchases again when the market reaches bottom and starts its upward trend. His is a special knowledge and skill that is a compound of many complex and variable factors, the net effect of which is reflected in short term swings in the market value of stocks. It involves an extensive knowledge of and ability to weigh the effects of such diverse factors as general economic conditions, the outcome of the next election, prospective government policies, and various world situations.

Now: The foregoing was first written almost twenty years ago. Until quite recently, it remained reasonably valid. Now, while the theory remains valid, or at least somewhat valid, the practice does not take place. Today, the stock market is the theater of operations for the institutional investor and the very large individual investor. Other types of investment vehicles are better suited to the small individual investor's needs. A great proliferation of *mutual funds, money market funds* and *money market certificates* compete vigorously for the small investor's dollar. Mutual funds, or investment funds

as they are also called, subdivide generally into growth fu which seek long-term profits in quality growth stocks, ine funds, which seek high present income from quality corp bonds, and tax exempt income funds which seek tax-fre come from investment in state and municipal bonds. M market funds emphasize safety by investing in federal go ment securities and federal government guaranteed secu and federal government guaranteed securities issued by a cies of the federal government, such as the "Fannie M securities discussed on page 211 which have become a fa ite of many of the money market funds. Money market tificates are generally term savings accounts offered by t and savings and loan associations at interest rates whic crease with the length of the term for which the money be left on deposit.

Stockholders' Rights

At least from the standpoint of a stockholder who has chased for investment purposes, his most important rig the right to dividends. Every stockholder has certain rights of greater or lesser importance, however.

Voting Rights: Unless otherwise provided in the articl incorporation, each share of stock is entitled to one vo However, as discussed earlier, voting rights are usually fined to common stock and may be confined to a parti class of common. The main exercise of the voting right the annual election of directors. However, as seen be there are other occasions on which the stockholder will reason to want to protect his rights by vote. Whatever matter voted upon, the stockholder may cast his ballot in son or by proxy. A *proxy* is a representative appointed stockholder to cast his vote for him, and *proxies* are wr instruments by which such representatives are appointed authorized.[83] A specimen form of proxy appears above.

Cumulative Voting: In the matter of voting for directo stockholder actually has more than one vote in the sense for each share he owns he may cast one vote for each o total number of directors to be elected. If five directors a be elected from those nominated—A, B, C, D, E, F, G, and J—the owner of one share has one vote each for the of his choice, so that he may cast one vote each for B, D G and H if they are his preferences. This is *ordinary* as tinguished from *cumulative* voting and, under it, his vo rights may be worthless for this reason: Suppose, as ag his one share and one vote, a second stockholder has shares and two votes. He casts two votes for each of A F, I and J. Each of them would win—two votes to one– he would have elected all of the directors. The stockho owning one share would have no representation on the bo

The idea of *cumulative voting* was conceived to pre such results. Cumulative voting enables minority stockho to gain some representation on the board. It permits a st holder to cast the total number of votes for one or more rectors that he might cast for all of the directors to be ele or, in terms of a mathematical formula, to cast for on more directors a number of votes equal to the number o shares multiplied by the number of directors to be electe In the hypothetical case above, the stockholder owning share cast one vote each for B, D, E, G and H, but rece no results from his five votes. Cumulative voting permits

---

[82]Corp. C. 700(a).

[83]Corp. C. 178. Note also §§ 705(a)(b), 702(a).

[84]Corp. C. 708(a).

PROXY

KNOW ALL MEN BY THESE PRESENTS: That I, the undersigned, being the owner of
............................shares of the capital stock of CALIFORNIA BRIDGE COMPANY, do hereby constitute and appoint J. B. Adams and M. C. Jones, or either of them, my true and lawful attorney for me and in my name, place and stead, to vote as my proxy upon the stock owned by me or standing in my name, at the annual meeting of the stockholders of said company to be held at 505 Skinner Building, San Francisco, California, on the 10th day of April, 1978, at 11 o'clock A. M., or on such other day as the meeting may thereafter be held by adjournment or otherwise, according to the number of votes I am now or may then be entitled to cast, hereby granting unto my said attorney full power and authority to act for me and in my name at said meeting or meetings in voting for directors of said company, or otherwise, and in the transaction of such other business as may properly come before the meeting, as fully as I could do if personally present, with full power of substitution and revocation, hereby ratifying and confirming all that my said attorney or substitute may do in my name, place and stead.

I hereby revoke all proxies heretofore given.

IN WITNESS WHEREOF, I have hereunto set my hand and seal this............................

day of ...., 1978

....(Seal)

....(Seal)

Witness:

....

---

ut his entire five votes on one or more candidates, which s him five votes to distribute as he sees fit, as against ten which the stockholder owning two shares may do the e thing. With his five votes, however, the stockholder ing one share will be able to elect two directors. To insure r election, the stockholder with ten votes may vote 3-3-3- r his candidates, A, C, F, and I. The stockholder with votes, on the other hand, can vote 3 and 2 for his cantes, B and D, and thereby elect them. Cumulative voting, , permits minority stockholders to obtain substantial repntation on the board of directors.

oting Trusts: A *voting trust* is a contract among a group tockholders to vote their stock as a unit. By this "orgad" voting, they can get the best results with the shares own, and such a voting trust may enable a minority group lect a majority of directors. It is for this purpose that most ng trusts are formed. In earlier years, voting trusts were n declared to be against public policy and void, but stat- in most states now permit them.[85] The voting trust argement is this: Those who join give an irrevocable proxy vote their shares to some person selected as *trustee,* and, he same time, turn over to him their stock certificates. He s them *voting trust certificates* in return to take the place heir stock certificates while the voting trust is in existence. trustee then votes the entire block of shares in such a way o gain maximum and, if possible, majority representation he board. By strategic voting, this unified group of votes gain majority control. Suppose a corporation with 1000 res and seven directors to be elected. Forty per cent of the res have formed a voting trust. Ten candidates are nomid for election. The voting trust, under cumulative voting, have 2800 votes, the remainder of the stock a total of 0 votes. The trustee of the voting trust apportions 700 s to each of four candidates. The remaining votes are ad out equally over seven candidates so as to give them votes each. The voting trust elects four of the seven dirs.

lass Votes—Amendment of Articles: Another voting rule esigned to protect minority stockholders. Suppose a cor- ation starts into business with a class of preferred stock

which is to get 7% cumulative dividends. At the time of formation, the corporation had to make this special offer to get the required capital. The corporation has operated for several years and is quite successful. The power to amend the articles of incorporation rests with the stockholders. The common stockholders have the voting rights. They hold a meeting and vote to amend the articles to reduce the dividend rate on the preferred stock from 12% to 10% in order to add this additional 2% to their own dividend rate. Just this has been done, and until the *class vote statute,* there was little that preferred stockholders could do about it.[86]

Class vote statutes in most states now prevent this type of unconscionable conduct by requiring that if a particular class of stock is to be adversely affected by an amendment of the articles, *that class* must vote approval of the amendment, which it would not do except in cases where it might be inclined to give up some of its rights to aid the corporation in time of difficulty. Corp. C. 903 is a representative class vote statute. Its subdivision (a)(4) would, for example, require approval of the majority of the class to be adversely affected by such important changes as reduction in dividend rate, conversion of cumulative preferred to non-cumulative, or reduction in the amount payable on liquidation.[87]

Organic Changes—Required Vote: As noted earlier, while the general powers of the corporation rest in the hands of the directors, certain organic or fundamental actions require approval of the stockholders. These include: (1) amendment of articles,[88] (2) increase or decrease of stock,[89] (3) consolidation or merger,[90] (4) sale of entire assets,[91] (5)

---

[86]In a clear cut case of fraudulent treatment of the preferred stockholders, they could have obtained equitable relief. Otherwise, there was nothing they could do.

[87]Corp. C. 903. Note also § 904.

[88]Corp. C. 902. Note §§ 903, 904 and § 910 re filing "Restated Articles of Incorporation."

[89]Corp. C. 903(a)(1). But note §§ 900(a), 202(e)(1) which permit the directors alone to increase the number of shares of a particular series if the articles give the directors authority to fix the number of shares of the series.

[90]Corp. C. 1201. Note §§ 1200, 1103. See page 301 re new California approach to mergers.

[91]Corp. C. 1001(a)(1).

[5]Corp. C. 2230. Note also § 706.

dissolution.[92] The percentage of stockholders required to approve such actions varies from state to state, ranging from a majority to two-thirds.

Preemptive Rights: It was the common law rule and is the general rule today that existing stockholders have the right to have the first opportunity to purchase new issues of stock in proportion to their existing holdings. This right is called the stockholder's *preemptive right*. Preemptive rights present an obstacle to new financing, and the tendency of modern statutes is to deny such rights unless expressly conferred by the articles of incorporation.[93] Where preemptive rights exist, a corporation which is about to issue new stock will send out *subscription warrants* or *stock warrants* to existing stockholders to enable them to exercise their preemptive rights. These stock warrants may be sold and often turn out to be a profitable incident of the original shares of stock. A new issue normally indicates that the corporation is succeeding. Usually, therefore, its stock will be desired by investors who will pay for the stock warrants to enable them to get it. The stock warrant then becomes something of an extra dividend to the stockholder.

Inspection of Records: Statutes usually give a stockholder the right to inspect and copy the books and records of the corporation at reasonable times for purposes reasonably related to his interests as a stockholder,[94] e.g., to determine whether or not the corporation is in condition to declare a dividend, but not for the purpose of conducting a mere "fishing expedition," as where token shares are purchased by a rival corporation for this purpose, or for such an ulterior purpose as getting a list of potential investors or customers. The books ordinarily required to be kept by a corporation and made available to its stockholders are (1) general books of account, (2) a book of minutes of directors' and stockholders' meetings, and (3) a share register showing names and addresses of stockholders and shares held.[95]

Annual Statement: Statutes usually require a corporation to send its stockholders an annual statement containing a balance sheet showing assets and liabilities, and a profit and loss statement for the year.[96]

Representative Suits: Where a corporation has a cause of action which the directors fail or refuse to prosecute, the stockholders, after demand upon the directors, may bring the action on behalf of the corporation. Such lawsuits are called *representative* or *derivative suits*. They may come about where directors pay a dividend when there is no proper fund. The directors become personally liable in such case and should, but would not, bring an action against themselves on behalf of the corporation.

Liability to Creditors

One of the important advantages of the corporate form of business organization is that its owners (stockholders) have *limited liability*—limited to their investment or agreed investment in the stock of the corporation. Ordinarily, therefore,

stockholders have no liability to unpaid creditors if the corporation fails. In two cases, stockholders have liability.

Partly Paid Shares: If stock is sold on the installment plan and the corporation becomes insolvent before the stock is fully paid for, the purchaser of the stock remains liable for the balance of the purchase price.[97] His contract is an asset of the corporation which creditors are entitled to have applied to the satisfaction of their claims.[98]

Watered Stock: Stock may be issued in exchange for property as well as for money. When this is to be done, it is for the board of directors to determine the value of the property for which the stock is to be issued. The directors may over-value the property, which will produce watered stock. The stockholder may become liable to creditors to the extent of the watering. If S owns property worth $40,000, and the directors fix its value as "$100,000" and issue stock of a par value of $100,000 for it, S may be liable to creditors for $60,000 if the corporation becomes insolvent.

● In some cases, the watering is clearly and intentionally fraudulent and these cause no problem. *Herron Co.* v. *Shaw*, 165 C. 668, 133 P. 488, is such a case. There, 695,000 shares of a par value of $1 each were issued to S in exchange for certain water rights, mining claims and mining machinery worth at best $69,500, or 1/10 the value of the stock issued therefor. The corporation became insolvent, with an unpaid deficit of $6000 to creditors. The creditors sued and were permitted to recover the $6000 from S.

● In other cases, a difficult problem may be presented. There are many cases where some amount of watering is "legitimate." Suppose that S owns property worth $50,000—an amount for which he could sell it for cash. C Corporation, newly formed, wants to buy S's property but would like to give him stock for it. S is willing to take stock but not $50,000 worth. It is one thing to sell for $50,000 cash and quite another to take $50,000 in stock. S may say, quite reasonably, "If you want my property in exchange for stock, you will have to give me $60,000 worth." The directors, realizing the reasonableness of this, resolve to issue to S $60,000 worth of stock in exchange for the property. May S be held for $10,000 if the corporation becomes insolvent? It depends on the rule of the particular state. There are two rules:

1. *"True Value Rule."* Some states say that directors may issue stock only to the extent of the true value of the property and that the stockholder is liable to the extent by which the true value of his property exceeds the value of the stock received by him—$10,000 in the instant case.

2. *"Good Faith Rule."* The great majority of states have adopted the *good faith rule*. Under this rule there is no liability of stockholder to creditors unless the overvaluation was fraudulent, which it would not have been in the instant case.

● Even though there is stock watering for which the stockholder is liable to creditors, the extent of liability depends on which of two rules is followed:

1. *"Trust Fund Theory."* This theory is that the amount of property or money which a corporation receives or should have received in exchange for its stock is in the nature of a *trust fund* held by the corporation for the benefit of its creditors. The corporation has no authority to deplete this fund which it does when it issues stock for property improperly

---

[92]Corp. C. 1900(a). Note §§ 1900(b), 1800(a).

[93]Corp. C. 406 so provides.

[94]Corp. C. 1601; 1600(c)(d).

[95]Corp. C. 16001601.

[96]Corp. C. 1501 makes this requirement but permits it to be waived in the bylaws in the case of a corporation with less than 100 shareholders.

[97]Corp. C. 410. Note § 412.

[98]Corp. C. 414.

[99]Corp. C. 409(e) would be considered to state this rule.

overvalued. The recipients of such stock having participated in this wrongful depletion of a trust fund are obligated to pay the difference between the fair value of the property and the face value of the stock received for it, i.e., to pay for the "water." Under this theory, it is held that creditors may recover from the stockholder whether they became creditors before or after the watering.

2. *"Fraud Theory."* The trust fund theory is followed in a majority of states as the legal basis for recovery from the recipient of watered stock. Some states have adopted another theory under which the watered stockholder's liability is less extensive. This is called the *fraud theory.* This treats stock watering as fraud in that it creates an ostensible capitalization which exceeds the real capitalization by an amount equal to the watering. Since creditors rely upon ostensible capitalization in extending credit, they are defrauded by the watering according to the reasoning of this rule. Since the watered stockholder has conspired with the corporation to perpetrate the fraud, he is liable to those damaged, the creditors. Under this rule, however, only creditors who became such *after* the watering would be entitled to recover from the stockholder since only they could have relied on and have been "deceived" by the misrepresented capitalization.[100]

Reorganization and Dissolution

In this section are grouped together and treated briefly the various things that bring about termination or complete or substantial change in the identity of a corporation.

Merger; Consolidation; Sale of Entire Assets

Merger, consolidation and sale by a corporation of its entire assets are a variety of devices for reorganization in which the shares of a new or expanded corporation are given in exchange for assets of a corporation which is absorbed and dissolved.

● Technically, *merger* is the purchase of one corporation by another. A Corporation buys out B Corporation which then becomes part of A, B being dissolved. *Consolidation,* by contrast, is the combination of two corporations to form a third, new and distinct corporation. A and B unite to form C Corporation. Both procedures ordinarily have as their purpose the creation of a larger corporate enterprise.

● The same thing may be accomplished by the sale by a corporation of its entire assets to a new corporation with a larger capitalization formed for the express purpose of buying the assets of the corporation to be absorbed, the new corporation then using its larger capitalization to expand upon the enterprise of the absorbed corporation.

● Under the new California code, any form of change in the identity of a corporation is a variety of *"reorganization."* Corp. C. 181 is basic. Section 181 conceives of three types of "reorganizations," as follows:

1. A merger of corporations pursuant to Corp. C. 1100-1111. Section 181 calls this a *"merger reorganization."*

2. The acquisition of one corporation by another by an exchange of stock of the acquiring corporation for the stock of the corporation acquired. Section 181 calls this an *"exchange reorganization."*

3. The acquisition of one corporation by another by an exchange of the stock of the acquiring corporation for the assets of the corporation acquired. Section 181 calls this a *"sale-of-assets reorganization."*

The new California code does not refer to "consolidation" and consolidation would presumably be a species of one of the three types of reorganization provided for by Section 181.

Note the concepts of "constituent corporation," "surviving corporation" and "disappearing corporation," defined in Sections 161, 190 and 165.

All of the Section 181 forms of reorganization must comply with the requirements of Sections 1200 and 1201. Section 1201 is, of course, designed to protect the shareholders of the corporations involved.

Dissolution and Winding Up

Dissolution of a solvent corporation ordinarily occurs only in connection with merger or consolidation designed to bring about a larger corporate enterprise. Otherwise, dissolution results from lack of success. Dissolution may be voluntary or involuntary and, so far as it is possible to make generalizations, the following may be made:

Voluntary Dissolution: Statutes provide for voluntary dissolution at any time by vote of some percentage of stockholders ranging from an even 50% to ⅔ Court approval of the dissolution and supervision of the winding up is generally not required.[101]

● Dissolution of a solvent, prosperous corporation may be enjoined by the minority stockholders where it is part of a scheme of the majority to "freeze out" the minority, e.g., where the majority intends to form a new corporation and buy up the assets of the corporation which they would dissolve.

Involuntary Dissolution: Involuntary or forced dissolution may generally be initiated by creditors of an insolvent corporation or by petition of some percentage of stockholders, ranging from 10% to 50%, for various causes—that directors have been guilty of fraud, mismanagement, abuse of authority or unfairness to minority stockholders; that the corporation's property is being wasted or misapplied; that there are deadlocked factions of directors and stockholders; or for such other reasons as may be prescribed.[102] Local statute may require appointment of a receiver to supervise the winding up of the corporation in this case or may give the court discretion to leave the matter in the hands of the directors.[103]

● To prevent abuse of the power of a minority to bring about dissolution, statutes in an increasing number of states give the majority stockholders a right to buy up at their fair value the shares of the minority who seek dissolution.[104]

Winding Up: In cases of voluntary dissolution, a certificate of election to dissolve is usually required to be filed with the Secretary of State after which the procedure of winding up takes place.[105] The corporation must immediately cease to do business except to the extent necessary to wind up its affairs. The directors must liquidate all or such of the assets as they deem necessary to effect the winding up.[106]

After all debts and liabilities have been paid or provided for, the directors must distribute the balance of assets among

---

[100]California follows the fraud theory. *Clark* v. *Tompkins,* 205 C. 373, 270 P. 946.

[101]Corp. C. 1900 et seq. Section 1900 requires approval of 50% of the voting shares.

[102]See Corp. C. 1800(a)(2)(3) re number of shareholders required to initiate proceedings; Corp. C. 1800(b) re grounds for involuntary dissolution.

[103]Corp. C. 1805(b), 1803.

[104]Corp. C. 2000.

[105]Corp. C. 1901.

[106]Corp. C. 2001.

the shareholders in accordance with their liquidation preferences, if any. Distribution may be made in money or in kind, i.e., in money or in property or securities if this can be done fairly and ratably.[107]

Upon completion of distribution, the directors must file with the Secretary of State a certificate showing that the corporation has been wound up, its liabilities satisfied, and the balance of assets distributed. At this point the corporate existence ceases.[108]

● In cases of involuntary dissolution, the court decrees dissolution and orders winding up by the directors under supervision of the court or by a receiver.[109] The procedure of liquidation, payment of debts and distribution of assets is the same as in the case of voluntary proceedings.

Foreign Corporations

Definition; "Doing Business"

The usual concept of *"foreign corporation"* is that it is a corporation incorporated under the laws of one state and doing business in another. Close questions arise as to when a corporation is "doing business" in another state so as to require it to qualify as a foreign corporation. Two California cases holding that business was being carried on within the state may be noted as illustrations. In *Millbank* v. *Standard Motor Co.*, 132 C.A. 67, 22 P.2d 271, a New Jersey corporation which sold engines to California purchasers out of New Jersey but which sent an employee to this state to service and maintain the engines was held to be doing "a substantial and important branch of its ordinary business" here. In *Thew Shovel Co.* v. *Superior Court*, 35 C.A.2d 183, 95 P.2d 149, a corporation which sold its products through distributors in this state was held to be doing business here despite provisions in the distributorship contracts to the effect that the distributors were independent contractors and not agents of the corporation.

---

[107]Corp. C. 2004.

[108]Corp. C. 1905. Note § 1907.

[109]Corp. C. 1804-1805, 1808-1809.

"Qualifying"

If "doing business" in another state, the corporation must *"qualify"* to do business there, one of the important requirements of which is that it must permit itself to be sued there. To that end, the corporation must file with the Secretary of State of the foreign state a copy of its articles together with a statement setting forth its home office and office within the foreign state, and the name and address of a person or corporation within the foreign state on whom legal process may be served in any legal action against the corporation. The statement must also consent to service of process upon the corporation by delivery to the Secretary of State if the agent named by the corporation cannot be found at the address given.[110]

Penalties

Penalties for not complying with the requirements for qualifying are (1) fine,[111] and (2) denial of use of the courts of the foreign state to enforce contracts.[112]

Even if a foreign corporation does not "qualify," it will be subject to suit in a state in which it engages in business activity if, according to the test laid down by the United States Supreme Court, it has such "minimum contacts" with the state as to make it fair to require it to submit to suit there. (*International Shoe Co.* v. *Washington*, 326 U.S. 310.)

New California Law

The new California Corporations Code would define a "foreign corporation" as a corporation formed under the laws of another state.[113] Corp. C. 2115 subjects a "foreign corporation" meeting this definition to much of the California General Corporation Law if, in effect, more than one-half of its stock is owned in California and more than 50% of its business is done in California and it is not exempted from the provisions of Section 2115 by the provision of Section 2115(e).

---

[110]Corp. C. 2105-2106.

[111]Corp. C. 2203.

[112]Corp. C. 2203(c).

[113]Corp. C. 170, 167.

CHAPTER 12

Insurance

History

California Insurance Code,[1] Section 22, says that "Insurance is a contract whereby one undertakes to indemnify another against loss, damage or liability arising from a contingent or unknown event." This definition covers the two general types of insurance which are: (1) Insurance designed to protect a person against loss to himself, such as fire insurance on property owned by him, or against loss to himself or his family, such as life or accident insurance protecting him or his family against the loss of his earning power by reason of his injury or death. (2) Insurance designed to place in another, an insurance company, one's responsibility for wrongful injury to a third person or his property—liability insurance.

Historically, insurances of the first type long preceded those of the second. The earliest insurance was on goods being transported from one place to another, the first vestiges of which are found as early as 3000 B.C. on the great caravan cargoes of the traders of that day. A thousand years later, the Phoenicians induced much of commerce and trading to the sea lanes and with this came the first beginnings of marine insurance, insurance on ships and their cargoes. Marine insurance has been with us ever since and is generally thought of as the first great field of insurance.

In the Roman era came the first forms of life insurance. Burials were expensive, and "burial societies" were formed into which the amount necessary for a proper funeral could be paid on the installment plan during life. Gradually these were widened in scope so that one could also pay in additional amounts which would go to his family upon his death and, so, became an antecedent of the mutual life insurance company of today. Actually, however, the most important form of life insurance of that earlier day was an incident of the ever-growing field of marine insurance. By way of minimizing their losses, those who furnished marine insurance in turn sought and obtained life insurance on the captains of the ships which they insured, so that if the ship sank and the marine insurer had to pay, he could recoup at least part of his loss by collecting insurance on the life of the captain who went down with the ship.

The modern history of insurance began in Lloyd's famous coffee house in London in the 17th century. Edward Lloyd's place, located in the heart of the city's maritime district, was the popular rendezvous of ships' officers and a natural clearing house of information on current shipping activities. Those who engaged in the business of insuring ships and their car-

goes soon gravitated there to be as close as possible to the scene of their activities. The procedure by which insurance came to be written was this: Suppose that the ship "Peerless" was about to sail with a cargo of textiles. The owners of the ship and its cargo would prepare a paper on the top half of which was set out all of the pertinent data—name of ship and its value, nature of cargo and its value, identity of captain and crew, itinerary, etc. This was passed among the assembled insurers who would write on the lower half of the paper the percentage of the risk that each was willing to assume until the entire amount of the risk was covered. Thus, if $45,000 of coverage was required, insurer A might take $20,000, insurer B $15,000 and insurer C the remaining $10,000. They would then fix a charge or *premium* for their agreement to insure. If the ship made its journey without mishap, they split this in proportion to the percentage of risk assumed. If the ship or its cargo were damaged or sank, they paid the loss in proportion to percentage of risk assumed. Originally, these various insurers were wealthy individuals or families, but before long many partnerships and joint stock companies became insurers. Because they made their insuring agreements by signing beneath the information relating to the ship and its cargo, they became known as *underwriters*, which is the historical derivation of that term.[2]

Somewhat ironically, it took the world's greatest fire to bring fire insurance into existence. This was the London fire of 1666, immediately after which the first fire insurance company of importance was formed.

The last noteworthy development in insurance in England was life insurance designed to serve the purposes primarily served by such insurance today—protection of the family in the event of death of the wage earner. Mutual life insurance societies for this purpose began to be formed in the 18th century and made rapid strides thereafter.

In this country, marine insurance was again the earliest form of insurance, dating back to as early as 1721. Fire insurance came a few decades later, although it took two major conflagrations—the New York and Chicago fires—to make the public really fire insurance conscious. The first known life insurance organization was the "Corporation for the Relief of Poor and Distressed Presbyterian Ministers and the Poor and Distressed Widows and Children of Presbyterian Ministers," formed in 1759, the purpose of which is self-evident. It is still in existence today.

Liability insurance was unknown until the 19th century. In the period from 1850 to 1900, the theory that industry should bear responsibility for industrial accidents, i.e., for the damages suffered by workmen injured on the job, became established, and employers sought and were furnished employer's liability or "workmen's compensation insurance" by which

---

[1]The insurance law of California was removed from the Civil Code and placed in a separate Insurance Code in 1935. This code covers the whole field of insurance—the general law; the various types of companies that are permitted, their capital, and other requirements; the various types of policies and provisions that must be contained in them; and qualifications of agents and brokers. This code is referred to throughout this chapter as "Ins. C." All forms of insurance companies in this state are under the supervision and regulation of the state Insurance Commissioner.

[2]In the insurance field today, an underwriter is one who evaluates risks and determines the premiums to be charged and/or decides whether insurance should be issued in particular cases or to particular persons.

the insurance company answered for an employer who became liable to an injured employee. (Workmen's compensation insurance is now called workers' compensation insurance in California.)

The 20th century brought the automobile, and the automobile brought automobile liability insurance, which indemnifies the owner or operator of an automobile against liability arising out of negligent operation. Other important forms of liability insurance also developed in this era: owners', landlords' and tenants' policies protecting these various classes of persons against liability for injuries suffered by third persons on the premises; products liability insurance indemnifying a manufacturer against liability to persons injured in connection with the use of his products; comprehensive personal liability policies indemnifying the individual against all forms of liability which might be incurred by reason of persons injured in his home or otherwise (except in the operation of motor vehicles); and comprehensive commercial liability policies in which all forms of liability which might be incurred by a businessperson or business organization were insured against in a single policy: liability for persons injured on the premises, for injuries suffered in connection with use of the product, for liability resulting from negligent operation of vehicles by employees, etc.

With the development of the railroad as a transporter of freight, insurance coverage became necessary. Having no other departments within themselves to handle this business, the insurance companies gave it to their marine departments with their experience in the insurance of ocean borne freight. For many years thereafter, all insurance on freight whether carried by ocean or inland transportation, was classified as marine insurance. As inland transportation began to outweigh its rival, however, ocean marine insurance became that on ocean freight, inland marine on inland freight.

Then, the whole cycle repeated itself. Until the late twenties, insurance on personal property was largely confined to that located on particular premises and was written as an incident to fire insurance on the property on which the personal property was located. Household furnishings were insured as an incident to fire insurance on the house, and business equipment and inventory as an incident to fire insurance on the business building. But, again, an insurance need arose and, as always, an insurance to accommodate it. Insurance was needed on goods and personal property wherever located—while temporarily stored at one place or another, while being moved about in the owner's vehicles, while being worn, etc. Having no other departments within themselves to which to give this business, the insurance companies gave it to the department to which it was most closely related, the inland marine department. These policies on personal property wherever located became and are known as *floaters* or floater policies, and a wide variety exist today—fur floaters, jewelry floaters, musical instruments floaters, etc., and comprehensive floaters covering all of one's personal property wherever located. All of these coverages are classified as inland marine insurance, but just as it was and is a misnomer to call insurance on freight carried by railroads and motor carriers inland "marine" insurance, so also is it to classify general personal property coverage as "inland marine."

Types of Insurance

The variety of particular types of insurance is infinite and ever increasing with new needs and demands. Ins. C. 100 says that insurance "is divided into the following classes," listing twenty-two—life, disability, marine, fire, plate glass, sprink-ler, boiler and machinery, burglary, liability, common carrier liability, automobile, aircraft, team and vehicle, workers' compensation, title, mortgage, mortgage guaranty, credit, insolvency, surety, legal, and miscellaneous. Sections 101-120 define each of these.[3] Section 120 is also designed to leave it open for any other legitimate form of insurance to be developed by permitting "any insurance not included in the foregoing classes, and which is a proper subject of insurance." The importance of these various classes of insurance and the policies issued in connection with them are treated in detail in sections that follow.

In the world of insurance, companies are formed to deal in only particular kinds of these various classes of insurance. Life companies deal exclusively with life and disability (accident and health) insurance. Companies may be formed to engage exclusively in the writing of marine and related lines and fire and related lines.[4] *Casualty* companies write the coverages which insure against accidents and, so, write all of the various lines of liability insurance.

All insurance however, may be classified as being either:

1. Insurance on the person—life, health and accident;
2. Insurance on property—fire, marine, inland marine, etc.; or
3. Liability insurance by which one indemnifies himself against liability to third persons for injury to such persons or their property: automobile liability, products liability, etc.

Types of Insurers

Stock Companies

These are simply private corporations formed to engage in the insurance business. As in the case of other corporations, the stock company obtains its original working capital from the sale of stock to stockholders who become its owners.

Mutual Companies

Theoretically at least, these are cooperative insurance plans operated solely for the benefit of the policyholders. A number of persons who agree to take out some minimum amount of insurance become associated, paying a premium which creates the original insurance fund. The basic insurance fund and the original working capital, then, are obtained directly from the policyholders, and there is no separate group of stockholders-owners who provide the capital as in the stock company. The

---

[3]*Credit* insurance is insurance against bad debt loss.

Insolvency insurance is insurance protecting against the failure of an insurance company to perform on its policies because of insolvency.

Mortgage insurance covers all loss sustained by a lender by virtue of nonpayment of a mortgage, whereas *mortgage guaranty* insurance is limited to payment of the top portion of the mortgage debt. Regarding mortgage guaranty insurance, see further Mortgage Guaranty Insurance Act, Ins.C. 12640.01 et seq.

Legal insurance reimburses the insured for certain kinds of expenses of legal services now being provided by legal services groups.

Miscellaneous insurance includes insurance against loss from damage done by lightning, windstorm, tornado or earthquake, and insurance indemnifying the producer of a theatrical or sporting event against loss by reason of postponement or cancellation due to death or illness of performers. It also includes any "proper subject of insurance," not otherwise provided for, as shown in the text, above.

[4]See the section on fire policies at page 313 for lines related to fire insurance.

"company," i.e., the recipient of these agreements and premiums, which issues the policies, may be and usually is a corporation. In the United States as a whole, mutual companies may now outnumber stock companies.

Reciprocals or Inter-Insurance Exchanges

These resemble mutual companies. A is appointed by some minimum number of persons as their agent to write contracts of insurance between each and every other one of their number. As their common agent, he then writes contracts between C and D, G and H, H and C, L and D, and so on, by which each reciprocally insures the other, each of them being issued a policy by A to show this. Each pays A a premium when they appoint him as their agent, and this becomes the insurance fund. A forms himself into a corporation, and this becomes the "company." Each new policyholder becomes a reciprocal insurer with all of the existing policyholders, and at all times the policyholders are simply insuring each other. The company's application forms will provide that each new applicant appoints the company as its *attorney in fact* (agent) to write contracts of insurance between the applicant and the existing policyholders and between him and all future applicants. The advantage of the inter-insurance exchange is that, like the mutual company, it can give lower premium rates. The disadvantage is that the policyholders are assessable until certain reserves are established. The inter-insurance exchange has enjoyed its greatest success in the automobile insurance field.[6]

Associations of Underwriters; Reinsurance

The Lloyd's of London type of insuring arrangement discussed previously, is referred to as an association of underwriters—the joinder of a group of individual insurers who split a risk among them and divide the premium received in proportion to the percentage of the risk assumed. We do not have organizations of this type in this country, but our insurance companies do largely the same thing by the process of reinsuring. Suppose that X Insurance Company is called upon to write a policy on a ten million dollar fire risk. Should the risk insured be destroyed and the policy become payable, X would suffer a severe loss. Hence, X will "farm out" a substantial portion of the risk to other companies with whom it has reinsuring arrangements, with each of perhaps four or five companies assuming a portion of the risk. X will reciprocate by taking portions of risks insured by these other companies.[7]

Federal and State Governments

The federal and state governments have entered the field of insurance to some extent. Old Age and Survivors' Insurance

provided for by the Social Security Act is an annuity and life insurance program set up by the federal government. The Federal Deposit Insurance Corporation plan permits banks to acquire stock in a corporation which in return indemnifies the bank's depositors against loss of deposits in the event of the bank's insolvency. Mortgage insurance, as provided for by the National Housing Act and the Servicemen's Readjustment Act, "insures" banks on loans made for home purchase and construction, although this is more accurately suretyship or guaranty rather than insurance, since what the government is actually doing is guaranteeing the payment of the purchase price by the individual.

● Every state now has a workers' compensation law which requires an employer to carry insurance that will compensate an employee for medical expenses and lost earnings during a period of incapacitation resulting from an on-the-job injury. Whenever a state makes a form of insurance mandatory, it becomes necessary for the state to set up a way in which the insurance can be obtained in case private companies are not willing to write it. For example, private companies may not wish to write compensation insurance for employees of a business which transports explosives. In California, Sections 11770 et seq. of the Insurance Code provide for a State Compensation Insurance Fund for this purpose. Any employer may obtain the required workers' compensation insurance from this organization whether or not private companies are willing to give it to him. This fund, then, is actually an insurance company operated by the state.

● Many states, including California, have made automobile liability insurance virtually mandatory by so-called financial responsibility acts.[8] Again, some method of making such insurance available to those whom private companies would consider substandard risks and would not insure voluntarily had to be set up. In California, this takes the form of the California Assigned Risk Plan under which the state rotates risks among the various private companies in this manner: A wishes insurance which a private company is not willing to give A voluntarily. A then applies to C.A.R.P. It has a list of private companies—M, N, O, P, Q, R and S. Assuming that it is O's turn, it assigns A's application to O, which must then furnish him with the minimum coverages required by the financial responsibility act. Next, B seeks insurance. His application is assigned to P, C's application to Q, and so on. Assignments are made in proportion to the premium volumes of the companies involved.

Self-Insurers

Large business organizations may find it advantageous to become *self-insurers*, i.e., to set up their own insurance funds within themselves, at least as respects certain types of insurance. Many large concerns are self-insurers, e.g., for workers' compensation insurance. Rather than paying premiums to an insurance company for such insurance, they set up their own fund, which must be approved by and is under the supervision of the Insurance Commissioner in the case of workers' compensation insurance.

---

[5][*Deleted*].

[6]Inter-insurance exchanges are covered by Ins. C. 12801530. Sections 1300, 1301, 1303 and 1305 are basic sections. Section 1300 provides that "Any persons may exchange reciprocal or inter-insurance contracts with one another providing insurance other than life . . ." Section 1301: "Such persons are termed subscribers." Section 1303: "The organization under which such subscribers so exchange contracts is termed a reciprocal or inter-insurance exchange." Section 1305: "Such contracts may be executed by an attorney-in-fact, agent or other representative duly authorized and acting for such subscribers under powers of attorney. Such authorized person is termed the attorney, and may be a corporation."

[7]Ins. C. 620-623 permit and provide for reinsurance. Section 620 defines reinsurance: "A contract of reinsurance is one by which an insurer procures a third person to insure him against loss or liability by reason of such original insurance."

---

[8]These provide that an uninsured person's driver's license shall be suspended, if he has an accident and does not post with the Department of Motor Vehicles a cash bond sufficient to cover damages to the other automobile. California's financial responsibility act is Sections 16000-16500 of the Vehicle Code. To be exempt from the application of these provisions one must carry $15,000 (one person injured)/30,000 (2 or more persons injured)/5,000 (property damage) insurance. Section 16056.

Types of Producers

Agents and brokers are the mediums through which insurance is sold, the *producers* of insurance as they are called.

Agents and Brokers

Agents are of various types and operate under various types of arrangements with the insurance companies for which they act. They all have one thing in common which is that they represent the insurance company in bringing about the insurance policy, and it is in this respect that they differ basically from brokers, who are agents of and represent the person seeking insurance.

● Agents are persons in business for themselves, on a commission basis. They may maintain their own places of business or work out of company offices. The "agency" consists entirely of an agency contract with the company such as that on page 59, which permits the agent to "*bind*" the company to a particular person desiring insurance, immediately, and pending issuance of a policy.[9] The agent, of course, receives commissions on insurance sold. The important advantage of agency over brokership is the power to bind, together with the fact that the agent may receive a higher rate of commission on insurance sold.

● Theoretically, a *broker* is one engaged to attempt to procure insurance for a person. He is the agent of the person seeking insurance from the company rather than the agent of the company seeking to sell insurance to the person. Like the agent, however, he is paid by the company in the form of commissions on insurance placed with a particular company. The same person may move in and out of the one category or the other. Suppose that M is an agent for X Automobile Insurance Company. T, a good risk, comes to M's place of business seeking insurance. M, in his capacity of agent, places it with X. Later, U, a bad risk, comes in for insurance. M knows X will not take U's insurance, so he tries to place it with a company which will take more speculative risks. In so doing, he acts as a broker on behalf of U. M may eventually have to place U's insurance with C.A.R.P., for which he will receive a small commission.

General Agents

General agencies are clearing houses for the efforts of agents and brokers. The general agent's powers vary with the insurance company and the general agency, and the general agency contract is a tailor-made one, some general agencies conferring broad authority and power upon the general agent, others very limited powers. A true general agency should have some degree of authority to pass upon applications, issue policies, adjust claims, and the like.

Application of Agency Law

Since agents and brokers are agents either for companies or persons seeking insurance, the ordinary rules of agency law apply to their actions. A variety of cases and situations may be noted in this respect.

● The principal will be liable for acts within the apparent scope of the agent's authority. Thus, in *Cronin* v. *Coyne and Mercer Casualty Co.*, 6 C.A.2d 205, 44 P.2d 385, a general

agency covered a taxicab company. The head office refused to approve the policy and so wired the general agent. Despite this, the general agency decided to leave the coverage in force until it could place the insurance with another company and, before this could be done, a claim arose on the policy. Held, the insurance company was liable. But in *Hargett* v. *Gulf Ins. Co.*, 12 C.A.2d 449, 55 P.2d 1258, where, in violation of policy provisions, a mortgage on property was not shown and the policy provided that provisions could not be waived without written indorsement upon or attached to the policy, it was held that the company was not liable; that not even a general agent could "waive" express provisions of the policy.

● The agency rule that notice to the agent is imputed to the principal often applies. Thus, in *Eagle Indem. Co.* v. *Ind. Acc. Comm.*, 92 C.A.2d 222, 206 P.2d 877, the company was held where, by mistake, there was a failure to issue a workers' compensation policy covering all employees of the particular employer, and the agent who had obtained the policy knew that one covering all employees had been requested. By contrast, in *Rizzuto* v. *Nat. Reserve Ins. Co.*, 92 C.A.2d 143, 206 P.2d 431, it was held that knowledge of a broker not disclosed to the company in the application (that the property, which was insured as a barber shop, was also used in part as a cleaning shop) was not imputed to the company since the broker was the agent of the person seeking insurance and not of the company.

● In one important respect, the misconduct of a broker may be charged to the insurance company rather than to the insured. Suppose that A goes to B, broker, for automobile insurance which B obtains from X Company. A may be given 30 or 60 days credit, i.e., such period of time within which to pay the premium. Thirty days later, A pays the premium to B for transmission to the company. B misappropriates this and other moneys received in the same way. It would seem that A would suffer the loss and would have to pay another premium. But, in many states, either by statute or by judicial interpretation of the situation, the broker is deemed to become the agent of the company for the purposes of collecting premiums in such cases.[10] Courts in such states say that while the broker is the agent of the person seeking insurance during the stage of procurement of the policy, the insurance company adopts him as its agent for collection of the premium where it issues the policy and authorizes him to collect the premium at the expiration of the credit period. Hence, the company suffers the loss and must leave the insurance paid for in force.

General Nature of Insurance Contracts

As stated in Ins. C. 22 on page 303, insurance is "a contract" and, like other contracts, must fulfill the essential elements required of all contracts.

Offer and Acceptance

The application for insurance is the *offer*.[11] Theoretically, issuance of a policy with intent for it to be operative is the *acceptance*. The effective date of coverage, however, may be considerably in advance of the date that the person to be insured actually receives the policy. In life insurance applications and policies, it is usually provided that the insurance

---

[9]This power of an agent to bind does not mean that the company must issue a policy, however. When it receives an application from the agent, it may decide that it does not wish to insure the applicant and may so notify him. The "bind" of the agent makes the company liable, however, until it notifies the applicant that it does not wish to insure him.

---

[10]The Insurance Commissioner has so held in California.

[11]This must not be taken too literally. In many forms of insurance, written applications are now often dispensed with and the only "application" may be a telephone call requesting the insurance.

shall take effect as of the date of the application provided that the first premium is paid at that time and/or the insured has not become an increased risk in the interim. So, a policy of life insurance applied for on May 1, will bear that date even though it is not delivered until June 15. In other forms of insurance where immediate coverage is needed, an immediate "bind" may be effected. Agents generally have binding authority for fire insurance, including the issuance, when needed by a lender, e.g., of a written binder or cover note such as the "binder" form on the following pages, signed by an employee of the company's local office authorized to issue binders. These are, in effect, interim or temporary policies giving the desired coverage until the company issues its regular policy.[12] Binding authority for automobile insurance is more restricted than for property insurance.

• A number of cases will bring out additional points on offer and acceptance: (1) Actual receipt of the policy is not necessary if the company has parted with possession of it with intention that it shall be operative. Thus, in *Paez* v. *Mutual Indem. Acc. H. & L. Ins. Co.*, 116 C.A. 654, 3 P.2d 69, the policy was in the mail from the local office of the company to the agent who had procured the insurance for delivery to the insured when the insured died. Held, the company was obligated to pay the policy since it was intended to be operative when it left the hands of the local office. (2) Where an application for insurance is received by the company, it must act upon it without undue delay—accept it by issuing a policy or reject it. If by mistake, procrastination or for other reason, the application is not acted upon, the company may be held to be estopped to deny liability if a loss occurs which would have been covered by the policy, since the applicant will have refrained from obtaining coverage elsewhere in the belief that he has obtained it from the company applied to, and that it is just a matter of time until he gets the policy. Thus, in *Travelers' Ins. Co.* v. *Taliaferro*, 176 Okla. 242, 54 P.2d 1069, the company was held where an application for workmen's compensation insurance was not acted upon within 10 days and an employee who would have been covered by the policy was injured. The company was also held in *Stark* v. *Pioneer Casualty Co.*, 139 C.A. 577, 34 P.2d 731, where an application for automobile insurance was mislaid in the selling agent's office. But in *Linnastruth* v. *Mut. Benefit H. & Acc. Assn.*, 22 C.2d 216, 137 P.2d 833, where it took 16 days to process a life policy and the injuries causing death were suffered 2 days before issuance of the policy, it was held that there was no estoppel upon which the company might be held.

Competent Parties

As respects the insured, ordinary contract rules apply. Thus, a minor may disaffirm a policy and get back the entire premium paid, or keep it in force and collect in event of loss.[13]

Consideration

Consideration, on the part of the insured, is the premium paid or agreed to be paid by him; on the part of the insurer, the promise of indemnity made by it.

Legal Purpose—Insurable Interest

The only problem of legality is that of insurable interest. In the case of insurance on property and on the person, it is *insurable interest* that makes the difference between an illegal wager and a valid contract of insurance.[14] If a person could "insure" the life of another person to whom he bore no family or business relationship, the "insurance" would be nothing more than a bet between parties as to how long the third person would live. Valid insurance requires a monetary interest to be protected, and it is the presence of this factor that constitutes an insurable interest in the person or thing insured. By way of distinguishing insurance from gambling, it is often said that a gambling contract creates a risk or contingency where none exists; that in an insurance contract a risk already exists against which the insurance contract merely protects.

Insurable Interest in Property: One has an *insurable interest in property* when he has a legal relationship to property such that loss of or damage to it may cause monetary loss to the insured.[15] This interest must be present both at the time the policy is taken out and at the time the loss occurs.[16]

• Legal relationships which give rise to an insurable interest in property are of two general types:

1. Legal or equitable ownership interests, as of fee simple owners, life tenants, mortgagors, trustors in deeds of trust, conditional buyers, pledgors, etc.

2. Security interests as of mortgagees, beneficiaries of deeds of trust, secured parties under Uniform Commercial Code security agreements, conditional sellers, pledgees, etc.[17] If the property which serves as security is damaged or destroyed, the secured party may suffer monetary loss by reason of the fact that the debtor has no other assets from which the amount owed may be recovered.

• The measure of a person's insurable interest in property is the extent of his monetary interest therein.[18] Thus, a mortgagee has an insurable interest only to the extent of the balance due on the note, the conditional seller to the extent of the balance due on the contract, etc. Where there are these divided interests in property, usually one policy will be issued for the full value of the property but protecting both parties— mortgagor and mortgagee, conditional seller and buyer, etc.— by the attachment of a *loss payable endorsement* providing that in the event of loss, the party having the security interest shall first be paid the balance owed him; or by making the policy payable to the parties "as their respective interests may appear," or on like terms which bring about the same result.

Insurable Interest in Persons: An *insurable interest in the person of another* exists when there is a legal relationship by blood, marriage or contract between the person taking out the

---

[12]Ins. C. 382, which calls them *covering notes,* permits issuance of binders for as long as 90 days.

[13]Ins. C. 10112 makes one exception—minors over 16 are bound on life and disability policies.

[14]Ins. C. 280: "If the insured has no insurable interest, the contract is void."

[15]Ins. C. 281 defines an insurable interest in property as follows: "Every interest in property, or any relation thereto, or liability in respect thereof, of such nature that a contemplated peril might directly damnify the insured, is an insurable interest."

[16]Ins. C. 286: "An interest in property insured must exist when the insurance takes effect, and when the loss occurs . . .; an interest in the life or health of a person must exist when the insurance takes effect, but need not exist thereafter or when the loss occurs."

[17]In *Hayward Lumber & Inv. Co.* v. *Lyders,* 139 C.A. 517, 34 P.2d 805, it was held that one having a mechanic's or materialman's lien had an insurable interest in the property on which the lien was held.

[18]Ins. C. 284: ". . . the measure of an insurable interest in property is the extent to which the insured might be damnified by loss or injury thereof."

CASUALTY INSURANCE ORDER BLANK
AND FIFTEEN DAY BINDER
No._____
(Separate blank may be used for each kind of insurance or for endorsements)

(1) Name of Applicant_____
                                                    (If Co-partnership give names)

_____

Owner_____

Receiver_____   Tenant_____

(2) Applicant is: Individual_____Co-partnership_____Corporation_____Trustee_____   Lessee_____

(3) P.O. or Business Address_____
                                     (No.)   (Street)   (City or Town)   (County)   (State)

(4) Business or Occupation_____

(5) Kind of Insurance and type of Policy Desired_____

(6) Location of Risk_____
                                     (No.)   (Street)   (City or Town)   (County)   (State)

(7)* Building is_____Portion Occupied_____
        (State whether business building or private residence, two-family house, apartment, hotel, boarding or lodging house)

(8)* If a residence, is business conducted in the portion of building occupied by applicant?_____

_____
                                                    (If so, describe)

(9) Coverage effective from_____Policy Term desired_____
                                     (Date)   (Hour)   (Years)

(10) Name of the Company last insuring this risk_____

(11) No Insurance of the applicant of the kind ordered herein has been cancelled or recalled, or renewal thereof declined by an Insurance Company during the past year within the knowledge of the applicant or the agent or broker placing this risk except as follows:_____

_____

(12)* Applicant has no Burglary, Robbery or Theft insurance except:_____

(13)* Applicant has not sustained, nor received indemnity for, any loss or damage by Burglary, Robbery or Theft within the last five years, except:_____

* Complete for Burglary, Robbery or Theft insurance only.

DESCRIPTION OF RISK
(Insert here details concerning kind of insurance desired)

C O V E R A G E				
BODILY INJURY		PROPERTY DAMAGE		BURGLARY
LIMITS	MEDICAL PAYMENTS	AMOUNT		AMOUNT
AGGREGATE		AGGREGATE		

This application is made with the understanding that the rates and rules applicable to the coverages desired are those contained in the manual in use by the Company on the date insurance becomes effective.

Submitted to_____
                                                    (Name of Company)

By_____
              (Agent or Broker)   (Address)

When accepted by the Company the applicant is insured in the above stated amount(s) in accordance with the binder on the back hereof.

Accepted by_____A.M.
                                                    (Date)   (Hour)   P.M.

(Reverse side of this form on following page)

Fifteen Day Binder

The Company accepting this risk acknowledges itself bound by the terms, conditions and limitations of the policy (or policies) of insurance in current use by the Company for the kind (or kinds) of insurance specifically ordered on the other side of this Binder from the effective date and hour specified therein and the insured accepts this Binder under such terms, conditions and limitations. Unless previously cancelled as hereinafter provided, this Binder shall terminate at 12:00 o'clock noon on the fifteenth day following the day upon which this Binder takes effect. Acceptance by the insured of a policy (or policies) as ordered in place hereof shall render this Binder null and void. This Binder may be cancelled at any time by the insured or by the broker or agent who placed the risk by notice to the Company or by the surrender of this Binder stating when thereafter such cancellation shall be effective. This Binder may be cancelled by the Company by written notice to the insured and to the agent or broker who placed the risk stating when, not before 12:00 o'clock noon of the third business day following the date of mailing, such cancellation shall be effective. A premium charge at the rates and in compliance with the rules of the Manual of Rates in use by the Company when this Binder becomes effective will be made for the time this Binder is in effect if no policy of insurance in place hereof is issued and accepted by the insured.

NOTE: Reference to time in this Binder shall mean Standard time at the place of issue.

---

insurance and the person insured, such that the person taking out the insurance may suffer monetary loss if the person insured dies or becomes incapacitated. As in the case of insurance on property, then, there are the two elements of legal relationship and potential monetary loss.

• Every person is deemed to have an insurable interest in his own life,[19] and since it is only the person taking out insurance who is required to have an insurable interest, any person may take out insurance on his own life and make anyone he wishes the beneficiary of the policy. Thus, while A cannot take out insurance on the life of B, a friend, since A would not have an insurable interest in B, B may take out insurance on his own life and name A as beneficiary of the policy. If this is a subterfuge to avoid the requirement of insurable interest, however, the policy will not be enforced. Thus, if A furnishes the money with which B pays premiums, with the whole thing being a scheme to avoid the insurable interest requirement, the policy will be illegal and not enforceable.

• An insurable interest in the person of another need exist only at the time insurance is taken out, and the policy may be continued and collected upon even though the insurable interest ceases.[20] So, if a wife takes out insurance on the life of her husband and, later, the marriage is dissolved, the wife may continue the policy and collect the proceeds on the husband's death. Or, if a corporation insures the life of its president who thereafter retires, the corporation may continue the policy and recover the proceeds upon his death. In modern insuring, this latter case is highly unlikely, however, since policies of this kind have an express provision for termination upon severance of the relationship which created the insurable interest.

BLOOD RELATIONSHIPS. This is the first of three general types of legal relationships that give rise to an insurable interest in the life of another. The general rule seems to be that the potential monetary loss which must accompany the relationship must rest upon a legal right to support or other monetary benefits from the person insured. Thus, a minor child has an insurable interest in the life of a parent because he has a legal right to be supported by the parent until he reaches the age of majority. And, conversely, a parent has an insurable

interest in the life of a minor child since the parent has a legal right to the services and earnings of the child until the child's majority. Under this general rule, however, an adult child would not have an insurable interest in the life of his parent since there is no longer any legal right to support from the parent; and for the same reason a sister would not have an insurable interest in the life of a brother. It makes no difference that the child or sister is in fact being supported by the parent or brother, since the test of insurable interest under the general rule is whether or not there is a legal right to such support.

• The rule is otherwise in many states, however, including California, where there is an extremely broad statute on the point. Ins. C. 10110(b) says that a person has an insurable interest in any person "on whom he depends wholly or in part for education or support." Thus, in California, support in fact is the test, not whether there is a legal right to it. So, in California and other states having a like rule, a sister could insure the life of her brother if she were being supported by him. And the California statute goes further. It eliminates the necessity of blood relationship, and it has been held that under the California statute, a person can insure the life of a friend if in fact he is receiving support from the friend.

MARITAL RELATIONSHIPS. That reciprocal insurable interests arise out of the marital relationship goes without saying. Each spouse is entitled to the support and services of the other and it is herein that potential monetary loss lies.

CONTRACT RELATIONSHIPS. There are two general types of contract relationships that give rise to insurable interests: *creditor-debtor relationships* and *business relationships*.

1. *Creditor-Debtor Relationships.* An unsecured creditor has an insurable interest in the life of his debtor to the extent of the amount of indebtedness existing at the time the insurance is taken out.[21] Death of the debtor and the consequent

---

[19]Ins. C. 10110: "Every person has an insurable interest in the life and health of: (a) Himself. . . ."

[20]See footnote 16.

[21]Ins. C. 10110: "Every person has an insurable interest in the life and health of: . . . (c) Any person under a legal obligation to him for the payment of money or respecting property or services, or which death or illness might delay or prevent the performance."

In *Jenkins* v. *Hill,* 35 C.A.2d 521, 96 P.2d 168, a woman agreed to care for a man during his last illness and to pay his funeral expenses. It was held that this imposed upon him a "legal obligation" to reimburse her and that, therefore, she had an insurable interest in his life.

termination of his earning power would result in the debt never being paid if the debtor had no other assets, and it is in this respect that there is potential monetary loss. Many lending agencies require such insurance, the usual arrangement being this: The borrower is required to take out and pay for term life insurance[22] on himself, the policy having a loss payable endorsement making the lender the beneficiary to the extent of the balance due on the debt, and with the remainder of the proceeds of the policy going to the family of the debtor.

2. *Business Relationships. Business policies* or *business life policies*, as they are called may be taken out by (a) corporations on their officers; (b) partners on copartners; and (c) sole proprietors on key employees.[23] The requirement of potential monetary loss is satisfied in each case by the fact that death of the particular person might deprive the business of an experienced person who could not readily be replaced, might deprive the business of an exceptional skill, might lose for the business a valuable personal following or clientele, etc., any or all of which would constitute loss.

• This last category, of business relationships, opens the way for discussion of one last point on insurable interest. The point is that where there is some legitimate social or economic purpose to be served by a particular insurance, the courts will not be too strict about compliance with the technicalities of the law of insurable interest. For example, within corporations, there are probably few instances of insuring officers as such. There is, however, a considerable amount of *closed corporation insurance*, which works in the same manner as the partnership insurance discussed earlier. Each of the perhaps five or six stockholders within a closed corporation may insure the life of another, with the proceeds to be used in every case for the purchase of the stock of a deceased stockholder. Technically, at least, there is not the contract relationship among stockholders that there is among partners, but no one has questioned the validity of such insurance.

Writing

Insurance contracts are not one of the types required by the statute of frauds to be in writing, but other statutes usually require this, and even though there may not be such statutes, the contract will always be in writing. The writing, of course, is the *policy.*[24] If there has been a written application, this may be incorporated by reference in and made a part of the policy.

Standard Form Policies: In many states, statutes require that certain standard forms of policies be used or that certain standard provisions be included in particular policies. In California, Ins. C. 2071 sets forth in full a standard form of fire insurance policy which must be used in this state.[25]

Component Parts of Policies: Policies may be broken down into the following component parts:

1. The *declaration* or face of the policy setting out the name of the insured, term of the policy, amount of coverage and location and description of the subject matter of the insurance.

2. The *contract of insurance* itself which breaks down into:

a. The *insuring agreement* which defines the coverage of the policy.

b. *Exclusions* and *exceptions*—provisions excluding from the coverage of the policy risks or causes of loss which would or might otherwise be held to come under the general coverage of the policy. Usually these are either things which are considered too hazardous to insure, such as the various valuables excluded from the coverage of the fire policy or things which are designed to be covered by other policies, e.g., theft, which is excluded from the coverage of the fire policy. They may be of other nature, however, based upon company policy or experience of the company, e.g., the suicide provision in life policies, or the exclusion in residence theft policies of thefts by relatives of the insured.

c. *Conditions* or provisions setting forth rights and obligations of the parties—obligations of insured in event of loss, rights of the parties to cancel the policy, and so on. There are stock provisions of this nature in all policies, some of which may be considered in greater detail at this point; others are treated in sections that follow, e.g., the right of the company to avoid the policy for misrepresentation and right of the insured to transfer the policy.

(1) *Notice and Proof of Loss.* The policy will usually require the insured to give the company *notice of loss* "without unnecessary delay" or "as soon as practicable," as in the specimen fire and automobile policies, and to give the company a "proof of loss" within some specified period, e.g., 60 days as in the aforementioned policies. The *proof of loss* is an itemized statement of the property lost or damaged and an estimation of its value.

(2) *Appraisal and Arbitration.* If the company feels that the amount of loss claimed by the insured is too high, the policy will give it the right to require appraisal and arbitration, in which case each party, the insured and the company, will be required to appoint an appraiser of the loss, the appraisers in turn selecting a third party or "umpire," as he may be called in the policy. The decision of the majority of these arbiters will be conclusive as to the amount of loss, i.e., as to the amount to be paid by the company on the policy.

(3) *Subrogation.* Suppose that A parks his car on a downtown street while transacting business. Operating his car negligently, B collides with A's car and does $500 damage. A has automobile insurance coverage with X Insurance Company. A has two directions in which he can go to recoup. He can sue B for $500 for the tort committed by B, or he can recover $500 from his (A's) insurance company. He will, of course, look to his insurance company for payment since this is why he has insurance. When one person answers for an obligation or liability of another, which is actually what the insurance company is doing in this case—answering for the wrong of B—that person "steps into the shoes" of the person to whom he answers and acquires all of his rights. This is called *subrogation*, and when his insurance company pays A, it is subrogated to his rights against B, which A did not use, to sue B for the $500. The insurance company may then sue and recover its loss from B. Policies expressly provide for the right of subrogation.

(4) *Cancellation.* All policies permit cancellation by the insured without any specific period of advance notice. If the company cancels, it must give notice to give the insured time to procure other insurance, e.g., 5 days to cancel automobile insurance, 30 days to cancel property insurance, and the company must refund a directly proportionate amount of the pre-

---

[22]See page 314 re term life insurance.

[23]These are called *corporation insurance, partnership insurance,* and *key man insurance.*

[24]Ins. C. 380: "The written instrument, in which a contract of insurance is set forth, is the policy."

[25]Ins. C. 10160 states provisions which must be included in life policies (the nonforfeiture provisions discussed on page 314). Ins.C. 11580-11580.2 state provisions which must be included in liability policies.

mium. Thus, if it is a one year policy at a $400 premium, and the company elects to cancel the policy after 3 months, it must refund $300, after 6 months $200, etc. If the insured wishes to cancel, he need not give notice for any particular period; his cancellation is effective as soon as the company is notified. The refund is computed differently, however. The insured is refunded only the amount called for by the customary *short rate table*, which is simply a schedule formulated by the insurance company of the amount of refund payable in such case. It runs considerably less than the directly proportionate amount and decreases in percentage with the age of the policy, e.g., taking the same policy and premium as above, if the insured cancelled after 3 months, he might get back only $240 on the short rate table, after 6 months only $140.

Endorsements: Endorsements are attachments to the policy for one of two general purposes: (1) To extend the coverage of the policy, e.g., the Dwelling and Contents Form and the Extended Coverage Endorsement on pages 333-335, which may be attached to the basic fire policy to give coverage for damage by explosion, windstorm, hail, etc., in the one case, and of the furnishings of a home in the other, neither of which are covered by the fire policy alone. (2) To cover the interests of two persons in the property: that of the "owner" and that of one who has a lien upon the property as security, such as a conditional seller or mortgagee.

Representations and Warranties; Concealment

In the earlier discussion of contracts, it was seen that they must be entered into without fraud, misrepresentation, mistake or other invalidating factor. Fraud, misrepresentation and mistake sometimes enter into insurance contracts. The extent to which mistake may enter and the consequences thereof are considered in the later section dealing with failure of the insured to read the policy. Fraud and misrepresentation are discussed here.

Representations and Warranties: In the field of insurance, any statement made or information furnished to the insurance company to induce it to issue the policy is classified as a *representation*. If there is a false representation, the question is whether it was *material*, i.e., whether it was of such importance that it may be said to have influenced the company in its decision as to whether or not to issue the policy, or, at least, in its decision as to the premium rate to be charged. Material misrepresentation permits the company to avoid the policy—refuse to pay on it.[26] The fact that the misrepresentation was unintentional on the part of the insured is immaterial if the misrepresentation was material as determined by the test above.

• The question of whether a misrepresentation was material may be a close one, and one which a court or jury could decide either way. It was to avoid the possibility that the court or jury might find that a representation was not material that the doctrine of warranty was conceived. A *warranty* is a representation that is made part of the policy. As defined in Ins.

C. 441, "A statement in a policy of a matter relating to the person or thing insured, or to the risk . . ." To *warrant* something is to *absolutely guarantee* it, as seen in connection with warranty deeds earlier, and this is what the law says an insured does with respect to representations which are made part of the policy. These become absolutely guaranteed representations, or warranties, on his part. Where something warranted proves to be untrue, the company may avoid the policy irrespective of whether or not the thing warranted was material, and the warranty concept permits the insurance company to avoid questions of materiality.

Thus, in *Craig* v. *United States Fidelity & Guaranty Co.*, 11 C.A.2d 644, 54 P.2d 486, statements made in an application for burglary insurance were made part of the policy and became warranties. One of the questions asked in the application was whether prior burglary insurance of the insured had been cancelled within 5 years, and this had been answered falsely. Held, "materiality" of the misrepresentation need not be considered; that "when a statement . . . is . . . a warranty, the falsity of such a statement voids the policy *ab initio*, and the question of the materiality of the false statement is removed from the consideration of the court. One of the principal reasons for such warranty is to preclude all controversy as to the materiality or immateriality of the statement."

Insurance companies have not abused the doctrine of warranty—have not attempted to escape policy liability because of the falsity of warranted matters of an inconsequential nature. In fact, they often pay claims that might be avoided, if for no other reason than to avoid the unfavorable publicity which litigation might bring. Nevertheless, the doctrine of warranty is potentially a harsh one, and in the last few decades many states have enacted statutes which require the warranted matter to be a material one before the policy can be avoided. The effect is to reduce warranties to the status of representations.

CALIFORNIA. Technically, the doctrine of warranty still applies in this state. If a matter is warranted, the policy may be avoided irrespective of its materiality. But Ins. C. 448 places an important limitation upon this by providing that "breach of an immaterial provision does not avoid the policy" unless the "policy declares" that it "shall avoid it." This requires an express stipulation in the policy that any "breach of warranty" shall avoid it, and modern policies seldom contain such provisions except in the field of life insurance, where they may still be found.[27]

Concealment: In the Contracts chapter, it was seen that it might not be necessary for a party to disclose special information which he had regarding the subject matter of the contract. In insurance contracts, however, the law requires a high degree of good faith dealing between the parties and, so, requires the person requesting insurance voluntarily to disclose facts material to the risk, if the information is of such a type as one party dealing in good faith with another "ought to communicate" to the other. Failure to make the requisite dis-

---

[26]Ins. C. 359: "If a representation is false in a material point . . . , the injured party is entitled to rescind the contract . . ." Ins. C. 360: "The materiality of a representation is determined by the same rule as the materiality of a concealment." With respect to materiality of a concealment, Ins. C. 334 says that it is to be determined by "the probable and reasonable influence of the facts upon the party to whom the communication is due, in forming his estimate of the disadvantages of the proposed contract, or in making his inquiries."

[27]About the nearest thing to a warranty provision to be found in most modern policies is that the company may avoid the policy if a statement is made to it "with intent to deceive," irrespective of materiality of the statement to the risk. Thus, in *Boyer* v. *United States Fidelity & Guaranty Co.*, 206 Cal. 273, 274 Pac. 57, it was held that the company could avoid the policy under such a provision where the insured stated that the named beneficiary of a life policy was her "Brother" when in fact he was only a friend.

closure constitutes *concealment* which permits the insurer to avoid the policy.[28] But, as stated in Ins. C. 333, the insured has no affirmative duty to mention things "of which [he] has no reason to suppose [the insurance company is] ignorant."

There are very few California cases involving the subject of concealment. The old case of *Hart* v. *British & Foreign Marine Ins. Co.*, 80 C. 440, is a rather interesting one but requires some background. In an earlier day, prior to telegraphic communication, it was the rule in the field of marine insurance that a policy could be taken out on a ship and cargo already at sea and that the policy was binding even though the ship had already sunk if neither party knew of the fact at the time that the insurance was contracted. In the *Hart* case, the insured procured a policy on a cargo being transported by ship down the coast of California. At the time of requesting and obtaining the policy, the insured had already heard a rumor that the ship had been sunk but did not inform the insurance company of this fact. The rumor proved to be true and, upon discovering the foregoing facts, the company refused to pay the policy. Held for the company on the ground that the insured was guilty of concealment.

In *Mirich* v. *Underwriters at Lloyd's London*, 64 C.A.2d 522, 149 P.2d 19, the application for a liability policy for a physician asked and was answered as follows: "I have not been sued or paid any sums for claims made against me for malpractice, error or mistake except as follows: 1 claim—7 yrs. ago—U.S.F. & G." This was the only *claim*, but lawsuits had been brought against the physician-applicant. Held for the company. This could be construed either as a concealment or as a positive representation that he had never been sued and, so, a material misrepresentation.

In *Strauss* v. *Dubuque F. & M. Ins. Co.*, 132 C.A. 283, 22 P.2d 582, it was held that failure to affirmatively disclose that substantial amounts of excelsior (highly inflammable) were handled in the business of the insured was concealment.

Other General Contract Aspects

Failure to Read Policy: It sometimes occurs that the policy does not give the insured the coverage requested or which he understood that it would give. He does not read the policy when it is received, and it is not until a loss occurs which the policy, as written, does not cover that he discovers the omission. Often, the courts have found some basis upon which to permit recovery by the insured, and they have consistently held that failure to read the policy is not such negligence as precludes or estops the insured from showing the mistake on his part. *Eagle Indem. Co.* v. *Ind. Acc. Comm.*, 92 C.2d 222, 206 P.2d 877, and *Golden Gate Motor Truck Co.* v. *Great American Indem. Co.*, 6 C.2d 439, 58 P.2d 374, are typical. In the *Eagle Indemnity Company* case, there was a failure by the insurance company to include all employees intended by the insured to be covered by a workers' compensation policy. The agent who sold the policy knew the coverage desired. Held, the insured was not required to read the policy where he relied upon an agent to obtain a policy providing a particular coverage. In the *Golden Gate Motor Truck Co.* case, it

was held that the insured's failure to read the policy to discover certain exceptions did not create an estoppel where he had requested from the company a policy giving full coverage on a fleet of vehicles, and the company sent a policy which purported to answer the request.

Assignment of Policy: Except in the case of life insurance, insurance policies contain express provisions forbidding assignment without consent of the company. Even without such provisions they would not be assignable because of the highly "personal" nature of the contract, in which the insurer relies upon the insured's personal past record for carefulness and for not having losses of the type insured against, in entering into the contract.

Rights of Third Persons: Because they are third party beneficiaries of the insurance contract, or for other reason, third persons may have rights in the policy or its proceeds.

BENEFICIARIES OF LIFE POLICIES. The persons named as beneficiaries of life policies are third party beneficiaries, as discussed in the chapter on Contracts, and are, of course, entitled to enforce the policy when it becomes payable. If the policy reserves to the insured the right to change beneficiaries, as it usually does, the beneficiaries are called *contingent beneficiaries*, and their rights are terminated by a change. Should the policy not reserve this right or if the insured makes a special contract giving up the right to change beneficiaries, then the beneficiaries are called *vested* and may not be changed. Occasionally, such a special contract is found in a property settlement agreement incidental to the dissolution of a marriage. The parties have a child, and the husband has a life insurance policy on his life. He agrees in the property settlement agreement to name the child as beneficiary of the policy, to file with the company an instrument waiving his right to change beneficiaries, and to pay the premiums on the policy. This would make the child a vested beneficiary. It is generally held that both vested and contingent beneficiaries can take over payment of the premiums if the insured discontinues payment.

CREDITORS IN LIFE POLICIES. Life insurance policies have a cash surrender value which the insured may recover if he elects to terminate the policy. This is an asset of the insured which may be reached by his creditors unless made exempt by statute. Most states have some kind of exemption statute.[29]

CREDITORS IN PROCEEDS OF FIRE POLICIES. Proceeds of a fire policy would also be an asset of the insured which creditors could reach. However, statutes in most states make one important exception. As seen earlier, a home may be homesteaded and in this way be made exempt from the claims of creditors. Statutes generally provide that proceeds of fire policies on homesteaded property are similarly exempt, with the insured being given some period of time within which to reinvest the proceeds in and homestead other property.[30]

MORTGAGEE IN FIRE POLICY ON MORTGAGED PREMISES. A mortgage always requires the mortgagor to carry insurance on the mortgaged property payable to the mortgagee to the extent of the balance due on the note. Should it occur that the mort-

---

[28]Ins. C. 330: "Neglect to communicate that which a party knows, and ought to communicate, is concealment." Section 331: "Concealment, whether intentional or unintentional, entitles the injured party to rescind insurance." Section 332: "Each party to a contract of insurance shall communicate to the other, in good faith, all facts within his knowledge which are or which he believes to be material to the contract and as to which he makes no warranty, and which the other has not the means of ascertaining."

[29]C.C.P. 690.9 exempts from creditors all benefits of life policies—the cash surrender value—where annual premiums do not exceed $500; the proportion which $500 bears to the whole premium where they do.

[30]California does not have a statute of this type, but it was held in *Houghton* v. *Lee*, 50 C. 101, that fire insurance proceeds on homesteaded property were exempt.

gagor procures insurance payable to himself only, he would be held to be a constructive trustee of the proceeds to the extent of the balance due on the note. Actually, however, the mortgagee would release its rights in the proceeds of the policy to permit the mortgagor to replace the improvements destroyed by fire. The lien of the mortgage would then attach to the replaced improvements.

INJURED PARTY AGAINST LIABILITY INSURER. There is a misconception to the effect that if a person is injured by the negligence of another, e.g., in an automobile accident, the injured party may "sue the insurance company" of the wrong-doer. This is not so unless statute gives some right of action directly against the insurance company, which Ins. C. 11580 does, but only after a judgment has been obtained against the insured (the wrongdoer). In the absence of such a statute, the insurance company's only relationship is with its insured and its only obligation is its contractual one to indemnify him against loss. This is made for the benefit of the insured, not for the benefit of third parties, and may not be enforced by them on a third party beneficiary theory.

Particular Policies

Fire Insurance Policies

Fire insurance policies are very much standardized, and the California Standard Form Fire Insurance Policy on pages 316-320 is a required form in this state. It is virtually the same as the New York statutory form. Certain aspects of it and of fire policies generally are noted.

Hostile Fire: The fire against which the policy insures is *hostile* fire as distinguished from *friendly* fire. A hostile fire is one which has escaped from the place to which it was intended to be confined, e.g., a spark which has escaped from the fireplace and has ignited a curtain and which thereby sets fire to the entire premises. Once a hostile fire is shown, recovery may be had for all damages directly traceable to it, e.g., damages from smoke or water.

Open vs. Valued Policies: Most policies on property are open policies. An *open policy* is one in which the company agrees to pay either replacement cost or "actual cash value" (fair market value) as in the policy form on page 317, up to the maximum face amount of the policy.[31]

● A *valued policy*, by contrast, is one in which the parties—insurer and insured—place a fixed value on the property at the time the policy is taken out[33] which the company agrees to pay in event of total destruction of the property, irrespective of actual replacement cost. Thus, if a value of $100,000 were placed upon a building and a valued policy issued, the company would have to pay $100,000 upon total loss even though replacement cost was only $90,000. In the event of anything less than total loss, the valued policy pays either replacement cost or actual cash value, i.e., operates in the same manner as an open policy.[34]

---

[31]Ins. C. 411: "An open policy is one in which the value of the subject matter is not agreed upon, but is left to be ascertained in case of loss."

[32][*Deleted*]

[33]Ins. C. 412: "A valued policy is one which expresses on its face an agreement that the thing insured shall be valued at a specified sum."

[34]Ins. C. 2054: ". . . a valued policy shall pay losses as follows: (a) In case of total loss, the whole amount insured . . . as stated in the policy . . . (b) In case of a partial loss the full amount of the partial loss."

The advantage of the valued policy is to the insured, since it eliminates any dispute over the value of the property in the event of total loss. Valued policies are rare, however. Companies do not like to write them because of the burden and expense of appraisal which they involve. For all practical purposes, valued policies are not written in California. The nearest thing to a valued policy in this state is insurance on scheduled personal property such as jewelry in which an item is declared to be "insured and valued at $......."

Average or Coinsurance Clauses: Suppose you have a building of steel construction worth $100,000. You may feel that the worst possible loss that could happen could be repaired for $20,000 and, so, to minimize premiums, take out only that amount of fire insurance. The insurance company response to this kind of thinking was the *average or co-insurance clause*, which operates in this way: Suppose you have a building worth $100,000 at the time of insuring. You elect to take out a policy with an 80% co-insurance clause. This means that you must take out $80,000 of insurance on the property, which you do. If you have a $60,000 loss, you will receive full payment, but if the property increases in value, you must take out additional insurance up to the stipulated 80% of coverage. Thus, if the building appreciates in value to $120,000, you must increase the insurance to $96,000. If you do not, you can recover only in accordance with this formula:

$$\frac{\text{Insurance carried}}{\text{Should be carried}} \times \text{loss} = \text{recovery (or)} \quad \frac{\$80,000}{96,000} \times 60,000 = \$50,000$$

By failing to maintain the proper percentage of coverage, you are penalized to the extent of the formula above, or become a *co-insurer* of the property to the extent that operation of the formula would require you to absorb some portion of the loss.

You may insure on a 60, 70, 80, 90 or 100% basis. To make it attractive for the insured to choose the higher percentages, the insured is given an increasingly lower rate per hundred dollars of insurance with each higher percentage. Thus, the premium per hundred on an 80% basis is lower than on a 70% basis, on a 90% basis lower than on an 80%, and so on.

Pro Rata Clause: The fire policy, and liability policies, will contain a clause providing that if there is other insurance covering the risk the insurer will be liable only for that portion of the loss which its insurance bears to the total insurance. See pages 317, 336, 343.

Mortgage Clauses: A mortgagee may be protected by a lender's loss payable endorsement or by a standard or union mortgage clause. The *standard or union mortgage clause* creates a separate contract between the insured and the mortgagee which is not subject to defenses which are good against the mortgagor. If there is merely a *loss payable endorsement*, the mortgage is subject to defenses which are good against the mortgagor.

Endorsements and Supplemental Coverages: Various endorsements and supplemental coverages are designed to complement that of the fire policy which insures only the house or building of the insured, and insures it only against fire. The following are important endorsements:

EXTENDED COVERAGE ENDORSEMENT. This covers loss by explosion, windstorm, hail, riot, aircraft, vehicles, and smoke.

WATER DAMAGE, EARTHQUAKE, ETC. Neither the fire policy nor the extended coverage endorsement covers various forms of water damage that may occur, and sprinkler insurance, rain insurance and general water damage insurance must be obtained to protect against these contingencies. The fire policy excludes loss by fire caused by attack or invasion of an enemy nation, and American companies generally do not offer any coverage against this peril.

DWELLING AND CONTENTS FORM. This covers household furnishings. See specimen form on page 318.

BUILDING, EQUIPMENT AND STOCK FORM. This is the business world counterpart of the dwelling and contents form. It covers equipment and inventory in a store or building.

BUSINESS INTERRUPTION INSURANCE. This covers lost profits during a period of suspended operation as the result of a fire, together with fixed charges—payroll, utilities, etc., which would continue during suspension of operations. See specimen form on page 321.

RENTAL INCOME FORM. This covers loss of rental income, e.g., of an apartment house, while the building is rendered untenantable as the result of fire damage.

LEASEHOLD INSURANCE. Destruction by fire of leased premises may result in termination of the lease with the lessee being required to seek new quarters. Leasehold insurance protects the lessee against increased rent, paying him the difference between the rent called for by the lease for the balance of its term and the amount required to be paid at the new location for the same period.

Homeowners Policies

For insuring residential property, the simple fire policy has been replaced by the "*homeowners policy*" which packages the homeowner's needs for fire coverage, various miscellaneous coverages and general personal liability coverage. (Space limitations do not permit the inclusion of a specimen homeowners policy.)

Life Insurance Policies

Life insurance may be written as 20- or 30-year life, i.e., insurance which is paid for in full in a certain period of time, called *limited payment life* insurance; or it may be written as *ordinary life* which is payable for life. Premiums per thousand dollars of coverage decrease with the increase in the duration of the premium payment period. Thus, 20-year life might be $22 per thousand a year, 30-year life $21 per thousand, and ordinary life $20 per thousand. Life insurance may also be *term insurance*. This has no savings or investment feature, i.e., no cash surrender value, and so has a very low premium rate.

● Certain standard provisions of life policies may be noted. A specimen life policy appears on page 324. It is an example of the newly-developing "plain language" policy form, designed to be understandable to the layperson.

Nonforfeiture Provisions: Most states have statutes protecting the insured against forfeiture of his equity in the policy where, after payment of premiums for a substantial period of time, he is compelled or elects to discontinue further payments. These non-forfeiture laws require the policy to have a *cash surrender value* plus one or more of the following privileges:

a. *Paid up insurance*—the company must give the insured a paid up policy in an amount determined by the period of time for which the policy has been maintained.[35]

---

[35]Ins. C. 10160 requires cash surrender value and paid up insurance provisions. As a practical matter, however, all policies contain all 4 types of provisions.

b. *Term insurance*—the company must give the insured term insurance in the original face amount of the policy for so long as the reserve value of the policy will purchase such insurance, the policy becoming terminated when this amount is exhausted.

c. *Reinstatement*—the company must permit the insured to reinstate the policy within a specified period of time after default by payment of delinquent premiums plus interest.

Military Service Exclusion: In time of war or imminency of war, life policies make an exclusion for death in the military service.

Suicide Provision: Life policies contain a suicide clause voiding the policy in event of self-destruction. Some of these extend throughout the life of the policy; others are limited to one or two years (see "Self-Destruction" provision on page 325).

Misstatement of Age Provision: Suppose in his application for life insurance A states his age to be 25 when in fact it is 26. This is by mistake or because of faulty birth records. At 25 the premium rate is slightly lower than at 26 and A has received the benefit of a lower premium rate than he should have received. The misstatement of age provision solves this problem by providing that the amount payable on the policy will be reduced to an amount which the premium paid would have purchased for the insured had his age been stated correctly. See page 331.

Incontestable Clause: Life policies contain a provision declaring that the policy may not be contested or avoided by the company on account of misrepresentation or for other reason after it has been in force for a specified period of time—one or two years. This is called the *incontestable clause*. It is the insured's antidote for the doctrine of warranty discussed earlier. It prevents avoidance of the policy for misrepresentations as to health, past medical history, etc., after the period of the incontestable clause has run. The general rule is that this is so even though the misrepresentation was intentional. Where the misinformation is a misstatement of age, the misstatement of age provision discussed above controls, and the incontestable clause does not apply. Also, the incontestable clause does not remedy the defect of lack of insurable interest. Where there is no insurable interest, there is no contract. The transaction is a complete nullity, and, since no contract comes into existence, no incontestable clause comes into existence.

Liability Policies

Two important types of liability policies are set out on pages 332-443, the standard automobile policy and the comprehensive liability policy.

Standard Automobile Policy: The automobile policy is actually 5 policies within one if all of the usual coverages are taken:

1. *Bodily Injury Liability.* This indemnifies the insured against liability to third persons injured through his negligent operation of an automobile. Thus, if the insured strikes a pedestrian in a crosswalk or negligently collides with another car and injures its driver, this is the coverage that protects him. It is written in combinations of $15,000 and $30,000, $50,000 and $100,000, and so on, which means that the company will pay a maximum of $15,000 or $50,000 if there is an accident in which only one person is injured; $30,000 or $100,000 if there is an accident in which two or more persons are injured.

Omnibus Clause. The Persons Insured clause of Part I of the policy on page 341 protects the insured against bodily injury liability where the car is being used by other persons with the permission of the insured. Such a provision is often referred to as an *omnibus clause*.

2. *Property Damage Liability*. This indemnifies the insured against liability for damage done to the vehicle or property of another in an accident. It may be written for as low as $5000.

3. *Medical Payments*. From here on, the policy ceases to be a liability policy and becomes insurance on the person as to this coverage, and insurance on property as to the remaining coverages. The medical payments coverage reimburses the insured and passengers in his car for medical expenses incurred as a result of an accident.

4. *Comprehensive*. This protects the insured against loss of car or contents by fire, theft, etc.

5. *Collision or Upset*. This reimburses the insured for damage to his car as a result of collision or upset. It is usually written as a "$100 deductible," or greater amount of deductible, which means that the insured must pay the first $100 of any damage incurred in an accident and that the company has no liability if the damage does not exceed this amount. This reduces the risk of the company and, hence, the premium for the coverage.

Uninsured Motorists Clause. Many states, including California,[36] now require an uninsured motorists clause to be included in an automobile policy. This indemnifies the insured against personal injuries suffered as the result of being struck

---

[36]Ins. C. 11580.2.

by an uninsured driver or an insured driver whose insurer is insolvent, or a hit-run driver who is not caught.

Comprehensive Liability Policy: This is designed to give a business organization broad form liability coverage in a single policy; hence, the name. The following important coverages are included:

1. Indemnity against liability to persons injured on the insured's premises.

2. Products liability—indemnifying a manufacturer against liability for injuries suffered by consumers in the use of the manufacturer's product.

3. Automobile liability—indemnifying the business against liability for injury to persons or damage to property caused by employees negligently operating vehicles in the course of employment.

"Umbrellas": Some insurers will provide a million or multimillion dollar *"umbrella"* policy for individual insureds. This supplements basic coverages that the insured is required to maintain for automobile liability insurance and for general personal liability insurance. Thus, if the insured is required to maintain $100,000/300,000 of automobile liability insurance to qualify for the umbrella, the umbrella gives him an additional million dollars of insurance coverage (or more if he has a larger umbrella) in case of an accident.

Workers' Compensation Insurance: The nature and requirements of workers' compensation laws have been discussed earlier. A business organization will need a workers' compensation or employer's liability policy to satisfy its obligations in this regard.

> ### CALIFORNIA
> ### STANDARD FORM FIRE INSURANCE POLICY

Insurance Company

CAPITAL STOCK COMPANY

Renewal of number:

Insured's
Name
and
Mailing
Address

AGENT

AND

CODE

Policy
Term: INCEPTION (Mo. Day Year)   EXPIRATION (Mo. Day Year)   YEARS

It is important that the written portions of all policies covering the same property read exactly alike. If they do not, they should be made uniform at once.

INSURANCE IS PROVIDED AGAINST ONLY THOSE PERILS AND FOR ONLY THOSE COVERAGES INDICATED BELOW BY A PREMIUM CHARGE AND AGAINST OTHER PERILS AND FOR OTHER COVERAGES ONLY WHEN ENDORSED HEREON OR ADDED HERETO.

Item No.	DESCRIPTION AND LOCATION OF PROPERTY COVERED Show address (No., Street, City, County, State, Zip Code) construction, type of roof and occupancy of building(s) covered or containing property covered. If occupied as a dwelling state if building is a seasonal or farm dwelling. If commercial state exact nature of product (and whether manufacturer, wholesaler or retailer) or the service or activity involved.	Pro-tection Class	Dwelling Business Only			
			No. of Families	Feet From Hydrant	Miles From Fire Dept.	Zone
1.						

Item No.	PERIL(S) INSURED AGAINST AND COVERAGE(S) PROVIDED (INSERT NAME OF EACH)	Per Cent of Co-Insurance Applicable	Deductible Amount	Amount of Insurance	Rate	Prepaid or Installment Premium Due At Inception	Installment Premium Due At Each Anniversary
1.	FIRE AND LIGHTNING			$		$	$
	EXTENDED COVERAGE			X X X X X X			
					TOTAL(S) $		$

TOTAL PREMIUM FOR POLICY TERM PAID IN INSTALLMENTS $

Countersignature Date   Agency at   Agent

(Form continued on following pages)

(A Capital Stock Company, herein called this Company)

IN CONSIDERATION OF THE PROVISIONS AND STIPULATIONS HEREIN OR ADDED HERETO AND OF the premium, this company, for the term of *years* from *inception date* At 12:01 a.m. (Standard Time) to *expiration date* At 12:01 a.m. (Standard Time) at location of property involved to an amount not exceeding the amount(s) specified in the Declarations, does insure *the insured named* in the Declarations and legal representatives, to the extent of the actual cash value of the property at the time of loss, but not exceeding the amount which it would cost to repair or replace the property with material of like kind and quality within a reasonable time after such loss, without allowance for any increased cost of repair or reconstruction by reason of any ordinance or law regulating construction or repair, and without compensation for loss resulting from interruption of business or manufacture, nor in any event for more than the interest of the insured, against all **LOSS BY FIRE, LIGHTNING AND BY REMOVAL FROM PREM-ISES ENDANGERED BY THE PERILS INSURED AGAINST IN THIS POLICY, EXCEPT AS HEREINAFTER PROVIDED**, to the property described herein while located or described in this policy, or pro rata for five days at each proper place to which any of the property shall necessarily be removed for preservation from the perils insured against in this policy, but not elsewhere.

Assignment of this policy shall not be valid except with the written consent of this Company.

This policy is made and accepted subject to the foregoing provisions and stipulations and those hereinafter stated, which are hereby made a part of this policy, together with such other provisions, stipulations and agreements as may be added hereto, as provided in this policy.

1 **Concealment, fraud.** This entire policy shall be void if, whether
2 before or after a loss, the insured has wilfully concealed or mis-
3 represented any material fact or circumstance concerning this
4 insurance or the subject thereof, or the interest of the insured
5 therein, or in case of any fraud or false swearing by the insured
6 relating thereto.
7 **Uninsurable and excepted property.** This policy shall not cover
8 accounts, bills, currency, deeds, evidences of debt, money or
9 securities; nor, unless specifically named hereon in writing,
10 bullion or manuscripts.
11 **Perils not included.** This company shall not be liable for loss by
12 fire or other perils insured against in this policy caused, directly
13 or indirectly, by: (a) enemy attack by armed forces, including
14 action taken by military, naval or air forces in resisting an actual
15 or an immediately impending enemy attack; (b) invasion;
16 (c) insurrection; (d) rebellion; (e) revolution; (f) civil war;
17 (g) usurped power; (h) order of any civil authority except acts
18 of destruction at the time of and for the purpose of preventing the
19 spread of fire, provided that such fire did not originate from any
20 of the perils excluded by this policy; (i) neglect of the insured to
21 use all reasonable means to save and preserve the property at
22 and after a loss, or when the property is endangered by fire in
23 neighboring premises; (j) nor shall this company be liable for
24 loss by theft.
25 **Other insurance.** Other insurance may be prohibited or the
26 amount of insurance may be limited by endorsement attached
27 hereto.
28 **Conditions suspending or restricting insurance.** Unless otherwise
29 provided in writing added hereto this company shall not be liable
30 for loss occurring (a) while the hazard is increased by any
31 means within the control or knowledge of the insured; or (b)
32 while a described building, whether intended for occupancy by
33 owner or tenant, is vacant or unoccupied beyond a period of
34 60 consecutive days; or (c) as a result of explosion or riot,
35 unless fire ensue, and in that event for loss by fire only.
36 **Other perils or subjects.** Any other peril to be insured against
37 or subject of insurance to be covered in this policy shall be by
38 endorsement in writing hereon or added hereto.
39 **Added provisions.** The extent of the application of insurance
40 under this policy and of the contribution to be made by this com-
41 pany in case of loss, and any other provision or agreement not in-
42 consistent with the provisions of this policy, may be provided for
43 in writing added hereto, but no provision may be waived except
44 such as by the terms of this policy or by statute is subject to
45 change.
46 **Waiver provisions.** No permission affecting this insurance shall
47 exist, or waiver of any provision be valid, unless granted herein
48 or expressed in writing added hereto. No provision, stipulation
49 or forfeiture shall be held to be waived by any requirement or
50 proceeding on the part of this company relating to appraisal or
51 to any examination provided for herein.
52 **Cancellation of policy.** This policy shall be canceled at any time
53 at the request of the insured, in which case this company shall,
54 upon demand and surrender of this policy, refund the excess of
55 paid premium above the customary short rates for the expired
56 time. This policy may be canceled at any time by this company
57 by giving to the insured a five days' written notice of cancellation
58 with or without tender of the excess of paid premium above the
59 pro rata premium for the expired time, which excess, if not ten-
60 dered, shall be refunded on demand. Notice of cancellation
61 shall state that said excess premium (if not tendered) will be
62 refunded on demand.
63 **Mortgagee interests and obligations.** If loss hereunder is made
64 payable, in whole or in part; to a designated mortgagee not
65 named herein as the insured, such interest in this policy may be
66 canceled by giving to such mortgagee a 10 days' written notice
67 of cancellation.
68   If the insured fails to render proof of loss such mortgagee, upon
69 notice, shall render proof of loss in the form herein specified
70 within sixty (60) days thereafter and shall be subject to the pro-
71 visions hereof relating to appraisal and time of payment and of
72 bringing suit. If this company shall claim that no liability existed
73 as to the mortgagor or owner, it shall, to the extent of payment
74 of loss to the mortgagee, be subrogated to all the mortgagee's
75 rights of recovery, but without impairing mortgagee's right to
76 sue; or it may pay off the mortgage debt and require an assign-
77 ment thereof and of the mortgage. Other provisions relating to
78 the interests and obligations of such mortgagee may be added
79 hereto by agreement in writing.

80 **Pro rata liability.** This company shall not be liable for a
81 greater proportion of any loss than the amount hereby insured
82 shall bear to the whole insurance covering the property against
83 the peril involved, whether collectible or not.
84 **Requirements in case loss occurs.** The insured shall give writ-
85 ten notice to this company of any loss without unnecessary de-
86 lay, protect the property from further damage, forthwith sepa-
87 rate the damaged and undamaged personal property, put it in
88 the best possible order, furnish a complete inventory of the de-
89 stroyed, damaged and undamaged property, showing in detail
90 quantities, costs, actual cash value and amount of loss claimed;
91 and within 60 days after the loss, unless such time is extended
92 in writing by this company, the insured shall render to this com-
93 pany a proof of loss, signed and sworn to by the insured, stating
94 the knowledge and belief of the insured as to the following: the
95 time and origin of the loss, the interest of the insured and of all
96 others in the property, the actual cash value of each item thereof
97 and the amount of loss thereto, all encumbrances thereon, all
98 other contracts of insurance, whether valid or not, covering any
99 of said property, any changes in the title, use, occupation, loca-
100 tion, possession or exposures of said property since the issuing of
101 this policy, by whom and for what purpose any building herein
102 described and the several parts thereof were occupied at the
103 time of loss and whether or not it then stood on leased ground,
104 and shall furnish a copy of all the descriptions and schedules in
105 all policies and, if required and obtainable, verified plans and
106 specifications of any building, fixtures or machinery de-
107 stroyed or damaged. The insured, as often as may be reason-
108 ably required, shall exhibit to any person designated by this
109 company all that remains of any property herein described, and
110 submit to examinations under oath by any person named by this
111 company, and subscribe the same; and, as often as may be rea-
112 sonably required, shall produce for examination all books of
113 account, bills, invoices and other vouchers, or certified copies
114 thereof if originals be lost, at such reasonable time and place as
115 may be designated by this company or its representative, and
116 shall permit extracts and copies thereof to be made.
117 **Appraisal.** In case the insured and this company shall fail to
118 agree as to the actual cash value of the amount of loss, then, on
119 the written demand of either, each shall select a competent and
120 disinterested appraiser and notify the other of the appraiser
121 selected within 20 days of such demand. The appraisers
122 shall first select a competent and disinterested umpire; and fail-
123 ing for 15 days to agree upon such umpire, then, on request of
124 the insured or this company, such umpire shall be selected by a
125 judge of a court of record in the state in which the property cov-
126 ered is located. The appraisers shall then appraise the loss,
127 stating separately actual cash value and loss to each item; and,
128 failing to agree, shall submit their differences, only, to the um-
129 pire. An award in writing, so itemized, of any two when filed
130 with this company shall determine the amount of actual cash
131 value and loss. Each appraiser shall be paid by the party
132 selecting him and the expenses of appraisal and umpire shall
133 be paid by the parties equally.
134 **Company's options.** It shall be optional with this company to
135 take all, or any part, of the property at the agreed or appraised
136 value, and also to repair, rebuild or replace the property
137 destroyed or damaged with other of like kind and quality
138 within a reasonable time, on giving notice of its intention so to
139 do within 30 days after the receipt of the proof of loss herein
140 required.
141 **Abandonment.** There can be no abandonment to this com-
142 pany of any property.
143 **When loss payable.** The amount of loss for which this com-
144 pany may be liable shall be payable 60 days after proof of
145 loss, as herein provided, is received by this company and ascer-
146 tainment of the loss is made either by agreement between the
147 insured and this company expressed in writing or by the filing
148 with this company of an award as herein provided.
149 **Suit.** No suit or action on this policy for the recovery of any
150 claim shall be sustainable in any court of law or equity unless
151 all the requirements of this policy shall have been complied
152 with, and unless commenced within 12 months next after
153 inception of the loss.
154 **Subrogation.** This company may require from the insured
155 an assignment of all right of recovery against any party for
156 loss to the extent that payment therefor is made by this
157 company.

DWELLING BUILDING(S) AND CONTENTS FORM

$100 DEDUCTIBLE APPLICABLE
(SEASONAL PROPERTY SHALL BE SO DESCRIBED IN THE POLICY)

Insurance attaches only to those items specifically described in this policy for which a specific amount is shown and, unless otherwise provided, all conditions of this form and the provisions of the policy to which it is attached shall apply separately to each item covered.

DEDUCTIBLE: THE SUM OF $100 SHALL BE DEDUCTED FROM THE AMOUNT OF LOSS TO ALL PROPERTY COVERED HEREUNDER IN ANY ONE OCCURRENCE RESULTING FROM THE PERILS INSURED AGAINST BY THIS POLICY, INCLUDING ENDORSEMENTS THERETO; EXCEPT, IF THIS POLICY COVERS MORE THAN ONE DWELLING THIS DEDUCTIBLE SHALL APPLY SEPARATELY TO THE AMOUNT OF LOSS TO EACH DWELLING INCLUDING PROPERTY APPERTAINING THERETO COVERED HEREUNDER.

This clause does not apply to rental value coverage, nor to the Earthquake Damage Assumption Endorsement if attached to this policy.

SECTION I — DESCRIPTION OF COVERAGE

A. DWELLING COVERAGE: Unless the occupancy is otherwise described on the first page of this policy, or by endorsement(s) attached thereto, the term "dwelling" shall mean a building occupied principally for dwelling purposes by the number of families stated in this policy, but in no event by more than 4 families.

When the insurance under this policy covers a dwelling, such insurance shall include additions in contact therewith; also, if the property of the owner of the described dwelling and when not otherwise covered, building equipment, fixtures and outdoor equipment, (BUT NOT LAWNS, TREES, SHRUBS OR PLANTS), all pertaining to the service of the described premises and while located thereon; also, materials and supplies located on the described premises or adjacent thereto, intended for use in construction, alteration or repair of such dwelling or private structures on the described premises.

B. PRIVATE STRUCTURES COVERAGE: When the insurance under this policy covers private structure(s) such insurance shall cover private structures (other than the described dwelling and additions in contact therewith) appertaining to the described premises and located thereon, BUT NOT STRUCTURES USED IN WHOLE OR IN PART FOR COMMERCIAL, MANUFACTURING OR FARMING PURPOSES. Structures used exclusively for private garage purposes shall not be deemed to be used for commercial, manufacturing or farming purposes.

C. CONTENTS COVERAGE: When the insurance under this policy covers contents, such insurance shall cover all household and personal property usual or incidental to the occupancy of the premises as a dwelling (EXCEPT ANIMALS, BIRDS, FISH, AIRCRAFT, MOTOR VEHICLES OTHER THAN MOTORIZED EQUIPMENT USED FOR MAINTENANCE OF THE PREMISES, AND BOATS OTHER THAN ROWBOATS AND CANOES); belonging to the Insured or members of the Insured's family of the same household, or for which the Insured may be liable, or, at the option of the Insured, belonging to a servant or guest of the Insured; all while on the described premises.

As to "Contents" —

(1) If, during the term of this policy, such property is removed to another location which is within this state and occupied in whole or in part as the Insured's residence, this policy shall cover such property while at such new location up to the amount applicable to contents and shall cease to cover at the former location, except that during the period of removal this policy shall cover at each location in the proportion that the value of such property at each location bears to the aggregate value at both locations.

(2) Loss shall be adjusted with and made payable to the named Insured unless other payee is specifically named.

D. RENTAL VALUE COVERAGE: When the insurance under this policy covers Rental Value, such insurance shall cover the fair rental value of the building(s) or parts thereof, as furnished and equipped by the owner whether rented or not. Loss of Rental Value shall be computed for the period of time, following damage to or destruction of the building(s) or equipment therein or on the described premises (caused by the peril(s) insured against) which would be required with the exercise of due diligence and dispatch, and not limited by the termination date of this policy, to restore the property to a tenantable condition, less such charges and expenses as do not continue.

SECTION II — PERILS INSURED AGAINST

This policy insures against all direct loss caused by:

1. FIRE AND LIGHTNING, EXCLUDING ANY LOSS RESULTING FROM ANY ELECTRICAL INJURY OR DISTURBANCE TO ELECTRICAL APPLIANCES, DEVICES, FIXTURES OR WIRING CAUSED BY ELECTRICAL CURRENTS ARTIFICIALLY GENERATED UNLESS FIRE ENSUES AND, IF FIRE DOES ENSUE, THIS COMPANY SHALL BE LIABLE ONLY FOR ITS PROPORTION OF LOSS CAUSED BY SUCH ENSUING FIRE.

2. REMOVAL, meaning loss by removal of the property covered hereunder from premises endangered by the perils insured against, and the amount of insurance applies prorata for 5 days at each proper place to which such property shall necessarily be removed for preservation from the perils insured against.

3. INHERENT EXPLOSION, meaning explosion occurring in the described dwelling or appurtenant private structures or in any structure containing property covered hereunder from hazards inherent therein.

Loss by explosion shall include direct loss resulting from the explosion of accumulated gases or unconsumed fuel within the firebox (or combustion chamber) of any fired vessel or within the flues or passages which conduct the gases of combustion therefrom.

THIS COMPANY SHALL NOT BE LIABLE FOR LOSS BY EXPLOSION OF STEAM BOILERS, STEAM PIPES, STEAM TURBINES OR STEAM ENGINES, IF OWNED BY, LEASED BY OR OPERATED UNDER THE CONTROL OF THE INSURED.

THE FOLLOWING ARE NOT EXPLOSIONS WITHIN THE INTENT OR MEANING OF THESE PROVISIONS (a) ELECTRIC ARCING, (b) RUPTURE OR BURSTING OF ROTATING OR MOVING PARTS OF MACHINERY CAUSED BY CENTRIFUGAL FORCE OR MECHANICAL BREAKDOWN, (c) WATER HAMMER, (d) RUPTURE OR BURSTING OF WATER PIPES, (e) RUPTURE, BURSTING OR OPERATION OF PRESSURE RELIEF DEVICES.

THIS POLICY IS EXTENDED TO INSURE AGAINST LOSS BY THE FOLLOWING PERILS AS HEREINAFTER PROVIDED, ONLY WHEN PREMIUM FOR EXTENDED COVERAGE IS INSERTED IN THE SPACE PROVIDED ON THE FIRST PAGE OF THIS POLICY OR ENDORSED HEREON.

4. WINDSTORM AND HAIL, EXCLUDING LOSS CAUSED DIRECTLY OR INDIRECTLY BY FROST OR COLD WEATHER, OR ICE (OTHER THAN HAIL), SNOW OR SLEET, WHETHER DRIVEN BY WIND OR NOT.

THIS COMPANY SHALL NOT BE LIABLE FOR LOSS TO THE INTERIOR OF THE BUILDING(S) OR THE PROPERTY COVERED THEREIN CAUSED: (a) BY RAIN, SNOW, SAND OR DUST, WHETHER DRIVEN BY WIND OR NOT, UNLESS THE BUILDING(S) COVERED OR CONTAINING THE PROPERTY COVERED SHALL FIRST SUSTAIN AN ACTUAL DAMAGE TO ROOF OR WALLS BY THE DIRECT ACTION OF WIND OR HAIL AND THEN SHALL BE LIABLE FOR LOSS TO THE INTERIOR OF THE BUILDING(S) OR THE PROPERTY COVERED THEREIN AS MAY BE CAUSED BY RAIN, SNOW, SAND OR DUST ENTERING THE BUILDING(S) THROUGH OPENINGS IN THE ROOF OR WALLS MADE BY DIRECT ACTION OF WIND OR HAIL; OR (b) BY WATER FROM SPRINKLER EQUIPMENT OR FROM OTHER PIPING, UNLESS SUCH EQUIPMENT OR PIPING BE DAMAGED AS A DIRECT RESULT OF WIND OR HAIL.

UNLESS AN ADDITIONAL PREMIUM IS CHARGED AND THIS POLICY IS SPECIFICALLY ENDORSED TO PROVIDE COVERAGE FOR WINDSTORM AND HAIL DAMAGE TO THE FOLLOWING PROPERTY, THIS COMPANY SHALL NOT BE LIABLE FOR WINDSTORM OR HAIL DAMAGE TO: (a) WINDMILLS, WIND PUMPS OR THEIR TOWERS; (b) CROP SILOS OR THEIR CONTENTS; (c) METAL SMOKESTACKS; OR (d) UNLESS WHOLLY WITHIN A BUILDING AND COMPLETELY ENCLOSED BY THE WALLS AND ROOF: (1) GRAIN, HAY, STRAW OR OTHER CROPS; (2) LAWNS, TREES, SHRUBS OR PLANTS; (3) AWNINGS OR CANOPIES (FABRIC OR SLAT), INCLUDING THEIR SUPPORTS; (4) SIGNS OR RADIO OR TELEVISION ANTENNAS, INCLUDING THEIR LEAD-IN WIRING, MASTS OR TOWERS.

5. EXPLOSION, including direct loss resulting from the explosion of accumulated gases or unconsumed fuel within the firebox (or combustion chamber) of any fired vessel or within the flues or passages which conduct the gases of combustion therefrom.

THIS COMPANY SHALL NOT BE LIABLE FOR LOSS BY EXPLOSION OF STEAM BOILERS, STEAM PIPES, STEAM TURBINES OR STEAM ENGINES, IF OWNED BY, LEASED BY OR OPERATED UNDER THE CONTROL OF THE INSURED.

(Form continued on following pages)

THE FOLLOWING ARE NOT EXPLOSIONS WITHIN THE INTENT OR MEANING OF THESE PROVISIONS:

(a) SHOCK WAVES CAUSED BY AIRCRAFT, GENERALLY KNOWN AS "SONIC BOOM",

(b) ELECTRIC ARCING,

(c) RUPTURE OR BURSTING OF ROTATING OR MOVING PARTS OF MACHINERY CAUSED BY CENTRIFUGAL FORCE OR MECHANICAL BREAKDOWN,

(d) WATER HAMMER,

(e) RUPTURE OR BURSTING OF WATER PIPES,

(f) RUPTURE OR BURSTING DUE TO EXPANSION OR SWELLING OF THE CONTENTS OF ANY BUILDING OR STRUCTURE, CAUSED BY OR RESULTING FROM WATER,

(g) RUPTURE, BURSTING OR OPERATION OF PRESSURE RELIEF DEVICES.

This Explosion provision, when effective, supersedes Inherent Explosion provision 3 herein.

6. RIOT, RIOT ATTENDING A STRIKE AND CIVIL COMMOTION, including direct loss by acts of striking employees of the owner or tenant(s) of the described building(s) while occupied by said striking employees and shall also include direct loss from pillage and looting occurring during and at the immediate place of a riot, riot attending a strike or civil commotion. UNLESS SPECIFICALLY ENDORSED HEREON, THIS COMPANY SHALL NOT BE LIABLE FOR LOSS RESULTING FROM DAMAGE TO OR DESTRUCTION OF THE DESCRIBED PROPERTY DUE TO CHANGE IN TEMPERATURE OR HUMIDITY OR INTERRUPTION OF OPERATIONS WHETHER OR NOT SUCH LOSS IS COVERED BY THIS POLICY AS TO OTHER PERILS.

7. AIRCRAFT AND VEHICLES, MEANING ONLY DIRECT LOSS RESULTING FROM ACTUAL PHYSICAL CONTACT OF AN AIRCRAFT OR A VEHICLE WITH THE PROPERTY COVERED HEREUNDER OR WITH THE BUILDING(S) CONTAINING THE PROPERTY COVERED HEREUNDER, except that loss by aircraft includes direct loss by objects falling therefrom. THIS COMPANY SHALL NOT BE LIABLE FOR LOSS: (a) BY ANY VEHICLE OWNED OR OPERATED BY AN INSURED OR BY ANY TENANT OF THE DESCRIBED PREMISES, (b) BY ANY VEHICLE TO FENCES, DRIVEWAYS, WALKS, OR, UNLESS WHOLLY WITHIN A BUILDING AND COMPLETELY ENCLOSED BY THE WALLS AND ROOF, TO LAWNS, TREES, SHRUBS OR PLANTS.

The term "vehicles," means vehicles running on land or tracks but not aircraft. The term "aircraft," shall include self-propelled missiles and spacecraft.

8. SMOKE, MEANING ONLY SMOKE DUE TO A SUDDEN, UNUSUAL AND FAULTY OPERATION OF ANY HEATING OR COOKING UNIT, ONLY WHEN SUCH UNIT IS CONNECTED TO A CHIMNEY BY A SMOKE PIPE OR VENT PIPE, AND WHILE IN OR ON THE DESCRIBED PREMISES BUT NOT SMOKE FROM FIREPLACES.

THIS POLICY IS EXTENDED TO INSURE AGAINST LOSS BY THE FOLLOWING PERILS AS HEREINAFTER PROVIDED, ONLY WHEN PREMIUM FOR EXTENDED COVERAGE AND VANDALISM AND MALICIOUS MISCHIEF IS INSERTED IN THE SPACE PROVIDED ON THE FIRST PAGE OF THIS POLICY OR ENDORSED HEREON.

9. VANDALISM AND MALICIOUS MISCHIEF, MEANING ONLY WILLFUL AND MALICIOUS DAMAGE TO OR DESTRUCTION OF THE PROPERTY COVERED HEREUNDER.

THIS COMPANY SHALL NOT BE LIABLE FOR LOSS:

(a) IF THE DESCRIBED BUILDING(S) HAD BEEN VACANT BEYOND A PERIOD OF THIRTY (30) CONSECUTIVE DAYS IMMEDIATELY PRECEDING THE LOSS, WHETHER OR NOT SUCH PERIOD COMMENCED PRIOR TO THE INCEPTION DATE OF THIS COVERAGE; BUT A BUILDING IN COURSE OF CONSTRUCTION SHALL NOT BE DEEMED VACANT.

(b) TO GLASS (OTHER THAN GLASS BUILDING BLOCKS) CONSTITUTING A PART OF A BUILDING, STRUCTURE OR AN OUTSIDE SIGN,

(c) BY PILFERAGE, THEFT, BURGLARY OR LARCENY, EXCEPT THAT THIS COMPANY SHALL BE LIABLE FOR WILFUL DAMAGE TO THE BUILDING(S) COVERED HEREUNDER CAUSED BY BURGLARS,

(d) BY EXPLOSION OF STEAM BOILERS, STEAM PIPES, STEAM TURBINES OR STEAM ENGINES, IF OWNED BY, LEASED BY OR OPERATED UNDER THE CONTROL OF THE INSURED; OR BY RUPTURE OR BURSTING OF ROTATING OR MOVING PARTS OF MACHINERY CAUSED BY CENTRIFUGAL FORCE OR MECHANICAL BREAKDOWN.

(e) FROM DEPRECIATION, DELAY, DETERIORATION OR LOSS OF MARKET; NOR, UNLESS SPECIFICALLY ENDORSED HEREON, FOR ANY LOSS RESULTING FROM CHANGE IN TEMPERATURE OR HUMIDITY.

SECTION III — EXTENSIONS OF COVERAGE

As respects the following Extensions of Coverage — IT IS A CONDITION OF THIS POLICY THAT IN THE EVENT THE INSURED ELECTS TO APPLY THE EXTENSIONS OF COVERAGE HEREIN, THIS COMPANY SHALL NOT BE LIABLE FOR A GREATER PROPORTION OF ANY LOSS THAN WOULD HAVE BEEN THE CASE IF ALL POLICIES COVERING THE DESCRIBED PROPERTY HAD CONTAINED IDENTICAL PROVISIONS AND THE SAME ELECTION WERE MADE UNDER ALL POLICIES.

A. PRIVATE STRUCTURES: The Insured may apply up to 10% of the amount of insurance applicable to the dwelling covered under this policy, not as an additional amount of insurance, to cover loss to private structures as defined in paragraph B of Section I. THIS EXTENSION OF COVERAGE SHALL NOT APPLY TO STRUCTURES (OTHER THAN STRUCTURES USED EXCLUSIVELY FOR PRIVATE GARAGE PURPOSES) WHICH ARE RENTED OR LEASED IN WHOLE OR IN PART, OR HELD FOR SUCH RENTAL OR LEASE, TO OTHER THAN A TENANT OF THE DESCRIBED DWELLING.

B. RENTAL VALUE: The Insured may apply up to 10% of the amount of insurance applicable to the dwelling covered under this policy, not as an additional amount of insurance, to cover rental value, as defined in paragraph D of Section I, BUT NOT EXCEEDING 1/12 OF SAID 10% FOR EACH MONTH THE DWELLING OR APPURTENANT PRIVATE STRUCTURES, OR PARTS THEREOF, ARE UNTENANTABLE.

THIS EXTENSION OF COVERAGE SHALL NOT APPLY TO LOSS RESULTING FROM DAMAGE TO OR DESTRUCTION OF BUILDINGS OR STRUCTURES USED IN WHOLE OR IN PART FOR COMMERCIAL, MANUFACTURING OR FARMING PURPOSES, OR STRUCTURES (OTHER THAN STRUCTURES USED EXCLUSIVELY FOR PRIVATE GARAGE PURPOSES) WHICH ARE RENTED OR LEASED IN WHOLE OR IN PART, OR HELD FOR SUCH RENTAL OR LEASE, TO OTHER THAN A TENANT OF THE DESCRIBED DWELLING.

C. OFF PREMISES CONTENTS: The Insured may apply up to 10% of the amount of insurance applicable to the contents covered under this policy, not as an additional amount of insurance, to cover loss to contents, as defined in paragraph C of Section I (EXCEPT ROWBOATS AND CANOES), belonging only to the Insured or members of the Insured's family of the same household, while elsewhere than on the described premises but within the limits of that part of Continental North America included within the United States of America and Canada, and in the State of Hawaii. THIS EXTENSION OF COVERAGE SHALL NOT INURE DIRECTLY OR INDIRECTLY TO THE BENEFIT OF ANY CARRIER OR OTHER BAILEE.

D. IMPROVEMENTS, ALTERATIONS AND ADDITIONS: The Insured, if not the owner of the described premises, may apply up to 10% of the amount of insurance applicable to the contents covered under this policy, not as an additional amount of insurance, to cover loss to improvements alterations and additions to the described dwelling and to private structures as defined in paragraph B of Section I.

E. DEBRIS REMOVAL: This insurance covers expense incurred in the removal of debris of the property covered hereunder, which may be occasioned by loss caused by any of the perils insured against in this policy.

THE TOTAL LIABILITY UNDER THIS POLICY FOR BOTH LOSS TO PROPERTY AND DEBRIS REMOVAL EXPENSE SHALL NOT EXCEED THE AMOUNT OF INSURANCE APPLYING UNDER THIS POLICY TO THE PROPERTY COVERED.

SECTION IV — GENERAL EXCLUSIONS

A. This policy does not insure against loss—

1. CAUSED BY, RESULTING FROM, CONTRIBUTED TO OR AGGRAVATED BY ANY OF THE FOLLOWING:

(a) FLOOD, SURFACE WATER, WAVES, TIDAL WATER OR TIDAL WAVE, OVERFLOW OF STREAMS OR OTHER BODIES OF WATER, OR SPRAY FROM ANY OF THE FOREGOING, ALL WHETHER DRIVEN BY WIND OR NOT;

(b) WATER WHICH BACKS UP THROUGH SEWERS OR DRAINS;

(c) WATER BELOW THE SURFACE OF THE GROUND INCLUDING THAT WHICH EXERTS PRESSURE ON OR FLOWS, SEEPS OR LEAKS THROUGH SIDEWALKS, DRIVEWAYS, FOUNDATIONS, WALLS, BASEMENT OR OTHER FLOORS, OR THROUGH DOORS, WINDOWS OR ANY OTHER OPENINGS IN SUCH SIDEWALKS, DRIVEWAYS, FOUNDATIONS, WALLS OR FLOORS;

UNLESS LOSS BY FIRE OR EXPLOSION AS INSURED AGAINST HEREUNDER ENSUES, AND THEN THIS COMPANY SHALL BE LIABLE FOR ONLY SUCH ENSUING LOSS.

2. CAUSED BY OR RESULTING FROM POWER, HEATING OR COOLING FAILURE, UNLESS SUCH FAILURE RESULTS FROM PHYSICAL DAMAGE TO POWER, HEATING OR COOLING EQUIPMENT SITUATED ON PREMISES WHERE THE PROPERTY COVERED IS LOCATED, CAUSED BY THE PERIL(S) INSURED AGAINST. THIS COMPANY SHALL NOT BE LIABLE FOR ANY LOSS SPECIFICALLY EXCLUDED UNDER (a) THE RIOT PERIL IN SECTION II, OR (b) THE VANDALISM AND MALICIOUS MISCHIEF PERIL IN SECTION II.

3. OCCASIONED DIRECTLY OR INDIRECTLY BY ENFORCEMENT OF ANY LOCAL OR STATE ORDINANCE OR LAW REGULATING THE CONSTRUCTION, REPAIR OR DEMOLITION OF BUILDING(S) OR STRUCTURE(S).

B. WAR RISK EXCLUSION CLAUSE (THIS CLAUSE APPLIES TO ALL PERILS INSURED AGAINST HEREUNDER EXCEPT THE PERILS OF FIRE AND LIGHTNING, WHICH ARE OTHERWISE PROVIDED FOR IN THIS POLICY): THIS COMPANY SHALL NOT BE LIABLE FOR LOSS CAUSED DIRECTLY OR INDIRECTLY BY (a) HOSTILE OR WARLIKE ACTION IN TIME OF PEACE OR WAR, INCLUDING ACTION IN HINDERING, COMBATING OR DEFENDING AGAINST AN ACTUAL, IMPENDING OR EXPECTED ATTACK, (1) BY ANY GOVERNMENT OR SOVEREIGN POWER (DE JURE OR DE FACTO), OR BY ANY AUTHORITY MAINTAINING OR USING MILITARY, NAVAL OR AIR FORCES; OR (2) BY MILITARY, NAVAL OR AIR FORCES; OR (3) BY AN AGENT OF ANY SUCH GOVERNMENT, POWER, AUTHORITY OR FORCES, IT BEING UNDERSTOOD THAT ANY DISCHARGE, EXPLOSION OR USE OF ANY WEAPON OF WAR EMPLOYING NUCLEAR FISSION OR FUSION SHALL BE CONCLUSIVELY PRESUMED TO BE SUCH A HOSTILE OR WARLIKE ACTION BY SUCH A GOVERNMENT, POWER, AUTHORITY OR FORCES; (b) INSURRECTION, REBELLION, REVOLUTION, CIVIL WAR, USURPED POWER, OR ACTION TAKEN BY GOVERNMENTAL AUTHORITY IN HINDERING, COMBATING OR DEFENDING AGAINST SUCH AN OCCURRENCE.

C. NUCLEAR CLAUSE: THE WORD "FIRE" IN THIS POLICY OR ENDORSEMENTS ATTACHED HERETO IS NOT INTENDED TO AND DOES NOT EMBRACE NUCLEAR REACTION OR NUCLEAR RADIATION OR RADIOACTIVE CONTAMINATION, ALL WHETHER CONTROLLED OR UNCONTROLLED, AND LOSS BY NU-CLEAR REACTION OR NUCLEAR RADIATION OR RADIOACTIVE CONTAMINATION IS NOT INTENDED TO BE AND IS NOT INSURED AGAINST BY THIS POLICY OR SAID ENDORSEMENTS, WHETHER SUCH LOSS BE DIRECT OR INDIRECT, PROXIMATE OR REMOTE, OR BE IN WHOLE OR IN PART CAUSED BY, CONTRIBUTED TO, OR AGGRAVATED BY "FIRE" OR ANY OTHER PERILS INSURED AGAINST BY THIS POLICY OR SAID ENDORSEMENTS; HOWEVER, SUBJECT TO THE FOREGOING AND ALL PROVISIONS OF THIS POLICY, DIRECT LOSS BY "FIRE" RESULTING FROM NUCLEAR REACTION OR NUCLEAR RADIATION OR RADIOACTIVE CONTAMINATION IS INSURED AGAINST BY THIS POLICY.

D. NUCLEAR EXCLUSION (THIS CLAUSE APPLIES TO ALL PERILS INSURED AGAINST HEREUNDER EXCEPT THE PERILS OF FIRE AND LIGHTNING, WHICH ARE OTHERWISE PROVIDED FOR IN THE NUCLEAR CLAUSE ABOVE): LOSS BY NUCLEAR REACTION OR NUCLEAR RADIATION OR RADIOACTIVE CONTAMINATION, ALL WHETHER CONTROLLED OR UNCONTROLLED, OR DUE TO ANY ACT OR CONDITION INCIDENT TO ANY OF THE FOREGOING, IS NOT INSURED AGAINST BY THIS POLICY, WHETHER SUCH LOSS BE DIRECT OR INDIRECT, PROXIMATE OR REMOTE, OR BE IN WHOLE OR IN PART CAUSED BY, CONTRIBUTED TO, OR AGGRAVATED BY ANY OF THE PERILS INSURED AGAINST BY THIS POLICY.

SECTION V — OTHER PROVISIONS

A. LOSS CLAUSE: Any loss hereunder shall not reduce the amount of this policy.

B. CONTROL OF PROPERTY: This insurance shall not be prejudiced by any act or neglect of any person (other than the named Insured), when such act or neglect is not within the control of the named Insured.

C. VACANCY AND UNOCCUPANCY: Permission granted for vacancy or unoccupancy without limit of time, EXCEPT FOR SECTION II, Peril 9, AND AS PROVIDED IN ANY ENDORSEMENT ATTACHED TO THIS POLICY.

D. OTHER OCCUPANCIES: Permission granted for other occupancies provided the dwelling building be principally occupied for dwelling house purposes, BUT EXCLUDING RETAIL AND WHOLESALE STORES AND COMMERCIAL MANUFACTURING OPERATIONS.

E. DESCRIPTION OF PROPERTY: This insurance shall not be prejudiced if any error is made in describing the location of the property covered.

F. SUBROGATION: This insurance shall not be invalidated should the Insured waive in writing prior to a loss any or all right of recovery against any party for loss occurring to the described property.

G. ALTERATIONS AND REPAIRS: Permission granted to make alterations, additions and repairs, and to complete structures in course of construction. In the event of loss hereunder, the Insured is permitted to make reasonable repairs, temporary or permanent, PROVIDED SUCH REPAIRS ARE CONFINED SOLELY TO THE PROTECTION OF THE PROPERTY FROM FURTHER DAMAGE AND PROVIDED FURTHER THAT THE INSURED SHALL KEEP AN ACCURATE RECORD OF SUCH REPAIR EXPENDITURES. The cost of any such repairs directly attributable to damage by any peril insured against shall be included in determining the amount of loss hereunder. NOTHING HEREIN CONTAINED IS INTENDED TO MODIFY THE POLICY REQUIREMENTS APPLICABLE IN CASE LOSS OCCURS, AND IN PARTICULAR THE REQUIREMENT THAT THE INSURED SHALL PROTECT THE PROPERTY FROM FURTHER DAMAGE.

H. LIBERALIZATION CLAUSE: If during the period that insurance is in force under this policy, or within 45 days prior to the inception date thereof, on behalf of this Company there be adopted, or filed with and approved or accepted by the insurance supervisory authorities, all in conformity with law, any changes in the form attached to this policy by which this form of insurance could be extended or broadened without increased premium charge by endorsement or substitution of form, then such extended or broadened insurance shall inure to the benefit of the Insured hereunder as though such endorsement or substitution of form had been made.

I. APPORTIONMENT: THIS COMPANY SHALL NOT BE LIABLE FOR A GREATER PROPORTION OF ANY LOSS LESS THE AMOUNT OF DEDUCTIBLE, IF ANY, FROM ANY PERIL OR PERILS INSURED AGAINST IN THIS FORM THAN (1) THE AMOUNT OF INSURANCE UNDER THIS POLICY BEARS TO THE WHOLE AMOUNT OF FIRE INSURANCE COVERING THE PROPERTY, OR WHICH WOULD HAVE COVERED THE PROPERTY EXCEPT FOR THE EXISTENCE OF THIS INSURANCE, WHETHER COLLECTIBLE OR NOT, AND WHETHER OR NOT SUCH OTHER FIRE INSURANCE INSURES AGAINST THE ADDITIONAL PERIL OR PERILS INSURED AGAINST HEREUNDER, NOR (2) FOR A GREATER PROPORTION OF ANY LOSS LESS THE AMOUNT OF DEDUCTIBLE, IF ANY, THAN THE AMOUNT HEREBY INSURED BEARS TO ALL INSURANCE WHETHER COLLECTIBLE OR NOT, COVERING IN ANY MANNER SUCH LOSS, OR WHICH WOULD HAVE COVERED SUCH LOSS EXCEPT FOR THE EXISTENCE OF THIS INSURANCE; EXCEPT IF ANY TYPE OF INSURANCE OTHER THAN FIRE EXTENDED TO COVER ADDITIONAL PERILS OR WINDSTORM INSURANCE APPLIES TO ANY LOSS TO WHICH THIS INSURANCE ALSO APPLIES, OR WOULD HAVE APPLIED TO ANY SUCH LOSS EXCEPT FOR THE EXISTENCE OF THIS INSURANCE, THE LIMIT OF LIABILITY OF EACH TYPE OF INSURANCE FOR SUCH LOSS, HEREBY DESIGNATED AS "JOINT LOSS", SHALL FIRST BE DETERMINED AS IF IT WERE THE ONLY INSURANCE, AND THIS TYPE OF INSURANCE SHALL BE LIABLE FOR NO GREATER PROPORTION OF JOINT LOSS THAN THE LIMIT OF ITS LIABILITY FOR SUCH LOSS BEARS TO THE SUM OF ALL SUCH LIMITS. THE LIABILITY OF THIS COMPANY (UNDER THIS FORM) FOR SUCH JOINT LOSS SHALL BE LIMITED TO ITS PROPORTIONATE PART OF THE AGGREGATE LIMIT OF THIS AND ALL OTHER INSURANCE OF THE SAME TYPE. THE WORDS "JOINT LOSS", AS USED IN THE FOREGOING, MEAN THAT PORTION OF THE LOSS IN EXCESS OF THE HIGHEST DEDUCTIBLE, IF ANY, TO WHICH THIS FORM AND OTHER TYPES OF INSURANCE ABOVE REFERRED TO BOTH APPLY.

J. DEFERRED PREMIUM PAYMENT: If the Insured elects to pay the premium in equal annual payments as indicated on the first page of this policy, the premium for this policy is hereby made so payable, provided that no payment shall be less than the Minimum Premium applicable.

If the Insured is in default of any such premium payment and this Company elects to cancel this policy, notice of cancellation shall be in accordance with the provisions of this policy. BUT IN SUCH CASE ANY PORTIONS OF THE PREMIUM PREVIOUSLY PAID SHALL BE EARNED BY THIS COMPANY.

BUSINESS INTERRUPTION FORM NO.3

GROSS EARNINGS FORM FOR MERCANTILE OR NON-MANUFACTURING RISKS

Insurance attaches to this item(s) only when "Business Interruption," a specific amount and a contribution (coinsurance) percentage are specified therefor in this policy, and, unless otherwise provided, all provisions and stipulations of this form and policy shall apply separately to each such item.

1. This policy insures against loss resulting directly from necessary interruption of business caused by damage to or destruction of real or personal property by the peril(s) insured against, during the term of this policy, on premises occupied by the Insured and situated as herein described.

2. In the event of such damage or destruction this Company shall be liable for the ACTUAL LOSS SUSTAINED by the Insured resulting directly from such interruption of business, BUT NOT EXCEEDING THE REDUCTION IN GROSS EARNINGS LESS CHARGES AND EXPENSES WHICH DO NOT NECESSARILY CONTINUE DURING THE INTERRUPTION OF BUSINESS, FOR ONLY SUCH LENGTH OF TIME AS WOULD BE REQUIRED WITH THE EXERCISE OF DUE DILIGENCE AND DISPATCH TO RE-BUILD, REPAIR OR REPLACE SUCH PART OF THE PROPERTY HEREIN DESCRIBED AS HAS BEEN DAMAGED OR DESTROYED, COMMENCING WITH THE DATE OF SUCH DAMAGE OR DESTRUCTION AND NOT LIMITED BY THE DATE OF EXPIRATION OF THIS POLICY. Due consideration shall be given to the continuation of normal charges and expenses, including payroll expense, to the extent necessary to resume operations of the Insured with the same quality of service which existed immediately preceding the loss.

3. **RESUMPTION OF OPERATIONS:** IT IS A CONDITION OF THIS INSURANCE THAT IF THE INSURED COULD REDUCE THE LOSS RESULTING FROM THE INTERRUPTION OF BUSINESS,

    (a) BY COMPLETE OR PARTIAL RESUMPTION OF OPERATION OF THE PROPERTY HEREIN DESCRIBED, WHETHER DAMAGED OR NOT, OR

    (b) BY MAKING USE OF MERCHANDISE OR OTHER PROPERTY AT THE LOCATION(S) DESCRIBED HEREIN OR ELSE-WHERE,

SUCH REDUCTION SHALL BE TAKEN INTO ACCOUNT IN ARRIVING AT THE AMOUNT OF LOSS HEREUNDER.

4. **EXPENSES RELATED TO REDUCING LOSS:** This policy also covers such expenses as are necessarily incurred for the purpose of reducing loss under this policy (EXCEPT EXPENSE INCURRED TO EXTINGUISH A FIRE), BUT IN NO EVENT SHALL THE AGGREGATE OF SUCH EXPENSES EXCEED THE AMOUNT BY WHICH THE LOSS OTHERWISE PAYABLE UNDER THIS POLICY IS THEREBY REDUCED. Such expenses shall not be subject to the application of the Contribution Clause.

5. **GROSS EARNINGS:** For the purposes of this insurance "Gross Earnings" are defined as the sum of:

    (a) Total net sales, and

    (b) Other earnings derived from operations of the business,

less the cost of:

    (c) Merchandise sold, including packaging materials therefor,

    (d) Materials and supplies consumed directly in supplying the service(s) sold by the Insured, and

    (e) Service(s) purchased from outsiders (not employees of the Insured) for resale which do not continue under contract.

No other costs shall be deducted in determining Gross Earnings.

In determining Gross Earnings due consideration shall be given to the experience of the business before the date of damage or destruction and the probable experience thereafter had no loss occurred.

6. **CONTRIBUTION CLAUSE:** IN CONSIDERATION OF THE RATE AND FORM UNDER WHICH THIS POLICY IS WRITTEN, THIS COMPANY SHALL BE LIABLE, IN THE EVENT OF LOSS, FOR NO GREATER PROPORTION THEREOF THAN THE AMOUNT HEREBY COVERED BEARS TO THE CONTRIBUTION (COINSURANCE) PERCENTAGE SPECIFIED ON THE FIRST PAGE OF THIS POLICY (OR ENDORSED HEREON) OF THE GROSS EARNINGS THAT WOULD HAVE BEEN EARNED (HAD NO LOSS OCCURRED) DURING THE 12 MONTHS IMMEDIATELY FOLLOWING THE DATE OF DAMAGE TO OR DESTRUCTION OF THE DESCRIBED PROPERTY.

7. **INTERRUPTION BY CIVIL AUTHORITY:** This policy is extended to include the actual loss sustained by the Insured, resulting directly from an interruption of business as covered hereunder, during the length of time, NOT EXCEEDING 2 CONSECUTIVE WEEKS, when, as a direct result of damage to or destruction of property adjacent to the premises herein described by the peril(s) insured against, access to such described premises is specifically prohibited by order of civil authority.

8. **LIMITATION—MEDIA FOR ELECTRONIC DATA PROCESSING:** WITH RESPECT TO LOSS RESULTING FROM DAMAGE TO OR DESTRUCTION OF MEDIA FOR, OR PROGRAMMING RECORDS PERTAINING TO, ELECTRONIC DATA PROCESSING OR ELECTRONICALLY CONTROLLED EQUIPMENT, INCLUDING DATA THEREON, BY THE PERIL(S) INSURED AGAINST, THE LENGTH OF TIME FOR WHICH THIS COMPANY SHALL BE LIABLE HEREUNDER SHALL NOT EXCEED —

    (a) 30 CONSECUTIVE CALENDAR DAYS; OR

    (b) THE LENGTH OF TIME THAT WOULD BE REQUIRED TO REBUILD, REPAIR OR REPLACE SUCH PROPERTY HEREIN DESCRIBED AS HAS BEEN DAMAGED OR DESTROYED (OTHER THAN MEDIA FOR, OR PROGRAMMING RECORDS PERTAINING TO, ELECTRONIC DATA PROCESSING OR ELECTRONICALLY CONTROLLED EQUIPMENT, INCLUDING DATA THEREON);

WHICHEVER IS THE GREATER LENGTH OF TIME.

9. **SPECIAL EXCLUSIONS:** THIS COMPANY SHALL NOT BE LIABLE FOR ANY INCREASE OF LOSS RESULTING FROM:

    (a) ENFORCEMENT OF ANY LOCAL OR STATE ORDINANCE OR LAW REGULATING THE CONSTRUCTION, REPAIR OR DEMOLITION OF BUILDINGS OR STRUCTURES; OR

(b) INTERFERENCE AT THE DESCRIBED PREMISES, BY STRIKERS OR OTHER PERSONS, WITH REBUILDING, RE-PAIRING OR REPLACING THE PROPERTY OR WITH THE RESUMPTION OR CONTINUATION OF BUSINESS; OR

(c) THE SUSPENSION, LAPSE OR CANCELLATION OF ANY LEASE, LICENSE, CONTRACT OR ORDER UNLESS SUCH SUSPENSION, LAPSE OR CANCELLATION RESULTS DIRECTLY FROM THE INTERRUPTION OF BUSINESS, AND THEN THIS COMPANY SHALL BE LIABLE FOR ONLY SUCH LOSS AS AFFECTS THE INSURED'S EARNINGS DURING, AND LIMITED TO, THE PERIOD OF INDEMNITY COVERED UNDER THIS POLICY;

NOR SHALL THIS COMPANY BE LIABLE FOR ANY OTHER CONSEQUENTIAL OR REMOTE LOSS.

10. **PRO RATA CLAUSE:** THE LIABILITY UNDER THIS POLICY SHALL NOT EXCEED THAT PROPORTION OF ANY LOSS WHICH THE AMOUNT OF INSURANCE HEREUNDER BEARS TO ALL INSURANCE, WHETHER COLLECTIBLE OR NOT, COVER-ING IN ANY MANNER THE LOSS INSURED AGAINST BY THIS POLICY.

11. **DEFINITION OF "NORMAL":** THE CONDITION THAT WOULD HAVE EXISTED HAD NO LOSS OCCURRED.

12. **LOSS CLAUSE:** Any loss hereunder shall not reduce the amount of this policy.

13. **METAL SMOKESTACKS:** If this policy is endorsed to insure against the perils of windstorm and hail and the endorse-ment specifically excludes loss resulting from damage to metal smokestacks, such exclusion is hereby deleted as respects this business interruption coverage.

14. **ALTERATIONS AND NEW BUILDINGS:** Permission granted to make alterations in or to construct additions to any building described herein and to construct new buildings on the described premises. This policy is extended to cover, subject to all its provisions and stipulations, loss resulting from damage to or destruction of such alterations, additions or new build-ings while in course of construction and when completed or occupied, provided that, in the event of damage to or destruction of such property (including building materials, supplies, machinery or equipment incident to such construction or occupancy while on the described premises or within one hundred (100) feet thereof) so as to delay commencement of business opera-tions of the Insured, the length of time for which this Company shall be liable shall be determined as otherwise provided herein but such determined length of time shall be applied and the loss hereunder calculated from the date that business operations would have begun had no damage or destruction occurred.

This clause does not waive or modify any of the conditions of the Automatic Sprinkler Clause, if any, attached to this policy.

15. **ELECTRICAL APPARATUS CLAUSE:** THIS COMPANY SHALL NOT BE LIABLE FOR ANY LOSS RESULTING FROM ANY ELECTRICAL INJURY OR DISTURBANCE TO ELECTRICAL APPLIANCES, DEVICES, FIXTURES OR WIRING CAUSED BY ELECTRI-CAL CURRENTS ARTIFICIALLY GENERATED UNLESS FIRE ENSUES AND, IF FIRE DOES ENSUE, THIS COMPANY SHALL BE LIABLE ONLY FOR ITS PROPORTION OF LOSS CAUSED BY SUCH ENSUING FIRE.

16. **EXTENSION CLAUSE:** This policy is extended (subject in all other respects to the provisions and stipulations of this policy) to cover actual loss sustained, as otherwise insured against by this policy, resulting from damage to or destruction of personal property of the named insured (a) while in, on or under sidewalks, streets, platforms, alleyways or open spaces, provided such property is located within 50 feet of the described premises; or (b) while in or on cars or vehicles within 300 feet of the described premises.

17. **PERMITS AND AGREEMENTS CLAUSE:** Permission granted (a) For such use of the premises as is usual and inci-dental to the business conducted therein and for existing and increased hazards and for change in use or occupancy except as to any specific hazard, use or occupancy prohibited by the express terms of this policy or by any endorsement thereto; (b) To keep and use all articles and materials, usual and incidental to said business, in such quantities as the exigencies of the business require. Nothing herein contained shall be construed to extend the term of this policy.

This insurance shall not be prejudiced: (1) By any act or neglect of the owner of the building(s) if the Insured is not the owner thereof, or by any act or neglect of any occupant of the building(s) (other than the named Insured), when such act or neglect of the owner or occupant is not within the control of the named Insured; (2) By failure of the named Insured to comply with any warranty or condition contained in any form, rider or endorsement attached to this policy with regard to any portion of the premises over which the named Insured has no control; nor (3) Shall this insurance be prejudiced by any error in stating the name, number, street or location of any building(s) and contents, the Business Interruption of which is covered hereunder.

18. **BREACH OF WARRANTY CLAUSE:** If a breach of any warranty or condition contained in any rider attached to or made a part of this policy shall occur, which breach by the terms of such warranty or condition shall operate to suspend or avoid the insurance hereunder, it is agreed that such suspension or avoidance due to such breach, shall be effective only during the continuance of such breach and then shall apply only with respect to such actual loss sustained as is directly and specifically attributable to damage to or destruction of the building, fire division, contents therein, or other separate location to which such warranty or condition has reference and in respect of which such breach occurs.

19. **SUBROGATION WAIVER CLAUSE:** This insurance shall not be invalidated should the Insured waive in writing any or all right of recovery against any party for loss, PROVIDED, HOWEVER, THAT IN THE EVENT THE INSURED WAIVES ONLY A PART OF HIS RIGHTS AGAINST ANY PARTICULAR THIRD PARTY, THIS COMPANY SHALL BE SUBROGATED WITH RESPECT TO ALL RIGHTS OF RECOVERY WHICH THE INSURED MAY RETAIN AGAINST ANY SUCH THIRD PARTY FOR LOSS FROM THE PERILS INSURED AGAINST TO THE EXTENT THAT PAYMENT THEREFOR IS MADE BY THIS COMPANY; ALL SUBJECT TO THE FOLLOWING ADDITIONAL PROVISIONS:

(a) If made before loss has occurred, such agreement may run in favor of any third party;

(b) IF MADE AFTER LOSS HAS OCCURRED, SUCH AGREEMENT MAY RUN ONLY IN FAVOR OF A THIRD PARTY FALLING WITHIN ONE OF THE FOLLOWING CATEGORIES AT THE TIME OF LOSS:

(1) A THIRD PARTY INSURED UNDER THIS POLICY; OR

(2) A CORPORATION, FIRM, OR ENTITY (a) OWNED OR CONTROLLED BY THE NAMED INSURED OR IN WHICH THE NAMED INSURED OWNS CAPITAL STOCK OR OTHER PROPRIETARY INTEREST, OR (b) OWNING OR CONTROLLING THE NAMED INSURED OR OWNING OR CONTROLLING CAPITAL STOCK OR OTHER PRO-PRIETARY INTEREST IN THE NAMED INSURED; OR

(Form continued on following page)

(3) A TENANT OF THE NAMED INSURED.

20. **LIBERALIZATION CLAUSE:** If during the period that insurance is in force under this policy, or within 45 days prior to the inception date thereof, on behalf of this Company there be adopted, or filed with and approved or accepted by the insurance supervisory authorities, all in conformity with law, any changes in the form attached to this policy by which this form of insurance could be extended or broadened without increased premium charge by endorsement or substitution of form, then such extended or broadened insurance shall inure to the benefit of the Insured hereunder as though such endorsement or substitution of form had been made.

21. **NUCLEAR CLAUSE:** THE WORD "FIRE" IN THIS POLICY OR ENDORSEMENTS ATTACHED HERETO IS NOT INTENDED TO AND DOES NOT EMBRACE NUCLEAR REACTION OR NUCLEAR RADIATION OR RADIOACTIVE CONTAMINATION, ALL WHETHER CONTROLLED OR UNCONTROLLED, AND LOSS BY NUCLEAR REACTION OR NUCLEAR RADIATION OR RADIOACTIVE CONTAMINATION IS NOT INTENDED TO BE AND IS NOT INSURED AGAINST BY THIS POLICY OR SAID ENDORSEMENTS, WHETHER SUCH LOSS BE DIRECT OR INDIRECT, PROXIMATE OR REMOTE, OR BE IN WHOLE OR IN PART CAUSED BY, CONTRIBUTED TO, OR AGGRAVATED BY "FIRE" OR ANY OTHER PERILS INSURED AGAINST BY THIS POLICY OR SAID ENDORSEMENTS; HOWEVER, SUBJECT TO THE FOREGOING AND ALL PROVISIONS OF THIS POLICY, LOSS BY "FIRE" RESULTING FROM NUCLEAR REACTION OR NUCLEAR RADIATION OR RADIOACTIVE CONTAMINATION IS INSURED AGAINST BY THIS POLICY.

22. **REQUIREMENTS IN CASE LOSS OCCURS:** THE INSURED SHALL GIVE IMMEDIATE WRITTEN NOTICE TO THIS COMPANY OF ANY BUSINESS INTERRUPTION LOSS AND PROTECT THE PROPERTY FROM FURTHER DAMAGE THAT MIGHT RESULT IN EXTENSION OF THE PERIOD OF INTERRUPTION; AND WITHIN 60 DAYS FOLLOWING THE DATE OF DAMAGE TO OR DESTRUCTION OF THE REAL OR PERSONAL PROPERTY DESCRIBED, UNLESS SUCH TIME IS EXTENDED IN WRITING BY THIS COMPANY, THE INSURED SHALL RENDER TO THIS COMPANY A PROOF OF LOSS, SIGNED AND SWORN TO BY THE INSURED, STATING THE KNOWLEDGE AND BELIEF OF THE INSURED AS TO THE FOLLOWING:

(a) THE TIME AND ORIGIN OF THE PROPERTY DAMAGE OR DESTRUCTION CAUSING THE INTERRUPTION OF BUSINESS,

(b) THE INTEREST OF THE INSURED AND OF ALL OTHERS IN THE BUSINESS,

(c) ALL OTHER CONTRACTS OF INSURANCE, WHETHER VALID OR NOT, COVERING IN ANY MANNER THE LOSS INSURED AGAINST BY THIS POLICY,

(d) ANY CHANGES IN THE TITLE, NATURE, LOCATION, ENCUMBRANCE OR POSSESSION OF SAID BUSINESS SINCE THE ISSUING OF THIS POLICY, AND

(e) BY WHOM AND FOR WHAT PURPOSE ANY BUILDING HEREIN DESCRIBED AND THE SEVERAL PARTS THEREOF WERE OCCUPIED AT THE TIME OF DAMAGE OR DESTRUCTION,

AND SHALL FURNISH A COPY OF ALL THE DESCRIPTIONS AND SCHEDULES IN ALL POLICIES, AND THE ACTUAL AMOUNT OF BUSINESS INTERRUPTION VALUE AND LOSS CLAIMED, ACCOMPANIED BY DETAILED EXHIBITS OF ALL VALUES, COSTS AND ESTIMATES UPON WHICH SUCH AMOUNTS ARE BASED.

THE INSURED, AS OFTEN AS MAY BE REASONABLY REQUIRED, SHALL EXHIBIT TO ANY PERSON DESIGNATED BY THIS COMPANY ALL THAT REMAINS OF ANY PROPERTY HEREIN DESCRIBED, AND SUBMIT TO EXAMINATIONS UNDER OATH BY ANY PERSON NAMED BY THIS COMPANY, AND SUBSCRIBE THE SAME; AND, AS OFTEN AS MAY BE REASONABLY REQUIRED, SHALL PRODUCE FOR EXAMINATION ALL BOOKS OF ACCOUNT, BILLS, INVOICES AND OTHER VOUCHERS, OR CERTIFIED COPIES THEREOF IF ORIGINALS BE LOST, AT SUCH REASONABLE TIME AND PLACE AS MAY BE DESIGNATED BY THIS COMPANY OR ITS REPRESENTATIVE, AND SHALL PERMIT EXTRACTS AND COPIES THEREOF TO BE MADE.

INSURANCE COMPANY

A STOCK COMPANY

Insured   **Amount Insured**

Contract Number   **Contract Date**

We are pleased to provide you the benefits of this Life Insurance Contract. Please read your contract and the copy of the application. We want to be sure that we have issued this contract correctly. If there is any error, tell us as soon as you can.   We will then make any change necessary.

APPLICANT'S RIGHT TO CANCEL

If this contract is returned to us at our office or to our agent to be cancelled within 10 days of its delivery, we will pay the Applicant, within 10 days after its return, all premium paid for this contract. After the contract is returned, it will be considered as never in effect.

This contract is issued in consideration of the application and the payment of the premium. It is subject to the terms and conditions stated on the attached pages, all of which are a part of it. It is made effective as stated in the application.

The entire contract between us and the Applicant consists of the policy, all attached pages, and the written application. All statements made in the application are considered to be to the best knowledge and belief of the Applicant and not as promises of truth. Unless it is contained in the written application, we will not use any statement to void this contract or to deny a claim.

No person other than one of our officers can, for us, alter or waive any terms or provisions of this contract.

Signed at

Secretary, LHFS   President

This is a Life Insurance Contract Providing Whole Life Insurance with Premiums that will not Change from those stated in the Contract and Without Dividends. Premiums are payable for a Specified Period or until the Insured's Prior Death.

(Form continued on following pages)

DEFINITIONS

. "We, us, our" means Insurance Company;

. "You, your" means the Owner;

. "Age" means age last birthday;

. "Contract years" means twelve month periods beginning with the Contract Date;

. "Contract month" means the twelve periods during the contract year, each of which begins on the Contract Date or the same date in any calendar month;

. "Basic contract" means this contract excluding any additional benefit for which a separate premium is charged;

. "Our office" means the Home Office,

or any other office which we may name for the purpose of administering this contract; and

8. "Proof of the Insured's death" means:

a. A copy of a certified death certificate; or

b. A copy of a certified decree of a court of competent jurisdiction as to the finding of death; or

c. A written statement by a medical doctor who attended the deceased; or

d. Any other proof satisfactory to us.

DEATH BENEFIT—BASIC CONTRACT

We will, on receiving proof of the Insured's death, pay the beneficiary the death benefit of the basic contract. The death benefit will be the Amount Insured, plus any premium paid for the basic contract beyond Contract Month in which the Insured died, less:

1. Any outstanding loan, secured by the basic contract, and made under its "Cash Loan" provision; and

2. Any premium due for the basic contract but not paid; and

3. Any amount payable to an assignee under a collateral assignment of the basic contract.

If the Insured commits suicide within two years of the Date of Issue, the Death Benefit will be limited by the "Suicide" provision. If the Insured's sex or date of birth was misstated in the Application, the Death Benefit will be limited by the "Sex and Age" provision. Our right to contest payment of any death benefit is limited by the "Contest" provision.

CONTRACT VALUES AND BENEFITS

Cash Values—
If all past due premiums have been paid to the end of the contract year, the Cash Value equals:

1. The then present value of future death benefits of the basic contract less;

2. The then present value of annual amounts equal to the cash value factors for the rest of the premium-paying period.

These Cash Values are shown in a table headed TABLE OF CONTRACT VALUES or an extension of that table. We will determine the Cash Value for any other time during a contract year by allowing for time which has passed in the year and any premium paid for the year.

If all past due premiums have not been paid to the end of the contract year, during the sixty days following the due date of any premium not paid, the Cash Value will be the same as on that date. After that, the Cash Value of benefits in the event premium is not paid is equal to the present value of future death benefits.

During the thirty days after the end of any contract year, the Cash Value will be at least equal to the Cash Value at the end of that contract year.

Cash Surrender Value—Cash Surrender Value means the Cash Value, less any outstanding loan on or secured by this contract.

Cash Surrender—We will pay the Cash Surrender Value to you, on written request and surrender of this contract, without the consent of any beneficiary unless irrevocably named. We may delay payment of the Cash Surrender Value for a period of not more than six months after we receive the request.

Loan Value—The Loan Value of this contract is equal to the Cash Value.

Cash Loans—We will, if you assign this contract to us while it is in effect other than as Extended Term Insurance, make a loan to you with this contract as security. We may defer the loan, other than one to pay premium due us, for no longer than six months after we receive the request for the loan at our office.

The maximum loan available will be the Loan Value at the end of the current contract year. We will deduct from the loan proceeds the amount of any outstanding loan. We may also deduct premium for this contract and interest on the loan to the end of the current contract year. Interest on the loan will be payable in advance, on the due dates of future premiums, at the rate shown on the CONTRACT SUMMARY. If no future premium is due, interest is payable at the beginning of each contract year. Interest not paid when due will be added to the loan and will bear interest at the same rate.

CONTRACT VALUES AND BENEFITS—(Continued)

All or part of any loan may be repaid while the Insured is living and the contract is in effect.

If the loan exceeds the Cash Value, this contract ends without value 31 days after we mail notice of termination to your, and any assignee's, last known address.

Automatic Premium Loan—This benefit is effective only if requested in the application or in writing to us while no premium remains not paid 31 days beyond its due date. If there is enough Loan Value, any premium for this contract not paid 31 days after its due date will be paid by a loan against this contract on the same terms as "Cash Loans." You may end this benefit by writing to our office.

If:

1. the Automatic Premium Loan is applied on the anniversary of the contract date; and

2. your contract has enough Cash Value available;

the Automatic Premium Loan will run for two consecutive contract years. After that, the basic contract will then continue:

1. as Extended Term Insurance, if available, or;

2. if not, as Paid-up Insurance.

If the Automatic Premium Loan is applied other than on the anniversary of the contract date and your contract has enough Cash Value, it will run for two contract years from the anniversary of the contract date next following the operation of the Automatic Premium Loan.

Benefits in the Event Premium Is Not Paid—If this contract has a Cash Surrender Value, you may, within 60 days after the due date of the first premium not paid, choose in writing one of the options below.

1. Extended Term Insurance (This option is only available if values for it are shown in the TABLE OF CONTRACT VALUES)—You may continue this contract as Extended Term Insurance:

a. in an amount equal to the Amount Insured less any outstanding loan secured by this contract; and

b. the term of the insurance will be what the Cash Surrender Value will buy as a net single premium, when applied on the due date of the first premium not paid at the then age of the Insured; or

2. Paid-up Insurance—You may continue this contract as Paid-up Insurance in an amount equal to what the Cash Surrender Value will buy as a net single premium when applied on the due date of the first premium not paid at the then age of the Insured; or

3. Cash—You may surrender this contract for its Cash Surrender Value determined as of the due date of the premium not paid.

We may defer the payment of the Cash Surrender Value for not more than six months after we receive notice of your choice of this option at our office.

If you do not make a choice within the 60-day period, the automatic option will be option 1 if available, otherwise option 2.

If either option 1 or 2 is effected, the insurance may be surrendered at any time for its Cash Surrender Value.

Cash Values, Extended Term Insurance, if any, and Paid-Up Life Insurance benefits are not less than the minimum required by the law of the state in which this contract is delivered.

Basis of Values and Benefits—The basis for all present values and net single premiums referred to under "CONTRACT VALUES AND BENEFITS" are shown on the TABLE OF CONTRACT VALUES.

OPTIONAL INCOME PROVISIONS

We will pay any amount payable under this contract under the terms of any Option if:

1. the amount is payable in one sum; and

2. the amount placed under an option is at least $5,000; and

3. the election is made:

a. in writing; and

b. by you, if the Insured is living; or

c. by the beneficiary, if the Insured has died.

Your election as to payments after the Insured dies is not

binding on the payee unless restricted in the election. If you have not made an election when the Insured dies, the person or persons entitled to the insurance proceeds may make the election. While the Insured is living, you may cancel an election you made:

1. before the Maturity Date if the contract is an endowment; or

2. before surrender if the contract has a cash value

unless you made the election irrevocable.

If you cancel an election and have not named a beneficiary under this contract when the Insured dies, the beneficiary is you, your executors, administrators, or assigns.

(Form continued on following pages)

OPTIONAL INCOME PROVISIONS (Continued)

Option 1—Payments of a Fixed Amount—We will make equal monthly payments of the amount elected until the amount placed under this option, with interest at a rate not less than 3½% per year, has been paid. The amount of each monthly payment must be at least $4.50 for each $1,000 of proceeds. The last payment will include any amount that is not enough to make another full payment.

Option 2—Payments for a Fixed Period—We will make equal monthly payments as shown in Table A, for the number of years elected.

Option 3—Amounts Held at Interest—We will keep amounts under this option and pay interest on them (monthly, quarterly, semi-annually, or annually, as elected) during the lifetime of the first payee, or for any other period agreed on. Interest will be at rates we set from time to time, but not less than 3½% per year. We will not make interest payments to any other payee after the 30th anniversary of the date this option first became payable. On the 30th anniversary we will pay any amounts being kept for any other payee in one sum. If the death of the first payee occurs on or after the 30th anniversary, we will pay the balance to the next payee in one sum.

Option 4—Monthly Life Income—We will make monthly payments, as shown in Table B, during the lifetime of the person on whose life the payments are based either:

1. with the number of payments assured for 60, 120, 180 or 240 months as elected; or

2. on the cash refund basis where, if at the death of that person payments have been made for less than the number of months elected, we will pay in one sum any amount used to provide this income that exceeds the sum of monthly payments already made.

Option 5—Joint and Survivor Level Amount Monthly Life Income—We will make monthly payments, as shown in Table C based on the lifetime of two persons. We will make monthly payments as long as either person lives.

payments will be either:

1. without payments assured (no payments will be made after the death of the survivor); or

2. with payments assured for 120 months.

Option 6—Joint and Survivor Monthly Life Income—Two-thirds to Survivor—We will make monthly payments, as shown in Table D, during the joint lifetime of two persons on whose lives payments are based. After the death of either, we will make payments of two-thirds the original amount during the lifetime of the survivor. No payments will be made after the death of the survivor.

Option 7—Joint and Last Survivor Monthly Life Income—Monthly Payment Reduces on Death of First Person Named—We will make monthly income payments, as shown in Table E, during the joint lifetime of two persons on whose lives payments are based. One of the two persons will be named the first person. The other will be named the second person. If the second person dies first, we will continue to make monthly payments during the life of the first person. These payments will be in the same amount that was payable during the joint lifetime of the two persons. If the first person dies first, we will continue to make monthly payments during the life of the second person in an amount equal to 50% of the payments we would have made during the lifetime of the first person. No payments will be made after the death of the survivor.

Option 8—Other Options—We will make any other arrangements for income payments as may be agreed on.

If any periodic payment due any payee is less than $50.00, we may make payments less often.

If, at the date the first payment under an option is due, we have declared a higher rate under an option, we will base the payments on the higher rate.

Payment Due—The first payment under an option, except Option 3, is due on the date the proceeds become payable under that option. Under Option 3 the first payment is due one month after that date.

Payee—We will make each payment under an elected option when due to the designated payee, with the designation applying at the due date of each payment. If two or more payees are to share payments under Option 3, we will divide the proceeds on which interest is payable in the proportions designated. Any rights of each payee will apply to each payee's share of the proceeds.

If any payee or the last surviving payee dies while receiving payments, we will pay in one sum:

1. any amounts not paid which remain (as to that payee) under the option; or

2. the present value of any remaining payments assured;

to the executors, administrators or assigns of that payee.

Rights of Payee—Unless restricted, a payee under Option 3 has the right to:

1. Elect Option 1, 2 or 4; but no election may be made under Option 1 or 2 which would continue payments past the 30th anniversary of the date the first payment was due;

2. Withdraw part or all of the proceeds at any time but not more than four times in any one calendar

OPTIONAL INCOME PROVISIONS (Continued)

year; after four times in a calendar year, the payee has the right to withdraw in one sum the entire amount not already paid.

Unless restricted, the payee under options 1, 2, 4, 5, 6, and 7 has:

1. the right to assign any payments under an option; and

2. has the right to receive the present value of future benefits.

A payee has no right to receive the present value of future benefits under a Life Income Option during the lifetime of the person on whose life the payments are based.

Any payee who has a right to withdraw or receive the present value of future benefits can exercise that right to the exclusion of the rights of any succeeding payee. The calculation of the present value of future benefits under a Life Income Option will be at an interest rate we determine.

If, at the time an option is elected, there is any outstanding loan on or secured by this contract, that loan may be repaid to us in whole or in part.

All amounts we hold and payments we make under an option are exempt from the claims of all creditors to the extent allowed by law. Amounts payable under any option are part of and invested in our general corporate funds.

Table A—Monthly Payments For Fixed Period Per $1,000 of Proceeds—3½%

Years	Monthly Instalment	Years	Monthly Instalment	Years	Monthly Instalment	Years	Monthly Instalment	Years	Monthly Instalment	Years	Monthly Instalment
1	$84.654	6	$15.350	11	$9.086	16	$6.763	21	$5.565	26	$4.842
2	43.055	7	13.376	12	8.464	17	6.465	22	5.393	27	4.732
3	29.194	8	11.899	13	7.939	18	6.201	23	5.236	28	4.630
4	22.268	9	10.751	14	7.490	19	5.966	24	5.093	29	4.535
5	18.115	10	9.835	15	7.101	20	5.755	25	4.963	30	4.447

Table B—Monthly Life Income Per $1,000 of Proceeds

Male

Age	Cash Ref.	60 Mo.	120 Mo.	180 Mo.	240 Mo.	Age	Cash Ref.	60 Mo.	120 Mo.	180 Mo.	240 Mo.	Age	Cash Ref.	60 Mo.	120 Mo.	180 Mo.	240 Mo.
20	3.35	3.39	3.38	3.37	3.36	44	4.06	4.20	4.18	4.14	4.09	68	6.10	6.87	6.52	6.01	5.44
21	3.37	3.40	3.39	3.38	3.37	45	4.11	4.26	4.24	4.19	4.13	69	6.26	7.09	6.68	6.11	5.49
22	3.38	3.42	3.41	3.40	3.39	46	4.16	4.32	4.30	4.25	4.18	70	6.42	7.31	6.85	6.21	5.53
23	3.40	3.44	3.43	3.42	3.41	47	4.21	4.39	4.36	4.30	4.23	71	6.60	7.55	7.02	6.30	5.57
24	3.43	3.47	3.46	3.45	3.44	48	4.26	4.45	4.42	4.36	4.28	72	6.79	7.81	7.19	6.40	5.61
25	3.45	3.49	3.48	3.47	3.46	49	4.32	4.53	4.49	4.42	4.33	73	6.99	8.08	7.37	6.48	5.64
26	3.47	3.51	3.50	3.49	3.48	50	4.38	4.60	4.56	4.48	4.39	74	7.20	8.37	7.56	6.57	5.66
27	3.49	3.54	3.53	3.52	3.51	51	4.44	4.68	4.63	4.55	4.44	75	7.44	8.67	7.74	6.65	5.69
28	3.52	3.56	3.55	3.54	3.53	52	4.50	4.76	4.70	4.61	4.49	76	7.67	8.99	7.92	6.72	5.70
29	3.54	3.59	3.58	3.57	3.56	53	4.57	4.84	4.78	4.68	4.55	77	7.94	9.33	8.11	6.79	5.72
30	3.57	3.61	3.60	3.59	3.58	54	4.64	4.93	4.86	4.76	4.61	78	8.24	9.69	8.29	6.85	5.73
31	3.60	3.64	3.63	3.62	3.61	55	4.71	5.03	4.95	4.83	4.67	79	8.53	10.07	8.47	6.90	5.74
32	3.62	3.67	3.66	3.65	3.64	56	4.79	5.12	5.04	4.91	4.73	80	8.87	10.46	8.64	6.95	5.74
33	3.65	3.71	3.70	3.69	3.67	57	4.87	5.23	5.13	4.99	4.79	81	9.26	10.88	8.81	6.99	5.75
34	3.68	3.74	3.73	3.72	3.70	58	4.95	5.34	5.23	5.07	4.85	82	9.62	11.31	8.97	7.02	5.75
35	3.71	3.78	3.77	3.75	3.74	59	5.04	5.45	5.34	5.15	4.91	83	10.08	11.77	9.11	7.04	5.75
36	3.75	3.81	3.80	3.79	3.77	60	5.14	5.58	5.44	5.24	4.98	84	10.52	12.24	9.25	7.06	5.75
37	3.78	3.85	3.84	3.83	3.80	61	5.23	5.70	5.56	5.33	5.04	85 and over	11.06	12.73	9.36	7.07	5.75
38	3.82	3.89	3.89	3.87	3.84	62	5.34	5.84	5.68	5.42	5.10						
39	3.85	3.94	3.93	3.91	3.88	63	5.45	5.99	5.80	5.52	5.16						
40	3.89	3.99	3.97	3.95	3.92	64	5.57	6.14	5.93	5.61	5.22						
41	3.93	4.04	4.02	4.00	3.96	65	5.69	6.31	6.07	5.71	5.28						
42	3.97	4.09	4.07	4.04	4.00	66	5.82	6.49	6.22	5.81	5.33						
43	4.02	4.14	4.12	4.09	4.04	67	5.96	6.67	6.36	5.91	5.39						

(Form continued on following pages)

Table B—Monthly Life Income Per $1,000 of Proceeds
Female

Age	Cash Ref.	60 Mo.	120 Mo.	180 Mo.	240 Mo.	Age	Cash Ref.	60 Mo.	120 Mo.	180 Mo.	240 Mo.	Age	Cash Ref.	60 Mo.	120 Mo.	180 Mo.	240 Mo.
20*	3.25	3.28	3.27	3.26	3.25	44	3.83	3.89	3.88	3.87	3.85	68	5.63	6.09	5.93	5.65	5.27
21	3.26	3.30	3.29	3.28	3.27	45	3.87	3.94	3.93	3.91	3.89	69	5.78	6.28	6.09	5.76	5.33
22	3.28	3.31	3.30	3.29	3.28	46	3.91	3.99	3.98	3.96	3.93	70	5.93	6.48	6.26	5.88	5.38
23	3.29	3.33	3.32	3.31	3.31	47	3.96	4.03	4.02	4.00	3.97	71	6.08	6.70	6.43	5.99	5.44
24	3.31	3.35	3.34	3.33	3.32	48	4.00	4.09	4.08	4.05	4.02	72	6.26	6.93	6.61	6.10	5.49
25	3.33	3.36	3.35	3.34	3.33	49	4.05	4.14	4.13	4.10	4.07	73	6.43	7.18	6.80	6.21	5.53
26	3.34	3.38	3.37	3.36	3.35	50	4.10	4.20	4.19	4.16	4.12	74	6.62	7.44	6.99	6.31	5.57
27	3.36	3.40	3.39	3.38	3.37	51	4.15	4.26	4.25	4.21	4.17	75	6.83	7.73	7.19	6.41	5.60
28	3.38	3.42	3.41	3.40	3.39	52	4.21	4.33	4.31	4.27	4.22	76	7.04	8.03	7.39	6.50	5.63
29	3.40	3.44	3.43	3.42	3.41	53	4.26	4.40	4.38	4.33	4.27	77	7.28	8.35	7.59	6.58	5.65
30	3.42	3.46	3.45	3.44	3.43	54	4.32	4.47	4.44	4.40	4.33	78	7.54	8.70	7.79	6.66	5.67
31	3.45	3.48	3.47	3.46	3.45	55	4.39	4.55	4.52	4.47	4.39	79	7.78	9.06	7.99	6.73	5.69
32	3.47	3.51	3.50	3.49	3.48	56	4.45	4.63	4.59	4.54	4.45	80	8.07	9.44	8.18	6.79	5.70
33	3.49	3.53	3.52	3.51	3.50	57	4.53	4.71	4.67	4.61	4.52	81	8.35	9.84	8.36	6.84	5.72
34	3.52	3.56	3.55	3.54	3.53	58	4.60	4.80	4.76	4.69	4.58	82	8.66	10.25	8.53	6.88	5.72
35	3.54	3.58	3.57	3.56	3.55	59	4.68	4.90	4.85	4.77	4.65	83	9.00	10.68	8.68	6.92	5.73
36	3.57	3.61	3.60	3.59	3.58	60	4.76	5.00	4.94	4.85	4.71	84	9.32	11.11	8.83	6.96	5.74
37	3.60	3.64	3.63	3.62	3.61	61	4.85	5.10	5.04	4.94	4.78	85 and over	9.69	11.55	8.96	6.98	5.74
38	3.63	3.67	3.66	3.65	3.64	62	4.94	5.22	5.15	5.03	4.85						
39	3.66	3.70	3.69	3.68	3.67	63	5.04	5.34	5.26	5.12	4.92						
40	3.69	3.74	3.73	3.72	3.70	64	5.15	5.47	5.38	5.22	4.99						
41	3.72	3.77	3.76	3.75	3.74	65	5.26	5.61	5.50	5.33	5.06						
42	3.76	3.81	3.80	3.79	3.77	66	5.38	5.76	5.64	5.43	5.13						
43	3.79	3.85	3.84	3.83	3.81	67	5.50	5.92	5.78	5.54	5.20						

*and under 20

Joint and Survivor Monthly Life Income Per $1,000 of Proceeds

Age and Sex		TABLE C—Level Amount										TABLE D—⅓ To Survivor				
		Age and Sex														
Male		50		55		60		65		70		50	55	60	65	70
	Fem.	55		60		65		70		75		55	60	65	70	75
		No Ref.	120 Mo.	No Ref.	120 Mo.	No Ref.	120 Mo.	No Ref.	120 Mo.	No Ref.	120 Mo.	No Ref.	No Ref.	No Ref.	No Ref.	No Ref.
50	55	$4.04	$4.03	$4.17	$4.16	$4.28	$4.27	$4.37	$4.36	$4.45	$4.44	$4.40	$4.58	$4.77	$4.98	$5.21
51	56	4.07	4.06	4.20	4.19	4.32	4.31	4.42	4.41	4.51	4.50	4.44	4.62	4.82	5.04	5.28
52	57	4.08	4.08	4.23	4.22	4.36	4.35	4.48	4.47	4.57	4.56	4.47	4.66	4.86	5.09	5.34
53	58	4.12	4.11	4.27	4.26	4.41	4.40	4.53	4.52	4.63	4.62	4.51	4.70	4.91	5.15	5.40
54	59	4.14	4.13	4.30	4.29	4.45	4.44	4.59	4.58	4.70	4.69	4.54	4.74	4.96	5.21	5.47
55	60	4.17	4.16	4.34	4.33	4.50	4.49	4.64	4.63	4.77	4.75	4.58	4.79	5.01	5.27	5.54
56	61	4.19	4.18	4.37	4.36	4.54	4.53	4.70	4.69	4.84	4.82	4.62	4.83	5.07	5.33	5.61
57	62	4.21	4.20	4.40	4.39	4.59	4.58	4.76	4.75	4.91	4.89	4.65	4.87	5.12	5.39	5.69
58	63	4.23	4.22	4.44	4.43	4.63	4.62	4.82	4.81	4.99	4.97	4.69	4.92	5.17	5.46	5.77
59	64	4.26	4.25	4.47	4.46	4.68	4.67	4.88	4.87	5.06	5.04	4.73	4.97	5.23	5.52	5.85
60	65	4.28	4.27	4.50	4.49	4.72	4.71	4.95	4.93	5.14	5.12	4.77	5.01	5.29	5.59	5.93
61	66	4.30	4.29	4.53	4.52	4.77	4.76	5.01	4.99	5.22	5.19	4.81	5.06	5.34	5.66	6.01
62	67	4.32	4.31	4.56	4.55	4.81	4.80	5.07	5.05	5.31	5.27	4.85	5.11	5.40	5.73	6.10
63	68	4.34	4.33	4.59	4.58	4.86	4.84	5.13	5.11	5.39	5.35	4.90	5.16	5.47	5.81	6.19
64	69	4.35	4.34	4.62	4.61	4.90	4.89	5.20	5.17	5.48	5.43	4.94	5.21	5.53	5.89	6.29
65	70	4.37	4.36	4.64	4.63	4.95	4.93	5.26	5.23	5.56	5.52	4.98	5.27	5.59	5.96	6.38

Table E—Joint and Last Survivor Monthly Life Income Per $1,000 of Proceeds
Monthly Payment Reduces on Death of First Person Named

Age and Sex			Age and Sex-Second Person Named				
Male			50	55	60	65	70
	Female		55	60	65	70	75
			No Ref.	No Ref.	No Ref.	No Ref.	No Ref.
First Person Named	50	55	$4.30	$4.37	$4.44	$4.49	$4.53
	51	56	4.35	4.43	4.50	4.55	4.60
	52	57	4.40	4.49	4.56	4.62	4.67
	53	58	4.45	4.54	4.62	4.69	4.75
	54	59	4.51	4.60	4.69	4.76	4.82
	55	60	4.56	4.66	4.76	4.84	4.91
	56	61	4.62	4.73	4.83	4.92	4.99
	57	62	4.67	4.79	4.90	5.00	5.08
	58	63	4.73	4.86	4.98	5.08	5.17
	59	64	4.79	4.93	5.05	5.17	5.27
	60	65	4.85	5.00	5.13	5.26	5.37
	61	66	4.92	5.07	5.22	5.36	5.48
	62	67	4.98	5.14	5.30	5.45	5.59
	63	68	5.05	5.22	5.39	5.56	5.70
	64	69	5.12	5.30	5.48	5.66	5.82
	65	70	5.19	5.38	5.58	5.77	5.95

We will furnish the amount of monthly income for other age combinations on request.
Age as used above means age when income begins.

ENDORSEMENTS

This endorsement is made a part of this contract at its Date of Issue.

The second paragraph of the provision entitled "Cash Loans" under "CONTRACT VALUE AND BENEFITS" is amended by the addition of the following:

The loan interest rate is 7.4% in advance.

INSURANCE COMPANY

Secretary

(Form continued on following page)

PREMIUM PAYMENT AND REINSTATEMENT

Premium—Each premium after the first is payable, as shown in the CONTRACT SUMMARY, to us at our office or to one of our authorized representatives. We will send you a receipt signed by one of our officers and properly countersigned.

We will allow a 31-day period after the due date for payment of any premium after the first. During this period this contract will be in full effect. If any premium past due is not paid during this period, this contract will, except as stated in the "Reinstatement" and the "Contract Values and Benefits" provisions, end. If the Insured dies during this period,

any premium not paid will be deducted from the death benefit.

Reinstatement—If any premium is not paid, then anytime within three years from the date to which premium was paid, we will restore this contract if it has not been surrendered for cash. Evidence of insurability acceptable to us is required. We also require payment of all premiums not paid and any outstanding loan on or secured by this contract, with interest at the reinstatement interest rate shown in the CONTRACT SUMMARY.

OWNERSHIP, ASSIGNMENT AND BENEFICIARY

Ownership—The original owner is shown in the application. You, during the Insured's lifetime, may, without the consent of any beneficiary unless irrevocably named, exercise all rights given in this contract.

Assignment—Ownership is transferable by assignment. No assignment is binding on us until we receive a copy of the written assignment at our office. We will not determine if an assignment is valid.

Proof of interest must be filed with any claim under a collateral assignment.

Beneficiary—The original beneficiary is stated in the

application. You may name a new beneficiary during the lifetime of the Insured and while this contract continues. Any change will be effective from the date you signed the notice of change, even if the Insured is not living when we receive it. We will have no further responsibility for any payment we make before we receive the notice at our office.

The interest of any beneficiary who is not living when the Insured dies will pass to you or your executors, administrators or assigns unless you have stated differently. The rights of any collateral assignee may affect the interest of the beneficiary.

GENERAL PROVISIONS

Contest—After the contract has been in effect during the Insured's lifetime for two years from its Date of Issue, we will not use misstatements made in the application to contest this contract.

Suicide—If the Insured commits suicide, while sane or insane, within two years from the Date of Issue, the death benefit will be limited to the premium paid.

Sex and Age—If the Insured's sex or date of birth was misstated in the application, all benefits of this contract

are what the premium paid would have purchased at the correct sex and age.

Proof of the Insured's age may be filed at any time at our office.

Changes—You may change this contract to another form or in amount, or both, with our consent and our requirements. We may reduce premiums or grant values or benefits greater than those stated in the contract.

Contract Payments—All payments we make will be paid at our office.

This is a Life Insurance Contract Providing Whole Life Insurance with Premiums that will not Change from those stated in the Contract and Without Dividends. Premiums are payable for a Specified Period or until the Insured's Prior Death.

ENDORSEMENTS

INSURANCE COMPANY

A Stock Insurance Company

DECLARATIONS   STANDARD AUTOMOBILE POLICY

ITEM 1.	**NAMED INSURED** AND ADDRESS (NUMBER, STREET, TOWN, COUNTY, STATE, ZIP)	INSURING COMPANY (SEE ABOVE)
	POLICY NUMBER	**THE NAMED INSURED IS** INDIVIDUAL □ PARTNERSHIP □ CORPORATION JOINT VENTURE □ OTHER _____
		BUSINESS OF THE **NAMED INSURED** IS

ITEM 2. POLICY PERIOD: FROM _____ TO _____ 12:01 A. M., STANDARD TIME AT THE ADDRESS OF THE NAMED INSURED AS STATED HEREIN.

ITEM 3. **SCHEDULE** AS OF EFFECTIVE DATE OF THIS INSURANCE—AS TO
(A) SECTIONS A, B AND C **OWNED AUTOMOBILES;**
(B) SECTION D—COVERED AUTOMOBILES   (INCLUDING NEWLY ACQUIRED VEHICLES: SUBJECT TO THE PROVISIONS OF PARAGRAPH **(b)** OF THE "COVERED AUTOMOBILE" DEFINITION)

(A.) DESCRIPTION; **PURPOSES OF USE**—(P & B = **PLEASURE AND BUSINESS;** C = COMMERCIAL)

AUTO	YEAR MODEL; TRADE NAME; BODY TYPE—CAPACITY (TRUCK LOAD, GALLONAGE, BUS SEATING); IDENTIFICATION (I), SERIAL (S), MOTOR (M) NO.; CYLINDERS (NO.); MODEL	PRINCIPALLY GARAGED IN (TOWN, STATE)	PURPOSE OF USE	CLASSIFICATION
1.				
2.				
3.				

(B.) FACTS RESPECTING PURCHASE

AUTO	LIST PRICE	ACTUAL COST	PURCHASED MO. & YEAR NEW USED (N) (U)	RATING SYMBOL	ANY LOSS UNDER COVERAGES OTHER THAN TOWING IS PAYABLE AS INTEREST MAY APPEAR TO THE NAMED INSURED AND THE LOSS PAYEE NAMED BELOW:
1.					
2.					
3.					

(C) AUTOMOBILE MEDICAL PAYMENTS COVERAGE	DESIGNATED PERSON INSURED	DESIGNATION OF AUTOMOBILE—DIVISION I
		AUTO NO.
(D) UNINSURED MOTORISTS COVERAGE	DESIGNATED PERSON INSURED	INSURED HIGHWAY VEHICLES
		AUTO NO.

ITEM 4. THE INSURANCE AFFORDED IS ONLY WITH RESPECT TO SUCH OF THE FOLLOWING COVERAGES, AND UNDER EACH SUCH SECTION D COVERAGE TO SUCH **COVERED** AUTOMOBILES, DESCRIBED IN THE SCHEDULE OF COVERED AUTOMOBILES, AS ARE INDICATED BY SPECIFIC PREMIUM CHARGE OR CHARGES. THE LIMIT OF THE COMPANY'S LIABILITY AGAINST EACH SUCH COVERAGE SHALL BE AS STATED HEREIN, SUBJECT TO ALL THE TERMS OF THIS INSURANCE HAVING REFERENCE THERETO.

SECTION	COVERAGES	LIMITS OF LIABILITY		PREMIUMS		
				AUTO 1	AUTO 2	AUTO 3
A	A. BODILY INJURY LIABILITY ★	$ _____ .000 EACH PERSON		$	$	$
		$ _____ .000 EACH OCCURRENCE				
	B. PROPERTY DAMAGE LIABILITY ★	$ _____ .000 EACH OCCURRENCE				
B	C. AUTOMOBILE MEDICAL PAYMENTS	$ _____ EACH PERSON				
C	D. UNINSURED MOTORISTS	$ _____ .000 EACH PERSON				
		.000 EACH ACCIDENT				
ENDORSEMENTS' ATTACHED		ENDORSEMENT PREMIUM				
		SUB-TOTAL		$	$	$
D	E. COMPREHENSIVE	ACTUAL CASH VALUE LESS $	DEDUCTIBLE	$	$	$
	F. COLLISION	ACTUAL CASH VALUE LESS $	DEDUCTIBLE			
	G. FIRE, LIGHTNING OR TRANSPORTATION	$				
	H. THEFT	$				
	I. COMBINED ADDITIONAL	$				
	J. TOWING	$25 FOR EACH DISABLEMENT				
ENDORSEMENTS ATTACHED		ENDORSEMENT PREMIUM				
		SUB-TOTAL		$	$	$
				TOTAL PREMIUM $		

ITEM 5. THE PREMIUM FOR THE POLICY INCLUDING INSTALLMENT CHARGES IS TO BE PAID ON THE DUE DATES AS FOLLOWS:

DUE DATE	_____	_____	_____	_____	TOTAL PREMIUM
AMOUNT	$	$	$	$	$

ITEM 6. EXCEPT WITH RESPECT TO BAILMENT LEASE, CONDITIONAL SALE, PURCHASE AGREEMENT, MORTGAGE OR OTHER ENCUMBRANCE, THE **NAMED INSURED** IS THE SOLE OWNER OF EVERY VEHICLE DESCRIBED IN ITEM 3 ABOVE, UNLESS OTHERWISE STATED HEREIN:

★**UNLESS A SPECIFIC PREMIUM CHARGE IS MADE FOR SECTION A COVERAGES, THIS POLICY DOES NOT PROVIDE BODILY INJURY OR PROPERTY DAMAGE LIABILITY INSURANCE AND DOES NOT COMPLY WITH ANY FINANCIAL RESPONSIBILITY LAW**

DATE OF ISSUE	COUNTERSIGNATURE OF AUTHORIZED AGENT

(Form continued on following pages)

THE COMPANY DESIGNATED ON THE DECLARATIONS PAGE

A Stock Insurance Company, herein called the Company

Agrees with the insured, named in the declarations made a part hereof, in consideration of the payment of the premium and in reliance upon the statements in the declarations and subject to all of the terms of this policy:

PART I — LIABILITY

Coverage A — Bodily Injury Liability;

Coverage B — Property Damage Liability

To pay on behalf of the insured all sums which the insured shall become legally obligated to pay as damages because of:

A. bodily injury, personal injury, sickness or disease, including death resulting therefrom, hereinafter called "bodily injury", sustained by any person;

B. injury to or destruction of property, including loss of use thereof, hereinafter called "property damage";

arising out of the ownership, maintenance or use of the owned automobile or any non-owned automobile, and the Company shall defend any suit alleging such bodily injury or property damage and seeking damages which are payable under the terms of this policy, even if any of the allegations of the suit are groundless, false or fraudulent; but the Company may make such investigation and settlement of any claim or suit as it deems expedient.

Supplementary Payments

To pay, in addition to the applicable limits of liability:

(a) all expenses incurred by the Company, all costs taxed against the insured in any such suit and all interest on the entire amount of any judgment therein which accrues after entry of the judgment and before the Company has paid or tendered or deposited in court that part of the judgment which does not exceed the limit of the Company's liability thereon;

(b) premiums on appeal bonds required in any such suit, premiums on bonds to release attachments for an amount not in excess of the applicable limit of liability of this policy, and the cost of bail bonds required of the insured because of accident or traffic law violation arising out of the use of an automobile insured hereunder, not to exceed $250 per bail bond, but without any obligation to apply for or furnish any such bonds;

(c) expenses incurred by the insured for such immediate medical and surgical relief to others as shall be imperative at the time of an accident involving an automobile insured hereunder and not due to war;

(d) all reasonable expenses, other than loss of earnings, incurred by the insured at the Company's request;

(e) for actual loss of earnings incurred by the insured while attending hearings or trials at the request of the Company in connection with any occurrence for which insurance is provided hereunder, subject to a maximum of $25 per day and a total of $500 for any such occurrence;

(f) in an amount not in excess of $50, for reasonable legal expenses, other than a fine or forfeiture of bail, incurred by the insured in the event of his arrest as a result of an accident for which insurance is provided under coverage A or B.

Persons Insured. The following are insureds under Part I:

(a) with respect to the owned automobile,

(1) the named insured and any resident of the same household,

(2) any other person using such automobile with the permission of the named insured, provided his actual operation or (if he is not operating) his other actual use thereof is within the scope of such permission, and

(3) any other person or organization but only with respect to his or its liability because of acts or omissions of an insured under (a) (1) or (2) above;

(b) with respect to a non-owned automobile,

(1) the named insured,

(2) any relative, but only with respect to a private passenger automobile or trailer,

provided his actual operation or (if he is not operating) the other actual use thereof is with the permission, or reasonably believed to be with the permission, of the owner and is within the scope of such permission, and

(3) any other person or organization not owning or hiring the automobile, but only with respect to his or its liability because of acts or omissions of an insured under (b) (1) or (2) above.

The insurance afforded under Part I applies separately to each insured against whom claim is made or suit is brought, but the inclusion herein of more than one insured shall not operate to increase the limits of the Company's liability.

Definitions

Under Part I:

"named insured" means the individual named in item 1 of the declarations and also includes his spouse, if a resident of the same household;

"insured" means a person or organization described under "Persons Insured";

"relative" means a relative of the named insured who is a resident of the same household;

"owned automobile" means (a) a private passenger, farm or utility automobile described in this policy for which a specific premium charge indicates that coverage is afforded, (b) a trailer owned by the named insured, (c) a private passenger, farm or utility automobile ownership of which is acquired by the named insured during the policy period, provided (1) it replaces an owned automobile as defined in (a) above, or (2) the Company insures under this policy all private passenger, farm and utility automobiles owned by the named insured on the date of such acquisition, or (3) that, if the Company does not insure under this policy all private passenger, farm and utility automobiles owned by the named insured on the date of such acquisition, the named insured notifies the Company within 30 days after the date of such acquisition of his election to make this and no other policy issued by the Company applicable to such automobile, or (d) a temporary substitute automobile;

"temporary substitute automobile" means any automobile or trailer, not owned by the named insured, while temporarily used with the permission of the owner as a substitute for the owned automobile or trailer when withdrawn from normal use because of its breakdown, repair, servicing, loss or destruction;

"non-owned automobile" means an automobile or trailer not owned by or furnished for the regular use of either the named insured or any relative, other than a temporary substitute automobile;

"private passenger automobile" means a four wheel private passenger, station wagon or jeep type automobile;

"farm automobile" means an automobile of the truck type with a load capacity of fifteen hundred pounds or less not used for business or commercial purposes other than farming;

"utility automobile" means an automobile, other than a farm automobile, with a load capacity of fifteen hundred pounds or less of the pick-up body, sedan delivery or panel truck type not used for business or commercial purposes;

"trailer" means a trailer designed for use with a private passenger automobile, if not being used for business or commercial purposes with other than a private passenger or utility automobile, or a farm wagon or farm implement while used with a farm automobile;

"automobile business" means the business or occupation of selling, repairing, servicing, storing or parking of automobiles;

"use" of an automobile includes the loading and unloading thereof;

"war" means war, whether or not declared, civil war, insurrection, rebellion or revolution, or any act or condition incident to any of the foregoing.

Exclusions

This policy does not apply under Part I:

(a) to any automobile while used as a public or livery conveyance, but this exclusion does not apply to the named insured with respect to bodily injury or property damage which results from the named insured's occupancy of a non-owned automobile other than as the operator thereof;

(b) to bodily injury or property damage caused intentionally by or at the direction of the insured;

(c) to bodily injury or property damage with respect to which an insured under the policy is also an insured under a nuclear energy liability policy issued by Nuclear Energy Liability Insurance Association, Mutual Atomic Energy Liability Underwriters or Nuclear Insurance Association of Canada, or would be an insured under any such policy but for its termination upon exhaustion of its limit of liability;

(d) to bodily injury or property damage arising out of the operation of farm machinery;

(e) to bodily injury to any employee of the insured arising out of and in the course of employment by the insured, but this exclusion does not apply with respect to any such injury arising out of and in the course of domestic employment by the insured unless benefits therefor are in whole or in part either payable or required to be provided under any workmen's compensation law;

(f) to bodily injury to any fellow employee of the insured injured in the course of his employment if such injury arises out of the use of an automobile in the business of his employer, but this exclusion does not apply to the named insured with respect to injury sustained by any such fellow employee;

(g) to an owned automobile while used by any person while such person is employed or otherwise engaged in the automobile business, but this exclusion does not apply to the named insured, a resident of the same household as the named insured, a partnership in which the named insured or such resident is a partner, or any partner, agent or employee of the named insured, such resident or partnership;

(h) to a non-owned automobile while maintained or used by any person while such person is employed or otherwise engaged in (1) the automobile business of the insured or of any other person or organization, or (2) any other business or occupation of the insured, but this exclusion (h) (2) does not apply to a private passenger automobile operated or occupied by the named insured or by his private chauffeur or domestic servant or a trailer used therewith or with an owned automobile;

(i) to injury to or destruction of property owned or transported by the insured or any automobile in charge of the insured;

(j) to the ownership, maintenance, operation, use, loading or unloading of an automobile ownership of which is acquired by the named insured during the policy period or any temporary substitute automobile therefor, if the named insured has purchased other automobile liability insurance applicable to such automobile for which a specific premium charge has been made.

PART II — EXPENSES FOR MEDICAL SERVICES

Coverage C — Medical Payments. To pay all reasonable expenses incurred within one year from the date of accident for necessary medical, surgical, X-ray and dental services, including prosthetic devices, and necessary ambulance, hospital, professional nursing and funeral services:

Division 1. To or for the named insured and each relative who sustains bodily injury, sickness or disease, including death resulting therefrom, hereinafter called "bodily injury", caused by accident, (a) while occupying the owned automobile, (b) while occupying a non-owned automobile, but only if such person has, or reasonably believes he has, the permission of the owner to use the automobile and the use is within the scope of such permission, or (c) through being struck by an automobile or by a trailer of any type;

Division 2. To or for any other person who sustains bodily injury, caused by accident, while occupying (a) the owned automobile, while being used by the named insured, by any resident of the same household or by any other person with the permission of the named insured; or (b) a non-owned automobile, if the bodily injury results from (1) its operation or occupancy by the named insured or its operation on his behalf by his private chauffeur or domestic servant, or (2) its operation or occupancy by a relative, provided it is a private passenger automobile or trailer, but only if such operator or occupant has, or reasonably believes he has, the permission of the owner to use the automobile and the use is within the scope of such permission.

Definitions. The definitions under Part I apply to Part II, and under Part II:

"occupying" means in or upon or entering into or alighting from.

Exclusions. This policy does not apply under Part II to bodily injury:

(a) sustained while occupying (1) an owned automobile while used as a public or livery conveyance, or (2) any vehicle while located for use as a residence or premises;

(b) sustained by the named insured or a relative while occupying or through being struck by (1) a farm type tractor or other equipment designed for use principally off public roads, while not upon public roads, or (2) a vehicle operated on rails or crawler-treads;

(c) sustained by any person other than the named insured or a relative, (1) while such person is occupying a non-owned automobile while used as a public or livery conveyance, or (2) resulting from the maintenance or use of a non-owned automobile by such person while employed or otherwise engaged in the automobile business, or (3) resulting from the maintenance or use of a non-owned automobile by such person while employed or otherwise engaged in any other business or occupation, unless the bodily injury results from the operation or occupancy of a private passenger automobile by the named insured or by his private chauffeur or domestic servant, or of a trailer used therewith or with an owned automobile;

(d) sustained by any person who is employed in the automobile business, if the accident arises out of the operation thereof and if benefits therefor are in whole or in part either payable or required to be provided under any workmen's compensation law;

(e) due to war.

PART III — PHYSICAL DAMAGE

Coverage D (1) — Comprehensive — excluding Collision
(2) — Personal Effects

(1) To pay for loss caused other than by collision to the owned automobile or to a non-owned automobile. For the purpose of this coverage, breakage of glass and loss caused by missiles, falling objects, fire, theft or larceny, explosion, earthquake, windstorm, hail, water, flood, malicious mischief or vandalism, riot or civil commotion, or colliding with a bird or animal, shall not be deemed to be loss caused by collision.

(2) To pay for loss caused other than by collision or by theft, larceny, robbery or pilferage, or attempt threat, to robes, wearing apparel and other personal effects which are the property of the named insured or a relative, while such effects are in or upon the owned automobile.

Coverage E — Collision. To pay for loss caused by collision to the owned automobile or to a non-owned automobile but only for the amount of each such loss in excess to the deductible amount stated in the declarations as applicable hereto. The deductible amount shall not apply to loss caused by a collision with another automobile insured by the Company.

Coverage F — Towing and Labor Costs. To pay for towing and labor costs necessitated by the disablement of the owned automobile or of any non-owned automobile, provided the labor is performed at the place of disablement.

Supplementary Payments. In addition to the applicable limit of liability:

(a) to reimburse the insured for transportation expenses incurred after a theft covered by this policy of the entire automobile has been reported to the Company and the police, and terminating when the automobile is returned to use or the Company pays for the loss; provided that the Company shall not be obligated to pay aggregate expenses in excess of $10 per day or totaling more than $300;

(b) to pay general average and salvage charges for which the insured becomes legally liable, as to the automobile being transported.

Definitions. The definitions of "named insured", "relative", "temporary substitute automobile", "private passenger automobile", "farm automobile", "utility automobile", "automobile business", "war", and "owned automobile" in Part I apply to Part III, but "owned automobile" does not include under Part III, (1) a trailer owned by the named insured on the effective date of this policy and not described herein, or (2) a trailer ownership of which is acquired during the policy period unless (a) the Company insures all private passenger, farm and utility automobiles and trailers owned by the named insured on the date of such acquisition, or (b) if the Company does not insure all such automobiles and trailers owned by the named insured on the date of such acquisition, the named insured notifies the Company within 30 days after the date of such acquisition of his election to make this and no other policy issued by the Company applicable to such trailer, and under Part III:

"insured" means (a) with respect to an owned automobile, (1) the named insured, and (2) any person or organization (other than a person or organization employed or otherwise engaged in the automobile business or as a carrier or other bailee for hire) maintaining, using or having custody of said automobile with the permission of the named insured and within the scope of such permission; (b) with respect to a non-owned automobile, the named insured and any relative while using such automobile, provided his actual operation or (if he is not operating) the other actual use thereof is with the permission, or reasonably believed to be with the permission, of the owner and is within the scope of such permission;

"non-owned automobile" means a private passenger automobile or trailer not owned by or furnished for the regular use of either the named insured or any relative, other than a temporary substitute automobile, while said automobile or trailer is in the possession or custody of the insured or is being operated by him;

"loss" means direct and accidental loss of or damage to (a) the automobile, including its equipment, or (b) other insured property;

"collision" means collision of an automobile covered by this policy with another object or with a vehicle to which it is attached or by upset of such automobile;

"trailer" means a trailer designed for use with a private passenger automobile, if not being used for business or commercial purposes with other than a private passenger, farm or utility automobile, and if not a home, office, store, display or passenger trailer.

Exclusions. This policy does not apply under Part III:

(a) to any automobile while used as a public or livery conveyance;

(b) to loss due to war;

(c) to loss to a non-owned automobile arising out of its use by the insured while he is employed or otherwise engaged in the automobile business;

(d) to loss to a private passenger, farm or utility automobile or trailer owned by the named insured and not described in this policy or to any temporary substitute automobile therefor, if the insured has other valid and collectible insurance against such loss;

(e) to damage which is due and confined to wear and tear, freezing, mechanical or electrical breakdown or failure, unless such damage results from a theft covered by this policy;

(f) to tires, unless damaged by fire, malicious mischief or vandalism, or stolen or unless the loss be coincident with and from the same cause as other loss covered by this policy;

(g) to loss due to radioactive contamination;

(h) under Coverage E, to breakage of glass if insurance with respect to such breakage is otherwise afforded.

(Form continued on following pages)

PART IV — PROTECTION AGAINST UNINSURED MOTORISTS

Coverage G—Uninsured Motorists (Damages for Bodily Injury). To pay all sums which the insured or his legal representative shall be legally entitled to recover as damages from the owner or operator of an uninsured automobile because of bodily injury, sickness or disease, including death resulting therefrom, hereinafter called "bodily injury", sustained by the insured, caused by accident and arising out of the ownership, maintenance or use of such uninsured automobile; provided, for the purposes of this coverage, determination as to whether the insured or such representative is legally entitled to recover such damages, and if so the amount thereof, shall be made by agreement between the insured or such representative and the Company or, if they fail to agree, by arbitration.

No judgment against any person or organization alleged to be legally responsible for the bodily injury shall be conclusive, as between the insured and the Company, of the issues of liability of such person or organization or of the amount of damages to which the insured is legally entitled unless such judgment is entered pursuant to an action prosecuted by the insured with the written consent of the Company.

Definitions. The definitions under Part I, except the definition of "insured", apply to Part IV, and under Part IV:

"insured" means:

(a) the named insured and any relative;

(b) any other person while occupying an insured automobile; and

(c) any person, with respect to damages he is entitled to recover because of bodily injury to which this Part applies sustained by an insured under (a) or (b) above.

The insurance afforded under Part IV applies separately to each insured, but the inclusion herein of more than one insured shall not operate to increase the limits of the Company's liability.

"insured automobile" means:

(a) an automobile described in the policy for which a specific premium charge indicates that coverage is afforded,

(b) a private passenger, farm or utility automobile, ownership of which is acquired by the named insured during the policy period, provided

(1) it replaces an insured automobile as defined in (a) above, or

(2) the Company insures under this coverage all private passenger, farm and utility automobiles owned by the named insured on the date of such acquisition, or

(3) the Company does not insure all such automobiles owned by the named insured on the date of such acquisition, provided further that the named insured notifies the Company within 30 days after the date of such acquisition of his election to make the Liability and Family Protection Coverages under this and no other policy issued by the Company applicable to such automobile,

(c) a temporary substitute automobile for an insured automobile as defined in (a) or (b) above, and

(d) a non-owned automobile while being operated by the named insured; and the term "insured automobile" includes a trailer while being used with an automobile described in (a), (b), (c) or (d) above, but shall not include:

(1) any automobile or trailer owned by a resident of the same household as the named insured,

(2) any automobile while used as a public or livery conveyance, or

(3) any automobile while being used without the permission of the owner.

"uninsured automobile" includes a trailer of any type and means:

(a) an automobile or trailer with respect to the ownership, maintenance or use of which there is, in at least the amounts specified by the financial responsibility law of the state in which the insured automobile is principally garaged, no bodily injury liability bond or insurance policy applicable at the time of the accident with respect to any person or organization legally responsible for the use of such automobile, or with respect to which there is a bodily injury liability bond or insurance policy applicable at the time of the accident but the Company writing the same denies coverage thereunder, or

(b) a hit-and-run automobile;

but the term "uninsured automobile" shall not include:

(1) an insured automobile or an automobile furnished for the regular use of the named insured or a relative,

(2) an automobile or trailer owned or operated by a self-insurer within the meaning of any motor vehicle financial responsibility law, motor carrier law or any similar law,

(3) an automobile or trailer owned by the United States of America, Canada, a state, a political subdivision of any such government or an agency of any of the foregoing,

(4) a land motor vehicle or trailer if operated on rails or crawler-treads or while located for use as a residence or premises and not as a vehicle, or

(5) a farm type tractor or equipment designed for use principally off public roads, except while actually upon public roads.

"hit-and-run automobile" means an automobile which causes bodily injury to an insured arising out of physical contact of such automobile with the insured or with an automobile which the insured is occupying at the time of the accident, provided:

(a) there cannot be ascertained the identity of either the operator or the owner of such "hit-and-run automobile"; (b) the insured or someone on his behalf shall have reported the accident within 24 hours to a police, peace or judicial officer or to the Commissioner of Motor Vehicles, and shall have filed with the Company within 30 days thereafter a statement under oath that the insured or his legal representative has a cause or causes of action arising out of such accident for damages against a person or persons whose identity is unascertainable, and setting forth the facts in support thereof; and (c) at the Company's request, the insured or his legal representative makes available for inspection the automobile which the insured was occupying at the time of the accident.

"occupying" means in or upon or entering into or alighting from.

"state" includes the District of Columbia, a territory or possession of the United States, and a province of Canada.

Exclusions. This policy does not apply under Part IV:

(a) to bodily injury to an insured while occupying an automobile (other than an insured automobile) owned by the named insured or a relative, or through being struck by such an automobile;

(b) to bodily injury to an insured with respect to which such insured, his legal representative or any person entitled to payment under this coverage shall, without written consent of the Company, make any settlement with any person or organization who may be legally liable therefor;

(c) so as to inure directly or indirectly to the benefit of any workmen's compensation or disability benefits carrier or any person or organization qualifying as a self-insurer under any workmen's compensation or disability benefits law or any similar law.

CONDITIONS

1. Policy Period, Territory. This policy applies only to accidents, occurrences and loss during the policy period and within North America or any territory or possession of the United States of America, or between ports thereof.

2. Premium. If the named insured disposes of, acquires ownership of, or replaces a private passenger, farm or utility automobile or, with respect to Part III, a trailer, any premium adjustment necessary shall be made as of the date of such change in accordance with the manuals in use by the Company. The named insured shall (a) notify the Company of any such acquisition not later than 30 days after the next anniversary date of the policy, if notice to the Company is not otherwise required under "owned automobile" **Definitions** in Parts I or III, and (b) upon request, furnish reasonable proof of the number of such automobiles or trailers and a description thereof.

3. Notice. In the event of an accident, occurrence or loss, written notice containing particulars sufficient to identify the insured and also reasonably obtainable information with respect to the time, place and circumstances thereof, and the names and addresses of the injured and of available witnesses, shall be given by or for the insured to the Company or any of its authorized agents as soon as practicable. In the event of theft the insured shall also promptly notify the police. If claim is made or suit is brought against the insured, he shall immediately forward to the Company every demand, notice, summons or other process received by him or his representative.

If, before the Company makes payment of loss under Part IV, the insured or his legal representative shall institute any legal action for bodily injury against any

person or organization legally responsible for the use of an automobile involved in the accident, a copy of the summons and complaint or other process served in connection with such legal action shall be forwarded immediately to the Company by the insured or his legal representative.

4. Limits of Liability

Part I. The limit of bodily injury liability stated in the declarations as applicable to "each person" is the limit of the Company's liability for all damages, including damages for care and loss of services, arising out of bodily injury sustained by one person as the result of any one occurrence; the limit of such liability stated in the declarations as applicable to "each occurrence" is, subject to the above provision respecting each person, the total limit of the Company's liability for all such damages arising out of bodily injury sustained by two or more persons as the result of any one occurrence. The limit of property damage liability stated in the declarations as applicable to "each occurrence" is the total limit of the Company's liability for all damages arising out of injury to or destruction of all property of one or more persons or organizations, including the loss of use thereof, as the result of any one occurrence.

Part II. The limit of liability for medical payments stated in the declarations as applicable to "each person" is the limit of the Company's liability for all expenses incurred by or on behalf of each person who sustains bodily injury as the result of any one accident.

Part III. The limit of the Company's liability for loss shall not exceed the actual cash value of the property, or if the loss is of a part thereof the actual cash value of such part, at time of loss, nor what it would then cost to repair or replace the property or such part thereof with other of like kind and quality, nor, with respect to an owned automobile described in this policy, the applicable limit of liability stated in the declarations; provided, however, the limit of the Company's liability (a) for loss to personal effects arising out of any one occurrence is $100, and (b) for loss to any trailer not owned by the named insured is $500.

Part IV. (a) The limit of liability for uninsured motorists coverage stated in the declarations as applicable to "each person" is the limit of the Company's liability for all damages, including damages for care or loss of services, because of bodily injury sustained by one person as the result of any one accident and, subject to the above provision respecting each person, the limit of liability stated in the declarations as applicable to "each accident" is the total limit of the Company's liability for all damages, including damages for care or loss of services, because of bodily injury sustained by two or more persons as the result of any one accident.

(b) Any amount payable under the terms of this Part because of bodily injury sustained in an accident by a person who is an insured under this Part shall be reduced by

(1) all sums paid on account of such bodily injury by or on behalf of (i) the owner or operator of the uninsured automobile and (ii) any other person or organization jointly or severally liable together with such owner or operator for such bodily injury including all sums paid under Coverage A, and

(2) the amount paid and the present value of all amounts payable on account of such bodily injury under any workmen's compensation law, disability benefits law or any similar law.

(c) Any payment made under this Part to or for any insured shall be applied in reduction of the amount of damages which he may be entitled to recover from any person insured under Coverage A.

(d) The Company shall not be obligated to pay under this Coverage that part of the damages which the insured may be entitled to recover from the owner or operator of an uninsured automobile which represents expenses for medical services paid or payable under Part II.

5. Two or More Automobiles — Parts I, II and III. When two or more automobiles are insured hereunder, the terms of this policy shall apply separately to each, but an automobile and a trailer attached thereto shall be held to be one automobile as respects limits of liability under Part I of this policy, and separate automobiles under Part III of this policy, including any deductible provisions applicable thereto.

6. Assistance and Cooperation of the Insured

Parts I and III. The insured shall cooperate with the Company and, upon the Company's request, assist in making settlements, in the conduct of suits and in enforcing any right of contribution or indemnity against any person or organization who may be liable to the insured because of bodily injury, property damage or loss with respect to which insurance is afforded under this policy; and the insured shall attend hearings and trials and assist in securing and giving evidence and obtaining the attendance of witnesses. The insured shall not, except at his own cost, voluntarily make any payment, assume any obligation or incur any expense other than for such immediate medical and surgical relief to others as shall be imperative at the time of accident.

Part IV. After notice of claim under Part IV, the Company may require the insured to take such action as may be necessary or appropriate to preserve his right to recover damages from any person or organization alleged to be legally responsible for the bodily injury; and in any action against the Company, the Company may require the insured to join such person or organization as a party defendant.

7. Action Against Company

Part I. No action shall lie against the Company unless, as a condition precedent thereto, the insured shall have fully complied with all the terms of this policy, nor until the amount of the insured's obligation to pay shall have been finally determined either by judgment against the insured after actual trial or by written agreement of the insured, the claimant and the Company.

Any person or organization or the legal representative thereof who has secured such judgment or written agreement shall thereafter be entitled to recover under this policy to the extent of the insurance afforded by this policy. No person or organization shall have any right under this policy to join the Company as a party to any action against the insured to determine the insured's liability, nor shall the Company be impleaded by the insured or his legal representative. Bankruptcy or insolvency of the insured or of the insured's estate shall not relieve the Company of any of its obligations hereunder.

Parts II, III and IV. No action shall lie against the Company unless, as a condition precedent thereto, there shall have been full compliance with all the terms of this policy nor, under Part III, until thirty days after proof of loss is filed and the amount of loss is determined as provided in this policy.

8. Financial Responsibility Laws — Part I. When this policy is certified as proof of financial responsibility for the future under the provisions of any motor vehicle financial responsibility law, such insurance as is afforded by this policy for bodily injury liability or for property damage liability shall comply with the provisions of such law to the extent of the coverage and limits of liability required by such law, but in no event in excess of the limits of liability stated in this policy.

9. Medical Reports; Proof and Payment of Claim — Part II. As soon as practicable the injured person or someone on his behalf shall give to the Company written proof of claim, under oath if required, and shall, after each request from the Company, execute authorization to enable the Company to obtain medical reports and copies of records. The injured person shall submit to physical examination by physicians selected by the Company when and as often as the Company may reasonably require.

The Company may pay the injured person or any person or organization rendering the services and such payment shall reduce the amount payable hereunder for such injury. Payment hereunder shall not constitute an admission of liability of any person or, except hereunder, of the Company.

10. Insured's Duties in Event of Loss

Part I. In the event of loss of earnings for which reimbursement is sought under paragraph (e) of "Supplementary Payments" the insured shall file with the Company, as soon as practicable after loss, his sworn proof of loss in such form and including such information as the Company may reasonably require and shall, upon the Company's request, exhibit earnings' statements or other related material and submit to examination under oath.

Part III. In the event of loss the insured shall:

(a) protect the automobile, whether or not the loss is covered by this policy, and any further loss due to the insured's failure to protect shall not be recoverable under this policy; reasonable expenses incurred in affording such protection shall be deemed incurred at the Company's request;

(b) file with the Company, as soon as practicable after loss, his sworn proof of loss in such form and including such information as the Company may reasonably require and shall, upon the Company's request, exhibit the damaged property and submit to examination under oath.

11. Proof of Claim; Medical Reports — Part IV. As soon as practicable, the insured or other person making claim shall give to the Company written proof of claim, under oath if required, including full particulars of the nature and extent of the injuries, treatment, and other details entering into the determination of the amount payable. The insured and every other person making claim shall submit to examinations under oath by any person named by the Company and subscribe the same, as often as may reasonably be required. Proof of claim shall be made upon forms furnished by the Company unless the Company shall have failed to furnish such forms within 15 days after receiving notice of claim.

The injured person shall submit to physical examinations by physicians selected by the Company when and as often as the Company may reasonably require and he, or in the event of his incapacity his legal representative, or in the event of his death his legal representative or the person or persons entitled to sue therefor, shall upon each request from the Company execute authorization to enable the Company to obtain medical reports and copies of records.

12. Appraisal — Part III. If the insured and the Company fail to agree as to the amount of loss, either may, within sixty days after proof of loss is filed, demand an appraisal of the loss. In such event the insured and the Company shall each select a competent appraiser, and the appraisers shall select a competent and disinterested umpire. The appraisers shall state separately the actual cash value and the amount of loss and failing to agree shall submit their differences to the umpire. An award in writing of any two shall determine the amount of loss. The insured and the Company shall each pay his chosen appraiser and shall bear equally the other expenses of the appraisal and umpire.

The Company shall not be held to have waived any of its rights by any act relating to appraisal.

13. Payment of Loss

Part III. The Company may pay for the loss in money; or may repair or replace the damaged or stolen property; or may, at any time before the loss is paid or the property is so replaced, at its expense return any stolen property to the named insured, or at its option to the address shown in the declarations, with payment for any resultant damage thereto; or may take all or such part of the property at the agreed or appraised value but there shall be no abandonment to the Company. The Company may settle any claim for loss either with the insured or the owner of the property.

Part IV. Any amount due is payable (a) to the insured, or (b) if the insured be a minor to his parent or guardian, or (c) if the insured be deceased to his surviving spouse, otherwise (d) to a person authorized by law to receive such payment or to a person legally entitled to recover the damages which the payment represents; provided, the Company may at its option pay any amount due in accordance with division (d) hereof.

14. No Benefit to Bailee — Part III. The insurance afforded by this policy shall not inure directly or indirectly to the benefit of any carrier or other bailee for hire liable for loss to the automobile.

15. Subrogation — Parts I and III. In the event of any payment under this policy, the Company shall be subrogated to all the insured's rights of recovery therefor against any person or organization and the insured shall execute and deliver instruments and papers and do whatever else is necessary to secure such rights. The insured shall do nothing after loss to prejudice such rights.

16. Other Insurance

Parts I and III. If the insured has other insurance against a loss covered by Part I or Part III of this policy, the Company shall not be liable under this policy for a greater proportion of such loss than the applicable limit of liability stated in the declarations bears to the total applicable limit of liability of all valid and collectible insurance against such loss; provided, however, the insurance shall be excess insurance over any other valid and collectible insurance with respect to (1) a temporary substitute automobile or a non-owned automobile, and (2) under Part I, loss against which the named insured has other insurance disclosed to the Company as in effect on the effective date of this policy and upon the basis of which the premium for the

(Form continued on following page)

insurance under this policy is modified, but in such event the insurance under this policy shall apply only in the amount by which the applicable limit of liability stated in the declarations exceeds the applicable limit of liability of such other insurance.

Part II. If there is other automobile medical payments insurance against a loss covered by Part II of this policy the Company shall not be liable under this policy for a greater proportion of such loss than the applicable limit of liability stated in the declarations bears to the total applicable limit of liability of all valid and collectible automobile medical payments insurance; provided, however, the insurance with respect to a temporary substitute automobile or non-owned automobile shall be excess insurance over any other valid and collectible automobile medical payments insurance.

Part IV. With respect to bodily injury to an insured while occupying an automobile not owned by the named insured, the insurance under Part IV shall apply only as excess insurance over any other similar insurance available to such insured and applicable to such automobile as primary insurance, and this insurance shall then apply only in the amount by which the limit of liability for this Coverage exceeds the applicable limit of liability of such other insurance.

Except as provided in the foregoing paragraph, if the insured has other similar insurance available to him and applicable to the accident, the damages shall be deemed not to exceed the higher of the applicable limits of liability of this insurance and such other insurance, and the Company shall not be liable for a greater proportion of any loss to which this Coverage applies than the limit of liability hereunder bears to the sum of the applicable limits of liability of this insurance and such other insurance.

17. Arbitration — Part IV. If any person making claim hereunder and the Company do not agree that such person is legally entitled to recover damages from the owner or operator of an uninsured automobile because of bodily injury to the insured, or do not agree as to the amount of payment which may be owing under this Part, then, upon written demand of either, the matter or matters upon which such person and the Company do not agree shall be settled by arbitration in accordance with the rules of the American Arbitration Association, and judgment upon the award rendered by the arbitrators may be entered in any court having jurisdiction thereof. Such person and the Company each agree to consider itself bound and to be bound by any award made by the arbitrators pursuant to this Part.

18. Trust Agreement — Part IV. In the event of payment to any person under this Part:

(a) the Company shall be entitled to the extent of such payment to the proceeds of any settlement or judgment that may result from the exercise of any rights of recovery of such person against any person or organization legally responsible for the bodily injury because of which such payment is made;

(b) such person shall hold in trust for the benefit of the Company all rights of recovery which he shall have against such other person or organization because of the damages which are the subject of claim made under this Part;

(c) such person shall do whatever is proper to secure and shall do nothing after loss to prejudice such rights;

(d) if requested in writing by the Company, such person shall take, through any representative designated by the Company, such action as may be necessary or appropriate to recover such payment as damages from such other person or organization, such action to be taken in the name of such person; in the event of a recovery, the Company shall be reimbursed out of such recovery for expenses, costs and attorneys' fees incurred by it in connection therewith;

(e) such person shall execute and deliver to the Company such instruments and papers as may be appropriate to secure the rights and obligations of such person and the Company established by this provision.

19. Changes. Notice to any agent or knowledge possessed by any agent or by any other person shall not effect a waiver or a change in any part of this policy or estop the Company from asserting any right under the terms of this policy; nor shall the terms of this policy be waived or changed, except by endorsement issued to form a part of this policy.

20. Assignment. Assignment of interest under this policy shall not bind the Company until its consent is endorsed hereon; if, however, the insured named in item 1 of the declarations, or his spouse if a resident of the same household, shall die, this policy shall cover (1) the survivor as named insured, (2) his legal representative as named insured but only while acting within the scope of his duties as such, (3) any person having proper temporary custody of an owned automobile, as an insured, until the appointment and qualification of such legal representative, and (4) under division 1 of Part II any person who was a relative at the time of such death.

21. Cancellation. This policy may be cancelled by the insured named in item 1 of the declarations by surrender thereof to the Company or any of its authorized agents or by mailing to the Company written notice stating when thereafter the cancellation shall be effective. This policy may be cancelled by the Company by mailing to the insured named in item 1 of the declarations at the address shown in this policy written notice stating when not less than ten days thereafter such cancellation shall be effective. The mailing of notice as aforesaid shall be sufficient proof of notice. The time of the surrender or the effective date and hour of cancellation stated in the notice shall become the end of the policy period. Delivery of such written notice either by such insured or by the Company shall be equivalent to mailing.

If such insured cancels, earned premium shall be computed in accordance with the customary short rate table and procedure. If the Company cancels, earned premium shall be computed pro rata. Premium adjustment may be made either at the time cancellation is effected or as soon as practicable after cancellation becomes effective, but payment or tender of unearned premium is not a condition of cancellation.

22. Cancellation by Company Limited — Part I. After this policy has been in effect for sixty days or, if the policy is a renewal, effective immediately, the Company shall not exercise its right to cancel the insurance afforded under Part I unless: (1) the named insured fails to discharge when due any of his obligations in connection with the payment of premium for this policy or any installment thereof whether payable directly or under any premium finance plan; or (2) the insurance was obtained through fraudulent misrepresentation; or (3) the insured violates any of the terms and conditions of the policy; or (4) the named insured or any other operator, either resident in the same household, or who customarily operates an automobile insured under the policy, (a) has had his driver's license suspended or revoked during the policy period, or (b) is or becomes subject to epilepsy or heart attacks, and such individual cannot produce a certificate from a physician testifying to his unqualified ability to operate a motor vehicle, or (c) is or has been convicted of or forfeits bail, during the 36 months immediately preceding the effective date of the policy or during the policy period, for: (1) any felony, or (2) criminal negligence resulting in death, homicide or assault, arising out of the operation of a motor vehicle, or (3) operating a motor vehicle while in an intoxicated condition or while under the influence of drugs, or (4) leaving the scene of an accident without stopping to report, or (5) theft of a motor vehicle, or (6) making false statements in an application for a driver's license, or (7) a third violation, committed within a period of 18 months, of (i) any ordinance or regulation limiting the speed of motor vehicles or (ii) any of the provisions in the motor vehicle laws of any state, the violation of which constitutes a misdemeanor, whether or not the violations were repetitions of the same offense or were different offenses.

23. Terms of Policy Conformed to Statute. Terms of this policy which are in conflict with the statutes of the state wherein this policy is issued are hereby amended to conform to such statutes.

24. Declarations. By acceptance of this policy, the insured named in item 1 of the declarations agrees that the statements in the declarations are his agreements and representations, that this policy is issued in reliance upon the truth of such representations and that this policy embodies all agreements existing between himself and the Company or any of its agents relating to this insurance.

IN WITNESS WHEREOF, the COMPANY has caused this policy to be signed by its President and Secretary, but the same shall not be binding upon the Company unless it has been countersigned on the declarations page by a duly authorized agent of the Company.

SECRETARY   PRESIDENT

INSURANCE COMPANY

A Stock Insurance Company

DECLARATIONS   COMPREHENSIVE LIABILITY POLICY

ITEM 1.	NAMED INSURED AND ADDRESS (NUMBER, STREET, TOWN, COUNTY, STATE, ZIP CODE)	ITEM 4.	BUSINESS OF THE NAMED INSURED IS

POLICY NUMBER

ITEM 5. LOCATIONS OF ALL PREMISES OWNED, RENTED OR CONTROLLED BY NAMED INSURED

(ENTER "SAME" IF SAME LOCATION AS ADDRESS SHOWN IN ITEM 1)

ITEM 6. INTEREST OF NAMED INSURED IN SUCH PREMISES

☐ OWNER   ☐ TENANT

☐ GENERAL LESSEE

ITEM 2.	POLICY PERIOD	ITEM 7.	PART OCCUPIED BY NAMED INSURED

FROM   TO

12:01 A.M., STANDARD TIME AT THE ADDRESS OF THE NAMED INSURED AS STATED HEREIN.

ITEM 8. AUDIT PERIOD: ANNUAL, UNLESS OTHERWISE STATED

ITEM 3.   THE NAMED INSURED IS

☐ INDIVIDUAL; ☐ PARTNERSHIP; ☐ CORPORATION; ☐ JOINT VENTURE;

☐ OTHER_____

ITEM 9. THE INSURANCE AFFORDED IS ONLY WITH RESPECT TO SUCH OF THE FOLLOWING PARTS AND COVERAGES AS ARE IN-DICATED BY SPECIFIC PREMIUM CHARGE OR CHARGES. THE LIMIT OF THE COMPANY'S LIABILITY AGAINST EACH SUCH COVERAGE SHALL BE AS STATED HEREIN, SUBJECT TO ALL THE TERMS OF THIS POLICY HAVING REFERENCE THERETO.

PART	COVERAGES		LIMITS OF LIABILITY			ESTIMATED PREMIUM
			EACH PERSON	EACH OCCURRENCE	AGGREGATE	
I	COMPREHENSIVE	A. BODILY INJURY LIABILITY	XXXXXXX	$,000	$,000	$
	GENERAL LIABILITY	B. PROPERTY DAMAGE LIABILITY	XXXXXXX	,000	,000	$
II	COMPREHENSIVE AUTOMOBILE	C. BODILY INJURY LIABILITY	,000	,000	XXXXXXX	$
	LIABILITY	D. PROPERTY DAMAGE LIABILITY	XXXXXXX	,000	XXXXXXX	$
AUTOMOBILE	COMPREHENSIVE		AS SHOWN IN SCHEDULE OF COVERAGE PART			$
PHYSICAL DAMAGE	COLLISION					$

ADDITIONAL COVERAGE PART(S)

FORM NUMBER	DESCRIPTION	
		$

ENDORSEMENTS (IDENTIFY BY FORM NUMBER) $

	TOTAL ESTIMATED PREMIUM	$
	ADVANCE PREMIUM ▶	$

DATE OF ISSUE	COUNTERSIGNATURE OF AUTHORIZED AGENT

THE COMPANY DESIGNATED ON THE DECLARATIONS PAGE
(A Stock Insurance Company, herein called the Company)

In consideration of the payment of the premium, in reliance upon the statements in the declarations made a part hereof and subject to all of the terms of this policy, agrees with the **named insured** as follows:

PART I. COMPREHENSIVE GENERAL LIABILITY INSURANCE

I. COVERAGE A—BODILY INJURY LIABILITY
COVERAGE B—PROPERTY DAMAGE LIABILITY

The Company will pay on behalf of the **insured** all sums which the **insured** shall become legally obligated to pay as damages because of

Coverage A. **bodily injury** or

Coverage B. **property damage**

to which this insurance applies, caused by an **occurrence**, and the Company shall have the right and duty to defend any suit against the **insured** seeking damages on account of such **bodily injury** or **property damage**, even if any of the allegations of the suit are groundless, false or fraudulent, and may make such investigation and settlement of any claim or suit as it deems expedient, but the Company shall not be obligated to pay any claim or judgment or to defend any suit after the applicable limit of the Company's liability has been exhausted by payment of judgments or settlements.

Exclusions

This insurance does not apply:

(a) to liability assumed by the **insured** under any contract or agreement except an **incidental contract**; but this exclusion does not apply to a warranty of fitness or quality of the **named insured's products** or a warranty that work performed by or on behalf of the **named insured** will be done in a workmanlike manner;

(b) to **bodily injury** or **property damage** arising out of the ownership, maintenance, operation, use, loading or unloading of

(1) any **automobile** or aircraft owned or operated by or rented or loaned to any **insured**, or

(2) any other **automobile** or aircraft operated by any person in the course of his employment by any **insured**;

but this exclusion does not apply to the parking of an **automobile** on premises owned by, rented to or controlled by the **named insured** or the ways immediately adjoining, if such **automobile** is not owned by or rented or loaned to any **insured**;

(c) to **bodily injury** or **property damage** arising out of (1) the ownership, maintenance, operation, use, loading or unloading of any **mobile equipment** while being used in any pre-arranged or organized racing, speed or demolition contest or in any stunting activity or in practice or preparation for any such contest or activity or (2) the operation or use of any snowmobile or trailer designed for use therewith;

(d) to **bodily injury** or **property damage** arising out of and in the course of the transportation of **mobile equipment** by an **automobile** owned or operated by or rented or loaned to any **insured**;

(e) to **bodily injury** or **property damage** arising out of the ownership, maintenance, operation, use, loading or unloading of

(1) any watercraft owned or operated by or rented or loaned to any **insured**, or

(2) any other watercraft operated by any person in the course of his employment by any **insured**;

but this exclusion does not apply to watercraft while ashore on premises owned by, rented to or controlled by the **named insured**;

(f) to **bodily injury** or **property damage** arising out of the discharge, dispersal, release or escape of smoke, vapors, soot, fumes, acids, alkalis, toxic chemicals, liquids or gases, waste materials or other irritants, contaminants or pollutants into or upon land, the atmosphere or any water course or body of water; but this exclusion does not apply if such discharge, dispersal, release or escape is sudden and accidental;

(g) to **bodily injury** or **property damage** due to war, whether or not declared, civil war, insurrection, rebellion or revolution or to any act or condition incident to any of the foregoing, with respect to

(1) liability assumed by the **insured** under an **incidental contract**, or

(2) expenses for first aid under the Supplementary Payments provision;

(h) to **bodily injury** or **property damage** for which the **insured** or his indemnitee may be held liable

(1) as a person or organization engaged in the business of manufacturing, distributing, selling or serving alcoholic beverages, or

(2) if not so engaged, as an owner or lessor of premises used for such purposes,

if such liability is imposed

(i) by, or because of the violation of, any statute, ordinance or regulation pertaining to the sale, gift, distribution or use of any alcoholic beverage, or

(ii) by reason of the selling, serving or giving of any alcoholic beverage to a minor or to a person under the influence of alcohol or which causes or contributes to the intoxication of any person; but part (ii) of this exclusion does not apply with respect to liability of the **insured** or his indemnitee as an owner or lessor described in (2) above;

(i) to any obligation for which the **insured** or any carrier as his insurer may be held liable under any workmen's compensation, unemployment compensation or disability benefits law, or under any similar law;

(j) to **bodily injury** to any employee of the **insured** arising out of and in the course of his employment by the **insured** or to any obligation of the **insured** to indemnify another because of damages arising out of such injury; but this exclusion does not apply to liability assumed by the **insured** under an **incidental contract**;

(k) to **property damage** to

(1) property owned or occupied by or rented to the **insured**,

(2) property used by the **insured**, or

(3) property in the care, custody or control of the **insured** or as to which the **insured** is for any purpose exercising physical control;

but parts (2) and (3) of this exclusion do not apply with respect to liability under a written sidetrack agreement and part (3) of this exclusion does not apply with respect to **property damage** (other than to **elevators**) arising out of the use of an **elevator** at premises owned by, rented to or controlled by the **named insured**;

(l) to **property damage** to premises alienated by the **named insured** arising out of such premises or any part thereof;

(m) to loss of use of tangible property which has not been physically injured or destroyed resulting from

(1) a delay in or lack of performance by or on behalf of the **named insured** of any contract or agreement, or

(2) the failure of the **named insured's products** or work performed by or on behalf of the **named insured** to meet the level of performance, quality, fitness or durability warranted or represented by the **named insured**;

but this exclusion does not apply to loss of use of other tangible property resulting from the sudden and accidental physical injury to or destruction of the **named insured's products** or work performed by or on behalf of the **named insured** after such products or work have been put to use by any person or organization other than an **insured**;

(n) to **property damage** to the **named insured's products** arising out of such products or any part of such products;

(o) to **property damage** to work performed by or on behalf of the **named insured** arising out of the work or any portion thereof, or out of materials, parts or equipment furnished in connection therewith;

(p) to damages claimed for the withdrawal, inspection, repair, replacement, or loss of use of the **named insured's products** or work completed by or for the **named insured** or of any property of which such products or work form a part, if such products, work or property are withdrawn from the market or from use because of any known or suspected defect or deficiency therein.

II. PERSONS INSURED

Each of the following is an **insured** under this insurance to the extent set forth below:

(a) if the **named insured** is designated in the declarations as an individual, the person so designated but only with respect to the conduct of a business of which he is the sole proprietor, and the spouse of the **named insured** with respect to the conduct of such a business;

(b) if the **named insured** is designated in the declarations as a partnership or joint venture, the partnership or joint venture so designated and any partner or member thereof but only with respect to his liability as such;

(c) if the **named insured** is designated in the declarations as other than an individual, partnership or joint venture, the organization so designated and any executive officer, director or stockholder thereof while acting within the scope of his duties as such;

(d) any person (other than an employee of the **named insured**) or organization while acting as real estate manager for the **named insured**; and

(e) with respect to the operation, for the purpose of locomotion upon a public highway, of **mobile equipment** registered under any motor vehicle registration law,

(i) an employee of the **named insured** while operating any such equipment in the course of his employment, and

(ii) any other person while operating with the permission of the **named insured** any such equipment registered in the name of the **named insured** and any person or organization legally responsible for such operation, but only if there is no other valid and collectible insurance available, either on a primary or excess basis, to such person or organization;

provided that no person or organization shall be an **insured** under this paragraph (e) with respect to:

(1) **bodily injury** to any fellow employee of such person injured in the course of his employment, or

(2) **property damage** to property owned by, rented to, in charge of or occupied by the **named insured** or the employer of any person described in subparagraph (ii).

This insurance does not apply to **bodily injury** or **property damage** arising out of the conduct of any partnership or joint venture of which the **insured** is a partner or member and which is not designated in this policy as a **named insured**.

III. LIMITS OF LIABILITY

Regardless of the number of (1) **insureds** under this policy, (2) persons or organizations who sustain **bodily injury** or **property damage**, or (3) claims made or suits brought on account of **bodily injury** or **property damage**, the Company's liability is limited as follows:

Coverage A — The total liability of the Company for all damages, including damages for care and loss of services, because of **bodily injury** sustained by one or more persons as the result of any one **occurrence** shall not exceed the limit of **bodily injury** liability stated in the declarations as applicable to "each **occurrence**."

Subject to the above provision respecting "each **occurrence**", the total liability of the Company for all damages because of (1) all **bodily injury** included within the **completed operations hazard** and (2) all **bodily injury** included within the **products hazard** shall not exceed the limit of **bodily injury** liability stated in the declarations as "aggregate".

Coverage B — The total liability of the Company for all damages because of all **property damage** sustained by one or more persons or organizations as the result of any one **occurrence** shall not exceed the limit of **property damage** liability stated in the declarations as applicable to "each **occurrence**".

Subject to the above provision respecting "each **occurrence**", the total liability of the Company for all damages because of all **property damage** to which this coverage applies and described in any of the numbered subparagraphs below shall not exceed the limit of **property damage** liability stated in the declarations as "aggregate":

(1) all **property damage** arising out of premises or operations rated on a remuneration basis or contractor's equipment rated on a receipts basis, including **property damage** for which liability is assumed under any **incidental contract** relating to such premises or operations, but excluding **property damage** included in subparagraph (2) below;

(2) all **property damage** arising out of and occurring in the course of operations performed for the **named insured** by independent contractors and general supervision thereof by the **named insured**, including any such **property damage** for which liability is assumed under any **incidental contract** relating to such operations, but this subparagraph (2) does not include **property damage** arising out of maintenance or repairs at premises owned by or rented to the **named insured** or structural alterations at such premises which do not involve changing the size of or moving buildings or other structures;

(3) all **property damage** included within the **products hazard** and all **property damage** included within the **completed operations hazard**.

Such aggregate limit shall apply separately to the **property damage** described in subparagraphs (1), (2) and (3) above, and under subparagraphs (1) and (2), separately with respect to each project away from premises owned by or rented to the **named insured**.

Coverages A and B — For the purpose of determining the limit of the Company's liability, all **bodily injury** and **property damage** arising out of continuous or repeated exposure to substantially the same general conditions shall be considered as arising out of one **occurrence**.

IV. POLICY TERRITORY

This insurance applies only to **bodily injury** or **property damage** which occurs within the **policy territory**.

PART II. COMPREHENSIVE AUTOMOBILE LIABILITY INSURANCE

I. COVERAGE C—BODILY INJURY LIABILITY
COVERAGE D—PROPERTY DAMAGE LIABILITY

The Company will pay on behalf of the **insured** all sums which the **insured** shall become legally obligated to pay as damages because of

Coverage C. **bodily injury** or

Coverage D. **property damage**

to which this insurance applies, caused by an **occurrence** and arising out of the ownership, maintenance or use, including loading and unloading, of any **automobile**, and the Company shall have the right and duty to defend any **suit** against the **insured** seeking damages on account of such **bodily injury** or **property damage**, even if any of the allegations of the suit are groundless, false or fraudulent, and may make such investigation and settlement of any claim or suit as it deems expedient, but the Company shall not be obligated to pay any claim or judgment or to defend any suit after the applicable limit of the Company's liability has been exhausted by payment of judgments or settlements.

Exclusions

This insurance does not apply:

(a) to liability assumed by the **insured** under any contract or agreement;

(b) to any obligation for which the **insured** or any carrier as his insurer may be held liable under any workmen's compensation, unemployment compensation or disability benefits law, or under any similar law;

(c) to **bodily injury** to any employee of the **insured** arising out of and in the course of his employment by the **insured** or to any obligation of the **insured** to indemnify another because of damages arising out of such injury; but this exclusion does not apply to any such injury arising out of and in the course of domestic employment by the **insured** unless benefits therefor are in whole or in part payable or required to be provided under any workmen's compensation law;

(d) to **property damage** to

(1) property owned or being transported by the **insured**, or

(2) property rented to or in the care, custody or control of the **insured**, or as to which the **insured** is for any purpose exercising physical control, other than **property damage** to a residence or private garage by a **private passenger automobile** covered by this insurance;

(Form continued on following pages)

(e) to **bodily injury** or **property damage** due to war, whether or not declared, civil war, insurrection, rebellion or revolution or to any act or condition incident to any of the foregoing, with respect to expenses for first aid under the Supplementary Payments provision;

(f) to **bodily injury** or **property damage** arising out of the discharge, dispersal, release or escape of smoke, vapors, soot, fumes, acids, alkalis, toxic chemicals, liquids or gases, waste materials or other irritants, contaminants or pollutants into or upon land, the atmosphere or any watercourse or body of water; but this exclusion does not apply if such discharge, dispersal, release or escape is sudden and accidental.

II. PERSONS INSURED

Each of the following is an **insured** under this insurance to the extent set forth below:

(a) the **named insured;**

(b) any partner or executive officer thereof, but with respect to a **non-owned automobile** only while such **automobile** is being used in the business of the **named insured;**

(c) any other person while using an **owned automobile** or a **hired automobile** with the permission of the **named insured**, provided his actual operation or (if he is not operating) his other actual use thereof is within the scope of such permission, but with respect to **bodily injury** or **property damage** arising out of the loading or unloading thereof, such other person shall be an **insured** only if he is:

(1) a lessee or borrower of the **automobile,** or

(2) an employee of the **named insured** or of such lessee or borrower;

(d) any other person or organization but only with respect to his or its liability because of acts or omissions of an **insured** under (a), (b) or (c) above.

None of the following is an **insured:**

(i) any person while engaged in the business of his employer with respect to **bodily injury** to any fellow employee of such person injured in the course of his employment;

(ii) the owner or lessee (of whom the **named insured** is a sublessee) of a **hired automobile** or the owner of a **non-owned automobile**, or any agent or employee of any such owner or lessee;

(iii) an executive officer with respect to an **automobile** owned by him or by a member of his household;

(iv) any person or organization, other than the **named insured**, with respect to:

(1) a motor vehicle while used with any **trailer** owned or hired by such person or organization and not covered by like insurance in the Company (except a **trailer** designed for use with a **private passenger automobile** and not being used for business purposes with another type motor vehicle), or

(2) a **trailer** while used with any motor vehicle owned or hired by such person or organization and not covered by like insurance in the Company;

(v) any person while employed in or otherwise engaged in duties in connection with an **automobile business**, other than an **automobile business** operated by the **named insured.**

This insurance does not apply to **bodily injury** or **property damage** arising out of (1) a **non-owned automobile** used in the conduct of any partnership or joint venture of which the **insured** is a partner or member and which is not designated in this policy as a **named insured**, or (2) if the **named insured** is a partnership, an **automobile** owned by or registered in the name of a partner thereof.

III. LIMITS OF LIABILITY

Regardless of the number of (1) **insureds** under this policy, (2) persons or organizations who sustain **bodily injury** or **property damage,** (3) claims made or suits brought on account of **bodily injury** or **property damage** or (4) **automobiles** to which this policy applies, the Company's liability is limited as follows:

Coverage C—The limit of **bodily injury** liability stated in the declarations as applicable to "each person" is the limit of the Company's liability for all damages, including damages for care and loss of services, because of **bodily injury** sustained by one person as the result of any one **occurrence;** but subject to the above provision respecting "each person", the total liability of the Company for all damages because of **bodily injury** sustained by two or more persons as the result of any one **occurrence** shall not exceed the limit of **bodily injury** liability stated in the declarations as applicable to "each **occurrence".**

Coverage D — The total liability of the Company for all damages because of all **property damage** sustained by one or more persons or organizations as the result of any one **occurrence** shall not exceed the limit of **property damage** liability stated in the declarations as applicable to "each **occurrence".**

Coverages C and D—For the purpose of determining the limit of the Company's liability, all **bodily injury** and **property damage** arising out of continuous or repeated exposure to substantially the same general conditions shall be considered as arising out of one **occurrence.**

IV. POLICY TERRITORY

This insurance applies only to **bodily injury** or **property damage** which occurs within the territory described in paragraph (1) or (2) of the definition of **policy territory.**

V. ADDITIONAL DEFINITIONS

When used in reference to this insurance (including endorsements forming a part of the policy):

"**automobile business**" means the business or occupation of selling, repairing, servicing, storing or parking **automobiles;**

"**hired automobile**" means an **automobile** not owned by the **named insured** which is used under contract in behalf of, or loaned to, the **named insured,** provided such **automobile** is not owned by or registered in the name of (a) a partner or executive officer of the **named insured** or (b) an employee or agent of the **named insured** who is granted an operating allowance of any sort for the use of such **automobile;**

"**non-owned automobile**" means an **automobile** which is neither an **owned automobile** nor a **hired automobile;**

"**owned automobile**" means an **automobile** owned by the **named insured;**

"**private passenger automobile**" means a four wheel private passenger or station wagon type **automobile;**

"**trailer**" includes semi-trailer but does not include **mobile equipment.**

VI. ADDITIONAL CONDITION

Excess Insurance—Hired and Non-Owned Automobiles

With respect to a **hired automobile** or a **non-owned automobile,** this insurance shall be excess insurance over any other valid and collectible insurance available to the **insured.**

SUPPLEMENTARY PAYMENTS

The Company will pay, in addition to the applicable limit of liability:

(a) all expenses incurred by the Company, all costs taxed against the **insured** in any suit defended by the Company and all interest on the entire amount of any judgment therein which accrues after entry of the judgment and before the Company has paid or tendered or deposited in court that part of the judgment which does not exceed the limit of the Company's liability thereon;

(b) premiums on appeal bonds required in any such suit, premiums on bonds to release attachments in any such suit for an amount not in excess of the applicable limit of liability of this policy, and the cost of bail bonds required of the **insured** because of accident or traffic law violation arising out of the use of any vehicle to which this policy applies, not to exceed $250 per bail bond, but the Company shall have no obligation to apply for or furnish any such bonds;

(c) expenses incurred by the **insured** for first aid to others at the time of an accident, for **bodily injury** to which this policy applies;

(d) reasonable expenses incurred by the **insured** at the Company's request in assisting the Company in the investigation or defense of any claim or suit, including actual loss of earnings not to exceed $25 per day.

DEFINITIONS

When used in this policy (including endorsements forming a part hereof):

"**automobile**" means a land motor vehicle, trailer or semitrailer designed for travel on public roads (including any machinery or apparatus attached thereto), but does not include **mobile equipment;**

"**bodily injury**" means bodily injury, sickness or disease sustained by any person which occurs during the policy period, including death at any time resulting therefrom;

"**completed operations hazard**" includes **bodily injury** and **property damage** arising out of operations or reliance upon a representation or warranty made at any time with respect thereto, but only if the **bodily injury** or **property damage** occurs after such operations have been completed or abandoned and occurs away from premises owned by or rented to the **named insured.** "Operations" include materials, parts or equipment furnished in connection therewith. Operations shall be deemed completed at the earliest of the following times:

(1) when all operations to be performed by or on behalf of the **named insured** under the contract have been completed,

(2) when all operations to be performed by or on behalf of the **named insured** at the site of the operations have been completed, or

(3) when the portion of the work out of which the injury or damage arises has been put to its intended use by any person or organization other than another contractor or subcontractor engaged in performing operations for a principal as a part of the same project.

Operations which may require further service or maintenance work, or correction, repair or replacement because of any defect or deficiency, but which are otherwise complete, shall be deemed completed.

The **completed operations hazard** does not include **bodily injury** or **property damage** arising out of

(a) operations in connection with the transportation of property, unless the **bodily injury** or **property damage** arises out of a condition in or on a vehicle created by the loading or unloading thereof,

(b) the existence of tools, uninstalled equipment or abandoned or unused materials, or

(c) operations for which the classification stated in the policy or in the Company's manual specifies "including completed operations";

"**elevator**" means any hoisting or lowering device to connect floors or landings, whether or not in service, and all appliances thereof including any car, platform, shaft, hoistway, stairway, runway, power equipment and machinery; but does not include an **automobile** servicing hoist, or a hoist without a platform outside a building if without mechanical power or if not attached to building walls, or a hod or material hoist used in alteration, construction or demolition operations, or an inclined conveyor used exclusively for carrying property or a dumbwaiter used exclusively for carrying property and having a compartment height not exceeding four feet;

"**incidental contract**" means any written (1) lease of premises, (2) easement agreement, except in connection with construction or demolition operations on or adjacent to a railroad, (3) undertaking to indemnify a municipality required by municipal ordinance, except in connection with work for the municipality, (4) sidetrack agreement, or (5) **elevator** maintenance agreement;

"**insured**" means any person or organization qualifying as an insured in the "Persons Insured" provision of the applicable insurance coverage. The insurance afforded applies separately to each **insured** against whom claim is made or suit is brought, except with respect to the limits of the Company's liability;

"**mobile equipment**" means a land vehicle (including any machinery or apparatus attached thereto), whether or not self-propelled, (1) not subject to motor vehicle registration, or (2) maintained for use exclusively on premises owned by or rented to the **named insured,** including the ways immediately adjoining, or (3) designed for use principally off public roads, or (4) designed or maintained for the sole purpose of affording mobility to equipment of the following types forming an integral part of or permanently attached to such vehicle: power cranes, shovels, loaders, diggers and drills; concrete mixers (other than the mix-in-transit type); graders, scrapers, rollers and other road construction or repair equipment; air-compressors, pumps and generators, including spraying, welding and building cleaning equipment; and geophysical exploration and well servicing equipment;

"**named insured**" means the person or organization named in Item 1. of the declarations of this policy;

"**named insured's products**" means goods or products manufactured, sold, handled or distributed by the **named insured** or by others trading under his name, including any container thereof (other than a vehicle), but "**named insured's products**" shall not include a vending machine or any property other than such container, rented to or located for use of others but not sold;

"**occurrence**" means an accident, including continuous or repeated exposure to conditions, which results in **bodily injury** or **property damage** neither expected nor intended from the standpoint of the **insured;**

"**policy territory**" means:

(1) the United States of America, its territories or possessions, or Canada, or

(2) international waters or air space, provided the **bodily injury** or **property damage** does not occur in the course of travel or transportation to or from any other country, state or nation, or

(3) anywhere in the world with respect to damages because of **bodily injury** or **property damage** arising out of a product which was sold for use or consumption within the territory described in paragraph (1) above, provided the original suit for such damages is brought within such territory;

"**products hazard**" includes **bodily injury** and **property damage** arising out of the **named insured's products** or reliance upon a representation or warranty made at any time with respect thereto, but only if the **bodily injury** or **property damage** occurs away from premises owned by or rented to the **named insured** and after physical possession of such products has been relinquished to others;

"**property damage**" means (1) physical injury to or destruction of tangible property which occurs during the policy period, including the loss of use thereof at any time resulting therefrom, or (2) loss of use of tangible property which has not been physically injured or destroyed provided such loss of use is caused by an **occurrence** during the policy period.

CONDITIONS

1. Premium. All premiums for this policy shall be computed in accordance with the Company's rules, rates, rating plans, premiums and minimum premiums applicable to the insurance afforded herein.

Premium designated in this policy as "advance premium" is a deposit premium only which shall be credited to the amount of the earned premium due at the end of the policy period. At the close of each period (or part thereof terminating with the end of the policy period) designated in the declarations as the audit period the earned premium shall be computed for such period and, upon notice thereof to the **named insured,** shall become due and payable. If the total earned premium for the policy period is less than the premium previously paid, the Company shall return to the **named insured** the unearned portion paid by the **named insured.**

The **named insured** shall maintain records of such information as is necessary for premium computation, and shall send copies of such records to the Company at the end of the policy period and at such times during the policy period as the Company may direct.

2. Inspection and Audit. The Company shall be permitted but not obligated to inspect the **named insured's** property and operations at any time. Neither the Company's right to make inspections nor the making thereof nor any report thereon shall constitute an undertaking, on behalf of or for the benefit of the **named insured** or others, to determine or warrant that such property or operations are safe or healthful, or are in compliance with any law, rule or regulation.

The Company may examine and audit the **named insured's** books

(Form continued on following page)

and records at any time during the policy period and extensions thereof and within three years after the final termination of this policy, as far as they relate to the subject matter of this insurance.

3. Financial Responsibility Laws. When this policy is certified as proof of financial responsibility for the future under the provisions of any motor vehicle financial responsibility law, such insurance as is afforded by this policy for **bodily injury** liability or for **property damage** liability shall comply with the provisions of such law to the extent of the coverage and limits of liability required by such law. The **insured** agrees to reimburse the Company for any payment made by the Company which it would not have been obligated to make under the terms of this policy except for the agreement contained in this paragraph.

4. Insured's Duties in the Event of Occurrence, Claim or Suit.

(a) In the event of an **occurrence**, written notice containing particulars sufficient to identify the **insured** and also reasonably obtainable information with respect to the time, place and circumstances thereof, and the names and addresses of the injured and of available witnesses, shall be given by or for the **insured** to the Company or any of its authorized agents as soon as practicable.

(b) If claim is made or suit is brought against the **insured**, the **insured** shall immediately forward to the Company every demand, notice, summons or other process received by him or his representative.

(c) The **insured** shall cooperate with the Company and, upon the Company's request, assist in making settlements, in the conduct of suits and in enforcing any right of contribution or indemnity against any person or organization who may be liable to the **insured** because of injury or damage with respect to which insurance is afforded under this policy; and the **insured** shall attend hearings and trials and assist in securing and giving evidence and obtaining the attendance of witnesses. The **insured** shall not, except at his own cost, voluntarily make any payment, assume any obligation or incur any expense other than for first aid to others at the time of accident.

5. Action Against Company. No action shall lie against the Company unless, as a condition precedent thereto, there shall have been full compliance with all of the terms of this policy, nor until the amount of the **insured's** obligation to pay shall have been finally determined either by judgment against the **insured** after actual trial or by written agreement of the **insured**, the claimant and the Company.

Any person or organization or the legal representative thereof who has secured such judgment or written agreement shall thereafter be entitled to recover under this policy to the extent of the insurance afforded by this policy. No person or organization shall have any right under this policy to join the Company as a party to any action against the **insured** to determine the **insured's** liability, nor shall the Company be impleaded by the **insured** or his legal representative. Bankruptcy or insolvency of the **insured** or of the **insured's** estate shall not relieve the Company of any of its obligations hereunder.

6. Other Insurance. The insurance afforded by this policy is primary insurance, except when stated to apply in excess of or contingent upon the absence of other insurance. When this insurance is primary and the **insured** has other insurance which is stated to be applicable to the loss on an excess or contingent basis, the amount of the Company's liability under this policy shall not be reduced by the existence of such other insurance. When both this insurance and other insurance apply to the loss on the same basis, whether primary, excess or contingent, the Company shall not be liable under this policy for a greater proportion of the loss than that stated in the applicable contribution provision below:

(a) **Contribution by Equal Shares.** If all of such other valid and collectible insurance provides for contribution by equal shares, the Company shall not be liable for a greater proportion of such loss than would be payable if each insurer contributes an equal share until the share of each insurer equals the lowest applicable limit of liability under any one policy or the full amount of the loss is paid, and with respect to any amount of loss not so paid the remaining insurers then continue to contribute equal shares of the remaining amount of the loss until each such insurer has paid its limit in full or the full amount of the loss is paid.

(b) **Contribution by Limits.** If any of such other insurance does not provide for contribution by equal shares, the Company shall not be liable for a greater proportion of such loss than the applicable limit of liability under this policy for such loss bears to the total applicable limit of liability of all valid and collectible insurance against such loss.

7. Subrogation. In the event of any payment under this policy, the Company shall be subrogated to all the **insured's** rights of recovery therefor against any person or organization and the **insured** shall execute and deliver instruments and papers and do whatever else is necessary to secure such rights. The **insured** shall do nothing after loss to prejudice such rights.

8. Changes. Notice to any agent or knowledge possessed by any agent or by any other person shall not effect a waiver or a change in any part of this policy or estop the Company from asserting any right under the terms of this policy; nor shall the terms of this policy be waived or changed, except by endorsement issued to form a part of this policy.

9. Assignment. Assignment of interest under this policy shall not bind the Company until its consent is endorsed hereon; if, however, the **named insured** shall die, such insurance as is afforded by this policy shall apply (1) to the **named insured's** legal representative, as the **named insured**, but only while acting within the scope of his duties as such, and (2) with respect to the property of the **named insured**, to the person having proper temporary custody thereof, as **insured**, but only until the appointment and qualification of the legal representative.

10. Three Year Policy. If this policy is issued for a period of **three** years any limit of the Company's liability stated in this policy as "aggregate" shall apply separately to each consecutive annual period thereof.

11. Cancellation. This policy may be cancelled by the **named insured** by surrender thereof to the Company or any of its authorized agents or by mailing to the Company written notice stating when thereafter the cancellation shall be effective. This policy may be cancelled by the Company by mailing to the **named insured** at the address shown in this policy, written notice stating when not less than ten days thereafter such cancellation shall be effective. The mailing of notice as aforesaid shall be sufficient proof of notice. The time of surrender or the effective date and hour of cancellation stated in the notice shall become the end of the policy period. Delivery of such written notice either by the **named insured** or by the Company shall be equivalent to mailing. If the **named insured** cancels, earned premium shall be computed in accordance with the customary short rate table and procedure. If the Company cancels, earned premium shall be computed pro rata. Premium adjustment may be made either at the time cancellation is effected or as soon as practicable after cancellation becomes effective, but payment or tender of unearned premium is not a condition of cancellation.

12. Declarations. By acceptance of this policy, the **named insured** agrees that the statements in the declarations are his agreements and representations, that this policy is issued in reliance upon the truth of such representations and that this policy embodies all agreements existing between himself and the Company or any of its agents relating to this insurance.

IN WITNESS WHEREOF, the COMPANY has caused this policy to be signed by its President and Secretary, but the same shall not be binding upon the Company unless it has been countersigned on the declarations page by a duly authorized agent of the Company.

SECRETARY　　　　　　　　　　PRESIDENT

CHAPTER 13

Suretyship and Guaranty

Introduction

Definitions

Suretyship is an agreement to answer for the debt, default or misconduct of another—to repay a loan made to another if he does not do so, to perform or pay the damages if he does not perform a contract, or to make restitution for his misappropriation or embezzlement.

● *Guaranty* is distinguished (a) in that it is thought of as being confined to an agreement to answer for a debt, and (b) in various technical particulars, the most important of which is that the surety must pay simply if the debtor does not, while the guarantor must pay only if the debtor cannot pay. This distinction is not of practical importance, however, because invariably the reason for nonpayment is an inability to pay. So much alike are suretyship and guaranty that the California Civil Code[1] has expressly abolished the distinction between them, which is also done in this chapter; what is said with respect to suretyship may be deemed to apply with equal force to guaranty. C.C. 2787 says that "The distinction between sureties and guarantors is hereby abolished. The terms and their derivatives, wherever used in this code or in any other statute or law of this State now in force or hereafter enacted, shall have the same meaning, as hereafter in this section defined. A surety or guarantor is one who promises to answer for the debt, default, or miscarriage of another, or hypothecates property as security therefor . . . continuing guaranties[2] are forms of suretyship obligations. . . ."

● *Insurance or indemnity* differs from *suretyship or guaranty* in that, whereas the surety or guarantor is not the ultimate obligor, the insurer or indemnitor may be. If the surety or guarantor is required to answer for the debt of the debtor, the surety or guarantor will have a right of recovery from the debtor, who, as between the two, is the ultimate obligor. If the insurer must pay the insured, the matter will stop there unless, as between the insured and the third party, the third party was guilty of fault and the insured was innocent of fault, in which case the insurer will be able to recover from the third person by virtue of subrogation to the right of the insured against the third person.[3] Thus, if A insures B with automobile insurance, and B has an accident with C, A will suffer the loss as between A and B unless C was responsible for the accident.

Types of Sureties and Suretyship Contracts

Suretyship contracts are of three general types: (1) those which guarantee a loan or extension of credit; (2) those which guarantee performance of a contract or of the duties imposed by a particular position; and (3) those which protect against the dishonesty of a person. The first of these is made exclusively by private individuals; the variables are too great to standardize such risks, and the professional sureties or bonding companies do not enter into this field. Just the opposite is true with respect to the second and third. They are made almost exclusively by professionals and take the form of a variety of *bonds*. Surety or bonding companies and insurance companies engaged in the bonding business—the largest writers of bonds—classify the second type as *surety bonds*, the third as *fidelity bonds*. Each of these is discussed in greater detail below.

Guarantees of Loans or Credit: If D wishes to borrow money from C bank or finance company and cannot give the security of a mortgage or pledge of property, the lending agency may settle for the security of a surety, i.e., the agreement of a responsible person to repay the loan if D does not. D, the borrower, will give his note for the amount of the loan and S, his surety, will simply sign or *indorse* a guarantee of payment. The parties to such a transaction are customarily referred to as the creditor (lender), debtor (borrower) and surety, as indicated by the alphabetical designations above. Practically all guarantees of loans take this form.

● Guarantees of credit may also be encountered. They take no particular form and may be simply a letter, as in *Kierulff* v. *Koping*, 94 C.A. 473, 271 P. 353, where the letter stated, "I hereby guarantee [D's] account to the amount of $500 five hundred dollars."

● Where the guaranty contemplates a series of extensions of credit, as it did in the *Kierulff* case, or a series of loans for which the guarantor is to be liable, e.g., where the guarantor is to be liable, "for all amounts up to $100,000 advanced to C by D during the year 1981," it is called a *continuing guaranty.*[4]

Surety Bonds: The suretyship contracts of insurance or bonding companies are called *bonds.* All bonds which guarantee performance of a contractual or other duty are classified as *surety bonds*, the most important particular types of which are as follows:

CONTRACT OR PERFORMANCE BONDS. These guarantee that a particular contract will be properly performed in all respects and that, if it is not, the surety will perform the contract or answer for the damages that result from nonperformance. The most common of these are bonds guaranteeing performance of building contracts and bonds guaranteeing payment of labor and for materials. Specimen forms follow. In these and other bonds, the parties are referred to as obligee, principal and surety, rather than as creditor, debtor and surety, as in guaranties of loans or credit. The obligee is the one in whose favor

---

[1]In California, suretyship and guaranty are covered by C.C. 2787-2854.

[2]Continuing guaranties are explained and discussed in subsequent sections.

[3]See page 321 for insurer's right of subrogation.

[4]C.C. 2814 defines a continuing guaranty: "A guaranty relating to a future liability of the principal, under successive transactions, which either continue his liability or from time to time renew it . . . is called a continuing guaranty."

the bond runs, i.e., the one to be protected by the bond,[5] the principal is the one whose performance or conduct is guaranteed, and the surety is the one guaranteeing it.

FIDUCIARY BONDS. These guarantee proper performance of his duties by a fiduciary—executor or administrator, guardian, or trustee.

PUBLIC OFFICIAL BONDS. These do the same thing with respect to public officials—assessors, auditors, county clerks, recorders, sheriffs, treasurers, etc.

LICENSE AND PERMIT BONDS. For the protection of the public, the state requires bonds for a wide variety of licenses and permits. Examples are bonds of insurance brokers, contractors, securities brokers, etc., or to insure payment of taxes as in the case of the sales tax bond required of persons engaged in business as retail sellers.

Fidelity Bonds: These protect employers against misappropriations or embezzlements of employees. According to the extent of coverage, they are classified as name bonds, position bonds, or blanket bonds. Name bonds cover only a named individual or individuals designated in the bond. A position bond covers a particular position or positions regardless of who occupies it. A blanket bond covers all employees and is the best and usual form where numerous employees handle money. If there is a misappropriation it would not be necessary for the employer to attribute it to a particular employee or position. An even broader form of blanket bond is often written for financial institutions, which combines insurance with the bond. This form of blanket bond covers not only embezzlement or misappropriation by employees, but also burglaries, robberies, forgeries, etc.

Formation and Termination of Contracts

Suretyship is a contract and must have the contract elements. Only those of offer and acceptance, consideration and writing are considered here. The extent to which the elements of competent parties, legal purpose and freedom from fraud or other invalidating factor are of significance is covered in the later section on defenses of the surety.

Offer, Acceptance and Consideration

In suretyship contracts, the surety is said to make the *offer*—to stand liable for the loan if the creditor will make it, to answer for misappropriations if the obligee-employer will employ or continue the employment of the principal-employee, etc. The creditor or obligee *accepts* by doing the thing requested—making the loan or employing or continuing the employment of the principal.

● Where the surety is a surety or bonding company, *consideration* presents no problem. Such sureties are paid a premium for assuming the responsibility, just as in insurance contracts, and the premium is the consideration. Where a premium is received, the surety is called a *compensated surety.*

● If the surety is a *gratuitous or accommodation surety*, by contrast, i.e., one who assumes responsibility as an accommodation and without receiving a monetary consideration, a technical application of the doctrine of consideration is adopted. Every suretyship situation involves two contracts. Suppose that C lends $1000 to D for which S becomes surety. D will give C a note in which he promises to make repayment at a specified future time. This contract—the contract between the creditor or obligee and the debtor or principal—is called the *principal contract.* Theoretically at least, the *suretyship contract* is a separate and distinct contract even though it consists of nothing more than the indorsement "Payment guaranteed," signed by the surety, on the back of the note. Consideration must be supplied for both of these contracts. That the principal contract is supported by consideration is clear—the $1000 loaned by C and the promise to repay a like sum with interest by D. In the suretyship contract, however, while S gives consideration—the promise to pay if D does not—he actually receives nothing in return. It is the rule, however, that a single consideration can support two promises made at the same time; that, therefore, the consideration of $1000 to D, which supports the principal contract, can run to and support the suretyship contract as well.[6]

Continuing Guaranties: A special problem of offer and acceptance arises when the surety is to stand liable throughout a series of transactions, i.e., makes a continuing guaranty. Suppose that S agrees to stand liable for all amounts up to $100,000 advanced by C to D during 1984. Assuming that S is doing this as an accommodation, his guaranty agreement is a *continuing offer* which, like other offers, may be revoked at any time[7] but which may be accepted any number of times prior to revocation. Each loan to D will be an acceptance by C and will give rise to a unilateral contract. Thus, if C lends $12,000 to D on January 15, 1984, another $8,000 to D on February 10, 1984, and another $15,000 on March 14, 1984, three unilateral contracts will have been formed between C and S. Now suppose that on March 15, 1984, S writes C advising C that he (S) will not be liable for further loans to D. When received by C, this notice would constitute revocation of S's continuing offer. However, it would not affect the unilateral contracts previously made. In the same vein, if S were to die on March 15, 1984, his continuing offer would be terminated, and the general rule is that this is so even though the creditor makes further advances without knowledge of the fact of the surety's death, and even though the suretyship contract expressly provides that death shall not terminate the surety's contract until the creditor knows of it.[8]

● The surety's liability on a continuing guaranty is not affected by the fact that credit in excess of the maximum amount guaranteed by the surety is extended to the debtor. The surety will remain liable to the extent of the guaranty. Thus, in *Kierulff* v. *Koping*, 94 C.A. 473, 271 P. 353, where the maximum guaranty was $500 but over $1000 of credit was extended, $600 of which was not satisfied by the debtor, the surety was held to be liable for $500.

Writing

Suretyship and guaranty contracts are one of the types required by the statute of frauds to be in writing.[9] But there are

(Continued on page 350)

---

[6]C.C. 2792: "Where a suretyship obligation is entered into at the same time with the original obligation, or with the acceptance of the latter by the creditor, and forms with that obligation a part of the consideration to him, no other consideration need exist. In all other cases there must be a consideration distinct from that of the original obligation."

[7]C.C. 2815: "A continuing guaranty may be revoked at any time by the guarantor, in respect to future transactions, unless there is a continuing consideration as to such transactions which he does not renounce."

[8]Restatement of Security, Sec. 87.

[9]See page 44. C.C. 2793, as part of the suretyship section of the code, also states that suretyship contracts must be in writing.

---

[5]See the specimen form on page 347.

PERFORMANCE BOND

Bond No. C-_____ ____ _____

The premium for this bond is $_____, payable in advance and subject to adjustment at current manual rates.

Insurance Company

KNOW ALL MEN BY THESE PRESENTS: That we,

_____

as Principal, and_____, a corporation organized under the laws of the State of _____ and duly authorized under the laws of the State of _____ to become sole surety on bonds and undertaking, as Surety, are held and firmly bound unto

as Obligee

in the full and just sum of

Dollars, ($), lawful money of the United States of America, to be paid to the said Obligee, successors or assigns; for which payment, well and truly to be made, we bind ourselves, our heirs, executors, successors, administrators and assigns, jointly and severally, firmly by these presents.

The Condition of the above Obligation is such that whereas the said Principal has entered into a contract of even date herewith with the said Obligee to do and perform the following work, to-wit:

as is more specifically set forth in said contract, to which contract reference is hereby made;

Now therefore, if the said Principal shall well and truly do the said work, and fulfill each and every of the covenants, conditions and requirements of the said contract in accordance with the plans and specifications, then the above obligation to be void, otherwise to remain in full force and virtue.

No right of action shall accrue under this bond to or for the use of any person other than the Obligee named herein.

Sealed with our seals and dated this   day of   19

_____
Principal

_____
Surety

By_____
Attorney-in-Fact

PAYMENT BOND — PUBLIC WORKS   Bond No. C-_____

Insurance Company

KNOW ALL MEN BY THESE PRESENTS:

That we,   as Principal,
and   and
                                              , incorporated under the laws of the State of
authorized to execute bonds and undertakings as sole surety, as Surety, are held and firmly bound unto any and all persons named
in California Civil Code Section 3181 whose claim has not been paid by the contractor, company or corporation, in the aggregate
total of

                                                                          Dollars, ($),

for the payment whereof, well and truly to be made, said Principal and Surety bind themselves, their heirs, administrators, successors
and assigns, jointly and severally, firmly by these presents.

The Condition of the foregoing obligation is such that; whereas the above bounden Principal has entered into a contract, dated
                                              , 19   , with the
to do the following work, to-wit:

Now, Therefore, if the above bounden Principal, contractor, person, company or corporation, or his or its sub-contractor, fails to pay
any claimant named in Section 3181 of the Civil Code of the State of California, or amounts due under the Unemployment Insurance
Code, with respect to work or labor performed by any such claimant, that, the Surety on this bond will pay the same, in an amount
not exceeding the aggregate sum specified in this bond, and also, in case suit is brought upon this bond, a reasonable attorney's fee,
which shall be awarded by the court to the prevailing party in said suit, said attorney's fee to be taxed as costs in said suit.

This bond shall inure to the benefit of any person named in Section 3181 of the Civil Code of the State of California so as to give a
right of action to them or their assignees in any suit brought upon this bond.

This bond is executed and filed to comply with the provisions of the act of Legislature of the State of California as designated in
Civil Code, Sections 3247-3252 inclusive, and all amendments thereto.

Signed and Sealed this   day of   , 19

_____
Principal

_____
Surety

By_____
Attorney-in-Fact

CONTINUING GUARANTY

To CITY BANK

(1) For valuable consideration, the undersigned (hereinafter called Guarantors) jointly and severally unconditionally guarantee and promise to pay to CITY BANK (hereinafter called Bank), or order, on demand, in lawful money

of the United States, any and all indebtedness of ....

.... (hereinafter called Borrowers) to Bank. The word "indebtedness" is used herein in its most comprehensive sense and includes any and all advances, debts, obligations and liabilities of Borrowers or any one or more of them, heretofore, now, or hereafter made, incurred or created, whether voluntary or involuntary and however arising, whether due or not due, absolute or contingent, liquidated or unliquidated, determined or undetermined, and whether Borrowers may be liable individually or jointly with others, or whether recovery upon such indebtedness may be or hereafter becomes barred by any statute of limitations, or whether such indebtedness may be or hereafter becomes otherwise unenforceable.

(2) The liability of Guarantors shall not exceed at any one time the sum of ....

.... Dollars ($ ....) for principal, together with all interest upon the indebtedness or upon such part thereof as shall not exceed the foregoing limitation. Notwithstanding the foregoing, Bank may permit the indebtedness of Borrowers to exceed Guarantors' liability. This is a continuing guaranty relating to any indebtedness, including that arising under successive transactions which shall either continue the indebtedness or from time to time renew it after it has been satisfied. This guaranty *shall not apply to any indebtedness created after actual receipt by Bank of written notice of its revocation as to future transactions.* Any payment by Guarantors shall not reduce their maximum obligation hereunder, unless written notice to that effect be actually received by Bank at or prior to the time of such payment.

(3) The obligations hereunder are joint and several, and independent of the obligations of Borrowers, and a separate action or actions may be brought and prosecuted against Guarantors whether action is brought against Borrowers or whether Borrowers be joined in any such action or actions; and Guarantors waive the benefit of any statute of limitations affecting their liability hereunder or the enforcement thereof.

(4) Guarantors authorize Bank, without notice or demand and without affecting their liability hereunder, from time to time to (a) renew, extend, accelerate or otherwise change the time for payment of, or otherwise change the terms of the indebtedness or any part thereof, including increase or decrease of the rate of interest thereon; (b) take and hold security for the payment of this guaranty or the indebtedness guaranteed, and exchange, enforce, waive and release any such security; (c) apply such security and direct the order or manner of sale thereof as Bank in its discretion may determine; and (d) release or substitute any one or more of the endorsers or guarantors. Bank may without notice assign this guaranty in whole or in part.

(5) Guarantors waive any right to require Bank to (a) proceed against Borrowers; (b) proceed against or exhaust any security held from Borrowers; or (c) pursue any other remedy in Bank's power whatsoever. Guarantors waive any defense arising by reason of any disability or other defense of Borrowers or by reason of the cessation from any cause whatsoever of the liability of Borrowers. Until all indebtedness of Borrowers to Bank shall have been paid in full, even though such indebtedness is in excess of Guarantors' liability hereunder, Guarantors shall have no right of subrogation, and waive any right to enforce any remedy which Bank now has or may hereafter have against Borrowers, and waive any benefit of, and any right to participate in any security now or hereafter held by Bank. Guarantors waive all presentments, demands for performance, notices of non-performance, protests, notices of protest, notices of dishonor, and notices of acceptance of this guaranty and of the existence, creation, or incurring of new or additional indebtedness.

(6) In addition to all liens upon, and rights of setoff against the moneys, securities or other property of Guarantors given to Bank by law, Bank shall have a lien upon and a right of setoff against all moneys, securities and other property of Guarantors now or hereafter in the possession of or on deposit with Bank, whether held in a general or special account or deposit, or for safekeeping or otherwise; and every such lien and right of setoff may be exercised without demand upon or notice to Guarantors. No lien or right of setoff shall be deemed to have been waived by any act or conduct on the part of Bank, or by any neglect to exercise such right of setoff or to enforce such lien, or by any delay in so doing, and every right of setoff and lien shall continue in full force and effect until such right of setoff or lien is specifically waived or released by an instrument in writing executed by Bank.

(7) Any indebtedness of Borrowers now or hereafter held by Guarantors is hereby subordinated to the indebtedness of Borrowers to Bank; and such indebtedness of Borrowers to Guarantors if Bank so request shall be collected, enforced and received by Guarantors as trustees for Bank and be paid over to Bank on account of the indebtedness of Borrowers to Bank but without reducing or affecting in any manner the liability of Guarantors under the other provisions of this guaranty.

(8) Where any one or more of Borrowers are corporations or partnerships it is not necessary for Bank to inquire into the powers of Borrowers or the officers, directors, partners or agents acting or purporting to act on their behalf, and any indebtedness made or created in reliance upon the professed exercise of such powers shall be guaranteed hereunder.

(9) Guarantors agree to pay a reasonable attorneys' fee and all other costs and expenses which may be incurred by Bank in the enforcement of this Guaranty.

(10) Any married woman who signs this guaranty hereby expressly agrees that recourse may be had against her separate property for all her obligations under this guaranty.

(11) In all cases where there is but a single Borrower or a single Guarantor, then all words used herein in the plural shall be deemed to have been used in the singular where the context and construction so require; and when there is more than one Borrower named herein, or when this guaranty is executed by more than one Guarantor, the word "Borrowers" and the word "Guarantors" respectively shall mean all and any one or more of them.

IN WITNESS WHEREOF the undersigned Guarantors have executed this guaranty this ...... day of .... 19 ......

....

....

a number of exceptions to or limitations upon the application of the statute which must be noted:[10]

1. *Promise Must be to Creditor.* It is only a promise to the creditor that is of suretyship character and must be made in writing. Thus, if A owes money to C, and A agrees to lend money to B if B will pay his (A's) debt to C, B's only promise and contract is to and with A and is not a suretyship contract. Whether it is oral or written, therefore, is immaterial. C may enforce it, not as a creditor against a surety, but as a third party beneficiary of a contract made for his benefit.

2. *Main Purpose Doctrine.* Perhaps the most important and only true exception is the *main purpose doctrine.* This is the doctrine that if the main purpose of the surety in becoming such is not to accommodate the debtor but to gain something for himself, he is bound even though his suretyship agreement is oral only. As an example, suppose that S, engaged in the canning business, orally agrees to stand liable for a loan to D, a farmer, which will enable D to raise a crop which D has promised to sell to S for canning purposes. Here, S's main purpose is not to accommodate D but rather to serve his own ends, and he will be held liable on his oral agreement when the foregoing facts are established. The justification of the exception is that an extrinsic fact supports or corroborates the likelihood that the suretyship contract claimed has been made. There is more than C's word alone to bear witness to the fact. As seen earlier, this has always been the basis of exception to the statute of frauds—that some extrinsic fact substantially increases the likelihood that the claimed oral contract has been made.[11]

3. *Del Credere Commitment of Factor.* In the chapter on Agency,[12] it was seen that a del credere factor or agent was one who took goods on consignment for resale and agreed that if any of his sales on credit were uncollectible, he would stand liable to his consignor for the deficiency of the defaulting purchaser. This appears to be a suretyship contract—an agreement to answer for the debt of another, the defaulting purchaser. But it is held not to be. The reason usually given is that there is no debt in existence at the time the factor makes his guaranty and that it is only when a promise is to answer for an existing debt or one coming into existence concurrently with the making of the guaranty that a suretyship contract is created. Hence, the factor's guaranty is binding though made orally.

Rights of Surety

If the debtor or principal does not fulfill the obligation when the time for performance comes due or the surety is compelled to answer for his default, the surety has certain legal rights as to the debtor and creditor and as against cosureties if others have jointly assumed suretyship liability with him.

Rights Against Debtor

Exoneration: As soon as the obligation falls due and is not satisfied by the debtor, the surety has the right to be exonerated by the debtor. This is the right to bring suit to compel the debtor to make payment and save the surety from being required to do so.[13] As a practical matter, however, it is an idle right which would seldom be resorted to because the sur-

---

[10]C.C. 2794 provides for these various exceptions.

[11]See discussion of this on page 44.

[12]At page 57.

[13]C.C. 2846: "A surety may compel his principal to perform the obligation when due."

ety must be able to show that the debtor has assets which he is wrongfully refusing to apply to the debt before the court will require the creditor to wait until completion of the action to get his money. Since the usual reason for nonpayment is that the debtor has no assets, this could seldom be shown.

Reimbursement or Indemnity: As soon as the surety has paid all or any part of the debt, he has the right to obtain reimbursement from the debtor.[14]

Rights Against Creditor

Exhaustion of Collateral Security: Suppose that D borrows $5000 from C who demands both collateral security from D and a surety. D pledges stock with C as the collateral security and gets S to sign as his surety. D does not repay the loan. Must C first sell the pledged stock to get his money and look for S only for the unpaid balance, or may he ignore the stock and demand payment of the $5000 from S? The general rule is that if there is no express stipulation in the suretyship contract that he must first sell the security, the creditor may ignore it and recover the full amount of the debt from the surety.[15] The reasoning is that the surety's promise is an unconditional promise to pay if the debtor does not so that it would be unjustly depriving the creditor of a right—to enforce that unconditional promise—if he were required first to sell the security; and that the surety is fully protected by the right of subrogation, next considered. In at least 20 states including California,[16] however, the rule is otherwise. In these states, the creditor must first sell and satisfy the debt as far as possible from the security and may look to the surety only if there is a deficiency.[17]

Subrogation: If the surety is required to pay the debt or fulfill the obligation of the debtor, he becomes subrogated to the position or "steps into the shoes of" the creditor and acquires all of his rights.[18] One example is where the debtor has pledged collateral with the creditor, as in the situation discussed in the preceding paragraph, and the creditor elects to ignore the security and look to the surety for payment.

---

[14]C.C. 2847: "If a surety satisfies the principal obligation, or any part thereof . . . the principal is bound to reimburse what he has disbursed, including necessary costs and expenses. . . ."

[15]It is highly unlikely, of course, that the creditor would do this. He would sell the security and then enforce his rights against the surety for any unpaid balance.

[16]C.C. 2854: "A creditor is entitled to the benefit of everything which a surety has received from the debtor by way of security for the performance of the obligation, and may, upon maturity of the obligation, compel the application of such security to its satisfaction."

[17]Even under the general rule it is held that if both the debtor and the surety mortgage or pledge property with the creditor as security, the creditor must sell the debtor's property first if that will place no undue burden on the creditor.

In California, C.C. 2845 provides broadly that "A surety may require the creditor . . . to proceed against the principal; or to pursue any other remedy in the creditor's power which the surety cannot pursue, and which would lighten the surety's burden; and if the creditor neglects to do so, the surety is exonerated to the extent to which the surety is thereby prejudiced."

[18]C.C. 2848: "A surety, upon satisfying the obligation of the principal, is entitled to enforce every remedy which the creditor then has against the principal to the extent of reimbursing what he has expended, and also to require all his cosureties to contribute thereto, without regard to the order of time in which they became such."

Upon paying, the surety would be entitled to an assignment of the security from the creditor and would have the right to sell it to get back his money.[19] As a practical matter, it would be a rare case in which the creditor would disregard the security and demand payment from the surety, and the usual application of the right of subrogation is of this nature: Suppose, again, that S becomes surety for D's obligation to C. D fails to pay and has gone into bankruptcy. C is a creditor of a type who is given a priority in the bankruptcy of his debtor.[20] C demands and S makes payment to him. S is then subrogated to C's position so as to get C's priority in D's bankruptcy. A surety is subrogated to all of the special rights and privileges of the creditor when he pays the creditor. The leading case on the point is *Bramwell* v. *United States Fidelity and Guaranty Co.*, 269 U.S. 483, 46 S.Ct. 176. There, S was surety on the bond of a bank insuring deposits of public funds by the state treasurer. The bank became insolvent and went into receivership. Had the state filed a claim in these proceedings it would have been entitled to payment before the other creditors of the bank. S was required to pay the state on its bond, and the question was whether or not it then succeeded to the state's priority. It was held that it did, and this is the general rule[21]—that a surety upon paying becomes subrogated even to the special priority of the United States, a state or other political subdivision.

Rights Against Cosureties

A creditor may require two or more sureties rather than merely one. As to each other, the sureties are cosureties. As to the creditor, however, each surety is severally liable for the full amount of the debt unless there is an express agreement to the contrary in the suretyship contract. It is for this reason that the right of contribution discussed below is important.

• Where several sureties guarantee the same obligation, it is generally held that they become cosureties with right of contribution despite the facts that one is a gratuitous surety and the other compensated, that they became sureties on different dates and by different instruments and/or that they did not know of each other's suretyship contracts. Thus, in *United States Fidelity & Guaranty Co.* v. *Naylor*, 237 Fed. 314, there were two sureties for deposits of county funds in a bank. One surety, S-1, was an insurance company which received a premium for its commitment. The other, S-2, was a group of individuals who became surety at a slightly later date by another instrument and without receiving compensation. S-1's and S-2's was a common obligation, however, the guaranty of repayment of county funds deposited for the period of the following year. The bank failed, and S-1 was required to reimburse the county for its lost deposits. S-1 then sued S-2 for contribution, and S-2 raised the defenses that the parties were not cosureties because one was compensated and the other was gratuitous and because they became sureties on different dates. Held, the parties were cosureties, and S-1 was entitled to contribution from S-2.

Said the court: "The test of cosuretyship is a common liability for the same debt or burden. This liability may arise at the same time or at different times, out of the same writing or many writings. A common interest and a common burden alone are required to create the relation, and to enable the cosurety who has paid more than his due proportion to claim contribution. . . . If several persons, or several sets of persons, become sureties for the same duty or debt, of, to, and for the same persons, though by different instruments, at different times, and without knowledge of the obligation of each other, they will be bound to mutual contribution." The court continued: "where some of the cosureties for a common debt have been compensated . . . for their suretyship, and others became cosureties for the accommodation of their principals, the fact is immaterial, and the compensated cosureties, who have paid more than their proportion of the common liability, are entitled to contribution from the accommodation cosureties. . . ."

Exoneration: A surety has the right to be exonerated by cosureties. He may bring an action to compel them to contribute their proportionate shares of the liability to protect himself from being required to pay the entire amount.

Contribution: As seen above to some extent, a surety who is compelled to pay all or some unpaid balance of the obligation is entitled to proportionate contribution from his cosureties.[22] Thus, if S-1 and S-2 are cosureties on a loan of $5000 by C to D and D fails to pay and S-1 is required to pay the entire $5000, S-1 may recover $2500 from S-2. (This assumes no special agreement between the sureties to the contrary. They may make any agreement they see fit and may agree that one surety shall bear a greater proportion of the liability than the other.) Taking the same case, if D had repaid $3000 of the loan, and S-1 had been required to pay only the $2000 balance, then S-1's right of contribution from S-2 would be the sum of $1000.

• If one of several cosureties becomes discharged of liability, then, under equitable rules of contribution, his share of the liability is redistributed among the remaining cosureties in accordance with their proportionate liabilities. Thus, if S-1, S-2 and S-3 become cosureties on a $10,000 debt and, after its maturity and nonpayment by D, S-3 goes into and is discharged of his suretyship obligation in bankruptcy, S-1 is entitled to $5000 contribution from S-2 if S-1 is compelled to pay the entire debt.

• Cosureties may expressly agree to bear other than equal shares of the ultimate liability. Such an agreement will be implied where they assume different maximum liabilities. This was the ultimate problem in *United States Fidelity & Guaranty* v. *Naylor*, discussed above. There, S-1, the compensated surety, had assumed liability for a maximum amount of $10,000. It was held that the contributive shares of the parties were in the ratio of 1 to 2 in view of the maximum liabilities assumed and, so, that S-2 was required to pay ⅔ of the loss, S-1 only ⅓.

Statute of Limitations

The statute of limitations begins to run on the surety's right to reimbursement from the debtor from the date that he makes payment to the creditor or contribution to a cosurety who has been compelled to answer for the debt.[23]

---

[19]Neither the creditor nor the surety may make any profit from the transaction, i.e., if the security is sold by one or the other and brings more than enough to satisfy the debt or reimburse the surety if he has paid it, the surplus must be paid over to the debtor.

[20]Creditors given priority in bankruptcy are discussed on page 362.

[21]83 A.L.R. 1131.

[22]See footnote 18.

[23]The statute of limitations is 4 years in California under C.C.P. 337(1).

Defenses of Surety

The surety may be able to escape responsibility on his suretyship contract by reason of various defenses. In general, these may be classified according to the time they arise as being defenses arising or existing at the time the suretyship contract is made, and defenses arising at some time subsequent to formation of the suretyship contract.

Arising or Existing When Contract Made

Incapacity of Surety: A suretyship contract made by a minor or mentally incompetent person is no more binding than other contracts made by such persons. Minority or mental incompetency of the principal or debtor, however, does not relieve the surety of liability.[24] This is one of the things which the creditor intends to guard against by requiring a surety.

Illegality or Invalidity of Principal Contract: The suretyship contract is an accessorial one—a contract which is incidental to and in support of another contract, the principal contract. This being so, it is held that if the principal contract is illegal or invalid and, so, not enforceable, the suretyship contract is not enforceable.[25] Examples of this are rare. One of the few cases is *Mound* v. *Barker*, 71 Vt. 253, 44 Atl. 346, where the surety guaranteed payment of rents on a lease. As between the lessor and lessee, it had been agreed that the premises could be used in a manner which violated the law. The lessee defaulted on the rent. It was held that the lessor could not recover rents from the lessee because of the illegality of the lease contract and that rents could not be collected from the surety for the same reason.

Lack of Writing: As discussed on pages 346 and 350, but with the exceptions noted there, the surety has a good defense if the suretyship contract is not in writing as required by the statute of frauds.

Fraud of Creditor Regarding Debtor: It is generally held that the creditor has no duty to advise the surety of financial weakness of the debtor known to the creditor. The surety is in a position to determine this for himself, and the fact that the creditor demands a surety gives warning of the creditor's fears. But the creditor does have a duty to inform the surety of known past dishonesties of the debtor, and failure to do so constitutes fraud in the form of nondisclosure which relieves the surety of liability to the creditor.

● Fraud of the *debtor* upon the surety does not relieve the surety of responsibility. Thus, if the debtor misrepresents his assets to induce the surety to become such, this does not give the surety a defense so long as the creditor did not participate in the fraud.

Arising Subsequent to Contract

Material Alteration of Principal Contract: A surety assumes responsibility for a particular contract in particular terms and between particular parties. If this contract is changed or enlarged upon in some respect, it would impose upon the surety a different or greater liability than he agreed to assume, which would not be fair to him. Hence, it is the rule that material alteration of the principal contract relieves the surety of liability.[26] Material alteration may take the form of a change in the terms of the principal contract or of the parties thereto.

Shuey v. *Bunney*, 4 C.A.2d 408, 40 P.2d 859, is an example of change in the terms of the contract releasing the surety. There, P agreed with O to raise a herd of approximately 700 head of cattle for a period of 5 years. At the end of that time P was to have the right to buy the herd at $30 a head, return it to O or sell all or any part of it and make payment to O at the rate of $30 a head. S was required to furnish a $5000 performance bond guaranteeing proper performance by P of his part of the contract. Thereafter, O and P made a "supplemental agreement" whereby the herd was to be increased to approximately 800 head and P's purchase price to $33 a head. At the end of the 5-year period, P sold a substantial portion of the herd but failed to account to O for the proceeds, and demand was made against S on its bond. Held, the supplemental agreement "was a change in the contract and we think such a change as comes within the provisions of the code sections by which a surety is released," the court having reference to C.C. 2819, in footnote 26.

● Concerning change of parties, suppose that S guarantees all credit extended by C to D for some period of time. D in this case is a partnership composed of A and B. During the period of the guaranty, B sells his interest to T who replaces B in the partnership. Thereafter, further extensions of credit are made to the partnership. Would S be liable for these? Or, framing the question as a legal one, would this constitute a change of parties—the debtor—such as would release S of further liability? It has been held that it would, and such holding is justified from S's standpoint. Change of debtor could increase the surety's risk. B could have been the tempering influence in the partnership, because of whom S was willing to become surety. T could be of a quite different nature, inclined, along with A, to overextend credit or to overstock with merchandise, creating, from S's point of view, a risk quite different from the risk originally bargained for by S.

There are, however, cases where change of the debtor or principal would not seem to affect the surety's liability. For example: S Insurance Co. writes a performance bond of the type on page 347, guaranteeing performance of a building job by P for O. P is a partnership consisting of A and B. During the course of the construction job, B sells his interest to T who replaces B in the partnership. P continues the job, receiving further labor and materials from various persons, which are not paid for. The labor and materialmen seek payment from S on its bond. It does not seem likely that S will be permitted to deny liability on the ground that there has been a change of debtor. Such bonds are recorded, and it is often entirely on the strength of them that materials are furnished to a contractor, the materialman feeling completely secure in the fact that he will have recourse against the bonding company if necessary. Materialmen will often check the public records for a bond or call the bonding company to see if a bond has been written before delivering materials on credit. It is the opinion of a number of persons in the bonding

---

[24]C.C. 2810: "A surety is liable, notwithstanding any mere personal disability of the principal, though the disability be such as to make the contract void against the principal; but he is not liable if for any other reason there is no liability on the part of the principal at the time of execution of the contract, or the liability of the principal thereafter ceases. . . ." The first half of this section covers the matter of incapacity. It says that the surety is liable even though the debtor is a minor or mental incompetent. The second half covers cases of illegality of the principal contract, as discussed in the next paragraph of the text.

[25]See footnote 24.

[26]C.C. 2819: "A surety is exonerated . . . if by any act of the creditor, without the consent of the surety, the original obligation of the principal is altered in any respect. . . ."

field that the bonding company would be held on the bond in such case on some policy theory or on estoppel grounds.

Extension of Time to or Release of Debtor: Suppose that on June 1, 1983, D borrows $5000 from C to be repaid on January 2, 1984. S becomes surety for repayment of the loan. On January 2, D is unable to pay. C agrees to give him an additional 3 months in which to make payment, S is not advised of this and has not consented to it. It is a general rule of law that an extension of time to the debtor releases the surety unless the surety consents to the extension or the creditor expressly reserves his rights against the surety.[27] The reasoning is that this prolongs the liability of the surety beyond the time agreed upon and, so, attempts to impose upon him a greater liability than he agreed to assume. Actually, however, he is being done a favor by the extension of time to the debtor. The debtor does not pay because he cannot. If the extension were not granted, the surety would be called upon to pay. Later courts began to see the matter more in this light and to limit the circumstances in which an extension would release the surety. As a result, these important limitations came to be imposed upon the rule that a surety was released by extension of time:

1. The extension must be a binding one, which requires (a) that it be for a definite period of time, and (b) that it be for a consideration. There is disagreement among the authorities as to whether the continued payment of interest at the same rate is sufficient consideration to make the extension binding.

2. Many courts hold that a compensated surety is not discharged unless he can show that he is actually prejudiced in some way by the extension.

3. As stated above, the extension does not release the surety if the creditor expressly reserves his rights against him. Several technical reasons are advanced for this rule. Perhaps the most understandable is this: The creditor's reservation of rights against the surety, being known to the debtor, implies assent by the debtor that the surety may pay the debt despite the extension and seek recovery from the debtor. Thus, the surety's rights, such as they are when the debtor cannot pay, are preserved intact in all respects, and the extension causes the surety no injury.

● How does the creditor reserve his rights against the surety? The best illustrative case is *Federal Trust Co.* v. *Central Trust Co.*, 244 Mass. 204, 138 N.E. 562. There, as would always be the case, the debt was represented by a note on which S had indorsed his guaranty. An extension was given at maturity of the note without the consent of the surety. The extension was made by a "renewal note" from the debtor to the creditor. The renewal note recited that the original note "with indorsements" was retained as security for the renewal note. Held, the retention of the original note "with indorsements" and, hence, with S's guaranty which was indorsed upon it, was a reservation of rights against the surety, S.

CALIFORNIA. Prior to 1939, California followed the general principles of law outlined above. In *Berkowitz* v. *Tyderko, Ltd.*, 13 C.A.2d 561, 57 P.2d 173, e.g., it was held that the surety was not released where a 6-month extension was given on a note but there was no consideration for it. In 1939, how-

ever, C.C. 2820 was amended to provide: "That a promise by a creditor is for any cause void, or voidable by him at his option, shall not prevent it from altering the obligation or suspending or impairing the remedy within the meaning of the last section." The "last section" is C.C. 2819 which discharges the surety if the principal contract is altered "or the remedies or rights of the creditor against the principal (are) in any way impaired or suspended." Under C.C. 2819, an extension of time would *suspend* the rights of the creditor against the debtor temporarily. Under C.C. 2820, the fact that the extension was not binding because, e.g., it was not for a definite time or was without consideration, would not stop the surety from becoming discharged under C.C. 2819. It is the rule in California, then, that a surety is discharged by an extension of time without his consent even though the extension is not a binding one—the opposite of the general rule.

● The question of *release* of the debtor as releasing the surety is apt to arise in a case such as this: D owes $5000 to A, $7000 to B and $8000 to C. S is surety on the debt to C. D has only $10,000 with which to pay his debts. He proposes a composition of creditors to A, B and C whereby they would each take 50 cents on the dollar and give D a release in full of his $20,000 of obligations to them, to which they agree. Unless C expressly reserves his rights against S, the surety, S will be discharged by C's release of D. The rule, as in the extension cases above, is that release of the debtor releases the surety as well unless the creditor expressly reserves his rights against the surety.

Non-disclosure of Facts Increasing Risk: Suppose that S Insurance Co. writes a position fidelity bond[28] in favor of O, an employer, protecting O against misappropriation by persons occupying the position of cashier in O's business. At the time the bond is issued, O has trusted persons in these positions. Later, one of O's cashiers leaves, and O decides to give a person previously convicted of embezzlement a chance at the job. Since it is a *position* bond, the surety will have consented in advance to changes in the occupancy of the position. Irrespective of this, however, the obligee has the duty to notify the surety of any fact occurring during the term of the suretyship contract which would materially increase the risk of the surety. This is to enable the surety to cancel the bond if it wishes to do so (which, of course, it would in a case such as this), all fidelity bonds containing the provision that they may be canceled by the surety company on some period of notice, usually 20 days or 30 days.

Bankruptcy of Surety: Ordinarily, discharge in bankruptcy of the surety will discharge him of suretyship liabilities along with his other debts and obligations. Should it be the case, however, that the surety goes through and is discharged in bankruptcy before maturity of a debt on which he is surety, this would not be so because the creditor would not have had a provable (enforceable) claim against the surety during the bankruptcy proceeding. Only when the debt matures and goes unpaid does the creditor have a claim against the surety. If this does not happen until after the surety's discharge in bankruptcy, the creditor would have had no provable claim in the bankruptcy proceeding, and one is discharged in bankruptcy only of claims which are provable against him in that proceeding.[29]

---

[27]As a practical matter, a principal obligation of a loan of money will always be represented by a note, and the note, if it is to be guaranteed, will contain an express provision that guarantors consent to any extensions of time that the creditor may see fit to give. This consent in advance is fully binding and eliminates any question of discharge of the guarantor on account of extension of time.

[28]See page 346 re position fidelity bonds.

[29]Discharge in bankruptcy of the *debtor* does not discharge the surety. This above all is the contingency that the creditor seeks to guard against. C.C. 2825 expressly provides this by stating that "A surety is not exonerated by the discharge of his principal by operation of law . . ."

Statute of Limitations: The creditor has no duty to sue the debtor to recover payment when maturity arrives and the debt goes unpaid,[30] and no duty to notify the surety of the debtor's failure to make payment where the debt has a fixed maturity so that it is within the surety's power, by inquiry, to determine whether or not the debt has been paid. Eventually, however, the statute of limitations will run on the creditor's right to recover from the surety, as it does on other rights. The statute

begins to run from the date of maturity of the debt or, if it is payable in installments, on each installment from the date it becomes due.[31]

---

[30]C.C. 2823: "Mere delay on the part of a creditor to proceed against the principal, or to enforce any other remedy, does not exonerate a surety."

---

[31]The statute of limitations may have run on the principal contract without having run on the suretyship contract. The principal contract may be oral if it does not come within the statute of frauds. In such case, in California, the statute of limitations is 2 years. The suretyship contract is always within the statute of frauds and therefore always required to be in writing and, in California, is therefore governed by a 4-year statute of limitations.

CHAPTER 14

Creditors' Rights and Bankruptcy

State Laws Protecting Creditors

In this chapter are discussed rights and remedies of creditors under state laws designed for their protection and under the federal Bankruptcy Act. The law has frequently been criticized as being overly protective of debtors, and unpaid creditors generally are in a rather unfavorable position. Legal proceedings are slow and expensive, much of the debtor's property is exempt from claims of creditors, and the door of the bankruptcy court is always open to the debtor to wipe out his obligations entirely. Consequently, creditors are usually willing to make any reasonable compromise which will give them some substantial portion of the amounts owed them, and the practical solution of compromise is a common one.

Attachment and Execution

These matters are discussed on pages 8-9, in connection with the steps in a legal proceeding. Note the exemptions set out in footnote 4 on page 8. The homestead exemption and the exemption of the debtor's wages succeed in removing most of the assets of the ordinary debtor from the reach of his creditors.

Fraudulent Conveyances

The law attempts to protect creditors against such fraudulent practices as "putting property in someone else's name" in anticipation of claims of creditors or after lawsuits to enforce such claims have been commenced. The law in this instance is the Uniform Fraudulent Conveyances Act set out in the Appendix.[1] It is aimed at two general types of "fraudulent conveyances"—those made with actual intent to defraud creditors and those made while insolvent or the effect of which will be to make the transferor insolvent or dangerously near to that condition. It permits creditors to have such transfers set aside.

1. *Transfers with intent to defraud.* U.F.C.A. 7 says that "Every conveyance made and every obligation incurred with actual intent . . . to hinder, delay or defraud either present and future creditors, is fraudulent as to both present and future creditors." To show "actual intent" to defraud is impossible without an admission of such intent by the transferor which, of course, he would not make, and the courts have always held that this intent may be inferred from the surrounding circumstances. Thus, in *Taylor* v. *Osborne-Fitzpatrick Finance Co.*, 57 C.A.2d 656, 135 P.2d 598, a woman transferred a certificate for 5,000 shares of stock while several lawsuits were pending against her. The transferee was aware of these circumstances, the transfer was not recorded on the books of the corporation, and such consideration as was given was nominal in relation to the value of the stock. Held, that the evidence was sufficient to permit a finding that the transfer was made with "actual intent" to defraud, the court saying that the "inference from circumstances surrounding the transaction" is sufficient proof of such intent.

2. *Transfers while insolvent, etc.* If the transfer is with actual intention to defraud, the fact that the transferor remains solvent after the transfer is immaterial. The remaining types of transfers covered by the Act are ones which are fraudulent because of their effect upon the solvency of the transferor, and in these cases his intention is immaterial. These are: (a) Transfers "without fair consideration" (consideration fairly equivalent in value to that of the property transferred) while insolvent or which will render the transferor insolvent.[2] The Act says that "A person is insolvent when the present fair salable value of his assets is less than the amount that will be required to pay his probable liability on his existing debts as they become absolute and matured."[3] (b) Transfers "without fair consideration when the person making it is engaged or is about to engage in a business or transaction for which the property remaining in his hands after the conveyance is an unreasonably small capital . . ."[4] (c) "Every conveyance made and every obligation incurred without fair consideration when the person making the conveyance or entering into the obligation intends or believes that he will incur debts beyond his ability to pay as they mature . . ."[5]

Bulk Transfers

Bulk transfers, the subject matter of Division 6 of the Uniform Commercial Code, are covered in Chapter 5, beginning at page 105.

Insolvency Proceedings

State laws provide for two general types of insolvency proceedings: assignments for the benefit of creditors and receivership proceedings.

● *Assignment for the benefit of creditors* is the transfer of his assets by an insolvent person to an "assignee," agreed upon between him and his creditors, who will liquidate the assets and distribute them pro rata to the creditors.[6] This will be combined with a *composition of creditors* agreement whereby each creditor will agree to give the debtor a full discharge in return for part payment so that, upon completion of the transaction, the debtor will be completely freed of his debts.[7] This obtains the benefits of bankruptcy proceedings without incurring the stigma of bankruptcy.

● Receiverships on account of insolvency are usually limited to cases of insolvency of corporations, as in California, where

---

[1] In California, the Uniform Fraudulent Conveyances Act is C.C. 3439-3439.12. In the Appendix, equivalent California Civil Code sections are shown in parentheses following the section numbers of the uniform act.

[2] U.F.C.A. 4.

[3] U.F.C.A. 2(a).

[4] U.F.C.A. 5.

[5] U.F.C.A. 6.

[6] C.C. 3449-3473 provide for assignments for the benefit of creditors.

[7] See page 33 for further discussion of composition of creditors.

C.C.P. 564(5) provides that a receiver may be appointed to take charge of the assets of a corporation when it "is insolvent or in imminent danger of insolvency."

Note on Boards of Trade

Most major cities have a board of trade which is a private institution established by wholesale and retail merchants and business firms to deal with and attempt to work out the problems of businesses or individuals having financial difficulties. The most common activity of such boards is to obtain extensions of time for payment of the debts of a business and then to supervise the operation of the business in order to restore it to solvency.

Federal Bankruptcy Act

Throughout the remainder of this chapter reference is made to "bankruptcy courts" and "bankruptcy judges," both of which were provided for in connection with the Bankruptcy Reform Act of 1978. Prior to the 1978 Act there were no such things as bankruptcy courts, as such, or bankruptcy judges. Prior to the 1978 Act, bankruptcy proceedings were commenced in federal district courts, the bottom tier of the federal court system, and then were administered by a referee appointed by the district court judge. At the conclusion of the administration of the case, the case was returned to the district court for discharge of the bankrupt in bankruptcy. Throughout the proceedings the referee, in carrying out his function, was regarded as acting as the agent or deputy of the district court judge. Article III, Section 1, of the United States Constitution, says that "The judicial Power of the United States shall be vested in one Supreme Court, and in such inferior Courts as the Congress may from time to time ordain and establish. The Judges, both of the Supreme and inferior Courts, shall hold their Offices during good Behaviour, and shall, at stated Times, receive for their Services, a Compensation, which shall not be diminished during their Continuance in Office." The second sentence of Section 1 is designed to protect federal judges against the possibility of outside influence. Since they are given life tenure, they have no constituency to bend to and since their salaries cannot be reduced they need not worry about this as a possible form of retaliation for unpopular or unwanted decisions. The bankruptcy judges created by 1978 law were not given these protections. They were given 14-year terms of office and the federal law creating them made their salaries subject to "adjustment." For these reasons, i.e., because the principle of independent adjudication commanded by Article III, Section 1, would not be satisfied, it was held in the 1981 United States Supreme Court case of Northern Pipeline Constr. Co. v. Marathon Pipe Line Co. (1981) __ U.S. __, 102 S.Ct. 2858, 73 L.Ed.2d 598, that they were not eligible to exercise federal jurisdiction, i.e., to serve as "judges" in the federal system.

Needless to say, this caused great consternation in the world of bankruptcy. At a time when bankruptcies were at their highest ever, the load of bankruptcy proceedings was cast back on already overloaded federal district courts. A solution to the problem has not yet been reached. One solution, not looked on favorably, however, would be to make bankruptcy judges federal district judges.

Since a solution must be forthcoming in the near future, it has seemed better to give this explanation and then, for the time being, allow the remainder of this chapter to continue to speak of "bankruptcy courts" and "bankruptcy judges."

● The bankruptcy law, being federal, is the exclusive law on the subject of bankruptcy throughout the United States. Where the Constitution confers upon the federal government the lawmaking power with respect to a given subject, the federal government has the exclusive lawmaking power in that field, and its enactment becomes the law everywhere. The Constitution gives the federal government the exclusive lawmaking power with respect to the "subject of bankruptcies."[8] The object was to insure a uniform law. Without such a law, one state could enact a law that was more advantageous to debtors than another, to the prejudice of persons of other states dealing with the debtor.

Congress passed a series of bankruptcy laws beginning in 1800. In 1898 the first permanent bankruptcy law was passed. The 1898 law was substantially revised and added to in 1938. The resultant body of law became known as the Bankruptcy Act of 1898 as amended by the Chandler Act of 1938 and continued to be the law of bankruptcy until the effective date of the Bankruptcy Reform Act of 1978. On November 6, 1978, the Bankruptcy Reform Act of 1978 was enacted by Congress, to become effective on October 1, 1979. The purposes of this new law were to simplify and modernize the law of bankruptcy. The United States Supreme Court is empowered to make rules of practice and procedure for the conduct of bankruptcy proceedings. Rules were made relative to the 1938 Act but new rules, for the 1978 Act, have not yet been made and the old rules will continue in force, so long as they are not in conflict with the new Act, until new rules are promulgated. This chapter is based on the Bankruptcy Reform Act of 1978, cited and referred to throughout the chapter as BRA. Extensive excerpts from the Bankruptcy Reform Act of 1978 are to be found in the Appendix.

Being a federal law, the bankruptcy law is administered exclusively in the federal courts, and all bankruptcy proceedings must be commenced in the bankruptcy court for the district in which the domicile, residence, principal place of business, in the United States, or principal assets, in the United States, of the person or entity that is the subject of the bankruptcy case have been located for the 180 days preceding commencement of the case, or the greater portion thereof.[9]

Overview

There are two basic kinds of bankruptcy proceedings: *liquidation proceedings* and *rehabilitation proceedings*.

● In *liquidation proceedings*, often called ordinary or "straight bankruptcy" proceedings, the debtor surrenders his nonexempt assets to his trustee in bankruptcy who liquidates the assets and distributes the proceeds pro rata to creditors. The debtor is then given a discharge in bankruptcy which discharges him from the unpaid balances of his debts. In this manner the debtor is given a new start in life.

BRA provides for liquidation proceedings in Chapter 7 and it has already become the practice to refer to BRA liquidation proceedings as *Chapter 7 proceedings*.

Chapter 7 proceedings may be *voluntary*, that is, initiated by the debtor against himself, or *involuntary*, that is, initiated by creditors against their debtor. A new feature of bankruptcy proceedings, introduced by BRA, is that husband and wife may initiate joint voluntary proceedings.

● *Rehabilitation proceedings*, by contrast with liquidation proceedings, are designed to allow a business enterprise or an

---

[8]U.S. Constitution, Art. 1, Section VIII(4). While the bankruptcy law is exclusively a federal one, it incorporates state law for certain purposes, as seen in this chapter, e.g. for the purpose of determining what may constitute exempt property.

[9]28 U.S.C. 1472.

individual debtor to attempt to rehabilitate itself or himself by scaling down indebtedness and paying the reduced amount of indebtedness over an extended period of time. Debt satisfaction will take place out of future earnings rather than out of existing assets, as in the case of liquidation proceedings, and creditors may be expected to get a greater percentage of satisfaction of their claims.

Chapters 11 and 13 of BRA, which had more limited counterparts under prior bankruptcy law, provide for rehabilitation proceedings. Under both Chapter 11 proceedings and Chapter 13 proceedings, the debtor, or creditors, must conceive and present a "plan" of rehabilitation which must be approved by creditors (Chapter 11) or the bankruptcy court (Chapter 13).

• *Chapter 11 proceedings* are apt to involve a relatively large scale debtor and therefore relatively large scale rehabilitation proceedings, while Chapter 13 proceedings will involve a relatively small scale debtor and relatively small scale rehabilitation proceedings.

Chapter 11 proceedings are designed to facilitate the rehabilitation of business organizations, up to the largest of corporations, by allowing such organizations to reorganize and restructure their debt and equity structures to manageable levels. Chapter 11 proceedings may be voluntary or involuntary. A trustee may be appointed only when such action is necessary for the protection of creditors and stockholders and in most cases the debtor will continue to be in conrol of its business. However the bankruptcy court may appoint an examiner to investigate the debtor and the Securities and Exchange Commission is given the right to participate in Chapter 11 proceedings for the protection of stockholders of the debtor.

• *Chapter 13 proceedings* are for "individual(s) with regular income," as defined in BRA 101(24) and 109(e), which means, roughly speaking, persons with stable income, and with unsecured debts of less than $100,000 and secured debts of less than $350,000.

Chapter 13 proceedings are available only to individuals, not partnerships or corporations, and only voluntary proceedings are provided for. However the individual may be engaged in the operation of a business and Chapter 13 proceedings will permit him to continue to operate the business while paying its debts. The debtor must present a debt-paying plan which must be confirmed by the bankruptcy court and which must ordinarily be completed within 3 years.

• Title 11 of the United States Code contains the substantive law of bankruptcy. Title 11 consists of 8 odd-numbered chapters (Chapters 1, 3, 5, 7, 9, 11, 13, 15). Chapters 1, 3 and 5 are general chapters, the rules of which apply to Chapters 7, 11 and 13. See BRA 103. Chapter 1 (General Provisions) contains an extensive list of across-the-board definitions.[10] Chapter 1 also declares who may be a debtor in liquidation and rehabilitation proceedings.[11] (BRA uses the term "debtor" throughout, rather than the term "bankrupt," and that practice will be followed in this book.) Chapter 3 (Case Administration) tells how and by whom voluntary and involuntary cases may be commenced[12] and states rules regarding the qualifications and compensation[13] of trustees, the call and conduct of meetings of creditors and stockholders,[14] and the use, sale and lease of property of the debtor's estate.[15] Chapter 5 (Creditors, Debtor and Estate) sets forth the rights and duties of creditors, debtors and trustees; what constitutes the estate of the debtor and what property is recoverable by the estate for the benefit of creditors; what property is exempt to the debtor; priorities given to various classes of unsecured creditors; and what kinds of claims are not discharged by BRA proceedings.

• Chapter 9 (Adjustment of Debts of Municipality) is designed to provide relief for insolvent local government units. Chapter 9 is beyond the scope of this book and will not receive further attention.

• Trustees serve various functions in bankruptcy proceedings. Traditionally, the trustee is *liquidator*, that is, one who takes possession of the nonexempt assets of the debtor, liquidates them and distributes the proceeds to creditors. However, under Chapter 11, the trustee may be an operating trustee rather than a liquidating trustee, operating the business of the debtor during the period of recovery. BRA experiments with still another kind of trustee, called a United States trustee. Chapter 15 of BRA is all about United States trustees.[16] Unlike the ordinary, private trustee whose functions have been described above, the United States trustee is a salaried federal official, appointed by the Attorney General, whose main function is to administer and supervise the panel of private trustees within the judicial district within which the United States trustee operates and thereby to relieve the bankruptcy judge of time-consuming chores.

The ordinary trustee is a private individual who has made it to the panel of private trustees established and maintained by the Director of the Administrative Office of the United States Courts. Upon the commencement of a Chapter 7 proceeding, the bankruptcy judge must appoint, from this panel, an "interim trustee" to serve at least temporarily as trustee.[17] The interim trustee becomes a permanent trustee unless, at the first meeting of creditors, creditors holding 20% in dollar amount of certain kinds of unsecured claims request the election of a trustee.[18] This eliminates the need for trustee election except in cases in which there is significant creditor interest in having such an election. In the judicial districts in which United States trustees have been appointed, the United States trustees will appoint interim trustees from the official panel and will receive from them final reports and final accountings at the conclusion of their administrations.

The United States trustee program is a 5-year pilot program being experimented with in 18 scattered federal judicial districts, including the Central District of California. United States trustees will not receive further discussion.

• While Title 11 of the United States Code (called Bankruptcy) contains the substantive law of bankruptcy, Title 28 of the United States Code (called the Judicial Code) contains the BRA's judicial legislation which creates a new and independent bankruptcy court.

Chapter 7 Liquidation

Procedural Outline of Chapter 7 Case

Chapter 7 cases are commenced by the filing, with the bankruptcy court, of a *voluntary or debtor's petition*, including a

---

[10]BRA 101(1)-(40).

[11]BRA 109.

[12]BRA 301-303.

[13]Private trustees receive very limited compensation under BRA (Section 326) and receive only $20 in a no-asset case. BRA 330(b). This may discourage persons from seeking to become trustees.

[14]BRA 341-343.

[15]BRA 363-365.

[16]Chapter 15 is not included in the Appendix.

[17]BRA 701.

[18]BRA 702.

joint petition of a husband and wife, or an *involuntary or creditors' petition.*[19] Forms of Chapter 7 petitions appear on pages 359-360, following.

• Bankruptcy proceedings require an eligible "debtor" which requires a person who resides in the United States or has a domicile, place of business or property in the United States.[20] Chapter 7 proceedings may be commenced by or against a partnership or corporation since such entities are "persons" by definition of BRA 101(30) but may not be commenced by banks, insurance companies or railroads[21] for whose liquidations separate forms of proceedings exist.

• Commencement of a voluntary Chapter 7 proceeding is less complicated than commencement of an involuntary Chapter 7 proceeding. For a voluntary proceeding all that is required is that there be an eligible debtor as defined above. Although normally it would be present, "insolvency" is not required for a Chapter 7 (or Chapter 11 or 13) voluntary proceeding. BRA 301 says that the "commencement of a voluntary case under a chapter of this title constitutes an *order for relief* under such chapter." (Italics supplied.) This is legalese for saying that, in voluntary proceedings, the proceeding is on as soon as the petition is filed. However, BRA 305(a) does permit the bankruptcy court to dismiss or suspend a case if "the interests of creditors and the debtor would be better served by such dismissal or suspension." Dismissal or suspension would be rare.

• Banks, insurance companies and railroads are excluded from involuntary Chapter 7 proceedings just as they are from voluntary Chapter 7 proceedings.[22] In addition, Chapter 7 (and Chapter 11) involuntary proceedings may not be commenced against farmers (because of the cyclical nature of their activity) or charitable corporations.[23] If the debtor has 12 or more unsecured creditors, involuntary proceedings must be commenced by 3 or more creditors holding unsecured claims totalling at least $5000.[24] Involuntary proceedings are not self-starting like voluntary proceedings are, that is, the filing of the petition does not constitute an "order for relief" like it does in a voluntary proceeding. In an involuntary proceeding, the debtor has the right to file an answer to the petition[25] and, if the debtor does so, there must be a hearing before the bankruptcy court which can "order relief" against the debtor only if one of two things is proven: (1) that the debtor is generally not paying his debts as they become due or (2) that within 120 days before the date of the filing of the petition a custodian took possession of all or substantially all of the debtor's property or was appointed to do so.[26] As in voluntary proceedings, the bankruptcy court can dismiss or suspend the proceedings if it is in the best interests of debtor and creditors to do so. This has more possibility in the case of an involuntary proceeding than in the case of a voluntary proceeding, e.g., where the debtor is already working with his creditors to try to solve his problems and is attempted to be forced into bankruptcy by a few impatient creditors.

• An important consequence of the filing of a bankruptcy petition is that it automatically "*stays*" debt collection efforts on the parts of creditors, e.g., prevents creditors from attaching or levying execution on the debtor's property. This allows an orderly liquidation of the debtor's property and, ultimately, the equality of treatment of creditors that bankruptcy is supposed to strive for.

• "Promptly after the order for relief" the bankruptcy court is required to appoint an "*interim trustee.*"[27] The interim trustee will ordinarily turn out to be the permanent trustee but the BRA does allow creditors in a Chapter 7 proceeding to elect a trustee if they are not satisfied with the appointed one. This will be elaborated.

• The debtor must file a *list of creditors*, together with a *schedule of assets and liabilities* and a *statement of financial affairs.*[28] *Notice* of the Chapter 7 proceeding must then be given to the listed creditors.[29] A *meeting of creditors* must be ordered within a reasonable time after the order for relief.[30] At the first meeting of creditors, creditors may elect a trustee to replace the interim trustee if the creditor interest required by BRA 702 is present. This is to insure that trustees are elected only when there is significant creditor interest in having an elected trustee. If a trustee is not elected, the interim trustee becomes the permanent trustee.

The principal function of the *trustee* in a Chapter 7 proceeding is to collect and liquidate the assets of the bankruptcy estate. See BRA 704. A Chapter 7 trustee can be given authority to operate the business of a debtor for a limited period.[31] Rules regarding eligibility to serve as a trustee, qualification as a trustee, the trustee's sale, employment of professional persons by the trustee and the trustee's compensation are set forth in BRA 321-327.

• At the first meeting of creditors, eligible creditors, as defined by BRA 705, may elect a *committee* to consult with the trustee in connection with the administration of the bankruptcy estate, make recommendations to the trustee regarding the performance of the trustee's duties, and submit to the bankruptcy court questions concerning the administration of the bankruptcy estate.[32]

• BRA does not say directly at least anything about how long the administration of the bankruptcy estate must or may continue. BRA 704 calls for the trustee to proceed to conclusion "expeditiously."

• When the trustee has done his job of liquidation, *distribution* must be made in accordance with the rules stated in BRA 726 and the debtor must be granted a *discharge* from his dischargeable debts unless an *objection to discharge*, as specified in BRA 727, exists. Objections to discharge are examined in a later section. Certain debts, specified in BRA 523, are not discharged. These will be seen later.

The Bankruptcy Estate

Property of the Estate: BRA 541 tells us that commencement of a bankruptcy proceeding "creates an estate" which consists of certain types of property. To water 541 down to manageable proportions, it tells us that these are general and

---

[19]BRA 301-303.

[20]BRA 109(a).

[21]BRA 109(b).

[22]BRA 109(b).

[23]BRA 303(a).

[24]BRA 303(b).

[25]BRA 303(d).

[26]BRA 303(h).

---

[27]BRA 701(a).

[28]BRA 521.

[29]BRA 342.

[30]BRA 341.

[31]BRA 721.

[32]BRA 704-705.

Form 1.—Voluntary Petition

UNITED STATES BANKRUPTCY COURT FOR THE
_____ DISTRICT OF _____

_____x
In re   :

_____,   :

Debtor [set forth here all names including   :   Case No. _____
trade names used by Debtor within last 6 years].
Social Security No. _____   :
or Employer's Tax Identification No. _____

_____x

Voluntary Petition

1. Petitioner's mailing address is _____.

2. Petitioner has resided [or has had his domicile or has had his principal place of business or has had his principal assets] within this district for the preceding 180 days [or for a longer portion of the preceding 180 days than in any other district].

3. Petitioner is qualified to file this petition and is entitled to the benefits of title 11, United States Code as a voluntary debtor.

4. [If appropriate] A copy of petitioner's proposed plan, dated _____, is attached [or Petitioner intends to file a plan pursuant to chapter 11 or chapter 13] of title 11, United States Code.

WHEREFORE, petitioner prays for relief in accordance with chapter 7 [or chapter 11 or chapter 13] of title 11, United States Code.

Signed: _____
Attorney for Petitioner.

Address: _____,

_____

[Petitioner signs if not
represented by attorney.]

_____,
Petitioner.

I, _____, the petitioner named in the foregoing petition, declare under penalty of perjury that the foregoing is true and correct.

Executed on _____.

Signature: _____
Petitioner.

Form No. 11.—Involuntary Case: Creditors' Petition

[Caption as in Form No. 1]

Involuntary Case: Creditors' Petition

    1. Petitioners, _____, of* _____, and
_____, of* _____, and
_____, of* _____,
are creditors of _____, of* _____,
holding claims against the debtor, not contingent as to liability, amounting in the aggregate, in
excess of the value of any lien held by them on the debtor's property securing such claims, to at
least $5000. The nature and amount of petitioners' claims are as follows: _____
_____.

    2. The debtor's principal place of business [or principal assets or domicile or residence]
has been within this district for the 180 days preceding the filing of this petition [or for a
longer portion of the 180 days preceding the filing of this petition than in any other district].

    3. The debtor is a person against whom an order for relief may be entered under title 11,
United States Code.

    4. [The debtor is generally not paying its debts as they become due as indicated by the
following _____.]
or [Within 120 days preceding the filing of this petition, a custodian was appointed for or has
taken possession of substantially all of the property of the debtor, as follows:
_____
_____.]

    WHEREFORE petitioners pray that an order of relief be entered against _____
_____ under chapter 7 [or 11] of title 11, United States Code.

                          Signed: _____,
                                     Attorneys for Petitioners
                         Address: _____

                         [Petitioners sign if not
                         represented by attorney]
                         _____,
                         _____,
                         _____,
                              Petitioners

    I, _____, one of the petitioners named in the foregoing petition,
declare under penalty of perjury that the foregoing is true and correct according to the best of
my knowledge, information and belief.

Executed on _____

                         Signature: _____
                                  Petitioner

    * State mailing address.

CREATORS' RIGHTS AND BANKRUPTCY

specific types of property which become part of the bankruptcy estate:

1. All legal or equitable interests of the debtor in property as of the commencement of the case.

2. Community property interests of the debtor.

3. Interests in property which the trustee has the right to recover because a fraudulent or preferential transfer has been made of the property.

4. An interest in property which the debtor acquires or becomes entitled to acquire within 180 days *after* the date of the filing of the bankruptcy petition (a) by will or inheritance; (b) as the result of a property settlement agreement or divorce decree; or (c) as the beneficiary of a life insurance policy or of a death benefit plan.

5. Proceeds of property of the estate which are not attributable to services performed by the debtor after commencement of the case.

6. Interests in property that the estate acquires after commencement of the case.

Exempt Property: We do not wipe out a debtor merely because he finds that he has to go through bankruptcy. We have always allowed him to keep basic necessities and a little more, sometimes a good deal more, e.g., the "grubstake exemption," discussed below. What he can keep is called *exempt property* and BRA considerably enlarges upon the concept of exempt property.

BRA 522 is the exempt property provision. It says, to begin with, that the debtor can choose between exemptions that BRA gives him in Section 522 and the exemptions his state's law gives him, e.g., the exemptions California gives a Californian as shown in footnote 4 on page 8. The debtor can't have both, or even a mix, and state law may deny him the federal alternative.[34] So the debtor, or his lawyer, must figure out what is best for the debtor, the debtor's state alternative or the federal alternative.

The *federal alternative* grants these exemptions in BRA 522(d):

1. *Exemptions limited as to amount*, based on the value of the debtor's interest or "equity" in the property:

a. $7500 homestead exemption.[35] Very importantly, to the extent that the debtor does not use the homestead exemption to exempt a residence, he may use it for other property (including money), along with a $400 unrestricted exemption that is given him by BRA 522(d)(5). Thus if the debtor does not have a home but has a motor boat worth $7800 he can fully exempt the motor boat by applying the full amount of the homestead exemption to it plus $300 of the unrestricted exemption. Or if the debtor has an income tax refund coming, he can use all or any part of his $7900 of exemption to save the refund for himself. The $7900 of exemption given by the combination of BRA 522(d)(1) and (d)(5) is now popularly known as the "*grubstake exemption*" in the obvious sense that it gives the debtor a $7900 grubstake for a new career.

b. $200 per item exemption on items of household furnishings, wearing apparel, and the like.[36] So the debtor can declare $200 exemptions on any number of tables, chairs, beds, dresses, etc.

c. $1200 car or car equity.[37]

d. $500 worth of personal jewelry.[38]

e. $750 worth of property used in the debtor's trade.[39]

f. $4000 cash value of life insurance.[40]

2. *Exemptions not limited as to amount*, which include, on the one hand, health aids;[41] on the other, such things as social security and veterans' benefits and disability and unemployment benefits.[42]

3. *Exemptions based on support needs of the debtor*, e.g., support and alimony payments and payments under life insurance policies to the extent that such payments are reasonably necessary for the support of the debtor.[43]

The debtor must file a list of exempt property.[44]

Executory Contracts and Unexpired Leases of the Debtor: BRA 365 gives the trustee the power, subject to court approval, to assume or reject executory contracts and unexpired leases of the debtor. In Chapter 7 cases the contract or lease is to be deemed to be rejected if the trustee does not act within 60 days after the order for relief.[45]

The trustee may assume and *retain* the contract or lease, e.g., retain a lease where it is in the best interests of the bankruptcy estate to continue temporarily a business of the debtor which is being operated on rented premises; or assume and *assign* the contract or lease, where this can be done at some profit to the bankruptcy estate, e.g., where a lease assignee would be willing to pay some amount of money for an assignment. For the protection of the non-bankrupt party to the contract or lease, the assignee must give the non-bankrupt party adequate assurance of performance of the contract or the balance of the lease.[46] Contracts and leases cannot be assigned if assignment would violate the common law rules against assignment of "personal" contracts[47] (page 52) but a "bankruptcy clause," i.e., a clause in a contract or lease permitting termination of the contract or lease because of bankruptcy of a party is made void by Section 365.[48]

Avoidable Transfers: Bankruptcy law attempts to obtain equality of distribution of the debtor's liquidated assets among his unsecured creditors. Consequently, bankruptcy has always disapproved of "preferential transfers" and has allowed their recovery by the trustee on behalf of the bankruptcy estate. Even more unfair to unsecured creditors is the "fraudulent transfer," i.e., a transfer by the debtor of property for "less than a reasonably equivalent value"[49] or other type of transfer that produces results that are fraudulent as to unsecured creditors as set forth in BRA 548. Fraudulent transfers can, of course, also be recovered by the trustee. The law of avoidable transfers is fairly complicated and only a fairly non-technical

---

[33][*Deleted*]

[34]BRA 522(b)(1). C.C.P. 703.130 permits California debtors to make a choice.

[35]BRA 522(d)(1).

[36]BRA 522(d)(3).

[37]BRA 522(d)(2).

[38]BRA 522(d)(4).

[39]BRA 522(d)(6).

[40]BRA 522(d)(8).

[41]BRA 522(d)(9).

[42]BRA 522(d)(10)(11).

[43]BRA 522(d)(10)(D), (11)(C).

[44]BRA 522(l).

[45]BRA 365(d)(1).

[46]BRA 365(f)(2)(B).

[47]BRA 365(c)(1)(A).

[48]BRA 365(e)(f).

[49]BRA 548(a)(2)(A).

discussion will be undertaken such as would seem to be consistent with the scope of this book.

PREFERENTIAL TRANSFERS: BRA 547(b) defines an avoidable *preferential transfer* as a transfer of property of the debtor (1) to or for the benefit of a creditor (2) for or on account of an antecedent debt (3) made while the debtor was insolvent (4) made within 90 days before the filing of the bankruptcy petition or within 90 days and 1 year before the filing of the petition to an "insider" who had reasonable cause to believe that the debtor was insolvent at the time of transfer *and* (5) which gives the creditor more than he would get in a Chapter 7 case.

To illustrate and expound upon the meaning of the foregoing requirements: (1) A gift made by an insolvent debtor 60 days before bankruptcy would constitute a fraudulent transfer but would not constitute a preferential transfer because it was not a transfer to a "creditor." (2) "Transfer" would include the creation of a security interest in property.[50] If, 30 days before bankruptcy, debtor borrows money and gives lender a mortgage on debtor's real property, the transaction is not a preferential transfer because it is not a transfer (mortgage) for an "*antecedent*" debt. (3) The requirement of "*insolvency*" on the date of transfer is simplified by the fact that BRA 547(f) "*presumes*" that the debtor was insolvent for the 90 days preceding bankruptcy. (4) "*Insider*" is a new concept, introduced by BRA. "Insider" is defined by BRA 101(25). Insiders know more about a debtor's business than "outsiders" and therefore ought to be held to a stricter standard of integrity in their dealings with the debtor than outsiders. BRA adopts this position and in effect imposes special obligations on insiders from place to place. (5) If, the day before bankruptcy, debtor pays creditor 20% of what debtor owes creditor and, as it turns out 20% is what all unsecured creditors will get in at the conclusion of the bankruptcy case, creditor has not been "*preferred*."

• BRA 547(c) states a number of transactions that are *exceptions* to the preferential transfer concept of 547(b). These include:

1. Substantially contemporaneous exchanges.[51] For example, May 1 C lends D money for which D promises to give C a mortgage as security. D gives the mortgage on May 5, then takes bankruptcy on May 10. This would be intended as and in fact be a substantially contemporaneous exchange, free therefore of the stamp of "preferential transfer."

2. Payment of ordinary-course-of-business debts.[52] For example, May 1 D receives the April phone bill for his business premises which D pays on May 5.

3. A security interest, evidenced by a written security agreement, which is given by the debtor-borrower to the creditor-lender to enable the debtor to acquire the property in which the security interest is given, provided the creditor perfects the security interest before 10 days after the security interest attaches.[53] For example, May 1 C lends D money to buy a new computer at which time D gives C a signed security agreement describing the computer as collateral for the loan. May 5 D uses the money to buy the computer. May 8 C perfects its security interest in the computer by filing a fi-

---

nancing statement. May 10 D takes bankruptcy. BRA 547(c)(3) would save the transaction.[54]

4. BRA 547(c)(4)-covered transactions. This BRA subsection says that if a creditor receives a preferential transfer but then makes an additional unsecured advance to the debtor, the creditor can offset the additional advance against what he is required to pay the trustee on account of the preferential transfer. For example, May 1 C lends D $25,000. June 5, while insolvent, D pays C $15,000 [a preferential transfer, by definition, under BRA 547(b)]. June 8 C lends D another $5,000, without security. June 10 D takes bankruptcy. D's trustee can recover $10,000 from C, i.e., the preferential transfer of $15,000 less the $5,000 additional advance.

5. Floating liens to the extent they are protected by BRA 547(c)(5). Essentially, BRA 547(c)(5) is designed to prevent a floating lien creditor (page 501) from improving its position during the 90-day period prior to bankruptcy. For example: C has a floating lien on D's inventory of goods. May 1 D takes bankruptcy. At that time D's debt to C is $100,000 and the value of D's inventory is $90,000. January 31 (90 days before bankruptcy) D owed C $110,000 and had inventory worth $80,000. Under BRA 547(c)(5)'s formula, C's secured claim would then be reduced to the sum of $70,000 [$90,000 − ((110,000 − 80,000) − (100,000 − 90,000))].

FRAUDULENT TRANSFERS. Suffice it to say here that if you look at BRA 548 you will see that the types of transfers that are declared fraudulent are essentially the same as those declared fraudulent by the Uniform Fraudulent Conveyances Act, as shown on page 479.

TRANSFERS NOT SEASONABLY PERFECTED. This is a very technical area of bankruptcy law which will be noted only very briefly. There can be a severe penalty for not recording a deed or mortgage without delay or filing an Article 9 financing statement or giving Article 6 bulk transfer notice. Section 544 is the applicable BRA section. Under Section 544, e.g., if in connection with a "bulk transfer" (sale of business) under a statute requiring personal notice of sale to be sent to the seller's creditors, the buyer of the business fails to give notice to one creditor, this will enable the sale to be avoided in its entirety by the seller's trustee in bankruptcy if, subsequently, the seller goes into bankruptcy. The bulk transfer is "fraudulent and void" against the creditor who was not given notice (see U.C.C. 6105, page 398) and can therefore be invalidated by the seller's trustee in bankruptcy under BRA 544(6).

Creditor's Claims and Priorities of Creditors

Creditor's Claims: "*Claim*" is all-encompassingly defined in BRA 101(4)(A) as a "right to payment, whether or not such right is reduced to judgment, liquidated, unliquidated, fixed, contingent, matured, unmatured, disputed, undisputed, legal, equitable, secured, or unsecured." Basically, claims are either *secured* or *unsecured*. Secured claims are claims protected by a contractual lien or a legal lien which is not subject to avoidance in bankruptcy.[55] The advantage of being a creditor with a valid secured claim is, of course, that the creditor is entitled to full satisfaction of his claim from his security. If there is anything left after this it goes to the lower ranks of creditors. Thus if D owes C $1000 for which C holds property worth $1000 as security, C is entitled to the entire value of the property even though this leaves nothing for other credi-

---

[50]See BRA 101(40).

[51]BRA 547(c)(1).

[52]BRA 547(c)(2).

[53]BRA 547(c)(3).

[54]Such a transaction is frequently called an "*enabling loan*."

[55]BRA 506(a).

tors. If D owes C only $700, then C gets full payment of $700 from the security and other ranks of creditors get to share in the remaining $300.

● A creditor establishes his claim by filing a *proof of claim*.[56] A proof of claim form appears on page 360. A proof of claim in a Chapter 7 or Chapter 13 case must be filed within 90 days after the date set for the first meeting of creditors. If proof of a claim which is dischargeable in the bankruptcy case is not seasonably filed, the claim is lost, i.e., the claimant does not share in the bankruptcy distribution. Some kinds of claims are not dischargeable in bankruptcy, as will be seen. A claimant having a nondischargeable claim has no need to file a claim in the bankruptcy case since he will continue to be able to collect on it after bankruptcy. This can work to the disadvantage of the debtor however. Suppose C has a $1000 nondischargeable claim against D. If C filed a proof of claim in D's bankruptcy, C would get 5 cents on the dollar, the amount D's unsecured creditors will get. So C would get $50 and C's post-bankruptcy claim would be reduced to $950. It is to D's advantage to have this be the case but it will not be the case if C doesn't file a claim. To make it be the case, BRA 501(c) allows D to file a claim on C's behalf.

● An unsecured claim must be "*allowed*" in order to qualify for distribution in the bankruptcy case.[57] A filed claim is "deemed allowed unless a party in interest . . . objects."[58] BRA 502(b) lists 9 grounds for objecting to claims. If a filed claim is contingent or unliquidated, it can still be allowed. If to await fixing or liquidation would unduly delay the closing of the bankruptcy case, BRA 502(c)(1) allows the court to estimate the amount of the claim for the purpose of allowance.

Priorities of Creditors: With respect to their priorities in obtaining satisfaction of their claims, creditors may be ranked as follows:

1. SECURED CREDITORS AND CREDITORS HAVING VALID SETOFFS. *Secured creditors* are entitled to full satisfaction from their security. If anything is left, it goes to the lower ranks of creditors. If the security is not sufficient to pay the debt, the creditor may claim as a general creditor for the balance.

● BRA 553 allows *setoffs*. C owes D $3000. D owes C $2000. D takes bankruptcy. C can set off C's $2000 claim against D against D's $3000 claim against C and thereby be required to pay D's trustee only $1000. BRA 553(a) disallows some kinds of setoffs; generally speaking, setoffs acquired by the creditor within 90 days of bankruptcy for the purpose of gaining unfair advantage over other creditors. Example: C owes D $6000. D owes T $5000. Bankruptcy is imminent for D. T doubts that he will be able to get more than $50 out of his claim in the bankruptcy case; therefore, within 90 days of the commencement of D's bankruptcy, T sells his claim to C for $100. C proposes to use the claim as an offset to C's $6000 debt to D, thereby making that debt only $1000. BRA 553(a) prevents C from doing this.

2. CREDITORS HAVING PRIORITY UNDER BRA 507. BRA 507 gives the following expenses and claims priority in the following order; each class of claims must be paid in full before there may be any payment to the next class and if there are insufficient funds to fully satisfy a class the members of that class share the available funds pro rata:

a. Administrative expenses.

b. In involuntary cases, claims arising in the ordinary course of the debtor's business or financial affairs after the commencement of the case but before the earlier of the appointment of a trustee and the order for relief.

c. Claims for wages, salaries or commissions, including vacation, severance and sick leave pay, earned by an individual within 90 days before the date of the filing of the petition or the date of the cessation of the debtor's business, whichever occurs first, to the extent of $2000 for each such individual.

d. Claims for contributions to employee benefit plans to the extent allowed by BRA 507(a)(4).

e. Claims of consumers, to the extent of $900 per consumer, for deposits made for goods or services which were not delivered.

f. Tax claims as specified in BRA 507(a)(6) which includes income taxes for the 3 years preceding bankruptcy and property taxes payable without penalty within 1 year prior to bankruptcy.

3. UNSECURED CREDITORS, i.e., creditors who do not have security or statutory priority under BRA 507. Unsecured creditors share in the leavings, if any, of which frequently there are none. BRA 726 sets up the following order of distribution to unsecured creditors:

a. Creditors having timely filed claims and creditors having claims which were filed tardily because the creditor did not have notice of the bankruptcy proceeding.

b. Creditors with notice of the bankruptcy proceeding who filed claims tardily.

c. Claims for fines, penalties and forfeitures on allowed claims and claims for punitive damages.

d. Claims for post-petition interest on BRA 507 priority claims and on unsecured claims.

Discharge

Unless there is a valid objection to the debtor's discharge, the debtor is entitled to a discharge at the conclusion of a Chapter 7 case, discharging the debtor of all dischargeable debts whether or not proofs of claim have been filed for such debts.[59]

Objections to Discharge: BRA 727(a) lists 10 objections to discharge, as follows:

1. Discharge granted only to individuals. Corporations do not require discharge since their owners are not liable for the corporation's debts.

2. Fraudulent transfer within 1 year prior to bankruptcy.

3. Concealment, destruction, mutilation, falsification or failure to keep or preserve financial records.

4. Dishonest and obstructive acts of the debtor, as follows: The filing of false claims; the giving or taking of bribes; and the withholding from the trustee of financial records.

5. Failure to explain satisfactorily the loss of assets.

6. Refusal to testify after grant of immunity.

7. Commission of any of acts 26, above, within 1 year prior to the date of the filing of the petition, or during the case, in connection with another case concerning an insider.

8. Discharge in Chapter 7 or 11 case within 6 years.

9. Discharge in Chapter 13 case within 6 years unless payments under the plan in such case totaled at least 100% of the allowed unsecured claims, or 70% of such claims and the plan was proposed by the debtor in good faith and was the debtor's best effort.

10. Court-approved written waiver of discharge.

---

[56]BRA 501(a).

[57]See BRA 726.

[58]BRA 502(a).

[59]BRA 727(a)(b).

Form No. 19.—Proof of Claim

[Caption as in Form No. 2]

Proof of Claim

1. [If claimant is an individual claiming for himself] The undersigned, _____
who is the claimant herein, resides at * _____ .
   [If claimant is a partnership claiming through a member] The undersigned, _____
_____ , who resides at * _____ , is a member of
of * _____ and doing business at * _____ , and is authorized
to make this proof of claim in behalf of the partnership.
   [If claimant is a corporation claiming through an authorized officer] The undersigned,
_____ , who resides at * _____ , is the _____ of
_____ , a corporation organized under the laws of _____
and doing business at * _____ , and is authorized to make this proof of
claim on behalf of the corporation.
   [If claim is made by agent] The undersigned, _____ , who resides at
* _____ , is the agent of _____ , of * _____ ,
and is authorized to make this proof of claim on behalf of the claimant.

2. The debtor was, at the time of the filing of the petition initiating this case, and still
is indebted [or liable] to this claimant, in the sum of $ _____ .

3. The consideration for this debt [or ground of liability] is as follows: _____
_____ .

4. [If the claim is founded on writing] The writing on which this claim is founded (or a
duplicate thereof) is attached hereto [or cannot be attached for the reason set forth in the
statement attached hereto].

5. [If appropriate] This claim is founded on an open account, which became [or will become]
due on _____ , as shown by the itemized statement attached hereto. Unless it is
attached hereto or in its absence is explained in an attached statement, no note or other negotiable instrument has been received for the account or any part of it.

6. No judgment has been rendered on the claim except _____ .

7. The amount of all payments on this claim has been credited and deducted for the purpose of
making this proof of claim.

8. This claim is not subject to any setoff or counterclaim except _____ .

9. No security interest is held for this claim except _____
[If security interest in property of the debtor is claimed] The undersigned claims the security
interest under the writing referred to in paragraph 4 hereof [or under a separate writing which
(or a duplicate of which) is attached hereto, or under a separate writing which cannot be
attached hereto for the reason set forth in the statement attached hereto]. Evidence of perfection of such security interest is also attached hereto.

10. This claim is a general unsecured claim, except to the extent that the security interest,
if any, described in paragraph 9 is sufficient to satisfy the claim. [If priority is claimed,
state the amount and basis thereof.] _____

    Dated: _____

                                              Signed: _____

    Penalty for Presenting Fraudulent Claim. Fine of not more than $5,000 or imprisonment for
not more than 5 years or both — Title 18, U.S.C., § 152.

* State mailing address.

Objection to discharge must be made by the trustee or a creditor.[60]

Exceptions to Discharge: Bankruptcy law has always excepted certain kinds of what for fairly obvious reasons are regarded as exceptional forms of debts from discharge, traditionally: tax debts; alimony and child support obligations; liabilities for moneys dishonestly obtained; and liabilities for aggravated forms of torts. BRA 523 continues such exceptions. Where there is a successful *objection* to discharge, the debtor is denied discharge from any of his debts. *Exception* to discharge, on the other hand, only denies him discharge from the excepted debt. BRA 523(a) declares these 9 exceptions to discharge:

1. Tax debts as specified in BRA 523(a)(1), which includes unpaid income taxes for 3 years prior to bankruptcy and longer if returns have not been filed or fraudulent returns have been filed.

2. Debts for money, property, services or credit obtained by fraud or by deliberate false financial statement.

3. Unscheduled debts to creditors who do not have notice or knowledge of the bankruptcy case.

4. Debts for embezzlement or larceny and for fraud or defalcation while acting in a fiduciary capacity.

5. Alimony and child support obligations.

6. Liabilities for willful and malicious injuries to the person or property of another.

7. Liabilities to governmental units for fines, penalties and forfeitures.

8. Debts for educational loans which become due within 5 years prior to bankruptcy unless excepting the debt from discharge would impose an undue hardship on the debtor and his dependents.

9. Debts that were or could have been listed or scheduled in a prior bankruptcy case in which the debtor did not obtain a discharge.

● A creditor seeking to have his claim excepted from discharge under grounds 2, 4 and 6, above, must apply to the bankruptcy court for a determination that the debtor is not entitled to be discharged from the debt.[61]

Discharge Hearing and Effect of Discharge: After the bankruptcy court has decided whether or not to grant a discharge, it must hold a hearing to inform the debtor of its decision.[62]

● Discharge does more than discharge the debtor of dischargeable debts. Under BRA 523(a), discharge voids judgments on discharged debts and operates as an injunction against legal or other action to collect discharged debts.

Chapter 11 Reorganization

The Chapter 11 Concept

Chapter 11 is the reorganization provision of the new bankruptcy law. Its purpose is to give a business organization which is in financial difficulty the opportunity to make an arrangement with creditors which will enable the business organization to keep going. The arrangement is called a "plan" and the plan is the heart of the Chapter 11 proceeding. The nature of the Chapter 11 plan is discussed below.

Chapter 11 proceedings are less standardized than Chapter 7 proceedings and it is not possible to discuss them with the

same degree of particularity. Therefore the discussion of Chapter 11 proceedings will be more general in nature.

Chapter 11 Procedure in General

A Chapter 11 proceeding may be *voluntary* or *involuntary*. Any person, except a stock or commodity broker, who is eligible to initiate a voluntary Chapter 7 case may initiate a voluntary Chapter 11 case. Insolvency is not required. The requirements for an involuntary Chapter 11 case are the same as for an involuntary Chapter 7 case.

● The bankruptcy court is supposed to appoint a *committee of unsecured creditors* as soon as is practicable after the order for relief.[63] A creditors' committee may already be in existence, from prior to the bankruptcy proceeding, and the court can merely continue it if it was fairly chosen and is representative of the different kinds of claims that need to be represented.[64] If such a pre-bankruptcy committee does not exist, the court is directed, under BRA 1102(b)(2), to appoint a committee consisting of the 7 largest unsecured creditors willing to serve. The court can appoint additional committees to represent creditors or stockholders if it is "necessary to assure adequate representation."[65] In the case of a large public corporation, for example, the court might feel obliged to appoint a committee representing unsecured bondholders and a committee representing stockholders. Important functions of a creditors' committee are to investigate the finances and business operation of the debtor, consult with the debtor's management regarding the proposed reorganization and participate in the preparation of the plan of reorganization.

● Chapter 11 seeks to continue the existence of a business rather than to liquidate it and therefore proceeds on the assumption that the business should ordinarily be left in the hands of its management rather than placed in the hands of a trustee. However, the court may appoint a *trustee* to take over the operation of the debtor's business, "for cause" such as fraud or gross mismanagement or because it is in the best interests of creditors and stockholders.[66] If the bankruptcy court does not appoint a trustee, it may still appoint an "*examiner*" to investigate and report on the affairs of the debtor.[67]

● As a public protection measure, the *SEC* is given the right to "raise and . . . appear and be heard on any issue in a case under this chapter."[68] If regarded as necessary for public protection, the SEC may move for the appointment of a trustee. It is considered to be a "party in interest" for this purpose.

The Plan

The "*plan*" of reorganization is at the heart of the Chapter 11 proceeding, or at the heart of the true Chapter 11 proceeding at least. The plan varies with the size and complexity of the problem to be solved.

General Nature of Plan: Plans range from grand scale to small scale. On the grand scale would be the large, public corporation with several classes of bondholders and stockholders and with large institutional creditors and various classes of small creditors. Here there might have to be a complete scaling down of interests in which bondholders become

---

[60]BRA 727(c).

[61]BRA 523(c).

[62]BRA 524(d).

[63]BRA 1102(a)(1).

[64]BRA 1102(b)(1).

[65]BRA 1102(a)(2).

[66]BRA 1104(a).

[67]BRA 1104(b).

[68]BRA 1109(a).

preferred stockholders, preferred stockholders become common stockholders, common stockholders become required to supply new capital and creditors become required to take some reduction in the amounts of their claims. In a smaller scale situation, the plan might be concerned only with creditors and not with stock or bondholders. Here, creditors under $200 might get full payment, creditors from $200-$1500, 80% payment, and the remaining, large, creditors get some other form of treatment. Frequently it is the goal of the debtor to get rid of small creditors and then work things out more flexibly with a half dozen or so large creditors.

Not all Chapter 11 proceedings will be genuine. Many will be staying actions designed to give the debtor time to complete a contract or bring in additional capital that has been subscribed, after which the debtor expects to be able to pay its debts in full.

Requirements of Plan: BRA 1123 specifies the requirements of a plan and the provisions that must and may be included. Included are the requirements that each class of claims be treated the same and that the plan contain adequate means for its execution according to criteria specified in subdivision (5) of BRA 1123.

Who May File: Unless a trustee has been appointed, the debtor is given the exclusive right to file a plan during the first 120 days of the proceeding.[69] If a trustee has been appointed or if the debtor does not file within 120 days or if the debtor files within 120 days but does not obtain acceptance of the plan within 180 days after commencement of the proceeding, then, in any of these events, any party in interest may file a plan.

Disclosure Requirements: Chapter 11 proceeds on the assumption that the primary responsibility for approving a plan should rest with those affected by it, i.e., the creditors and stockholders of the debtor. Therefore the bankruptcy court does not approve the plan in advance of its presentation to creditors and stockholders. However Chapter 11 concerns itself with the ability of creditors and stockholders to make an informed judgment and therefore sets up the *disclosure statement* requirement of BRA 1125.

Before the debtor can solicit acceptances of the proposed plan, it must supply each of the creditors and stockholders to be affected with (1) a copy of the plan or a summary of the plan and (2) "a written disclosure statement approved, after notice and a hearing, by the court as containing adequate information" to enable the creditor or stockholder to make its informed judgment.[70]

Acceptance of Plan: A class of claims accepts a plan when ⅔ in amount and more than ½ in number of the allowed claims of the class accept.[71] A class of "interests" such as stockholders accepts a plan when ⅔ in amount of the allowed interests of the class accept.[72]

Confirmation of Plan: The bankruptcy court must hold a hearing to determine whether or not the plan should be confirmed.[73] If every class of claims and interests has accepted the plan, the court must confirm the plan if all of the requirements of BRA 1129(a) have been met.

A plan cannot be confirmed unless at least one class of claims has accepted it[74] but, if this is so, then it may be confirmed even though other classes of claims or interests do not accept it. This is by virtue of the *"cram down" provision* of the Act, BRA 1129(b), which requires merely that "the plan does not discriminate unfairly, and is fair and equitable with respect to each class of claims or interests that is impaired under, and has not accepted, the plan."

Effect of Confirmation: Upon confirmation of the plan, the debtor becomes bound by the plan and becomes discharged from debts that arose before the date of confirmation.[75]

Conversion to Chapter 7 Proceeding

Frequently the Chapter 11 debtor cannot provide an acceptable plan. In such case, the debtor may convert to a Chapter 7 liquidation proceeding unless a trustee has been put in possesion of the debtor's business or the case is an involuntary case originally commenced under Chapter 11.[76] A Chapter 11 case may also be converted to a Chapter 7 case on the grounds shown in BRA 1112(b).

Chapter 13 Debt Adjustment

The Chapter 13 Concept

Roughly speaking, Chapter 13 is to small debtors as Chapter 11 is to large debtors. Like Chapter 11, Chapter 13 is a rehabilitation proceeding, at the heart of which is the "plan" of rehabilitation. The plan will combine a reduction in the amount of indebtedness with an extension of time to pay. The obligaton incurred by the plan will be funded by future earnings of the debtor so that, if the plan is successfully fulfilled, creditors will receive more than they would have received in a Chapter 7 liquidation proceeding.

Eligibility

Chapter 13 is available only to (1) an *individual*, and therefore not a partnership or corporation, (2) a debtor who has a *"regular income,"* per BRA 101(24) definition, and (3) a debtor who has *unsecured debts in an amount less than $100,000* and *secured debts in an amount less than $350,000.*[77] *Spouses* may file a joint proceeding but are jointly limited to the $100,000/$350,000 limitations even though both have regular incomes.[78] Only one spouse is required to have a regular income.[79]

Regular income does not mean regular salary or wages but may consist of a stable income from any source such as investments or the operation of a sole proprietorship business.[80] Thus a small business debtor may initiate a Chapter 13 proceeding and will ordinarily be permitted to continue the operation of the business.[81]

Procedure

Chapter 13 is *voluntary* only.[82] As in all BRA proceedings, the proceeding is commenced by the filing of a petition.[83] A

---

[69]BRA 1121(b).

[70]BRA 1125(b).

[71]BRA 1126(c).

[72]BRA 1126(d).

[73]BRA 1128.

[74]BRA 1129(a)(10).

[75]BRA 1141(a)(d).

[76]BRA 1112(a).

[77]BRA 109(e).

[78]BRA 109(e).

[79]BRA 109(e).

[80]BRA 101(24).

[81]BRA 1304(b).

[82]BRA 303(a).

[83]BRA 301,302(a).

Chapter 7 or 11 case may be converted to a Chapter 13 case.[84] A trustee must be appointed in every case, whose chief function is to serve as a disbursing agent, receiving the plan funds from the debtor and disbursing them to the creditors in accordance with the terms of the plan.[85]

The Plan

Only the debtor may file a plan.[86] Great flexibility is afforded by the Act with respect to the plan. There are only three *requirements*: (1) The plan must provide for submission to the trustee of such amount of the income of the debtor as is necessary for the execution of the plan; (2) the plan must provide for full payment of all BRA 507 priority claims; and (3) if the plan classifies claims, it must provide the same treatment for each claim within a particular class.[87] BRA 1322(b) lists *optional provisions*, including a provision modifying the rights of holders of *secured* claims other than a claim secured by a security interest in the real property constituting the debtor's principal residence.[88] The plan must ordinarily be consummated in 3 years.[89]

● The plan will ordinarily combine an extension of time to pay debts with a reduction in the amount to be paid.

Confirmation of the Plan

Only holders of secured claims are required to accept the plan.[90] Approval of unsecured creditors is not required; only bankruptcy court approval.[91] The bankruptcy court is required to confirm the plan if the requirements of BRA 1325 are met. BRA 1325 includes the requirement that, as of the effective date of the plan, the unsecured creditors will receive at least as much as they would receive under a Chapter 7 liquidation[92]

and the requirement of a finding that the debtor will be able to make the payments required by the plan.[93]

● If a secured claimholder does not accept the plan, BRA 1325(5)(B) is a *"cram down" provision* which allows the bankruptcy court to confirm the plan despite the creditor's dissent if the plan offers the creditor payment of the actual value of the security.

Discharge

Upon completion of the payments called for by the plan, the debtor receives a *discharge*[94] which discharges him from all unsecured debts provided for by the plan except longterm debts provided for by the plan which are not made payable within the time limits of the plan[95] and alimony and child support obligations.[96] A so-called *"hardship discharge"* may be granted to a debtor who fails to complete the payments called for by the plan if failure was due to circumstances for which the debtor should not be held accountable and the payments made equal what creditors would have received under a Chapter 7 proceeding.[97] If the debtor has to settle for for a hardship discharge, all of the BRA 523(a) types of claims survive.[98]

A Chapter 7 discharge cannot be obtained within 6 years after a Chapter 13 discharge has been obtained unless payments under the plan in the Chapter 13 case totaled at least 70% of unsecured claims and the plan was proposed by the debtor in good faith and respresented his best effort.[99]

Conversion to Chapter 7 Case

The debtor may convert a Chapter 13 case to a Chapter 7 case at any time[100] and creditors may request such a conversion on the grounds set forth in BRA 1307(c) which include delay in filing a Chapter 13 plan and material default in a term of the plan.

---

[84]BRA 706(a);1112(d).

[85]BRA 1302(a)(b).

[86]BRA 1321.

[87]BRA 1322(a).

[88]BRA 1322(b)(2).

[89]BRA 1322(c).

[90]See BRA 1325(a)(5).

[91]BRA 1325.

[92]BRA 1325(a)(4).

[93]BRA 1325(a)(6).

[94]BRA 1328(a).

[95]BRA 1328(a)(1).

[96]BRA 1328(a)(2).

[97]BRA 1328(b).

[98]BRA 1328(c)(2).

[99]BRA 727(a)(9).

[100]BRA 1307(a).

NOTES

CALIFORNIA UNIFORM COMMERCIAL CODE

DIVISION 1

GENERAL PROVISIONS

CHAPTER 1

SHORT TITLE, CONSTRUCTION, APPLICATION AND SUBJECT MATTER OF THE CODE

Sec. 1101. **Short Title.** This code shall be known and may be cited as Uniform Commercial Code.

Sec. 1102. **Purposes; Rules of Construction; Variation by Agreement.** (1) This code shall be liberally construed and applied to promote its underlying purposes and polices.

(2) Underlying purposes and policies of this code are

(a) To simplify, clarify and modernize the law governing commercial transactions;

(b) To permit the continued expansion of commercial practices through custom, usage and agreement of the parties;

(c) To make uniform the law among the various jurisdictions.

(3) The effect of provisions of this code may be varied by agreement, except as otherwise provided in this code and except that the obligations of good faith, diligence, reasonableness and care prescribed by this code may not be disclaimed by agreement but the parties may by agreement determine the standards by which the performance of such obligations is to be measured if such standards are not manifestly unreasonable.

(4) The presence in certain provisions of this code of the words "unless otherwise agreed" or words of similar import does not imply that the effect of other provisions may not be varied by agreement under subdivision (3).

(5) In this code unless the context otherwise requires

(a) Words in the singular number include the plural, and in the plural include the singular;

(b) Words of the masculine gender include the feminine and the neuter, and when the sense so indicates words of the neuter gender may refer to any gender.

Sec. 1103. **Supplementary General Principles of Law Applicable.** Unless displaced by the particular provisions of this code, the principles of law and equity, including the law merchant and the law relative to capacity to contract, principal and agent, estoppel, fraud, misrepresentation, duress, coercion, mistake, bankruptcy, or other validating or invalidating cause shall supplement its provisions.

Sec. 1104. **Construction Against Implicit Repeal.** This code being a general act intended as a unified coverage of its subject matter, no part of it shall be deemed to be impliedly repealed by subsequent legislation if such construction can reasonably be avoided.

Sec. 1105. **Territorial Application of the Act; Parties' Power to Choose Applicable Law.** (1) Except as provided hereafter in this section, when a transaction bears a reasonable relation to this State and also to another state or nation the parties may agree that the law either of this State or such other state or nation shall govern their rights and duties. Failing such agreement this code applies to transactions bearing an appropriate relation to this State.

(2) Where one of the following provisions of this code specifies the applicable law, that provision governs and a contrary agreement is effective only to the extent permitted by the law (including the conflict of laws rules) so specified.

Rights of creditors against sold goods. Section 2402.

Applicability of the division on bank deposits and collections. Section 4102.

Bulk transfers subject to the division on bulk transfers. Section 6102.

Applicability of the division on investment securities. Section 8106.

Perfection provisions of the division on secured transactions. Section 9103.

Sec. 1106. **Remedies to Be Liberally Administered.** (1) The remedies provided by this code shall be liberally administered to the end that the aggrieved party may be put in as good a position as if the other party had fully performed but neither consequential or special nor penal damages may be had except as specifically provided in this code or by other rule of law.

(2) Any right or obligation declared by this code is enforceable by action unless the provision declaring it specifies a different and limited effect.

Sec. 1107. **Waiver or Renunciation of Claim or Right After Breach.** Any claim or right arising out of an alleged breach can be discharged in whole or in part without consideration by a written waiver or renunciation signed and delivered by the aggrieved party.

Sec. 1108. **Severability.** If any provision or clause of this code or application thereof to any person or circumstances is held invalid, such invalidity shall not affect other provisions or applications of the code which can be given effect without the invalid provision or application, and to this end the provisions of this code are declared to be severable.

CHAPTER 2

GENERAL DEFINITIONS AND PRINCIPLES OF INTERPRETATION

Sec. 1201. **General Definitions.** Subject to additional definitions contained in the subsequent divisions of this code which are applicable to specific divisions or chapters thereof, and unless the context otherwise requires, in this code:

(1) "Action" in the sense of a judicial proceeding includes recoupment, counterclaim, setoff, suit in equity and any other proceedings in which rights are determined.

(2) "Aggrieved party" means a party entitled to resort to a remedy.

(3) "Agreement" means the bargain of the parties in fact as found in their language or by implication from other circumstances including course of dealing or usage of trade or course of performance as provided in this code (Sections 1205 and 2208). Whether an agreement has legal consequences is determined by the provisions of this code, if applicable; otherwise by the law of contracts (Section 1103). (Compare "contract.")

(4) "Bank" means any person engaged in the business of banking.

(5) "Bearer" means the person in possession of an instrument, document of title, or security payable to bearer or indorsed in blank.

(6) "Bill of lading" means a document evidencing the receipt of goods for shipment issued by a person engaged in the business of transporting or forwarding goods, and which, by its terms, evidences the intention of the issuer that the person entitled under the document (Section 7403(4) has the right to receive, hold and dispose of the document and the goods it covers. Designation of a document by the issuer as a "bill of lading" is conclusive evidence of such intention. "Bill of lading" includes an airbill. "Airbill" means a document serving for air transportation as a bill of lading does for marine or rail transportation, and includes an air consignment note or air waybill.

(7) "Branch" includes a separately incorporated foreign branch of a bank.

(8) "Burden of establishing" a fact means the burden of persuading the triers of fact that the existence of the fact is more probable than its nonexistence.

(9) "Buyer in ordinary course of business" means a person who in good faith and without knowledge that the sale to him is in violation of the ownership rights or security interest of a third party in the goods buys in ordinary course from a person in the business of selling goods of that kind but does not include a pawnbroker. All persons who sell minerals or the like (including oil and gas) at wellhead or mineralhead shall be deemed to be persons in the business of selling goods of that kind. "Buying" may be for cash or by exchange of other property or on secured or unsecured credit and includes receiving goods or documents of title under a preexisting contract for sale but does not include a transfer in bulk or as security for or in total or partial satisfaction of a money debt.

(10) "Conspicuous." A term or clause is conspicuous when it is so written that a reasonable person against whom it is to operate ought to have noticed it. A printed heading in capitals (as: NONNEGOTIABLE BILL OF LADING) is conspicuous. Language in the body of a form is "conspic-

uous" if it is in larger or other contrasting type or color. But in a telegram any stated term is "conspicuous." Whether a term or clause is "conspicuous" or not is for decision by the court.

(11) "Contract" means the total legal obligation which results from the parties' agreement as affected by this code and any other applicable rules of law. (Compare "agreement.")

(12) "Creditor" includes a general creditor, a secured creditor, a lien creditor and any representative of creditors, including an assignee for the benefit of creditors, a trustee in bankruptcy, a receiver in equity and an executor or administrator of an insolvent debtor's or assignor's estate.

(13) "Defendant" includes a person in the position of defendant in a cross-action or counterclaim.

(14) "Delivery" with respect to instruments, documents of title, chattel paper or securities means voluntary transfer of possession.

(15) "Document of title" includes bill of lading, dock warrant, dock receipt, warehouse receipt, gin ticket, compress receipt, and also any other document which in the regular course of business or financing is treated as adequately evidencing that the person entitled under the document (Section 7403(4)) has the right to receive, hold and dispose of the document and the goods it covers. To be a document of title a document must purport to be issued by a bailee and purport to cover goods in the bailee's possession which are either identified or are fungible portions of an identified mass.

(16) "Fault" means wrongful act, omission or breach.

(17) "Fungible" with respect to goods or securities means goods or securities of which any unit is, by nature or usage of trade, the equivalent of any other like unit. Goods which are not fungible shall be deemed fungible for the purposes of this code to the extent that under a particular agreement or document unlike units are treated as equivalents.

(18) "Genuine" means free of forgery or counterfeiting.

(19) "Good faith" means honesty in fact in the conduct or transaction concerned.

(20) "Holder" means a person who is in possession of a document of title or an instrument or an investment security drawn, issued or indorsed to him or to his order or to bearer or in blank.

(21) To "honor" is to pay or to accept and pay, or where a credit so engages to purchase or discount a draft complying with the terms of the credit.

(22) "Insolvency proceedings" includes any assignment for the benefit of creditors or other proceedings intended to liquidate or rehabilitate the estate of the person involved.

(23) A person is "insolvent" who either has ceased to pay his debts in the ordinary course of business or cannot pay his debts as they become due or is insolvent within the meaning of the federal bankruptcy law.

(24) "Money" means a medium of exchange authorized or adopted by a domestic or foreign government as a part of its currency.

(25) A person has "notice" of a fact when

(a) He has actual knowledge of it; or

(b) He has received a notice or notification of it; or

(c) From all the facts and circumstances known to him at the time in question he has reason to know that it exists.

A person "knows" or has "knowledge" of a fact when he has actual knowledge of it. "Discover" or "learn" or a word or phrase of similar import refers to knowledge rather than to reason to know. The time and circumstances under which a notice or notification may cease to be effective are not determined by this code.

(26) A person "notifies" or "gives" a notice or notification to another by taking such steps as may be reasonably required to inform the other in ordinary course whether or not such other actually comes to know of it. A person "receives" a notice or notification when

(a) It comes to his attention; or

(b) It is duly delivered at the place of business through which the contract was made or at any other place held out by him as the place for receipt of such communications.

(27) Notice, knowledge or a notice or notification received by an organization is effective for a particular transaction from the time when it is brought to the attention of the individual conducting that transaction, and in any event from the time when it would have been brought to his attention if the organization had exercised due diligence. An organization exercises due diligence if it maintains reasonable routines for communicating significant information to the person conducting the transaction and there is reasonable compliance with the routines. Due diligence does not require an individual acting for the organization to communicate information unless such communication is part of his regular duties or unless he has reason to know of the transaction and that the transaction would be materially affected by the information.

(28) "Organization" includes a corporation, government or governmental subdivision or agency, business trust, estate, trust, partnership or association, two or more persons having a joint or common interest, or any other legal or commercial entity.

(29) "Party" as distinct from "third party," means a person who has engaged in a transaction or made an agreement within this division.

(30) "Person" includes an individual or an organization. (See Section 1102.)

(32) "Purchase" includes taking by sale, discount negotiation, mortgage, pledge, lien, issue or reissue, gift or any other voluntary transaction creating an interest in property.

(33) "Purchaser" means a person who takes by purchase.

(34) "Remedy" means any remedial right to which an aggrieved party is entitled with or without resort to a tribunal.

(35) "Representative" includes an agent, an officer of a corporation or association, and a trustee, executor or administrator of an estate, or any other person empowered to act for another.

(36) "Rights" includes remedies.

(37) "Security interest" means an interest in personal property or fixtures which secures payment or performance of an obligation. The retention or reservation of title by a seller of goods notwithstanding shipment or delivery to the buyer (Section 2401) is limited in effect to a reservation of a "security interest." The term also includes any interest of a buyer of accounts or chattel paper which is subject to Division 9. The special property interest of a buyer of goods on identification of such goods to a contract for sale under Section 2501 is not a "security interest," but a buyer may also acquire a "security interest" by complying with Division 9. Unless a lease or consignment is intended as security, reservation of title thereunder is not a "security interest" but a consignment is in any event subject to the provisions on consignment sales (Section 2326). Whether a lease is intended as security is to be determined by the facts of each case; however, (a) the inclusion of an option to purchase does not of itself make the lease one intended for security, and (b) an agreement that upon compliance with the terms of the lease the lessee shall become or has the option to become the owner of the property for no additional consideration or for a nominal consideration does make the lease one intended for security.

(38) "Send" in connection with any writing or notice means to deposit in the mail or deliver for transmission by any other usual means of communication with postage or cost of transmission provided for and properly addressed and in the case of an instrument to an address specified thereon or otherwise agreed, or if there be none to any address reasonable under the circumstances. The receipt of any writing or notice within the time at which it would have arrived if properly sent has the effect of a proper sending. When a writing or notice is required to be sent by registered or certified mail, proof of mailing is sufficient, and proof of receipt by the addressee is not required unless the words "with return receipt requested" are also used.

(39) "Signed" includes any symbol executed or adopted by a party with present intention to authenticate a writing.

(40) "Surety" includes guarantor.

(41) "Telegram" includes a message transmitted by radio, teletype, cable, any mechanical method of transmission, or the like.

(42) "Term" means that portion of an agreement which relates to a particular matter.

(43) "Unauthorized" signature or indorsement means one made without actual, implied or apparent authority and includes a forgery.

(44) "Value." Except as otherwise provided with respect to negotiable instruments and bank collections (Sections 3303, 4208 and 4209) a person gives "value" for rights if he acquires them

(a) In return for a binding commitment to extend credit or for the extension of immediately available credit whether or not drawn upon and whether or not a chargeback is provided for in the event of difficulties in collection; or

(b) As security for or in total or partial satisfaction of a preexisting claim; or

(c) By accepting delivery pursuant to a pre-existing contract for purchase; or

(d) Generally, in return for any consideration sufficient to support a simple contract.

(45) "Warehouse receipt" means a document evidencing the receipt of goods for storage issued by warehouseman (Section 7102), and which, by its terms, evidences the intention of the issuer that the person entitled under the document (Section 7403(4)) has the right to receive, hold and dispose of the document and the goods it covers. Designation of a document by the issuer as a "warehouse receipt" is conclusive evidence of such intention.

(46) "Written" or "writing" includes printing, typewriting or any other intentional reduction to tangible form.

Sec. 1202. Bill of lading: Insurance policy: Weigher's certificate: Consular invoice: Admissibility to prove facts stated: Contract actions: Presumption of authenticity of document: Presumption of truth of facts stated. (1) A bill of lading, policy or certificate of insurance, official weigher's or inspector's certificate, consular invoice, or any other document authorized or required by the contract to be issued by a third party is admissible as evidence of the facts stated in the document by the third party in any action arising out of the contract which authorized or required the document.

(2) In any action arising out of the contract which authorized or required the document referred to in subdivision (1):

(a) A document in due form purporting to be the document referred to in subdivision (1) is presumed to be authentic and genuine. This presumption is a presumption affecting the burden of producing evidence.

(b) If the document is found to be authentic and genuine, the facts stated in the document by the third party are presumed to be true. This presumption is a presumption affecting the burden of proof.

Sec. 1203. Obligation of Good Faith. Every contract or duty within this code imposes an obligation of good faith in its performance or enforcement.

Sec. 1204. Time; Reasonable Time; "Seasonably." (1) Whenever this code requires any action to be taken within a reasonable time, any time which is not manifestly unreasonable may be fixed by agreement.

(2) What is a reasonable time for taking any action depends on the nature, purpose and circumstances of such action.

(3) An action is taken "seasonably" when it is taken at or within the time agreed or if no time is agreed at or within a reasonable time.

Sec. 1205. Course of Dealing and Usage of Trade. (1) A course of dealing is a sequence of previous conduct between the parties to a particular transaction which is fairly to be regarded as establishing a common basis of understanding for interpreting their expressions and other conduct.

(2) A usage of trade is any practice or method of dealing having such regularity of observance in a place, vocation or trade as to justify an expectation that it will be observed with respect to the transaction in question. The existence and scope of such a usage are to be proved as facts. If it is established that such a usage is embodied in a written trade code or similar writing the interpretation of the writing is for the court.

(3) A course of dealing between parties and any usage of trade in the vocation or trade in which they are engaged or of which they are or should be aware give particular meaning to and supplement or qualify terms of an agreement.

(4) The express terms of an agreement and an applicable course of dealing or usage of trade shall be construed wherever reasonable as consistent with each other; but when such construction is unreasonable express terms control both course of dealing and usage of trade and course of dealing controls usage of trade.

(5) An applicable usage of trade in the place where any part of performance is to occur shall be used in interpreting the agreement as to that part of the performance.

(6) Evidence of a relevant usage of trade offered by one party is not admissible unless and until he has given the other party such notice as the court finds sufficient to prevent unfair surprise to the latter.

Sec. 1206. Statute of Frauds for Kinds of Personal Property Not Otherwise Covered. (1) Except in the cases described in subdivision (2) of this section a contract for the sale of personal property is not enforceable by way of action or defense beyond five thousand dollars ($5,000) in the amount of value of remedy unless there is some writing which indicates that a contract for sale has been made between the parties at a defined or stated price, reasonably identifies the subject matter, and is signed by the party against whom enforcement is sought or by his authorized agent.

(2) Subdivision (1) of this section does not apply to contracts for the sale of goods (Section 2201) nor of securities (Section 8319) nor to security agreements (Section 9203).

Sec. 1207. Performance or Acceptance Under Reservation of Rights. A party who with explicit reservation of rights performs or promises performance or assents to performance in a manner demanded or offered by the other party does not thereby prejudice the rights reserved. Such words as "without prejudice," "under protest" or the like are sufficient.

Sec. 1208. Option to Accelerate at Will. A term providing that one party or his successor in interest may accelerate payment or performance or require collateral or additional collateral "at will" or "when he deems himself insecure" or in words of similar import shall be construed to mean that he shall have power to do so only if he in good faith believes that the prospect of payment or performance is impaired. The burden of establishing lack of good faith is on the party against whom the power has been exercised.

Sec. 1209. Subordinated obligations: Interest Created: Construction of section. An obligation may be issued as subordinated to payment of another obligation of the person obligated, or a creditor may subordinate his right to payment of an obligation by agreement with either the person obligated or another creditor of the person obligated. Such a subordination does not create a security interest as against either the common debtor or a subordinated creditor. This section shall be construed as declaring the law as it existed prior to the enactment of this section and not as modifying it.

Sec. 1210. Presumptions: Burden of Proof. Except as otherwise provided in Section 1202, the presumptions established by this code are presumptions affecting the burden of producing evidence.

DIVISION 2

SALES

CHAPTER 1

SHORT TITLE, GENERAL CONSTRUCTION AND SUBJECT MATTER

Sec. 2101. Short Title. This division shall be known and may be cited as Uniform Commercial Code—Sales.

Sec. 2102. Scope; Certain Security and Other Transactions Excluded From This Article. Unless the context otherwise requires, this division applies to transactions in goods; it does not apply to any transaction which although in the form of an unconditional contract to sell or present sale is intended to operate only as a security transaction nor does this division impair or repeal any statute regulating sales to consumers, farmers or other specified classes of buyers.

Sec. 2103. Definitions and Index of Definitions. (1) In this division unless the context otherwise requires

(a) "Buyer" means a person who buys or contracts to buy goods.

(b) "Good faith" in the case of a merchant means honesty in fact and the observance of reasonable commercial standards of fair dealing in the trade.

(c) "Receipt" of goods means taking physical possession of them.

(d) "Seller" means a person who sells or contracts to sell goods.

(2) Other definitions applying to this division or to specified chapters thereof, and the sections in which they appear are:

"Acceptance." Section 2606.
"Banker's credit." Section 2325.
"Between merchants." Section 2104.
"Cancellation." Section 2106(4).
"Commercial unit." Section 2105.
"Confirmed credit." Section 2325.
"Conforming to contract." Section 2106.
"Contract for sale." Section 2106.
"Cover." Section 2712.
"Entrusting." Section 2403.

"Financing agency." Section 2104.
"Future goods." Section 2105.
"Goods." Section 2105.
"Identification." Section 2501.
"Installment contract." Section 2612.
"Letter of Credit." Section 2325.
"Lot." Section 2105.
"Merchant." Section 2104.
"Overseas." Section 2323.
"Person in position of seller." Section 2707.
"Present sale." Section 2106.
"Sale." Section 2106.
"Sale on approval." Section 2326.
"Sale or return." Section 2326.
"Termination." Section 2106.

(3) The following definitions in other divisions apply to this division:
"Check." Section 3104.
"Consignee." Section 7102.
"Consignor." Section 7102.
"Consumer goods." Section 9109.
"Dishonor." Section 3507.
"Draft." Section 3104.

(4) In addition Division 1 contains general definitions and principles of construction and interpretation applicable throughout this division.

Sec. 2104. **Definitions: "Merchant"; "Between Merchants"; "Financing Agency."** (1) "Merchant" means a person who deals in goods of the kind or otherwise by his occupation holds himself out as having knowledge or skill peculiar to the practices or goods involved in the transaction or to whom such knowledge or skill may be attributed by his employment of an agent or broker or other intermediary who by his occupation holds himself out as having knowledge or skill.

(2) "Financing agency" means a bank, finance company or other person who in the ordinary course of business makes advances against goods or documents of title or who by arrangement with either the seller or the buyer intervenes in ordinary course to make or collect payment due or claimed under the contract for sale, as by purchasing or paying the sellers' draft or making advances against it or by merely taking it for collection whether or not documents of title accompany the draft. "Financing agency" includes also a bank or other person who similarly intervenes between persons who are in the position of seller and buyer in respect to the goods (Section 2707.)

(3) "Between merchants" means in any transaction with respect to which both parties are chargeable with the knowledge or skill of merchants.

Sec. 2105. **Definitions: Transferability; "Goods"; "Future" Goods; "Lot"; "Commercial Unit."** (1) "Goods" means all things (including specially manufactured goods) which are movable at the time of identification to the contract for sale other than the money in which the price is to be paid, investment securities (Division 8) and things in action. "Goods" also includes the unborn young of animals and growing crops and other identified things attached to realty as described in the section on goods to be severed from realty (Section 2107).

(2) Goods must be both existing and identified before any interest in them can pass. Goods which are not both existing and identified are "future" goods. A purported present sale of future goods or of any interest therein operates as a contract to sell.

(3) There may be a sale of a part interest in existing identified goods.

(4) An undivided share in an identified bulk of fungible goods is sufficiently identified to be sold although the quantity of the bulk is not determined. Any agreed proportion of such a bulk or any quantity thereof agreed upon by number, weight or other measure may to the extent of the seller's interest in the bulk be sold to the buyer who then becomes an owner in common.

(5) "Lot" means a parcel or a single article which is the subject matter of a separate sale or delivery, whether or not it is sufficient to perform the contract.

(6) "Commercial unit" means such a unit of goods as by commercial usage is a single whole for purposes of sale and division of which materially impairs its character or value on the market or in use. A commercial unit may be a single article (as a machine) or a set of articles (as a suite of furniture or an assortment of sizes) or a quantity (as a bale, gross, or carload) or any other unit treated in use or in the relevant market as a single whole.

Sec. 2106. **Definitions: "Contract"; "Agreement"; "Contract for Sale"; "Sale"; "Present Sale"; "Conforming to Contract"; "Termination"; "Cancellation."** (1) In this division unless the context otherwise requires "contract" and "agreement" are limited to those relating to the present or future sale of goods. "Contract for sale" includes both a present sale of goods and a contract to sell goods at a future time. A "sale" consists in the passing of title from the seller to the buyer for a price (Section 2401). A "present sale" means a sale which is accomplished by the making of the contract.

(2) Goods or conduct including any part of a performance are "conforming" or conform to the contract when they are in accordance with the obligations under the contract.

(3) "Termination" occurs when either party pursuant to a power created by agreement or law puts an end to the contract otherwise than for its breach. On "termination" all obligations which are still executory on both sides are discharged but any right based on prior breach or performance survives.

(4) "Cancellation" occurs when either party puts an end to the contract for breach by the other and its effect is the same as that of "termination" except that the cancelling party also retains any remedy for breach of the whole contract or any unperformed balance.

Sec. 2107. **Goods to Be Severed From Realty; Recording.** (1) A contract for the sale of minerals or the like (including oil and gas) or a structure or its materials to be removed from realty is a contract for the sale of goods within this division if they are to be severed by the seller but until severance a purported present sale thereof which is not effective as a transfer of an interest in land is effective only as a contract to sell.

(2) A contract for the sale apart from the land of growing crops or other things attached to realty and capable of severance without material harm thereto but not described in subdivision (1) or of timber to be cut is a contract for the sale of goods within this division whether the subject matter is to be severed by the buyer or by the seller even though it forms part of the realty at the time of contracting, and the parties can by identification effect a present sale before severance.

(3) The provisions of this section are subject to any third party rights provided by the law relating to realty records, and the contract for sale may be executed and recorded in the same manner as a document transferring an interest in land and shall then constitute notice to third parties of the buyer's rights under the contract for sale.

CHAPTER 2

FORM, FORMATION AND READJUSTMENT OF CONTRACT

Sec. 2201. **Formal Requirements; Statute of Frauds.** (1) Except as otherwise provided in this section a contract for the sale of goods for the price of $500 or more is not enforceable by way of action or defense unless there is some writing sufficient to indicate that a contract for sale has been made between the parties and signed by the party against whom enforcement is sought or by his authorized agent or broker. A writing is not insufficient because it omits or incorrectly states a term agreed upon but the contract is not enforceable under this paragraph beyond the quantity of goods shown in such writing.

(2) Between merchants if within a reasonable time a writing in confirmation of the contract and sufficient against the sender is received and the party receiving it has reason to know its contents, it satisfies the requirements of subdivision (1) against such party unless written notice of objection to its contents is given within 10 days after it is received.

(3) A contract which does not satisfy the requirements of subdivision (1) but which is valid in other respects is enforceable

(a) If the goods are to be especially manufactured for the buyer and are not suitable for sale to others in the ordinary course of the seller's business and the seller, before notice of repudiation is received and under circumstances which reasonably indicate that the goods are for the buyer, has made either a substantial beginning of their manufacture or commitments for their procurement; or

(c) With respect to goods for which payment has been made and accepted or which have been received and accepted (Section 2606).

Sec. 2202. **Final Written Expression; Parol or Extrinsic Evidence.** Terms with respect to which the confirmatory memoranda of the parties agree or which are otherwise set forth in a writing intended by the parties as a final expresssion of their agreement with respect to such terms as are included therein may not be contradicted by evidence of any prior agreement or of a contemporaneous oral agreement but may be explained or supplemented

(a) By course of dealing or usage of trade (Section 1205) or by course of performance (Section 2208); and

(b) By evidence of consistent additional terms unless the court finds the writing to have been intended also as a complete and exclusive statement of the terms of the agreement.

Sec. 2203. **Reserved.**

Sec. 2204. **Formation in General.** (1) A contract for sale of goods may be made in any manner sufficient to show agreement, including conduct by both partes which recognizes the existence of such a contract.

(2) An agreement sufficient to constitute a contract for sale may be found even though the moment of its making is undetermined.

(3) Even though one or more terms are left open a contract for sale does not fail for indefiniteness if the parties have intended to make a contract and there is a reasonably certain basis for giving an appropriate remedy.

Sec. 2205. **Firm Offers; offers to supply goods to contractors.** (a) An offer by a merchant to buy or sell goods in a signed writing which by its terms gives assurance that it will be held open is not revocable, for lack of consideration, during the time stated or if no time is stated for a reasonable time, but in no event may such period of irrevocability exceed three months; but any such term of assurance on a form supplied by the offeree must be separately signed by the offeror.

(b) Notwithstanding subdivision (a), when a merchant renders an offer, oral or written, to supply goods to a contractor licensed pursuant to the provisions of Chapter 9 (commencing with Section 7000) of Division 3 of the Business and Professions Code or a similar contractor's licensing law of another state, and the merchant has actual or imputed knowledge that the contractor is so licensed, and that the offer will be relied upon by the contractor in the submission of its bid for a construction contract with a third party, the offer relied upon shall be irrevocable, notwithstanding lack of consideration, for 10 days after the awarding of the contract to the prime contractor, but in no event for more than 90 days after the date the bid or offer was rendered by the merchant; except that an oral bid or offer, when for a price of two thousand five hundred dollars ($2,500) or more, shall be confirmed in writing by the contractor or his or her agent within 48 hours after it is rendered. Failure by the contractor to confirm such offer in writing shall release the merchant from his or her offer. Nothing in this subdivision shall prevent a merchant from providing that the bid or offer will be held open for less than the time provided for herein.

Sec. 2206. **Offer and Acceptance in Formation of Contract.** (1) Unless otherwise unambiguously indicated by the language or circumstances

(a) An offer to make a contract shall be construed as inviting acceptance in any manner and by any medium reasonable in the circumstances;

(b) An order or other offer to buy goods for prompt or current shipment shall be construed as inviting acceptance either by a prompt promise to ship or by the prompt or current shipment of conforming or nonconforming goods, but such a shipment of nonconforming goods does not constitute an acceptance if the seller seasonably notifies the buyer that the shipment is offered only as an accommodation to the buyer.

(2) Where the beginning of a requested performance is a reasonable mode of acceptance an offeror who is not notified of acceptance within a reasonable time may treat the offer as having lapsed before acceptance.

Sec. 2207. **Additional Terms in Acceptance or Confirmation.** (1) A definite and seasonable expression of acceptance or a written confirmation which is sent within a reasonable time operates as an acceptance even though it states terms additional to or different from those offered or agreed upon, unless acceptance is expressly made conditional on assent to the additional or different terms.

(2) The additional terms are to be construed as proposals for addition to the contract. Between merchants such terms become part of the contract unless:

(a) The offer expressly limits acceptance to the terms of the offer;

(b) They materially alter it; or

(c) Notification of objection to them has already been given or is given within a reasonable time after notice of them is received.

(3) Conduct by both parties which recognizes the existence of a contract is sufficient to establish a contract for sale although the writings of the parties do not otherwise establish a contract. In such case the terms of the particular contract consist of those terms on which the writings of the parties agree, together with any supplementary terms incorporated under any other provisions of this code.

Sec. 2208. **Course of Performance or Practical Construction.** (1) Where the contract for sale involves repeated occasions for performance by either party with knowledge of the nature of the performance and opportunity for objection to it by the other, any course of performance accepted or acquiesced in without objection shall be relevant to determine the meaning of the agreement.

(2) The express terms of the agreement and any such course of performance, as well as any course of dealing and usage of trade, shall be construed whenever reasonable as consistent with each other; but when such construction is unreasonable, express terms shall control course of performance and course of performance shall control both course of dealing and usage of trade (Section 1205).

(3) Subject to the provisions of the next section on modification and waiver, such course of performance shall be relevant to show a waiver or modification of any term inconsistent with such course of performance.

Sec. 2209. **Modification, Rescission and Waiver.** (1) An agreement modifying a contract within this division needs no consideration to be binding.

(2) A signed agreement which excludes modification or rescission except by a signed writing cannot be otherwise modified or rescinded, but except as between merchants such a requirement on a form supplied by the merchant must be separately signed by the other party.

(3) The requirements of the statute of frauds section of this division (Section 2201) must be satisfied if the contract as modified is within its provisions.

(4) Although an attempt at modification or rescission does not satisfy the requirements of subdivision (2) or (3), it can operate as a waiver.

(5) A party who has made a waiver affecting an executory portion of the contract may retract the waiver by reasonable notification received by the other party that strict performance will be required of any term waived, unless the retraction would be unjust in view of a material change of position in reliance on the waiver.

Sec. 2210. **Delegation of Performance; Assignment of Rights.** (1) A party may perform his duty through a delegate unless otherwise agreed or unless the other party has a substantial interest in having his original promisor perform or control the acts required by the contract. No delegation or performance relieves the party delegating of any duty to perform or any liability for breach.

(2) Unless otherwise agreed all rights of either seller or buyer can be assigned except where the assignment would materially change the duty of the other party, or increase materially the burden or risk imposed on him by his contract, or impair materially his chance of obtaining return performance. A right to damages for breach of the whole contract or a right arising out of the assignor's due performance of his entire obligation can be assigned despite agreement otherwise.

(3) Unless the circumstances indicate the contrary a prohibition of assignment of "the contract" is to be construed as barring only the delegation to the assignee of the assignor's performance.

(4) An assignment of "the contract" or of "all my rights under the contract" or an assignment in similar general terms is an assignment of rights and unless the language or the circumstances (as in an assignment for security) indicate the contrary, it is a delegation of performance of the duties of the assignor and its acceptance by the assignee constitutes a promise by him to perform those duties. This promise is enforceable by either the assignor or the other party to the original contract.

(5) The other party may treat any assignment which delegates performance as creating reasonable grounds for insecurity and may without prejudice to his rights against the assignor demand assurances from the assignee (Section 2609).

CHAPTER 3

GENERAL OBLIGATION AND CONSTRUCTION OF CONTRACT

Sec. 2301. **General Obligations of Parties.** The obligation of the seller is to transfer and deliver and that of the buyer is to accept and pay in accordance with the contract.

Sec. 2302. **Reserved.**

Sec. 2303. **Allocation or Division of Risks.** Where this division allocates a risk or a burden as between the parties "unless otherwise agreed," the agreement may not only shift the allocation but may also divide the risk or burden.

Sec. 2304. Price Payable in Money, Goods, Realty, or Otherwise. (1) The price can be made payable in money or otherwise. If it is payable in whole or in part in goods each party is a seller of the goods which he is to transfer.

(2) Even though all or part of the price is payable in an interest in realty the transfer of the goods and the seller's obligations with reference to them are subject to this division, but not the transfer of the interest in realty or the transferor's obligations in connection therewith.

Sec. 2305. Open Price Term. (1) The parties if they so intend can conclude a contract for sale even though the price is not settled. In such a case the price is a reasonable price at the time for delivery if

(a) Nothing is said as to price; or

(b) The price is left to be agreed by the parties and they fail to agree; or

(c) The price is to be fixed in terms of some agreed market or other standard as set or recorded by a third person or agency and it is not so set or recorded.

(2) A price to be fixed by the seller or by the buyer means a price for him to fix in good faith.

(3) When a price left to be fixed otherwise than by agreement of the parties fails to be fixed through fault of one party the other may at his option treat the contract as canceled or himself fix a reasonable price.

(4) Where, however, the parties intend not to be bound unless the price be fixed or agreed and it is not fixed or agreed there is no contract. In such a case the buyer must return any goods already received or if unable so to do must pay their reasonable value at the time of delivery and the seller must return any portion of the price paid on account.

Sec. 2306. Output, Requirements and Exclusive Dealings. (1) A term which measures the quantity by the output of the seller or the requirements of the buyer means such actual output or requirements as may occur in good faith, except that no quantity unreasonably disproportionate to any stated estimate or in the absence of a stated estimate to any normal or otherwise comparable prior output or requirements may be tendered or demanded.

(2) A lawful agreement by either the seller or the buyer for exclusive dealin g in the kind of goods concerned imposes unless otherwise agreed an obligation by the seller to use best efforts to supply the goods and by the buyer to use best efforts to promote their sale.

Sec. 2307. Delivery in Single Lot or Several Lots. Unless otherwise agreed all goods called for by a contract for sale must be tendered in a single delivery and payment is due only on such tender but where the circumstances give either party the right to make or demand delivery in the lots the price if it can be apportioned may be demanded for each lot.

Sec. 2308. Absence of Specified Place for Delivery. Unless otherwise agreed

(a) The place for delivery of goods is the seller's place of business or if he has none his residence; but

(b) In a contract for sale of identified goods which to the knowledge of the parties at the time of contracting are in some other place, that place is the place for their delivery; and

(c) Documents of title may be delivered through customary banking channels.

Sec. 2309. Absence of Specific Time Provisions; Notice of Termination. (1) The time for shipment or delivery or any other action under a contract if not provided in this division or agreed upon shall be a reasonable time.

(2) Where the contract provides for successive performances but is indefinite in duration it is valid for a reasonable time but unless otherwise agreed may be terminated at any time by either party.

(3) Termination of a contract by one party except on the happening of an agreed event requires that reasonable notification be received by the other party and an agreement dispensing with notification is invalid if its operation would be unconscionable.

Sec. 2310. Open Time for Payment or Running of Credit; Authority to Ship Under Reservation. Unless otherwise agreed

(a) Payment is due at the time and place at which the buyer is to receive the goods even though the place of shipment is the place of delivery; and

(b) If the seller is authorized to send the goods he may ship them under reservation, and may tender the documents of title, but the buyer may inspect the goods after their arrival before payment is due unless such inspection is inconsistent with the terms of the contract (Section 2513); and

(c) If delivery is authorized and made by way of documents of title otherwise than by subdivision (b) then payment is due at the time and place at which the buyer is to receive the documents regardless of where the goods are to be received; and

(d) Where the seller is required or authorized to ship the goods on credit the credit period runs from the time of shipment but post-dating the invoice or delaying its dispatch will correspondingly delay the starting of the credit period.

Sec. 2311. Options and Cooperation Respecting Performance. (1) An agreement for sale which is otherwise sufficiently definite (subdivision (3) of Section 2204) to be a contract is not made invalid by the fact that it leaves particulars of performance to be specified by one of the parties. Any such specification must be made in good faith and within limits set by commercial reasonableness.

(2) Unless otherwise agreed specifications relating to assortment of the goods are at the buyer's option and except as otherwise provided in subdivisions (1)(c) and (3) of Section 2319 specifications or arrangements relating to shipment are at the seller's option.

(3) Where such specification would materially affect the other party's performance but is not seasonably made or where one party's co-operation is necessary to the agreed performance of the other but is not seasonably forthcoming, the other party in addition to all remedies

(a) Is excused for any resulting delay in his own performance; and

(b) May also either proceed to perform in any reasonable manner or after the time for a material part of his own performance treat the failure to specify or to co-operate as a breach by failure to deliver or accept the goods.

Sec. 2312. Warranty of Title and Against Infringement; Buyers Obligation Against Infringement. (1) Subject to subdivision (2) there is in a contract for sale a warranty by the seller that

(a) The title conveyed shall be good, and its transfer rightful; and

(b) The goods shall be delivered free from any security interest or other lien or encumbrance of which the buyer at the time of contracting has no knowledge.

(2) A warranty under subdivision (1) will be excluded or modified only by specific language or by circumstances which give the buyer reason to know that the person selling does not claim title in himself or that he is purporting to sell only such right or title as he or a third person may have.

(3) Unless otherwise agreed a seller who is a merchant regularly dealing in goods of the kind warrants that the goods shall be delivered free of the rightful claim of any third person by way of infringement or the like but a buyer who furnishes specifications to the seller must hold the seller harmless against any such claim which arises out of compliance with the specifications.

Sec. 2313. Express Warrants by Affirmation, Promise, Description, Sample. (1) Express warranties by the seller are created as follows:

(a) Any affirmation of fact or promise made by the seller to the buyer which relates to the goods and becomes part of the basis of the bargain creates an express warranty that the goods shall conform to the affirmation or promise.

(b) Any description of the goods which is made part of the basis of the bargain creates an express warranty that the goods shall conform to the description.

(c) Any sample or model which is made part of the basis of the bargain creates an express warranty that the whole of the goods shall conform to the sample or model.

(2) It is not necessary to the creation of an express warranty, that the seller use formal words such as "warrant" or "guarantee" or that he have a specific intention to make a warranty, but an affirmation merely of the value of the goods or a statement purporting to be merely the seller's opinion or commendation of the goods does not create a warranty.

Sec. 2314. Implied Warranty: Merchantability; Usage of Trade. (1) Unless excluded or modified (Section 2316), a warranty that the goods shall be merchantable is implied in a contract for their sale if the seller is a merchant with respect to goods of that kind. Under this section the serving for value food or drink to be consumed either on the premises or elsewhere is a sale.

(2) Goods to be merchantable must be at least such as

(a) Pass without objection in the trade under the contract description; and

(b) In the case of fungible goods, are of fair average quality within the description; and

(c) Are fit for the ordinary purposes for which such goods are used; and

(d) Run, within the variations permitted by the agreement, of even kind, quality and quantity within each unit and among all units involved; and

(e) Are adequately contained, packaged, and labeled as the agreement may require; and

(f) Conform to the promises or affirmations of fact made on the container or label if any.

(3) Unless excluded or modified (Section 2316) other implied warranties may arise from course of dealing or usage of trade.

Sec. 2315. Implied Warranty: fitness for Particular Purpose.

Where the seller at the time of contracting has reason to know any particular purpose for which the goods are required and that the buyer is relying on the seller's skill or judgment to select 'or furnish suitable goods, there is unless excluded or modified under the next section an implied warranty that the goods shall be fit for such purpose.

Sec. 2316. Exclusion or Modification of Warranties.

(1) Words or conduct relevant to the creation of an express warranty and words or conduct tending to negate or limit warranty shall be be construed wherever reasonable as consistent with each other; but subject to the provisions of this division on parol or extrinsic evidence (Section 2202) negation or limitation is inoperative to the extent that such construction is unreasonable.

(2) Subject to subdivision (3), to exclude or modify the implied warranty of merchantability or any part of it the language must mention merchantability and in case of a writing must be conspicuous, and to exclude or modify any implied warranty of fitness the exclusion must be by a writing and conspicuous. Language to exclude all implied warranties of fitness is sufficient if it states, for example, that "There are no warranties which extend beyond the description on the face hereof."

(3) Notwithstanding subdivision (2)

(a) Unless the circumstances indicate otherwise, all implied warranties are excluded by expressions like "as is," "with all faults" or other language which in common understanding calls the buyer's attention to the exclusion of warranties and makes plain that there is no implied warranty; and

(b) When the buyer before entering into the contract has examined the goods or the sample or model as fully as he desired or has refused to examine the goods there is no implied warranty with regard to defects which an examination ought in the circumstances to have revealed to him; and

(c) An implied warranty can also be excluded or modified by course of dealing or course of performance or usage of trade.

(4) Remedies for breach of warranty can be limited in accordance with the provisions of this division on liquidation or limitation of damages and on contractual modification of remedy (Sections 2718 and 2719).

Sec. 2317. Cumulation and Conflict of Warranties Express or Implied.

Warranties whether express or implied shall be construed as consistent with each other and as cumulative, but if such construction is unreasonable the intention of the parties shall determine which warranty is dominant. In ascertaining the intention the following rules apply:

(a) Exact or technical specifications displace an inconsistent sample or model or general language of description.

(b) A sample from an existing bulk displaces inconsistent general language of description.

(c) Express warranties displace inconsistent implied warranties other than an implied warranty of fitness for a particular purpose.

Sec. 2318. Reserved.

Sec. 2319. F.O.B. and F.A.S. Terms.

(1) Unless otherwise agreed the term F.O.B. (which means "free on board") at a named place, even though used only in connection with the stated price, is a delivery term under which

(a) When the term is F.O.B. the place of shipment, the seller must at that place ship the goods in the manner provided in this division (Section 2504) and bear the expense and risk of putting them into the procession of the carrier; or

(b) When the term is F.O.B. the place of destination, the seller must at his own expense and risk transport the goods to that place and there tender delivery of them in the manner provided in this division (Section 2503);

(c) When under either (a) or (b) the term is also F.O.B. vessel, car or other vehicle, the seller must in addition at his own expense and risk load the goods on board. If the term is F.O.B. vessel the buyer must name the vessel and in an appropriate case the seller must comply with the provisions of this division on the form of bill of lading (Section 2323).

(2) Unless otherwise agreed the term F.A.S. vessel (which means "free alongside") at a named port, even though used only in connection with the stated price, is a delivery term under which the seller must

(a) At his own expense and risk deliver the goods alongside the vessel in the manner usual in that port or on a dock designated and provided by the buyer; and

(b) Obtain and tender a receipt for the goods in exchange for which the carrier is under a duty to issue a bill of lading.

(3) Unless otherwise agreed in any case falling within subdivision (1)(a) or (c) or subdivision (2) the buyer must seasonably give any needed instructions for making delivery, including when the term is F.A.S. or F.O.B. the loading berth of the vessel and in an appropriate case its name and sailing date. The seller may treat the failure of needed instructions as a failure of cooperation under this division (Section 2311). He may also at his option move the goods in any reasonable manner preparatory to delivery or shipment.

(4) Under the term F.O.B. vessel or F.A.S. unless otherwise agreed the buyer must make payment against tender of the required documents and the seller may not tender nor the buyer demand delivery of the goods in substitution for the documents.

Sec. 2320. C.I.F. and C. & F. Terms.

(1) The term C.I.F. means that the price includes in a lump sum the cost of the goods and the insurance and freight to the named destination. The term C. & F. or C.F. means that the price so includes cost and freight to the named destination.

(2) Unless otherwise agreed and even though used only in connection with the stated price and destination, the term C.I.F. destination or its equivalent requires the seller at his own expense and risk to

(a) Put the goods into the possession of a carrier at the port for shipment and obtain a negotiable bill or bills of lading covering the entire transportation to the named destination; and

(b) Load the goods and obtain a receipt from the carrier (which may be contained in the bill of lading) showing that the freight has been paid or provided for; and

(c) Obtain a policy or certificate of insurance, including any war risk insurance, of a kind and on terms then current at the port of shipment in the usual amount, in the currency of the contract, shown to cover the same goods covered by the bill of lading and providing for payment of loss to the order of the buyer or for the account of whom it may concern; but the seller may add to the price the amount of the premium for any such war risk insurance; and

(d) Prepare an invoice of the goods and procure any other documents signed to effect shipment or to comply with the contract; and

(e) Forward and tender with commercial promptness all the documents in due form and with any indorsement necessary to perfect the buyer's rights.

(3) Unless otherwise agreed the term C. & F. or its equivalent has the same effect and imposes upon the seller the same obligations and risks as a C.I.F. term except the obligation as to insurance.

(4) Under the term C.I.F. or C. & F. unless otherwise agreed the buyer must make payment against tender of the required documents and the seller may not tender nor the buyer demand delivery of the goods in substitution for the documents.

Sec. 2321. C.I.F. or C. & F.: "Net Landed Weights"; "Payment on Arrival"; Warranty of Condition on Arrival.

Under a contract containing a term C.I.F. or C. & F.

(1) Where the price is based on or is to be adjusted according to "net landed weights," "delivered weights," "out turn" quantity or quality or the like, unless otherwise agreed the seller must reasonably estimate the price. The payment due on tender of the documents called for by the contract is the amount so estimated, but after final adjustment of the price a settlement must be made with commerical promptness.

(2) An agreement described in subdivision (1) or any warranty of quality or condition of the goods on arrival places upon the seller the risk of ordinary deterioration, shrinkage and the like in transportation but has no

effect on the place or time of identification to the contract for sale or delivery or on the passing of the risk of loss.

(3) Unless otherwise agreed where the contract provides for payment on or after arrival of the goods the seller must before payment allow such preliminary inspection as is feasible; but if the goods are lost delivery of the documents and payment are due when the goods should have arrived.

Sec. 2322. **Delivery "Ex-Ship."** (1) Unless otherwise agreed a term for delivery of goods "ex-ship" (which means from the carrying vessel) or in equivalent language is not restricted to a particular ship and requires delivery from a ship which has reached a place at the named port of destination where goods of the kind are usually discharged.

(2) Under such a term unless otherwise agreed

(a) The seller must discharge all liens arising out of the carriage and furnish the buyer with a direction which puts the carrier under a duty to deliver the goods; and

(b) The risk of loss does not pass to the buyer until the goods leave the ship's tackle or are otherwise properly unloaded.

Sec. 2323. **Form of Bill of Lading Required in Overseas Shipment; "Overseas."** (1) Where the contract contemplates overseas shipment and contains a term C.I.F. or C. & F. or F.O.B. vessel, the seller unless otherwise agreed must obtain a negotiable bill of lading stating that the goods have been loaded on board or, in the case of a term C.I.F. or C. & F., received for shipment.

(2) Where in a case within subdivision (1) a bill of lading has been issued in a set of parts, unless otherwise agreed if the documents are not to be sent from abroad the buyer may demand tender of the full set; otherwise only one part of the bill of lading need be tendered. Even if the agreement expressly requires a full set

(a) Due tender of a single part is acceptable within the provisions of this division on cure of improper delivery (subdivision (1) of Section 2508); and

(b) Even though the full set is demanded, if the documents are sent from abroad the person tendering an incomplete set may nevertheless require payment upon furnishing an indemnity which the buyer in good faith deems adequate.

(3) A shipment by water or by air or a contract contemplating such shipment is "overseas" insofar as by usage of trade or agreement it is subject to the commercial, financing or shipping practices characteristic of international deepwater commerce.

Sec. 2324. **"No Arrival, No Sale" Term.** Under a term "no arrival no sale" or terms of like meaning, unless otherwise agreed.

(a) The seller must properly ship conforming goods and if they arrive by any means he must tender them on arrival but he assumes no obligation that the goods will arrive unless he has caused the nonarrival; and

(b) Where without fault of the seller the goods are in part lost or have so deteriorated as no longer to conform to the contract or arrive after the contract time, the buyer may proceed as if there had been casualty to identified goods (Section 2613).

Sec. 2325. **"Letter of Credit" Term; "Confirmed Credit."** (1) Failure of the buyer seasonably to furnish an agreed letter of credit is a breach of the contract for sale.

(2) The delivery to seller of a proper letter of credit suspends the buyer's obligation to pay. If the letter of credit is dishonored, the seller may on seasonable notification to the buyer require payment directly from him.

(3) Unless otherwise agreed the term "letter of credit" or "banker's credit" in a contract for sale means an irrevocable credit issued by a financing agency of good repute. The term "confirmed credit" means that the credit must also carry the direct obligation of such an agency which does business in the seller's financial market.

Sec. 2326. **Sale on Approval and Sale or Return; Consignment Sales and Rights of Creditors.** (1) Unless otherwise agreed, if delivered goods may be returned by the buyer even though they conform to the contract, the transaction is

(a) A "sale on approval" if the goods are delivered primarily for use, and

(b) A "sale or return" if the goods are delivered primarily for resale.

(2) Except as provided in subdivision (3), goods held on approval are not subject to the claims of the buyer's creditors until acceptance; goods held on sale or return are subject to such claims while in the buyer's possession.

(3) Where goods are delivered to a person for sale and such person maintains a place of business at which he deals in goods of the kind involved, under a name other than the name of the person making delivery, then with respect to claims of creditors of the person conducting the business the goods are deemed to be on sale or return. The provisions of this subdivision are applicable even though an agreement purports to reserve title to the person making delivery until payment or resale or uses such words as "on consignment" or "on memorandum." However, this subdivision is not applicable if the person making delivery

(b) Establishes that the person conducting the business is generally known by his creditors to be substantially engaged in selling the goods of others, or

(c) Complies with the filing provisions of the division on secured transactions (Division 9),

(4) Any "or return" term of a contract for sale is to be treated as a separate contract for sale within the statute of frauds section of this division (Section 2201) and as contradicting the sale aspect of the contract within the provisions of this division on parol or extrinsic evidence (Section 2202).

Sec. 2327. **Special Incidents of Sale on Approval and Sale or Return.** (1) Under a sale on approval unless otherwise agreed

(a) Although the goods are identified to the contract the risk of loss and the title do not pass to the buyer until acceptance; and

(b) Use of the goods consistent with the purpose of trial is not acceptance but failure seasonably to notify the seller of election to return the goods is acceptance, and if the goods conform to the contract acceptance of any part is acceptance of the whole; and

(c) After due notification of election to return, the return is at the seller's risk and expense but a merchant buyer must follow any reasonable instructions.

(2) Under a sale or return unless otherwise agreed

(a) The option to return extends to the whole or any commercial unit of the goods while in substantially their original condition, but must be exercised seasonably; and

(b) The return is at the buyer's risk and expense.

Sec. 2328. **Sale by Auction.** (1) In a sale by auction if goods are put up in lots each lot is the subject of a separate sale.

(2) A sale by auction is complete when the auctioneer so announces by the fall of the hammer or in other customary manner. Where a bid is made while the hammer is falling in acceptance of a prior bid the auctioneer may in his discretion reopen the bidding or declare the goods sold under the bid on which the hammer was falling.

(3) Such a sale is with reserve unless the goods are in explicit terms put up without reserve. In an auction with reserve the auctioneer may withdraw the goods at any time until he announces completion of the sale. In an auction without reserve, after the auctioneer calls for bids on an article or lot, that article or lot cannot be withdrawn unless no bid is made within a reasonable time. In either case a bidder may retract his bid until the auctioneer's announcement of completion of the sale, but a bidder's retraction does not revive any previous bid.

(4) If the auctioneer knowingly receives a bid on the seller's behalf or the seller makes or procures such a bid, and notice has not been given that liberty for such bidding is reserved, the buyer may at his option avoid the sale or take the goods at the price of the last good faith bid prior to the completion of the sale. This subdivision shall not apply to any bid at a forced sale.

CHAPTER 4

TITLE, CREDITORS AND GOOD FAITH PURCHASERS

Sec. 2401. **Passing of Title; Reservation for Security; Limited Application of This Section.** Each provision of this division with regard to the rights, obligations and remedies of the seller, the buyer, purchasers or other third parties applies irrespective of title to the goods except where the provision refers to such title. Insofar as situations are not covered by the other provisions of this division and matters concerning title become material the following rules apply:

(1) Title to goods cannot pass under a contract for sale prior to their identification to the contract (Section 2501), and unless otherwise explicitly agreed the buyer acquires by their identification a special property as limited by this code. Any retention or reservation by the seller of the title (property) in goods shipped or delivered to the buyer is limited in effect to a reservation of a security interest. Subject to these provisions and to

the provisions of the division on secured transactions (Division 9), title to goods passes from the seller to the buyer in any manner and on any conditions explicitly agreed on by the parties.

(2) Unless otherwise explicitly agreed title passes to the buyer at the time and place at which the seller completes his performance with reference to the physical delivery of the goods, despite any reservation of a security interest and even though a document of title is to be delivered at a different time or place; and in particular and despite any reservation of a security interest by the bill of lading.

(a) If the contract requires or authorizes the seller to send the goods to the buyer but does not require him to deliver them at destination, title passes to the buyer at the time and place of shipment; but

(b) If the contract requires delivery at destination, title passes on tender there.

(3) Unless otherwise explicitly agreed where delivery is to be made without moving the goods,

(a) If the seller is to deliver a document of title, title passes at the time when and the place where he delivers such documents; or

(b) If the goods are at the time of contracting already identified and no documents are to be delivered, title passes at the time and place of contracting.

(4) A rejection or other refusal by the buyer to receive or retain the goods, whether or not justified, or a justified revocation of acceptance revests title to the goods in the seller. Such revesting occurs by operation of law and is not a "sale."

Sec. 2402. **Rights of Seller's Creditors Against Sold Goods.** (1) Except as provided in subdivisions (2) and (3), rights of unsecured creditors of the seller with respect to goods which have been identified to a contract for sale are subject to the buyer's rights to recover the goods under this division (Sections 2502 and 2716).

(2) A creditor of the seller may treat a sale or an identification of goods t o a contract for sale as void if as against him a retention of possession by the seller is fraudulent under any rule of law of the state where the goods are situated, except that retention of possession in good faith and current course of trade by a merchant-seller for a commercially reasonable time after a sale or identification is not fraudulent.

(3) Nothing in this division shall be deemed to impair the rights of creditors of the seller

(a) Under the provisions of the division on secured transactions (Division 9); or

(b) Where identification to the contract or delivery is made not in current course of trade but in satisfaction of or as security for a pre-existing claim for money, security or the like and is made under circumstances which under any rule of law of the state where the goods are situated would apart from this division constitute the transaction a fraudulent transfer or voidable preference.

Sec. 2403. **Power to Transfer; Good Faith Purchase of Goods; "Entrusting."** (1) A purchaser of goods acquires all title which his transferor had or had power to transfer except that a purchaser of a limited interest acquires rights only to the extent of the interest purchased. A person with voidable title has power to transfer a good title to a good faith purchaser for value. When goods have been delivered under a transaction of purchase the purchaser has such power even though

(a) The transferor was deceived as to the identity of the purchaser, or

(b) The delivery was in exchange for a check which is later dishonored, or

(c) It was agreed that the transaction was to be a "cash sale," or

(d) The delivery was procured through fraud punishable as larcenous under the criminal law.

(2) Any entrusting of possession of goods to a merchant who deals in goods of that kind gives him power to transfer all rights of the entruster to a buyer in ordinary course of business.

(3) "Entrusting" includes any delivery and any acquiescence in retention of possession for the purpose of sale, obtaining offers to purchase, locating a buyer, or the like, regardless of any condition expressed between the parties to the delivery or acquiescence and regardless of whether the procurement of the entrusting or the possessor's disposition of the goods have been such as to be larcenous under the criminal law.

(4) The rights of other purchasers of goods and of lien creditors are governed by the divisions on secured transactions (Division 9), bulk transfers (Division 6) and documents of title (Division 7).

Chapter 5

PERFORMANCE

Sec. 2501. **Insurable Interest in Goods; Manner of Identification of Goods.** (1) The buyer obtains a special property and an insurable interest in goods by identification of existing goods as goods to which the contract refers even though the goods so identified are nonconforming and he has an option to return or reject them. Such identification can be made at any time and in any manner explicitly agreed to by the parties. In the absence of explicit agreement identification occurs

(a) When the contract is made if it is for the sale of goods already existing and identified;

(b) If the contract is for the sale of future goods other than those described in paragraph (c), when the goods are shipped, marked or otherwise designated by the seller as goods to which the contract refers;

(c) If the contract is for the sale of unborn young or future crops, when the crops are planted or otherwise become growing crops or the young are conceived.

(2) The seller retains an insurable interest in goods so long as title to or any security interest in the goods remains in him and where the identification is by the seller alone he may until default or insolvency or notification to the buyer that the identification is final substitute other goods for those identified.

(3) Nothing in this section impairs any insurable interest recognized under any other statute or rule of law.

Sec. 2502. **Buyer's Right to Goods on Seller's Insolvency.** (1) Subject to subdivision (2) and even though the goods have not been shipped a buyer who has paid a part or all of the price of goods in which he has a special property under the provisions of the immediately preceding section may on making and keeping good a tender of any unpaid portion of their price recover them from the seller if the seller becomes insolvent within 10 days after receipt of the first installment on their price.

(2) If the identification creating his special property has been made by the buyer he acquires the right to recover the goods only if they conform to the contract for sale.

Sec. 2503. **Manner of Seller's Tender of Delivery.** (1) Tender of delivery requires that the seller put and hold conforming goods at the buyer's disposition and give the buyer any notification reasonably necessary to enable him to take delivery. The manner, time and place for tender are determined by the agreement and this division, and in particular

(a) Tender must be at reasonable hour, and if it is of goods they must be kept available for the period reasonably necessary to enable the buyer to take possession but

(b) Unless otherwise agreed the buyer must furnish facililties reasonably suited to the receipt of the goods.

(2) Where the case is within the next section respecting shipment tender requires that the seller comply with its provisions.

(3) Where the seller is required to deliver at a particular destination tender requires that he comply with subdivision (1) and also in any appropriate case tender documents as described in subdivisions (4) and (5) of this section.

(4) Where goods are in the possession of a bailee and are to be delivered without being moved

(a) Tender requires that the seller either tender a negotiable document of title covering such goods or procure acknowledgment by the bailee of the buyer's right to possession of the goods; but

(b) Tender to the buyer of a nonnegotiable document of title or of a written direction to the bailee to deliver is sufficient tender unless the buyer seasonably objects, and receipt by the bailee of notification of the buyer's rights fixes those rights as against the bailee and all third persons; but risk of loss of the goods and of any failure by the bailee to honor the nonnegotiable document of title or to obey the direction remains on the seller until the buyer has had a reasonable time to present the document or direction, and a refusal by the bailee to honor the document or to obey the direction defeats the tender.

(5) Where the contract requires the seller to deliver documents

(a) He must tender all such documents in correct form, except as provided in this division with respect to bills of lading in a set (subdivision (2) of Section 2323); and

(b) Tender through customary banking channels is sufficient and dishonor of a draft accompanying the documents constitutes nonacceptance or rejection.

Sec. 2504. Shipment by Seller. Where the seller is required or authorized to send the goods to the buyer and the contract does not require him to deliver them at a particular destination, then unless otherwise agreed he must

(a) Put the goods in the possession of such a carrier and make such a contract for their transportation as may be reasonable having regard to the nature of the goods and other circumstances of the case; and

(b) Obtain and promptly deliver or tender in due form any document necessary to enable the buyer to obtain possession of the goods or otherwise required by the agreement or by usage or trade; and

(c) Promptly notify the buyer of the shipment.

Failure to notify the buyer under paragraph (c) or to make a proper contract under paragraph (a) is a ground for rejection only if material delay or loss ensues.

Sec. 2505. Shipment Under Reservation. (1) Where the seller has identified goods to the contract by or before shipment:

(a) His procurement of a negotiable bill of lading to his own order or otherwise reserves in him a security interest in the goods. His procurement of the bill to the order of a financing agency or of the buyer indicates in addition only the seller's expectation of transfering that interest to the person named.

(b) A nonnegotiable bill of lading to himself or his nominee reserves possession of the goods as security but except in a case of conditional delivery (subdivision (2) of Section 2507) a nonnegotiable bill of lading naming the buyer as consignee reserves no security interest even though the seller retains possession of the bill of lading.

(2) When shipment by the seller with reservation of a security interest is in violation of the contract for sale it constitutes an improper contract for transportation within the preceding section but impairs neither the rights given to the buyer by shipment and identification of the goods to the contract nor the seller's powers as a holder of a negotiable document.

Sec. 2506. Rights of Financing Agency. (1) A financing agency by paying or purchasing for value a draft which relates to a shipment of goods acquires to the extent of the payment or purchase and in addition to its own rights under the draft and any document of title securing it any rights of the shipper in the goods including the right to stop delivery and the shipper's right to have the draft honored by the buyer.

(2) The right to reimbursement of a financing agency which has in good faith honored or purchased the draft under commitment to or authority from the buyer is not impaired by subsequent discovery of defects with reference to any relevant document which was apparently regular on its face.

Sec. 2507. Effect of Seller's Tender; Delivery on Condition. (1) Tender of delivery is a condition to the buyer's duty to accept the goods and, unless otherwise agreed, to his duty to pay for them. Tender entitles the seller to acceptance of the goods and to payment according to the contract.

(2) Where payment is due and demanded on the delivery to the buyer of goods or documents of title, his right as against the seller to retain or dispose of them is conditional upon his making the payment due.

Sec. 2508. Cure by Seller of Improper Tender or Delivery; Replacement. (1) Where any tender or delivery by the seller is rejected because nonconforming and the time for performance has not yet expired, the seller may seasonably notify the buyer of his intention to cure and may then within the contract time make a conforming delivery.

(2) Where the buyer rejects a nonconforming tender which the seller had reasonable grounds to believe would be acceptable with or without money allowance the seller may if he seasonably notifies the buyer have a further reasonable time to substitute a confirming tender.

Sec. 2509. Risk of Loss in the Absence of Breach. (1) Where the contract requires or authorizes the seller to ship the goods by carrier

(a) If it does not require him to deliver them at a particular destination, the risk of loss passes to the buyer when the goods are duly delivered to the carrier even though the shipment is under reservation (Section 2505); but

(b) If it does require him to deliver them at a particular destination and the goods are there duly tendered while in the possession of the carrier, the risk of loss passes to the buyer when the goods are there duly so tendered as to enable the buyer to take delivery.

(2) Where the goods are held by a bailee to be delivered without being moved, the risk of loss passes to the buyer

(a) On his receipt of a negotiable document of title covering the goods; or

(b) On acknowledgment by the bailee of the buyer's right to possession of the goods; or

(c) After his receipt of a nonnegotiable document of title or other written direction to deliver, as provided in subdivision (4)(b) of Section 2503.

(3) In any case not within subdivision (1) or (2), the risk of loss passes to the buyer on his receipt of the goods if the seller is a merchant; otherwise the risk passes to the buyer on tender of delivery.

(4) The provisions of this section are subject to contrary agreement of the parties and to the provisions of this division on sale on approval (Section 2327) and on effect of breach on risk of loss (Section 2510).

Sec. 2510. Effect of Breach on Risk of Loss. (1) Where a tender or delivery of goods so fails to conform to the contract as to give a right of rejection the risk of their loss remains on the seller until cure or acceptance.

(2) Where the buyer rightfully revokes acceptance he may to the extent of any deficiency in his effective insurance coverage treat the risk of loss as having rested on the seller from the beginning.

(3) Where the buyer as to conforming goods already identified to the contract for sale repudiates or is otherwise in breach before risk of their loss has passed to him, the seller may to the extent of any deficiency in his effective insurance coverage treat the risk of loss as resting on the buyer for a commercially reasonable time.

Sec. 2511. Tender of Payment by Buyer; Payment by Check. (1) Unless otherwise agreed tender of payment is a condition to the seller's duty to tender and complete any delivery.

(2) Tender of payment is sufficient when made by any means or in any manner current in the ordinary course of business unless the seller demands payment in legal tender and gives any extension of time reasonably necessary to procure it.

(3) Subject to the provisions of this code on the effect of an instrument on an obligation (Section 3802), payment by check is conditional and is defeated as between the parties by dishonor of the check on due presentment.

Sec. 2512. Payment by Buyer Before Inspection. (1) Where the contract requires payment before inspection nonconformity of the goods does not excuse the buyer from so making payment unless (a) the nonconformity appears without inspection.

(2) Payment pursuant to subdivision (1) does not constitute an acceptance of goods or impair the buyer's right to inspect or any of his remedies.

Sec. 2513. Buyer's Right to Inspection of Goods. (1) Unless otherwise agreed and subject to subdivision (3), where goods are tendered or delivered or identified to the contract for sale, the buyer has a right before payment or acceptance to inspect them at any reasonable place and time and in any reasonable manner. When the seller is required or authorized to send the goods to the buyer, the inspection may be after their arrival.

(2) Expenses of inspection must be borne by the buyer but may be recovered from the seller if the goods do not conform and are rejected.

(3) Unless otherwise agreed and subject to the provisions of this division on C.I.F. contracts (subdivision (3) of Section 2321), the buyer is not entitled to inspect the goods before payment of the price when the contract provides

(a) For delivery "C.O.D." or on other like terms; or

(b) For payment against documents of title, except where such payment is due only after the goods are to become available for inspection.

(4) A place or method of inspection fixed by the parties is presumed to be exclusive but unless otherwise expressly agreed it does not postpone identification or shift the place for delivery or for passing the risk of loss. If compliance becomes impossible, inspection shall be provided in this section, unless the place or method fixed was clearly intended as an indispensable condition failure of which avoids the contract.

Sec. 2514. When Documents Deliverable on Acceptance; When on Payment. Unless otherwise agreed documents against which a draft is drawn are to be delivered to the drawee on acceptance of the draft if it is payable more than three days after presentment; otherwise, only on payment.

Sec. 2515. Preserving Evidence of Goods in Dispute. In furtherance of the adjustment of any claim or dispute

(a) Either party on reasonable notification to the other and for the purpose of ascertaining the facts and preserving evidence has the right to inspect, test and sample the goods including such of them as may be in the possession or control of the other; and

(b) The parties may agree to a third party inspection or survey to determine the conformity or condition of the goods and may agree that the findings shall be binding upon them in any subsequent litigation or adjustment.

CHAPTER 6

BREACH, REPUDIATION AND EXCUSE

Sec. 2601. Buyer's Rights on Improper Delivery. Subject to the provisions of this division on breach in installment contracts (Section 2612) and unless otherwise agreed under the sections on contractual limitations of remedy (Sections 2718 and 2719), if the goods or the tender of delivery fail in any respect to conform to the contract, the buyer may

(a) Reject the whole; or

(b) Accept the whole; or

(c) Accept any commercial unit or units and reject the rest.

Sec. 2602. Manner and Effect of Rightful Rejection. (1) Rejection of goods must be within a reasonable time after their delivery or tender. It is ineffective unless the buyer seasonably notifies the seller.

(2) Subject to the provisions of the two following sections on rejected goods (Sections 2603 and 2604),

(a) After rejection any exercise of ownership by the buyer with respect to any commercial unit is wrongful as against the seller; and

(b) If the buyer has before rejection taken physical possession of goods in which he does not have a security interest under the provisions of this division (subdivision (3) of Section 2711), he is under a duty after rejection to hold them with reasonable care at the seller's disposition for a time sufficient to permit the seller the remove them; but

(c) The buyer has no further obligations with regard to goods rightfully rejected.

(3) The seller's rights with respect to goods wrongfully rejected are governed by the provisions of this division on seller's remedies in general (Section 2703).

Sec. 2603. Merchant Buyer's Duties as to Rightfully Rejected Goods. (1) Subject to any security interest in the buyer (subdivision (3) of Section 2711), when the seller has no agent or place of business at the market of rejection a merchant buyer is under a duty after rejection of goods in his possession or control to follow any reasonable instructions received from the seller with respect to the goods and in the absence of such instructions to make reasonable efforts to sell them for the seller's account if they are perishable or threaten to decline in value speedily. Instructions are not reasonable if on demand indemnity for expenses is not forthcoming.

(2) When the buyer sells goods under subdivision (1), he is entitled to reimbursement from the seller or out of the proceeds for reasonable expenses of caring for and selling them, and if the expenses include no selling commission then to such commission as is usual in the trade or if there is none to a reasonable sum not exceeding 10 percent on the gross proceeds.

(3) In complying with this section the buyer is held only to good faith and good faith conduct hereunder is neither acceptance nor conversion nor the basis of an action for damages.

Sec. 2604. Buyer's Options as to Salvage of Rightfully Rejected Goods. Subject to the provisions of the immediately preceding section on perishables if the seller gives no instructions within a reasonable time after notification of rejection the buyer may store the rejected goods for the seller's account or reship them to him or resell them for the seller's account with reimbursement as provided in the preceding section. Such action is not acceptance or conversion.

Sec. 2605. Waiver of Buyer's Objections by Failure to Particularize. (1) The buyer's failure to state in connection with rejection a particular defect which is ascertainable by reasonable inspection precludes him from relying on the unstated defect to justify rejection or to establish breach

(a) Where the seller could have cured it if stated seasonably; or

(b) Between merchants when the seller has after rejection made a request in writing for a full and final written statement of all defects on which the buyer proposes to rely.

(2) Payment against documents made without reservation of rights precludes recovery of the payment for defects apparent on the face of the documents.

Sec. 2606. What Constitutes Acceptance of Goods. (1) Acceptance of goods occurs when the buyer

(a) After a reasonable opportunity to inspect the goods signifies to the seller that the goods are conforming or that he will take or retain them in spite of their nonconformity; or

(b) Fails to make an effective rejection (subdivision (1) of Section 2602), but such acceptance does not occur until the buyer has had a reasonable opportunity to inspect them; or

(c) Does any act inconsistent with the seller's ownership; but if such act is wrongful as against the seller it is an acceptance only if ratified by him.

(2) Acceptance of a part of any commercial unit is acceptance of that entire unit.

Sec. 2607. Effect of Acceptance; Notice of Breach; Burden Establishing Breach After Acceptance; Notice of Claim or Litigation to Person Answerable Over. (1) The buyer must pay at the contract rate for any goods accepted.

(2) Acceptance of the goods by the buyer precludes rejection of the goods accepted and if made with knowledge of a nonconformity cannot be revoked because of it unless the acceptance was on the reasonable assumption that the nonconformity would be seasonably cured but acceptance does not of itself impair any other remedy provided by this division for nonconformity.

(3) Where a tender has been accepted

(a) The buyer must within a reasonable time after he discovers or should have discovered any breach notify the seller of breach or be barred from any remedy; and

(b) If the claim is one for infringement or the like (subdivision (3) of Section 2312) and the buyer is sued as a result of such a breach he must so notify the seller within a reasonable time after he receives notice of the litigation or be barred from any remedy over for liability established by the litigation.

(4) The burden is on the buyer to establish any breach with respect to the goods accepted.

(5) Where the buyer is sued for breach of a warranty or other obligation for which his seller is answerable over

(a) He may give his seller written notice of the litigation. If the notice states that the seller may come in and defend and that if the seller does not do so he will be bound in any action against him by his buyer by any determination of fact common to the two litigations, then unless the seller after seasonable receipt of the notice does come in and defend he is so bound.

(b) If the claim is one for infringement or the like (subdivision (3) of Section 2312) the orignal seller may demand in writing that his buyer turn over to him control of the litigation including settlement or else be barred from any remedy over and if he also agrees to bear all expense and to satisfy any adverse judgment, then unless the buyer after seasonable receipt of the demand does turn over control the buyer is so barred.

(6) The provisions of subdivision (3), (4) and (5) apply to any obligation of a buyer to hold the seller harmless against infringement or the like (subdivision (3) of Section 2312).

Sec. 2608. Revocation of Acceptance in Whole or in Part. (1) The buyer may revoke his acceptance of a lot or commercial unit whose nonconformity substantially impairs its value to him if he has accepted it

(a) On the reasonable assumption that its nonconformity would be cured and it has not been seasonably cured; or

(b) Without discovery of such nonconformity if his acceptance was reasonably induced either by the difficulty of discovery before acceptance or by the seller's assurances.

(2) Revocation of acceptance must occur within a reasonable time after the buyer discovers or should have discovered the ground for it and before any substantial change in condition of the goods which is not caused by their own defects. It is not effective until the buyer notifies the seller of it.

(3) A buyer who so revokes has the same rights and duties with regard to the goods involved as if he had rejected them.

Sec. 2609. Right to Adequate Assurance of Performance. (1) A contract for sale imposes an obligation of each party that the other's expectation of receiving due performance will not be impaired. When reasonable grounds for insecurity arise with respect to the performance of either party the other may in writing demand adequate assurance of due performance and until he receives such assurance may if commercially reasonable suspend any performance for which he has not already received the agreed return.

(2) Between merchants the reasonableness of grounds for insecurity and the adequacy of any assurance offered shall be determined according to commercial standards.

(3) Acceptance of any improper delivery or payment does not prejudice the aggrieved party's right to demand adequate assurance of future performance.

(4) After receipt of a justified demand failure to provide within a reasonable time not exceeding 30 days such assurance of due performance as is adequate under the circumstances of the particular case is a repudiation of the contract.

Sec. 2610. Anticipatory Repudiation. When either party repudiates the contract with respect to a performance not yet due the loss of which will substantially impair the value of the contract to the other, the aggrieved party may

(a) For a commercially reasonable time await performance by the repudiating party; or

(b) Resort to any remedy for breach (Section 2703 or Section 2711), even though he has notified the repudiating party that he would await the latter's performance and has urged retraction; and

(c) In either case suspend his own performance or proceed in accordance with the provisions of this division on the seller's right to identify goods to the contract notwithstanding breach or to salvage unfinished goods (Section 2704).

Sec. 2611. Retraction of Anticipatory Repudiation. (1) Until the repudiating party's next performance is due he can retract his repudiation unless the aggrieved party has since the repudiation canceled or materially changed his position or otherwise indicated that he considers the repudiation final.

(2) Retraction may be by any method which clearly indicates to the aggrieved party that the repudiating party intends to perform, but must include any assurance justifiably demanded under the provisions of this division (Section 2609).

(3) Retraction reinstates the repudiating party's rights under the contract with due excuse and allowance to the aggrieved party for any delay occasioned by the repudiation.

Sec. 2612. "Installment Contract"; Breach. (1) An "installment contract" is one which requires or authorizes the delivery of goods in separate lots to be separately accepted, even though the contract contains a clause "each delivery is a separate contract" or its equivalent.

(2) The buyer may reject any installment which is nonconforming if the nonconformity substantially impairs the value of that installment and cannot be cured or if the nonconformity is a defect in the required documents; but if the nonconformity does not fall within subdivision (3) and the seller gives adequate assurance of its cure the buyer must accept that installment.

(3) Whenever nonconformity or default with respect to one or more installments substantially impairs the value of the whole contract there is a breach of the whole. But the aggrieved party reinstates the contract if he accepts a nonconforming installment without seasonably notifying of cancellation or if he brings an action with respect only to past installments or demands performance as to future installments.

Sec. 2613. Casualty to Identified Goods. Where the contract requires for its performance goods identified when the contract is made, and the goods suffer casualty without fault of either party before the risk of loss passes to the buyer, or in a proper case under a "no arrival, no sale" term (Section 2324) then

(a) If the loss is total the contract is avoided; and

(b) If the loss is partial or the goods have so deteriorated as no longer to conform to the contract the buyer may nevertheless demand inspection and at his option either treat the contract as avoided or accept the goods with due allowance from the contract price for the deterioration or the deficiency in quantity but without further right against the seller.

Sec. 2614. Substituted Performance. (1) Where without fault of either party the agreed type of carrier becomes unavailable or the agreed manner of delivery otherwise becomes commercially impracticable but a commercially reasonable substitute is available, such substitute performance must be tendered and accepted.

(2) If the agreed means or manner of payment fails because of domestic or foreign governmental regulation, the seller may withhold or stop delivery unless the buyer provides a means or manner of payment which is commercially a substantial equivalent. If delivery has already been taken, payment by the means or in the manner provided by the regulation discharges the buyer's obligation unless the regulation is discriminatory, oppressive or predatory.

Sec. 2615. Excuse by Failure of Presupposed Conditions. Except so far as a seller may have assumed a greater obligation and subject to the preceding section on substituted performance:

(a) Delay in delivery or nondelivery in whole or in part by a seller who complies with paragraphs (b) and (c) is not a breach of his duty under a contract for sale if performance as agreed has been made impracticable by the occurrence of a contingency the nonoccurrence of which was a basic assumption on which the contract was made or by compliance in good faith with any applicable foreign or domestic governmental regulation or order whether or not it later proves to be invalid.

(b) Where the causes mentioned in paragraph (a) affect only a part of the seller's capacity to perform, he must allocate production and deliveries among his customers but may at his own option include regular customers not then under contract as well as his own requirements for further manufacture. He may so allocate in any manner which is fair and reasonable.

(c) The seller must notify the buyer seasonably that there will be delay or nondelivery and, when allocation is required under paragraph (b), of the estimated quota thus made available for the buyer.

Sec. 2616. Procedure on Notice Claiming Excuse. (1) Where the buyer receives notification of a material indefinite delay or an allocation justified under the preceding section he may by written notification to the seller as to any delivery concerned, and where the prospective deficiency substantially impairs the value of the whole contract under the provisions of this division relating to breach of installment contracts (Section 2612), then also as to the whole,

(a) Terminate and thereby discharge any unexecuted portion of the contract; or

(b) Modify the contract by agreeing to take his available quota in substitution.

(2) If after receipt of such notification from the seller the buyer fails so to modify the contract within a reasonable time not exceeding 30 days the contract lapses with respect to any deliveries affected.

(3) The provisions of this section may not be negated by agreement except insofar as the seller has assumed a greater obligation under the preceding section.

CHAPTER 7

REMEDIES

Sec. 2701. Remedies for Breach of Collateral Contracts Not Impaired. Remedies for breach of any obligation or promise collateral or ancillary to a contract for sale are not impaired by the provisions of this division.

Sec. 2702. Seller's Remedies on Discovery of Buyer's Insolvency. (1) Where the seller discovers the buyer to be insolvent he may refuse delivery except for cash including payment for all goods theretofore delivered under the contract, and stop delivery under this division (Section 2705).

(2) Where the seller discovers that the buyer has received goods on credit while insolvent he may reclaim the goods upon demand made within 10 days after the receipt, but if misrepresentation of solvency has been made to the particular seller in writing within three months before delivery the 10-day limitation does not apply. Except as provided in this subdivision the seller may not base a right to reclaim goods on the buyer's fraudulent or innocent misrepresentation of solvency or of intent to pay.

(3) The seller's right to reclaim under subdivision (2) is subject to the rights of a buyer in ordinary course or other good faith purchaser under this division (Section 2403). Successful reclamation of goods excludes all other remedies with respect to them.

Sec. 2703. Seller's Remedies in General. Where the buyer wrongfully rejects or revokes acceptance of goods or fails to make a payment due on or before delivery or repudiates with respect to a part or the whole, then with respect to any goods directly affected and, if the breach is of the whole contract (Section 2612), then also with respect to the whole undelivered balance, the aggrieved seller may

(a) Withhold delivery of such goods;

(b) Stop delivery by any bailee as hereinafter provided (Section 2705);

(c) Proceed under the next section respecting goods still unidentified to the contract;

(d) Resell and recover damages as hereafter provided (Section 2706);

(e) Recover damages for nonacceptance (Section 2708) or in a proper case the price (Section 2709);

(f) Cancel.

Sec. 2704. Seller's Right to Identify Goods to the Contract Notwithstanding Breach or to Salvage Unfinished Goods. (1) An aggrieved seller under the preceding section may

(a) Identify to the contract conforming goods not already identified if at the time he learned of the breach they are in his possession or control;

(b) Treat as the subject of resale goods which have demonstrably been intended for the particular contract even though those goods are unfinished.

(2) Where the goods are unfinished an aggrieved seller may in the exercise of reasonable commercial judgment for the purposes of avoiding loss and of effective realization either complete the manufacture and wholly identify the goods to the contract or cease manufacture and resell for scrap or salvage value or proceed in any other reasonable manner.

Sec. 2705. Seller's Stoppage of Delivery in Transit or Otherwise. (1) The seller may stop delivery of goods in the possession of a carrier or other bailee when he discovers the buyer to be insolvent (Section 2702) and may stop delivery of carload, truckload, planeload or larger shipments of express or freight when the buyer repudiates or fails to make a payment due before delivery or if for any other reason the seller has a right to withhold or reclaim the goods.

(2) As against such buyer the seller may stop delivery until

(a) Receipt of the goods by the buyer; or

(b) Acknowledgment to the buyer by any bailee of the goods except a carrier that the bailee holds the goods for the buyer; or

(c) Such acknowledgment to the buyer by a carrier by reshipment or as warehouseman; or

(d) Negotiation to the buyer of any negotiable document of title covering the goods.

(3) (a) To stop delivery the seller must so notify as to enable the bailee by reasonable diligence to prevent delivery of the goods.

(b) After such notification the bailee must hold and deliver the goods according to the directions of the seller but the seller is liable to the bailee for any ensuing charges or damages.

(c) If a negotiable document of title has been issued for goods the bailee is not obliged to obey a notification to stop until surrender of the document.

(d) A carrier who has issued a nonnegotiable bill of lading is not obliged to obey a notification to stop received from a person other than the consignor.

Sec. 2706. Seller's Resale Including Contract for Resale. (1) Under the conditions stated in Section 2703 on seller's remedies, the seller may resell the goods concerned or the undelivered balance thereof. Where the resale is made in good faith and in a commercially reasonable manner the seller may recover the difference between the resale price and the contract price together with any incidental damages allowed under the provisions of this division (Section 2710), but less expenses saved in consequence of the buyer's breach.

(2) Except as otherwise provided in subdivision (3) or unless otherwise agreed resale may be at public or private sale including sale by way of one or more contracts to sell or of identification to an existing contract of the seller. Sale may be as a unit or in parcels and at any time and place and on any terms but every aspect of the sale including the method, manner, time, place and terms must be commercially reasonable. The resale must be reasonably identified as referring to the broken contract, but it is not necessary that the goods be in existence or that any or all of them have been identified to the contract before the breach.

(3) Where the resale is at private sale the seller must give the buyer reasonable notification of his intention to resell.

(4) Where the resale is at public sale

(a) Only identified goods can be sold except where there is a recognized market for a public sale of futures in goods of the kind; and

(b) It must be made at a usual place or market for public sale if one is reasonably available and except in the case of goods which are perishable or threaten to decline in value speedily the seller must give the buyer reasonable notice of the time and place of the resale; and

(c) If the goods are not to be within the view of those attending the sale the notification of sale must state the place where the goods are located and provide for their reasonable inspection by prospective bidders and

(d) The seller may buy.

(5) A purchaser who buys in good faith at a resale takes the goods free of any rights of the original buyer even though the seller fails to comply with one or more of the requirements of this section.

(6) The seller is not accountable to the buyer for any profit made on any resale. A person in the position of a seller (Section 2707) or a buyer who has rightfully rejected or justifiably revoked acceptance must account for any excess over the amount of his security interest, as hereinafter defined (subdivision (3) of Section 2711).

Sec. 2707. "Person in the Position of a Seller." (1) A "person in the position of a seller" includes as against a principal an agent who has paid or become responsible for the price of goods on behalf of his principal or anyone who otherwise holds a security interest or other right in goods similar to that of a seller.

(2) A person in the position of a seller may as provided in this division withhold or stop delivery (Section 2705) and resell (Section 2706) and recover incidental damages (Section 2710).

Sec. 2708. Seller's Damages for Non-acceptance or Repudiation. (1) Subject to subdivision (2) and to the provisions of this division with respect to proof of market price (Section 2723), the measure of damages for nonacceptance or repudiation by the buyer is the difference between the market price at the time and place for tender and the unpaid contract price together with any incidental damages provided in this division (Section 2710), but less expenses saved in consequence of the buyer's breach.

(2) If the measure of damages provided in subdivision (1) is inadequate to put the seller in as good a position as performance would have done then the measure of damages is the profit (including reasonable overhead) which the seller would have made from full performance by the buyer, together with any incidental damages provided in this division (Section 2710), due allowance for costs reasonably incurred and due credit for payments or proceeds of resale.

Sec. 2709. Action for the Price. (1) When the buyer fails to pay the price as it becomes due the seller may recover, together with any incidental damages under the next section, the price

(a) Of goods accepted or of conforming goods lost or damaged within a commercially reasonable time after risk of their loss has passed to the buyer; and

(b) Of goods identified to the contract if the seller is unable after reasonable effort to resell them at a reasonable price or the circumstances reasonably indicate that such effort will be unavailing.

(2) Where the seller sues for the price he must hold for the buyer any goods which have been identified to the contract and are still in his control except that if resale becomes possible he may resell them at any time prior to the collection of the judgment. The net proceeds of any such resale must be credited to the buyer and payment of the judgment entitles him to any goods not resold.

(3) After the buyer has wrongfully rejected or revoked acceptance of the goods or has failed to make a payment due or has repudiated (Section 2610), a seller who is held not entitled to the price under this section shall nevertheless be awarded damages for nonacceptance under the preceding section.

Sec. 2710. Seller's Incidental Damages. Incidental damages to an aggrieved seller include any commercially reasonable charges, expenses or commissions incurred in stopping delivery, in the transportation, care and custody of goods after the buyers' breach, in connection with return or resale of the goods or otherwise resulting from the breach.

Sec. 2711. Buyer's Remedies in General; Buyer's Security Interest in Rejected Goods. (1) Where the seller fails to make delivery or repudiates or the buyer rightfully rejects or justifiably revokes acceptance then with respect to any goods involved, and with respect to the whole if the breach goes to the whole contract (Section 2612), the buyer may cancel and whether or not he has done so may in addition to recovering so much of the price as has been paid

(a) "Cover" and have damages under the next section as to all the goods affected whether or not they have been identified to the contract; or

(b) Recover damages for nondelivery as provided in this division (Section 2713).

(2) Where the seller fails to deliver or repudiates the buyer may also

(a) If the goods have been identified recover them as provided in this division (Section 2502); or

(b) In a proper case obtain specific performance or replevy the goods as provided in this division (Section 2716).

(3) On rightful rejection or justifiable revocation of acceptance a buyer has a security interest in goods in his possession or control for any payments made on their price and any expenses reasonably incurred in their inspection, receipt, transportation, care and custody and may hold such goods and resell them in like manner as an aggrieved seller (Section 2706).

Sec. 2712. "Cover"; Buyer's Procurement of Substitute Goods.

(1) After a breach within the preceding section the buyer may "cover" by making in good faith and without unreasonable delay any reasonable purchase of or contract to purchase goods in substitution for those due from the seller.

(2) The buyer may recover from the seller as damages the difference between the cost of cover and the contract price together with any incidental or consequential damages as hereinafter defined (Section 2715), but less expenses saved in consequence of the seller's breach.

(3) Failure of the buyer to effect cover within this section does not bar him from any other remedy.

Sec. 2713. Buyer's Damages for Non-Delivery or Repudiation.

Subject to the provisions of this division with respect to proof of market price (Section 2723), the measure of damages for nondelivery or repudiation by the seller is the difference between the market price at the time when the buyer learned of the breach and the contract price together with any incidental and consequential damages provided in this division (Section 2715), but less expenses saved in consequence of the seller's breach.

(2) Market price is to be determined as of the place for tender or, in cases of rejection after arrival or revocation of acceptance, as of the place of arrival.

Sec. 2714. Buyer's Damages for Breach in Regard to Accepted Goods.

(1) Where the buyer has accepted goods and given notification (Subdivision (3) of Section 2607) he may recover as damages for any nonconformity of tender the loss resulting in the ordinary course of events from the seller's breach as determined in any manner which is reasonable.

(2) The measure of damages for breach of warranty is the difference at the time and place of acceptance between the value of the goods accepted and the value they would have had if they had been as warranted, unless special circumstances show proximate damages of a different amount.

(3) In a proper case any incidental and consequential damages under the next section may also be recovered.

Sec. 2715. Buyer's Incidental and Consequential Damages.

(1) Incidental damages resulting from the seller's breach include expenses reasonably incurred in inspection, receipt, transportation and care and custody of goods rightfully rejected, any commercially reasonable charges, expenses or commissions in connection with effecting cover and any other reasonable expense incidental to the delay or other breach.

(2) Consequential damages resulting from the seller's breach include

(a) Any loss resulting from general or particular requirements and needs of which the seller at the time of contracting had reason to know and which could not reasonably be prevented by cover or otherwise; and

(b) Injury to person or property proximately resulting from any breach of warranty.

Sec. 2716. Buyer's Right to Specific Performance or Replevin.

(1) Specific performance may be decreed where the goods are unique or in other proper circumstances.

(2) The decree for specific performance may include such terms and conditions as to payment of the price, damages, or other relief as the court may deem just.

(3) The buyer has a right of replevin for goods identified to the contract if after reasonable effort he is unable to effect cover for such goods or the circumstances reasonably indicate that such effort will be unavailing or if the goods have been shipped under reservation and satisfaction of the security interest in them has been made or tendered.

Sec. 2717. Deduction of Damages From the Price.

The buyer on notifying the seller of his intention to do so may deduct all or any part of the damages resulting from any breach of the contract from any part of the price still due under the same contract.

Sec. 2718. Liquidation or Limitation of Damages; Deposits.

(1) Damages for breach by either party may be liquidated in the agreement but only at an amount which is reasonable in the light of the anticipated or actual harm caused by the breach, the difficulties of proof of loss, and the inconvenience or nonfeasiblity of otherwise obtaining an adequate remedy. A term fixing unreasonably large liquidated damages is void as a penalty.

(2) Where the seller justifiably withholds delivery of goods because of the buyer's breach, the buyer is entitled to restitution of any amount by which the sum of his payments exceeds

(a) The amount to which the seller is entitled by virtue of terms liquidating the seller's damages in accordance with subdivision (1), or

(b) In the absence of such terms, 20 percent of the value of the total performance for which the buyer is obligated under the contract or five hundred dollars ($500), whichever is smaller.

(3) The buyer's right to restitution under subdivision (2) is subject to offset to the extent that the seller establishes

(a) A right to recover damages under the provisions of this chapter other than subdivision (1), and

(b) The amount or value of any benefits received by the buyer directly or indirectly by reason of the contract.

(4) Where a seller has received payment in goods their reasonable value or the proceeds of their resale shall be treated as payments for the purposes of subdivision (2); but if the seller has notice of the buyer's breach before reselling goods received in part performance, his resale is subject to the conditions laid down in this division on resale by an aggrieved seller (Section 2706).

Sec. 2719. Contractual Modification or Limitation or Remedy.

(1) Subject to the provisions of subdivisions (2) and (3) of this section and of the preceding section on liquidation and limitation of damages,

(a) The agreement may provide for remedies in addition to or in substitution for those provided in this division and may limit or alter the measure of damages recoverable under this division, as by limiting the buyer's remedies to return of the goods and repayment of the price or to repair and replacement of nonconforming goods or parts; and

(b) Resort to a remedy as provided is optional unless the remedy is expressly agreed to be exclusive, in which case it is the sole remedy.

(2) Where circumstances cause an exclusive or limited remedy to fail of its essential purpose, remedy may be had as provided in this code.

(3) Consequential damages may be limited or excluded unless the limitation or exclusion is unconscionable. Limitation of consequential damages for injury to the person in the case of consumer goods is invalid unless it is proved that the limitation is not unconscionable. Limitation of consequential damages where the loss is commerical is valid unless it is proved that the limitation is unconscionable.

Sec. 2720. Effect of "Cancellation" or "Rescission" on Claims for Antecedent Breach.

Unless the contrary intention clearly appears, expressions of "cancellation" or "rescission" of the contract or the like shall not be construed as a renunciation or discharge of any claim in damages for an antecedent breach.

Sec. 2721. Remedies for Fraud.

Remedies for material misrepresentation or fraud include all remedies available under this division for nonfraudulent breach. Neither rescission or a claim for rescission of the contract for sale nor rejection or return of the goods shall bar or be deemed inconsistent with a claim for damages or other remedy.

Sec. 2722. Who Can Sue Third Parties for Injury to Goods.

Where a third party so deals with goods which have been identified to a contract for sale as to cause actionable injury to a party to that contract

(a) A right of action against the third party is in either party to the contract for sale who has title to or a security interest or a special property or an insurable interest in the goods; and if the goods have been destroyed or converted a right of action is also in the party who either bore the risk of loss under the contract for sale or has since the injury assumed that risk as against the other;

(b) If at the time of the injury the party plaintiff did not bear the risk as against the other party to the contract for sale and there is no arrangement between them for disposition of the recovery, his suit or settlement is, subject to his own interest, as a fiduciary for the other party to the contract;

(c) Either party may with the consent of the other sue for the benefit of whom it may concern.

Sec. 2723. Proof of Market Price; Time and Place. (1) If an action based on anticipatory repudiation comes to trial before the time for performance with respect to some or all of the goods, any damages based on market price (Section 2708 or Section 2713) shall be determined according to the price of such goods prevailing at the time when the aggrieved party learned of the repudiation.

(2) If evidence of a price prevailing at the times or places described in this division is not readily available the price prevailing within any reasonable time before or after the time described or at any other place which in commercial judgment or under usage of trade would serve as a reasonable substitute for the one described may be used, making any proper allowance for the cost of transporting the goods to or from such other place.

(3) Evidence of a relevant price prevailing at a time or place other than the one described in this division offered by one party is not admissible unless and until he has given the other party such notice as the court finds sufficient to prevent unfair surprise.

Sec. 2724. Admissibility of Market Quotations. Whenever in prevailing price of value of any goods regularly bought and sold in any established commodity market is in issue, reports in official publications or trade journals or in newspapers or periodicals of general circulation published as the reports of such market shall be admissible in evidence. The circumstances of the preparation of such a report may be shown to affect its weight but not its admissibility.

Sec. 2725. Breach of contract for sale: Limitations of actions: Accrual of action: Time for bringing second action: Retrospective operation of section. (1) An action for breach of any contract for sale must be commenced within four years after the cause of action has accrued. By the original agreement the parties may reduce the period of limitation to not less than one year but may not extend it.

(2) A cause of action accrues when the breach occurs, regardless of the aggrieved party's lack of knowledge of the breach. A breach of warranty occurs when tender of delivery is made, except that where a warranty explicitly extends to future performance of the goods and discovery of the breach must await the time of such performance the cause of action accrues when the breach is or should have been discovered.

(3) Where an action commenced within the time limited by subdivision (1) is so terminated as to leave available a remedy by another action for the same breach such other action may be commenced after the expiration of the time limited and within six months after the termination of the first action unless the termination resulted from voluntary discontinuance or from dismissal for failure or neglect to prosecute.

(4) This section does not alter the law on tolling of the statute of limitations nor does it apply to causes of action which have accrued before this code becomes effective.

CHAPTER 8

RETAIL SALES

Sec. 2800. As used in this chapter "goods" means goods used or bought for use primarily for personal, family or household purposes.

Sec. 2801. In any retail sale of goods, if the manufacturer or seller of the goods issues a written warranty or guarantee to the condition or quality of all or part of the goods which requires the buyer to complete and return any form to the manufacturer or seller as proof of the purchase of the goods, such warranty or guarantee shall not be unenforceable solely because the buyer fails to complete or return the form. This section does not relieve the buyer from proving the fact of purchase and the date thereof in any case in which such a fact is in issue.

The buyer must agree in writing to any waiver of this section for the waiver to be valid. Any waiver by the buyer of the provisions of this section which is not in writing is contrary to public policy and shall be unenforceable and void.

DIVISION 3

COMMERCIAL PAPER

CHAPTER 1

SHORT TITLE FORM AND INTERPRETATION

Sec. 3101. Short Title. This division shall be known and may be cited as Uniform Commercial Code—Commercial Paper.

Sec. 3102. Definitions and Index Definitions. (1) In this division unless the context otherwise requires

(a) "Issue" means the first delivery of an instrument to a holder or a remitter.

(b) An "order" is a direction to pay and must be more than an authorization or request. It must identify the person to pay with reasonable certainty. It may be addressed to one or more such persons jointly or in the alternative but not in succession.

(c) A "promise" is an undertaking to pay and must be more than an acknowledgment of an obligation.

(d) "Secondary party" means a drawer or endorser.

(e) "Instrument" means a negotiable instrument.

(2) Other definitions applying to this division and the sections in which the y appear are:

"Acceptance." Section 3140.
"Accommodation party." Section 3415.
"Alteration." Section 3407.
"Certification of deposit." Section 3104.
"Certification." Section 3411.
"Check." Section 3104.
"Definite Time." Section 3109.
"Dishonor." Section 3507.
"Draft." Section 3104.
"Holder in due course." Section 3302.
"Negotiation." Section 3202.
"Note." Section 3104.
"Notice of dishonor." Section 3508.
"On demand." Section 3108.
"Presentment." Section 3504.
"Protest." Section 3509.
"Restrictive indorsement." Section 3205.
"Signature." Section 3401.

(3) The following definitions in other divisions apply to this division:

"Account." Section 4104.
"Banking Day." Section 4104.
"Clearinghouse." Section 4104.
"Collecting bank." Section 4105.
"Customer." Section 4104.
"Depositary bank." Section 4105.
"Documentary draft." Section 4104.
"Intermediary bank." Section 4105.
"Item." Section 4104.
"Midnight deadline." Section 4104.
"Payor bank." Section 4105.

(4) In addition Division 1 contains general definitions and principles of construction and interpretation applicable throughout this division.

Sec. 3103. Limitations on Scope of Article. (1) This division does not apply to money, documents of title or investment securities.

(2) The provisions of this division are subject to the provisions of this division on bank deposits and collections (Division 4) and secured transactions (Division 9).

Sec. 3104. Form of Negotiable Instruments; "Draft"; "Check"; "Certificate of Deposit"; "Note." (1) Any writing to be a negotiable instrument within this division must

(a) Be signed by the maker or drawer; and

(b) Contain an unconditional promise or order to pay a sum certain in money and no other promise, order, obligation or power given by the maker or drawer except as authorized by this division; and

(c) Be payable on demand or at a definite time; and

(d) Be payable to order or to bearer.

(2) A writing which complies with the requirements of this section is

(a) A "draft" ("bill of exchange") if it is an order;

(b) A "check" if it is a draft drawn on a bank and payable on demand;

(c) A "certificate of deposit" if it is an acknowledgment by a bank of receipt of money with an engagement to repay it;

(d) A "note" if it is a promise other than a certificate of deposit.

(3) As used in other divisions of this code, and as the context may require, the terms "draft," "check," "certificate of deposit" and "note" may refer to instruments which are not negotiable within this division as well as to instruments which are so negotiable.

Sec. 3105. **When Promise or Order Unconditional.** (1) A promise or order otherwise unconditional is not made conditional by the fact that the instrument

(a) Is subject to implied or constructive conditions; or

(b) States its considerations, whether performed or promised, or the transaction which gave rise to the instrument, or that the promise or order is made to the instrument matures in accordance with or "as per" such transaction; or

(c) Refers to or states that it arises out of a separate agreement or refers to a separate agreement for rights as to prepayment or acceleration; or

(d) States that it is drawn under a letter of credit; or

(e) States that it is secured, whether by mortgage, reservation of title or otherwise; or

(f) Indicates a particular account to be debited or any other fund or sources from which reimbursement is expected; or

(g) Is limited to payment out of a particular fund or the proceeds of a particular source, if the instrument is issued by a government or governmental agency or unit; or

(h) Is limited to payment out of the entire assets of a partnership, unincorporated association, trust or estate by or on behalf of which the instrument is issued.

(2) A promise or order is not unconditional if the instrument

(a) States that it is subject to or governed by any other agreement; or

(b) States that it is to be paid only out of a particular fund or source except as provided in this section.

Sec. 3106. **Sum Certain.** (1) The sum payable is a sum certain even though it is to be paid

(a) With stated interest or by stated installments; or

(b) With stated different rates of interest before and after default or a specified date; or

(c) With a stated discount or addition if paid before or after the date fixed for payment; or

(d) With exchange or less exchange, whether at a fixed rate or at the current rate; or

(e) With costs of collection or an attorney's fee or both upon default.

(2) Nothing in this section shall validate any term which is otherwise illegal.

Sec. 3107. **Money.** (1) An instrument is payable in money if the medium of exchange in which it is payable is money at the time the instrument is made. An instrument payable in "currency" or "current funds" is payable in money.

(2) A promise or order to pay a sum stated in a foreign currency is for a sum certain in money and, unless a different medium of payment is specified in the instrument, may be satisfied by payment of that number of dollars which the stated foreign currency will purchase at the buying sight rate for that currency on the day on which the instrument is payable or, if payable on demand, on the day of demand. If such an instrument specifies a foreign currency as the medium of payment the instrument is payable in that currency.

Sec. 3108. **Payable on Demand.** Instruments payable on demand include those payable at sight or on presentation and those in which no time for payment is stated.

Sec. 3109. **Definite Time.** (1) An instrument is payable at a definite time if by its terms it is payable

(a) On or before a stated date or at a fixed period after a stated date; or

(b) At a fixed period after sight; or

(c) At a definite time subject to any acceleration; or

(d) At a definite time subject to extension at the option of the holder or to extension to a further definite time at the option of the maker or acceptor or automatically upon or after a specific act or event.

(2) An instrument which by its terms is otherwise payable only upon an act or event uncertain as to time of occurrence is not payable at a definite time and even though the act or event has occurred.

Sec. 3110. **Payable Order.** (1) An instrument is payable to order when by its terms it is payable to the order or assigns of any person therein specified with reasonable certainty, or to him or his order, or when it is conspicuously designated on its face as "exchange" or the like and names a payee. It may be payable to the order of

(a) The maker or drawer; or

(b) The drawee; or

(c) A payee who is not maker, drawer or drawee; or

(d) Two or more payees together or in the alternative; or

(e) An estate, trust or fund, in which case it is payable to the order of the representative of such estate, trust or fund or his successors; or

(f) An office, or an officer by his title as such in which case it is payable to the principal but the incumbent of the office or his successors may act as if he or they were the holder; or

(g) A partnership or unincorporated association, in which case it is payable to the partnership or association and may be indorsed or transferred by any person thereto authorized.

(2) An instrument not payable to order is not made so payable by such words as "payable upon return of this instrument properly indorsed."

(3) An instrument made payable both to order and to bearer is payable to order unless the bearer words are handwritten or typewritten.

Sec. 3111. **Payable to Bearer.** An instrument is payable to bearer when by its terms it is payable to

(a) Bearer or the order of bearer; or

(b) A specified person or bearer; or

(c) "Cash" or the order of "cash," or any other indication which does not purport to designate a specific payee.

Sec. 3112. **Terms and Omissions Not Affecting Negotiability.** (1) The negotiability of an instrument is not affected by

(a) The omission of a statement of any consideration or of the place where the instrument is drawn or payable; or

(b) A statement that collateral has been given to secure obligations either on the instrument or otherwise or of an obligor on the instrument or that in the case of default on those obligations the holder may realize on or dispose of the collateral; or

(c) A promise or power to maintain or protect collateral, to furnish financia l information or to do or refrain from doing any other act for the protection of the obligation expressed in the instrument not involving the payment of money on account of the indebtedness evidenced by the instrument; or

(d) A term authorizing a confession of judgment on the instrument if it is not paid when due; or

(e) A term purporting to waive the benefit of any law intended for the advantage or protection of any obligor; or

(f) A term in a draft providing that the payee by indorsing or cashing it acknowledges full satisfaction of an obligation of the drawer; or

(g) A statement in a draft drawn in a set of parts (Section 3801) to the effect that the order is effective only if no other part has been honored.

(2) Nothing in this section shall validate any term which is otherwise illegal.

Sec. 3113. **Seal.** An instrument otherwise negotiable is within this division even though it is under a seal.

Sec. 3114. **Date, Antedating, Postdating.** (1) The negotiability of an instrument is not affected by the fact that it is undated, antedated or postdated.

(2) Where an instrument is antedated or postdated the time when it is payable is determined by the stated date if the instrument is payable on demand or at a fixed period after date.

(3) Where the instrument or any signature thereon is dated, the date is presumed to be correct.

Sec. 3115. **Incomplete Instruments.** (1) When a paper whose contents at the time of signing show that it is intended to become an instrument is signed while still incomplete in any necessary respect it cannot be enforced until completed, but when it is completed in accordance with authority given it is effective as completed.

(2) If the completion is unauthorized the rules as to material alteration apply (Section 3407), even though the paper was not delivered by maker

or drawer; but the burden of establishing that any completion is unauthorized is on the party so asserting.

Sec. 3116. Instruments Payable to Two or More Persons. An instrument payable to the order of two or more persons

(a) If in the alternative is payable to any one of them and may be negotiated, discharged or enforced by any of them who has possession of it;

(b) If not in the alternative is payable to all of them and may be negotiated, discharged or enforced only by all of them.

Sec. 3117. Instruments Payable With Words of Description. An instrument made payable to a named person with the addition of words describing him

(a) As agent or officer of a specified person is payable to his principal but the agent or officer may act as if he were the holder;

(b) As any other fiduciary for a specified person or purpose is payable to the payee and may be negotiated, discharged or enforced by him;

(c) In any other manner is payable to the payee unconditionally and the additional words are without effect on subsequent parties.

Sec. 3118. Ambiguous Terms and Rules of Construction. The following rules apply to every instrument:

(a) Where there is doubt whether the instrument is a draft or a note the holder may treat it as either. A draft drawn on the drawer is effective as a note.

(b) Handwritten terms control typewritten and printed terms, and typewritten control printed.

(c) Words control figures except that if the words are ambiguous figures control.

(d) Unless otherwise specified a provision for interest means interest at the judgment rate at the place of payment from the date of the instrument, or if it is undated from the date of issue.

(e) Unless the instrument otherwise specifies two or more persons who sign as maker, acceptor or drawer or indorser and as a part of the same transaction are jointly and severally liable even though the instrument contains such words as "I promise to pay."

(f) Unless otherwise specified consent to extension authorizes a single extension for not longer than the original period. A consent to extension, expressed in the instrument, is binding on secondary parties and accommodation makers. A holder may not exercise his option to extend an instrument over the objection of a maker or acceptor or other party who in accordance with Section 3604 tenders full payment when the instrument is due.

Sec. 3119. Other Writings Affecting Instrument. (1) As between the obligor and his immediate obligee or any transferee the terms of an instrument may be modified or affected by any other written agreement executed as a part of the same transaction, except that a holder in due course is not affected by any limitation of his rights arising out of the separate written agreement if he had no notice of the limitation when he took the instrument.

(2) A separate agreement does not affect the negotiability of an instrument.

Sec. 3120. Instruments "Payable Through" Bank. An instrument which states that it is "payable through" a bank or the like designates that bank as a collecting bank to make presentment but does not of itself authorize the bank to pay the instrument.

Sec. 3121. Instruments Payable at Bank. An instrument which states that it is payable at a bank is not of itself an order of authorization to the bank to pay it unless the bank is the drawee.

Sec. 3122. Accrual of Cause of Action. (1) A cause of action against a maker or an acceptor accrues

(a) In the case of a time instrument on the day after maturity;

(b) In the case of a demand instrument upon its date or, if no date is stated, on the date of issue.

(2) A cause of action against the obligor of a demand or time certificate of deposit accrues upon demand, but demand on a time certificate may not be made until on or after the date of maturity.

(3) A cause of action against a drawer of a draft or an indorser of any instrument accrues upon demand following dishonor of the instrument. Notice of dishonor is a demand.

(4) Unless an instrument provides otherwise, interest runs at the rate provided by law for a judgment.

(a) In the case of a maker, acceptor or other primary obligor of a demand instrument, from the date of demand;

(b) In all other cases from the date of accrual of the cause of action.

Sec. 3123. Maturity; Optional Bank Holidays. (1) Every instrument is payable at the time fixed therein without grace. When the day of maturity falls upon Sunday, Saturday or a holiday, the instrument is payable on the next succeeding business day which is not a Saturday. Where the day of maturity of the instrument falls on an optional bank holiday or the instrument would except for the foregoing provision be payable on an optional bank holiday and it is payable by or at a banking house or any branch or separate office thereof, and the particular banking house or branch or separate office thereof by or at which the instrument is payable is open for the transaction of business on such optional bank holiday, the holder of the instrument may at his option present the instrument for payment at the banking house or branch or separate office thereof by or at which the instrument is payable on the optional bank holiday or on the next succeeding business day which is not a Saturday. An instrument payable on demand is not to be presented for payment on Sunday, Saturday, or a holiday but is to be presented for payment on the next succeeding business day which is not a Saturday, except that where the instrument is payable by or at a banking house or branch or separate office thereof and the particular banking house or branch or separate office thereof by or at which the instrument is payable is open for the transaction of business on an optional bank holiday, the holder of the instrument may at his option present the instrument for payment at the banking house or branch or separate office thereof by or at which the instrument is payable on such optional bank holiday or on the next succeeding business day which is not a Saturday.

(2) For the purpose of this section "holiday" includes, if July 4th, September 9th, or December 25th falls on a Saturday, the preceding Friday.

(3) For the purpose of this section "optional bank holiday" means any closing of a bank because of an emergency, as that term is defined in the Bank Extraordinary Situation Closing Act (Chapter 20 commencing with Section 3600) of Division 1 of the Financial Code), Good Friday commencing at 3 p.m. and every holiday referred to in Sections 6700 and 6701 of the Government Code, except the following:

(a) January 1st.

(b) July 4th.

(c) September 9th, known as "Admission Day."

(d) December 25th.

(e) Any Monday following any Sunday on which January 1st, July 4th, September 9th or December 25th falls.

(f) The last Monday in May.

(g) The first Monday in September.

(h) Good Friday from 12 noon until 3 p.m.

(i) The Thursday in November appointed as Thanksgiving Day.

(j) Every Sunday.

CHAPTER 2

TRANSFER AND NEGOTIATION

Sec. 3201. Transfer; Right to Indorsement. (1) Transfer of an instrument vests in the transferee such rights as the transferor has therein, except that a transferee who has himself been a party to any fraud or illegality affecting the instrument or who as a prior holder had notice of a defense or claim against it cannot improve his position by taking from a later holder in due course.

(2) A transfer of a security interest in an instrument vests the foregoing rights in the transferee to the extent of the interest transferred.

(3) Unless otherwise agreed any transfer for value of an instrument not then payable to bearer gives the transferee the specifically enforceable right to have the unqualified indorsement of the transferor. Negotiation takes effect only when the indorsement is made and until that time there is no presumption that the transferee is the owner.

Sec. 3202. Negotiation. (1) Negotiation is the transfer of an instrument in such form that the transferee becomes a holder. If the instrument is payable to order it is negotiated by delivery with any necessary indorsement; if payable to bearer it is negotiated by delivery.

(2) An indorsement must be written by or on behalf of the holder and on the instrument or on a paper so firmly affixed thereto as to become a part thereof. An indorsement on a paper so affixed shall be valid and effective even though there is sufficient space on the instrument to write the indorsement.

(3) An indorsement is effective for negotiation only when it conveys the entire instrument or any unpaid residue. If it purports to be of less it operates only as a partial assignment.

(4) Words of assignment, condition, waiver, guaranty, limitation or disclaimer or liability and the like accompanying an indorsement do not affect its character as an indorsement.

Sec. 3203. Wrong or Misspelled Name. Where an instrument is made payable to a person under a misspelled name or one other than his own he may indorse in that name or his own or both; but signature in both names may be required by a person paying or giving value for the instrument.

Sec. 3204. Special Indorsement; Blank Indorsement. (1) A special indorsement specifies the person to whom or to whose order it makes the instrument payable. Any instrument specially indorsed becomes payable to the order of the special indorsee and may be further negotiated only by his endorsement.

(2) An indorsement in blank specifies no particular indorsee and may consist of a mere signature. An instrument payable to order and indorsed in blank becomes payable to bearer and may be negotiated by delivery alone until specially indorsed.

(3) The holder may convert a blank indorsement into a special indorsement by writing over the signature of the indorser in blank any contract consistent with the character of the indorsement.

Sec. 3205. Restrictive Indorsements. An indorsement is restrictive which either

(a) Is conditional; or

(b) Purports to prohibit further transfer of the instrument; or

(c) Includes the words "for collection," "for deposit," "pay any bank," or like terms signifying a purpose of deposit or collection; or

(d) Otherwise states that is is for the benefit or use of the indorser or of another person.

Sec. 3206. Effect of Restrictive Indorsement. (1) No restrictive indorsement prevents further transfer or negotiation of the instrument.

(2) An intermediary bank, or a payor bank which is not the depositary bank, is neither given notice nor otherwise affected by a restrictive indorsement of any person except the bank's immediate transferor or the person presenting for payment.

(3) Except for an intermediary bank, any transferee under an indorsement which is conditional or includes the words "for collection," "for deposit," "pay any bank," or like terms (paragraphs (a) and (c) of Section 3205) must pay or apply any value given by him for or on the security of the instrument consistently with the indorsement and to the extent that he does so he becomes a holder for value. In addition such transferee is a holder in due course if he otherwise complies with the requirements of Section 3302 on what constitutes a holder in due course.

(4) The first taker under an indorsement for the benefit of the indorser or another person (paragraph (d) of Section 3205) must pay or apply any value given by him for or on the security of the instrument consistently with the indorsement and to the extent that he does so he becomes a holder for value. In addition such taker is a holder in due course if he otherwise complies with the requirements of Section 3302 on what constitutes a holder in due course. A later holder for value is neither given notice nor otherwise affected by such restrictive indorsement unless he has knowledge that a fiduciary or other person has negotiated the instrument in any transaction for his own benefit or otherwise in breach of duty (subdivision (2) of Section 3304).

Sec. 3207. Negotiation Effective Although It May Be Rescinded. (1) Negotiation is effective to transfer the instrument although the negotiation is

(a) Made by an infant, a corporation exceeding its powers, or any other perso n without capacity; or

(b) Obtained by fraud, duress or mistake of any kind; or

(c) Part of an illegal transaction; or

(d) Made in breach of duty.

(2) Except as against a subsequent holder in due course such negotiation is in an appropriate case subject to rescission, the declaration of a constructive trust or any other remedy permitted by law.

Sec. 3208. Reacquisition. Where an instrument is returned to or reacquired by a prior party he may cancel any indorsement which is not necessary to his title and reissue or further negotiate the instrument, but any intervening party is discharged as against the reacquiring party and subsequent holders not in due course and if his indorsement has been cancelled is discharged as against subsequent holders in due course as well.

CHAPTER 3

RIGHTS OF A HOLDER

Sec. 3301. Rights of a Holder. The holder of an instrument whether or not he is the owner may transfer or negotiate it and, except as otherwise provided in Section 3603 on payment or satisfaction, discharge it or enforce payment in his own name.

Sec. 3302. Holder in Due Course. (1) A holder in due course is a holder who takes the instrument

(a) For value; and

(b) In good faith; and

(c) Without notice that it is overdue or has been dishonored or of any defense against or claim to it on the part of any person.

(2) A payee may be a holder in due course.

(3) A holder does not become a holder in due course of an instrument:

(a) By purchase of it at judicial sale or by taking it under legal process; or

(b) By acquiring it in taking over an estate; or

(c) By purchasing it as part of a bulk transaction not in regular course of business of the transferor.

(4) A purchaser of a limited interest can be a holder in due course only to the extent of the interest purchased.

Sec. 3303. Taking for Value. A holder takes the instrument for value

(a) To the extent that the agreed consideration has been performed or that he acquires a security interest in or a lien on the instrument otherwise than by legal process; or

(b) When he takes the instrument in payment of or as security for an antecedent claim against any person whether or not the claim is due; or

(c) When he gives a negotiable instrument for it or makes an irrevocable commitment to a third person.

Sec. 3304. Notice to Purchaser. (1) The purchaser has notice of a claim or defense if

(a) The instrument is so incomplete, bears such visible evidence of forgery or alteration, or is otherwise so irregular as to call into question its validity, terms or ownership or to create an ambiguity as to the party to pay; or

(b) The purchaser has notice that the obligation of any party is voidable in whole or in part, or that all parties have been discharged.

(2) The purchaser has notice of a claim against the instrument when he has knowledge that a fiduciary has negotiated the instrument in payment of or as security for his own debt or in any transaction for his own benefit or otherwise in breach of duty.

(3) The purchaser has notice that an instrument is overdue if he has reason to know

(a) That any part of the principal amount is overdue or that there is an uncured default in payment of another instrument of the same series; or

(b) That acceleration of the instrument has been made; or

(c) That he is taking a demand instrument after demand has been made or more than a reasonable length of time after its issue. A reasonable time for a check drawn and payable within the states and territories of the United States and the District of Columbia is presumed to be 30 days.

(4) Knowledge of the following facts does not of itself give the purchaser notice of a defense or claim

(a) That the instrument is antedated or postdated;

(b) That it was issued or negotiated in return for an executory promise or accompanied by a separate agreement, unless the purchaser has notice that a defense or claim has arisen from the terms thereof;

(c) That any party has signed for accommodation;

(d) That an incomplete instrument has been completed, unless the purchaser has notice of any improper completion;

(e) That any person negotiating the instrument is or was a fiduciary;

(f) That there has been default in payment of interest on the instrument or in payment of any other instrument, except one of the same series.

(5) The filing or recording of a document does not of itself constitute notice within the provisions of this division to a person who would otherwise be a holder in due course.

(6) To be effective notice must be received at such time and in such manner as to give a reasonable opportunity to act on it.

Sec. 3305.　**Rights if a Holder in Due Course.**　To the extent that a holder is a holder in due course he takes the instrument free from

(1) All claims to it on the part of any person; and

(2) All defenses of any party to the instrument with whom the holder has not dealt except

(a) Infancy, to the extent that it is a defense to a simple contract; and

(b) Such other incapacity, or duress, or illegality of the transaction, as renders the obligation of the party a nullity; and

(c) Such misrepresentation as has induced the party to sign the instrument with neither knowledge nor reasonable opportunity to obtain knowledge of its character or its essential terms; and

(d) Discharge in insolvency proceedings; and

(e) Any other discharge of which the holder has notice when he takes the instrument.

Sec. 3306.　**Rights of One Not Holder in Due Course.**　Unless he has the rights of a holder in due course any person takes the instrument subject to

(a) All valid claims to it on the part of any person; and

(b) All defenses of any party which would be available in an action on a simple contract; and

(c) The defenses of want or failure of consideration (Section 3408), nonperformance of any condition precedent, nondelivery, or delivery for a special purpose; and

(d) The defense that he or a person through whom he holds the instrument acquired it by theft, or that payment or satisfaction to such holder would be inconsistent with the terms of a restrictive indorsement. The claim of any third person to the instrument is not otherwise available as a defense to any party liable thereon unless the third person himself defends the action for such party.

Sec. 3307.　**Burden of Establishing Signatures, Defenses and Due Course.**　(1) Unless specifically denied in the pleading each signature on an instrument is admitted. When the effectiveness of a signature is put in issue

(a) The burden of establishing it is on the party claiming under the signature; but

(b) The signature is presumed to be genuine or authorized except where the action is to enforce the obligation of a purported signer who has died or become incompetent before proof is required.

(2) When signatures are admitted or established, production of the instrument entitles a holder to recover on it unless the defendant establishes a defense.

(3) After it is shown that a defense exists a person claiming the rights of a holder in due course has the burden of establishing that he or some person under whom he claims is in all respects a holder in due course.

CHAPTER 4

LIABILITY OF PARTIES

Sec. 3401.　**Signature.**　(1) No person is liable on an instrument unless his signature appears thereon.

(2) A signature is made by use of any name, including any trade or assumed name, upon an instrument, or by any word or mark used in lieu of a written signature.

Sec. 3402.　**Signature in Ambiguous Capacity.**　Unless the instrument clearly indicates that a signature is made in some other capacity it is an indorsement.

Sec. 3403.　**Signature by Authorized Representative.**　(1) A signature may be made by an agent or other representative, and his authority to make it may be established as in other cases of representation. No particular form of appointment is necessary to establish such authority.

(2) An authorized representative who signs his own name to an instrument

(a) Is personally obligated if the instrument neither names the person represented nor shows that the representative signed in a representative capacity;

(b) Except as otherwise established between the immediate parties, is personally obligated if the instrument names the person represented but does not show that the representative signed in a representative capacity, or if the instrument does not name the person represented but does show that the representative signed in a representative capacity.

(3) Except as otherwise established the name of an organization preceded or followed by the name and office of an authorized individual is a signature made in a representative capacity.

Sec. 3404.　**Unauthorized Signatures.**　(1) Any unauthorized signature is wholly inoperative as that of the person whose name is signed unless he ratifies it or is precluded from denying it; but it operates as the signature of the unauthorized signer in favor of any person who in good faith pays the instrument or takes it for value.

(2) Any unauthorized signature may be ratified for all purposes of this division. Such ratification does not of itself affect any rights of the person ratifying against the actual signer.

Sec. 3405.　**Imposters; Signature in Name of Payee.**　(1) An indorsement by any person in the name of a named payee is effective if

(a) An imposter by use of the mails or otherwise has induced the maker or drawer to issue the instrument to him or his confederate in the name of the payee; or

(b) A person signing as or on behalf of a maker or drawer intends the payee to have no interest in the instrument; or

(c) An agent or employee of the maker or drawer has supplied him with the name of the payee intending the latter to have no such interest.

(2) Nothing in this section shall affect the criminal or civil liability of the person so indorsing.

Sec. 3406.　**Negligence Contributing to Alteration or Unauthorized Signature.**　Any person who by his negligence substantially contributes to a material alteration of the instrument or to the making of an unauthorized signature is precluded from asserting the alteration or lack of authority against a holder in due course or against a drawee or other payor who pays the instrument in good faith and in accordance with the reasonable commercial standards of the drawee's or payor's business.

Sec. 3407.　**Alteration.**　(1) Any alteration of an instrument is material which changes the contract of any party thereto in any respect, including any such change in

(a) The number or relations of the parties; or

(b) An incomplete instrument, by completing it otherwise than as authorized; or

(c) The writing as signed, by adding to it or by removing any part of it.

(2) As against any person other than a subsequent holder in due course

(a) Alteration by the holder which is both fraudulent and material discharges any party whose contract is thereby changed unless that party assents or is precluded from asserting the defense;

(b) No other alteration discharges any party and the instrument may be enforced according to its original tenor, or as to incomplete instruments according to the authority given.

(3) A subsequent holder in due course may in all cases enforce the instrument according to its original tenor, and when an incomplete instrument has been completed, he may enforce it as completed.

Sec. 3408.　**Consideration.**　Want or failure of consideration is a defense as against any person not having the rights of a holder in due course (Section 3302), except that no consideration is necessary for an instrument or obligation thereon given in payment of or as security for an antecedent obligation of any kind. Nothing in this section shall be taken to displace any statute outside this code under which a promise is enforceable notwithstanding lack or failure of consideration. Partial failure of consideration is a defense pro tanto whether or not the failure is in an ascertained or liquidated amount.

Sec. 3409.　**Draft Not an Assignment.**　(1) A check or other draft does not of itself operate as an assignment of any funds in the hands of the drawee available for its payment, and the drawee is not liable on the instrument until he accepts it.

(2) Nothing in this section shall affect any liability in contract, tort or otherwise arising from any letter of credit or other obligation or representation which is not an acceptance.

Sec. 3410.　**Definition and Operation of Acceptance.**　Acceptance is the drawee's signed engagement to honor the draft as presented. It must be written on the draft, and may consist of his signature alone. It becomes operative when completed by delivery or notification.

(2) A draft may be accepted although it has not been signed by the drawer or is otherwise incomplete or is overdue or has been dishonored.

(3) Where the draft is payable at a fixed period after sight and the acceptor fails to date his acceptance the holder may complete it by supplying a date in good faith.

Sec. 3411. Certification of a Check.
(1) Certification of a check is acceptance. Where a holder procures certification the drawer and all prior indorsers are discharged.

(2) Unless otherwise agreed a bank has no obligation to certify a check.

(3) A bank may certify a check before returning it for lack of proper indorsement. If it does so the drawer is discharged.

Sec. 3412. Acceptance Varying Draft.
(1) Where the drawee's proffered acceptance in any manner varies the draft as presented the holder may refuse the acceptance and treat the draft as dishonored in which case the drawee is entitled to have his acceptance canceled.

(2) The terms of the draft are not varied by an acceptance to pay at any particular bank or place in the United States, unless the acceptance states that the draft is to be paid only at such bank or place.

(3) Where the holder assents to an acceptance varying the terms of the draft each drawer and indorser who does not affirmatively assent is discharged.

Sec. 3413. Contract of Maker, Drawer and Acceptor.
(1) The maker or acceptor engages that he will pay the instrument according to its tenor at the time of his engagement or as completed pursuant to Section 3115 on incomplete instruments.

(2) The drawer engages that upon dishonor of the draft and any necessary notice of dishonor or protest he will pay the amount of the draft to the holder or to any indorser who takes it up. The drawer may disclaim this liability by drawing without recourse.

(3) By making, drawing or accepting the party admits as against all subsequent parties including the drawee the existence of the payee and his then capacity to indorse.

Sec. 3414. Contract of Indorser; Order of Liability.
(1) Unless the indorsement otherwise specifies (as by such words as "without recourse") every indorser engages that upon dishonor and any necessary notice of dishonor and protest he will pay the instrument according to its tenor at the time of his indorsement to the holder or to any subsequent indorser who takes it up, even though the indorser who takes it up was not obligated to do so.

(2) Unless they otherwise agree indorsers are liable to one another in the order in which they indorse, which is presumed to be the order in which their signatures appear on the instrument.

Sec. 3415. Contract of Accommodation Party.
(1) An accommodation party is one who signs the instrument in any capacity for the purpose of lending his name to another party to it.

(2) When the instrument has been taken for value before it is due the accommodation party is liable in the capacity in which he has signed even though the taker knows of the accommodation.

(3) As against a holder in due course and without notice of the accommodation oral proof of the accommodation is not admissible to give the accommodation party the benefit of discharges dependent on his character as such. In other cases the accommodation character may be shown by oral proof.

(4) An indorsement which shows that it is not in the chain of title is notice of its accommodation character.

(5) An accommodation party is not liable to the party accommodated, and if he pays the instrument has a right of recourse on the instrument against such party.

Sec. 3416. Contract of Guarantor.
(1) "Payment guaranteed" or equivalent words added to a signature mean that the signer engages that if the instrument is not paid when due he will pay it according to its tenor without resort by the holder to any other party.

(2) "Collection guaranteed" or equivalent words added to a signature mean that the signer engages that if the instrument is not paid when due he will pay it according to its tenor, but only after the holder has reduced his claim against the maker or acceptor to judgment and execution has been returned unsatisfied, or after the maker or acceptor has become insolvent or it is otherwise apparent that it is useless to proceed against him.

(3) Words of guaranty which do not otherwise specify guarantee payment.

(4) No words of guaranty added to the signature of a sole maker or acceptor affect his liability on the instrument. Such words added to the signature of one of two or more makers or acceptors create a presumption that the signature is for the accommodation of the others.

(5) When words of guaranty are used presentment, notice of dishonor and protest are not necessary to charge the user.

(6) Any guaranty written on the instrument is enforceable notwithstanding any statute of frauds.

Sec. 3417. Warranties on Presentment and Transfer.
(1) Any person who obtains payment or acceptance and any prior transferor warrants to a person who in good faith pays or accepts that

(a) He has a good title to the instrument or is authorized to obtain payment or acceptance on behalf of one who has a good title; and

(b) He has no knowledge that the signature of the maker or drawer is unauthorized, except that this warranty is not given by a holder in due course acting in good faith

(i) To a maker with respect to the maker's own signature; or

(ii) To a drawer with respect to the drawer's own signature, whether or not the drawer is also the drawee; or

(iii) To an acceptor of a draft if the holder in due course took the draft after the acceptance or obtained the acceptance without knowledge that the drawer's signature was unauthorized; and

(c) The instrument has not been materially altered, except that this warranty is not given by a holder in due course acting in good faith

(i) To the maker of a note; or

(ii) To the drawer of a draft whether or not the drawer is also the drawee; or

(iii) To the acceptor of a draft with respect to an alteration made prior to the acceptance if the holder in due course took the draft after the acceptance, even though the acceptance provided "payable as originally drawn" or equivalent terms; or

(iv) To the acceptor of a draft with respect to an alteration made after the acceptance.

(2) Any person who transfers an instrument and receives consideration warrants to his transferee and if the transfer is by indorsement to any subsequent holder who takes the instrument in good faith that

(a) He has a good title to the instrument or is authorized to obtain payment or acceptance on behalf of one who has a good title and the transfer is otherwise rightful; and

(b) All signatures are genuine or authorized; and

(c) The instrument has not been materially altered; and

(d) No defense of any party is good against him; and

(e) He has no knowledge of any insolvency proceeding instituted with respect to the maker or acceptor or the drawer of an unaccepted instrument.

(3) By transferring "without recourse" the transferor limits the obligation stated in subdivision (2)(d) to a warranty that he has no knowledge of such a defense.

(4) A selling agent or broker who does not disclose the fact that he is acting only as such gives the warranties provided in this section, but if he makes such disclosure warrants only his good faith and authority.

Sec. 3418. Finality of Payment or Acceptance.
Except for recovery of bank payments as provided in the division on bank deposits and collections (Division 4) and except for liability for breach of warranty on presentment under the preceding section, payment or acceptance of any instrument is final in favor of a holder in due course, or a person who has in good faith changed his position in reliance on the payment.

Sec. 3419. Conversion of Instrument; Innocent Representative.
(1) An instrument is converted when

(a) A drawee to whom it is delivered or acceptance refuses to return it on demand; or

(b) Any person to whom it is delivered for payment refuses on demand either to pay or to return it; or

(c) It is paid on a forged indorsement.

(2) In any action under subdivision (1), the measure of liability is presumed to be the face amount of the instrument.

(3) Subject to the provisions of this code concerning restrictive indorsements a representative, including a depositary or collecting bank, who has in good faith and in accordance with the reasonable commercial standards applicable to the business of such representative dealt with an instrument or its proceeds on behalf of one who was not the true owner is not liable in conversion or otherwise to the true owner beyond the amount of any proceeds remaining in his hands.

(4) An intermediary bank or payor bank which is not a depositary bank is not liable in conversion solely by reason of the fact that proceeds of an item indorsed restrictively (Sections 3205 and 3206) are not paid or

applied consistently with the restrictive indorsement of an indorser other than its immediate transferor.

CHAPTER 5

PRESENTMENT, NOTICE OF DISHONOR AND PROTEST

Sec. 3501. When Presentment, Notice of Dishonor, and Protest Necessary or Permissible. (1) Unless excused (Section 3511) presentment is necessary to charge secondary parties as follows:

(a) Presentment for acceptance is necessary to charge the drawer and indorsers of a draft where the draft so provides, or is payable elsewhere than at the residence or place of business of the drawee, or its date of payment depends upon such presentment. The holder may at his option present for acceptance any other draft payable at a stated date;

(b) Presentment for payment is necessary to charge any indorser;

(c) In the case of any drawer, the acceptor of a draft payable at a bank or the maker of a note payable at a bank, presentment for payment is necessary, but failure to make presentment discharges such drawer, acceptor or maker only as stated in Section 3502(1)(b).

(2) Unless excused (Section 3511)

(a) Notice of any dishonor is necessary to charge any indorser;

(b) In the case of any drawer, the acceptor of a draft payable at a bank or the maker of a note payable at a bank, notice of any dishonor is necessary, but failure to give such notice discharges such drawer, acceptor or maker only as stated in Section 3502(1)(b).

(3) Unless excused (Section 3511) protest of any dishonor is necessary to charge the drawer and indorsers of any draft which on its face appears to be drawn or payable outside of the states and territories of the United States and the District of Columbia. The holder may at his option make protest of any dishonor of any other instrument and in the case of a foreign draft may on insolvency of the acceptor before maturity make protest for better security.

(4) Notwithstanding any provision of this section, neither presentment nor notice of dishonor nor protest is necessary to charge an indorser who has indorsed an instrument after maturity.

Sec. 3502. Unexcused Delay; Discharge. (1) Where without excuse any necessary presentment or notice of dishonor is delayed beyond the time when it is due

(a) Any indorser is discharged; and

(b) Any drawer or the acceptor of a draft payable at a bank or the maker of a note payable at a bank who because the drawee or payor bank becomes insolvent during the delay is deprived of funds maintained with the drawee or payor bank to cover the instrument may discharge his liability by written assignment to the holder of his rights against the drawee or payor bank in respect of such funds, but such drawer, acceptor or maker is not otherwise discharged.

(2) Where without excuse a necessary protest is delayed beyond the time when it is due any drawer or indorser is discharged.

Sec. 3503. Time of Presentment. (1) Unless a different time is expressed in the instrument the time for any presentment is determined as follows:

(a) Where an instrument is payable at or a fixed period after a stated date any presentment for acceptance must be made on or before the date it is payable;

(b) Where an instrument is payable after sight it must either be presented for acceptance or negotiated within a reasonable time after date or issue whichever is later;

(c) Where an instrument shows the date on which it is payable presentment for payment is due on that date;

(d) Where an instrument is accelerated presentment for payment is due within a reasonable time after the acceleration;

(e) With respect to the liability of any secondary party presentment for acceptance or payment of any other instrument is due within a reasonable time after such party becomes liable thereon.

(2) A reasonable time for presentment is determined by the nature of the instrument, any usage of banking or trade and the facts of the particular case. In the case of an uncertified check which is drawn and payable within the United States and which is not a draft drawn by a bank the following are presumed to be reasonable periods within which to present for payment or to initiate bank collection:

(a) With respect to the liability of the drawer, 30 days after date or issue whichever is later; and

(b) With respect to the liability of an indorser, seven days after his indorsement.

(3) Where any presentment is due on a day which is not a full business day for either the person making presentment or the party to pay or accept, presentment is due on the next following day which is a full business day for both parties.

(4) Presentment to be sufficient must be made at a reasonable hour, and if at a bank during its banking day.

Sec. 3504. How Presentment Made. (1) Presentment is a demand for acceptance or payment made upon the maker, acceptor, drawee or other payor by or on behalf of the holder.

(2) Presentment may be made

(a) By mail, in which event the time of presentment is determined by the time of receipt of the mail; or

(b) Through a clearinghouse or a place designated by the party who is to pay or accept; or

(c) At the place of acceptance or payment specified in the instrument or if there be none at the place of business or residence of the party to accept or pay. If neither the party to accept or pay nor anyone authorized to act for him is present or accessible at such place presentment is excused.

(3) It may be made

(a) To any one of two or more makers, acceptors, drawees or other payors; or

(b) To any person who has authority to make or refuse the acceptance or payment.

(4) A draft accepted or a note made payable at a bank in the United States must be presented at the separate office or branch of the bank at which such instrument was made payable.

(5) In the cases described in Section 4210 presentment may be made in the manner and with the result stated in that section.

Sec. 3505. Rights of Party to Whom Presentment Is Made. (1) The party to whom presentment is made may without dishonor require

(a) Exhibition of the instrument; and

(b) Reasonable identification of the person making presentment and evidence of his authority to make it if made for another; and

(c) That the instrument be produced for acceptance or payment at a place specified in it, or if there be none at any place reasonable in the circumstances; and

(d) A signed receipt on the instrument for any partial or full payment and its surrender upon full payment.

(2) Failure to comply with any such requirement invalidates the presentment but the person presenting has a reasonable time in which to comply and the time for acceptance or payment runs from the time of compliance.

Sec. 3506. Time Allowed for Acceptance or Payment. (1) Acceptance may be deferred without dishonor until the close of the next business day following presentment. The holder may also in a good faith effort to obtain acceptance and without either dishonor of the instrument or discharge of secondary parties allow postponement of acceptance for an additional business day.

(2) Except as a longer time is allowed in the case of documentary drafts drawn under a letter of credit, and unless an earlier time is agreed to by the party to pay, payment of an instrument may be deferred without dishonor pending reasonable examination to determine whether it is properly payable, but payment must be made in any event before the close of business on the day of presentment.

Sec. 3507. Dishonor; Holder's Right of Recourse; Term Allowing Re-Presentment. (1) An instrument is dishonored when

(a) A necessary or optional presentment is duly made and due acceptance or payment is refused or cannot be obtained within the prescribed time or in case of bank collections the instrument is seasonably returned by the midnight deadline (Section 4301); or

(b) Presentment is excused and the instrument is not duly accepted or paid.

(2) Subject to any necessary notice of dishonor and protest, the holder has upon dishonor an immediate right of recourse against the drawers and indorsers.

(3) Return of an instrument for lack of proper indorsement is not dishonor.

(4) A term in a draft or an indorsement thereof allowing a stated time for re-presentment in the event of any dishonor of the draft by nonacceptance if a time draft or by nonpayment if a sight draft gives the holder

as against any secondary party bound by the term an option to waive the dishonor without affecting the liability of the secondary party and he may present again up to the end of the stated time.

Sec. 3508. Notice of Dishonor. (1) Notice of dishonor may be given to any person who may be liable on the instrument by or on behalf of the holder or any party who has himself received notice, or any other party who can be compelled to pay the instrument. In addition an agent or bank in whose hands the instrument is dishonored may give notice to his principal or customer or to another agent or bank from which the instrument was received.

(2) Any necessary notice must be given by a bank before its midnight deadline and by any other person before midnight of the third business day after dishonor or receipt of notice of dishonor.

(3) Notice may be given in any reasonable manner. It may be oral or written and in any terms which identify the instrument and state that it has been dishonored. A misdescription which does not mislead the party notified does not vitiate the notice. Sending the instrument bearing a stamp, ticket or writing stating that acceptance or payment has been refused or sending a notice of debt with respect to the instrument is sufficient.

(4) Written notice is given when sent although it is not received.

(5) Notice to one partner is notice to each although the firm has been dissolved.

(6) When any party is in insolvency proceedings instituted after the issue of the instrument notice may be given either to the party or to the representative of his estate.

(7) When any party is dead or incompetent notice may be sent to his last known address or given to his personal representative.

(8) Notice operates for the benefit of all parties who have rights on the instrument against the party notified.

Sec. 3509. Protest; Noting for Protest. (1) A protest is a certificate of dishonor made under the hand and seal of a United States consul or vice consul or a notary public or other person authorized to certify dishonor by the law of the place where dishonor occurs. It may be made upon information satisfactory to such person.

(2) The protest must identify the instrument and certify either that due presentment has been made or the reason why it is excused and that the instrument has been dishonored by nonacceptance or nonpayment.

(3) The protest may also certify that notice of dishonor has been given to all parties or to specified parties.

(4) Subject to subdivision (5) any necessary protest is due by the time that notice of dishonor is due.

(5) If, before protest is due, an instrument has been noted for protest by the officer to make protest, the protest may be made at any time thereafter as of the date of the noting.

Sec. 3510. Evidence of Dishonor and Notice of Dishonor. The following are admissible as evidence and create a presumption of dishonor and of any notice of dishonor therein shown:

(a) A document regular in form as provided in the preceding section which purports to be a protest;

(b) The purported stamp or writing of the drawee, payor bank or presenting bank on the instrument or accompanying it stating that acceptance or payment has been refused for reasons consistent with dishonor;

(c) Any book or record of the drawee, payor bank, or any collecting bank kept in the usual course of business which shows dishonor, even though there is no evidence of who made the entry.

Sec. 3511. Waived or Excused Presentment, Protest or Notice of Dishonor or Delay Therein. (1) Delay in presentment, protest or notice of dishonor is excused when the party is without notice that it is due or when the delay is caused by circumstances beyond his control and he exercises reasonable diligence after the cause of the delay ceases to operate.

(2) Presentment or notice or protest as the case may be is entirely excused when

(a) The party to be charged has waived it expressly or by implication either before or after it is due; or

(b) Such party has himself dishonored the instrument or has countermanded payment or otherwise has no reason to expect or right to require that the instrument be accepted or paid; or

(c) By reasonable diligence the presentment or protest cannot be made or the notice given.

(3) Presentment is also entirely excused when

(a) The maker, acceptor or drawee of any instrument except a documentary draft is dead or in insolvency proceedings instituted after the issue of the instrument; or

(b) Acceptance or payment is refused but not for want of proper presentment.

(4) Where a draft has been dishonored by nonacceptance a later presentment for payment and any notice of dishonor and protest for nonpayment are excused unless in the meantime the instrument has been accepted.

(5) A waiver of protest is also a waiver of presentment and of notice of dishonor even though protest is not required.

(6) Where a waiver of presentment or notice of protest is embodied in the instrument itself it is binding upon all parties; but where it is written above the signature of an indorser it binds him only.

CHAPTER 6

DISCHARGE

Sec. 3601. Discharge of Parties. (1) The extent of the discharge of any party from liability on an instrument is governed by the sections on

(a) Payment or satisfaction (Section 3603); or

(b) Tender of payment (Section 3604); or

(c) Cancellation or renunciation (Section 3605); or

(d) Impairment of right of recourse or of collateral (Section 3606); or

(e) Reacquisition of the instrument by a prior party (Section 3208); or

(f) Fraudulent and material alteration (Section 3407); or

(g) Certification of a check (Section 3411); or

(h) Acceptance varying a draft (Section 3412); or

(i) Unexcused delay in presentment or notice of dishonor or protest (Section 3502).

(2) Any party is also discharged from his liability on an instrument to another party by any other act or agreement with such party which would discharge his simple contract for the payment of money.

(3) The liability of all parties is discharged when any party who has himself no right of action or recourse on the instrument

(a) Reacquires the instrument in his own right; or

(b) Is discharged under any provision of this division, except as otherwise provided with respect to discharge for impairment of recourse or of collateral (Section 3606).

Sec. 3602. Effect of Discharge Against Holder in Due Course. No discharge of any party provided by this division is effective against a subsequent holder in due course unless he has notice thereof when he takes the instrument.

Sec. 3603. Payment or Satisfaction. (1) The liability of any party is discharged to the extent of his payment or satisfaction to the holder even though it is made with knowledge of a claim of another person to the instrument unless prior to such payment or satisfaction the person making the claim either supplies indemnity deemed adequate by the party seeking the discharge or enjoins payment or satisfaction by order of a court of competent jurisdiction in an action in which the adverse claimant and the holder are parties. This subdivision does not, however, result in the discharge of the liability

(a) Of a party who in bad faith pays or satisfies a holder who acquired the instrument by theft or who (unless having the rights of a holder in due course) holds through one who so acquired it; or

(b) Of a party (other than an intermediary bank or a payor bank which is not a depositary bank) who pays or satisfies the holder of an instrument which has been restrictively indorsed in a manner not consistent with the terms of such restrictive indorsement.

(2) Payment or satisfaction may be made with the consent of the holder by any person including a stranger to the instrument. Surrender of the instrument to such a person gives him the rights of a transferee (Section 3201).

Sec. 3604. Tender of Payment. (1) Any party making tender of full payment to a holder when or after it is due is discharged to the extent of all subsequent liability for interest, costs and attorney's fees.

(2) The holder's refusal of such tender wholly discharges any party who has a right of recourse against the party making the tender.

(3) Where the maker or acceptor of an instrument payable otherwise than on demand is able and ready to pay at every place of payment specified in the instrument when it is due, it is equivalent to tender.

Sec. 3605. **Cancellation and Renunciation.** (1) The holder of an instrument may even without consideration discharge any party

(a) In any manner apparent on the face of the instrument or the indorsement, as by intentionally canceling the instrument or the party's signature by destruction or mutilation, or by striking out the party's signature; or

(b) By renouncing his rights by a writing signed and delivered or by surrender of the instrument to the party to be discharged.

(2) Neither cancellation nor renunciation without surrender of the instrument affects the title thereto.

Sec. 3606. **Impairment of Recourse or of Collateral.** (1) The holder discharges any party to the instrument to the extent that without such party's consent the holder

(a) Without express reservation of rights releases or agrees not to sue any person against whom the party has to the knowledge of the holder a right of recourse or agrees to suspend the right to enforce against such person the instrument or collateral or otherwise discharges such person, except that failure or delay in effecting any required presentment, protest or notice of dishonor with respect to any such person does not discharge any party as to whom presentment, protest or notice of dishonor is effective or unnecessary; or

(b) Unjustifiably impairs any collateral for the instrument given by or on behalf of the party or any person against whom he has a right of recourse.

(2) By express reservation of rights against a party with a right of recourse the holder preserves

(a) All his rights against such party as of the time when the instrument was originally due; and

(b) The right of the party to pay the instrument as of that time; and

(c) All rights of such party to recourse against others.

CHAPTER 7

ADVICE OF INTERNATIONAL SIGHT DRAFT

Sec. 3701. **Letter of Advice of International Sight Draft.** (1) A "letter of advice" is a drawer's communication to the drawee that a described draft has been drawn.

(2) Unless otherwise agreed when a bank receives from another bank a letter of advice of an international sight draft the drawee bank may immediately debit the drawer's account and stop the running of interest pro tanto. Such a debit and any resulting credit to any account covering outstanding draft leaves in the drawer full power to stop payment or otherwise dispose of the amount and creates no trust or interest in favor of the holder.

(3) Unless otherwise agreed and except where a draft is drawn under a credit issued by the drawee, the drawee of an international sight draft owes the drawer no duty to pay an unadvised draft but if it does so and the draft is genuine, may appropriately debit the drawer's account.

CHAPTER 8

MISCELLANEOUS

Sec. 3801. **Drafts in a Set.** (1) Where a draft is drawn in a set of parts, each of which is numbered and expressed to be an order only if no other part has been honored, the whole of the parts constitutes one draft but a taker of any part may become a holder in due course of the draft.

(2) Any person who negotiates, indorses or accepts a single part of a draft drawn in a set thereby becomes liable to any holder in due course of that part as if it were the whole set, but as between different holders in due course to whom different parts have been negotiated the holder whose title first accrues has all rights to the draft and its proceeds.

(3) As against the drawee the first presented part of a draft drawn in a set is the part entitled to payment, or if a time draft to acceptance and payment. Acceptance of any subsequently presented part renders the drawee liable thereon under subdivision (2). With respect both to a holder and to the drawer payment of a subsequently presented part of a draft payable at sight has the same effect as payment of a check notwithstanding an effective stop order (Section 4407).

(4) Except as otherwise provided in this section, where any part of a draft in a set is discharged by payment or otherwise the whole draft is discharged.

Sec. 3802. **Effect of Instrument on Obligation for Which It Is Given.** (1) Unless otherwise agreed where an instrument is taken for an underlying obligation

(a) The obligation is pro tanto discharged if a bank is drawer, maker or acceptor of the instrument and there is no recourse on the instrument against the underlying obligor; and

(b) In any other case the obligation is suspended pro tanto until the instrument is due or if it is payable on demand until its presentment. If the instrument is dishonored action may be maintained on either the instrument or the obligation; discharge of the underlying obligor on the instrument also discharges him on the obligation.

(2) The taking in good faith of a check which is not postdated does not of itself so extend the time on the original obligation as to discharge a surety.

Sec. 3803. **Notice to Third Party.** Where a defendant is sued for breach of an obligation for which a third person is answerable over under this division he may give the third person written notice of the litigation, and the person notified may then give similar notice to any other person who is answerable over to him under this division. If the notice states that the person notified may come in and defend and that if the person notified does not do so he will in any action against him by the person giving the notice be bound by any determination of fact common to the two litigations, then unless after seasonable receipt of the notice the person notified does come in and defend he is so bound.

Sec. 3804. **Lost, Destroyed or Stolen Instruments.** The owner of an instrument which is lost, whether by destruction, theft or otherwise, may maintain an action in his own name and recover from any party liable thereon upon due proof of his ownership, the facts which prevent his production of the instrument and its terms. The court shall require a sufficient indemnity bond indemnifying the defendant against loss by reason of further claims on the instrument.

Sec. 3805. **Instruments Not Payable to Order or to Bearer.** This division applies to any instrument whose terms do not preclude transfer and which is otherwise negotiable within this division but which is not payable to order or to bearer, except that there can be no holder in due course of such an instrument.

DIVISION 4

BANK DEPOSITS AND COLLECTIONS

CHAPTER 1

GENERAL PROVISIONS AND DEFINITIONS

Sec. 4101. **Short Title.** This division shall be known and may be cited as Uniform Commercial Code Bank Deposits and Collections.

Sec. 4102. **Applicability.** (1) To the extent that items within this division are also within the scope of Divisions 3 and 8, they are subject to the provisions of those divisions. In the event of conflict the provisions of this division govern those of Division 3 but the provisions of Division 8 govern those of this division.

(2) The liability of a bank for action or nonaction with respect to any item handled by it for purposes of presentment, payment or collection is governed by the law of the place where the bank is located. In the case of action or nonaction by or at a branch or separate office of a bank, its liability is governed by the law of the place where the branch or separate office is located.

Sec. 4103. **Variation by Agreement; Measure of Damages; Certain Action Constituting Ordinary Care.** (1) The effect of the provisions of this division may be varied by agreement except that no agreement can disclaim a bank's responsibility for its own lack of good faith or failure to exercise ordinary care or can limit the measure of damages for such lack or failure; but the parties may by agreement determine the standards by which such responsibility is to be measured if such standards are not manifestly unreasonable.

(2) Federal Reserve regulations and operating letters, clearinghouse rules, and the like, have the effect of agreements under subdivision (1), whether or not specifically assented to by all parties interested in items handled.

(3) Action or nonaction approved by this division or pursuant to Federal Reserve regulations or operating letters constitutes the exercise of ordinary care and, in the absence of special instructions, action or nonaction consistent with clearinghouse rules and the like or with a general banking usage not disapproved by this division, prima facie constitutes the exercise of ordinary care.

(4) The specification or approval of certain procedures by this division does not constitute disapproval of other procedures which may be reasonable under the circumstances.

(5) The measure of damages for failure to exercise ordinary care in handling an item is the amount of the item reduced by an amount which could not have been realized by the use of ordinary care, and where there is bad faith it includes other damages, if any, suffered by the party as a proximate consequence.

Sec. 4104. **Definitions and Index of Definitions.** (1) In this division unless the context otherwise requires

(a) "Account" means any account with a bank and includes a checking, time, interest or savings account;

(b) "Afternoon" means the period of a day between noon and midnight;

(c) "Banking day" means that part of any day on which a bank is open to the public for carrying on substantially all of its banking functions;

(d) "Clearinghouse" means any association of banks or other payors regularly clearing items;

(e) "Customer" means any person having an account with a bank or for whom a bank has agreed to collect items and includes a bank carrying an account with another bank;

(f) "Documentary draft" means any negotiable or nonnegotiable draft with accompanying documents, securities or other papers to be delivered against honor of the draft;

(g) "Item" means any instrument for the payment of money even though it is not negotiable but does not include money;

(h) "Midnight deadline" with respect to a bank is midnight on its next banking day following the banking day on which it receives the relevant item or notice or from which the time for taking action commences to run, whichever is later;

(i) "Properly payable" includes the availability of funds for payment at the time of decision to pay or dishonor;

(j) "Settle" means to pay in cash by clearinghouse settlement, in a charge or credit or by remittance, or otherwise as instructed. A settlement may be either provisional or final;

(k) "Suspends payments" with respect to a bank means that it has been closed by order of the supervisory authorities, that a public officer has been appointed to take it over or that it ceases or refuses to make payments in the ordinary course of business.

(2) Other definitions applying to this division and the sections in which they appear are:

"Collecting bank." Section 4105.
"Depositary bank." Section 4105.
"Intermediary bank." Section 4105.
"Payor bank." Section 4105.
"Presenting bank." Section 4105.
"Remitting bank." Section 4105.

(3) The following definitions in other divisions apply to this division:

"Acceptance." Section 3410.
"Certificate of deposit." Section 3104.
"Certification." Section 3411.
"Check." Section 3104.
"Draft." Section 3104.
"Holder in due course." Section 3302.
"Notice of dishonor." Section 3508.
"Presentment." Section 3504.
"Protest." Section 3509.
"Secondary party." Section 3102.

(4) In addition Division 1 contains general definitions and principles of construction and interpretation applicable throughout this division.

Sec. 4105. **"Depositary Bank"; "Intermediary Bank" "Collecting Bank"; "Payor Bank"; "Presenting Bank"; "Remitting Bank."** In this division unless the context otherwise requires:

(a) "Depositary bank" means the first bank to which an item is transferred for collection even though it is also the payor bank;

(b) "Payor bank" means a bank by which an item is payable as drawn or accepted;

(c) "Intermediary bank" means any bank to which an item is transferred in course of collection except the depositary or payor bank;

(d) "Collecting bank" means any bank handling the item for collection except the payor bank;

(e) "Presenting bank" means any bank presenting an item except a payor bank;

(f) "Remitting bank" means any payor or intermediary bank remitting for an item.

(g) Each branch or separate office of a bank shall be deemed a separate bank for the purpose of the definitions in this section.

Sec. 4106. **Separate Office of Bank.** A branch or separate office of a bank is a separate bank for the purpose of computing the time within which and determining the place at or to which action may be taken or notices or orders shall be given under this division and under Division 3, and the receipt of any notice or order by, or the knowledge of, one branch or separate office of a bank is not actual or constructive notice to or knowledge of any other branch or separate office of the same bank and does not impair the right of such other branch or separate office to be a holder in due course of an item.

Sec. 4107. **Time of Receipt of Items.** (1) For the purpose of allowing time to process items, prove balances and make the necessary entries on its books to determine its position for the day, a bank may fix an afternoon hour of 2 p.m. or later as a cutoff hour for the handling of money and items and the making of entries on its books.

(2) Any item or deposit of money received on any day after a cutoff hour so fixed or after the close of the banking day may be treated as being received at the opening of the next banking day.

Sec. 4108. **Delays.** (1) Unless otherwise instructed, a collecting bank in a good faith effort to secure payment may, in the case of specific items and with or without the approval of any person involved, waive, modify or extend time limits imposed or permitted by this code for a period not in excess of an additional bank day without discharge of secondary parties and without liability to its transferor or any prior party.

(2) Delay by a collecting bank or payor bank beyond time limits prescribed or permitted by this code or by instructions is excused if caused by interruption of communication facilities, suspension of payments by another bank, war, emergency conditions or other circumstances beyond the control of the bank provided it exercises such diligence as the circumstances require.

CHAPTER 2

COLLECTION OF ITEMS: DEPOSITARY AND COLLECTING BANKS

Sec. 4201. **Presumption and Duration of Agency Status of Collecting Banks and Provisional Status of Credits; Applicability of Article; Item Indorsed "Pay Any Bank."** (1) Unless a contrary intent clearly appears and prior to the time that a settlement given by a collecting bank for an item is or becomes final (subdivision (3) of Section 4211 and Sections 4212 and 4213) the bank is an agent or subagent of the owner of the item and any settlement given for the item is provisional. This provision applies regardless of the form of indorsement or lack of indorsement and even though credit given for the item is subject to immediate withdrawal as of right or is in fact withdrawn; but the continuance of ownership of an item by its owner and any rights of the owner to proceeds of the item are subject to rights of a collecting bank such as those resulting from outstanding advances on the item and valid rights of setoff. When an item is handled by banks for purposes of presentment, payment and collection, the relevant provisions of this division apply even though action of parties clearly establishes that a particular bank has purchased the item and is the owner of it.

(2) After an item has been indorsed with the words "pay any bank" or the like, only a bank may acquire the rights of a holder

(a) Until the item has been returned to the customer initiating collection; or

(b) Until the item has been specially endorsed by a bank to a person who is not a bank.

Sec. 4202. Responsibility for Collection; When Action Seasonable. (1) A collecting bank must use ordinary care in

(a) Presenting an item or sending it for presentment; and

(b) Sending notice of dishonor or nonpayment or returning an item other than a documentary draft to the bank's transferor after learning that the item has not been paid or accepted, as the case may be; and

(c) Settling for an item when the bank receives final settlement; and

(d) Making or providing for any necessary protest; and

(e) Notifying its transferor of any loss or delay in transit within a reasonable time after discovery thereof.

(2) A collecting bank taking proper action before its midnight deadline following receipt of an item, notice or payment acts seasonably; taking proper action within a reasonably longer time may be seasonable but the bank has the burden of so establishing.

(3) Subject to subdivision (1)(a), a bank is not liable for the insolvency, neglect, misconduct, mistake or default of another bank or person or for loss or destruction of or inability to obtain repossession of an item in transit or in the possession of others.

Sec. 4203. Effect of Instructions. Subject to the provisions of Division 3 concerning conversion of instruments (Section 3419) and the provisions of both Division 3 and this division concerning restrictive indorsements only a collecting bank's transferor can give instructions which affect the bank or constitute notice to it and a collecting bank is not liable to prior parties for any action taken pursuant to such instructions or in accordance with any agreement with its transferor.

Sec. 4204. Methods of Sending and Presenting; Sending Direct to Payor Bank. (1) A collecting bank must send items by reasonably prompt method taking into consideration any relevant instructions, the nature of the item, the number of such items on hand, and the cost of collection involved and the method generally used by it or others to present such items.

(2) A collecting bank may send

(a) Any item direct to the payor bank;

(b) Any item to any nonbank payor if authorized by its transferor;

(c) Any item other than documentary drafts to any nonbank payor, if authorized by Federal Reserve regulation or operating letter, clearinghouse rule or the like;

(d) Any item to any Federal Reserve bank; and

(e) Any item to any other bank or agency thereof.

Items may be sent to the place of business of, or to any place designated by, those to whom items may be sent under paragraphs (a), (b), (c), (d) or (e).

Sec. 4205. Supplying Missing Indorsement; No Notice from Prior Indorsement. (1) A depositary bank which has taken an item for collection may supply any indorsement of the customer which is necessary to title unless the item contains the words "payee's indorsement required" or the like. In the absence of such a requirement a statement placed on the item by the depositary bank to the effect that the item was deposited by a customer or credited to his account is effective as the customer's indorsement.

(2) An intermediary bank, or payor bank which is not a depositary bank, is neither given notice nor otherwise affected by a restrictive indorsement of any person except the bank's immediate transferor.

Sec. 4206. Transfer Between Banks. Any agreed method which identifies the transferor bank is sufficient for the item's further transfer to another bank.

Sec. 4207. Warranties of Customer and Collecting Bank on Transfer or Presentment of Items; Time for Claims. (1) Each customer or collecting bank who obtains payment or acceptance of an item and each prior customer and collecting bank warrants to the payor bank or other payor who in good faith pays or accepts the item that

(a) He has a good title to the item or is authorized to obtain payment or acceptance on behalf of one who has a good title; and

(b) He has no knowledge that the signature of the maker or drawer is unauthorized, except that this warranty is not given by any customer or collecting bank that is a holder in due course and acts in good faith

(i) To a maker with respect to the maker's own signature; or

(ii) To a drawer with respect to the drawer's own signature, whether or not the drawer is also the drawee; or

(iii) To an acceptor of an item if the holder in due course took the item after the acceptance or obtained the acceptance without knowledge that the drawer's signature was unauthorized; and

(c) The item has not been materially altered, except that this warranty is not given by any customer or collecting bank that is a holder in due course and acts in good faith

(i) To the maker of a note; or

(ii) To the drawer of a draft whether or not the drawer is also the drawee; or

(iii) To the acceptor of an item with respect to an alteration made prior to the acceptance if the holder in due course took the item after the acceptance, even though the acceptance provided "payable as originally drawn" or equivalent terms; or

(iv) To the acceptor of an item with respect to an alteration made after the acceptance.

(2) Each customer and collecting bank who transfers an item and receives a settlement or other consideration for it warrants to his transferee and to any subsequent collecting bank who takes the item in good faith that

(a) He has a good title to the item or is authorized to obtain payment or acceptance on behalf of one who has a good title and the transfer is otherwise rightful; and

(b) All signatures are genuine or authorized; and

(c) The item has not been materially altered; and

(d) No defense of any party is good against him; and

(e) He has no knowledge of any involvency proceeding instituted with respect to the maker or acceptor or the drawer of an unaccepted item.

In addition each customer and collecting bank so transferring an item and receiving a settlement or other consideration engages that upon dishonor and any necessary notice of dishonor and protest he will take up the item.

(3) The warranties and the engagement to honor set forth in the two preceding subdivisions arise notwithstanding the absence of indorsement or words of guaranty or warranty in the transfer or presentment and a collecting bank remains liable for their breach despite remittance to its transferor. Damages for breach of such warranties or engagement to honor shall not exceed the consideration received by the customer or collecting bank responsible plus finance charges and expenses related to the item, if any.

(4) Unless a claim for breach of warranty under this section is made within a reasonable time after the person claiming learns of the breach, the person liable is discharged to the extent of any loss caused by the delay in making claim.

Sec. 4208. Security Interest of Collecting Bank in Items, Accompanying Documents and Proceeds. (1) A bank has a security interest in an item and any accompanying documents or the proceeds of either

(a) In case of an item deposited in an account to the extent to which credit given for the item has been withdrawn or applied;

(b) In case of an item for which it has given credit available for withdrawal as of right, to the extent of the credit given whether or not the credit is drawn upon and whether or not there is a right of chargeback; or

(c) If it makes an advance on or against the item.

(2) When credit which has been given for several items received at one time or pursuant to a single agreement is withdrawn or applied in part the security interest remains upon all the items and any accompanying documents or the proceeds of either. For the purpose of this section, credits first given are first withdrawn.

(3) Receipt by a collecting bank of a final settlement for an item is a realization on its security interest in the item, accompanying documents and proceeds. To the extent and so long as the bank does not receive final settlement for the item or give up possession of the item or accompanying documents for purposes other than collection, the security interest continues and is subject to the provisions of Division 9 except that

(a) No security agreement is necessary to make the security interest enforceable (subdivision (1)(b)of Section 9203); and

(b) No filing is required to perfect the security interest; and

(c) The security interest has priority over conflicting perfected security interests in the item, accompanying documents or proceeds.

Sec. 4209. When Bank Gives Value for Purposes of Holder in Due Course. For purposes of determining its status as a holder in due course, the bank has given value to the extent that it has a security interest in an item provided that the bank otherwise complies with the requirements of Section 3302 on what constitutes a holder in due course.

Sec. 4210. Presentment by Notice of Item Not Payable by, Through or at a Bank; Liability of Secondary Parties. (1) Unless otherwise instructed, a collecting bank may present an item not payable by, through or at a bank by sending to the party to accept or pay a written notice that the bank holds the item for acceptance or payment. The notice must be sent in time to be received on or before the day when presentment is due and the bank must meet any requirement of the party to accept or pay under Section 3505 by the close of the bank's next banking day after it knows of the requirement.

(2) Where presentment is made by notice and neither honor nor request for compliance with a requirement under Section 3505 is received by the close of business on the day after maturity or in the case of demand items by the close of business on the third banking day after notice was sent, the presenting bank may treat the item as dishonored and charge any secondary party by sending him notice of the facts.

Sec. 4211. Media of Remittance; Provisional and Final Settlement in Remittance Cases.
(1) A collecting bank may take in settlement of an item

(a) A check of the remitting bank or of another bank on any bank except the remitting bank; or

(b) A cashier's check or similar primary obligation of a remitting bank which is a member of or clears through a member of the same clearing-house or group as the collecting bank; or

(c) Appropriate authority to charge an account of the remitting bank or of another bank with the collecting bank; or

(d) If the item is drawn upon or payable by a person other than a bank, a cashier's check, certified check or other bank check or obligation; or

(e) Credit on the books of any federal reserve bank or of any bank designated as a depositary by the collecting bank; or

(f) Money.

(2) If before its midnight deadline the collecting bank properly dishonors a remittance check or authorization to charge on itself or presents or forwards for collection a remittance instrument of or on another bank which is of a kind approved by subdivision (1) or has not been authorized by it, the collecting bank is not liable to prior parties in the event of the dishonor of such check, instrument or authorization.

(3) A settlement for an item by means of a remittance instrument or authorization to charge is or becomes a final settlement as to both the person making and the person receiving the settlement

(a) If the remittance instrument or authorization to charge is of a kind approved by subdivision (1) or has not been authorized by the person receiving the settlement and in either case the person receiving the settlement acts seasonably before its midnight deadline in presenting, forwarding for collection or paying the instrument or authorization—at the time the remittance instrument or authorization is finally paid by the payor by which it is payable;

(b) If the person receiving the settlement has authorized remittance by a nonbank check or obligation or by a cashier's check or similar primary obligation of or a check upon the payor or other remitting bank which is not of a kind approved by subdivision (1)(b)—at the time of the receipt of such remittance check or obligation; or

(c) If in a case not covered by paragraphs (a) or (b) the person receiving the settlement fails to seasonably present, forward for collection, pay or return a remittance instrument or authorization to it to charge before its midnight deadline—at such midnight deadline.

Sec. 4212. Right of Charge-Back or Refund.
(1) If a collecting bank has made provisional settlement with its customer for an item and itself fails by reason of dishonor, suspension of payments by a bank or otherwise to receive a settlement for the item which is or becomes final, the bank may revoke the settlement given by it, charge back the amount of any credit given for the item to its customer's account or obtain refund from its customer whether or not it is able to return the items if by its midnight deadline or within a longer reasonable time after it learns the facts it returns the item or sends notification of the facts. These rights to revoke, charge back and obtain refund terminate if and when a settlement for the item received by the bank is or becomes final (subdivision (3) of Section 4211 and subdivisions (2) and (3) of Section 4213).

(2) [Reserved.]

(3) A depositary bank which is also the payor may charge back the amount of an item to its customer's account or obtain refund in accordance with the section governing return of an item received by a payor bank for credit on its books (Section 4301).

(4) The right to charge back is not affected by

(a) Prior use of the credit given for the item; or

(b) Failure by any bank to exercise ordinary care with respect to the item but any bank so failing remains liable.

(5) A failure to charge back or claim refund does not affect other rights of the bank against the customer or any other party.

(6) If credit is given in dollars as the equivalent of the value of an item payable in a foreign currency the dollar amount of any chargeback or refund shall be calculated on the basis of the buying sight rate for the foreign currency prevailing on the day when the person entitled to the chargeback or refund learns that it will not receive payment in ordinary course.

(7) The right to obtain refund is not affected by

(a) Prior use of the credit given for the item; or

(b) Failure by any bank to exercise ordinary care with respect to the item except to the extent of the bank's liability therefor.

Sec. 4213. Final Payment of Item by Payor Bank; When Provisional Debits and Credits Become Final; When Certain Credits Become Available for Withdrawal.
(1) An item is finally paid by a payor bank when the bank has done any of the following, whichever happens first:

(a) Paid the item in cash; or

(b) Settled for the item without having a right to revoke the settlement under any of the following: statute, clearinghouse rule, agreement, or reservation thereof; or

(c) [Reserved.]

(d) Settled for the item having a right to revoke the settlement under any one or more of the following: statute, clearinghouse rule, agreement or reservation thereof, and failed to revoke the settlement in the time and manner permitted under such right.

Upon final payment under paragraphs (b) or (d) the payor bank shall be accountable for the amount of the item.

(2) If provisional settlement for an item between the presenting and payor banks is made through a clearinghouse or by debits or credits in an account between them, then to the extent that provisional debits or credits for the item are entered in accounts between the presenting and payor banks or between the presenting and successive prior collecting banks seriatim, they become final upon final payment of the item by the payor bank.

(3) If a collecting bank receives a settlement for an item which is or becomes final (subdivision (3) of Section 4211, subdivision (2) of this section) the bank is accountable to its customer for the amount of the item and any provisional credit given for the item in an account with its customer becomes final.

(4) Subject to any right of the bank to apply the credit to an obligation of the customer, credit given by a bank for an item in an account with its customer becomes available for withdrawal as of right

(a) In any case where the bank has received a provisional settlement for the item—when such settlement becomes final and the bank has had a reasonable time to learn that the settlement is final;

(b) In any case where the bank is both a depositary bank and a payor bank and the item is finally paid at the opening of the bank's second banking day following receipt of the item.

(5) A deposit of money in a bank is final when made but, subject to any right of the bank to apply the deposit to an obligation of the customer, the deposit becomes available for withdrawal as of right at the opening of the bank's next banking day following receipt of the deposit.

Sec. 4214. Insolvency and Preference.
(1) Any item in or coming into the possession of a payor collecting bank which suspends payment and which item is not finally paid shall be returned by the receiver, trustee or agent in charge of the closed bank to the presenting bank or the closed bank's customer.

(2) If a payor bank finally pays an item and suspends payments without making a settlement for the item with its customer or the presenting bank which settlement is or becomes final, the owner of the item has a preferred claim against the payor bank.

(3) If a payor bank gives or a collecting bank gives or receives a provisional settlement for an item and thereafter suspends payments, the suspension does not prevent or interfere with the settlement becoming final if such finality occurs automatically upon the lapse of certain time or the happening of certain events (subdivision (3) of Section 4211, subdivisions (1)(d), (2) and (3) of Section 4213).

(4) If a collecting bank receives from subsequent parties settlement for an item which settlement is or becomes final and suspends payments without making a settlement for the item with its customer which is or becomes final, the owner of the item has a preferred claim against such collecting bank.

CHAPTER 3

COLLECTION OF ITEMS: PAYOR BANKS

Sec. 4301. Deferred Posting; Recovery of Payment by Return of Items; Time of Dishonor. (1) Where an authorized settlement for a demand item (other than a documentary draft) received by a payor bank otherwise than for immediate payment over the counter has been made before midnight of the banking day of receipt the payor bank may revoke the settlement and recover any payment if before it has made final payment (subdivision (1) of Section 4213) and before its midnight deadline it

(a) Returns the item; or

(b) Sends written notice of dishonor or nonpayment if the item is held for protest or is otherwise unavailable for return.

(2) If a demand item is received by a payor bank for credit on its books it may return such item or send notice of dishonor and may revoke any credit given or recover the amount thereof withdrawn by its customer, if it acts within the time limit and in the manner specified in the preceding subdivision.

(3) Unless previous notice of dishonor has been sent an item is dishonored at the time when for purposes of dishonor it is returned or notice sent in accordance with this section.

(4) An item is returned:

(a) As to an item received through a clearinghouse, when it is delivered to the presenting or last collecting bank or to the clearinghouse or is sent or delivered in accordance with its rules; or

(b) In all other cases, when it is sent or delivered to the bank's customer or transferor or pursuant to his instructions.

Sec. 4302. Payor Bank's Responsibility for Late Return of Item. In the absence of a valid defense such as breach of a presentment warranty (subdivision (1) of section 4207), settlement effected or the like, if an item is presented on and received by a payor bank the bank is accountable for the amount of

(a) A demand item other than a documentary draft whether properly payable or not if the bank, in any case where it is not also the depositary bank, retains the item beyond midnight of the banking day of receipt without settling for it or, regardless of whether it is also the depositary bank, does not pay or return the item or send notice of dishonor until after its midnight deadline; or

(b) Any other properly payable item unless within the time allowed for acceptance or payment of that item the bank either accepts or pays the item or returns it and accompanying documents.

Sec. 4303. When Items Subject to Notice, Stop-Order, Legal Process or Setoff; Order in Which Items May Be Charged or Certified. (1) Any knowledge, notice or stop order received by, legal process served upon or setoff exercised by a payor bank, whether or not effective under other rules of law to terminate, suspend or modify the bank's right or duty to pay an item or to charge its customer's account for the item, comes too late to so terminate, suspend or modify such right or duty if the knowledge, notice, stop order or legal process is received or served and the bank does not have a reasonable time to act thereon before, or the setoff is exercised after the happening of any of the following:

(a) The bank has accepted or certified the item;

(b) The bank has paid the item in cash;

(c) The bank has settled for the item without having a right to revoke the settlement under any of the following: statute, clearinghouse rule, agreement, or reservation thereof;

(d) The cutoff hour (Section 4107) or the close of the banking day if no cutoff hour is fixed on the day on which the bank received the item;

(e) The bank has become accountable for the amount of the item under subdivision (1)(d) of Section 4213 and Section 4302 dealing with the payor bank's responsibility for late return of items; or

(f) The item has been deposited or received for deposit for credit in an account of a customer with the payor bank.

(2) Subject to the provisions of subdivision (1) items may be accepted, paid, certified or charged to the indicated account of its customer in any order convenient to the bank and before or after its regular banking hours. A bank is under no obligation to determine the time of day an item is received and without liability may withhold the amount thereof pending a determination of the effect, consequence or priority of any knowledge, notice, stop order or legal process concerning the same, or interplead such amount and the claimants thereto.

CHAPTER 4

RELATIONSHIP BETWEEN PAYOR BANK AND ITS CUSTOMER

Sec. 4401. When Bank May Charge Customer's Account. (1) As against its customer, a bank may charge against his account any item which is otherwise properly payable from that account even though the charge creates an overdraft and in such event recover or obtain refund of the amount of the overdraft.

(2) A bank which in good faith makes payment to a holder may charge the indicated account of its customer according to

(a) The original tenor of his altered item; or

(b) The tenor of his completed item, even though the bank knows the item has been completed unless the bank has notice that the completion was improper.

Sec. 4402. Bank's Liability to Customer for Wrongful Dishonor. A payor bank is liable to its customer for damages proximately caused by the wrongful dishonor of an item. When the dishonor occurs through mistake liability is limited to actual damages proved.

Sec. 4403. Customer's Right to Stop Payment; Burden of Proof of Loss. (1) A customer, or any customer if there is more than one, or any person authorized to sign checks or make withdrawals thereon may stop payment of any item payable for or drawn against such customer's or customers' account but the bank may disregard the same unless the order is in writing, is signed by such customer or authorized person, describes with certainty the item on which payment is to be stopped, and is received by the bank in such time and in such manner as to afford the bank a reasonable opportunity to act on it prior to the happening of any of the events described in Section 4303.

(2) An order may be disregarded by the bank six months after receipt unless renewed in writing.

(3) The bank is liable to its customer for the actual loss incurred by him resulting from the payment of an item contrary to a binding stop payment order, not exceeding the amount of the item unless the bank is guilty of negligence. The burden of establishing the fact and amount of loss resulting from the payment of an item contrary to a binding stop payment order is on the customer.

Sec. 4404. Bank Not Obligated to Pay Check More Than Six Months Old. A bank is under no obligation to a customer having a checking account to pay a check, other than a certified check, which is presented more than six months after its date, but it may charge its customer's account for a payment made thereafter.

Sec. 4405. Death or Incompetence of Customer. (1) A payor or collecting bank's authority to accept, pay or collect an item or to account for proceeds of its collection if otherwise effective is not rendered ineffective by incompetence of a customer of either bank existing at the time the item is issued or its collection is undertaken if the bank does not know of an adjudication of incompetence. Neither death nor incompetence of a customer revokes such authority to accept, pay, collect or account until the bank knows of the fact of death or of an adjudication of incompetence and has reasonable opportunity to act on it.

(2) Even with knowledge of the death of a customer or of any person authorized to sign checks or make withdrawals a bank may, for 10 days after the date of death, pay or certify checks drawn by the decedent on or prior to that date unless the bank has received notice pursuant to Section 852 or Section 952 of the Financial Code.

(3) Even with knowledge of the incompetence of a customer, whether adjudicated or not, a bank may, if the item would have been effective prior to such incompetence, accept, pay, collect and account for the proceeds of any item drawn by any other customer or person authorized by such other customer, unless the bank has received notice pursuant to Section 852 or Section 952 of the Financial Code.

(4) A bank may refuse to pay a check, draft or other order for the withdrawal of money from an account, whether commercial or savings, if it believes or receives an affidavit stating that the person drawing, indorsing or presenting the instrument is or was at the time of signing, indorsing or presenting it so under the influence of liquor or drugs or so mentally or physically disabled as to raise doubt whether such person is or was competent to transact business. No damages shall be awarded in any action against the bank, or its officers or other employees, for refusing in good faith to pay any such instrument for that reason or in relying upon such affidavit.

Sec. 4406. Customer's Duty to Discover and Report Unauthorized Signature or Alteration. (1) When a bank sends to its customer a statement of account accompanied by items paid in good faith in support of the debit entries or holds the statement and items pursuant to a request or instructions of its customer or otherwise in a reasonable manner makes the statement and items available to the customer, the customer must exercise reasonable care and promptness to examine the statement and items to discover his unauthorized signature or any alteration on an item and must notify the bank promptly after the discovery thereof.

(2) If the bank establishes that the customer failed with respect to an item to comply with the duties imposed on the customer by subdivision (1) the customer is precluded from asserting against the bank

(a) His unauthorized signature or any alteration on the item if the bank also establishes that it suffered a loss by reason of such failure; and

(b) An unauthorized signature or alteration by the same wrongdoer on any other item paid in good faith by the bank after the first item and statement was available to the customer for a reasonable period not exceeding 14 calendar days and before the bank receives notification from the customer of any such unauthorized signature or alteration.

(3) The preclusion under subdivision (2) does not apply if the customer establishes lack of ordinary care on the part of the bank in paying the item(s).

(4) Without regard to care or lack of care of either the customer or the bank a customer who does not within one year from the time the statement and items are made available to the customer (subdivision (1)) discover and report his unauthorized signature or any alteration on the face or back of the item or any unauthorized indorsement, and if the bank so requests exhibit the item to the bank for inspection, is precluded from asserting against the bank such unauthorized signature or indorsement or such alteration. The burden of establishing the fact of such unauthorized signature or indorsement or such alteration is on the customer.

(5) If under this section a payor bank has a valid defense against a claim of a customer upon or resulting from payment of an item and waives or fails upon request to assert the defense the bank may not assert against any collecting bank or other prior party presenting or transferring the item a claim based upon the unauthorized signature or alteration giving rise to the customer's claim.

Sec. 4407. Payor Bank's Right to Subrogation on Improper Payment. If a payor bank has paid an item over the stop payment order of the drawer or maker or otherwise under circumstances giving a basis for objection by the drawer or maker, to prevent unjust enrichment and only to the extent necessary to prevent loss to the bank by reason of its payment of the item, the payor bank shall be subrogated to the rights

(a) Of any holder in due course on the item against the drawer or maker; and

(b) Of the payee or any other holder of the item against the drawer or making either on the item or under the transaction out of which the item arose; and

(c) Of the drawer or maker against the payee or any other holder of the item with respect to the transaction out of which the item arose.

CHAPTER 5

COLLECTION OF DOCUMENTARY DRAFTS

Sec. 4501. Handling of Documentary Drafts; Duty to Send for Presentment and to Notify Customer of Dishonor. A bank which takes a documentary draft for collection must present or send the draft and accompanying documents for presentment and upon learning that the draft has not been paid or accepted in due course must seasonably notify its customer of such fact even though it may have discounted or bought the draft or extended credit available for withdrawal as of right.

Sec. 4502. Presentment of "On Arrival" Drafts. When a draft or the relevant instructions require presentment "on arrival," "when goods arrive" or the like, the collecting bank need not present until in its judgment a reasonable time for arrival of the goods has expired. Refusal to pay or accept because the goods have not arrived is not dishonor; the bank must notify its transferor of such refusal but need not present the draft again until it is instructed to do so or learns of the arrival of the goods.

Sec. 4503. Responsibility of Presenting Bank for Documents and Goods; Report of Reasons for Dishonor; Referee in Case of Need. Unless otherwise instructed and except as provided in Division 5 a bank presenting a documentary draft

(a) Must deliver the documents to the drawee on acceptance of the draft if it is payable more than three days after presentment; otherwise, only on payment; and

(b) Upon dishonor, either in the case of presentment for acceptance or presentment for payment, may seek and follow instructions from any referee in case of need designated in the draft or if the presenting bank does not choose to utilize his services it must use diligence and good faith to ascertain the reason for dishonor, must notify its transferor of the dishonor and of the results of its effort to ascertain the reasons therefor and must request instructions.

But the presenting bank is under no obligation with respect to goods represented by the document except to follow any reasonable instructions seasonably received; it has a right to reimbursement for any expense incurred in following instructions and to prepayment of or indemnity for such expenses.

Sec. 4504. Privilege of Presenting Bank to Deal With Goods; Security Interest for Expenses. (1) A presenting bank which, following the dishonor of a documentary draft, has seasonably requested instructions but does not receive them within a reasonable time may store, sell, or otherwise deal with the goods in any reasonable manner.

(2) For its reasonable expenses incurred by action under subdivision (1) the presenting bank has a lien upon the goods or their proceeds, which may be foreclosed in the same manner as an unpaid seller's lien.

DIVISION 5

LETTERS OF CREDIT

Sec. 5101. Short Title. This division shall be known and may be cited as Uniform Commercial Code—Letters of Credit.

Sec. 5102. Scope. (1) This division applies

(a) To a credit issued by a bank if the credit requires a documentary draft or a documentary demand for payment; and

(b) To a credit issued by a person other than a bank if the credit requires that the draft or demand for payment be accompanied by a document of title; and

(c) To a credit issued by a bank or other person if the credit is not within paragraph (a) or (b) but conspicuously states that it is a letter of credit or is conspicuously so entitled.

(2) Unless the engagement meets the requirements of subdivision (1), this division does not apply to engagements to make advances or to honor drafts or demands for payment, to authorities to pay or purchase, to guarantees or to general agreements.

(3) This division deals with some but not all of the rules and concepts of letters of credit as such rules or concepts have developed prior to this act or may hereafter develop. The fact that this division states a rule does not by itself require, imply or negate application of the same or a converse rule to a situation not provided for or to a person not specified by this division.

Sec. 5103. Definitions. (1) In this division unless the context otherwise requires

(a) "Credit" or "letter of credit" means an engagement by a bank or other person made at the request of a customer and of a kind within the scope of this division (Section 5102) that the issuer will honor drafts or other demands for payment upon compliance with the conditions specified in the credit. A credit may be either revocable or irrevocable. The engagement may be either an agreement to honor or a statement that a bank or other person is authorized to honor.

(b) A "documentary draft" or a "documentary demand for payment" is one honor of which is conditioned upon the presentation of a document or documents. "Document" means any paper including document of title, security, invoice, certificate, notice of default and the like.

(c) An "issuer" is a bank or other person issuing a credit.

(d) A "beneficiary" of a credit is a person who is entitled under its terms to draw or demand payment.

(e) An "advising bank" is a bank which gives notification of the issuance of a credit by another bank.

(f) A "confirming bank" is a bank which engages either that it will itself honor a credit already issued by another bank or that such a credit will be honored by the issuer or a third bank.

(g) A "customer" is a buyer or other person who causes an issuer to issue a credit. The term also includes a bank which procures issuance or confirmation on behalf of that bank's customer.

(2) Other definitions applying to this division and the sections in which they appear are:

"Notation of credit." Section 5108.

"Presenter." Section 5112(3).

(3) Definitions in other divisions applying to this division and the sections in which they appear are:

"Accept" or "acceptance." Section 3410.

"Contract for sale." Section 2106.

"Draft." Section 3104.

"Holder in due course." Section 3302.

"Midnight deadline." Section 4104.

"Security." Section 8102.

(4) In addition, Division 1 contains general definitions and principles of construction and interpretation applicable throughout this division.

Sec. 5104. Formal Requirements; Signing.

(1) Except as otherwise required in subdivision (1)(c) of Section 5102 on scope, no particular form of phrasing is required for a credit. A credit must be in writing and signed by the issuer and a confirmation must be in writing and signed by the confirming bank. A modification of the terms of a credit or confirmation must be signed by the issuer or confirming bank.

(2) A telegram may be a sufficient signed writing if it identifies its sender by an authorized authentication. The authentication may be in code and the authorized naming of the issuer in an advice of credit is a sufficient signing.

Sec. 5105. Consideration.

No consideration is necessary to establish a credit or to enlarge or otherwise modify its terms.

Sec. 5106. Time and Effect of Establishment of Credit.

(1) Unless otherwise agreed a credit is established

(a) As regards the customer as soon as a letter of credit is sent to him or the letter of credit or an authorized written advice of its issuance is sent to the beneficiary; and

(b) As regards the beneficiary when he receives a letter of credit or an authorized written advice of its issuance.

(2) Unless otherwise agreed once an irrevocable credit is established as regards the customer it can be modified or revoked only with the consent of the customer and once it is established as regards the beneficiary it can be modified or revoked only with his consent.

(3) Unless otherwise agreed after a revocable credit is established it may be modified or revoked by the issuer without notice to or consent from the customer or beneficiary.

(4) Notwithstanding any modification or revocation of a revocable credit any person authorized to honor or negotiate under the terms of the original credit is entitled to reimbursement for or honor of any draft or demand for payment duly honored or negotiated before receipt of notice of the modification or revocation and the issuer in turn is entitled to reimbursement from its customer.

Sec. 5107. Advice of Credit; Confirmation; Error in Statement of Terms.

(1) Unless otherwise specified an advising bank by advising a credit issued by another bank does not assume any obligation to honor drafts drawn or demands for payment made under the credit but it does assume obligation for the accuracy of its own statement.

(2) A confirming bank by confirming a credit becomes directly obligated on the credit to the extent of its confirmation as though it were its issuer and acquires the rights of an issuer.

(3) Even though an advising bank incorrectly advises the terms of a credit it has been authorized to advise the credit is established as against the issuer to the extent of its original terms.

(4) Unless otherwise specified the customer bears as against the issuer all risks of transmission and reasonable translation or interpretation of any message relating to a credit.

Sec. 5108. "Notation Credit"; Exhaustion of Credit.

(1) A credit which specifies that any person purchasing or paying drafts drawn or demands for payment made under it must note the amount of the draft or demand on the letter or advice of credit is a "notation credit."

(2) Under a notation credit

(a) A person paying the beneficiary or purchasing a draft or demand for payment from him acquires a right to honor only if the appropriate notation is made and by transferring or forwarding for honor the documents under the credit such a person warrants to the issuer that the notation has been made; and

(b) Unless the credit or a signed statement that an appropriate notation has been made accompanies the draft or demand for payment the issuer may delay honor until evidence of notation has been procured which is satisfactory to it but its obligation and that of its customer continue for a reasonable time not exceeding 30 days to obtain such evidence.

(3) If the credit is not a notation credit

(a) The issuer may honor complying drafts or demands for payment presented to it in the order in which they are presented and is discharged pro tanto by honor of any such draft or demand;

(b) As between competing good faith purchasers of complying drafts or demands the person first purchasing has priority over a subsequent purchaser even though the later purchased draft or demand has been first honored.

Sec. 5109. Issuer's Obligation to Its Customer.

(1) An issuer's obligation to its customer includes good faith and observance of any general banking usage but unless otherwise agreed does not include liability or responsibility

(a) For performance of the underlying contract for sale or other transaction between the customer and the beneficiary; or

(b) For any act or omission of any person other than itself or its own branch or for loss or destruction of a draft, demand or document in transit or in the possession of others; or

(c) Based on knowledge or lack of knowledge of any usage of any particular trade.

(2) An issuer must examine documents with care so as to ascertain that on their face they appear to comply with the terms of the credit but unless otherwise agreed assumes no liability or responsibility for the genuineness, falsification or effect of any document which appears on such examination to be regular on its face.

(3) A nonbank issuer is not bound by any banking usage of which it has no knowledge.

Sec. 5110. Availability of Credit in Portions; Presenter's Reservation of Lien or Claim.

(1) Unless otherwise specified a credit may be used in portions in the discretion of the beneficiary.

(2) Unless otherwise specified a person by presenting a documentary draft or demand for payment under a credit relinquishes upon its honor all claims to the documents and a person by transferring such draft or demand or causing such presentment authorizes such relinquishment. An explicit reservation of claim makes the draft or demand noncomplying.

Sec. 5111. Warranties on Transfer and Presentment.

(1) Unless otherwise agreed the beneficiary by transferring or presenting a documentary draft or demand for payment warrants to all interested parties that the necessary conditions of the credit have been complied with. This is in addition to any warranties arising under Divisions 3, 4, 7, and 8.

(2) Unless otherwise agreed a negotiating, advising, confirming, collecting or issuing bank presenting or transferring a draft or demand for payment under a credit warrants only the matters warranted by a collecting bank under Division 4 and any such bank transferring a document warrants only the matters warranted by an intermediary under Divisions 7 and 8.

Sec. 5112. Time Allowed for Honor or Rejection; Withholding Honor or Rejection by Consent; "Presenter."

(1) A bank to which a documentary draft or demand for payment is presented under a credit may without dishonor of the draft, demand or credit

(a) Defer honor until the close of the third banking day following receipt of the documents; and

(b) Further defer honor if the presenter has expressly or impliedly consented thereto.

Failure to honor within the time here specified constitutes dishonor of the draft or demand and of the credit.

(2) Upon dishonor the bank may unless otherwise instructed fulfill its duty to return the draft or demand and the documents by holding them at the disposal of the presenter and sending him an advice to that effect.

(3) "Presenter" means any person presenting a draft or demand for payment for honor under a credit even though that person is a confirming bank or other correspondent which is acting under an issuer's authorization.

Sec. 5113. Indemnities.

(1) A bank seeking to obtain (whether for itself or another) honor, negotiation or reimbursement under a credit may give an indemnity to induce such honor, negotiation or reimbursement.

(2) An indemnity agreement inducing honor, negotiation or reimbursement unless otherwise explicitly agreed applies to defects in the documents but not in the goods.

Sec. 5114. **Issuer's Duty and Privilege to Honor; Right to Reimbursement.** (1) An issuer must honor a draft or demand for payment which complies with the terms of the relevant credit regardless of whether the goods or documents conform to the underlying contract for sale or other contract between the customer and the beneficiary. The issuer is not excused from honor of such a draft or demand by reason of an additional general term that all documents must be satisfactory to the issuer, but an issuer may require that specified documents must be satisfactory to it.

(2) Unless otherwise agreed when documents appear on their face to comply with the terms of a credit but a required document does not in fact conform to the warranties made on negotiation or transfer of a document of title (Section 7507) or of a security (Section 8306) or is forged or fraudulent or there is fraud in the transaction

(a) The issuer must honor the draft or demand for payment if honor is demande d by a negotiating bank or other holder of the draft or demand which has taken the draft or demand under the credit and under circumstances which would make it a holder in due course (Section 3302) and in an appropriate case would make it a person to whom a document of title has been duly negotiated (Section 7501) or a bona fide purchaser of a security (Section 8302); and

(b) In all other cases as against its customer, an issuer acting in good faith may honor the draft or demand for payment despite notification from the customer of fraud, forgery or other defect not apparent on the face of the documents.

(3) Unless otherwise agreed an issuer which has duly honored a draft or demand for payment is entitled to immediate reimbursement of any payment made under the credit and to be put in effectively available funds not later than the day before maturity of any acceptance made under the credit.

Sec. 5115. **Remedy for Improper Dishonor or Anticipatory Repudiation.** (1) When an issuer wrongfully dishonors a draft or demand for payment presented under a credit the person entitled to honor has with respect to any documents the rights of a person in the position of a seller (Section 2707) and may recover from the issuer the face amount of the draft or demand together with incidental damages under Section 2710 on seller's incidental damages and interest but less any amount realized by resale or other use or disposition of the subject matter of the transaction. In the event no resale or other utilization is made the documents, goods or other subject matter involved in the transaction must be turned over to the issuer on payment of judgment.

(2) When an issuer wrongfully cancels or otherwise repudiates a credit before presentment of a draft or demand for payment drawn under it the beneficiary has the rights of a seller after anticipatory repudiation by the buyer under Section 2610 if he learns of the repudiation in time reasonably to avoid procurement of the required documents. Otherwise the beneficiary has an immediate right of action for wrongful dishonor.

Sec. 5116. **Transfer and Assignment.** (1) The right to draw under a credit can be transferred or assigned only when the credit is expressly designated as transferable or assignable.

(2) Even though the credit specifically states that it is nontransferable or nonassignable the beneficiary may before performance of the conditions of the credit assign his right to proceeds. Such an assignment is an assignment of an account under Division 9 on secured transactions and is governed by that division except that

(a) The assignment is ineffective until the letter of credit or advice of credit is delivered to the assignee which delivery constitutes perfection of the security interest under Division 9; and

(b) The issuer may honor drafts or demands for payment drawn under the credit until it receives a notification of the assignment signed by the beneficiary which reasonably identifies the credit involved in the assignment and contains a request to pay the assignee; and

(c) After what reasonably appears to be such a notification has been received the issuer may without dishonor refuse to accept or pay even to a person otherwise entitled to honor until the letter of credit or advice of credit is exhibited to the issuer.

(3) Except where the beneficiary has effectively assigned his right to draw or his right to proceeds, nothing in this section limits his right to transfer or negotiate drafts or demands drawn under the credit.

Sec. 5117. **Insolvency of Bank Holding Funds for Documentary Credit.** (1) Where an issuer or an advising or confirming bank or a bank which has for a customer procured issuance of a credit by another bank becomes insolvent before final payment under the credit and the credit is one to which this division is made applicable by paragraph (a)

or (b) of Section 5102(1) on scope, the receipt or allocation of funds or collateral to secure or meet obligations under the credit shall have the following results:

(a) To the extent of any funds or collateral turned over after or before the insolvency as indemnity against or specifically for the purpose of payment of drafts or demands for payment drawn under the designated credit; the drafts or demands are entitled to payment in preference over depositors or other general creditors of the issuer or bank; and

(b) On expiration of the credit or surrender of the beneficiary's rights under it unused any person who has given such funds or collateral is similarly entitled to return thereof; and

(c) A charge to a general or current account with a bank if specifically consented to for the purpose of indemnity against or payment of drafts or demands for payment drawn under the designated credit falls under the same rules as if the funds had been drawn out in cash and then turned over with specific instructions.

(2) After honor or reimbursement under this section the customer or other person for whose account the insolvent bank has acted is entitled to receive the documents involved.

DIVISION 6

BULK TRANSFERS

Sec. 6101. **Short Title.** This division shall be known and may be cited as Uniform Commercial Code—Bulk Transfers.

Sec. 6102. **"Bulk Transfers"; Transfers of Equipment; Enterprises Subject to This Article; Bulk Transfers Subject to This Article.** (1) A "bulk transfer" is any transfer in bulk and not in the ordinary course of the transferor's business of a substantial part of the materials, supplies, merchandise, or other inventory (Section 9109) of an enterprise subject to this division.

(2) A transfer of a substantial part of the equipment (Section 9109) of such an enterprise is also a bulk transfer.

(3) The enterprises subject to this division are all those whose principal business is the sale of merchandise, including those who manufacture what they sell, or that of a baker, cafe or restaurant owner, garage owner, cleaner and dyer, or retail or wholesale merchant.

(4) Except as limited by the following section all bulk transfers of goods located within this State are subject to this division.

(5) The word "transfer" as used in this division includes the creation of a security interest.

Sec. 6103. **Transfers Excepted From This Article.** The following transfers are not subject to this division:

(1) A transfer subject to subdivision (h) of Section 3441 of the Civil Code;

(2) Assignments for the benefit of all the creditors of the transferor, and subsequent transfers by the assignee thereunder;

(3) Transfers of property subject to a lien or other security interest in settlement or realization of such lien or other security interest;

(4) Sales by executors, administrators, receivers, trustees in bankruptcy, or any public officer under judicial process;

(5) Sales made in the course of judicial or administrative proceedings for the dissolution or reorganization of a corporation and of which notice is sent to the creditors of the corporation pursuant to order of the court or administrative agency;

(6) Transfers of property which is exempt from enforcement of a money judgment;

(7) The transfer of goods in a warehouse where a warehouse receipt has been issued therefor by a warehouseman (Section 7102) and a copy of such receipt is kept at the principal place of business of the warehouseman and at the warehouse in which said goods are stored;

(8) A transfer which is subject to and complies with Article 5 (commencing with Section 24070) of Chapter 6 of Division 9 of the Business and Professions Code, except that such transfer shall be subject to subdivision (1) of Section 6105 insofar as it refers to Section 6107, Section 6107 other than paragraph (e) of subdivision (1) thereof, and subdivision (a) of Section 6111.

Sec. 6104. **Reserved.**

Sec. 6105. **Notice to Creditors; Noticed Sale Date.** (1) Any bulk transfer subject to this division except one made by auction sale (Section 6108) is fraudulent and void against any creditor of the transferor unless the transferee gives notice of the transfer in the manner and within the time hereafter provided (subdivision (6) of Section 6106, where applicable, and Section 6107).

(2) The term "notice sale date" as used in this division means the date set forth in the notice provided for in subdivision (1) of Section 6107 on or after which the bulk transfer may be consummated.

Sec. 6106. **Payment of Consideration to Satisfy Claims of Transferor's Creditors; Disputed Claims; Attachment; Interpleader; Notice; Security Interests.** (1) This section applies only to a bulk transfer where the consideration is less than one million dollars ($1,000,000) and is substantially all cash or an obligation of the transferee to pay cash in the future to the transferor or a combination thereof.

(2) Upon every bulk transfer subject to this section except one made by sale at auction it is the duty of the transferee (or, if the transaction is handled through an escrow, the escrow agent) to apply the consideration in accordance with the provisions of this section so far as necessary to pay those debts of the transferor for which claims are due and payable on or before the noticed sale date and are filed in writing on or prior to the date specified as the last date to file claims with the person designated in the notice to receive claims. This duty of the transferee or escrow agent runs to each creditor timely filing such a claim.

(3) If the transferor disputes whether a claim is due and payable on the noticed sale date or the amount of any claim, the transferee or escrow agent shall withhold from distribution the amount thereof (or the pro rata amount under subdivision (2) of Section 6106.1) and shall send a written notice to the claimant filing the claim on or before two business days after the distribution that the amount will be paid to the transferor (or to the other claimants in accordance with subdivision (2) of Section 6106.1, as the case may be) unless attached within 25 days from the mailing of the notice. Any portion of the amount withheld which is not attached by the claimant within such time shall be paid by the transferee or escrow agent to the transferor (or to the other claimants in accordance with subdivision (2) of Section 6106.1 if they have not been paid in full). An attachment of any amount so withheld shall be limited in its effect to the amount withheld for the attaching claimant and shall give the attaching claimant no greater priority or rights with respect to his claim than the claimant would have had if the claim had not been disputed. For purposes of this subdivision, a claimant may obtain the issuance of an attachment for a claim which is less than five hundred dollars ($500) and which otherwise meets the requirements of Section 483.010 of the Code of Civil Procedure or which is a secured claim or lien of the type described in Section 483.010 of the Code of Civil Procedure. The remedy in this subdivision shall be in addition to any other remedies the claimant may have, including any right to attach the property intended to be transferred or any other property.

(4) If the cash consideration payable is not sufficient to pay all of the claims filed in full, where no escrow has been established pursuant to Section 6106.1 the transferee shall follow the procedures specified in subdivisions (1) through (3) of Section 6106.1.

(5) The transferee or escrow agent, as the case may be, shall within 45 days after the transferee takes legal title to any of the goods either pay to the extent of the cash consideration the claims filed and not disputed (or the applicable portion thereof to the extent of the cash consideration under subdivision (2) of Section 6106.1) or institute an action in interpleader pursuant to subdivision (b) of Section 386 of the Code of Civil Procedure and deposit the consideration with the clerk of the court pursuant to subdivision (c) of that section. Such action shall be brought in the appropriate court for the county where the transferor had its principal place of business in this state. Sections 386.1 and 386.6 of the Code of Civil Procedure shall apply in such action.

(6) The notice shall state, in addition to the matters required by Section 6107, the name and address of the person with whom claims may be filed and the last date for filing claims, which shall be the business day before the noticed sale date. Claims shall be deemed timely filed only if actually received by the person designated in the notice to receive claims before the close of business on the day specified in the notice as the last date for filing claims.

(7) Nothing contained in this section shall release any security interest or other lien on the property which is the subject of the bulk transfer except upon the voluntary release thereof by the secured party or lienholder.

Sec. 6106.1. **Escrow; Filing Claims; Distribution; Notice.** In any case where the notice of a bulk transfer subject to Section 6106 states that claims may be filed with a person who is an escrow agent, the intended transferee shall deposit with the escrow agent the full amount of the purchase price or consideration. If at the time the transfer is otherwise ready to be consummated the amount of cash deposited or agreed to be deposited at or prior to consummation in the escrow is insufficient to pay in full all of the claims filed with the escrow agent, the escrow agent shall:

(1) (a) Delay the distribution of the consideration and the passing of legal title for a period of not less than 25 days nor more than 30 days from the date the notice required in paragraph (b) of this subdivision is mailed; and

(b) Within five business days after the time the transfer would otherwise have been consummated, send a written notice to each claimant who has filed a claim stating the total consideration deposited or agreed to be deposited in the escrow, the name of each claimant who filed a claim against the escrow and the amount of each claim, the amount proposed to be paid to each claimant, the new date scheduled for the passing of legal title pursuant to paragraph (a) of this subdivision and the date on or before which distribution will be made to claimants which shall not be more than five days after the new date specified for the passing of legal title.

(c) If no written objection to the distribution described in the notice required by paragraph (b) of this subdivision is received by the transferee or escrow agent, as the case may be, prior to the new date specified in such notice for the passing of legal title, the transferee or escrow agent, as the case may be, shall not be liable to any person to whom the notice required by paragraph (b) was sent for any good faith error which may have been committed in allocating and distributing the consideration as stated in such notice.

(2) Distribute the consideration in the following order of priorities:

(a) All obligations owing to the United States, to the extent given priority by federal law.

(b) Secured claims, including statutory and judicial liens, to the extent of the consideration fairly attributable to the value of the properties securing such claims and in accordance with the priorities provided by law; provided, however, that a secured creditor shall participate in the distribution pursuant to this subdivision only if a release of lien is deposited by such secured creditor conditioned only upon receiving an amount equal to such distribution.

(c) Escrow and professional charges and broker's fees attributable directly to the sale.

(d) Wage claims given priority by Section 1205 of the Code of Civil Procedure.

(e) All other tax claims.

(f) All other unsecured claims pro rata, including any deficiency claims of partially secured creditors.

(3) To the extent that an obligation of the transferee to pay cash in the future is a part of the consideration and the cash consideration is not sufficient to pay all claims filed in full, apply all principal and interest received on such obligation to the payment of claims in accordance with subdivision (2) until they are paid in full before making any payment to the transferor. In such case, the notice pursuant to subdivision (1) shall state the amount, terms and due dates of the obligation and the portion of the claims expected to be paid thereby.

No funds shall be drawn from the escrow, prior to the actual closing and completion of the escrow, for the payment, in whole or in part, of any commission, fee or other consideration as compensation for a service which is contingent upon the performance of any act, condition, or instruction set forth in an escrow.

Sec. 6107. **The Notice.** (1) The notice to creditors (Section 6105) shall state:

(a) That a bulk transfer is about to be made; and

(b) The names and business addresses of the transferor and, except in the case of a sale at auction, the transferee, and all other business names and addresses used by the transferor within three years last past so far as known to the transferee;

(c) The location and general description of the property to be transferred;

(d) The place, and the date on or after which, the bulk transfer is to be consummated; and

(e) Whether or not the bulk transfer is subject to Section 6106, and if so subject, the matters required by subdivision (6) of Section 6106.

(2) The notice shall be

(a) Recorded in the office of the county recorder in the county or counties in which the property to be transferred is located at least 12 business days before the bulk transfer is to be consummated or the sale by auction is to be commenced; and

(b) Published at least once in a newspaper of general circulation published (i) in the judicial district in which the property is located and (ii) in the judicial district, if different, in which the chief executive office of the transferor, or, if the chief executive office is not in California, the principal business office in California, is located, if in either case there is one, and if there is none, then in a newspaper of general circulation in the county embracing such judicial district, at least 12 business days before the bulk transfer is to be consummated or the sale by auction is to be commenced; and

(c) Delivered or sent by registered or certified mail at least 12 business days before the bulk transfer is to be consummated or the sale by auction is to be commenced to the county tax collector in the county or counties in which the property to be transferred is located.

If the property to be transferred is located in more than one judicial district, the publication required by paragraph (b) of subdivision (2) shall be in a newspaper published in the judicial district where a greater portion of the property is located, on the date the notice is published, than in any other judicial district, or in the county embracing such judicial district, as the case may be. As used in this section "business day" means any day other than a Saturday, Sunday or a day observed as a holiday by the California state government.

Sec. 6108. **Auction Sales; "Auctioneer."** (1) A bulk transfer is subject to this division even though it is by sale at auction, but only in the manner and with the results stated in this section.

(2) The person or persons other than the transferor who direct, control or are responsible for the auction are collectively called the "auctioneer." The auctioneer shall be responsible for giving the notice of the transfer (Section 6107). In the case of a sale by auction, in addition to the matters specified in 6107, the notice shall state that the sale is to be by auction, the name of the auctioneer, and the time and place of the auction.

(3) Failure of the auctioneer to give the notice of the transfer does not affect the validity of the sale to or the title of the purchasers, but such failure renders the auctioneer liable to the creditors of the transferor as a class for the sums owing to them from the transferor up to but not exceeding the reasonable value of the assets sold. If the auctioneer consists of several persons their liability is joint and several.

Sec. 6109. **What Creditors Protected.** The creditors of the transferor mentioned in this division are those holding claims based on transactions or events occurring before the bulk transfer.

Sec. 6110. **Subsequent Transfers.** When the title of a transferee to property is subject to a defect by reason of his noncompliance with the requirements of this division, then:

(1) A purchaser of any such property from such transferee who pays no value or who takes with notice of such noncompliance takes subject to such defect, but

(2) A purchaser for value in good faith and without such notice takes free of such defect.

Sec. 6111. **Limitation of Actions and Levies.** (a) No action under this division shall be brought nor levy made more than one year after the date on which the transferee took possession of the goods unless the transfer has been concealed. If the transfer has been concealed, an action may be brought or levy made within one year after its discovery by the creditor bringing such action or making such levy or after it should have been discovered by such creditor in the exercise of reasonable diligence, whichever first occurs.

(b) If a bulk transfer is subject to and complies with Section 6106, no levy shall be made by a creditor of the transferor on the proceeds of sale in the hands of the transferee or escrow agent after the transferee takes legal title to the goods, except to the extent of that creditor's share of the proceeds pursuant to Section 6106 and 6106.1.

DIVISION 7

WAREHOUSE RECEIPTS, BILLS OF LADING AND OTHER DOCUMENTS OF TITLE

CHAPTER 1

GENERAL

Sec. 7101. **Short Title.** This division shall be known and may be cited as Uniform Commercial Code Documents of Title.

Sec. 7102. **Definitions and Index of Definitions.** (1) In this division, unless the context otherwise requires:

(a) "Bailee" means the person who by a warehouse receipt, bill of lading or other document of title acknowledges possession of goods and contracts to deliver them.

(b) "Consignee" means the person named in a bill to whom or to whose order the bill promises delivery.

(c) "Consignor" means the person named in a bill as the person from whom the goods have been received for shipment.

(e) "Document" means document of title as defined in the general definitions in Division 1 (Section 1201).

(f) "Goods" means all things which are treated as movable for the purposes of a contract of storage or transportation.

(g) "Issuer" means a bailee who issues a document. Issuer includes any person for whom an agent or employee purports to act in issuing a document if the agent or employee has real or apparent authority to issue documents, notwithstanding that the issuer received no goods or that the goods were misdescribed or that in any other respect the agent or employee violated his instructions.

(h) "Warehouseman" is a person engaged in the business of storing goods for hire.

(2) Other definitions applying to this division or to specified chapters thereof, and the sections in which they appear are:

"Duly negotiate." Section 7501.

"Person entitled under the document." Section 7403(4).

(3) Definitions in other divisions applying to this division and the sections in which they appear are:

"Contract for sale." Section 2106.

"Overseas." Section 2323.

"Receipt" of goods. Section 2103.

(4) In addition Division 1 contains general definitions and principles of construction and interpretation applicable throughout this division.

Sec. 7103. **Relation of Article to Treaty, Statute, Tariff, Classification or Regulation.** To the extent that any treaty or statute of the United States, regulatory statute of this State, or tariff, classification or regulation filed or issued pursuant thereto is applicable, the provisions of this division are subject thereto.

Sec. 7104. **Negotiable and Non-Negotiable Warehouse Receipt, Bill of Lading or Other Document of Title.** (1) A warehouse receipt, bill of lading or other document of title is negotiable

(a) If by its terms the goods are to be delivered to bearer or to the order of a named person; or

(b) Where recognized in overseas trade, if it runs to a named persons or assigns.

(2) Any other document is nonnegotiable. A bill of lading in which it is stated that the goods are consigned to a named person is not made negotiable by a provision that the goods are to be delivered only against a written order signed by the same or another named person.

(3) A nonnegotiable warehouse receipt and a nonnegotiable bill of lading must be conspicuously (Section 1201) marked "nonnegotiable." In case of the bailee's failure to do so, a holder of the document who purchased it for value supposing it to be negotiable may, at his option, treat such document as imposing upon the bailee the same liabilities he would have incurred had the document been negotiable.

Sec. 7105. **Construction Against Negative Implication.** The omission from either Chapter 2 or Chapter 3 of this division of a provision corresponding to a provision made in the other chapter does not imply that a corresponding rule of law is not applicable.

CHAPTER 2

WAREHOUSE RECEIPTS: SPECIAL PROVISIONS

Sec. 7201. Who May Issue a Warehouse Receipt; Storage Under Government Bond. (1) A warehouse receipt may be issued by any warehouseman.

(2) Where goods including distilled spirits and agricultural commodities are stored under a statute requiring a bond against withdrawal or a license for the issuance of receipts in the nature of warehouse receipts, a receipt issued for the goods has like effect as a warehouse receipt even though issued by a person who is the owner of the goods and is not a warehouseman.

Sec. 7202. Form of Warehouse Receipt; Essential Terms; Optional Terms. (1) A warehouse receipt need not be in any particular form.

(2) Unless a warehouse receipt embodies within its written or printed terms each of the following, the warehouseman is liable for damages caused by the omission to a person injured thereby:

(a) The location of the warehouse where the goods are stored;

(b) The date of issue of the receipt;

(c) The consecutive number of the receipt;

(d) A statement whether the goods received will be delivered to the bearer, to a specified person, or to a specified person or his order;

(e) The rate of storage and handling charges, except that where goods are stored under a field warehousing arrangement a statement of that fact is sufficient on a nonnegotiable receipt and except that where goods are stored in a public utility warehouse having a lawful tariff on file with the Public Utilities Commission, a statement that the rate of storage and handling charges are as provided in such tariff is sufficient;

(f) A description of the goods or of the packages containing them;

(g) The signature of the warehouseman, which may be made by his authorized agent;

(h) If the receipt is issued for goods of which the warehouseman is owner, either solely or jointly or in common with others, the fact of such ownership; and

(i) A statement of the amount of advances made and of liabilities incurred for which the warehouseman claims a lien or security interest (Section 7209). If the precise amount of such advances made or of such liabilities incurred is, at the time of the issue of the receipt, unknown to the warehouseman or to his agent who issues it, a statement of the fact that advances have been made or liabilities incurred and the purpose thereof is sufficient.

(3) A warehouseman may insert in his receipt any other terms which are not contrary to the provisions of this code and do not impair his obligation of delivery (Section 7403) or his duty of care (Section 7204). Any contrary provisions shall be ineffective.

Sec. 7203. Liability for Non-Receipt or Misdescription. A party to or purchaser for value in good faith of a document of title other than a bill of lading relying in either case upon the description therein of the goods may recover from the issuer damages caused by the nonreceipt or misdescription of the goods, except to the extent that the document conspicuously indicates that the issuer does not know whether any part or all of the goods in fact were received or conform to the description, as where the description is in terms of marks or labels or kind, quantity or condition, or the receipt or description is qualified by "contents, condition and quality unknown," "said to contain" or the like, if such indication be true, or the party or purchaser otherwise has notice.

Sec. 7204. Duty of Care; Contractual Limitation of Warehouseman's Liability. (1) A warehouseman is liable for damages for loss of or injury to the goods caused by his failure to exercise such care in regard to them as a reasonably careful man would exercise under like circumstances but unless otherwise agreed he is not liable for damages which could not have been avoided by the exercise of such care.

(2) Damages may be limited by a term in the warehouse receipt or storage agreement limiting the amount of liability in case of loss or damage, and setting forth a specific liability per article or item, or value per unit of weight, beyond which the warehouseman shall not be liable; provided, however, that such liability may on written request of the bailor at the time of signing such storage agreement or within a reasonable time after receipt of the warehouse receipt be increased on part or all of the goods thereunder, in which event increased rates may be charged based on such increased valuation, but that no such increase shall be permitted contrary to a lawful limitation of liability contained in the warehouseman's tariff, if any, nor permit recovery in excess of the actual value of the goods. No such limitation is effective with respect to the warehouseman's liability for conversion to his own use.

(3) Reasonable provisions as to the time and manner of presenting claims and instituting actions based on the bailment may be included in the warehouse receipt or tariff.

(4) This section does not impair or repeal Section 1630 of the Civil Code nor any of the provisions of the Public Utilities Code or the Agricultural Code or any lawful regulations issued thereunder.

Sec. 7205. Title Under Warehouse Receipt Defeated in Certain Cases. A buyer in the ordinary course of business of fungible goods sold and delivered by a warehouseman who is also in the business of buying and selling such goods takes free of any claim under a warehouse receipt even though it has been duly negotiated.

Sec. 7206. Termination of Storage at Warehouseman's Option. (1) A warehouseman may on notifying the person on whose account the goods are held and any other person known to claim an interest in the goods require payment of any charges and removal of the goods from the warehouse at the termination of the period of storage fixed by the document, or, if no period is fixed, within a stated period not less than 30 days after the notification. If the goods are not removed before the date specified in the notification, the warehouseman may sell them in accordance with the provisions of the section on enforcement of a warehouseman's lien (Section 7210).

(2) If a warehouseman in good faith believes that the goods are about to deteriorate or decline in value to less than the amount of his lien within the time prescribed in subdivision (1) for notification, advertisement and sale, the warehouseman may specify in the notification any reasonable shorter time for removal of the goods and in case the goods are not removed, may sell them at public sale held not less than one week after a single advertisement or posting.

(3) If as a result of a quality or condition of the goods of which the warehouseman had no notice at the time of deposit the goods are a hazard to other property or to the warehouse or to persons, the warehouseman may sell the goods at public or private sale without advertisement on reasonable notification to all persons known to claim an interest in the goods. If the warehouseman after a reasonable effort is unable to sell the goods he may dispose of them in any lawful manner and shall incur no liability by reasons of such disposition.

(4) The warehouseman must deliver the goods to any person entitled to them under this division upon due demand made at any time prior to sale or other disposition under this section and payment of any amount necessary to satisfy the warehouseman's lien and reasonable expenses incurred under this section.

(5) The warehouseman may satisfy his lien from the proceeds of any sale or disposition under this section but must hold the balance for delivery on the demand of any person to whom he would have been bound to deliver the goods.

Sec. 7207. Goods Must Be Kept Separate; Fungible Goods. (1) Unless the warehouse receipt otherwise provides, a warehouseman must keep separate the goods covered by each receipt so as to permit at all times identification and delivery of those goods except that different lots of fungible goods may be commingled.

(2) Fungible goods so commingled are owned in common by the persons entitled thereto and the warehouseman is severally liable to each owner for that owner's share. Where because of overissue a mass of fungible goods is insufficient to meet all the receipts which the warehouseman has issued against it, the persons entitled include all holders to whom overissued receipts have been duly negotiated.

Sec. 7208. Altered Warehouse Receipts. Where a blank in a negotiable warehouse receipt has been filled in without authority, a purchaser for value and without notice of the want of authority may treat the insertion as authorized. Any other unauthorized alteration leaves any receipt enforceable against the issuer according to its original tenor.

Sec. 7209. Lien of Warehouseman. (1) A warehouseman has a lien against the bailor on the goods deposited or on the proceeds thereof in his possession for charges for storage, processing incidental to storage, or transportation, including demurrage and terminal charges, insurance, labor, or charges present or future in relation to the goods, and for expenses necessary for preservation of the goods or reasonably incurred in their sale pursuant to law. If the person on whose account the goods are held is liable for like charges or expenses in relation to other goods whenever deposited, the warehouseman also has a lien against him for such charges and expenses whether or not the other goods have been delivered by the warehouseman. But against a person to whom a negotiable warehouse receipt is duly negotiated a warehouseman's lien is limited to charges specified on the receipt or if no charges are so specified then to a reasonable charge for storage of the goods covered by the receipt subsequent to the date of the receipt.

(2) The warehouseman may also reserve a security interest against the bailor for charges other than those specified in subdivision (1), such as for money advanced and interest, but if a receipt is issued for the goods such a security interest is not valid as against third persons without notice unless the maximum amount thereof is conspicuously specified (Section 1201) on the receipt. Such a security interest is governed by the division on secured transactions (Division 9).

(3) (a) A warehouseman's lien for charges and expenses under subdivision (1) or a security interest under subdivision (2) is also effective against any person who so entrusted the bailor with possession of the goods that a pledge of them by him to a good faith purchaser for value would have been valid but is not effective against a person as to whom the document confers no right in the goods covered by it under Section 7503.

(b) A warehouseman's lien on household goods for charges and expenses in relation to the goods under subdivision (1) is also effective against all persons if the depositor was the legal processor of the goods at the time of deposit. "Household goods" means furniture, furnishings and personal effects used by the depositor in a dwelling.

(4) A warehouseman loses his lien on any goods which he voluntarily delivers or which he unjustifiably refuses to deliver.

Sec. 7210. Enforcement of Warehouseman's Lien.

(1) Except as provided in subdivision (2), a warehouseman's lien may be enforced by public or private sale of the goods in bloc or in parcels, at any time or place and on any terms which are commercially reasonable, after notifying all persons known to claim an interest in the goods. Such notification must include a statement of the amount due, the nature of the proposed sale and the time and place of any public sale. The fact that a better price could have been obtained by a sale at a different time or in a different method from that selected by the warehouseman is not of itself sufficient to establish that the sale was not made in a commercially reasonable manner. If the warehouseman either sells the goods in the usual manner in any recognized market therefor, or if he sells at the price current in such market at the time of his sale, or if he has otherwise sold in conformity with commercially reasonable practices among dealers in the type of goods sold, he has sold in a commercially reasonable manner. A sale of more goods than apparently necessary to be offered to insure satisfaction of the obligation is not commercially reasonable except in cases covered by the preceding sentence.

(2) A warehouseman's lien on goods other than goods stored by a merchant in the course of his business may be enforced only as follows:

(a) All persons known to claim an interest in the goods must be notified.

(b) The notification must be delivered in person or sent by registered or certified letter to the last known address of any person to be notified.

(c) The notification must include an itemized statement of the claim, a description of the goods subject to the lien, a demand for payment within a specified time not less than 10 days after receipt of the notification, and a conspicuous statement that unless the claim is paid within that time the goods will be advertised for sale and sold by auction at a specified time and place.

(d) The sale must conform to the terms of the notification.

(e) The sale must be held at the nearest suitable place to that where the goods are held or stored.

(f) After the expiration of the time given in the notification, an advertisement of the sale must be published once a week for two weeks consecutively in a newspaper of general circulation published in the judicial district where the sale is to be held. The advertisement must include a description of the goods, the name of the person on whose account they are being held, and the time and place of the sale. The sale must take place at least 15 days after the first publication. If there is no newspaper of general circulation published in the judicial district where the sale is to be held, the advertisement must be posted at least 10 days before the sale in not less than six conspicuous places in the neighborhood of the proposed sale.

(3) Before any sale pursuant to this section any person claiming a right in the goods may pay the amount necessary to satisfy the lien and the reasonable expenses incurred under this section. In that event the goods must not be sold, but must be retained by the warehouseman subject to the terms of the receipt and this division.

(4) The warehouseman may buy at any public sale pursuant to this section.

(5) A purchaser in good faith of goods sold to enforce a warehouseman's lien takes the goods free of any rights of persons against whom the lien was valid, despite noncompliance by the warehouseman with the requirements of this section.

(6) The warehouseman may satisfy his lien from the proceeds of any sale pursuant to this section but must hold the balance, if any, for delivery on demand to any person to whom he would have been bound to deliver the goods.

(7) The rights provided by this section shall be in addition to all other rights allowed by law to a creditor against his debtor.

(8) Where a lien is on goods stored by a merchant in the course of his business the lien may be enforced in accordance with either subdivision (1) or (2).

(9) The warehouseman is liable for damages caused by failure to comply with the requirements for sale under this section and in case of willful violation is liable for conversion.

Chapter 3

BILLS OF LADING: SPECIAL PROVISIONS

Sec. 7301. Liability for Non-Receipt or Misdescription; "Said to Contain"; "Shipper's Load and Count"; Improper Handling.

(1) A consignee of a nonnegotiable bill who has given value in good faith or a holder to whom a negotiable bill has been duly negotiated relying in either case upon the description therein the goods, or upon the date therein shown, may recover from the issuer damages caused by the misdating of the bill or the nonreceipt or misdescription of the goods, except to the extent that the document indicates that the issuer does not know whether any part or all of the goods in fact were received or conform to the description, as where the description is in terms of marks or labels or kind, quantity, or condition or the receipt or description is qualified by "contents or condition of contents of packages unknown," "said to contain," "shipper's weight, load and count" or the like, if such indication be true.

(2) When goods are loaded by an issuer who is a common carrier, the issuer must count the packages or goods if package freight and ascertain the kind and quantity if bulk freight. In such cases "shipper's weight, load and count" or other words indicating that the description was made by the shipper are ineffective except as to freight concealed by packages.

(3) When bulk freight is loaded by a shipper who makes available to the issuer adequate facilities for weighing such freight, an issuer who is a common carrier must ascertain the kind and quantity within a reasonable time after receiving the written request of the shipper to do so. In such cases "shipper's weight" or other words of like purport are ineffective.

(4) The issuer may by inserting in the bill the words "shipper's weight, load and count" or other words of like purport indicate that the goods were loaded by the shipper; and if such statement be true the issuer shall not be liable for damages caused by the improper loading. But their omission does not imply liability for such damages.

(5) The shipper shall be deemed to have guaranteed to the issuer the accuracy at the time of shipment of the description, marks, labels, number, kind, quantity, condition and weight, as furnished by him; and the shipper shall indemnify the issuer against damage caused by inaccuracies in such particulars. The right of the issuer to such indemnity shall in no way limit his responsibility and liability under the contract of carriage to any person other than the shipper.

Sec. 7302. Through Bills of Lading and Similar Documents.

(1) The issuer of a through bill of lading or other documents embodying an undertaking to be performed in part by persons acting as its agents or by connecting carriers is liable to anyone entitled to recover on the document for any breach by such other persons or by a connecting carrier of its obligation under the document but to the extent that the bill covers an undertaking to be performed overseas or in territory not contiguous to the continental United States or an undertaking including matters other than transportation this liability may be varied by agreement of the parties.

(2) Where goods covered by a through bill of lading or other document embodying an undertaking to be performed in part by persons other than the issuer are received by any such person, he is subject with respect to his own performance while the goods are in his possession to the obligation of the issuer. His obligation is discharged by delivery of the goods to another such person pursuant to the document, and does not include liability for breach by any other such persons or by the issuer.

(3) The issuer of such through bill of lading or other document shall be entitled to recover from the connecting carrier or such other person in possession of the goods when the breach of the obligation under the document occurred, the amount it may be required to pay to anyone entitled to recover on the document therefor, as may be evidenced by any receipt, judgment, or transcript thereof, and the amount of any expense reasonably incurred by it in defending any action brought by anyone entitled to recover on the document therefor.

Sec. 7303. Diversion; Reconsignment; Change of Instructions. (1) Unless the bill of lading otherwise provides, the carrier may deliver the goods to a person or destination other than that stated in the bill or may otherwise dispose of the goods on instructions from

(a) The holder of a negotiable bill; or

(b) The consignor on a nonnegotiable bill notwithstanding contrary instructions from the consignee; or

(c) The consignee on a nonnegotiable bill in the absence of contrary instructions from the consignor, if the goods have arrived at the billed destination or if the consignee is in possession of the bill; or

(d) The consignee on a nonnegotiable bill if he is entitled as against the consignor to dispose of them.

(2) Unless such instructions are noted on a negotiable bill of lading, a person to whom the bill is duly negotiated can hold the bailee according to the original terms.

Sec. 7304. Bills of Lading in a Set. (1) Except where customary in overseas transportation, a bill of lading must not be issued in a set of parts. The issuer is liable for damages caused by violation of this subdivision.

(2) Where a bill of lading is lawfully drawn in a set of parts, each of which is numbered and expressed to be valid only if the goods have not been delivered against any other part, the whole of the parts constitute one bill.

(3) Where a bill of lading is lawfully issued in a set of parts and different parts are negotiated to different persons, the title of the holder to whom the first due negotiation is made prevails as to both the document and the goods even though any later holder may have received the goods from the carrier in good faith and discharged the carrier's obligation by surrender of his part.

(4) Any person who negotiates or transfers a single part of a bill of lading drawn in a set is liable to holders of that part as if it were the whole set.

(5) The bailee is obliged to deliver in accordance with Chapter 4 of this division against the first presented part of a bill of lading lawfully drawn in a set. Such delivery discharges the bailee's obligation on the whole bill.

Sec. 7305. Destination Bills. (1) Instead of issuing a bill of lading to the consignor at the place of shipment a carrier may at the request of the consignor procure the bill to be issued at destination or at any other place designated in the request.

(2) Upon request of anyone entitled as against the carrier to control the goods while in transit and on surrender of any outstanding bill of lading or other receipt covering such goods, the issuer may procure a substitute bill to be issued at any place designated in the request.

Sec. 7306. Altered Bills of Lading. An unauthorized alteration or filling in of a blank in a bill of lading leaves the bill enforceable according to its original tenor.

Sec. 7307. Lien of Carrier. (1) A carrier has a lien on the goods covered by a bill of lading for charges subsequent to the date of its receipt of the goods for storage or transportation (including demurrage and terminal charges) and for expenses necessary for preservation of the goods incident to their transportation or reasonably incurred in their sale pursuant to law. But against a purchaser for value of a negotiable bill of lading a carrier's lien is limited to charges stated in the bill or the applicable tariffs, or if no charges are stated then to a reasonable charge.

(2) A lien for charges and expenses under subdivision (1) on goods which the carrier was required by law to receive for transportation is effective against the consignor or any person entitled to the goods unless the carrier had notice that the consignor lacked authority to subject the goods to such charges and expenses. Any other lien under subdivision (1) is effective against the consignor and any person who permitted the bailor to have control or possession of the goods unless the carrier had notice that the bailor lacked such authority.

(3) A carrier loses his lien on any goods which he voluntarily delivers or which he unjustifiably refuses to deliver.

Sec. 7308. Enforcement of Carrier's Lien. (1) A carrier's lien may be enforced by public or private sale of the goods, in bloc or in parcels, at any time or place and on any terms which are commercially reasonable, after notifying all persons known to claim an interest in the goods. Such notification must include a statement of the amount due, the nature of the proposed sale and the time and place of any public sale. The fact that a better price could have been obtained by a sale at a different time or in a different method from that selected by the carrier is not of itself sufficient to establish that the sale was not made in a commercially reasonable manner. If the carrier either sells the goods in the usual manner in any recognized market therefor or if he sells at the price current in such market at the time of his sale or if he has otherwise sold in conformity with commercially reasonable practices among dealers in the type of goods sold he has sold in a commercially reasonable manner. A sale of more goods than apparently necessary to be offered to ensure satisfaction of the obligation is not commercially reasonable except in cases covered by the preceding sentence.

(2) Before any sale pursuant to this section any person claiming a right in the goods may pay the amount necessary to satisfy the lien and the reasonable expenses incurred under this section. In that event the goods must not be sold, but must be retained by the carrier subject to the terms of the bill and this division.

(3) The carrier may buy at any public sale pursuant to this section.

(4) A purchaser in good faith of goods sold to enforce a carrier's lien takes the goods free of any rights of persons against whom the lien was valid, despite noncompliance by the carrier with the requirements of this section.

(5) The carrier may satisfy his lien from the proceeds of any sale pursuant to this section but must hold the balance, if any, for delivery on demands to any person to whom he would have been bound to deliver the goods.

(6) The rights provided by this section shall be in addition to all other rights allowed by law to a creditor against his debtor.

(7) A carrier's lien may be enforced in accordance wtih either subdivision (1) or the procedure set forth in subdivision (2) of Section 7210.

(8) The carrier is liable for damages caused by failure to comply with the requirements for sale under this section and in case of willful violation is liable for conversion.

Sec. 7309. Duty of Care; Contractual Limitation of Carriers' Liability. (1) A carrier who issues a bill of lading whether negotiable or nonnegotiable must exercise the degree of care in relation to the goods which a reasonably careful man would exercise under like circumstances. This subdivision does not repeal or change any law or rule of law which imposes liability upon a common carrier for damages not caused by its negligence.

(2) Damages may be limited by a provision that the carrier's liability shall not exceed a value stated in the document if the carrier's rates are dependent upon value and the consignor by the carrier's tariff is afforded an opportunity to declare a higher value or a value as lawfully provided in the tariff, or where no tariff is filed he is otherwise advised of such opportunity; but no such limitation is effective with respect to the carrier's liability for conversion to its own use.

(3) Reasonable provisions as to the time and manner of presenting claims and instituting actions based on the shipment may be included in a bill of lading or tariff.

CHAPTER 4

WAREHOUSE RECEIPTS AND BILLS OF LADING: GENERAL OBLIGATIONS

Sec. 7401. Irregularities in Issue of Receipt or Bill or Conduct of Issuer. The obligations imposed by this division on an issuer apply to a document of title regardless of the fact that

(a) The document may not comply with the requirements of this division or of any other law or regulation regarding its issue, form or content; or

(b) The issuer may have violated laws regulating the conduct of his business; or

(c) The goods covered by the document were owned by the bailee at the time the document was issued; or

(d) The person issuing the document does not come within the definition of warehouseman if it purports to be a warehouse receipt.

Sec. 7402. **Duplicate Receipt or Bill; Overissue.** Neither a duplicate nor any other document of title purporting to cover goods already represented by an outstanding document of the same issuer confers any right in the goods, except as provided in the case of bills in a set, overissue of documents for fungible goods and substitutes for lost, stolen or destroyed documents. But the issuer is liable for damages caused by his overissue or failure to identify a duplicate document as such by conspicuous notation on its face.

Sec. 7403. **Obligation of Warehouseman or Carrier to Deliver; Excuse.** (1) The bailee must deliver the goods to a person entitled under the document who complies with subdivisions (2) and (3), unless and to the extent that the bailee establishes any of the following:

(a) Delivery of the goods to a person whose receipt was rightful as against the claimant;

(b) Damage to or delay, loss or destruction of the goods for which the bailee is not liable, but the burden of establishing negligence in case of damage or destruction by fire is on the person entitled under the document;

(c) Previous sale or other disposition of the goods in lawful enforcement of a lien or on warehouseman's lawful termination of storage;

(d) The exercise by a seller of his right to stop delivery pursuant to the provisions of the division on sales (Section 2705);

(e) A diversion, reconsignment or other disposition pursuant to the provisions of this division (Section 7303) or tariff regulating such right;

(f) Release, satisfaction or any other fact affording a personal defense against the claimant;

(g) Any other lawful excuse.

(2) A person claiming goods covered by a document of title must satisfy the bailee's lien where the bailee so requests or where the bailee is prohibited by law from delivering the goods until the charges are paid.

(3) Unless the person claiming is one against whom the document confers no right under subdivision (1) of Section 7503, he must surrender for cancellation or notation of partial deliveries any outstanding negotiable document covering the goods, and the bailee must cancel the document or conspicuously note the partial delivery thereon or be liable to any person to whom the document is duly negotiated.

(4) "Person entitled under the document" means holder in the case o f a negotiable document, or the person to whom delivery is to be made by the terms of or pursuant to written instructions under a nonnegotiable document.

Sec. 7404. **No Liability for Good Faith Delivery Pursuant to Receipt or Bill.** A bailee who in good faith including observance of reasonable commercial standards has received goods and delivered or otherwise disposed of them according to the terms of the document of title or pursuant to this division is not liable therefor. This rule applies even though the person from whom he received the goods had no authority to procure the document or to dispose of the goods and even though the person to whom he delivered the goods had no authority to receive them.

CHAPTER 5

WAREHOUSE RECEIPTS AND BILLS OF LADING: NEGOTIATION AND TRANSFER

Sec. 7501. **Form of Negotiation and Requirements of "Due Negotiation."** (1) A negotiable document of title running to the order of a named person is negotiated by his indorsement and delivery. After his indorsement in blank or to bearer any person can negotiate it by delivery alone.

(2) (a) A negotiable document of title is also negotiated by delivery alone when by its original terms it runs to bearer.

(b) When a document running to the order of a named person is delivered to him the effect is the same as if the document had been negotiated.

(3) Negotiation of a negotiable document of title after it has been indorsed to a specified person requires indorsement by the special indorsee as well as delivery.

(4) A negotiable document of title is "duly negotiated" when it is negotiated in the manner stated in this section to a holder who purchases it in good faith without notice of any defense against or claim to it on the part of any person and for value.

(5) Indorsement of a nonnegotiable document neither makes it negotiable nor adds to the transferee's rights.

(6) The naming in a negotiable bill of a person to be notified of the arrival of the goods does not limit the negotiability of the bill nor constitute notice to a purchaser thereof of any interest of such person in the goods.

Sec. 7502. **Rights Acquired by Due Negotiation.** (1) Subject to the following section and to the provisions of Section 7205 on fungible goods, a holder to whom a negotiable document of title has been duly negotiated acquires thereby:

(a) Title to the document;

(b) Title to the goods;

(c) All rights accruing under the law of agency or estoppel, including rights to goods delivered to the bailee after the document was issued; and

(d) The direct obligation of the issuer to hold or deliver the goods according to the terms of the document free of any defense or claim by him except those arising under the terms of the document or under this division.

(2) Subject to the following section, title and rights so acquired are not defeated by any stoppage of the goods represented by the document or by surrender of such goods by the bailee, and are not impaired even though the negotiation or any prior negotiation constituted a breach of duty or even though any person has been deprived of possession of the document by misrepresentation, fraud, accident, mistake, duress, loss, theft or conversion, or even though a previous sale or other transfer of the goods or document has been made to a third person.

Sec. 7503. **Document of Title to Goods Defeated in Certain Cases.** (1) A document of title confers no right in goods against a person who before issuance of the document had a legal interest or a perfected security interest in them and who neither

(a) Delivered nor entrusted them nor any document of title covering them to the bailor or his nominee with actual or apparent authority to ship, store or sell or with power to obtain delivery under this division (Section 7403) or with power of disposition under this code (Sections 2403 and 9307) or other statute or rule of law, nor

(b) Acquiesced in the procurement by the bailor or his nominee of any document of title.

(2) Title to goods based upon a bill of lading issued to a freight forwarder is subject to the rights of anyone to whom a bill issued by the freight forwarder is duly negotiated; but delivery by the carrier in accordance with Chapter 4 of this division pursuant to its own bill of lading discharges the carrier's obligation to deliver.

Sec. 7504. **Rights Acquired in the Absence of Due Negotiation; Effect of Diversion; Seller's Stoppage of Delivery.** (1) A transferee of a document, whether negotiable or nonnegotiable, to whom the document has been delivered but not duly negotiated, acquires the title and rights which his transferor had or had actual authority to convey.

(2) In the case of a nonnegotiable document, until but not after the bailee receives notification of the transfer, the rights of the transferee may be defeated

(a) By those creditors of the transferor who could treat the sale as void under Section 2402; or

(b) By a buyer from the transferor in ordinary course of business if the bailee has delivered the goods to the buyer or received notification of his rights; or

(c) As against the bailee by good faith dealings of the bailee with the transferor.

(3) A diversion or other change of shipping instructions by the consignor in a nonnegotiable bill of lading which causes the bailee not to deliver to the consignee defeats the consignee's title to the goods if they have been delivered to a buyer in ordinary course of business and in any event defeats the consignee's rights against the bailee.

(4) Delivery pursuant to a nonnegotiable document may be stopped by a seller under Section 2705, and subject to the requirement of due notification there provided. A bailee honoring the seller's instructions is entitled to be indemnified by the seller against any resulting loss or expense.

Sec. 7505. **Indorser Not a Guarantor for Other Parties.** The indorsement of a document of title issued by a bailee does not make the indorser liable for any default by the bailee or by previous indorsers.

Sec. 7506. **Delivery Without Indorsement: Right to Compel Indorsement.** The transferee of a negotiable document of title has a specifically enforceable right to have his transferor supply any necessary indorsement but the transfer becomes a negotiation only as of the time the indorsement is supplied.

Sec. 7507. **Warranties on Negotiation or Transfer of Receipt or Bill.** Where a person negotiates or transfers a document of title for value otherwise than as a mere intermediary under the next following section, then unless otherwise agreed he warrants to his immediate purchaser only in addition to any warranty made in selling the goods

(a) That the document is genuine; and

(b) That he has no knowledge of any fact which would impair its validity or worth; and

(c) That his negotiation or transfer is rightful and fully effective with respect to the title to the document and the goods it represents.

Sec. 7508. Warranties of Collecting Bank as to Documents. A collecting bank or other intermediary known to be entrusted with documents on behalf of another or with collection of a draft or other claim against delivery of documents warrants by such delivery of the documents only its own good faith and authority. This rule applies even though the intermediary has purchased or made advances against the claim or draft to be collected.

Sec. 7509. Receipt or Bill: When Adequate Compliance With Commercial Contract. The question whether a document is adequate to fulfill the obligations of a contract for sale or the conditions of a credit is governed by the divisions on sales (Division 2) and on letters of credit (Division 5).

CHAPTER 6

WAREHOUSE RECEIPTS AND BILLS OF LADING: MISCELLANEOUS PROVISIONS

Sec. 7601. Lost and Missing Documents. (1) If a document has been lost, stolen or destroyed, a court may order delivery of the goods or issuance of a substitute document and the bailee may without liability to any person comply with such order. If the document was negotiable the claimant must post an undertaking approved by the court to indemnify any person who may suffer loss as a result of nonsurrender of the document. If the document was not negotiable, an undertaking may be required at the discretion of the court. The court may also in its discretion order payment of the bailee's reasonable costs and counsel fees.

(2) A bailee who without court order delivers goods to a person claiming under a missing negotiable document is liable to any person injured thereby, and if the delivery is not in good faith becomes liable for conversion. Delivery in good faith is not conversion if made in accordance with a filed classification or tariff or, where no classification or tariff is filed, if the claimant posts an undertaking with the bailee in an amount at least double the value of the goods at the time of posting to indemnify any person injured by the delivery who files a notice of claim within one year after the delivery.

Sec. 7602. Attachment of Goods Covered by a Negotiable Document. Except where the document was originally issued upon delivery of the goods by a person who had no power to dispose of them, no lien attaches by virtue of any judicial process to goods in the possession of a bailee for which a negotiable document of title is outstanding unless the document be first surrendered to the bailee or its negotiation enjoined, and the bailee shall not be compelled to deliver the goods pursuant to process until the document is surrendered to him or impounded by the court. One who purchases the document for value without notice of the process or injunction takes free of the lien imposed by judicial process.

Sec. 7603. Conflicting Claims; Interpleader. If more than one person claims title or possession of the goods, the bailee or warehouseman is excused from delivery until he has had a reasonable time to ascertain the validity of the adverse claims or to bring an action to compel all claimants to interplead and may compel such interpleader, either in defending an action for nondelivery of the goods, or by original action, whichever is appropriate.

DIVISION 8

INVESTMENT SECURITIES

CHAPTER 1

SHORT TITLE AND GENERAL MATTERS

Sec. 8101. Short Title. This division shall be known and may be cited as Uniform Commercial Code—Investment Securities.

Sec. 8102. Definitions and Index of Definitions. (1) In this division unless the context otherwise requires

(a) A "security" is an instrument which

(i) Is issued in bearer or registered form; and

(ii) Is of a type commonly dealt in upon securities exchanges or markets or commonly recognized in any area in which it is issued or dealt in as a medium for investment; and

(iii) Is either one of a class or series or by its terms is divisible into a class or series of instruments; and

(iv) Evidences a share, participation or other interest in property or in an enterprise or evidences an obligation of the issuer.

(b) A writing which is a security is governed by this division and not by Uniform Commercial Code—Commercial Paper even though it also meets the requirements of that division. This division does not apply to money.

(c) A security is in "registered form" when it specifies a person entitled to the security or to the rights it evidences and when its transfer may be registered upon books maintained for that purpose by or on behalf of an issuer or the security so states.

(d) A security is in "bearer form" when it runs to bearer according to its terms and not by reason of any indorsement.

(2) A "subsequent purchaser" is a person who takes other than by original issue.

(3) A "clearing corporation" is a corporation:

(a) At least 90 percent of the capital stock of which is held by or for one or more persons (other than individuals), each of whom

(i) Is subject to supervision or regulation pursuant to the provisions of federal or state banking laws or state insurance laws, or

(ii) Is a broker or dealer or investment company registered under the Securities Exchange Act of 1934 or the Investment Company Act of 1940, or

(iii) Is a national securities exchange or association registered under a statute of the United States such as the Securities Exchange Act of 1934, and none of whom, other than a national securities exchange or association, holds in excess of 20 percent of the capital stock of such corporation.

(b) Any remaining capital stock of which is held by individuals who have purchased such capital stock at or prior to the time of their taking office as directors of such corporation and who have purchased only so much of such capital stock as may be necessary to permit them to qualify as such directors.

(4) A "custodian bank" is any bank or trust company which is supervised by state or federal authority having supervision over banks and which is acting as custodian for a clearing corporation.

(5) Other definitions applying to this division or to specified chapters thereof and the sections in which they appear are:

"Adverse claim." Section 8301.

"Bona fide purchaser." Section 8302.

"Broker." Section 8303.

"Guarantee of the signature." Section 8402.

"Intermediary bank." Section 4105.

"Issuer." Section 8201.

"Overissue." Section 8104.

(6) In addition Division 1 (commencing with Section 1101) contains general definitions and principles of construction and interpretation applicable throughout this division.

Sec. 8103. Issuer's Lien. A lien upon a security in favor of an issuer thereof is ineffective unless noted conspicuously on the security, except against a transferee with actual knowledge of it. For the purpose of this section, a transferee includes a purchaser from the corporation.

Sec. 8104. Effect of Overissue; "Overissue." (1) The provisions of this division which validate a security or compel its issue or reissue do not apply to the extent that validation, issue or reissue would result in overissue; but

(a) If an identical security which does not constitute an overissue is reasonably available for purchase, the person entitled to issue or validation may compel the issuer to purchase and deliver such a security to him against surrender of the security, if any, which he holds; or

(b) If a security is not so available for purchase, the person entitled to issue or validation may recover from the issuer the price he or the last purchaser for value paid for it with interest from the date of his demand.

(2) "Overissue" means the issue of securities in excess of the amount which the issuer has corporate power to issue.

Sec. 8105. **Burden of Establishing Signature, Defense or Defect.**
(1) Securities governed by this division are negotiable instruments.
(2) In any action on a security
(a) Unless specifically denied in the pleadings, each signature on the security or in a necessary indorsement is admitted;
(b) When the effectiveness of a signature is put in issue the burden of establishing it is on the party claiming under the signature but the signature is presumed to be genuine or authorized;
(c) When signatures are admitted or established production of the instrument entitles a holder to recover on it unless the defendant establishes a defense or a defect going to the validity of the security; and
(d) After it is shown that a defense or defect exists the plaintiff has the burden of establishing that he or some person under whom he claims is a person against whom the defense or defect is ineffective (Section 8202).

Sec. 8106. **Law Governing Validity of Security and Duty of Issuer To Register Transfer; Applicability of Division.** The validity of a security and the duty of an issuer to register a transfer (Section 8401) are governed by the law of the jurisdiction of organization of the issuer or, in the case of any national bank or other corporation organized under the laws of the United States, by the law of the jurisdiction in which such bank or other corporation has its principal place of business. (See Section 8107.)

Sec. 8107. **Right to Deliver Equivalent of Securities, Under Obligation; Seller's Remedy.** (1) Unless otherwise agreed, a person obligated to deliver securities may deliver a like number of units of any securities which by nature or usage of trade are the equivalent of the securities he is obligated to deliver.
(2) Where, pursuant to the contract to sell or a sale, a security has been delivered or tendered to the purchaser, and the purchaser wrongfully fails to pay for the security according to the terms of the contract or the sale, the seller may as an alternative to any other remedy recover the agreed price of the security. This subsection does not affect the remedy of a seller if the security has not been delivered or tendered.

Sec. 8108. **Other Codes Not Modified.** Nothing in this division shall be construed to modify any of the provisions of the Corporate Securities Law, the Insurance Code, the Financial Code, or the Public Utilities Code.

CHAPTER 2

ISSUE—ISSUER

Sec. 8201. **"Issuer."** (1) With respect to obligations on or defenses to a security "issuer" includes a person who
(a) Places or authorizes the placing of his name on a security (otherwise than as authenticating trustee, registrar, transfer agent or the like) to evidence that it represents a share, participation or other interest in his property or in an enterprise or to evidence his duty to perform an obligation evidenced by the security; or
(b) Directly or indirectly creates fractional interests in his rights or property which fractional interests are evidenced by securities; or
(c) Becomes responsible for or in place of any other person described as an issuer in this section.
(2) With respect to obligations on or defenses to a security a guarantor is an issuer to the extent of his guaranty whether or not his obligation is noted on the security.
(3) With respect to registration of transfer (Chapter 4 of this division) "issuer" means a person on whose behalf transfer books are maintained.

Sec. 8202. **Issuer's Responsibility and Defenses; Notice of Defect or Defense.** (1) Even against a purchaser for value and without notice, the terms of a security include those stated on the security and those made part of the security by reference to another instrument, indenture or document or to a constitution, statute, ordinance, rule, regulation, order or the like to the extent that the terms so referred to do not conflict with the stated terms.

Such a reference does not of itself charge a purchaser for value with notice of a defect going to the validity of the security even though the security expressly states that a person accepting it admits such notice.
(2) (a) A security other than one issued by a government or governmental agency or unit even though issued with a defect going to its validity is valid in the hands of a purchaser for value and without notice of the particular defect unless the defect involves a violation of constitutional provisions in which case the security is valid in the hands of a subsequent purchaser for value and without notice of the defect;
(b) The rule of paragraph (a) applies to an issuer which is a government or governmental agency or unit only if either there has been substantial compliance with the legal requirements governing the issue or the issuer has received a substantial consideration for the issue as a whole or for the particular security and a stated purpose of the issue is one for which the issuer has power to borrow money or issue the security.
(3) Except as otherwise provided in the case of certain unauthorized signatures on issue (Section 8205), lack of genuineness of a security is a complete defense even against a purchaser for value and without notice.
(4) All other defenses of the issuer including nondelivery and conditional delivery of the security are ineffective against a purchaser for value who has taken without notice of the particular defense.

Sec. 8203. **Staleness as Notice of Defects or Defenses.** (1) After an act or event which creates a right to immediate performance of the principal obligation evidenced by the security or which sets a date on or after which the security is to be presented or surrendered for redemption or exchange, a purchaser is charged with notice of any defect in its issue or defense of the issuer
(a) If the act or event is one requiring the payment of money or the delivery of securities or both on presentation or surrender of the security and such funds or securities are available on the date set for payment or exchange and he takes the security more than one year after that date; and
(b) If the act or event is not covered by paragraph (a) and he takes the security more than two years after the date set for surrender or presentation or the date on which such performance became due.
(2) A call which has been revoked is not within subdivision (1).

Sec. 8204. **Effect of Issuer's Restrictions on Transfer.** Unless noted conspicuously on the security a restriction on transfer imposed by the issuer even though otherwise lawful is ineffective except against a person with actual knowledge of it. For the purpose of this section, a transferee includes a purchaser from the corporation.

Sec. 8205. **Effect of Unauthorized Signature on Issue.** An unauthorized signature placed on a security prior to or in the course of issue is ineffective except that the signature is effective in favor of a purchaser for value and without notice of the lack of authority if the signing has been done by
(a) An authenticating trustee, registrar, transfer agent or other person entrusted by the issuer with the signing of the security or of similar securities or their immediate preparation for signing; or
(b) An employee of the issuer or of any of the foregoing entrusted with responsible handling of the security.

Sec. 8206. **Completion or Alteration of Instrument.** (1) Where a security contains the signatures necessary to its issue or transfer but is incomplete in any other respect
(a) Any person may complete it by filling in the blanks as authorized; and
(b) Even though the blanks are incorrectly filled in, the security as completed is enforceable by a purchaser who took it for value and without notice of such incorrectness.
(2) A complete security which has been improperly altered even though fraudulently remains enforceable but only according to its original terms.

Sec. 8207. **Rights of Issuer With Respect to Registered Owners.** (1) Prior to due presentment for registration of transfer of a security in registered form the issuer or indenture trustee may treat the registered owner as the person exclusively entitled to vote, to receive notifications and otherwise to exercise all the rights and powers of an owner.
(2) Nothing in this division shall be construed to affect the liability of the registered owner of a security for calls, assessments or the like.

Sec. 8208. **Effect of Signature of Authenticating Trustee, Registrar or Transfer Agent.** (1) A person placing his signature upon a security as authenticating trustee, registrar, transfer agent or the like warrants to a purchaser for value without notice of the particular defect that

(a) The security is genuine; and

(b) His own participation in the issue of the security is within his capacity and within the scope of the authorization received by him from the issuer; and

(c) He has reasonable grounds to believe that the security is in the form and within the amount the issuer is authorized to issue.

(2) Unless otherwise agreed, a person by so placing his signature does not assume responsibility for the validity of the security in other respects.

CHAPTER 3

PURCHASE

Sec. 8301. **Rights Acquired by Purchaser; "Adverse Claim"; Title Acquired by Bona Fide Purchaser.** (1) Upon delivery of a security the purchaser acquires the rights in the security which his transferor had or had actual authority to convey except that a purchaser who has himself been a party to any fraud or illegality affecting the security or who as a prior holder had notice of an adverse claim cannot improve his position by taking from a later bona fide purchaser. "Adverse claim" includes a claim that a transfer was or would be wrongful or that a particular adverse person is the owner of or has an interest in the security.

(2) A bona fide purchaser in addition to acquiring the rights of a purchaser also acquires the security free of any adverse claim.

(3) A purchaser of a limited interest acquires rights only to the extent of the interest purchased.

Sec. 8302. **"Bona Fide Purchaser."** A "bona fide purchaser" is a purchaser for value in good faith and without notice of any adverse claim who takes delivery of a security in bearer form or of one in registered form issued to him or indorsed to him or in blank.

Sec. 8303. **"Broker."** "Broker" means a person engaged for all or part of his time in the business of buying and selling securities, who in the transaction concerned acts for, or buys a security from or sells a security to a customer. Nothing in this division determines the capacity in which a person acts for purposes of any other statute or rule to which such person is subject.

Sec. 8304. **Notice to Purchaser of Adverse Claims.** (1) A purchaser (including a broker for the seller or buyer but excluding an intermediary bank) of a security is charged with notice of adverse claims if

(a) The security whether in bearer or registered form has been indorsed "for collection" or "for surrender" or for some other purpose not involving transfer; or

(b) The security is in bearer form and has on it an unambiguous statement that it is the property of a person other than the transferor. The mere writing of a name on a security is not such a statement.

(2) The fact that the purchaser (including a broker for the seller or buyer) has notice that the security is held for a third person or is registered in the name of or indorsed by a fiduciary does not create a duty of inquiry into the rightfulness of the transfer or constitute notice of adverse claims. If, however, the purchaser (excluding an intermediary bank) has knowledge that the proceeds are being used or that the transaction is for the individual benefit of the fiduciary or otherwise in breach of duty, the purchaser is charged with notice of adverse claims.

Sec. 8305. **Staleness as Notice of Adverse Claims.** An act or event which creates a right to immediate performance of the principal obligation evidenced by the security or which sets a date on or after which the security is to be presented or surrendered for redemption or exchange does not of itself constitute any notice of adverse claims except in the case of a purchase

(a) After one year from any date set for such presentment or surrender for redemption or exchange; or

(b) After six months from any date set for payment of money against presentation or surrender of the security if funds are available for payment on that date.

Sec. 8306. **Warranties on Presentment and Transfer.** (1) A person who presents a security for registration of transfer or for payment or exchange warrants to the issuer that he is entitled to the registration, payment or exchange. But a purchaser for value without notice of adverse claims who receives a new, reissued or reregistered security on registra-

tion of transfer warrants only that he has no knowledge of any unauthorized signature (Section 8311) in a necessary indorsement.

(2) A person by transferring a security to a purchaser for value warrants onl y that

(a) His transfer is effective and rightful; and

(b) The security is genuine and has not been materially altered; and

(c) He knows no fact which might impair the validity of the security.

(3) Where a security is delivered by an intermediary known to be entrusted with delivery of the security on behalf of another or with collection of a draft or other claim against such delivery, the intermediary by such delivery warrants only his own good faith and authority even though he has purchased or made advances against the claim to be collected against the delivery.

(4) A pledge or other holder for security who redelivers the security received, or after payment and on order of the debtor delivers that security to a third person makes only the warranties of an intermediary under subdivision (3).

(5) A broker gives to his customer and to the issuer and a purchaser the warranties provided in this section and has the rights and privileges of a purchaser under this section. The warranties of and in favor of the broker acting as an agent are in addition to applicable warranties given by and in favor of his customer.

Sec. 8307. **Effect of Delivery Without Indorsement; Right to Compel Indorsement.** Where a security in registered form has been delivered to a purchaser without a necessary indorsement he may become a bona fide purchaser only as of the time the indorsement is supplied, but against the transferor the transfer is complete upon delivery and the purchaser has a specifically enforceable right to have any necessary indorsement supplied.

Sec. 8308. **Indorsement, How Made; Special Indorsement; Indorser Not a Guarantor; Partial Assignment.** (1) An indorsement of a security in registered form is made when an appropriate person signs on it or on a separate document an assignment or transfer of the security or a power to assign or transfer it or when the signature of such person is written without more upon the back of the security.

(2) An indorsement may be in blank or special. An indorsement in blank includes an indorsement to bearer. A special indorsement specifies the person to whom the security is to be transferred, or who has power to transfer it. A holder may convert a blank indorsement into a special indorsement.

(3) "An appropriate person" in subdivision (1) means

(a) The person specified by the security or by special indorsement to be entitled to the security; or

(b) Where the person so specified is described as a fiduciary but is no longer serving in the described capacity—either that person or his successor; or

(d) Where the person so specified is an individual and is without capacity to act by virtue of death, incompetence, infancy or otherwise—his executor, administrator, guardian or like fiduciary; or

(e) Where the security or indorsement so specifies more than one person as tenants by the entirety or with right of survivorship and by reason of death all cannot sign—the survivor or survivors; or

(f) A person having power to sign under applicable law or controlling instrument; or

(g) To the extent that any of the foregoing persons may act through an agent—his authorized agent.

(4) Unless otherwise agreed the indorser by his indorsement assumes no obligation that the security will be honored by the issuer.

(5) An indorsement purporting to be only of part of a security representing units intended by the issuer to be separately transferable is effective to the extent of the indorsement.

(6) Whether the person signing is appropriate is determined as of the date of signing and an indorsement by such a person does not become unauthorized for the purposes of this division by virtue of any subsequent change of circumstances.

(7) Failure of a fiduciary to comply with a controlling instrument or with the law of the state having jurisdiction of the fiduciary relationship, including any law requiring the fiduciary to obtain court approval of the transfer, does not render his endorsement unauthorized for the purposes of this division.

Sec. 8309. **Effect of Indorsement Without Delivery.** An indorsement of a security whether special or in blank does not constitute a transfer until delivery of the security on which it appears or if the indorsement is on a separate document until delivery of both the document and the security.

Sec. 8310. Indorsement of Security in Bearer Form. An indorsement of a security in bearer form may give notice of adverse claims (Section 8304) but does not otherwise affect any right to registration the holder may possess.

Sec. 8311. Effect of Unauthorized Indorsement. Unless owner has ratified an unauthorized indorsement or is otherwise precluded from asserting its ineffectiveness

(a) He may assert its ineffectiveness against the issuer or any purchaser other than a purchaser for value and without notice of adverse claims who has in good faith received a new, reissued or reregistered security on registration of transfer; and

(b) An issuer who registers the transfer of a security upon the unauthorized indorsement is subject to liability for improper registration (Section 8404).

Sec. 8312. Effect of Guaranteeing Signature or Indorsement. (1) Any person guaranteeing a signature of an indorser of a security warrants that at the time of signing

(a) The signature was genuine; and

(b) The signer was an appropriate person to indorse (Section 8308); and

(c) The signer has legal capacity to sign.

But the guarantor does not otherwise warrant the rightfulness of the particular transfer.

(2) Any person may guarantee an indorsement of a security and by so doing warrants not only the signature (subdivision 1) but also the rightfulness of the particular transfer in all respects. But no issuer may require a guarantee of indorsement as a condition to registration of transfer.

(3) The foregoing warranties are made to any person taking or dealing with the security in reliance on the guarantee and the guarantor is liable to such person for any loss resulting from breach of the warranties.

Sec. 8313. When Delivery to the Purchaser Occurs; Purchaser's Broker as Holder; Notice of Adverse Claim. (1) Delivery to a purchaser occurs when

(a) He or a person designated by him acquires possession of a security; or

(b) His broker acquires possession of a security specially indorsed to or issued in the name of the purchaser; or

(c) His broker sends him confirmation of the purchase and also by book entry or otherwise identifies a specific security in the broker's possession as belonging to the purchaser; or

(d) With respect to an identified security to be delivered while still in the possession of a third person when that person acknowledges that he holds for the purchaser; or

(e) Appropriate entries on the books of a clearing corporation are made under Section 8320.

(2) The purchaser is the owner of a security held from him by his broker, but is not the holder except as specified in paragraphs (b), (c) and (e) of subdivision (1) of this section. Where a security is part of a fungible bulk, the purchaser is the owner of a proportionate property interest in the fungible bulk.

(3) Notice of an adverse claim received by the broker or by the purchaser after the broker takes delivery as a holder for value is not effective either as to the broker or as to the purchaser. However, as between the broker and the purchaser the purchaser may demand delivery of an equivalent security as to which no notice of an adverse claim has been received.

Sec. 8314. Duty to Deliver, When Completed. (1) Unless otherwise agreed where a sale of a security is made on an exchange or otherwise through brokers

(a) The selling customer fulfills his duty to deliver when he places such a security in the possession of the selling broker or of a person designated by the broker or if requested causes an acknowledgment to be made to the selling broker that it is held for him; and

(2) Except as otherwise provided in this section and unless otherwise agreed, a transferor's duty to deliver a security under a contract of purchase is not fulfilled until he places the security in form to be negotiated by the purchaser in the possession of the purchaser or of a person designated by him or at the purchaser's request causes an acknowledgment to be made to the purchaser that it is held for him. Unless made on an exchange sale to a broker purchasing for his own account is within this subdivision and not within subdivision (1).

Sec. 8315. Action Against Purchaser Based Upon Wrongful Transfer. (1) Any person against whom the transfer of a security is wrongful for any reason, including lack of delivery or his incapacity, may against any purchaser except a bona fide purchaser reclaim possession of the security or obtain possession of any new security evidencing all or part of the same rights or have damages.

(2) If the transfer is wrongful because of an unauthorized indorsement, the owner may also reclaim or obtain possession of the security or new security even from a bona fide purchaser if the ineffectiveness of the purported indorsement can be asserted against him under the provisions of this division on unauthorized indorsements (Section 8311).

(3) The right to obtain or reclaim possession of a security may be specifically enforced and its transfer enjoined and the security impounded pending the litigation.

Sec. 8316. Purchaser's Right to Requisites for Registration of Transfer on Books. Unless otherwise agreed the transferor must on due demand supply his purchaser with any proof of his authority to transfer or with any other requisite which may be necessary to obtain registration of the transfer of the security but if the transfer is not for value a transferor need not do so unless the purchaser furnishes the necessary expenses. Failure to comply with a demand made within a reasonable time gives the purchaser the right to reject or rescind the transfer.

Sec. 8317. Attachment or Levy Upon Security. (1) No attachment or levy upon a security or any share or other interest evidenced thereby which is outstanding shall be valid until: (a) the security is actually seized by the officer making the attachment or levy, or (b) in the case of a security held in escrow pursuant to the provisions of the Corporate Securities Law, a copy of the writ and a notice that the securities are attached or levied upon in pursuance of such writ is served upon the escrow holder; but a security which has been surrendered to the issuer may be attached or levied upon at the source.

(2) A creditor whose debtor is the owner of a security shall be entitled to such aid from courts of appropriate jurisdiction, by injunction or otherwise, in reaching such security or in satisfying the claim by means thereof as is allowed at law or in equity in regard to property which cannot readily be attached or levied upon by ordinary legal process.

Sec. 8318. No Conversion by Good Faith Delivery. An agent or bailee who in good faith (including observance of reasonable commercial standards if he is in the business of buying, selling or otherwise dealing with securities) has received securities and sold, pledged or delivered them according to the instructions of his principal is not liable for conversion or for participation in breach of fiduciary duty although the principal had no right to dispose of them.

Sec. 8319. Statute of Frauds. (1) A contract for the sale of securities is not enforceable by way of action or defense unless

(a) There is some writing signed by the party against whom enforcement is sought or by his authorized agent or broker sufficient to indicate that a contract has been made for sale of a stated quantity of described securities at a defined or stated price; or

(b) Delivery of the security has been accepted or payment has been made but the contract is enforceable under this provision only to the extent of such delivery or payment; or

(c) Within a reasonable time a writing in confirmation of the sale or purchase and sufficient against the sender under paragraph (a) has been received by the party against whom enforcement is sought and he has failed to send written objection to its contents within 10 days after its receipt.

(2) A contract relating to the purchase or sale of securities between a broker acting as an agent and his principal is not subject to the provisions of this section.

Sec. 8320. Transfer or Pledge by Book Entry. (1) If a security

(a) Is in the custody of a clearing corporation or of a custodian bank or a nominee of either subject to the instructions of the clearing corporation; and

(b) Is in bearer form or indorsed in blank by an appropriate person or registered in the name of the clearing corporation or custodian bank or a nominee of either; and

(c) Is shown on the account of a transferor or pledgor on the books of the clearing corporation;

then, in addition to other methods, a transfer or pledge of the security or any interest therein may be effected by the making of appropriate entries on the books of the clearing corporation reducing the account of the transferor or pledgor and increasing the account of the transferee or pledgee by the amount of the obligation or the number of shares or rights transferred or pledged.

(2) Under this section entries may be with respect to like securities or interests therein as a part of a fungible bulk and may refer merely to a quantity of a particular security without reference to the name of the registered owner, certificate or bond number or the like and, in appropriate cases, may be on a net basis taking into account other transfers or pledges of the same security.

(3) A transfer or pledge under this section has the effect of a delivery of a security in bearer form or duly indorsed in blank (Section 8301) representing the amount of the obligation or the number of shares or rights transferred or pledged and if a pledge or the creation of a security interest is intended, the making of entries has the effect of a taking of delivery by the pledgee or a secured party (Sections 9304 and 9305). A transferee or pledgee under this section is a holder.

(4) A transfer or pledge under this section does not constitute a registratio n of transfer under Chapter 4 of this division.

(5) That entries made on the books of the clearing corporation as provided in subdivision (1) are not appropriate does not affect the validity or effect of the entries nor the liabilities or obligations of the clearing corporation to any person adversely affected thereby.

CHAPTER 4

REGISTRATION

Sec. 8401. Duty of Issuer to Register Transfer. (1) Where a security in registered form is presented to the issuer with a request to register transfer, the issuer is under a duty to register the transfer as requested if

(a) The security is indorsed by the appropriate person or persons (Section 8308); and

(b) Reasonable assurance is given that those indorsements are genuine and effective (Section 8402); and

(c) The issuer has no duty to inquire into adverse claims or has discharged any such duty (Section 8403); and

(d) Any applicable law relating to the collection of taxes has been complied with.

(2) Where an issuer is under a duty to register a transfer of a security the issuer is liable to the person presenting it for registration or his principal for loss resulting from any unreasonable delay in registration or from failure or refusal to register the transfer, but in any such case the plaintiff must allege and prove that the transfer requested was in fact rightful or that he was a bona fide purchaser.

Sec. 8402. Assurance That Indorsements Are Effective. (1) The issuer may require the following assurance that each necessary indorsement (Section 8308) is genuine and effective.

(a) In all cases, a guarantee of the signature (subdivision (1) of Section 8312) of the person indorsing; and

(b) Where the indorsement is by an agent, appropriate assurance of authority to sign;

(c) Where the indorsement is by a fiduciary, appropriate evidence of appointment or incumbency;

(d) Where there is more than one fiduciary, reasonable assurance that all who are required to sign have done so;

(e) Where the indorsement is by a person not covered by any of the foregoing assurance appropriate to the case corresponding as nearly as may be to the foregoing.

(2) A "guarantee of the signature" in subdivision (1) means a guarantee signed by or on behalf of a person reasonably believed by the issuer to be responsible. The issuer may adopt standards with respect to responsibility provided such standards are not manifestly unreasonable.

(3) "Appropriate evidence of appointment or incumbency" in subdivision (1) means

(a) In the case of a fiduciary appointed or qualified by a court, a certificate issued by or under the direction or supervision of that court or an officer thereof and dated within 60 days before the date of presentation for transfer; or

(b) In any other case, a copy of a document showing the appointment or a certificate issued by or on behalf of a person reasonably believed by the issuer to be responsible or, in the absence of such a document or certificate, other evidence reasonably deemed by the issuer to be appropriate. The issuer may adopt standards with respect to such evidence provided such standards are not manifestly unreasonable. The issuer is

not charged with notice of the contents of any document obtained pursuant to this paragraph (b) except to the extent that the contents relate directly to the appointment or incumbency.

Sec. 8403. Limited Duty of Inquiry. (1) An issuer to whom a security is presented for registration is under a duty to inquire into adverse claims if

(a) A written notification of an adverse claim is received at a time and in a manner which affords the issuer a reasonable opportunity to act on it prior to the issuance of a new, reissued or reregistered security and the notification identifies the claimant, the registered owner and the issue of which the security is a part and provides an address for communications directed to the claimant.

(2) The issuer may discharge any duty of inquiry by any reasonable means, including notifying an adverse claimant by registered or certified mail at the address furnished by him or if there be no such address at his residence or regular place of business that the security has been presented for registration of transfer by a named person, and that the transfer will be registered unless within 30 days from the date of mailing the notification, either

(a) An appropriate restraining order, injunction or other process issues from a court of competent jurisdiction; or

(b) An indemnity bond sufficient in the issuer's judgment to protect the issuer and any transfer agent, registrar or other agent of the issuer involved, from any loss which it or they may suffer by complying with the adverse claim is filed with the issuer.

(3) Unless an issuer receives notification of an adverse claim under subdivision (1) of this section, where a security presented for registration is indorsed by the appropriate person or persons the issuer is under no duty to inquire into adverse claims.

(4) An issuer registering a security in the name of a person who is a fiduciary or who is described as a fiduciary is not bound to inquire into the existence, extent, or correct description of the fiduciary relationship and thereafter the issuer may assume without inquiry that the newly registered owner continues to be the fiduciary until the issuer receives written notice that the fiduciary is no longer acting as such with respect to the particular security.

(5) An issuer registering transfer on an indorsement by a fiduciary is not bound to inquire whether the transfer is made in compliance with a controlling instrument or with the law of the state having jurisdiction of the fiduciary relationship, including any law requiring the fiduciary to obtain court approval of the transfer, even though the transfer is made on the indorsement of a fiduciary to the fiduciary himself or his nominee.

(6) The issuer is not charged with notice of the contents of any court record or file or other recorded or unrecorded document even though the document is in its possession and even though the transfer is made on the indorsement of a fiduciary to the fiduciary himself or to his nominee.

(7) (a) No person who participates in the acquisition, disposition, assignme nt or transfer of a security by or to a fiduciary including a person who guarantees the signature of the fiduciary is liable for participation in any breach of fiduciary duty by reason of failure to inquire whether the transaction involves such a breach unless it is shown that he acted with knowledge that the proceeds were being used or that the transaction was wrongfully for the individual benefit of the fiduciary or otherwise in breach of duty.

(b) If a corporation or transfer agent makes a transfer pursuant to an assignment by a fiduciary, a person who guaranteed the signature of the fiduciary is not liable on the guarantee to any person to whom the corporation or transfer agent by reason of subdivision (1) of Section 8404 incurs no liability.

(c) This subdivision (7) does not impose any liability upon the corporation or its transfer agent.

Sec. 8404. Liability and Non-Liability for Registration. (1) Except as otherwise provided in any law relating to the collection of taxes, the issuer is not liable to the owner or any other person suffering loss as a result of the registration of a transfer of a security if

(a) There were on or with the security the necessary indorsements (Section 8308); and

(b) The issuer had no duty to inquire into adverse claims or has discharged any such duty (Section 8403).

(2) Where an issuer has registered a transfer of a security to a person not entitled to it the issuer on demand must deliver a like security to the true owner unless

(a) The registration was pursuant to subdivision (1); or

(b) The owner is precluded from asserting any claim for registering the transfer under subdivision (1) of the following section; or

(c) Such delivery would result in overissue, in which case the issuer's liability is governed by Section 8104.

Sec. 8405. Lost, Destroyed and Stolen Securities. (1) Where a security has been lost, apparently destroyed or wrongfully taken and the owner fails to notify the issuer of that fact within a reasonable time after he has notice of it and the issuer registers a transfer of the security before receiving such a notification, the owner is precluded from asserting against the issuer any claim for registering the transfer under the preceding section or any claim to a new security under this section.

(2) Where the owner of a security claims that the security has been lost, destroyed or wrongfully taken, the issuer must issue a new security in place of the original security if the owner

(a) So requests before the issuer has notice that the security has been acquired by a bona fide purchaser; and

(b) Files with the issuer a sufficient indemnity bond; and

(c) Satisfies any other reasonable requirements imposed by the issuer.

(3) If, after the issue of the new security, a bona fide purchaser of the original security presents it for registration of transfer, the issuer must register the transfer unless registration would result in overissue, in which event the issuer's liability is governed by Section 8104. In addition to any rights on the indemnity bond, the issuer may recover the new security from the person to whom it was issued or any person taking under him except a bona fide purchaser.

Sec. 8406. Duty of Authenticating Trustee, Transfer Agent or Registrar. (1) Where a person acts as authenticating trustee, transfer, agent, registrar, or other agent for an issuer in the registration of transfers of its securities or in the issue of new securities or in the cancellation of surrendered securities

(a) He is under a duty to the issuer to exercise good faith and due diligence in performing his functions; and

(b) He has with regard to the particular functions he performs the same obligation to the holder or owner of the security and has the same rights and privileges as the issuer has in regard to those functions.

(2) Notice to an authenticating trustee, transfer agent, registrar or other such agent is notice to the issuer with respect to the functions performed by the agent.

DIVISION 9

SECURED TRANSACTIONS; SALES OF ACCOUNTS AND CHATTEL PAPER

CHAPTER 1

SHORT TITLE, APPLICABILITY AND DEFINITIONS

Sec. 9101. Short Title. This division shall be known and may be cited as Uniform Commercial Code—Secured Transactions.

Sec. 9102. Policy and Scope of Division. (1) Except as otherwise provided in Section 9104 on excluded transactions, this division applies

(a) To any transaction (regardless of its form) which is intended to create a security interest in personal property or fixtures including goods, documents, instruments, general intangibles, chattel paper or accounts; and also

(b) To any sale of accounts or chattel paper.

(2) This division applies to security interests created by contract including pledge, assignment, chattel mortgage, chattel trust, trust deed, inventory lien, equipment trust, conditional sale, trust receipt, other lien or title retention contract and lease or consignment intended as security. This division does not apply to statutory lien except as provided in Section 9310.

(3) The application of this division to a security interest in a secured obligation is not affected by the fact that the obligation is itself secured by a transaction or interest to which this division does not apply.

(4) Notwithstanding anything to the contrary in this division, no nonpossessory security interest, other than a purchase money security interest, may be given or taken in or to the inventory of a retail merchant held for sale, except in or to inventory consisting of durable goods having a unit retail value of at least five hundred dollars ($500) or motor vehicles, house trailers, semitrailers, farm and construction machinery and repair parts thereof, or aircraft. A cooperative association organized pursuant to Chapter 1 (commencing with Section 54001), Division 20 of the Food and Agricultural Code (Agricultural Cooperative Associations) or Part 3 (commencing with Section 13200), Division 3, Title 1 of the Corporations Code (Fish Marketing Act) is not to be deemed a merchant within the meaning of this subdivision. The phrase "purchase money security interest" as used in this subdivision does not extend to any after-acquired property other than the initial property sold by a secured party or taken by a lender as security as provided in Section 9107. This subdivision does not apply to the inventory of a person whose sales for resale exceeded 75 percent in dollar volume of his total sales of all goods during the 12 months preceding the attachment of the security interest. For the purpose of the preceding sentence, a sale of goods to a contractor, who is required to be licensed, for the purpose of incorporating such goods at any time into improvements or repairs to real property, is a sale for resale.

Sec. 9103. Laws Governing Perfection of Security Interests. (1) (a) This subdivision applies to documents and instruments and to goods other than those covered by a certificate of title described in subdivision (2), mobile goods described in subdivision (3), and minerals described in subdivision (5).

(b) Except as otherwise provided in this subdivision, perfection and the effect of perfection or nonperfection of a security interest in collateral are governed by the law of the jurisdiction where the collateral is when the last event occurs on which is based the assertion that the security interest is perfected or unperfected.

(c) If the parties to a transaction creating a purchase money security interest in goods in one jurisdiction understand at the time that the security interest attaches that the goods will be kept in another jurisdiction, then the law of the other jurisdiction governs the perfection and the effect of perfection or nonperfection of the security interest from the time it attaches until 30 days after the debtor receives possession of the goods and thereafter if the goods are taken to the other jurisdiction before the end of the 30-day period.

(d) When collateral is brought into and kept in this state while subject to a security interest perfected under the law of the jurisdiction from which the collateral was removed, the security interest remains perfected, but if action is required by Chapter 3 of this division to perfect the security interest,

(i) If the action is not taken before the expiration of the period of perfection in the other jurisdiction or the end of four months after the collateral is brought into this state, whichever period first expires, the security interest becomes unperfected at the end of that period and is thereafter deemed to have been unperfected as against a person who became a purchaser after removal;

(ii) If the action is taken before the expiration of the period specified in subparagraph (i), the security interest continues perfected thereafter;

(iii) For the purpose of priority over a buyer of consumer goods (subdivision (2) of Section 9307), the period of the effectiveness of a filing in the jurisdiction from which the collateral is removed is governed by the rules with respect to perfection in subparagraphs (i) and (ii).

(e) If goods are or become fixtures (Section 9313(1)(a)) in relation to real estate located in this state, the conflicting interest of an encumbrancer or owner of the real estate is governed by Section 9313.

(2) (a) This subdivision applies to goods covered by a certificate of title issued under a statute of this state or another jurisdiction under the law of which indication of a security interest on the certificate is required as a condition of perfection whether such certificate is designated a "certificate of title," "certificate of ownership," or otherwise.

(b) Except as otherwise provided in this subdivision, perfection and the effect of perfection or nonperfection of the security interest are governed by the law (including the conflict of laws rules) of the jurisdiction issuing the certificate until four months after the goods are removed from that jurisdiction and thereafter until the goods are registered in another jurisdiction, but in any event not beyond surrender of the certificate. After the expiration of that period, the goods are not covered by the certificate of title within the meaning of this section.

(c) Except with respect to the rights of a buyer described in the next paragraph, a security interest, perfected in another jurisdiction otherwise than by notation on a certificate of title, in goods brought into this state and thereafter covered by a certificate of title issued by this state is subject to the rules stated in paragraph (d) of subdivision (1).

(d) If goods are brought into this state while a security interest therein is perfected in any manner under the law of the jurisdiction from which the goods are removed and a certificate of title is issued by this state and the certificate does not show that the goods are subject to the security interest or that they may be subject to security interest not shown on the certificate, the security interest is subordinate to the rights of a buyer of the goods who is not in the business of selling goods of that kind to the extent that he gives value and receives delivery of the goods after issuance of the certificate and without knowledge of the security interest.

(3) (a) This subdivision applies to accounts (other than an account described in subdivision (5) on minerals) and general intangibles and to goods which are mobile and which are of a type normally used in more than one jurisdiction, such as motor vehicles, trailers, rolling stock, airplanes, shipping containers, roadbuilding and construction machinery and commercial harvesting machinery and the like, if the goods are equipment or are inventory leased or held for lease by the debtor to others, and are not covered by a certificate of title described in subdivision (2).

(b) The law (including the conflict of laws rules) of the jurisdiction in which the debtor is located governs the perfection and the effect of perfection or nonperfection of the security interest.

(c) If, however, the debtor is located in a jurisdiction which is not a part of the United States, and which does not provide for perfection of the security interest by filing or recording in that jurisdiction, the law of the jurisdiction in the United States in which the debtor has its major executive office in the United States governs the perfection and the effect of perfection or nonperfection of the security interest through filing. In the alternative, if the debtor is located in a jurisdiction which is not a part of the United States or Canada and the collateral is accounts or general intangibles for money due or to become due, the security interest may be perfected by notification to the account debtor. As used in this paragraph, "United States" includes its territories and possessions and the Commonwealth of Puerto Rico.

(d) A debtor shall be deemed at his place of business if he has one, at his chief executive office if he has more than one place of business, otherwise at his residence. If, however, the debtor is a foreign air carrier under the Federal Aviation Act of 1958, as amended, it shall be deemed located at the designated office of the agent upon whom service of process may be made on behalf of the foreign air carrier.

(e) A security interest perfected under the law of the jurisdiction of the location of the debtor is perfected until the expiration of four months after a change of the debtor's location to another jurisdiction, or until perfection would have ceased by the law of the first jurisdiction, whichever period first expires. Unless perfected in the new jurisdiction before the end of that period, it become unperfected thereafter and is deemed to have been unperfected as against a person who became a purchaser after the change.

(4) The rules stated for goods in subdivision (1) apply to a possessory security interest in chattel paper. The rules stated for accounts in subdivision (3) apply to a nonpossessory security interest in chattel paper, but the security interest may not be perfected by notification to the account debtor.

(5) Perfection and the effect of perfection or nonperfection of a security interest which is created by a debtor who has an interest in minerals or the like (including oil and gas) before extraction and which attaches thereto as extracted, or which attaches to an account resulting from the sale thereof at the wellhead or minehead are governed by the law (including the conflict of laws rules) of the jurisdiction wherein the wellhead or minehead is located.

Sec. 9104. **Transactions Excluded From Division.** This division does not apply

(a) To a security interest subject to any statute of the United States to the extent that such statute governs the rights of parties to and third parties affected by transactions in particular type of property; or

(c) To a lien given by statute or other rule of law for services or materials except as provided in Section 9310 on priority of such liens; or

(d) To a transfer of a claim for wages, salary or other compensation of an employee; or

(e) To a transfer, including creation of a security interest, by a government or governmental subdivision or agency; or

(f) To a sale of accounts or chattel paper as part of a sale of the business out of which they arose, or an assignment of accounts or chattel paper which is for the purpose of collection only, or a transfer of a right to payment under a contract on to an assignee who is also to do the performance under the contract or a transfer of a single account to an assignee in whole or partial satisfaction of a preexisting indebtedness; or

(g) To any loan made by an insurance company pursuant to the provisions of a policy or contract issued by it and upon the sole security of such policy or contract; or

(h) To a right represented by a judgment (other than a judgment taken in a right to payment which was collateral); or

(i) To any right of setoff; or

(j) Except to the extent that provision is made for fixtures in Section 9313, to the creation or transfer of an interest in or lien on real estate, including a lease or rents thereunder and to any interest of a lessor and lessee in any such lease or rents; or

(k) To a transfer in whole or in part of any claim arising out of tort.

(l) To any security interest created by the assignment of the benefits of any public constructions contract under the Improvement Act of 1911 (Division 7 (commencing with Section 5000), Streets and Highways Code).

Sec. 9105. **Definitions and Index of Definitions.** (1) In this division unless the context otherwise requires:

(a) "Account debtor" means the person who is obligated on an account, chattel paper or general intangible;

(b) "Chattel paper" means a writing or writings which evidence both a monetary obligation and a security interest in or a lease of specific goods, but a charter or other contract involving the use or hire of a vessel is not chattel paper. When a transaction is evidenced both by such a security agreement or a lease and by an instrument or a series of instruments, the group of writings taken together constitutes chattel paper;

(c) "Collateral" means the property subject to a security interest, and includes accounts and chattel paper which have been sold;

(d) "Debtor" means the person who owes payment or other performance of the obligation secured, whether or not he owns or has rights in the collateral, and includes the seller of accounts or chattel paper. Where the debtor and the owner of the collateral are not the same person, the term "debtor" means the owner of the collateral in any provision of the division dealing with the collateral, the obligor in any provision dealing with the obligation, and may include both where the context so requires;

(e) "Deposit account" means a demand, time, savings, passbook or like account maintained with a bank, savings and loan association, credit union or like organization, other than an account evidenced by a negotiable certificate of deposit;

(f) "Document" means document of title as defined in the general definitions of Division 1 (Section 1201), and a receipt of the kind described in subdivision (2) of Section 7201;

(g) "Encumbrance" includes real estate mortgages and other liens on real estate and all other rights in real estate that are not ownership interests;

(h) "Goods" includes all things which are movable at the time the security interest attaches or which are fixtures (Section 9313), but does not include money, documents, instruments, accounts, chattel paper, general intangibles or minerals or the like (including oil and gas) before extraction. "Goods" also includes standing timber which is to be cut and removed under a conveyance or contract for sale, the unborn young of animals, and growing crops;

(i) "Instrument" means a negotiable instrument (defined in Section 3104), or a security (defined in Section 8102) or any other writing which evidences a right to the payment of money and is not itself a security agreement or lease and is of a type which is in ordinary course of business transferred by delivery with any necessary indorsement or assignment;

(j) "Mortgage" means a consensual interest created by a real estate mortgage, a trust deed on real estate, or the like;

(k) An advance is made "pursuant to commitment" if the secured party has bound himself to make it, whether or not a subsequent event of default or other event not within his control has relieved or may relieve him from his obligation;

(l) "Security agreement" means an agreement which creates or provides for a security interest;

(m) "Secured party" means a lender, seller or other person in whose favor there is a security interest, including a person to whom accounts or chattel paper have been sold. When the holders of obligations issues under an indenture of trust, equipment trust agreement or the like are represented by a trustee or other person, the representative is the secured party.

(n) "Transmitting utility" means any person primarily engaged in the railroad, street railway or trolley bus business, the electric or electronics communications transmission business, the transmission of goods by pipeline, or the transmission or the production and transmission of electricity, steam, gas or water, or the provision of sewer service.

(o) "New value" includes new advances or loans made, or new obligations incurred, or the release of a valid and existing security interest, or the release of a claim to proceeds; but "new value" shall not be construed to include extension or renewals of existing obligations of the debtor, nor obligations substituted for such existing obligations.

(2) Other definitions to this division and the sections in which they appear are:

"Account." Section 9106.
"Attach." Section 9203.
"Consumer goods." Section 9109(1).
"Construction mortgage." Section 9313(1).
"Equipment." Section 9109(2).
"Farm products." Section 9109(3).
"Fixture." Section 9313(1).
"Fixture filing." Section 9313(1).
"General intangibles." Section 9106.
"Inventory." Section 9109(4).
"Lien creditor." Section 9301(3).
"Proceeds." Section 9306(1).
"Purchase money security interest." Section 9107.
"United States." Section 9103.

(3) The following definitions in other divisions apply to this division:
"Check." Section 3104.
"Contract for sale." Section 2106.
"Holder in due course." Section 3302.
"Note." Section 3104.
"Sale." Section 2106.

(4) In addition Division 1 contains general definitions and principles of construction and interpretation applicable throughout this division.

Sec. 9106.   Definitions: "Account"; "General Intangibles."   "Account" means any right to payment for goods sold or leased or for services rendered which is not evidenced by an instrument or chattel paper, whether or not it has been earned by performance. "General intangibles" means any personal property (including things in action) other than goods, accounts, chattel paper, documents, instruments and money . . . .

Sec. 9107.   Definitions: "Purchase Money Security Interest."   A security interest is a "purchase money security interest" to the extent that it is

(a) Taken or retained by the seller of the collateral to secure all or part of its price; or

(b) Taken by a person who by making advances or incurring an obligation gives value to enable the debtor to acquire rights in or the use of collateral is such value is in fact so used.

Sec. 9108.   When After-Acquired Collateral Not Security for Antecedent Debt.   Where a secured party makes an advance, incurs an obligation, releases a perfected security interest, or otherwise gives new value which is to be secured in whole or in part by afteracquired property his security interest in the afteracquired collateral shall be deemed to be taken for new value and not as security for an antecedent debt if the debtor acquires his rights in such collateral either in the ordinary course of his business or under a contract of purchase made pursuant to the security agreement within a reasonable time after new value is given.

Sec. 9109.   Classification of Goods; "Consumer Goods"; "Equipment"; "Farm Products"; "Inventory."   Goods are

(1) "Consumer goods" if they are used or bought for use primarily for personal, family or household purposes;

(2) "Equipment" if they are used or bought for use primarily in business (including farming or a profession) or by a debtor who is a nonprofit organization or a governmental subdivision or agency or if the goods are not included in the definitions of inventory, farm products or consumer goods;

(3) "Farm products" if they are crops or livestock or supplies used or produced in farming operations or if they are products of crops or livestock in their unmanufactured states (such as ginned cotton, wool clip, maple syrup, milk and eggs), and if they are in the possession of a debtor engaged in raising, fattening, grazing or other farming operations. If goods are farm products they are neither equipment nor inventory;

(4) "Inventory" if they are held by a person who holds them for sale or lease or to be furnished under contract of service or if he has so leased or furnished them, or if they are raw materials, work in process or materials used or consumed in a business. Inventory of a person is not to be classified as his equipment.

Sec. 9110.   Sufficiency of Description.   For the purposes of this division any description of personal property or real estate is sufficient whether or not it is specific if it reasonably identifies what is described. Personal Property may be referred to by general kind or class if the property can be reasonably identified as falling within such kind or class or if it can be so identified when it is acquired by the debtor.

Sec. 9111.   Applicability of Bulk Transfer Laws.   The creation of a security interest under this division may be a bulk transfer under Division 6, except as specified in subdivision (1) of Section 6103.

Sec. 9112.   Where Collateral Is Not Owned by Debtor.   Unless otherwise agreed, when a secured party knows that collateral is owned by a person who is not the debtor, the owner of the collateral is entitled to receive from the secured party any surplus under Section 9502(2) or under Section 9504(1), and is not liable for the debt or for any deficiency after resale, and he has the same right as the debtor

(a) To receive statements under Section 9208;

(b) To receive notice of and to object to a secured party's proposal to retain the collateral in satisfaction of the indebtedness under Section 9505;

(c) To redeem the collateral under Section 9506;

(d) To obtain injunctive or other relief under Section 9507(1); and

(e) To recover losses caused to him under Section 9208(2).

Sec. 9113.   Security Interests Arising Under Article on Sales.   A security interest arising solely under the division on sales (Division 2) is subject to the provisions of this division except that to the extent that and so long as the debtor does not have or does not lawfully obtain possession of the goods

(a) No security agreement is necessary to make the security interest enforceable; and

(b) No filing is required to perfect the security interest; and

(c) The rights of the secured party on default by the debtor are governed by the division on sales (Division 2).

Sec. 9114.   Priority of Consignment Not a Security Interest.   (1) A person who delivers goods under a consignment which is not a security interest and who would be required to file under this division by paragraph (3)(c) of Section 2326 has priority over a secured party who is or becomes a creditor of the consignee and who would have a perfected security interest in the goods if they were the property of the consignee, and also has priority with respect to identifiable cash proceeds received on or before delivery of the goods to a buyer, if

(a) The consignor complies with the filing provision of the division on sales with respect to consignments (paragraph (3)(c) of Section 2326) before the consignee receives possession of the goods; and

(b) The consignor gives notification in writing to the holder of the security interest if the holder has filed a financing statement covering the same types of goods before the date of the filing made by the consignor; and

(c) The holder of the security interest receives the notification within five years before the consignee receives possession of the goods; and

(d) The notification states that the consignor expects to deliver goods on consignment to the consignee describing the goods by item or type.

(2) In the case of a consignment which is not a security interest and in which the requirements of the preceding subdivision have not been met, a person who delivers goods to another is subordinate to a person who would have a perfected security interest in the goods if they were the property of the debtor.

CHAPTER 2

VALIDITY OF SECURITY AGREEMENT AND RIGHTS OF PARTIES THERETO

Sec. 9201.   General Validity of Security Agreement.   Except as otherwise provided by this code a security agreement is effective according to its terms between the parties, against purchasers of the collateral and against creditors. Nothing in this division validates any charge or practice illegal under any statute or regulation thereunder governing usury, small loans, retail installment sales, or the like or extends the application of any such statute or regulation to any transaction not otherwise subject thereto.

Sec. 9202. Title to Collateral Immaterial. Each provision of this division with regard to rights, obligations and remedies applies whether title to collateral is in the secured party or in the debtor.

Sec. 9203. Enforceability of Security Interest; Attachment; Proceeds; Formal Requisites. (1) Subject to the provisions of Section 4208 on the security interest of a collecting bank and Section 9113 on a security interest arising under the division on sale, a security interest is not enforceable against the debtor or third parties with respect to the collateral and does not attach unless

(a) The collateral is in the possession of the secured party pursuant to agreement, or the debtor has signed a security agreement which contains a description of the collateral and in addition, when the security interest covers crops growing or to be grown or timber to be cut, a description of the land concerned; and

(b) Value has been given; and

(c) The debtor has rights in the collateral.

(2) A security interest attaches when it becomes enforceable against the debtor with respect to the collateral. Attachment occurs as soon as all of the events specified in subdivision (1) have taken place unless explicit agreement postpones the time of attaching.

(3) Unless otherwise agreed a security agreement gives the secured party the rights to proceeds provided by Section 9306.

(4) A transaction, although subject to this division, is also subject to the Retail Installment Sales Act, Title 2 (commencing at Section 1801) of Part 4, Division 3 of the Civil Code; the Automobile Sales Finance Act, Chapter 2b (commencing at Section 2981) of Title 14, Part 4, Division 3 of the Civil Code; the Industrial Loan Law, Division 7 (commencing at Section 18000) of the Financial Code; the Pawnbroker Law, Division 8 (commencing at Section 21000) of the Financial Code; the Personal Property Brokers Law, Division 9 (commencing at Section 22000) of the Financial Code; and the Commercial Finance Lenders Law, Division 11 (commencing with Section 26000) of the Financial Code, and in the case of conflict between the provisions of this division and any such statute, the provisions of such statute control. Failure to comply with any applicable statute has only the effect which is specified therein.

Sec. 9204. After-Acquired Collateral; Future Advances. (1) Except as provided in subdivision (2) a security agreement may provide that any or all obligations covered by the security agreement are to be secured by afteracquired collateral.

(2) No security interest attaches under an afteracquired property clause to consumer goods other than accessions (Section 9314) when given as additional security unless the debtor acquires rights in them within 10 days after the secured party gives value.

(3) Obligations covered by a security agreement may include future advances or other value whether or not the advances or value are given pursuant to commitment (subdivision (1) of Section 9105).

Sec. 9205. Use or Disposition of Collateral Without Accounting Permissible. A security interest is not invalid or fraudulent against creditors by reason of liberty in the debtor to use, commingle or dispose of all or part of the collateral (including returned or repossessed goods) or to collect or compromise accounts or chattel paper, or to accept the return of goods or make repossessions, or to use, commingle or dispose of proceeds, or by reason of the failure of the secured party to require the debtor to account for proceeds or replace collateral. This section does not relax the requirements of possession where perfection of a security interest depends upon possession of the collateral by the secured party or by a bailee.

Sec. 9206. Agreement Not to Assert Defenses Against Assignee; Modification of Sales Warranties Where Security Agreement Exists. (1) Subject to any statute or decision which establishes a different rule for buyers or lessees of consumer goods, an agreement by a buyer or lessee that he will not assert against an assignee any claim or defense which he may have against the seller or lessor is enforceable by any assignee who takes his assignment for value, in good faith and without notice of a claim or defense, except as to defenses of a type which may be asserted against a holder in due course of a negotiable instrument under the division on commercial paper (Division 3). A buyer who as part of one transaction signs both a negotiable instrument and a security agreement makes such an agreement.

(2) When a seller retains a purchase money security interest in goods the division on sales (Division 2) governs the sale and any disclaimer, limitation or modification of the seller's warranties.

Sec. 9207. Rights and Duties When Collateral Is in Secured Party's Possession. (1) A secured party must use reasonable care in the custody and preservation of collateral in his possession. In the case of an instrument or chattel paper reasonable care includes taking necessary steps to preserve rights against prior parties unless otherwise agreed.

(2) Unless otherwise agreed, when collateral is in the secured party's possession

(a) Reasonable expenses (including the cost of any insurance and payment of taxes or other charges) incurred in the custody, preservation, use or operation of the collateral are chargeable to the debtor and are secured by the collateral;

(b) The risk of accidental loss or damage is on the debtor to the extent of any deficiency in any effective insurance coverage;

(c) The secured party may hold as additional security any increase or profits (except money) received from the collateral, but money so received, unless remitted to the debtor, shall be applied in reduction of the secured obligation;

(d) The secured party must keep the collateral identifiable but fungible collateral may be commingled;

(e) The secured party may repledge the collateral upon terms which do not impair the debtor's right to redeem it.

(3) A secured party is liable for any loss caused by his failure to meet any obligation imposed by the preceding subdivisions but does not lose his security interest.

(4) A secured party may use or operate the collateral for the purpose of preserving the collateral or its value or pursuant to the order of a court of appropriate jurisdiction or, except in the case of consumer goods, in the manner and to the extent provided in the security agreement.

Sec. 9208. Request for Statement of Account or List of Collateral. (1) A debtor may sign a statement indicating what he believes to be the aggregate amount of unpaid indebtedness as of a specified date and may send it to the secured party with a request that the statement be approved or corrected and returned to the debtor. When the security agreement or any other record kept by the secured party identifies the collateral a debtor may similarly request the secured party to approve or correct a list of the collateral.

(2) The secured party must comply with such a request within two weeks after receipt by sending a written correction or approval. If the secured party claims a security interst in all of a particular type of collateral owned by the debtor he may indicate that fact in his reply and need not approve or correct an itemized list of such collateral. If the secured party without reasonable excuse fails to comply he is liable for any loss caused to the debtor thereby; and if the debtor has properly included in his request a good faith statement of the obligation or a list of the collateral or both the secured party may claim a security interest only as shown in the statement against persons misled by his failure to comply. If he no longer has an interest in the obligation or collateral at the time the request is received he must disclose the name and address of any successor in interest known to him and he is liable for any loss caused to the debtor as a result of failure to disclose. A successor in interest is not subject to this section until a request is received by him.

(3) A debtor is entitled to such a statement once every six months without charge. The secured party may require payment of a charge not exceeding ten dollars ($10) for each additional statement furnished.

(4) If the secured party is an organization maintaining branches or branch offices the requests herein provided for shall be sent to the branch or branch office at which the security transaction was entered into or at which the debtor is to make payment of his obligation, and the secured party's statement, unless otherwise specified, shall be deemed to apply only to indebtedness entered into at or payable to such branch or branch office and to any collateral taken by such branch or branch office.

CHAPTER 3

RIGHTS OF THIRD PARTIES; PERFECTED AND UNPERFECTED SECURITY INTERESTS; RULES OF PRIORITY

Sec. 9301. Persons Who Take Priority Over Unperfected Security Interests; "Lien Creditor"; Service of Judgment Lien on Personal Property. (1) Except as otherwise provided in subdivision (2), an unperfected security interest is subordinate to the rights of

(a) Persons entitled to priority under Section 9312;

(b) A person who becomes a lien creditor before the security interest is perfected;

(c) In the case of goods, instruments, documents, and chattel paper, a person who is not a secured party and who is a transferee in bulk or other buyer not in ordinary course of business to the extent that he gives value and receives delivery of the collateral without knowledge of the security interest and before it is perfected;

(d) In the case of accounts and general intangibles, a person who is not a secured party and who is a transferee to the extent that he gives value without knowledge of the security interest and before it is perfected.

(2) If the secured party files with respect to a purchase money security interest before or within 10 days after the debtor receives possession of the collateral, he takes priority over the rights of a transferee in bulk or of a lien creditor which arise between the time the security interest attaches and the time of filing.

(3) A "lien creditor" means a creditor who has acquired a lien on the property involved by attachment, levy or the like, or by filing a notice of judgment lien on personal property, and includes an assignee for benefit of creditors from the time of assignment, and a trustee in bankruptcy from the date of the filing of the petition or a receiver in equity from the time of appointment.

(4) A person who becomes a lien creditor while a security interest is perfected takes subject to the security interest only to the extent that it secures advances made before he becomes a lien creditor or within 45 days thereafter or made without knowledge of the lien or pursuant to a commitment entered into without knowledge of the lien.

(5) For the purpose of subdivision (4), a secured party shall be deemed not to have knowledge of a judgment lien on personal property acquired pursuant to Section 697.510 of the Code of Civil Procedure until the time the judgment creditor serves a copy of the notice of judgment lien on the secured party personally or by mail pursuant to Chapter 4 (commencing with Section 684.010) of Division 1 of Title 9 of Part 2 of the Code of Civil Procedure. If service on the secured party is by mail, it shall be sent to the secured party at the address shown in the financing statement or security agreement.

Sec. 9302.   When Filing Is Required to Perfect Security Interest; Security Interests to Which Filing Provisions of This Article Do Not Apply.   (1) A financing statement must be filed to perfect all security interests except the following:

(a) A security interest in collateral in possession of the secured party under Section 9305;

(b) A security interest temporarily perfected in instruments or documents without delivery under Section 9304 or in proceeds for a 10-day period under Section 9306;

(c) A security interest created by an assignment of a beneficial interest in a trust or a decedent's estate;

(d) A purchase money security interest in consumer goods; but filing is required for a motor vehicle or boat required to be registered; and fixture filing is required for priority over conflicting interests in fixtures to the extent provided in Section 9313;

(e) A security interest of a collecting bank (Section 4208) or arising under the division on sales (see Section 9113) or covered in subdivision (3) of this section;

(f) An assignment for the benefit of all the creditors of the transferor, and subsequent transfers by the assignee thereunder;

(g) A security interest in a deposit account. Such a security interest is perfected:

(1) As to a deposit account maintained with the security party when the security agreement is executed;

(2) As to a deposit account not described in subparagraph (1) when notice thereof is given in writing to the organization with whom the deposit account is maintained.

(h) A security interest in or claim in or under any policy of insurance including unearned premiums. Such interest shall be perfected when notice thereof is given in writing to the insurer.

(2) If a secured party assigns a perfected security interest, no filing under this division is required in order to continue the perfected status of the security interest against creditors of and transferees from the original debtor.

(3) The filing of a financing statement otherwise required by this division is not necessary or effective to perfect a security interest in property subject to any of the following:

(a) A statute or treaty of the United States which provides for a national or international registration or a national or international certificate of title or which specifies a place of filing different from that specified in this division for filing of the security interest.

(b) The provisions of the Vehicle Code which require registration of a vehicle or boat, or provisions of the Health and Safety Code which re-

quire registration of a mobilehome or commercial coach; but during any period in which collateral is inventory held by a person who is in the business of selling such vehicles or boats, or both, as the case may be, the filing provisions of this division (Chapter 4) apply to a security interest in that collateral.

(c) A certificate of title statute of another jurisdiction under the law of which indication of a security interest on the certificate is required as a condition of perfection (Subdivision (2) of Section 9103).

(d) The provisions of the Health and Safety Code which require registration of all interests in approved air contaminant emission reductions (Sections 40709 to 40713, inclusive, of the Health and Safety Code).

(4) Compliance with a statute or treaty described in subdivision (3) is equivalent to the filing of a financing statement under this division and a security interest in property subject to the statute or treaty can be perfected only by compliance therewith except as provided in Section 9103 on multiple state transactions. Duration and renewal of perfection of a security interest perfected by compliance with the statute or treaty are governed by the provisions of the statute or treaty; in other respects the security interest is subject to this division.

Sec. 9303.   When Security Interest Is Perfected; Continuity of Perfection.   (1) A security interest is perfected when it has attached and when all of the applicable steps required for perfection have been taken. Such steps are specified in Sections 9302, 9304, 9305 and 9306. If such steps are taken before the security interest attaches, it is perfected at the time when it attaches.

(2) If a security interest is originally perfected in any way permitted under this division and is subsequently perfected in some other way under this division, without an intermediate period when it was unperfected, the security interest shall be deemed to be perfected continuously for the purposes of this division.

Sec. 9304.   Perfection of Security Interest in Instruments, Documents, and Goods Covered by Documents; Perfection by Permissive Filing; Temporary Perfection Without Filing or Transfer of Possession; Third-Party Claims in Certain Proceeds.   (1) A security interest in chattel paper or negotiable documents may be perfected by filing. A security interest in money or instruments (other than instruments which constitute part of chattel paper) can be perfected only by the secured party's taking possession, except as provided in subdivisions (4), (5), and (7) of this section and subdivisions (2) and (3) of Section 9306 on proceeds.

(2) During the period that goods are in the possession of the issuer of a negotiable document therefor, a security interest in the goods is perfected by perfecting a security interest in the document, and any security interest in the goods otherwise perfected during such period is subject thereto.

(3) A security interest in goods in the possession of a bailee other than one who has issued a negotiable document therefor is perfected by issuance of a document in the name of the secured party or by the bailee's receipt of notification of the secured party's interest or by filing as to the goods.

(4) A security interest in instruments or negotiable document is perfected without filing or the taking of possession for a period of 21 days from the time it attaches to the extent that it arises for new value given under a written security agreement.

(5) A security interest remains perfected for a period of 21 days without filing where a secured party having a perfected security interest in an instrument, a negotiable document or goods in possession of a bailee other than one who has issued a negotiable document therefor

(a) Makes available to the debtor the goods or documents representing the goods for the purpose of ultimate sale or exchange or for the purpose of loading, unloading, storing, shipping, trans-shipping, manufacturing, processing or otherwise dealing with them in a manner preliminary to their sale or exchange, but priority between conflicting security interests in the goods is subject to subdivision 3 of Section 9312; or

(b) Delivers the instrument to the debtor for the purpose of ultimate sale or exchange or of presentation, collection, renewal or registration of transfer.

(6) After the 21-day period in subdivisions (4) and (5) perfection depends upon compliance with applicable provisions of this division.

(7) If an instrument claimed as proceeds (other than cash proceeds) under Section 9306 is in the custody of a levying officer, a secured party may perfect a security interest in such instrument by filing a third-party claim with the levying officer pursuant to Chapter 3 (commencing with Section 720.210) of Division 4 of Title 9 of Part 2 of the Code of Civil Procedure within the 10-day period allowed under Section 9306.

Sec. 9305. **When Possession by Secured Party Perfects Security Interest Without Filing.** A security interest in letters of credit and advices of credit (paragraph (2)(a) of Section 5116), goods, instruments, money, negotiable documents or chattel paper may be perfected by the secured party's taking possession of the collateral. If such collateral other than goods covered by a negotiable document is held by a bailee, the secured party is deemed to have possession from the time the bailee receives notification of the secured party's interest. A security interest is perfected by possession from the time possession is taken without relation back and continues only so long as possession is retained, unless otherwise specified in this division. The security interest may be otherwise perfected as provided in this division before or after the period of possession by the secured party.

Sec. 9306. **"Proceeds"; Secured Party's Rights on Disposition of Collateral.** (1) "Proceeds" includes whatever is received upon the sale, exchange, collection or other disposition of collateral or proceeds. Insurance payable by reason of loss or damage to the collateral is proceeds, except to the extent that it is payable to a person other than a party to the security agreement. Money, checks, deposit accounts, and the like are "cash proceeds." All other proceeds are "noncash proceeds."

(2) Except where this division otherwise provides, a security interest continues in collateral notwithstanding sale, exchange or other disposition thereof unless the disposition was authorized by the secured party in the security agreement or otherwise, and also continues in any identifiable proceeds including collections received by the debtor.

(3) The security interest in proceeds is a continuously perfected security interest if the interest in the original collateral was perfected but it ceases to be a perfected security interest and becomes unperfected 10 days after receipt of the proceeds by the debtor unless

(a) A filed financing statement covers the original collateral and the proceeds are collateral in which a security interest may be perfected by filing in the office or offices where the financing statement has been filed and, if the proceeds are acquired with cash proceeds, the description of collateral in the financing statement indicates the types of property constituting the proceeds; or

(b) A filed financing statement covers the original collateral and the proceeds are identifiable cash proceeds; or

(c) The security interest in the proceeds is perfected before the expiration of the 10-day period.

Except as provided in this section, a security interest in proceeds can be perfected only by the methods or under the circumstances permitted in this division for original collateral of the same type.

(4) In the event of insolvency proceedings instituted by or against a debtor, a secured party with a perfected security interest in proceeds has a perfected security interest only in the following proceeds

(a) In identifiable noncash proceeds and in a separate deposit account containing only proceeds;

(b) In identifiable cash proceeds in the form of money which is neither commingled with other money nor deposited in a deposit account prior to the insolvency proceedings;

(c) In identifiable cash proceeds in the form of checks and the like which are not deposited in a deposit account prior to the insolvency proceedings; and

(d) In all cash and deposit accounts of the debtor in which proceeds have been commingled with other funds, but the perfected security interest under this paragraph (d) is

(i) Subject to any right of setoff; and

(ii) Limited to an amount not greater than the amount of any cash proceeds received by the debtor within 10 days before the institution of the insolvency proceedings less the sum of (I) the payments to the secured party on account of cash proceeds received by the debtor during such period and (II) the cash proceeds received by the debtor during such period to which the secured party is entitled under paragraphs (a) through (c) of this subdivision (4).

(5) If a sale of goods results in an account or chattel paper which is transferred by the seller to a secured party, and if the goods are returned to or are repossessed by the seller or the secured party, the following rules determine priorities:

(a) If the goods were collateral at the time of sale, for an indebtedness of the seller which is still unpaid, the original security interest attaches again to the goods and continues as a perfected security interest if it was perfected at the time when the goods were sold. If the security interest was originally perfected by a filing which is still effective, nothing further is required to continue the perfected status; in any other case, the secured party must take possession of the returned or repossessed goods or must file.

(b) An unpaid transferee of the chattel paper has a security interest in the goods against the transferor. Such security interest is prior to a security interest asserted under paragraph (a) to the extent that the transferee of the chattel paper was entitled to priority under Section 9308.

(c) An unpaid transferee of the account has a security interest in the goods against the transferor. Such security interest is subordinate to a security interest asserted under paragraph (a).

(d) A security interest of an unpaid transferee asserted under paragraph (b) or (c) must be perfected for protection against creditors of the transferor and purchasers of the returned or repossessed goods.

(6) Cash proceeds retain their character as cash proceeds while in the possession of a levying officer pursuant to Title 6.5 (commencing with Section 481.010) or Title 9 (commencing with Section 680.010) of Part 2 of the Code of Civil Procedure.

Sec. 9307. **Protection of Buyers of Goods.** (1) A buyer in ordinary course of business (subdivision (9) of Section 1201) takes free of a security interest created by his seller even though the security interest is perfected and even though the buyer knows of its existence.

(3) A buyer other than a buyer in ordinary course of business (subdivision (1) of this section) takes free of a security interest to the extent that it secures future advances made after the secured party acquires knowledge of the purchase, unless made pursuant to a commitment entered into without knowledge of the purchase.

Sec. 9308. **Priority of Purchasers of Chattel Paper Giving New Value and Taking Possession in Ordinary Course of Business.** A purchaser of chattel paper or an instrument who gives new value and takes possession of it in the ordinary course of his business has priority over a security interest in the chattel paper or instrument

(a) Which is perfected under Section 9304 (permissive filing and temporary perfection) or under Section 9306 (perfection as to proceeds) if he acts without knowledge that the specific paper or instrument is subject to a security interest; or

(b) Which is claimed merely as proceeds of inventory subject to a security interest (Section 9306) even though the he knows that the specific paper or instrument is subject to the security interest.

Sec. 9309. **Protection of Purchasers of Instruments and Documents.** Nothing in this division limits the rights of a holder in due course of a negotiable instrument (Section 3302) or a holder to whom a negotiable document of title has been duly negotiated (Section 7501) or a bona fide purchaser of a security (Section 8301) and such holders or purchasers take priority over an earlier security interest even though perfected. Filing under this division does not constitute notice of the security interest to such holders or purchasers.

Sec. 9310. **Priority of Certain Liens Arising by Operation of Law.** When a person in the ordinary course of his business furnishes services or materials with respect to goods subject to a security interest, a lien upon goods in the possession of such person given by statute or rule of law for such materials or services takes priority over a perfected security interest unless the lien is statutory and the statute expressly provides otherwise.

Sec. 9311. **Alienability of Debtor's Rights: Judicial Process.** The debtor's rights in collateral may be voluntarily or involuntarily transferred (by way of sale, creation of a security interest, attachment, levy, garnishment or other judicial process) notwithstanding a provision in the security agreement prohibiting any transfer but a provision in the security agreement making the transfer constitute a default is valid.

Sec. 9312. **Priorities Among Conflicting Security Interests in the Same Collateral.** (1) The rules of priority stated in other sections of this chapter and in the following sections shall govern where applicable: Section 4208 with respect to the security interest of collecting banks in items being collected, accompanying documents and proceeds; Section 9103 on security interests related to other jurisdictions; Section 9114 on consignments.

(3) A perfected purchase money security interest in inventory has priority over a conflicting security interest in the same inventory and also has priority in identifiable cash proceeds received on or before the delivery of the inventory to a buyer if

(a) The purchase money security interest is perfected at the time and debtor receives possession of the inventory; and

(b) The purchase money secured party gives notification in writing to the holder of the conflicting security interest if the holder had filed a financing statement covering the same types of inventory (i) before the date of the filing made by the purchase money secured party, or (ii) before the beginning of the 21-day period where the purchase money security interest is temporarily perfected without filing or possession (subdivision (5) of Section 9304); and

(c) The holder of the conflicting security interest receives the notification within five years before the debtor receives possession of the inventory; and

(d) The notification states that the person giving the notice has or expects to acquire a purchase money security interest in inventory of the debtor, describing such inventory by item or type.

(4) A purchase money security interest in collateral other than inventory has priority over a conflicting security interest in the same collateral or its proceeds if the purchase money security interest is perfected at the time the debtor receives possession of the collateral or within 10 days thereafter.

(5) In all cases not governed by other rules in this section (including cases of purchase money security interests which do not qualify for the special priorities set forth in subdivisions (3) and (4)), priority between conflicting security interests in the same collateral shall be determined according to the following rules:

(a) Conflicting security interests rank according to priority in time of filing or perfection. Priority dates from the time a filing is first made covering the collateral or the time the security interest is first perfected, whichever is earlier, provided that there is no period thereafter when there is neither filing nor perfection.

(b) So long as conflicting security interests are unperfected, the first to attach has priority.

(6) For the purposes of subdivision (5) a date of filing or perfection as to collateral is also a date of filing or perfection as to proceeds.

(7) If future advances are made while a security interest is perfected by filing or the taking of possession, the security interest has the same priority for the purposes of subdivision (5) with respect to the future advances as it does with respect to the first advance. If a commitment is made before or while the security interest is so perfected, the security interest has the same priority with respect to advances made pursuant thereto. In other cases a perfected security interest has priority from the date the advance is made.

Sec. 9313. Priority of Security Interests in Fixtures. (1) In this section and in the provisions of Chapter 4 (commencing with Section 9401) referring to fixture filing, unless the context otherwise requires

(a) Goods are "fixtures" when they become so related to particular real estate that an interest in them arises under real estate law.

(b) A "fixture filing" is the filing in the office where a mortgage on the real estate would be recorded of a financing statement covering goods which are or are to become fixtures and conforming to the requirements of subdivision (5) of Section 9402.

(c) A mortgage is a "construction mortgage" to the extent that it secures an obligation incurred for the construction of an improvement on land including the acquisition cost of the land, if the recorded writing so indicates.

(2) A security interest under this division may be created in goods which are fixtures or may continue in goods which become fixtures, but no security interest exists under this division in ordinary building materials incorporated into an improvement on land.

(3) This division does not prevent creation of an encumbrance upon fixtures pursuant to real estate law.

(4) A perfected security interest in fixtures has priority over the conflicting interest of an encumbrancer or owner of the real estate where

(a) The security interest is a purchase money security interest, the interest of the encumbrancer or owner arises before the goods become fixtures, a fixture filing covering the fixtures is filed before the goods become fixtures or within 10 days thereafter, and the debtor has an interest of record in the real estate or is in possession of the real estate; or

(b) A fixture filing covering the fixtures is filed before the interest of the encumbrancer or owner is of record, the security interest has priority over any conflicting interest of a predecessor in title of the encumbrancer or owner, and the debtor has an interest of record in the real estate or is in possession of the real estate; or

(c) The fixtures are readily removable factory or office machines or readily removable replacements of domestic appliances which are consumer goods; or

(d) The conflicting interest is a lien on the real estate obtained by legal or equitable proceedings after the security interest was perfected by any method permitted by this division.

(5) A security interest in fixtures, whether or not perfected, has priority over the conflicting interest of an encumbrancer or owner of the real estate where

(a) The encumbrancer or owner has consented in writing to the security interest or has disclaimed an interest in the goods as fixtures; or

(b) The debtor has a right to remove the goods as against the encumbrancer or owner. If the debtor's right terminates, the priority of the security interest continues for a reasonable time.

(6) Notwithstanding paragraph (a) of subdivision (4) but otherwise subject to subdivisions (4) and (5), a security interest in fixtures is subordinate to a construction mortgage recorded before the goods become fixtures if the goods become fixtures before the completion of the construction. To the extent that it is given to refinance a construction mortgage, a mortgage has this priority to the same extent as the construction mortgage.

(7) In the cases not within the preceding subdivisions, a security interest in fixtures is subordinate to the conflicting interest of an encumbrancer or owner of the related real estate who is not the debtor.

(8) When the secured party has priority over all owners and encumbrancers of the real estate, he may, on default, subject to the provisions of Chapter 5 (commencing with Section 9501), remove his collateral from the real estate but he must reimburse any encumbrancer or owner of the real estate who is not the debtor and who has not otherwise agreed for the cost of repair of any physical injury, but not for any diminution in value of the real estate caused by the absence of the goods removed or by any necessity of replacing them. A person entitled to reimbursement may refuse permission to remove until the secured party gives adequate security for the performance of this obligation.

Sec. 9314. Accessions. (1) A security interest in goods which attaches before they are installed in or affixed to other goods takes priority as to the goods installed or affixed (called in this section "accessions") over the claims of all persons to the whole except as stated in subdivision (3) and subject to Section 9315(1).

(2) A security interest which attaches to goods after they become part of a whole is valid against all persons subsequently acquiring interests in the whole except as stated in subdivision (3) but is invalid against any person with an interest in the whole at the time the security interest attaches to the goods who has not in writing consented to the security interest or disclaimed an interest in the goods as part of the whole.

(3) The security interests described in subdivsiions (1) and (2) do not take priority over

(a) A subsequent purchaser for value of any interest in the whole; or

(b) A creditor with a lien on the whole subsequently obtained by judicial proceedings; or

(c) A creditor with a prior perfected security interest in the whole to the extent that he makes subsequent advances if the subsequent purchase is made, the lien by judicial proceedings obtained or the subsequent advance under the prior perfected security interest is made or contracted for without knowledge of the security interest and before it is perfected. A purchaser of the whole at a foreclosure sale other than the holder of a perfected security interest purchasing at his own foreclosure sale is a subsequent purchaser within this section.

(4) When under subdivisions (1) or (2) and (3) a secured party has an interest in accessions which has priority over the claims of all persons who have interests in the whole, he may on default subject to the provisions of Chapter 5 remove his collateral from the whole but he must reimburse any encumbrancer or owner of the whole who is not the debtor and who has not otherwise agreed for the cost of repair of any physical injury but not for any diminution in value of the whole caused by the absence of the goods removed or by any necessity for replacing them. A person entitled to reimbursement may refuse permission to remove until the secured party gives adequate security for the performance of this obligation.

Sec. 9315. Priority When Goods are Commingled or Processed. (1) If a security interest in goods was perfected and subsequently the goods or a part thereof have become part of a product or mass, the security interest continues in the product or mass if

(a) The goods are so manufactured, processed, assembled or commingled that their identity is lost in the product or mass; or

(b) A financing statement covering the original goods also covers the product into which the goods have been manufactured, processed or assembled.

In a case to which paragraph (b) applies, no separate security interest in that part of the original goods which has been manufactured, processed or assembled into the product may be claimed under Section 9314.

(2) When under subdivision (1) more than one security interest attaches to the product or mass, they rank equally according to the ratio that the cost of the goods to which each interest originally attached bears to the cost of the total product or mass.

Sec. 9316. Priority Subject to Subordination. Nothing in this division prevents subordination by agreement by any person entitled to priority.

Sec. 9317. Secured Party Not Obligated on Contract of Debtor. The mere existence of a security interest or authority given to the debtor to dispose of or use collateral does not impose contract or tort liability upon the secured party for the debtor's acts or omissions.

Sec. 9318. Defenses Against Assignee; Modification of Contract After Notification of Assignment; Term Prohibiting Assignment Ineffective: Identification and Proof of Assignment. (1) Unless an account debtor has made an enforceable agreement not to assert defenses or claims arising out of a sale as provided in Section 9206 the rights of an assignee are subject to

(a) All the terms of the contract between the account debtor and assignor and any defense or claim arising therefrom; and

(b) Any other defense or claim of the account debtor against the assignor which accrues before the account debtor receives notification of the assignment.

(2) So far as the right to payment or a part thereof under an assigned contract has not been fully earned by performance, and notwithstanding notification of the assignment, any modification of or substitution for the contract made in good faith and in accordance with reasonable commercial standards is effective against an assignee unless the account debtor has otherwise agreed but the assignee acquired corresponding rights under the modified or substituted contract. The assignment may provide that such modification or substitution is a breach by the assignor.

(3) The account debtor is authorized to pay the assignor until the account debtor receives notification that the amount due or to become due has been assigned and that payment is to be made to the assignee. A notification which does not reasonably identify the rights assigned is ineffective. If requested by the account debtor, the assignee must seasonably furnish reasonable proof that the assignment has been made and unless he does so the account debtor may pay the assignor.

(4) A term in any contract between an account debtor and an assignor is ineffective if it prohibits assignment of an account or prohibits creation of a security interest in a general intangible for money due or to become due or requires the account debtor's consent to such assignment or security interest.

CHAPTER 4

FILING

Sec. 9401. Place of Filing; Erroneous Filing; Removal of Collateral. (1) The proper place to file an order to perfect a security interest is as follows:

(a) When the collateral is consumer goods, then in the office of the county recorder in the county of the debtor's residence or if the debtor is not a resident of this state, then in the office of the county recorder of the county in which the goods are kept;

(b) When the collateral is crops growing or to be grown, timber to be cut or is minerals or the like (including oil and gas) or accounts subject to subdivision (5) of Section 9103, then in the office where a mortgage on the real estate would be recorded.

(c) In all other cases, in the office of the Secretary of State.

(2) A filing which is made in good faith in an improper place or not in all o f the places required by this section is nevertheless effective with regard to any collateral as to which the filing complied with the requirements of this division and is also effective with regard to collateral covered by the financing statement against any person who has knowledge of the contents of such financing statement.

(3) A filing which is made in the proper place in this state continues effective even though the debtor's residence or place of business or the location of the collateral or its use, whichever controlled the original filing, is thereafter changed.

(4) The rules stated in Section 9103 determines whether filing is necessary in this state.

(5) Notwithstanding subdivision (1), and subject to subdivision (3) of Section 9302, the proper place to file an order to perfect a security interest in collateral, including fixtures, of a transmitting utility is the office of the Secretary of State. This filing also constitutes a fixture filing (Section 9313) as to the collateral described therein which is or is to become fixtures.

(6) For the purposes of this section, the residence of an organization is its place of business if it has one or its chief executive office if it has more than one place of business.

(7) The proper place to file a financing statement filed as a fixture is in the office where a mortgage on the real estate would be recorded.

Sec. 9402. Formal Requisites of Financing Statement; Amendments; Mortgage as Financing Statement. (1) A financing statement is sufficient if it gives the names of the debtor and the secured party, is signed by the debtor, gives an address of the secured party from which information concerning the security interest may be obtained, gives a mailing address of the debtor and contains a statement indicating the types, or describing the items, of collateral. A financing statement should include the debtor's trade name or style, if any, if known to the secured party, but a failure to include such trade name or style shall not under any circumstances affect the validity of the financing statement. A financing statement may be filed before a security agreement is made or a security interest otherwise attaches. When the financing statement covers crops growing or to be grown, the statement must also contain a description of the real estate concerned. When the financing statement covers timber to be cut or covers minerals or the like (including oil and gas) or accounts subject to subdivision (5) of Section 9103, or when the financing statement is filed as a fixture filing (Section 9313) and the collateral is goods which are or are to become fixtures, the statement must also comply with subdivision (5). A copy of the security agreement is sufficient as a financing statement if it contains the above information and is signed by the debtor. A certified copy of a financing statement or security agreement is sufficient as a financing statement if the original thereof was filed in this state.

(2) A financing statement which otherwise complies with subdivision (1) is sufficient when it is signed by the secured party instead of the debtor if it is filed to perfect a security interest in or as a fixture filing covering:

(a) Collateral already subject to a security interest in another jurisdiction when it is brought into this state or when the debtor's location is changed to this state. Such a financing statement must state that the collateral was brought into this state or that the debtor's location was changed to this state under such circumstances; or

(b) Proceeds under Section 9306, if the security interest in the original collateral was perfected. Such a financing statement must describe the original collateral and give the date of filing and the file number of the prior financing statement; or

(c) Collateral as to which the filing has lapsed. Such a financing statement must include a statement to the effect that the prior financing statement has lapsed and give the date of filing and the file number of the prior financing statement; or

(d) Collateral acquired after a change of name, identity or corporate structure of the debtor (subdivision (7)). Such a financing statement must include a statement that the name, identity or corporate structure of the debtor has been changed and give the date of filing and the file number of the prior financing statement and the name of the debtor as shown in the prior financing statement.

(3) A form substantially as follows is sufficient to comply with subdivision (1):

Name of debtor (or assignor) ....

Address ....

Name of secured party (or assignee) ....

Address ....

Debtor's trade name or style, if any ....

1. This financing statement covers the following types (or items) of property: (Describe) ....

2. (If collateral is crops) The above-described crops are growing or are to be grown on: (Describe real estate) ....

3. (If applicable) The above goods are or are to become fixtures on * (Describe real estate) ....
and this financing statement is to be recorded in the real estate records. (If the debtor does not have an interest of record) (If the debtor does not have an interest of record) The name of a record owner is ....

4. (If products of collateral are claimed) Products of the collateral are also covered.

(Use ....
whichever   Signature of debtor (or assignor)
is
applicable) ....
                Signature of Secured party (or assignee)

*Where appropriate substitute either "The above timber is standing on
. . . . ." or "The above mineral or the like (including oil and gas) or
accounts will be financed at the wellhead or minehead of the well or mine
located on . . . . ."

(4) A financing statement may be amended by filing a writing signed
by both the debtor and the secured party, or by the secured party alone
in the case of an amendment pursuant to subivision (7). An amendment
does not extend the period of effectiveness of a financing statement. If
any amendment adds collateral, it is effective as to the added collateral
only from the filing date of the amendment. In this division, unless the
context otherwise requires, the term "financing statement" means the
original financing statement and any amendments.

(5) A financing statement covering timber to be cut or covering minerals or the like (including oil and gas) or accounts subject to subdivision
(5) of Section 9103, or a financing statement filed as a fixture filing (Section 9313) where the debtor is not a transmitting utility, must show that
it covers this type of collateral, must recite that it is to be recorded in the
real estate records, and the financing statement must contain a description
of the real estate sufficient if it were contained in a mortgage of the real
estate to give constructive notice of the mortgage under the law of this
state. If the debtor does not have an interest of record in the real estate,
the financing statement must show the name of a record owner. A financing statement filed as a fixture filing (Section 9313) where the debtor
is not a transmitting utility must also recite either that it is filed as a
fixture filing or that it covers goods which are or are to become fixtures.

(6) A mortgage is effective as a financing statement as a fixture filing
from the date of its recording if

(a) The goods are described in the mortgage by item or type; and

(b) The goods are or are to become fixtures related to the real estate
described in the mortgage; and

(c) The mortgage complies with the requirements for a financing statement in this section other than a recital that it is to be filed in the real
estate records; and

(d) The mortgage is duly recorded.

No fee with reference to the financing statement is required other than
the regular recording and satisfaction fees with respect to the mortgage.

(7) A financing statement substantially complying with the requirements of this section is effective even though it contains minor errors
which are not seriously misleading.

(8) A financing statement substantially complying with the requirements of this section is effective even though it contains minor errors
which are not seriously misleading. A financing statement filed as a fixture filing (Section 9313) where the debtor is not a transmitting utility is
not effective if it does not recite that it is to be recorded in the real estate
records and either that it is filed as a fixture filing or that it covers goods
which are or are to become fixtures.

(9) A financing statement substantially complying with the requirements of this section creates a security interest only to the extent of the
interest of the debtor.

(10) No person or entity acting for or on behalf of the parties to a
financing statement shall incur any liability for the consequences of
recording a financing statement in the real estate records, and no action
may be brought or maintained against any such person or entity as a result
of the recordation.

Sec. 9403. **What Constitutes Filing; Duration of Filing; Effect of
Lapsed Filing; Continuation Statement; Duties of Filing Officer; Fees;
Recordation and Indexing.** (1) Presentation for filing of a financing
statement, tender of the filing fee and acceptance of the statement by the
filing officer constitutes filing under this division.

(2) Except as provided in subdivision (6), a filed financing statement
is effective for a period of five years from the date of filing. The effectiveness of a filed financing statement lapses on the expiration of such
five-year period unless a continuation statement is filed prior to the lapse.
If a security interest perfected by a filing exists at the time insolvency
proceedings are commenced by or against the debtor, the security interest
remains perfected until termination of the insolvency proceedings and
thereafter for a period of 60 days or until expiration of the five-year
period, whichever occurs later. Upon such lapse the security interest becomes unperfected unless it is perfected without filing. If the security
interest becomes unperfected upon lapse, it is deemed to have been un-

perfected as against a person who became a purchaser or lien creditor
before lapse. If a fixture filing is effective at the time insolvency proceedings are commenced by or against the debtor, the fixture filing remains effective until termination of the insolvency proceedings and thereafter for a period of 60 days or until expiration of the five-year period or
termination pursuant to subdivision (6), whichever occurs later. Upon
lapse of a fixture filing, it is deemed to have been ineffective as against
a person who became a purchaser or lien creditor before lapse.

(3) A continuation statement may be filed by the secured party of
record within six months prior to the expiration of the five-year period
specified in subdivision (2). Any such continuation statement must be
signed by the secured party of record, identify the original statement by
giving the date and the names of the parties thereto and the file number
thereof and state that the original statement is continued. A continuation
statement filed to continue the effectiveness of a financing statement filed
as a fixture filing (Section 9313) is not effective unless the following
requirements are met:

(a) If the debtor did not have an interest of record in the real estate as
of the date of the filing of the original statement, the continuation statement shall contain the name of a record owner of the real estate as of the
date of the filing of the original statement.

(b) The continuation statement shall contain substantially the following
statement: "This continuation statement is filed to continue the effectiveness of a financing statement filed as a fixture filing"; provided, that such
statement shall clearly indicate the intent to continue the effectiveness of
a financing statement as a fixture filing.

Upon timely filing of the continuation statement, the effectiveness of
the original statement is continued for five years after the last date to
which the filing was effective whereupon it lapses in the same manner as
provided in subdivision (2) unless another continuation statement is filed
prior to such lapse. Succeeding continuation statements may be filed in
the same manner to continue the effectiveness of the original statement.
The filing officer may remove a lapsed financing statement and related
filings from the files and destroy them immediately if he has retained a
microfilm or other photographic record, or in other cases after one year
after the lapse. The filing officer shall so arrange matters by physical
annexation of financing statements to continuation statement or other related filings, or by other means, that if he physically destroys the financing statements of a period more than five years past, those which have
been continued by a continuation statement or which are still effective
under subdivision (6) shall be retained. The filing officer shall not destroy
a financing statement and related filings as to which he has received written notice that there is an action pending relative thereto or that insolvency proceedings have been commenced by or against the debtor.

(4) Except as provided in subdivision (7) a filing officer shall mark
each financing statement with a consecutive file number and with the date
and time of filing and shall hold the statement or a microfilm or other
photographic copy thereof for public inspection. In addition, the filing
officer shall index the statement according to the name of the debtor and
shall note in the index the file number and the address of the debtor given
in this statement. The filing officer shall mark each continuation statement
with the date and time of filing and shall index the same under the file
number of the original financing statement.

(5) The uniform fee for filing, indexing and furnishing filing data (subdivision 1 of Section 9407) for an original financing statement, an amendment or a continuation statement shall be three dollars ($3) if the state-
ment is in the standard form prescribed by the Secretary of State and
otherwise shall be four dollars ($4).

(6) If the debtor is a transmitting utility (subdivision (5) of Section
9401) and a filed financing statement so states, it is effective until a termination statement is filed. A real estate mortgage which is effective as
a fixture filing under subdivision (6) of Section 9402 remains effective as
a fixture filing until the mortgage is released or satisfied of record or its
effectiveness otherwise terminates as to the real estate.

(7) A financing or continuation statement covering collateral described
in paragraph (b) of subdivision (1) of Section 9401 or filed as a fixture
filing shall be recorded and indexed by the filing officer in the real property index of grantors under the name of the debtor and any owner of
record shown on the financing statement. A financing or continuation
statement so recorded and indexed and containing a description of real
property affected thereby shall constitute constructive notice from the
time of its acceptance for recording to any purchaser or encumbrancer of
the real property of the security interest in such collateral.

Sec. 9403.1. **Destruction of Financing Statement Index.** The
county recorder may destroy any index of financing statements, including
any amendments, releases, continuations, terminations, assignments, any

other document relating to an original financing statement, if the last entry in the index is six or more years old.

Sec. 9404. Termination Statement. (1) Whenever there is no outstanding secured obligation and no commitment to make advances, incur obligations or otherwise give value, the secured party of record must on written demand by the debtor send the debtor a statement that he no longer claims a security interest under the financing statement, which shall be identified by date, names of parties thereto and file number. If the affected secured party of record fails to send such a termination statement within 10 days after proper demand therefor he shall be liable to the debtor for all actual damages suffered by the debtor by reason of such failure, and if the failure is in bad faith for a penalty of one hundred dollars ($100).

(2) The filing officer shall mark each such termination statement with the date and time of filing and shall index the same under the name of the debtor and under the file number of the original financing statement.

If the filing officer has a microfilm or other photographic record of the financing statement and related filings, he may remove the originals from the files at any time after receipt of the termination statement and destroy them, or if he has not such record, he may remove them from his files at any time after one year after receipt of the termination statement and destroy them.

(3) The uniform fee for filing, indexing and furnishing filing data (subdivision (1) of Section 9407) for a termination statement shall be three dollars ($3) if the statement is in the standard form prescribed by the Secretary of State and otherwise shall be four dollars ($4).

Sec. 9405. Release of Security Interest. (1) A secured party of record may by a writing release his security interest in all or a part of the collateral covered by a filed financing statement. A statement of release is sufficient if it is signed by the secured part of record, contains a statement describing the collateral being released, the name and address of the debtor, and the file number of the original financing statement.

(2) The filing officer shall mark each such statement with the date and time of filing and index the same under the name of the debtor and under the file number of the original financing statement.

(3) The uniform fee for filing, indexing and furnishing filing data (subdivision (1) of Section 9407) for a statement of release on a form conforming to standards prescribed by the Secretary of State shall be three dollars ($3) or, if such a statement otherwise conforms to the requirements of this section, four dollars ($4).

Sec. 9406. Assignment of Security Interest; Duties of Filing Officer; Fees. (1) If a secured party assigns or transfers his security interest in any collateral as to which a financing statement has been filed, a statement of such assignment may be filed. Such a statement shall be signed by the secured party, describe the collateral as to which the security interest has been assigned, give the name and mailing address of the assignee or transferee, the name and address of the debtor and the file number of the original financing statement.

(2) The filing officer shall mark each such statement of assignment or transfer with the date and time of filing and shall index the same under the name of the debtor and under the file number of the original financing statement.

(3) A statement of assignment may be filed at the time of the filing of the financing statement, in which event the filing officer shall first file the financing statement and index the assignment under the name of the debtor and under the file number given the financing statement. An assignment endorsed on the financing statement before it is filed with the filing officer need not be indexed by him.

(4) The uniform fee for filing, indexing and furnishing filing data (subdivision (1) of Section 9407) for a separate statement of assignment on a form conforming to standards prescribed by the Secretary of State shall be three dollars ($3) or, if such a statement otherwise conforms to the requirements of this section, four dollars ($4).

(5) Whenever a continuation statement, an amendment to a financing statement, a termination statement, a statement of release or a statement of assignment signed by one other than the secured party of record is presented for filing it must be accompanied by a statement of assignment signed by the secured party of record covering the collateral of which such continuation statement, amendment, termination statement, release, or assignment applies.

(6) Wherever in this code reference is made to the secured party of record it means the secured party named in the original financing statement or, if a statement of assignment has been filed, or an assignee has been named in the financing statement before it is filed, the assignee or

transferee of the security interest in the collateral affected. Any continuation statement, amendment to a financing statement, termination statement, statement of release or statement of assignment signed by one other than the secured party of record as to the collateral affected thereby shall be ineffective for any purpose except as between the parties thereto.

Sec. 9407. Information From Filing Officer. (1) If the person filing any financing statement, amendment, termination statement, statement of assignment, continuation statement, or statement of release, furnishes the filing officer a copy thereof, the filing officer shall upon request note upon the copy of a financing statement the file number and upon the copy of any such statements the date and time of the filing of the original and deliver or send the copy to such person.

(2) Upon request of any person, the filing office shall issue his or her certificate showing whether there is on file on the date and time stated therein, any presently effective financing statement naming a particular debtor and any statement of assignment thereof and if there is, giving the date and time of filing of each such statement and the names and addresses of each secured party therein. The certificate shall not include any statement as to the possibility of insolvency proceedings which might have the effect of preventing the lapse of effectiveness of a filed financing statement pursuant to Section 9403 whether actual insolvency proceedings are known or unknown to the filing officer. The uniform fee for such a certificate shall be set by the filing officer in an amount which covers actual costs but which in no event exceeds fifteen dollars ($15). Upon request the filing officer shall furnish a copy of any filed financing statement or related filings for a uniform fee of one dollar ($1) for the first page and fifty cents ($0.50) for each page thereafter.

(3) Fees to be charged by the Secretary of State for daily or less frequent summaries or compilations of filings, which he or she may furnish, shall be sufficient to pay at least the actual cost of such service. Fees shall be determined by the Secretary of State with the approval of the Department of Finance. Such summaries or compilations may be in the form of microfilm copies of such other form as may be provided for the required information.

Sec. 9407.1. Record of Papers in Lieu of Filing; Microphotography System. In lieu of filing all financing statements, termination statements, partial releases, assignments, or other related papers falling under this code, the filing officer may record such papers. He may employ a system of microphotography. All film used in the microphotography process shall comply with minimum standards of quality approved by the United States Bureau of Standards and the American National Standards Institute. A true copy of the microfilm shall be kept in a safe and separate place for security purposes.

Sec. 9407.2. Financing Statements and Related Papers Marked with File Number: Index. Should the filing officer choose to record rather than file all financing statements and related papers, he shall mark each statement with a consecutive file number. All other related papers affecting such financing statement shall thereafter bear the same file number. He shall index the same under the name of the debtor (or assignor or seller) in a separate index or in his general index, and under the file number of the original statement.

Sec. 9407.3. Originals or Copy Returned Upon Recording. Upon recording the financing statement or other related papers, the originals or copy of the same shall be returned to the parties entitled thereto.

Sec. 9408. Effect of Using Different Terms in Financing Statements. A consignor or lessor of goods may file a financing statement using the terms "consignor," "consignee," "lessor," "lessee" or the like instead of the terms specified in Section 9402. The provisions of this part shall apply as appropriate to such a financing statement but its filing shall not of itself be a factor in determining whether or not the consignment or lease is intended as security (Section 1201(37)). However, if it is determined for other reasons that the consignment or lease is so intended, a security interest of the consignor or lessor which attaches to the consigned or leased goods is perfected by such filing.

Sec. 9409. Combined Certificate (a) Upon request of any person, the Secretary of State shall issue a combined certificate showing the information as to financing statements as specified in Section 9407 of this code, the information as to state tax liens as specified in Section 7226 of the Government Code, the information as to attachment liens as specified in Sections 488.375 and 488.405 of the Code of Civil Procedure, the information as to judgment liens as specified in Section 697.580 of the Code of Civil Procedure, and, if the name requested appears to be other than an individual, the information as to federal liens as specified in Section 2103 of the Code of Civil Procedure. The fee for such a combined certificate is five dollars ($5).

(b) The Secretary of State shall construe a request for a certificate as one for a combined certificate pursuant to this section unless the request is specifically limited to federal liens, state tax liens, judgment liens, or attachment liens.

CHAPTER 5

DEFAULT

Sec. 9501. Default; Procedure When Security Agreement Covers Both Real and Personal Property. (1) When a debtor is in default under a security agreement, a secured party has the rights and remedies provided in this chapter and except as limited by subdivision (3) those provided in the security agreement. He may reduce his claim to judgment, foreclose or otherwise enforce the security interest by any available judicial procedure. If the collateral is documents the secured party may proceed either as to the documents or as to the goods covered thereby. A secured party in possession has the rights, remedies and duties provided in Section 9207. The rights and remedies referred to in this subdivision are cumulative.

(2) After default, the debtor has the rights and remedies provided in this chapter, those provided in the security agreement and those provided in Section 9207.

(3) To the extent that they give rights to the debtor and impose duties on the secured party, the rules stated in the subdivisions referred to below may not be waived or varied except as provided with respect to compulsory disposition of collateral (subdivision (3) of Section 9504 and Section 9405) and with respect to redemption of collateral (Section 9506) but the parties may by agreement determine the standards by which the fulfillment of these rights and duties is to be measured if such standards are not manifestly unreasonable:

(a) Subdivision (2) of Section 9502 and subdivision (2) of Section 9504 insofar as they require accounting for surplus proceeds of collateral;

(b) Subdivision (3) of Section 9504 and subdivision (1) of Section 9505 which deal with disposition of collateral;

(c) Subdivision (2) of Section 9505 which deals with acceptance of collateral as discharge of obligation;

(d) Section 9506 which deals with redemption of collateral; and

(e) Subdivision (1) of Section 9507 which deals with the secured party's liability for failure to comply with this chapter.

(4) If the security agreement covers both real and personal property or fixtures (Section 9313(1)(a)), the secured party may proceed under this chapter as to the personal property or fixtures or he may proceed as to both the real property and the personal property or fixtures in accordance with his rights and remedies in respect of the real property in which case the provisions of this chapter do not apply.

(5) When a secured party has reduced his claim to judgment the lien of any levy which may be made upon his collateral by virtue of any execution based upon the judgment shall relate back to the date of the perfection of the security interest in such collateral. A judicial sale, pursuant to such execution, is a foreclosure of the security interest by judicial procedure within the meaning of this section, and the secured party may purchase at the sale and thereafter hold the collateral free of any other requirements of this division.

Sec. 9502. Collection Rights of Secured Party. (1) When so agreed and in any event on default the secured party is entitled to notify an account debtor or the obligor on an instrument to make payment to him whether or not the assignor was therefore making collection on the collateral, and also to take control of any proceeds to which he is entitled under Section 9306.

(2) A secured party who by agreement is entitled to charge back uncollected collateral or otherwise to full or limited recourse against the debtor and who undertakes to collect from the account debtors or obligors must proceed in a commercially reasonable manner and may deduct his reasonable expenses of realization from the collections. If the security agreement secures an indebtedness, the secured party must account to the debtor for any surplus, and unless otherwise agreed, the debtor is liable for any deficiency. But, if the underlying transaction was a sale of accounts or chattel paper, the debtor is entitled to any surplus or is liable for any deficiency only if the security agreement so provides.

Sec. 9503. Secured Party's Right to Take Possession After Default. Unless otherwise agreed a secured party has on default the right to take possession of the collateral. In taking possession a secured party may proceed without judicial process if this can be done without breach of the peace or may proceed by action. If the security agreement so provides the secured party may require the debtor to assemble the collateral and make it available to the secured party at a place to be designated by the secured party which is reasonably convenient to both parties. Without removal a secured party may render equipment unusable, and may dispose of collateral on the debtor's premises under Section 9504.

Sec. 9504. Secured Party's Right to Dispose of Collateral After Default; Effect of Disposition. (1) A secured party after default may sell, lease or otherwise dispose of any or all of collateral in its then condition or following any commercially reasonable preparation or processing. Any sale of goods is subject to the division on sales (Division 2). The proceeds of disposition shall be applied in the order following to

(a) The reasonable expenses of retaking, holding, preparing for sale or lease, selling, leasing and the like and, to the extent provided for in the agreement and not prohibited by law, the reasonable attorneys' fees and legal expenses incurred by the secured party;

(b) The satisfaction of indebtedness secured by the security interest under which the disposition is made;

(c) The satisfaction of indebtedness secured by any subordinate security interest in the collateral if written notification of demand therefor is received before distribution of the proceeds is completed and to the satisfaction of any subordinate attachment lien or execution lien pursuant to subdivision (b) of Section 701.040 of the Code of Civil Procedure if notice of the levy of attachment or execution is received before distribution of the proceeds is completed. If requested by the secured party, the holder of a subordinate security interest must seasonably furnish reasonable proof of his interest, and unless he does so, the secured party need not comply with his demand.

(2) If the security interest secures an indebtedness, the secured party must account to the debtor for any surplus except as provided in Section 701.040 of the Code of Civil Procedure, and unless otherwise agreed, the debtor is liable for any deficiency. But if the underlying transaction was a sale of accounts or chattel paper, the debtor is entitled to any surplus or is liable for any deficiency only if the security agreement so provides and the provisions of Section 701.040 of the Code of Civil Procedure relating to payment of proceeds and the liability of the secured party apply only if the security agreement provides that the debtor is entitled to any surplus.

(3) A sale or lease of collateral may be as a unit or in parcels, at wholesale or retail and at any time and place and on any terms, provided the secured party acts in good faith and in a commercially reasonable manner. Unless collateral is perishable or threatens to decline speedily in value or is of a type customarily sold on a recognized market, the secured party must give to the debtor, if he has not signed after default a statement renouncing or modifying his right to notification of sale, and to any other person who has a security interest in the collateral and who has filed with the secured party a written request for notice giving his address (before that secured party sends his notification to the debtor or before debtor's renunciation of his rights), a notice in writing of the time and place of any public sale or of the time on or after which any private sale or other intended disposition is to be made. Such notice must be delivered personally or be deposited in the United States mail postage prepaid addressed to the debtor at his address as set forth in the financing statement or as set forth in the security agreement or at such other address as may have been furnished to the secured party in writing for this purpose, or, if no address has been so set forth or furnished, at his last known address, and to any other secured party at the address set forth in his request for notice, at least five days before the date fixed for any public sale or before the date on or after which any private sale or other disposition is to be made. Notice of the time and place of a public sale shall also be given at least five days before the date of sale by publication once in a newspaper of general circulation published in the county in which the sale is to be held. Any public sale shall be held in the county or place specified in the security agreement, or if no county or place is specified in the security agreement, in the county in which the collateral or any part thereof is located or in the county in which the debtor has his residence or chief place of business, or in the county in which the secured party has his residence or a place of business if the debtor does not have a residence or chief place of business within this State. If the collateral is located outside of this State or has been removed from this State, a public sale may be held in the locality in which the collateral is located. Any public sale may be postponed from time to time by public announcement at the time and place last scheduled for the sale. The secured party may buy at any public sale and if the collateral is customarily sold in a recognized

market or is the subject of widely or regularly distributed standard price quotations he may buy at private sale. Any sale of which notice is delivered or mailed and published as herein provided and which is held as herein provided is a public sale.

(4) When collateral is disposed of by a secured party after default, the disposition transfer to a purchaser for value all of the debtor's rights therein, discharges the security interest under which it is made and any security interest or lien subordinate thereto. The purchaser takes free of all such rights and interest even though the secured party fails to comply with the requirements of this chapter or of any judicial proceedings

(a) In the case of a public sale, if the purchaser has no knowledge of any defects in the sale and if he does not buy in collusion with the secured party, other bidders or the person conducting the sale; or

(b) In any other case, if the purchaser acts in good faith.

(5) A person who is liable to a secured party under a guaranty, indorsement, repurchase agreement or the like and who receives a transfer of collateral from the secured party or is subrogated to his rights has thereafter the rights and duties of the secured party. Such a transfer of collateral is not a sale or disposition of the collateral under this division.

Sec. 9505. Debtor's Recovery Where Disposal of Collateral Mandated; Notice of Intent to Retain Collateral.

(1) If the debtor has paid 60 percent of the cash price in the case of a purchase money security interest in consumer goods or 60 percent of the loan in the case of another security interest in consumer goods, and has not signed after default a statement renouncing or modifying his rights under this chapter a secured party who has taken possession of collateral must dispose of it under Section 9504 and if he fails to do so within 90 days after he takes possession or within a reasonable time after such 90-day period, the debtor at his option may recover in conversion or under Section 9507(1) on secured party's liability.

(2) In any other case involving consumer goods or any other collateral a secured party in possession may, after default, propose to retain the collateral in satisfaction of the obligation. Written notice of such proposal shall be sent to the debtor if he has not signed after default a statement renouncing or modifying his rights under this subdivision. In the case of consumer goods no other notice need be given. In other cases notice shall be sent to any other secured party from whom the secured party has received (before sending his notice to the debtor or before the debtor's renunciation of his rights) written notice of a claim of an interest in the collateral. If the secured party receives objection in writing from a person entitled to receive notification while 21 days after the notice was sent, the secured party must dispose of the collateral under Section 9504. In the absence of such written objection the secured party may retain the collateral in satisfaction of the debtor's obligation.

Sec. 9506. Debtor's Rights to Redeem Collateral.

At any time before the secured party has disposed of collateral or entered into a contract for its disposition under Section 9504 or before the obligation has been discharged under Section 9505(2) the debtor or any other secured party may unless otherwise agreed in writing after default redeem the collateral by tendering fulfillment of all obligations secured by the collateral as well as the expenses reasonably incurred by the secured party in retaking, holding and preparing the collateral for disposition, in arranging for the sale, and to the extent provided in the agreement and not prohibited by law, his reasonable attorneys' fees and legal expenses.

Sec. 9507. Secured Party's Liability for Failure to Comply With This Chapter.

(1) If it is established that the secured party is not proceeding in accordance with the provisions of this chapter disposition may be ordered or restrained on appropriate terms and conditions. If the disposition has occurred the debtor or any person entitled to notification or whose security interest has been made known to the secured party prior to the disposition has a right to receover from the secured party any loss caused by a failure to comply with the provisions of this chapter.

(2) The fact that a better price could have been obtained by a sale at a different time or in a different method from that selected by the secured party is not of itself sufficient to establish that the sale was not made in a commercially reasonable manner. If the secured party either sells the collateral in the usual manner in any recognized market therefor or if he sells at the price current in such market at the time of his sale or if he has otherwise sold in conformity with reasonable commercial practices among dealers in the type of property sold he has sold in a commercially reasonable manner. The principles stated in the two preceding sentences with respect to sales also apply as may be appropriate to other types of disposition. A disposition which has been approved in any judicial proceeding or by any bona fide creditors' committee or representative of creditors shall conclusively be deemed to be commercially reasonable, but this sentence does not indicate that any such approval must be obtained in any case nor does it indicate that any disposition not so approved is not commercially reasonable.

Sec. 9508. Enforceability of Debtor's Renunciations.

No renunciation or modification by the debtor of any of his rights under this chapter as to consumer goods shall be valid or enforceable unless the renunciation or modification is in consideration of a waiver by the secured party of any right to a deficiency on the debt.

UNIFORM PARTNERSHIP ACT

Note: In California, the Uniform Partnership Act is sections 15001-15045 of the Corporation Code. The California code follows the same numerical sequence as the uniform act—Corp. C. 15001 is U.P.A. 1, Corp. C. 15002 is U.P.A. 2, Corp. C. 15020 is U.P.A. 20, and so on throughout the 45 sections. Such being the case, only the California code section numbers are shown. California has amended U.P.A. 10 and U.P.A. 25(e) and has added Corp. C. 15010.5 and Corp. C. 15035.5 which are not contained in the uniform act. A "Note" following Corp. C. 15010 and Corp. C. 15025(e) shows the manner in which California has amended the uniform act. California also adds Corp. C. 15700, set out at the end of the Uniform Limited Partnership Act.

Sec. 15001. Name of act. This chapter may be cited as "Uniform Partnership Act."

Sec. 15002. Definition of terms. In this act, "Court" includes every court and judge having jurisdiction in the case.

"Business" includes every trade, occupation, or profession.

"Person" includes individuals, partnerships, corporations, and other associations.

"Bankrupt" includes a debtor under Chapter 7 of the federal bankruptcy law or an insolvent under any state insolvent act.

"Conveyance" includes every assignment, lease, mortgage, or encumbrance.

"Real property" includes land and any interest or estate in land.

Sec. 15003. "Knowledge" and "notice" defined. (1) A person has "knowledge" of a fact within the meaning of this act not only when he has actual knowledge thereof, but also when he has knowledge of such other facts as in the circumstances shows bad faith.

(2) A person has "notice" of a fact within the meaning of this act when the person who claims the benefit of the notice

(a) States the fact to such person, or

(b) Delivers through the mail, or by other means of communication, a written statement of the fact to such person or to a proper person at his place of business or residence.

Sec. 15004. Rules of construction. (1) The rule that statutes in derogation of the common law are to be strictly construed shall have no application to this act.

(2) The law of estoppel shall apply under this act.

(3) The law of agency shall apply under this act.

(4) This act shall be so interpreted and construed as to effect its general purpose to make uniform the law of those states which enact it.

(5) This act shall not be construed so as to impair the obligations of any contract existing when the act goes into effect, nor to affect any action or proceedings begun or right accrued before this act takes effect.

Sec. 15005. Cases not provided for in act. In any case not provided for in this act the rules of law and equity, including the law merchant, shall govern.

Sec. 15006. Partnership defined. (1) A partnership is an association of two or more persons to carry on as co-owners a business for profit.

(2) But any association formed under any other statute of this State, or any statute adopted by authority, other than the authority of this State, is not a partnership in this State prior to the adoption of this act; but this act shall apply to limited, special, and mining partnerships except insofar as the statutes relating to such partnerships are inconsistent herewith.

Sec. 15007. Rules for determining existence of partnership. In determining whether a partnership exists, these rules shall apply:

(1) Except as provided by Section 15016 persons who are not partners as to each other are not partners as to third persons.

(2) Joint tenancy, tenancy in common, tenancy by the entireties, joint property, common property, or part ownership does not of itself establish a partnership, whether such co-owners do or do not share any profits made by the use of the property.

(3) The sharing of gross returns does not of itself establish a partnership, whether or not the persons sharing them have a joint or common right or interest in any property from which the returns are derived.

(4) The receipt by a person of a share of the profits of a business is prima facie evidence that he is a partner in the business, but no such inference shall be drawn if such profits were received in payment:

(a) As a debt by installments or otherwise.

(b) As wages of an employee or rent to a landlord.

(c) As an annuity to a surviving spouse or representative of a deceased partner.

(d) As interest on a loan, though the amount of payment vary with the profits of the business.

(e) As the consideration for the sale of a good will of a business or other property by installments or otherwise.

Sec. 15008. Partnership property. (1) All property originally brought into the partnership stock or subsequently acquired by purchase or otherwise, on account of the partnership, is partnership property.

(2) Unless the contrary intention appears, property acquired with partnership funds is partnership property.

(3) Any estate in real property may be acquired in the partnership name. Title so acquired can be conveyed only in the partnership name.

(4) A conveyance to a partnership in the partnership name, though without words of inheritance, passes the entire estate of the grantor unless a contrary intent appears.

Sec. 15009. Agency of partner for partnership: Limitation of authority of partner. (1) Every partner is an agent of the partnership for the purpose of its business, and the act of every partner, including the execution in the partnership name of any instrument, for apparently carrying on in the usual way the business of the partnership of which he is a member binds the partnership, unless the partner so acting has in fact no authority to act for the partnership in the particular matter, and the person with whom he is dealing has knowledge of the fact that he has no such authority.

(2) An act of a partner which is not apparently for carrying on of the business of the partnership in the usual way does not bind the partnership unless authorized by the other partners.

(3) Unless authorized by the other partners or unless they have abandoned the business, one or more but less than all the partners have no authority to:

(a) Assign the partnership property in trust for creditors or on the assignee's promise to pay the debts of the partnership.

(b) Dispose of the good will of the business.

(c) Do any other act which would make it impossible to carry on the ordinary business of a partnership.

(d) Confess a judgment.

(e) Submit a partnership claim or liability to arbitration or reference.

(4) No act of a partner in contravention of a restriction on authority shall bind the partnership to persons having knowledge of the restriction.

Sec. 15010. Conveyances of partnership real property: Passing of title. (1) Where title to real property is in the partnership name, any partner may convey title to such property by a conveyance executed in the partnership name; but the partnership may recover such property unless the partner's act binds the partnership under the provisions of paragraph (1) of Section 15009, or unless such property has been conveyed to a bona fide purchaser for value without knowledge that the partner in executing the conveyance has exceeded his authority.

(2) Where title to real property is in the name of the partnership, a conveyance executed by a partner, in his own name, passes the equitable interest of the partnership, provided the act is one within the authority of the partner under the provisions of paragraph (1) of Section 15009.

(3) Where title to real property is in the name of one or more of the partners, whether or not the record discloses the right of the partnership, the partners in whose name the title stands may convey title to such property, but the partnership may recover such property unless the partner's act binds the partnership under the provisions of paragraph (1) of Section 15009, or unless the property has been conveyed to a bona fide purchaser for value without knowledge that the partner in executing the conveyance has exceeded his authority.

(4) Where the title to real property is in the name of one or more or all the partners, or in a third person in trust for the partnership, a conveyance executed by a partner in the partnership name, or in his own name, passes the equitable interest of the partnership, provided the act is one within the authority of the partner under the provisions of paragraph (1) of Section 15009.

(5) Where the title to real property is in the names of all the partners a conveyance executed by all the partners passes all their rights in such property.

NOTE: Section 10 of the Uniform Partnership Act reads as follows:

"(1) Where title to real property is in the partnership name, any partner may convey title to such property by a conveyance executed in the partnership name; but the partnership may recover such property unless the partner's act binds the partnership under the provisions of paragraph (1) of section 9, or unless such property has been conveyed *by the grantee or a person claiming through such grantee to a holder for value* without knowledge that the partner, in making the conveyance, has exceeded his authority.

"(2) Where title to real property is in the name of the partnership, a conveyance executed by a partner, in his own name, passes the equitable interest of the partnership, provided the act is one within the authority of the partner under the provisions of paragraph (1) of section 9.

"(3) Where title to real property is in the name of one or more but not all the partners, and the record does *not disclose the right of the partnership*, the partners in whose name the title stands may convey title to such property, but the partnership may recover such property *if the partners act does not bind the partnership under the provisions of paragraph (1) of section (9), unless the purchaser or his assignee, is a holder for value, without knowledge.*"

U.P.A. 10(4)(5) are the same as Corp. C. 15010(4)(5).

Sec. 15010.5. **Recording statement of partnership: Presumption as to members of partnership: Definitions.** (1) A statement of partnership, in the name of the partnership, signed, acknowledged and verified by two or more of the partners, or such a statement signed by two or more of the partners as individuals, acknowledged and verified by each signing partner, may be recorded in the office of the county recorder of any county. Such recorded statement, or a copy thereof certified by any recorder in whose office it or a copy thereof so certified is recorded, may be recorded in any other county or counties. The statement shall set forth the name of the partnership and the name of each of the partners, and shall state the partners named are all of the partners. If a partnership is not dissolved by the death or by the withdrawal of a partner by reason of an agreement provided for in subdivision (4) or (7) of Section 15031 the statement or amended statement may state the name and date of death or withdrawal of such deceased or withdrawing (whether voluntarily or involuntarily according to the terms of the agreement) partner and that the partnership was not dissolved by reason of such death or withdrawal because of the existence of such agreement.

It shall be conclusively presumed, in favor of any bona fide purchaser for value of the partnership real property located in a county in which such statement or such certified copy thereof has been recorded, that the persons named as partners therein are members of the partnership and that any partner stated to be dead is deceased, and any partner stated to have withdrawn therefrom, and that the partnership was not dissolved by reason of such death or withdrawal, unless there is recorded by anyone claiming to be a partner, or a personal representative, whether executor, administrator, guardian or conservator, of such partner, a statement of partnership, verified and acknowledged by the person executing it, which shall set forth the name of the partnership, a statement that such person claims to be a member of such partnership, or a personal representative of such member, or a statement that any of the persons named in previously recorded statement of partnership are not members of such partnership.

(2) As used in this section and in Section 15010, "conveyance" includes every instrument in writing by which any estate or interest in real estate is created, aliened, mortgaged, or encumbered, or by which the title to any real property may be effected, except wills; "convey" includes the execution of any such instrument; and "purchaser" includes any person acquiring an interest under any such instrument.

Sec. 15010.6. **Recording partnership statement after death of partner.** Where no statement of partnership as provided in Section 15010.5 has been recorded prior to the death of one or more of the partners, such statement may be signed, acknowledged and verified by two or more of the surviving partners, in the form and manner specified in said section; provided that if all of the partners except one are deceased, the statement may be signed, acknowledged and verified by the last survivor of the partners only; and provided further that such statement shall specify the date of creation of the partnership, which of the partners are deceased and the date of death of each deceased partner.

Nothing in this section shall be construed to affect the provisions of Section 15031 of this code.

Sec. 15011. **Partnership bound by admission or representation of partner.** An admission or representation made by any partner concerning partnership affairs within the scope of his authority as conferred by this act is evidence against the partnership.

Sec. 15012. **Partnership charged with knowledge of or notice to partner.** Notice to any partner of any matter relating to partnership affairs, and the knowledge of the partner acting in the particular matter, acquired while a partner or then present to his mind, and the knowledge of any other partner who reasonably could and should have communicated it to the acting partner, operate as notice to or knowledge of the partnership, except in the case of a fraud on the partnership committed by or with the consent of that partner.

Sec. 15013. **Partnership bound by partner's wrongful act or omission.** Where, by any wrongful act or omission of any partner acting in the ordinary course of the business of the partnership or with the authority of his copartners, loss or injury is caused to any person, not being a partner in the partnership, or any penalty is incurred, the partnership is liable therefor to the same extent as the partner so acting or omitting to act.

Sec. 15014. **Partnership bound by partner's breach of trust.** The partnership is bound to make good the loss:

(a) Where one partner acting within the scope of his apparent authority receives money or property of a third person and misapplies it; and

(b) Where the partnership in the course of its business receives money or property of a third person and the money or property so received is misapplied by any partner while it is in the custody of the partnership.

Sec. 15015. **Nature of partner's liability.** All partners are liable

(a) Jointly and severally for everything chargeable to the partnership under Section 15013 and 15014.

(b) Jointly for all other debts and obligations of the partnership; but any partner may enter into a separate obligation to perform a partnership contract.

Sec. 15016. **Partner by estoppel.** (1) When a person, by words spoken or written or by conduct, represents himself, or consents to another representing him to any one, as a partner in an existing partnership or with one or more persons not actual partners, he is liable to any such person to whom such representation has been made, who has, on the faith of such representation, given credit to the actual or apparent partnership, and if he has made such representation or consented to its being made in a public manner he is liable to such person, whether the representation has or has not been made or communicated to such person so giving credit by or with the knowledge of the apparent partner making the representation or consenting to its being made.

(a) When a partnership liability results, he is liable as though he were an actual member of the partnership.

(b) When no partnership liability results, he is liable jointly with the other persons, if any, so consenting to the contract or representation as to incur liability, otherwise separately.

(2) When a person has been thus represented to be a partner in an existing partnership, or with one or more persons not actual partners, he is an agent of the persons consenting to such representation to bind them to the same extent and in the same manner as though he were a partner in fact, with respect to persons who rely upon the representation. Where all the members of the existing partnership consent to the representation, a partnership act or obligation results; but in all other cases it is the joint act or obligation of the person acting and the persons consenting to the representation.

Sec. 15017. **Liability of incoming partner.** A person admitted as a partner into an existing partnership is liable for all the obligations of the partnership arising before his admission as though he had been a partner when such obligations were incurred, except that this liability shall be satisfied only out of partnership property.

Sec. 15018. **Rules determining rights and duties of partners.** The rights and duties of the partners in relation to the partnership, shall be determined subject to any agreement between them, by the following rules:

(a) Each partner shall be repaid his contributions, whether by way of capital or advances to the partnership property and share equally in the profits and surplus remaining after all liabilities, including those to partners, are satisfied; and must contribute towards the losses whether of capital or otherwise, sustained by the partnership according to his share of the profits.

(b) The partnership must indemnify every partner in respect of payments made and personal liabilities reasonably incurred by him in the ordinary and proper conduct of its business, or for the preservation of its business or property.

(c) A partner, who in aid of the partnership makes any payment or advance beyond the amount of the capital which he agreed to contribute, shall be paid interest from the date of the payment or advance.

(d) A partner shall receive interest on the capital contributed by him only from the date when repayment should be made.

(e) All partners have equal rights in the management and conduct of the partnership business.

(f) No partner is entitled to remuneration for acting in the partnership business, except that a surviving partner is entitled to reasonable compensation for his sevices in winding up the partnership affairs.

(g) No person can become a member of a partnership without the consent of all the partners.

(h) Any difference arising as to ordinary matters connected with the partnership business may be decided by a majority of the partners; but no act in contravention of any agreement between the partners may be done rightfully with out the consent of all the partners.

Sec. 15019. Partnership books. The partnership books shall be kept, subject to any agreement between the partners, at the principal place of business of the partners, and every partner shall at all times have access to and may inspect and copy any of them.

Sec. 15020. Duty of partners to render information. Partners shall render on demand true and full information of all things affecting the partnership to any partner of the legal representative of any deceased partner or partner under legal disability.

Sec. 15021. Partner accountable as a fiduciary. (1) Every partner must account to the partnership for any benefit, and hold as trustee for it any profits derived by him without the consent of the other partners from any transaction connected with the formation, conduct, or liquidation of the partnership or from any use by him of its property.

(2) This section applies also to the representatives of a deceased partner engaged in the liquidation of the affairs of the partnership as the personal representative of the last surviving partner.

Sec. 15022. Right to an account. Any partner shall have the right to a formal account as to partnership affairs:

(a) If he is wrongfully excluded from the partnership business or possession of its property by his copartners,

(b) If the right exists under the terms of any agreement,

(c) As provided by Section 15021,

(d) Whenever other circumstances render it just and reasonable.

Sec. 15023. Continuation of partnership beyond fixed term. (1) When a partnership for a fixed term or particular undertaking is continued after the termination of such term or particular undertaking without any express agreement, the rights and duties of the partners remain the same as they were at such termination, so far as is consistent with a partnership at will.

(2) A continuation of a business by the partners or such of them as habitually acted therein during the term, without any settlement or liquidation of the partnership affairs, is prima facie evidence of a continuation of the partnership.

Sec. 15024. Extent of property rights of a partner. The property rights of a partner as (1) his rights in specific partnership property, (2) his interest in the partnership, and (3) his right to participate in the management.

Sec. 15025. Nature of a partner's right in specific partnership property. (1) A partner is coowner with the other partners of specific partnership property holding as a tenant in partnership.

(2) The incidents of this tenancy are such that:

(a) A partner, subject to the provisions of this chapter and to any agreement between the partners, has an equal right with the other partners to possess specific partnership property for partnership purposes; but a partner has no right to possess such property for any other purpose without the consent of the other partners.

(b) A partner's right in specific partnership property is not assignable except in connection with the assignments of rights of all the partners in the same property.

(c) A partner's right in specific partnership property is not subject to enforcement of a money judgment, except on a claim against the partnership. When partnership property is levied upon for a partnership debt the partners, or any of them, or the representatives of a deceased partner, cannot claim any right under the exemption laws.

(d) On the death of a partner the partner's right in specific partnership property vests in the surviving partner or partners, except where the deceased was the last surviving partner, when the deceased partner's right in such property vests in his or her legal representative. Such surviving partner or partners, or the legal representative of the last surviving partner, has no right to possess the partnership property for any but a partnership purpose.

(e) A partner's right in specific partnership property is not subject to dower, curtesy, or allowances to widows, heirs, or next of kin, and is not community property.

NOTE: Section 25(e) of the Uniform Partnership Act does not contain the words, "*and is not community property*," added to the end of Corp. C. 15025(e) above because of the adoption of the community property law in this state.

Sec. 15026. Nature of partner's interest in the partnership. A partner's interest in the partnership is his share of the profits and surplus, and the same is personal property.

Sec. 15027. Assignment of partner's interest. (1) A conveyance by a partner of his interest in the partnership does not itself dissolve the partnership, nor, as against the other partners in the absence of agreement, entitle the assignee, during the continuance of the partnership, to interfere in the management or administration of the partnership business or affairs, or to require any information or account of partnership transactions, or to inspect the partnership books; but it merely entitles the assignee to receive in accordance with his contract the profits to which the assigning partner would otherwise be entitled.

(2) In the case of a dissolution of the partnership, the assignee is entitled to receive his assignor's interest and may require an account from the date only of the last account agreed to by all the partners.

Sec. 15028. Partner's interest subject to charging order. (1) On due application to a competent court by any judgment creditor of a partner, the court which entered the judgment, order, or decree, or any other court, may charge the interest of the debtor partner with payment of the unsatisfied amount of such judgment debt with interest thereon; and may then or later appoint a receiver of his share of the profits, and of any other money due or to fall due to him in respect of the partnership, and make all other orders, directions, accounts, and inquiries which the debtor partner might have made, or which the circumstances of the case may require.

(2) The interest charged may be redeemed at any time before foreclosure, or in case of a sale being directed by the court may be purchased without thereby causing a dissolution:

(a) With separate property, by any one or more of the partners, or

(b) With partnership property, by any one or more of the partners with the consent of all the partners whose interests are not so charged or sold.

(3) Nothing in this act shall be held to deprive a partner of his right, if any, under the exemption laws, as regards his interest in the partnership.

Sec. 15029. Dissolution defined. The dissolution of a partnership is the change in the relation of the partners caused by any partner ceasing to be associated in the carrying on as distinguished from the winding up of the business.

Sec. 15030. Partnership not terminated by dissolution. On dissolution the partnership is not terminated, but continues until the winding up of partnership affairs is completed.

Sec. 15031. Causes of dissolution. Dissolution is caused:

(1) Without violation of the agreement between the partners,

(a) By the termination of the definite term of particular undertaking specified in the agreement,

(b) By the express will of any partner when no definite term or particular undertaking is specified,

(c) By the express will of all the partners who have not assigned their interest or suffered them to be charged for their separate debts, either before or after the termination of any specified term or particular undertaking,

(d) By the expulsion of any partner from the business bona fide in accordance with such a power conferred by the agreement between the partners;

(2) In contravention of the agreement between the partners, where the circumstances do not permit a dissolution under any other provision of this section, by the express will of any partner at any time;

(3) By any event which makes it unlawful for the business of the partnership to be carried on or for the members to carry it on in partnership;

(4) By the death of any partner unless otherwise provided in an agreement in writing signed by all the partners before such death;

(5) By the bankruptcy of any partner or the partnership;

(6) By decree of court under Section 15032.

(7) By withdrawal of a partner of admission of a new partner unless otherwise provided in an agreement in writing signed by all of the partners, including any such withdrawing partner or any such newly admitted partner, before such withdrawal or admission; provided that in the case of a newly admitted partner he may become a party to any such pre-existing agreement by signing the same upon such admission.

None of the provisions of any other section of this chapter shall prevent, or impair the effect or enforceability of, any agreement in writing that a partnership will not be dissolved as provided for in subdivision (4) or (7) of this section.

Sec. 15032. **Dissolution by decree of court.** (1) On application by or for a partner the court shall decree a dissolution whenever:

(a) A partner has been declared a lunatic in any judicial proceeding or is shown to be of unsound mind,

(b) A partner becomes in any other way incapable of performing his part of the partnership contract,

(c) A partner has been guilty of such conduct as tends to affect prejudicially the carrying on of the business,

(d) A partner wilfully or persistently commits a breach of the partnership agreement, or otherwise so conducts himself in matters relating to the partnership business that it is not reasonably practicable to carry on the business in partnership with him.

(e) The business of the partnership can only be carried on at a loss.

(f) Other circumstances render a dissolution equitable.

(2) On the application of the purchaser of a partner's interest under Section 15027 and 15028:

(a) After the termination of the specified term or particular undertaking,

(b) At any time if the partnership was a partnership at will when the interest was assigned or when the charging order was issued.

Sec. 15033. **General effect of dissolution on authority of partner.** Except so far as may be necessary to wind up partnership affairs or to complete transactions begun but not then finished, dissolution terminates all authority of any partner to act for the partnership,

(1) With respect to the partners,

(a) When the dissolution is not by the act, bankruptcy or death of a partner; or

(b) When the dissolution is by such act, bankruptcy or death of a partner in cases where Section 15034 so requires;

(2) With respect to persons not partners, as declared in Section 15035.

Sec. 15034. **Right of partner to contribution from copartners after dissolution.** Where the dissolution is caused by the act, death or bankruptcy of a partner, each partner is liable to his copartners for his share of any liability created by any partner acting for the partnership as if the partnership had not been dissolved unless

(a) The dissolution being by act of any partner, the partner acting for the partnership had knowledge of the dissolution, or

(b) The dissolution being by the death or bankruptcy of a partner, the partner acting for the partnership had knowledge or notice of the death or bankruptcy.

Sec. 15035. **Power of partner to bind partnership to third person after dissolution.** (1) After dissolution a partner can bind the partnership except as provided in paragraph three,

(a) By any act appropriate for winding up partnership affairs or completing transactions unfinished at dissolution;

(b) By any transaction which would bind the partnership if dissolution had not taken place, provided, the other party to the transaction:

I. Had extended credit to the partnership prior to dissolution and had no knowledge or notice of the dissolution; or

II. Though he had not so extended credit, had nevertheless known of the partnership prior to dissolution, and, having no knowledge of notice of dissolution, the fact of dissolution had not been advertised in a newspaper or general circulation in the place (or in each place if more than one) at which the partnership business was regularly carried on.

(2) The liability of a partner under paragraph (1b) shall be satisfied out of partnership assets alone when such partner had been prior to dissolution:

(a) Unknown as a partner to the person with whom the contract is made; and

(b) So far unknown and inactive in partnership affairs that the business reputation of the partnership could not be said to have been in any degree due to his connection with it.

(3) The partnership is in no case bound by any act of a partner after dissolution

(a) Where the partnership is dissolved because it is unlawful to carry on the business, unless the act is appropriate for winding up partnership affairs; or

(b) Where the partner has become bankrupt; or

(c) Where the partner has no authority to wind up partnership affairs; except by a transaction with one who

I. Had extended credit to the partnership prior to dissolution and had no knowledge or notice of his want of authority; or

II. Had not extended credit to the partnership prior to dissolution, and, having no knowledge or notice of his want of authority, the fact of his want of authority has not been advertised in the manner provided for advertising the fact of dissolution in paragraph (1bII).

(4) Nothing in this section shall affect the liability under Section 15016 of any person who after dissolution represents himself or consents to another representing him as a partner in a partnership engaged in carrying on business.

Sec. 15035.5. **Publication of notice of dissolution.** Whenever a partnership is dissolved, a notice of the dissolution shall be published at least once in a newspaper of general circulation in the place, or in each place if more than one, at which the partnership business was regularly carried on, and an affidavit showing the publication of such notice shall be filed with the county clerk within thirty days after such publication.

Sec. 15036. **Effect of dissolution on partner's existing liability.** (1) The dissolution of the partnership does not of itself discharge the existing liability of any partner.

(2) A partner is discharged from any existing liability upon dissolution of the partnership by an agreement to that effect between himself, the partnership creditor and the person or partnership continuing the business; and such agreement may be inferred from the course of dealing between the creditor having knowledge of the dissolution and the person or partnership continuing the business.

(3) Where a person agrees to assume the existing obligations of a dissolved partnership, the partners whose obligations have been assumed shall be discharged from any liability to any creditor of the partnership who, knowing of the agreement, consents to a material alteration in the nature or time of payment of such obligations.

(4) The individual property of a deceased partner shall be liable for all obligations of the partnership incurred while he was a partner but subject to the prior payment of his separate debts.

Sec. 15037. **Right to wind up.** Unless otherwise agreed the partners who have not wrongfully dissolved the partnership or the legal representative of the last surviving partner, not bankrupt, has the right to wind up the partnership affairs; provided, however, that any partner, his legal representative, or his assignee, upon cause shown, may obtain winding up by the court.

Sec. 15038. **Rights of partners upon dissolution.** (a) When dissolution is caused in any way, except in contravention of the partnership agreement, each partner, as against the copartners and all persons claiming through them in respect of their interests in the partnership, unless otherwise agreed, may have the partnership property applied to discharge its liabilities, and the surplus applied to pay in cash the net amount owing to the respective partners. But if dissolution is caused by expulsion of a partner, bona fide under the partnership agreement and if the expelled partner is discharged from all partnership liabilities, either by payment or agreement under Section 15036(2), the expelled partner shall receive in cash only the net amount due from the partnership.

(b) When dissolution is caused in contravention of the partnership agreement the rights of the partners shall be as follows:

(1) Each partner who has not caused dissolution wrongfully shall have,

(A) All the rights specified in subdivision (a),

(B) The right as against each partner who has caused the dissolution wrongfully, to damages for breach of the agreement.

(2) The partners who have not caused the dissolution wrongfully, if they all desire to continue the business in the same name, either by themselves or jointly with others, may do so, during the agreed term for the partnership and for that purpose may possess the partnership property; provided, they secure the payment by bond or pay to any partner who has caused the dissolution wrongfully, the value of the partner's interest in the partnership at the dissolution, less any damages recoverable under subdivision (b) (1) (B), and in like manner indemnify him against all present or future partnership liabilities.

(3) A partner who has caused the dissolution wrongfully shall have:

(A) If the business is not continued under the provisions of subdivision (b)(2), all the rights of a partner under paragraph (a), subject to subdivision (b)(1)(B).

(B) If the business is continued under subdivision (b)(2) the right as against the copartners and all claiming through them in respect of their interests in the partnership, to have the value of the partner's interest in the partnership, less any damages caused to his copartners by the dissolution, ascertained and paid to the partner in cash, or the payment secured by bond, and to be released from all existing liabilities of the partnership; but in ascertaining the value of the partner's interest the value of the good will of the business shall not be considered.

Sec. 15039. Rights where partnership is dissolved for fraud or misrepresentation.

Where a partnership contract is rescinded on the ground of the fraud or misrepresentation of one of the parties thereto the party entitled to rescind is, without prejudice to any other right, entitled,

(a) To a lien on, or right of retention of, the surplus of the partnership property after satisfying the partnership liabilities to third persons for any sum of money paid by him for the purchase of an interest in the partnership and for any capital or advances contributed by him; and

(b) To stand, after all liabilities to third persons have been satisfied, in the place of the creditors of the partnership for any payments made by him in respect of the partnership liabilities; and

(c) To be indemnified by the person guilty of the fraud or making the representation against all debts and liabilities of the partnership.

Sec. 15040. Rules for distribution.

In settling accounts between the partners after dissolution, the following rules shall be observed, subject to any agreement to the contrary:

(a) The assets of the partnership are:

I. The partnership property,

II. The contributions of the partners necessary for the payment of all the liabilities specified in clause (b) of this paragraph.

(b) The liabilities of the partnership shall rank in order of payment, as follows:

I. Those owing to creditors other than partners,

II. Those owing to partners other than for capital and profits,

III. Those owing to partners in respect of capital,

IV. Those owing to partners in respect of profits.

(c) The assets shall be applied in the order of their declaration in clause (a) of this paragraph to the satisfaction of the liabilities.

(d) The partners shall contribute, as provided by Section 15018(a) the amount necessary to satisfy the liabilities; but if any, but not all, of the partners are insolvent, or, not being subject to process, refuse to contribute, the other partners shall contribute their share of the liabilities, and, in the relative proportion in which they share the profits, the additional amount necessary to pay the liabilities.

(e) An assignee for the benefit of creditors or any person appointed by the court shall have the right to enforce the contributions specified in clause (d) of this paragraph.

(f) Any partner or his legal representative shall have the right to enforce the contributions specified in clause (d) of this paragraph, to the extent of the amount which he has paid in excess of his share of the liability.

(g) The individual property of a deceased partner shall be liable for the contributions specified in clause (d) of this paragraph.

(h) When partnership property and the individual properties of the partners are in possession of a court for distribution, partnership creditors shall have priority on partnership property and separate creditors on individual property, saving the rights of lien or secured creditors as heretofore.

(i) Where a partner has become bankrupt or his estate is insolvent the claims against his separate property shall rank in the following order:

I. Those owing to separate creditors.

II. Those owing to partnership creditors.

III. Those owing to partners by way of contribution.

Sec. 15041. Liability of persons continuing the business in certain cases.

(1) When any new partner is admitted into an existing partnership, or when any partner retires and assigns (or the representative of the deceased partner assigns) his rights in partnership property to two or more of the partners, or to one or more of the partners and one or more third persons, if the business is continued without liquidation of the partnership affairs, creditors of the first or dissolved partnership are also creditors of the partnershp so continuing the business.

(2) When all but one partner retire and assign (or the representative of a deceased partner assigns) their rights in partnership property to the remaining partner, who continues the business without liquidation of partnership affairs, either alone or with others, creditors of the dissolved partnership are also creditors of the person or partnership so continuing the business.

(3) When any partner retires or dies and the business of the dissolved partnership is continued as set forth in paragraphs (1) and (2) of this section, with the consent of the retired partners or the representative of the deceased partner, but without any assignment of his right in partnership property, rights of creditors of the dissolved partnership and of the creditors of the person or partnership continuing the business shall be as if such assignment had been made.

(4) When all the partners or their representatives assign their rights in partnership property to one or more third persons who promise to pay the debts and who continue the business of the dissolved partnership, creditors of the dissolved partnership are also creditors of the person or partnership continuing the business.

(5) When any partner wrongfully causes a dissolution and the remaining partners continue the business under the provisions of Section 15038(2b), either alone or with others, and without liquidation of the partnership affairs, creditors of the dissolved partnership are also creditors of the person or partnership continuing the business.

(6) When a partner is expelled and the remaining partners continue the business either alone or with others, without liquidation of the partnership affairs, creditors of the dissolved partnership are also creditors of the person or partnership continuing the business.

(7) The liability of a third person becoming a partner in the partnership continuing the business, under this section, to the creditors of the dissolved partnership shall be satisfied out of partnership property only.

(8) When the business of a partnership after dissolution is continued under any conditions set forth in this section the creditors of the dissolved partnership, as against the separate creditors of the retiring or deceased partner or the representative of the deceased partner, have a prior right to any claim of the retired partner or the representative of the deceased partner against the person or partnership continuing the business, on account of the retired or deceased partner's interest in the dissolved partnership or an account of any consideration promised for such interest or for his right in partnership property.

(9) Nothing in this section shall be held to modify any right of creditors to set aside any assignment on the ground of fraud.

(10) The use by the person or partnership continuing the business of the partnership name, or the name of a deceased partner as part thereof, shall not of itself make the individual property of the deceased partner liable for any debts contracted by such person or partnership.

Sec. 15042. Rights of retiring partner or estate of deceased partner when the business is continued.

When any partner retires or dies, and the business is continued under any of the conditions set forth in Section 15041(1, 2, 3, 5, 6), or Section 15038(2b) without any settlement of accounts as between him or his estate and the person or partnership continuing the business, unless otherwise agreed, he or his legal representative as against such persons or partnership may have the value of his interest at the date of dissolution ascertained, and shall received as an ordinary creditor an amount equal to the value of his interest in the dissolved partnership with interest, or, at his option or at the option of his legal representative, in lieu of interest, the profits attributable to the use of his right in the property of the dissolved partnership; provided, that the creditors of the dissolved partnership as against the separate creditors, or the representative of the retired or deceased partner, shall have priority on any claim arising under this section, as provided by Section 15041(8) of this act.

Sec. 15043. **Accrual of actions.** The right to an account of his interest shall accrue to any partner, or his legal representative, as against the winding up partners or the surviving partners or the person or partnership continuing the business, at the date of dissolution, in the absence of any agreement to the contrary.

CALIFORNIA REVISED LIMITED PARTNERSHIP ACT

Sec. 15611. **Definitions.** As used in this chapter, unless the context otherwise requires:

(a) "Acknowledged" means that an instrument is either of the following:

(1) Formally acknowledged as provided in Article 3 (commencing with Section 1180) of Chapter 4 of Title 4 of Part 4 of Division 2 of the Civil Code.

(2) Accompanied by a declaration in writing signed by the person executing it that the declarant is that person and that the instrument is the act and deed of the person executing it.

Any certificate of acknowledgment taken without this state before a notary public or a judge or clerk of a court of record having an official seal need not be further authenticated.

(b) "Capital account" of a partner, unless otherwise provided in the partnership agreement, means the amount of the capital interest of that partner in the partnership consisting of that partner's original contribution, as (1) increased by any additional contributions and by that partner's share of the partnership's profits and (2) decreased by any distribution to that partner and by that partner's share of the partnership's losses.

(c) "Certificate of limited partnership" or "certificate" means the certificate referred to in Section 15621, and the certificate as amended.

(d) "Contribution" means any money, property or services rendered, or a promissory note or other binding obligation to contribute money or property, or to render services as permitted in this chapter, which a partner contributes to a limited partnership as capital in that partner's capacity as a partner pursuant to an agreement between the partners, including an agreement as to value.

(e) "Distribution" means the transfer of money or property by a partnership to its partners without consideration.

(f) "Foreign limited partnership" means a partnership formed under the laws of any state other than this state or under the laws of a foreign country and having as partners one or more general partners and one or more limited partners (or their equivalents under any name).

(g) "General partner" means a person who has been admitted to a limited partnership as a general partner in accordance with the partnership agreement or a person who has been admitted as a general partner pursuant to Section 15641.

(h) "Interests of limited partners" means the aggregate interests of all limited partners in the current profits derived from business operations of the partnership.

(i) "Limited partner" means a person who has been admitted to a limited partnership as a limited partner in accordance with the partnership agreement or an assignee of a limited partnership interest who has become a limited partner pursuant to Section 15674.

(j) "Limited partnership" and "domestic limited partnership" mean a partnership formed by two or more persons under the laws of this state and having one or more general partners and one or more limited partners.

(k) "Mail," unless otherwise provided in the partnership agreement, means first-class mail, postage prepaid, unless registered mail is specified. Registered mail includes certified mail.

(*l*) "Majority-in-interest of the limited partners," unless otherwise provided in the partnership agreement, means more than 50 percent of the interests of limited partners.

(m) "Partner" means a limited or general partner.

(n) "Partnership agreement" means any valid written agreement of the partners as to the affairs of a limited partnership and the conduct of its business, including all amendments thereto.

(o) "Person" means an individual, partnership, limited partnership (domestic or foreign), trust, estate, association, corporation, or other entity.

(p) "Proxy" means a written authorization signed by a partner or the partner's attorney-in-fact giving another person the power to vote with respect to the interest of that partner. "Signed," for the purpose of this section, means the placing of the partner's name on the proxy (whether by manual signature, typewriting, telegraphic transmission, or otherwise) by the partner or partner's attorney-in-fact.

(q) "Return of capital," unless otherwise provided in the partnership agreement, means any distribution to a partner to the extent that the partner's capital account, immediately after the distribution, is less than the amount of that partner's contributions to the partnership as reduced by prior distributions which were a return of capital.

(r) "State" means a state, territory, or possession of the United States, the District of Columbia, or the Commonwealth of Puerto Rico.

(s) "Time a notice is given or sent," unless otherwise expressly provided, means the time a written notice to a partner or the limited partnership is deposited in the United States mails; or the time any other written notice is personally delivered to the recipient or is delivered to a common carrier for transmission, or actually transmitted by the person giving the notice by electronic means, to the recipient; or the time any oral notice is communicated, in person or by telephone or wireless, to the recipient or to a person at the office of the recipient who the person giving the notice has reason to believe will promptly communicate it to the recipient.

Sec. 15612. **Partnership name.** The name of each limited partnership as set forth in its certificate of limited partnership:

(a) Shall contain without abbreviation the words "a California limited partnership" at the end of its name.

(b) May not contain the name of a limited partner unless (1) it is also the name of a general partner or the corporate name of a corporate general partner, or (2) the business of the limited partnership had been carried on under that name before the admission of that limited partner.

(c) May not be the same as, or resemble so closely as to tend to deceive (1) a name which is under reservation for another limited partnership pursuant to Section 15613 or (2) the name of any limited partnership which has previously filed a certificate pursuant to Section 15621 or of a foreign limited partnership registered pursuant to Section 15692.

(d) May not contain the words "bank," "insurance," "trust" or "trustee."

Sec. 15613. **Certificate of reservation of name.** Any applicant may, upon payment of the fee prescribed therefor in the Government Code, obtain from the Secretary of State a certificate of reservation of any name not prohibited by Section 15612, and upon the issuance of the certificate the name stated therein shall be reserved for a period of 60 days. The Secretary of State shall not, however, issue certificates reserving the same name for two or more consecutive 60-day periods to the same applicant or for the use or benefit of the same person; nor shall consecutive reservations be made by or for the use or benefit of the same person of names so similar as to fall within the prohibitions of subdivision (c) of Section 15612.

Sec. 15614. **Required office and agent for service of process.** Each limited partnership shall continuously maintain in this state each of the following:

(a) An office, which may be, but need not be, a place of its business in this state, at which shall be kept the records required by Section 15615 to be maintained.

(b) An agent for service of process on the limited partnership.

Sec. 15615. **Required documents, books and records.** Each limited partnership shall keep at the office referred to in subdivision (a) of Section 15614 all of the following:

(a) A current list of the full name and last known business or residence address of each partner set forth in alphabetical order together with the contribution and the share in profits and losses of each partner.

(b) A copy of the certificate of limited partnership and all certificates of amendment thereto, together with executed copies of any powers of attorney pursuant to which any certificate has been executed.

(c) Copies of the limited partnership's federal, state, and local income tax or information returns and reports, if any, for the six most recent taxable years.

(d) Copies of the original partnership agreement and all amendments thereto.

(e) Financial statements of the limited partnership agreement and all amendments thereto.

(e) Financial statements of the limited partnership for the six most recent fiscal years.

(f) The partnership's books and records for at least the current and past three fiscal years.

Sec. 15616. **Conductible business.** A limited partnership may carry on any business that a partnership without limited partners may carry on except the banking, insurance or trust company business.

Sec. 15617. **Partner-partnership business transactions.** Except as otherwise provided in the partnership agreement, a partner may lend money to and transact other business with the limited partnership and, subject to other applicable law, has the same rights and obligations with respect thereto as a person who is not a partner.

Sec. 15621. **Certificate of limited partnership; etc.** (a) In order to form a limited partnership the partners shall execute a partnership agreement and the general partners shall execute, acknowledge and file a certificate of limited partnership. The certificate shall be filed in the office of, and on a form prescribed by, the Secretary of State and shall set forth all of the following:

(1) The name of the limited partnership.

(2) (A) The street address of the principal executive office.

(B) If the principal executive office is not in this state, the street address of an office in this state.

(3) The names and addresses of the general partners.

(4) The name and address of the agent for service of process required to be maintained by Section 15614, unless a corporate agent is designated, in which case only the name of such agent shall be set forth.

(5) The term for which the partnership is to exist.

(6) Any other matters the general partners determine to include.

(b) A limited partnership is formed at the time of the filing of the certificate of limited partnership in the office of the Secretary of State.

(c) For all purposes, a copy of the certificate of limited partnership duly certified by the Secretary of State is conclusive evidence of the formation of a limited partnership and prima facie evidence of its existence.

(d) A limited partnership may record in the office of the county recorder of any county in this state a certified copy of the certificate of limited partnership, or any amendment thereto, which has been filed by the Secretary of State. A foreign limited partnership may record in the office of the county recorder of any county in the state a certified copy of the application for registration, together with the certificate of registration, referred to in Section 15692, or any amendment thereto, which has been filed by the Secretary of State. The recording shall create a conclusive presumption in favor of any bona fide purchaser or encumbrancer for value of the partnership real property located in the county in which the certified copy has been recorded, that the persons named as general partners therein are the general partners of the partnership named and that they are all of the general partners of the partnership, and the recording shall also create such other presumptions as provided in Section 15010.5.

Sec. 15622. **Amendment of certificate.** (a) A certificate of limited partnership is amended by filing a certificate of amendment thereto executed and acknowledged by all general partners (unless a lesser number is provided in the certificate of limited partnership) in the office of, and on a form prescribed by, the Secretary of State. The certificate of amendment shall set forth all of the following:

(1) The name and the Secretary of State's file number of the limited partnership.

(2) The text of the amendment to the certificate.

(b) The general partners shall cause to be filed, within 30 days after the happening of any of the following events, an amendment to a certificate of limited partnership reflecting the occurrence of any of the following events:

(1) A change in name of the limited partnership.

(2) A change in either of the following:

(A) The street address of the principal executive office.

(B) If the principal executive office is not in this state, the street address of an office in this state.

(3) A change in the address of or the withdrawal of a general partner, or a change in the address of the agent for service of process, unless a corporate agent is designated, or appointment of a new agent for service of process.

(4) The admission of a general partner and that partner's address.

(5) The discovery by any of the general partners of any false or erroneous material statement contained in the certificate or any amendment thereto.

(c) A certificate of limited partnership may also be amended at any time in any other respect that the general partners determine.

(d) Any general partner, or any limited partner executing a certificate pursuant to Section 15633 or a certificate of amendment pursuant to Section 15625 or a certificate of dissolution pursuant to paragraph (1) of subdivision (a) of Section 15623 or a certificate of cancellation of certificate of limited partnership pursuant to paragraph (1) of subdivision (b)

of Section 15623, shall be liable for any statement materially inconsistent with the partnership agreement or any material misstatement of fact contained in the certificate or the certificate of amendment if the partner knew or should have known that the statement was false when made or became false and an amendment required by subdivision (b) was not filed, and the person suffering the loss relied on the statement or misstatement.

(e) No person has any liability because an amendment to a certificate of limited partnership has not been filed to reflect the occurrence of any event referred to in subdivision (b) if the amendment is filed within the time specified in subdivision (b).

(f) Except as provided in subdivision (d), no limited partner shall incur any liability for any misstatement contained in the certificate or for the failure to file an amendment to a certificate of limited partnership pursuant to subdivision (b).

Sec. 15623. **Requirement of certificate of dissolution.** (a) (1) The general partners shall cause to be filed in the office of, and on a form prescribed by, the Secretary of State, a certificate of dissolution upon the dissolution of the limited partnership pursuant to Article 8 (commencing with Section 15681), unless the event causing the dissolution is that specified in subdivision (c) of Section 15681, in which case the limited partners conducting the winding up of the partnership affairs under Section 15683 shall have the obligation to file the certificate of dissolution.

(2) The certificate of dissolution shall set forth all of the following:

(A) The name of the limited partnership and the Secretary of State's file number.

(B) The event causing, and the date of, the dissolution.

(b) (1) The general partners shall cause to be filed in the office of, and on a form prescribed by, the Secretary of State, a certificate of cancellation of certificate of limited partnership upon the completion of the winding up of the affairs of the limited partnership, pursuant to Article 8 (commencing with Section 15681), unless the event causing the dissolution is that specified in subdivision (c) of Section 15681, in which case the limited partners conducting the winding up of the partnership affairs under Section 15683 shall have the obligation to file the certificate of cancellation of certificate of limited partnership.

(2) The certificate of cancellation of certificate of limited partnership shall set forth all of the following:

(A) The name of the limited partnership and the Secretary of State's file number.

(B) Any other information the partners filing the certificate of cancellation of certificate of limited partnership determine to include.

Sec. 15624. **Manner of execution of certificates.** (a) Each certificate required by this article to be filed in the office of the Secretary of State shall be executed in the following manner:

(1) A certificate referred to in Section 15621 shall be executed by all general partners, unless filed by a limited partner pursuant to Section 15633.

(2) A certificate of amendment shall be executed by all general partners (or a lesser number provided in the certificate of limited partnership) and by each general partner designated in the certificate as a new partner, unless filed by a limited partner pursuant to Section 15625.

(3) A certificate of dissolution shall be executed by all general partners (or a lesser number provided in the certificate of limited partnership) unless filed by a limited partner pursuant to paragraph (1) of subdivision (a) of Section 15623.

(4) A certificate of cancellation of certificate of limited partnership shall be executed by all general partners (or a lesser number provided in the certificate of limited partnership) unless filed by a limited partner pursuant to paragraph (1) of subdivision (b) of Section 15623.

(5) A certificate filed by a limited partner pursuant to Section 15633 or a certificate of amendment filed by a limited partner pursuant to Section 15625 or a certificate of dissolution filed by a limited partner pursuant to paragraph (1) of subdivision (a) of Section 15623 or a certificate of cancellation of certificate of limited partnership filed by a limited partner pursuant to paragraph (1) of subdivision (b) of Section 15623 shall be signed by the limited partner.

(b) Any person may execute a certificate referred to in Section 15621 or any certificate of amendment thereto by an attorney-in-fact.

Sec. 15625. **Failure or refusal to execute or file certificate of amendment.** If a general partner required by this article to execute or file a certificate of amendment fails after demand to do so within a reasonable time or refuses to do so, any other partner may prepare, execute, and file with the Secretary of State an appropriate certificate of amendment.

Sec. 15626. **Effect of filing certificate of amendment or cancellation.** Upon the filing of a certificate of amendment in the office of the Secretary of State, the certificate of limited partnership is amended as set forth therein, and upon the filing of a certificate of cancellation of certificate of limited partnership pursuant to paragraph (1) of subdivision (b) of Section 15623, the certificate of limited partnership is canceled.

Sec. 15627. **Service of process.** (a) In addition to the provisions of Chapter 4 (commencing with Section 413.10) of Title 5 of Part 2 of the Code of Civil Procedure, process may be served upon limited partnerships and foreign limited partnerships as provided in this section.

(b) Personal service of a copy of any process against the limited partnership or the foreign limited partnership by delivery (1) to any individual designated by it as agent or, if a limited partnership, to any general partner or (2) if the designated agent or, if a limited partnership, general partner is a corporation, to any person named in the latest certificate of the corporate agent filed pursuant to Section 1505 at the office of the corporate agent or to any officer of the general partner, shall constitute valid service on the limited partnership or the foreign limited partnership. No change in the address of the agent for service of process or appointment of a new agent for service of process shall be effective (1) for a limited partnership until an amendment to the certificate of limited partnership is filed pursuant to paragraph (3) of subdivision (b) of Section 15622 or (2) for a foreign limited partnership until an amendment to the application for registration is filed pursuant to Section 15695.

(c) (1) If an agent for service of process has resigned and has not been replaced or if the agent designated cannot with reasonable diligence be found at the address designated for personal delivery of the process, and it is shown by affidavit to the satisfaction of the court that process against a limited partnership or foreign limited partnership cannot be served with reasonable diligence upon the designated agent or, if a foreign limited partnership, upon any general partner by hand in the manner provided in Section 415.10, subdivision (a) of Section 415.20 or subdivision (a) of Section 415.30. of the Code of Civil Procedure, the court may make an order that the service shall be made upon a domestic limited partnership which has filed a certificate pursuant to Section 15621 or upon a registered foreign limited partnership by delivering by hand to the Secretary of State, or to any person employed in the Secretary of State's office in the capacity of assistant or deputy, one copy of the process for each defendant to be served, together with a copy of the order authorizing the service. Service in this manner shall be deemed complete on the 10th day after delivery of the process to the Secretary of State.

(2) Upon receipt of any such copy of process and the fee therefor, the Secretary of State shall give notice of the service of the process to the limited partnership or foreign limited partnership, at its principal executive office, by forwarding to that office, by registered mail with request for return receipt, the copy of the process.

(3) The Secretary of State shall keep a record of all process served upon the Secretary of State under this chapter and shall record therein the time of service and the Secretary of State's action with reference thereto. A certificate under the Secretary of State's official seal, certifying to the receipt of process, the giving of notice thereof to the limited partnership or foreign limited partnership, and the forwarding of the process pursuant to this section, shall be competent and prima facie evidence of the matters stated therein.

(d) (1) The certificate of a limited partnership and the application for registration of a foreign limited partnership shall designate, as the agent for service of process, an individual residing in this state or a corporation which has complied with Section 1505 and whose capacity to act as an agent has not terminated. If an individual is designated, the statement shall set forth that person's complete business or residence address in this state.

(2) An agent designated for service of process may file with the Secretary of State a signed and acknowledged written statement of resignation as an agent. Thereupon the authority of the agent to act in that capacity shall cease and the Secretary of State forthwith shall give written notice of the filing of the statement of resignation by mail to the limited partnership or foreign limited partnership addressed to its principal executive office.

(3) If an individual who has been designated agent for service of process dies or resigns or no longer resides in the state or if the corporate agent for that purpose, resigns, dissolves, withdraws from the state, forfeits its right to transact intrastate business, has its corporate rights, powers and privileges suspended or ceases to exist, (A) the limited partnership shall promptly file an amendment to the certificate pursuant to paragraph (3) of subdivision (b) of Section 15622 designating a new agent or (B) the foreign limited partnership shall promptly file an amendment to the application for registration pursuant to Section 15695.

Sec. 15628. **Filing with Secretary of State.** Upon receipt of any instrument accompanied by the fee prescribed therefor in the Government Code by the Secretary of State for filing pursuant to this chapter, it shall be filed by, and in the office of, the Secretary of State and the date of filing endorsed thereon. The date of filing shall be the date the instrument is received by the Secretary of State unless withheld from filing for a period of time not to exceed 90 days pursuant to a request by the party submitting it for filing or unless in the judgment of the Secretary of State the filing is intended to be coordinated with the filing of some other document which cannot be filed. The Secretary of State shall file a document as of any requested future date not more than 90 days after its receipt, including a Saturday, Sunday or legal holiday, if that document is received in the Secretary of State's office at least one business day prior to the requested date of filing. Upon receipt and after filing of any document under this chapter the Secretary of State may microfilm or reproduce by other techniques any such filings or documents and destroy the original filing or document. The microfilm or other reproduction of any document under the provision of this section shall be admissible in any court of law.

Sec. 15631. **Admission of additional limited partner.** (a) After the filing of a certificate referred to in Section 15621, a person may become a limited partner:

(1) In the case of a person acquiring a limited partnership interest directly from the limited partnership, upon the compliance with the partnership agreement or, if the partnership agreement does not so provide, upon the written consent of the partners.

(2) In the case of an assignee of a partnership interest, upon compliance with subdivision (a) of Section 15674.

(b) In each case under subdivision (a), the person acquiring the partnership interest shall be added by the general partners as a limited partner to the list required by subdivision (a) of Section 15615.

Sec. 15632. **Liability of limited partner to third parties.** (a) Except as provided in subdivision (d), a limited partner is not liable for any obligation of a limited partnership unless named as a general partner in the certificate or, in addition to the exercise of the rights and powers of a limited partner, the limited partner participates in the control of the business. If a limited partner participates in the control of the business without being named as a general partner, that partner is nevertheless not liable to persons who transact business with the limited partnership unless they do so with actual knowledge of that partner's participation in control and reasonably believing that partner to be a general partner.

(b) A limited partner does not participate in the control of the business within the meaning of subdivision (a) solely by doing one or more of the following:

(1) Being a contractor for or an agent or employee of the limited partnership or of a general partner, or an officer, director or shareholder of a corporate general partner.

(2) Consulting with and advising a general partner with respect to the business of the limited partnership.

(3) Acting as surety for the limited partnership or guaranteeing one or more specific debts of the limited partnership.

(4) Approving or disapproving an amendment to the partnership agreement.

(5) Voting on one or more of the following matters:

(A) The dissolution and winding up of the limited partnership.

(B) The sale, exchange, lease, mortgage, pledge, or other transfer of all or a substantial part of the assets of the limited partnership other than in the ordinary course of its business.

(C) The incurrence of indebtedness beyond the limited partnership other than in the ordinary course of its business.

(D) A change in the nature of the business.

(E) Transactions in which the general partners have an actual or potential conflict of interest with the limited partners or the partnership.

(F) The removal of a general partner.

(G) An election to continue the business of the limited partnership other than under the circumstances described in subparagraph (I) or (J) of this paragraph (5).

(H) The admission of a general partner other than under the circumstances described in subparagraph (I) or (J) of this paragraph (5).

(I) The admission of a general partner or an election to continue the business of the limited partnership after a general partner ceases to be a general partner other than by removal where there is no remaining or surviving general partner.

(J) The admission of a general partner or an election to continue the business of the limited partnership after the removal of a general partner where there is no remaining or surviving general partner.

(6) Winding up the partnership pursuant to Section 15683.

(7) Executing and filing a certificate pursuant to Section 15633 or a certificate of amendment pursuant to Section 15625 or a certificate of dissolution pursuant to paragraph (1) of subdivision (a) of Section 15623 or a certificate of cancellation of certificate of limited partnership pursuant to paragraph (1) of subdivision (b) of Section 15623.

(8) Serving on an audit committee or committee performing the functions of an audit committee.

(c) The enumeration in subdivision (b) does not mean that any other conduct or the possession or exercise of any other power by a limited partner constitutes participation by the limited partner in the control of the business of the limited partnership.

(d) A limited partner who knowingly permits that partner's name to be used in the name of the limited partnership, except under circumstances permitted by subdivision (b) of Section 15612, is liable for all obligations of the limited partnership to persons without actual knowledge or notice that the limited partner is not a general partner.

Sec. 15633. **Partner erroneously believing himself limited partner.** (a) Except as provided in subdivision (b), if a certificate of limited partnership has not been filed, a person who makes a contribution to the purported limited partnership and in good faith believes that that person has become a limited partner is not liable for the obligations of the purported limited partnership, if, on ascertaining that the certificate has not been filed and after a failure of the general partner or partners to file the certificate within a reasonable time after request, that person promptly files the certificate of limited partnership.

(b) A person who makes a contribution to the purported limited partnership and in good faith believes that that person has become a limited partner is liable only to any third party who transacted business with the purported limited partnership before the certificate is filed and who reasonably believed that the person was a general partner at the time of the transaction.

Sec. 15634. **Rights to information, inspect and copy records, copies of tax returns; etc.** (a) Upon the request of a limited partner, the general partners shall promptly deliver to the limited partner, at the expense of the partnership, a copy of the information required to be maintained by subdivision (a), (b), or (d) of Section 15615.

(b) Each limited partner has the right upon reasonable request to each of the following:

(1) Inspect and copy during normal business hours any of the partnership records required to be maintained by Section 15615.

(2) Obtain from the general partners, promptly after becoming available, a copy of the limited partnership's federal, state and local income tax or information returns for each year.

(c) In the case of any limited partnership with more than 35 limited partners:

(1) The general partners shall cause an annual report to be sent to each of the partners not later than 120 days after the close of the fiscal year. That report shall contain a balance sheet as of the end of the fiscal year and an income statement and statement of changes in financial position for the fiscal year.

(2) Limited partners representing at least 5 percent of the interests of limited partners may make a written request to a general partner for an income statement of the limited partnership for the initial three-month, six-month, or nine-month period of the current fiscal year ended more than 30 days prior to the date of the request and a balance sheet of the partnership as of the end of that period. The statement shall be delivered or mailed to the limited partners within 30 days thereafter.

(3) The financial statements referred to in this section shall be accompanied by the report thereon, if any, of the independent accountants engaged by the partnership or, if there is no such report, the certificate of a general partner of the partnership that such financial statements were prepared without audit from the books and records of the limited partnership.

(d) The general partners shall promptly furnish to a limited partner a copy of any amendment to the partnership agreement executed by a general partner pursuant to a power of attorney from the limited partner.

(e) The general partners shall send to each of the partners within 90 days after the end of each taxable year such information as is necessary to complete federal and state income tax or information returns, and, in the case of a limited partnership with 35 or fewer limited partners, a copy of the limited partnership's federal, state, and local income tax or information returns for the year.

(f) In addition to any other remedies, a court of competent jurisdiction may enforce the duty of making and mailing or delivering the information and financial statements required by this section and, for good cause shown, may extend the time therefor.

(g) In any action under this section, if the court finds the failure of the partnership to comply with the requirements of this section to have been without justification, the court may award an amount sufficient to reimburse the partners bringing the action for the reasonable expenses incurred by the partners, including attorneys' fees, in connection with the action or proceeding.

(h) Any waiver by a partner of the rights provided in this section shall be unenforceable.

Sec. 15635. **Complaint to Attorney General upon failure to afford rights.** (a) The Attorney General, upon complaint that a limited partnership is failing to comply with the provisions of Section 15634, or to afford to the partners rights given to them in the partnership agreement, may in the name of the people of the State of California send to the principal executive office, as specified pursuant to paragraph (2) of subdivision (a) of Section 15621, notice of the complaint.

(b) If the answer of the limited partnership is not received within 30 days of the date the notice was transmitted, or if the answer is not satisfactory, and if the enforcement of the rights of the aggrieved persons by private civil action, by class action or otherwise, would be so burdensome or expensive as to be impracticable, the Attorney General may institute, maintain, or intervene in their suits, actions or proceedings in any court of competent jurisdiction or before any administrative agency for relief by way of injunction, the dissolution of entities, the appointment of receivers, or any other temporary, preliminary, provisional, or final remedies as may be appropriate to protect the rights of partners or to restore the position of the partners for the failure to comply with the requirements of Section 15634 or the partnership agreement. In any such action, suit, or proceeding there may be joined as parties all persons and entities responsible for or affected by the activity.

Sec. 15636. **Rights and duties of partners.** The rights and duties of the partners in relation to the limited partnership shall be determined, subject to any provision of the partnership agreement to the contrary, by the following rules:

(a) No limited partner shall be required to make any additional contribution to the limited partnership.

(b) No limited partner shall have a priority over any other limited partner, as to return of contributions or as to compensation as a limited partner by way of income.

(c) The obligation of a partner to make a contribution or return money or property distributed in violation of this chapter may be compromised only by the written consent of all the partners.

(d) No limited partner shall have the right to receive property other than money upon any distribution.

(e) A partner may not be compelled to accept a distribution of any asset in kind from a limited partnership in lieu of a proportionate distribution of money being made to other partners.

(f) The limited partners shall have the right to vote on all matters specified in subparagraphs (A) to (G), inclusive, of paragraph (5) of subdivision (b) of Section 15632 and the actions specified therein may be taken by the general partners only with the affirmative vote of a majority in interest of the limited partners. The limited partners shall also have the right to vote on matters specified in subparagraphs (H) and (I) of paragraph (5) of subdivision (b) of Section 15632. Notwithstanding any other provision of this chapter or any provision of the partnership agreement to the contrary, the actions specified in that subparagraph (H) may only be taken by the affirmative vote of a majority in interest of the limited partners, and the actions specified in that subparagraph (I) may only be taken by the affirmative vote of all of the limited partners.

Sec. 15637. **Meetings; Procedure.** (a) Meetings of partners may be held at any place within or without this state as may be stated in or fixed in accordance with the partnership agreement. If no other place is stated or so fixed, partners' meetings shall be held at the principal executive office of the partnership, or if the principal executive office is not in this state, at the street address of an office in this state as set forth in the certificate.

(b) A meeting of the partners may be called by the general partners or by limited partners representing more than 10 percent of the interests of limited partners for any matters on which the limited partners may vote.

(c) (1) Whenever partners are required or permitted to take any action at a meeting, a written notice of the meeting shall be given not less than 10, nor more than 60, days before the date of the meeting to each partner entitled to vote at the meeting. The notice shall state the place, date, and hour of the meeting and the general nature of the business to be transacted, and no other business may be transacted.

(2) Notice of a partners' meeting or any report shall be given either personally or by mail or other means of written communication, addressed to the partner at the address of the partner appearing on the books of the partnership or given by the partner to the partnership for the purpose of notice, or, if no address appears or is given, at the place where the principal executive office of the partnership is located or by publication at least once in a newspaper of general circulation in the county in which the principal executive office is located. The notice or report shall be deemed to have been given at the time when delivered personally or deposited in the mail or sent by other means of written communication. An affidavit of mailing of any notice or report in accordance with the provisions of this article, executed by a general partner, shall be prima facie evidence of the giving of the notice or report.

If any notice or report addressed to the partner at the address of the partner appearing on the books of the partnership is returned to the partnership by the United States Postal Service marked to indicate that the United States Postal Service is unable to deliver the notice or report to the partner at the address, all future notices or reports shall be deemed to have been duly given without further mailing if they are available for the partner at the principal executive office of the partnership for a period of one year from the date of the giving of the notice or report to all other partners.

(3) Upon written request to the general partners by any person entitled to call a meeting of partners, the general partners immediately shall cause notice to be given to the partners entitled to vote that a meeting will be held at a time requested by the person calling the meeting, not less than 10, nor more than 60, days after the receipt of the request. If the notice is not given within 20 days after receipt of the request, the person entitled to call the meeting may give the notice or the superior court of the proper county shall summarily order the giving of the notice, after notice to the partnership giving it an opportunity to be heard. The procedure provided in subdivision (c) of Section 305 of the Corporations Code shall apply to the application. The court may issue any order as may be appropriate, including, without limitation, an order designating the time and place of the meeting, the record date for determination of partners entitled to vote, and the form of notice.

(d) When a partners' meeting is adjourned to another time or place, unless the partnership agreement otherwise requires and, except as provided in this subdivision, notice need not be given of the adjourned meeting if the time and place thereof are announced at the meeting at which the adjournment is taken. At the adjourned meeting the partnership may transact any business which might have been transacted at the original meeting. If the adjournment is for more than 45 days or if after the adjournment a new record date is fixed for the adjourned meeting, a notice of the adjourned meeting shall be given to each partner of record entitled to vote at the meeting.

(e) The transactions of any meeting of partners, however called and noticed, and wherever held, are as valid as though had at a meeting duly held after regular call and notice, if a quorum is present either in person or by proxy, and if, either before or after the meeting, each of the persons entitled to vote, not present in person or by proxy, signs a written waiver of notice or a consent to the holding of the meeting or an approval of the minutes thereof. All waivers, consents, and approvals shall be filed with the partnership records or made a part of the minutes of the meeting. Attendance of a person at a meeting shall constitute a waiver of notice of the meeting, except when the person objects, at the beginning of the meeting to the transaction of any business because the meeting is not lawfully called or convened and except that attendance at a meeting is not a waiver of any right to object to the consideration of matters required by this chapter to be included in the notice but not so included, if the objection is expressly made at the meeting. Neither the business to be transacted at nor the purpose of any meeting of partners need be specified in any written waiver of notice, unless otherwise provided in the partnership agreement, except as provided in subdivision (f).

(f) Any partner approval at a meeting, other than unanimous approval by those entitled to vote, pursuant to paragraph (5) of subdivision (b) of Section 15632 shall be valid only if the general nature of the proposal so approved was stated in the notice of meeting or in any written waiver of notice.

(g) (1) Unless otherwise provided in the partnership agreement, a majority in interest of the limited partners represented in person or by proxy shall constitute a quorum at a meeting of partners.

(2) The partners present at a duly called or held meeting at which a quorum is present may continue to transact business until adjournment notwithstanding the withdrawal of enough partners to leave less than a quorum, if any action taken (other than adjournment) is approved by the requisite percentage of interests of limited partners specified in this chapter or in the partnership agreement.

(3) In the absence of a quorum, any meeting of partners may be adjourned from time to time by the vote of a majority of the interests represented either in person or by proxy, but no other business may be transacted, except as provided in paragraph (2).

(h) Unless otherwise provided in the partnership agreement, any action which may be taken at any meeting of the partners may be taken without a meeting if a consent in writing, setting forth the action so taken, shall be signed by partners having not less than the minimum number of votes that would be necessary to authorize or take that action at a meeting at which all entitled to vote thereon were present and voted. In the event the limited partners are requested to consent on a matter without a meeting, each partner shall be given notice of the matter to be voted upon in the same manner as described in subdivision (c). In the event any general partner, or limited partners representing more than 10 percent of the interests of the limited partners, request a meeting for the purpose of discussing or voting on the matter, the notice of a meeting shall be given in accordance with subdivision (c) and no action shall be taken until the meeting is held. Unless delayed in accordance with the provisions of the preceding sentence, any action taken without a meeting will be effective 15 days after the required minimum number of voters have signed the consent, however, the action will be effective immediately if all general partners and limited partners representing at least 90 percent of the interests of the limited partners have signed the consent.

(i) The use of proxies in connection with this section will be governed in the same manner as in the case of corporations formed under the General Corporation Law.

(j) In order that the limited partnership may determine the partners entitled to notices of any meeting or to vote, or entitled to receive any distribution or to exercise any rights in respect of any other lawful action, the general partners, or limited partners representing more than 10 percent of the interests of limited partners, may fix, in advance, a record date, which is not more than 60 nor less than 10 days prior to the date of the meeting nor more than 60 days prior to any other action. If no record date is fixed:

(1) The record date for determining partners entitled to notice of or to vote at a meeting of partners shall be at the close of business on the business day next preceding the day on which notice is given or, if notice is waived, at the close of business on the business day next preceding the day on which the meeting is held.

(2) The record date for determining partners entitled to give consent to partnership action in writing without a meeting shall be the day on which the first written consent was given.

(3) The record date for determining partners for any other purpose shall be at the close of business on the day on which the general partners adopt it, or the 60th day prior to the date of the other action, whichever is later.

(4) The determination of partners of record entitled to notice of or to vote at a meeting of partners shall apply to any adjournment of the meeting unless the general partners, or the limited partners who called the meeting, fix a new record date for the adjourned meeting, but the general partners, or the limited partners who called the meeting, shall fix a new record date if the meeting is adjourned for more than 45 days from the date set for the original meeting.

Sec. 15641. **Admission of additional general partner.**   Unless otherwise provided in the partnership agreement, after the filing of a certificate referred to in Section 15621, a general partner in accordance with the provisions of subdivision (f) of Section 15636 or (b) with the written consent of each partner in accordance with the provisions of subdivision (c) of Section 15681.

Sec. 15642. **When partner ceases to be general partner.**   A person ceases to be a general partner of a limited partnership upon the happening of any of the following events:

(a) The general partner withdraws from the limited partnership.

(b) The general partner is removed as a general partner.

(c) Unless otherwise provided in the partnership agreement, an order for relief against the general partner is entered under Chapter 7 of the federal bankruptcy law, or the general partner: (1) makes a general assignment for the benefit of creditors, (2) files a voluntary petition under the federal bankruptcy law, (3) files a petition or answer seeking for that partner any reorganization, arrangement, composition, readjustment, liquidation, dissolution or similar relief under any statute, law, or regulation, (4) files an answer or other pleading admitting or failing to contest the material allegations of a petition filed against that partner in any proceeding of this nature, or (5) seeks, consents to, or acquiesces in the appointment of a trustee, receiver, or liquidator of the general partner or of all or any substantial part of that partner's properties.

(d) Unless otherwise provided in the partnership agreement, 60 days after the commencement of any proceeding against the general partner seeking reorganization, arrangement, composition, readjustment, liquidation, dissolution or similar relief under any statute, law, or regulation, the proceeding has not been dismissed, or if within 60 days after the appointment without that partner's consent or acquiescence of a trustee, receiver, or liquidator of the general partner or of all or any substantial part of that partner's properties, the appointment is not vacated or stayed, or within 60 days after the expiration of any such stay, the appointment is not vacated.

(e) In the case of a general partner who is an individual, either of the following:

(1) The death of that partner.

(2) The entry by a court of competent jurisdiction of an order adjudicating the partner incompetent to manage the general partner's person or estate.

(f) Unless otherwise provided in the partnership agreement, in the case of a general partner who is acting as a general partner by virtue of being a trustee of a trust, the termination of the trust (but not merely the substitution of a new trustee, in which case the new trustee automatically becomes the new general partner).

(g) Unless otherwise provided in the partnership agreement, in the case of a general partner that is a separate partnership, the dissolution of the separate partnership.

(h) In the case of a general partner that is a corporation, the filing of a certificate of dissolution, or its equivalent, for the corporation.

(i) In the case of a general partner that is an estate, the distribution by the fiduciary of the estate's entire interest in the limited partnership.

Sec. 15643. **Rights and liabilities of general partner.** (a) Except as otherwise provided in this chapter or in the partnership agreement, a general partner of a limited partnership has the rights and powers and is subject to the restrictions of a partner in a partnership without limited partners.

(b) Except as provided in this chapter, a general partner of a limited partnership has the liabilities of a partner in a partnership without limited partners to persons other than the partnership and the other partners. Except as provided in this chapter or in the partnership agreement, a general partner of a limited partnership has the liabilities of a partner in a partnership without limited partners to the partnership and to the other partners.

Sec. 15644. **Partner serving as both general and limited partner.** A general partner of a limited partnership may make contributions to the limited partnership and share in the profits and losses of, and in distributions from, the limited partnership as a general partner. A general partner also may make contributions, and share in the profits and losses and distributions, as a limited partner, if the general partner's interest as a limited partner is separately designated in the partnership agreement. A person who is both a general partner and a limited partner has the rights and powers, and is subject to the restrictions and liabilities, of a general partner and, except as otherwise provided in the partnership agreement, also has the powers, and is subject to the restrictions, of a limited partner to the extent of his participation in the limited partnership as a limited partner.

Sec. 15651. **Form of contribution.** The contribution of a partner may be in money, property, or services rendered, or a promissory note or other obligation to contribute money or property or to render services. A limited partner may not make a contribution of an obligation to render future services in consideration of the receipt of a partnership interest.

Sec. 15652. **Right to enforce original obligation on claim compromised under Section 15536.** Notwithstanding the compromise of a claim referred to in subdivision (c) of Section 15636, a person whose claim against a limited partnership arises before the receipt of notice of the compromise may enforce the original obligation.

Sec. 15653. **Sharing of profits and losses.** The profits and losses of a limited partnership shall be allocated among the partners in the manner provided in the partnership agreement. If the partnership agreement does not so provide, profits and losses shall be allocated in proportion to the contribution of each partner.

Sec. 15654. **Sharing of distributions.** Distributions of the money or property of a limited partnership shall be made to the partners in the manner provided in the partnership agreement. If the partnership agreement does not so provide, distributions which are a return of capital shall be made in proportion to the contributions of each partner and distributions which are not a return of capital shall be made in proportion to the allocation of profits.

Sec. 15661. **Right to distributions prior to withdrawal of dissolution.** Except as provided in this article, a partner is entitled to receive distributions from a limited partnership before the withdrawal of that partner from the limited partnership and before the dissolution and winding up thereof, subject to the limitations contained in Section 15666, to the extent and at the times or upon the happening of the events specified in the partnership agreement.

Sec. 15662. **Withdrawal of general partner.** (a) A general partner may withdraw from a limited partnership at any time by giving written notice to the other partners, but if the withdrawal violates the partnership agreement the limited partnership may recover from the withdrawing general partner damages for breach of the partnership agreement and, in addition to any other remedies, shall have the right to offset the damages against any amounts otherwise distributable to the general partner. Unless otherwise provided in the partnership agreement, in the case of a partnership for a fixed term, a withdrawal by a general partner prior to the expiration of that term is a breach of the partnership agreement.

(b) Unless otherwise provided in the partnership agreement, and subject to the liability created under subdivision (a), a general partner who ceases to be a general partner under Section 15642 shall:

(1) Retain the same interest in that partner's capital account, profits, losses, and distributions, but that interest shall be that of a limited partner.

(2) Not be personally liable for partnership debts incurred after the person ceases to be a general partner.

(3) Be entitled to vote as a limited partner on all matters except the admission and compensation of a general partner.

(4) Have the partner's interest in profits, losses, and distributions reduced pro rata with all other partners to provide compensation, or an interest in the partnership, or both, to a new general partner.

Sec. 15663. **Withdrawal of limited partner.** A limited partner may withdraw from a limited partnership at the time or upon the happening of events specified in the partnership agreement. If the partnership agreement does not specify the time or the events upon the happening of which a limited partner may withdraw or a definite time for the dissolution and winding up of the limited partnership, a limited partner may withdraw upon not less than six months' prior written notice to each general partner at his address set forth in the certificate.

Sec. 15664. **Right of limited partner to distribution upon withdrawal.** Upon withdrawal, any withdrawing limited partner is entitled to receive any distribution to which that partner is entitled under the partnership agreement and, if not otherwise provided in the partnership agreement, the limited partner is entitled to receive, within a reasonable time after withdrawal, the fair value of the limited partner's interest in the limited partnership as of the date of withdrawal based upon the limited partner's right to share in distributions from the limited partnership.

Sec. 15665. **Partner as creditor upon acquiring right to distribution.** Subject to Section 15684, at the time a partner becomes entitled to receive a distribution, that partner has the status of, and is entitled to all remedies available to a creditor of the limited partnership with respect to the distribution.

Sec. 15666. **Obligation to return distribution.** A partner is obligated to return a distribution from a limited partnership to the extent that, after giving effect to the distribution, and notwithstanding the compromise of a claim referred to in subdivision (c) of Section 15636, all liabilities of the limited partnership, other than liabilities to partners on account of their interest in the limited partnership and liabilities as to which recourse of creditors is limited to specified property of the limited partnership, exceed the fair salable value of the partnership assets other than those assets which are subject to liabilities as to which recourse of creditors is so limited.

Sec. 15671. **Nature of partnership interest.** An interest in a limited partnership is personal property and a partner has no interest in specific partnership property.

Sec. 15672. **Assignment of limited partnership interest.** Except as otherwise provided in the partnership agreement, a limited partnership interest is assignable in whole or in part. An assignment of a limited partnership interest does not dissolve a limited partnership or entitle the assignee to become or to exercise any rights of a partner. An assignment entitles the assignee to receive, to the extent assigned, only the distributions to which the assignor would be entitled. A limited partner remains a partner upon assignment of all or part of the limited partner's limited partnership interest, subject to the assignee becoming a limited partner pursuant to subdivision (a) of Section 15674.

Sec. 15673. **Right of creditor to charge limited partnership interest.** On application to a court of competent jurisdiction by any judgment creditor of a partner, the court may charge the limited partnership interest of the partner with payment of the unsatisfied amount of the judgment with interest. To the extent so charged, the judgment creditor has only the rights of an assignee of the limited partnership interest. This chapter does not deprive any partner of the benefit of any exemption laws applicable to the partner's limited partnership interest.

Sec. 15674. **Rights and liabilities of assignee of limited partnership interest.** (a) An assignee of a limited partnership interest may become a limited partner if and to the extent that (1) the partnership agreement so provides or (2) all partners consent.

(b) An assignee who has become a limited partner has, to the extent assigned, the rights and powers, and is subject to the restrictions and liabilities, of a limited partner under the partnership agreement and this chapter. An assignee who becomes a limited partner also is liable for the obligations of the assignor to make contributions as provided in Article 5 (commencing with Section 15651). However, the assignee is not obligated for liabilities unknown to the assignee at the time the assignee became a limited partner and which could not be ascertained from the partnership agreement.

(c) If an assignee of a limited partnership interest becomes a limited partner, the assignor is not released from the assignor's liability to the limited partnership under subdivision (d) of Section 15622, and Sections 15652 and 15666.

Sec. 15675. **Right to represent deceased limited partner.** If a limited partner who is an individual dies or a court of competent jurisdiction adjudges the limited partner to be incompetent to manage the limited partner's person or property, the partner's executor, administrator, guardian, conservator, or other legal representative may exercise all the partner's rights for the purpose of settling the partner's estate or administering the partner's property.

Sec. 15681. **Nonjudicial dissolution.** A limited partnership is dissolved and its affairs shall be wound up upon the happening of the first to occur of the following:

(a) At the time or upon the happening of events specified in the partnership agreement.

(b) Except as otherwise provided in the partnership agreement, written consent of all general partners and a majority in interest of the limited partners.

(c) A general partner ceases to be a general partner under Section 15642 (other than by removal), unless (1) at the time there is at least one other general partner and the partnership agreement permits the business of the limited partnership to be continued by the remaining general partner or partners, if any, and such partner or partners do so, or (2) all partners agree in writing to continue the business of the limited partnership and to admit one or more general partners.

(d) Entry of a decree of judicial dissolution under Section 15682.

Sec. 15682. **Judicial dissolution.** Pursuant to an action filed by a partner, a court of competent jurisdiction may decree the dissolution of a limited partnership whenever any of the following occurs:

(a) It is not reasonably practicable to carry on the business in conformity with the partnership agreement.

(b) The general partners have been guilty of or have knowingly countenanced persistent and pervasive fraud or abuse of authority or persistent unfairness toward any partner, or the property of the limited partnership is being misapplied or wasted by the general partners.

(c) Dissolution is reasonably necessary for the protection of the rights or interest of the complaining partners.

Sec. 15683. **Winding up.** In the event of a dissolution of a limited partnership:

(a) Except as provided in the partnership agreement, the general partners who have not wrongfully dissolved a limited partnership or, if none, the limited partners, may wind up the limited partnership's affairs, unless the dissolution occurs pursuant to subdivision (d) of Section 15681, in which even the winding up shall be conducted in accordance with the decree of dissolution.

(b) Upon the petition of limited partners representing 5 percent or more of the interests of limited partners, or three or more creditors, a court of competent jurisdiction may enter a decree ordering the winding up of the limited partnership if that appears necessary for the protection of any parties in interest. The decree shall designate the partners who are to wind up the limited partnership's affairs.

(c) Unless otherwise provided in the partnership agreement, the limited partners winding up the affairs of the partnership pursuant to this section, shall be entitled to reasonable compensation.

Sec. 15684. **Distribution of assets.** Upon the winding up of a limited partnership, the assets shall be distributed in the following order:

(a) To creditors, including partners who are creditors to the extent permitted by law, in satisfaction of liabilities of the limited partnership other than liabilities for distributions to partners under Section 15661, 15664 or 15665.

(b) Except as provided in the partnership agreement, to partners and former partners in satisfaction of liabilities for distributions under Sections 15661, 15664, and 15665.

(c) To partners in accordance with their rights under the partnership agreement and Section 15636.

Sec. 15685. **Binding partnership after dissolution.** After dissolution, a general partner can bind the partnership as follows:

(a) By any act appropriate for winding up partnership affairs or completing transactions unfinished at dissolution.

(b) By any transaction which would bind the partnership if dissolution had not taken place, if the other party to the transaction:

(1) Had extended credit to the partnership prior to dissolution and had no actual knowledge or notice of the dissolution.

(2) Though not so extending credit, had nevertheless known of the partnership prior to dissolution, and, had no actual knowledge of notice of dissolution, and a certificate of dissolution has not been filed as provided in subdivision (a) of Section 15623.

Sec. 15691. **Foreign limited partnership; law governing.** Subject to Section 15694, (a) the laws of the state or country under which a foreign limited partnership is organized govern its organization and internal affairs and the liability of its limited partners, and (b) a foreign limited partnership may not be denied registration by reason of any difference between those laws and the laws of this state.

Sec. 15692. **Registration requirement.** Before transacting intrastate business in this state, a foreign limited partnership shall register with the Secretary of State. In order to register, a foreign limited partnership shall submit to the Secretary of State an application for registration as a foreign limited partnership, signed and acknowledged by a general partner on a form prescribed by the Secretary of State and setting forth all of the following:

(a) The name of the foreign limited partnership and, if different, the name under which it proposes to register and transact business in this state.

(b) The state or country and date of its formation and a statement that the foreign limited partnership is authorized to exercise its powers and privileges in such state or country of formation.

(c) The name and address of an agent for service of process on the foreign limited partnership meeting the qualifications specified in paragraph (1) of subdivision (d) of Section 15627.

(d) A statement that the Secretary of State is appointed the agent of the foreign limited partnership for service of process if the agent has resigned and has not been replaced or if the agent cannot be found or served with the exercise of reasonable diligence.

(e) The address of the principal executive office of the foreign limited partnership and of its principal office in this state, if any.

(f) The names and business or residence addresses of the general partners.

Sec. 15693. Issuance of certificate of registration. If the Secretary of State finds that an application for registration conforms to law and all requisite fees have been paid, the Secretary of State shall issue a certificate of registration to transact intrastate business in this state. However, no certificate of registration shall be issued for a foreign limited partnership to transact intrastate business in this state under a name which falls within the prohibitions of subdivision (c) of Section 15612.

Sec. 15694. Right to information of resident limited partners. If the limited partners of a foreign limited partnership residing in this state represent 25 percent or more of the interests of limited partners of that partnership, those limited partners shall be entitled to all information and rights provided in Section 15634.

Sec. 15695. Amendment of application for registration. If any statement in the application for registration of a foreign limited partnership was false when made or any statements made have become erroneous, the foreign limited partnership shall promptly file in the office of the Secretary of State an amendment to the application for registration, signed and acknowledged by a general partner, amending the statement.

Sec. 15696. Cancellation of registration. A foreign limited partnership may cancel its registration by filing with the Secretary of State a certificate of cancellation signed and acknowledged by a general partner. A cancellation does not terminate the authority of the Secretary of State to accept service of process on the foreign limited partnership with respect to causes of action arising out of the transaction of business in this state.

Sec. 15697. Transaction of intrastate business without registration. (a) A foreign limited partnership transacting intrastate business in this state without registration is subject to a penalty of twenty dollars ($20) for each day that such unauthorized intrastate business is transacted, up to a maximum of ten thousand dollars ($10,000). An action to recover such penalty may be brought, and any recovery shall be paid, as provided in Section 2258.

(c) The failure of a foreign limited partnership to register in this state does not impair the validity of any contract or act of the foreign limited partnership or prevent the foreign limited partnership from defending any action, suit, or proceeding in any court of this state.

(d) A limited partner of a foreign limited partnership is not liable as a general partner of the foreign limited partnership solely by reason of its having transacted intrastate business in this state without registration.

(e) A foreign limited partnership, transacting intrastate business in this state without registration, appoints the Secretary of State as its agent for service of process with respect to causes of action arising out of the transaction of business in this state.

Sec. 15698. Action by Attorney General. The Attorney General may bring an action to restrain a foreign limited partnership from transacting intrastate business in this state in violation of this article.

Sec. 15701. Right of limited partner to bring class action. Any limited partner may bring a class action on behalf of all or a class of limited partners to enforce any claim common to those limited partners against a domestic or foreign partnership or any or all general partners, without regard to the number of those limited partners, but each of those limited partners shall be given an opportunity to procure exclusion from the class.

Sec. 15702. Derivative actions. (a) No action may be instituted or maintained in right of any domestic or foreign limited partnership by any partner of the limited partnership unless both of the following conditions exist:

(1) The plaintiff alleges in the complaint that plaintiff was a partner of record or beneficially, at the time of the transaction or any part thereof of which plaintiff complains or that plaintiff's interest thereafter devolved upon plaintiff by operation of law from a partner who was a partner at the time of the transaction or any part thereof complained of. Any partner who does not meet these requirements may nevertheless be allowed in the discretion of the court to maintain the action or a preliminary showing to and determination by the court, by motion and after a hearing at which the court shall consider any evidence, by affidavit or testimony, as it deems material, that (A) there is a strong prima facie case in favor of the claim asserted on behalf of the limited partnership, (B) no other similar action has been or is likely to be instituted, (C) the plaintiff acquired the interest before there was disclosure to the public or to the plaintiff of the wrongdoing of which plaintiff complains, (D) unless the action can be maintained the defendant may retain a gain derived from defendant's willful breach of a fiduciary duty, and (E) the requested relief will not result in unjust enrichment of the limited partnership or any partner of the limited partnership.

(2) The plaintiff alleges in the complaint with particularity plaintiff's efforts to secure from the general partners such action as plaintiff desires or the reasons for not making that effort, and alleges further that plaintiff has either informed the limited partnership or the general partners in writing of the ultimate facts of each cause of action against each defendant or delivered to the limited partnership or the general partners a true copy of the complaint which plaintiff proposes to file.

(b) In any action referred to in subdivision (a), at any time within 30 days after service of summons upon the limited partnership or upon any defendant who is a general partner of the limited partnership or held that position at the time of the acts complained of, the limited partnership or the defendant may move the court for an order, upon notice and hearing, requiring the plaintiff to furnish security as hereinafter provided. The motion shall be based upon one or both of the following grounds:

(1) That there is no reasonable possibility that the prosecution of the cause of action alleged in the complaint against the moving party will benefit the limited partnership or its partners.

(2) That the moving party, if other than the limited partnership, did not participate in the transaction complained of in any capacity. The court on application of the limited partnership or any defendant may, for good cause shown, extend the 30-day period for an additional period not exceeding 60 days.

(c) At the hearing upon any motion pursuant to subdivision (b), the court shall consider evidence, written or oral, by witnesses or affidavit, as may be material (1) to the ground upon which the motion is based, or (2) to a determination of the probable reasonable expenses, including attorney's fees, of the limited partnership and the moving party which will be incurred in the defense of the action. If the court determines after hearing the evidence adduced by the parties, that the moving party has established a probability in support of any of the grounds upon which the motion is based, the court shall fix the nature and amount of security, not to exceed fifty thousand dollars ($50,000), to be furnished by the plaintiff for reasonable expenses, including attorneys' fees, which may be incurred by the moving party and the limited partnership in connection with the action. A ruling by the court on the motion shall not be a determination of any issue in the action or of the merits thereof. The amount of the security may thereafter be increased or decreased in the discretion of the court upon a showing that the security provided has or may become inadequate or is excessive, but the court may not in any event increase the total amount of the security beyond fifty thousand dollars ($50,000) in the aggregate for all defendants. If the court, upon any such motion, makes a determination that security shall be furnished by the plaintiff as to any one or more defendants, the action shall be dismissed as to such defendant or defendants, unless the security required by the court shall have been furnished within any reasonable time as may be fixed by the court. The limited partnership and the moving party shall have recourse to the security in such amount as the court shall determine upon the termination of the action.

(d) If the plaintiff shall, either before or after a motion is made pursuant to subdivision (b), or any order or determination pursuant to such motion, post good and sufficient bond or bonds in the aggregate amount of fifty thousand dollars ($50,000) to secure the reasonable expenses of the parties entitled to make the motion, the plaintiff has complied with the requirements of this section and with any order for security theretofore made pursuant hereto, and any such motion then pending shall be dismissed and no further or additional bonds or other security shall be required.

(e) If a motion is filed pursuant to subdivision (b), no pleadings need be filed by the limited partnership or any other defendant and the prosecution of the action shall be stayed until 10 days after the motion has been disposed of.

Sec. 15711. Prior limited partnerships; continuation under prior law. Except as provided in Section 15712, this Chapter 3 shall not apply to any limited partnership organized under the laws of this state and existing on the effective date, which shall continue to be governed by the law previously applicable to it.

Sec. 15712. **Prior limited partnership; election as to applicable law; etc.** A limited partnership organized under the laws of this state and existing on the effective date:

(a) (1) Shall be governed by the law previously applicable to it unless it elects to be governed by this chapter instead of by the law previously applicable to it. Such election shall be made by the written consent of all partners, or of the lesser number provided by the partnership agreement for this election. The election shall be prospective only and shall not affect preexisting rights of third parties.

(2) Shall file a certificate as provided by subdivision (a) of Section 15621, including therein the date that the limited partnership filed under the law previously applicable to it, and shall thereafter be governed by the provisions of Article 2 (commencing with Section 15621), and not by the law previously applicable to it relating to filing requirements.

(3) Shall not be subject to the requirement of subdivision (a) of Section 15612 or to the limitations of subdivision (c) of Section 15612 if a certificate as required by paragraph (2) of this subdivision is filed prior to July 1, 1985.

(4) May not maintain any action, suit, or proceeding in any court of this state until it has filed a certificate as required by paragraph (2) of this subdivision.

(b) To the extent that the provisions of the certificate filed under the law previously applicable to a limited partnership governed the rights and obligations of the partners and the limited partnership among each other, those provisions will continue to govern those rights and obligations except (i) as they may subsequently be affected by amendments to the partnership agreement or by the terms of a certificate filed pursuant to paragraph (6) of subdivision (a) of Section 15621 or by the terms of a certificate or amendment filed pursuant to subdivision (c) of Section 15622, and (ii) for the effect upon those rights and obligations of an election to be governed by this chapter pursuant to this Section 15712.

Sec. 15713. **Operative date and application of certain provisions.** (a) A foreign limited partnership existing on the effective date shall not be subject to the limitation of subdivision (c) of Section 15612 if a certificate of registration referred to in Section 15693 is issued prior to July 1, 1975.

(b) The provisions of subdivision (b) of Section 15697 shall not be operative until July 1, 1975.

Sec. 15714. **Effective date.** As used in this article, "effective date" means July 1, 1984.

Sec. 15721. **Short title.** This chapter may be cited as the California Revised Limited Partnership Act.

Sec. 15722. **Rules for cases not provided for in this chapter.** In any case not provided for in this chapter, the provisions of the Uniform Partnership Act, Chapter 1 (commencing with Section 15001), govern.

Sec. 15723. **Alteration or repeal of provisions; rights of partners subject to reservation.** All provisions of this chapter and all provisions that may hereafter be added to this chapter may be altered from time to time or repealed and all rights of partners are subject to this reservation.

Sec. 15800. **Foreign partnership to designate process agent: Evidence of appointment: Service to agent, Secretary of State or deputy secretary of state.** Every partnership, other than a commercial or banking partnership established and transacting business in a place without the United States, which is domiciled without this state and has no regular place of business within this state, shall, within 40 days from the time it commences to do business in this state, file a statement in the office of the Secretary of State in accordance with Section 24003 designating some natural person or corporation as the agent of the partnership upon whom process issued by authority of or under any law of this state directed against the partnership may be served. A copy of such designation, duly certified by the Secretary of State, is sufficient evidence of such appointment.

Such process may be served in the manner provided in subdivision (e) of Section 24003 on the person so designated, or, in the event that no such person has been designated, or if the agent designated for the service of process is a natural person and cannot be found with due diligence at the address stated in the designation, or if such agent is a corporation and no person can be found with due diligence to whom the delivery authorized by subdivision (e) of Section 24003 may be made for the purpose of delivery to such corporate agent, or if the agent designated is no longer authorized to act, then service may be made by personal delivery to the Secretary of State, Assistant Secretary of State or a Deputy Secretary of State of the process, together with a written statement signed by the party to the action seeking such service, or by his attorney, setting forth the last-known address of the partnership and a service fee of five dollars ($5). The Secretary of State shall forthwith give notice of such service to the partnership by forwarding the process to it by registered mail, return receipt requested, at the address given in the written statement.

Service on the person designated, or personal delivery of the process and statement of address together with a service fee of five dollars ($5) to the Secretary of State, Assistant Secretary of State or a Deputy Secretary of State, pursuant to this section is a valid service on the partnership. The partnership so served shall appear within 30 days after service on the person designated or within 30 days after delivery of the process to the Secretary of State, Assistant Secretary of State or a Deputy Secretary of State.

FEES OF SECRETARY OF STATE

Govt. C. 12213. The fee for filing a certificate of limited partnership or an application for registration as a foreign limited partnership is seventy dollars ($70).

Govt. C. 12214. The fee for filing an amendment to the certificate of limited partnership or to the application for registration of a foreign limited partnership is fifteen dollars ($15). There is no fee for filing a certificate of dissolution or certificate of cancellation by a limited partnership, either domestic or foreign.

CALIFORNIA CORPORATIONS CODE—
GENERAL CORPORATION LAW

TITLE I

CORPORATIONS

DIVISION I

GENERAL CORPORATION LAW

CHAPTER 1

GENERAL PROVISIONS AND DEFINITIONS

Sec. 110. **Effective date of filing instruments with Secretary of State.** (a) Upon receipt of any instrument by the Secretary of State for filing pursuant to this division, if it conforms to law, it shall be filed by, and in the office of, the Secretary of State and the date of filing endorsed thereon. Except for instruments filed pursuant to Sections 1502 and 2108, the date of filing shall be the date the instrument is received by the Secretary of State unless withheld from filing for a period of time pursuant to a request by the party submitting it for filing or unless in the judgment of the Secretary of State the filing is intended to be coordinated with the filing of some other corporate document which cannot be filed. The Secretary of State shall file a document as of any requested future date not more than 90 days after its receipt, including a Saturday, Sunday or legal holiday, if the document is received in the Secretary of State's office at least one business day prior to the requested date of filing. An instrument does not fail to conform to law because it is not accompanied by the full filing fee if the unpaid portion of such fee does not exceed the limits established by the policy of the Secretary of State for extending credit in such cases.

(b) If the Secretary of State determines that an instrument submitted for filing or otherwise submitted does not conform to law and returns it to the person submitting it, the instrument may be resubmitted accompanied by a written opinion of the member of the State Bar of California submitting the instrument, or representing the person submitting it, to the effect that the specific provision of the instrument objected to by the Secretary of State does conform to law and stating the points and authorities upon which the opinion is based. The Secretary of State shall rely, with respect to any disputed point of law (other than the application of Sections 201, 2101 and 2106), upon such written opinion in determining whether the instrument conforms to law. The date of filing in such case shall be the date the instrument is received on resubmission.

(c) Any instrument filed with respect to a corporation (other than original articles) may provide that it is to become effective not more than 90 days subsequent to its filing date. In case such a delayed effective date is specified, the instrument may be prevented from becoming effective by a certificate stating that by appropriate corporate action it has been revoked and is null and void, executed in the same manner as the original instrument and filed before the specified effective date. In the case of a merger agreement, such certificate revoking the earlier filing need only be executed on behalf of one of the constituent corporations. If no such revocation certificate is filed, the instrument becomes effective on the date specified.

Sec. 111. **Voting of shares includes voting of other securities.** All references in this division to the voting of shares include the voting of other securities given voting rights in the articles pursuant to subdivision (a)(7) of Section 204.

Sec. Sec.114. **Preparation of accounting statements in accordance with generally accepted accounting principles.** All references in this division to financial statements, balance sheets, income statements and statements of changes in financial position of a corporation and all references to assets, liabilities, earnings, retained earnings and similar accounting items of a corporation mean such financial statements or such items prepared or determined in conformity with generally accepted accounting principles then applicable, and fairly presenting in conformity with generally accepted accounting principles the matters which they purport to present, subject to any specific accounting treatment required by a particular section of this division. Unless otherwise expressly stated, all references in this division to such financial statements mean, in the case of a corporation which has subsidiaries, consolidated statements of the corporation and such of its subsidiaries as are required or permitted to be included in such consolidated statements under generally accepted accounting principles then applicable and all references to such accounting items mean such items determined on a consolidated basis in accordance with such consolidated financial statements. Financial statements other than annual statements may be condensed or otherwise presented as permitted by authoritative accounting pronouncements.

Sec. 115. **"Independent accountant."** As used in this division, independent accountant means a certified public accountant or public accountant who is independent of the corporation as determined in accordance with generally accepted auditing standards and who is engaged to audit financial statements of the corporation or perform other accounting services.

Sec. 117. **"Vote of each class of outstanding shares."** Any requirement in this division for a vote of each class of outstanding shares means such a vote regardless of limitations or restrictions upon the voting rights thereof, unless expressly limited to voting shares.

Sec. 149. **"Acknowledged."** "Acknowledged" means that an instrument is either:

(a) Formally acknowledged as provided in Article 3 (commencing with Section 1180) of Chapter 4 of Title 4 of Part 4 of Division 2 of the Civil Code, or

(b) Accompanied by a declaration in writing signed by the persons executing the same that they are such persons and that the instrument is the act and deed of the person or persons executing the same.

Any certificate of acknowledgment taken without this state before a notary public or a judge or clerk of a court of record having an official seal need not be further authenticated.

Sec. 150. **"Affiliate" or "affiliated."** A corporation is an "affiliate" of, or a corporation is "affiliated" with, another specified corporation if it directly, or indirectly through one or more intermediaries, controls, is controlled by or is under common control with the other specified corporation.

Sec. 151. **"Approved by the board."** "Approved by (or approval of) the board" means approved or ratified by the vote of the board or by the vote of a committee authorized to exercise the powers of the board, except as to matters not within the competence of the committee under Section 311.

Sec. 152. "Approved by the outstanding shares." "Approved by (or approval of) the outstanding shares" means approved by the affirmative vote of a majority of the outstanding shares entitled to vote. Such approval shall include the affirmative vote of a majority of the outstanding shares of each class or series entitled, by any provision of the articles or of this division, to vote as a class or series on the subject matter being voted upon and shall also include the affirmative vote of such greater proportion (including all) of the outstanding shares of any class or series if such greater proportion is required by the articles or this division.

Sec. 153. "Approved by the shareholders." "Approved by (or approval of) the shareholders" means approved or ratified by the affirmative vote of a majority of the shares represented and voting at a duly held meeting at which a quorum is present (which shares voting affirmatively also constitute at least a majority of the required quorum) or by the written consent of shareholders (Section 603) or by the affirmative vote or written consent of such greater proportion (including all) of the shares of any class or series as may be provided in the articles or in this division for all or any specified shareholder action.

Sec. 154. "Articles." "Articles" includes the articles of incorporation, amendments thereto, amended articles, restated articles, certificate of incorporation and certificates of determination. All references in this division to a vote required by the "articles" include, in the case of a close corporation (Section 158), any vote required by a shareholders' agreement.

Sec. 155. "Board." "Board" means the board of directors of the corporation.

Sec. 156. "Certificate of determination." "Certificate of determination" means a certificate executed and filed pursuant to Section 401.

Sec. 158. "Close corporation." (a) "Close corporation" means a corporation whose articles contain, in addition to the provisions required by Section 202, a provision that all of the corporation's issued shares of all classes shall be held of record by not more than a specified number of persons, not exceeding 35, and a statement "This corporation is a close corporation."

(b) The special provisions referred to in subdivision (a) may be included in the articles by amendment, but if such amendment is adopted after the issuance of shares only by the affirmative vote of all of the issued and outstanding shares of all classes.

(c) The special provisions referred to in subdivision (a) may be deleted from the articles by amendment, or the number of shareholders specified may be changed by amendment, but if such amendment is adopted after the issuance of shares only by the affirmative vote of at least two-thirds of each class of the outstanding shares; provided, however, that the articles may provide for a lesser vote, but not less than a majority of the outstanding shares, or may deny a vote to any class, or both.

(d) In determining the number of shareholders for the purposes of the provision in the articles authorized by this section, a husband and wife and the personal representative of either shall be counted as one regardless of how shares may be held by either or both of them, a trust or personal representative of a decedent holding shares shall be counted as one regardless of the number of trustees or beneficiaries and a partnership or corporation or business holding shares shall be counted as one (except that any such trust or entity the primary purpose of which was the acquisition or voting of the shares shall be counted according to the number of beneficial interests therein).

(e) A corporation shall cease to be a close corporation upon the filing of an amendment to its articles pursuant to subdivision (c) or if it shall have more than the maximum number of holders of record of its shares specified in its articles as a result of an inter vivos transfer of shares which is not void under subdivision (d) of Section 418, the transfer of shares on distribution by will or pursuant to the laws of descent and distribution, the dissolution of a partnership or corporation or business association or the termination of a trust which holds shares, by court decree upon dissolution of a marriage or otherwise by operation of law. Promptly upon acquiring more than the specified number of holders of record of its shares, a close corporation shall execute and file an amendment to its articles deleting the special provisions referred to in subdivision (a) and deleting any other provisions not permissible for a corpora-

tion which is not a close corporation, which amendment shall be promptly approved and filed by the board and need not be approved by the outstanding shares.

(f) Nothing contained in this section shall invalidate any agreement among the shareholders to vote for the deletion from the articles of the special provisions referred to in subdivision (a) upon the lapse of a specified period of time or upon the occurrence of a certain event or condition or otherwise.

(g) The following sections contain specific references to close corporations: 186, 202, 204, 300, 418, 421, 706, 1111, 1201, 1800 and 1904.

Sec. 159. "Common shares." "Common shares" means shares which have no preference over any other shares with respect to distribution of assets on liquidation or with respect to payment of dividends.

Sec. 160. "Control." (a) Except as provided in subdivision (b), "control" means the possession, direct or indirect, of the power to direct or cause the direction of the management and policies of a corporation.

(b) "Control" in Sections 181, 1001 and 1200 means the ownership directly or indirectly of shares possessing more than 50 percent of the voting power.

Sec. 161. "Constituent corporation." "Constituent corporation" means a corporation which is merged with one or more other corporations and includes the surviving corporation.

Sec. 162. "Corporation." "Corporation," unless otherwise expressly provided, refers only to a corporation organized under this division or a corporation subject to this division under the provisions of subdivision (a) of Section 102.

Sec. 164. "Directors." "Directors" means natural persons designated in the articles as such or elected by the incorporators and natural persons designated, elected or appointed by any other name or title to act as directors, and their successors.

Sec. 165. "Disappearing corporation." "Disappearing corporation" means a constituent corporation which is not the surviving corporation.

Sec. 166. "Distribution to its shareholders." "Distribution to its shareholders" means the transfer of cash or property by a corporation to its shareholders without consideration, whether by way of dividend or otherwise, except a dividend in shares of the corporation, or the purchase or redemption of its shares for cash or property, including such transfer, purchase or redemption by a subsidiary of the corporation. The time of any distribution by way of dividend shall be the date of declaration thereof and the time of any distribution by purchase or redemption of shares shall be the date cash or property is transferred by the corporation, whether or not pursuant to a contract of an earlier date; provided, that where a negotiable debt security (as defined in subdivision (1) of Section 8102 of the Commercial Code) is issued in exchange for shares the time of the distribution is the date when the corporation acquires the shares in such exchange. In the case of a sinking fund payment, cash or property is transferred within the meaning of this section at the time that it is delivered to a trustee for the holders of preferred shares to be used for the redemption of such shares or physically segregated by the corporation in trust for that purpose.

Sec. 167. "Domestic corporation." "Domestic corporation" means a corporation formed under the laws of this state.

Sec. 168. "Equity security." "Equity security" in Sections 181, 1200 and 1201 means any share, any security convertible, with or without consideration, into shares or any warrant or right to subscribe to or purchase any of the foregoing.

Sec. 169. "Filed." "Filed," unless otherwise expressly provided, means filed in the office of the Secretary of State.

Sec. 170. "Foreign association." "Foreign association" means a business association organized as a trust under the laws of a foreign jurisdiction.

Sec. 171. "Foreign corporation." "Foreign corporation" means any corporation other than a domestic corporation and, when used in Section 191, Section 201, Section 2203, Section 2258 and Section 2259 and Chapter 21, includes a foreign association, unless otherwise stated. "Foreign corporation" as used in Chapter 21 does not include a corporation or association chartered under the laws of the United States.

Sec. 172. **"Liquidating price" or "liquidation preference."** "Liquidation price" or "liquidation preference" means amounts payable on shares of any class upon voluntary or involuntary dissolution, winding up or distribution of the entire assets of the corporation, including any cumulative dividends accrued and unpaid, in priority to shares of another class or classes.

Sec. 173. **"Officers' certificate."** "Officers' certificate" means a certificate signed and verified by the chairman of the board, the president or any vice president and by the secretary, the chief financial officer, the treasurer or any assistant secretary or assistant treasurer.

Sec. 174. **"On the certificate."** "On the certificate" means that a statement appears on the face of a share certificate or on the reverse thereof with a reference thereto on the face.

Sec. 175. **"Parent."** Except as used in Sections 1001, 1101 and 1200, a "parent" of a specified corporation is an affiliate controlling such corporation directly or indirectly through one or more intermediaries. In Sections 1001 and 1101, "parent" means a person in control of a corporation as defined in subdivision (b) of Section 160.

Sec. 176. **"Preferred shares."** "Preferred shares" means shares other than common shares.

Sec. 177. **"Proper county."** "Proper county" means the county where the principal executive office of the corporation is located or, if the principal executive office of the corporation is not located in this state, or the corporation has no such office, the County of Sacramento.

Sec. 178. **"Proxy."** "Proxy" means a written authorization signed by a shareholder or the shareholder's attorney in fact giving another person or persons power to vote with respect to the shares of such shareholder. "Signed" for the purpose of this section means the placing of the shareholder's name on the proxy (whether by manual signature, typewriting, telegraphic transmission or otherwise) by the shareholder or the shareholder's attorney in fact.

Sec. 179. **"Proxyholder."** "Proxyholder" means the person or persons to whom a proxy is given.

Sec. 180. **"Redemption price."** "Redemption price" means the amount or amounts (in cash, property or securities, or any combination thereof) payable on shares of any class or series upon the redemption of the shares. Unless otherwise expressly provided, the redemption price is payable in cash.

Sec. 181. **"Reorganization."** "Reorganization" means:
(a) A merger pursuant to Chapter 11 (commencing with Section 1100) other than a short-form merger (a "merger reorganization");
(b) The acquisition by one corporation in exchange in whole or in part for its equity securities (or the equity securities of a corporation which is in control of the acquiring corporation) of shares of another corporation if, immediately after the acquisition, the acquiring corporation has control of such other corporation (an "exchange reorganization"); or
(c) The acquisition by one corporation in exchange in whole or in part for its equity securities (or the equity securities of a corporation which is in control of the acquiring corporation) or for its debt securities (or debt securities of a corporation which is in control of the acquiring corporation) which are not adequately secured and which have a maturity date in excess of five years after the consummation of the reorganization, or both, of all or substantially all of the assets of another corporation (a "sale-of-assets reorganization").

Sec. 182. **"Reverse stock split."** "Reverse stock split" means the pro rata combination of all the outstanding shares of a class into a smaller number of shares of the same class by an amendment to the articles stating the effect on outstanding shares.

Sec. 183. **"Series" of shares.** "Series" of shares means those shares within a class which have the same rights, preferences, privileges and restrictions but which differ in one or more rights, preferences, privileges or restrictions from other shares within the same class.

Sec. 184. **"Shares."** "Shares" means the units into which the proprietary interests in a corporation are divided in the articles.

Sec. 185. **"Shareholder."** "Shareholder" means one who is a holder of record of shares.

Sec. 186. **"Shareholders' agreement."** "Shareholders' agreement" means a written agreement among all of the shareholders of a close corporation, or if a close corporation has only one shareholder between such shareholder and the corporation, as authorized by subdivision (b) of Section 300.

Sec. 187. **"Short-form merger."** "Short-form merger" means a merger pursuant to Section 1110.

Sec. 188. **"Stock split."** "Stock split" means the pro rata division, otherwise than by a share dividend, of all the outstanding shares of a class into a greater number of shares of the same class by an amendment to the article stating the effect on outstanding shares.

Sec. 189. **"Subsidiary."** (a) Except as provided in subdivision (b), "subsidiary" of a specified corporation means a corporation shares of which possessing more than 50 percent of the voting power are owned directly or indirectly through one or more subsidiaries by the specified corporation.
(b) For the purpose of Section 703, "subsidiary" of a specified corporation means a corporation shares of which possessing more than 25 percent of the voting power are owned directly or indirectly through one or more subsidiaries as defined in subdivision (a) by the specified corporation.

Sec. 190. **"Surviving corporation."** "Surviving corporation" means a corporation into which one or more other corporations are merged.

Sec. 191. **"Transact intrastate business."** (a) For the purposes of Chapter 21 (commencing with Section 2100), "transact intrastate business" means entering into repeated and successive transactions of its business in this state, other than interstate or foreign commerce.
(b) A foreign corporation shall not be considered to be transacting intrastate business merely because its subsidiary transacts intrastate business.
(c) Without excluding other activities which may not constitute transacting intrastate business, a foreign corporation shall not be considered to be transacting intrastate business within the meaning of subdivision (a) solely by reason of carrying on in this state any one or more of the following activities:
(1) Maintaining or defending any action or suit or any administrative or arbitration proceeding, or effecting the settlement thereof or the settlement of claims or disputes.
(2) Holding meetings of its board or shareholders or carrying on other activities concerning its internal affairs.
(3) Maintaining bank accounts.
(4) Maintaining offices or agencies for the transfer, exchange and registration of its securities or depositaries with relation to its securities.
(5) Effecting sales through independent contractors.
(6) Soliciting or procuring orders, whether by mail or through employees or agents or otherwise, where such orders require acceptance without this state before becoming binding contracts.
(7) Creating evidences of debt or mortgages, liens or security interests on real or personal property.
(8) Conducting an isolated transaction completed within a period of 180 days and not in the course of a number of repeated transactions of like nature.
(d) Without excluding other activities which may not constitute transacting intrastate business, any foreign lending institution, including, but not limited to: any foreign banking corporation, any foreign corporation all of the capital stock of which is owned by one or more foreign banking corporations, any foreign savings and loan association, any foreign insurance company or any foreign corporation or association authorized by its charter to invest in loans secured by real and personal property, whether organized under the laws of the United States or of any other state, district or territory of the United States, shall not be considered to be doing, transacting or engaging in business in this state solely by reason of engaging in any or all of the following activities either on its own behalf or as a trustee of a pension plan, employee profit sharing or re-

tirement plan, testamentary or inter vivos trust, or in any other fiduciary capacity.

(1) The acquisition by purchase, by contract to purchase, by making of advance commitments to purchase or by assignment of loans, secured or unsecured, or any interest therein, if such activities are carried on from outside this state by the lending institution.

(2) The making by an officer or employee of physical inspections and appraisals of real or personal property securing or proposed to secure any loan, if the officer or employee making any physical inspection or appraisal is not a resident of and does not maintain a place of business for such purpose in this state.

(3) The ownership of any loans and the enforcement of any loans by trustee's sale, judicial process or deed in lieu of foreclosure or otherwise.

(4) The modification, renewal, extension, transfer or sale of loans or the acceptance of additional or substitute security therefor or the full or partial release of the security therefor or the acceptance of substitute or additional obligors thereon, if the activities are carried on from outside this state by the lending institution.

(5) The engaging by contractual arrangement of a corporation, firm or association, qualified to do business in this state, which is not a subsidiary or parent of the lending institution and which is not under common management with the lending institution to make collections and to service loans in any manner whatsoever, including the payment of ground rents, taxes, assessments, insurance and the like and the making, on behalf of the lending institution, of physical inspections and appraisals of real or personal property securing any loans or proposed to secure any loans, and the performance of any such engagement.

(6) The acquisition of title to the real or personal property covered by any mortgage, deed of trust or other security instrument by trustee's sale, judicial sale, foreclosure or deed in lieu of foreclosure, or for the purpose of transferring title to any federal agency or instrumentality as the insurer or guarantor of any loan, and the retention of title to any real or personal property so acquired pending the orderly sale or other disposition thereof.

(7) The engaging in activities necessary or appropriate to carry out any of the foregoing activities.

Nothing contained in this subdivision shall be construed to permit any foreign banking corporation to maintain an office in this state otherwise than as provided by the laws of this state or to limit the powers conferred upon any foreign banking corporation as set forth in the laws of this state or to permit any foreign lending institution to maintain an office in this state except as otherwise permitted under the laws of this state.

Sec. 192. **"Vacancy."** "Vacancy" when used with respect to the board means any authorized position of director which is not then filled by a duly elected director, whether caused by death, resignation, removal, change in the authorized number of directors (by the board or the shareholders) or otherwise.

Sec. 193. **"Verified."** "Verified" means that the statements contained in a certificate or other document are declared to be true of the own knowledge of the persons executing the same in either:

(a) An affidavit signed by them under oath before an officer authorized by the laws of this state or of the place where it is executed to administer oaths, or

(b) A declaration in writing executed by them "under penalty of perjury" and stating the date and place (whether within or without this state) of execution.

Any affidavit sworn to without this state before a notary public or a judge or clerk of a court of record having an official seal need not be further authenticated.

Sec. 194. **"Vote" includes written consent.** "Vote" includes authorization by written consent, subject to the provisions of subdivision (c) of Section 307 and subdivision (d) of Section 603.

Sec. 194.5. **"Voting power."** "Voting power" means the power to vote for the election of directors at the time any determination of voting power is made and does not include the right to vote upon the happening of some condition or event which has not yet occurred. In any case where different classes of shares are entitled to vote as separate classes for different members of the board, the determination of percentage of voting power shall be made on the basis of the percentage of the total authorized directors which the shares in question (whether of one or more classes) have the power to elect in an election at which all shares then entitled to vote for the election of any directors are voted.

CHAPTER 2

ORGANIZATION AND BYLAWS

Sec. 200. **Formation by execution and filing of articles.** (a) One or more natural persons, partnerships, associations or corporations, domestic or foreign, may form a corporation under this division by executing and filing articles of incorporation.

(b) If initial directors are named in the articles, each director named in the articles shall sign and acknowledge the articles; if initial directors are not named in the articles, the articles shall be signed by one or more persons described in subdivision (a) who thereupon are the incorporators of the corporation.

(c) The corporate existence begins upon the filing of the articles and continues perpetually, unless otherwise expressly provided by law or in the articles.

Sec. 201. **Prohibited names; reservation of names.** (a) The Secretary of State shall not file articles setting forth a name in which "bank," "trust," "trustee" or related words appear, unless the certificate of approval of the Superintendent of Banks is attached thereto. This subdivision does not apply to the articles of any corporation subject to the Banking Law on which is endorsed the approval of the Superintendent of Banks.

(b) The Secretary of State shall not file articles which set forth a name which is likely to mislead the public or which is the same as, or resembles so closely as to tend to deceive, the name of a domestic corporation, the name of a foreign corporation which is authorized to transact intrastate business or has registered its name pursuant to Section 2101, a name which a foreign corporation has assumed under subdivision (b) of Section 2106, a name which will become the record name of a domestic or foreign corporation upon the effective date of a filed corporate instrument where there is a delayed effective date pursuant to subdivision (c) of Section 110 or subdivision (c) of Section 5508, or a name which is under reservation for another corporation pursuant to this section, Section 5122, Section 7122, or Section 9122, except that a corporation may adopt a name that is substantially the same as an existing domestic corporation or foreign corporation which is authorized to transact intrastate business or has registered its name pursuant to Section 2101, upon proof of consent by such domestic or foreign corporation and a finding by the Secretary of State that under the circumstances the public is not likely to be misled.

The use by a corporation of a name in violation of this section may be enjoined notwithstanding the filing of its articles by the Secretary of State.

(c) Any applicant may, upon payment of the fee prescribed therefor in the Government Code, obtain from the Secretary of State a certificate of reservation of any name not prohibited by subdivision (b), and upon the issuance of the certificate the name stated therein shall be reserved for a period of 60 days. The Secretary of State shall not, however, issue certificates reserving the same name for two or more consecutive 60-day periods to the same applicant or for the use or benefit of the same person, partnership, firm or corporation; nor shall consecutive reservations be made by or for the use or benefit of the same person, partnership, firm or corporation of names so similar as to fall within the prohibitions of subdivision (b).

Sec. 202. **Articles: Required provisions.** The articles of incorporation shall set forth:

(a) The name of the corporation; provided, however, that in order for the corporation to be subject to the provisons of this division applicable to a close corporation (Section 158), the name of the corporation must contain the word "corporation," "incorporated" or "limited" or an abbreviation of one of such words.

(b) (1) The applicable one of the following statements:

(i) The purpose of the corporation is to engage in any lawful act or activity for which a corporation may be organized under the General Corporation Law of California other than the banking business or the practice of a profession permitted to be incorporated by the California Corporations Code; or

(ii) The purpose of the corporation is to engage in the profession of . . . . . (with the insertion of a profession permitted to be incorporated by the California Corporations Code) and any other lawful activities (other than the banking or trust company business) not prohibited to a corporation engaging in such profession by applicable laws and regulations.

(2) In case the corporation is a corporation subject to the Banking Law, the articles shall set forth a statement of purpose which is prescribed in the applicable provision of the Banking Law.

(3) In case the corporation is a corporation subject to the Insurance Code as an insurer, the articles shall additionally state that the business of the corporation is to be an insurer.

The articles shall not set forth any further or additional statement with respect to the purposes or powers of the corporation, except by way of limitation or except as expressly required by any law of this state other than this division or any federal or other state or regulation (including the Internal Revenue Code and regulations thereunder as a condition of acquiring or maintaining a particular status for tax purposes).

(c) The name and address in this state of the corporation's initial agent for service of process in accordance with subdivision (b) of Section 1502.

(d) If the corporation is authorized to issue only one class of shares, the total number of shares which the corporation is authorized to issue.

(e) If the corporation is authorized to issue more than one class of shares, or if any class of shares is to have two or more series:

(1) The total number of shares of each class the corporation is authorized to issue, and the total number of shares of each series which the corporation is authorized to issue or that the board is authorized to fix the number of shares of any such series;

(2) The designation of each class, and the designation of each series or that the board may determine the designation of any such series; and

(3) The rights, preferences, privileges and restrictions granted to or imposed upon the respective classes or series of shares or the holders thereof, or that the board, within any limits and restrictions stated, may determine or alter the rights, preferences, privileges and restrictions granted to or imposed upon any wholly unissued class of shares or any wholly unissued series of any class of shares. As to any series the number of shares of which is authorized to be fixed by the board, the articles may also authorize the board, within the limits and restrictions stated therein or stated in any resolution or resolutions of the board originally fixing the number of shares constituting any series, to increase or decrease (but not below the number of shares of such series then outstanding) the number of shares of any such series subsequent to the issue of shares of the series. In case the number of shares of any series shall be so decreased, the shares constituting such decrease shall resume the status which they had prior to the adoption of the resolution originally fixing the number of shares of such series.

Sec. 203. **Distinctions between classes or series of shares.** Except as specified in the articles or in any shareholders' agreement, no distinction shall exist between classes or series of shares or the holders thereof.

Sec. 204. **Articles: Optional provisions.** The articles of incorporation may set forth:

(a) Any or all of the following provisions, which shall not be effective unless expressly provided in the articles:

(1) Granting, with or without limitations, the power to levy assessments upon the shares or any class of shares;

(2) Granting to shareholders preemptive rights to subscribe to any or all issues of shares or securities;

(3) Special qualifications of persons who may be shareholders;

(4) A provision limiting the duration of the corporation's existence to a specified date;

(5) A provision requiring, for any or all corporate actions (except as provided in Section 303, subdivision (b) of Section 402.5, subdivision (c) of Section 708 and Section 1900) the vote of a larger proportion or of all of the shares of any class or series, or the vote or quorum for taking action of a larger proportion or of all of the directors, than is otherwise required by this division;

(6) A provision limiting or restricting the business in which the corporation may engage or the powers which the corporation may exercise or both;

(7) A provision conferring upon the holders of any evidences of indebtedness, issued or to be issued by the corporation, the right to vote in the election of directors and on any other matters on which shareholders may vote;

(8) A provision conferring upon shareholders the right to determine the consideration for which shares shall be issued.

(9) A provision requiring the approval of the shareholders (Section 153) or the approval of the outstanding shares (Section 152) for any corporate action, even though not otherwise required by this division.

Notwithstanding this subdivision, in the case of a close corporation any of the provisions referred to above may be validly included in a shareholders' agreement. Notwithstanding this subdivision, bylaws may require for all or any actions by the board the affirmative vote of a majority of the authorized number of directors. Nothing contained in this subdi-

vision shall affect the enforceability, as between the parties thereto, of any lawful agreement not otherwise contrary to public policy.

(b) Reasonable restrictions upon the right to transfer or hypothecate shares of any class or classes or series, but no restriction shall be binding with respect to shares issued prior to the adoption of the restriction unless the holders of such shares voted in favor of the restriction.

(c) The names and addresses of the persons appointed to act as initial directors.

(d) Any other provision, not in conflict with law, for the management of the business and for the conduct of the affairs of the corporation, including any provision which is required or permitted by this division to be stated in the bylaws.

Sec. 205. **Value of authorized shares for purposes of taxes or fees.** Solely for the purpose of any statute or regulation imposing any tax or fee based upon the capitalization of a corporation, all authorized shares of a corporation organized under this division shall be deemed to have a nominal or par value of one dollar ($1) per share. If any federal or other statute or regulation applicable to a particular corporation requires that the shares of such corporation have a par value, such shares shall have the par value determined by the board in order to satisfy the requirements of such statute or regulation.

Sec. 206. **Permissible business activities.** Subject to any limitation contained in the articles and to compliance with any other applicable laws, any corporation other than a corporation subject to the Banking Law or a professional corporation may engage in any business activity; and a corporation subject to the Banking Law or a professional corporation may engage in any business activity not prohibited by the respective statutes and regulations to which it is subject.

Sec. 207. **Corporate powers.** Subject to any limitations contained in the articles and to compliance with other provisions of this division and any other applicable laws, a corporation shall have all of the powers of a natural person in carrying out its business activities, including, without limitation, the power to:

(a) Adopt, use and at will alter a corporate seal, but failure to affix a seal does not affect the validity of any instrument.

(b) Adopt, amend and repeal bylaws.

(c) Qualify to do business in any other state, territory, dependency or foreign country.

(d) Subject to the provisions of Section 510, issue, purchase, redeem, receive, take or otherwise acquire, own, hold, sell, lend, exchange, transfer or otherwise dispose of, pledge, use and otherwise deal in and with its own shares, bonds, debentures and other securities.

(e) Make donations, regardless of specific corporate benefit, for the public welfare or for community fund, hospital, charitable, educational, scientific, civic or similar purposes.

(f) Pay pensions, and establish and carry out pension, profit-sharing, share bonus, share purchase, share option, savings, thrift and other retirement, incentive and benefit plans, trusts and provisions for any or all of the directors, officers and employees of the corporation or any of its subsidiary or affiliated corporations, and to indemnify and purchase and maintain insurance on behalf of any fiduciary of such plans, trusts or provisions.

(g) Subject to the provisions of Section 315, assume obligations, enter into contracts, including contracts of guaranty or suretyship, incur liabilities, borrow and lend money and otherwise use its credit, and secure any of its obligations, contracts or liabilities by mortgage, pledge or other encumbrance of all or any part of its property, franchises and income.

(h) Participate with others in any partnership, joint venture or other association, transaction or arrangement of any kind, whether or not such participation involves sharing or delegation of control with or to others.

Sec. 208. **Ultra vires transactions.** (a) No limitation upon the business, purposes or powers of the corporation or upon the powers of the shareholders, officers or directors, or the manner of exercise of such powers, contained in or implied by the articles or by Chapters 18, 19 and 20 or by any shareholders' agreement shall be asserted as between the corporation or any shareholder and any third person, except in a proceeding (1) by a shareholder or the state to enjoin the doing or continuation of unauthorized business by the corporation or its officers, or both, in cases where third parties have not acquired rights thereby, or (2) to dissolve the corporation or (3) by the corporation or by a shareholder suing in a representative suit against the officers or directors of the corporation for violation of their authority.

(h) Any contract or conveyance made in the name of a corporation which is authorized or ratified by the board, or is done within the scope of the authority, actual or apparent, conferred by the board or within the agency power of the officer executing it, except as the board's authority is limited by law other than this division, binds the corporation, and the corporation acquires rights thereunder, whether the contract is executed or wholly or in part executory.

(c) This section applies to contracts and conveyances made by foreign corporations in this state and to all conveyances by foreign corporations of real property situated in this state.

Sec. 209. Certified copy of articles as proof of corporate existence. For all purposes other than an action in the nature of quo warranto, a copy of the articles of a corporation duly certified by the Secretary of State is conclusive evidence of the formation of the corporation and prima facie evidence of its corporate existence.

Sec. 210. Power of incorporators to complete incorporation pending election of directors. If initial directors have not been named in the articles, the incorporator or incorporators, until the dirctors are elected, may do whatever is necessary and proper to perfect the organization of the corporation, including the adoption and amendment of bylaws of the corporation and the election of directors and officers.

Sec. 211. Bylaws: Adoption, amendment, or repeal. Bylaws may be adopted, amended or repealed either by approval of the out standing shares (Section 152) or by the approval of the board, except as provided in Section 212. Subject to subdivision (a)(5) of Section 204, the articles or bylaws may restrict or eliminate the power of the board to adopt, amend or repeal any or all bylaws.

Sec. 212. Bylaws: Provisions. (a) The bylaws shall set forth (unless such provision is contained in the articles, in which case it may only be changed by an amendment of the articles) the number of directors of the corporation; or that the number of directors shall be not less than a stated minimum nor more than a stated maximum (which in no case shall be greater than two times the stated minimum minus one), with the exact number of directors to be fixed, within the limits specified, by approval of the board or the shareholders (Section 153) in the manner provided in the bylaws, subject to paragraph (5) of subdivision (a) of Section 204. The number or minimum number of directors shall not be less than three; provided, however, that (1) before shares are issued, the number may be one, (2) before shares are issued, the number may be two, (3) so long as the corporation has only one shareholder, the number may be one, (4) so long as the corporation has only one shareholder, the number may be two, and (5) so long as the corporation has only two shareholders, the number may be two. After the issuance of shares, a bylaw specifying or changing a fixed number of directors or the maximum or minimum number or changing from a fixed to a variable board or vice versa may only be adopted by approval of the outstanding shares (Section 152); provided, however, that a bylaw or amendment of the articles reducing the fixed number or the minimum number of directors to a number less than five cannot be adopted if the votes cast against its adoption at a meeting or the shares not consenting in the case of action by written consent are equal to more than 16% percent of the outstanding shares entitled to vote.

(b) The bylaws may contain any provision, not in conflict with law or the articles for the management of the business and for the conduct of the affairs of the corporation, including but not limited to:

(1) Any provision referred to in subdivision (b), (c) or (d) of Section 204.

(2) The time, place and manner of calling, conducting and giving notice of shareholders', directors' and committee meetings.

(3) The manner of execution, revocation and use of proxies.

(4) The qualifications, duties and compensation of directors; the time of their annual election; and the requirements of a quorum for directors' and committee meetings.

(5) The appointment and authority of committees of the board.

(6) The appointment, duties, compensation and tenure of officers.

(7) The mode of determination of holders of record of its shares.

(8) The making of annual reports and financial statements to the shareholders.

Sec. 213. Location and right of inspection. Every corporation shall keep at its principal executive office in this state, or if its principal executive office is not in this state at its principal business office in this state, the original or a copy of its bylaws as amended to date, which shall be open to inspection by the shareholders at all reasonable times during office hours. If the principal executive office of the corporation is outside this state and the corporation has no principal business office in this state, it shall upon the written request of any shareholder furnish to such shareholder a copy of the bylaws as amended to date.

CHAPTER 3

DIRECTORS AND MANAGEMENT

Sec. 300. Corporate powers to be exercised by or under direction of board; exception for close corporations. (a) Subject to the provisions of this division and any limitations in the articles relating to action required to be approved by the shareholders (Section 153) or by the outstanding shares (Section 152), or by a less than majority vote of a class or series of preferred shares (Section 402.5), the business and affairs of the corporation shall be managed and all corporate powers shall be exercised by or under the direction of the board. The board may delegate the management of the day-to-day operations of the business of the corporation to a management company or other person provided that the business and affairs of the corporation shall be managed and all corporate powers shall be exercised under the ultimate direction of the board.

(b) Notwithstanding subdivision (a) or any other provision of this division, but subject to subdivision (c), no shareholders' agreement, which relates to any phase of the affairs of a close corporation, including but not limited to management of its business, division of its profits or distribution of its assets on liquidation, shall be invalid as between the parties thereto on the ground that it so relates to the conduct of the affairs of the corporation as to interfere with the discretion of the board or that it is an attempt to treat the corporation as if it were a partnership or to arrange their relationships in a manner that would be appropriate only between partners. A transferee of shares covered by such an agreement which is filed with the secretary of the corporation for inspection by any prospective purchaser of shares, who has actual knowledge thereof or notice thereof by a notation on the certificate pursuant to Section 418, is bound by its provisions and is a party thereto for the purposes of subdivision (d). Original issuance of shares by the corporation to a new shareholder who does not become a party to the agreement terminates the agreement, except that if the agreement so provides it shall continue to the extent it is enforceable apart from this subdivision. The agreement may not be modified, extended or revoked without the consent of such a transferee, subject to any provision of the agreement permitting modification, extension or revocation by less than unanimous agreement of the parties. A transferor of shares covered by such an agreement ceases to be a party thereto upon ceasing to be a shareholder of the corporation unless the transferor is a party thereto other than as a shareholder. An agreement made pursuant to this subdivision shall terminate when the corporation ceases to be a close corporation, except that if the agreement so provides it shall continue to the extent it is enforceable apart from this subdivision. This subdivision does not apply to an agreement authorized by subdivision (a) of Section 706.

(c) No agreement entered into pursuant to subdivision (b) may alter or waive any of the provisions of Sections 158, 417, 418, 500, 501, and 1111, subdivision (e) of Section 1201, Sections 2009, 2010, and 2011, or of Chapters 15 (commencing with Section 1500), 16 (commencing with Section 1600), 18 (commencing with Section 1800), and 22 (commencing with Section 2200). All other provisions of this division may be altered or waived as between the parties thereto in a shareholders' agreement, except the required filing of any document with the Secretary of State.

(d) An agreement of the type referred to in subdivision (b) shall, to the extent and so long as the discretion or powers of the board in its management of corporate affairs is controlled by such agreement, impose upon each shareholder who is a party thereto liability for managerial acts performed or omitted by such person pursuant thereto that is otherwise imposed by this division upon directors, and the directors shall be relieved to that extent from such liability.

(e) The failure of a close corporation to observe corporate formalities relating to meetings of directors or shareholders in connection with the management of its affairs, pursuant to an agreement authorized by subdivision (b), shall not be considered a factor tending to establish that the shareholders have personal liability for corporate obligations.

Sec. 301. Election and term of office of directors. (a) At each annual meeting of shareholders, directors shall be elected to hold office until the next annual meeting. The articles may provide for the election of one or more directors by the holders of the shares of any class or series voting as a class or series.

(b) Each director, including a director elected to fill a vacancy, shall hold office until the expiration of the term for which elected and until a successor has been elected and qualified.

Sec. 302. **Removal of director for cause.** The board may declare vacant the office of a director who has been declared of unsound mind by an order of court or convicted of a felony.

Sec. 303. **Removal of director without cause.** (a) Any or all of the directors may be removed without cause if such removal is approved by the outstanding shares (Section 152), subject to the following:

(1) No director may be removed (unless the entire board is removed) when the votes cast against removal, or not consenting in writing to such removal, would be sufficient to elect such director if voted cumulatively at an election at which the same total number of votes were cast (or, if such action is taken by written consent, all shares entitled to vote were voted) and the entire number of directors authorized at the time of the director's most recent election were then being elected; and

(2) When the provisions of the articles the holders of the shares of any class or series, voting as a class or series, are entitled to elect one or more directors, any director so elected may be removed only by the applicable vote of the holders of the shares of that class or series.

(b) Any reduction of the authorized number of directors does not remove any director prior to the expiration of such director's term of office.

(c) Except as provided in this section and Sections 302 and 304, a director may not be removed prior to the expiration of such director's term of office.

Sec. 304. **Removal of director by shareholders' suit.** The superior court of the proper county may, at the suit of shareholders holding at least 10 percent of the number of outstanding shares of any class, remove from office any director in case of fraudulent or dishonest acts or gross abuse of authority or discretion with reference to the corporation and may bar from reelection any director so removed for a period prescribed by the court. The corporation shall be made a party to such action.

Sec. 305. **Filling vacancies.** (a) Unless otherwise provided in the articles or bylaws and except for a vacancy created by the removal of a director, vacancies on the board may be filled by a majority of the directors then in office, whether or not less than a quorum, or by a sole remaining director. Unless the articles or a bylaw adopted by the shareholders provide that the board may fill vacancies occurring in the board by reason of the removal of directors, such vacancies may be filled only by approval of the shareholders (Section 153).

(b) The shareholders may elect a director at any time to fill any vacancy not filled by the directors. Any such election by written consent other than to fill a vacancy created by removal requires the consent of a majority of the outstanding shares entitled to vote.

(c) If, after the filling of any vacancy by the directors, the directors then in office who have been elected by the shareholders shall constitute less than a majority of the directors then in office,

(1) Any holder or holders of an aggregate of 5 percent or more of the total number of shares at the time outstanding having the right to vote for such directors may call a special meeting of shareholders, or

(2) The superior court of the proper county shall, upon application of such shareholder or shareholders, summarily order a special meeting of shareholders, to be held to elect the entire board. The term of office of any director shall terminate upon such election of a successor.

The hearing on any application filed pursuant to this subdivision shall be held on not less than 10 business days notice to the corporation. If the corporation intends to oppose the application, it shall file with the court a notice of opposition not later than five business days prior to the date set for the hearing. The application and any notice of opposition shall be supported by appropriate affidavits and the court's determination shall be made on the basis of the papers in the record; but, for good cause shown, the court may receive and consider at the hearing additional evidence, oral or documentary, and additional points and authorities. The hearing shall take precedence over all other matters not of a similar nature pending on the date set for the hearing.

(d) Any director may resign effective upon giving written notice to the chairman of the board, the president, the secretary or the board of directors of the corporation, unless the notice specifies a later time for the effectiveness of such resignation. If the resignation is effective at a future time, a successor may be elected to take office when the resignation becomes effective.

Sec. 306. **Appointment of directors by superior court.** If a corporation has not issued shares and all the directors resign, die or become incompetent, the superior court of any county may appoint directors of the corporation upon application by any party in interest.

Sec. 307. **Regular and special meetings of board of directors; quorum.** (a) Unless otherwise provided in the articles or (subject to paragraph (5) of subdivision (a) of Section 204) in the bylaws:

(1) Meetings of the board may be called by the chairman of the board or the president or any vice president or the secretary or any two directors.

(2) Regular meetings of the board may be held without notice if the time and place of such meetings are fixed by the bylaws or the board. Special meetings of the board shall be held upon four days' notice by mail or 48 hours' notice delivered personally or by telephone or telegraph. The articles or bylaws may not dispense with notice of a special meeting. A notice, or waiver of notice, need not specify the purpose of any regular or special meeting of the board.

(3) Notice of a meeting need not be given to any director who signs a waiver of notice or a consent to holding the meeting or an approval of the minutes thereof, whether before or after the meeting, or who attends the meeting without protesting, prior thereto or at its commencement, the lack of notice to such director. All such waivers, consents and approvals shall be filed with the corporate records or made a part of the minutes of the meeting.

(4) A majority of the directors present, whether or not a quorum is present, may adjourn any meeting to another time and place. If the meeting is adjourned for more than 24 hours, notice of any adjournment to another time or place shall be given prior to the time of the adjourned meeting to the directors who were not present at the time of the adjournment.

(5) Meetings of the board may be held at any place within or without the state which has been designated in the notice of the meeting or, if not stated in the notice or there is no notice, designated in the bylaws or by resolution of the board.

(6) Members of the board may participate in a meeting through use of conference telephone or similar communications equipment, so long as all members participating in such meeting can hear one another. Participation in a meeting pursuant to this subdivision constitutes presence in person at such meeting.

(7) A majority of the authorized number of directors constitutes a quorum of the board for the transaction of business. The articles or bylaws may not provide that a quorum shall be less than one-third the authorized number of directors or less than two, whichever is larger, unless the authorized number of directors is one, in which case one director constitutes a quorum.

(8) Every act or decision done or made by a majority of the directors present at a meeting duly held at which a quorum is present is the act of the board, subject to the provisions of Section 310 and subdivision (e) of Section 317. The articles or bylaws may not provide that a lesser vote than a majority of the directors present at a meeting is the act of the board. A meeting at which a quorum is initially present may continue to transact business notwithstanding the withdrawal of directors, if any action taken is approved by at least a majority of the required quorum for such meeting.

(b) Any action required or permitted to be taken by the board may be taken without a meeting, if all members of the board shall individually or collectively consent in writing to such action. Such written consent or consents shall be filed with the minutes of the proceedings of the board. Such action by written consent shall have the same force and effect as a unanimous vote of such directors.

(c) The provisions of this section apply also to committees of the board and incorporators and action by such committees and incorporators, mutatis mutandis.

Sec. 308. **Court appointment of provisional director.** (a) If a corporation has an even number of directors who are equally divided and cannot agree as to the management of its affairs, so that its business can no longer be conducted to advantage or so that there is danger that its property and business will be impaired or lost, the superior court of the proper county may, notwithstanding any provisions of the articles or bylaws and whether or not an action is pending for an involuntary winding up or dissolution of the corporation, appoint a provisional director pursuant to this section. Action for such appointment may be brought by any director or by the holders of not less than 33⅓ percent of the voting power.

(b) If a corporation has an uneven number of directors and the shareholders are deadlocked so that they cannot elect a successor board at an annual meeting of shareholders, the superior court of the proper county may, notwithstanding any provisions of the articles or bylaws, upon petition of a shareholder or shareholders holding 50 percent of the voting power, appoint a provisional director or directors pursuant to this section or order such other equitable relief as the court deems appropriate.

(c) A provisional director shall be an impartial person, who is neither a shareholder nor a creditor of the corporation, nor related by consanguinity or affinity within the third degree according to the common law to any of the other directors of the corporation or to any judge of the court by which such provisional director is appointed. A provisional director shall have all the rights and powers of a director until the deadlock in the board or among shareholders is broken or until such provisional director is removed by order of the court or by approval of the outstanding shares (Section 152). Such person shall be entitled to such compensation as shall be fixed by the court unless otherwise agreed with the corporation.

(d) This section does not apply to corporations subject to the Public Utilities Act (Part 1 (commencing with Section 201 of Division 1 of the Public Utilities Code)).

Sec. 309. **Duties and liabilities of directors.** (a) A director shall perform the duties of a director, including duties as a member of any committee of the board upon which the director may serve, in good faith, in a manner such director believes to be in the best interests of the corporation and with such care, including reasonable inquiry, as an ordinarily prudent person in a like position would use under similar circumstances.

(b) In performing the duties of a director, a director shall be entitled to rely on information, opinions, reports or statements, including financial statements and other financial data, in each case prepared or presented by:

(1) One or more officers or employees of the corporation whom the director believes to be reliable and competent in the matters presented.

(2) Counsel, independent accountants or other persons as to matters which the director believes to be within such person's professional or expert competence, or

(3) A committee of the board upon which the director does not serve, as to matters within its designated authority, which committee the director believes to merit confidence, so long as, in any such case, the director acts in good faith, after reasonable inquiry when the need therefor is indicated by the circumstances and without knowledge that would cause such reliance to be unwarranted.

(c) A person who performs the duties of a director in accordance with subdivisions (a) and (b) shall have no liability based upon any alleged failure to discharge the person's obligations as a director.

Sec. 310. **Transaction between corporation and director or between corporation and another corporation in which director has material financial interest.** (a) No contract or other transaction between a corporation and one or more of its directors, or between a corporation and any corporation, firm or association in which one or more of its directors has a material financial interest, is either void or voidable because such director or directors or such other corporation, firm or association are parties or because such director or directors are present at the meeting of the board or a committee thereof which authorizes, approves or ratifies the contract or transaction, if

(1) The material facts as to the transaction and as to such director's interest are fully disclosed or known to the shareholders and such contract or transaction is approved by the shareholders (Section 153) in good faith, with the shares owned by the interested director or directors not being entitled to vote thereon, or

(2) The material facts as to the transaction and as to such director's interest are fully disclosed or known to the board or committee, and the board or committee authorizes, approves or ratifies the contract or transaction in good faith by a vote sufficient without counting the vote of the interested director or directors and the contract or transaction is just and reasonable as to the corporation at the time it is authorized, approved or ratified, or

(3) As to contracts or transactions not approved as provided in paragraph (1) or (2) of this subdivision, the person asserting the validity of the contract or transaction sustains the burden of proving that the contract or transaction was just and reasonable as to the corporation at the time it was authorized, approved or ratified.

A mere common directorship does not constitute a material financial interest within the meaning of this subdivision. A director is not interested within the meaning of this subdivision in a resolution fixing the compensation of another director as a director, officer or employee of the cor-

poration, notwithstanding the fact that the first director is also receiving compensation from the corporation.

(b) No contract or other transaction between a corporation and any corporatio n or association of which one or more of its directors are directors is either void or voidable because such director or directors are present at the meeting of the board or a committee thereof which authorizes, approves or ratifies the contract or transaction, if

(1) The material facts as to the transaction and as to such director's other directorship are fully disclosed or known to the board or committee, and the board or committee authorizes, approves or ratifies the contract or transaction in good faith by a vote sufficient without counting the vote of the common director or directors or the contract or transaction is approved by the shareholders (Section 153) in good faith, or

(2) As to contracts or transactions not approved as provided in paragraph (1) of this subdivision, the contract or transaction is just and reasonable as to the corporation at the time it is authorized, approved or ratified.

This subdivision does not apply to contracts or transactions covered by subdivision (a).

(c) Interested or common directors may be counted in determining the presence of a quorum at a meeting of the board or a committee thereof which authorizes, approves or ratifies a contract or transaction.

Sec. 311. **Committees.** The board may, by resolution adopted by a majority of the authorized number of directors, designate one or more committees, each consisting of two or more directors, to serve at the pleasure of the board. The board may designate one or more directors as alternate members of any committee, who may replace any absent member at any meeting of the committee. The appointment of members or alternate members of a committee requires the vote of a majority of the authorized number of directors. Any such committee, to the extent provided in the resolution of the board or in the bylaws, shall have all the authority of the board, except with respect to:

(a) The approval of any action for which this division also requires shareholders' approval (Section 153) or approval of the outstanding shares (Section 152).

(b) The filling of vacancies on the board or in any committee.

(c) The fixing of compensation of the directors for serving on the board or on any committee.

(d) The amendment or repeal of bylaws or the adoption of new bylaws.

(e) The amendment or repeal of any resolution of the board which by its express terms is not so amendable or repealable.

(f) A distribution (Section 166), except at a rate, in a periodic amount or within a price range set forth in the articles or determined by the board.

(g) The appointment of other committees of the board or the members thereof.

Sec. 312. **Corporate officers.** (a) A corporation shall have a chairman of the board or a president or both, a secretary, a chief financial officer and such other officers with such titles and duties as shall be stated in the bylaws or determined by the board and as may be necessary to enable it to sign instruments and share certificates. The president, or if there is no president the chairman of the board, is the general manager and chief executive officer of the corporation, unless otherwise provided in the articles or bylaws. Any number of offices may be held by the same person unless the articles or bylaws provide otherwise.

(b) Except as otherwise provided by the articles or bylaws, officers shall be chosen by the board and serve at the pleasure of the board, subject to the rights, if any, of an officer under any contract of employment. Any officer may resign at any time upon written notice to the corporation without prejudice to the rights, if any, of the corporation under any contract to which the officer is a party.

Sec. 313. **Apparent authority of signing officers.** Subject to the provisions of subdivision (a) of Section 208, any note, mortgage, evidence of indebtedness, contract, share certificate, conveyance or other instrument in writing, and any assignment or endorsement thereof, executed or entered into between any corporation and any other person, when signed by the chairman of the board, the president or any vice president and the secretary, any assistant secretary, the chief financial officer or any assistant treasurer of such corporation, is not invalidated as to the corporation by any lack of authority of the signing officers in the absence of actual knowledge on the part of the other person that the signing officers had no authority to execute the same.

Sec. 314. **Proof of adoption of bylaws and of corporate proceedings.** The original or a copy of the bylaws or of the minutes of any incorporators', shareholders', directors', committee or other meeting or of any resolution adopted by the board or a committee thereof, or shareholders, certified to be a true copy by a person purporting to be the secretary or an assistant secretary of the corporation, is prima facie evidence of the adoption of such bylaws or resolution or of the due holding of such meeting and of the matters stated therein.

Sec. 315. **Loans or guarantees of obligations of directors, officers or other persons.** (a) A corporation shall not make any loan of money or property to, or guarantee the obligation of, any director or officer of the corporation or its parent or subsidiary, unless the transaction or an employee benefit plan authorizing such loans or guaranties, after disclosure of the right under such a plan to include officers or directors (1) is approved by the shareholders (Section 153), with the shares owned by the director or officer, or by the directors or officers then eligible to participate in such plan not being entitled to vote thereon or (2) is approved by the unanimous vote of the shareholders.

(b) Notwithstanding subdivision (a), if the corporation has outstanding shares held of record by 100 or more persons (determined as provided in Section 605) on the date of approval by the board, and has a bylaw approved by the outstanding shares (Section 152) authorizing the board alone to approve such a loan or guaranty to an officer, whether or not a director, or an employee benefit plan authorizing such a loan or guaranty to an officer, such a loan or guaranty or employee benefit plan may be approved by the board alone by a vote sufficient without counting the vote of any interested director or directors if the board determines that such a loan or guaranty or plan may reasonably be expected to benefit the corporation.

(c) A corporation shall not make any loan of money or property to, or guarantee the obligation of, any person upon the security of shares of the corporation or of its parent, unless the loan or guaranty is (1) otherwise adequately secured, (2) made pursuant to an employee benefit plan permitted by Section 408, (3) approved by the shareholders (Section 153) with the shares owned by the borrower not entitled to vote, or (4) approved by unanimous vote of the shareholders.

(d) Notwithstanding subdivision (a) a corporation may advance money to a director or officer of the corporation or of its parent or any subsidiary for any expenses reasonably anticipated to be incurred in the performance of the duties of such director or officer, provided that in the absence of such advance such director or officer would be entitled to be reimbursed for such expenses by such corporation, its parent or any subsidiary.

(e) The provisions of subdivision (a) do not apply to the payment of premiums in whole or in part by a corporation on a life insurance policy on the life of a director or officer so long as repayment to the corporation of the amount paid by it is secured by the proceeds of the policy and its cash surrender value.

(f) This section does not apply to any corporation subject to the Banking Law or to industrial loan companies or credit unions or to loans permitted under any statute regulating any special class of corporations.

Sec. 316. **Liability of directors for distributions and for loans or guarantees.** (a) Subject to the provisions of Section 309, directors of a corporation who approve any of the following corporate actions shall be jointly and severally liable to the corporation for the benefit of all of the creditors or shareholders entitled to institute an action under subdivision (c):

(1) The making of any distribution to its shareholders to the extent that it is contrary to the provisions of Sections 500 to 503, inclusive.

(2) The distribution of assets to shareholders after institution of dissolution proceedings of the corporation, without paying or adequately providing for all known liabilities of the corporation, excluding any claims not filed by creditors within the time limit set by the court in a notice given to creditors under Chapter 18 (commencing with Section 1800), 19 (commencing with Section 1900) and 20 (commencing with Section 2000).

(3) The making of any loan or guaranty contrary to Section 315.

(b) A director who is present at a meeting of the board, or any committee thereof, at which action specified in subdivision (a) is taken and who abstains from voting shall be considered to have approved the action.

(c) Suit may be brought in the name of the corporation to enforce the liability (1) under paragraph (1) of subdivision (a) against any or all directors liable by the persons entitled to sue under subdivision (b) of Section 506, (2) under paragraph (2) or (3) of subdivision (a) against any or all directors liable by any one or more creditors of the corporation whose debts or claims arose prior to the time of any of the corporate actions specified in paragraph (2) or (3) of subdivision (a) and who have not consented to the corporate action, whether or not they have reduced their claims to judgment, or (3) under paragraph (3) of subdivision (a) against any or all directors liable by any one or more holders of shares outstanding at the time of any corporate action specified in paragraph (3) of subdivision (a) who have not consented to the corporate action, without regard to the provisions of Section 800.

(d) The damages recoverable from a director under this section shall be the amount of the illegal distribution or the loss suffered by the corporation as a result of the illegal loan or guaranty, as the case may be, but not exceeding the liabilities of the corporation owed to nonconsenting creditors at the time of the violation and the injury suffered by nonconsenting shareholders, as the case may be.

(e) Any director sued under this section may implead all other directors liable and may compel contribution, either in that action or in an independent action against directors not joined in that action.

(f) Directors liable under this section shall also be entitled to be subrogated to the rights of the corporation:

(1) With respect to paragraph (1) of subdivision (a), against shareholders who received the distribution.

(2) With respect to paragraph (2) of subdivision (a), against shareholders who received the distribution of assets.

(3) With respect to paragraph (3) of subdivision (a), against the person who received the loan or guaranty.

Any director sued under this section may file a cross-complaint against the person or persons who are liable to such director as a result of the subrogation provided for in this subdivision or may proceed against them in an independent action.

Sec. 317. **Indemnification of corporate "agent."** (a) For the purposes of this section, "agent" means any person who is or was a director, officer, employee or other agent of the corporation, or is or was serving at the request of the corporation as a director, officer, employee or agent of another foreign or domestic corporation, partnership, joint venture, trust or other enterprise, or was a director, officer, employee or agent of a foreign or domestic corporation which was a predecessor corporation of the corporation or of another enterprise at the request of such predecessor corporation; "proceeding" means any threatened, pending or completed action or proceeding, whether civil, criminal, administrative or investigative; and "expenses" includes without limitation attorneys' fees and any expenses of establishing a right to indemnification under subdivision (d) or paragraph (3) of subdivision (e).

(b) A corporation shall have power to indemnify any person who was or is a party or is threatened to be made a party to any proceeding (other than an action by or in the right of the corporation to procure a judgment in its favor) by reason of the fact that such person is or was an agent of the corporation, against expenses, judgments, fines, settlements and other amounts actually and reasonably incurred in connection with such proceeding if such person acted in good faith and in a manner such person reasonably believed to be in the best interests of the corporation and, in the case of a criminal proceeding, had no reasonable cause to believe the conduct of such person was unlawful. The termination of any proceeding by judgment, order, settlement, conviction or upon a plea of nolo contendere or its equivalent shall not, of itself, create a presumption that the person did not act in good faith and in a manner which the person reasonably believed to be in the best interests of the corporation or that the person had reasonable cause to believe that the person's conduct was unlawful.

(c) A corporation shall have power to indemnify any person who was or is a party or is threatened to be made a party to any threatened, pending or completed action by or in the right of the corporation to procure a judgment in its favor by reason of the fact that such person is or was an agent of the corporation, against expenses actually and reasonably incurred by such person in connection with the defense or settlement of such action if such person acted in good faith, in a manner such person believed to be in the best interests of the corporation and with such care, including reasonable inquiry, as an ordinarily prudent person in a like position would use under similar circumstances. No indemnification shall be made under this subdivision (c):

(1) In respect of any claim, issue or matter as to which such person shall have been adjudged to be liable to the corporation in the performance of such person's duty to the corporation, unless and only to the extent that the court in which such proceeding is or was pending shall determine upon application that, in view of all the circumstances of the case, such person is fairly and reasonably entitled to indemnity for the expenses which such court shall determine;

(2) Of amounts paid in settling or otherwise disposing of a threatened or pending action, with or without court approval; or

(3) Of expenses incurred in defending a threatened or pending action which is settled or otherwise disposed of without court approval.

(d) To the extent that an agent of a corporation has been successful on the merits in defense of any proceeding referred to in subdivision (b) or (c) or in defense of any claim, issue or matter therein, the agent shall be indemnified against expenses actually and reasonably incurred by the agent in connection therewith.

(e) Except as provided in subdivision (d), any indemnification under this section shall be made by the corporation only if authorized in the specific case, upon a determination that indemnification of the agent is proper in the circumstances because the agent has met the applicable standard of conduct set forth in subdivision (b) or (c), by:

(1) A majority vote of a quorum consisting of directors who are not parties to such proceedings;

(2) Approval of the shareholders (Section 153), with the shares owned by the person to be indemnified not being entitled to vote thereon; or

(3) The court in which such proceeding is or was pending upon application made by the corporation or the agent or the attorney or other person rendering services in connection with the defense, whether or not such application by the agent, attorney or other person is opposed by the corporation.

(f) Expenses incurred in defending any proceeding may be advanced by the corporation prior to the final disposition of such proceeding upon receipt of an undertaking by or on behalf of the agent to repay such amount unless it shall be determined ultimately that the agent is entitled to be indemnified as authorized in this section.

(g) No provision made by a corporation to indemnify its or its subsidiary's directors or officers for the defense of any proceeding, whether contained in the articles, bylaws, a resolution of shareholders or directors, an agreement or otherwise, shall be valid unless consistent with this section. Nothing contained in this section shall affect any right to indemnification to which persons other than such directors and officers may be entitled by contract or otherwise.

(h) No indemnification or advance shall be made under this section, except as provided in subdivision (d) or paragraph (3) of subdivision (e), in any circumstance where it appears:

(1) That it would be inconsistent with a provision of the articles, bylaws, a resolution of the shareholders or an agreement in effect at the time of the accrual of the alleged cause of action asserted in the proceeding in which the expenses were incurred or other amounts were paid, which prohibits or otherwise limits indemnification; or

(2) That it would be inconsistent with any condition expressly imposed by a court in approving a settlement.

(i) A corporation shall have power to purchase and maintain insurance on behalf of any agent of the corporation against any liability asserted against or incurred by the agent in such capacity or arising out of the agent's status as such whether or not the corporation would have the power to indemnify the agent against such liability under the provisions of this section.

(j) This section does not apply to any proceeding against any trustee, investment manager or other fiduciary of an employee benefit plan in such person's capacity as such, even though such person may also be an agent as defined in subdivision (a) of the employer corporation. A corporation shall have power to indemnify such a trustee, investment manager or other fiduciary to the extent permitted by subdivision (f) of Section 207.

CHAPTER 4

SHARES AND SHARE CERTIFICATES

Sec. 400. **Issuance of classes or series of shares; limitations on distinctions as to rights.** (a) A corporation may issue one or more classes or series of shares or both, with full, limited or no voting rights and with such other rights, preferences, privileges and restrictions as are stated or authorized in its articles. No denial or limitation of voting rights shall be effective unless at the time one or more classes or series of outstanding shares or debt securities, singly or in the aggregate, are entitled to full voting rights; and no denial or limitation of dividend or liquidation rights shall be effective unless at the time one or more classes or series of outstanding shares, singly or in the aggregate, are entitled to unlimited dividend and liquidation rights.

(b) All shares of any one class shall have the same voting, conversion and redemption rights and other rights, preferences, privileges and restrictions, unless the class is divided into series. If a class is divided into series, all the shares of any one series shall have the same voting, conversion and redemption rights and other rights, preferences, privileges and restrictions.

Sec. 401. **Issuance of shares with preferences and restrictions set by resolution of board; filing of certificate of determination.** (a) Before any corporation issues any shares of any class or series of which the rights, preferences, privileges and restrictions, or any of them, or the number of shares constituting any series or the designation of such series, are not set forth in its articles but are fixed in a resolution adopted by the board pursuant to authority given by its articles, an officers' certificate setting forth a copy of the resolution, the number of shares of the class or series and that none of the shares of such class or series has been issued shall be executed and filed.

(b) After any certificate of determination has been filed, but before the corporation issues any shares of the class or series covered thereby, the board may alter or revoke any right, preference, privilege or restriction fixed or determined by the resolution set forth therein by the adoption of another resolution appropriate for that purpose and the execution and filing of an officers' certificate setting forth a copy of the resolution, and stating that none of the shares of the class or the series affected has been issued. No right, preference, privilege or restriction may be altered or revoked after the issue of any shares of the class or series specifically affected other than by amendment to the articles pursuant to Chapter 9.

(c) After any certificate of determination has been filed, the board may, if authorized in the articles pursuant to subdivision (e) of Section 202, increase or decrease the number of shares constituting any series, by the adoption of another resolution appropriate for that purpose and the execution and filing of an officers' certificate setting forth a copy of such resolution, the number of shares of such series then outstanding and the increase or decrease in the number of shares constituting such series. If any such certificate of determination has been incorporated in restated articles filed pursuant to Section 910, the action authorized by this subdivision may, notwithstanding Section 902, be accomplished by an amendment of the articles approved by the board alone.

Sec. 402. **Redeemable shares.** (a) A corporation may provide in its articles for one or more classes or series of shares which are redeemable, in whole or in part, (1) at the option of the corporation or (2) to the extent and upon the happening of one or more specified events, and not otherwise except as herein provided. A corporation may provide in its articles for one or more classes or series of preferred shares which are redeemable, in whole or in part, (1) as specified above, (2) at the option of the holder, or (3) upon the vote of at least a majority of the outstanding shares of the class or series to be redeemed. An open end investment company registered under the United States Investment Company Act of 1940 may, if its articles so provide, issue shares which are redeemable at the option of the holder at a price approximately equal to the shares' proportionate interest in the net assets of the corporation and a shareholder may compel redemption of such shares in accordance with their terms.

(b) Any such redemption shall be effected at such price or prices, within such time and upon such terms and conditions as are stated in the articles. When the articles permit partial redemption of a class or series of shares, the articles shall prescribe the method of selecting the shares to be redeemed, which may be pro rata, by lot, at the discretion of, or in a manner approved by, the board or upon such other terms as are specified in the articles.

(c) No redeemable common shares, other than (1) shares issued by an open end investment company registered under the United States Investment Company Act of 1940, (2) shares of a corporation which has a license or franchise from a governmental agency to conduct its business or is a member corporation of a national securities exchange registered under the United States Securities Exchange Act of 1934, which license, franchise or membership is conditioned upon some or all of the holders of its stock possessing prescribed qualifications, to the extent necessary to prevent the loss of such license, franchise or membership or to reinstate it, or (3) shares of a professional corporation as defined in Part 4 (commencing with Section 13400) of Division 3 of Title 1, shall be issued or redeemed unless the corporation at the time has outstanding a class of common shares that is not subject to redemption.

(d) Any redemption by a corporation of its shares shall be subject to the provisions of Chapter 5 (commencing with Section 500). Nothing in this section shall prevent a corporation from creating a sinking fund or similar provision for, or entering into an agreement for, the redemption or purchase of its shares to the extent permitted by Chapter 5, but unless such purchase or redemption is permitted under Chapter 5, the holder of shares to be so purchased or redeemed shall not become a creditor of the corporation.

Sec. 402.5. **Preferred shares: optional provisions.** The rights, preferences, privileges, and restrictions granted to or imposed upon a class or series of preferred shares (Section 176) the designation of which includes either the word "preferred" or the word "preference" may:

(a) Notwithstanding paragraph (9) of subdivision (a) of Section 204, include a provision requiring a vote of a specified percentage or proportion of the outstanding shares of the class or series that is less than a majority of the class or series to approve any corporate action, except where the vote of a majority or greater proportion of the class or series is required by this division, regardless of restrictions or limitations on the voting rights thereof.

(b) Notwithstanding paragraph (5) of subdivision (a) of Section 204, provide that in addition to the requirement of subdivision (a) of Section 1900 the corporation may voluntarily wind up and dissolve only upon the vote of a specified percentage (which shall not exceed 66⅔ percent) of such class or series.

(c) Provide that Section 502 or 503 not apply in whole or in part with respect to distributions on shares junior to the class or series.

Sec. 403. **Convertible shares and debt securities.** (a) When so provided in the articles, a corporation may issue shares convertible within such time or upon the happening of one or more specified events and upon such terms and conditions as are stated in the articles:

(1) At the option of the holder or automatically upon either the vote of at least a majority of the outstanding shares of the class or series to be converted or upon the happening of one or more specified events, into shares of any class or series; or

(2) If it is a corporation which has a license or franchise from a governmental agency to conduct its business or a member corporation of a national securities exchange registered under the United States Securities Exchange Act of 1934, the license, franchise or membership of which is conditioned upon some or all of the holders of its stock possessing prescribed qualifications, to the extent necessary to prevent the loss of such license, franchise or membership or to reinstate it, at the option of the corporation, into shares of any class or series or into any other security of the corporation.

(b) Unless otherwise provided in the articles, a corporation may issue its debt securities convertible into other debt securities or into shares of the corporation within such time or upon the happening of one or more specified events and upon such terms and conditions as are fixed by the board.

Sec. 404. **Options.** Either in connection with the issue, subscription or sale of any of its shares, bonds, debentures, notes or other securities or independently thereof, a corporation may grant options to purchase or subscribe for shares of any class or series upon such terms and conditions as may be deemed expedient. Option rights may be transferable or nontransferable and separable or inseparable from other securities of the corporation.

Sec. 405. **Authorization of additional shares for satisfaction of option and conversion rights.** (a) If at the time of granting option or conversion rights or at any later time the corporation is not authorized by its articles to issue all the shares required for the satisfaction of the rights, if and when exercised, the additional number of shares required to be issued upon the exercise of such option or conversion rights shall be authorized by an amendment to the articles.

(b) If a corporation has obtained approval of the outstanding shares (Section 152) for the issue of options to purchase shares or of securities convertible into shares of the corporation, the board may, without further approval of the outstanding shares (Section 152), amend the articles to increase the authorized shares of any class or series to such number as will be sufficient from time to time, when added to the previously authorized but unissued shares of such class or series, to satisfy any such option or conversion rights.

Sec. 406. **Securities having conversion or option rights—prior offer to shareholders not required.** Unless the articles provide otherwise, the board may issue shares, options or securities having conversion or option rights without first offering them to shareholders of any class.

Sec. 407. **Fractional shares.** A corporation may, but is not required to, issue fractions of a share originally or upon transfer. If it does not issue fractions of a share, it shall in connection with any original issuance of shares (a) arrange for the disposition of fractional interests by those entitled thereto, (b) pay in cash the fair value of fractions of a share as of the time when those entitled to receive such fractions are determined or (c) issue scrip or warrants in registered or bearer form which shall entitle the holder to receive a certificate for a full share upon the surrender of such scrip or warrants aggregating a full share; provided, however, that, if the fraction of a share which any person would otherwise be entitled to receive in a merger or reorganization is less than one-half of 1 percent of the total shares such person is entitled to receive, a merger or reorganization agreement may provide that fractions of a share will be disregarded or that shares issuable in the merger will be rounded off to the nearest whole share; and provided, further, that a corporation may not pay cash for fractional shares if such action would result in the cancellation of more than 10 percent of the outstanding shares of any class. A determination by the board of the fair value of fractions of a share shall be conclusive in the absence of fraud. A certificate for a fractional share shall, but scrip or warrants shall not unless otherwise provided therein, entitle the holder to exercise voting rights, to receive dividends thereon and to participate in any of the assets of the corporation in the event of liquidation. The board may cause scrip or warrants to be issued subject to the condition that they shall become void if not exchanged for certificates representing full shares before a specified date or that the shares for which scrip or warrants are exchangeable may be sold by the corporation and the proceeds thereof distributed to the holder of the scrip or warrants or any other condition which the board may impose.

Sec. 408. **Employee stock purchase or stock option plans.** (a) A corporation may adopt and carry out a stock purchase plan or agreement or stock option plan or agreement providing for the issue and sale for such consideration as may be fixed of its unissued shares, or of issued shares acquired or to be acquired, to one or more of the employees or directors of the corporation or of a subsidiary or parent thereof or to a trustee on their behalf and for the payment for such shares in installments or at one time, and may provide for aiding any such persons in paying for such shares by compensation for services rendered, promissory notes or otherwise.

(b) A stock purchase plan or agreement or stock option plan or agreement may include, among other features, the fixing of eligibility for participation therein, the class and price of shares to be issued or sold under the plan or agreement, the number of shares which may be subscribed for, the method of payment therefor, the reservation of title until full payment therefor, the effect of the termination of employment, an option or obligation on the part of the corporation to repurchase the shares upon termination of employment, subject to the provisions of Chapter 5, restrictions upon transfer of the shares and the time limits of and termination of the plan.

(c) Sections 406 and 407 of the Labor Code shall not apply to shares issued by any foreign or domestic corporation to the following persons:

(1) Any employee of the corporation or of any parent or subsidiary thereof, pursuant to a stock purchase plan or agreement or stock option plan or agreement provided for in subdivision (a).

(2) In any transaction in connection with securing employment, to a persons who is or is about to become an officer of the corporation or of any parent or subsidiary thereof.

Sec. 409. **Consideration for issuance of shares; issuance prior to full payment; resolution determining fair market value of consideration other than money.** (a) Shares may be issued:

(1) For such consideration as is determined from time to time by the board, or by the shareholders if the articles so provide, consisting of any or all of the following: money paid; labor done; services actually rendered to the corporation or for its benefit or in its formation or reorganization; debts or securities canceled; and tangible or intangible property actually received either by the issuing corporation or by a wholly owned subsidiary; but neither promissory notes of the purchaser (unless adequately secured by collateral other than the shares acquired or unless permitted by Section 408) nor future services shall constitute payment or part payment for shares of the corporation; or

(2) As a share dividend or upon a stock split, reverse stock split, reclassification of outstanding shares into shares of another class, conversion of outstanding shares into shares of another class, exchange of outstanding shares for shares of another class or other change affecting outstanding shares.

(b) Except as provided in subdivision (d), shares issued as provided in this section or Section 408 shall be declared and taken to be fully paid stock and not liable to any further call nor shall the holder thereof be liable for any further payments under the provisions of this division. In the absence of fraud in the transaction, the judgment of the directors as to the value of the consideration for shares shall be conclusive.

(c) If the articles reserve to the shareholders the right to determine the consideration for the issue of any shares, such determination shall be made by approval of the outstanding shares (Section 152).

(d) A corporation may issue the whole or any part of its shares as partly paid and subject to call for the remainder of the consideration to be paid therefor. On the certificate issued to represent any such partly paid shares the total amount of the consideration to be paid therefor and the amount paid thereon shall be stated. Upon the declaration of any dividend on fully paid shares, the corporation shall declare a dividend upon partly paid shares of the same class, but only upon the basis of the percentage of the consideration actually paid thereon.

(e) The board shall state by resolution its determination of the fair value to the corporation in monetary terms of any consideration other than money for which shares are issued. This subdivision does not affect the accounting treatment of any transaction, which shall be in conformity with generally accepted accounting principles.

Sec. 410. **Liability of subscribers and issuees for payment.** (a) Every subscriber to shares and every other person to whom shares are originally issued is liable to the corporation for the full consideration agreed to be paid for the shares.

(b) The full agreed consideration for shares shall be paid prior to or concurrently with the issuance thereof, unless the shares are issued as partly paid pursuant to subdivision (d) of Section 409, in which case the consideration shall be paid in accordance with the agreement of subscription or purchase.

Sec. 411. **Liability of transferee without knowledge of nonpayment.** A transferee of shares for which the full agreed consideration has not been paid to the issuing corporation, who acquired them in good faith, without knowledge that they were not paid in full or to the extent stated on the certificate representing them, is liable only for the amount shown by the certificate to be unpaid on the shares represented thereby, until the transferee transfers the shares to one who becomes liable therefor; provided that the transferor shall remain personally liable if so provided on the certificate or agreed upon in writing. The liability of any holder of such shares who derives title through such a transferee and who is not a party to any fraud affecting the issue of the shares is the same as that of the transferee through whom title is derived.

Sec. 412. **Liability of transferee with knowledge of nonpayment.** Every transferee of partly paid shares who acquired them under a certificate showing the fact of part payment, and every transferee of such shares (other than a transferee who derives title through a holder in good faith without knowledge and who is not a party to any fraud affecting the issue of such shares) who acquired them with actual knowledge that the full agreed consideration had not been paid to the extent stated on the certificate therefor, is personally liable to the corporation for installments of the amount unpaid becoming due until the shares are transferred to one who becomes liable therefor; provided that the transferor shall remain personally liable if so provided on the certificate or agreed upon in writing.

Sec. 413. **Liability of representative or fiduciary for nonpayment.** A person holding shares as pledgee, executor, administrator, guardian, conservator, trustee, receiver or in any representative or fiduciary capacity is not personally liable for any unpaid balance of the subscription price of the shares because the shares are so held but the estate and funds in the hands of such fiduciary or representative are liable and the shares are subject to sale therefor.

Sec. 414. **Creditor's action to reach and apply shareholder's liability.** (a) No action shall be brought by or on behalf of any creditor to reach and apply the liability, if any, of a shareholder to the corporation to pay the amount due on such shareholder's shares unless final judgment has been rendered in favor of the creditor against the corporation and execution has been returned unsatisfied in whole or in part or unless such proceedings would be useless.

(b) All creditors of the corporation, with or without reducing their claims to judgment, may intervene in any such creditor's action to reach and apply unpaid subscriptions and any or all shareholders who hold partly paid shares may be joined in such action. Several judgments may be rendered for and against the parties to the action or in favor of a receiver for the benefit of the respective parties thereto.

(c) All amounts paid by any shareholder in any such action shall be credited on the unpaid balance due the corporation upon such shareholder's shares.

Sec. 415. **Remedies for fraud or illegality.** Nothing in this division shall be construed as a derogation of any rights or remedies which any

creditor or shareholder may have against any promoter, shareholder, director, officer or the corporation because of participation in any fraud or illegality practiced upon such creditor or shareholder by any such person or by the corporation in connection with the issue or sale of shares or other securities or in derogation of any rights which the corporation may have by rescission, cancellation or otherwise because of any fraud or illegality practiced on it by any such person in connection with the issue or sale of shares or other securities.

Sec. 416. **Right to share certificate.** (a) Every holder of shares in a corporation shall be entitled to have a certificate signed in the name of the corporation by the chairman or vice chairman of the board or the president or a vice president and by the chief financial officer or an assistant treasurer or the secretary or any assistant secretary, certifying the number of shares and the class or series of shares owned by the shareholder. Any or all of the signatures on the certificate may be facsimile. In case any officer, transfer agent or registrar who has signed or whose facsimile signature has been placed upon a certificate shall have ceased to be such officer, transfer agent or registrar before such certificate is issued, it may be issued by the corporation with the same effect as if such person were an officer, transfer agent or registrar at the date of issue.

(b) Notwithstanding subdivision (a), a corporation which is the issuer of securities registered under the United States Securities Exchange Act of 1934 or which is registered under the United States Investment Company Act of 1940 may adopt a system of issuance, recordation and transfer of its shares by electronic or other means not involving any issuance of certificates, including provisions for notice to purchasers in substitution for the required statements on certificates under Sections 417 and 418, which system has been approved by the Commissioner of Corporations or the United States Securities and Exchange Commission or which is authorized in any statute of the United States.

Sec. 417. **Required statements on certificates involving classified shares.** If the shares of the corporation are classified or if any class of shares has two or more series, there shall appear on the certificate one of the following:

(a) A statement of the rights, preferences, privileges and restrictions granted to or imposed upon each class or series of shares authorized to be issued and upon the holders thereof.

(b) A summary of such rights, preferences, privileges and restrictions with reference to the provisions of the articles and any certificates of determination establishing the same.

(c) A statement setting forth the office or agency of the corporation from which shareholders may obtain, upon request and without charge, a copy of the statement referred to in subdivision (a).

Sec. 418. **Additional statements when applicable; close corporations.** (a) There shall also appear on the certificate (unless stated or summarized under subdivision (a) or (b) of Section 417) the statements required by all of the following clauses to the extent applicable:

(1) The fact that the shares are subject to restrictions upon transfer.

(2) If the shares are assessable or are not fully paid, a statement that they are assessable or the statements required by subdivision (d) of Section 409 if they are not fully paid.

(3) The fact that the shares are subject to a voting agreement under subdivision (a) of Section 706 or an irrevocable proxy under subdivision (e) of Section 705 or restrictions upon voting rights contractually imposed by the corporation.

(4) The fact that the shares are redeemable.

(5) The fact that the shares are convertible and the period for conversion.

Any such statement or reference thereto (Section 174) on the face of the certificate required by paragraph (1) or (2) shall be conspicuous.

(b) Unless stated on the certificate as required by subdivision (a) , no restriction upon transfer, no liability to assessment or for the unpaid portion of the subscription price, no right of redemption and no voting agreement under subdivision (a) of Section 706 nor irrevocable proxy under subdivision (e) of Section 705 nor voting restriction imposed by the corporation shall be enforceable against a transferee of the shares without actual knowledge of such restriction, liability, right, agreement or proxy. For the purpose of this subdivision, transferee includes a purchaser from the corporation.

(c) All certificates representing shares of a close corporation shall contain, in addition to any other statements required by this section, the following conspicuous legend on the face thereof: "This corporation is a close corporation. The number of holders of record of its shares of all classes cannot exceed . . . [a number not in excess of 35]. Any attempted voluntary inter vivos transfer which would violate this requirement is void. Refer to the articles, bylaws and any agreements on file with the secretary of the corporation for further restrictions."

(d) Any attempted voluntary inter vivos transfer of the shares of a close corporation which would result in the number of holders of record of its shares exceeding the maximum number specified in its articles is void if the certificate contains the legend required by subdivision (c).

Sec. 419. Lost, stolen or destroyed certificates.

(a) A domestic or foreign corporation may issue a new share certificate or a new certificate for any other security in the place of any certificate theretofore issued by it, alleged to have been lost, stolen or destroyed, and the corporation may require the owner of the lost, stolen or destroyed certificate or the owner's legal representative to give the corporation a bond (or other adequate security) sufficient to indemnify it against any claim that may be made against it (including any expense or liability) on account of the alleged loss, theft or destruction of any such certificate or the issuance of such new certificate.

(b) If a corporation refuses to issue a new share certificate or other certificate in place of one theretofore issued by it, or by any corporation of which it is the lawful successor, alleged to have been lost, stolen or destroyed, the owner of the lost, stolen or destroyed certificate or the owner's legal representative may bring an action in the superior court of the proper county for an order requiring the corporation to issue a new certificate in place of the one lost, stolen or destroyed.

(c) If the court is satisfied that the plaintiff is the lawful owner of the number of shares or other securities, or any part thereof, described in the complaint and that the certificate therefor has been lost, stolen or destroyed, and no sufficient cause has been shown why a new certificate should not be issued in place thereof, it shall make an order requiring the corporation to issue and deliver to the plaintiff a new certificate for such shares or other securities. In its order the court shall direct that, prior to the issuance and delivery to the plaintiff of such new certificate, the plaintiff give the corporation a bond (or other adequate security) as to the court appears sufficient to indemnify the corporation against any claim that may be made against it (including any expense or liability) on account of the alleged loss, theft or destruction of any such certificate or the issuance of such new certificate.

Sec. 420. Liability for transfer of shares on books of corporation.

Neither a domestic nor foreign corporation nor its transfer agent or registrar is liable:

(a) For transferring or causing to be transferred on the books of the corporation to the surviving joint tenant or tenants any share or shares or other securities issued to two or more persons in joint tenancy, whether or not the transfer is made with actual or constructive knowledge of the existence of any understanding, agreement, condition or evidence that the shares or securities were held other than in joint tenancy or of a breach of trust by any joint tenant.

(b) To a minor or incompetent person in whose name shares or other securities are of record on its books or to any transferee of or transferor to either for transferring the shares or other securities on its books at the instance of or to the minor or incompetent or for the recognition of or dealing with the minor or incompetent as a shareholder or security holder, whether or not the corporation, transfer agent or registrar had notice, actual or constructive, of the nonage or incompetency, unless a guardian or conservator of the property of the minor or incompetent has been appointed and the corporation, transfer agent or registrar has received written notice thereof.

(c) To any married person or to any transferee of such person for transferring shares or other securities on its books at the instance of the person in whose name they are registered, without the signature of such person's spouse and regardless of whether the registration indicates that the shares or other securities are community property, in the same manner as if such person were unmarried.

(d) For transferring or causing to be transferred on the books of the corporation shares or other securities pursuant to a judgment or order of a court which has been set aside, modified or reversed unless, prior to the registration of the transfer on the books of the corporation, written notice is served upon the corporation or its transfer agent in the manner provided by law for the service of a summons in a civil action, stating that an appeal or other further court proceeding has been or is to be taken from or with regard to such judgment or order. After the service of such notice neither the corporation nor its transfer agent has any duty to register the requested transfer until the corporation or its transfer agent has received a certificate of the county clerk of the county in which the judg-

ment or order was entered or made, showing that the judgment or order has become final.

(e) The provisions of the California Commercial Code shall not affect the limitations of liability set forth in this section. Section 5125 of the Civil Code shall be subject to the provisions of this section and shall not be construed to prevent transfers, or result in liability to the corporation, transfer agent or registrar permitting or effecting transfers, which comply with this section.

Sec. 421. Restriction on transfer of shares of close corporation.

Each holder of shares of a close corporation, whether original or subsequent, by accepting the certificates for the shares which contain the legend required by subdivision (c) of Section 418 agrees and consents that such holder cannot make any transfer of shares which would violate the provisions of subdivision (d) of Section 418 and waives any right which such holder might otherwise have under any other law to sell such shares to a greater number of purchasers or to demand any registration thereof under the Securities Act of 1933, as now or hereafter amended, or as provided in any statute adopted in substitution therefor, or otherwise, so long as the corporation is a close corporation.

Sec. 422. Compulsory exchange of certificates.

(a) When the articles are amended in any way affecting the statements contained in the certificates for outstanding shares, or it becomes desirable for any reason, in the discretion of the board, to cancel any outstanding certificate for shares and issue a new certificate therefor conforming to the rights of the holder, the board may order any holders of outstanding certificates for shares to surrender and exchange them for new certificates within a reasonable time to be fixed by the board.

(b) The order may provide that a holder of any certificates so ordered to be surrendered is not entitled to vote or to receive dividends or exercise any of the other rights of shareholders until the holder has complied with the order, but such order operates to suspend such rights only after notice and until compliance. The duty of surrender of any outstanding certificates may also be enforced by civil action.

Sec. 423. Assessment of shares.

(a) Shares are not assessable except as provided in this section or as otherwise provided by a statute other than this division. If the articles expressly confer such authority upon the corporation or the board, and subject to any limitations therein contained, the board may in its discretion levy and collect assessments upon all shares of any or all classes made subject to assessment by the articles. This authority is in addition to the right of the corporation to recover the unpaid subscription price of shares or the remainder of the consideration to be paid therefor.

(b) Every levy of an assessment shall: specify the amount thereof and to whom and where it is payable; fix, or if proceedings or filings with any governmental or other agency for any qualification, permit, registration or exemption therefrom are required as a condition precedent to the levy or payment of an assessment provide for the establishment of, a date on which the assessment is payable; fix a date, not less than 30 nor more than 60 days from the date on which the assessment is payable, on which such assessment becomes delinquent if not paid; and fix a date, not less than 15 nor more than 60 days from the date on which the unpaid assessment becomes delinquent, for the sale of delinquent shares The levy also shall fix the hour and place of sale, which place shall be in the county where the corporation is required to keep a copy of its bylaws pursuant to Section 213, or if there is no such county, in Sacramento.

(c) On or before the date an assessment is payable, the secretary of the corporation shall give notice thereof in substantially the following form:

(Name of corporation in full. Location of principal executive office.)

Notice is hereby given that the board of directors on (date) has levied an assessment of (amount) per share upon the (name or designation of class or series of shares) of the corporation payable (to whom and where). Any shares upon which this assessment remains unpaid on (date fixed) will be delinquent. Unless payment is made prior to delinquency, the said shares, or as many of them as may be necessary, will be sold at (particular place) on (date) at (hour) of such day, to pay the delinquent assessment, together with a penalty of 5 percent of the amount of the assessment on such shares, or be forfeited to the corporation. (Name of secretary with location of office.)

(d) The notice shall be served personally upon each holder of record of shares assessed; provided, however, that in lieu of personal service the notice may be mailed to each such shareholder addressed to the last address of the shareholder appearing on the books of the corporation or given by the shareholder to the corporation for the purpose of notice, or if no such address appears or is given, at the place where the principal executive office of the corporation is located, and published once in some newspaper of general circulation in the county in which the principal executive office of the corporation is located. If there is no such newspaper in such county, the publication shall be made in some newspaper of general circulation in an adjoining county.

(e) The assessment is a lien upon the shares assessed from the time of personal service or the publication of the notice of assessment, unless the articles provide for such lien from the time of the levy. Unless otherwise provided by law, a transfer of the shares on the books of the corporation after the lien of an assessment has attached is a waiver of the lien unless a conspicuous legend is placed on the face of any certificate issued upon such transfer setting forth the information contained in the notice required by subdivision (c). Such legend shall be removed if the assessment on the shares evidenced by the certificate is paid or if the shares are sold to pay the assessment or forfeited for nonpayment.

(f) The date of sale of delinquent shares fixed in any levy of an assessment may be extended from time to time for not more than 30 days at a time by order of the board entered on the records of the corporation, or when the sale is restrained by order of a court. Notice of such extension shall be given by announcement by the secretary, or other person authorized to conduct the sale, made at the time and place of sale last theretofore fixed.

If a date of sale of delinquent shares is extended for more than five days the corporation shall cause a notice to be mailed to the shareholder or shareholders whose shares are to be the subject of such sale setting forth the date and time to which the date of sale has been extended.

(g) If payment is made after delinquency and before the sale, the shareholder shall pay a penalty of 5 percent of the amount of the assessment on the shares in addition to the assessment.

(h) At the place and time appointed in the notice of levy any officer or an agent of the corporation, shall, unless otherwise ordered by the board, sell or cause to be sold to the highest bidder for cash as many shares of each delinquent holder of the assessed shares as may be necessary to pay the assessment and charges thereon according to the notice.

The person offering at the sale to pay the assessment and penalty for the smallest number of shares is the highest bidder. The shares purchased shall be transferred to the highest bidder on the share register of the corporation on the payment of the assessment and penalty and a new certificate therefor issued to such highest bidder. A corporation is not required to accept an offer for a fraction of a share.

(i) If no bidder offers to pay the amount due on the shares, together with the penalty of 5 percent thereof, the shares shall be forfeited to the corporation in satisfaction of the assessment and penalty thereon.

(j) After a sale or forfeiture of shares for nonpayment of an assessment, the holder or owner of delinquent shares shall surrender the certificate for such shares to the corporation for cancellation. This duty may be enforced by order or decree of court and such holder or owner shall be liable for damages to the corporation for failure to surrender the certificate for cancellation upon demand without good cause or excuse.

Any certificate not so surrendered forthwith becomes null and void and ceases to be evidence of the right or title of the holder or any transferee to the shares purporting to be represented thereby, and neither the corporation nor the purchaser of such shares incurs any liability thereon to any such transferee.

The purchaser of any shares, at a sale for delinquent assessments thereon, whenever made, is entitled to the issue of a new certificate representing the shares so purchased.

(k) The certificate of the secretary or assistant secretary of the corporation is prima facie evidence of the time and place of sale and any postponement thereof, of the quantity and particular description of the shares sold, to whom, for what price, and of the fact of payment of the purchase money. The certificate shall be filed in the office of the corporation, and copies of the certificate, certified by the secretary or an assistant secretary of the corporation, are prima facie evidence of the facts therein stated.

(l) An assessment is not invalidated by a failure to publish the notice of assessment, nor by the nonperformance of any act required in order to enforce the payment of the assessment; but in case of any substantial error or omission in the course of proceedings for collection of an assessment on any shares, all previous proceedings, except the levy of the assessment, are void as to such shares, and shall be taken anew.

(m) No action shall be maintained to recover shares sold for delinquent assessments, upon the ground of irregularity in the assessment, irregularity or defect of the notice of sale, or defect or irregularity in the sale, unless the party seeking to maintain the action first pays or tenders to the corporation, or the party holding the shares sold, the sum for which the shares were sold, together with all subsequent assessments which may

have been paid thereon and interest on such sums from the time they were paid. No such action shall be maintained unless it is commenced by the filing of a complaint and the issuing of a summons thereon within six months after the sale was made.

(n) The only remedy for the collection of an assessment on fully paid shares is sale or forfeiture of the shares unless (1) remedy by action is expressly authorized in the original articles or by an amendment of the articles adopted before August 21, 1933, or by an amendment adopted on or after August 21, 1933, by unanimous consent of the shareholders, and (2) unless a statement of such remedy appears on the face of any share certificate issued on or after August 21, 1933.

CHAPTER 5

DIVIDENDS AND REACQUISITIONS OF SHARES

Sec. 500. Distributions: Retained Earnings and Assets Requirements. Neither a corporation nor any of its subsidiaries shall make any distribution to the corporation's shareholders (Section 166) unless:

(a) The amount of the retained earnings of the corporation immediately prior thereto equals or exceeds the amount of the proposed distribution; or

(b) Immediately after giving effect thereto:

(1) The sum of the assets of the corporation (exclusive of goodwill, capitalized research and development expenses and deferred charges) would be at least equal to 1¼ times its liabilities (not including deferred taxes, deferred income and other deferred credits); and

(2) The current assets of the corporation would be at least equal to its current liabilities or, if the average of the earnings of the corporation before taxes on income and before interest expense for the two preceding fiscal years was less than the average of the interest expense of the corporation for such fiscal years, at least equal to 1¼ times its current liabilities; provided, however, that in determining the amount of the assets of the corporation profits derived from an exchange of assets shall not be included unless the assets received are currently realizable in cash; and provided, further, that for the purpose of this subdivision "current assets" may include net amounts which the board has determined in good faith may reasonably be expected to be received from customers during the 12-month period used in calculating current liabilities pursuant to existing contractual relationships obligating such customers to make fixed or periodic payments during the term of the contract or, in the case of public utilities, pursuant to service connections with customers, after in each case giving effect to future costs not then included in current liabilities but reasonably expected to be incurred by the corporation in performing such contracts or providing service to utility customers. The amount of any distribution payable in property shall, for the purpose of this chapter, be determined on the basis of the value at which such property is carried on the corporation's financial statements in accordance with generally accepted accounting principles. Paragraph (2) of subdivision (b) is not applicable to a corporation which does not classify its assets into current and fixed under generally accepted accounting principles. For the purpose of applying this section to a distribution by a corporation of cash or property in payment in whole or in part of an obligation incurred by the corporation in connection with the purchase of its shares, there shall be added to retained earnings any amount that had been deducted therefrom at the time the obligation was incurred, but not in excess of the principal of the obligation which remains unpaid immediately prior to the distribution and there shall be deducted from liabilities any amount which had been added thereto at the time the obligation was incurred, but not in excess of the principal of the obligation which will remain unpaid after the distribution.

Sec. 501. Distribution resulting in corporate insolvency. Neither a corporation nor any of its subsidiaries shall make any distribution to the corporation's shareholders (Section 166) if the corporation or the subsidiary making the distribution is, or as a result thereof would be, likely to be unable to meet its liabilities (except those whose payment is otherwise adequately provided for) as they mature.

Sec. 502. Distributions to junior shares affecting liquidation preferences of shares having liquidation preferences. Neither a corporation nor any of its subsidiaries shall make any distribution to the corporation's shareholders (Section 166) or any shares of its stock of any class or series which are junior to outstanding shares of any other class or series with respect to distribution of assets on liquidation if, after giving effect thereto, the excess of its assest (exclusive of goodwill, capitalized research and development expenses and deferred charges) over its liabilities (not including deferred taxes, deferred income and other deferred credits) would be less than the liquidation preference of all shares having a preference on liquidation over the class or series to which the distribution is made; provided, however, that for the purpose of applying this section to a distribution by a corporation of cash or property in payment in whole or in part of an obligation incurred by the corporation in connection with the purchase of its shares, there shall be deducted from liabilities any amount which had been added thereto at the time the obligation was incurred, but not in excess of the principal of the obligation which will remain unpaid after the distribution.

Sec. 503. Distributions to junior shares affecting cumulative dividends on shares having dividend preferences.   Neither a corporation or any of its subsidiaries shall make any distribution to the corporation's shareholders (Section 166) on any shares of its stock of any class or series which are junior to outstanding shares of any other class or series with respect to payment of dividends unless the amount of the retained earnings of the corporation immediately prior thereto equals or exceeds the amount of the proposed distribution plus the aggregate amount of the cumulative dividends in arrears on all shares having a preference with respect to payment of dividends over the class or series to which the distribution is made; provided, however, that for the purpose of applying this section to a distribution by a corporation of cash or property in payment in whole or in part of an obligation incurred by the corporation in connection with the purchase of its shares, there shall be added to retained earnings any amount that had been deducted therefrom at the time the obligation was incurred, but not in excess of the principal of the obligation which remains unpaid immediately prior to the distribution.

Sec. 504. Regulated investment company dividends; registered open-end investment company redemptions.   The provisions of Section 500 do not apply to any dividend declared by a regulated investment company, as defined in the United States Internal Revenue Code, to the extent that the dividend is necessary to maintain the status of the corporation as a regulated investment company under the provisions of that code. The provisions of this chapter do not apply to any purchase or redemption of shares redeemable at the option of the holder by a registered open-end investment company under the United States Investment Company Act of 1940, so long as the right of redemption remains unsuspended under the provisions of that statute and the articles and bylaws of the corporation.

Sec. 505. Additional restrictions on distributions in articles, bylaws, indentures or agreements.   Nothing in this chapter prohibits additional restrictions upon the declaration of dividends or the purchase or redemption of a corporation's own shares by provision in the articles or bylaws or in any indenture or other agreement entered into by the corporation.

Sec. 506. Liability of shareholders receiving prohibited distributions.   (a) Any shareholder who receives any distribution prohibited by this chapter with knowledge of facts indicating the impropriety thereof is liable to the corporation for the benefit of all of the creditors or shareholders entitled to institute an action under subdivision (b) for the amount so received by such shareholder with interest thereon at the legal rate on judgments until paid, but not exceeding the liabilities of the corporation owed to nonconsenting creditors at the time of the violation and the injury suffered by nonconsenting shareholders, as the case may be.

(b) Suit may be brought in the name of the corporation to enforce the liability (1) to creditors arising under subdivision (a) for a violation of Section 500 or 501 against any or all shareholders liable by any one or more creditors of the corporation whose debts or claims arose prior to the time of the distribution to shareholders and who have not consented thereto, whether or not they have reduced their claims to judgment, or (2) to shareholders arising under subdivision (a) for a violation of Section 502 or 503 against any or all shareholders liable by any one or more holders of preferred shares outstanding at the time of the distribution who have not consented thereto, without regard to the provisions of Section 800.

(c) Any shareholder sued under this section may implead all other shareholders liable under this section and may compel contribution, either in that action or in an independent action against shareholders not joined in that action.

(d) Nothing contained in this section affects any liability which any shareholder may have under Sections 3439 to 3439.12, inclusive, of the Civil Code.

Sec. 507. Notice of source of dividend.   Each dividend other than one chargeable to retained earnings shall be identified in a notice to shareholders as being made from a source other than retained earnings, stating the accounting treatment thereof. The notice shall accompany the dividend or shall be given within three months after the end of the fiscal year in which the dividend is paid.

Sec. 508. Chapter not applicable to corporate dissolutions.   This chapter does not apply in connection with any proceeding for winding up and dissolution under Chapter 18 or 19.

Sec. 509. Manner of redemption of shares.   (a) A corporation may redeem any or all shares which are redeemable at its option by (1) giving notice of redemption, and (2) payment or deposit of the redemption price of the shares as provided in its articles or deposit of the redemption price pursuant to subdivision (d).

(b) Subject to any provisions in the articles with respect to the notice required for redemption of shares, the corporation may give notice of the redemption of any or all shares subject to redemption by causing a notice of redemption to be published in a newspaper of general circulation in the county in which the principal executive office of the corporation is located at least once a week for two successive weeks, in each instance on any day of the week, commencing not earlier than 60 nor later than 20 days before the date fixed for redemption. The notice of redemption shall set forth all of the following:

(1) The class or series of shares or part of any class or series of shares to be redeemed.

(2) The date fixed for redemption.

(3) The redemption price.

(4) The place at which the shareholders may obtain payment of the redemption price upon surrender of their share certificates.

(c) If the corporation gives notice of redemption pursuant to subdivision (b), it shall also mail a copy of the notice of redemption to each holder of record of shares to be redeemed as of the date of mailing or record date fixed in accordance with Section 701, addressed to the holder at the address of such holder appearing on the books of the corporation or given by the holder to the corporation for the purpose of notice, or if no such address appears or is given at the place where the principal executive office of the corporation is located, not earlier than 60 nor later than 20 days before the date fixed for redemption. Failure to comply with this subdivision does not invalidate the redemption of the shares.

(d) If, on or prior to any date fixed for redemption of redeemable shares, the corporation deposits with any bank or trust company in this state as a trust fund a sum sufficient to redeem, on the date fixed for redemption thereof, the shares called for redemption, with irrevocable instructions and authority to the bank or trust company to publish the notice of redemption thereof (or to complete such publication if theretofore commenced) and to pay, on and after the date fixed for redemption or prior thereto, the redemption price of the shares to their respective holders upon the surrender of their share certificates, then from and after the date of the deposit (although prior to the date fixed for redemption) the shares so called shall be redeemed and dividends on those shares shall cease to accrue after the date fixed for redemption. The deposit shall constitute full payment of the shares to their holders and from and after the date of the deposit the shares shall no longer be outstanding and the holders thereof shall cease to be shareholders with respect to such shares and shall have no rights with respect thereto except the right to receive from the bank or trust company payment of the redemption price of the shares without interest, upon surrender of their certificates therefor, and any right to convert the shares which may exist and then continue for any period fixed by its terms.

Sec. 510. Reissuance of redeemed shares.   (a) When a corporation purchases or redeems or otherwise acquires its own shares, such shares are restored to the status of authorized but unissued shares, unless the articles prohibit the reissuance thereof.

(b) If the articles prohibit the reissue of shares upon acquisition thereof by the corporation, then upon such acquisition the authorized number of shares of the class and series, if any, to which such shares belonged is reduced by the number of shares so acquired. Thereupon the articles shall be amended to reflect such reduction in authorized shares and, if all of the authorized shares of any class or series are acquired and their reissue is prohibited by the articles, then the articles shall also be amended to eliminate therefrom any statement of rights, preferences, privileges and restrictions relating solely to such class or series. A certificate of amendment shall be filed in accordance with the requirements of Chapter 9, except that approval by the outstanding shares (Section 152) shall not be required to adopt any such amendment.

CHAPTER 6

SHAREHOLDERS' MEETINGS AND CONSENTS

Sec. 600. Place and time of annual and special meetings; failure to hold annual meeting. (a) Meetings of shareholders may be held at such place within or without this state as may be stated in or fixed in accordance with the bylaws. If no other place is stated or so fixed, shareholder meetings shall be held at the principal executive office of the corporation.

(b) An annual meeting of shareholders shall be held for the election of directors on a date and at a time stated in or fixed in accordance with the bylaws. Any other proper business may be transacted at the annual meeting.

(c) If there is a failure to hold the annual meeting for a period of 60 days after the date designated therefor or, if no date has been designated, for a period of 15 months after the organization of the corporation or after its last annual meeting, the superior court of the proper county may summarily order a meeting to be held upon the application of any shareholder after notice to the corporation giving it an opportunity to be heard. The shares represented at such meeting, either in person or by proxy, and entitled to vote thereat shall constitute a quorum for the purpose of such meeting, notwithstanding any provision of the articles or bylaws or in this division to the contrary. The court may issue such orders as may be appropriate, including, without limitation, orders designating the time and place of such meeting, the record date for determination of shareholders entitled to vote and the form of notice of such meeting.

(d) Special meetings of the shareholders may be called by the board, the chairman of the board, the president or the holders of shares entitled to cast not less than 10 percent of the votes at the meeting or such additional persons as may be provided in the articles or bylaws.

Sec. 601. Notice of meeting; waiver of notice. (a) Whenever shareholders are required or permitted to take any action at a meeting a written notice of the meeting shall be given not less than 10 (or, if sent by third class mail, 30) nor more than 60 days before the date of the meeting to each shareholder entitled to vote thereat. Such notice shall state the place, date and hour of the meeting and (1) in the case of a special meeting, the general nature of the business to be transacted, and no other business may be transacted, or (2) in the case of the annual meeting, those matters which the board, at the time of the mailing of the notice, intends to present for action by the shareholders, but subject to the provisions of subdivision (f) any proper matter may be presented at the meeting for such action. The notice of any meeting at which directors are to be elected shall include the names of nominees intended at the time of the notice to be presented by the board for election.

(b) Notice of a shareholders' meeting or any report shall be given either personally or by first class mail, or, in the case of a corporation with outstanding shares held of record by 500 or more persons (determined as provided in Section 605) on the record date for the shareholders' meeting, notice may be sent third class mail, or other means of written communication, addressed to the shareholder at the address of such shareholder appearing on the books of the corporation or given by the shareholder to the corporation for the purpose of notice; or if no such address appears or is given, at the place where the principal executive office of the corporation is located or by publication at least once in a newspaper of general circulation in the county in which the principal executive office is located. The notice or report shall be deemed to have been given at the time when delivered personally or deposited in the mail or sent by other means of written communication. An affidavit of mailing of any notice or report in accordance with the provisions of this division, executed by the secretary, assistant secretary or any transfer agent, shall be prima facie evidence of the giving of the notice or report.

If any notice or report addressed to the shareholder at the address of such shareholder appearing on the books of the corporation is returned to the corporation by the United States Postal Service marked to indicate that the United States Postal Service is unable to deliver the notice or report to the shareholder at such address, all future notices or reports shall be deemed to have been duly given without further demand of the shareholder at the principal executive office of the corporation for a period of one year from the date of the giving of the notice or report to all other shareholders.

(c) Upon request in writing to the chairman of the board, president, vice president or secretary by any person (other than the board) entitled to call a special meeting of shareholders, the officer forthwith shall cause notice to be given to the shareholders entitled to vote that a meeting will be held at a time requested by the person or persons calling the meeting, not less than 35 nor more than 60 days after the receipt of the request. If the notice is not given within 20 days after receipt of the request, the persons entitled to call the meeting may give the notice or the superior court of the proper county shall summarily order the giving of the notice, after notice to the corporation giving it an opportunity to be heard. The procedure provided in subdivision (c) of Section 305 shall apply to such application. The court may issue such orders as may be appropriate, including, without limitation, orders designating the time and place of the meeting, the record date for determination of shareholders entitled to vote and the form of notice.

(d) When a shareholders' meeting is adjourned to another time or place, unless the bylaws otherwise require and except as provided in this subdivision, notice need not be given of the adjourned meeting if the time and place thereof are announced at the meeting at which the adjournment is taken. At the adjourned meeting the corporation may transact any business which might have been transacted at the original meeting. If the adjournment is for more than 45 days or if after the adjournment a new record date is fixed for the adjourned meeting, a notice of the adjourned meeting shall be given to each shareholder of record entitled to vote at the meeting.

(e) The transactions of any meeting of shareholders, however called and noticed, and wherever held, are as valid as though had at a meeting duly held after regular call and notice, if a quorum is present either in person or by proxy, and if, either before or after the meeting, each of the persons entitled to vote, not present in person or by proxy, signs a written waiver of notice or a consent to the holding of the meeting or an approval of the minutes thereof. All such waivers, consents and approvals shall be filed with the corporate records or made a part of the minutes of the meeting. Attendance of a person at a meeting shall constitute a waiver of notice of and presence at such meeting, except when the person objects, at the beginning of the meeting, to the transaction of any business because the meeting is not lawfully called or convened and except that attendance at a meeting is not a waiver of any right to object to the consideration of matters required by this division to be included in the notice but not so included, if such objection is expressly made at the meeting. Neither the business to be transacted at nor the purpose of any regular or special meeting of shareholders need be specified in any written waiver of notice, consent to the holding of the meeting or approval of the minutes thereof, unless otherwise provided in the articles or bylaws, except as provided in subdivision (f).

(f) Any shareholder approval at a meeting, other than unanimous approval by those entitled to vote, pursuant to Section 310, 902, 1201, 1900 or 2007 shall be valid only if the general nature of the proposal so approved was stated in the notice of meeting or in any written waiver of notice.

Sec. 602. Quorum of shareholders. (a) Unless otherwise provided in the articles, a majority of the shares entitled to vote, represented in person or by proxy, shall constitute a quorum at a meeting of the shareholders, but in no event shall a quorum consist of less than one-third (or, in the case of a mutual water company, 20 percent) of the shares entitled to vote at the meeting or, except in the case of a close corporation, of more than a majority of the shares entitled to vote at the meeting. Except as provided in subdivision (b), the affirmative vote of a majority of the shares represented and voting at a duly held meeting at which a quorum is present (which shares voting affirmatively also constitute at least a majority of the required quorum) shall be the act of the shareholders, unless the vote of a greater number or voting by classes is required by this division or the articles.

(b) The shareholders present at a duly called or held meeting at which a quorum is present may continue to transact business until adjournment notwithstanding the withdrawal of enough shareholders to leave less than a quorum, if any action taken (other than adjournment) is approved by at least a majority of the shares required to constitute a quorum.

(c) In the absence of a quorum, any meeting of shareholders may be adjourned from time to time by the vote of a majority of the shares represented either in person or by proxy, but no other business may be transacted, except as provided in subdivision (b).

Sec. 603. Consent in writing as validating action without meeting. (a) Unless otherwise provided in the articles, any action which may be taken at any annual or special meeting of shareholders may be taken without a meeting and without prior notice, if a consent in writing, setting forth the action so taken, shall be signed by the holders of outstanding shares having not less than the minimum number of votes that would be necessary to authorize or take such action at a meeting at which all shares entitled to vote thereon were present and voted.

(b) Unless the consents of all shareholders entitled to vote have been solicited in writing,

(1) Notice of any shareholder approval pursuant to Section 310, 317, 1201 or 2007 without a meeting by less than unanimous written consent shall be given at least 10 days before the consummation of the action authorized by such approval, and

(2) Prompt notice shall be given of the taking of any other corporate action approved by shareholders without a meeting by less than unanimous written consent, to those shareholders entitled to vote who have not consented in writing. Subdivision (b) of Section 601 applies to such notice.

(c) Any shareholder giving a written consent, or the shareholder's proxyholders, or a transferee of the shares or a personal representative of the shareholder or their respective proxyholders, may revoke the consent by a writing received by the corporation prior to the time that written consents of the number of shares required to authorize the proposed action have been filed with the secretary of the corporation, but may not do so thereafter. Such revocation is effective upon its receipt by the secretary of the corporation.

(d) Notwithstanding subdivision (a), subject to subdivision (b) of Section 305 directors may not be elected by written consent except by unanimous written consent of all shares entitled to vote for the election of directors.

Sec. 604. Requirements for request for shareholder proxy by corporation. (a) Any form of proxy or written consent distributed to 10 or more shareholders of a corporation with outstanding shares held of record by 100 or more persons shall afford an opportunity on the proxy or form of written consent to specify a choice between approval and disapproval of each matter or group of related matters intended to be acted upon at the meeting for which the proxy is solicited or by such written consent, other than elections to office, and shall provide, subject to reasonable specified conditions, that where the person solicited specifies a choice with respect to any such matter the shares will be voted in accordance therewith.

(b) In any election of directors, any form of proxy in which the directors to be voted upon are named therein as candidates and which is marked by a shareholder "withhold" or otherwise marked in a manner indicating that the authority to vote for the election of directors is withheld shall not be voted for the election of a director.

(c) Failure to comply with this section shall not invalidate any corporate action taken, but may be the basis for challenging any proxy at a meeting and the superior court may compel compliance therewith at the suit of any shareholder.

(d) This section does not apply to any corporation with an outstanding class of securities registered under Section 12 of the Securities Exchange Act of 1934 or whose securities are exempted from such registration by Section 12(g)(2) of that act.

Sec. 605. Determination of whether shares "held of record" by 100 or more persons. (a) For the purpose of determining whether a corporation has outstanding shares held of record by 100 or more persons, shares shall be deemed to be "held of record" by each person who is identified as the owner of such shares on the record of shareholders maintained by or on behalf of the corporation, subject to the following:

(1) In any case where the record of shareholders has not been maintained in accordance with accepted practice, any additional person who would be identified as such an owner on such record if it had been maintained in accordance with accepted practice shall be included as a holder of record.

(2) Shares identified as held of record by a corporation, a partnership, a trust, whether or not the trustees are named, or other organization shall be included as so held by one person.

(3) Shares identified as held of record by one or more persons as trustees, executors, guardians, conservators, custodians or in other fiduciary capacities with respect to a single trust, estate or account shall be included as held of record by one person.

(4) Shares held by two or more persons as co-owners shall be included as held by one person.

(5) Shares registered in substantially similar names, where the corporation (or other person soliciting proxies) has reason to believe because of the address or other indications that such names represent the same person, may be included as held of record by one person.

(b) Notwithstanding subdivision (a):

(1) Shares held, to the knowledge of the corporation (or other person soliciting proxies), subject to a voting trust, deposit agreement or similar arrangement shall be included as held of record by the recordholders of the voting trust certificates, certificates of deposit, receipts or similar evidences of interest in such securities; provided, however, that the corporation (or other person soliciting proxies) may rely in good faith on such information as is received in response to its request from a nonaffiliated issuer of the certificates or evidences of interest.

(2) If the corporation (or other person soliciting proxies) knows or has reason to know that the form of holding shares of record is used primarily to circumvent the provisions of this section, the beneficial owners of such shares shall be deemed to be the record owners thereof.

CHAPTER 7

VOTING OF SHARES

Sec. 700. One vote per share; right to split votes. (a) Except as provided in Section 708 and except as may be otherwise provided in the articles, each outstanding share, regardless of class, shall be entitled to one vote on each matter submitted to a vote of shareholders.

(b) Any holder of shares entitled to vote on any matter may vote part of the shares in favor of the proposal and refrain from voting the remaining shares or vote them against the proposal, other than elections to office, but, if the shareholder fails to specify the number of shares such shareholder is voting affirmatively, it will be conclusively presumed that the shareholder's approving vote is with respect to all shares such shareholder is entitled to vote.

Sec. 701. Record date for shareholders of record. (a) In order that the corporation may determine the shareholders entitled to notice of any meeting or to vote or entitled to receive payment of any dividend or other distribution or allotment of any rights or entitled to exercise any rights in respect of any other lawful action, the board may fix, in advance, a record date, which shall not be more than 60 nor less than 10 days prior to the date of such meeting nor more than 60 days prior to any other action.

(b) If no record date is fixed:

(1) The record date for determining shareholders entitled to notice of or to vote at a meeting of shareholders shall be at the close of business on the business day next preceding the day on which notice is given or, if notice is waived, at the close of business on the business day next preceding the day on which the meeting is held.

(2) The record date for determining shareholders entitled to give consent to corporate action in writing without a meeting, when no prior action by the board has been taken, shall be the day on which the first written consent is given.

(3) The record date for determining shareholders for any other purpose shall be at the close of business on the day on which the board adopts the resolution relating thereto, or the 60th day prior to the date of such other action, whichever is later.

(c) A determination of shareholders of record entitled to notice of or to vote at a meeting of shareholders shall apply to any adjournment of the meeting unless the board fixes a new record date for the adjourned meeting, but the board shall fix a new record date if the meeting is adjourned for more than 45 days from the date set for the original meeting.

(d) Shareholders at the close of business on the record date are entitled to notice and to vote or to receive the dividend, distribution or allotment of rights or to exercise the rights, as the case may be, notwithstanding any transfer of any shares on the books of the corporation after the record date, except as otherwise provided in the articles or by agreement or in this division.

Sec. 702. Voting by representatives, fiduciaries, receivers, pledgees, minors. (a) Subject to subdivision (c) of Section 703, shares held by an administrator, executor, guardian, conservator or custodian may be voted by such holder either in person or by proxy, without a transfer of such shares into the holder's name; and shares standing in the name of a trustee may be voted by the trustee, either in person or by proxy, but no trustee shall be entitled to vote shares held by such trustee without a transfer of such shares into the trustee's name.

(b) Shares standing in the name of a receiver may be voted by such receiver; and shares held by or under the control of a receiver may be voted by such receiver without the transfer thereof into the receiver's name if authority to do so is contained in the order of the court by which such receiver was appointed.

(c) Subject to the provisions of Section 705 and except where otherwise agreed in writing between the parties, a shareholder whose shares are pledged shall be entitled to vote such shares until the shares have been transferred into the name of the pledgee, and thereafter the pledgee shall be entitled to vote the shares so transferred.

(d) Shares standing in the name of a minor may be voted and the corporation may treat all rights incident thereto as exercisable by the minor, in person or by proxy, whether or not the corporation has notice, actual or constructive, of the nonage, unless a guardian of the minor's property has been appointed and written notice of such appointment given to the corporation.

Sec. 703. Voting by corporate shareholders.

(a) Shares standing in the name of another corporation, domestic or foreign, may be voted by such officer, agent or proxyholder as the bylaws of such other corporation may prescribe or, in the absence of such provision, as the board of such other corporation may determine or, in the absence of such determination, by the chairman of the board, president or any vice president of such other corporation, or by any other person authorized to do so by the chairman of the board, president or any vice president of such other corporation. Shares which are purported to be voted or any proxy purported to be executed in the name of a corporation (whether or not any title of the person signing is indicated) shall be presumed to be voted or the proxy executed in accordance with the provisions of this subdivision, unless the contrary is shown.

(b) Shares of a corporation owned by its subsidiary shall not be entitled to vote on any matter.

(c) Shares held by the issuing corporation in a fiduciary capacity, and shares of an issuing corporation held in a fiduciary capacity by its subsidiary, shall not be entitled to vote on any matter, except to the extent that the settlor or beneficial owner possesses and exercises a right to vote or to give the corporation binding instructions as to how to vote such shares.

Sec. 704. Voting by shares standing in names of two or more persons.

If shares stand of record in the names of two or more persons, whether fiduciaries, members of a partnership, joint tenants, tenants in common, husband and wife as community property, tenants by the entirety, voting trustees, persons entitled to vote under a shareholder voting agreement or otherwise, or if two or more persons (including proxyholders) have the same fiduciary relationship respecting the same shares, unless the secretary of the corporation is given written notice to the contrary and is furnished with a copy of the instrument or order appointing them or creating the relationship where in it is so provided, their acts with respect to voting shall have the following effect:

(1) If only one votes, such act binds all;

(2) If more than one vote, the act of the majority so voting binds all;

(3) If more than one vote, but the vote is evenly split on any particular matter, each faction may vote the securities in question proportionately.

If the instrument so filed or the registration of the shares shows that any such tenancy is held in unequal interests, a majority or even split for the purpose of this section shall be a majority or even split in interest.

Sec. 705. Proxies.

(a) Every person entitled to vote shares may authorize another person or persons to act by proxy with respect to such shares. Any proxy purporting to be executed in accordance with the provisions of this division shall be presumptively valid.

(b) No proxy shall be valid after the expiration of 11 months from the date thereof unless otherwise provided in the proxy. Every proxy continues in full force and effect until revoked by the person executing it prior to the vote pursuant thereto, except as otherwise provided in this section. Such revocation may be effected by a writing delivered to the corporation stating that the proxy is revoked or by a subsequent proxy executed by the person executing the prior proxy and presented to the meeting, or as to any meeting by attendance at such meeting and voting in person by the person executing the proxy. The dates contained on the forms of proxy presumptively determine the order of execution, regardless of the postmark dates on the envelopes in which they are mailed.

(c) A proxy is not revoked by the death or incapacity of the maker unless, before the vote is counted, written notice of such death or incapacity is received by the corporation.

(d) Except when other provision shall have been made by written agreement between the parties, the recordholder of shares which such person holds as pledgee or otherwise as security or which belong to another shall issue to the pledgor or to the owner of such shares, upon

demand therefor and payment of necessary expenses thereof, a proxy to vote or take other action thereon.

(e) A proxy which states that it is irrevocable is irrevocable for the period specified therein (notwithstanding subdivision (c)) when it is held by any of the following or a nominee of any of the following:

(1) A pledgee;

(2) A person who has purchased or agreed to purchase or holds an option to purchase the shares or a person who has sold a portion of such person's shares in the corporation to the maker of the proxy;

(3) A creditor or creditors of the corporation or the shareholder who extended or continued credit to the corporation or the shareholder in consideration of the proxy if the proxy states that it was given in consideration of such extension or continuation of credit and the name of the person extending or continuing credit;

(4) A person who has contracted to perform services as an employee of the corporation, if a proxy is required by the contract of employment and if the proxy states that it was given in consideration of such contract of employment, the name of the employee and the period of employment contracted for; or

(5) A person designated by or under an agreement under Section 706.

(6) A beneficiary of a trust with respect to shares held by the trust.

Notwithstanding the period of irrevocability specified, the proxy becomes revocable when the pledge is redeemed, the option or agreement to purchase is terminated or the seller no longer owns any shares of the corporation or dies, the debt of the corporation or the shareholder is paid, the period of employment provided for in the contract of employment has terminated or the agreement under Section 706 has terminated, or the person ceases to be a beneficiary of the trust. In addition to the foregoing clauses (1) through (5), a proxy may be made irrevocable (notwithstanding subdivision (c)) if it is given to secure the performance of a duty or to protect a title, either legal or equitable, until the happening of events which, by its terms, discharge the obligations secured by it.

(f) A proxy may be revoked, notwithstanding a provision making it irrevocable, by a transferee of shares without knowledge of the existence of the provision unless the existence of the proxy and its irrevocability appears on the certificate representing such shares.

Sec. 706. Voting agreement by shareholders of close corporation; voting trust agreements.

(a) Notwithstanding any other provision of this division, an agreement between two or more shareholders of a close corporation, if in writing and signed by the parties thereto, may provide that in exercising any voting rights the shares held by them shall be voted as provided by the agreement, or as the parties may agree or as determined in accordance with a procedure agreed upon by them, and the parties may transfer the shares covered by such an agreement to a third party or parties with authority to vote them in accordance with the terms of the agreement. Such an agreement shall not be denied specific performance by a court on the ground that the remedy at law is adequate or on other grounds relating to the jurisdiction of a court of equity. An agreement made pursuant to this subdivision between shareholders of a close corporation shall terminate when the corporation ceases to be a close corporation, except that if the agreement so provides it shall continue to the extent it is enforceable apart from this subdivision.

(b) Shares in any corporation may be transferred by written agreement to trustees in order to confer upon them the right to vote and otherwise represent the shares for such period of time, not exceeding 10 years, as may be specified in the agreement. The validity of a voting trust agreement, otherwise lawful, shall not be affected during a period of 10 years from the date when it was created or last extended as hereinafter provided by the fact that under its terms it will or may last beyond such 10-year period. At any time within two years prior to the time of expiration of any voting trust agreement as originally fixed or as last extended as provided in this subdivision, one or more beneficiaries under the voting trust agreement may, by written agreement and with the written consent of the voting trustee or trustees, extend the duration of the voting trust agreement with respect to their shares for an additional period not exceeding 10 years from the expiration date of the trust as originally fixed or as last extended as provided in this subdivision. A duplicate of the voting trust agreement and any extension thereof shall be filed with the secretary of the corporation and shall be open to inspection by a shareholder, a holder of a voting trust certificate or the agent of either, upon the same terms as the record of shareholders of the corporation is open to inspection.

(c) No agreement made pursuant to subdivision (a) shall be held to be invalid or unenforceable on the ground that it is a voting trust which does not comply with subdivision (b).

(d) This section shall not invalidate any voting or other agreement among shareholders or any irrevocable proxy complying with subdivision (e) of Section 705, which agreement or proxy is not otherwise illegal.

Sec. 707. **Appointment of inspectors of election; duties.** (a) In advance of any meeting of shareholders the board may appoint inspectors of election to act at the meeting and any adjournment thereof. If inspectors of election are not so appointed, or if any persons so appointed fail to appear or refuse to act, the chairman of any meeting of shareholders may, and on the request of any shareholder or a shareholder's proxy shall, appoint inspectors of election (or persons to replace those who so fail or refuse) at the meeting. The number of inspectors shall be either one or three. If appointed at a meeting on the request of one or more shareholders or proxies, the majority of shares represented in person or by proxy shall determine whether one or three inspectors are to be appointed.

(b) The inspectors of election shall determine the number of shares outstanding and the voting power of each, the shares represented at the meeting, the existence of a quorum and the authenticity, validity and effect of proxies, receive votes, ballots or consents, hear and determine all challenges and questions in any way arising in connection with the right to vote, count and tabulate all votes or consents, determine when the polls shall close, determine the result and do such acts as may be proper to conduct the election or vote with fairness to all shareholders.

(c) The inspectors of election shall perform their duties impartially, in good faith, to the best of their ability and as expeditiously as is practical. If there are three inspectors of election, the decision, act or certificate of a majority is effective in all respects as the decision, act or certificate of all. Any report or certificate made by the inspectors of election is prima facie evidence of the facts stated therein.

Sec. 708. **Election of directors; cumulative voting.** (a) Every shareholder complying with subdivision (b) and entitled to vote at any election of directors may cumulate such shareholder's votes and give one candidate a number of votes equal to the number of directors to be elected multiplied by the number of votes to which the shareholder's shares are normally entitled, or distribute the shareholder's votes on the same principle among as many candidates as the shareholder thinks fit.

(b) No shareholder shall be entitled to cumulate votes (i.e., cast for any candidate a number of votes greater than the number of votes which such shareholder normally is entitled to cast) unless such candidate or candidates' names have been placed in nomination prior to the voting and the shareholder has given notice at the meeting prior to the voting of the shareholder's intention to cumulate the shareholder's votes. If any one shareholder has given such notice, all shareholders may cumulate their votes for candidates in nomination.

(c) In any election of directors, the candidates receiving the highest number of affirmative votes of the shares entitled to be voted for them up to the number of directors to be elected by such shares are elected; votes against the director and votes withheld shall have no legal effect.

(d) Subdivision (a) applies to the shareholders of any mutual water company organized or existing for the purpose of delivering water to its shareholders at cost on lands located within the boundaries of one or more reclamation districts now or hereafter legally existing in this state and created by or formed under the provisions of any statute of this state, but does not otherwise apply to the shareholders of mutual water companies unless their articles or bylaws so provide.

(e) Elections for directors need not be by ballot unless a shareholder demands election by ballot at the meeting and before the voting begins or unless the bylaws so require.

Sec. 709. **Action to determine validity of election.** (a) Upon the filing of an action therefor by any shareholder or by any person who claims to have been denied the right to vote, the superior court of the proper county shall try and determine the validity of any election or appointment of any director of any domestic corporation, or of any foreign corporation if the election was held or the appointment was made in this state. In the case of a foreign corporation the action may be brought at the option of the plaintiff in the county in which the corporation has its principal office in this state or in the county in which the election was held or the appointment was made.

(b) Upon the filing of the complaint, and before any further proceedings are had, the court shall enter an order fixing a date for the hearing, which shall be within five days unless for good cause shown a later date is fixed, and requiring notice of the date for the hearing and a copy of the complaint to be served upon the corporation and upon the person whose purported election or appointment is questioned and upon any per-

son (other than the plaintiff) whom the plaintiff alleges to have been elected or appointed, in the manner in which a summons is required to be served, or, if the court so directs, by registered mail; and the court may make such further requirements as to notice as appear to be proper under the circumstances.

(c) The court may determine the person entitled to the office of director or may order a new election to be held or appointment to be made, may determine the validity, effectiveness and construction of voting agreements and voting trusts, the validity of the issuance of shares and the right of persons to vote and may direct such other relief as may be just and proper.

CHAPTER 8

SHAREHOLDER DERIVATIVE ACTIONS

Sec. 800. **Conditions to maintenance of shareholder's action; requirement of furnishing security.** (a) As used in this section, "corporation" includes an unincorporated association; "board" includes the managing body of an unincorporated association; "shareholder" includes a member of an unincorporated association; and "shares" includes memberships in an unincorporated association.

(b) No action may be instituted or maintained in right of any domestic or foreign corporation by any holder of shares or of voting trust certificates of the corporation unless both of the following conditions exist:

(1) The plaintiff alleges in the complaint that plaintiff was a shareholder, of record or beneficially, or the holder of voting trust certificates at the time of the transaction or any part thereof of which plaintiff complains or that plaintiff's shares or voting trust certificates thereafter devolved upon plaintiff by operation of law from a holder who was a holder at the time of the transaction or any part thereof complained of; provided, that any shareholder who does not meet these requirements may nevertheless be allowed in the discretion of the court to maintain the action on a preliminary showing to and determination by the court, by motion and after a hearing, at which the court shall consider such evidence, by affidavit or testimony, as it deems material, that (i) there is a strong prima facie case in favor of the claim asserted on behalf of the corporation, (ii) no other similar action has been or is likely to be instituted, (iii) the plaintiff acquired the shares before there was disclosure to the public or to the plaintiff of the wrongdoing of which plaintiff complains, (iv) unless the action can be maintained the defendant may retain a gain derived from defendant's willful breach of a fiduciary duty, and (v) the requested relief will not result in unjust enrichment of the corporation or any shareholder of the corporation; and

(2) The plaintiff alleges in the complaint with particularity plaintiff's efforts to secure from the board such action as plaintiff desires, or the reasons for not making such effort, and alleges further that plaintiff has either informed the corporation or the board in writing of the ultimate facts of each cause of action against each defendant or delivered to the corporation or the board a true copy of the complaint which plaintiff proposes to file.

(c) In any action referred to in subdivision (b), at any time within 30 days after service of summons upon the corporation or upon any defendant who is an officer or director of the corporation, or held such office at the time of the acts complained of, the corporation or the defendant may move the court for an order, upon notice and hearing, requiring the plaintiff to furnish a bond as hereinafter provided. The motion shall be based upon one or both of the following grounds:

(1) That there is no reasonable possibility that the prosecution of the cause of action alleged in the complaint against the moving party will benefit the corporation or its shareholders.

(2) That the moving party, if other than the corporation, did not participate in the transaction complained of in any capacity.

The court on application of the corporation or any defendant may, for good cause shown, extend the 30-day period for an additional period or periods not exceeding 60 days.

(d) At the hearing upon any motion pursuant to subdivision (c), the court shall consider such evidence, written or oral, by witnesses or affidavit, as may be material (1) to the ground or grounds upon which the motion is based, or (2) to a determination of the probable reasonable expenses, including attorneys' fees, of the corporation and the moving party which will be incurred in the defense of the action. If the court determines, after hearing the evidence adduced by the parties, that the moving party has established a probability in support of any of the grounds upon which the motion is based, the court shall fix the amount of the bond, not to exceed fifty thousand dollars ($50,000), to be furnished by the plaintiff for reasonable expenses, including attorneys' fees, which may be incurred by the moving party and the corporation in connection with the action, including expenses for which the corporation may become liable pursuant to Section 317. A ruling by the court on the motion shall not be a determination of any issue in the action or of the merits thereof. If the court, upon the motion, makes a determination that a bond shall be furnished by the plaintiff as to any one or more defendants, the action shall be dismissed as to the defendant or defendants, unless the bond required by the court has been furnished within such reasonable time as may be fixed by the court.

(e) If the plaintiff shall, either before or after a motion is made pursuant to subdivision (c), or any order or determination pursuant to the motion, furnish a bond in the aggregate amount of fifty thousand dollars ($50,000) to secure the reasonable expenses of the parties entitled to make the motion, the plaintiff has complied with the requirements of this section and with any order for a bond theretofore made, and any such motion then pending shall be dismissed and no further or additional bond shall be required.

(f) If a motion is filed pursuant to subdivision (c), no pleadings need be filed by the corporation or any other defendant and the prosecution of the action shall be stayed until 10 days after the motion has been disposed of.

CHAPTER 9

AMENDMENT OF ARTICLES

Sec. 900. **Permissible amendments of articles.** (a) By complying with the provisions of this chapter, a corporation may amend its articles from time to time, in any and as many respects as may be desired, so long as its articles as amended contain only such provisions as it would be lawful to insert in original articles filed at the time of the filing of the amendment and, if a change in shares or the rights of shareholders or an exchange, reclassification or cancellation of shares or rights of shareholders is to be made, such provisions as may be necessary to effect such change, exchange, reclassification or cancellation. It is the intent of the Legislature in adopting this section to exercise to the fullest extent the reserve power of the state over corporations and to authorize any amendment of the articles covered by the preceding sentence regardless of whether any provision contained in the amendment was permissible at the time of the original incorporation of the corporation.

(b) A corporation shall not amend its articles to alter any statement which may appear in the original articles of the names and addresses of the first directors, nor the name and address of the initial agent, except to correct an error in the statement or to delete either after the corporation has filed a statement under Section 1502.

Sec. 901. **Amendments before issuance of shares.** Before any shares have been issued, any amendment of the articles may be adopted by a writing signed by a majority of the incorporators, if directors were not named in the original articles and have not been elected, or, if directors were named in the original articles or have been elected, by a majority of the directors.

Sec. 902. **Amendments after issuance of shares.** (a) After any shares have been issued, amendments may be adopted if approved by the board and approved by the outstanding shares (Section 152), either before or after the approval by the board.

(b) Notwithstanding subdivision (a), an amendment extending the corporate existence or making the corporate existence perpetual may be adopted by a corporation organized prior to August 14, 1929, with approval by the board alone.

(c) Notwithstanding subdivision (a), unless the corporation has more than one class of shares outstanding, an amendment effecting only a stock split (including an increase in the authorized number of shares in proportion thereto) may be adopted with approval by the board alone.

(d) Notwithstanding subdivision (a), an amendment deleting the names and addresses of the first directors or the name and address of the initial agent may be adopted with approval by the board alone.

(e) Whenever the articles require for corporate action the vote of a larger proportion or of all of the shares of any class or series, or of a larger proportion or of all of the directors, than is otherwise required by this division, the provision in the articles requiring such greater vote shall not be altered, amended or repealed except by such greater vote unless otherwise provided in the articles.

(f) Notwithstanding subdivision (a), any amendment reducing the vote required for an amendment pursuant to subdivision (c) of Section 158

may not be adopted unless approved by the affirmative vote of at least two-thirds of each class of outstanding shares or such other vote as may then be specified by the articles of the corporation.

Sec. 903. **Approval of amendments adversely affecting class of shares.** (a) A proposed amendment must be approved by the outstanding shares (Section 152) of a class, whether or not such class is entitled to vote thereon by the provisions of the articles, if the amendment would:

(1) Increase or decrease the aggregate number of authorized shares of such class, other than an increase incident to a stock split or as provided in Section 405(b).

(2) Effect an exchange, reclassification or cancellation of all or part of the shares of such class, other than a stock split.

(3) Effect an exchange, or create a right of exchange, of all or part of the shares of another class into the shares of such class.

(4) Change the rights, preferences, privileges or restrictions of the shares of such class.

(5) Create a new class of shares having rights, preferences or privileges prior to the shares of such class, or increase the rights, preferences or privileges or the number of authorized shares of any class having rights, preferences or privileges prior to the shares of such class.

(6) In the case of preferred shares, divide the shares of any class into series having different rights, preferences, privileges or restrictions or authorize the board to do so.

(7) Cancel or otherwise affect dividends on the shares of such class which have accrued but have not been paid.

(b) Different series of the same class shall not constitute different classes for the purpose of voting by classes except when a series is adversely affected by an amendment in a different manner than other shares of the same class.

(c) In addition to approval by a class as provided in subdivision (a), a proposed amendment must also be approved by the outstanding voting shares (Section 152).

Sec. 904. **Amendment making shares assessable.** If any amendment of the articles would make shares assessable or would authorize remedy by action for the collection of an assessment on fully paid shares, it must be approved by all of the outstanding shares affected regardless of limitations or restrictions on the voting rights thereof.

Sec. 905. **Certificate of amendment for amendment adopted after issuance of shares.** In the case of amendments adopted after the corporation has issued any shares, the corporation shall file a certificate of amendment, which shall consist of an officers' certificate stating:

(a) The wording of the amendment or amended articles in accordance with Section 907;

(b) That the amendment has been approved by the board;

(c) If the amendment is one for which the approval of the outstanding shares (Section 152) is required, that the amendment was approved by the required vote of shareholders in accordance with Section 902, 903 or 904; the total number of outstanding shares of each class entitled to vote with respect to the amendment; and that the number of shares of each class voting in favor of the amendment equaled or exceeded the vote required, specifying the percentage vote required of each class entitled to vote; and

(d) If the amendment is one which may be adopted with approval by the board alone, a statement of the facts entitling the board alone to adopt the amendment.

In the event of an amendment of the articles pursuant to a merger, the filing of the officers' certificate and agreement pursuant to Section 1103 or a certificate of ownership pursuant to subdivision (d) of Section 1110 shall be in lieu of any filing required under this chapter.

Sec. 906. **Certificate of amendment for amendment adopted before issuance of shares.** In the case of amendments adopted by the incorporators or the board under Section 901, the corporation shall file a certificate of amendment signed and verified by a majority of the incorporators or of the board, as the case may be, which shall state that the signers thereof constitute at least a majority of the incorporators or of the board, that the corporation has issued no shares and that they adopt the amendment or amendments therein set forth. In the case of amendments adopted by the incorporators, the certificate shall also state that directors were not named in the original articles and have not been elected.

In the case of amendments adopted by the board under Section 901, the corporation may file a certificate of amendment pursuant to Section 905 in lieu of a certificate of amendment pursuant to this section.

Sec. 907. **Form of certificate of amendment.** The certificate of amendment shall establish the wording of the amendment or amended articles by one or more of the following means:

(a) By stating that the articles shall be amended to read as therein set forth in full.

(b) By stating that any provision of the articles, which shall be identified by the numerical or other designation given it in the articles or by stating the wording thereof, shall be stricken from the articles or shall be amended to read as set forth in the certificate.

(c) By stating that the provisions set forth therein shall be added to the articles.

If the purpose of the amendment is to effect a stock split or reverse stock split or to reclassify, cancel, exchange, or otherwise change outstanding shares, the amended articles shall state the effect thereof on outstanding shares.

Sec. 908. **Effective date of amendment.** Upon the filing of the certificate of amendment, the articles shall be amended in accordance with the certificate and any stock split, reverse stock split, reclassification, cancellation, exchange or other change in shares shall be effected, and a copy of the certificate, certified by the Secretary of State, is prima facie evidence of the performance of the conditions necessary to the adoption of the amendment.

Sec. 909. **Amendment extending term of corporate existence.** A corporation formed for a limited period may at any time subsequent to the expiration of the term of its corporate existence, if it has continuously acted as a corporation and done business as such, extend the term of its existence by an amendment to its articles removing any provision limiting the term of its existence and providing for perpetual existence. If the filing of the certificate of amendment providing for perpetual existence would be prohibited if it were original articles by the provisions of Section 201, the Secretary of State shall not file such certificate unless by the same or a concurrently filed certificate of amendment the articles of such corporation are amended to adopt a new available name. For the purpose of the adoption of any such amendment, persons who have been functioning as directors of such corporation shall be considered to have been validly elected even though their election may have occurred after the expiration of the original term of the corporate existence. The certificate of amendment shall set forth that the corporation continuously acted as a corporation and did business as such from the expiration of its term of corporate existence to the date of the amendment.

Sec. 910. **Restated articles.** (a) A corporation may restate in a single certificate the entire text of its articles as amended by filing an officers' certificate entitled "Restated Articles of Incorporation of (insert name of corporation)" which shall set forth the articles as amended to the date of the filing of the certificate, except that the signatures and acknowledgments of the incorporators and any statements regarding the effect of any prior amendment upon outstanding shares and any provisions of agreements of merger (other than amendments to the articles of the surviving corporation) and the names and addresses of the first directors and of the initial agent for service of process shall be omitted. Such omissions are not alterations or amendments of the articles. The certificate may also itself alter or amend the articles in any respect, in which case the certificate must comply with Section 905 or 906, as the case may be, and Section 907.

(b) If the certificate does not itself alter or amend the articles in any respect, it shall be approved by the board and shall be subject to the provisions of this chapter relating to an amendment of the articles not requiring any approval of the outstanding shares (Section 152). If the certificate does itself alter or amend the articles, it shall be subject to the provisions of this chapter relating to the amendment or amendments so made.

(c) Certificates of determination are a part of the articles within the meaning of this section. The provisions of such a certificate shall be given an article designation in the restated articles.

(d) Restated articles of incorporation filed pursuant to this section shall supersede for all purposes the original articles and all amendments and certificates of determination filed prior thereto.

Sec. 911. **Conversion to a nonprofit corporation.** (a) A corporation may, by amendment of its articles pursuant to this section, convert to a nonprofit public benefit corporation, nonprofit mutual benefit corporation or, nonprofit religious corporation.

(b) The amendment of the articles shall revise the statement of purpose, delete the authorization for shares and any other provisions relating to authorized or issued shares, make such other changes as may be necessary or desired, and, if any shares have been issued, provide either for the cancellation of such shares or for the conversion of such shares to memberships of the nonprofit corporation.

(c) If shares have been issued, the amendment shall be approved by all of the outstanding shares of all classes regardless of limitations or restrictions on the voting rights thereof.

(d) If an amendment pursuant to this section is included in a merger agreement, the provisions of this section apply, except that any provision for cancellation or conversion of shares shall be in the merger agreement rather than in the amendment of the articles.

CHAPTER 10
SALES OF ASSETS

Sec. 1000. **Board's authority to hypothecate corporate property.** Any mortgage, deed of trust, pledge or other hypothecation of all or any part of the corporation's property, real or personal, for the purpose of securing the payment or performance of any contract or obligation may be approved by the board. Unless the articles otherwise provide, no approval of shareholders (Section 153) or of the outstanding shares (Section 152) shall be necessary for such action.

Sec. 1001. **Disposition of entire assets.** (a) A corporation may sell, lease, convey, exchange, transfer or otherwise dispose of all or substantially all of its assets when the principal terms are

(1) Approved by the board, and

(2) Unless the transaction is in the usual and regular course of its business, approved by the outstanding shares (Section 152), either before or after approval by the board and before or after the transaction.

A transaction constituting a reorganization (Section 181) is subject to the provisions of Chapter 12 (commencing with Section 1200) and not this section (other than subdivision (d) hereof).

(b) Notwithstanding approval of the outstanding shares (Section 152), the board may abandon the proposed transaction without further action by the shareholders, subject to the contractual rights, if any, of third parties.

(c) Such sale, lease, conveyance, exchange, transfer or other disposition may be made upon such terms and conditions and for such consideration as the board may deem in the best interests of the corporation. The consideration may be money, property or securities of any other corporation, domestic or foreign, or any of them.

(d) If the buyer in a sale of assets pursuant to subdivision (a) of this section or subdivision (g) of Section 2001 is in control of or under common control with the seller, the principal terms of the sale must be approved by at least 90 percent of the voting power unless the sale is to a domestic or foreign corporation in consideration of the nonredeemable common shares of the purchasing corporation or its parent.

(e) Subdivision (d) does not apply to any transaction if the Commissioner of Corporations, the Superintendent of Banks, the Insurance Commissioner or the Public Utilities Commission has approved the terms and conditions of the transaction and the fairness of such terms and conditions pursuant to Section 25142, Section 696.5 of the Financial Code, Section 838.5 of the Insurance Code or Section 822 of the Public Utilities Code.

Sec. 1002. **Certificate of secretary.** Any deed or instrument conveying or otherwise transferring any assets of a corporation may have annexed to it the certificate of the secretary or an assistant secretary of the corporation, setting forth that the transaction has been validly approved by the board and (a) stating that the property described in said deed or instrument is less than substantially all of the assets of the corporation or that the transfer is in the usual and regular course of the business of the corporation, if such be the case, or (b) if such property constitutes all or substantially all of the assets of the corporation and the transfer is not in the usual and regular course of the business of the corporation, stating the fact of approval thereof by the outstanding shares (Section 152) pursuant to this chapter or Chapter 12, as the case may be, or that such approval is not required by Chapter 12. Such certificate is prima facie evidence of the existence of the facts authorizing such conveyance or other transfer of the assets and conclusive evidence in favor of any innocent purchaser or encumbrancer for value.

CHAPTER 11
MERGER

Sec. 1100. **Authority to merge.** Any two or more corporations may be merged into one of such corporations pursuant to this chapter.

Sec. 1101. **Contents of agreement of merger.** The board of each corporation which desires to merge shall approve an agreement of merger. The constituent corporations shall be parties to the agreement of merger and other persons, including a parent party corporation (Section 1200), may be parties to the agreement of merger. The agreement shall state:

(a) The terms and conditions of the merger;

(b) The amendments, subject to Sections 900 and 907, to the articles of the surviving corporation to be effected by the merger, if any; if any amendment changes the name of the surviving corporation the new name may be the same as or similar to the name of a disappearing domestic or foreign corporation, subject to subdivision (b) of Section 201;

(c) The name and place of incorporation of each constituent corporation and which of the constituent corporations is the surviving corporation;

(d) The manner of converting the shares of each of the constituent corporations into shares or other securities of the surviving corporation and, if any shares of any of the constituent corporations are not to be converted solely into shares or other securities of the surviving corporation, the cash, property, rights or securities of any corporation which the holders of such shares are to receive in exchange for such shares, which cash, property, rights or securities of any corporation may be in addition to or in lieu of shares or other securities of the surviving corporation; and

(e) Such other details or provisions as are desired, if any, including, without limitation, a provision for the payment of cash in lieu of fractional shares or for any other arrangement with respect thereto consistent with the provisions of Section 407.

Each share of the same class, or series of any constituent corporation (other than the cancellation of shares held by a constituent corporation or its parent or a wholly owned subsidiary of either in another constituent corporation) shall, unless all shareholders of the class or series consent and except as provided in Section 407, be treated equally with respect to any distribution of cash, property, rights or securities. Notwithstanding subdivision (d), except in a short-form merger, the nonredeemable common shares of a constituent corporation may be converted only into nonredeemable common shares of the surviving corporation or a parent party if a constituent corporation or its parent owns, directly or indirectly, shares of another constituent corporation representing more than 50 percent of the voting power of the other constituent corporation prior to the merger, unless all of the shareholders of the class consent and except as provided in Section 407.

Sec. 1102. **Execution of agreement.** Each corporation shall sign the agreement by its chairman of the board, president or a vice president and secretary or an assistant secretary acting on behalf of their respective corporations.

Sec. 1103. **Filing agreement and certificate with secretary of state.** After approval of a merger by the board and any approval of the outstanding shares (Section 152) required by Chapter 12 (commencing with Section 1200), the surviving corporation shall file a copy of the agreement of merger with an officers' certificate of each constituent corporation attached stating the total number of outstanding shares of each class entitled to vote on the merger, that the principal terms of the agreement in the form attached were approved by that corporation by a vote of a number of shares of each class which equaled or exceeded the vote required, specifying each class entitled to vote and the percentage vote required of each class, or that the merger agreement was entitled to be and was approved by the board alone under the provisions of Section 1201. If equity securities of a parent of a constituent corporation are to be issued in the merger, the officers' certificate of that constituent corporation shall state either that no vote of the shareholders of the parent was required or that the required vote was obtained. The merger and any amendment of the articles of the surviving corporation contained in the merger agreement shall thereupon be effective (subject to subdivision (c) of Section 110 and subject to the provisions of Section 1108) and the several parties thereto shall be one corporation. The agreement shall not be filed, however, until there has been filed by or on behalf of each corporation taxed under the Bank and Corporation Tax Law (Part 11 (commencing with Section 23001) of Division 2 of the Revenue and Taxation Code), the existence of which is terminated by the merger, the certificate of satisfaction of the Franchise Tax Board that all taxes imposed by said law have been paid or secured. The Secretary of State may certify a copy of the merger agreement separate from the officers' certificates attached thereto.

Sec. 1104. **Amendments to agreement.** Any amendment to the agreement may be adopted and the agreement so amended may be ap-

proved by the board and, if it changes any of the principal terms of the agreement, by the outstanding shares (Section 152) (if required by Chapter 12) of any constituent corporation in the same manner as the original agreement. If the agreement so amended is approved by the board and the outstanding shares (if required) of each of the corporations, the agreement so amended shall then constitute the agreement of merger.

Sec. 1105. **Abandonment of merger.** The board may, in its discretion, abandon a merger, subject to the contractual rights, if any, of third parties, including other constituent corporations, without further approval by the outstanding shares (Section 152), at any time before the merger is effective.

Sec. 1106. **Certified copy of agreement as evidence.** A copy of an agreement of merger certified on or after the effective date by an official having custody thereof has the same force in evidence as the original and, except as against the state, is conclusive evidence of the performance of all conditions precedent to the merger, the existence on the effective date of the surviving corporation and the performance of the conditions necessary to the adoption of any amendment to the articles contained in the agreement of merger.

Sec. 1107. **Effect of merger.** (a) Upon merger pursuant to this chapter the separate existence of the disappearing corporations ceases and the surviving corporation shall succeed, without other transfer, to all the rights and property of each of the disappearing corporations and shall be subject to all the debts and liabilities of each in the same manner as if the surviving corporation had itself incurred them.

(b) All rights of creditors and all liens upon the property of each of the constituent corporations shall be preserved unimpaired, provided that such liens upon property of a disappearing corporation shall be limited to the property affected thereby immediately prior to the time the merger is effective.

(c) Any action or proceeding pending by or against any disappearing corporation may be prosecuted to judgment, which shall bind the surviving corporation, or the surviving corporation may be proceeded against or substituted in its place.

Sec. 1108. **Merger of domestic and foreign corporations.** (a) The merger of any number of domestic corporations with any number of foreign corporations may be effected if the foreign corporations are authorized by the laws under which they are formed to effect such a merger. The surviving corporation may be any one of the constituent corporations and shall continue to exist under the laws of the state or place of its incorporation.

(b) If the surviving corporation is a domestic corporation, the merger proceedings with respect to that corporation and any domestic disappearing corporation shall conform to the provisions of this chapter governing the merger of domestic corporations, or to Section 1110, but if the surviving corporation is a foreign corporation, then, subject to the requirements of subdivision (d) and of Section 407 and Chapters 12 (commencing with Section 1200) and 13 (commencing with Section 1300) (with respect to any domestic constituent corporations), the merger proceedings may be in accordance with the laws of the state or place of incorporation of the surviving corporation.

(c) If the surviving corporation is a domestic corporation, the agreement and the officers' certificate of each domestic or foreign constituent corporation shall be filed as provided in Section 1103 and thereupon, subject to subdivision (c) of Section 110, the merger shall be effective as to each domestic constituent corporation; and each foreign disappearing corporation which is qualified for the transaction of intrastate business shall by virtue of the filing automatically surrender its right to transact intrastate business.

(d) Subject to Section 1110, if the surviving corporation is a foreign corporation, the merger shall become effective in accordance with the law of the jurisdiction in which it is organized, but shall be effective as to any domestic disappearing corporation as of the time of effectiveness in such foreign jurisdiction upon the filing in this state as required by this subdivision. There shall be filed as to the domestic disappearing corporation or corporations a copy of the agreement, certificate or other document filed by the surviving foreign corporation in the state or place of its incorporation for the purpose of effecting the merger, which copy shall be certified by the public officer having official custody of the original or, in lieu thereof, either an executed counterpart of such agreement, certificate or other document or, in case of a merger by agreement of merger, a copy of the agreement of merger with an officers' certificate of each constituent corporation attached as prescribed in Section 1103;

and each foreign disappearing corporation which is qualified for the transaction of intrastate business shall automatically by such filing surrender its right to transact intrastate business.

(e) The provisions of the last two sentences of Section 1101 and Chapters 12 (commencing with Section 1200) and 13 (commencing with Section 1300) apply to the rights of the shareholders of any of the constituent corporations which are domestic corporations and of any domestic corporation which is a parent party of any foreign constituent corporation.

Sec. 1109. **Establishing ownership of real property of disappearing corporation.** Whenever a domestic or foreign corporation having any real property in this state merges or consolidates with another corporation pursuant to the laws of this state or of the state or place in which any constituent corporation was incorporated, and the laws of the state or place of incorporation (including this state) of any disappearing corporation provide substantially that the making and filing of the agreement of merger or consolidation or certificate of ownership or certificate of merger vests in the surviving or consolidated corporation all the real property of any disappearing corporation, the filing for record in the office of the county recorder of any county in this state in which any of the real property of such disappearing corporation is located of either (a) a certificate prescribed by the Secretary of State, or (b) a copy of the agreement of merger or consolidation or certificate of ownership or certificate of merger, certified by the Secretary of State or an authorized public official of the state or place pursuant to the laws of which the merger or consolidation is effected, shall evidence record ownership in the surviving or consolidated corporation of all interest of such disappearing corporation in and to the real property located in that county.

Sec. 1110. **Merger of subsidiary corporation.** (a) If a domestic corporation owns all the outstanding shares of a corporation or corporations, domestic or foreign, the merger of the subsidiary corporation or corporations into the parent corporation may be effected by a resolution adopted by the board of the parent corporation and the filing of a certificate of ownership as provided in subdivision (d). The resolution shall provide for the merger and shall provide that the parent corporation assumes all the liabilities of each subsidiary corporation.

(b) If a domestic corporation owns less than all the outstanding shares but at least 90 percent of the outstanding shares of each class of a corporation or corporations, domestic or foreign, the merger of the subsidiary corporation or corporations into the parent corporation may be effected by resolutions adopted by the boards of the parent and each subsidiary corporation and the filing of a certificate of ownership as provided in subdivision (d). The resolution of the board of the parent corporation shall provide for the merger, shall provide that the parent corporation assumes all the liabilities of each subsidiary corporation and shall set forth the securities, cash, property or rights to be issued, paid, delivered or granted by the parent corporation upon surrender of each share of each subsidiary corporation not owned by the parent corporation. The resolution of the board of each subsidiary corporation shall approve the fairness of the consideration to be received for each share of the subsidiary corporation not owned by the parent corporation.

(c) In any merger pursuant to this section, the parent corporation may change its name, subject to Section 201, regardless of whether the name so adopted is the same as or similar to that of one of the disappearing corporations. In such case the resolution shall provide for the amendment of articles to change the name and shall establish the wording of the amendment as provided in Section 907.

(d) After adoption of the resolution or resolutions of merger, a certificate of ownership consisting of an officers' certificate of the parent corporation shall be filed, and a copy thereof for each domestic and qualified foreign disappearing corporation shall also be filed. The certificate of ownership shall:

(1) Identify the parent and subsidiary corporation or corporations.

(2) Set forth the share ownership by the parent corporation of each subsidiary corporation as 100 percent of the outstanding shares or as at least 90 percent of the outstanding shares of each class, as the case may be.

(3) Set forth the resolution adopted by the board of the parent corporation, including the resolution for change of name if applicable.

(4) Set forth the resolution adopted by the board of each subsidiary corporation, if required.

(e) The certificate of ownership shall not be filed, however, until there has been filed by or on behalf of each subsidiary corporation taxed under the Bank and Corporation Tax Law (Part 11 (commencing with Section 23001) of Division 2 of the Revenue and Taxation Code), the existence of which is terminated by the merger, the certificate of satisfaction of the

Franchise Tax Board that all taxes imposed by such law have been paid or secured.

(f) Upon the filing of the certificate of ownership, the merger shall be effective and any amendment of the articles of the surviving corporation set forth in the certificate shall be effective.

(g) A merger pursuant to this section may be effected if the parent corporation is a foreign corporation and if at least one subsidiary corporation is a domestic corporation but in such a case the certificate of ownership prepared as in subdivision (d) or the document required by subdivision (d) of Section 1108 shall be filed as to each domestic and qualified foreign subsidiary corporation, but no filing shall be made as to the foreign parent corporation.

(h) A foreign subsidiary corporation may not be merged as in this section provided and a foreign parent corporation may not act as in this section provided unless the laws of the state or place of its incorporation permit such action.

(i) In the event all of the outstanding shares of a subsidiary domestic corporation party to a merger effected under this section are not owned by the parent corporation immediately prior to the merger, the parent corporation shall, at least 20 days before the effective date of the merger, give notice to each shareholder of such subsidiary corporation that the merger will become effective on or after a specified date, which notice shall contain a copy of the resolutions of the boards of the parent and the subsidiary required by subdivision (b) and the information required by subdivision (a) of Section 1301. The notice shall be sent by mail addressed to the shareholder at the address of such shareholder as it appears on the records of the corporation. Any such shareholder shall have the right to demand payment of cash for the shares of such shareholder pursuant to the provisions of Chapter 13 (commencing with Section 1300).

Sec. 1111. **Merger of close corporation.** If any disappearing corporation in a merger is a close corporation and the surviving corporation is not a close corporation, the merger shall be approved by the affirmative vote of at least two-thirds of each class of the outstanding shares of such disappearing corporation; provided, however, that the articles may provide for a lesser vote, but not less than a majority of the outstanding shares of each class.

CHAPTER 12

REORGANIZATIONS

Sec. 1200. **Board approval.** A reorganization (Section 181) shall be approved by the board of:

(a) Each constituent corporation in a merger reorganization;

(b) The acquiring corporation in an exchange reorganization;

(c) The acquiring corporation and the corporation whose property and assets are acquired in a sale-of-assets reorganization; and

(d) The corporation in control of any constituent or acquiring corporation under subdivision (a), (b) or (c) and whose equity securities are issued or transferred in the reorganization (a "parent party").

Sec. 1201. **Shareholder approval.** (a) The principal terms of a reorganization shall be approved by the outstanding shares (Section 152) of each class of each corporation the approval of whose board is required under Section 1200, except as provided in subdivision (b) and except that (unless otherwise provided in the articles) no approval of any class of outstanding preferred shares of the surviving or acquiring corporation or parent party shall be required if the rights, preferences, privileges and restrictions granted to or imposed upon such class of shares remain unchanged (subject to the provisions of subdivision (c)). For the purpose of this subdivision, two classes of common shares differing only as to voting rights shall be considered as a single class of shares.

(b) No approval of the outstanding shares (Section 152) is required by subdivision (a) in the case of any corporation if such corporation, or its shareholders immediately before the reorganization, or both, shall own (immediately after the reorganization) equity securities, other than any warrant or right to subscribe to or purchase such equity securities, of the surviving or acquiring corporation or a parent party (subdivision (d) of Section 1200) possessing more than five-sixths of the voting power of the surviving or acquiring corporation or parent party. In making the determination of ownership by the shareholders of a corporation, immediately after the reorganization, of equity securities pursuant to the preceding sentence, equity securities which they owned immediately before the reorganization as shareholders of another party to the transaction shall be disregarded. For the purpose of this section only, the voting power of a corporation shall be calculated by assuming the conversion of all equity securities convertible (immediately or at some future time) into shares entitled to vote but not assuming the exercise of any warrant or right to subscribe to or purchase such shares.

(c) Notwithstanding the provisions of subdivision (b), a reorganization shall be approved by the outstanding shares (Section 152) of the surviving corporation in a merger reorganization if any amendment is made to its articles which would otherwise require such approval.

(d) Notwithstanding the provisions of subdivision (b), a reorganization shall be approved by the outstanding shares (Section 152) of any class of a corporation which is a party to a merger or sale-of-assets reorganization if holders of shares of that class receive shares of the surviving or acquiring corporation or parent party having different rights, preferences, privileges or restrictions than those surrendered. Shares in a foreign corporation received in exchange for shares in a domestic corporation have different rights, preferences, privileges and restrictions within the meaning of the preceding sentence.

(e) Notwithstanding the provisions of subdivisions (a) and (b), a reorganization shall be approved by the affirmative vote of at least two-thirds of each class of the outstanding shares of any close corporation if the reorganization would result in their receiving shares of a corporation which is not a close corporation; provided, however, that the articles may provide for a lesser vote, but not less than a majority of the outstanding shares of each class.

(f) Any approval required by this section may be given before or after the approval by the board. Notwithstanding approval required by this section, the board may abandon the proposed reorganization without further action by the shareholders, subject to the contractual rights, if any, of third parties.

CHAPTER 13

DISSENTERS' RIGHTS

Sec. 1300. **Shareholders having right to require purchase of shares.** (a) If the approval of the outstanding shares (Section 152) of a corporation is required for a reorganization under subdivisions (a) and (b) or subdivision (e) of Section 1201, each shareholder of such corporation entitled to vote on the transaction and each shareholder of a disappearing corporation in a short-form merger may, by complying with this chapter, require the corporation in which the shareholder holds shares to purchase for cash at their fair market value the shares owned by the shareholder which are dissenting shares as defined in subdivision (b). The fair market value shall be determined as of the day before the first announcement of the terms of the proposed reorganization or short-form merger, excluding any appreciation or depreciation in consequence of the proposed action, but adjusted for any stock split, reverse stock split or share dividend which becomes effective thereafter.

(b) As used in this chapter, "dissenting shares" means shares which come within all of the following descriptions:

(1) Which were not immediately prior to the reorganization or short-form merger either (i) listed on any national securities exchange certified by the Commissioner of Corporations under subdivision (o) of Section 25100 or (ii) listed on the list of OTC margin stocks issued by the Board of Governors of the Federal Reserve System, and the notice of meeting of shareholders to act upon the reorganization summarizes the provisions of this section and Sections 1301, 1302, 1303 and 1304; provided, however, that this provision does not apply to any shares with respect to which there exists any restriction on transfer imposed by the corporation or by any law or regulation; and provided, further, that this provision does not apply to any class of shares described in clause (i) or (ii) if demands for payment are filed with respect to 5 percent or more of the outstanding shares of that class.

(2) Which were outstanding on the date for the determination of shareholders entitled to vote on the reorganization and (i) were not voted in favor of the reorganization or, (ii) if described in clause (i) or (ii) of paragraph (1) (without regard to the provisos in that paragraph), were voted against the reorganization, or which were held of record on the effective date of a short-form merger; provided, however, that clause (i) rather than clause (ii) of this paragraph applies in any case where the approval required by Section 1201 is sought by written consent rather than at a meeting.

(3) Which the dissenting shareholder has demanded that the corporation purchase at their fair market value, in accordance with Section 1301.

(4) Which the dissenting shareholder has submitted for endorsement, in accordance with Section 1302.

(c) As used in this chapter, "dissenting shareholder" means the record-holder of dissenting shares and includes a transferee of record.

Sec. 1301. **Demand for purchase.** (a) If, in the case of a reorganization, any shareholders of a corporation have a right under Section 1300, subject to compliance with paragraphs (3) and (4) of subdivision (b) thereof, to require the corporation to purchase their shares for cash, such corporation shall mail to each such shareholder a notice of the approval of the reorganization by its outstanding shares (Section 152) within 10 days after the date of such approval, accompanied by a copy of Sections 1300, 1302, 1303, 1304 and this section, a statement of the price determined by the corporation to represent the fair market value of the dissenting shares, and a brief description of the procedure to be followed if the shareholder desires to exercise the shareholder's right under such sections. The statement of price constitutes an offer by the corporation to purchase at the price stated any dissenting shares as defined in subdivision (b) of Section 1300, unless they lose their status as dissenting shares under Section 1309.

(b) Any shareholder who has a right to require the corporation to purchase the shareholder's shares for cash under Section 1300, subject to compliance with paragraphs (3) and (4) of subdivision (b) thereof, and who desires the corporation to purchase such shares shall make written demand upon the corporation for the purchase of such shares and payment to the shareholder in cash of their fair market value. The demand is not effective for any purpose unless it is received by the corporation or any transfer agent thereof (1) in the case of shares described in clause (i) or (ii) of paragraph (1) of subdivision (b) of Section 1300 (without regard to the provisos in that paragraph), not later than the date of the shareholders' meeting to vote upon the reorganization, or (2) in any other case within 30 days after the date on which the notice of the approval by the outstanding shares pursuant to subdivision (a) or the notice pursuant to subdivision (i) of Section 1110 was mailed to the shareholder.

(c) The demand shall state the number and class of the shares held of record by the shareholder which the shareholder demands that the corporation purchase and shall contain a statement of what such shareholder claims to be the fair market value of those shares as of the day before the announcement of the proposed reorganization or short-form merger. The statement of fair market value constitutes an offer by the shareholder to sell the shares at such price.

Sec. 1302. **Surrender of shares.** Within 30 days after the date on which notice of the approval by the outstanding shares or the notice pursuant to subdivision (i) of Section 1110 was mailed to the shareholder, the shareholder shall submit to the corporation at its principal office or at the office of any transfer agent thereof the shareholder's certificates representing any shares which the shareholder demands that the corporation purchase, to be stamped or endorsed with a statement that the shares are dissenting shares or to be exchanged for certificates of appropriate denomination so stamped or endorsed. Upon subsequent transfers of the dissenting shares on the books of the corporation the new certificates issued therefor shall bear a like statement, together with the name of the original dissenting holder of the shares.

Sec. 1303. **Agreement regarding price; payment.** (a) If the corporation and the shareholder agree that the shares are dissenting shares and agree upon the price of the shares, the dissenting shareholder is entitled to the agreed price with interest thereon at the legal rate on judgments from the date of the agreement. Any agreements fixing the fair market value of any dissenting shares as between the corporation and the holders thereof shall be filed with the secretary of the corporation.

(b) Subject to the provisions of Section 1306, payment of the fair market value of dissenting shares shall be made within 30 days after the amount thereof has been agreed or within 30 days after any statutory or contractual conditions to the reorganization are satisfied, whichever is later, upon surrender of the certificates therefor, unless provided otherwise by agreement.

Sec. 1304. **Action to require payment.** (a) If the corporation denies that the shares are dissenting shares, or the corporation and the shareholder fail to agree upon the fair market value of the shares, then the shareholder demanding purchase of such shares as dissenting shares or any interested corporation, within six months after the date on which notice of the approval by the outstanding shares (Section 152) or notice pursuant to subdivision (i) of Section 1110 was mailed to the shareholder, but not thereafter, may file a complaint in the superior court of the proper county praying the court to determine whether the shares are dissenting shares or the fair market value of the dissenting shares or both or may intervene in any action pending on such a complaint.

(b) Two or more dissenting shareholders may join as plaintiffs or be joined as defendants in any such action and two or more such actions may be consolidated.

(c) On the trial of the action, the court shall determine the issues. If the status of the shares as dissenting shares is in issue, the court shall first determine that issue. If the fair market value of the dissenting shares is in issue, the court shall determine, or shall appoint one or more impartial appraisers to determine, the fair market value of the shares.

Sec. 1305. **Judicial determination of fair market value.** (a) If the court appoints an appraiser or appraisers, they shall proceed forthwith to determine the fair market value per share. Within the time fixed by the court, the appraisers, or a majority of them, shall make and file a report in the office of the clerk of the court. Thereupon, on the motion of any party, the report shall be submitted to the court and considered on such evidence as the court considers relevant. If the court finds the report reasonable, the court may confirm it.

(b) If a majority of the appraisers appointed fail to make and file a report within 10 days from the date of their appointment or within such further time as may be allowed by the court or the report is not confirmed by the court, the court shall determine the fair market value of the dissenting shares.

(c) Subject to the provisions of Section 1306, judgment shall be rendered against the corporation for payment of an amount equal to the fair market value of each dissenting share multiplied by the number of dissenting shares which any dissenting shareholder who is a party, or who has intervened, is entitled to require the corporation to purchase, with interest thereon at the legal rate from the date on which judgment was entered.

(d) Any such judgment shall be payable only upon the endorsement and delivery to the corporation of the certificates for the shares described in the judgment. Any party may appeal from the judgment.

(e) The costs of the action, including reasonable compensation to the appraisers to be fixed by the court, shall be assessed or apportioned as the court considers equitable, but, if the appraisal exceeds the price offered by the corporation, the corporation shall pay the costs (including in the discretion of the court attorneys' fees, fees of expert witnesses and interest at the legal rate on judgments from the date of compliance with Sections 1300, 1301 and 1302 if the value awarded by the court for the shares is more than 125 percent of the price offered by the corporation under subdivision (a) of Section 1301.

Sec. 1306. **Dissenting shareholder as creditor.** To the extent that the provisions of Chapter 5 prevent the payment to any holders of dissenting shares of their fair market value, they shall become creditors of the corporation for the amount thereof together with interest at the legal rate on judgments until the date of payment, but subordinate to all other creditors in any liquidation proceeding, such debt to be payable when permissible under the provisions of Chapter 5.

Sec. 1307. **Dividends paid as credit against payment.** Cash dividends declared and paid by the corporation upon the dissenting shares after the date of approval of the reorganization by the outstanding shares (Section 152) and prior to payment for the shares by the corporation shall be credited against the total amount to be paid by the corporation therefor.

Sec. 1308. **Continuing rights and privileges of dissenting shareholders.** Except as expressly limited in this chapter, holders of dissenting shares continue to have all the rights and privileges incident to their shares, until the fair market value of their shares is agreed upon or determined. A dissenting shareholder may not withdraw a demand for payment unless the corporation consents thereto.

Sec. 1309. **Events causing termination of dissenting shareholder status.** Dissenting shares lose their status as dissenting shares and the holders thereof cease to be dissenting shareholders and cease to be entitled to require the corporation to purchase their shares upon the happening of any of the following:

(a) The corporation abandons the reorganization. Upon abandonment of the reorganization, the corporation shall pay on demand to any dissenting shareholder who has initiated proceedings in good faith under this chapter all necessary expenses incurred in such proceedings and reasonable attorneys' fees.

(b) The shares are transferred prior to their submission for endorsement in accordance with Section 1302 or are surrendered for conversion into shares of another class in accordance with the articles.

(c) The dissenting shareholder and the corporation do not agree upon the status of the shares as dissenting shares or upon the purchase price of the shares, and neither files a complaint or intervenes in a pending action as provided in Section 1304, within six months after the date on which

notice of the approval by the outstanding shares or notice pursuant to subdivision (i) of Section 1110 was mailed to the shareholder.

(d) The dissenting shareholder, with the consent of the corporation, withdraws the shareholder's demand for purchase of the dissenting shares.

Sec. 1310. **Suspension of proceedings for payment pending litigation.** If litigation is instituted to test the sufficiency or regularity of the votes of the shareholders in authorizing a reorganization, any proceedings under Sections 1304 and 1305 shall be suspended until final determination of such litigation.

Sec. 1311. **Exempt shares.** This chapter does not apply to classes of shares whose terms and provisions specifically set forth the amount to be paid in respect to such shares in the event of a reorganization or merger.

Sec. 1312. **Attacking validity of reorganization or merger.** (a) No shareholder of a corporation who has a right under this chapter to demand payment of cash for the shares held by the shareholder shall have any right at law or in equity to attack the validity of the reorganization or short-form merger, or to have the reorganization or short-form merger set aside or rescinded, except in an action to test whether the number of shares required to authorize or approve the reorganization have been legally voted in favor thereof; but any holder of shares of a class whose terms and provisions specifically set forth the amount to be paid in respect to them in the event of a reorganization or short-form merger is entitled to payment in accordance with those terms and provisions.

(b) If one of the parties to a reorganization or short-form merger is directly or indirectly controlled by, or under common control with, another party to the reorganization or short-form merger, subdivision (a) shall not apply to any shareholder of such party who has not demanded payment of cash for such shareholder's shares pursuant to this chapter; but if the shareholder institutes any action to attack the validity of the reorganization or short-form merger or to have the reorganization or short-form merger set aside or rescinded, the shareholder shall not thereafter have any right to demand payment of cash for the shareholder's shares pursuant to this chapter. The court in any action attacking the validity of the reorganization or short-form merger or to have the reorganization or short-form merger set aside or rescinded shall not restrain or enjoin the consummation of the transaction except upon 10-days prior notice to the corporation and upon a determination by the court that clearly no other remedy will adequately protect the complaining shareholder or the class of shareholders of which such shareholder is a member.

(c) If one of the parties to a reorganization or short-form merger is directly or indirectly controlled by, or under common control with, another party to the reorganization or short-form merger, in any action to attack the validity of the reorganization or short-form merger or to have the reorganization or short-form merger set aside or rescinded, (1) a party to a reorganization or short-form merger which controls another party to the reorganization or short-form merger shall have the burden of proving that the transaction is just and reasonable as to the shareholders of the controlled party, and (2) a person who controls two or more parties to a reorganization shall have the burden of proving that the transaction is just and reasonable as to the shareholders of any party so controlled.

CHAPTER 14

BANKRUPTCY REORGANIZATIONS AND ARRANGEMENTS

Sec. 1400. **Authority to effectuate plan of reorganization or arrangement under federal statute.** (a) Any domestic corporation with respect to which a proceeding has been initiated under any applicable statute of the United States, as now existing or hereafter enacted, relating to reorganizations or arrangements of corporations, has full power and authority to put into effect and carry out any plan of reorganization or arrangement and the orders of the court or judge entered in such proceeding and may take any proceeding and do any act provided in the plan or directed by such orders, without further action by its board or shareholders. Such power and authority may be exercised and such proceedings and acts may be taken, as may be directed by such orders, by the trustee or trustees of such corporation appointed in the reorganization or arrangement proceeding (or a majority thereof), or if none is appointed and acting, by officers of the corporation designated or a master or other representative appointed by the court or judge, with like effect as if exercised and taken by unanimous action of the board and shareholders of the corporation.

(b) Such corporation may, in the manner provided in subdivision (a), but without limiting the generality or effect of subdivision (a), alter, amend or repeal its bylaws; constitute or reconstitute its board and name, constitute or appoint directors and officers in place of or in addition to all or some of the directors or officers then in office; amend its articles; make any change in its capital stock; make any other amendment, change, alteration or provision authorized by this division; be dissolved, transfer all or part of its assets or merge as permitted by this division, in which case, however, no shareholder shall have any statutory dissenter's rights; change the location of its principal executive office or remove or appoint an agent to receive service of process; authorize and fix the terms, manner and conditions of the issuance of bonds, debentures or other obligations, whether or not convertible into shares of any class or bearing warrants or rights to purchase or subscribe to shares of any class; or lease its property and franchises to any corporation, if permitted by law.

Sec. 1401. Certificate of reorganization. (a) A certificate of any amendment, change or alteration or of dissolution or any agreement of merger made by such corporation pursuant to Section 1400 and executed as provided in subdivision (b), shall be filed and shall thereupon become effective in accordance with its terms and the provisions of this chapter.

(b) Such certificate, agreement of merger or other instrument shall be signed and verified, as may be directed by such orders of the court or judge, by the trustee or trustees appointed in the reorganization or arrangement proceeding (or a majority thereof) or, if none is appointed and acting, by officers of the corporation designated or by a master or other representative appointed by the court or judge, and shall state that provision for the making of such certificate, agreement or instrument is contained in an order, identifying the same, of a court or judge having jurisdiction of a proceeding under a statute of the United States for the reorganization or arrangement of such corporation.

CHAPTER 15

RECORDS AND REPORTS

Sec. 1500. Requirement of keeping books and records. Each corporation shall keep adequate and correct books and records of account and shall keep minutes of the proceedings of its shareholders, board and committees of the board and shall keep at its principal executive office, or at the office of its transfer agent or registrar, a record of its shareholders, giving the names and addresses of all shareholders and the number and class of shares held by each. Such minutes shall be kept in written form. Such other books and records shall be kept either in written form or in any other form capable of being converted into written form.

Sec. 1501. Annual report to shareholders. (a) The board shall cause an annual report to be sent to the shareholders not later than 120 days after the close of the fiscal year, unless in the case of a corporation with less than 100 holders of record of its shares (determined as provided in Section 605) this requirement is expressly waived in the bylaws. Such report shall contain a balance sheet as of the end of that fiscal year and an income statement and statement of changes in financial position for that fiscal year, accompanied by any report thereon of independent accountants or, if there is no such report, the certificate of an authorized officer of the corporation that the statements were prepared without audit from the books and records of the corporation.

Unless so waived, the report shall be sent to the shareholders at least 15 (or, if sent by third-class mail, 35) days prior to the annual meeting of shareholders to be held during the next fiscal year, but this requirement shall not limit the requirement for holding an annual meeting as required by Section 600.

Notwithstanding Section 114, the financial statements of any corporation with fewer than 100 holders of record of its shares (determined as provided in Section 605) required to be furnished by this subdivision and subdivision (c) of this section are not required to be prepared in conformity with generally accepted accounting principles if they reasonably set forth the assets and liabilities and the income and expense of the corporation and disclose the accounting basis used in their preparation.

(b) In addition to the financial statements required by subdivision (a), the annual report of any corporation having 100 or more holders of record of its shares (determined as provided in Section 605) and having no class of securities registered under Section 12 of the Securities Exchange Act of 1934, or exempted from such registration by Section 12(g)(2) of that act, shall also describe briefly:

(1) Any transaction (excluding compensation of officers and directors) during the previous fiscal year involving an amount in excess of forty thousand dollars ($40,000) (other than contracts let at competitive bid or services rendered at prices regulated by law) to which the corporation or its parent or subsidiary was a party and in which any director or officer of the corporation or of a subsidiary or (if known to the corporation or its parent or subsidiary) any holder of more than 10 percent of the outstanding voting shares of the corporation had a direct or indirect material interest, naming the person and stating the person's relationship to the corporation, the nature of such person's interest in the transaction and, where practicable, the amount of such interest; provided, that in the case of a transaction with a partnership of which such person is a partner, only the interest of the partnership need be stated; and provided, further that no such report need be made in the case of any transaction approved by the shareholders (Section 153).

(2) The amount and circumstances of any indemnification or advances aggregating more than ten thousand dollars ($10,000) paid during the fiscal year to any officer or director of the corporation pursuant to Section 317; provided, that no such report need be made in the case of indemnification approved by the shareholders (Section 153) under paragraph (2) of subdivision (e) of Section 317.

(c) If no annual report for the last fiscal year has been sent to shareholders, the corporation shall, upon the written request of any shareholder made more than 120 days after the close of such fiscal year, deliver or mail to the person making the request within 30 days thereafter the financial statements required by subdivision (a) for that year. A shareholder or shareholders holding at least 5 percent of the outstanding shares of any class of a corporation may make a written request to the corporation for an income statement of the corporation for the three-month, six-month or nine-month period of the current fiscal year ended more than 30 days prior to the date of the request and a balance sheet of the corporation as of the end of such period and, in addition, if no annual report for the last fiscal year has been sent to shareholders, the statements referred to in subdivision (a) for the last fiscal year. The statements shall be delivered or mailed to the person making the request within 30 days thereafter. A copy of the statements shall be kept on file in the principal office of the corporation for 12 months and they shall be exhibited at all reasonable times to any shareholder demanding an examination of them or a copy shall be mailed to such shareholder.

(d) The quarterly income statements and balance sheets referred to in this section shall be accompanied by the report thereon, if any, of any independent accountants engaged by the corporation or the certificate of an authorized officer of the corporation that such financial statements were prepared without audit from the books and records of the corporation.

(e) In addition to the penalties provided for in Section 2200, the superior court of the proper county shall enforce the duty of making and mailing or delivering the information and financial statements required by this section and, for good cause shown, may extend the time therefor.

(f) In any action or proceeding under this section, if the court finds the failure of the corporation to comply with the requirements of this section to have been without justification, the court may award an amount sufficient to reimburse the shareholder for the reasonable expenses incurred by the shareholder, including attorneys' fees, in connection with such action or proceeding.

(g) This section applies to any domestic corporation and also to a foreign corporation having its principal executive office in this state or customarily holding meetings of its board in this state.

Sec. 1502. Annual filing with Secretary of State. (a) Every corporation shall file, within 90 days after the filing of its original articles and annually thereafter during the applicable filing period in each year, file, on a form prescribed by the Secretary of State, a statement containing: (1) the presently authorized number of its directors; (2) the names and complete business or residence addresses of its incumbent directors; (3) the names and complete business or residence addresses of its chief executive officer, secretary and chief financial officer; (4) the street address of its principal executive office; (5) if the address of its principal executive office is not in this state, the street address of its principal business office in this state, if any; and (6) a statement of the general type of business which constitutes the principal business activity of the corporation (for example, manufacturer of aircraft; wholesale liquor distributor; retail department store).

(b) The statement required by subdivision (a) shall also designate, as the agent of such corporation for the purpose of service of process, a natural person residing in this state or a corporation which has complied with Section 1505 and whose capacity to act as such agent has not terminated. If a natural person is designated, the statement shall set forth such person's complete business or residence address. If a corporate agent is designated, no address for it shall be set forth.

(c) If there has been no change in the information in the last filed statement of the corporation on file in the Secretary of State's office, the corporation may, in lieu of filing the statement required by subdivisions (a) and (b), advise the Secretary of State, on a form prescribed by the Secretary of State, that no changes in the required information have occurred during the applicable filing period.

(d) For the purposes of this section, the applicable filing period for a corporation shall be the calendar month during which its original articles were filed and the immediately preceding five calendar months. The Secretary of State shall mail a form for compliance with this section to each corporation approximately three months prior to the close of the applicable filing period. The form shall state the due date thereof and shall be mailed to the last address of the corporation according to the records of the Secretary of State. The failure of the corporation to receive the form is not an excuse for failure to comply with this section.

(e) Whenever any of the information required by subdivision (a) is changed, the corporation may file a current statement containing all the information required by subdivisions (a) and (b). In order to change its agent for service of process or the address of the agent, the corporation must file a current statement containing all the information required by subdivisions (a) and (b). Whenever any statement is filed pursuant to this section, it supersedes any previously filed statement and the statement in the articles as to the agent for service of process and the address of the agent.

(f) The Secretary of State may destroy or otherwise dispose of any statement filed pursuant to this section after it has been superseded by the filing of a new statement.

(g) This section shall not be construed to place any person dealing with the corporation on notice of, or under any duty to inquire about, the existence or content of a statement filed pursuant to this section.

Sec. 1503. Resignation of agent for service of process by filing statement of resignation. An agent designated for service of process pursuant to Section 1502 or 2105 or 2107 may file a signed and acknowledged written statement of resignation as such agent. Thereupon the authority of the agent to act in such capacity shall cease and the Secretary of State forthwith shall give written notice of the filing of the statement of resignation by mail to the corporation addressed to its principal executive office.

Sec. 1504. Designation of new agent for service of process. If a natural person who has been designated agent for service of process pursuant to Section 1502 or 2105 or 2107 dies or resigns or no longer resides in the state or if the corporate agent for such purpose resigns, dissolves, withdraws from the state, forfeits its right to transact intrastate business, has its corporate rights, powers and privileges suspended or ceases to exist, the corporation shall forthwith file a designation of a new agent conforming to the requirements of Section 1502 or 2107.

Sec. 1505. Filing of certificate by corporation undertaking to qualify as agent for service of process. (a) Any domestic or foreign corporation, before it may be designated as the agent for the purpose of service of process of any domestic or foreign corporation pursuant to Section 1502 or 2105 or 2107 or 6210 or 8210 or Section 6210 as made applicable pursuant to Section 9660 shall file a certificate executed in the name of the corporation by an officer thereof stating:

(1) The complete address of its office or offices in this state, wherein any corporation designating it as such agent may be served with process.

(2) The name of each person employed by it at each such office to whom it authorizes the delivery of a copy of any such process.

(3) Its consent that delivery thereof to any such person at the office where such person is employed shall constitute delivery of any such copy to it, as such agent.

(b) Any corporation which has filed the certificate provided for in subdivision (a) may file any number of supplemental certificates containing all the statements provided for in subdivision (a), which, upon the filing thereof, shall supersede the statements contained in the original or in any supplemental certificate previously filed.

(c) No domestic or foreign corporation may file a certificate pursuant to this section unless it is currently authorized to engage in business in this state and is in good standing on the records of the Secretary of State.

CHAPTER 16

RIGHTS OF INSPECTION

Sec. 1600. Shareholders having right to inspect and obtain copy of record of shareholders. (a) A shareholder or shareholders holding at least 5 percent in the aggregate of the outstanding voting shares of a corporation or who hold at least 1 percent of such voting shares and have filed a Schedule 14B with the United States Securities and Exchange Commission (or, in case the corporation is a bank the deposits of which are insured in accordance with the Federal Deposit Insurance Act, a Form F-6 with the appropriate federal bank regulatory agency) relating to the election of directors of the corporation shall have an absolute right to do either or both of the following: (1) inspect and copy the record of shareholders' names and addresses and shareholdings during usual business hours upon five business days' prior written demand upon the corporation, or (2) obtain from the transfer agent for the corporation, upon written demand and upon the tender of its usual charges for such a list (the amount of which charges shall be stated to the shareholder by the transfer agent upon request), a list of the shareholders' names and addresses, who are entitled to vote for the election of directors, and their shareholdings, as of the most recent record date for which it has been compiled or as of a date specified by the shareholder subsequent to the date of demand. The list shall be made available on or before the later of five business days after the demand is received or the date specified therein as the date as of which the list is to be compiled. A corporation shall have the responsibility to cause its transfer agent to comply with this subdivision.

(b) Any delay by the corporation or the transfer agent in complying with a demand under subdivision (a) beyond the time limits specified therein shall give the shareholder or shareholders properly making the demand a right to obtain from the superior court, upon the filing of a verified complaint in the proper county and after a hearing, notice of which shall be given to such persons and in such manner as the court may direct, an order postponing any shareholders' meeting previously noticed for a period equal to the period of such delay. Such right shall be in addition to any other legal or equitable remedies to which the shareholder may be entitled.

(c) The record of shareholders shall also be open to inspection and copying by any shareholder or holder of a voting trust certificate at any time during usual business hours upon written demand on the corporation, for a purpose reasonably related to such holder's interests as a shareholder or holder of a voting trust certificate.

(d) Any inspection and copying under this section may be made in person or by agent or attorney. The rights provided in this section may not be limited by the articles or bylaws. This section applies to any domestic corporation and to any foreign corporation having its principal executive office in this state or customarily holding meetings of its board in this state.

Sec. 1601. Shareholder's right to inspect books and records. (a) The accounting books and records and minutes of proceedings of the shareholders and the board and committees of the board of any domestic corporation, and of any foreign corporation keeping any such records in this state or having its principal executive office in this state, shall be open to inspection upon the written demand on the corporation of any shareholder or holder of a voting trust certificate at any reasonable time during usual business hours, for a purpose reasonably related to such holder's interests as a shareholder or as the holder of such voting trust certificate. The right of inspection created by this subdivision shall extend to the records of each subsidiary of a corporation subject to this subdivision.

(b) Such inspection by a shareholder or holder of a voting trust certificate may be made in person or by agent or attorney, and the right of inspection includes the right to copy and make extracts. The right of the shareholders to inspect the corporate records may not be limited by the articles or bylaws.

Sec. 1602. Director's right to inspect books, records and physical properties of corporation. Every director shall have the absolute right at any reasonable time to inspect and copy all books, records and documents of every kind and to inspect the physical properties of the corporation of which such person is a director and also of its subsidiary corporations, domestic or foreign. Such inspection by a director may be made in person or by agent or attorney and the right of inspection includes the right to copy and make extracts. This section applies to a director of any foreign corporation having its principal executive office in this state or customarily holding meetings of its board in this state.

464   BUSINESS LAW   Corp.C. §§ 1603-1801

Sec. 1603. **Action to enforce right of inspection.** (a) Upon refusal of a lawful demand for inspection, the superior court of the proper county, may enforce the right of inspection with just and proper conditions or may, for good cause shown, appoint one or more competent inspectors or accountants to audit the books and records kept in this state and investigate the property, funds and affairs of any domestic corporation or any foreign corporation keeping records in this state and of any subsidiary corporation thereof, domestic or foreign, keeping records in this state and to report thereon in such manner as the court may direct.

(b) All officers and agents of the corporation shall produce to the inspectors or accountants so appointed all books and documents in their custody or power, under penalty of punishment for contempt of court.

(c) All expenses of the investigation or audit shall be defrayed by the applicant unless the court orders them to be paid or shared by the corporation.

Sec. 1604. **Reimbursement of expenses.** In any action or proceeding under Section 1600 or Section 1601, if the court finds the failure of the corporation to comply with a proper demand thereunder was without justification, the court may award an amount sufficient to reimburse the shareholder or holder of a voting trust certificate for the reasonable expenses incurred by such holder, including attorneys' fees, in connection with such action or proceeding.

Sec. 1605. **Requirement that records be maintained in written form.** If any record subject to inspection pursuant to this chapter is not maintained in written form, a request for inspection is not complied with unless and until the corporation at its expense makes such record available in written form.

CHAPTER 17

SERVICE OF PROCESS

Sec. 1700. **Methods of service.** In addition to the provisions of Chapter 4 (commencing with Section 413.10) of Title 5 of Part 2 of the Code of Civil Procedure, process may be served upon domestic corporations as provided in this chapter.

Sec. 1701. **Valid service.** Delivery by hand of a copy of any process against the corporation (a) to any natural person designated by it as agent or (b), if a corporate agent has been designated, to any person named in the latest certificate of the corporate agent filed pursuant to Section 1505 at the office of such corporate agent shall constitute valid service on the corporation.

Sec. 1702. **Service on Secretary of State.** (a) If an agent for the purpose of service of process has resigned and has not been replaced or if the agent designated cannot with reasonable diligence be found at the address designated for personally delivering the process, or if no agent has been designated, and it is shown by affidavit to the satisfaction of the court that process against a domestic corporation cannot be served with reasonable diligence upon the designated agent by hand in the manner provided in Section 415.10, subdivision (a) of Section 415.20 or subdivision (a) of Section 415.30 of the Code of Civil Procedure or upon the corporation in the manner provided in subdivision (a), (b) or (c) of Section 416.10 or subdivision (a) of Section 416.20 of the Code of Civil Procedure, the court may make an order that the service be made upon the corporation by delivering by hand to the Secretary of State, or to any person employed in the Secretary of State's office in the capacity of assistant or deputy, one copy of the process for each defendant to be served, together with a copy of the order authorizing such service. Service in this manner is deemed complete on the 10th day after delivery of the process to the Secretary of State.

(b) Upon the receipt of any such copy of process and the fee therefor, the Secretary of State shall give notice of the service of the process to the corporation at its principal executive office, by forwarding to such office, by registered mail with request for return receipt, the copy of the process or, if the records of the Secretary of State do not disclose an address for its principal executive office, by forwarding such copy in the same manner to the last designated agent for service of process who has not resigned. If the agent for service of process has resigned and has not been replaced and the records of the Secretary of State do not disclose an address for its principal executive office, no action need be taken by the Secretary of State.

(c) The Secretary of State shall keep a record of all process served upon the Secretary of State under this chapter and shall record therein the time of service and the Secretary of State's action with reference thereto. The certificate of the Secretary of State, under the Secretary of State's official seal, certifying to the receipt of process, the giving of notice thereof to the corporation and the forwarding of such process pursuant to this section, shall be competent and prima facie evidence of the matters stated therein.

CHAPTER 18

INVOLUNTARY DISSOLUTION

Sec. 1800. **Persons entitled to file complaint; grounds.** (a) A verified complaint for involuntary dissolution of a corporation on any one or more of the grounds specified in subdivision (b) may be filed in the superior court of the proper county by any of the following persons:

(1) One-half or more of the directors in office.

(2) A shareholder or shareholders who hold shares representing not less than 33⅓ percent of (i) the total number of outstanding shares (assuming conversion of any preferred shares convertible into common shares) or (ii) the outstanding common shares or (iii) the equity of the corporation, exclusive in each case of shares owned by persons who have personally participated in any of the transactions enumerated in paragraph (4) of subdivision (b), or any shareholder or shareholders of a close corporation.

(3) Any shareholder if the ground for dissolution is that the period for whic h the corporation was formed has terminated without extension thereof.

(4) Any other person expressly authorized to do so in the articles.

(b) The grounds for involuntary dissolution are that:

(1) The corporation has abandoned its business for more than one year.

(2) The corporation has an even number of directors who are equally divided and cannot agree as to the management of its affairs, so that its business can no longer be conducted to advantage or so that there is danger that its property and business will be impaired or lost, and the holders of the voting shares of the corporation are so divided into factions that they cannot elect a board consisting of an uneven number.

(3) There is internal dissension and two or more factions of shareholders in the corporation are so deadlocked that its business can no longer be conducted with advantage to its shareholders or the shareholders have failed at two consecutive annual meetings at which all voting power was exercised, to elect successors to directors whose terms have expired or would have expired upon election of their successors.

(4) Those in control of the corporation have been guilty of or have knowingly countenanced persistent and pervasive fraud, mismanagement or abuse of authority or persistent unfairness toward any shareholders or its property is being misapplied or wasted by its directors or officers.

(5) In the case of any corporation with 35 or fewer shareholders (determined as provided in Section 605), liquidation is reasonably necessary for the protection of the rights or interests of the complaining shareholder or shareholders.

(6) The period for which the corporation was formed has terminated without extension of such period.

(c) At any time prior to the trial of the action any shareholder or creditor may intervene therein.

(d) This section does not apply to any corporation subject to the Banking Law (Division 1 (commencing with Section 99) of the Financial Code), the Public Utilities Act (Part 1 (commencing with 201) of Division 1 of the Public Utilities Code), the Savings and Loan Association Law (Division 2 (commencing with Section 5000) of the Financial Code) or Article 14 (commencing with Section 1010) of Chapter 1 of Part 2 of Division 1 of the Insurance Code.

(e) For the purposes of this section, "shareholder" includes a beneficial owner of shares who has entered into an agreement under Section 300 or 706.

Sec. 1801. **Action by Attorney General.** (a) The Attorney General may bring an action against any domestic corporation or purported domestic corporation in the name of the people of this state, upon the Attorney General's own information or upon complaint of a private party, to procure a judgment dissolving the corporation and annulling, vacating or forfeiting its corporate existence upon any of the following grounds:

(1) The corporation has seriously offended against any provision of the statutes regulating corporations.

(2) The corporation has fraudulently abused or usurped corporate privileges or powers.

(3) The corporation has violated any provision of law by any act or default which under the law is a ground for forfeiture of corporate existence.

(4) The corporation has failed to pay to the Franchise Tax Board for a period of five years any tax imposed upon it by the Bank and Corporation Tax Law.

(b) If the ground of the action is a matter or act which the corporation has done or omitted to do that can be corrected by amendment of its articles or by other corporate action, such suit shall not be maintained unless (1) the Attorney General, at least 30 days prior to the institution of suit, has given the corporation written notice of the matter or act done or omitted to be done and (2) the corporation has failed to institute proceedings to correct it within the 30-day period or thereafter fails to prosecute such proceedings.

(c) In any such action the court may order dissolution or such other or partial relief as it deems just and expedient. The court also may appoint a receiver for winding up the affairs of the corporation or may order that the corporation be wound up by its board subject to the supervision of the court.

(d) Service of process on the corporation may be made pursuant to Chapter 17 or by written notice to the president or secretary of the corporation at the address indicated in the corporation's last tax return filed pursuant to the Bank and Corporation Tax Law. The Attorney General shall also publish one time in a newspaper of general circulation in the proper county a notice to the shareholders of the corporation.

Sec. 1802. Appointment of provisional director to break deadlock.
If the ground for the complaint for involuntary dissolution of the corporation is a deadlock in the board as set forth in subdivision (b)(2) of Section 1800, the court may appoint a provisional director. The provisions of subdivision (c) of Section 308 apply to any such provisional director so appointed.

Sec. 1803. Appointment of receiver.
If, at the time of the filing of a complaint for involuntary dissolution or at any time thereafter, the court has reasonable grounds to believe that unless a receiver of the corporation is appointed the interests of the corporation and its shareholders will suffer pending the hearing and determination of the complaint, upon the application of the plaintiff, and after a hearing upon such notice to the corporation as the court may direct and upon the giving of security pursuant to Sections 566 and 567 of the Code of Civil Procedure, the court may appoint a receiver to take over and manage the business and affairs of the corporation and to preserve its property pending the hearing and determination of the complaint for dissolution.

Sec. 1804. Decree of winding up and dissolution.
After hearing the court may decree a winding up and dissolution of the corporation if cause therefor is shown or, with or without winding up and dissolution, may make such orders and decrees and issue such injunctions in the case as justice and equity require.

Sec. 1805. Cessation of business activities on commencement of proceeding.
(a) Involuntary proceedings for winding up a corporation commence when the order for winding up is entered under Section 1804.

(b) When an involuntary proceeding for winding up has commenced, the board shall conduct the winding up of the affairs of the corporation, subject to the supervision of the court, unless other persons are appointed by the court, on good cause shown, to conduct the winding up. The directors or such other persons may, subject to any restrictions imposed by the court, exercise all their powers through the executive officers without any order of court.

(c) When an involuntary proceeding for winding up has commenced, the corporation shall cease to carry on business except to the extent necessary for the beneficial winding up thereof and except during such period as the board may deem necessary to preserve the corporation's goodwill or going-concern value pending a sale of its business or assets, or both, in whole or in part. The directors shall cause written notice of the commencement of the proceeding for involuntary winding up to be given by mail to all shareholders and to all known creditors and claimants whose addresses appear on the records of the corporation, unless the order for winding up has been stayed by appeal therefrom or otherwise or the proceeding or the execution of the order has been enjoined.

Sec. 1806. Jurisdiction of court.
When an involuntary proceeding for winding up has been commenced, the jurisdiction of the court includes:

(a) The requirement of the proof of all claims and demands against the corporation, whether due or not yet due, contingent, unliquidated or sounding only in damages, and the barring from participation of creditors and claimants failing to make and present claims and proof as required by any order.

(b) The determination or compromise of all claims of every nature against the corporation or any of its property, and the determination of the amount of money or assets required to be retained to pay or provide for the payment of claims.

(c) The determination of the rights of shareholders and of all classes of shareholders in and to the assets of the corporation.

(d) The presentation and filing of intermediate and final accounts of the directors or other persons appointed to conduct the winding up and hearing thereon, the allowance, disallowance or settlement thereof and the discharge of the directors or such other persons from their duties and liabilities.

(e) The appointment of a commissioner to hear and determine any or all matters, with such power or authority as the court may deem proper.

(f) The filling of any vacancies on the board which the directors or shareholders are unable to fill.

(g) The removal of any director if it appears that the director has been guilty of dishonesty, misconduct, neglect or abuse of trust in conducting the winding up or if the director is unable to act. The court may order an election to fill the vacancy so caused, and may enjoin, for such time as it considers proper, the reelection of the director so removed; or the court, in lieu of ordering an election, may appoint a director to fill the vacancy caused by such removal. Any director so appointed by the court shall serve until the next annual meeting of shareholders or until a successor is elected or appointed.

(h) Staying the prosecution of any suit, proceeding or action against the corporation and requiring the parties to present and prove their claims in the manner required of other creditors.

(i) The determination of whether adequate provision has been made for payment or satisfaction of all debts and liabilities not actually paid.

(j) The making of orders for the withdrawal or termination of proceedings to wind up and dissolve, subject to conditions for the protection of shareholders and creditors.

(k) The making of an order, upon the allowance or settlement of the final accounts of the directors or such other persons, that the corporation has been duly wound up and is dissolved. Upon the making of such order, the corporate existence shall cease except for purposes of further winding up if needed.

(l) The making of orders for the bringing in of new parties as the court deems proper for the determination of all questions and matters.

Sec. 1807. Creditors' claims; notice to creditors.
(a) All creditors and claimants may be barred from participation in any distribution of the general assets if they fail to make and present claims and proofs within such time as the court may direct, which shall not be less than four nor more than six months after the first publication of notice to creditors unless it appears by affidavit that there are no claims, in which case the time limit may be three months. If it is shown that a claimant did not receive notice because of absence from the state or other cause, the court may allow a claim to be filed or presented at any time before distribution is completed.

(b) Such notice to creditors shall be published not less than once a week for three consecutive weeks in a newspaper of general circulation published in the county in which the proceeding is pending or, if there is no such newspaper published in that county, in such newspaper as may be designated by the court, directing creditors and claimants to make and present claims and proofs to the person, at the place and within the time specified in the notice. A copy of the notice shall be mailed to each person shown as a creditor or claimant on the books of the corporation, at such person's last known address.

(c) Holders of secured claims may prove for the whole debt in order to realize any deficiency. If such creditors fail to present their claims they shall be barred only as to any right to claim against the general assets for any deficiency in the amount realized on their security.

(d) Before any distribution is made the amount of any unmatured, contingent or disputed claim against the corporation which has been presented and has not been disallowed, or such part of any such claim as the holder would be entitled to if the claim were due, established or absolute, shall be paid into court and there remain to be paid over to the party when the party becomes entitled thereto or, if the party fails to establish a claim, to be paid over or distributed with the other assets of the corporation to those entitled thereto; or such other provision for the full payment of such claim, if and when established, shall be made as the court may deem adequate. A creditor whose claim has been allowed but is not yet due shall be entitled to its present value upon distribution.

(e) Suits against the corporation on claims which have been rejected shall be commenced within 30 days after written notice of rejection thereof is given to the claimant.

Sec. 1808. Dissolution order. (a) Upon the final settlement of the accounts of the directors or other persons appointed pursuant to Section 1805 and the determination that the corporation's affairs are in condition for it to be dissolved, the court may make an order declaring the corporation duly wound up and dissolved. The order shall declare:

(1) That the corporation has been duly wound up, that any tax or penalty due under the Bank and Corporation Tax Law has been paid or secured and that its other known debts and liabilities have been paid or adequately provided for, or that such taxes, penalties, debts and liabilities have been paid as far as its assets permitted, as the case may be. If there are known debts or liabilities for payment of which adequate provision has been made, the order shall state what provision has been made, setting forth the name and address of the corporation, person or governmental agency that has assumed or guaranteed the payment, or the name and address of the depositary with which deposit has been made or such other information as may be necessary to enable the creditor or other person to whom payment is to be made to appear and claim payment of the debt or liability.

(2) That its known assets have been distributed to the persons entitled thereto or that it acquired no known assets, as the case may be.

(3) That the accounts of directors or such other persons have been settled and that they are discharged from their duties and liabilities to creditors and shareholders.

(4) That the corporation is dissolved. The court may make such additional orders and grant such further relief as it deems proper upon the evidence submitted.

(b) Upon the making of the order declaring the corporation dissolved, corporate existence shall cease except for the purposes of further winding up if needed; and the directors or such other persons shall be discharged from their duties and liabilities, except in respect to completion of the winding up.

Sec. 1809. Filing copy of order with Secretary of State. Whenever a corporation is dissolved or its existence forfeited by order, decree or judgment of a court, a copy of the order, decree or judgment, certified by the clerk of court, shall forthwith be filed in the office of the Secretary of State. Notwithstanding Section 23334 of the Revenue and Taxation Code, when the order is based on an action for involuntary dissolution brought by the Attorney General pursuant to Section 1801, there need not be filed in the office of the Secretary of State the certificate of satisfaction of the Franchise Tax Board that all taxes have been paid or secured.

CHAPTER 19

VOLUNTARY DISSOLUTION

Sec. 1900. When voluntary dissolution permitted. (a) Any corporation may elect voluntarily to wind up and dissolve by the vote of shareholders holding shares representing 50 percent or more of the voting power.

(b) Any corporation which comes within one of the following descriptions may elect by approval by the board to wind up and dissolve:

(1) A corporation as to which an order for relief has been entered under Chapter 7 of the federal bankruptcy law.

(2) A corporation which has disposed of all of its assets and has not conducted any business for a period of five years immediately preceding the adoption of the resolution electing to dissolve the corporation.

(3) A corporation which has issued no shares.

Sec. 1901. Filing of certificate of election. (a) Whenever a corporation has elected to wind up and dissolve a certificate evidencing such election shall forthwith be filed.

(b) The certificate shall be an officers' certificate or shall be signed and verified by at least a majority of the directors then in office or by one or more shareholders authorized to do so by shareholders holding shares representing 50 percent or more of the voting power and shall set forth:

(1) That the corporation has elected to wind up and dissolve.

(2) If the election was made by the vote of shareholders, the number of shares voting for the election and that the election was made by shareholders representing at least 50 percent of the voting power.

(3) If the certificate is executed by a shareholder or shareholders, that the subscribing shareholder or shareholders were authorized to execute the certificate by shareholders holding shares representing at least 50 percent of the voting power.

(4) If the election was made by the board pursuant to subdivision (b) of Section 1900, the certificate shall also set forth the circumstances showing the corporation to be within one of the categories described in said subdivision.

Sec. 1902. Revocation of election to dissolve. (a) A voluntary election to wind up and dissolve may be revoked prior to distribution of any assets by the vote of shareholders holding shares representing a majority of the voting power, or by approval by the board if the election was by the board pursuant to subdivision (b) of Section 1900. Thereupon a certificate evidencing the revocation shall be signed, verified and filed in the manner prescribed by Section 1901.

(b) The certificate shall set forth:

(1) That the corporation has revoked its election to wind up and dissolve.

(2) That no assets have been distributed pursuant to the election.

(3) If the revocation was made by the vote of shareholders, the number of shares voting for the revocation and the total number of outstanding shares the holders of which were entitled to vote on the revocation.

(4) If the election and revocation was by the board, that shall be stated.

Sec. 1903. Cessation of business activities on commencement of proceeding. (a) Voluntary proceedings for winding up the corporation commence upon the adoption of the resolution of shareholders or directors of the corporation electing to wind up and dissolve, or upon the filing with the corporation of a written consent of shareholders thereto.

(b) When a voluntary proceeding for winding up has commenced, the board shall continue to act as a board and shall have full powers to wind up and settle its affairs, both before and after the filing of the certificate of dissolution.

(c) When a voluntary proceeding for winding up has commenced, the corporation shall cease to carry on business except to the extent necessary for the beneficial winding up thereof and except during such period as the board may deem necessary to preserve the corporation's goodwill or going-concern value pending a sale of its business or assets, or both, in whole or in part. The board shall cause written notice of the commencement of the proceeding for voluntary winding up to be given by mail to all shareholders (except no notice need be given to the shareholders who voted in favor of winding up and dissolving the corporation) and to all known creditors and claimants whose addresses appear on the records of the corporation.

Sec. 1904. Assumption of jurisdiction by court. If a corporation is in the process of voluntary winding up, the superior court of the proper county, upon the petition of (a) the corporation, or (b) a shareholder or shareholders who hold shares representing 5 percent or more of the total number of any class of outstanding shares, or (c) any shareholder or shareholders of a close corporation, or (d) three or more creditors, and upon such notice to the corporation and to other persons interested in the corporation as shareholders and creditors as the court may order, may take jurisdiction over such voluntary wind-ing up proceeding if that appears necessary for the protection of any parties in interest. The court, if it assumes jurisdiction, may make such orders as to any and all matters concerning the winding up of the affairs of the corporation and for the protection of its shareholders and creditors as justice and equity may require. The provisions of Chapter 18 (commencing with Section 1800) (except Sections 1800 and 1801) shall apply to such court proceedings.

Sec. 1905. Certificate of dissolution; filing. (a) When a corporation has been completely wound up without court proceedings therefor, a majority of the directors then in office shall sign and verify a certificate of dissolution stating:

(1) That the corporation has been completely wound up.

(2) That its known debts and liabilities have been actually paid, or adequately provided for, or paid or adequately provided for as far as its assets permitted, or that it has incurred no known debts or liabilities, as the case may be. If there are known debts or liabilities for payment of which adequate provision has been made, the certificate shall state what provision has been made, setting forth the name and address of the corporation, person or governmental agency that has assumed or guaranteed the payment, or the name and address of the depositary with which deposit has been made or such other information as may be necessary to

enable the creditor or other person to whom payment is to be made to appear and claim payment of the debt or liability.

(3) That its known assets have been distributed to the persons entitled thereto or that it acquired no known assets, as the case may be.

(4) That the corporation is dissolved.

(b) The certificate of dissolution shall be filed and thereupon the corporate existence shall cease, except for the purpose of further winding up if needed. However, before any corporation taxed under the Bank and Corporation Tax Law (Part 11 (commencing with Section 23001) of Division 2 of the Revenue and Taxation Code) may file a certificate of dissolution it shall file or cause to be filed the certificate of satisfaction of the Franchise Tax Board that all taxes imposed under the Bank and Corporation Tax Law have been paid or secured.

Sec. 1906. **Termination for expiration of term of existence.** Except as otherwise provided by law, if the term of existence for which any corporation was organized expires without renewal or extension thereof, the board shall terminate its business and wind up its affairs; and when the business and affairs of the corporation have been wound up a majority of the directors shall execute and file a certificate conforming to the requirements of Section 1905.

Sec. 1907. **Petition for order declaring corporation wound up and dissolved in lieu of filing certificate of dissolution.** (a) The board, in lieu of filing the certificate of dissolution, may petition the superior court of the proper county for an order declaring the corporation duly wound up and dissolved. Such petition shall be filed in the name of the corporation.

(b) Upon the filing of the petition, the court shall make an order requiring all persons interested to show cause why an order should not be made declaring the corporation duly wound up and dissolved and shall direct that the order be served by notice to all creditors, claimants and shareholders in the same manner as the notice given under subdivision (b) of Section 1807.

(c) Any person claiming to be interested as shareholder, creditor or otherwis e may appear in the proceeding at any time before the expiration of 30 days from the completion of publication of the order to show cause and contest the petition, and upon failure to appear such person's claim shall be barred.

(d) Thereafter an order shall be entered and filed and have the effect as prescribed in Sections 1808 and 1809.

CHAPTER 20

GENERAL PROVISIONS RELATING TO DISSOLUTION

Sec. 2000. **Avoidance of dissolution by purchase of shares of moving parties.** (a) Subject to any contrary provision in the articles, in any suit for involuntary dissolution, or in any proceeding for voluntary dissolution initiated by the vote of shareholders representing only 50 percent of the voting power, the corporation or, if it does not elect to purchase, the holders of 50 percent or more of the voting power of the corporation (the "purchasing parties") may avoid the dissolution of the corporation and the appointment of any receiver by purchasing for cash the shares owned by the plaintiffs or by the shareholders so initiating the proceeding (the "moving parties") at their fair value. The fair value shall be determined on the basis of the liquidation value but taking into account the possibility, if any, of sale of the entire business as a going concern in a liquidation. In fixing the value, the amount of any damages resulting if the initiation of the dissolution is a breach by any moving party or parties of an agreement with the purchasing party or parties may be deducted from the amount payable to such moving party or parties, unless the ground for dissolution is that specified in paragraph (4) of subdivision (b) of Section 1800. The election of the corporation to purchase may be made by the approval of the outstanding shares (Section 152) excluding shares held by the moving parties.

(b) If the purchasing parties (1) elect to purchase the shares owned by the moving parties, and (2) are unable to agree with the moving parties upon the fair value of such shares, and (3) give bond with sufficient security to pay the estimated reasonable expenses (including attorneys' fees) of the moving parties if such expenses are recoverable under subdivision (c), the court upon application of the purchasing parties, either in the pending action or in a proceeding initiated in the superior court of the proper county by the purchasing parties in the case of a voluntary election to wind up and dissolve, shall stay the winding up and dissolution

proceeding and shall proceed to ascertain and fix the fair value of the shares owned by the moving parties.

(c) The court shall appoint three disinterested appraisers to appraise the fair value of the shares owned by the moving parties, and shall make an order referring the matter to the appraisers so appointed for the purpose of ascertaining such value. The order shall prescribe the time and manner of producing evidence, if evidence is required. The award of the appraisers or of a majority of them, when confirmed by the court, shall be final and conclusive upon all parties. The court shall enter a decree which shall provide in the alternative for winding up and dissolution of the corporation unless payment is made for the shares within the times specified by the decree. If the purchasing parties do not make payment for the shares within the time specified, judgment shall be entered against them and the surety or sureties on the bond for the amount of the expenses (including attorneys' fees) of the moving parties. Any shareholder aggrieved by the action of the court may appeal therefrom.

(d) If the purchasing parties desire to prevent the winding up and dissolution, they shall pay to the moving parties the value of their shares ascertained and decreed within the time specified pursuant to this section, or, in case of an appeal, as fixed on appeal. On receiving such payment or the tender thereof, the moving parties shall transfer their shares to the purchasing parties.

(e) For the purposes of this section, "shareholder" includes a beneficial owner of shares who has entered into an agreement under Section 300 or 706.

Sec. 2001. **Powers and duties of directors after commencement of dissolution proceedings.** The powers and duties of the directors (or other persons appointed by the court pursuant to Section 1805) and officers after commencement of a dissolution proceeding include, but are not limited to, the following acts in the name and on behalf of the corporation:

(a) To elect officers and to employ agents and attorneys to liquidate or wind up its affairs.

(b) To continue the conduct of the business insofar as necessary for the disposal or winding up thereof.

(c) To carry out contracts and collect, pay, compromise and settle debts and claims for or against the corporation.

(d) To defend suits brought against the corporation.

(e) To sue, in the name of the corporation, for all sums due or owing to the corporation or to recover any of its property.

(f) To collect any amounts remaining unpaid on subscriptions to shares or to recover unlawful distributions.

(g) To sell at public or private sale, exchange, convey or otherwise dispose of all or any part of the assets of the corporation for cash in an amount deemed reasonable by the board without compliance with the provisions of Section 1001 (except subdivision (d) thereof), or (subject to compliance with the provisions of Sections 1001, 1200 and 1201, but Chapter 13 (commencing with Section 1300) shall not be applicable thereto) upon such other terms and conditions and for such other considerations as the board deems reasonable or expedient; and to execute bills of sale and deeds of conveyance in the name of the corporation.

(h) In general, to make contracts and to do any and all things in the name of the corporation which may be proper or convenient for the purposes of winding up, settling and liquidating the affairs of the corporation.

Sec. 2002. **Filling vacancies on board of directors.** A vacancy on the board may be filled during a winding up proceeding in the manner provided in Section 305.

Sec. 2003. **Proceedings to determine or appoint directors to wind up corporation's affairs.** When the identity of the directors or their right to hold office is in doubt, or if they are dead or unable to act, or they fail or refuse to act or their whereabouts cannot be ascertained, any interested person may petition the superior court of the proper county to determine the identity of the directors or, if there are no directors, to appoint directors to wind up the affairs of the corporation, after hearing upon such notice to such persons as the court may direct.

Sec. 2004. **Distribution of assets to shareholders.** After determining that all the known debts and liabilities of a corporation in the process of winding up have been paid or adequately provided for, the board shall distribute all the remaining corporate assets among the shareholders according to their respective rights and preferences or, if there are no shareholders, to the persons entitled thereto. If the winding up is by court proceeding or subject to court supervision, the distribution shall not be made until after the expiration of any period for the presentation of claims which has been prescribed by order of the court.

Sec. 2005. What constitutes adequate provision for payment of debts or liabilities. The payment of a debt or liability, whether the whereabouts of the creditor is known or unknown, has been adequately provided for if the payment has been provided for by either of the following means:

(a) Payment thereof has been assumed or guaranteed in good faith by one or more financially responsible corporations or other persons or by the United States government or any agency thereof, and the provision (including the financial responsibility of such corporations or other persons) was determined in good faith and with reasonable care by the board to be adequate at the time of any distribution of the assets by the board pursuant to this chapter.

(b) The amount of the debt or liability has been deposited as provided in Section 2008.

This section does not prescribe the exclusive means of making adequate provision for debts and liabilities.

Sec. 2006. Manner and time of distribution. Distribution may be made either in money or in property or securities and either in installments from time to time or as a whole, if this can be done fairly and ratably and in conformity with the provisions of the articles and the rights of the shareholders, and shall be made as soon as reasonably consistent with the beneficial liquidation of the corporate assets.

Sec. 2007. Plan of distribution; right of preferred shareholders to obtain cash payment. (a) If the corporation in process of winding up has both preferred and common shares outstanding, a plan of distribution of the shares, obligations or securities of any other corporation, domestic or foreign, or assets other than money which is not in accordance with the liquidation rights of the preferred shares as specified in the articles may nevertheless be adopted if approved by (a) the board and (b) by approval of the outstanding shares (Section 152) of each class. The plan may provide that such distribution is in complete or partial satisfaction of the rights of any of such shareholders upon distribution and liquidation of the assets.

(b) A plan of distribution so approved shall be binding upon all the shareholders except as provided in subdivision (c). The board shall cause notice of the adoption of the plan to be given by mail within 20 days after its adoption to all holders of shares having a liquidation preference.

(c) Shareholders having a liquidation preference who dissent from the plan of distribution are entitled to be paid the amount of their liquidation preference in cash if they file written demand for payment with the corporation within 30 days after the date of mailing of the notice of the adoption of the plan of distribution, unless the plan of distribution is abandoned. The demand shall state the number and class of the shares held of record by the shareholder in respect of which the shareholder claims payment.

(d) If any such demand for cash payment is filed, the board in its discretion may abandon the plan without further approval by the outstanding shares (Section 152), and all shareholders shall then be entitled to distribution according to their rights and liquidation preferences in the process of winding up.

Sec. 2008. Deposits with State Treasurer. (a) If any shareholders or creditors are unknown or fail to refuse to accept their payment, dividend or distribution in cash or property or their whereabouts cannot be ascertained after diligent inquiry, or the existence or amount of a claim of a creditor or shareholder is contingent, contested or not determined, or if the ownership of any shares of stock is in dispute, the corporation may deposit any such payment, dividend, distribution or the maximum amount of such claim with the State Treasurer or with a bank or trust company in this state in trust for the benefit of those lawfully entitled thereto. Such payment, dividend or distribution shall be paid over by the depositary to the lawful owners, their representatives or assigns, upon satisfactory proof of title.

(b) For the purpose of providing for the transmittal, receipt, accounting for, claiming, management and investment of all money or other property deposited in the State Treasury under the provisions of subdivision (a), such money or other property shall be deemed to be paid or delivered for deposit in the State Treasury under the provisions of Chapter 7 (commencing with Section 1500) of Title 10 of Part 3 of the Code of Civil Procedure, and may be recovered in the manner prescribed therein.

Sec. 2009. Recovery of improper distribution. (a) Whenever in the process of winding up a corporation any distribution of assets has been made, otherwise than under an order of court, without prior payment or adequate provision for payment of any of the debts and liabilities of the corporation, any amount so improperly distributed to any shareholder may be recovered by the corporation. Any of such shareholders may be joined as defendants in the same action or brought in on the motion of any other defendant.

(b) Suit may be brought in the name of the corporation to enforce the liability under subdivision (a) against any or all shareholders receiving the distribution by any one or more creditors of the corporation, whether or not they have reduced their claims to judgment.

(c) Shareholders who satisfy any liability under this section shall have the right of ratable contribution from other distributees similarly liable. Any shareholder who has been compelled to return to the corporation more than the shareholder's ratable share of the amount needed to pay the debts and liabilities of the corporation may require that the corporation recover from any or all of the other distributees such proportion of the amounts received by them upon the improper distribution as to give contribution to those held liable under this section and make the distribution of the assets fair and ratable, according to the respective rights and preferences of the shares, after payment or adequate provision for payment of all the debts and liabilities of the corporation.

(d) As used in this section, "process of winding up" includes proceedings under Chapters 18 and 19 and also any other distribution of assets to shareholders made in contemplation of termination or abandonment of the corporate business.

Sec. 2010. Continued existence of dissolved corporation. (a) A corporation which is dissolved nevertheless continues to exist for the purpose of winding up its affairs, prosecuting and defending actions by or against it and enabling it to collect and discharge obligations, dispose of and convey its property and collect and divide its assets, but not for the purpose of continuing business except so far as necessary for the winding up thereof.

(b) No action or proceeding to which a corporation is a party abates by the dissolution of the corporation or by reason of proceedings for winding up and dissolution thereof.

(c) Any assets inadvertently or otherwise omitted from the winding up continue in the dissolved corporation for the benefit of the persons entitled thereto upon dissolution of the corporation and on realization shall be distributed accordingly.

Sec. 2011. Suit on cause of action arising prior to dissolution. (a) In all cases where a corporation has been dissolved, the shareholders may be sued in the corporate name of such corporation upon any cause of action against the corporation arising prior to its dissolution. This section is procedural in nature and is not intended to determine liability.

(b) Summons or other process against such a corporation may be served by delivering a copy thereof to an officer, director or person having charge of its assets or, if no such person can be found, to any agent upon whom process might be served at the time of dissolution. If none of such persons can be found with due diligence and it is so shown by affidavit to the satisfaction of the court, then the court may make an order that summons or other process be served upon the dissolved corporation by personally delivering a copy thereof, together with a copy of the order, to the Secretary of State or an assistant or deputy secretary of state. Service in this manner is deemed complete on the 10th day after delivery of the process to the Secretary of State.

(c) Every such corporation shall survive and continue to exist indefinitely for the purpose of being sued in any quiet title action. Any judgment rendered in any such action shall bind each and all of its shareholders or other persons having any equity or other interest in such corporation, to the extent of their interest therein, and such action shall have the same force and effect as an action brought under the provisions of Sections 410.50 and 410.60 of the Code of Civil Procedure. Service of summons or other process in any such action may be made as provided in Chapter 4 (commencing with Section 413.10) of Title 5 of Part 2 of the Code of Civil Procedure or as provided in subdivision (b).

(d) Upon receipt of such process and the fee therefor, the Secretary of State forthwith shall give notice to the corporation as provided in Section 1702.

CHAPTER 21

FOREIGN CORPORATIONS

Sec. 2100. Application of chapter. This chapter applies only to foreign corporations transacting intrastate business, except as otherwise expressly provided.

Sec. 2101. Registration of name of foreign corporation not transacting intrastate business. (a) Any foreign corporation (other than a foreign association) not transacting intrastate business may register its corporate name with the Secretary of State, provided its corporate name would be available pursuant to Section 201 to a new corporation organized under this division at the time of such registration.

(b) Such registration may be made by filing (1) an application for registration signed by a corporate officer stating the name of the corporation, the state or place under the laws of which it is incorporated, the date of its incorporation, and that it desires to register its name under this section; and (2) a certificate of an authorized public official of the state or place in which it is organized stating that such corporation is in good standing under those laws. Such registration shall be effective until the close of the calendar year in which the application for registration is filed.

(c) A corporation which has in effect a registration of its corporate name may renew such registration from year to year by annually filing an application for renewal setting forth the facts required to be set forth in an original application for registration and a certificate of good standing as required for the original registration between the first day of October and the 31st day of December in each year. Such renewal application shall extend the registration for the following calendar year.

Sec. 2105. Certificate of qualification. (a) A foreign corporation shall not transact intrastate business without having first obtained from the Secretary of State a certificate of qualification. To obtain such certificate it shall file, on a form prescribed by the Secretary of State, a statement and designation signed by a corporate officer stating:

(1) Its name and the state or place of its incorporation or organization.

(2) The address of its principal executive office.

(3) The address of its principal office within this state.

(4) The name of an agent upon whom process directed to the corporation may be served within this state. Such designation shall comply with the provisions of subdivision (b) of Section 1502.

(5) Its irrevocable consent to service of process directed to it upon the agent designated and to service of process on the Secretary of State if the agent so designated or the agent's successor is no longer authorized to act or cannot be found at the address given.

(6) If it is a corporation which will be subject to the Insurance Code as an insurer, it shall so state such fact.

(b) Annexed to such statement and designation shall be a certificate by an authorized public official of the state or place of incorporation of the corporation to the effect that such corporation is an existing corporation in good standing in that state or place or, in the case of an association, an officers' certificate stating that it is a validly organized and existing business association under the laws of a specified foreign jurisdiction.

(c) Before it may be designated by any foreign corporation as its agent for service of process, any corporate agent must comply with Section 1505.

Sec. 2106. Issuance of certificates; limitations on use of name. (a) Subject to the provisions of subdivision (b), upon payment of the fees required by law the Secretary of State shall file the statement and designation prescribed in Section 2105 and shall issue to the corporation a certificate of qualification stating the date of filing of said statement and designation and that the corporation is qualified to transact intrastate business, subject, however, to any licensing requirements otherwise imposed by the laws of this state.

(b) No foreign corporation having a name which would not be available pursuant to subdivision (b) of Section 201 to a new corporation organized under this division shall transact intrastate business in this state or qualify to do so under this chapter or file an amended statement and designation containing such name unless either: (1) it obtains and files an order from a court of competent jurisdiction permanently enjoining the other corporation having a conflicting name from doing business in this state under that name; or (2) the Secretary of State finds, upon proof by affidavit or otherwise as the Secretary of State may determine, that the business to be conducted in this state by the foreign corporation is not the same as or similar to the business being conducted by the corporation (or to be conducted by the proposed corporation) with whose name it may conflict and that the public is not likely to be deceived, and the foreign corporation agrees that it will transact business in this state under an assumed name disclosed to the Secretary of State and that it will use such assumed name in all of its dealings with the Secretary of State and in the conduct of its affairs in this state. Such assumed name may be its name with the addition of some distinguishing word or words acceptable to the Secretary of State or a name available for the name of a domestic corporation pursuant to subdivision (b) of Section 201. A corporation which

has made such an agreement with the Secretary of State shall not do business in this state except under the name agreed upon, so long as the agreement remains in effect.

This subdivision shall not apply to any corporation which is subject to the Insurance Code as an insurer unless the insurer has first obtained from the Insurance Commissioner a certificate approving the assumed name.

Sec. 2107. Amended statement and designation. (a) If any foreign corporation qualified to transact intrastate business shall change its name, the address of its principal office in this state, the address of its principal executive office or its agent for the service of process, or if the stated address of any natural person designated as agent is changed, it shall file, on a form prescribed by the Secretary of State, an amended statement and designation signed by a corporate officer setting forth the change or changes made. In the case of a change of name, the amended statement and designation shall set forth the name relinquished as well as the new name assumed and there shall be annexed to the amended statement and designation a certificate of an authorized public official of its state or place of incorporation that such change of name was made in accordance with the laws of that state or place or, in the case of an association, an officers' certificate stating that such change of name was made in accordance with its declaration of trust.

(b) If the change includes a change of name, or a change affecting a fictitious name pursuant to Section 2106, upon the filing of the amended statement and designation the Secretary of State shall issue a new certificate of qualification.

(c) If the change includes a change of name of an insurer subject to the Insurance Code, the form shall include a statement that the corporation is such an insurer if it does not already so appear.

Sec. 2108. Annual certificate of financial information. Each foreign corporation (other than a foreign association) qualified to transact intrastate business and each foreign parent corporation subject to Section 2115 shall file annually within three months and 15 days after the close of its income year ending on or after December 31, 1976 or within 30 days after the filing of its franchise tax return with the Franchise Tax Board if an extension of time for filing the return was granted, an officers' certificate setting forth:

(1) The percentage of its outstanding voting securities held of record, as of the last record date for a shareholder's meeting by persons having addresses in this state calculated as provided in Section 2115 and either

(2) That all the income of the corporation was taxable for California franchise tax purposes or that such income would have been so taxable if the corporation had had sufficient income to be subject to more than the minimum franchise tax; or

(3) Its property factor, payroll factor and sales factor computed as provided in Section 2115.

This subdivision does not apply to a foreign corporation described in subdivision (e) of Section 2115. If the percentage in response to paragraph (1) is 40 percent or less, the officers' certificate need not include the information required by paragraph (2) or (3).

(b) The Secretary of State shall mail a form for compliance with this section to each foreign corporation qualified to transact intrastate business in reasonably sufficient time for such compliance. The form shall state the due date thereof and shall be mailed to the last address of the corporation according to the records of the Secretary of State. Neither the failure of the Secretary of State to mail the form nor the failure of corporation to receive it is an excuse for failure to comply with this section.

(c) The Secretary of State need not mail a form to a foreign corporation exempted from subdivision (a) or a foreign corporation whose right to exercise its corporate powers, rights and privileges in this state were forfeited by the Franchise Tax Board pursuant to Section 23301 or 23301.5 of the Revenue and Taxation Code more than six months prior to the date the Secretary of State would otherwise have mailed the form pursuant to subdivision (b) and which right has not been revived on or prior to such date of mailing.

(d) The Secretary of State shall forfeit the right of any foreign corporation to transact intrastate business if it fails to file the statement required by this section for a period of six months after notice given to it by the Secretary of State that such filing is delinquent and that it will have its right to transact intrastate business forfeited unless it complies with this section.

(e) Neither the report required by this section nor the computation provided by Section 2115 shall have any effect with respect to the basis upon which the corporation reports its income for franchise tax purposes.

Sec. 2109. **Reinstatement of corporation disqualified from transacting business because of failure to file annual certificate of financial information.** (a) Any foreign corporation which has suffered the forfeiture provided for in subdivision (d) of Section 2108 may be relieved therefrom upon making application therefor in writing to the Secretary of State and upon filing the officers' certificate prescribed in Section 2108 for each taxable year for which such certificate was required to be filed and has not been filed.

(b) The Secretary of State shall not grant the relief if the name of the foreign corporation would not meet the requirements of subdivision (b) of Section 2106. Notwithstanding subdivision (d) of Section 2108, a foreign corporation which has forfeited its right to transact intrastate business may file an amended statement and designation to change its name or to establish an assumed name pursuant to subdivision (b) of Section 2106.

(c) The Secretary of State shall promptly notify the foreign corporation of the relief from forfeiture of the right to transact intrastate business but such relief shall not affect any forfeiture under other provisions of law.

Sec. 2110. **Service of process on foreign corporation.** Delivery by hand of a copy of any process against a foreign corporation (a) to any officer of the corporation or its general manager in this state, or if the corporation is a bank to a cashier or an assistant cashier, (b) to any natural person designated by it as agent for the service of process, or (c), if the corporation has designated a corporate agent, to any person named in the latest certificate of such corporate agent filed pursuant to Section 1505 shall constitute valid service on the corporation. A copy of the statement and designation, certified by the Secretary of State, is sufficient evidence of the appointment of an agent for the service of process.

Sec. 2111. **Service on Secretary of State.** (a) If the agent designated for the service of process is a natural person and cannot be found with due diligence at the address stated in the designation or if such agent is a corporation and no person can be found with due diligence to whom the delivery authorized by Section 2110 may be made for the purpose of delivery to such corporate agent, or if the agent designated is no longer authorized to act, or if no agent has been designated and if no one of the officers or agents of the corporation specified in Section 2110 can be found after diligent search and it is so shown by affidavit to the satisfaction of the court, then the court may make an order that service be made by personal delivery to the Secretary of State or to an assistant or deputy secretary of state of two copies of the process together with two copies of the order, except that if the corporation to be served has not filed the statement required to be filed by Section 2105 then only one copy of the process and order need be delivered but the order shall include and set forth an address to which such process shall be sent by the Secretary of State. Service in this manner is deemed complete on the 10th day after delivery of the process to the Secretary of State.

(b) Upon receipt of the process and order and the fee therefor the Secretary of State forthwith shall give notice to the corporation of the service of the process by forwarding by registered mail, with request for return receipt, a copy of the process and order to the address specified in the order if the corporation has not filed the statement required by Section 2105 or to the two offices of the corporation the addresses of which are set forth in the latest such statement filed.

(c) The Secretary of State shall keep a record of all process served upon the Secretary of State and shall record therein the time of service and the Secretary of State's action with respect thereto. The certificate of the Secretary of State, under the Secretary of State's official seal, certifying to the receipt of process, the giving of notice thereof to the corporation and the forwarding of such process pursuant to this section, shall be competent and prima facie evidence of the matters stated therein.

Sec. 2112. **Certificate of surrender of right to transact business.** Subject to Section 2113, a foreign corporation which has qualified to transact intrastate business may surrender its right to engage in such business within this state by filing a certificate of surrender signed by a corporate officer stating:

(a) The name of the corporation as shown on the records of the Secretary of State, and the state or place of incorporation or organization.

(b) That it revokes its designation of agent for service of process.

(c) That it surrenders its authority to transact intrastate business.

(d) That it consents that process against it in any action upon any liability or obligation incurred within this state prior to the filing of the certificate of withdrawal may be served upon the Secretary of State.

(e) A post office address to which the Secretary of State may mail a copy of any process against the corporation that is served upon the Sec-

retary of State, which address or the name to which the process should be sent may be changed from time to time by filing a statement signed by a corporate officer stating the new address or name or both.

Sec. 2115. **Foreign corporations subject to provisions of general corporation law.** (a) A foreign corporation (other than a foreign association or foreign nonprofit corporation but including a foreign parent corporation even though it does not itself transact intrastate business) is subject to this section if the average of the property factor, the payroll factor and the sales factor (as defined in Sections 25129, 25132 and 25134 of the Revenue and Taxation Code) with respect to it is more than 50 percent during its latest full income year and if more than one-half of its outstanding voting securities are held of record by persons having addresses in this state. The property factor, payroll factor and sales factor shall be those used in computing the portion of its income allocable to this state in its franchise tax return or, with respect to corporations the allocation of whose income is governed by special formulas or which are not required to file separate or any tax returns, which would have been so used if they were governed by such three-factor formula. The determination of these factors with respect to any parent corporation shall be made on a consolidated basis, including in a unitary computation (after elimination of intercompany transactions) the property, payroll and sales of the parent and all of its subsidiaries in which it owns directly or indirectly more than 50 percent of the outstanding shares entitled to vote for the election of directors, but deducting a percentage of such property, payroll and sales of any subsidiary equal to the percentage minority ownership, if any, in such subsidiary. For the purpose of this subdivision, any securities held to the knowledge of the issuer in the names of broker-dealers or nominees for broker-dealers shall not be considered outstanding.

(b) The following chapters and sections of this division shall apply to a foreign corporation subject to this section (to the exclusion of the law of the jurisdiction in which it is incorporated):

Chapter 1 (general provisions and definitions), to the extent applicable to the following provisions;

Section 301 (annual election of directors);

Section 303 (removal of directors without cause);

Section 304 (removal of directors by court proceedings);

Section 305, subdivision (c) (filling of director vacancies where less than a majority in office elected by shareholders);

Section 309 (directors' standard of care);

Section 316 (excluding paragraph (3) of subdivision (a) and paragraph (3) of subdivision (f) (liability of directors for unlawful distributions);

Section 317 (indemnification of directors, officers and others);

Sections 500 to 505, inclusive (limitations on corporate distributions in cash or property);

Section 506 (liability of shareholder who receives unlawful distribution);

Section 600, subdivisions (b) and (c) (requirement for annual shareholders' meeting and remedy if same not timely held);

Section 708, subdivisions (a), (b) and (c) (shareholder's right to cumulate votes at any election of directors);

Section 1001, subdivision (d) (limitations on sale of assets);

Section 1101 (provisions following subdivision (e)) (limitations on merger);

Chapter 12 (commencing with Section 1200) (reorganizations);

Chapter 13 (commencing with Section 1300) (dissenters' rights);

Sections 1500 and 1501 (records and reports);

Section 1508 (action by Attorney General);

Chapter 16 (commencing with Section 1600)(rights of inspection).

(c) Subdivision (a) shall become applicable to any foreign corporation only upon the first day of the first income year of the corporation commencing on or after the 30th day after the filing by it of the report pursuant to Section 2108 showing that the tests referred to in subdivision (a) have been met or upon the entry of a final order by a court of competent jurisdiction declaring that such tests have been met.

(d) Subdivision (a) shall cease to be applicable at the end of any income year during which a report pursuant to Section 2108 shall have been filed showing that at least one of the tests referred to in subdivision (a) is not met or a final order shall have been entered by a court of competent jurisdiction declaring that one of such tests is not met, provided that such filing or order shall be ineffective if a contrary report or order shall be made or entered before the end of such income year.

(e) This section does not apply to any corporation with outstanding securities listed on any national securities exchange certified by the Commissioner of Corporations under subdivision (o) of Section 25100, or to any corporation if all of its voting shares (other than directors' qualifying shares) are owned directly or indirectly by a corporation not subject to this section.

FEES OF SECRETARY OF STATE AND COUNTY CLERK

SECRETARY OF STATE

(Government Code, Sections 12199-12207.)

Sec. 12199.　The fee for issuing a certificate of reservation of corporate name is four dollars ($4).

Sec. 12200.　The fee for filing articles of incorporation or agreements of consolidation not providing for shares is fifteen dollars ($15).

Sec. 12201.　The fee for filing articles of incorporation or agreements of consolidation providing for shares is sixty-five dollars ($65).

Sec. 12202.　The fee for filing an agreement of merger is sixty-five dollars ($65). This section does not apply where the articles of incorporation of each domestic corporation party to the merger do not provide for shares nor where the surviving corporation is a foreign corporation.

Sec. 12203.　The fee for filing certificates pursuant to Section 40110 of the Corporations Code is included in the fee for filing the agreement of merger or consolidation.

Sec. 12204.　The fee for filing the statement and designation upon the qualification of a foreign nonprofit nonstock corporation, and of a foreign corporation organized for educational, religious, scientific, or charitable purposes, and not issuing shares, is fifteen dollars ($15).
The fee for filing the statement and designation upon the qualification of any other foreign corporation is three hundred fifty dollars ($350).
The fees in this section include the fee for designating an agent.

Sec. 12205.　Unless another fee is specified by law, the fee for filing any instrument by or on behalf of a corporation is fifteen dollars ($15).
This section is not applicable to a certificate showing the surrender of the right of a foreign corporation to transact intrastate business.

Sec. 12206.　**Acceptance of copies of process against corporation, firm, partnership, business trust or natural person.**　Unless another fee is specified by law or the law specifies that no fee is to be charged, the fee for acceptance of copies of process against a corporation, firm, partnership, association, business trust or natural person is five dollars ($5) for each corporation, firm, partnership, association, business trust or natural person upon whom service is sought.

Sec. 12207.　Unless another fee is specified by law:
(a) The fee for affixing the certificate and seal of State is two dollars ($2).
(b) The fee for issuing certificate of filing of any document not otherwise provided for is three dollars ($3).

TITLE 4

SECURITIES

Division 1.　Corporate Securities Law of 1968, Secs. 25000-25804.

DIVISION 1

CORPORATE SECURITIES LAW OF 1968

PART 1

DEFINITIONS

Sec. 25000.　**Division title.**　This division may be known as the "Corporate Securities Law of 1968."

Sec. 25005.　**"Commissioner."**　"Commissioner" means the Commissioner of Corporations.

Sec. 25011.　**"Nonissuer transaction."**　"Nonissuer transaction" means any transaction not directly or indirectly for benefit of the issuer. A transaction is indirectly for the benefit of the issuer if any portion of the purchase price of any securities involved in the transaction will be received indirectly by the issuer. An offering which involves both an issuer transaction and a nonissuer transaction shall be treated for the purposes of Chapters 2 (commencing with Section 25110) and 4 (commencing with Section 25130) of Part 2 of this division as an issuer transaction, but for the purposes of Chapter 1 (commencing with Section 25100) of Part 2 of this division they shall be treated as separate transactions.

Sec. 25017.　**"Sale, sell, offer, offer to sell."**　(a) "Sale" or "sell" includes every contract of sale of, contract to sell, or disposition of, a security or interest in a security for value. "Sale" or "sell" includes any exchange of securities and any change in the rights, preferences, privileges, or restrictions of or on outstanding securities.
(b) "Offer" or "offer to sell" includes every attempt or offer to dispose of, or solicitation of an offer to buy, a security or interest in a security for value.
(c) Any security given or delivered with, or as a bonus on account of, any purchase of securities or any other thing constitutes a part of the subject of the purchase and is considered to have been offered and sold for value.
(d) A purported gift of assessable stock involves an offer and sale.
(e) Every sale or offer of a warrant or right to purchase or subscribe to another security of the same or another issuer, as well as every sale or offer of a security which gives the holder a present or future right or privilege to convert the security into another security of the same or another issuer, includes an offer and sale of the other security only at the time of the offer or sale of the warrant or right or convertible security; but neither the exercise of the right to purchase or subscribe or to convert nor the issuance of securities pursuant thereto is an offer or sale.
(f) The terms defined in this section do not include: (1) any bona fide secured transaction in or loan of outstanding securities; (2) any stock dividend payable with respect to common stock of a corporation solely (except for any cash or scrip paid for fractional shares) in shares of such common stock, if the corporation has no other class of voting stock outstanding; provided, that shares issued in any such dividend shall be subject to any conditions previously imposed by the commissioner applicable to the shares with respect to which they are issued; or (3) any act incident to a judicially approved arrangement or reorganization in which securities are issued and exchanged for one or more outstanding securities, claims or property interests, or partly in such exchange and partly for cash.

Sec. 25019.　**"Security."**　"Security" means any note; stock; treasury stock; membership in an incorporated or unincorporated association; bond; debenture; evidence of indebtedness; certificate of interest or participation in any profit-sharing agreement; collateral trust certificate; preorganization certificate or subscription; transferable share; investment contract; voting trust certificate; certificate of deposit for a security; certificate of interest or participation in an oil, gas or mining title or lease or in payments out of production under such a title or lease; any beneficial interest or other security issued in connection with a funded employees' pension, profit sharing, stock bonus, or similar benefit plan; or, in general, any interest or instrument commonly known as a "security"; or any certificate of interest or participation in, temporary or interim certificate for, receipt for, guarantee of, or warrant or right to subscribe to or purchase, any of the foregoing. All of the foregoing are securities whether or not evidenced by a written document. "Security" does not include: (1) any beneficial interest in any voluntary inter vivos trust which is not created for the purpose of carrying on any business or solely for the purpose of voting, or (2) any beneficial interest in any testamentary trust, or (3) any insurance or endowment policy or annuity contract under which an insurance company admitted in this state promises to pay a sum of money (whether or not based upon the investment performance of a segregated fund) either in a lump sum or periodically for life or some other specified period, or (4) any franchise subject to registration under the Franchise Investment Law, or exempted from such registration by Section 31100 or 31101 of that law.

Part 2

QUALIFICATION OF THE SALE OF SECURITIES

Chapter 1

EXEMPTIONS

Sec. 25100. **Exempt issuer securities.** The following securities are exempted from the provisions of Sections 25110, 25120, and 25130: Domestic and foreign government securities; bank or trust company securities; savings and loan association securities; insurance, public utility, real estate securities; subdivision securities; credit union securities; interstate common carrier or public utility securities; nonprofit corporation securities; life income contracts; short term commercial paper; agricultural cooperative securities; pension or profit-sharing plans.

* * * * *

(o) Any security listed or approved for listing upon notice of issuance on a national securities exchange certified by rule or order of the commissioner and any warrant or right to purchase or subscribe to any such security.

Such certification of an exchange shall be made by the commissioner upon the written request of the exchange if he finds that the exchange, in acting on applications for listing of common stock substantially applies each of the minimum standards set forth in subparagraph (1) below, and in considering suspension or removal from listing, substantially applies each of the criteria set forth in subparagraph (2) below.

(1) Listing standards:

(i) Net tangible assets of at least two million dollars ($2,000,000).

(ii) Net income of at least two hundred fifty thousand dollars ($250,000) after all charges including federal income taxes in the fiscal year immediately preceding the filing of a listing application and net income before such taxes of at least five hundred thousand dollars ($500,000).

(iii) Minimum public distribution of 250,000 shares excluding the holdings of officers, directors, controlling shareholders and other concentrated or family holdings among not less than 900 holders including not less than 600 holders of lots of 100 shares or more, with a corresponding requirement that such securities not be largely held in blocks by institutional investors.

(iv) Minimum price of four dollars ($4) per share for reasonable period of time prior to the filing of a listing application.

(v) An aggregate market value for publicly held shares of at least one million five hundred thousand dollars ($1,500,000).

(2) Criteria for consideration of suspension or removal from listing:

(i) If a company which (A) has net tangible assets of less than one million dollars ($1,000,000) has sustained net losses in each of its two most recent fiscal years, or (B) has net tangible assets of less than three million dollars ($3,000,000) and has sustained net losses in three of its four most recent fiscal years.

(ii) If the number of shares publicly held (excluding the holdings of officers, directors, controlling shareholders and other concentrated or family holdings) is less than 150,000.

(iii) If the total number of shareholders of record is less than 450 or if the number of shareholders of lots of 100 shares or more is less than 300.

(iv) If the aggregate market value of shares publicly held is less than seven hundred fifty thousand dollars ($750,000).

(v) If shares of common stock sell at a price of less than four dollars ($4) per share for a substantial period of time and the issuer shall fail to effectuate a reverse stock split of such shares within a reasonable period of time after being requested by the exchange to take such action.

The commissioner after appropriate notice and opportunity for hearing in accordance with the provisions of the Administrative Procedure Act, Chapter 5 (commencing with Section 11500) of Part I of Division 3 of Title 2 of the Government Code, made by rule or order, decertify any exchange previously certified which ceases substantially to apply the standards or criteria as set forth above. A rule or order of certification shall conclusively establish that any security listed or approved for listing upon notice of issuance on any exchange named in a rule or order of certification and any warrant or right to purchase or subscribe to any such security is exempt under this subdivision until the adoption of any rule or order decertifying such exchange.

(p) A promissory note secured by a lien on real property, which is neither one of a series of notes of equal priority secured by interests in the same real property nor a note in which beneficial interests are sold to more than one person or entity.

Sec. 25101. **Exempt nonissuer securities.** The following securities are exempt from the provisions of Section 25130:

(a) Any security issued by a person which is the issuer of any security listed on a national securities exchange certified by rule or order of the commissioner.

(b) Any security (except limited or general partnership interests) issued by a person which (i) is the issuer of any security listed on a national securities exchange which is not certified by the commissioner pursuant to subdivision (a) hereof, (ii) is the issuer of any security registered under Section 12(g) of the Securities Exchange Act of 1934 or is exempt from registration under such Section 12 by Section 12(g)(2)(G) of that act, or (iii) is registered under the Investment Company Act of 1940, if in any such case, there has been filed with the commissioner a notice in such form as the commissioner shall specify by rule setting forth the following:

(1) The name of the issuer, the date of its organization, and the jurisdiction under whose laws it is organized;

(2) The issuer's taxpayer identification number as assigned by the federal Department of Internal Revenue and, if applicable, the issuer's file number under the Securities Exchange Act of 1934 or the Investment Company Act of 1940 as assigned by the federal Securities and Exchange Commission or other appropriate federal regulatory agency;

(3) A statement that the issuer has a currently effective registration under Section 12 of the Securities Exchange Act of 1934 (specifying the subsection thereof) or the Investment Company Act of 1940, or that it is exempt from registration under such Section 12 by Section 12(g)(2)(G) thereof;

(4) A statement that the issuer has a class of equity securities held by 500 or more persons and has total assets exceeding one million dollars ($1,000,000), determined in such manner as is provided by rule of the commissioner or, in the absence of such rule, in accordance with generally accepted accounting principles;

(5) A description of each security of the issuer which is to be exempted pursuant to this subdivision, and a statement that each class of common stock described in such notice, if any, possesses full voting rights equal per share to the voting rights possessed by any other class of common stock of the issuer;

(6) An undertaking to file a supplemental notice if any of the facts stated in the notice previously filed with the commissioner shall, to the knowledge of the filer of such notice, cease to be true.

(7) The name and address of the person filing the notice, the signature of such person or of the authorized principal officer of such person (and the name of such principal officer), and a verification to the best knowledge or belief of the person signing the notice of all of the information contained in such notice.

The notice provided for herein may be filed by the issuer, any broker-dealer registered under this law or any holder of record or beneficially of any of the securities covered by such notice. Except in the case of a notice filed by an issuer, the exemption provided by this subdivision shall lapse 13 months after the filing of the notice.

(c) The exemption provided by subdivision (a) or (b) of this section shall not apply to any of the following:

(1) Securities offered pursuant to a registration under the Securities Act of 1933 or pursuant to the exemption afforded by Regulation A under such act if the aggregate offering price of the securities offered pursuant to such exemption exceeds fifty thousand dollars ($50,000);

(2) Securities which the commissioner has found, after notice and, if requested as hereinafter provided, hearing, to be the subject of a notice or supplemental notice filed pursuant to subdivision (b) which contains any statement which is, or which was at the time of filing, materially untrue. Notice hereunder shall be given to the person named pursuant to paragraph (7) of subdivision (b), to the issuer unless the notice or supplemental notice was filed by the issuer, and to licensed broker-dealers. The notice shall state the reasons for the issuance of the notice and that the exemption pursuant to this section for the security identified therein may be terminated unless, within 10 business days, either a notice or supplemental notice is filed in accordance with subdivision (b) or a written request for hearing is received, such hearing to commence within 15 business days of the receipt of such notice unless the commissioner consents to a later date. An order terminating an exemption pursuant to this paragraph shall be effective when issued or at such time thereafter as the commissioner may provide.

(3) All securities of an issuer when the commissioner has found the issuer has ceased to have any securities registered under Section 12 of the Securities Exchange Act of 1934 or the issuer of which has ceased to have a class of equity securities held by 500 or more persons or total assets exceeding one million dollars ($1,000,000). An order may be issued under this paragraph without notice of hearing if the facts on which it is based are stated in a notice or supplemental notice filed pursuant to subdivion (b) or are stated in a certificate filed with the Securities and Exchange Commission pursuant to Section 12(g)(4) of the Securities Exchange Act of 1934; otherwise, such order shall be issued only as provided in paragraph (2) of this subdivision.

Sec. 25102. **Exempt issuer transactions.** The following transactions are exempted from the provisions of Section 25110:

(a) Any offer (but not a sale) not involving any public offering and the execution and delivery of any agreement for the sale of securities pursuant to such offer if (1) the agreement contains substantially the following provisions: "The sale of the securities which are the subject of this agreement has not been qualified with the Commissioner of Corporations of the State of California and the issuance of such securities or the payment or receipt of any part of the consideration therefor prior to such qualification is unlawful. The rights of all parties to this agreement are expressly conditioned upon such qualification being obtained"; and (2) no part of the purchase price is paid or received and none of the securities are issued until the sale of such securities is qualified under this law.

(b) Any offer (but not a sale) of a security for which a registration statement has been filed under the Securities Act of 1933 but has not yet become effective, if no stop order or refusal order is in effect and no public proceeding or examination looking toward such an order is pending under Section 8 of such act and no order under Section 25140 or subdivision (a) of Section 25143 is in effect under this law.

(h) Any offer or sale of voting common stock by a corporation incorporated in any state if, immediately after the proposed sale and issuance, there will be only one class of stock of such corporation outstanding which is owned beneficially by no more than 10 persons, provided all of the following requirements have been met:

(1) All such stock shall be evidenced by certificates which shall have stamped or printed prominently on their face a legend in a form to be prescribed by rule of the commissioner restricting transfer of such stock in such manner as the rule provides.

(2) The offer and sale of such stock is not accompanied by the publication of any advertisement, and no selling expenses have been given, paid, or incurred in connection therewith.

(3) The consideration to be received by the issuer for the stock to be issued shall consist of (i) only assets (which may include cash) of an existing business enterprise transferred to the issuer upon its initial organization, of which all of the persons who are to receive the stock to be issued pursuant to this exemption were owners during, and such enterprise was operated for, a period of not less than one year immediately preceding the proposed issuance, and the ownership of such enterprise immediately prior to such proposed issuance was in the same proportions as the shares of stock are to be issued, or (ii) only cash or cancellation of indebtedness for money borrowed or both upon the initial organization of the issuer, provided all such stock is issued for the same price per share, or (iii) only cash, provided the sale is approved in writing by each of the existing shareholders and the purchaser or purchasers are existing shareholders, or (iv), in a case where after the proposed issuance there will be only one owner of the stock of the issuer, any legal consideration.

(4) No promotional consideration has been given, paid, or incurred in connection with such issuance. Promotional consideration means any consideration paid directly or indirectly to a person who, acting alone or in conjunction with one or more other persons, takes the initiative in founding and organizing the business or enterprise of an issuer, for services rendered in connection with such founding or organizing.

(5) A notice in a form prescribed by rule of the commissioner, signed by an active member of the State Bar of California shall be filed with or mailed for filing to the commissioner not later than 10 business days after receipt of consideration for the securities by the issuer which notice shall contain an opinion of such member of the State Bar of California that the exemption provided by this subdivision is available for the offer and sale of the securities. Such notice, except when filed on behalf of a California corporation, shall be accompanied by an irrevocable consent, in such form as the commissioner by rule prescribes, appointing the commissioner or his successor in office to be the issuer's attorney to receive service of any lawful process in any noncriminal suit, action, or proceeding against it or its successor which arises under this law or any rule or order hereunder after the consent has been filed, with the same force and validity as if served personally on the issuer. An issuer on whose behalf a consent has been filed in connection with a previous qualification or exemption from qualification under this law (or application for a permit under any prior law if the application or notice under this law states that such consent is still effective) need not file another. Service may be made by leaving a copy of the process in the office of the commissioner but it is not effective unless (1) the plaintiff, who may be the commissioner in a suit, action or proceeding instituted by him forthwith sends notice of the service and a copy of the process by registered or certified mail to the defendant or respondent at its last address on file with the commissioner, and (2) the plaintiff's affidavit of compliance with this section is filed in the case on or before the return day of the process, if any, or within such further time as the court allows.

For the purposes of this subdivision, all securities held by a husband and wife, whether or not jointly, shall be considered to be owned by one person, and all securities held by a corporation which has issued stock pursuant to this exemption shall be considered to be held by the shareholders to whom it has issued such stock.

Sec. 25104. **Exempt nonissuer transactions.** The following transactions are exempted from the provisions of Section 25130:

(a) Any offer or sale of a security by the bona fide owner thereof for his own account if the sale (1) is not accompanied by the publication of any advertisement and (2) is not effected by or through a broker-dealer in a public offering.

(f) Any transaction by an executor, administrator, sheriff, marshal, receiver, trustee in bankruptcy, guardian or conservator.

(g) Any offer (but not a sale) of a security for which a registration statement has been filed under the Securities Act of 1933 but has not yet become effective, if no stop order or refusal order is in effect and no public proceeding or examination looking toward such an order is pending under Section 8 of that act and no order under Section 25140 or subdivision (a) of Section 25143 is in effect under this law.

Sec. 25105. **Exempt transactions by rule of commissioner.** There shall be exempted from the provisions of Section 25110, 25120 or 25130 any other transaction which the commissioner by rule exempts as not being comprehended within the purposes of this law and the qualification of which he finds is not necessary or appropriate in the public interest or for the protection of investors.

CHAPTER 2

ISSUER TRANSACTIONS

Sec. 25110. **Requirement of qualification by issuer.** It is unlawful for any person to offer or sell in this state any security in an issuer transaction (other than in a transaction subject to Section 25120), whether or not by or through underwriters, unless such sale has been qualified under Section 25111, 25112 or 25113 (and no order under Section 25140 or subdivision (a) of Section 25143 is in effect with respect to such qualification) or unless such security or transaction is exempted under Chapter 1 (commencing with Section 25100) of this part.

Sec. 25111. **Qualification by coordination—Securities Act of 1933.**
(a) Any security for which a registration statement has been filed under the Securities Act of 1933 in connection with the same offering may be qualified by coordination under this section either in an issuer or nonissuer transaction.

(b) An application for qualification under this section shall contain the following information and be accompanied by the following documents, in addition to the information specified in Section 25160 and the consent to service of process required by Section 25165: (1) a copy of the registration statement under the Security Act of 1933, together with all exhibits (other than exhibits incorporated by reference and those specified by rule of the commissioner, unless requested by the commissioner); (2) an undertaking to forward to the commissioner all future amendments to the registration statement under the Securities Act of 1933, other than an amendment which merely delays the effective date of the registration statement, promptly and in any event not later than the first business day after the day they are forwarded to or filed with the Securities and Exchange Commission, whichever first occurs; and (3) such other information as may be required to evidence compliance with any rules of the commissioner. Such application must be filed with the commissioner not later than the fifth business day following filing of the registration statement with the Securities and Exchange Commission, unless such time is extended by rule or order of the commissioner.

Sec. 25112. **Qualification by notification.** Securities Exchange Act of 1934 Investment Company Act of 1940.

(a) Any security issued by a person which is the issuer of any security registered under Section 12 of the Securities Exchange Act of 1934 or issued by an investment company registered under the Investment Company Act of 1940, and which is not eligible for qualification under Section 25111, may be qualified by notification under this section.

(b) An application for qualification under this section shall contain such information and be accompanied by such documents as shall be required by rule of the commissioner, in addition to the information specified in Section 25160 and the consent to service of process required by Section 25165. For this purpose, the commissioner may classify issuers and types of securities.

Sec. 25113. **Qualification by permit—all securities.** (a) All securities, whether or not eligible for qualification by coordination under Section 2511 or qualification by notification under Section 25112, may be qualified by permit under this section.

(b) An application for a permit under this section shall contain such information and be accompanied by such documents as shall be required by rule of the commissioner, in addition to the information specified in Section 25160 and the consent to service of process required by Section 25165. For this purpose, the commissioner may classify issuers and types of securities.

(c) Qualification of securities under this section becomes effective upon the commissioner issuing a permit authorizing the issuance of such securities.

Sec. 25114. **Term of qualification.** Every qualification under this chapter is effective for 12 months from its effective date, unless the commissioner by order or rule specifies a different period, except during the time an order under Section 25140 or subdivision (a) of Section 25143 is in effect.

Sec. 25115. **Execution of application.** Every application of qualification of an issuer transaction under this chapter shall be signed and verified by the issuer; every application for qualification of a nonissuer transaction under Section 25111 shall be signed and verified by the person on whose behalf the offering is being made or by the issuer on behalf of such person.

CHAPTER 4

NONISSUER TRANSACTIONS

Sec. 25130. **Requirement of qualification by nonissuer—transfers.** It is unlawful for any person to offer or sell any security in this state in any nonissuer transaction unless it is qualified for such sale under this chapter or under Section 25111 or 25113 of Chapter 2 (commencing with Section 25110) of this part (and no order under Section 25140 or subdivision (a) of Section 25143 is in effect with respect to such qualification) or unless such security or transaction is exempted under Chapter 1 (commencing with Section 25100) of this part.

Sec. 25131. **Method of qualification.** (a) The securities to be offered or sold in a nonissuer transaction, which are not eligible for qualification under Section 25111 or 25113, shall be qualified by notification under this section; provided however that securities offered in a nonissuer transaction pursuant to an exemption under Regulation A under the Securities Act of 1933 shall be qualified under Section 25113.

(b) The application for qualification by notification under this section shall be signed and verified by the person on whose behalf the offering is being made or by the issuer or by any broker-dealer and shall contain such information and be accompanied by such documents as shall be required by rule of the commissioner, in addition to the information specified in Section 25160 and the consent to service of process required by Section 25165. For this purpose, the commissioner may classify issuers and types of securities.

Sec. 25133. **Transfer of securities in escrow or under legend condition.** It is unlawful for any person without the written consent of the commissioner to consummate the sale or transfer of any securities heretofore or hereafter placed in escrow pursuant to a condition ordered by the commissioner and which have not been released from escrow, or which are subject to a currently effective legend condition requiring such consent (except as permitted therein), or which are issued pursuant to the

exemption in subdivision (h) of Section 25102 (except as permitted by rule or order of the commissioner), or con-cerning which the commissioner has issued a written notice to the holders thereof pursuant to Section 25534 ordering the certificates evidencing such securities to be stamped or printed with a legend as provided in such section.

CHAPTER 5

AUTHORITY OF THE COMMISSIONER

Sec. 25140. **Application of fair, just, and equitable standard by commissioner.** (a) The commissioner may issue a stop order denying effectiveness to, or suspending or revoking the effectiveness of, any qualification of securities under Section 25111, 25112 or 25131 or may suspend or revoke any permit issued under Section 25113 or 25122 if he finds (1) that the order is in the public interest and (2) that the proposed plan of business of the issuer or the proposed issuance or sale of securities is not fair, just, or equitable, or that the issuer does not intend to transact its business fairly and honestly, or that the securities proposed to be issued or the method to be used in issuing them will tend to work a fraud upon the purchaser thereof.

(b) The commissioner may refuse to issue a permit under Section 25113 unless he finds that the proposed plan of business of the applicant and the proposed issuance of securities are fair, just, and equitable, that the applicant intends to transact its business fairly and honestly, and that the securities which it proposes to issue and the methods to be used by it in issuing them are not such as, in his opinion, will work a fraud upon the purchaser thereof.

Sec. 25141. **Conditions of qualification—escrow, legend, impound, expense limitation, waiver of rights.** The commissioner may impose as a condition of qualification under Chapter 2 (commencing with Section 25110) or Chapter 3 (commencing with Section 25120) of this part conditions requiring the deposit in escrow of securities, imposing a legend condition restricting the transferability thereof, impounding the proceeds from the sale thereof, limiting the expense in connection with the sale thereof, requiring the waiver of assets, dividends or voting rights by the holders of promotional securities, or any other condition if the commissioner finds that without such condition the offering will be unfair, unjust or inequitable. The commissioner may in his discretion modify or remove any such conditions or any legend condition imposed by subdivision (h) of Section 25102 when in his opinion they are no longer necessary or appropriate.

Sec. 25142. **Issuance of securities in exchange for other securities or property approval of terms and conditions.** When application is made for a permit to issue securities or to deliver other consideration (whether or not the security or transaction is exempt from qualification or not required to be qualified) in exchange for one or more bona fide outstanding securities, claims, or security interests, or partly in such exchange and partly for cash, the commissioner is expressly authorized to approve the terms and conditions of such issuance and exchange or such delivery and exchange and the fairness of such terms and conditions, and is expressly authorized to hold a hearing upon the fairness of such terms and conditions, at which all persons to whom it is proposed to issue securities or to deliver such other consideration in such exchange have the right to appear. The application for a permit to deliver consideration other than securities shall be in such form, contain such information and be accompanied by such documents as shall be required by rule of the commissioner or, in the absence thereof, in substantially the form of an application filed pursuant to Section 25121.

Sec. 25143. **Stop orders—notice and hearing.** (a) The commissioner may by order summarily postpone or suspend the effectiveness of any qualification pending final determination of any proceeding under this chapter. Upon the entry of the order, the commissioner shall promptly notify each person specified in subdivision (b) of this section that it has been entered and of the reasons therefor and that upon the receipt of a written request the matter will be set down for hearing to commence within 15 business days after such receipt unless the applicant consents to a later date. If no hearing is requested and none is ordered by the commissioner the order will remain in effect until it is modified or vacated by the commissioner. If a hearing is requested or ordered, the commissioner, after notice and hearing in accordance with subdivision (b) of this section, may modify or vacate the order or extend it until final determination.

(b) No stop order may be entered under this chapter except under subdivision (a) of this section without appropriate prior notice to the applicant, the issuer, and the person on whose behalf the securities are to be or have been offered and hearing in accordance with the provisions of the Administrative Procedure Act, Chapter 5 (commencing with Section 11500) of Part 1 of Division 3 of Title 2 of the Government Code, in connection with which the commissioner shall have all of the powers granted thereunder. In the case of qualification by permit, such hearing shall be held upon such notice within 20 business days after a written request therefor by the applicant unless the permit is issued prior to the expiration of such period or the applicant consents to a later date.

Sec. 25144. Stop orders—vacation or modification. The commissioner may vacate or modify a stop order if he finds that the conditions which caused its entry have changed or that it is otherwise in the public interest to do so.

Sec. 25145. Records and reports of sales and proceeds. Every issuer qualifying securities for sale in this state shall at all times keep and maintain a complete set of books, records, and accounts of such sales and the disposition of the proceeds thereof, and shall thereafter, at such times as are required by the commissioner, make and file in the office of the commissioner a report, setting forth the securities sold by it under such qualification, the proceeds derived therefrom and the disposition thereof.

Sec. 25146. Semiannual reports. For a period of 18 months after the qualification is effective, the commissioner may by rule or order require an issuer who has filed an application to file reports not more often than semiannually for the purpose of keeping reasonably current the information contained in the application; provided, that the commissioner may not require the filing of any such report after completion of the offering if a nonissuer transaction in the security would be entitled to exemption under subdivision (a) of Section 25101.

Sec. 25147. Subscription or sale contract. The commissioner may by rule or order require as a condition of qualification that any security qualified under Section 25113 be sold only on a specified form of subscription or sale contract, and that a signed or conformed copy of each contract be preserved for any period up to three years specified in the rule or order.

Sec. 25148. Requirement of prospectus or proxy statement. Except in cases where the delivery of a prospectus or proxy statement is required under the Securities Act of 1933 or the Securities Exchange Act of 1934, the commissioner may by rule or order require as a condition of qualification under Section 25112, 25113, 25122 or 25131 that a prospectus or proxy statement containing any designated part of the information required in the application be sent or given to each person to whom an offer is made before the sale of the security to be issued under the permit or order.

Sec. 25149. Commissioner as escrow holder. The commissioner may act as escrow holder for securities required to be deposited in escrow by his order.

Sec. 25151. Consent to transfer securities under escrow or legend condition. Upon the filing of a written request for the consent to transfer securities referred to in Section 25133, accompanied by such information and documents as the commissioner may by rule require, the commissioner shall issue such consent if he finds that the transfer requested will be fair, just, and equitable to the proposed transferees, and otherwise he shall deny such consent.

PART 4

ADVERTISING SECURITIES

Sec. 25300. Filing advertising with commissioner—exceptions. (a) No person shall publish any advertisement in this state concerning any security sold or offered for sale in this state unless a true copy of the advertisement has first been filed in the office of the commissioner at least three business days prior to the publication or such shorter period as the commissioner may by rule or order allow.

(b) Subdivision (a) of this section does not apply to:

(1) Any advertisement for any security published by a licensed broker-dealer if he is not effecting transactions in such security as an underwriter or other participant in a distribution for the issuer;

(2) Any advertisement for any security published by an issuer or any underwriter or other participant in a distribution for the issuer if the security or transaction is exempted by the provisions of Chapter 1 (commencing with Section 25100) of Part 2 of this division;

(3) Any advertisement for any security in a nonissuer transaction if the security is exempted by Section 25100 or an offer of the security is exempted by subdivision (g) of Section 25104;

(4) Any advertisement permitted or required by Section 5(b)(2) or Section 2(10)(b) of the Securities Act of 1933 with respect to a security which has been registered under the Securities Act of 1933 and qualified for sale in this state; or

(5) Any other advertisement exempted by rule of the commissioner.

Sec. 25301. Approval of advertising by responsible supervising official. All advertisements published by any broker-dealer which are exempted from filing by clause (1) or clause (5) of subdivision (b) of Section 25300 shall be approved prior to use by signature or initial of an officer, partner, or responsible supervisory official of such broker-dealer and such signed or initialed copy shall be retained by such broker-dealer in an appropriate file for a period of three years, subject to examination by the commissioner.

Sec. 25302. Order against misleading advertising—rescission of order. (a) No person shall publish any advertisement concerning any security in this state after the commissioner finds that the advertisement contains any statement that is false or misleading or omits to make any statement necessary in order to make the statements made, in the light of the circumstances under which they were made, not misleading and so notifies the person in writing. Such notification may be given summarily without notice or hearing. At any time after the issuance of a notification under this section, the person desiring to use the advertisement may in writing request that the order be rescinded. Upon the receipt of such a written request, the matter shall be set down for hearing to commence within 15 business days after such receipt unless the person making the request consents to a later date. After such hearing, which shall be conducted in accordance with the provisions of the Administrative Procedure Act, Chapter 5 (commencing with Section 11500) of Part 1 of Division 3 of Title 2 of the Government Code, the commissioner shall determine whether to affirm and continue or to rescind such order, and the commissioner shall have all of the powers granted under such act.

(b) This section does not apply to any advertisement for any security which is subject to the supervision, regulation or examination of any of the following:

(1) The Insurance Commissioner.

(2) The Savings and Loan Commissioner.

(3) The Superintendent of Banks.

(4) The Public Utilities Commission.

(5) The Federal Home Loan Bank Board.

(6) The Federal Savings and Loan Insurance Corporation.

(7) The Comptroller of the Currency of the United States.

(8) The Federal Deposit Insurance Corporation.

(9) The Board of Governors of the Federal Reserve System.

PART 5

FRAUDULENT AND PROHIBITED PRACTICES

Sec. 25400. Manipulation of prices or appearance of trading. It is unlawful for any person, directly or indirectly, in this state:

(a) For the purpose of creating a false or misleading appearance of active trading in any security or a false or misleading appearance with respect to the market for any security, (1) to effect any transaction in a security which involves no change in the beneficial ownership thereof, or (2) to enter an order or orders for the purchase of any security with the knowledge that an order or orders of substantially the same size, at substantially the same time and at substantially the same price, for the sale of any such security, has been or will be entered by or for the same or different parties, or (3) to enter an order or orders for the sale of any security with the knowledge that an order or orders of substantially the same size, at substantially the same time and at substantially the same price, for the purchase of any such security, has been or will be entered by or for the same or different parties.

(b) To effect, alone or with one or more other persons, a series of transactions in any security creating actual or apparent active trading in such security or raising or depressing the price of such security, for the purpose of inducing the purchase or sale of such security by others.

(c) If such person is a broker-dealer or other person selling or offering for sale or purchasing or offering to purchase the security, to induce the purchase or sale of any security by the circulation or dissemination of information to the effect that the price of any such security will or is likely to rise or fall because of market operations of any one or more persons conducted for the purpose of raising or depressing the price of such security.

(d) If such person is a broker-dealer or other person selling or offering for sale or purchasing or offering to purchase the security, to make, for the purpose of inducing the purchase or sale of such security by others, any statement which was, at the time and in the light of the circumstances under which it was made, false or misleading with respect to any material fact, or which omitted to state any material fact necessary in order to make the statements made, in the light of the circumstances under which they were made, not misleading, and which he knew or had reasonable ground to believe was so false or misleading.

(e) For a consideration, received directly or indirectly from a broker-dealer or other person selling or offering for sale or purchasing or offering to purchase the security, to induce the purchase or sale of any security by the circulation or dissemination of information to the effect that the price of such security will or is likely to rise or fall because of the market operations of any one or more persons conducted for the purpose of raising or depressing the price of such security.

Sec. 25401. **Misrepresentation of material facts.** It is unlawful for any person to offer or sell a security in this state or buy or offer to buy a security in this state by means of any written or oral communication which includes an untrue statement of a material fact or omits to state a material fact necessary in order to make the statements made, in the light of the circumstances under which they were made, not misleading.

Sec. 25402. **Unlawful insider trading.** It is unlawful for an issuer or any person who is an officer, director or controlling person of an issuer or any other person whose relationship to the issuer gives him access, directly or indirectly, to material information about the issuer not generally available to the public, to purchase or sell any security of the issuer in this state at a time when he knows material information about the issuer gained from such relationship which would significantly affect the market price of that security and which is not generally available to the public, and which he knows is not intended to be so available, unless he has reason to believe that the person selling to or buying from him is also in possession of the information.

PART 6

ENFORCEMENT

CHAPTER 1

CIVIL LIABILITY

Sec. 25500. **Damages for price manipulation.** Any person who willfully participates in any act or transaction in violation of Section 25400 shall be liable to any other person who purchases or sells any security at a price which was affected by such act or transaction for the damages sustained by the latter as a result of such act or transaction. Such damages shall be the difference between the price at which such other person purchased or sold securities and the market value which such securities would have had at the time of his purchase or sale in the absence of such act or transaction, plus interest at the legal rate.

Sec. 25501. **Rescission or damages for misrepresentation—defenses.** Any person who violates Section 25401 shall be liable to the person who purchases a security from him or sells a security to him, who may sue either for rescission or for damages (if the plaintiff or the defendant, as the case may be, no longer owns the security), unless the defendant proves that the plaintiff knew the facts concerning the untruth or omission or that the defendant exercised reasonable care and did not know (or if he had exercised reasonable care would not have known) of the untruth or omission. Upon rescission, a purchaser may recover the consideration paid for the security, plus interest at the legal rate, less the amount of any income received on the security, upon tender of the security. Upon rescission, a seller may recover the security, upon tender of the consideration paid for the security plus interest at the legal rate, less the amount of any income received by the defendant on the security. Damages recoverable under this section by a purchaser shall be an amount equal to

the difference between (a) the price at which the security was bought plus interest at the legal rate from the date of purchase and (b) the value of the security at the time it was disposed of by the plaintiff plus the amount of any income received on the security by the plaintiff. Damages recoverable under this section by a seller shall be an amount equal to the difference between (1) the value of the security at the time of the filing of the complaint plus the amount of any income received by the defendant on the security and (2) the price at which the security was sold plus interest at the legal rate from the date of sale. Any tender specified in this section may be made at any time before entry of judgment.

Sec. 25502. **Damages for insider trading—defenses.** Any person who violates Section 25402 shall be liable to the person who purchases a security from him or sells a security to him, for damages equal to the difference between the price at which such security was purchased or sold and the market value which such security would have had at the time of the purchase or sale if the information known to the defendant had been publicly disseminated prior to that time and a reasonable time had elapsed for the market to absorb the information, plus interest at the legal rate, unless the defendant proves that the plaintiff knew the information or that the plaintiff would have purchased or sold at the same price even if the information had been revealed to him.

Sec. 25503. **Rescission or damages for failure to qualify securities.** Any person who violates Section 25110, 25130 or 25133, or a condition of qualification under Chapter 2 (commencing with Section 25110) of this part, imposed pursuant to Section 25141, or an order suspending trading issued pursuant to Section 25219, shall be liable to any person acquiring from him the security sold in violation of such section, who may sue to recover the consideration he paid for such security with interest thereon at the legal rate, less the amount of any income received therefrom, upon the tender of such security, or for damages, if he no longer owns the security, of if the consideration given for the security is not capable of being returned. Damages, if the plaintiff no longer owns the security, shall be equal to the difference between (a) his purchase price plus interest at the legal rate from the date of purchase and (b) the value of the security at the time it was disposed of by the plaintiff plus the amount of any income received therefrom by the plaintiff.

Damages, if the consideration given for the security is not capable of being returned, shall be equal to the value of that consideration plus interest at the legal rate from the date of purchase, provided the security is tendered; and if the plaintiff no longer owns the security, damages in such case shall be equal to the difference between (a) the value of the consideration given for the security plus interest at the legal rate from the date of purchase and (b) the value of the security at the time it was disposed of by the plaintiff plus the amount of any income received therefrom by the plaintiff. Any person who violates Section 25120 or a condition of qualification under Chapter 3 (commencing with Section 25120) of this part imposed pursuant to Section 25141, shall be liable to any person acquiring from him the security sold in violation of such section who may sue to recover the difference between (a) the value of the consideration received by the seller and (b) the value of the security at the time it was received by the buyer, with interest thereon at the legal rate from the date of purchase. Any person on whose behalf an offering is made and any underwriter of the offering, whether on a best efforts or a firm commitment basis, shall be jointly and severally liable under this section, but in no event shall any underwriter (unless such underwriter shall have knowingly received from the issuer for acting as an underwriter some benefit, directly or indirectly, in which all other underwriters similarly situated did not share in proportion to their respective interest in the underwriting) be liable in any suit or suits authorized under this section for damages in excess of the total price at which the securities underwritten by him and distributed to the public were offered to the public. Any tender specified in this section may be made at any time before entry of judgment. No person shall be liable under this section for violation of Section 25110, 25120 or 25130 if the sale of the security is qualified prior to the payment or receipt of any part of the consideration for the security sold, even though an offer to sell or a contract of sale may have been made or entered into without qualification.

CHAPTER 2

POWERS OF THE COMMISSIONER

Sec. 25530. **Civil actions by commissioner.** (a) Whenever it appears to the commissioner that any person has engaged or is about to engage in any act or practice constituting a violation of any provision of this law or any rule or order hereunder, the commissioner may in the commissioner's discretion bring an action in the name of the people of the State of California in the superior court to enjoin the acts or practices or to enforce compliance with this law or any rule or order hereunder. Upon a proper showing a permanent or preliminary injunction, restraining order, or writ of mandate shall be granted and a receiver or conservator may be appointed for the defendant or the defendant's assets, or such other ancillary relief may be granted as appropriate.

A receiver or conservator appointed by the superior court pursuant to this section may, with the approval of the court, exercise all of the powers of the defendant's officers, directors, partners, trustees or persons who exercise similar powers and perform similar duties, including the filing of a petition for bankruptcy. No action at law or in equity may be maintained by any party against the commissioner, or a receiver or conservator, by reason of their exercising such powers or performing such duties pursuant to the order of, or with the approval of, the superior court.

(b) If the commissioner determines it is in the public interest, the commissioner may include in any action authorized by subdivision (a) a claim for ancillary relief, including but not limited to, a claim for restitution or damages under Chapter 1 (commencing with Section 25500) of this part on behalf of the persons injured by the act or practice constituting the subject matter of the action, and the court shall have jurisdiction to award such additional relief.

Sec. 25531. **Investigations and judicial powers.** (a) The commissioner in his discretion (1) may make such public or private investigations within or outside of this state as he deems necessary to determine whether any person has violated or is about to violate any provision of this law or any rule or order hereunder or to aid in the enforcement of this law or in the prescribing of rules and forms hereunder, and (2) may publish information concerning any violation of this law or any rule or order hereunder.

(b) In making any investigation authorized by subdivision (a) of this section, the commissioner may, for a reasonable time not exceeding 30 days, take possession of the books, records, accounts and other papers pertaining to the business of any broker-dealer or investment adviser and place a keeper in exclusive charge of them in the place where they are usually kept. During such possession no person shall remove or attempt to remove any of the books, records, accounts, or other papers except pursuant to a court order or with the consent of the commissioner; but the directors, officers, partners, and employees of the broker-dealer or investment adviser may examine them, and employees shall be permitted to make entries therein reflecting current transactions.

(c) For the purpose of any investigation or proceeding under this law, the commissioner or any officer designated by him may administer oaths and affirmations, subpoena witnesses, compel their attendance, take evidence, and require the production of any books, papers, correspondence, memoranda, agreements, or other documents or records which the commissioner deems relevant or material to the inquiry.

(d) In case of contumacy by, or refusal to obey a subpoena issued to, any person, the superior court, upon application by the commissioner, may issue to the person an order requiring him to appear before the commissioner, or the officer designated by him, there to produce documentary evidence, if so ordered, or to give evidence touching the matter under investigation or in question. Failure to obey the order of the court may be punished by the court as a contempt.

(e) No person is excused from attending and testifying or from producing any document or record before the commissioner, or in obedience to the subpoena of the commissioner or any officer designated by him, or in any proceeding instituted by the commissioner, on the ground that the testimony or evidence (documentary or otherwise) required of him may tend to incriminate him or subject him to a penalty or forfeiture; but no individual may be prosecuted or subjected to any penalty or forfeiture for or on account of any transaction, matter, or thing concerning which he is compelled, after validly claiming his privilege against self-incrimination, to testify or produce evidence (documentary or otherwise), except that the individual testifying is not exempt from prosecution and punishment for perjury or contempt committed in testifying.

Sec. 25532. **Order to desist and refrain from activity until qualified or licensed: Hearing.** (a) If in the opinion of the commissioner the sale of any security is subject to qualification under this law and it is being or has been offered or sold without first being qualified, the commissioner may order the issuer or offeror of such security to desist and refrain from the further offer or sale of such security unless and until qualification has been made under this law.

(b) If in the opinion of the commissioner any person is acting as a broker-dealer or investment adviser in violation of Section 25210 or 25230, the commissioner may order such person to desist and refrain from such activity unless and until the person has been licensed as such under this law.

(c) If, after an order has been made under subdivision (a) or (b), a request for hearing is filed in writing by the person to whom such order was directed, a hearing shall be held in accordance with the provisions of the Administrative Procedure Act, Chapter 5 (commencing with Section 11500) of Part 1 of Division 3 of Title 2 of the Government Code, and the commissioner shall have all of the powers granted thereunder; unless such hearing is commenced within 15 business days after the request is made (or the person affected consents to a later date), such order is rescinded.

Sec. 25533. **Reference of violation to district attorney.** The commissioner may refer such evidence as is available concerning any violation of this law or of any rule or order hereunder to the district attorney of the county in which the violation occurred, who may, with or without such a reference, institute appropriate criminal proceedings under this law. The commissioner and his counsel, deputies, or assistants may, upon request of the district attorney, assist the district attorney in presenting the law or facts at the trial.

Sec. 25534. **Order imposing legend condition on issued securities.** Whenever any securities are issued which the commissioner determines were offered or sold in violation of Section 25110, 25120, or 25130, the commissioner may, by written order to the issuer and notice to the holders of such securities, require certificates evidencing such securities to have stamped or printed prominently on their face a legend, in the form prescribed by rule of the commissioner, restricting the transfer of such securities. Upon receipt of the order, the issuer shall stamp or print such legend prominently on the face of all outstanding certificates subject to the order. If, after such order or notice has been given, a request for a hearing is filed in writing by the person or persons to whom such order or notice was addressed, a hearing shall be held in accordance with the provisions of the Administrative Procedure Act, Chapter 5 (commencing with Section 11500) of Part 1 of Division 3 of Title 2 of the Government Code, and the commissioner shall have all the powers granted thereunder; unless such hearing is commenced within 15 business days after the request for hearing is received by the commissioner (or the person or persons affected and the issuer consent to a later date), such order and notice are rescinded.

CHAPTER 3

CRIMES

Sec. 25540. **Penalty for violation of law or rule.** Any person who willfully violates any provision of this law, or who willfully violates any rule or order under this law; shall upon conviction be fined not more than ten thousand dollars ($10,000) or imprisoned in the state prison, or in a county jail for not more than one year, or be punished by both such fine and imprisonment; but no person may be imprisoned for the violation of any rule or order if he proves that he had no knowledge of the rule or order.

Sec. 25541. **Penalty for fraud or deceit.** Any person who willfully employs, directly or indirectly, any device, scheme, or artifice to defraud in connection with the offer, purchase, or sale of any security or willfully engages, directly or indirectly, in any act, practice, or course of business which operates or would operate as a fraud or deceit upon any person in connection with the offer, purchase, or sale of any security shall upon conviction be fined not more than ten thousand dollars ($10,000) or imprisoned in the state prison, or in a county jail for not more than one year, or be punished by both such fine and imprisonment.

Sec. 25542. **Punishment of crimes under other statutes.** Nothing in this law limits the power of the state to punish any person for any conduct which constitutes a crime under any other statute.

CHAPTER 4

SERVICE OF PROCESS

Sec. 25550. **Service of process on commissioner authorized.** When any person, including any nonresident of this state, engages in conduct prohibited or made actionable by this law or any rule or order hereunder, whether or not he has filed a consent to service of process under subdivision (h) of Section 25102, Section 25165 or Section 25240, and personal jurisdiction over him cannot otherwise be obtained in this state, that conduct shall be considered equivalent to his appointment of the commissioner or his successor in office to be his attorney to receive service of any lawful process in any non-criminal suit, action, or proceeding against him or his successor, executor, or administrator which grows out of that conduct and which is brought under this law or any rule or order hereunder, with the same force and validity as if served on him personally. Service may be made by leaving a copy of the process in the office of the commissioner, but it is not effective unless (a) the plaintiff, who may be the commissioner in a suit, action, or proceeding instituted by him, forthwith sends notice of the service and a copy of the process by registered or certified mail to the defendant or respondent at his last known address or takes other steps which are reasonably calculated to give actual notice, and (b) the plaintiff's affidavit of compliance with this section is filed in the case on or before the return day of the process, if any, or within such further time as the court allows.

UNIFORM FRAUDULENT CONVEYANCE ACT

(Equivalent California Civil Code section numbers follow the U.F.C.A. section numbers in parentheses. California has added "or encumbrancer" throughout U.F.C.A. 9, as indicated by those words in parentheses in that section, and has added subdivision (b) to U.F.C.A. 9.)

Sec. 1. (3439.01) **Definition of Terms.** In this act "Assets" of a debtor means property not exempt from liability for his debts. To the extent that any property is liable for any debts of the debtor, such property shall be included in his assets.

"Conveyance" includes every payment of money, assignment, release, transfer, lease mortgage or pledge of tangible or intangible property, and also the creation of any lien or encumbrance.

"Creditor" is a person having any claim, whether matured or unmatured, liquidated or unliquidated, absolute, fixed or contingent.

"Debt" includes any legal liability, whether matured or unmatured liquidated or unliquidated, absolute, fixed or contingent.

Sec. 2. (3439.02) **Insolvency.** (1) A person is insolvent when the present fair salable value of his assets is less than the amount that will be required to pay his probable liability on his existing debts as they become absolute and matured.

(2) In determining whether a partnership is insolvent there shall be added to the partnership property the present fair salable value of the separate assets of each general partner in excess of the amount probably sufficient to meet the claims of his separate creditors, and also the amount of any unpaid subscription to the partnership of each limited partner, provided the present fair salable value of the assets of such limited partner is probably sufficient to pay his debts, including such unpaid subscription.

Sec. 3. (3439.03) **Fair Consideration.** Fair consideration is given for property, or obligation,

(a) When in exchange for such property, or obligation, as a fair equivalent therefor, and in good faith, property is conveyed or an antecedent debt is satisfied, or

(b) When such property, or obligation is received in good faith to secure a present advance or antecedent debt in amount not disproportionately small as compared with the value of the property, or obligation obtained.

Sec. 4. (3439.04) **Conveyances by Insolvent.** Every conveyance made and every obligation incurred by a person who is or will be thereby rendered insolvent is fraudulent as to creditors without regard to his actual intent if the conveyance is made or the obligation is incurred without a fair consideration.

Sec. 5. (3439.05) **Conveyances by Persons in Business.** Every conveyance made without fair consideration when the person making it is engaged or is about to engage in a business or transaction for which the property remaining in his hands after the conveyance is an unreasonably small capital, is fraudulent as to creditors and as to other persons who become creditors during the continuance of such business or transaction without regard to his actual intent.

Sec. 6. (3439.06) **Conveyances by a Person About to Incur Debts.** Every conveyance made and every obligation incurred without fair consideration when the person making the conveyance or entering into the obligation intends or believes that he will incur debts beyond his ability to pay as they mature, is fraudulent as to both present and future creditors.

Sec. 7. (3439.07) **Conveyance Made With Intent to Defraud.** Every conveyance and every obligation incurred with actual intent, as distinguished from intent presumed in law, to hinder, delay, or defraud either present or future creditors, is fraudulent as to both present and future creditors.

Sec. 8. (3439.08) **Conveyance of Partnership Property.** Every conveyance of partnership property and every partnership obligation incurred when the partnership is or will be thereby rendered insolvent, is fraudulent as to partnership creditors, if the conveyance is made or obligation is incurred,

(a) To a partner, whether with or without a promise by him to pay partnership debts, or

(b) To a person not a partner without fair compensation to the partnership as distinguished from consideration to the individual partners.

Sec. 9. (3439.09) **Rights of Creditors Whose Claims Have Matured.** (a) Where a conveyance or obligation is fraudulent as to a creditor, such creditor, when his claim has matured, may, as against any person except a purchaser (or encumbrancer) for fair consideration without knowledge of the fraud at the time of the purchase, or one who has derived title immediately or mediately from such a purchaser (or encumbrancer):

(1) Have the conveyance set aside or obligation annulled to the extent necessary to satisfy his claim, or

(2) Disregard the conveyance and attach or levy execution upon the property conveyed.

(b) An assignee of a general assignment for the benefit of creditors, as defined in Section 393.010 of the Code of Civil Procedure, may exercise any or all of the rights specified in subdivision (a) if and to the extent they are available to any one or more creditors of the assignor who are beneficiaries of the assignment.

(c) A purchaser (or encumbrancer) who without actual fraudulent intent has given less than a fair consideration for the conveyance or obligation, may retain the property or obligation as security for repayment.

Sec. 10. (3439.10) **Rights of Creditors Whose Claims Have Not Matured.** Where a conveyance made or obligation incurred is fraudulent as to a creditor whose claim has not matured he may proceed to a court of competent jurisdiction against any person against whom he could have proceeded had his claim matured, and the court may,

(a) Restrain the defendant from disposing of his property,

(b) Appoint a receiver to take charge of the property,

(c) Set aside the conveyance or annul the obligation, or

(d) Make any order which the circumstances of the case may require.

Sec. 11. (3439.11) **Cases Not Provided for in Act.** In any case not provided for in this act the rules of law and equity including the law merchant, and in particular the rules relating to the law of principal and agent, and the effect of fraud, misrepresentation, duress or coercion, mistake, bankruptcy or other invalidating cause shall govern.

Sec. 12. (3439.12) **Construction of Act.** This act shall be so interpreted and construed as to effectuate its general purpose to make uniform the law of those states which enact it.

Sec. 13. (3439) **Name of Act.** This act may be cited as the Uniform Fraudulent Conveyance Act.

BANKRUPTCY REFORM ACT OF 1978

(Selected Provisions)

TITLE II

BANKRUPTCY

CHAPTER 1

GENERAL PROVISIONS

Sec. 101. **Definitions.** In this title (1) "accountant" means authorized under applicable law to practice public accounting, and includes professional accounting association, corporation, or partnership, if so authorized;

(2) "affiliate" means

(A) entity that directly or indirectly owns, controls, or holds with power to vote, 20 percent or more of the outstanding voting securities of the debtor, other than an entity that holds such securities

(i) in a fiduciary or agency capacity without sole discretionary power to vote such securities; or

(ii) solely to secure a debt, if such entity has not in fact exercised such power to vote;

(B) corporation 20 percent or more of whose outstanding voting securities are directly or indirectly owned, controlled, or held with power to vote, by the debtor, or by an entity that directly or indirectly owns, controls, or holds with power to vote, 20 percent or more of the outstanding voting securities of the debtor, other than an entity that holds such securities

(i) in a fiduciary or agency capacity without sole discretionary power to vote such securities; or

(ii) solely to secure a debt, if such entity has not in fact exercised such power to vote;

(C) person whose business is operated under a lease or operating agreement by a debtor, or person substantially all of whose property is operated under an operating agreement with the debtor; or

(D) entity that operates the business or all or substantially all of the property of the debtor under a lease or operating agreement;

(3) "attorney" means attorney, professional law association, corporation, or partnership, authorized under applicable law to practice law;

(4) "claim" means

(A) a right to payment, whether or not such right is reduced to judgment, liquidated, unliquidated, fixed, contingent, matured, unmatured, disputed, undisputed, legal, equitable, secured, or unsecured; or

(B) right to an equitable remedy for breach of performance if such breach gives rise to a right to payment, whether or not such right to an equitable remedy is reduced to judgment, fixed, contingent, matured, unmatured, disputed, undisputed, secured, or unsecured;

(5) "commodity broker" means futures commission merchant, foreign futures commission merchant, clearing organization, leverage transaction merchant, or commodity options dealer, as defined in Section 761 of this title, with respect to which there is a customer, as defined in section 761(9) of this title;

(6) "community claim" means claim that arose before the commencement of the case concerning the debtor for which property of the kind specified in Section 541(a)(2) of this title is liable, whether or not there is any such property at the time of the commencement of the case;

(7) "consumer debt" means debt incurred by an individual primarily for a personal, family, or household purpose;

(8) "corporation"

(A) includes

(i) association having a power or privilege that a private corporation, but not an individual or a partnership, possesses;

(ii) partnership association organized under a law that makes only the capital subscribed responsible for the debts of such association;

(iii) joint-stock company;

(iv) unincorporated company or association; or

(v) business trust; but

(B) does not include limited partnership;

(9) "creditor" means

(A) entity that has a claim against the debtor that arose at the time of or before the order for relief concerning the debtor;

(B) entity that has a claim against the estate of a kind specified in Section 502 (f), 502 (g), 502 (h) or 502 (i) of this title; or

(C) entity that has a community claim;

(10) "custodian" means

(A) receiver or trustee of any of the property of the debtor, appointed in a case or proceeding not under this title;

(B) assignee under a general assignment for the benefit of the debtor's creditors; or

(C) trustee, receiver, or agent under applicable law, or under a contract, that is appointed or authorized to take charge of property of the debtor for the purpose of enforcing a lien against such property, or for the purpose of general administration of such property for the benefit of the debtor's creditors;

(11) "debt" means liability on a claim;

(12) "debtor" means person or municipality concerning which a case under this title has been commenced;

(13) "disinterested person" means person that

(A) is not a creditor, an equity security holder, or an insider;

(B) is not and was not an investment banker for any outstanding security of the debtor;

(C) has not been, within three years before the date of the filing of the petition, an investment banker for a security of the debtor, or an attorney for such an investment banker in connection with the offer, sale, or issuance of a security of the debtor;

(D) is not and was not, within two years before the date of the filing of the petition, a director, officer, or employee of the debtor or of an investment banker specified in subparagraph (B) or (C) of this paragraph; and

(E) does not have an interest materially adverse to the interest of the estate or of any class of creditors or equity security holders, by reason of any direct or indirect relationship to, connection with, or interest in, the debtor or an investment banker specified in subparagraph (B) or (C) of this paragraph, or for any other reason;

(14) "entity" includes person, estate, trust, government unit;

(15) "equity security" means

(A) share in a corporation, whether or not transferable or denominated "stock" or similar security;

(B) interest of a limited partner in a limited partnership; or

(C) warrant or right, other than a right to convert, to purchase, sell, or subscribe in a share, security, or interest of a kind specified in subparagraph (A) or (B) of this paragraph;

(16) "equity security holder" means holder of an equity security of the debtor;

(17) "farmer" means person that received more than 80 percent of such person's gross income during the taxable year of such person immediately preceding the taxable year of such person during which the case under this title concerning such person was commenced from a farming operation owned or operated by such person;

(18) "farming operation" includes farming, tillage of the soil, dairy farming, ranching, production or raising of crops, poultry or livestock, and production of poultry or livestock products in an unmanufactured state;

(19) "foreign proceeding" means proceeding, whether judicial or administrative and whether or not under bankruptcy law, in a foreign country in which the debtor's domicile, residence, principal place of business, or principal assets were located at the commencement of such proceeding, for the purpose of liquidating an estate, adjusting debts by composition, extension, or discharge, or effecting a reorganization;

(20) "foreign representative" means duly selected trustee, administrator, or other representative of an estate in a foreign proceeding;

(21) "governmental unit" means United States; State; Commonwealth; District; Territory; municipality; foreign state; department, agency, or instrumentality of the United States, a State, a Commonwealth, a District, a Territory, a municipality, or a foreign state; or other foreign or domestic government;

(22) "indenture" means mortgage, deed of trust, or indenture, under which there is outstanding a security, other than a voting-trust certificate, constituting a claim against the debtor, a claim secured by a lien on any of the debtor's property, or an equity security of the debtor;

(23) "indenture trustee" means trustee under an indenture;

(24) "individual with regular income" means individual whose income is sufficiently stable and regular to enable such individual to make payments under a plan under chapter 13 of this title, other than a stock broker or a commodity broker;

(25) "insider" includes

(A) if the debtor is an individual

(i) relative of the debtor or of a general partner of the debtor;

(ii) partnership in which the debtor is a general partner

(iii) general partner of the debtor; or

(iv) corporation of which the debtor is a director, officer, or person in control;

(B) if the debtor is a corporation

(i) director of the debtor;

(ii) officer of the debtor;

(iii) person in control of the debtor;

(iv) partnership in which the debtor is a general partner;

(v) general partner of the debtor; or

(vi) relative of a general partner, director, officer, or person in control of the debtor;

(C) if the debtor is a partnership

(i) general partner in the debtor;

(ii) relative of a general partner in, general partner of, or person in control of the debtor;

(iii) partnership in which the debtor is a general partner;

(iv) general partner of the debtor; or

(v) person in control of the debtor;

(D) if the debtor is a municipality, elected official of the debtor or relative of an elected official of the debtor;

(E) affiliate, or insider of an affiliate as if such affiliate were the debtor; and

(F) managing agent of the debtor;

(26) "insolvent" means

(A) with reference to an entity other than a partnership, financial condition such that the sum of such entity's debts is greater than all of such entity's property, as a fair valuation, exclusive of

(i) property transferred, concealed, or removed with intent to hinder, delay, or defraud such entity's creditors; and

(ii) property that may be exempted from property of the estate under section 522 of this title; and

(B) with reference to a partnership, financial condition such that the sum of such partnership's debts is greater than the aggregate of, at a fair valuation

(i) all of such partnership's property, exclusive of property of the kind specified in subparagraph (A)(i) of this paragraph; and

(ii) the sum of the excess of the value of each general partner's separate property, exclusive of property of the kind specified in subparagraph (A)(ii) of this paragraph, over such partner's separate debts;

(27) "judicial lien" means lien obtained by judgment, levy, sequestration, or other legal or equitable process or proceeding;

(28) "lien" means charge against or interest in property to secure payment of a debt or performance of an obligation;

(29) "municipality" means political subdivision or public agency or instrumentality of a State;

(30) "person" includes individual, partnership, and corporation, but does not include governmental unit;

(31) "petition" means petition filed under section 301, 302, 303, or 304 of this title, as the case may, commencing a case under this title;

(32) "purchaser" means transferee of a voluntary transfer, and includes immediate or mediate transferee of such a transferee;

(33) "railroad" means common carrier by railroad engaged in the transportation of individuals or property or owner of trackage facilities leased by such a common carrier;

(34) "relative" means individual related by affinity or consanguinity within the third degree as determined by the common law, or individual in a step or adoptive relationship within such third degree;

(35) "securities clearing agency" means person that is registered as a clearing agency under section 17A of the Securities Exchange Act of 1934 (15 U.S.C. 78q-1) or whose business is confined to the performance of functions of a clearing agency with respect to exempted securities, as defined in section 3(a)(12) of such Act (15 U.S.C. 78c(12)) for the purpose of such section 17A;

(36) "security"

(A) includes

(i) note;

(ii) stock;

(iii) treasury stock;

(iv) bond;

(v) debenture;

(vi) collateral trust certificate;

(vii) pre-organization certificate or subscription;

(viii) transferable share;

(ix) voting-trust certificate;

(x) certificate of deposit

(xi) certificate of deposit for security;

(xii) investment contract or certificate of interest or participation in a profit-sharing agreement or in an oil, gas, or mineral royalty or lease, if such contract or interest is required to be the subject of a registration statement filed with the Securities and Exchange Commission under the provisions of the Securities Act of 1933 (15 U.S.C. 77a et seq.), or is exempt under section 3(b) of such Act (15 U.S.C. 77c(b)) from the requirement to file such a statement;

(xiii) interest of a limited partner in a limited partnership;

(xiv) other claim or interest commonly known as "security"; and

(xv) certificate of interest or participation in, temporary or interim certificate for, receipt for, or warrant or right to subscribe to or purchase or sell, a security; but

(B) does not include

(i) currency, check, draft, bill of exchange, or bank letter of credit;

(ii) leverage transaction, as defined in section 761 (13) of this title;

(iii) commodity futures contract or forward commodity contract;

(iv) option, warrant, or right to subscribe to or purchase or sell a commodity futures contract;

(v) option to purchase or sell a commodity;

(vi) contract or certificate specified in clause (xii) of subparagraph (A) of this paragraph that is not the subject of such a registration statement filed with the Securities and Exchange Commission and is not exempt under section 3 (b) of the Securities Act of 1933 (15 U.S.C. 77c (b)) from the requirement to file such a statement; or

(vii) debt or evidence of indebtedness for goods sold and delivered or services rendered;

(37) "security agreement" means agreement that creates or provides for a security interest;

(38) "security interest" means lien created by an agreement;

(39) "statutory lien" means lien arising solely by force of a statute on specified circumstances or conditions or lien of distress for rent, whether or not statutory, but does not include security interest or judicial lien, whether or not such interest or lien is provided by or is dependent on a statute and whether or not such interest or lien is made fully effective by statute;

(40) "stockbroker" means person

(A) with respect to which there is a customer, as defined in section 741(2) of this title; and

(B) that is engaged in the business of effecting transactions in securities

(i) for the account of others; or

(ii) with members of the general public, from or for such person's own account;

(41) "transfer" means every mode, direct or indirect, absolute or conditional, voluntary or involuntary, of disposing of or parting with property or with an interest in property, including retention of title as a security interest.

Sec. 109. **Who may be a debtor.** (a) Notwithstanding any other provision of this section, only a person that resides in the United States, or has a domicile, a place of business, or property in the United States, or a municipality, may be a debtor under this title.

(b) A person may be a debtor under chapter 7 of this title only if such person is not

(1) a railroad;

(2) a domestic insurance company, bank, savings bank, cooperative bank, savings and loan association, building and loan association, homestead association, or credit union; or

4

(3) a foreign insurance company, bank, savings bank, cooperative bank, savings and loan association, building and loan association, homestead associaiton, or credit union, engaged in such business in the United States.

(c) An entity may be a debtor under chapter 9 of this title if and only if such entity

(1) is a municipality;

(2) is generally authorized to be a debtor under such chapter by State law, or by a governmental officer or organization empowered by State law to authorize such entity to be a debtor under such chapter;

(3) is insolvent or unable to meet such entity's debts as such debts mature;

(4) desires to effect a plan to adjust such debts; and

(5) (A) has obtained the agreement of creditors holding at least a majority in amount of the claims of each class that such entity intends to impair under a plan in a case under such chapter;

(B) has negotiated in good faith with creditors and has failed to obtain the agreement of creditors holding at least a majority in amount of the claims of each class that such entity intends to impair under a plan in a case under such chapter;

(C) is unable to negotiate with creditors because such negotiation is impracticable; or

(D) reasonably believes that a creditor may attempt to obtain a preference.

(d) Only a person that may be a debtor under chapter 7 of this title, except a stockholder or a commodity broker, and a railroad may be a debtor under chapter 11 of this title.

(e) Only an individual with regular income that owes, on the date of the filing of the petition, noncontingent, liquidated, unsecured debts of less than $100,000 and noncontingent, liquidated, secured debts of less than $350,000, or an individual with regular income and such individual's spouse, except a stockbroker or a commodity broker, that owe, on the date of the filing of the petition, noncontingent, liquidated, unsecured debts that aggregate less than $100,000 and noncontingent, liquidated, secured debts of less than $350,000 may be a debtor under chapter 13 of this title.

CHAPTER 3

CASE ADMINISTRATION

SUBCHAPTER I—COMMENCEMENT OF A CASE

Sec. 301. Voluntary cases. A voluntary case under a chapter of this title is commenced by the filing with the bankruptcy court of a petition under such chapter by an entity that may be a debtor under such chapter. The commencement of a voluntary case under a chapter of this title constitutes an order for relief under such chapter.

Sec. 302. Joint cases. (a) A joint case under a chapter of this title is commenced by the filing with the bankruptcy court of a single petition under such chapter by an individual that may be a debtor under such chapter and such individual's spouse. The commencement of a joint case under a chapter of this title constitutes an order for relief under such chapter.

(b) After the commencement of a joint case, the court shall determine the extent, if any, to which the debtors' estates shall be consolidated.

Sec. 303. Involuntary cases. (a) An involuntary case may be commenced only under chapter 7 or 11 of this title, and only against a person, except a farmer or a corporation that is not a moneyed, business, or commercial corporation, that may be a debtor under the chapter under which such case is commenced.

(b) An involuntary case is commenced by the filing with the bankruptcy court of a petition under chapter 7 or 11 of this title

(1) by three or more entities, each of which is either a holder of a claim against such person that is not contingent as to liability or an indenture trustee representing such a holder, if such claims aggregate at least $5,000 more than the value of any lien on property of the debtor securing such claims held by the holders of such claims;

(2) if there are fewer than 12 such holders, excluding any employee or insider of such person and any transferee of a transfer that is voidable under section 544, 545, 547, 548, 549, or 724(a) of this title, by one or more of such holders that hold in the aggregate at least $5,000 of such claims;

(3) if such person is a partnership

(A) by fewer than all of the general partners in such partnership; or

(B) if relief has been ordered under this title with respect to all of the general partners in such partnership, by a general partner in such partnership, the trustee of such a general partner, or a holder of a claim against such partnership; or

(4) by a foreign representative of the estate in a foreign proceeding concerning such person.

(c) After the filing of a petition under this section but before the case is dismissed or relief is ordered, a creditor holding an unsecured claim that is not contingent, other than a creditor filing under subsection (b) of this section, may join in the petition with the same effect as if such joining creditor were a petitioning creditor under subsection (b) of this section.

(d) The debtor, or a general partner in a partnership debtor that did not join in the petition, may file an answer to a petition under this section.

(e) After notice and a hearing, and for cause, the court may require the petitioners under this section to file a bond to indemnify the debtor for such amounts as the court may later allow under subsection (i) of this section.

(f) Notwithstanding section 363 of this title, except to the extent that the court orders otherwise, and until an order for relief in the case, any business of the debtor may continue to operate, and the debtor may continue to use, acquire, or dispose of property as if an involuntary case concerning the debtor had not been commenced.

(g) At any time after the commencement of an involuntary case under chapter 7 of this title but before an order for relief in the case, the court, on request of a party in interest, after notice to the debtor and a hearing, and if necessary to preserve the property of the estate or to prevent loss to the estate, may appoint an interim trustee under section 701 of this title to take possession of the property of the estate and to operate any business of the debtor. Before an order for relief, the debtor may regain possession of property in the possession of a trustee ordered appointed under this subsection if the debtor files such bond as the court requires, conditioned on the debtor's accounting for and delivering to the trustee, if there is an order for relief in the case, such property, or the value, as of the date the debtor regains possession, of such property.

(h) If the petition is not timely controverted, the court shall order relief against the debtor in an involuntary case under the chapter under which the petition was filed. Otherwise, after trial, the court shall order relief against the debtor in an involuntary case under the chapter under which the petition was filed, only if

(1) the debtor is generally not paying such debtor's debts as such debts become due; or

(2) within 120 days before the date of the filing of the petition, a custodian, other than a trustee, receiver, or agent appointed or authorized to take charge of less than substantially all of the property of the debtor for the purpose of enforcing a lien against such property, was appointed or took possession.

Sec. 305. Abstention. (a) The court, after notice and a hearing, may dismiss a case under this title, or may suspend all proceedings in a case under this title, at any time if

(1) the interests of creditors and the debtor would be better served by such dismissal or suspension; or

(2) (A) there is pending a foreign proceeding: and

(B) the factors specified in section 304(c) of this title warrant such dismissal or suspension.

SUBCHAPTER II—OFFICERS

Sec. 321. Eligibility to serve as trustee. (a) A person may serve as trustee in a case under this title only if such person is

(1) an individual that is competent to perform the duties of trustee and, in a case under chapter 7 or 13 of this title, resides or has an office in the judicial district within which the case is pending, or in any judicial district adjacent to such district; or

(2) a corporation authorized by such corporation's charter or bylaws to act as trustee, and, in a case under chapter 7 or 13 of this title, having an office in at least one of such districts.

(b) A person that has served as an examiner in a case may not serve as trustee in the case.

Sec. 322. Qualification of trustee. (a) A person selected under section 701, 702, 703, 1104, 1163, or 1302 of this title to serve as trustee in a case under this title qualifies if before five days after such selection, and before beginning official duties, such person has filed with the court a bond in favor of the United States conditioned on the faithful performance of such official duties.

(b) The court shall determine

(1) the amount of a bond filed under subsection (a) of this section; and

(2) the sufficiency of the surety on such bond.

Sec. 323. Role and capacity of trustee. (a) The trustee in a case under this title is the representative of the estate.

(b) The trustee in a case under this title has capacity to sue and be sued.

Sec. 326. Limitation on compensation of trustee. (a) In a case under chapter 7 or 11, the court may allow reasonable compensation under section 330 of this title of the trustee for the trustee's services, payable after the trustee renders such services, not to exceed fifteen percent on the first $1,000 or less, six percent on any amount in excess of $1,000 but not in excess of $3,000, three percent on any amount in excess of $3,000 but not in excess of $20,000, two percent on any amount in excess of $20,000 but not in excess of $50,000, and one percent on any amount in excess of $50,000, upon all moneys disbursed or turned over in the case by the trustee to parties in interest, excluding the debtor, but including holders of secured claims.

(b) In a case under chapter 13 of this title, the court may not allow compensation for services or reimbursement of expenses of a standing trustee appointed under section 1302(d) of this title, but may allow reasonable compensation under section 330 of this title of a trustee appointed under section 1302(a) of this title for the trustee's services, payable after the trustee renders such services, not to exceed five percent upon all payments under the plan.

Sec. 327. Employment of professional persons. (a) Except as otherwise provided in this section, the trustee, with the court's approval, may employ one or more attorneys, accountants, appraisers, auctioneers, or other professional persons, that do not hold or represent an interest adverse to the estate, and that are disinterested persons, to represent or assist the trustee in carrying out the trustee's duties under this title.

(b) If the trustee is authorized to operate the business of the debtor under section 721 or 1108 of this title, and if the debtor has regularly employed attorneys, accountants, or other professional persons on salary, the trustee may retain or replace such professional persons if necessary in the operation of such business.

SUBCHAPTER III—ADMINISTRATION

Sec. 341. Meetings of creditors and equity security holders. (a) Within a reasonable time after the order for relief in a case under this title, there shall be a meeting of creditors.

(b) The court may order a meeting of equity security holders.

(c) The court may not preside at, and may not attend, any meeting under this section.

Sec. 342. Notice. There shall be given such notice as is appropriate of an order for relief in a case under this title.

Sec. 343. Examination of the debtor. The debtor shall appear and submit to examination under oath at the meeting of creditors under section 341(a) of this title. Creditors, any indenture trustee, or any trustee or examiner in the case may examine the debtor.

Sec. 344. Self-incrimination; immunity. Immunity for persons required to submit to examination, to testify, or to provide information in a case under this title may be granted under part V of title 18.

SUBCHAPTER IV—ADMINISTRATIVE POWERS

Sec. 362. Automatic stay. (a) Except as provided in subsection (b) of this section, a petition filed under section 301, 302, or 303 of this title operates as a stay, applicable to all entities, of

(1) the commencement or continuation, including the issuance or employment of process, of a judicial, administrative, or other proceeding against the debtor that was or could have been commenced before the commencement of the case under this title, or to recover a claim against the debtor that arose before the commencement of the case under this title;

(2) the enforcement, against the debtor or against property of the estate, of a judgment obtained before the commencement of the case under this title;

(3) any act to obtain possession of property of the estate or of property from the estate;

(4) any act to create, perfect, or enforce any lien against property of the estate;

(5) any act to create, perfect, or enforce against property of the debtor any lien to the extent that such lien secures a claim that arose before the commencement of the case under this title;

(6) any act to collect, assess, or recover a claim against the debtor that arose before the commencement of the case under this title;

(7) the setoff of any debt to the debtor that arose before the commencement of the case under this title against any claim against the debtor; and

Sec. 363. Use, sale, or lease of property. (a) In this section, "cash collateral" means cash, negotiable instruments, documents of title, securities, deposit accounts, or other cash equivalents in which the estate and an entity other than the estate have an interest.

(b) The trustee, after notice and a hearing, may use, sell, or lease, other than in the ordinary course of business, property of the estate.

Sec. 365. Executory contracts and unexpired leases. (a) Except as provided in sections 765 and 766 of this title and in subsections (b), (c), and (d) of this section, the trustee, subject to the court's approval, may assume or reject any executory contract or unexpired lease of the debtor.

(b) (1) If there has been a default in an executory contract or unexpired lease of the debtor, the trustee may not assume such contract or lease unless, at the time of assumption of such contract or lease, the trustee

(A) cures, or provides adequate assurance that the trustee will promptly cure, such default;

(B) compensates, or provides adequate assurance that the trustee will promptly compensate, a party other than the debtor to such contract or lease, for any actual precuniary loss to such party resulting from such default; and

(C) provides adequate assurance of future performance under such contract or lease.

(2) Paragraph (1) of this subsection does not apply to a default that is a breach of a provision relating to

(A) the insolvency or financial condition of the debtor at any time before the closing of the case;

(B) the commencement of a case under this title; or

(C) the appointment of or taking possession by a trustee in a case under this title or a custodian before such commencement.

(3) For the purposes of paragraph (1) of this section, adequate assurance of future performance of a lease of real property in a shopping center includes adequate assurance

(A) of the source of rent and other consideration due under such lease;

(B) that any percentage rent due under such lease will not decline substantially;

(C) that assumption or assignment of such lease will not breach substantially any provision, such as a radius, location, use, or exclusivity provision, in any other lease, financing agreement, or master agreement relating to such shopping center; and

(D) that assumption or assignment of such lease will not disrupt substantially any tenant mix or balance in such shopping center.

(4) Notwithstanding any other provision of this section, if there has been a default in an unexpired lease of the debtor, other than a default of a kind specified in paragraph (2) of this subsection, the trustee may not require a lessor to provide services or supplies incidental to such lease before assumption of such lease unless the lessor is compensated under the terms of such lease for any services and supplies provided under such lease before assumption of such lease.

(c) The trustee may not assume or assign an executory contract or unexpired lease of the debtor, whether or not such contract or lease prohibits or restricts assignment of rights or delegation of duties, if

(1) (A) applicable law excuses a party, other than the debtor, to such contract or lease from accepting performance from or rendering performance to the trustee or to an assignee of such contract or lease, whether or not such contract or lease prohibits or restricts assignment of rights or delegation of duties; and

(B) such party does not consent to such assumption or assignment; or

(2) such contract is a contract to make a loan, or extend other debt financing or financial accommodations, to or for the benefit of the debtor, or to issue a security of the debtor.

(d) (1) In a case under chapter 7 of this title, if the trustee does not assume or reject an executory contract or unexpired lease of the debtor within 60 days after the order for relief, or within such additional time as the court, for cause, within such 60-day period, fixes, then such contract or lease is deemed rejected.

(?) In a case under chapter 9, 11, or 13 of this title, the trustee may assume or reject an executory contract or unexpired lease of the debtor at any time before the confirmation of a plan, but the court, on request of any party to such contract or lease, may order the trustee to determine within a specified period of time whether to assume or reject such contract or lease.

(e) (1) Notwithstanding a provision in an executory contract or unexpired lease, or in applicable law, an executory contract or unexpired lease of the debtor may not be terminated or modified, and any right or obligation under such contract or lease may not be terminated or modified, at any time after the commencement of the case solely because of a provision in such contract or lease that is conditioned on

(A) The involvency or financial condition of the debtor at any time before the closing of the case;

(B) the commencement of a case under this title; or

(C) the appointment of or taking possession by a trustee in a case under this title or a custodian before such commencement.

(2) Paragraph (1) of this subsection does not apply to an executory contract or unexpired lease of the debtor, whether or not such contract or lease prohibits or restricts assignment of rights or delegation of duties, if

(A) (i) applicable law excuses a party, other than the debtor, to such contract or lease from accepting performance from or rendering performance to the trustee or to an assignee of such contract or lease, whether or not such contract or lease prohibits or restricts assignment of rights or delegation of duties; and

(ii) such party does not consent to such assumption or assignment; or

(B) such contract is a contract to make a loan, or extend other debt financing or financial accommodations, to or for the benefit of the debtor, or to issue a security of the debtor.

(f) (1) Except as provided in subsection (c) of this section, notwithstanding a provision in an executory contract or unexpired lease of the debtor, or in applicable law, that prohibits, restricts, or conditions the assignment of such contract or lease, the trustee may assign such contract or lease under paragraph (2) of this subsection.

(2) The trustee may assign an executory contract or unexpired lease of the debtor only if

(A) the trustee assumes such contract or lease in accordance with the provisions of this section; and

(B) adequate assurance of future performance by the assignee of such contract or lease is provided, whether or not there has been a default in such contract or lease.

(3) Notwithstanding a provision in an executory contract or unexpired lease of the debtor, or in applicable law that terminates or modifies, or permits a party other than the debtor to terminate or modify, such contract or lease or a right or obligation under such contract or lease on account of an assignment of such contract or lease, such contract, lease, right, or obligation may not be terminated or modified under such provision because of the assumption or assignment of such contract or lease by the trustee.

(g) Except as provided in subsections (h)(2) and (i)(2) of this section, the rejection of an executory contract or unexpired lease of the debtor constitutes a breach of such contract or lease

(1) if such contract or lease has not been assumed under this section or under a plan confirmed under chapter 9, 11, or 13 of this title, immediately before the date of the filing of the petition; or

(2) if such contract or lease has been assumed under this section or under a plan confirmed under chapter 9, 11, or 13 of this title

(A) if before such rejection the case has not been converted under section 1112 or 1307 of this title, at the time of such rejection; or

(B) if before such rejection the case has been converted under section 1112 or 1307 of this title

(i) immediately before the date of such conversion, if such contract or lease was assumed before such conversion; or

(ii) at the time of such rejection, if such contract or lease was assumed after such conversion.

(h) (1) If the trustee rejects an unexpired lease of real property of the debtor under which the debtor is the lessor, the lessee under such lease may treat the lease as terminated by such rejection, or, in the alternative, may remain in possession for the balance of the term of such lease and any renewal or extension of such term that is enforceable by such lessee under applicable nonbankruptcy law.

(2) If such lessee remains in possession, such lessee may offset against the rent reserved under such lease for the balance of the term after the date of the rejection of such lease, and any such renewal or extension, any damages occurring after such date caused by the nonperformance of any obligation of the debtor after such date, but such lessee does not have

any rights against the estate on account of any damages arising after such date from such rejection, other than such offset.

(i) (1) If the trustee rejects an executory contract of the debtor for the sale of real property under which the purchaser is in possession, such purchaser may treat such contract as terminated, or, in the alternative, may remain in possession of such real property.

(2) If such purchaser remains in possession

(A) such purchaser shall continue to make all payments due under such contract, but may, offset against such payments any damages occurring after the date of the rejection of such contract caused by the nonperformance of any obligaiton of the debtor after such date, but such purchaser does not have any rights against the estate on account of any damages arising after such date from such rejection, other than such offset; and

(B) the trustee shall deliver title to such purchaser in accordance with the provisions of such contract, but is relieved of all other obligations to perform under such contract.

(k) Assignment by the trustee to an entity of a contract or lease assumed under this section relieves the trustee and the estate from any liability for any breach of such contract or lease occurring after such assignment.

CHAPTER 5

CREDITORS, THE DEBTOR, AND THE ESTATE

SUBCHAPTER I—CREDITORS AND CLAIMS

Sec. 501. **Filing of proofs of claims or interests.** (a) A creditor or an indenture trustee may file a proof of claim. An equity security holder may file a proof of interest.

(b) If a creditor does not timely file a proof of such creditor's claim, an entity that is liable to such creditor with the debtor, or that has secured such creditor, may file a proof of such claim.

(c) If a creditor does not timely file a proof of such creditor's claim, the debtor or the trustee may file a proof of such claim.

(d) A claim of a kind specified in section 502(f), 502(g), 502(h) or 502(i) of this title may be filed under subsection (a), (b), or (c) of this section the same as if such claim were a claim against the debtor and had arisen before the date of the filing of the petition.

Sec. 502. **Allowance of claims or interests.** (a) A claim or interest, proof of which is filed under section 501 of this title, is deemed allowed, unless a party in interest including a creditor of a partner in a partnership that is a debtor in a case under chapter 7 of this title, objects.

(c) There shall be estimated for purpose of allowance under this section

(1) any contingent or unliquidated claim, fixing or liquidation of which, as the case may be, would unduly delay the closing of the case; or

(2) any right to an equitable remedy for breach of performance if such breach gives rise to a right to payment.

Sec. 507. **Priorities.** (a) The following expenses and claims have priority in the following order:

(1) First, administrative expenses allowed under section 503(b) of this title, and any fees and charges assessed against the estate under chapter 123 of title 28.

(2) Second, unsecured claims allowed under section 502(f) of this title.

(3) Third, allowed unsecured claims for wages, salaries, or commissions, including vacation, severance and sick leave pay

(A) earned by an individual within 90 days before the date of the filing of the petition or the date of the cessation of the debtor's business, whichever occurs first; but only

(B) to the extent of $2,000 for each such individual.

(i) entered for consumption within one year before the date of the filing of the petition;

(ii) covered by an entry liquidated or reliquidated within one year before the date of the filing of the petition; or

(iii) entered for consumption within four years before the date of the filing of the petition but unliquidated on such date, if the Secretary of the Treasury certifies that failure to liquidate such entry was due to an investigation pending on such date into assessment of antidumping or countervailing duties or fraud, or if information needed for the proper appraisement or classification of such merchandise was not available to the appropriate customs officer before such date; or

(4) Fourth, allowed unsecured claims for contributions to employee benefit plans

(A) arising from services rendered within 180 days before the date of the filing of the petition or the date of the cessation of the debtor's business, whichever occurs first; but only

(B) for each such plan, to the extent of

(i) the number of employees covered by such plan multiplied by $2,000; less

(ii) the aggregate amount paid to such employees under paragraph (3) of this subsection, plus the aggregate amount paid by the estate on behalf of such employees to any other employee benefit plan.

(5) Fifth, allowed unsecured claims of individuals, to the extent of $900 for each such individual, arising from the deposit, before the commencement of the case, of money in connection with the purchase, lease, or rental of property, or the purchase of services, for the personal, family, or household use of such individuals, that were not delivered or provided.

(6) Sixth, allowed unsecured claims of governmental units, to the extent that such claims are for

(A) a tax on or measured by income or gross receipts

(i) for a taxable year ending on or before the date of the filing of the petition for which a return, if required, is last due, including extensions, after three years before the date of the filing of the petition;

(ii) assessed within 240 days, plus any time plus 30 days during which an offer in compromise with respect to such tax that was made within 240 days after such assessment was pending, before the date of the filing of the petition; or

(iii) other than a tax of a kind specified in section 523(a)(1)(B) or 523(a)(1)(C) of this title, not assessed before, but assessable, under applicable law or by agreement, after, the commencement of the case;

(B) a property tax assessed before the commencement of the case and last payable without penalty after one year before the date of the filing of the petition;

(C) a tax required to be collected or withheld and for which the debtor is liable in whatever capacity;

(D) an employment tax on a wage, salary, or commission of a kind specified in paragraph (3) of this subsection earned from the debtor before the date of the filing of the petition, whether or not actually paid before such date, for which a return is last due, under applicable law or under any extension, after three years before the date of the filing of the petition;

(E) an excise tax on

(i) a transaction occurring before the date of the filing of the petition for which a return, if required, is last due, under applicable law or under any extension, after three years before the date of the filing of the petition; or

(ii) if a return is not required, a transaction occurring during the three years immediately preceding the date of the filing of the petition;

(F) a customs duty arising out of the importation of merchandise.

(G) a penalty related to a claim of a kind specified in this paragraph and in compensation for actual pecuniary loss.

SUBCHAPTER II—DEBTOR'S DUTIES AND BENEFITS

Sec. 521. **Debtor's duties.** The debtor shall

(1) file a list of creditors, and unless the court orders otherwise, a schedule of assets and liabilities, and a statement of the debtor's financial affairs;

(2) if a trustee is serving in the case, cooperate with the trustee as necessary to enable the trustee to perform the trustee's duties under this title;

(3) if a trustee is serving in the case, surrender to the trustee all property of the estate and any recorded information, including books, documents, records, and papers, relating to property of the estate; and

(4) appear at the hearing required under section 524(d) of this title.

Sec. 522. **Exemptions.** (a) In this section

(1) "dependent" includes spouse, whether or not actually dependent; and

(2) "value" means fair market value as of the date of the filing of the petition.

(b) Notwithstanding section 541 of this title, an individual debtor may exempt from property of the estate either

(1) property that is specified under subsection (d) of this section, unless the State law that is applicable to the debtor under paragraph (2)(A) of this subsection specifically does not so authorize; or, in the alternative,

(2) (A) any property that is exempt under Federal law, other than subsection (d) of this section, or State or local law that is applicable on the date of the filing of the petition at the place in which the debtor's domicile has been located for the 180 days immediately preceding the date of the filing of the petition, or for a longer portion of such 180-day period than in any other place; and

(B) any interest in property in which the debtor had, immediately before the commencement of the case, an interest as a tenant by the entirety or joint tenant to the extent that such interest as a tenant by the entirety or joint tenant is exempt from process under applicable nonbankruptcy law.

(c) Unless the case is dismissed, property exempted under this section is not liable during or after the case for any debt of the debtor that arose, or that is determined under section 502 of this title as if such claim had arisen before the commencement of the case, except

(1) a debt of a kind specified in seciton 523(a)(1) or section 523(a)(5) of this title; or

(2) a lien that is

(A) not avoided under section 544, 545, 547, 548, 549, or 724(a) of this title;

(B) not voided under section 506(d) of this title; or

(C) (i) a tax lien, notice of which is properly filed; and

(ii) avoided under section 545(2) of this title.

(d) The following property may be exempted under subsection (b)(1) of this section:

(1) The debtor's aggregate interest, not to exceed $7,500 in value, in real property or personal property that the debtor or a dependent of the debtor uses as a residence, in a cooperative that owns property that the debtor or a dependent of the debtor uses as a residence, or in a burial plot for the debtor or a dependent of the debtor.

(2) The debtor's interest, not to exceed $1,200 in value, in one motor vehicle.

(3) The debtor's interest, not to exceed $200 in value in any particular item, in household furnishings, household goods, wearing apparel, appliances, books, animals, crops, or musical instruments, that are held primarily for the personal, family, or household use of the debtor or a dependent of the debtor.

(4) The debtor's aggregate interest, not to exceed $500 in value, in jewelry held primarily for the personal, family, or household use of the debtor or a dependent of the debtor.

(5) The debtor's aggregate interest, not to exceed in value $400 plus any unused amount of the exemption provided under paragraph (1) of this subsection, in any property.

(6) The debtor's aggregate interest, not to exceed $750 in value, in any implements, professional books, or tools, of the trade of the debtor or the trade of a dependent of the debtor.

(7) Any unmatured life insurance contract owned by the debtor, other than a credit life insurance contract.

(8) The debtor's aggregate interest, not to exceed in value $4,000 less any amount of property of the estate transferred in the manner specified in section 542(d) of this title, in any accrued dividend or interest under, or loan value of, any unmatured life insurance contract owned by the debtor under which the insured is the debtor or an individual of whom the debtor is a dependent.

(9) Professionally prescribed health aids for the debtor or a dependent of the debtor.

(10) The debtor's right to receive

(A) a social security benefit, unemployment compensation, or a local public assistance benefit;

(B) a veteran's benefit;

(C) a disability, illness, or unemployment benefit;

(D) alimony, support, or separate maintenance, to the extent reasonably necessary for the support of the debtor and and dependent of the debtor;

(E) a payment under a stock bonus, pension, profitsharing, annuity, or similar plan or contract on account of illness, disability, death, age, or length of service, to the extent reasonably necessary for the support of the debtor and any dependent of the debtor, unless

(i) such plan or contract was established by or under the auspices of an insider that employed the debtor at the time the debtor's rights under such plan or contract arose;

(ii) such payment is on account of age or length of service; and

(iii) such plan or contract does not qualify under section 401(a), 403(a), 403(b), 408, or 409 of the Internal Revenue Code of 1954 (26 U.S.C. 401(a), 403(a), 403(b), 408, or 409).

(11) The debtor's right to receive, or property that is traceable to

(A) an award under a crime victim's reparation law;

(B) a payment on account of the wrongful death of an individual of whom the debtor was a dependent, to the extent reasonably necessary for the support of the debtor and any dependent of the debtor;

(C) a payment under a life insurance contract that insured the life of an individual of whom the debtor was a dependent on the date of such individual's death, to the extent reasonably necessary for the support of the debtor and any dependent of the debtor;

(D) a payment, not to exceed $7,500, on account of personal bodily injury, not including pain and suffering or compensation for actual pecuniary loss, of the debtor or an individual of whom the debtor is a dependent; or

(E) a payment in compensation of loss of future earnings of the debtor or an individual of whom the debtor is or was a dependent, to the extent reasonably necessary for the support of the debtor and any dependent of the debtor.

(e) A waiver of exemptions executed in favor of a creditor that holds an unsecured claim against the debtor is unenforceable in a case under this title with respect to such claim against property that the debtor may exempt under subsection (b) of this section. A waiver by the debtor of a power under subsection (f) or (h) of this section to avoid a transfer, under subsection (g) or (i) of this section to exempt property, or under subsection (i) of this section to recover property or to preserve a transfer, is unenforceable in a case under this title.

(f) Notwithstanding any waiver of exemptions, the debtor may avoid the fixing of a lien on an interest of the debtor in property to the extent that such lien impairs an exemption to which the debtor would have been entitled under subsection (b) of this section, if such lien is

(1) a judicial lien; or

(2) a nonpossessory, nonpurchase-money security interest in any

(A) household furnishings, household goods, wearing apparel, appliances, books, animals, crops, musical instruments, or jewelry that are held primarily for the personal, family, or household use of the debtor or a dependent of the debtor;

(B) implements, professional books, or tools, of the trade of the debtor or the trade of a dependent of the debtor; or

(C) professionally prescribed health aids for the debtor or a dependent of the debtor.

(g) Notwithstanding sections 550 and 551 of this title, the debtor may exempt under subsection (b) of this section property that the trustee recovers under section 510(c)(2), 542, 543, 550, 551, or 553 of this title, to the extent that the debtor could have exempted such property under subsection (b) of this section if such property had not been transferred, if

(1) (A) such transfer was not a voluntary transfer of such property by the debtor; and

(B) the debtor did not conceal such property; or

(2) the debtor could have avoided such transfer under subsection (f)(2) of this section.

(h) The debtor may avoid a transfer of property of the debtor or recover a setoff to the extent that the debtor could have exempted such property under subsection (g)(1) of this section if the trustee had avoided such transfer, if

(1) such transfer is avoidable by the trustee under section 544, 545, 547, 548, 549, or 724(a) of this title or recoverable by the trustee under section 553 of this title; and

(2) the trustee does not attempt to avoid such transfer.

(i) (1) If the debtor avoids a transfer or recovers a setoff under subsection (f) or (h) of this section, the debtor may recover in the manner prescribed by, and subject to the limitations of, section 550 of this title, the same as if the trustee had avoided such transfer, and may exempt any property so recovered under subsection (b) of this section.

(2) Notwithstanding section 551 of this title, a transfer avoided under section 544, 545, 547, 548, 549, or 724(a) of this title, under subsection (f) or (h) of this section, or property recovered under section 553 of this title, may be preserved for the benefit of the debtor to the extent that the debtor may exempt such property under subsection (g) of this section or paragraph (1) of this subsection.

(j) Notwithstanding subsections (g) and (i) of this section, the debtor may exempt a particular kind of property under subsections (g) and (i) of this section only to the extent that the debtor has exempted less property in value of such kind than that to which the debtor is entitled under subsection (b) of this section.

(k) Property that the debtor exempts under this section is not liable for payment of any administrative expense except

(1) the aliquot share of the costs and expenses of avoiding a transfer of property that the debtor exempts under subsection (g) of this section, or of recovery of such property, that is attributable to the value of the portion of such property exempted in relation to the value of the property recovered; and

(2) any costs and expenses of avoiding a transfer under subsection (f) or (h) of this section, or of recovery of property under subsection (i)(1) of this section, that the debtor has not paid.

(1) The debtor shall file a list of property that the debtor claims as exempt under subsection (b) of this section. If the debtor does not file such a list, a dependent of the debtor may file such a list, or may claim property as exempt from property of the estate on behalf of the debtor. Unless a party in interest objects, the property claimed as exempt on such list is exempt.

(m) This section shall apply separately with respect to each debtor in a joint case.

Sec. 523. **Exceptions to discharge.** (a) A discharge under section 727, 1141, or 1328(b) of this title does not discharge an individual debtor from any debt

(1) for a tax or a customs duty

(A) of the kind and for the periods specified in section 507(a)(2) or 502(a)(6) of this title, whether or not a claim for such tax was filed or allowed;

(B) with respect to which a return, if required

(i) was not filed; or

(ii) was filed after the date on which such return was last due, under applicable law or under any extension, and after two years before the date of the filing of the petition; or

(C) with respect to which the debtor made a fraudulent return or willfully attempted in any manner to evade or defeat such tax;

(2) for obtaining money, property, services, or an extension, renewal, or refinance of credit, by

(A) false pretenses, a false representation, or actual fraud, other than a statement respecting the debtor's or an insider's financial condition; or

(B) use of a statement in writing

(i) that is materially false;

(ii) respecting the debtor's or an insider's financial condition;

(iii) on which the creditor to whom the debtor is liable for obtaining such money, property, services, or credit reasonably relied; and

(iv) that the debtor caused to be made or published with intent to deceive;

(3) neither listed nor scheduled under section 521(1) of this title, with the name, if known to the debtor, of the creditor to whom such debt is owed, in time to permit

(A) if such debt is not of a kind specified in paragraph (2), (4), or (6) of this subsection, timely filing of a proof of claim, unless such creditor had notice or actual knowledge of the case in time for such timely filing; or

(B) if such debt is of a kind specified in paragraph (2), (4), or (6) of this subsection, timely filing of a proof of claim and timely request for a determination of dischargeability of such debt under one of such paragraphs, unless such creditor had notice or actual knowledge of the case in time for such timely filing and request;

(4) for fraud or defalcation while acting in a fiduciary capacity, embezzlement, or larceny;

(5) to a spouse, former spouse, or child of the debtor, for alimony to, maintenance for, or support of such spouse or child, in connection with a separation agreement, divorce decree, or property settlement agreement, but not to the extent that

(A) such debt is assigned to another entity, voluntarily, by operation of law, or otherwise; or

(B) such debt includes a liability designated as alimony, maintenance, or support, unless such liability is actually in the nature of alimony, maintenance, or support;

(6) for willful and malicious injury by the debtor to another entity or to the property of another entity;

(7) to the extent such debt is for a fine, penalty, or forfeiture payable to an for the benefit of a governmental unit, and is not compensation for actual pecuniary loss, other than a tax penalty

(A) relating to a tax of a kind not specified in paragraph (1) of this subsection; or

(B) imposed with respect to a transaction or event that occurred before three years before the date of the filing of the petition;

(8) to a governmental unit, or a nonprofit institution of higher education, for an educational loan, unless

(A) such loan first became due before five years before the date of the filing of the petition; or

(B) excepting such debt from discharge under this paragraph will impose an undue hardship on the debtor and the debtor's dependents; or

(9) that was or could have been listed or scheduled by the debtor in a prior case concerning the debtor under this title or under the Bankruptcy

Act in which the debtor waived discharge, or was denied a discharge under section 727(a) (2), (3), (4), (5), (6), or (7) of this title, or under section 14c(1), (2), (3), (4), (6), or (7), of such Act.

(b) Notwithstanding subsection (a) of this section, a debt that was excepted from discharge under subsection (a)(1), (a)(3), or (a)(8) of this section, under section 17a(1), 17a(3), or 17a(5) of the Bankruptcy Act, under section 439A of the Higher Education Act of 1965 (20 U.S.C. 1087-3), or under section 733(g) of the Public Health Services Act (42 U.S.C. 294f) in a prior case concerning the debtor under this title, or under the Bankruptcy Act, is dischargeable in a case under this title unless, by the terms of subsection (a) of this section, such debt is not dischargeable in the case under this title.

(c) Except as provided in subsection (a)(3)(B) of this section, the debtor shall be discharged from a debt specified in paragraph (2), (4), or (6) of subsection (a) of this section, unless, on request of the creditor to whom such debt is owed, and after notice and a hearing, the court determines such debt to be excepted from discharge under paragraph (2), (4), or (6), as the case may be, of subsection (a) of this section.

(d) If a creditor requests a determination of dischargeability of a consumer debt under subsection (a)(2) of this section, and such debt is discharged, the court shall grant judgment against such creditor and in favor of the debtor for the costs of, and a reasonable attorney's fee for, the proceeding to determine dischargeability, unless such granting of judgment would be clearly inequitable.

Sec. 524. **Effect of discharge.** (a) A discharge in a case under this title

(1) voids any judgment at any time obtained, to the extent that such judgment is a determination of the personal liability of the debtor with respect to any debt discharged under section 727, 944, 1141, or 1328 of this title, whether or not discharge of such debt is waived;

(2) operates as an injunction against the commencement or continuation of an action, the employment of process, or any act, to collect, recover or offset any such debt as a personal liability of the debtor, or from property of the debtor, whether or not discharge of such debt is waived; and

(3) operates as an injunction against the commencement or continuation of an action, the employment of process, or any act, to collect or recover from, or offset against, property of the debtor of the kind specified in sections 541(a)(2) of this title that is acquired after the commencement of the case, on account of any allowable community claim, except a community claim that is excepted from discharge under section 523 or 1328(c)(1) of this title, or that would be so excepted, determined in accordance with the provisions of sections 523(c) and 523(d) of this title, in a case concerning the debtor's spouse commenced on the date of the filing of the petition in the case concerning the debtor, whether or not discharge of the debt based on such community claim is waived.

(b) Subsection (a)(3) of this section does not apply if

(1) (A) the debtor's spouse is a debtor in a case under this title, or a bankrupt or a debtor in a case under the Bankruptcy Act, commenced within six years of the date of the filing of the petition in the case concerning the debtor; and

(B) the court does not grant the debtor's spouse a discharge in such case concerning the debtor's spouse; or

(2) (A) the court would not grant the debtor's spouse a discharge in a case under chapter 7 of this title concerning such spouse commenced on the date of the filing of the petition in the case concerning the debtor; and

(B) a determination that the court would not so grant such discharge is made by the bankruptcy court within the time and in the manner provided for a determination under section 727 of this title of whether a debtor is granted a discharge.

(c) An agreement between a holder of a claim and the debtor, the consideration for which, in whole or in part, is based on a debt that is dischargeable in a case under this title is enforceable only to any extent enforceable under applicable nonbankruptcy law, whether or not discharge of such debt is waived, only if

(1) such agreement was made before the granting of the discharge under section 727, 1141, or 1328 of this title;

(2) the debtor has not rescinded such agreement within 30 days after such agreement becomes enforceable;

(3) the provisions of subsection (d) of this section have been complied with; and

(4) in a case concerning an individual, to the extent that such debt is a consumer debt that is not secured by real property of the debtor, the court approves such agreement as

(A) (i) not imposing an undue hardship on the debtor or a dependent of the debtor; and

(ii) in the best interest of the debtor; or

(B) (i) entered into in good faith; and

(ii) in settlement of litigation under section 523 of this title, or providing for redemption under section 722 of this title.

(d) In a case concerning an individual, when the court has determined whether to grant or not to grant a discharge under section 727, 1141, or 1328 of this title, the court shall hold a hearing at which the debtor shall appear in person. At such hearing, the court shall inform the debtor that a discharge has been granted or the reason why a discharge has not been granted. If a discharge has been granted and if the debtor desires to make an agreement of the kind specified in subsection (c) of this section, then at such hearing the court shall

(1) inform the debtor

(A) that such an agreement is not required under this title, under nonbankruptcy law, or under any agreement not made in accordance with the provisions of subsection (c) of this section; and

(B) of the legal effect and consequences of

(i) an agreement of the kind specified in subsection (c) of this section; and

(ii) a default under such an agreement;

(2) determine whether the agreement that the debtor desires to make complies with the requirements of subsection (c)(4) of this subsection, if the consideration for such agreement is based in whole or in part on a consumer debt that is not secured by real property of the debtor.

(e) Except as provided in subsection (a)(3) of this section, discharge of a debt of the debtor does not affect the liability of any other entity on, or the property of any other entity for, such debt.

SUBCHAPTER III—THE ESTATE

Sec. 541. **Property of the estate.** (a) The commencement of a case under under section 301, 302, or 303 of this title creates an estate. Such estate is comprised of all the following property, wherever located:

(1) Except as provided in subsections (b) and (c)(2) of this section, all legal or equitable interests of the debtor in property as of the commencement of the case.

(2) All interests of the debtor and the debtor's spouse in community property as of the commencement of the case that is

(A) under the sole, equal, or joint management and control of the debtor; or

(B) liable for an allowable claim against the debtor, or for both an allowable claim against the debtor and an allowable claim against the debtor's spouse, to the extent that such interest is so liable.

(3) Any interest in property that the trustee recovers under section 543, 550, 553, or 723 of this title.

(4) Any interest in property preserved for the benefit of or ordered transferred to the estate under section 510(c) or 551 of this title.

(5) An interest in property that would have been property of the estate if such interest had been an interest of the debtor on the date of the filing of the petition, and that the debtor acquires or becomes entitled to acquire within 180 days after such date

(A) by bequest, devise, or inheritance;

(B) as a result of a property settlement agreement with the debtor's spouse, or of an interlocutory or final divorce decree; or

(C) as a beneficiary of a life insurance policy or of a death benefit plan.

(6) Proceeds, product, offspring, rents, and profits of or from property of the estate, except such as are earnings from services performed by an individual debtor after the commencement of the case.

(7) Any interest in property that the estate acquires after the commencement of the case.

(b) Property of the estate does not include any power that the debtor may only exercise solely for the benefit of an entity other than the debtor.

(c) (1) Except as provided in paragraph (2) of this subsection, an interest of the debtor in property becomes property of the estate under subsection (a)(1), (a)(2), or (a)(5) of this section notwithstanding any provision

(A) that restricts or conditions transfer of such interest by the debtor; or

(B) that is conditioned on the insolvency or financial condition of the debtor, on the commencement of a case under this title, or on the appointment of or the taking possession by a trustee in a case under this title or a custodian, and that effects or gives an option to effect a forfeiture, modification, or termination of the debtor's interest in property.

(2) A restriction on the transfer of a beneficial interest of the debtor in a trust that is enforceable under applicable nonbankruptcy law is enforceable in a case under this title.

Sec. 544. Trustee as lien creditor and as successor to certain creditors and purchasers. (a) The trustee shall have, as of the commencement of the case, and without regard to any knowledge of the trustee or of any creditor, the rights and powers of, or may avoid any transfer of property of the debtor or any obligation incurred by the debtor that is voidable by

(1) a creditor that extends credit to the debtor at the time of the commencement of the case, and that obtains, at such time and with respect to such credit, a judicial lien on all property on which a creditor on a simple contract could have obtained a judicial lien, whether or not such a creditor exists;

(2) a creditor that extends credit to the debtor at the time of the commencement of the case, and obtains, at such time and with respect to such credit, an execution against the debtor that is returned unsatisfied at such time, whether or not such a creditor exists; and

(3) a bona fide purchaser of real property from the debtor, against whom applicable law permits such transfer to be perfected, that obtains the status of a bona fide purchaser at the time of the commencement of the case, whether or not such a purchaser exists.

(b) The trustee may avoid any transfer of an interest of the debtor in property or any obligation incurred by the debtor that is voidable under applicable law by a creditor holding an unsecured claim that is allowable under section 502 of this title or that is not allowable only under section 502(e) of this title.

Sec. 545. **Statutory liens.** The trustee may avoid the fixing of a statutory lien on property of the debtor to the extent that such lien

(1) first becomes effective against the debtor

(A) when a case under this title concerning the debtor is commenced;

(B) when an insolvency proceeding other than under this title concerning the debtor is commenced;

(C) when a custodian is appointed or takes possession;

(D) when the debtor becomes insolvent;

(E) when the debtor's financial condition fails to meet a specified standard; or

(F) at the time of an execution against property of the debtor levied at the instance of an entity other than the holder of such statutory lien;

(2) is not perfected or enforceable on the date of the filing of the petition against a bona fide purchaser that purchases such property on the date of the filing of the petition, whether or not such a purchaser exists;

(3) is for rent; or

(4) is a lien of distress for rent.

Sec. 547. **Preferences.** (a) In this section

(1) "inventory" means personal property leased or furnished, held for sale or lease, or to be furnished under a contract for service, raw materials, work in process, or materials used or consumed in a business, including farm products such as crops or livestock, held for sale or lease;

(2) "new value" means money or money's worth in goods, services, or new credit, or release by a transferee of property previously transferred to such transferee in a transaction that is neither void nor voidable by the debtor or the trustee under any applicable law, but does not include an obligation substituted for an existing obligation;

(3) "receivable" means right to payment, whether or not such right has been earned by performance; and

(4) a debt for a tax is incurred on the day when such tax is last payable, including any extension, without penalty.

(b) Except as provided in subsection (c) of this section, the trustee may avoid any transfer of property of the debtor

(1) to or for the benefit of a creditor;

(2) for or on account of an antecedent debt owed by the debtor before such transfer was made;

(3) made while the debtor was insolvent;

(4) made

(A) on or within 90 days before the date of the filing of the petition; or

(B) between 90 days and one year before the date of the filing of the petition, if such creditor, at the time of such transfer

(i) was an insider; and

(ii) had reasonable cause to believe the debtor was insolvent at the time of such transfer; and

(5) that enables such creditor to receive more than such creditor would receive if

(A) the case were a case under chapter 7 of this title;

(B) the transfer had not been made; and

(C) such creditor received payment of such debt to the extent provided by the provisions of this title.

(c) The trustee may not avoid under this section a transfer

(1) to the extent that such transfer was

(A) intended by the debtor and the creditor to or for whose benefit such transfer was made to be a contemporaneous exchange for new value given to the debtor; and

(B) in fact a substantially contemporaneous exchange;

(2) to the extent that such transfer was

(A) in payment of a debt incurred in the ordinary course of business or financial affairs of the debtor and the transferee;

(B) made not later than 45 days after such debt was incurred;

(C) made in the ordinary course of business or financial affairs of the debtor and the transferee; and

(D) made according to ordinary business terms;

(3) of a security interest in property acquired by the debtor

(A) to the extent such security interest secures new value that was

(i) given at or after the signing of a security agreement that contains a description of such property as collateral;

(ii) given by or on behalf of the secured party under such agreement;

(iii) given to enable the debtor to acquire such property; and

(iv) in fact used by the debtor to acquire such property; and

(B) that is perfected before 10 days after such security interest attaches;

(4) to or for the benefit of a creditor, to the extent that, after such transfer, such creditor gave new value to or for the benefit of the debtor

(A) not secured by an otherwise unavoidable security interest; and

(B) on account of which new value the debtor did not make an otherwise unavoidable transfer to or for the benefit of such creditor;

(5) of a perfected security interest in inventory or a receivable or the proceeds of either, except to the extent that the aggregate of all such transfers to the transferee caused a reduction, as of the date of the filing of the petition and to the prejudice of other creditors holding unsecured claims, of any amount by which the debt secured by such security interest exceeded the value of all security interest for such debt on the later of

(A) (i) with respect to a transfer to which subsection (b)(4)(A) of this section applies, 90 days before the date of the filing of the petition; or

(ii) with respect to a transfer to which subsection (b)(4)(B) of this section applies, one year before the date of the filing of the petition; and

(B) the date on which new value was first given under the security agreement creating such security interest; or

(6) that is the fixing of a statutory lien that is not avoidable under section 545 of this title.

(e) (1) For the purposes of this section

(A) a transfer of real property other than fixtures, but including the interest of a seller or purchaser under a contract for the sale of real property, is perfected when a bona fide purchaser of such property from the debtor against whom applicable law permits such transfer to be perfected cannot acquire an interest that is superior to the interest of the transferee; and

(B) a transfer of a fixture or property other than real property is perfected when a creditor on a simple contract cannot acquire a judicial lien that is superior to the interest of the transferee.

(2) For the purposes of this section, except as provided in paragraph (3) of this subsection, a transfer is made

(A) at the time such transfer takes effect between the transferor and the transferee, if such transfer is perfected at, or within 10 days after, such time;

(B) at the time such transfer is perfected, if such transfer is perfected after such 10 days; or

(C) immediately before the date of the filing of the petition, if such transfer is not perfected at the later of

(i) the commencement of the case; and

(ii) 10 days after such transfer takes effect between the transferor and the transferee.

(3) For the purposes of this section, a transfer is not made until the debtor has acquired rights in the property transferred.

(f) For the purposes of this section, the debtor is presumed to have been insolvent on and during the 90 days immediately preceding the date of the filing of the petition.

Sec. 548. **Fraudulent transfers and obligations.** (a) The trustee may avoid any transfer of an interest of the debtor in property, or any obligation incurred by the debtor, that was made or incurred on or within one year before the date of the filing of the petition, if the debtor

(1) made such transfer or incurred such obligation with actual intent to hinder, delay, or defraud any entity to which the debtor was or became, on or after the date that such transfer occurred or such obligation was incurred, indebted; or

(2) (A) received less than a reasonably equivalent value in exchange for suc h transfer or obligation; and

(B) (i) was insolvent on the date that such transfer was made or such obligation was incurred, or became insolvent as a result of such transfer or obligation;

(ii) was engaged in business, or was about to engage in business or a transaction, for which any property remaining with the debtor was an unreasonably small capital; or

(iii) intended to incur, or believe that the debtor would incur, debts that would be beyond the debtor's ability to pay as such debts matured.

(b) The trustee of a partnership debtor may avoid any transfer of an interest of the debtor in property, or any obligation incurred by the debtor, that was made or incurred on or within one year before the date of the filing of the petition, to a general partner in the debtor, if the debtor was insolvent on the date such transfer was made or such obligation was incurred, or became insolvent as a result of such transfer or obligation.

(c) Except to the extent that a transfer or obligation voidable under this section is voidable under section 544, 545, or 547 of this title, a transferee or obligee of such a transfer or obligation that takes for value and in good faith has a lien on any interest transferred, may retain any lien transferred, or many enforce any obligation incurred, as the case may be, to the extent that such transferee or obligee gave value to the debtor in exchange for such transfer or obligation.

(d) (1) For the purpose of this section, a transfer is made when such transfer becomes so far perfected that a bona fide purchaser from the debtor against whom such transfer could have been perfected cannot acquire an interest in the property transferred that is superior to the interest in such property of the transferee, but if such transfer is not so perfected before the commencement of the case, such transfer occurs immediately before the date of the filing of the petition.

(2) In this section

(A) "value" means property, or satisfaction or securing of a present or antecedent debt of the debtor, but does not include an unperformed promise to furnish support to the debtor or to a relative of the debtor; and

(B) a commodity broker or forward contract merchant that receives a margin payment, as defined in section 761(15) of this title, takes for value.

Sec. 549. **Postpetition transactions.** (a) Except as provided in subsection (b) and (c) of this section, the trustee may avoid a transfer of property of the estate

(1) that occurs after the commencement of the case; and

(2) (A) that is authorized under section 303(f) or 542(c) of this title; or

(B) that is not authorized under this title or by the court.

(b) In an involuntary case, a transfer that occurs after the commencement of such case but before the order for relief is valid against the trustee to the extent of any value, including services, but not including satisfaction or securing of a debt that arose before the commencement of the case, given after the commencement of the case in exchange for such transfer, notwithstanding any notice or knowledge of the case that the transferee has.

(c) The trustee may not avoid under subsection (a) of this section a transfer , to a good faith purchaser without knowledge of the commencement of the case and for present fair equivalent value or to a purchaser at a judicial sale, of real property located other than in the county in which the case is commenced, unless a copy of the petition was filed in the office where conveyances of real property in such county are recorded before such transfer was so far perfected that a bona fide purchaser of such property against whom applicable law permits such transfer to be perfected cannot acquire an interest that is superior to the interest of such good faith or judicial sale purchaser. A good faith purchaser, without knowledge of the commencement of the case and for less than present fair equivalent value, of real property located other than in the county in which the case is commenced, under a transfer that the trustee may avoid under this section, has a lien on the property transferred to the extent of any present value given, unless a copy of the petition was so filed before such transfer was so perfected.

Sec. 553. **Setoff.** (a) Except as otherwise provide in this section and in sections 362 and 363 of this title, this title does not affect any right of a creditor to offset a mutual debt owing by such creditor to the debtor that arose before the commencement of the case under this title against a claim of such creditor against the debtor that arose before the commencement of the case, except to the extent that

(1) the claim of such creditor against the debtor is disallowed other than under 502(b)(3) of this title;

(2) such claim was transferred, by an entity other than the debtor, to such creditor

(A) after the commencement of the case; or

(B) (i) after 90 days before the date of the filing of the petition; and

(ii) while the debtor was insolvent; or

(3) the debt owed to the debtor by such creditor was incurred by such creditor

(A) after 90 days before the date of the filing of the petition;

(B) while the debtor was insolvent; and

(C) for the purpose of obtaining a right of setoff against the debtor.

(b) (1) Except with respect to a setoff of a kind described in section 362(b)(6) or 365(h)(1) of this title, if a creditor offsets a mutual debt owing to the debtor against a claim against the debtor on or within 90 days before the date of the filing of the petition, then the trustee may recover from such creditor the amount so offset to the extent that any insufficiency on the date of such setoff is less than the insufficiency on the later of

(A) 90 days before the date of the filing of the petition; and

(B) the first date during the 90 days immediately preceding the date of the filing of the petition on which there is an insufficiency.

(2) In this subsection, "insufficiency" means amount, if any, by which a claim against the debtor exceeds a mutual debt owing to the debtor by the holder of such claim.

(c) For the purposes of this section, the debtor is presumed to have been insolvent on and during the 90 days immediately preceding the date of the filing of the petition.

CHAPTER 7

LIQUIDATION

SUBCHAPTER I—OFFICERS AND ADMINISTRATION

Sec. 701. **Interim trustee.** (a) Promptly after the order for relief under this chapter, the court shall appoint one disinterested person that is a member of the panel of private trustees established under section 604(f) of title 28 or that was serving as trustee in the case immediately before the order for relief under this chapter to serve as interim trustee in the case.

(b) The service of an interim trustee under this section terminates when a trustee elected or designated under section 702 of this title to serve as trustee in the case qualifies under section 322 of this title.

(c) An interim trustee serving under this section is a trustee in a case under this title.

Sec. 702. **Election of trustee.** (a) A creditor may vote for a candidate for trustee only if such creditor

(1) holds an allowable, undisputed, fixed, liquidated, unsecured claim of a kind entitled to distribution under section 726(a)(2), 726(a)(3), or 726(a)(4) of this title;

(2) does not have an interest materially adverse, other than an equity interest that is not substantial in relation to such creditor's interest as a creditor, to the interest of creditors entitled to such distribution; and

(3) is not an insider.

(b) At the meeting of creditors under section 341 of this title, creditors may elect one person to serve as trustee in the case if election of a trustee is requested by creditors that may vote under subsection (a) of this section, and that hold at least 20 percent in amount of the claims specified in subsection (a)(1) of this section that are held by creditors that may vote under subsection (a) of this section.

(c) A candidate for trustee is elected trustee if

(1) creditors holding at least 20 percent in amount of the claims specified in subsection (a)(1) of this section that are held by creditors that may vote under subsection (a) of this section vote; and

(2) such candidate receives the votes of creditors holding a majority in amount of claims specified in subsection (a)(1) of this section that are held by creditors that vote for trustee.

(d) If a trustee is not elected under subsection (c) of this section, then the interim trustee shall serve as trustee in the case.

Sec. 704. **Duties of trustee.** The trustee shall

(1) collect and reduce to money the property of the estate for which such trustee serves, and close up such estate as expeditiously as is compatible with the best interests of parties in interest;

(2) be accountable for all property received;

(3) investigate the financial affairs of the debtor;

(4) if a purpose would be served, examine proofs of claims and object to the allowance of any claim that is improper;

(5) if advisable, oppose the discharge of the debtor;

(6) unless the court orders otherwise, furnish such information concerning the estate and the estate's administration as is requested by a party in interest;

(7) if the business of the debtor is authorized to be operated, file with the court and with any governmental unit charged with responsibility for collection or determination of any tax arising out of such operation, periodic reports and summaries of the operation of such business, including a statement of receipts and disbursements, and such other information as the court requires; and

(8) make a final report and file a final account of the administration of the estate with the court.

Sec. 705. Creditor's committee. (a) At the meeting under section 341(a) of this title, creditors that may vote for a trustee under section 702(a) of this title may elect a committee of not fewer than three, and not more than eleven, creditors, each of whom holds an allowable unsecured claim of a kind entitled to distribution under section 726(a)(2) of this title.

(b) A committee elected under subsection (a) of this section may consult with the trustee in connection with the administration of the estate, make recommendations to the trustee respecting the performance of the trustee's duties, and submit to the court any question affecting the administration of the estate.

Sec. 706. Conversion. (a) The debtor may convert a case under this chapter to a case under chapter 11 or 13 of this title at any time, if the case has not been converted under section 1112 or 1307 of this title. Any waiver of the right to convert a case under this subsection is unenforceable.

(b) On request of a party in interest and after notice and a hearing, the court may convert a case under this chapter to a case under chapter 11 of this title at any time.

(c) The court may not convert a case under this chapter to a case under chapter 13 of this title unless the debtor requests such conversion.

(d) Notwithstanding any other provision of this section, a case may not be converted to a case under another chapter of this title unless the debtor may be a debtor under such chapter.

Sec. 707. Dismissal. The court may dismiss a case under this chapter only after notice and a hearing and only for cause, including

(1) unreasonable delay by the debtor that is prejudicial to creditors; and

(2) nonpayment of any fees and charges required under chapter 123 of title 28.

SUBCHAPTER II—COLLECTION, LIQUIDATION, AND DISTRIBUTION OF THE ESTATE

Sec. 721. Authorization to operate business. The court may authorize the trustee to operate the business of the debtor for a limited period, if such operation is in the best interest of the estate and consistent with the orderly liquidation of the estate.

Sec. 726. Distribution of property of the estate. (a) Except as provided in section 510 of this title, property of the estate shall be distributed

(1) first, in payment of claims of the kind specified in, and in the order specified in, section 507 of this title;

(2) second, in payment of any allowed unsecured claim, other than a claim of a kind specified in paragraph (1), (3), or (4) of this subsection, proof of which is

(A) timely filed under section 501(a) of this title;

(B) timely filed under section 501(b) or 501(c) of this title; or

(C) tardily filed under section 501(a) of this title, if

(i) the creditor that holds such claim did not have notice or actual knowledge of the case in time for timely filing of a proof of such claim under section 501(a) of this title; and

(ii) proof of such claim is filed in time to permit payment of such claim;

(3) third, in payment of any allowed unsecured claim proof of which is tardily filed under section 501(a) of this title, other than a claim of the kind specified in paragraph (2)(C) of this subsection;

(4) fourth, in payment of any allowed claim, whether secured or unsecured, for any fine, penalty, or forfeiture, or for multiple, exemplary, or punitive damages, arising before the earlier of the order for relief or the appointment of a trustee, to the extent that such fine, penalty, forfeiture, or damages are not compensation for actual pecuniary loss suffered by the holder of such claim;

(5) fifth, in payment of interest at the legal rate from the date of the filing of the petition, on any claim paid under paragraph (1), (2), (3), or (4) of this subsection; and

(6) sixth, to the debtor.

(b) Payment on claims of a kind specified in paragraph (1), (2), (3), (4), (5), or (6) of section 507(a) of this title, or in paragraph (2), (3), (4), or (5) of subsection (a) of this section, shall be made pro rata among claims of the kind specified in a particular paragraph, except that in a case that has been converted to this chapter under section 1112 or 1307 of this title, administrative expenses incurred under this chapter after such conversion have priority over administrative expenses incurred under any other chapter of this title or under this chapter before such conversion and over any expenses of a custodian superseded under section 543 of this title.

(c) Notwithstanding subsections (a) and (b) of this section, if there is property of the kind specified in section 541(a)(2) of this title, or proceeds of such property, in the estate, such property or proceeds shall be segregated from other property of the estate, and such property or proceeds and other property of the estate shall be distributed as follows:

(1) Administrative expenses shall be paid either from property of the kind specified in section 541(a)(2) of this title, or from other property of the estate, as the interest of justice requires.

(2) Claims other than for administrative expenses shall be paid in the order specified in subsection (a) of this section, and, with respect to claims of a kind specified in a particular paragraph of section 507 of this title or subsection (a) of this section, in the following order and manner:

(A) First, community claims against the debtor or the debtor's spouse shall be paid from property of the kind specified in section 541(a)(2) of this title, except to the extent that such property is solely liable for debts of the debtor.

(B) Second, to the extent that community claims against the debtor are not paid under subparagraph (A) of this paragraph, such community claims shall be paid from property of the kind specified in section 541(a)(2) of this title that is solely liable for debts of the debtor.

(C) Third, to the extent that all claims against the debtor including community claims against the debtor are not paid under subparagraph (A) or (B) of this paragraph such claims shall be paid from property of the estate other than property of the kind specified in section 541(a)(2) of this title.

(D) Fourth, to the extent that community claims against the debtor or the debtor's spouse are not paid under subparagraph (A), (B), or (C) of this paragraph, such claims shall be paid from all remaining property of the estate.

Sec. 727. Discharge. (a) The court shall grant the debtor a discharge, unless

(1) the debtor is not an individual;

(2) the debtor, with intent to hinder, delay, or defraud a creditor or an officer of the estate charged with custody of property under this title, has transferred, removed, destroyed, mutilated, or concealed, or has permitted to be transferred, removed, destroyed, mutilated, or concealed

(A) property of the debtor, within one year before the date of the filing of the petition; or

(B) property of the estate, after the date of the filing of the petition;

(3) the debtor has concealed, destroyed, mutilated, falsified, or failed to keep or preserve any recorded information, including books, documents, records, and papers from which the debtor's financial condition or business transactions might be ascertained, unless such act or failure to act was justified under all the circumstances of the case;

(4) the debtor knowingly and fraudulently, in or in connection with the case

(A) made a false oath or account;

(B) presented or used a false claim;

(C) gave, offered, received, or attempted to obtain money, property, or advantage, or a promise of money, property, or advantage, for acting or forbearing to act; or

(D) withheld from an officer of the estate entitled to possession under this title, any recorded information, including books, documents, records, and papers, relating to the debtor's property or financial affairs;

(5) the debtor has failed to explain satisfactorily, before determination of denial of discharge under this paragraph, any loss of assets or deficiency of assets to meet the debtor's liabilities;

(6) the debtor has refused, in the case

(A) to obey any lawful order of the court, other than an order to respond to a material question or to testify;

(B) on the ground of privilege against self-incrimination, to respond to a material questions approved by the court or to testify, after the debtor has been granted immunity with respect to the matter concerning which such privilege was invoked; or

(C) on a ground other than the property invoked privilege against self-incrimination, to respond to a material question approved by the court or to testify;

(7) the debtor has committed any act specified in paragraph (2), (3), (4), (5), or (6) of this subsection, on or within one year before the date of the filing of the petition, or during the case, in connection with another case concerning an insider;

(8) the debtor has been granted a discharge under this section, under section 1141 of this title, or under section 14, 371 or 476 of the Bankruptcy Act, in a case commenced within six years before the date of the filing of the petition;

(9) the debtor has been granted a discharge under section 1328 of this title, or under section 660 or 661 of the Bankruptcy Act, in a case commenced within six years before the date of the filing of the petition, unless payments under the plan in such case totaled at least

(A) 100 percent of the allowed unsecured claims in such case; or

(B) (i) 70 percent of such claims; and

(ii) the plan was proposed by the debtor in good faith, and was the debtor's best effort; or

(10) the court approves a written waiver of discharge executed by the debtor after the order for relief under this chapter.

(b) Except as provided in section 523 of this title, a discharge under subsection (a) of this section discharges the debtor from all debts that arose before the date of the order for relief under this chapter, and any liability on a claim that is determined under section 502 of this title as if such claim had arisen before the commencement of the case, whether or not a proof of claim based on any such debt or liability is filed under section 501 of this title, and whether or not a claim based on any such debt or liability is allowed under section 502 of this title.

(c) (1) The trustee or a creditor may object to discharge under subsection (a) of this section.

(2) On request of a party in interest, the court may order the trustee to examine the acts and conduct of the debtor to determine whether a ground exists for denial of discharge.

(d) On request of the trustee or a creditor, and after notice and a hearing, the court shall revoke a discharge granted under subsection (a) of this section if

(1) such discharge was obtained through the fraud of the debtor, and the requesting party did not know of such fraud until after the granting of such discharge;

(2) the debtor acquired property that is property of the estate, or became entitled to acquire property that would be property of the estate, and knowingly and fraudulently failed to report the acquisition of, or entitlement to, such property, or to deliver or surrender such property to the trustee; or

(3) the debtor committed an act specified in subsection (a)(6) of this section.

(e) The trustee or a creditor may request a revocation of a discharge

(1) under subsection (d)(1) of this section, within one year after such discharge was granted; or

(2) under subsection (d)(2) or (d)(3) of this section, before the later of

(A) one year after the granting of such discharge; and

(B) the date the case is closed.

CHAPTER 11

REORGANIZATION

SUBCHAPTER I—OFFICERS AND ADMINISTRATION

Sec. 1101. **Definitions for this chapter.** In this chapter

(1) "debtor in possession" means debtor except when a person that has qualified under section 322 of this title is serving as trustee in the case;

(2) "substantial consummation" means

(A) transfer of all or substantially all of the property proposed by the plan to be transferred;

(B) assumption by the debtor or by the successor to the debtor under the plan of the business or of the management of all or substantially all of the property dealt with by the plan; and

(C) commencement of distribution under the plan.

Sec. 1102. **Creditors' and equity security holders' committees.** (a) (1) As soon as practicable after the order for relief under this chapter, the court shall appoint a committee of creditors holding unsecured claims.

(2) On request of a party in interest, the court may order the appointment of additional committees of creditors or of equity security holders if necessary to assure adequate representation of creditors or of equity security holders. The court shall appoint any such committee.

(b) (1) A committee of creditors appointed under subsection (a) of this section shall ordinarily consist of the persons, willing to serve, that hold the seven largest claims against the debtor of the kinds represented on such committee, or of the members of a committee organized by creditors before the order for relief under this chapter, if such committee was fairly chosen and is representative of the different kinds of claims to be represented.

(2) A committee of equity security holders appointed under subsection (a)(2) of this section shall ordinarily consist of the persons, willing to serve, that hold the seven largest amounts of equity securities of the debtor of the kinds represented on such committee.

(c) On request of a party in interest and after notice and a hearing, the court may change the membership or the size of a committee appointed under subsection (a) of this section if the membershp of such committee is not representative of the different kinds of claims or interests to be represented.

Sec. 1103. **Powers and duties of committees.** (a) At a scheduled meeting of a committee appointed under section 1102 of this title, at which a majority of the members of such committee are present, and with the court's approval, such committee may select and authorize the employment by such committee of one or more attorneys, accountants, or other agents, to represent or perform services for such committee.

(b) A person employed to represent a committee appointed under section 1102 of this title may not, while employed by such committee, represent any other entity in connection with the case.

(c) A committee appointed under section 1102 of this title may

(1) consult with the trustee or debtor in possession concerning the administration of the case;

(2) investigate the acts, conduct, assets, liabilities, and financial condition of the debtor, the operation of the debtor's business and the desirability of the continuance of such business, and any other matter relevant to the case or to the formation of a plan;

(3) participate in the formulation of a plan, advise those represented by such committee of such committee's recommendations as to any plan formulated, and collect and file with the court acceptances of a plan;

(4) request the appointment of a trustee or examiner under section 1104 of this title, if a trustee or examiner, as the case may be, has not previously been appointed under this chapter in the case; and

(5) perform such other services as are in the interest of those represented.

(d) As soon as practicable after the appointment of a committee under section 1102 of this title, the trustee shall meet with such committee to transact such business as may be necessary and proper.

Sec. 1104. **Appointment of trustee or examiner.** (a) At any time after the commencement of the case but before confirmation of a plan, on request of a party in interest, and after notice and a hearing, the court shall order the appointment of a trustee

(1) for cause, including fraud, dishonesty, incompetence, or gross mismanagement of the affairs of the debtor by current management, either before or after the commencement of the case, or similar cause, but not including the number of holders of securities of the debtor or the amount of assets or liabilities of the debtor; or

(2) if such appointment is in the interests of creditors, any equity security holders, and other interests of the estate, without regard to the number of holders of securities of the debtor or the amount of assets or liabilities of the debtor.

(b) If the court does not order the appointment of a trustee under this section, then at any time before the confirmation of a plan, on request of a party in interest, and after notice and a hearing, the court shall order the appointment of an examiner to conduct such an investigation of the debtor as is appropriate, including an investigation of any allegations of fraud, dishonesty, incompetence, misconduct, mismanagement, or irregularity in the management of the affairs of the debtor or or by current or former management of the debtor, if

(1) such appointment is in the interests of creditors, any equity security holders, and other interests of the estate; or

(2) the debtor's fixed, liquidated, unsecured debts, other than debts for goods, services, or taxes, or owing to an insider, exceed $5,000,000.

(c) If the court orders the appointment of a trustee or an examiner, if a trustee or an examiner dies or resigns during the case or is removed under section 324 of this title, or if a trustee fails to qualify under section 322 of this title, then the court shall appoint one disinterested person to serve as trustee or examiner, as the case may be, in the case.

Sec. 1105. Termination of trustee's appointment.

At any time before confirmation of a plan, on request of a party in interest, and after notice and a hearing, the court may terminate the trustee's appointment and restore the debtor to possession and management of the property of the estate, and operation of the debtor's business.

Sec. 1106. Duties of trustee and examiner.

(a) A trustee shall

(1) perform the duties of a trustee specified in sections 704(2), 704(4), 704(6), 704(7), and 704(8) of this title;

(2) if the debtor has not done so, file the list, schedule, and statement required under section 521(1) of this title;

(3) except to the extent that the court orders otherwise, investigate the acts, conduct, assets, liabilities, and financial condition of the debtor, the operation of the debtor's business and the desirability of the continuance of such business, and any other matter relevant to the case or to the formulation of a plan;

(4) as soon as practicable

(A) file a statement of any investigation conducted under paragraph (3) of this subsection, including any fact ascertained pertaining to fraud, dishonesty, incompetence, misconduct, mismanagement, or irregularity in the management of the affairs of the debtor, or to a cause of action available to the estate; and

(B) transmit a copy or a summary of any such statement to any creditors' committee or equity security holders' committee, to any indenture trustee, and to such other entity as the court designates;

(5) as soon as practicable, file a plan under section 1121 of this title, file a report of why the trustee will not file a plan, or recommend conversion of the case to a case under chapter 7 or 13 of this title or dismissal of the case;

(6) for any year for which the debtor has not filed a tax return required by law, furnish, without personal liability, such information as may be required by the governmental unit with which such tax return was to be filed, in light of the condition of the debtor's books and records and the availability of such information; and

(7) after confirmation of a plan, file such reports as are necessary or as the court orders.

(b) An examiner appointed under section 1104(c) of this title shall perform the duties specified in paragraphs (3) and (4) of subsection (a) of this section, and any other duties of the trustee that the court orders the debtor in possession not to perform.

Sec. 1107. Rights, powers, and duties of debtor in possession.

(a) Subject to any limitations on a trustee under this chapter, and to such limitations or conditions as the court prescribes, a debtor in possession shall have all the rights, other than the right to compensation under section 330 of this title, and powers, and shall perform all the functions and duties, except the duties specified in sections 1106(a) (2), (3), and (4) of this title, of a trustee serving in a case under this chapter.

(b) Notwithstanding section 327(a) of this title, a person is not disqualified for employment under section 327 of this title by a debtor in possession solely because of such person's employment by or representation of the debtor before the commencement of the case.

Sec. 1108. Authorization to operate business.

Unless the court orders otherwise, the trustee may operate the debtor's business.

Sec. 1109. Right to be heard.

(a) The Securities and Exchange Commission may raise and may appear and be heard on any issue in a case under this chapter, but the Securities and Exchange Commission may not appeal from any judgment, order, or decree entered in the case.

(b) A party in interest, including the debtor, the trustee, a creditors' committee, an equity security holders' committee, a creditor, an equity security holder, or any indenture trustee, may raise and may appear and be heard on any issue in a case under this chapter.

Sec. 1112. Conversion or dismissal.

(a) The debtor may convert a case under this chapter to a case under chapter 7 of this title unless

(1) the debtor is not a debtor in possession;

(2) the case is an involuntary case originally commenced under this chapter; or

(3) the case was converted to a case under this chapter on other than the debtor's request.

(b) Except as provided in subsection (c) of this section, on request of a party in interest, and after notice and a hearing, the court may convert a case under this chapter to a case under chapter 7 of this title or may dismiss a case under this chapter, whichever is in the best interest of creditors and the estate, for cause, including

(1) continuing loss to or diminution of the estate and absence of a reasonable likelihood of rehabilitation;

(2) inability to effectuate a plan;

(3) unreasonable delay by the debtor that is prejudicial to creditors;

(4) failure to propose a plan under section 1121 of this title within any time fixed by the court;

(5) denial of confirmation of every proposed plan and denial of additional time for filing another plan or a modification of a plan;

(6) revocation of an order of confirmation under section 1144 of this title, and denial of confirmation of another plan or a modified plan under section 1129 of this title;

(7) inability to effectuate substantial consummation of a confirmed plan;

(8) material default by the debtor with respect to a confirmed plan; and

(9) termination of a plan by reason of the occurrence of a condition specified in the plan.

(c) The court may not convert a case under this chapter to a case under chapter 7 of this title if the debtor is a farmer or a corporation that is not a moneyed, business, or commercial corporation, unless the debtor requests such conversion.

(d) The court may convert a case under this chapter to a case under chapter 13 of this title only if

(1) the debtor requests such conversion; and

(2) the debtor has not been discharged under section 1141(d) of this title.

(e) Notwithstanding any other provision of this section, a case may not be converted to a case under another chapter of this title unless the debtor may be a debtor under such chapter.

SUBCHAPTER II—THE PLAN

Sec. 1121. Who may file a plan.

(a) The debtor may file a plan with a petition commencing a voluntary case, or at any time in a voluntary case or an involuntary case.

(b) Except as otherwise provided in this section, only the debtor may file a plan until after 120 days after the date of the order for relief under this chapter.

(c) Any party in interest, including the debtor, the trustee, a creditors' committee, an equity security holders' committee, a creditor, an equity holder, or any indenture trustee, may file a plan if and only if

(1) a trustee has been appointed under this chapter;

(2) the debtor has not filed a plan before 120 days after the date of the order for relief under this chapter; or

(3) the debtor has not filed a plan that has been accepted, before 180 days after the date of the order for relief under this chapter, by each class the claims or interests of which are impaired under the plan.

(d) On request of a party in interest and after notice and a hearing, the court may for cause reduce or increase the 120-day period or the 180-day period referred to in this section.

Sec. 1122. Classification of claims or interests.

(a) Except as provided in subsection (b) of this section, a plan may place a claim or an interest in a particular class only if such claim or interest is substantially similar to the other claims or interests of such class.

(b) A plan may designate a separate class of claims consisting only of every unsecured claim that is less than or reduced to an amount that the court approves as reasonable and necessary for administrative convenience.

Sec. 1123. Contents of plan.

(a) A plan shall

(1) designate, subject to section 1122 of this title, classes of claims other than claims of a kind specified in section 507(a)(1), 507(a)(2), or 507(a)(6) of this title and classes of interests;

(2) specify any class of claims or interests that is not impaired under the plan;

(3) shall specify the treatment of any class of claims or interests that is impaired under the plan;

(4) provide the same treatment for each claim or interest of a particular class, unless the holder of a particular claim or interest agrees to a less favorable treatment of such particular claim or interest;

(5) provide adequate means for the plan's execution, such as

(A) retention by the debtor of all or any part of the property of the estate;

(B) transfer of all or any part of the property of the estate to one or more entities, whether organized before or after the confirmation of such plan;

(C) merger or consolidation of the debtor with one or more persons;

(D) sale of all or any part of the property of the estate, either subject to or free of any lien, or the distribution of all or any part of the property of the estate among those having an interest in such property of the estate;

(E) satisfaction or modification of any lien;

(F) cancellation or modification of any indenture or similar instrument;

(G) curing or waiving any default;

(H) extension of a maturity date or a change in an interest rate or other term of outstanding securities;

(I) amendment of the debtor's charter; or

(J) issuance of securities of the debtor, or of any entity referred to in subparagraph (B) or (C) of this paragraph, for cash, for property, for existing securities, or in exchange for claims or interests, or for any other appropriate purpose;

(6) provide for the inclusion in the charter of the debtor, if the debtor is a corporation, or of any corporation referred to in paragraph (5)(B) or (5)(C) of this subsection, of a provision prohibiting the issuance of non-voting equity securities, and providing, as to the several classes of securities possessing voting power, an appropriate distribution of such power among such classes, including, in the case of any class of equity securities having a preference over another class of equity securities with respect to dividends, adequate provisions for the election of directors representing such preferred class in the event of default in the payment of such dividends; and

(7) contain only provisions that are consistent with the interests of creditors and equity security holders and with public policy with respect to the manner of selection of any officer, director, or trustee under the plan and any successor to such officer, director, or trustee.

(b) Subject to subsection (a) of this section, a plan may

(1) impair or leave unimpaired any class of claims, secured or unsecured, or of interests;

(2) subject to section 365 of this title, provide for the assumption or rejection of any executory contract or unexpired lease of the debtor not previously rejected under section 365 of this title;

(3) provide for

(A) the settlement or adjustment of any claim or interest belonging to the debtor or to the estate; or

(B) the retention and enforcement by the debtor, by the trustee, or by a representative of the estate appointed for such purpose, of any such claim or interest;

(4) provide for the sale of all or substantially all of the property of the estate, and the distribution of the proceeds of such sale among holders of claims or interests; and

(5) include any other appropriate provision not inconsistent with the applicable provisions of this title.

(c) In a case concerning an individual, a plan proposed by an entity other than the debtor may not provide for the use, sale, or lease of property exempted under section 522 of this title, unless the debtor consents to such use, sale, or lease.

Sec. 1124. **Impairment of claims or interests.** Except as provided in section 1123(a)(4) of this title, a class of claims or interests is impaired under a plan unless, with respect to each claim or interest of such class, the plan

(1) leaves unaltered the legal, equitable, and contractual rights to which such claim or interest entitles the holder of such claim or interest;

(2) notwithstanding any contractual provision or applicable law that entitles the holder of such claim or interest to demand or receive accelerated payment of such claim or interest after the occurrence of a default

(A) cures any such default, other than a default of a kind specified in section 365(b)(2) of this title, that occurred before or after the commencement of the case under this title;

(B) reinstates the maturity of such claim or interest as such maturity existed before such default;

(C) compensates the holder of such claim or interest for any damages incurred as a result of any reasonable reliance by such holder on such contractual provision or such applicable law; and

(D) does not otherwise alter the legal, equitable, or contractual rights to which such claim or interest entitles the holder of such claim or interest; or

(3) provides that, on the effective date of the plan, the holder of such claim or interest receives, on account of such claim or interest, cash equal to

(A) with respect to a claim, the allowed amount of such claim; or

(B) with respect to an interest, if applicable, the greater of

(i) any fixed liquidation preference to which the terms of any security representing such interest entitle the holder of such interest; and

(ii) any fixed price at which the debtor, under the terms of such security, may redeem such security from such holder.

Sec. 1125. **Postpetition disclosure and solicitation.** (a) In this section

(1) "adequate information" means information of a kind, and in sufficient detail, as far as is reasonably practicable in light of the nature and history of the debtor and the condition of the debtor's books and records, that would enable a hypothetical reasonable investor typical of holders of claims or interests of the relevant class to make an informed judgment about the plan; and

(2) "investor typical of holders of claims or interests of the relevant class" means investor having

(A) a claim or interest of the relevant class;

(B) such a relationship with debtor as the holders of other claims or interests of such class generally have; and

(C) such ability to obtain such information from sources other than the disclosure required by this section as holders claims or interests in such class generally have.

(b) An acceptance or rejection of a plan may not be solicited after the commencement of the case under this title from a holder of a claim or interest with respect to such claim or interest, unless, at the time of or before such solicitation, there is transmitted to such holder the plan or a summary of the plan, and a written disclosure statement approved, after notice and a hearing, by the court as containing adequate information. The court may approve a disclosure statement without a valuation of the debtor or an appraisal of the debtor's assets.

(c) The same disclosure statement shall be transmitted to each holder of a claim or interest of a particular class, but there may be transmitted different disclosure statements, differing in amount, detail, or kind of information, as between classes.

(d) Whether a disclosure statement contains adequate information is not governed by any otherwise applicable nonbankruptcy law, rule, or regulation, but an agency or official whose duty is to administer or enforce such a law, rule, or regulation may be heard on the issue of whether a disclosure statement contains adequate information. Such an agency or official may not appeal from an order approving a disclosure statement.

(e) A person that solicits, in good faith and in compliance with the applicable provisions of this title, or that participates, in good faith and in compliance with the applicable provisions of this title, in the offer, issuance, sale, or purchase of a security, offered or sold under the plan, of the debtor, of an affiliate participating in a joint plan with the debtor, or of a newly organized successor to the debtor under the plan, is not liable, on account of such solicitation or participation, for violation of any applicable law, rule, or regulation governing the offer, issuance, sale, or purchase of securities.

Sec. 1126. **Acceptance of plan.** (a) The holder of a claim or interest allowed under section 502 of this title may accept or reject a plan. If the United States is a creditor or equity security holder, the Secretary of the Treasury may accept or reject the plan on behalf of the United States.

(b) For the purpose of subsections (c) and (d) of this section, a holder of a claim or interest that has accepted or rejected the plan before the commencement of the case under this title is deemed to have accepted or rejected such plan, as the case may be, if

(1) the solicitation of such acceptance or rejection was in compliance with any applicable nonbankruptcy law, rule, or regulation governing the adequacy of disclosure in connection with such solicitation; or

(2) if there is not any such law, rule, or regulation, such acceptance or rejection was solicited after disclosure to such holder of adequate information, as defined in section 1125 (a)(1) of this title.

(c) A class of claims has accepted a plan if such plan has been accepted by creditors, other than any entity designated under subsection (e) of this section, that hold at least two-thirds in amount and more than one half in number of the allowed claims of such class held by creditors, other than may any entity designated under subsection (e) of this section, that have accepted or rejected such plan.

(d) A class of interests has accepted a plan if such plan has been accepted by holders of such interests other than any entity designated under subsection (e) of this section, that hold at least two-thirds in amount of the allowed interests of such class held by holders of such interests, other than any entity designated under subsection (e) of this section, that have accepted or rejected such plan.

(e) On request of a party in interest, and after notice and a hearing, the court may designate any entity whose acceptance or rejection of such plan was not in good faith, or was not solicited or procured in good faith or in accordance with the provisions of this title.

(f) Notwithstanding any other provision of this section, a class that is not impaired under a plan is deemed to have accepted the plan, and solicitation of acceptances with respect to such class from the holders of claims or interest of such class is not required.

(g) Notwithstanding any other provision of this section, a class is deemed not to have accepted a plan if such plan provides that the claims or interests of such class do not entitle the holders of such claims or interests to any payment or compensation under the plan on account of such claims or interests.

Sec. 1128. **Confirmation hearing.** (a) After notice, the court shall hold a hearing on confirmation of a plan.

(b) A party in interest may object to confirmation of a plan.

Sec. 1129. **Confirmation of plan.** (a) The court shall confirm a plan only if all of the following requirements are met:

(1) The plan complies with the applicable provisions of this chapter.

(2) The proponent of the plan complies with the applicable provisions of this chapter.

(3) The plan has been proposed in good faith and not by any means forbidden by law.

(4) (A) Any payment made or promised by the proponent, by the debtor, or by a person issuing securities or acquiring property under the plan, for services or for costs and expenses in, or in connection with, the case, or in connection with the plan and incident to the case, has been disclosed to the court; and

(B) (i) any such payment made before confirmation of the plan is reasonable; or

(ii) if such payment is to be fixed after confirmation of the plan, such payment is subject to the approval of the court as reasonable.

(5) (A) (i) The proponent of the plan has disclosed the identity and affiliations of any individual proposed to serve, after confirmation of the plan, as a director, officer, or voting trustee of the debtor, an affiliate of the debtor participating in a joint plan with the debtor, or a successor to the debtor under the plan; and

(ii) the appointment to, or continuance in, such office of such individual, is consistent with the interests of creditors and equity security holders and with public policy.

(B) The proponent of the plan has disclosed the identity of any insider that will be employed or retained by the reorganized debtor, and the nature of any compensation for such insider.

(6) Any regulatory commission with jurisdiction, after confirmation of the plan, over the rates of the debtor has approved any rate change provided for in the plan, or such rate change is expressly conditioned on such approval.

(7) With respect to each class

(A) each holder of a claim or interest of such class

(i) has accepted the plan; or

(ii) will receive or retain under the plan on account of such claim or interest property of a value, as of the effective date of the plan, that is not less than the amount that such holder would so receive or retain if the debtor were liquidated under chapter 7 of this title on such date; or

(B) if section 1111(b)(2) of this title applies to the claims of such class, each holder of a claim of such class will receive or retain under the plan on account of such claim property of a value, as of the effective date of the plan, that is not less than the value of such creditor's interest in the estate's interest in the property that secures such claims.

(8) With respect to each class

(A) such class has accepted the plan; or

(B) such class is not impaired under the plan.

(9) Except to the extent that the holder of a particular claim has agreed to a different treatment of such claim, the plan provides that

(A) with respect to a claim of a kind specified in section 507(a)(1) or 507(a)(2) of this title, on the effective date of the plan, the holder of such claim will receive on account of such claim cash equal to the allowed amount of such claim;

(B) with respect to a class of claims of a kind specified in section 507(a)(3), 507(a)(4), or 507(a)(5) of this title, each holder of a claim of such class will receive

(i) if such class has accepted the plan, deferred cash payments of a value, as of the effective date of the plan, equal to the allowed amount of such claim; or

(ii) if such class has not accepted the plan, cash on the effective date of the plan equal to the allowed amount of such claim; and

(C) with respect to a claim of a kind specified in section 507(a)(6) of this title, the holder of such claim will receive on account of such claim deferred cash payments, over a period not exceeding six years after the date of assessment of such claim, of a value, as of the effective date of the plan, equal to the allowed amount of such claim.

(10) At least one class of claims has accepted the plan, determined without including any acceptance of the plan by any insider holding a claim of such class.

(11) Confirmation of the plan is not likely to be followed by the liquidation, or the need for further financial reorganization, of the debtor or any successor to the debtor under the plan, unless such liquidation or reorganization is proposed in the plan.

(b) (1) Notwithstanding section 510(a) of this title, if all of the applicable requirements of subsection (a) of this section other than paragraph (8) are met with respect to a plan, the court, on request of the proponent of the plan, shall confirm the plan notwithstanding the requirements of such paragraph if the plan does not discriminate unfairly, and is fair and equitable, with respect to each class of claims or interests that is impaired under, and has not accepted, the plan.

(2) For the purpose of this subsection, the condition that a plan be fair and equitable with respect to a class includes the following requirements:

(A) With respect to a class of secured claims, the plan provides

(i) (I) that the holders of such claims retain the lien securing such claims, whether the property subject to such lien is retained by the debtor or transferred to another entity, to the extent of the allowed amount of such claims; and

(II) that each holder of a claim of such class receive on account of such claim deferred cash payments totaling at least the allowed amount of such claim, of a value, as of the effective date of the plan, of at least the value of such holder's interest in the estate's interest in such property;

(ii) for the sale, subject to section 363(k) of this title, of any property that is subject to the lien securing such claims, free and clear of such lien, with such lien to attach to the proceeds of such sale, and the treatment of such lien on proceeds under clause (i) or (iii) of this subparagraph; or

(iii) for the realization by such holders of the indubitable equivalent of such claims.

(B) With respect to a class of unsecured claims

(i) the plan provides that each holder of a claim of such class receive or retain on account of such claim property of a value, as of the effective date of the plan, equal to the allowed amount of such claim; or

(ii) the holder of any claim or interest that is junior to the claims of such class will not receive or retain on account of such junior claim or interest any property.

(C) With respect to a class of interests

(i) the plan provides that each holder of an interest of such class receive or retain on account of such claim property of a value, as of the effective date of the plan, equal to the greatest of the allowed amount of any fixed liquidation preference to which such holder is entitled, any fixed redemption price to which such holder is entitled, and the value of such interest; or

(ii) the holder of any interest that is junior to the interests of such class will not receive or retain under the plan on account of such junior interest any property.

(c) Notwithstanding subsections (a) and (b) of this section and except as provided in section 1127(b) of this title, the court may confirm only one plan, unless the order of confirmation in the case has been revoked under section 1144 of this title. If the requirements of subsections (a) and (b) of this section are met with respect to more than one plan, the court shall consider the preferences of creditors and equity security holders in determining which plan to confirm.

(d) Notwithstanding any other provision of this section, on request of a party in interest that is a governmental unit, the court may not confirm a plan if the principal purpose of the plan is the avoidance of taxes or the avoidance of section 5 of the Securities Act of 1933 (15 U.S.C. 77e).

SUBCHAPTER III—POSTCONFIRMATION MATTERS

Sec. 1141. **Effect of confirmation.** (a) Except as provided in subsections (d)(2) and (d)(3) of this section, the provisions of a confirmed plan bind the debtor, any entity issuing securities under the plan, any entity acquiring property under the plan, and any creditor or equity security holder of, or general partner in, the debtor, whether or not the claim or interest of such creditor, equity security holder, or general partner is impaired under the plan and whether or not such creditor, equity security holder, or general partner has accepted the plan.

(b) Except as otherwise provided in the plan or the order confirming the plan, the confirmation of a plan vests all of the property of the estate in the debtor.

(c) After confirmation of a plan, the property dealt with by the plan is free and clear of all claims and interests of creditors, of equity security holders, and of general partners in the debtor, except as otherwise provided in the plan or in the order confirming the plan.

(d) (1) Except as otherwise provided in this subsection, in the plan, or in the order confirming the plan, the confirmation of a plan

(A) discharges the debtor from any debt that arose before the date of such confirmation, and any debt of a kind specified in section 502(g), 502(h), or 502(i) of this title, whether or not

(i) a proof of the claim based on such debt is filed or deemed filed under section 501 of this title;

(ii) such claim is allowed under section 502 of this title; or

(iii) the holder of such claim has accepted the plan; and

(B) terminates all rights and interests of equity security holders and general partners provided for by the plan.

(2) The confirmation of a plan does not discharge an individual debtor from any debt excepted from discharge under section 523 of this title.

(3) The confirmation of a plan does not discharge a debtor if

(A) the plan provides for the liquidation of all or substantially all of the property of the estate;

(B) the debtor does not engage in business after consummation of the plan; and

(C) the debtor would be denied a discharge under section 727(a) of this title if the case were a case under chapter 7 of this title.

(4) The court may approve a written waiver of discharge executed by the debtor after the order for relief under this chapter.

CHAPTER 13

ADJUSTMENT OF DEBTS OF AN INDIVIDUAL WITH REGULAR INCOME

SUBCHAPTER I—OFFICERS, ADMINISTRATION, AND THE ESTATE

Sec. 1301. **Stay of action against codebtor.** (a) Except as provided in subsections (b) and (c) of this section, after the order for relief under this chapter, a creditor may not act, or commence or continue any civil action, to collect all or any part of a consumer debt of the debtor, from any individual that is liable on such debt with the debtor, or that secured such debt, unless

(1) such individual became liable on or secured such debt in the ordinary course of such individual's business; or

(2) the case is closed, dismissed, or converted to a case under chapter 7 or 11 of this title.

(b) A creditor may present a negotiable instrument, and may give notice of dishonor of such an instrument.

(c) On request of a party in interest and after notice and a hearing, the court shall grant relief from the stay provided by subsection (a) of this section with respect to a creditor, to the extent that

(1) as between the debtor and the individual protected under subsection (a) of this section, such individual received the consideration for the claim held by such creditor;

(2) the plan filed by the debtor proposes not to pay such claim; or

(3) such creditor's interest would be irreparably harmed by such stay.

Sec. 1302. **Trustee.** (a) If the court has appointed an individual under subsection (d) of this section to serve as standing trustee in cases under this chapter and if such individual qualifies under section 322 of this title, then such individual shall serve as trustee in the case. Otherwise, the court shall appoint a person to serve as trustee in the case.

(b) The trustee shall

(1) perform the duties specified in sections 704(2), 704(3), 704(4), 704(5), 704(6), and 704(8) of this title;

(2) appear and be heard at any hearing that concerns

(A) the value of property subject to a lien;

(B) confirmation of a plan; or

(C) modification of the plan after confirmation; and

(3) advise, other than on legal matters, and assist the debtor in performance under the plan.

(c) If the debtor is engaged in business, then in addition to the duties specified in subsection (b) of this section, the trustee shall perform the duties specified in sections 1106(a)(3) and 1106(a)(4) of this title.

Sec. 1303. **Rights and powers of debtor.** Subject to any limitations on a trustee under this chapter, the debtor shall have, exclusive of the trustee, the rights and powers of a trustee under sections 363(b), 363(d), 363(e), 363(f), and 363(l), of this title.

Sec. 1304. **Debtor engaged in business.** (a) A debtor that is self-employed and incurs trade credit in the production of income from such employment is engaged in business.

(b) Unless the court orders otherwise, a debtor engaged in business may operate the business of the debtor, and, subject to any limitations on a trustee under sections 363(c) and 364 of this title and to such limitations or conditions as the court prescribes, shall have, exclusive of the trustee, the rights and powers of the trustee under such sections.

(c) A debtor engaged in business shall perform the duties of the trustee specified in section 704(7) of this title.

Sec. 1306. **Property of the estate.** (a) Property of the estate includes, in addition to the property specified in section 541 of this title

(1) all property of the kind specified in such section that the debtor acquires after the commencement of the case but before the case is closed, dismissed, or converted to a case under chapter 7 or 11 of this title, whichever occurs first; and

(2) earnings from services performed by the debtor after the commencement of the case but before the case is closed, dismissed, or converted to a case under chapter 7 or 11 of this title, whichever occurs first.

(b) Except as provided in a confirmed plan or order confirming a plan, the debtor shall remain in possession of all property of the estate.

Sec. 1307. **Conversion or dismissal.** (a) The debtor may convert a case under this chapter to a case under chapter 7 of this title at any time. Any waiver of the right to convert under this subsection is unenforceable.

(b) On request of the debtor at any time if the case has not been converted under section 706 or 1112 of this title, the court shall dismiss a case under this chapter. Any waiver of the right to dismiss under this subsection is unenforceable.

(c) Except as provided in subsection (e) of this section, on request of a party in interest and after notice and a hearing, the court may convert a case under this chapter to a case under chapter 7 of this title, or may dismiss a case under this chapter, whichever is in the best interests of creditors and the estate, for cause, including

(1) unreasonable delay by the debtor that is prejudicial to creditors;

(2) nonpayment of any fees and charges required under chapter 123 of title 28;

(3) failure to file a plan timely under section 1321 of this title;

(4) denial of confirmation of a plan under section 1325 of this title and denial of additional time for filing another plan or a modification of a plan;

(5) material default by the debtor with respect to a term of a confirmed plan;

(6) revocation of the order of confirmation under section 1330 of this title, and denial of confirmation of a modified plan under section 1329 of this title; and

(7) termination of a confirmed plan by reason of the occurrence of a condition specified in the plan.

(d) Except as provided in subsection (e) of this section, at any time before the confirmation of a plan under section 1325 of this title, on request of a party in interest and after notice and a hearing, the court may convert a case under this chapter to a case under chapter 11 of this title.

(e) The court may not convert a case under this chapter to a case under chapter 7 or 11 of this title if the debtor is a farmer, unless the debtor requests such conversion.

(f) Notwithstanding any other provision of this section, a case may not be converted to a case under another chapter of this title unless the debtor may be a debtor under such chapter.

SUBCHAPTER II—THE PLAN

Sec. 1321. Filing of plan. The debtor shall file a plan.

Sec. 1322. Contents of plan. (a) The plan shall

(1) provide for the submission of all or such portion of future earnings or other future income of the debtor to the supervision and control of the trustee as is necessary for the execution of the plan;

(2) provide for the full payment, in deferred cash payments of all claims entitled to priority under section 507 of this title, unless the holder of a particular claim agrees to a different treatment of such claim; and

(3) if the plan classifies claims, provide the same treatment for each claim within a particular class.

(b) Subject to subsections (a) and (c) of this section, the plan may

(1) designate a class or classes of unsecured claims, as provided in section 1122 of this title, but may not discriminate unfairly against any class so designated;

(2) modify the rights of holders of secured claims, other than a claim secured only by a security interest in real property that is the debtor's principal residence, or of holders of unsecured claims;

(3) provide for the curing or waiving of any default;

(4) provide for payments on any unsecured claim to be made concurrently with payments on any secured claim or any unsecured claim;

(5) notwithstanding paragraph (2) of this subsection, provide for the curing of any default within a reasonable time and maintenance of payments while the case is pending on any unsecured claim or secured claim on which the last payment is due after the date on which the final payment under the plan is due;

(6) provide for the payment of all or any part of any claim allowed under section 1305 of this title;

(7) provide for the assumption or rejection of any executory contract or unexpired lease of the debtor not previously rejected under section 365 of this title;

(8) provide for the payment of all or any part of a claim against the debtor from property of the estate or property of the debtor;

(9) provide for the vesting of property of the estate, on confirmation of the plan or at a later time, in the debtor or in any other entity; and

(10) include any other appropriate provision not inconsistent with this title.

(c) The plan may not provide for payments over a period that is longer than three years, unless the court, for cause, approves a longer period, but the court may not approve a period that is longer than five years.

Sec. 1324. Confirmation hearing. After notice, the court shall hold a hearing on the confirmation of the plan. A party in interest may object to the confirmation of the plan.

Sec. 1325. Confirmation of plan. (a) The court shall confirm a plan if

(1) the plan complies with the provisions of this chapter and with other applicable provisions of this title;

(2) any fee, charge, or amount required under chapter 123 of title 28, or by the plan, to be paid before confirmation, has been paid;

(3) the plan has been proposed in good faith and not by any means forbidden by law;

(4) the value, as of the effective date of the plan, of property to be distributed under the plan on account of each allowed unsecured claim is not less than the amount that would be paid on such claim if the estate of the debtor were liquidated under chapter 7 of this title on such date;

(5) with respect to each allowed secured claim provided for by the plan

(A) the holder of such claim has accepted the plan;

(B) (i) the plan provides that the holder of such claim retain the lien securing such claim; and

(ii) the value, as of the effective date of the plan, of property to be distributed under the plan on account of such claim is not less than the allowed amount of such claim; or

(C) the debtor surrenders the property securing such claim to such holder; and

(6) the debtor will be able to make all payments under the plan and to comply with the plan.

Sec. 1327. Effect of confirmation. (a) The provisions of a confirmed plan bind the debtor and each creditor, whether or not the claim of such creditor is provided for by the plan, and whether or not such creditor has objected to, has accepted, or has rejected the plan.

(b) Except as otherwise provided in the plan or the order confirming the plan, the confirmation of a plan vests all of the property of the estate in the debtor.

(c) Except as otherwise provided in the plan or in the order confirming the plan, the property vesting in the debtor under subsection (b) of this section is free and clear of any claim or interest of any creditor provided for by the plan.

Sec. 1328. Discharge. (a) As soon as practicable after completion by the debtor of all payments under the plan, unless the court approves a written waiver of discharge executed by the debtor after the order for relief under this chapter, the court shall grant the debtor a discharge of all debts provided for by the plan or disallowed under section 502 of this title, except any debt

(1) provided for under section 1322(b)(5) of this title; or

(2) of the kind specified in section 523(a)(5) of this title.

(b) At any time after the confirmation of the plan and after notice and a hearing, the court may grant a discharge to a debtor that has not completed payments under the plan only if

(1) the debtor's failure to complete such payments is due to circumstances for which the debtor should not justly be held accountable;

(2) the value, as of the effective date of the plan, of property actually distributed under the plan on account of each allowed unsecured claim is not less than the amount that would have been paid on such claim if the estate of the debtor had been liquidated under chapter 7 of this title on such date; and

(3) modification of the plan under section 1329 of this title is not practicable.

(c) A discharge granted under subsection (b) of this section discharges the debtor from all unsecured debts provided for by the plan or disallowed under section 502 of this title, except any debt

(1) provided for under section 1322(b)(5) of this title; or

(2) of a kind specified in section 523(a) of this title.

(d) Notwithstanding any other provision of this section, a discharge granted under this section does not discharge the debtor from any debt based on an allowed claim filed under section 1305(a)(2) of this title if prior approval by the trustee of the debtor's incurring such debt was practicable and was not obtained.

(e) On request of a party in interest before one year after a discharge under this section is granted, and after notice and a hearing, the court may revoke such discharge only if

(1) such discharge was obtained through fraud; and

(2) knowledge of such fraud came to the requesting party after such discharge was granted.

INDEX

NOTE: For Forms, See Table of Forms on Page xv